Some Georgia County Records

Vol. 4

96 – 1219

BEING SOME OF THE LEGAL RECORDS
OF
BURKE, BUTTS, COLUMBIA, EMANUEL,
GREENE, HANCOCK, JASPER, MORGAN
AND RICHMOND COUNTIES, GEORGIA

COMPILED BY:
   THE REV. SILAS EMMETT LUCAS, JR.
PUBLISHED BY:
   SOUTHERN HISTORICAL PRESS

SOUTHERN HISTORICAL PRESS, INC.
c/o The Rev. Silas Emmett Lucas, Jr.
275 West Broad Street
Greenville, South Carolina 29601

ISBN 0-89308- 685-1

Table of Contents

Publisher's Preface

The records found in this Volume 4 of *Some Georgia County Records* are, for the majority, taken from the back issues of the *Georgia Genealogical Magazine* between 1970 and 1985.

The reader will note that upon occasion some of these legal records are not complete but may end midway in the particular book being abstracted. The reason for this is that different persons abstracted these records and for some reason were unable to complete the entire book under consideration.

It should be further pointed out to the reader that we have used records already appearing in the *Georgia Genealogical Magazine* because our experience has shown that people who purchase genealogical books generally do not subscribe to quarterly genealogical magazines such as the "GGM," and, likewise, people who subscribe to quarterlies do not often purchase genealogical books. It is our desire to make these records available to as many people as we can. Hence, this Volume 4 is a series of at least six volumes on abstracts of legal records from various counties in Georgia.

The Rev. Emmett Lucas, Jr.

SOME EARLY RESIDENTS BURKE COUNTY, GEORGIA 1786-1819

Since the Burke County Courthouse at Waynesborough was burned in 1856, practically all the records before that year were lost. Some pettitions and other records that had once been stored in the basement of the Capitol at Milledgeville, have found their way to the University of Georgia, Athens where they are now in the Manuscript Collection. Others are in the Georgia Department of Archives and History, Atlanta. The names of Burke County residents in these records have been published. 1/ Newspapers furnish information on some other residents of Burke Co. The Georgia Gazette and the Augusta Chronicle has been searched for the years 1787 through 1794. Nearly 400 additional names are listed below. Very few of them are duplicated in the March 1966 National Genealogical Society Quarterly. The marriage and death items have been copied from Marriages and Deaths, 1763-1820, by Mary Warren, 1968, and are in addition to those previous published in the Quarterly.

Grand Jury, October 18, 1786

Beal, Henry	Harvey, Charles	Robinson, William
Burton, Thomas	Jones, Batt	Sharp, John
Byne, Edward, Foreman	Lambert, James	Spight, Moses
Cox, Caleb	McNiel, Daniel	Whitehead, Amos
Fryer, Zackariah L.	Martin, William	Yarbrough, Thomas
Greene, Benjamin	Patterson, Robert	Davies, J., Clerk of Court
Hadden, William	Patterson, William	

Members to the General Assembly from Burke Co., Dec. 29, 1787

Bayne, Edward	Lewis, Thomas, Jr.	Powell, John
Emanuel, David	Lawson, Hugh	Perry, Isaac
Jones, John	Morrison, John	Wagnon, John Peter
Lewis, Jacob		

Delegates to State Convention, Dec. 15, 1787 2/

Telfair, Edward	Dr. (Henry?) Todd	George Walton

Tax Defaulters, 1787-89, 1792-1793

The defaulters were persons who had not paid their county taxes for the preceeding year. The lists for 1790,1793,1796,1804,1805, and 1806 have been published. When the present lists are compared with those already published, there were only 31 duplications. This indicates that many of the persons listed, had already moved out of Burke Co. A few of the present lists were "non-resident." These have been indicated by an*. Sales of their property were advertised by the Sheriff. A few of these sales notices will be found in the section following this one.

To save space, the tax districts have been numbered as follows:

1787

Bickham	1	Blasingham Harvey	11	Hudson Whitaker	18
Gray	2	(Daniel) Evans	12	Wm. Green	19
(John) McKenzie	3	Michael Sharp	13	Wm. Little	20
Dell Sapp	4			Benj. Whitaker	21
		1789		Elias. Harvey	22
1788				Jas. Harvey	23
		Wynne	14	Wm. Fussell	24
Wynne	5	Whitaker	15	John Emanuel	25
Woodburn	6	Evans	16		
Reuben Lott	7	Fussell	17	**1793**	
Dell Sapp	8				
(Wm.) Fussell	9	**1792**		John Lasiter 3/	26
(Willis) Watson	10			Bell	27
				Lt. Roberts	28
				Wynne	29

1/See the N.G.S. Quarterly, June 1962, p. 69; and March 1966, pp. 3-54.
2/This convention was called to write a State Constitution, Augusta, Ga.
3/The captains for 15 districts for 1793 were given in March 1966 Quarterly.

Four new districts as listed in the Augusta newspapers, are added below.

Defaulters

Adams, Elcy	28	Dudlass, Robt.	11	Lowe, John		13
Allbritton, Isaac	19	Dunn, John	27	McCalrey, Jas.,		
Allen, David	4	Eaterkin, Wm.	1	heirs of*		6
Anderson, Elisha	13	Elliott, Wm.	13	McCormick, Samuel		28
Aueiau, Nicholas	4	Eubanks, Daniel	22	McKee, Samuel		21
(Cavena-?)		Evans, John	11	McMurray, Wm.		11
Cason, John	19	Fail, Thos.	11	McNiel, James		22
Carpenter, Baily	13	Fields, Jas.	19	Maclimore, Milly		19
Ballard, Edward	20	Finney, John	27	Maitland, Thos.*		2
Barron, Joseph	16	Frederick, Thos.	10	Moon, Arthur		7
Barron, Wm.	5	Martin, Clem	28	Moore, Andrew		13
Bartholomey, John	5	Martin, Oliver	1	Moore, Sam.*4/		26
Bass, Matthews 4/	7,15	Merrell, Arthur	16	Nichols, David		15
Battle, Thos. *4/	2	Grass, Solomon	18	Norrill, Samuel		23
Bigham, Wm.	21	Griffin, James	21	Nounder, Jonas		8
Black, Wm.	17	Guirm, James	2	Odan, Rich.		17
Bonds, Wm.	23	Hallwell, Luther	8	Odom, Elizabeth		13
Booth, Dread.	27	Hamilton, And. 4/	6	Oliver, Thos.		27
Boyd, David	16	Hammock, David	11	Oston, Harris		1
Brantley, James	16	Hammock, old Mrs.	11	Parsons, Jos.		21
Brantly, Jos.	16	Handbury, John	29	Pearson, Wm.		9
Brice, Miles	5	Harrell, Elisha	27	Peoples, Ephraim	5,23	
Carver, Joseph, Sr.	23	Harris, Jas.	1	Peoples, Thos.		13
Carver, Jos., Jr.	23	Harvey, Blas. 5/	11	Permentor, John 4/		8
Carver, Thos.	23	Harvey, Capt.		Phillips, Isom		11
Freeman, John	4	Blasingame	11	Phillips, John		20
Gaines, James	13	Heatherington,		Phillips, Stephen		7
Gates, Samuel	11	Martha	6	Pior, Robert		1
Glass, Wm.	11	Hendrick, Alex.	5	Pitman, Philip		23
Gray, Hezekiah	11	Henery, Chas.	20	Poythress, Thos.		5
Briggs, Samuel	1	Higdon, Robt.	28	Price, Jas.		19
Brinson, Moses	1	Hilliard, Henry	19	Rae, John		11
Brown, Elijah 4/	6	Hillis, Wm.*	12	Rawls, Jas.		5
Bruce, Townley	11	Hinson, Lewis	10	Recdick, Jacob		10
Bruster, Hugh	11	Hobbs, John	11	Recdick, Peter		10
Bryant, Henry	4	Hooker, Elisha	19	Redick, Shadrick		28
Bunt, Stephen	24	Howell, Daniel Sr.	2	Reeves, Benj.		13
Burney, David	11	Howell, Wm.	26	Richards, John Jr.		14
Burney, Richard	11	Huggins, Wm. 4/	5	Roberts, Thos.		23
Buthey, Zachariah	16	Hunter, John	2	Robertson, Moses		23
Canada, John	9	Inman, Joshua	13	Robinson, Archibald	14	
Cannon, Willoughby	7	Richardson, Burrel	7	Rogers, Rich.		28
Cartian, Jas.	16	Richardson, Wm.	18	Sackett, Simon		13
Irby, Edward	7	Roberts, Mary	1	Samfort, Samuel		16
Jenkins, Aquilla		Johnson, James	7	Sapp, Capt. Dell		4
Cavanah	19	Johnston, Bellom	8	Sapp, Doalin		4
Jenkins, Chas.		Johnston, Ramon	19	Sapp, John		4
Cavanah	19	Johnston, Samson	19	Sapp, Levi		8
Cavaritt, Bright	23	Jones, David	18,26	Sapp, Luke		8
Chambers, James	10	Jones, Francis	9	Sapp, Philip 4/		4
Chance, Henry	2	Jones, Jas.	10	Sartin, James		19
Chance, Philemon	2	Jordon, Chas.	21	Scarborough, Wm.		6
Chaplin, Jos.	16	Kelly, Wm., heir		Schley, Rich.		27
Cherry, Nathan*	5	of 4/	6	Shaffer, Henry		22
Chisolm, Thos. 4/	7,13	Keys, Hugh	25	Shelman, John		11
Clyma, Peter	11	Kilpatrick, Partick*	2	Shipard, Andrew		28
Coates, Susannah	13	Lefever, Abraham	23	Shipard, John		28
Comber, John	5	Lassiter, David, Sr.	13	Shorrs, Rich.		11
Corker, John	9	Leveston, Michael	8	Simpson, Eliza		7
Davis, Jos.	3	Liptrot, Bowling	7	Simpson, Elizabeth		
Dean, James	26	Liptrot, Jeptha	19	4/		15
Dennis, Abraham	11	Lodge, Josiah	19	Sneed, Robt.		23
Douglass, James	19	Lott, Arthur	7	Spell, Celia		19
Draighan, Bial	28	Lowe, Edmond	13	Spence, Robt.		23
Dridon, Jesse	18	Lowe, Henry	13	Spight, Jos.		19

2

Spivey, Eliza	7	Thompson, Jas. 4/	6	Wesh, Wm.	11
Stokeley, Peter	5	Tillman, Geo.	1	White, James	13
Stradley, David	19	Tillman, Robt.*	17	Willey, Jas.	19
Stradley, Mi(?)rod	19	Tomlin, Atom	11	Williamson, Jno.	19
Strauder, Rich.	9	Underwood, Sarah	1	Wilson, John	11
Stubbs, James	11	Vickers, Abraham	6	Wilson, Robt.	11
Sumelin, Thos.	16	Vickers, Joshua	11	Womack, Jesse	17
Swain, Stephen	16	Wealch, Joseph	10	Womack, Johnston	13
Taylor, Chas.	10	Wells, Absolem	9	Wynne, John	28
Taylor, Jordan	28	Wells, Julius	5,25	Young, Henry*	7
Thompson, Ann	5	Wells, John	14		

Sheriff and Tax Sales

Bass, Matthew, heirs of; 200 acres Ogeechee Riv. & Buckhead, tax sale, 5/22/1790.

Battle, Thomas; 200 acres, sheriff sale, Oct. 1793.

Brown, Elijah; 100 acres, next John Person & Thos. Beaty, tax sale, May 1790.

Burton, Thomas, decd.; 345 acres, sheriff sale, 7/1/1793.

Caid, John; 2 lives out of state, sheriff sale, 3/21/1790.

Carr, Patrick; 1150 acres, next Jas. Howard, tax sale (1793 taxes), 4/1/1794.

Chisolm, Thomas, decd.; 850 acres, sheriff sale, 8/1/1793.

Edward, Benjamin, decd.; 200 acres, sheriff sale, Oct. 1793.

Elliott, Thomas; 118 acres, tax sale, 1/7/1794.

Green, John; 300 acres, sheriff sale, July 1793.

Hamilton, Andrew; 100 acres, Lambert's Cr., next Jas. Hadden, Wm. Hadden, Math. Moore, 5/22/1790.

Harvey, Blasingame, Jr.; 150 acres, Rocky Comfort Cr., next Blas. Harvey, Sr., Daniel Thomas, sheriff sale, 7/1/1793.

Harvey, James; 400 acres, tax sale, 1/7/1794.

Higgins, William; 100 acres, tax sale, 1/7/1794.

Holmes, David, decd.; 450 acres, sheriff sale, July 1791.

Horn, Henry; 200 acres, tax sale, 1/7/1794.

Hydrick, George; 97 acres, next Philip Lightfoot, sheriff sale, Oct. 1793.

Kelly, William S., Jr., decd., heirs of; 100 acres, Lambert's Big Cr., next Robt. Gordon & Jas. Beaty, tax sale, 5/22/1790.

Kennedy, William; 200 acres, tax sale, 1/7/1794.

Little, Thomas; 200 acres (where he now lives), sheriff sale, 2/6/1794.

McKay, Samuel; town house & lot, Louisville, sheriff sale, Oct. 1793.

Miller, Nathaniel, decd; 450 acres (where Sarah Miller lives), sheriff sale, Oct. 1793.

Moore, Samuel; 200 acres, next Jas. Jones, sheriff sale, Oct. 1793.

Paris, Francis; 3100 acres, saw mill, 10 slaves, sheriff sale, 4/1/1794.

Permenter, John; 100 acres, tax sale, 1/7/1794.

Redding, Wm., decd.; (where John Miller now lives), sheriff sale, 7/2/1793.

Rogers, Peleg; 200 acres, Washington Co., tax sale, 1/7/1794.

Sapp, Philip; 200 acres (where Philip lives), sheriff sale, 2/6/1794.

Sharp, John, Sr.; 1 slave, sheriff sale, 2/6/1794.

Simpson, Elizabeth (or her heirs); 850 acres, Ogeechee Riv. & Buckhead Dr., tax sale, 5/22/1790.

Thomson, James; 100 acres, Rocky Cr., next Thos. Beaty, John Manson & John Bartholomew, tax sale, 5/22/1790.

Wade, Hezekiah; 3 slaves, sheriff sale, 4/1/1794.

Worrel, William's estate; 100 acres between Bryer & McBean Creeks, tax sale, 5/22/1790.

Marriages 5/

4/ See Sheriff and Tax Sales section which follows.

Broome, Capt. John and Miss Precilla Matthews, both of Burke Co., on 2/14/1802.

Bugg, Samuel and Miss Nancy Jones, Burke Co., on 2/26/1807.

Burch, Joel and Keziah Gray, both of Burke Co., on 9/30/1813.

Byne, Enoch (son of Gen. W. Byne) and Miss Mary Hughes (dau. of Capt. Henry Hughes, decd.), on 7/2/1816.

Byne, Miss Mary (dau. of Gen. Byne), Burke Co. and Capt. Peter Lequieux, on 5/15/1817.

Caswell, Alexander and Miss Mary Palmer, on 3/11/1813.

Davis, Col. John, Burke Co. and Miss Maria Ingram, Burke Co., on 6/26/1804.

Davis, Thomas W. of Walburg, Burke Co., and Miss Sarah Ann Jones, Savannah, on 5/19/1819.

Douglass, William and Miss Whitehead, dau. of Amos, on Briar Cr., on 4/11/1787.

Fryer, Zackariah and Miss Sarah Matthews, both of Burke Co., on 1/27/1814.

Gaines, Geo. G., merchant, Savannah, and Miss Peggy Duhart, Burke Co., on 7/15/1800.

Gray, James, St. Geo. Par., and Miss Polly Tobler in Savannah on 4/2/1770.

Gresham, John, Jr., Oglethorpe Co. and Miss Martha Lumpkin, Burke Co., on 7/7/1808.

Henderson, James, Burke Co., and Miss Ann Barbara Vince, Barnwell Co., S. C., on 10/25/1810.

Iverson, Col. Robert, Burke Co. and Miss Margaret J. Harris on 3/27/1808.

Johnson, Elijah, Burke Co. and Miss Sally Collins, Richmond Co. on 11/26/1808.

Johnston, Moses and Miss Nancy Palmer on 11/27/1808.

Knapen, Thomas and Miss Emily Hughes (eldest dau. of Capt. Henry Hughes) on 8/26/1813.

Marbury, William and Miss Mary Anne Armstrong Milton on 5/28/1807.

Navey, Wilson and Mrs. Charlotte Gordon, both of Burke Co. on 7/10/1817.

Neyland, Capt. Gilbert and Mrs. Charlotte S. Gibbons on 6/25/1810.

Shirly, John and Miss Mary Snead, both of Burke Co. on 3/25/1813.

Stone, William, merchant, and Miss Mary Carter (dau. of Isaiah Carter, Waynesboro) on 9/20/1808.

Vining, Ben, Louisville and Miss Polly King, Burke Co. on ?. (L.G. 1/13/1802).

Walker, Capt. Reuben, Richmond Co. and Martha Evans, dau. of Col. Daniel Evans, Burke, on 10/20/1814.

Whitehead, Amos, Waynesboro and Miss Zemala Creswell, dau. of Col. David Creswell, Jackson Co. on 7/23/1812 in Richmond Co.

Whitehead, Amos P. and Miss Elizabeth Walker, dau. of Major Isaac Walker on 8/19/1813.

5/ Abstracted from Marriages and Deaths 1763-1820, by Mary Warren, 1968.

Deaths 6/

Anderson, Mrs. Sarah, age 40, wife of Elisha Anderson, d. 9/3/1805.

Baduly, William, Clerk of Court of Ordinary, Burke Co., d. Waynesborough 2/14/1806.

Bostick, Columbus Washington, 11 mo., son of H. G. Bostick, d. 5/6/1809.

Broadnax, Mrs. Jane, age 39, wife of Dr. Robt. E. Broadnax. d. 10/19/1819.

Bynem, Mrs., wife of Rich. Byne, Burke Co. & dau. of John Gresham, Oglethorpe Co., d. 1/12/1816.

Byne, Rev. Edmund, Rev. soldier, died a few days ago. (AC 2/10/1814).

Byne, Mrs. Martha, wife of Lewis Byne, d. 7/14/1817, leaving 5 children alive, 7 dead.

Byne, Mrs. Milly, age 53, wife of Edward Byne, d. 4/28/1806.

Caldwell, Rev. Ebenezer B., late of Mass., pastor Cong. Church & Rector of Academy, Waynesborough, d. 8/6/1819 at Bath, Richmond Co., leaving wife & infant son.

Carswell, Alexander, age 74, d. 2/11/1808; native of Ireland; in Burke Co. 35 years.

Carswell, Mrs. Sarah, wife of Capt. Carswell, d. 11/12/1808.

Chisolm, Mrs. Mary, wife of Thomas Chisolm, d. ? . (GG. 7/24/1783).

Chisolm, Thomas, late Major, Cont. Line of Ga., d. 10/21/1789.

Cornelius, ----- (Benj.?), postmaster, Burke Co., d. ?. (AC 12/10/1808).

4

Devine, John, age 37, d. 2/7/1812, leaving wife & infant.
Divis, Rev. Benj., d. 10/11/1802, leaving wife & 11 children.
Emanuel, Col. David, age 65, d. 2/19/1808, Rev. Sol. in Ga. Legislature.
Gray, James, age 62, d. at Mt. Hope, Burke Co., 2/20/1804; native Aberdeen, Scotland; member of firm of James & John Gray, merchants, Savannah.
Green, William, member, Executive Council from Burke Co., d. Augusta, 4/18/1787.
Hillyer, Trueman, lawyer, d. 8/29/1802 at Jefferson Baths.
Hughes, Thos. G., age 26, d. 12/4/1814.
Jones, James, lawyer, d. 1/9/1810.
Lark, Dr. Dennis, age 43, d. 12/18/1818.
Leavitt, Mrs. Mary, age 39, wife of Dr. Thomas Leavitt, d. 12/12/1815.
Lewis, Col. Thomas, d. 11/4/1800, Rev. Sol., member Gen. Assembly.
McNorell, Mackay, shot 2/4/1806.
Milton, Fabire Maximus, age 22, son of Col. John Milton, d. 12/27/1813.
Milton, Col. John, age 61, d. 10/19/1817, Rev. Sol., 20 yrs., Secry of State.
Milton, Julius Ceasar, youngest son of Col. John Milton, d. 5/14/1801.
Mitchell, John, d. lately in Burke Co. (GG. 2/12/1801).
Mitchell, William, age 13, son of the late Capt. John Mitchell, d. 4/19/1812.
Morrison, Mrs. Elizabeth, widow of Gen. John Morrison, d. 12/21/1816.
Neyland, Rev. Gilbert, age 41, d. 3/11/1818.
Patterson, Miss Theodore, age 26, d. on Francis Well's plantation, Burke Co., 8/12/1802.
Phillips, Absolem W., age 21, d. 7/26/1818; M.E. circuit preacher.
Pooler, Burke, age 22, d. 5/20/1808.
Royal, William, age 69, d. 3/29/1818.
Shubert, Capt. Frederick, age 34, d. 1/28/1809; b. in Penn.
Shubert, Caroline Jane, dau. of Capt. Fred Shubert, d. 1/29/1801, in Augusta, Ga.
Taylor, James, age 80, b. co. Tyron, Ireland; d. 2/26/1815; leaving widow & 7 children.
Tharpe, Dr. James B., d. 1/6/1801.
Whitehead, Amos, age 68, came from Md.; d. 3/15/1812, leaving widow & 7 children.
Wyche, Robert, age 46, d. 2/6/1815.
Wynn, Augustus E., age 3, only son of Hamilton Wynn, d. 11/15/1806.

Administration of Estates

Butler, Joseph; John Connor, Admin., asked for dismissal, 4/6/1793.
Chisolm, Thomas; Exec. John Milton, Wm. Few, 11/27/1789.
Edwards, Benjamin; Samuel Clarke, Admin., asked for dismissal, 3/9/1793.
Lyon, Henry; Isaac Pollock, Judith Minis, Admin. to sell property, 4/11/1792.
Jones, Philip; Philip Jones, Elizabeth Jones, guardians, to sell property, 10/25/1790.
Jones, William; Wm. Jones, Admin., claimed a slave taken by Tories during Rev. War, 9/5/1791.
NesSmith, James; Mary & Thos. Innes, Admin., 4/23/1788.
Ratclift, Benjamin; Jas. Babcock, Admin., 11/10/1793.
Scott, James; Admins.: Thos. B. Scott, Wilkes Co.; Reuben Coleman, Rich. Co.; Jas. Stubbs, Burke Co., 1/1/1789.
Simms, Thomas; Elizabeth Simms, Admin. to sell 100 acres, 12/20/1792.
Todd, Henry; Admins.: Apphia Todd, Edmund Byne, Isaac Walker, to sell prop., 5/2/1788.
Williams, Susannah; Benj. Greene, Admin., 12/29/1792.

Legal Notices

Grand Jury indictments, October 1786: for being drunk: Thomas Fussell and Col. James McKay; for mal-administration in office - William Sapp, accuser, John Green.

Miscellaneous Items

5

James Gray, decd., bought land from William Rhoads before the Revolution. Has lost the deed, so his Admin. refiled, Feb. 1791.

William Jones claimed that he bought 200 acres on Dry Branch, Ogeechee River from John Smith before the Revolution, but has lost deed. Smith since decd. Apr. 6, 1789.

William Little, Jr., member of Legislature in 1782 and 1787, stated that he had been imprisoned in 1780 by the British in Savannah. (GG. 7/6/1788).

James Oliver advertises that his wife Priscilla had eloped with David Pricehay, 8/31/1787.

John Sharp, Sr., claimed that he had lost a slave, 5/27/1790.

Thomas Wolfington advertises that his wife Eleanor has left him, 5/4/1792.

BURKE COUNTY MILITIA, FEBRUARY 25, 1819

The following rosters of the Burke County, Ga. militia, February 25, 1819, are taken from volume four of "Georiga Military Affairs," a series of WPA, indexed, typescripts at the Georgia Department of Archives and History. The original of the rosters used here could not be located.

Under the Act of December 19, 1818, every ablebodied, white, male citizen and alien in Georgia between the ages of over eighteen and under forty-five was enrolled in the county militia. Officers were elected and sergeants and corporals were appointed or drawn from names placed in a hat. Officers were to wear blue uniforms identical to those of the regular U. S. Army, with whatever special additions their company chose.

The classes described on the following rolls are of no special significance. Classes were simply a means of dividing the militia into thirds so that in an emergency a county's militia could be called out in shifts. No distinction was made with regards to age or military fitness in classes.

For more information on these Burke County men see Robert S. Davis, Jr., The Families of Burke County, 1755-1855, A Census (Southern Historical Press, 1981).

A Muster Roll of the first Class of the 2nd Brigade of the 1st Division Georgia Militia:

1st Company

Capt. John Bell
Lieut. John Davis
Ensign Mathew Dunn

Henry Turner
John Wornock
John Smith
Charles Turner
James Tindal
Nixon Lester
Stephen Brookins
Jonah Aldsy
William Brack
Menches Gray
John Barefield
Jacob Joiner
Abner Stringer
John Wallace
Thos. Joiner
Adam Brinson
Danl. Lester
James Parnell
Henry Parnell
James Edwards
James Anderson
Redding Metts
Solomon Daniel
Smith Stringer
Wm Bonnell

Chas. Bonnell
Rablin Davis
Stephen Floyd
Jas Kimball
Joseph Kimball
William Lewis
Stephen Murray Snr.
David Murray
John Murray
Timothy Murray

7th Regiment
(Burke Co.)

Francis Parris
Stephen Royal
John Rollins
John Sapp Snr.
James Sapp
Wiley Sap
William Thompson
Moses Thompson
Arthur White
Danl Thompson
Joseph Attoway
Robert Dixon
Wm. McNat
Baldy Moore
Harley Attoway
Edward Burch
David Attoway
John Saxon

Mathew Bidgood
Thomas Ward
Isaac Stephens
Abram. Floyd
Henry Bell
John Lugs
Emery Lasiter
Hamilton Wynn
James Russel
Joshua Myrick
Cotton Merrit
Gro. Hener
Edward Rogers
John Allmond
Archd. Warren
Reubin Chance
Joniah Holten
Wm Caldwell
Thos. Syhes
Arthur Bell
John Allen
Isaac Lambert
Robert Skinner
William Bell
Dempsy Bell
Richd. Moore
Randal McDowell
John Tennison
John Elliot
Harvey Andrews
Lewis Coady
Lewis Dunn

John Clarke   86

2nd Company

Capt. Elijah Powell
Lieut. Wm. Gunn
Ensign Jno. Daniel

John Brown
Thos. Sorsbee
Reubin Moore
Spivy Reaves
William Walton
William Haymons
William Jones
Miles Woodard
Robert Fryer
Wm. Hester
Henry McNorrell
James Rees
William Gordon
Jas. Salsbury
John Sykes
Cisas Odam
John Jones
Abrm. Green
Solomon Salsbury
John Davis
Harris Tomlin
Hillory Bostick
Henry Hurst
John Dillard
George Gaugh
James Rowland
Hugh McCan
Moses Johnson
Elija Johnson
Richard Irwin
Benj Dye
Hampton Hudson
Ischabad Ledbetter
Wilson Hester
Eli Hester
Aaron Weaver
Wiley Nilloms
Wm. Greenaway
Wm. Shirley
Jesse Wiggins
Hugh Volletin
Mathew Lively
Zach Wimberly
John Brockston
Reubin Lively
Jno Griffin
William Moors
Benj Mobley
Jacob Ellison
Needham Wimborly
Seth Royal
John Spears
Mathew Goodwin
Job Griffin
John Glisson
Wm Buxton
Alfred Godbee
George Wllison
Stephen Miller
Benj Buxton
John Tatman

John Platt
David Livecord
William Wages
Benj Guest
John Stallings
Michael Mixon
William Coulson
Dempsy Knight
James Cook
Samuel Bugg
James Butler
William Wimpey
Holmes G. Bostick
Geo. W. Pierce
John Gray
Robert Walton
Thomas Tabb
Salta Knight
Levy Crain
William Stewart
Wm. Cox
John Tomlin
Joshua Stephens
David Daniel
Simon Parker
William Bealt

Capt. James Tarrence
Lieut. Benj Seagar
Ensign Malachi Mond

Lewis Byne
George Cogbourne
Elijah Byne
Verity Farmer
Benj Davis
Lewis Emanuel
Benj Smith
Gilbert Neyland
Conway Hughes
Moses Davis
David Lewis, Jr.
John Handberry
Simeon Roberts
Cade Sharp
William Brown
John Kilpatrick
Azariah Dakes
Charles Baxter
Drurey Dukes
Daniel Dukes
Graystock Roberts
John Owens
William Tremble
James Marsh
Berry Hutchins
William Moxley
Rolla Rollins
John Rollins
Charles Coleman
Robert Tremble
James Moxley
James Gordy

========================

8th Regiment
(Burke Co.)

Everet Walton

Arthur Mock
Daniel Moxley
Thomas Hart
Jehu Marsh
Francis Hodges
David -ears
Thomas Justies
Bird Hudson
William West
Elam Young
Archy Bird
Thomas Weekes
Robert Patterson Jr.
Francis Martin
Edward Poyhress
Amos Nichols
Lewis Spence
Thomas Wyche
Jas. Liptrott
Moses Morris
Adam Brinson
William Clifton
Levy Spain
Stephen Smith
Malicha Warren
Benj Sherwood
Wiley Belcher
Jonathan Bass
William Wynne
John Brown
Zach. Cowart
Isaac Wimberly
Levy Cahoon
Danl. White
Jno. Magruder
Miles Adams
John Bass
Ephraim Bass
Silas Scarbrough
Silas Burnet
Jesse Parker
Noah Adams
Isaac Stephens
David Fitzjareld
Elisha Coleman
James Fields
Ezekiel Hull
Jesse Bass
Joel Scarbrough
Thomas Moore
Richard Lane
Thomas Holliday
Jonas Procter
Stephen Harvard
Seth Eson
Wiott Arnold
Jacob Peterson
Elias Nichols
Jesse Danford
Barzilla Pope
Simeon Spain
John Welsh
James Cravy   98

========================

2nd class
1st Company

Capt. William Dewolf
Lieut. Andrew Russel

7

Ensign John Lamb

John Moore
Benj Wornock
William Burke
Absolam Turner
Joshua Gray
Martin Thomas
John Lester
Stephen Brinson
Ezekial Lester
Francis Floyd
Stiving Wallace
William Wallace
Newton Perkins
Bassil Shepherd
John Landing
Thomas Brinson
James Shepherd
William Sapp
David Perkins
William Gilstrap
Samuel Proctor
David Robinson
Thomas Hampton
Henry Chance
James Ratliff
Jesse Chance
Benj Bargeron
Michael Burns
William Boon
William Bryan
Wade Bryan
Elias Daniel

7th Regiment
(Burke Co.)

John Lambert
Robert Lambert
Claudius Lard
Furney Maye
Hardee Parker
Arthur Powell
John Royal
Arthur Royal
Willoughby Mercer
Philip Sapp
*Robert White
Samuel White
George Johnson
James McCroan
Samuel Saxon
A. P. Whitehead
Richd. Rogers
Jacob Bostick
William Davis
William Steptoe
Kindred Pace
Elisha Baker
John Walker
George Tilly
Reddick Ballard
Thomas Bell
Wm. M. Scruggs
Aaron Williams
Robert McNat
William Plythress

Alexander M. Allen
*Edmond Gray
Adam Hener
*John Sapp Junr.
Elija Sapp
*Isaac Holten
Richard Ihley
Fountain Moss
Hazel Wornock
John Wynn
Elija Harrell
Samuel Mattock
Joshua Odam
Delson B. Sapp
*William Lassiter
William Thompson
John Grice
Murrel Finney
William Taylor
Joab. Rowell
Richd. Brack
William Crozier
Joshua Freadwell
John Crozier
Benj Buckley
William Dunkin
Peter Allday
Gideon Odam

=====

2nd Company

Capt. Jeremiah Lewis
Lieut. Charles-Clark
Ensign Peter Lyon

Peter Milton
John Prescot
Jacob Lamb
Anthony Prescot
Samuel Davis
Spencer Kilpatrick
James Tilly
Zach. L. Fryer
James Kirton
John A. Godley
*William Sapp
William Umphreys
Robert Jones
Robert B. Mason
Parks Goodall
Samuel Wilds
Philip M. Cobb
Allen Whittenton
Abner Moore
John Saucer
George Shandler
Zachariah Tomlin
Lewis Powell
Bud Caisey
William White
Jonathan Ashbery
*Amos Wiggins
Philip Dillard
Richard Hines
Robert Palmer
William Mahone
Robert Irwin
David Owens

Jacob Springs
Jesse Waller
Martin M. Dye
James Brown
John Roberts
John Bradshaw
John Shirley
Samuel Taylor
John Knight
Samuel Tarver
James Holland
Samuel Godbe
Abram. Heath
Dennis Glisson
William Royal
John Royal
George Griffin
*Richd. Wiggins
Artemew Powell
George McCoy
Samuel Allegood
Gideon McCail
Samuel Prescot
Daniel Horseford
Henry G. Shields
John McCarrell
Willis Hillis
Emanuel Sheftall
John Buckhalter
Samuel Heath
James Babcock
James Heath
David Platt
James Godbee
Abraham Cook
James Todd
John Price
Lewis Collins
Thomas Hatcher
Ezekiel Rachels
David Hall
Barges Wall
Elijah Hill
Robert Wyche
Gillam Hill
George Martin
Silas Odam
John Moore
David Ward
William Rogers
Charles Ward
James M. Dye
Edward Hatcher
Joseph Daniel
George Mixon

=====

Capt. George Jones
Lieut. Tolliver Dillard
Ensign Job. Gresham

George Byne
David Bedingfield
Moses Walker
Samuel Davis
William Tilly
Isaac Farmer Jr.
David Farmer
Isaac Welsh

8

John Hudson
Isaac Farmer Senr.
Reading D. Bryant
Henry Neyland
Richd. Madray
James Madray
Watkins Hart
John Gregory
Green Dukes
Green Roberts
Turner Dukes
Alexander Sloan
Ben Lindsey
Saml. Jenkins
Jesse Owens
Ralph Penrose
John Liptrott
William Bryant
Allen Page
Solomon Page
Jacob Bryant
Josiah Cornet
Jas. McMullen
Andrew Ronaldson
Robert Jones

8th Regiment
(Burke Co.)

Benj Nixon
Dempsey Barnes
John Finley
Jno. M. Smilie
John Kenedy
Francis Kenedy
Edwd. Ballard Jr.
Thomas Archer
James Nail
Hardy Bedingfield
James Blount
Edward Ballard Snr.
Saml. Patterson
Caleb. Baxley
Richd. Thomas
Jesse Waltom
Hugh Gordon
George Philips
George Gordy
*Danl. Green
Ezekial Inman
John Farnell
Wright Murphree
Harris Johnson
Benj Farnell
Thomas Floyd
John Spence
John Colliday
Jno. Boatwright
Thomas Grubs
Wm. Murphree
William White
Willougby Drew
David Stephens
*Robert Pugh
Eli Bass
Danl. Medows
James Mercer
Kendal Huislip
John Skinner

Danl. McDaniel
Jno. Mulkey
Elias Drake
John Haislip
Isaac Cross
Stephen Hines
Abel Parmer
William Stephens
Jordon Baker
Seth Fields Jr.
Wm. Scarborough
Abram. Belcher
Marcus Stokes
Wm. Barefield
Vincent Barefield
James Ealy
Drury Stokes
Bat. Barnes
Henry J. Jones
Jesse Tilman
Mathew Brinson
Henry P. Jones
Hugh Cravy
Jeremiah Outlaw
Wm. Stancell
Ferney Holliday

===

3rd Class
1st Company

Capt. Thomas Burke
Lieut. Hezekiah Lewis
Ensign Jesse Carpenter

Collin Barefield
John Alday
John Thomas
Jacob Smith
Mathew Lewis
James Smith
Mathew Burke
Joseph Shepherd
Henry Sapp
Sterling Brinson
Abraham Belcher
Robert Wilson Junr.
William Reynolds
William Gray
John Clarke
Samuel Brookins
Jacob Tipton
Joseph Chance
Sterling Jenkins
Andrew Hardrich
Philip Lightfoot
Robert Atkinson
Abishai Jenkins
Philip Hardrich
David Daniel
Arther Bell Junr.
Henry Cravy
Ernst. W. Zyer
John Hannah
Jacob Hollingsworth
Martin Herrington
Charles Kimball
Stephen Murray, Jr.

7th Regiment
(Burke Co.)

Asa Royal
Nathan Rackley
Aley Sapp
Addin Sapp
John Sapp
Isaac Sapp
Aaron Thompson
Jesse White
David Coavy
Arthur Robins
Dempsy Davis
Archd. Bell
Augustin Hewlit
Littleberry Burch
Jesse Johns
Willson Pace
Benj Wyat
Caleb. Taylor
William Douglass
William Attoway
William M. Hobbs
William Saxon
Samuel Garlick
Solomon Ellis
Green Bell
Ferguson Cook
John Banyan
Isaac Tilly
John Rowell
Mathew Bell
Francis Ward Jr.
George Poythress
John Ward
Edward Bird
Charles Scott
Richard Wynn
John Crain
Thomas Red
Thimothy Page
Nathan Bell
Joseph Bell
Laban Odam
Charles Reheyney
Jacob Thompson
Lewis Johnson
Charles Skinner
Wiley Shores
John Taylor
Turner B. Moore
Jordan Taylor
John Boykin
John Treadwell
Thomas Crozier
Samuel Wilds
William Robinson

===

2nd Company

Capt. Wm. Godbee
Lieut. Hardy Hay
Ensign Joseph Shumake

David Hasmer
David G. Salsberry
Charles Jones

9

John Boyt
James Stringer
Aaron Barrow
James Tilly
Josiah Mathews
James Cook
John Catlett
John Thompson
Jas. Speight
James Boyt Snr.
Stephen Boyt
Benjamin Davis
William Cook
James Boyt
Nathanl. Harris
Thomas Saunders
John Fryer
Sumner Sumner
Samuel Williams
Isham Stephens
Elbert Douglass
James Roberts
Enock Womble
Harman Hurst
Saml. Greenaway
Peter Wiggins
Churchwell Hines
*Alexander Carswell
Arther Sykes
James Anderson
William Owens
Bartholomew Springs
Seaborn Collins
Willis Hister
Jared Wright
Eli Holly
Thomas Byne
Risdon Oliver
James Hay
Silas Brockston
John Wimberly
Alexr. Mobley
James Henderson
*Thomas Walls
Charles Granville
Richard Dove
Thos. Scarborough
Hezekiah Wade
Gabriel Clemments
Moses Overstreet
Beniah Nicks
Jeremiah Cuise
Thos. Adkinson
Thomas Francis
Joseph Ellison
Mark Radcliff
Mark Lively
James Clary
Edward Young
William Griffin
William B. Ennis
William Young
Thomas Holiday
Buckner Gray
William Weathers

Thos. H. Jones
Benj Cook
David Green
James Red
Nehemiah Johnson
William Rachels
Joshua Gray
Israel Cook
John Fulcher
Peter Mathews
Edward Tabb
Warren Clark
Richd. Evans Jr.
Midling Hall
John Seagar
John Taylor

=================

Capt. Jonan. Scarborough
Lieut. John Cason
Ensign John Hines

─────────────────

Archd. Baker
Marmaduke Hobby
Warren Welsh
Jno. M. Dye
Edmond Pyor
Jno. McCullers
Reubin Diamond
Needham Bedingfield
Joseph Neyland
James Moore
John Baker
Isaac Dillard
Edmond Madray
George Kirby
Jared E. Bass
Jno. Andleton
John Dukes
Wm. Pugh Snr.
Wm. Roberts
Mark McClammy
Williard Roberts
Jno. Roberts
Doles Dukes
William Rollins
Reubin Marsh
*James McMahon
Wm. Carothers
Eli Gordy
Cader Wyatt
James Marshall
James Hayes
*James McBride
Eli Cornet

─────────────────

8th Regiment
(Burke Co.)

Jno. Moxley
James Beatys Snr.
Thos. Waltom
Jeremiah Kimbel

Henry Bird
Jas. Beaty Jr.
Wm. Nichols
Charles Oats
Redding Pate
James Young
John Dixon
James Butts
John Holliman
James Archer
Duncan Gaines
Rhesy Bostick
Henry Turner, Jr.
Josiah Murphree
Hardy Wooten
Elisha Anderson
William Pugh Jr.
Miles Scarborough
Wm. Metcalf
Archy Mathews
Eli Wooten
Chas. Nichols
Joseph Munroe
Alford Inman
Carolus Anderson
Robert Allen
Lewis Tilman
John Cox
Curtis Cobb
Joab Scarborough
Harmon Stephens
Stephen Monroe
Joshua Johnson
Mathew Albritton
Miles Parker
Levin Collins
William Cahoon
George Bass
Esau Bass
Richd. Sconyers
Henry Gay
Josiah Scutchins
Henry Lynch
Haywood Alford
Danl. King
D. Noals
Lawrence Camp
Wm. Stewart
James Magee
Martin Stokes
Ad. Scarborough
Nathan Vickers
Lewis Heath
Mathew Floyd
John Lane
Harden Brack
Palemon Floyd
Drury Forehand
Anthony Mitcalf
John Floyd
WZT. Floyd

I Do. Certify that the foregoing muster Rolls of the several Classes of
Militia within the Second Brigade of the first Division, are Correct and
true agreabley to the returns made to me ---
J. M. Berrien; 2nd Brigade Georgia Militia

Louisville 25. February 1819

Genl. Bynes Brigade

Muster Roll

Of the 2nd Class from

2nd Brigade 1st

Division Georgia Militia

SOME BURKE COUNTY RESIDENTS IN THE EARLY 1820's

The estate records of Wiley Belcher of Burke County, Ga., were not lost in Burke County's several court house fires. They were spared because they were recorded in Henry County, Ga. The estate sales, held January 23-25, 1821, are recorded in Henry County Inventories and Appraisements (1821-1838), on microfilm reel 8-66 at the Georgia Archives, pp. 1-19. The inventory is in Inventory and Appraisements (1823-1840), pp. 16-19, on the same reel, and the annual returns for 1820-1824 are in Inventories, Appraisements, and Annual Returns (1821-1835), pp. 1-7 and 9-22, on microfilm reel 8-65 at the Georgia Archives. Reproduced below is a list of the names found in these records, some of which appear several times and almost all of which can be found in the Annual Returns. This list forms a sort of mini-census for a section of Burke County for the early 1820's. The administrators of this estate were Martha Belcher (securities John Cock and Warren Green) and Abner Belcher (securities Jesse Cox and Lewellin Spain). The appraisors were John Cock, Daniel Inman, William Murphree, Eleazor Lewis, Mathew Albritton.

James O. Abbott
Noah Adams
Mathew Albritton
H. Alford/Haywood Alfred
Alexander M. Allen
Eason Allen
James Allen
Carolus Anderson
Sherrod Arrington/Arronton
Babcock and Posh
Estate of Doct. Bailey (?)
Holden Barber
Jesse Bass
S. & W. Battey
John Beaty
Abner Belcher
Daniel Belcher
J. Abner Belcher, adm.
Martha Belcher
Phillip Belcher
S. W. Blount
Charles F. Bochrist
Hellory Bostick
William Bostwick
Miller Bradley
Jacob Briant/Bryon
Absalom Bright
Adam Brinson
Miller Broddy
Brooks & Holf
Burrel Brown
Charles Brown
E. B. Browning
Jacob Bryan
Nedham Bryan
Moses Bryant
S. J. & J. J. Bryant
Amos Bullard

Henry Bullard
Camack & Hines
Levi Colhoun/Calhoun
E. H. Callaway
John Campbell
James Chaison
Samuel Clark
John Cock (Cox?) Jr.
Isaac Coleman
Jesse Coleman
Milly Coleman
William Collerson
Patrick P. Connelly
John Cook
Stephen Corker
Stephen Corkins (?)
John W. Coward
Zachariah Coward
Jesse Cox
John Cock/Cox
John Cock Jr.
John R. Daniel
Mary Daniel
William Darden/Durden
John Davenport
Elnathan Davis
Jesse H. Davis
Robert Dellon
Jesse Denson
Stephen Devenport
Elias Drake
Acy Drew
John Dunbar
Henry Durden
Jacob Durdin
Sterling Eason
Miles Fields
Robert Fleming

11

James Floyd
Margaret Floyd
Joseph Floyd
Samuel Garlick
John Gindrat
James Gordeys
Daniel Graves (Greens?)
Benjamin Green Jr., adm.
Warren Green
Francis H. Godfreys
James Grubbs
Ely Gurdys/Gerdy
George Gurdy/Gerdy
Nancy Gurdy/Gerdy
Thomas Gurdy/Thomas Gurdy Sr.
James Hancock
Edward J. Harden
Thomas M. Harden
Blass Harvey
Caleb P. Harvey (?)
Galphin B. Harvey
Edward Hatcher
John Henning
John Herbay
James and Jane Hilliard
Henry Hilliard, excr.
Joseph Hines
Hines & Camack
Joseph Hinson
Abner Holloway
E. H. Holloway
Elizabeth Hutchins
Daniel Inman
Eliza Inman
Robert Jervin
Charloth Johnson
James Johnston (?)
Henry P. Jones
Thomas Jones
William Jones
James Kenyon
Daniel King
J. M. Lambert
Edward Lane
James Leaptrot
John Leaptrot
Media Leaiuve
Benjamin Leggate/Logget
Jordan Legate
Daniel Lemlo (?)
Sion Lennington
John Leaptrot
James Leptrot
Ezekiel Lester
John Lestee/Lester
Eleazer Lewis
John Liptrot
John Lodge
Ruth Lodges
Samuel Loudandale
John Love
Andrew Low & Co.
Simon Lowrey
William Lynches/Linches
Anthony Madcalf
Mahary & Roff
Thomas Mallery
Alexander Mars
Littleberry Marsh
Ennis McDaniel (?)

John McGill
John M. Gruder/Gouder/McGruder
David Memse
Loisesa Miles
John Miller
J. Mills
David Monrow/Monroe
Joseph Monrow
William Murphree
Wright Murphree
John Nayworthy
Frederick Nichere
Malcom Nicholson
Zachariah Noles
John Norworthy
David Oaten
Bryant O'Banion
Jacob Parker
Lewis Parker
Miles Parker
James Patterson
William Patterson
B. G. Paulett
Rebecaah Peacock
John G. Polhill
Est. of Bailey Pro.
Andrew Proudfit
Robert Pugh
Whitson Pugh
Henry Richards
John Richardson
John Roberds/Roberts
Mathew Robertson/Roberson
Charles F. Rochrist/Bochrist
Roff & Mahary
Hudson Rose
William Ross
Reddick Rutland
Nathan T. Sandford
Elizabeth Scarborough
Jonathan Scarborough
William Scarborough
John Schleys
Phillip T. Schley
Josiah Scrutchens/Scratchens
Shefferd & Turner
J. W. L. Simmons
John M. Smiley
Lily Smith
Dudley Sneed
Samuel M. Sneed/Samuel Sneed
Levi Spain
Ledston Spence
Littleton Spence
Bluford Spencer
Greenville Spencer
Littleton (Littleberry?) Spivey
Wm. R. Stancil
James Stephens
Mathew Stephens
William Stephens
James Stephenson
Samuel and N. L. Stingers
James Stores (Steves?)
Thomas Street
Abner Stringer
Turner & Shefferd
E. & J. W. Vanhookis
Arthur Vickers
Frederick Vickers

Nathan Vickers
Low Wallace
Henry Wamble
J. R. Warren/Warner
William Whigham
Mrs. Constance White
Daniel White
Henry White (?)

William White
Henry Whitson
William (?) Whitson
T. H. (F.H.?) Williams
F. H. Wilman
Mrs. Casey Wimberly
Barnes Woodard
Joshua Woodard

WAR OF 1812 ROSTERS
BURKE COUNTY, GEORGIA

Georgia Militia Rosters, War of 1812, Record Group 94, National Archives, Washington, D. C.

The following rosters were selected from the above collection because they are known to have contained the names of at least some Burke County soldiers. The rosters also include the names of militiamen from Jefferson and probably other nearby counties. The following are all taken from muster rolls although pay rolls and contemporary copies of these same muster rolls were also found in this collection, for exactly the same period.

The author would like to express his thanks to Captain Gordon B. Smith of Savannah for identifying the Burke County rolls for this project.

A Roll of a Company of Georgia Volunteers under the Command of Captain R.L. Gamble in the service of the United States Commanded by Major Robert Bowling from the 24th Day of March 1814 the time when first Mustered.

NAMES	RANK	DATE VOLUNTEERING	TO WHAT TIME ENGAGED	REMARKS
1. R.L. Gamble	Capt.	26 March 1814	26 Sept. 1814	

1. Benamud Bower	1st Lieut.
1. Micl Burke	2nd Lieut.
1. John Gamble	3rd Lieut.
1. John Chambers	Ensign
1. Micl. Lamp	1st Sgt.
1. Isaac Welch	2nd Sgt.
1. John Laidler	3rd Sgt.
1. John Rutledge	4th Sgt.
1. Lewis Lamp	1st Corp.
1. Thomas Grant	2nd Corp.
1. Redding D. Bryant	3rd Corp.
1. Wm. Baggs	4th Corp.
1. John Bothwell	Private
2. John W. Bothwell	
3. John R. Cook	
4. Robinson Askew	
5. Tandy Jones	
6. Samuel Pomroy	
7. Chars. Ferrell	
8. Jno. Brackett	
9. Uriah Pipkin	
10. Jno. Arrington	
11. Saml. Walden	
12. John Baggs	
13. Daniel Smith	
14. William Wren	
15. Wm. Streetman	
16. Jno. Kelly	
17. John Johnston	
18. Readon Colie	
19. Wm. Arrington	

20. Wm. Evans
21. Norris Smith
22. John Olief
23. Laird B. Fleming
24. John Caulir
25. Saml. Ford
26. James Hayley
27. Benjn. Olief
28. Stephn. Overstreet
29. Jackson Scarbro
30. Jno. Mason
31. Wm. Ross
32. John Mitchell
33. Faney Deal
34. James Cobb
35. David Jordon
36. Nathn. Rowland
37. Aaron Gardner
38. Joseph Miller
39. Wiley Godding
40. Chars. French
41. Stephen Godden
42. Saml. Gregory
43. Moses Herrington
44. Wm. Cato
45. Adm. Lamb (Redding Metts
    subs. for Abm. Lamb)
46. Wm. Lankford
47. Moses Davis
48. Zachr. Noles
49. Theophilus Gains
50. Danl. Walton
51. Danl. Umphreys
52. John Spence
53. John Coliday
54. John Bird

55. Jas. Bird (Rejected in consequence
    of a sore leg)
56. Joseph Floyd
57. John Gooding
58. Dd. Bryant
59. Levy Glass
60. Benjn. Stephens
61. Isaac Spence
62. Moses Morris
63. Jas. Carvy
64. Jno. Handbury
65. Nimrod Lewis
66. Henry Wester
67. McCullars Kirkling
68. John Coleman
69. Isaac Coleman
70. Robert Frence
71. John Cunningham
72. Rease French (Turned over to Capt.
    Cone by order of Major Bowling)
73. James Maddrey.

I have inspected and organized the
number of men of which has rendez-
voused agreeabley to an order from
His Excellency Governor Early upon
the requisition of General Pinckney
into such parts as seem best, but for
the want of men I could not organize
them agreeably to the Regulations of
the Army.

/s/ Robert Bowling
Major Commanding
Detachment of Georgia
Militia.

Georgia Militia Rosters, War of 1812, Including some Burke County Troops.
Record Group 94, National Archives, Washington, D. C.

Muster Roll of a Company of Volunteer Georgia Militia under the Command
of Capt. Roger L. Gamble Commanded by Major Robert Bowling from the 26th
March the time when first mustered to 31st May 1814.

NAMES	RANK	DATE OF VOLUNTEERING	TO WHAT TIME ENGAGED	REMARKS
1. Roger L. Gamble	Captain	26th Mar.1814	26th Sept.1814	
2. Benamund Bower	1st Lieut.	"	"	
3. Michl. Burke	2nd Lieut.	"	"	Promoted from an Ensign 14 Apr.1814
4. John Gamble	3rd Lieut.	"	"	Prom. from private 11th Apr. 1814
5. John Chambers	Ensign	"	"	Prom. from Sgt. 11 Apr. 1814 on Command at Camp Pinckney
1. Isaac Welch	1st Sergt.	"	"	Prom. from Private 12 Apr. 1814
2. Michl Lamb	2nd Sergt.	"	"	
3. John Ladler	3rd Sergt.	"	"	Prom. from Pvt. 7 Apr. 1814 - sick

14

NAMES	RANK	DATES OF VOLUNTEERING	TO WHAT TIME ENGAGED	REMARKS
4. John Rutledge	4th Sgt.	"	"	Prom. from Pvt. 6th Apr. 1814
1. Lewis Lamp	1st Corpl.	"	"	
2. Thomas Grant	2nd Corpl.	"	"	
3. Redding Bryant	3rd Corpl.	"	"	Prom. from Pvt. 6th Apr. 1814
4. Wm. Baggs	4th Corpl.	"	"	Prom. from Pvt. 6th Apr. 1814
1. Askew Robinson	Private	"	"	In confine-ment
2. Arrington, William	"	"	"	
3. Arrington, John	"	"	"	In confine-ment
4. Bracket, John	"	"	"	In Confine-ment
5. Bird, John	"	"	"	Sick
6. Baggs, John	"	"	"	
7. Bayley, James	"	"	"	
8. Bothwell, John	"	"	"	On command Camp Pinckney
9. Bryant, David	"	"	"	On command Camp Pinckney
10. Caulie, Reason	"	"	"	
11. Caulie, John	"	"	"	In confine-ment
12. Cato, William	"	"	"	On command Camp Pinckney
13. Coleman, John	"	"	"	In Confine-ment
14. Coleman, Wade	"	"	"	"
15. Cobb, James	"	"	"	"
16. Colliday, John	"	"	"	
17. Cook, John	"	"	"	
18. Davis, Moses	"	"	"	Sick
19. Deal, Ferney	"	"	"	In confine-ment
20. Evins, William	"	"	"	Waiting on sick
21. Ford, Samuel	"	"	"	
22. Floyd, Joseph	"	"	"	Sick & in con-finement
23. French, Robert	"	"	"	In confine-ment
24. French, Charles	"	"	"	"
25. French, Rease	"	"	"	"
26. Fleming, L.B.	"	"	"	"
27. Ferrel, Charles	"	"	"	
28. Gregnorey, Saml.	"	"	"	On command at Camp Pinckney
29. Gains, Theophilus	"	"	"	In confine-ment
30. Glass, Levy	"	"	"	
31. Gardner, Aaron	"	"	"	
32. Goding, Wiley	"	"	"	
33. Goding, Stephen	"	"	"	Unfit for service
34. Gooding, John	"	"	"	
35. Herrington, Moses	"	"	"	On command at Camp Pinckney
36. Hanberry, John	"	"	"	
37. Johnston, Jared	"	"	"	In confine-ment
38. Jones, Tandy C.	"	"	"	
39. Johnston, John	"	"	"	"

NAMES	RANK	DATES OF VOLUNTEERING	TO WHAT TIME ENGAGED	REMARKS
40. Jordan, David	"	"	"	
41. Kelly, John	"	"	"	Sick
42. Lewis, Nemrod	"	"	"	
43. Lankford, Wm.	"	"	"	In confinement
44. Mettz, Redding	"	"	"	
45. Madry, James	"	"	"	Sick
46. Mason, John	"	"	"	
47. Mitchell, John	"	"	"	Sick
48. Mallory, Thomas	"	"	"	On command at Camp Pinckney
49. Mallory, James	"	"	"	"
50. Miller, Joseph	"	"	"	"
51. Morris, Moses	"	"	"	"
52. Overstreet, Stephn.	"	"	"	
53. Olief, John	"	"	"	
54. Olief, Benjamin	"	"	"	
55. Pipkin, Uriah	"	"	"	
56. Pomroy, Samuel	"	"	"	
57. Ross, William	"	"	"	In Confinement
58. Rowland, Nathan	"	"	"	Sick
59. Stephens, Benjamin	"	"	"	Sick
60. Spence, Isaac	"	"	"	Sick
61. Spence, John	"	"	"	
62. Smith, Daniel	"	"	"	In confinement
63. Smith, Norris	"	"	"	Sick
64. Scarborough, Jackson	"	"	"	In confinement
65. Streetman, Wm.	"	"	"	On command at Camp Pinckney
66. Umphries, Danl.	"	"	"	
67. Walton, Danl.	"	"	"	
68. Wester, Henry	"	"	"	
69. Wren, William	"	"	"	On command at Camp Pinckney
70. Walding, Saml.	"	"	"	"

I do certify on honour that the within Muster Roll exhibits a true and correct statement of the volunteer company under my command as is taken this 31 May 1814.

/s/ Roger L. Gamble
Capt. V.G.M.

We certify upon honour that the within muster roll exhibits a true and correct statement of Captain Gamble's Company of Georgia Volunteers and the remarks set opposite the men's names are accurate and just as mustered by me at Camp Point Petre this 31st May 1814.

/s/ Chisolm Cap.
8 Infy. Comdy.
Charles Lewis
Regimt S.M. 8 Infy.

Muster Roll of a Company of Volunteer Georgia Militia under the Command of Captain Roger L. Gamble Commanded by Major Robert Bowling from the 31st May to the 31st July 1814.
(Only information not found on the previous roll is included below. All other information on this roll is omitted by the editor to save space.)

Michl Burke	2nt Lieut.	On Command at Camp Pinckney
John Gamble	3rd Lieut.	Deceased on the 21st July 1814*
Wm. Baggs	4th Corpl.	In Confinement
Wilson Curl	Private	Sick substituted for Nathan Rowland
William Cato	Private	Deserted on the 1st of June 1814
Laird B. Fleming	Private	

16

Wiley Goden	Private	
Stephen Goden	Private	Unfit for service
Aaron Gardener	Private	On Command at Camp Pinckney
John Gooden	Private	On Command at Camp Pinckney
Saml. Gregeorey	Private	Deserted on the 1st of June 1814
Danl. Humphrey	Private	
John Jordan	Private	Substitute for Reason Caulie
James Nobles	Private	Substitute for Henry Wester
Daniel Smith	Private	Sick
Samuel Wester	Private	On Command at Camp Pinckney

Officers Private Waiters
Parris and Hannibel

I do certify on honour that the within muster Roll exhibits a true and correct statement of the Volunteer Company Under my Command as is taken this 31 July, 1814.

/s/ Benj. Bowers 1st Lieut.
U. S. Quoto G M

We Certify upon honour that the within muster Roll exhibits a true and correct Statement of Captain Gambles Company of Georgia Volunteers and the remarks set opposite the men's names are accurate & just as mustered by us at Camp Point Petre 31st July 1814

/s/ Roger L. Gamble Capt.
U S Q G M Commanding
T M Rallenden Ast. Surys MF ?

*NOTE: John Gamble, previous page - On a duplicate roll the date is given as 21 June 1814. However, on the payrolls the date is also shown as 21 July 1814.

Muster Roll of Captain R.L. Gambles Company of Infantry belonging to a detachment of Militia of the State of Georgia in the Service of the United States Commanded by Major Robert Bowling from the 31st of July when last mustered to the 12th of September 1814.

(Only information not found on the preceeding rolls is included in the following. All other information is omitted to avoid repitition.)

Wm. Cato	Private	A Deserter who surrendered on the 20th August 1814
Saml. Gregory	Private	A Deserter who surrendered on the 20th August 1814
John Johnston	Private	Sick
Wm. Lankford	Private	Died on the 5th September 1814
John Madry	Private	Died on the 10th September 1814
Saml. Pomeroy	Private	On Command at Camp Pinckney
Norris Smith	Private	Sick

I Certify on honor the above muster roll exhibits the true state of the Company under my command and that the remarks set opposite the mens names are accurate and just.

/s/ Roger L. Gamble Capt. U.S.M.
Commanding Company

I certify on honor the above muster roll exhibits a true statement of Captain R.L. Gambles Company of Georgia Militia in the service of the United States as Mustered by me this 12th day of Sept. 1814.

/s/ M.G. Waage
Asst. Insp. Genl.

Muster Roll of Capt. Roger L. Gambles Company of Infantry belonging to a detachment of Militia in the State of Georgia in the Service of the United States Commanded by Major Robert Bowling from the 12th September when mustered last to the 26th September 1814.

(Only information not found on the preceeding rolls is included in the following abstracts. All other information has been omitted by the editor).

Ben Bower	1st Lieut.	Sick
John R. Cook	Private	Sick
Samuel Gregory	Private	Sick
Robert French	Private	Sick
John Jordon	Private	Sick
Daniel Smith	Private	Dead - Deceased the 24th Sept.1814

I do certify on honor that the above muster roll exhibits a true statement of the company under my command and that the remarks set opposite
their names are just and true.

/s/ Roger L. Gamble Capt.
Georgia Militia Comdy. Compy.

We certify on honor that the above muster roll exhibits a true statement
of Capt. R.L. Gamble's Company of Georgia Militia in the service of the
United States as mustered by us this 25th day September 1814 at Point
Petre Georgia.

/s/ Art Majors Capt.
1st Rifle Regt.
Comm.

Muster Roll of Field and Staff officers of Volunteer Militia of the
State of Georgia in the Service of the United States from the Commencement of Service to the 25th September 1814.

NAME	RANK	COME. OF SERV.	FOR THE TIME ENGAGED	NAMES PRESENT
Robert Bowling	Major	26 Mar.1814	6 months	Robert Bowling
Elias		REMARKS: Servant of Major Bowling		

I Certify on honour the above Muster roll Exhibits The true State of the
Staff Officers of a detachment of Georgia Militia under my Command and
Remarks set oposit the names are accurate and just.

/s/ Robert Bowling
Majr. Commd. detachment

I Certify on honour that the above Muster Roll exhibits a true Statement
of the Field and Staff officers of a Detachment of Georgia Militia Under
the Command of Major Bowling As Mustered by me this 25th of September
1814 at Fort Jackson Georgia.

/s/ M.G. Waage
Asst. Insp. Genl.

Muster Roll of Lieut Cones Company militia in the Service of the U.
States Commanded by Major R. Bowling the 26th March (1814).

NAMES	RANK	TIME OF ENTERING SERV.	FOR WHAT TIME ENGAGED	REMARKS
1. Peter Cone	1st Lieut.	March 26th	6 months	
2. John Rawls	2nd Lieut.	"	"	
3. Thos. Hall	3rd Lieut.	"	"	
4. Cuyler Lovet	Ensign	"	"	
5. Joseph Hagan	Srgts.	"	"	
6. James G. Conner	"	"	"	
7. Thos. Stanly	"	"	"	
8. H. H. Hand	"	"	"	
9. Wm. Burns		"	"	
10. Henry Goodman	Corporal	"	"	
11. Alexr. Stewart	"	"	"	
12. James Scott	"	"	"	
13. Jos. Hitchcock	"	"	"	
14. Seaborn Miller	Private	"	"	
15. Wm. Fisher	"	"	"	
16. Henry Cook	"	"	"	

18

NAME	RANK	TIME OF ENTERING SERV.	FOR WHAT TIME ENGAGED	REMARKS
17. Moses Wright	Private	March 26th	6 months	
18. Moses Sugs	"	"	"	
19. Wm. Carne	"	"	"	
20. Joseph Rawls	"	"	"	
21. John Scott	"	"	"	
22. John Coward	"	"	"	
23. John Roberts	"	"	"	
24. James Pye	"	"	"	
25. Amos Emanuel	"	"	"	
26. William Pierce	"	"	"	
27. John Hendrix	"	"	"	
28. Mikel Gaines	"	"	"	
29. Samuel Craps	"	"	"	
30. Lewis Green	"	"	"	
31. Elisha Stringfield	"	"	"	
32. Wilson King	"	"	"	
33. Wm. House	"	"	"	Unfit for Service
34. Daniel Green	"	"	"	
35. David Sumeral	"	"	"	"
36. Simeon Driggers	"	"	"	
37. Rash Cobb	"	"	"	
38. John Williams	"	"	"	
39. Jacob Bess	"	"	"	
40. Wm. Bess	"	"	"	
41. Jacob Carter	"	"	"	
42. Dred Newborn	"	"	"	
43. Elisha Green	"	"	"	
44. Redick Thornton	"	"	"	
45. James Wilkinson	"	"	"	
46. William Whiddon	"	"	"	
47. Solomon Hiers	"	"	"	
48. Elias Johnson	"	"	"	
James Bennet	"	"	"	
49. Wm. Waters	"	"	"	
50. Wm. Shepherd	"	"	"	
51. Kirkland McCullers	"	"	"	
52. Robert Cotheron	"	"	"	

I do Certify on Honor that the foregoing muster Roll & recapitulation
Exhibits a true Statement of a Company of Militia and my Command the
26th March 1814.

/s/ P. Cone Lieut.

Muster Roll of Lieut Cones Detachment of Volunteer Militia Infantry of
the State of Georgia belonging to a detachment under the Command of
Major Robert Bowling in the Service of the US from the commencement of
their service to the 25th of Sept. 1814.

(Only information not found on the preceeding roll is included below.)

Peter Cone	1st Lieut.	Sick at Sunbury Georgia
Thos. C. Lovett	Ensign	Commissioned in 8th Regt. US Infantry 4th of June
John Waldron	Sergeant	Promoted on the 2nd July 1814; Sick at Savannah
Elexander Stewart	Corporal	Sick at Sunbury
John B. Sheppard	Musician	Sick at Savannah Reported
William Sheppard	Musician	Musician 13 May 1814; sick at Sunbury
Jacob Best	Private	Nursing the sick at Sunbury
William Best	Private	Sick at Sunbury
Jacob Carter	Private	Sick at Sunbury
William Conner	Private	Sick at Savannah
Samuel Craps	Private	Sick at Savannah
Lewis Green	Private	Sick at Savannah
Henry Goodman	Private	Reduced to private 8th August 1814

John Hendrix	Private	Sick at Savannah	
H. Henry Hand	Private	Sick on furlough, failed to arrive July 2nd 1814	
Solomon Hiers	Private	Sick at Savannah	
William House	Private	Sick at Savannah	
Michael James	Private	Sick at Savannah	
Wilson King	Private	Sick at Savannah	
Seaborn Miller	Private	Sick at Savannah	
Dred Newbern	Private	Sick at Savannah	
William Pierce	Private	Sick at Savannah	
Robert Scott	Private	Also shown on this roll & the pre-previous roll as John Scott	
William Watters	Private	Sick at Savannah	
James Wilkerson	Private	Sick at Savannah	
William Whidden	Private	Attending the Sick at Sunbury	

I do Certify on honor that the above Muster Roll exhibits a true Statement of the detachment under my Command and that the remarks set opposite
the names are accurate and Just.

/s/ John Rawls Lieut Commanding detach.

I do Certify, on honor that the above Muster Roll exhibits a true statement of Lieut. Cones detachment of Volunteer militia Infantry of the
State of Georgia in the Service of the U. States as mustered by me this
25th Sept. 1814 at Fort Jackson near Savannah.

/s/ M.G. Wagge
Asst. Inspr. Genl.

Muster Roll of Captain David Clarkes Company of Georgia Artillery in the
Service of the United States at Fort Jackson the 25th of March when first
Mustered.

NAMES	RANK	COMMENCEMENT SERVICE	TO WHAT TIME ENGAGED	REMARKS
1. David Clarke	Capt.	26 Mar.1814	25 Sept.1814	
2. Alexander Meriwether	1st Lieut.	"	"	
3. Leon H. Marks	2nd Lieut.	"	"	On Command as adjuct-ant
4. James Clarke	3rd Lt.	"	"	
1. Michael Schley	1st Sgt.	"	"	
2. Alexr. G. Raiford	2nd Sgt.	"	"	
3. Etheldred Moore	3rd Sgt.	"	"	
4. Phenias Coyne	4th Sgt.	"	"	
5. William Shirley	5th Sgt.	"	"	
1. James Gordon	1st Corp.	"	"	
2. James Bigham	2nd Corp.	"	"	
3. Seth S. Langston	3rd Corp.	"	"	
4. Littleton Spivy	4th Corp.	"	"	
1. Edward T. Satter	Artificer	"	"	
2. James Sample	"	"	"	
3. Jacob McCollough	"	"	"	
4. Andrew Crosby	"	"	"	
5. Caswell Moore	"	"	"	
6. Josep Kirk	"	"	"	
7. Josep Darny	"	"	"	
8. John Woods	"	"	"	
1. William Starling	Fifer	"	"	
2. Thomas Hendley	"	"	"	
1. Dennis Goodman	Private	"	"	
2. Abram Robinson	"	"	"	Sick at Louisville
3. Jed Hilton	"	"	"	
4. Willie Webb	"	"	"	
5. Aldridge Moore	"	"	"	
6. John Ford	"	"	"	
7. Shadi Fokes	"	"	"	
8. Allen Coursey	"	"	"	

NAMES	RANK	COMMENCEMENT SERVICE	TO WHAT TIME ENGAGED	REMARKS
9. William Woods	Private	26 Mar.1814	25 Sept.1814	
10. John Trimble	"	"	"	Officers cook
11. John Trimble	"	"	"	
12. Danl. Hammond	"	"	"	
13. William Sample	"	"	"	
14. Isaac Mathers	"	"	"	
15. Miles Fields	"	"	"	
16. Aaug. Moore	"	"	"	
17. John Drew	"	"	"	
18. Reddick Scarber	"	"	"	
19. James Kemp	"	"	"	
20. David Mimms	"	"	"	
21. William White	"	"	"	
22. John Hall	"	"	"	
23. Reuben Boatright	"	"	"	
24. Jesse Riggs	"	"	"	
25. Josiah Register	"	"	"	
26. Starling Parker	"	"	"	
27. Asa Baker	"	"	"	
28. Levi Lee	"	"	"	
29. John Marshall	"	"	"	
30. William Deloach	"	"	"	
31. William Morrison	"	"	"	
32. Jesse Owens	"	"	"	
33. Lewis Tyre	"	"	"	
34. Joseph Davis	"	"	"	
35. John Birch	"	"	"	Sick in Bulloch Co.
36. Stephen Boyd	"	"	"	
37. William Stone	"	"	"	
38. James Drawdy	"	"	"	
39. Benniah Boyd	"	"	"	
40. James Boyd	"	"	"	
41. Aaron Haw	"	"	"	
42. William Bragg	"	"	"	
43. John Tyre	"	"	"	
44. Joseph Sasson	"	"	"	
45. John Olive	"	"	"	
46. John Jeffers	"	"	"	
47. Isaac Conner	"	"	"	
48. Charles Butler	"	"	"	
49. David Reddy	"	"	"	
50. George Waters	"	"	"	
51. William Vickery	"	"	"	
52. Robert Long	"	"	"	
53. William Donaldson	"	"	"	
54. David Wilde	"	"	"	
55. J. M. Norman	"	"	"	
56. A. B. Norman	"	"	"	
57. Isaac Simonson	"	"	"	
58. Robert Raiford	"	"	"	Absent with leave
59. William Patterson	"	"	"	

I do Certify on honor that the within muster roll and foregoing recapitulation exhibits a true and correct statement of the Company under my
Command, and that the remarks sit oppoiste the mens names are correct to
the best of my knowledge.

/s/ Dd. Clarke Capt.
Geo. art. In U.S. service
at Fort Jackson

Muster Roll of Captain David Clarke's Company of Georgia Artillery in
the Service of the United States Stationed at Fort Jackson from the 26th
day of March 1814 when last Mustered to the 30th June 1814.

NAMES	RANK	COMMENCEMENT OF SERVICE	TO WHAT TIME ENGAGED	REMARKS
1. David Clarke	Capt.	26 Mar. 1814	26 Sep.1814	
2. A. Meriwether	1st Lt.	"	"	
3. Leon H. Marks	2nd Lt.	"	"	
4. James Clarke	3rd Lt.	"	"	
Michael Schley	1st Sergt	"	"	Substituted by E. Moy 26th May
1. Alexr. G. Raiford	2d Sergt	"	"	Promoted to 1st Sgt.
2. Ethelred Moore	3rd Sergt	"	"	Promoted to 2nd Sergt
Phenias Coyne	4th Sergt	"	"	Reduced to the line /?/ 1st June
3. William S. Sherley	5th Sergt.	"	"	Promoted
1. James Gordon	1st (Corp?)	"	"	Prom.to Sgt. 26 May 1814
2. James Begham	2nd Corp.	"	"	Prom.to 1st Corporal
3. Seth S. Langston	3rd Corp.	"	"	Prom. to 2nd Corporal
4. Littleton Spivy	4th Corp.	"	"	Prom. to 3rd Corp. On furlough
1. E.T. Salter	Artla	"	"	
2. James Sample	"	"	"	
3. Jacob McCulloigh	"	"	"	Reduced to lines 26 May
4. Andrew Crossby	"	"	"	
5. Caswell Moore	"	"	"	
6. Joseph Kirk	"	"	"	
7. Joseph Darsey	"	"	"	
8. John Woods	"	"	"	
1. William Starling	Musn.	"	"	
2. Thomas Hendley	"	"	"	
1. Dennis Goldware	Private	"	"	
2. Abram Robinson	"	"	"	Substituted by Zach Noles 1st May
2. Jeremiah Hilton	"	"	"	
3. Willie Webb	"	"	"	
4. Aldridge Moore	"	"	"	
5. John Ford	"	"	"	
6. Shadi Folkes	"	"	"	
7. Allen Causey	"	"	"	
8. William Woods	"	"	"	
9. John McNelly	"	"	"	
10. John Trimble	"	"	"	
11. Daniel Hammond	"	"	"	
12. William Sample	"	"	"	
13. Isaac Mathirs	"	"	"	
14. Miles Fields	"	"	"	
15. Augustus Moore	"	"	"	
16. John Duce	"	"	"	
Reddick Scarber	"	"	"	Substituted by Owen Sanderlin June 1st
17. James Kemp	"	"	"	
18. David Mims	"	"	"	
19. William White	"	"	"	Sick in Hospital
20. John Hall	"	"	"	
21. Jesse Heggs	"	"	"	
Reubin Boatright	"	"	"	Substituted by Saml. Stone 1 May

NAMES	RANK	COMMENCEMENT OF SERVICE	TO WHAT TIME ENGAGED	REMARKS
22. Josiah Register	Private	26 Mar.1814	26 Sept.1814	
23. Starling Parker	"	"	"	
24. Asa Baker	"	"	"	Sick in Hospital
25. Levi Lee	"	"	"	
26. John Marshall	"	"	"	Appointed artifr. 26th May
27. William Deloach	"	"	"	
28. William Morrison	"	"	"	
29. Jesse Owens	"	"	"	
30. Lewis Tyre	"	"	"	
31. John Bert	"	"	"	
32. William Stone	"	"	"	
Stephen Boyd	"	"	"	Substituted by George Spires 1 May
James Deawday	"	"	"	Substituted by Henry Stone 1 May
33. Baniah Boyd	"	"	"	
34. James Boyt	"	"	"	
Aaron Haw (Ham?)	"	"	"	Substituted by C.S.Dokes (Cokes?)
William Bragg	"	"	"	Substituted by William Goodman
35. John Tyre	"	"	"	
36. Joseph Sasser	"	"	"	
Joseph Oliver	"	"	"	Substituted by Samuel Bandy
37. John Jeffers	"	"	"	
38. Isaac Conner	"	"	"	
39. Charles Butler	"	"	"	
40. George Waters	"	"	"	
41. William Pickery (Vickery?)	"	"	"	Sick in Hospital
42. Robert Lang	"	"	"	
43. William Donaldson	"	"	"	
44. David Wilde	"	"	"	
45. James M. Norman	"	"	"	
46. A.B. Norman	"	"	"	
47. Isaac Simonson	"	"	"	Deserted
48. James Norris	"	"	"	Substitute for Robt. Raiford
49. David Boles	"	"	"	Substitute for Wm. Patterson
50. David Reddy	"	"	"	
51. Joseph Davis	"	"	"	Sick in Hospital
52. Thomas Berryhill	"	"	"	
53. Samuel Randy	"	"	"	Substitute for John Oliver
54. William Goodman	"	"	"	Substitute for Wm.Bragg; sick in hosp.
55. Campbell S. Dokes	"	"	"	Substitute for Aaron Haw
56. Henry Stone	"	"	"	Substitute for Jas. Drawdy

23

NAMES	RANK	COMMENCEMENT OF SERVICE	TO WHAT TIME ENGAGED	REMARKS
57. George Spires	Private	26 Mar.1814	25 Sept.1814	Substitute for Stephen Boyd
58. Samuel	"	"	"	Substitute for Reuben Botright
59. Owen Sanderlin	"	"	"	Substitute for Reddick Sarborough
60. Zach Noles	"	"	"	Substitute for Abram Robinson
61. Phenias Coyne	"	"	"	Reduced 1st June 3rd Sep.
62. Edwin Moy	"	"	"	Substitute for M.Schley
63. Jacob McCullogh	"	"	"	Reduced 20 May 1814
1. June	Waiter	1st Apr.1814	"	To Captain
2. Lettuce	"	"	"	To three sublaterns

I certify on honour that the within Muster Roll and foregoing Recapitulation exhibits a true and correct statement of the Company under my
Command and that the remarks set opposite the Mens names are accurate
and Just.

/s/ Dd. Clarke
Capt. of Arty U.S. Quota
Commdg. Fort Jackson

We Certify on honor that the above Muster Roll exhibits a true statement of Captain David Clarkes Company of Georgia Artillery as Mustered
by us this 30th day of June 1814.

/s/ Art. Massee /?/ Capt.
1 Rifle Regmt. Commd.
U.S. Troops Savannah

Muster Roll of Captain David Clarkes Company of Volunteer Militia Lt.
Artillery of the State of Georgia in the Service of the United States
from the 30th June when last Mustered to the 7th Day of September 1814.

(Note: Only information not found on the previous roll is abstracted and
included here.)

Leon H. Marks	2nd Lieut.	Conductor of artillery appd. June 12th 1814, by general or-der
James Clarke	3rd Lieut.	Sick absent
Alexander G. Raiford	1st Sergt.	
Ethelred Moore	2nd Sergt.	Sick
William S. Sherley	3rd Sergt.	Sick
James Gordon	4th Sergt.	
Seth S. Langston	5th Sergt.	Promoted from Corpl. 7th July 1814
Littleton Spivy	1st Corpl.	
James Begham	2nd Corp.	Sick in Hospital
Shadrick Fokes	3rd Corpl.	Promoted 1st July 1814
Miles Fields	4th Corpl.	Promoted 1st July 1814
E. T. Salter	Artil.	Sick
Joseph Darsey	Artil.	Sick in Hospital
William Starling	Musc.	Sick in Hospital
Thomas Handley	Musc.	Sick in Hospital
Joseph Sasser	Musc.	
Baker, Asa	Private	Sick in Hospital
Birt, John	Private	Sick
Boyd, Bania	Private	Sick; absent

24

```
Butler, Charles          Private          Sick in Hospital
Boles, David             Private          Sick
Coyne, Phenias           Private          Sick
Conner, Isaac            Private          Sick in Hospital
Deloach, William         Private          Sick; absent
Dokes, Campbell S.       Private          Sick in Hospital
Lee, Levi                Private          Sick in Hospital
Moore, Aldridge          Private          Sick
Moyne, Edwin             Private          Commenced Service 26 May 1814
Parker, Starling         Private          Sick in Hospital
Register, Josiah         Private          Sick in Hospital
Reddy, David             Private          Sick in Hospital
Stone, Henry             Private          Sick; absent
Stone, William           Private          Sick; absent
Vickery, William         Private          Sick; absent
Wilde, David             Private          Sick in Hospital
White, William           Private          Sick in Hospital
```

Servants Serving the Officers of the Company:

```
Lettuce                           Commenced Service June 1, 1814
June                              Commenced Service June 1, 1814
```

I certify on honor that the above muster Roll exhibits the true state
of the Company under my Command and that the Remarks set opposite the
names are accurate and Just.

/s/ D. Clarke Capt.
Commdg.

I certify on honor that the above Muster Roll exhibits a true statement
of Captain David Clarkes Company of Volunteer Light Artillerists of the
State of Geogia in the Service of the United States as mustered by me
this 7th day of September 1814 at Fort Jackson near Savannah Georgia.

/s/ M.G. Waage
Asst. Inspr. Genl.

Muster Roll of Captain David Clarkes Company of Volunteer Militia Light
Artillerist of the State of Georgia belonging to a detachment under the
Command of Major Robert Bowling and in the Service of the United States
from the Commencement of the Service until the 25th of September 1814.

(Only information not found on the preceeding rolls is included in the
abstracts below.)

```
William S. Shirley       3rd Sergt.       Promoted from Corpl. 26th May
James Gordon             4th Sergt.       Promoted 1st June
Seth S. Langston         5th Sergt.       Promoted 1st June
Littleton Spivey         1st Corp.        Promoted 1st June
James Bigham             2nd Corp.        Sick; absent
Shadrack Fokes           3rd Corp.        Promoted 1st June
Miles Fields             4th Corp.        Promoted 1st June
Andrew Crossby           Artificer        Sick in hospital
John Marshall            Artificer        Appointed 26 May 1814
Joseph Sasser            Musician         Sick in hospital
Charles Butler           Private          Died 8th September 1814
Allen Causey             Private          In hospital
Isaac Mathis             Private          Sick
Augustus Moore           Private          Sick
Josiah Register          Private          Died 11th Septr. 1814
David Wilde              Private          Sick but present
Willie Webb              Private          Sick but present
```

I certify on honor that the above muster roll exhibits a true state of
the Company under my command and that the remarks set opposite the names
are accurate and Just.

/s/ Dd. Clarke Captn.
Arty. U.S. Qo. Comdg. Company

I Certify on honor that the above Muster Roll exhibits a true statement
of Captain David Clarkes Company of volunteer light artillerists of the

militia of the State of Georgia in the service of the United States as mustered by me this 25th day of September 1814 at Fort Jackson near Savannah Georgia.

/s/ M.G. Waage
Asst. Inspr. Genl.

Muster Roll of Captn. Stephen W. Blount's Company of Volunteer Infantry Georgia Militia in the Service of the U. States belonging to a regiment Commanded by Lieut. Col. Jas. Johnson from the Commencement of their Service to the 17th day of Feb. 1815.

NAMES	RANK	DATES OF JOINING	TERM OF SERVICE	REMARKS
1. Stephen W. Blount	Capt.	30 Jan.1815	Six Mos.	Sick in City
1. Hardy Perry	1st Lieut.	"	"	
1. Beverly Randolph	Ensign	"	"	
1. Lewis, Evan	Sergt.	"	"	
2. Scott, Andrew	"	"	"	
3. Tipton, Reuben	"	"	"	Sick in City
4. Tipton, Jonathan	"	"	"	
1. Scruggs, Abisha	"	"	"	
2. Forth, Joel L.	"	"	"	Sick in City
3. Lewis, Josiah	"	"	"	Sick in City
4. Lewis, Nimrod	"	"	"	Sick in City
1. Baxter, Charles	Musician	"	"	
1. Boyd, Thomas	Private	"	"	
2. Daniel, David	"	"	"	Sick in City
3. Duke, Willis	"	"	"	
4. Farnel, Benjamin	"	"	"	
5. Futch, John	"	"	"	
6. Farley, William	"	"	"	
7. Gaines, Duncan	"	"	"	
8. Hampton, John	"	"	"	Sick in City
9. Hobbs, William	"	"	"	
10. Hester, William	"	"	"	Sick in City
11. Hester, Willis	"	"	"	
12. Hampton, James	"	"	"	
13. Hester, Tapley	"	"	"	Sick in City
14. Justin, Thomas	"	"	"	
15. Jordan, Daniel	"	"	"	
16. Lane, Thomas	"	"	"	
17. Moss, Fountain	"	"	"	
18. Thomas, Red	"	"	"	
19. Stafford, William	"	"	"	
20. Stevens, Henry	"	"	"	
21. Sherley, Richard	"	"	"	
22. Sherley, William	"	"	"	
23. Tabb, Davis	"	"	"	
24. Ward, James	"	"	"	
25. Williams, James	"	"	"	
26. Wroten, Leaven	"	"	"	
27. Warnock, David	"	"	"	

We do certify on honor that this Muster Roll exhibits a true Statement of Captain Stephen W. Blount's Company of the Regiment of Georgia Militia in the Service of the United States Commanded by Lieutenant Colonel James Johnson for the period therein mentioned, and that the mark set opposite the names of the men are accurate and just. Mustered the Seventeenth day of February 1815 at Savannah Georgia.

/s/ SW Blount Capt.
Wm. R. Bootz Inspr. Genl.

26

Muster Roll of Capt. S.W. Blounts Company of Volunteer Infantry Georgia Militia in the Service of the United States belonging to a regiment Commanded by Lieut Colonel James Johnson from the 17 of February to the first day of March 1815.

(Note: Only information not included on the preceeding roll is abstracted here.)

Andrew Scott	2nd Sgt.	Absent with Leave
Reuben, Tipton	3rd Sgt.	Absent with leave
Jonathan Tipton	4th Sgt.	Absent with leave
Willis Dukes	Private	Absent with leave
John Hampton	Private	Absent with leave
James Hampton	Private	Absent with leave
Daniel Jordon	Private	Absent with leave
Thomas Lane	Private	Absent with leave
Davis Tabb	Private	Absent with leave
James Ward	Private	Absent with leave

We do Certify on honor that this muster Roll exhibits a true statement of Captain Stephen W. Blounts Company of the Regiment of Georgia Militia in the Service of the United States Commanded by Lieut Colonel James Johnston for the period herein mentioned and that the remarks set opposit the names of the men are accurate and just Mustered this First day of March 1815 at Savannah Geo.

/s/ S.W. Blount Capt.
John B. Hobkirk Lt. 8th Infy.
Inspecting Officer

INDEX TO 1820 BURKE COUNTY CENSUS

27

Beal, Nathaniel	38	
Beaty, James	3	
Beck, John B.	37	
Bedgood, Matthew	11	
Bedingfield, Martha	34	
Belcher, Abner	24	
" Mary	33	
" Mournin	30	
" Wiley	24	
Bell, Archd.	22	
" Arthur	20	
" Benjamin	23	
" Elisha	22	
" Green	11	
" Henry	22	
" James		
" John	9	
" Jordan	22	
" Martha	22	
" Richard	21	
" Thomas	10	
" William	21	
Bergeron, Abigail	28	
" Elijah	35	
" Elizabeth	35	
Blount, James	6	
" S. W.	11	
Bolton, James	36	
Bonnell, Anthony	28	
Bostick, Jacob (overseer for)	38	
" J. (overseer for)	5	
" Thomas	12	
Bothwell, James J.	3	
Bourks, Edward	15	
" also see Burke		
Boyt, Abraham	19	
" James Jr.	19	
" James Sr.	19	
" John	37	
" Stephen	5	
Brack, Benjamin	31	
" Mary	21	
" Richard	31	
" William	21	
Bradshow, John	14	
Brantly, Mary	35	
Brigham, John	24	
Bright, Absalom	33	
Brinson, Cypron	33	
" John	33	
" John Jr.	30	
" Mary	12	
" Shepherd	29	
" Stephen	33	
" Thomas	33	
Brodnax, R. E.	10	
Brookins, Samuel	31	
Brown, Benjamin	26	
" Burrel	31	
" Charles	31	
" James	19	
" James B.	14	
" Richard	9	
" William	8	
" William	31	
Broxton, John	35	
" Silas	34	
" Thomas	35	
Bruce, Nancy	26	
Bryan, Jacob	18	

Bryan, James H.	28	
" Lewis	19	
" Moses	24	
" Needham	25	
" Reading D.	27	
" William	18	
Buckley, Bartlet	22	
" Benjamin	21	
Bullard, Amos	32	
" Henry	32	
Bunn, Moses	30	
Burch, Jessee	12	
" Lb. (Laban?)	16	
Burke, Matthew	13	
" Thomas	21	
" also see Bourks		
Burnell also see Bonnell		
Burnes, F. J.	9	
Burnet, Feriby	32	
Burton, Charles	21	
" William	22	
" also see Buxton		
Bush, David F.	37	
" Joseph	37	
" Levi	14	
Buxton, Benjamin	23	
" William	24	
Byne, Elijah	10	
" Enoch	34	
" George	27	
" Henry	34	
" John	16	
" Lewis	33	
" Richard	15	
" Thomas	15	
" William	34	
Byrd, Harmon	7	
" John	20	
" Nathan	13	
" Samuel	32	
Cain also see Cato		
Caldwell, Mary	3	
Calhoun, Levi	26	
Carpenter, Bailey	20	
" Bailey Sr.	21	
" John	9	
Carroll also see McCarrol		
Carswell, Alexander	14	
" Elizabeth	15	
" Matthew	15	
Carter, Alexander	10	
Caruthers, Nancy	18	
" William	18	
Cates, James	5	
" John	16	
Catlet, Polly	38	
Cato, Jinny	37	
Causey, Philip	25	
Caustin, Hester	17	
Cessums, Patrick	16	
Chance, Henry	12	
" Jesse	12	
" Joseph	6	
" Reuben	10	
" Stephen	12	
" William	32	
Chandler, George	9	
Chapman, Israel	35	
Clagg, David	28	

28

Clark, Christopher 21
Clarke, Charles 14
" Charles 16
" John 21
" Fanny 13
Clements, Jacob 34
" Mary A. 23
Cobb, Briton 26
Cock, John 32
Cohn also see McColen
Coil, Gideon M. 35
Cole also see Coleman
Coleman, Charles 25
" Elisha 24
" Jesse 25
Collins, John 24
" Levin 26
Conner, John 16
" Mary 17
Connor, Nancy 3
Coody, Lewis 23
Cook, Abram 8
" James 8
" James 37
Cooper, Joseph 26
Coosa, Hugh 29
Corker, Stephen 29
Cornet, Eli 7
Cotton, Pleasant 9
Coulson, John 8
" William 8
Coutteau, Charles 23
Covennah, Charles 22
" Lb. (Leban?) 21
Cowart, Zachariah 21
Cox, Aaron 6
" Jesse 25
" Milly 9
" Moses 32
" Peggy 39
" William 31
Craft, Jesse 12
Crane, John 8
" Levi 8
" Moses 20
Crew, Elbert 9
" Henry 28
Croan also see McCroan
Crocket, Floyd 8
Cross, Isaac 25
" Stephen 25
" William 24
Crozier, Nancy 22
" Thomas 20
Cruce, John 32

Daniel, Annis M. 25
" Joseph 12
" Martha 13
" Mary 38
" Robert C. 15
" also see McDaniel
Darsy, John 5
Davies, William W. or H/N 16
Davis, Celia 22
" Elnathan 33
" Robbin 28
" Samuel 18
" Samuel 27
" Sarah 23

Davis, Simeon 21
" Thomas W. 10
" William 16
Dawson, Briton 3
Deal, Ezekiel 32
Devenport, Stephen 38
Dillard, Elizabeth 15
" Isaac 27
" Philip 15
" William 15
Dillon, Tolliver 39
Dixon, Robert 6
Douglas, W. B. 7
Dove, Richard 28
Dowlin, Thomas P. 7
Dowse, Samuel 38
Doyle, William (overseer for) 5
Drake, Elias 25
Drew, Asa 30
" Josiah 25
" William 32
" Wilson 25
Dudly, Kinchen C. 13
Dugas, L. P. 36
Duke, Azariah 6
" Daniel 6
" Drewry 6
" James 7
" Mary 5
" Turner 6
Dunford, Daniel 29
" Susannah 29
Dunn, Jane 23
" John 22
" Mary 11
Dye, Avery 14
" Benjamin 14
" Hopkin 14
" Martin M. 14

Edmunds, William 33
Elliby, Dick 37
" Elizabeth 20
" Elizabeth 23
Elliott, Drewry 21
" John 21
" Silas 20
Elliston, George 35
" Joseph 35
" Robert 35
Ellotson, Jacob 23
Ennis, Peggy 35
Erwin, Richard 15
" Robert 15
Evans, Daniel 8
" Daniel J. 8
" George W. 18
" Richard 15
" Richard H. 9

Faircloth, Reddin 34
Farmer, Isaac 27
" James 39
" Nancy 27
" Verity 39
Farrel, Bender 12
Farrow, Jesse 5
Fields, Mary 25
" Miles 24
Findley, John 5

29

Finny, Sarah	21
Fitzgerald, David	32
" John	25
Floyd, James	25
" John	31
" Matthew	30
" Thomas	32
Folds, Richard	20
Forehand, Drewry	29
Forth, Joel L.	17
" John T.	17
" Thomas	5
Foster, Richard	8
Fountain, Dempsy	16
Frost, James	27
Fryer, Fielding	38
" John	7
" Robert	19
" Winnifred	19
" Zachariah L.	19
Fulcher, John	8
Gabard, Thomas	7
Gaines, Duncan	5
" Theophilus	6
Galloway (no first name)	37
Garet, Mary	20
Garlick, Samuel	9
Gay, Joel	18
" Mary	18
" Thomas	17
George, David	20
Gilstrap, Henry	13
" William	13
Glascock, E. (overseer for)	5
Glisson, Dennis	36
" Lydia	36
" Pheroh	23
" Tilly	36
Godbee, Alfred A.	35
" Elbert	36
" Henry	35
" James	24
" Mary	36
" Stephen	36
" William	36
Godfrey, Enoch	35
Golphin, Frances	37
Goodwin, Charles	38
" Matthews	23
" William	14
Gordon, Robert	18
" William	18
" William	19
Gordy, Eli	18
" Elizabeth	26
" James	18
" Moses	32
Goulding, Peter I.	12
Grace, Elizabeth	18
Graham, Andrew	3
" Sarah	3
Grant, Isaac	28
" Mary	24
Gray, Bazil	7
" Edmund	6
" Gibson	12
" John	7
" Mincha	29
" William	29

Green, Abram	11
" David E.	9
" Moses	29
" W. D.	8
" Warren	31
Greenway, Lucretia	13
" William	15
Gregory, Hardy	17
" Martha	12
Gresham, Job	27
Griffin, John	37
" Mary (struck out and Sarah entered lightly)	23
" Noah	19
" Sarah	39
Grubbs, Thomas	31
Guest, Benjamin	23
" E. B.	36
Gunn, William	7
Gwynn, William	33
Hadley, Elizabeth	37
" John	20
Hail, Tharp	32
Hall, Davis	18
" James	30
" Sarah	5
" Sarah	8
" Zilphay	39
Hamm, Aaron	20
Hampton, James	11
" Simeon	11
" Thomas	11
Hancock, Nero	37
Hand, John J.	24
Handburg, Israel	25
Hannah, John	23
Hardin, Isaac B.	16
Hardwick, Andrew	11
Hargrove, Jacob	28
Harlow, Southworth	10
Harris, Benjamin	11
" Gideon	10
Hart, Thomas	6
Harvy, Blassingame	13
" G. B.	13
Harwell, Absalom	18
Hatcher, Edward	18
" Josiah	20
Hawes, Sabra	30
Hay, Hardy	23
Hayes, Richard	18
Hayman, Stephen	19
" William	19
Hayslip, John	26
" Kendal C. or G.	26
" Susannah	25
Heath, Drucilla	35
" Henry	35
" James	24
" Jordan	23
" Richard	34
" Samuel	35
Heislar, Samuel	5
Henderson, George	36
Henior, John	11
" Mary	11
Herrington, Martin	33
Hester, David	14
" William	14

Hickman, Stephen	35	Jones, Batt	30
Hicky, James	9	" Charles	37
Hill, Elijah	38	" Henry T.	29
" Gilham	7	" James W.	10
" Granberry	8	" Jane	30
Hilliard, Henry	29	" Jemima	8
" Jane	31	" John	33
Hillis, Jane	36	" John M.	38
" John	36	" Robert	38
" William	36	" Seaborn H.	10
Hines, James	24	" Simon	39
" John Jr.	24	" Smith (Estate)	21
" John Sr.	26	" Thomas	30
" Joseph	26	" Thomas H.	7
" Stephen 2	26	" William (overseer for)	15
Hinly, Mary	11	" William	37
Hodges, Elizabeth	5	Jordan, Daniel	16
" Nancy	17	Josey, Willis	8
Holland, Daniel	24		
" Jeremiah	24	Kelly, Jesse	37
Holliday, Abner	30	" John	37
" Ferny	30	" Susannah	20
" Joseph	30	Kersy, Bud	20
" Milner	30	" John	26
" Thomas	13	Key, William	13
" William	33	Keyland, Jane	23
Holloway, David	14	" also see Neyland	
Holly, James	14	Kidd, Henry	9
" John	16	Kilpatrick, John	12
Holton, Isaac	11	" Spencer	19
" James	27	Kimball, James	27
" Josiah	11	" James W.	29
" Thomas	12	" Joseph	27
Hooks, William	32	" Joshua	27
Howard, William	31	" Mary	28
Hudson, John	7	" William	28
Hughes, Jane	34	Kimbell, Charles	23
Hull, Ezekiel	17	King, Ephraim	25
Humphries also see Umphries		Kirsy also see Kersy	
Hurst, Jesse	35	Knight see Night	
" John	35		
" Major	35	Lamb, Barnaba	12
" William	35	" Jacob	37
Hust(?), Harmon	27	Lambert, James	28
Huston, Frances	37	Lancaster, Mahala	14
Hutchens, Elizabeth	18	Landing, John	33
" William	26	Lane, James	30
		" John	30
Inman, Alfred	31	" Thomas	5
" Daniel	31	" Thomas	11
" Ezekiel	31	Lassiter, Edward	21
Ishley, Marah	11	" Lemuel	7
		" Mary	17
Jackson, James or Jarvis	7	" William	22
" Obed.	36	Lawson, A. J.	10
Jarvis, Patrick	38	" S. B.	3
Jenkins, Sampson	13	Ledbetter, Mary	14
" Stephen	13	Lee, John C.	39
Johns, Jesse	5	Leggit, Benjamin	31
Johnson, Charlotte	17	" David	31
" Elijah	27	" also see Legget	
" Elizabeth	17	Lenoir, Robert C.	29
" George	17	Lequoux, Peter	26
" Jacob	31	Lester, Ezekiel Jr.	13
" James J.	29	" Ezekiel Sr.	22
" Jared	38	" John	33
" Moses	15	" Neel (Noel?)	12
" Sarah	15	Leverett, Elizabeth	34
Johnston, Moses	15	Levett, Thomas	10
Joiner, Thomas	34	Lewis, A. P.	7

Lewis, Abel	27
Abram	33
Eleazar	32
Hezekiah	16
James	33
John C.	27
Jonathan	6
Josiah	16
Littleberry	38
William	28
Ligget, Jordan	25
" also see Legget	
Liggin, Marshall	8
Lightfoot, Philip	7
Liptrot, James	32
" John	17
" Nelly	32
" Sarah	17
Lissenby, William	29
Little, Elizabeth	14
Lively, Elizabeth	35
" James D.	5
" Matthew	37
Livingston, Peter L.	27
Lodge, John	25
" Levi	24
" Lewis	26
" Ruth	25
Lowery, Simeon	30
Lumpkin, Edmund W.	38
" Philip	38
Lynch, Henry	24
Lyon, Peter	22
McBride, James	18
McCarroll, John	36
McClaney, Barbara	32
" Thomas	18
McClendon, Jesse	20
McCroan, Zilphay	17
McCullers, John	26
" Matthew C.	31
McDaniel, John	35
" Randal	10
" also see Daniel	
McKay, George	36
McMahon, Moses	18
McNatt, Benjamin L.	38
" Robert	5
" William	5
McNealy, Esther	18
McNorrell, Fielding	19
" Henry	7
McTyre, Frizel	14
Macon, Catherine	15
" Margaret	14
Madray, Joseph	27
Madry, Benjamin	6
Magruder, John	25
Mainor, Hardy	12
Malden, Elias	20
Mallard, John	13
Mallory, Thomas	13
Marsh, John	17
" Lb.	17
Marshall, Matthew	3
" William S.	17
Martin, David	8
" Rovisa	11

Matthews, Henry	22
" Josiah	19
" Peter	7
Maund, Elizabeth	29
" Mallicai	29
Meadow, Daniel	26
Mercer, Stephen	29
" Williby	28
Meredith, William H.	34
Merit, Abscilla	11
" Cotton	10
" Jesse	5
Metcalf, Anthony	32
" Isaac	31
" William	31
Miles, Levisa	34
Miller, John	32
Millin, George	37
" James H.	36
Mills, Anthony	28
" Elizabeth	28
Milton, Hannah E.	12
" Peter	20
Mixon, George	9
" Michael	9
" Nancy	9
Mobly, Benjamin	35
" Sarah	36
Mock, Arthur	6
Monroe, David	32
" Joseph	32
Moore, Elizabeth	20
" James	29
" John R.	20
" Pleasant	19
" Sarah	22
" Thomas	29
" Turner B.	21
" William	36
" Winfred	29
Morris, James E.	10
Morrison, John B.	16
Mosley also see Moxley	
Moxley, Benjamin	17
" Daniel	3
" Nathaniel	3
Mulford, William B.	23
Mulky, Isaac	23
" Moses	23
" William	7
Murphy, James	31
" John	31
" John W.	38
" Josiah	32
" William	31
" William	5
" Wright	31
Murray, David	27
" James	28
" John	28
" Mary	28
" Mary	29
" Timothy	28
Nares, (?) John	35
Navy, Wilson	18
Nazworthy, John	24
" Ogburn	26
Nelms, Mary	14
Nesmith, Charles	36

Rollins, Raleigh 18
" Samuel 18
" William 18
Rowel, Joab 21
Rowland, James 14
Royal, Asa 28
" John 24
" John S. 23
" Mary 23
" Saml. 24
" Seaborn L. 24
Runnels, Betsy 37
Runnelson, Andrew 17
Russel, James 10
Rutledge, John 27

Salisbury, James G. 19
Sanders, Alexander 32
Sandyford, N. T. 32
" William 10
Sapp, Addison 29
" Elizabeth 34
" Everet 28
" Hardy C. 34
" Isaiah 22
" James 28
" John 22
" John 33
" Luke Jr. 13
" Luke Sr. 34
" Wiley 22
" William 34
" William 33
" William Jr. 28
" William Sr. 29
Savage, Daniel (overseer for) 5
Saxon, John 16
" Samuel 17
" William 10
Scarborough, Joel 30
" Samuel 26
" Silas 24
" Thomas 36
" William 25
Sconyers see Skonvers
Scott, Andrew 11
" Charles 38
Scruggs, Abishae 16
Scrutchens, Josiah 26
Segar, Benjamin 18
" Charles T. 10
" Joab 38
" Samuel 37
Sessions see Cessiom
Sevier, John 34
Sharp, Basdil 30
" Cade 7
" Clemy 6
" Polly 5
Shepherd, Bazil 34
" James 34
Shepherdson, Elizabeth 36
Shumake, Joseph 21
Sillivan, Dennis 13
Sills, Nancy 15
Simmons, Pheriby 36
Skinner, Charles 21
" John 10
" John 22
" Jonas 18

Skinner, Robert 21
" Sarah 22
" Uriah 10
Skonyers, Celia 26
" Richard 26
Slain, Matthew 3
Slone, Sally 7
Smith, Benjamin 26
" David 8
" James J. 27
" John 30
" Joseph A. 12
" Noah 15
" William 15
Snead, Dudley 30
" Leaston 29
" Philip 33
" Samuel 31
Soursby, Thomas 19
Spain, Levi 30
" Luellen 30
" Matthew 30
Spann, James B. 34
Spears, John 37
Spence, Harris 32
" Mary 31
" Nancy 32
Spikes, Jinny 37
Spivy, Littleton 24
Stallings, John Jr. 9
Stevens, Henry 19
" James 25
Stewart see Stuart
Stobo, Nancy 23
Stockdale, John 13
Stokes, Mark 29
" Martha 30
Stringer, Abner 13
" James 20
" Smith 12
Stuart, Anna 38
" James 14
" James 17
" Isaac 8
Stubblefield, William S. 11
Sturgis, Samuel 9
Suggs, John 22
Sullivan see Sillivan
Sumner, Sumner 38
Sykes, Arthur 13
" John 5
" Sarah 15
" Thomas 23

Tabb, Davis 8
" Edward 9
Tarver, Samuel B. 14
Taylor, Caleb 16
" Catherine 21
" David 16
" William 6
Tedder, James 22
Telfair, Alexn. 37
Thomas, Absolom 37
" Etheldred 3
" Joseph D. 19
" Richard 5
" Roberts 8
Thompson, Aaron 28
" Artemus 21

Thompson, Benjamin	34	Ward, James	20
" Charity	28	" James	37
" Daniel	27	" Jane	23
" Eady	33	" John	13
" Jane	34	" M. B.	10
" John	16	" Thomas	9
" Martha	23	Warnock, Bazil	3
" Solomon	21	" Benjamin	33
" William	28	Warren, Carlos	7
Tillinghast, Stutely	15	Watkins, Rhoda	11
Tilly, Betsy	12	Weeks, Thomas	3
" George	12	Welch, James	27
" Isaac	12	West, Arthur	18
" Joseph	12	" Gibson	22
" William	19	" William	17
Tindall, James Jr.	13	" William	22
Tinnison, John	11	Wetherby, Caroline	36
Tipton, Amy	11	Wheeler, Lott	30
" Jonathan	11	White, Arthur	28
" Reuben	29	" Constant	33
Toedwell, F. S.	20	" Ezekiel	29
Toler, Daniel	21	" Henry	26
Tomlin, Harris	19	" Jesse	9
" John	18	" Robert	28
Tootle, Robert	8	" William	29
Torrence, James	29	Whitehead, Amos P.	11
Tosey see Josey		" James	38
Trimble, John	17	" John Sr.	16
Trowel, James	21	" John	39
Turner, Absolom	34	Whitfield, Bryan	19
" Henry	27	" Lewis	38
" John	7	Wiggins, Amos	15
" Reuben	3	" Jesse	14
Turning, Lucius	26	" Michael	21
		" William	13
Umphries, William	20	Wilkinson, John	35
Urquhart, William	38	Williams, Aaron	13
Utley, Elisha H.	5	" Arthur	24
" Henry	19	" Charlotte	14
" Henry (overseer for		" Hester: see	
Alex Telfair)	37	" William	
		" Jane	19
Vollotton, Francis S.	15	" John	36
" Rachel	15	" Samuel	34
Vann, Josiah	8	" Thomas	12
Vaughn, James	9	" Wright	34
" William	9	Williamson, Sarah	36
Vickers, Frederick	26	Wilson, James	9
" Nathan	30	" Solomon	34
" Penelope	30	Wimberly, John	34
Vincent, Richard	27	" Lewis	8
		" Lucretia	32
Waley, William	31	" Needham	34
Walker, A.	39	" Wiley	9
" Bathiah	38	" William	3
" Elijah	15	" Zachr.	35
" F. (overseer)	38	Wimpy, John	38
" Moses	27	Wiot, Margaret	39
" V. (overseer for)	9	Wise, William	38
Wall, Thomas	15	Woodard, Joshua	25
Wallace, John	34	" Lemuel	25
" Josiah	34	Woods, Thomas	18
" Pheriby	34	Wooton, Jerusa	32
" Stirling	33	" Mournin	33
" William	13	Wynn, Thomas P.	27
Walton, Daniel	3	" William	31
" Everet	6	Wynne, Emily	16
" Jesse	6	Young, Alexander	35
Ward, David	9	" Zilphay	23
" Francis	11	Youngblood, Abraham	27

GROOM	BRIDE	DATE
Addison, Thomas	Sarah Lawson	17 Nov. 1857
Alday, Joseph	Rebecca Bell	17 Jan. 1856
Allday, Charles	Sarah Clark	18 Mar. 1858
Allen, Young J.	Mary Hairston	22 Jul. 1858
Allen, Elisha E.	Flora M. Catchett	17 Mar. 1863
Allen, Handy	Easter Simpson	22 Jul. 1866
Allen, Peter	Phillis Brown	13 Dec. 1868
Allen, John G.	Eva M. Gunder	11 Jun. 1869
Allen, Peter	Minor Roberson	15 Sep. 1869
Allen, Oliver	Eliza Reynolds	29 Dec. 1869
Andrews, Thomas	Pollena Jeppson	26 Jul. 1858
Armstrong, John	Harriett Walker	6 May 1869
Atkinson, William F.	Emiley C. Daniel	30 Jan. 1861
Atkinson, John	Susan McCuller	15 Jan. 1868
Attaway, Ezekiel	Armaminta Cates	22 Jan. 1856
Attaway, William	Josie Baer	30 Sep. 1861
Attaway, John J.	Virginia Messex	19 Jan. 1863
Attaway, Amos	Sarah Proctor	31 Dec. 1865
Atteberry, Darling C.	Julia Tabb	12 Sep. 1861
Auret, Nathaniel	Mary E. Sikes	29 Dec. 1867
Bailey, David Jr.	Elizabeth Skinner	19 Dec. 1855
Bailey, David C.	Martha Farmell	12 Oct. 1865
Baldwin, John	Sara Corly	19 Jun. 1869
Bar, Clark	Betsey Gray	27 Oct. 1867
Barber, Augustus	Joanna Lively	9 Feb. 1856
Barefield, James J.	Virginia Hampton	7 Dec. 1856
Barefield, John	May Ann Conner	16 Dec. 1860
Bargeron, Benjamin	Elizabeth Sapp	27 Aug. 1857
Bargeron, William	Nancy A. Hargrove	20 May 1858
Bargeron, Robert	Joanna L. Hurst	7 May 1861
Bargeron, William	Louisa Wimberly	27 Sep. 1864
Bargeron, George W.	Frances Royal	31 Jan. 1866
Bargeron, Benjamin F.	Nancy Herrington	7 Nov. 1867
Bareron, Jack	Betsey Williams	15 Nov. 1868
Barron, Tom	Melvina Jinkins	22 Sep. 1867
Barrow, Benjamin L.	Elizabeth Cox	11 Oct. 1860
Barrow, Charles W.	Sarah A. Holton	2 Sep. 1862
Barrow, Homer V.	Emma E. Stone	3 Jan. 1867
Barry, Thomas H.	Emily F. Tabb	7 Mar. 1865
Bartley, Henry C.	Sarah H. Saxon	14 Dec. 1865
Barton, William	Amanda Murray	1 Jan. 1860
Barton, Willoughby	Anna E. Etter	22 Dec. 1867
Baston, C. B.	Grarey Wiggins (sic)	5 Nov. 1863
Baston, Martin V.	Mary Ann Hines	22 Jun. 1867
Baston, Luther	Adaline Lockhart	27 Feb. 1869
Bates, John F.	Eugenia Herrington	10 May 1867
Bates, Joseph W.	Alice P. Pollock	20 Aug. 1868
Baxley, Dr. William	Rebecca E. Ward	4 Sep. 1856
Beale, John W.	Lizzie Chance	22 Sep. 1857
Beale, John	Hetty Skinner	7 Jul. 1866
Bearfield, James I.	Frances Moore	19 Apr. 1860
Beckam, Camel	Frances Turner	23 Sep. 1863
Becton, Andrew F.	Ropey Ann Dickey	7 Feb. 1856
Bedson, George W.	Lizzy Seals	10 Aug. 1862
Belcher, James	Elizabeth Lightfoot	6 Dec. 1860
Bell, Seaborn	Sarah Quinn	5 Nov. 1856
Bell, Hendy J.	Kesiah Sapp	23 Dec. 1856
Bell, Joseph W. H.	Sarah Allen	20 Jan. 1859
Bell, James W.	Martha C. Brookins	20 Oct. 1859
Bell, James K.	Julianna Hines	2 Mar. 1864
Bell, Amos	Nancy Clark	10 Nov. 1864
Bell, Malcomb	Rachel Bell	24 Jun. 1866
Bell, Joseph R.	Georgia W.A. Carpenter	8 Nov. 1866
Bell, John W.	Ellefair Burton (sic)	15 Nov. 1866
Bell, Lemuel	Louisa Clark	27 Dec. 1866

Bell, Moses	Ester Reeves	29 Feb. 1868
Bell, Albert	Ellen Thorn	4 Feb. 1869
Bell, John	Sanoline Cooper	21 Feb. 1869
Bell, Jacob	Parthenia Dent	15 May 1869
Bennett, Alex	Ella Perkins	21 Mar. 1869
Benson, William	Amelia Godbee	10 Dec. 1868
Benton, Thomas J.	Sarah J. Shewmaker	29 Nov. 1860
Berrian, Aleck	Livey Harris	15 Jun. 1867
Beverly, Alexander	Cheny Jone	15 May 1869
Blackwell, William	Josephine L. Gray	10 Jun. 1867
Blocker, Barkley M.	Sarah M. Hiates	16 Jul. 1868
Blount, Edwin F.	Margaret H. Allen	3 Nov. 1859
Blount, Robert B.	Louisa A. Dillard	22 Dec. 1859
Blount, Stephen W.	Rosa C. White	20 Aug. 1865
Blount, Henry	Mary Curtis	3 Jun. 1868
Boan, Isaac	Sarah Salsbury	20 Jun. 1867
Boatwright, Andrew J.	Civility Mobley	1 Jun. 1857
Boatwright, James H.	Margaret Mason	2 Feb. 1862
Bonnell, John C.	Lydia Bailey	30 Mar. 1858
Bonnell, James H.	Elizabeth Reed	18 Apr. 1860
Bonnell, Charles E.	Louisa Bargeron	6 Mar. 1861
Bostwick, Westley	Frances Wallace	24 Feb. 1866
Bostwick, Joseph	Amelia Brown	21 Jun. 1866
Bostwick, Peter	Janett McKinna	5 Oct. 1867
Boyd, Abraham	Anna S. E. Smith	26 Jul. 1860
Boyed, John R.	Martha Scott	18 Jul. 1866
Branch, William A.	Anna E. Fetts	28 Mar. 1866
Branch, Albert H.	Yallulah Beal (sic)	21 Mar. 1869
Brigham, Calvin	Rosa Ellison	25 Feb. 1869
Brinson, Isaac M.	Esther M. Clark	13 Jul. 1856
Brinson, Middleton F.	Alvina Bell	1 Feb. 1858
Brinson, Simion C.	Mary A. E. Brinson	15 May 1860
Brinson, Jasper L.	Joanna M. Hargrove	4 Oct. 1860
Brinson, William T.	Susan E. Hargrove	8 Jun. 1865
Brown, Allen T.	Elizabeth Atwell	20 Aug. 1857
Brown, Jerry	Maria An Roberson	14 Apr. 1866
Brown, Thomas	Mary Ann Carter	4 Apr. 1867
Brown, Patrick	Emma Cook	15 Jun. 1867
Brown, William H.	Zilpha A. Smith	7 Mar. 1868
Brown, Alfred	Emma Thompson	24 Dec. 1868
Brown, Henry	Ann Hines	24 Dec. 1868
Brown, Teaac	Tilda Johnson	2 Jan. 1869
Brown, William A.	Amelia Glisson	26 Jan. 1869
Brown, Harrison	Esther Preston	2 Mar. 1869
Brown, Washington	Charlotte Roberts	18 Sep. 1869
Brown, John	Chaney Dickson	23 Dec. 1869
Brown, Alek	Henretta Thorn	25 Dec. 1869
Brown, David	Adaline Morse	27 Dec. 1869
Bryant, Berrien	Sarah Jane Handberry	20 Aug. 1856
Bryant, James	Rutha Clark	29 Mar. 1859
Burch, Jesse	Sarah Roberson	13 Sep. 1866
Burton, Thomas J.	Sarah J. Shewmaker	29 Nov. 1860
Burton, Frances M.	Ella Herrington	8 Mar. 1866
Burton, Uriah	Isabell L. Devant	25 Oct. 1866
Bush, Charles	Matilda Williams	28 Dec. 1866
Bush, John	Ella Sapp	3 Jan. 1869
Buxton, Samuel H.	Josephine R. Dixon	15 Aug. 1862
Buxton, Jefferson L.	Martha L. Graham	31 May 1866
Byne, John S.	Margaret J. Murphree	26 Nov. 1856
Byne, Henry	Dicey Collins	26 Dec. 1866
Byne, Edward	Ellen Sapp	6 Jun. 1867
Byne, David	Virginia Prior	10 Aug. 1867
Byne, Glascow	Clarra Levign	5 Oct. 1867
Cain, Emerson	Savannah Lacy	23 Oct. 1869
Callyer, Abram	Anna Woodfall	22 Jul. 1869
Canel, Hector	Rosetta Carrell	30 Sep. 1866
Canley, George W.	Jane Messex	15 Jul. 1858
Carmet, Fredrick A.	Amanda M. Moore	24 Jun. 1858
Carnel, Wright	Faniel Martin	27 Jun. 1867
Carpenter, Lewis	Emma Bell	20 Jul. 1867

37

Carroll, Hector	Amanda Sapp	25 Dec. 1869
Carroll, Hector	Lucy Carrole	25 Dec. 1869

(He took the license to marry Lucy Carrole on 23 Dec. 1869, but he married Amanda Sapp on the above date with the same license.)

Carson, Edward	Raze Jones	21 Jun. 1866
Carswell, John D.	Linda M. Royal	22 Feb. 1866
Carswell, Cudjai Golding	Hetty Hines	23 Dec. 1866
Carter, Isiah W.	Electa A. Varnes	12 Nov. 1856
Carter, Lewis	Tena Morris	1 Apr. 1866
Carter, John	Lizzie Lewis	27 Mar. 1869
Carter, Edward A.	Augusta L. Lawson	17 Nov. 1869
Case, Harmon H.	Lou Wimberly	21 Feb. 1867
Cates, John	Nancy Maynor	31 Aug. 1859
Cates, Thomas W.	Jane E. Knight	12 Aug. 1860
Cates, Thomas	Julia C. Ruff	10 Oct. 1861
Chambers, Thomas	Eliza Carter	13 Nov. 1869
Chamblers, A.	Dinah Jones	21 Aug. 1869
Chance, Augustus	Elizabeth Huseton	26 Nov. 1856
Chance, William	Ellen Kimbrel	11 Dec. 1856
Chance, Benjamin	Sarah Kimble	2 May 1858
Chance, Alfred W.	Martha M. Tennerson	15 Dec. 1859
Chance, Willoughby	Dici Davis	23 Jan. 1868
Chance, Granville	Florence Attaway	25 Jun. 1869
Chandler, Robert	Sarah E. Smith	1 Aug. 1867
Chester, John A.	Martha D. Jerrers	19 Jan. 1868
Chester, W. G.	Christian Williams	22 Nov. 1868
Chew, John C.	A.H.E. Stephens	14 --- 1866
Churchill, George	Ruth Anderson	10 Jul. 1869
Clark, John	Charlotte Godbee	24 Jul. 1859
Clark, George W.	Susan Eviline Burke	12 Jul. 1863
Clark, Phillip	Lydia Irwin	5 Aug. 1866
Clark, Edward	M. B. Allen	27 Feb. 1868
Clarke, William E.	Harriet C. Fulcher	23 Dec. 1865
Clauden, Chaly	Dallie Jones	23 Jun. 1867
Claxton, William	Jane Skinner	28 Dec. 1865
Clinton, D. W.	Savannah V. Bull	30 Aug. 1869
Clutsion, Hensian	Julia B. Holt	26 Jul. 1863
Cochrane, James J.	Amanda Buxton	28 Dec. 1859
Cogland, Edward	Mary Caughlin	4 Nov. 1858
Cole, Bud G.	Frances C. Sikes	8 Dec. 1867
Collier, Clinch	Adalaid Grubbs	23 Dec. 1869
Cook, George R.	Magga F. Jordin	15 Apr. 1868
Cosnahan, Charles A.	Mary Jane Parker	21 Oct. 1868
Cox, William	Lauria Heath	29 May 1856
Cox, William	Amelia Halcomb	31 Jan. 1861
Cox, Thomas R.	Laura E. Rodgers	3 Mar. 1864
Cox, Seaborn J. M.	Hellen J. Cox	27 Jun. 1866
Cox, Dunkin P.	Alana Fulcher	21 Feb. 1867
Cox, Daniel	Lizzy Young	25 Dec. 1869
Crain, Reesy	Virginia Redd	28 Oct. 1869
Crane, Resey	Margarett Jeffers	1 May 1864
Crawford, Henry	Lona Robinson	18 Oct. 1868
Crawford, Henry	Martha Hankerson	25 Dec. 1869
Cue, James	Ely Shingle	28 Jul. 1867
Cullens, Thomas W.	Elizabeth J. Brookins	23 Apr. 1856
Cunneley, Daniel	Laura Green	22 Jul. 1866
Daniel, Zachariah	Elizabeth Miller	23 Jan. 1866
Dauggin, John	Mary F. Jeffers	5 Apr. 1863
Davis, Asa A.	Ann Guest	31 Mar. 1857
Davis, Wilson O.	Amarentha E. Gaines	20 Jan. 1858
Davis, John E.	Catherine Owen	20 Apr. 1864
Davis, Tober	Annie Sapp	10 Jan. 1867
Davis, Henry	Ann Jones	28 Dec. 1867
Dawson, James B.	Eugenia C. Patterson	20 Dec. 1866
Deason, William	Laura Mills	1 May 1865
Dickerson, Alic	Rhoda Patterson	11 Aug. 1867
Dickerson, Augustus	Becky Branch	22 Dec. 1867
Dickerson, Emanuel	Elsey Caminaings	27 Dec. 1868
Dickerson, Jessie	Verlinda Young	13 Oct. 1869
Dickerson, Fred	Chaney Perry	19 Feb. 1869

Dickey, M. M.	S. J. Moore	26 Feb.	1869
Dillard, Tolliver	Anna Jones Cook	15 Jul.	1862
Dillon, George W.	Laura Bennett	6 Jun.	1855
Dixon, James	Elizabeth Pollack	8 May	1856
Dixon, Weames R.	Frances Dilks	15 Dec.	1858
Dixon, Dennis B.	Narcissa Hillis	13 Nov.	1861
Dixon, Carter	Eliza Lassiter	16 Sep.	1867
Dorset, J. F.	Savannah Buxtor	29 Jan.	1866
Daughtey, Simeon C.	Sarah L. Brinson	19 Dec.	1858
Douglass, Jacob	Fanny Brown	1 Aug.	1869
Dove, William	Mary Allums	24 Feb.	1867
Dowse, Charles	Emma Jone	25 Dec.	1867
Drayton, Peter	Nancy Burgess	17 Feb.	1869
Drayton, Ned	Sarah Berrien	6 Nov.	1869
Drew, Josiah	Priscilla Holton	3 Feb.	1859
Dukes, Elbert	Charlotte Robinson	28 Feb.	1869
Duvelle, George W.	Jannie L. Gray	15 Sep.	1858
Dye, William	Louisa Buss	21 Sep.	1858
Dye, Benjamin G.	Sarah F. Gordon	30 Dec.	1863
Egerton, John William	Elmira Cox	11 Dec.	1856
Ellison, Laban	Mary Parris	2 Sep.	1866
Ellison, T. J.	Teresa C. Lovett	13 Aug.	1869
Ethridge, J. F.	Rachel Jainer	10 Feb.	1869
Etter, Godfrey DeGilse	Eugenia C. Barton	25 Nov.	1869
Fair, Gilmore	Adaline Wooten	14 Mar.	1869
Felder, Thomas B.	M. E. Jones	2 Dec.	1869
Feutral, John J.	Sarah S. Penrow	5 Apr.	1860
Fickling, Mortimore C.	Avey Griffin	6 Jun.	1861
Fleming, Peter L.	Annie F. Fulcher	15 Oct.	1868
Foalds, Ferney	Aramitta Newnus (sic)	19 Dec.	1867
Forehand, Berrien A.	Harriet E. Brinson	13 Nov.	1856
Forehand, W. H.	Emily Hills	5 Feb.	1868
Fortner, Thomas	Virginia Nasworthy	13 Jun.	1869
Francis, James C.	Sarah G. Whitehead	17 Feb.	1864
Franklin, Augustus F.	Alla G. Hughes	19 Jul.	1864
Freeman, Rerrick	Frances Rainy	18 May	1867
Fulcher, John W.	Annie Syms	21 Jun.	1869
Fullerwood, Jim	Mary Malone	9 Oct.	1869
Gaines, Seaborn	Louisa Ricker	16 Jan.	1861
Gaines, Nunroe (sic)	Susannah Green	20 Apr.	1869
Gamaway, Edward	Violet McElmurray	8 May	1869
Garlinton, Benjamin	Rosaline E. Helmley	18 Jul.	1861
Garner, Sam	Rhoda Bell	16 May	1869
Garvin, John	Phillis Pryor	5 Aug.	1866
Gaulding, Cnojo (sic)	Amanda Lowery	14 May	1869
Gay, Jacob	Dilsey Adams	23 Sep.	1869
George, Silas	Mariann Mathis	16 Mar.	1867
George, Jacob	Martha Thomen	8 Aug.	1869
Gilstrap, Mingo	Margaret Kilpatrick	24 Nov.	1867
Glisson, James T.	Mrs. Aby Young	13 Dec.	1856
Glisson, Evan C.	Cellinise M. Carpenter	30 Jul.	1863
Glisson, Dennis T.	Mary Jane E. Hillis	9 Jan.	1868
Glisson, J. W.	Alice Houston	9 Dec.	1869
Godbee, Stephen	Jane M. Bargeron	15 Apr.	1855
Godbee, Jason	Carrie Parris	14 Aug.	1856
Godbee, James M.	Sarah Mulkey	6 Nov.	1856
Godbee, Alfred A.	Ursula Holland	5 Jan.	1862
Godbee, Carswell G.	Josie A. Royal	11 Jul.	1864
Godbee, James W.	Ellen J. Harley	1 May	1865
Godbee, Homer V.	Eliza Lewis	30 Nov.	1865
Godbee, Charles	Savannah Elliott	20 Jul.	1866
Godbee, Rayford	Mary J. Godbee	1 Nov.	1866
Godbee, Dave	Sarah Darlington	27 Dec.	1866
Godbee, Ezekiel S.	Sarah A. Herrington	26 Mar.	1868
Godbee, Coper (sic)	Mattie Homes	7 Jan.	1869
Godby, Elippey P.	Winnie Valloton	3 Sep.	1861
Golden, Lankuter	Lovey Jackson	3 Oct.	1869
Gorden, Robert	E. A. Powell	15 Jun.	1865
Gordon, John	Sophia Smith	30 Nov.	1869
Gray, Portus	Chaney Colson	27 Nov.	1869

Green, Jesse P.	Mary J. Gresham	17 Feb. 1859
Green, Sam	Emma Cuyles	8 Sep. 1867
Green, Toby	Hannah Thomas	4 Jul. 1868
Green, John	Dianah Tomlon	15 Feb. 1869
Green, Riley	Susan Smith	26 Dec. 1869
Gresham, J. Jones	Ella Ulla Lasseter	1 Jul. 1868
Griffin, Benjamin F.	Sarah M. Godbee	2 Mar. 1859
Griffin, Jefferson L.	Sydney Ann Holland	2 Jan. 1859
Griffin, Dewey	Lettie Jones	16 Apr. 1868
Griffin, Joe	Lindy Boyd	19 Sep. 1869
Griffin, Royal	Harriet Williams	23 Oct. 1869
Grubbs, James	Jane C. Hoyle	20 Nov. 1856
Grubbs, Daniel G.	Georgia Messex	3 Jul. 1866
Hale, Benning T.	Amanda Royal	2 Dec. 1869
Hall, Verdree	Virginia Lovell	12 Aug. 1857
Hall, Benning J.	Susan Godbee	24 Oct. 1860
Hall, Berryan	Catherine Holland	6 Sep. 1866
Hanberg, Solomon	Nancy Bell	23 Dec. 1855
Harper, Henry	Moselle Lavine	12 Feb. 1869
Harrell, John D.	Annie E. Owens	23 Feb. 1863
Harris, La Fayette	Susan Chance	12 Jan. 1860
Harris, Franklin	Bassheba Jenkins	24 Oct. 1860
Harrison, John P.	Linda Saxon	11 Feb. 1869
Hatcher, Leonidas B.	Ann Powell	3 Jan. 1861
Hatcher, Dr. Edward	Augusta V. Churchill	10 Jan. 1861
Hatcher, Berry	Selina Hilton	17 Jun. 1863
Hatcher, N. J.	Sarah M. Boyd	22 Oct. 1869
Haws, Joseph W.	Susan Perkins	11 Nov. 1860
Hayman, Elisha	Roscian Snider	15 Dec. 1865
Hayman, Everett	Elizabeth Coonaman	30 Jan. 1866
Hayne, Orrin L.	Emily Owen	20 Nov. 1857
Haynes, James B.	Mrs. Julia E. Anderson	26 Feb. 1857
Haynes, Edward	Amanda Brooks	6 Sep. 1867
Haywood, Luke	Sarah Hunter	3 Aug. 1869
Heath, Washington	Ann Godbee	27 Oct. 1858
Heath, Judson L.	Mary Jane Covender	10 Feb. 1864
Heath, George W.	Sarah McCain	18 Feb. 1865
Heath, Homer V.	Octavia Godbee	9 Mar. 1865
Heath, Juluis V.	Melvina Oden	21 Dec. 1865
Heath, Justin B.	Mary Rowse	9 May 1867
Heath, Samuel J.	Amelia Buxton	16 May 1867
Heath, Samuel L.	Leonora Buxton	1 Nov. 1868
Heath, Jim	Sarah Allen	4 Sep. 1869
Henderson, W. N.	Emily Truett	1 May 1867
Henson, Sut	Serena Jackson	13 Jun. 1869
Herrington, Stephen M.	Caroline L. Bostwick	25 Oct. 1860
Herrington, Daniel	Hetty Bell	23 Jun. 1867
Herrington, Crawford	Abbie A. Reeves	19 Dec. 1867
Herrington, Martin E.	Lou Carpenter	12 Nov. 1868
Hickman, William	Nancy Oglesbee	24 Dec. 1865
Hickman, Andrew	Rebecca Royals	24 Sep. 1868
Hickman, Henry A.	Eliza E. Spears	21 Oct. 1868
Higgins, Nathan	Sarah Ann Douglas	6 Jul. 1869
Hill, Pleasant	Mary A. Murray	12 Aug. 1863
Hill, Benjamin	Sallie L. Turner	28 Sep. 1865
Hill, William J.	Lucy Casnahan	12 Nov. 1865
Hill, B. D.	Eliza Lovett	21 May 1866
Hill, John G.	Julia B. Godbee	19 Feb. 1867
Hill, Jacob	Mariah Crockett	16 Jun. 1867
Hillis, Alexander	Jane Frances Kelly	18 Jan. 1861
Hillis, Henry	Mary Stacy	7 Nov. 1861
Hillis, Jacob	Frances Daniel	17 Nov. 1864
Hillis, Simeon	Mariah Jane Breuson	12 Jul. 1866
Hilton, Joseph	Joanna Boyd	28 Jan. 1869
Holland, Seaborn	Celia Kent	12 Jul. 1855
Holland, Iasiah	Polly Ann Godbee	9 Feb. 1859
Holland, George W., Esq.	Frances E. Houston	18 Jan. 1860
Holland, Marion	Louisa Bargeron	28 Mar. 1861
Holmes, George	Rachel Williams	20 Dec. 1868
Holton, George J.	Martha Bearrow	21 Oct. 1860

Holton, Benjamin	Harriet Randle	12 Aug. 1866
Horn, William	Frances Jones	29 Dec. 1866
Houston, Augustus	Avery Ann Burke	5 Dec. 1858
Houston, Rufus	Joicis Wilkins (sic)	5 Jul. 1866
Houston, E. N.	Florence A. Godbee	27 Aug. 1869
Howard, John Gordon	Julia A. Whitehead	19 Apr. 1858
Howell, James	Maria Marshall	30 Oct. 1869
Howell, Green	Susan Sampson	22 Dec. 1869
Huggins, George W.	Sarah E. Griffin	10 Oct. 1866
Hughes, Augustus B.	Alice G. Cates	26 Oct. 1858
Hughes, Charles T.	Mrs. Agnes E. Hughes	3 Feb. 1866
Hughes, West	Hannah Glover	28 Dec. 1867
Hughes, Robert	Lottie Roberts	5 Dec. 1869
Hughes, Ward H.	Anna A. Roberts	22 Dec. 1869
Hurst, Seaborn E.	Lydia D. Clarke	13 Jun. 1861
Hurst, Moses	Melisia Brigham	18 Mar. 1869
Inman, Alfred G.	Mary J. Grubbs	12 May 1868
Iram, John	Easter Whitehead	29 Jul. 1866
Jackson, Stephen A.	Sarah Skinner	23 Jun. 1858
Jackson, Hezekiah	Rebecca Barrow	8 Jan. 1862
Jackson, Lemuel	Anna Davis	1 Mar. 1868
Jackson, Will	Lizzie Walton	26 Jan. 1869
Jackson, Wm. Jasper	Leah Wilson	27 Mar. 1869
Jackson, George	Scilla Green	25 Dec. 1869
Jackson, Ned	Violet Blount	27 Dec. 1869
Jawers, John H.	Sarah A. Perry	28 Mar. 1866
Jeffers, W. William	Lucretia Barefield	12 Jul. 1855
Jeffers, James M.	Josephine Wallace	16 May 1866
Jeffers, Johnathan	Mary Hall	2 Aug. 1866
Jenkins, Iqatus (sic)	Lavina Proctor	17 Apr. 1856
Jenkins, Phillip	Ellen Raney	May 1867
Jenkins, Spane	Hannah Hall	8 May 1869
Jenkins, Charles J.	Catherine M. Attaway	13 Oct. 1869
Johnson, James	Elizabeth Johnson	31 Aug. 1858
Johnson, Dr. L. D.	Branka J. Rollins	15 Oct. 1861
Johnson, Parish	Jane Shaw	22 Mar. 1868
Johnson, John	Amanda Brown	27 Sep. 1868
Johnson, Bradus	Phebe Mills	23 Jun. 1869
Jones, Malcomb D.	Virginia L. Inman	10 Apr. 1860
Jones, Batt	Caraline E. Hines	24 Jun. 1858
Jones, Thomas	Rosalina O. Randle	18 Apr. 1860
Jones, George W.	Elizabeth Bullard	8 Oct. 1865
Jones, Seaborn	Louisa Barton	15 Mar. 1866
Jones, Ross	Caroline Johnson	13 May 1866
Jones, David	Rebecca Carswell	11 Jun. 1866
Jones, Augustus	Martha Jones	6 Oct. 1866
Jones, James	Patsey Davis	18 Nov. 1866
Jones, Forney	Mary Stewart	19 Nov. 1866
Jones, Alfred	Nancy Lane	4 May 1867
Jones, Samuel	Julia Stewart	4 May 1867
Jones, Simeon	Rachel Jones	25 May 1867
Jones, Jerry	Nancy Huse	16 Jun. 1867
Jones, Isam	Eliza Rheney	24 Nov. 1867
Jones, John	Judy Whitehead	18 Mar. 1868
Jones, Henry	Jane Skinner	13 Mar. 1869
Jones, Thomas Reed	Dinah Lawson	2 Mar. 1869
Jones, Serm (sic)	Louisa Marshall	10 Apr. 1869
Jones, Preston	Frances Doyle	12 May 1869
Jones, George	Betsey Ann Kilpatrick	3 Sep. 1869
Jones, Charles	Matilda Hughes	14 Nov. 1869
Jones, Morris	Carrie Hammond	25 Dec. 1869
Jordon, James	Fanny Mack	1 Feb. 1868
Kelly, John	Law M. Symms	4 Mar. 1866
Kelly, John W.	Florida Pickering	26 Feb. 1868
Kelsey, Robert	Milly Jones	5 Dec. 1866
Kennady, William F.	Araminta C. Utley	15 Jan. 1868
Kenyan, John L.	Virginia M. Gray	22 Aug. 1866
Kimbrell, Dallis	Mary Rackley	28 Dec. 1864
Kimbrell, Simeon	Chloe Watkins	10 Aug. 1869
Kirk, Rollin H.	Julia L. Cox	12 Jul. 1866

Knight, John D.	Mary Cross	24 Dec.	1868
Knight, John	Fanny Bartley	23 Sep.	1869
Knight, Soloman	Ella Lawson	31 Dec.	1869
Lake, William P.	Ellen J. Wallace	14 Feb.	1867
Lamb, Charles R.	Rebecca Chance	19 Mar.	1856
Lambert, John	Nancy Ann Hurd	7 Mar.	1856
Lambert, Jermiah E.	Lousia Godbee	28 Dec.	1865
Lambert, George A.	Mary E. Watkins	20 Dec.	1868
Lanor, Benjamin	Susan Carter	5 Aug.	1866
Landing, David M. M.	Harriet Belcher	24 Dec.	1856
Landing, Ransom L.	Elvira Brinson	16 Jun.	1867
Lane, Daniel	Mary Clark	8 May	1864
Lane, George	Ellen Belcher	26 Dec.	1867
Lanier, Thomas W.	Nancy Lovett	29 May	1862
Lasseter, William E.	Margaret E. Caldwell	8 Dec.	1857
Lasseter, Middleton T.	Dilly Moore	28 Oct.	1866
Lasseter, Pad	Nancy Mills	23 Dec.	1866
Lassiter, Thomas H.	Patenice P. Tabb (sic)	24 Jan.	1856
Law, Dick	Amey Walton	26 Jan.	1869
Lawson, Moses	Susan Bennefield	7 Feb.	1869
Lawson, Nathan	Phillis Washington	16 May	1869
Lester, John A.	Sallie Rodgers	8 Oct.	1868
Lewis, Henry S.	Olive McCoy	11 Jan.	1857
Lewis, John	Nancy A. Perkins	29 Oct.	1857
Lewis, Thomas	Sabra McCoy	22 Dec.	1857
Lewis, Barnett B.	Frances M. Chance	5 Jun.	1859
Lewis, Alfred	Charlotte Ward	25 Mar.	1866
Lewis, Ned	Georgia Ann Royal	8 Nov.	1868
Lewis, Bill	Lucy Blount	29 Dec.	1868
Lightfoot, James	Beda Ann Love	24 Apr.	1856
Lightfoot, Archa	Polly Adkinson	17 Nov.	1859
Lightfoot, James	Josephine Massey	25 Nov.	1866
Lightfoot, Moses	Elizabeth Perry	7 Feb.	1869
Linch, Robert	Frances Foster	25 Mar.	1866
Lipsey, William	Roxey Ann Anderson	25 Sep.	1856
Lively, John G.	Julia Ann Holland	18 Jan.	1861
Lively, Alexander	Elizabeth Kimbrel	10 Jun.	1862
Lively, Green B.	Mary Jane Elliot	10 Sep.	1866
Lively, George P.	Clara N. Powell	2 Apr.	1867
Lockhart, Andrew	Charity Burton	3 Mar.	1869
Long, William	Mary E. Stacey	8 Mar.	1869
Lovette, Alex	Lizzie Small	27 Mar.	1869
Lucky, Marcus A.	Fanny Modisda	5 Jun.	1868
Lumkin, Joseph L.	Sarah J. Grimes	5 Oct.	1865
Lumkin, Joseph S.	Ann Eliza Cole	30 Oct.	1856
Lynch, Alfred	Ann Garvin	21 Feb.	1869
Mabyn, Daniel Webster	Charlotte Murray	26 Jun.	1869
Madden, James M.	Maria M. McIntosh	13 Feb.	1868
Madiset, Charles M.	Sarah H. Gregory	18 Feb.	1864
Malabar, John	Martha Godbee	27 Jul.	1859
Mannd, Calhoun	Balsora C. McCan	22 Dec.	1859
Mares, James H.	Elifare L. Adam	2 Oct.	1861
Marsh, Isaac M.	Georgia S. Walton	22 Jan.	1857
Martin, James	Mary Ann Smith	21 Aug.	1860
Martin, Jerry	Leticia Smith	2 Apr.	1867
Mathis, Taney	Sarah Colson	7 Mar.	1869
Maund, Calhoun	Balsora C. McCon	22 Dec.	1859
Maynor, Simeon	Virginia Tabb	25 Dec.	1855
Mays, Edward S.	A. E. Mary Jones	7 Dec.	1858
Merry, Bradford, Esq.	Sarah H. Palmer	1 Aug.	1866
Messex, Jesse	Lenora Lawrence	11 Jun.	1857
Milican, John A.	Josephine A. Hines	8 Apr.	1868
Miller, William K.	Emily Murphee	1 Feb.	1859
Miller, Henry	Nancy Cosnahan	15 Nov.	1860
Miller, William, Esq.	Dinah Sexton	14 Oct.	1866
Miller, Alfred	Adaline Schley	4 Mar.	1867
Miller, William K.	Fanny H. Williams	20 Jul.	1869
Mills, Solomon K.	Sarah M. Ellison	19 Sep.	1860
Mills, Randall	Nancy Roberson	17 Jan.	1869
Mills, Costell	Creasy Kimbell	11 Dec.	1869

Mims, Thomas S.	Emma Ellison	12 Feb.	1866
Mitchell, Newton	Mandy Crummond	4 Dec.	1869
Mixon, John	Josephine Stephens	20 Jan.	1867
Moncrief, Seaborn L.	Virginia L. Rhodes	30 Apr.	1867
Moocsett, Lewis Y.	Celeslia V. Clark	6 Jun.	1869
Moody, Walter F.	Jane Adalade Dixon	26 Dec.	1865
Moore, Thomas	Mary Ann Peal	25 Feb.	1857
Moore, John	Sarah Skinner	27 Sep.	1860
Moore, Thomas	Mary Sharp	26 Dec.	1866
Moore, W. E.	J. D. Hatch	25 Dec.	1868
Morgan, Christopher C.	Jane Mary Moore (sic)	24 Oct.	1857
Morris, Coly	Caroline Plumer	4 Nov.	1866
Munnerlyn, John D.	Annie R. Mandell	14 Dec.	1865
Murphy, William R.	Sarah J. Jones	15 Oct.	1856
Murphy, Robert A.	Henry S. Jones	15 Oct.	1856
Murray, Enoch	Mary Boyd	17 Jan.	1863
Murry, Caleb	Myram A. Jenkins	12 Mar.	1863
McCarthan, Rias	Amelia Hosey	24 Nov.	1867
McCatharine, Walker, Esq.	Sallie Chandler	23 Feb.	1868
McCaughlin, John	Emily Bailey	15 Jul.	1858
McCollough, John T.	Mary E. Wooding	29 Dec.	1859
McCoy, William	Mary Ann Bryant	19 Oct.	1856
McCoy, George M.	Eliza Wheeler	23 Aug.	1869
McCroan, Rhesa H. C.	Florence C. Roberson	27 May	1863
McElmurry, Thomas J.	Louisa E. Barron	5 Mar.	1861
McElmurry, John F.	Annie E. Shewmaker	7 Sep.	1865
McHenry, Edward A. L.	Anna J. Hill	19 Sep.	1865
McKenzie, James	Laura Palmer	25 Dec.	1867
McKensey, Isum	Harriet Conley	17 Jan.	1867
McNat, Moses	Rose McNat	16 Mar.	1867
McNarrell, Kinchen P.	Mary V. Fulcher	17 Jan.	1865
Nasworthy, Thomas J.	Queen Elizabeth Drake	20 Jul.	1865
Nasworthy, John	Martha Godbee	28 Mar.	1867
Nasworthy, Mitchell O.	Willie Jones	7 Nov.	1869
Nealy, James M.	Caroline Alexander	7 Feb.	1861
Netherland, William P.	Mary Jane Robertson	18 Oct.	1866
O'Banion, John	Martha Lively	16 Dec.	1855
O'Cheler, John F.	Joanna Williams	1 Jun.	1858
Odum, James P.	Matilda Sapp	24 Feb.	1864
Oglesby, Henry	Elizabeth Jenkins	11 May	1856
Oglesby, John	Adaline Murray	2 Mar.	1865
Oglesby, B. J.	Mary H. Oliver	10 Dec.	1869
Oglesby, Richard	Louisa Jenkins	19 Dec.	1869
Oliver, Charles T.	Nancy A. Reeves	1 May	1867
Osborn, Moses	Huldy Barton	6 Jun.	1869
Owen, John B.	Katie M. Mackenzie	18 Feb.	1857
Owen, Alexander	Martha Cates	14 Oct.	1858
Owens, Lancaster	Eister Warnock (sic)	13 Dec.	1866
Owens, James	Mary Ann Jinkins	29 Jan.	1868
Pace, Andrew	Savannah Rhodes	14 Apr.	1866
Pallock, George W.	Usula E. Wood	2 Aug.	1868
Palmer, George A.	Mary Davis	4 Oct.	1860
Palmer, Edwin N.	Ella E. Ballard	17 Jan.	1867
Palmer, Elbert	Emily Palmer	16 Nov.	1867
Paris, Mose	Grace Lovette	13 Jun.	1869
Parker, Thomas	Harriet E. Jones	15 Nov.	1860
Parker, Henry	Emma Miller	20 Jun.	1869
Parramore, Robert R.	Nancy J. Brinson	27 Jan.	1857
Pee, Peter	Nancy Brinson	14 Jun.	1867
Peel, Thomas	Sarah Ann Dickey	14 Sep.	1856
Peel, Robert D.	Milly Joiner	22 Jul.	1858
Peel, Henry	Susan Wallace	26 Mar.	1865
Peel, William M.	Olive Dickey	13 Nov.	1865
Penny, Joshua E.	Mary E. Lightfoot	12 Jul.	1863
Penro, Martin A.	Carnelai S. Hopkins	1 Mar.	1866
Perkins, Newton	Sarah Reynolds	17 May	1857
Perkins, David M.	Sarah Ann Sapp	27 May	1858
Perkins, George W.	Susannah Brinson	6 Dec.	1859
Perkins, Andrew J.	Pauline V. Perkins	24 Apr.	1862
Perkins, George W.	Mary Ann Wallace	28 Sep.	1865

Perkins, Randale	Norah McElmurray	20 Dec.	1866
Perry, Joseph D.	Martha Warnock	23 May	1861
Perry, Heman H.	Charlotte E. Carter	15 Apr.	1868
Perry, Charles	Eliza Sherrod	31 Dec.	1868
Peterson, Seaborn H.	Francis Wiggins	28 Jul.	1857
Phillips, John A.	Elizabeth F. Warnock	7 Aug.	1862
Phillups, Isach	Eliza Williams	9 May	1869
Pickering, G. F. P.	S. Z. Cosnohan	1 Dec.	1869
Pierce, William L.	Savannah A. Drake	24 Dec.	1857
Pinckard, Alvin W.	Isabella Perry	23 Feb.	1862
Pool, W. B.	Willie Vaughn	21 Mar.	1869
Port, Basil	Barbara Floyd	23 Dec.	1869
Powell, Barry	Joicy Perden (sic)	20 Mar.	1864
Powell, John	Augustus Ann Royal	12 Jul.	1860
Powell, LaFayette	Sophia A. Murphy	3 Jan.	1862
Prescott, Thomas	Mattie A. Dukes	28 May	1868
Prescott, Anderson Augustus	Louisa O'Bannion	7 Jun.	1869
Preskitt, Britton	Elizabeth A. Syms	17 Dec.	1868
Prince, Dennis	Manda Dixon	5 Aug.	1869
Proctor, William P.	Margaret P. Hurst	5 Dec.	1858
Quick, Cameron	Radaskey Heath (sic)	24 Jan.	1858
Randall, Abram	Hannah Barnes	23 Dec.	1869
Reese, John T. A.	Elizabeth Elliot	31 Jan.	1866
Reese, Toby	Eliza Peel	14 Jun.	1868
Reeves, Dand	Amelia Corke	24 Feb.	1867
Reeves, John T.	Florence M. Chance	14 Nov.	1867
Reeves, George W.	Kittia Prescott	18 Dec.	1868
Revill, William T.	Alice A. Ledbetter	16 Jul.	1863
Reynolds, Amelius W.	Martha Ann Forehand	10 Jan.	1856
Reynolds, John W.	Mary L. Shewmaker	23 Nov.	1865
Reynolds, Charles	Lucy Roberson	15 May	1869
Reynolds, William M.	Josephine Perkins	22 Dec.	1867
Rhaney, Anthony	Laurah Perry	21 May	1867
Rhodes, Elbert	Maude Scales	14 Apr.	1866
Rhodes, Simon	Patsey McCollum	15 May	1869
Rhodes, Arnor	Jimmis Garvin	27 Oct.	1869
Roberson, Lamb	Susan Mills	23 Oct.	1862
Roberson, Mack	Venus Grant	24 Dec.	1866
Roberson, Fortson	Annie Genings	17 Feb.	1867
Roberson, Ceasar	Sarah Wise	30 Jun.	1867
Roberson, John T.	Emily Scott	2 Jan.	1868
Roberson, William	Savannah Lively	17 Oct.	1869
Roberts, George D.	Susan R. McElmurray	12 Nov.	1863
Roberts, William	Missouri Barber	18 Jan.	1868
Roberts, Jacob	Emily Whitfield	26 Jun.	1869
Robertson, David	Frances Cook	24 Feb.	1867
Robinson, Nathan	Mary Harris	5 Jun.	1869
Rodgers, Aloheus M.	Martha Virginia Blount	8 Feb.	1860
Rogers, Enoch Jr.	Anna J. Hughes	10 Nov.	1859
Rogers, Richard W.	Frances A. Robertson	11 Jun.	1862
Rogers, Rufus J.	Nancy Buxton	17 Sep.	1862
Rogers, Benjamin F.	Earnist G. Brown	26 Jan.	1865
Rosier, Daniel	Elivira Green	10 Dec.	1869
Routzahn, L. H.	Florence V. Byne	4 Jul.	1867
Rowland, Charles A.	Cathrine B. Whitehead	13 Jun.	1860
Rowland, James M.	Victoria Buxton	9 Dec.	1862
Rowland, Robert A.	Martha Wooding	7 Jan.	1864
Rowland, James M.	Savannah Odom	5 Oct.	1865
Rowls, Hesekiah	Cameral Zimon Sapp	30 Jul.	1863
Royal, Franklin	Christanna Prescott	5 Mar.	1856
Royal, William P.	Jane D. Odem	28 Dec.	1865
Royal, James W.	Elmina C. Oglesbee	21 Jan.	1866
Royal, Guilford	Frances G. Perry	10 Feb.	1869
Royal, Sam	Susan Brinson	3 Jul.	1869
Royal, George	Anaby Jones	19 Sep.	1869
Ruder, Shadick	Gracy Hodson	13 Apr.	1867
Salmon, Jefferson D.	Amelia M. Davant	31 Jan.	1867
Sanders, Jarvis W.	Emily E. Mears	10 Sep.	1856
Sapp, Enos	Mary Elliott	24 Feb.	1856
Sapp, Seaborn	Narcissa Scarbough	13 Nov.	1857

Sapp, Peter	Jane Bostick	27 May 1866
Sapp, Solomon	Easter Hankerson	29 Dec. 1866
Sapp, Madison	Edney Lewis	2 Jun. 1867
Sapp, Henderson	Deana Chandler	7 Sep. 1867
Sapp, Allen	Junny Shewmaker	19 Dec. 1867
Sapp, John	Mary Sapp	14 Jun. 1868
Sapp, Henderson	Jane Sapp	28 Jan. 1869
Sapp, Minock	Lizzie Roberts	28 Mar. 1869
Sapp, Jonen	Hitty Nesmith	30 Dec. 1869
Saxon, John	Milly Madray	15 Apr. 1857
Saxon, Augustus A.	Mary Frances Bearfield	25 Jun. 1866
Saxon, Ranson Y.	Lucky A. W. Tabb	11 Oct. 1866
Saxon, William H.	Clara C. Goddwin	7 Feb. 1867
Saxon, Albert B.	Susan Carpenter	19 Apr. 1868
Scaffield, William	Barney Proctor	20 Sep. 1865
Scales, Barney	Chaney Ward	26 Dec. 1865
Scaffner, John F.	Mary J. Dillard	16 Jul. 1857
Schley, Henry	Luch Skinner	13 Jan. 1867
Schley, Ned	Hannah Nathan	13 Jun. 1869
Scott, Henry	Alhee Cook	15 Dec. 1867
Scott, George	Sarah Griffin	4 Dec. 1868
Scott, Willis	Betsey Smith	14 Jan. 1869
Sew, Alfred Roath	Susannah C. Mobley	2 Jun. 1857
Shepard, William B.	Lavina Forehand	4 Feb. 1857
Shewmaker, Saxon	Maria Brown	31 Oct. 1867
Shewmaker, George	Viney Scott	26 Dec. 1869
Shubert, Abram	Sarah Allen	16 Aug. 1868
Sikes, James	Harriet M. Belcher	1 Jul. 1858
Sikes, Edward	Martha Melvina Cole	14 Aug. 1867
Singleton, Grandison	Caroline Singleton	13 Mar. 1869
Skinner, Uriah	Lavinia L. Lane	13 Aug. 1857
Skinner, Simeion G.	Jane Sarah Ann Barrow	8 Jan. 1858
Skinner, Unah	Ivena Chance	10 Mar. 1859
Skinner, Simeon	Mary Oglesby	26 Jul. 1863
Smith, John B.	Mary Wilkins	15 Mar. 1858
Smith, Ebenzer	Jane Brown	5 Sep. 1858
Smith, William	Martha Jenkins	10 Apr. 1859
Smith, Charles M.	Florence M. Harris	6 May 1862
Smith, Alfred B.	Malissa Godbee	20 May 1862
Smith, James R.	Sallie A. Dawson	11 Sep. 1863
Smith, Nathan	Nancy Ann Bargeron	14 Feb. 1866
Smith, W. J.	Susan Randon	22 Oct. 1867
Smith, Luke Nee	Ann Newton	7 Aug. 1869
Smith, Bill	Jane Jones	29 Aug. 1869
Smith, Calvin	Louisa Carter	7 Sep. 1869
Smith, Alek	Mary Boyd	17 Oct. 1869
Snead, Walter	Olive Bostick	21 Jan. 1869
Snead, Prince	Phillis West	3 Jul. 1869
Stephens, Hezekiah	Mary Ann Wimberly	14 Aug. 1856
Stephens, General P.	Sarah J. Barrow	30 Jul. 1861
Stevens, Daniel J.	Dealpha M. W. Jeffers	20 Sep. 1857
Stewart, Vincent	Eliza J. Skinner	3 May 1863
Stewart, Vincent	Elizabeth Morris	9 Aug. 1866
Stokes, James M.	Louisa C. Heath	8 Mar. 1863
Stone, James G.	Laura A. Tarver	19 Jan. 1864
Stone, Robert R.	Drucilla Jackson	8 Jul. 1869
Stringer, William F. M.	Ann C. Fulcher	25 Jun. 1857
Sumner, Robert	Julia Blackburn	22 Feb. 1866
Sykes, William	Virginia W. McClennand	2 Oct. 1864
Syll, Thomas	Elizy Franklin	26 May 1867
Symes, Robert	Edy Osburn	31 May 1866
Tabb, Robert	Emily Gray	8 Nov. 1860
Taylor, Abram	Mary Wheeler	2 Feb. 1868
Templeton, John C.	Mary E. McCullough	27 Dec. 1867
Tenison, John L.	Cynthia Harrel	18 Dec. 1867
Tessier, Rush E.	Elizabeth A. Heath	1 May 1861
Tessier, Madison M.	Lamira L. Griffin	11 May 1862
Tessier, Madison M.	Charlotte Godbee	1 May 1866
Thomas, Robert F.	Marie Louisa Gordon	4 Mar. 1860
Thomas, John R.	Sarah Louisa McNorrill	6 Jun. 1861

Thomas, Joseph A.	Geraldine A. Gordon	15 Jul. 1862
Thomas, Charles	Jane Davis	26 May 1867
Thompson, R. E. J.	Frances Packard	1 Jan. 1867
Thompson, John	Jane Walls	9 Dec. 1860
Thompson, Nathan	Louisa Thompson	23 Jun. 1867
Tomlin, John	Lou Caine	4 Apr. 1867
Tree, Lovett Rason	Annie Palmer	24 Jul. 1869
Tucker, S. J.	Hester Brinson	30 Dec. 1866
Turner, William E.	Louisa M. Collins	8 Sep. 1858
Turner, Moses	Lucindy Turner	1 Jan. 1868
Turner, Sam	Jane Matthews	19 Jun. 1869
Twiggs, Abram	Henrietta Jones	22 Dec. 1867
Utley, Henry L.	Mariah Godbee	2 Nov. 1865
Vaughn, McDonald	Martha Ward	24 Apr. 1856
Vaughn, McDaniel	Rosaline Duke	8 Feb. 1866
Vaugn, Jeremiah	Sarah A. Carson	6 May 1866
Vickory, Hesekiah	Margarett Jenkins	20 Feb. 1863
Videtta, Payton L.	Eliza A. M. Rackley	3 Sep. 1867
Viditto, Henry A.	Mary L. Graham	11 Jul. 1864
Walker, John	Lavina Attaway	5 Oct. 1859
Walker, William	Lucinda Lightfoot	10 Nov. 1866
Walker, Abram	Elizabeth Cummings	10 Apr. 1869
Walker, Capers	Fanny Hatcher	16 Jun. 1869
Walker, Wanen	Mary Jinkins	31 Jul. 1869
Walker, Stephen	Leah Jackson	28 Dec. 1869
Wallace, Stying C.	Mary D. Perkins	1 Nov. 1860
Wallace, William B.	Sarah J. Daughtery	18 Aug. 1861
Wallace, Newton S.	Virginia Brinson	23 Oct. 1866
Wallace, W. Simeon	Mary Holloway	5 Jan. 1868
Wallace, Semion (sic)	Sarah F. Perkins	22 Sep. 1868
Walton, William F.	Ida O. Gordon	13 Nov. 1865
Walton, Robert	Lucy West	12 Feb. 1869
Walton, Emory S.	June Cawley	15 Jul. 1869
Ward, Edwin L. A.	Amanda Hutchens	19 Apr. 1864
Ward, Joseph	Anna Bell	28 Oct. 1866
Ward, Henry C.	Caroline E. Sapp	22 Aug. 1867
Warner, Samuel	Amanda F. Colson	16 Jun. 1864
Warnock, Simeon	Lucy Ann Lamb	17 Jul. 1856
Washington, George	Rosa Lewis	25 Nov. 1866
Washington, Andrew	Lucinon Matthews	20 Dec. 1868
Washington, George	Adeline Johnson	12 Jun. 1869
Washington, Shippeord	Harriette Davis	25 Dec. 1869
Watkins, Stephen	Mary Byne	7 Feb. 1869
Way, Jim	Harriet Wiley	6 Jun. 1869
Weaver, Henry C.	Fannie R. Ruddell	18 Dec. 1866
Welch, Nicholas S.	Mary Diemond	9 Mar. 1859
Welch, Handy	Jane Peterson	5 Aug. 1866
Whitehead, Augustus	Harriet Sapp	3 Jan. 1869
Whitehead, Prines	Affie Jones	26 Sep. 1869
Whitfield, Bryant W.	Rebecca Bonnell	25 Apr. 1860
Whitfield, Arter	Dolly Barnes	4 Jan. 1868
Whitfield, Friday	Rosa Dickson	9 Jan. 1869
Whitfield, Henry	Jane Kelsey	21 Aug. 1869
Whitfield, Asa B.	Mary Thompson	29 Oct. 1869
Wilde, Richard D.	Annie Whitehead	29 Apr. 1856
Williams, James	Mahaly Pennington	17 Jul. 1859
Williams, Samuel M.	Mary Proctor	15 Sep. 1859
Williams, Herrington	Harriet Ward	25 Feb. 1866
Williams, Henry	Henretta Jenkins	7 Jun. 1866
Williams, Prasper	Mary Virges	5 Aug. 1866
Williams, Thomas	Ludia S. Lovett	21 Oct. 1866
Williams, Frank R.	Laura C. Wood	6 Dec. 1866
Williams, Peter	Aby Whitehead	29 Dec. 1866
Williams, Bedford	Charlota Hatcher	24 Feb. 1867
Williams, Richmond	Maria Duke	7 Mar. 1867
Williams, Henry H.	Ann Lewis	27 May 1867
Williams, Randolph	Ella Weaver	27 Oct. 1867
Williams, Ed	Caroline Evans	18 Jan. 1868
Williams, Emit	Royals Condus	28 Jan. 1868
Williams, Richard	Anna Lewis	5 Jan. 1869

Williams, Scott	Lucinda Green	10 Mar. 1869
Williams, Olliver	July Byne	26 Apr. 1869
Williams, Well	Edie Jones	22 May 1869
Williams, Floyd T.	S. O. Gray	26 Aug. 1869
Wilson, John B.	Delila Ann Peel	5 Feb. 1863
Wilson, Mike	Becky Jones	26 Dec. 1868
Wilson, Cupid	Ann Oliver	18 Apr. 1869
Wimberley, Richard C.	Georgia Bell	28 Nov. 1867
Wimberly, Simeon	Ally Chadler	13 Dec. 1855
Wimberly, Mackey W.	Maria E. Brickest	29 Oct. 1863
Wimberly, William T.	Edla C. Powell	9 Mar. 1865
Wimberly, Jesse	Alice M. Wimberly	2 Nov. 1865
Winskey, William	Georgia Jinkins	11 Jan. 1866
Winter, John W.	S. J. Rosier	26 Nov. 1867
Witherspoon, Samuel	Laura Scales	14 Apr. 1866
Woodward, Welcom	Mary Baxter	28 Sep. 1869
Wright, Ambrose R.	Carrie C. Hazlehurst	3 Sep. 1857
Wright, Augustus	Jesse Wallace	24 Nov. 1867
Wright, Crawford	Laura Cummings	24 Jan. 1869
Wright, George	Polly Abenter	26 Jan. 1869
Wyett, Benjamin	Tenah Bullard	22 Sep. 1865
Young, Stanley	Amarintha Perry	11 Apr. 1866
Young, Robert	Jane Cooper	6 Dec. 1868
Young, Wade	Adeline Brown	20 Mar. 1869
Youngblood, John T.	Mary Green Carson	22 Oct. 1856
Youngblood, Davis	Elefair Overstreet	18 Oct. 1866
Youngblood, Harry	Dinah Cook	11 Apr. 1869

1830 CENSUS OF BURKE COUNTY, GEORGIA

Sometimes there are several page numbers on a page. The official one recognized by the National Archives is the one STAMPED in the top right corner, and is the one used here.

Page 117

Fitzpatrick, John
Turner, John Jr.
Gregory, John
Sharp, Abeda
Hickman, Paschal
Applewhite, Stephen
Lightfoot, Benjamin
Duke, Azariah
Duke, James
Daniell, Moses
Applewhite, Peter
Attaway, Candacy
Jeffers, Jonathan
Turner, John Jr.
Mainor, Willis
Cox, Esther
Byrd, Nathan
Sharp, Cader
Brinson, William
Luke, Edward
Duke, Elisha
Madray, George
Owen, John
Johns, Jesse
Hasty, Willis
Parker, Zilpha
Applewhite, John

Page 118

Hodges, Elizabeth

Page 118 cont.

Duke, Mary Sr.
Duke, Nancy
Duke, Christiana
Allen, Andrew T. J.
Lewis, Jonathan
Roberts, John
Dailey, Mary
Gunn, Thomas G.
Baxter, Charles
Roberts, Delilah
Duke, Mary Jr.
Dixon, Robert
Woods, Archibald
Moxley, John
Cross, William
Mills, Wm. H. C.
Douglass, Wm. B.

Page 119

Ballard, Milley
Davenport, Stephen
Trapnell, Elijah
Hull, Ezekiel
Hutchins, Elizabeth
Caruthers, Nancy
Caruthers, James
Knight, Nealy
Woods, Thomas
Murphy, Malachi
Moxley, Wm. Sr.

Page 119 cont.

Rollins, Wm.
Penrow, Ralph
Moxley, Wm.
Randleson, Andrew
Moxley, Matthew
Gay, Nancy
Warnock, Sarah
Gordon, James Sr.
West, William
Sloan, Sarah
Bryan, Wm.
Deall, Ezekiel
Cole, John
Allen, Jeremiah
Marsh, L. B.
Skinner, Jesse

Page 120

Skinner, Jonas
Rollins, John
Rollins, Roley
Caruthers, Samuel
Evans, Wm. E.
Gordon, James Jr.
McNeily, Esther
McCowan, Nancy
Patterson, William
Liptrott, Hopkin
Moxley, Benjamin
Evans, George W.

Page 120 cont.

Seegar, Benjamin
Phillips, Joseph J.
Clark, William
Allen, James P.
Ruff, Lemmon
Bennett, William
Cates, James
Bostwick, Rhesa
Stephens, Fielding
Forth, John T.
Seegar, Samuel
Seegar, Charles F.
Forth, Joel L.
Carson, Andrew

Page 121

Barnes, Dempsey
Farrow, Fanney
Barnes, William
Barnes, David
Vaughan, John
Thomas, Richard
Desaleaye, Mark
Saxon, Benjamin Y.
Vaughan, John
Farrow, Frances
McCoy, Alexander
Skinner, Jacob
Boyt, Elbert
Nichols, Amelia A.
Roberts, Absalom
Ballard, Mary
Gough, George
Dawson, Mary
Turner, John
Moore, Rowland
Walton, Daniel
Turner, Reuben
Knight, Robert
Taylor, Sir. Wm.
Turner, Henry
Smith, Richard
Taylor, Wm. P.

Page 122

Lumpkin, E. W.
Boyt, Stephen
Walker, Thomas P.
Byne, Elijah
Magee, John
Travis, David D.
Taylor, Elizabeth
Attaway, Elijah
Gordon, William
Patterson, John
Marshall, Wm. S.
Patterson, Mary
Lawson, A. B.
Oates, Charles
Moxley, Daniel
Slatter, Horatio
Robinson, James
Gaines, Duncan
Murphey, William
Weeks, Thomas
Futerell, Joel

Page 122 cont.

Lambert, John N.
Murphey, John
Saxon, John
Cates, Joseph
Blount, Stephen M.
Finley, John

Page 123

Heislar, Samuel
Barrow, John
Bowen, William
Ross, James
Woodward, Abedea
Prior, Robert
Haslip, Lott W.
Haslip, Jonas
Scarborough, Silas
Bryant, Anna
Hines, John H.
Brown, Elizabeth
Cross, Isaac
Parker, Jacob
Albritton, Matthew
Albritton, Robert L.
Coleman, Jesse
Hutchins, Nancy
Drake, Sarah
Scrutchins, Josiah
Hines, John Sr.
Thersey, Mary
Magruder, John
Lodge, Simeon
Pierce, John
Monroe, David

Page 124

Hutchins, Daniel
Bass, John
Cross, Joseph
Linch, Henry
Green, Daniel
Hines, John Jr.
Cross, James
Cross, Sardis E.
Bass, Jesse
Cobb, Jacob
Scarborough, Turner
Lodge, John
Ross, William
Cook, John
Bryant, Needham
Paul, Andrew
Green, Benjamin
Sconiers, Richard
Woodward, Joshua
Spence, Joseph
Sconiers, John
Sconiers, Richard B.
Sconiers, Jehu
Sconiers, Noah
Noles, Ephraim
Garner, Richard
Allen, Wm. P.

Page 125
Cross, Thomas

Page 125 cont.

Nichols, Charles
Meddows, Daniel
Jones, Francis
Burnett, Jsma
Cobb, Curtis
Nasworthy, William
Coleman, Charles
Pierce, Cader
Monroe, Stephen
Scarborough, William
Cox, Jesse
Spence, Greenville
Coleman, Elisha
Corker, Stephen
Williams, Thomas
Grubbs, John
McCullers, Matthew
Anderson, Jane
Lipsey, William
Collins, Andrew
Tyson, Mary A.
Maund, William W.
Barber, Holding
Jones, Matthew
Johns, Jonathan

Page 126

Fountain, Brinson
Schley, O. William
Inman, Daniel
Inman, Alfred
Murphree, Josiah
Leggett, David
Cruse, John
Prescott, James
Lewis, Eleazer
Wootten, Jerusa
Wotten, Mourning
Holloday, Dennis L.
Holliday, Abner E.
Sneed, Leaston
Powell, Mary
Hooks, Michael
Brown, Burrel
Brown, James
Chance, John
Bullard, Amos
Monroe, Joseph
Bunn, Moses
Brown, Benjamin
Jeffers, Thomas
Bullard, James
Murphree, Wright
Belanger, William

Page 127

Bright, Absalom
Johnston, Jared
Grubbs, James
Holliday, Ashley
Spence, Mary
Drew, Mary
Liptroot, James
Hale, Drusilla
Murphree, William
Hale, Tharpe

Johnston, Isaiah
Gordy, Elijah
Scarborough, Reddick
Brinson, Stiring
Anderson, Aug. H.
Lowrey, Simeon
Hall, Edwin
Hall, Irwin
Hines, William
Eason, Seth
Burton, Charles
Killpatrick, J.H.T.
Lewis, Thomas
Hall, Henry H.
Spain, Matthew
Inman, Allen

Page 128

Randolph, Beverley
Jones, Henry S.
Jones, Abraham
Davis, John F.
Torrance, James
Martin, Jesse
Wallace, Stiring B.
Perkins, John S.
Dunford, Susannah
Lane, John
Jones, Henry P.
Verdery, M. P.
Farrow, Sheldon
Moore, Winfield
Forehand, Drewry
Belcher, Mourning
Martin, James
Holliday, Furney
Lewis, Daniel
Brinson, Shepherd
Scarborough, Sarah
Brinson, John Jr.
Lane, Wiley
Holliday, Thomas
Saunders, Alexander
Hall, Eli
Brown, Charles

Page 129

Brookings, Samuel
Bragden, John
Peterson, Seaborn H.
Corker, Drewry
Farnell, Theresa
Hines, James E.
Jenkins, Sterling
Proctor, Samuel
Hampton, Sally
Jeffers, Elizabeth
Anderson, James
Jenkins, Isaitus
Tipton, Joseph
Glisson, John B.
Chance, Henry
Lane, Thomas
Mainor, Sarah
Gilstrap, Henry
Jenkins, Abishal

Page 129 cont.

Mussa, Polley
Gilstrap, William
Jackson, William
Thersey, Haney
Hampton, James
Thorn, William
Thincey, Absalom

Page 130

Coudy, A. B.
Burke, Matthew
Howell, Joab T.
Thompson, Elihu
Perkins, David
Dicky, Joseph
Brinson, Stephen
Atkinson, John
Joiner, Thomas
Brinson, Cyprian
Brinson, Mary
Harvey, Elizabeth
Brinson, Benjamin
Turner, Absalom
Lewis, James
Lewis, John
Gray, Minchey Jr.
Reynolds, John W.
Hampton, Simeon
Burch, L. B.
Mitchell, John
Nunn, Hiram
Phillips, Benjamin
Stokes, Mark
Barefield, Jesse
Malding, Elias
Ward, John

Page 131

Lane, Etheldred
Tindale, Wiley
Tindale, James Sr.
Tindale, James Jr.
Barefield, John
Reese, Wesley W.
Jenkins, Samuel
Jenkins, Stephen
Bell, Jordan
Sharp, Elizabeth
Lester, Ezekiel
Lester, Elizabeth Jr.
Perkins, Newton
Perkins, Newton Jr.
Maund, Hardy C.
Shepherd, James
Brinson, John Sr.
Landing, John
Atkinson, Sarah
Wallace, William
McCoy, John
Wallace, Adam
Reynolds, William
Perkins, Brinson
Wallace, John
Smith, John
Peterson, Mary

Page 132

Sykes, Thomas
Cox, James
Andrews, Samuel
Ursery, Elizabeth
Carpenter, Bailey Sr.
Taylor, Mary
Crozier, John
Andrews, John
Reddick, John
Bell, Delaey
Elliott, Drewry
Elliott, John
Sapp, Charles
Allen, James
Rutledge, John
Somersett, Mary H.
Taylor, Catharine
Gray, Joshua
Collins, Sarah
Allen, James S.
Lassiter, William
Cavenah, Charles
Burke, Thomas Sr.
Bell, Elias
Bell, Frederick
Reeves, Spius
Bell, Dempsey

Page 133

Tilley, Isaac
Barron, William Jr.
Andrews, Harvey
Goodwin, John
Skinner, John
Skinner, Rebeccah
Bostwick, Thomas
Reddick, Nicholas
Bell, Hiram
Allday, John P.
Allday, Josiah
Allday, Peter
Lewis, Ransom
Allday, Nancy
Heath, Rigdon
Carpenter, Bailey Jr.
Bell, Archibald
Clark, Christopher
Skinner, Robert
Lambert, Thomas
Bell, Simeon
Skinner, Charles
Shewmake, Joseph
Holton, Isaac
Smith, John C.
Crozier, Thomas
Reddick, Sarah

Page 134

Leveritt, Maston
Bargeron, Elisha
Bargeron, Abigail
Hust, James
Mobley, James
Rawlings, Elizabeth
Murray, Henry
Thompson, Daniel
Minchev, Sarah

Kimball, Joshua
Murray, James
Ellison, Benjamin
Thompson, William
Thompson, Charity
Murray, Timothy
Murray, Jeremiah
Rackley, Joel
Kimball, William
Parris, Henry A.
Thompson, Nichodemus
Sapp, William
Davis, Roblin
Dunn, Jane
Barefield, Cullen
Barefield, Vinson
Elliott, Mary
Bailey, Davis

Allen, James P.
Allen, Thomas
Allen, Hugh
Sapp, Hardy C.
Sapp, Theophilus
Herrington, Martin
Sapp, Zilpha
Sapp, Dennis
Sapp, John
Hargrove, Henry
Hargrove, Jacob
Sapp, Isaiah
Thompson, Aaron
Sapp, James
Lewis, William
Mills, Elizabeth
Mills, Archibald
Mulford, William B.
Mills, Anthony
Burton, William
Lord, Mary
West, Gibson
Finney, Sarah
Sapp, Everitt
Bonnell, Archibald
Sapp, Pehnicy
Leveritt, John B.

Byne, Mary
Evans, Richard Sr.
Harris, John T.
Tarver, Mark
Gordon, Duncan
Smith, Noah
Greenway, John
Tarver, William
Taylor, James W.
Vollotton, Francis
Daniell, Robert C.
Wyse, Thomas
Rodgers, James
Wiggins, Amos
Wall, Isaac D.
Walker, Robert T.
Owen, John

Murphey, Alexander
Walker, Amos

Clark, Charles
Smith, Daniel
Johnson, Moses
Johnson, Elhannon
Byne, Richard
Byne, William
Proctor, Moses T.
Daniell, Christopher
Sills, Nancy
Steptoe, John
Stockdale, Nancy
Dillard, John
Polhill, Nathaniel
Polhill, Rebeccah
Ponder, Ephraim
Ponder, Ephraim Jr.
Lingo, Peter
Staveley, Elizabeth
Greenway, William
Roberts, Josiah
Roberts, James
Farmer, John
Davis, Thomas
Carswell, Alexander
McCann, Anna
Carswell, Matthew
Pritchett, Guilford

Holly, Eli
Bradshaw, John
Dye, Martin M.
Brown, Samuel J.
Hester, David
Gainus, John
Gainus, Cooperur
Hester, William
Cawley, James
Palmer, Benjamin
Jones, Thomas J.
Palmer, William
Washington, Sophia
Templeton, Matthew
Tarver, Allen
Lyons, Beersheba
Tarver, Robert
Springs, Bartholemew
Brown, James B.
Watkins, Rhoda
McCann, Charles
Dye, Avery
Ponder, Richard
Owen, William
Seales, John
Harrell, Elisha
Greenway, Samuel

Williams, Jane
McClendon, Jesse
Whitfield, William

Whitfield, Lewis Sr.
Tabb, Davis
Mulkev, Homer V.
Pearce, George W.
Melton, Peter
Rogers, William
Pemberton, Alton
Whitfield, Bryan
Cooke, John D.
Thomas, Absalom
Tomlin, L. L. F.
Tilley, William
Fryer, Fielding
Griffin, Stephen
Bush, Joseph
Brown, Wade
Jones, John M.
Jones, Charles
Stephens, Isaac
Whitfield, Lewis
Griffin, Mary
Barton, Stephen
Bryant, Sarah
Davis, Arthur

Utley, Henry
Red, Holland
Nunes, Robert (col.)
Young, Allen (colored)
Elliley, Dick (col.)
Nunes, Charles (col.)
Mason, Isaac (colored)
Young, Jesse (col.)
Nunes, Joseph (col.)
Hancock, Nero (col.)
Nunes, Janet (col.)
Waters, Charles W.
Atkerson, R. R.
Killpatrick, Spencer
Tomlin, Mary
Foster, Sterling
Garrott, Mary
Folks, John
Allen, Robert A.
Ganter, Joseph
Killpatrick, Robert
Wilkins, Whit (col.)
Reece, James
Fann, Milley
Pierce, William
Folds, Richard
Boyt, James

Powell, Lewis T.
Sumner, Clarissa
Powell, Elizabeth
Haymond, Elizabeth
Harrell, Thomas
Haymond, Stephen
Haymond, Elisha
Broxton, Thomas
Mulkey, Moses
Godbee, James
Evans, Jacob

Page 141 cont.

Williams, Ezekiel
Thomas, Joseph D.
Tilley, John
Prescott, John
Boyt, Abraham Sr.
Williams, Margaret
Chandler, George
Brown, Elizabeth
Sumner, Elizabeth
Few, Emily
Garvin, Ignatius P.
Hutchinson, James
Perry, Hardy
Bryant, Selina
Barrow, Isaiah
Barrow, Aaron

Page 142

Thompson, Tabitha
Banion, John O.
Broom, William
Treadwell, J. L.
Gordon, John
Tabb, Thomas
Tilley, Joseph
Few, Benjamin
Robinson, Lemuel
Fryer, John
McNorrell, Henry
Crockett, Floyd
McElmurray, James R.
Cosnahan, Thomas
Taylor, Margaret
Bush, John B.
Ward, Mary
Ward, Charles
Ward, James
Goodson, Jacob
Ward, Robert
Hancock, Joseph
Walton, Robert
Clark, William
Clark, Warren

Page 143

Smith, Henry
Palmer, Edmund
Colson, William
Hill, Frederick
Stallings, John
Mixon, George
Mixon, William
Verdery, B. F.
Rawles, Hosea
Tabb, Edward
Foster, Samuel
Daniell, David
Martin, Nicholas
Knight, Margaret
Barton, David
Nelson, Anna
Dyus, Moses
Rhoney, Morris G.
Smith, Morris
Knight, Jesse
Smith, David

Page 143 cont.

Red, Hiram
Green, Jesse P.
Lambert, Thomas
Gray, Barbary
Wimpey, John
Green, David E.

Page 144

Tomlin, John
Stewart, David
Hatcher, Sarah
Mixon, Michael
Cooke, Arthur S.
Evans, Richard H.
Hickey, James
Evans, Daniel G.
Shaw, John
Grumbles, John S.
Mitchell, William
Dyus, John
Greene, William B.
Evans, Robert H.
Hill, Gillium
Red, William
Hill, Elijah
Beall, Nathaniel
Tutle, Robert
Evans, William G.
Lovell, William
Cooke, Abraam
Cooke, James
Rachels, Ezekiel
Gunn, William
Gunn, David
Rachels, William

Page 145

Burkes, Nimrod
McNair, James
Grumbles, George
Green, Elizabeth E.
Huckaboo, Joel
Kidd, Augustus
Wiggins, William
Dillard, John G.
Tabb, John
Walton, John
Wimberley, Wiley
Wimberley, Zachariah
Wimberley, Lewis Jr.
Wimberley, Lewis Sr.
Moore, Mourning
Fulcher, John
Matthews, Peter
Ward, Nancy
McCollum, Joseph
Stewart, Milley
Davies, James J.
Hatcher, Edward
Godbee, Alfred A.
Griffin, Moses

Page 146

Hall, Joshua
Bohan, Joseph

Page 146 cont.

Buxton, William
Mobley, Benjamin
Leveritt, Pherobe
Hickman, Stephen
Coulteau, Mary
Prescott, Benijah
Hust, John
Norris, William C.
Long, Elizabeth
Hust, Jesse
Hilliss, John
Godbee, Samuel
Hall, David
Godbee, Drusilla
Royal, Sarah
Guest, Sarah
Lively, Matthew
Lively, Luke
Goodwin, Matthew
Brigham, John
Holland, Civility
Royal, John
Odum, Laban
Heath, Jordan Jr.
Heath, James

Page 147

Roberts, Tammey
Heath, Moses
Coile, Elizabeth
Bonnell, Archibald
Houston, Frances
Mobley, Sarah
Godbee, James
Godbee, Moses
Wimberley, John
Goodbee, Henry Sr.
Godbee, Margaret
Goodbee, Albert
Prescott, Nancy
Perkins, Thomas (col.)
Griffin, George
Bargeron, Elijah
Holland, James
Prescott, Moses
Tessier, Lewis P.
Williamson, John
Speers, Charlotte
Holland, Anna
Godbee, Mary
Godbee, Henry Jr.
Hand, John
Mallard, John

Page 148

Dixon, Robert J.
Nessmith, Charles R.
Garlington, Ann
Kelly, Abraham
Mobley, William
Barley, Celia
Glisson, Evan C.
Perry, George S.
Prescott, Sarah
McCay, George
Glisson, Dennis

INDEX TO 1840 CENSUS OF BURKE COUNTY, GEORGIA

52

Blount, Hester
" William
Bush, Joseph
Butler, Jolton
Buxton, William
Byne, Elijah
" Enoch
" William
Byon, Sarah
Byrd, Elizabeth

Calliday, A. F.
Cardwick, Jesse F.
Carpenter, Bailey
Carson, Andrew
Carswell, Alexander
" John
" Matthew
Carter, Edward
" Matilda
" Sarah
Caruthers, Samuel
Cates, James
" Joseph L.
" Thomas
Caughlin, James
Cavennet, Sarah
Cetchrews, W. F. (?)
Chance, Betha
" Edward
" Henry
" Jacob
" James
" John
" John B.
" Mary
Chandler, Susannah
Churchill, Calvin B.
Clarke, Charles
" E.
" James
" Joseph
" Sarah
" Sarah
" Warren
Claton, Daniel W.
Clayton, I. I.
Clinton, Angelina
Coleman, Milly
" Nancy
" Nancy
Collins, Jacob
" John
Colson, William
Colter, George
Cook, Andrew L.
" Sherod A.
Cooper, William
Corker, Drewry
" Stephen
Coward, Andrew I.
Cox, John
" Mary
" Seborn
Crews, John
Cross, Euron
" Frances
" Isaac
" Joseph
" Littleton

Cross, Thomas
Curruthers, James
" William

Daily, Mary
Daniel, Chesley
" Matthew
" Robert
" Major
" Zacharriah
Dance, Gedeon
Darlington, Martha
Davenport, Uriah
David, Arthur
" Evas
" H.
" Moses
" Robbin
" Samuel
" Sarah Ann
" Thomas
Davison, Henry
Deal, Argent
" James
DeLoach, Sarah S.
Dickey, John
" Joseph W.
" Mary
Dillard, John
" Joseph
" Toliver
Dixon, Robert
" Thomas
" William
Dodd, William L.
Douglass, Tilmon
" William B.
Dowde, Nancy
" Samuel
Drake, Milly
" Thomas
" William
Dudley, Kinchen
" Kinchen C.
Duke, James H.
" John
" Nancy
" Reuben
" William
Dunford, Adison
Dye, Avery
" D. C.

Eason, E.
Eates, Joseph I.
Elliot, John
Ellison, Benjamin
" Robert
" Thomas
Ellisor, Sarah
Elsey, M.
Evans, George W.
" Jacob
" William
Everitt, James
Everstreet, William

Fabb, Davis
Farmer, Isaac
" Verity

Farrow, Daniel
" Mary
" Sheldon
Fenison, Joseph
Ficklin, Samuel
Fitch, I. D.
Floyd, Andrew
Flynn, John
" John
Folds, George
" John Richard
Foster, Samuel
Fountain, Brinson
Foyd, John
Francis, Thomas
Fryer, A. G.
" Fielding
" John
Fulcher, James A.
Fulford, Caroline
Futch, O.
Futral, Mary

Gaines, Charles
" Duncan
" John
" John L.
" Sarah
Gardner, James
" William
Garlick, Edward
Gidens, Ali
Gilstrap, Benjamin E.
" R. W.
Gipson, S. C.
Glisson, Dennis
Godbee, Alfred A.
" E.
" Eliza
" Freeman
" Henry
" James
" James F.
" James H.
" Margaret
" Martin
" Mary
" Merchant
" Milledge
" Moses
" Samuel
" Simeon
Goodwin, John
Gordin, William
Gordon, Elency
" John B.
Gordy, Elijah
" Peter
Gough, George
Goulding, William
Graham, Anson B.
Grant, Mary
Gray, Joshua
" Minthe
" Robert R.
" William
Green, Jesse P.
" William
Gregory, Nancy
Gresham, Edward

53

Gresham, John
Griffin, Aaron
" Elizabeth
" Isaac
" James
" Joseph
" Moses
" T. W.
" William
" William
Grineway, James
" William
Grubbs, James
" John
" William
Grumbles, John S.
Guen, Sarah
" William
Gullet, Rebecca
Guthrie, Alfred

Hail, Thorp
Hall, David
" Henry
" Martha
Hallow, William L.
Ham, Nancy
Hampton, James
" Simon
Hanberry, A.
Hand, John J.
Hardwick, Hannah
" Nancy
Hargroves, Elisha
" Henry
Harlow, Rebecca
Harold, Elijah
Harrell, P. O.
" Thomas
Harrington, Martin
Harris, George H.
" Mary Ann
Hasty, Willis
Hatcher, Edward
" William
Haymon, Clay
" James
" Sarah
Hayslip, Elijah
" James
" John
" Lott
Heath, Henry
" Isaac J.
" James
" John
" Jordan
" Moses
" Mrs.
" Rigdon
Henderson, Nobby
" William
Hickman, Stephen
Hicks, James M.
Hill, A.
" B. D.
" Frederick
" H. G.
" John
" Sarah

Hillis, John
" William
Hines, James P.
" John H.
Hoger, Elton
Holland, Elizabeth
" James
" Joseph
" W. A.
Holliday, Ceville
Holloman, Elijah
Holly, Elizabeth
Holton, Isaac
Hooks, Michael
Howard, John
Hudson, S.
Hughs, William H.
Hughston, Lewis
Hull, Delila
Hures, Stephen
Hurst, Elizabeth
" George W.
" Harmon
" Needham
" Susan
" W.
" Willis
Huston, Lewis
" Zach.
Hutchins, Matthew

Iepsev, Thomas
Inman, Alford
" Allen
" Jeremiah
" Middy

Jackson, Abraham
" Casey
" Mrs. E.
" James W.
Jeffers, Johnathan
" Josiah
" Thomas
" William
Jenkins, Izatus
" John
" Starling
" Stephen
" William
Joiner, Mathew
" Thomas
Johns, Jesse
Johnson, Joseph
" Mary Ann
" Moses
" Mrs.
" Sarah
" William
Jones, Abraham
" Elizabeth
" Henry P.
" J. M.
" James W.
" John
" L. H.
" Margaret
" Vinson
" William

Keen, E.
Kelly, John
" Sarah
Kersey, Wesley
Key, Joshua
" Joshua Jr.
Kid, Edward
Kilpatrick, Eliza
" Spencer
Kimbrell, William
Kirkland, B. L.
Knight, Demcy
" Ellen
" Jesse
" John

Lamb, Elijah
Lamberth, A.
" James
" Thomas
" Thomas
Landing, Brison L.
" J.
" John
Landsford, Zilphey
Lane, Thomas
Lassiter, William
Law, George
Lawson, A. B.
" James
Leggett, Daniel
Legnex, Martha
Legur, Emanuel
Lester, Ezekiel
Leverett, A.
" Ferriby
" Martin
Levett, A. L.
" George
" James
" Payne
" Samuel
Lewis, Abel
" Alexander
" Benjamin
" Elam B.
" Gillford
" Henry
" John
" Josiah
" Rachel
" Ransom
" Thomas
" William
Lightfoot, Archer
" C.
Linch, Benjamin
Lindsey, Reason
Liptrot, Elijah
" J. A.
" James
" Loven
Lively, Elizabeth
" Emily
" John
" Lewis
" Mark
London, Dr. J. W.
Long, Elizabeth
Loper, Charles

Loper, Mrs. Lapsy
Lovett, Payne
Lowery, Osborn
Luke, Edward
Lumpkin, Edmund
Lumus, Elizabeth
Lyons, Benjamin

McCatherine, David
McClendon, Jesse
McClanary, G.
McColum, Jordan
McCoy, Mary
McCram, Eli
"   Rhessa
McCraney, Martha
"   Richard
McCroan, James I.
McCullers, Matthew
McGowen, Nancy
McKinnie, John
McNat, A.
McNorrel, M.

Macy, Charlotte
Magruder, James
Marsh, L. B.
"   Mallford
"   Martin
Martin, James
"   William
Massey, Isaac
Maynor, Jesse
"   William
Meddey, Daniel
Merrit, Comfort
"   George W.
Miles, Dr. L. M.
Miller, D. B. B.
Mills, Anthony
"   Archibald
"   Elizabeth
"   Stephen
"   William
Milton, Peter
Minchey, Hill
"   Sarah
Mixon, George
"   Jep or Jes
"   Michael
Mobley, Benjamin
"   James A.
"   James R.
"   Mary
Monelia, Esther
Monroe, John
"   Joseph
"   Nancy
Moore, Abner R.
"   John
"   Josiah
"   Thomas
Morley, William
Morris, William T.
Moxley, Benjamin
"   Daniel
"   John
"   Mather
Mulford, Thomas
Mulkey, Isaac

Mulkey, Homer V.
"   Mockey
"   Moses
"   Washington
Murdock, Thomas P.
Murphree, Alexander
"   William
"   Wright
Murphrey, Josiah
Murry, Henry
"   Sepey (Susey ?)
Myer, L. B.

Nasworthy, George
"   Uriah
"   William
Nelson, Anna
Nessmith, Charles
Netherland, L. B.
Nickles, Morris
Noland, A.
Noles, Ephraim
Norris, John
Numis, Jesse
"   Joseph

Obanion, John
Odom, Labon
Oglesby, Daniel
"   Elijah
Oliver, Quilpha
O'Neal, Daniel
Owens, John
"   John

Palmer, Mrs. Ann
"   Benjamin
"   Edmund
Parmer, William
Parnell, James
Parsons, John A.
"   Dr. Thomas A.
Patterson, Mary
"   William
Peel, James
"   Levi
"   Mills
Pemberton, Alton
Pennington, Thomas
Penroe, Eli M.
"   William
Perkins, Brinson
"   David
"   Newton
"   Newton
Perry, A. J.
"   Joseph
"   Joseph W.
Peterson, Eliza
Philips, Gathery
Pierce, John Sr.
"   John Jr.
"   Rebecca
"   William
Ponder, H.
Powell, Cader R.
"   L. F.
Poythress, John
Prescott, John
"   Moses

Prescott, Willis
Prior, Robert
Pryer, Elijah
Proctor, Abraham
"   Thomas

Quinn, Bryant O.

Rackley, Joel
Rainey, Charles
"   John W.
" also see Rhaney
Randolson, Marget
Rector, Sampson
Red, Allen B.
"   Barbara
"   Green B.
"   Holland
"   Noah
"   Welcome
"   William
Reddick, Mary Ann
"   Nicholas
"   Sarah
Reece, James
Reeves, Anna
"   Speous
Reynolds, James M.
"   Sarah
Rhaney, Sarah
" also see Rainey
Roberts, Charles
"   Greer
"   Jeff
"   John A.
"   Madison
"   Miles
"   Tameny
Robertson, T.
Robinson, Philip
"   Philip Jr.
"   William A.
Roe, A. H.
"   Joseph A.
Rogers, John
"   Mary
"   Thomas
Roland, Robert A.
Rollins, Eliza
"   John
"   John Jr.
"   Samuel
"   William
Rowell, Elizabeth
"   William B.
Rowland, James
Royal, Mrs. J. J.
"   James
"   Mary
"   Moses
"   Moses
"   Samuel
"   Seth

Sally, Samuel
Sanderford, Hill
Sanders, Martha
Sapp, Dennis
"   Everett
"   John

55

Sapp, John
" Joiah
" Luke
" Pendleton
" William
Saxon, Celia
" Joshua
" Mary
Scarbrough, A.T.
Sconges, I.
" Isaac
" Jane
" Richard
" T.
Scott, Charles
" John
Seaborn, Rachel
Seals, John
Sharp, M. M.
" Micajah
Shepard, Gathers
Shoemaker, Joseph
Sikes, Thomas
Skinner, A. R.
" Charles
" Henry
" Jane
" John R.
" Jonas
" Jonas Jr.
" Lottey
" Rebecca
" Robert
" Uriah
" William
" William
Smith, Ann
" David
" Elizabeth
" H.
" J. D.
" James
" John
" Mary
" Mrs. N.
" Nancy
" Nathaniel
" Susannah
" Thomas
" William T.
Speers, Mrs. C.
Springer, William
Stephens, Isaac
Stewart, Rebecca
" William
Stokes, Mark
Strain, Isaac
Stringer, M. W.
Suggs, John
Sumner, Hollin

Tabb, Edward
" John
" William
Tailer, E. D.
Tant, John
Tarver, Mark
Taver, William
Taylor, Jeremiah
" William
" William
" Sir William
Telfair, Lewis O.
Tennison, John
Thomas, Joseph D.
" Richard
Thompson, Benjamin
" Daniel
" Elihu
" Seborn
" Solomon
" T.
Thorn, Middleton
Tilley, John
" Levi
" William
Tinson, William
Tisdel, James
" Sampson
" William H.
Tomlin, John
" John Sr.
" Mary
" Y. L.
Torrence, Martha
Trapnell, Elijah
Triggs, John I.
Tucker, William S.
Turner, John
Twer, N.

Urquhart, Alex.
Utley, William

Vollintine, Francis

Wade, William
Wadkins, Benjamin
Walker, Elizabeth
" Dr. Frances I.
" John A.
" Moses
Wall, Robert
Wallace, Adam
" Adam
" John
" S. B.
" Simeon
" William
" William
Walton, David

Walton, Hugh
Ward, Charles
" David
Ware, James
" Nancy
Warnock, Ella
" John
" Sarah
Waters, Charles
Weathers, Nancy
Weeks, Benjamin L.
Wells, Mrs.
West, Gibson
" Martha K.
" William R.
Whinkley, John
White, Daniel
" Henry
Whitehead, Amos G.
" Charles
" J. C.
" Dr. J.
" John Sr.
Whitfield, Lewis
Wiggins, Amos
Williams, Aaron
" Ezekiel
" Hezekiah
" John
" L.
Wimberly, Allen
" Henry
" Isaac
" John
" Lewis
" R.
" Randal
" Wylly
Woodard, Bedy
Woods, Archy
" David
" Martha
" Mathew W.
" Thomas
Wooten, Eli
" James
Wright, Lucy
Wyatt, Elizabeth
" Martha

Young, Allen
Youngblood, Abram

1850 MORTALITY CENSUS OF BURKE COUNTY, GEORGIA.

(This consists of deaths occurring from July 1, 1849 - July 1, 1850, as reported to the census enumerator. Month of Death, Married/Widowed.)

Name	Age	Sex	Place	Month	M/W
Warnock, Elizabeth	37	F	Ga.	Apr.	M
Allen, Sarah Ann	28	F	Ga.	Nov.	M
Johns, Sarah	50	F	Ga.	Feb.	W
Perry, James D.	6	M	Ga.	Nov.	
Pierce, Rebecca	60	F	Ga.	Nov.	W
Flanagan, Mary J.	2/12	F	Ga.	Dec.	
Koneman, Sarah C.	1	F	Ga.	Mar.	
Barron, William	54	M	Ga.	Oct.	M
Bele, Rufus	8/12	M	Ga.	Oct.	
Skinner, Thomas	10 da	M	Ga.	Oct.	
Hampton, William E.	3/12	M	Ga.		
Taylor, George D.	40	M	Va.	Jan.	M
Clarke, Sarah	44	F	Ga.	Feb.	M
Ganey, Benjamin	1/12	M	Ga.	Dec.	
Tindale, Lourania	55	F	Ga.	Aug.	M
Tindale, James	65	M	Ga.	Sep.	W
Tindale, William	38	M	Ga.	Oct.	
Baxter, R. infant	1 wk.	M	Ga.	Aug.	
Anthony, Margaret C.	4/12	F	Ga.	May	
Lewis, Julia	23	F	Ga.	Oct.	
Belsher, A. infant	7 mo.				
Brinson, Cyprian	16	M	Ga.	Apr.	
Peel, Fereby	30	F	Ga.	May	M
Brown, Mary A.	28	F	Ga.	Jul.	M
Brown, Mary T.	3/12	F	Ga.	Jul.	
Hill, Gilleem	28	M	Ga.	May	
Foster, John W.	2/12	M	Ga.	Oct.	
Ponder, Sarah Y.	18	F	Ga.	Oct.	
Mobley, Christopher	1/12	M	Ga.	Jul.	
Hatcher, Ellington	9/12	M	Ga.	Oct.	
Perry, Eliza C.	1	F	Ga.	Jul.	
Perry, Julia C.	7/12	F	Ga.	Jul.	
Lawson, Fannie J.	9/12	F	Ga.	May	
Springer, Oriman V.	5/12	F	Ga.	Jul.	
Springer, Webster A.	1 mo.	M	Ga.	Jul.	
Blount, Leroy	1/12	M	Ala.	Oct.	
Tompkins, James M.	15 da.	M	Ga.	May	
Gaines, Levi	31	M	Ga.	Jan.	
Futrel, Levi	21	M	Ga.	Feb.	
Lewis, Benjamin S.	4	M	Ga.	Sep.	
Lewis, Elam B's infant	1/12	M	Ga.	Sep.	
Firth, Zachery	8/12	M	Ga.	Sep.	
Oates, John S.	3	M	Ga.	Apr.	
Burnett, Zoe	3	F	Ga.	Sep.	
Rosier, Jane E.	30	F	Ga.	Jan.	
Whitehead, Mary A.	2	F	Ga.	Mar.	
Roberts, Matison	38	M	Ga.	Mar.	M
White, Daniel	58	M	SC	Mar.	M
Moore, Daniel L.	6	M	Ga.	Jul.	
Coop (Coos?), Samuel J.	6	M	Ga.	Sep.	
Saxon, Margaret	32	F	Ga.	Oct.	M
Strain, Isaac	52	M	SC	Feb.	M
Sharpe, William	33	M	PA	Jan.	
Jones, James M.	24	M	Ga.	Jul.	
Archer, Thomas	2/12	M	Ga.	Dec.	
Murphree, Emily V.	1	F	Ga.	Dec.	
Inman, Mary E. E.	4/12	F	Ga.	Apr.	
Bunn, Moses	1	M	Ga.	Sep.	
Ham, Martha A. E.	8/12	F	Ga.	Oct.	
Turner, Mourning	78	F	NC	Jul.	W
Lewis, Eugenia	8	F	Ga.	Feb.	
Lewis, Savannah	7	F	Ga.	Feb.	
Feeloy, James	40	M	Ire.	Nov.	

```
Owens, Elizabeth              63   F   SC   Jan.   M
Ataway, Paralee                6   F   SC   Oct.
Attaway, William W.         1/12   M   SC   Jan.
Roberts, John W.            5/12   M   SC   Jul.   SC
Clark, Elizabeth              29   F   SC   Aug.   M
Martin, Ann E. E.             11   F   SC   Mar.
Ward, Mary                    21   F   Ga.  Mar.
Weathersly, William          31   M   SC   Feb.   M
Nelson, Julia V.              1   F   Ga.  Feb.
Sapp, Everett                 46   M   Ga.  Oct.   M
Dodd, Jane                    35   F   Ga.  Jun.   M
Darlington, Martha            43   F   SC   Apr.   W
Hankerson, Wm B's infant  3 da.   M   Ga.  Apr.
Godbee, Palmyra V.             2   F   Ga.  Mar.
Godbee, James H.              76   M   Ga.  Oct.   W
Wilkins, Mary             2 wk.   F   Ga.  Aug.
Roe, Joseph A.                33   M   Ga.  Feb.   M
Hillis, William P.          1/12   M   Ga.  Jun.
Roe, Elizabeth                 5   F   Ga.  Nov.
Royall, Alexr. T.           6/12   M   Ga.  Oct.
Daniel, Simeon                17   M   Ga.  Feb.
Overstreet, Eliza             10   F   Ga.  May    M
Henderson, Sabra              60   F   SC   Feb.   W
Dixon, Delaware                2   M   Ga.  Aug.
Godbee, Mary                  85   F   Ga.  Apr.   W
Godbee, James A.              24   M   Ga.  Oct.
Spears, Lavina              8/12   F   Ga.  Dec.
Godbee, Samuel                59   F   Ga.  Mar.   M
Godbee, Henry                 47   M   Ga.  Feb.   M
```

BUTTS COUNTY, DEED BOOK B

Page 1 is missing.

Date Unknown, Green Pennell to George Pennell, 112 acres, 9th Dist.,
Henry Co. Wit: Parham Lindsay, J.P., J. M. Pearson, J.P. Page 2.

January 20, 1829, Abel L. Robinson to John McMichael for $150, 50 3/4
part of Lot #105, 1st Dist., Henry Co. (now Butts). Wit: R. Pound,
Silas Elliott, J.P. Page 4.

January 10, 1829, Robert Smith to William Smith, Monroe Co., (now Butts)
Lot #29-attested to by Hamlin Freeman and Leonard Roan before John
McMichael, JIC. Page 5.

November 28, 1828, Jeremiah Mulloy to John Reeves, 101 acres, Henry Co.,
now Butts, Lot #28. Wit: Leonard Roan, Hamlin Freeman. Pages 5-6.

January 23, 1829, Richard Pound to John Hall, 100 acres, Henry Co. (now
Butts), Lot #123. Pages 6-7.

January 8, 1829, Receipt to Alexander Hunter for $290. for negro woman,
Lucy, belonging to the estate of Arthur C. Atkinson, late of Clarke Co.,
signed by: Thomas P. Atkinson, Washington G. Atkinson, Executors of
Arthur Atkinson. Wit: J. J. Pelham, Eleazer Mobley, J.P. Page 7.

September 13, 1828, Receipt of Robert M. Hunter for $360 for negro boy
(or man) George, 21 years old from Charles Allen. Wit: John S. Cobb.
Page 8.

Robert W. Hunter receipt to Alexander Hunter $101.00 for negro girl be-
longing to Elijah Fuller, sold publicly, (negress Elizabeth). R. W.
Hunter, highest bidder. Wit: James V. Hogg, John Hendrick, JIC. Page 8.

March 8, 1828, Moses Cox of Henry Co. to Greenlee Holly of Butts Co.,
107 acres in Henry Co. (now Butts). Wit: Ephraim Cox, W. G. Ray, Jr.
Pages 8-9.

January 22, 1829, Deed headed Wilkes Co. Samuel (X) Jones to Cornelius Slaton, Wilkes Co., for 202½ acres, Lot #132, Henry Co., (now Butts). Wit: A. B. Linton, George W. Johnson, J.P. Page 9.

(Note: 2 pages are numbered "9")

January 24, 1829, James Bently to Lawrence Gahagan, security on notes. Endorsing note by James Merewither and James Bently. Wit: Benjamin Tucker, William V. Buny. Pages 9-10.

April 7, 1827, James Osburn to Eldred M. Hibbles, one-half of Lot #6, Henry Co. (now Butts). Wit: Alexander Hall, Alexander Urquhart. Page 11.

September 27, 1827, John F. Davis, Wilkinson Co. to Ledford Edwards, Lot #172, Monroe Co. (now Butts). Page 12.

June 4, 1828, Benjamin F. Tucker to Elijah Fuller, Lot #181. Pages 12-13.

February 4, 1829, A. L. Robinson to Samuel Gee of South Carolina, Anderson District, Lot #34, Henry Co. (now Butts). Wit: E. Case, James H. Stark, Henry Hately. Pages 13-14.

February 5, 1828, Fifas against James Morris of Marion Co. for Taxes, 1826, Thomas Malone, Tax Collector of County, Lot #21, sold publicly. Solomon Leat, highest bidder. Wit: William P. Henry, Allen Powel, J.P. Pages 14-15.

January 7, 1829, Jeremiah Evans to William Reeves, both of Butts Co., Monroe Co., (now Butts) Lot #140. Wit: Levi Martin, Jonathan Nichols, George McLain, J.P. Pages 15-16.

December 13, 1829, William Byars to William Redman, 101 acres, Henry Co. (now Butts), Lot #28. Wit: Azariah Reams, A. L. Robinson, Clerk. Page 16.

December 3, 1828, Thomas Robinson to Daniel Slay, Lot #206, Henry Co. (now Butts). Wit: Lewis Moore, A. L. Robinson, Clerk. Page 17.

August 5, 1828, Robert W. Harkness, Sheriff, sells Lot #77, Henry Co. (now Butts) property of Samuel Clay, on account of fifas issued Justice Court of Butts County at instance of Trustees of Jackson Academy against Edward Butler, A.B. Pope and Samuel Clay, Pleasant G. Clay, highest bidder. Wit: E. Case, Ezekiel Walker, J.P. Pages 17-18.

January 16, 1829, William Byars to Thomas Thomas, (Note: Sometime spelled "Tomas") 50 acres, Lot #129, Henry Co. (now Butts). Wit: David Byars, William Barkley. Pages 18-19.

January 24, 1828, James Bentley to Thomas Johnson for Lot #12, Henry Co. (now Butts). Wit: John McCord, Abel L. Robinson, Clerk. Page 19.

September 19, 1828, Thomas (X) Tucker to James Bentley, Lot #12, Henry Co. (now Butts). Wit: Alexander Hall, William Barkley, J.P. Page 20.

December 6, 1824, Jesse Little of Pike Co. to James Bunkley of Butts Co., Lot #195, Henry Co. (now Butts). Wit: Robert Little, Bushwood Johnston, John G. Wood. January 19, 1829, Signatures sworn to by Bushwood Johnston before Eli E. Gather, J.P. Pages 20-21.

July 11, 1827, Woody Dozier of Jasper Co. to Joseph Sentell of Troup Co. for Lot #93, Monroe Co. (now Butts) on Little Sandy Creek. Wit: Willie B. Ector, John Howard, JIC. Pages 21-22.

January 22, 1828, Susannah (X) Permenter to Pharris Permenter, her son, 101¼ acres, for good will and regard, in Monroe Co. (now Butts) Lot #38. Wit: William F. McTyne, R. S. Cargile, Edward Weaver, J.P. Pages 22-23.

October 17, 1825, Sarah (X) Woodard to James Morris, Lot #21 in Henry Co. (now Butts). Wit: John L. Woodard, Silvanus S. Bryan, & David B. Gilson. Pages 23-24.

November 5, 1825, Affidavit of John L. Woodard as to signatures before
E. G. Brown, J.P. Page 24.

February 4, 1829, David Tingle to Young R. Norrice, Lot #8, 50 acres.
Wit: John M. Norrice, Samuel (X) Clark. Page 24.

February 10, 1829, Affidavit of signatures by John M. Norris before O. P.
Cheatham, J.P. Page 25.

November 20, 1828, Abraham M. Jackson of Jackson County to A. L. Robinson,
part of Lot #105, cont. 50 acres in Henry Co. (now Butts). Wit: John
Robinson, John McMichael, JIC. Page 25.

October 2, 1827, Luke Robinson to William Barron of Newton Co., part of
Lot #85, cont. 127½ acres in Henry Co. (now Butts). Wit: John Barron,
Susan (X) Barron. Page 26.

March 8, 1828, John Barron's affidavit as to signatures before Ezekiel
Walker, J.P. Page 26.

December 15, 1828, John Connal of Henry Co. to Aaron Woodward-half of Lot
#29, Henry Co. (now Butts). Wit: W. V. Beeney, A. L. Robinson, Clerk
SCBC. Page 27.

December 15, 1828, John Connel of Henry Co. to Aaron Woodward sells one
negro woman, 35, Nann; one negro girl, Bett, 16 years old; one negro boy,
Lewis, 13 years old; Daniel, 10 yrs., one hundred bbls corn, 5000# fodder, 50 heads hogs, 18 or 20 cattle, one sorrel mare, one gray mare, one
colt, household and kitchen furniture, Con. $3625.00. Wit: A. L. Robin-
son. Page 28.

January 30, 1829, James (X) Sartin of Madison Co. to Samuel Collins,
101¼ acres, part of Lot #67 in Henry Co. (now Butts). Wit: Moses Rosser,
David Kimbril, Joshua J. Evans, J.P. Page 28.

May 31, 1828, Receipt of James Thurman to James Thurman, Jr. $1000 for
five negroes: Aggy, a woman 60 years old; Early, a girl 16 years old;
Loisham, a boy 8 years of age; Clar a girl 6 years of age. Wit: John
Lemmons. Pages 29-30.

August 1, 1828, Silas Cheek of Coweta Co. to Robert Smith, Senior, of
Butts Co. Lot #27, 14th Dist., Monroe Co. (now Butts) adjoining William
Smith and William Higgins. Wit: J. C. Dunsieth, David Smith. Page 30.

February 14, 1829, James C. Dunsieth makes affidavit as to signatures before Elijah McMichael, J.P. Page 30.

February 9, 1829, John Witcher of Newton Co. signs receipt for $300 from
Robert Brown for 1 negro woman, Sally, sound and healthy. Wit: John
Bass. Page 30.

January 24, 1828, Wilson Magee to Jacob Gardner-Lot #20, 1st Dist. Henry
Co. (now Butts) for $750.00. Wit: Ignatius Rusel, Willis Jarel. Page
31.

Ignatius Russel makes affidavit as to signatures before Samuel P. Burford, J.P. Page 32.

February 10, 1829, John McMichael, John Hall, Henry Hately, Justices of
the Inferior Court to Barnaby Woolbute of Morgan Co. for $65.45, Lot in
town of Jackson, Lot #4, Square #12. Wit: Henry Jackson, J.P. Pages
32-33.

March 2, 1829, Justices of Inferior Court to Augustus B. Pope for $60.50
for town lot #3, cont. 2 acres. Wit: John Robinson, John Lofton, J.P.
Pages 33-34.

December 17, 1828, Andrew Rhea to James V. Hogg, 1 feather bed purchased
from Mrs. Beak, at 50¢ lb. to remain in Rhea's possession until his dau.,
Susan marries. Page 34.

May 7, 1828, William Giles to Spencer Maddox for $100, 101½ acres, south half of Lot #35, 9th Dist., Henry Co. (now Butts). Wit: G. T. Speake, Ebenezer Maddox. Page 36.

February 14, 1829, Ebeneazer Maddox makes affidavit as to signatures before George T. Speake, J.P. Page 35.

February 14, 1829, Spencer (X) Maddox to James T. Maddox for $100, 101 acres, south half Lot #37, 9th Dist., Henry (now Butts) Co. Wit: Archibald Fincher, George T. Speake, J.P. Page 36.

February 16, 1829, Spencer (X) Maddox gives receipt to Ebenezar Maddox for $75.00 for 1 sorrel mare, 9 years old, 10 head cattle, 2 beds and bedding, 6 cupboards, 6 chairs. Wit: Archibald Fincher, George T. Speake, J.P. Page 36.

March 13, 1827, to John V. Dunn by Samuel D. Echols for $300, (Newton Co.) 3rd Dist., Monroe (now Butts) Co., Lot #238, where Yelverton Thaxton lives. Wit: William Griffith, Archibald Rich, J.P. Page 37.

October 9, 1827, John V. Dunn to Wiley Thaxton for $300.00-3rd Dist., Monroe (now Butts) Co., Lot #238. Wit: A. Branch, Samuel Bellah, J.P. Page 38.

October 8, 1823, Deed Headed Twiggs Co. Alexander Williams of Putnam Co. to Hezekiah Browin of Laurens Co. for $100.00-Lot #74, 1st Dist. Henry Co. (now Butts). Wit: Moses Gaston, John Grayton, J.P. Pages 38-39.

February 5, 1828, Deed Headed Morgan Co. John Bellah, Tax Collector for Morgan Co., sold property of Dickson Parham for 1825 Taxes in Morgan Co. Joseph T. Camp, John Malcom, William Stallings, highest bidder. 3rd Dist., Monroe (now Butts) Co. Lot #171. Wit: John C. Reese, Joshua Echols, J.P. Pages 39-40.

December 17, 1825, John Murkison to B. Fluker, both of Washington Co., for $350 - Lot #68, 1st Dist., Henry Co. (now Butts). Wit: Andrew B. Griffin, Robert Williams, William Gilbert, J.P. Page 41.

March 5, 1829, Hezekiah Brown of Houston Co. to Henry Burt of Walton Co. for $200.00, 1st Dist., Henry Co. (now Butts), Lot #74. Wit: Elizabeth (X) Saidlen, John Saidlen, JIC. Pages 41-42.

March 12, 1829, Henry Burt of Walton Co. to Joseph Summerlin and Abel L. Robinson, $400, 1st Dist., Henry Co. (now Butts), Lot #74; John Hall, JIC. Pages 42-43.

January 27, 1829, Henry J. Bailey to Kinney Smith of Oglethorpe Co., $100 for better security on account, claim bond to Charles Bailey and bond to William Lumpkin, Sheriff of Oglethorpe Co., the first claim up 34 head of fattening hogs, levied on as property of Henry Bailey, by heirs and distributees of William Bailey, deceased, said by Charles Bailey, last bond of delivery for property when called on for it by Sheriff. Claim bond $400, delivery bond $600, Kinney being on bond, makes over to Kinney the following negroes: York, a man 22 yrs. old, George, a boy 11 years old, Ephraim, a man, 20 years, Wyett, a boy 14 years. If Henry J. Bailey or Charles Bailey make claims good, then present instrument void. Wit: F. A. Combs.

November 8, 1828, William L. Wilson and Simeon Lovejoy to John P. Force of City of Augusta, $200.00, Monroe Co. (now Butts) 4th Dist., Lot #39, granted to John Nance. Wit: Ezekiel Walker, J.P., Lawson Gahagan. Page 45.

March 13, 1829, Burrell Bridges to Lucinda Schackleford (widow) Exec. and Benjamin White, Executor of John Shackleford, dec'd. Morgan Co., $300.00, 1st Dist., Henry Co. (now Butts) ½ of Lot #168. Wit: James H. Edwards, Henry Halebey, JIC. Page 46.

April 24, 1828, Charles J. McDonald to Adam G. Saffold of Morgan Co. for $200., 1st Dist., Henry Co., Lot #8 granted to John Florey, 3-2-1822.

Wit: William Hatcher, David Ralston, JIC. Page 47.

February 14, 1829, John Andrews of Pike Co. to James Waller of Hancock Co. for $350., 14th Dist., Monroe Co. (now Butts). Wit: David Andrews, Robert Humber. (Footnote added: James Waller, son of Captain James Waller.) Page 48.

April 6, 1829, Affidavit of Robert Humber as to signatures 'fore O.P. Cheatham, J.P. Page 49.

March 16, 1828, James Bently gives receipt to Samuel Clay for $400 for negro man, Gage, 30 years old. Wit: T. L. Spencer, Thomas Johnson. Page 49.

April 7, 1829, Affidavit of Thomas Johnson as to signatures before Eleazer Mobley, J.P. Page 49.

January 3, 1829, Major Stanley to Sippy Alford of Morgan Co. $450., 8th Dist., Henry Co. (now Butts) Lot #166, drawn by James South of Kittle Dist., Wilkinson Co. Wit: James H. Roberts, Geo. S. Thompson, J.P. Page 50.

May 13, 1828, John P. Flake to Emanuel Shivers and Wilson Shivers of Warren Co., $150., 1st Dist., Monroe Co., Lot #109, drawn by John P. Flake. G.W.C. Shivers, JIC. Wit: William B. Hundley, James Shivers. Page 51.

April 15, 1829, Abel L. Robinson to Samuel Gee, of South Carolina, Anderson District, Lot #39, 1st Dist., Henry (now Butts) Co. $250. Witness: James H. Stark, John Hall, JIC. Page 52.

March 12, 1829, Zechariah Deason to John Hall, promissory note $113.33 on, or before, 12-25-1829, on receipt of $5.00 Deason deeds 126 acres, 1st Dist. Henry Co., part of Lot #126. If note paid with lawful interest, then above deed void. Wit: John McCord, Henry Jackson, J.P. Pages 52-54.

December 10, 1828, Samuel Parker (name is Sanders Parker) to James Thompson of Jasper Co. for $130., 4th Dist. Monroe Co. (now Butts) part of Lot #20. Wit: J. M. McLendon, Jesse McLendon, C. M. Coody, J.P. Page 54.

January 30, 1829, James (X) Sartin of Madison Co. to Sterling Camp of Butts Co. $225, 2nd Dist., north half of Lot #67. Wit: Moses Rosser, David Kimball, Joshua J. Evans, J.P. Page 55.

April 8, 1829, Howell Holly of Walton Co. to Robert Brown of Butts Co. for $600.00 town of Jackson, Lot #1, Square #12. Wit: Eli Conger, John McMichael, JIC. Pages 55-56.

Dated Feb. 10, 1829, Thomas W. Collier to Robert F. Benton on account of being security for Collier, 2 promissory notes, $30 each, dated 1-12-1829, due 11-1-1829, payable to Burrell P. Key, assigns following property: 1 bay mare, 10 years; 1 cow & calf; 1 heifer; 27 head hogs of different size; 2 trunks; 1 featherbed & bedstead, furniture; a looking glass; 1 loom & spinning wheel; 1 clock; 1 man's saddle and bridle; 1 four gallon jug; 1 large pot; 2 tubs; if money due is paid with lawful interest, above mortgage void. Wit: Benjamin F. Collier, Wm. W. Kannon. Pages 56-57.

January 10, 1828, Cornelius Atkinson, John N. Robey and Hiram Glazier are bonded to Ordinary's Court for $5500. Condition: Cornelius Atkinson, apptd gdn. to Susan & Martha Patrick, now Susan McCune. John Tarpley, CCO. Pages 57-58.

March 2, 1829, Charles Bailey, Henry J. Bailey, Gustavus Hendrick and Armistead Branch for $18,000. Charles Bailey aptd. gdn. to John M. D. Taylor, Mary Taylor, Noah Taylor; if Chas. Bailey demean himself as gdn. agreeable to letters of guardianship, then above bond void. John McCord, CCO. Page 58.

January 6, 1829, Robert W. Harkness on account of fifas from Court of

Wilkes Co. by Augustus Binns against C. Bryant, A. Bryant, B. Bryant, sells west ½ of lot #105, 1st Dist., Henry Co. (now Butts), 101½ acres, property of Bryants, Henry McCoy highest bidder. Wit: Cyrus Phillips, John McMichael, JIC. Pages 59-60.

May 2, 1829, Mary (X) Harris of Putnam Co. for love and affection for granddaughter, Mary Kimbrough, daughter of John Kimbrough of Butts Co., gives featherbed and furniture, one chest, now in possession of John Kimbrough. Wit: Joel Bailey, C. M. Coody, J.P. Page 60.

April 14, 1826, William Reeves gives receipt to Jemima Lovejoy for $125. payment for negro girl, Charlotte, fourteen years of age, and warrants same. Page 60.

February 14, 1826, Ann F. Cox and Asa Cox of Bryan Co. to Allan Rawles of Bulloch Co. $300., 1st Dist., Henry Co. (now Butts) Lot #62. Wit: Rebuen R. Stone, Peter Cone. Page 61.

February 16, 1826, Peter Cone of Bryan Co. makes affidavit to foregoing signatures before Solomon Smith, JIC. Page 62.

October 17, 1828, Randall Robinson of Coweta Co. to Robert Andrews of Butts Co. $1000., 2nd Dist., Henry (now Butts) Co., Lot #31, granted to Figgs. Wit: Hugh Goin, Samuel Bellah, J.P. Page 62.

May 9, 1829, William Smith, Sr. to William Smith, Jr. for $230., Lot #29, 14th Dist., Monroe Co. (now Butts). Wit: Elijah McMichael, J.P., James C. Smith. Page 63.

January 17, 1829, Robert Curry of Coweta Co. to David Lawson of Butts Co., $580.00, 9th Dist., Henry (now Butts) Co., Lot #66. Granted to Franklin. Wit: Jonathan S. Lawson, Joseph Key, J.P. Page 64.

January 4, 1826, Thomas Hancock to Obediah P. Cheatham, $5000.00, 1st Dist., Henry Co. (now Butts), Lot #13, on waters of Sandy Creek, granted to James Adam. Wit: Josiah Rounsaville, James Carroll, William Nieda, J.P. Page 65.

May 16, 1829, Obediah P. Cheatham to Thomas Johnson, $250.00, SW part of Lot #12, 1st Dist., Henry Co. (now Butts), 100 acres, granted to Jonathan Barney, on 2-5-1822. Wit: George Owen, Edward Weaver, J.P. Pages 66-67.

July 24, 1826, Hugh Hamil to Phinias Kell, $200, 202½ acres, part of Lots #15 & 16, Henry Co. (now Butts), 1st Dist. drawn by James McCay and Thomas Underwood. Wit: John Glenn, Samuel Bellah, J.P. Pages 67-68.

----- 23, 1829, Henry Hately, John McMichael, John Hall, John Hendrick, Justices of Inferior Court, Butts Co. to William Hitchcock of Jasper Co., $122.25, Lots #14, Square 11, #2, Square #9, and No. 4, Square 16, Town of Jackson. Wit: John Tarpley, Abel L. Robinson, Clerk SCBC. Pages 68-69.

May 29, 1829, Henry Hately, John McMichael, John Hall, and John Hendrick Justices of Inferior Court, Butts Co. to William Hichcock of Jasper Co., $336.00 for Lots #16, 22, 23, 24, 25, & 14. Wit: John Tarpley, Abel L. Robinson, Clerk SCBC. Pages 69-70.

February 23, 1829, Henry Hately, John Hall, John Hendrick, Justices Inferior Ct. Butts Co., to John Robinson, Abel L. Robinson, $550. Lot #3, Square 2, Lot #2, Square #2, town of Jackson, fronting public square. Wit: John Tarpley, William Hitchcock. Pages 71-72.

May 3, 1829, Henry Hately, John McMichael, John Hall, John Hendrick, Justices ICBC to Abel L. Robinson, $673., Lot #1, Sq #3, Lot #20, larger size Lot #7, Lot #19, large size. Wit: John Tarpley, James Willson. Page 73.

May 15, 1829, James C. Dunsieth, William Smith and Robert Smith bonded in Ordinary's Court for $3000. Condt: Dunsieth apptd. gdn. of Louisa C. Flewellen. John McCord, CCO. Pages 73-74.

June 2, 1829, Abel L. Robinson to Richard Bailey for $54.00, west half of lot in town of Jackson, 1 3/4 acres, Lot #19. Also ½ fence between that and the half belonging to William Bardley. Wit: Stephen Bailey, John M. Hall, JIC. Pages 74-75.

April 24, 1829, Kinney Smith states mortgages satisfied. Wit: Richard Bailey. Page 75.

August 31, 1826, Frederick A. Bailey, relinquishes to Henry J. Bailey right in following negroes: Hannah, a woman 25 or 26 years old; and her three children, which he sold to Ezekiel Gilham of Oglethorpe Co., Henry J. Bailey security to Gilham for title to negroes. Frederick being under age at the time. Pages 75-76.

May 13, 1829, Jeremiah Maxey to James Harrison for fifty cents paid to Maxey, for note 3-12-1829, due 12-25-1829 for $12.00, conveys the following - 2 head cattle, 3 years old. (1 brindle bull with swallow fork in right ear, 1 red and white pided, 2 years old). Page 76.

June 10, 1829, Michael Summerlin makes affidavit as to signatures before John Lofton, J.P. Page 77.

January 30, 1827, Henry Hately to John D. Swift, $300.00, Lot #1, Sq. #14, town of Jackson. Wit: Robert W. Harkness, B. F. Tucker, J.P. Page 77.

March 25, 1829, Thomas Beardin to O. P. Cheatham, $50.00, 67½ acres part of Lot #13, 4th Dist., Monroe (now Butts) Co. Wit: R. C. Chapman, Edward Weaver, J.P. Page 78.

June 9, 1829, Deed headed Newton Co., John D. Swift of Newton Co. to James L. Bankston of State of Virginia, $500.00, improved lot in town of Jackson, Lot #1, Sq. #14, formerly property of Henry Hately. Wit: Wm. A. Swift, McCoranch Noel, J.I.C. Page 79.

April 17, 1829, John Lumsden (Rev. Sol.) of Putnam Co. from Nathan Barnett of Butts Co., $962.00 note dated 4-17-1829 due 3-1-1830 or before with lawful interest for $5.00 from Lumsden, makes deed to Lumsden, 2 tracts land 405 acres, Lots #68 & #69, 9th Dist., Henry Co. (now Butts) on Tussahaw Creek, whereon saw & grist mill. If notes paid, then above deed void. Wit: James Dudley, Joseph Key, J.P. Pages 79-81.

February 11, 1828, Richard (X) Griffin of Hancock Co. to Thomas Kinney of Butts Co. for $250.00, 3rd Dist., Monroe Co., 302½ acres, Lot #243, granted to Richard Griffin by Gov. Troup. Wit: John Hall, Yelverton Thaxton, JIC. Page 81.

September 23, 1827, Britton (X) Alford of Pike Co. to Henry Hately for $300., 1st Dist., Henry Co. (now Butts) 202½ acres, Lot #23. Wit: John (X) Brown, Green Moody, John McMichael, JIC. Page 82.

June 13, 1829, Henry Hately to John Hall for $300., 1st Dist., Henry Co. (now Butts), 202½ acres, Lot #23, joining William Hearst. Wit: John McCord, Henry Jackson, J.P. Page 82.

May 23, 1829, Henry Hately, John McMichael, John Hendrick, Justices of Inferior Court, to John Hall for $29.25, Lot #1, Sq #17, town of Jackson. Wit: Lawrence Gahagan, A. L. Robinson, Clerk, SCBC. Pages 82-84.

Deed headed Jefferson Co. George (Rev. Sol.) Eubanks, Senior of Jefferson Co. to George Eubanks, Jr., Butts Co., $300., half of lot #21, 4th Dist., Monroe Co. (now Butts) drawn by Lewis Martin of Hall's Dist., Jefferson Co. Wit: John Murphy, Asa Holt, Jr., JIC. Pages 84-87.

April 11, 1829, David M. Maddox to Henry Summerlin for $5.00, from Summerlin, for 5 notes given by Maddox dated 3-29-1829, due one day after date, $23.46¼, $10.08 due 12-25-1829, $25 attested by Smith Bolling, $27.62½ due 12-25-1829, deed 150 acres, drawn by Davis M. Maddox, 8th Dist., Henry Co. (now Butts), 50 acres having been sold to Jesse & Green Maddox, Lot #189. If note paid, then deed void. Wit: Michael Summerlin, Stephen

D. Crane. Pages 87-88.

May 16, 1829, Michael Summerline makes affidavit as to signatures before George S. Thompson, J.P. Page 89.

October 28, 1828, Deed headed DeKalb Co., John Carter, DeKalb Co. to Aristotle G. Duke, $400.00 Henry Co., 1st Dist., Lot #217, 202½ acres. Wit: Samuel Barber, Wesley Camp, J.P. Pages 89-90.

July 6, 1829, Gideon Matthews and Wiley Thaxton give bond to Ordinary's office for $500.00. Condition: Gideon Matthews gdn. for Charles Gideon Thaxton. John McCord, CCO. Page 90.

October 22, 1828, Thomas Folds to John Folds of Jasper Co., 101¼ acres, west half of lot #204, 3rd Dist., Monroe Co., now Butts. Granted to Hardy Hart, $100.00. Witness: Jeremiah Evans, J.P. Page 91.

July 7, 1829, Zachariah Deason to John Hall promissory note for $18.52½ due 12-25-1829, by $5.00 from John Hall, Deason deed 101¼ acres, 1st Dist., Henry Co., part of Lot #126. If note paid deed void. Wit: John McCord, Henry Jackson, J.P. Pages 91-93.

March 10, 1828, E. M. C. Daniel signs receipt to John Lofton and John H. McDaniel for negro boy, Allen, before Daniel Parkman & Matthew Mayes, Senior. Page 93.

July 14, 1829, John H. McDaniel assigns to John Lofton his interest in negro boy, Allen, before R. S. Mason. Page 93.

July 16, 1829, Yelverton Thaxton to Mary Thaxton, wife of deceased son, Charles Thaxton, for Charles Gideon, only heir of Mary Thaxton, and Charles Thaxton, places in hands of Gideon Matthews, father of Mary Thaxton, wife of son Charles Gideon Thaxton, notes to amount to $260. to be collected and placed at interest for 4 yrs. or longer, to purchase a negro girl for Mary, during her lifetime, or until she marries again, then to go to Charles Gideon Thaxton, only child of deceased son Charles Thaxton. Wit: A. L. Robinson, C. F. Knight, J.P. Pages 93-94.

July 8, 1829, Zechariah Deason to John Hall for $500.00, Henry Co. (Yellow Water Creek), 202½ acres, Lot #125, 1st Dist. (now Butts). Wit: John McCord, James Willson, Joseph Key, J.P. Page 95.

December 25, 1828, Francis Miller, Henry Co. to John Lofton, $980.00, 8th Dist. Henry Co. (now Butts), north half of Lot #254, near Spring used by Robert Watson, near Littleberry Johnson. Wit: John Goodman, John Hendrick, JIC. Page 96.

December 2, 1822, Deed headed Morgan Co. Thomas Glass to Joshua Boon for $200.00, 9th Dist., Henry Co., Lot #67. Wit: W. M. Reed, E. Duke, J.P. Page 97.

April 4, 1827, Josiah (X) Jones, Burton's Dist., Richmond Co., to William Glover of Augusta, for $50.00, 202½ acres, Henry Co., 1st Dist., Lot #36. Wit: John Lamkins, James Cliatt, Roberts Thomas, J.P. Pages 98-99.

December 29, 1828, Deed headed Jasper Co. This indenture made this 29th day of December, in the year of our Lord, one thousand eight hundred and twenty-eight, between Thomas Key and Sarah Key, his wife, of the State and County aforesaid of the one part and a Thomas Cook, Henry Vanbibber, James Clayton, Joseph C. Atkins (Adkins) of the county of Newton and State aforesaid, Trustees in trust for the use and purpose herein after mentioned of the other part, witnesseth that the said Thomas Key and Sarah Key, his wife, for and in consideration of the sum of one dollar to them in hand paid at and upon the sealing and delivery of these presents the receipt whereof is hereby acknowledged hath given granted bargained sold released confined and conveyed and by these doth give grant bargain sell or lease confirm and convey unto them the said Thomas Cook, Henry Vanvibber, James Clayton, Joseph C. Adkins, Richard Shepperd, and their successors. (Trustees in trust for the use and purpose herein

65

after mentioned and declared all the estate rights title, interest property claim and demand whatsoever either in Law or Equity which he the
said Thomas Key and Sarah Key, his wife, hath or have unto or upon all
and singular a certain lot or peace of land cituate lying and being in
the first district of Henry now Butts County being part of No. 256, and
State aforesaid. Bounded and butted as follows to wit: Beginning at a
spring by the road running thence west to a post oak 148 yards thence
down the old line to a post oak 122 yards thence to a red oak 91 yards
from said red oak to the beginning of the spring 120 yards containing
and laid out for three acres, more or less of land, together with all and
singular the houses woods waters ways privileges and appertaining thereto belonging or in any wise pertaining to have and to hold all and singular the above mentioned and described Lot or peace of land cituate
lying and as aforesaid. Together with all and singular the houses woods
waters ways and privileges thereto belonging or in any wise appertaining
unto them the said Thomas Cook, Henry Vanbibber, James Clayton, Joseph
C. Adkins, Richard Shepherd and Their successors in office forever in
trust that they shall erect and build or cause to be erected, and built
thereon a house or place of worship for the use of the members of the
Methodist Episcopal Church in the United States of America, according to
the Rules and Dissiplin which from time to time may be agreed upon and
adopted by the Ministers and preachers of the said church, at their
general conferences in the United States of America, and in further Trust
& confidence that they shall at all times forever hereafter permit such
ministers and preachers belonging to the said church as shall from time
to time be duly authorized by the General Conferences of the Ministers
& Preachers of the said Methodist Episcopal Church, or by the Annual
Conferences authorized by the said General Conference to preach and ex-
pound God's holly word therein and in further trust and confidence that
as often as any one or more of the trustees herein before mentioned shall
die or cease to be a member or members of said church according to the
Rules & Disciplin as aforesaid then and in such cases it shall be the
duty of the Stationed Ministers or Preachers (authorized as aforesaid)
who shall have the pastoral charge of the members of the said Church to
call a meeting of the remaining Trustees as soon as conveniently may be
and when so met the said minister or preacher shall proceede to nominate
one or more persons to fill the place or places of him or them whose
offices has or have been vacated as aforesaid; provided the person or
persons so nominated shall have been one year a member or members of the
said Church immediately preceeding such nomination and be at least twenty
one years of age and the said Trustees so Assembled shall procede to
elect and by a majority of votes appoint the person or persons so nominated to fill such vancany or vancancies in order to keep up the number
of five trustees forever and in case of an equal number of votes for and
against the said nomination the stationed minister or preacher shall
have the casting vote provided never the less that the said Trustees or
any of them or their successors have advanced or shall advance any sum
or sums of money or are or shall be responsible for any sum or sums of
money on account of the said premises and they the said Trustees or their
successors be obliged to pay the said sums of money they or a majority
of them shall be authorized to raise the said sums of money by mortgage
or the said premises or by selling the said premises after notice given
to the pastor or preacher who has the oversight of the Congregation
attending Devine service on the said premises if the money due be not
paid to the said Trustees or their successors within one year after such
notice given and if such sale take place the said trustees or their
successors after paying the debt and other expenses which are due from
the money arising from such sale shall deposit the remainder of the
money produced by the said sale in the hands of the Steward or Stewards
of the society belonging to or attending Devine service on said premises
which surplus of the produce of such sale so deposited in the hands of
the said steward or stewards shall be at the disposal of the next annual
conference authorized as aforesaid which said annual conference shall
dispose of the said money according to the best of their judgement for
the use of the said society; and the said Thomas Key and Sarah Key, his
wife, doth by these presents warrant and forever defend all singular the
aforementioned and described lot or piece of land with the appertenances
thereto belonging unto them the said Thomas Cook, Henry Vanbibber, James
Clayton, Joseph C. Adkins, Richard Shepherd and their successors chosen
and appointed as aforesaid from the claim or claims of him the said

Thomas Key and Sarah Key, his wife, their heirs and assigns and from the claim or claims of all persons whatsoever. In Testimony whereof the said Thomas Key and Sarah Key, his wife have hereunto set their hands and seals the day and date aforesaid. Pages 100-103.

Sealed and delivered in the presence   Thomas Key (L.S.)
of us, James S. Brown,   Sarah Key (L.S.)
Thomas Wilson, J.P.

August 19, 1828, Augustine B. Pope, Ermine Case & Lawrence Gahagan give bond to Court of Ordinary for $400. Cond: Augustin B. Pope, Adm. of Estate of Walter T. Knight, late of Co., deceased. John McCord, CCO. Page 103.

July 21, 1829, Stephen Kight, of Meriwether Co. to James Pridgen of Butts Co., $450.00, south half of Lot #39, 9th Dist., Henry Co., (now Butts). Wit: J. M. D. Bond, John McMichael, JIC. Page 104.

July 9, 1828, Jeremiah S. Walker of Jasper Co., to Francis Ward of Putnam Co., Ga., $600.00, 107 acres, part of fraction of Lot #21, 14th Dist., Monroe Co., near Adams Ferry on the Ocmulgee, granted by Governor on 7-8-1828. Wit: Joel W. Terrill, Zach. Butler, J.P. Page 105.

August 5, 1824, Robert Kimbell of Henry Co. to David Kimbell of Oglethrope Co. for $250. by David Kimbell Jr., part of Lot #94, 2nd Dist., Henry Co. on Indian Creek, 90 acres, on south side of tract adjoining Lot #67. Wit: Robert Davis, Enoch McLendon, J.P. Page 106.

September 7, 1829, Samuel R. Nutt, Jane (X) Barkley, Samuel Nutt & Andrew Barkley give bond to Ordinary's Court for $4500.00, condition: Samuel R. Nutt, Adm. and Jane Barkley, Admnx. of estate of John Barkley, late of this county, deceased. John McCord, CCO. Pages 107-108.

October 20, 1828, Deed headed, Oglethorpe Co., Henry Bailey of Oglethorpe Co. for love and affection for daughter, Mary Ann Bailey, gives 1 negro girl, Judy, 12 or 13 years old. Wit: Robert Bailey, Thomas B. Bailey, Stephen Bailey. Page 108.

September 25, 1829, David Lawson to John Lawson for $100.00, fraction of land in 9th Dist., Henry Co. (now Butts), Lot #55, 183 acres. Wit: John McCord, John Hall, JIC. Page 108.

September 22, 1825, Thomas Hampton of Monroe Co. to Charles Heard for $600., 4th Dist., Lot #1, drawn by Thomas Hampton, running with Reynolds line. Wit: John Heard, W. W. Baget, J.P. (Monroe Co.) Page 109.

September 25, 1829, Thomas (X) Hampton of Troup Co. to Charles Heard of Butts Co. for $300.00, part of Lot #2, 14th Dist., Monroe Co. (now Butts), cont. 50 acres, northeast corner of lot. Wit: George Heard, Elijah McMichael, J.P. Page 110.

September 1, 1829, John Bellah, T. C., Morgan Co., seized property of John M. Davenport, Rebecca Caroline Davenport, highest bidder, for $16.50. Bellah made deed for 1st Dist., Henry Co., Lot #75, 202½ acres. Wit: Sibbert Wilson, Roanck Leonard, JIC. (T.C. - tax collector added). Page 111.

Deed headed Morgan Co., Joshua Boon of Butts Co. to Adam G. Saffold of Morgan Co., for $400., 9th Dist., Henry Co., 202½ acres, Lot #67, granted 11-30-1822 to Thomas Glass, by John Clark, Governor of Ga. Wit: A. K. Leonard, William Porter, JIC. Pages 112-113.

December 18, 1828, William Barkley to Joel Baley for $100, 120 acres, part of fraction of Lot #55, Henry Co., 9th Dist. (now Butts). Wit: S. P. Baley, P. Payne, J.P. Page 114.

February 6, 1829, William Barkley to Joel Bailey for $1100, 202½ acres, 9th Dist., Henry Co. (now Butts), Lot #43, granted to Nathaniel Sledge, Putnam Co. Wit: O. P. King, Stephen P. Bailey. Page 115.

October 9, 1829, O. P. King made affidavit as to signatures before Henry
Jackson, J.P. Pages 115-116.

December 6, 1828, William Barkley to Joel Bailey for $800., 202½ acres,
Lot #35, 9th Dist. Henry Co. (now Butts) drawn by John Gillespie of
Captain Loyd's Dist., Hancock Co. Wit: S. P. Bailey, O. P. Payne, J.P.
Page 116.

December 6, 1828, William Barkley for $300.00 to Joel Bailey, 75 3/4 a.
NE corner of Lot #36, 9th Dist., Henry Co. (now Butts). Wit: S. P.
Bailey, O. P. Payne, J.P. Page 117.

December 6, 1828, William Barkley to Joel Bailey for $400.00, Lot #7,
9th Dist., Henry Co. (now Butts), 202½ acres, drawn by B. F. Chew of
Chatham Co. Wit: S. P. Bailey, P. Payne, J.P. Page 118.

April 9, 1828, Deed headed Henry Co., William J. Torier, (Note: maybe
Tavier) Marion Co., Tennessee to George Brown, Chesire Co., New Hampshire
on account of note by Torier (Tovier ?) to Brown for $314.75 due 3-1-
1829 for $5.00, to Tavies (Tovier, Torier ?) deeds Lot #225, 202½ acres,
1st Dist., Henry Co. to secure same. Wit: Henry Loyless, Williard
Boynton. Pages 119-120.

April 12, 1828, Deed headed Twiggs Co., Willard Boynton makes affidavit
as to signatures before Thomas Dozier, J.P. Page 120.

April 21, 1829, John Phillips to Robert White, Lot #84, 1st Dist., Henry
(now Butts) Co. for $300. Wit: James S. Meek, Reuben Phillips. Page
120.

October 17, 1829, Affidavit of James S. Meek as to signatures before
Eleazer Mobley, J.P. Page 121.

February 19, 1829, Deed headed DeKalb Co., William R. Anderson to
William Gresham of DeKalb Co. for $10.00 to secure note 4-1-1828 for
$260.00. Note dated 2-19-1829, $65.00 land where Anderson now lives,
Lot #80, 202½ acres, 4th Dist., Monroe Co. (now Butts) also Lot #82, 4th
Dist., Monroe Co. (now Butts). Wit: William J. Howard, James Lemon, JIC.
Pages 121 - 122.

February 24, 1829, Mansel J. Smith, Baldwin Co. and Anderson Brown of
Jasper Co. to Smith Barron of Butts Co., 1st Dist., Henry Co. (now Butts)
Lot #186, 202½ acres, for $250. Wit: Abel L. Robinson, John Hendrick,
JIC. Page 123.

February 20, 1829, Mansel J. Smith authorized Anderson Brown to sign his
name to deed, for Lot #186, 1st Dist., Henry Co. (now Butts). Page 123.

----- 17, 1829, Thomas Robinson to Alpheus Slay of Meriwether Co. for
$300.00, 1st Dist., Henry Co., Lot #172, 202½ acres. Wit: David J.
Bailey, Abel L. Robinson, Clerk SCBC. Page 124.

March 3, 1829, Luke Robinson to Thomas Robinson for $650., 1st Dist.,
Henry Co. (now Butts) for Lot #184. Wit: James V. Hogg, Abel L. Robinson, Clerk, SCBC. Page 124.

November 5, 1828, Richard Pound to Jacob Wise for $275.00 for part of
Lot #36, cont. 80 acres. Wit: John McCord, Hugh Wise, Creed Wise.
Page 125.

January 13, 1828, Henry H. Baker of Fayette Co. to Jacob Wise for $150.
for south half of Lot #23, 9th Dist., Henry Co. (now Butts), bounded by
Joseph Wright & others. Wit: Augustine B. Pope, Benjamin F. Tucker, J.P.
Page 126.

October 5, 1829, James Bunkley to Caswell Ethridge for $500.00, west side
Macon Road, part of Lot #195, 1st Dist., Henry (now Butts) Co., cont. 30
acres. Wit: Gustavus Hendrick, Silas Eliott, J.P. Page 127.

September 29, 1829, Augustin B. Pope to Hamlin Freeman for $550, town

Lot #3, cont. 2 acres in plan of town of Jackson. Wit: Thomas R. Barker, Henry Hately, JIC. Page 128.

December 8, 1828, Parmour A. Higgins & William Higgins to Ebenezer Smith for $280.00, 140 acres, west part of Lot #5, 14th Dist., Monroe Co. (now Butts). Wit: Ferdinand Smith, O. Pain, J.P. Page 129.

October 10, 1827, William C. Swain, of Warren Co. for $110.00, to Jacob Wise, north half of Lot #23, 9th Dist., Henry Co. (now Butts), 101¼ acres. Wit: Richard Swain, John Burge, John L. Swain. Page 130.

December 1, 1828, William Reeves of Butts Co. to Reuben Bankston of Pike Co. for $300.00, 3rd Dist., Monroe Co. (now Butts) south half, Lot #144. Wit: Levi Martin, William Martin. Page 131.

January 15, 1830. Edward Weaver to Jarrett Weaver of Wilkes Co. for (note for) $252.50 due December 25, 1830, on receipt of $5.00 from Jarrett Weaver, Lot #43, 4th District Monroe Co. 202½ acres as security on note. Wit: David Evans, George T. Speake, J.P. Pages 147-148.

October 31, 1828. James Alexander of Bryan Co., to James McClure of Butts Co., $150.00, 1st District Henry Co. (now Butts) Lot #100, drawn by Sarah Wannah (widow) November 21, 1823. Wit: James McClure, Silas Elliott, J.P. Pages 149-150.

May 28, 1828. Joseph Sentell of Meriwether Co., to Robert Smith of Butts Co. for $1500, Lot #61, 14th District Monroe Co. (now Butts) 202½ a. (on Little Sandy Creek). Wit: A. R. Bickerstaff, J. Word. Page 150.

September 13, 1828. A. R. Bickerstaff makes affidavit as to signatures before Parham Lindsay, J.P. Page 151.

January 22, 1827. William Hamlett to John Castleberry, $160.00, 4th District Monroe Co. (now Butts) Lot #14, granted to Sarah Morris. Wit: C. Butler, John Reeves, Allen Cleveland. Page 151.

December 29, 1829. Allen Cleveland makes affidavit to signatures before Henry Haytly, J.I.C. Page 152.

September 10, 1829. Joseph Carmichael to James Carmichael for $250.00, 101½ a. on waters of Towaliga River, 2nd Dist., Henry Co. (now Butts), S half of lot #34 where James Carmichael now lives, granted to Valentine Crewse, February 7, 1829. Wit: Elizabeth (X) Tillery, Samuel Bellah, J.P. Pages 152-153.

December 8, 1829. George T. Anderson to Smith Wilkerson for $23.00 promissory note dated November 12, 1829, payable to William H. Goldsmith, Lot #67, 4th District, Monroe Co. (now Butts) and for $5.00 to George T. Anderson. If Anderson pays note to Wilkerson, February 1, 1830, then deed void. Wit: Thomas A. Barker, Samuel R. Nutt.

February 15, 1830. Samuel R. Nutt makes affidavit to signatures before John Hall, JIC. Page 155.

December 11, 1829. Isaac Burson of Warren Co. to Isaac Nolen of Butts Co., for $60.00, 4th District Monroe Co., Lot #52 granted to Isaac Burson. Wit: Leroy Sale, Robert Cochran, Stanley Crews, C. M. Coody, J.P. Page 155.

August 4, 1827. Samuel Straham to Isaac Nolen for $400.00 4th District of Monroe Co. (now Butts) Lot #34. Wit: Wm. H. Strahan & Eli Conger, J.I.C. Page 156.

February 16, 1830. William Burford to John B. Burford, a negro and child, Edd and Lucy Edd, about 18 mos. old, $500.00. Wit: Joseph Harmon, Thos. B. Burford. Page 157.

February 17, 1830. Thos. B. Burford made affidavit before John M. Pearson, J.P. Page 157.

January 27, 1830. John M. Pearson to William P. Hill relinquishes
right and title to four negroes to William P. Hill, eldest named Lydia
and Robert and Robert and Davy. Does not warrant negroes, as Pearson
took title to accommodate Polly Hill. Wit: E. R. Goodrich, John Hall,
J.I.C. Page 157.

February 16, 1830. Henry Hately, John Hall and John McMichael, J.I.C.
for $383.50 to John Hendrick, Lots Nos. 1 & 2, Square #7, each one
hundred feet square, in the town of Jackson. Wit: Henry McCoy, A. L.
Robinson, C.S.C.B.C.   Page 158.

October 13, 1829. John Goodman to John Hendrick for $350.00, 1st Dist.,
Henry Co., Lot #191. Wit: E. Butler, John Lofton, J.P. Page 159.

February 13, 1830. John Hendrick to James Bunkley for $350.00, 1st
Dist., Henry Co. (now Butts), Lot #191. Wit: John Tarpley, A. L. Robinson, Clerk S.C.B.C. Page 159.

December 1, 1829. Sampson Russell to William T. Lyon for $225.00, 1st
Dist., Henry Co. (now Butts), 101¼ acres S half of lot #7 on Sandy
Creek. Wit: Hamlin Freeman, Robert W. Harkness. Page 160.

December 29, 1829. Affidavit of Hamlin Freeman as to signatures before
Silas Elliott, J.P. (Clark Co.) Page 161.

November 24, 1829. John McMichael to Henry McCoy for $100.00, 300 acres,
part of Lot 105, 1st Dist., Henry Co. (now Butts), west side of east
half of lot. Wit: A. L. Robinson, John Hall, J.I.C. Pages 161-162.

August 12, 1828. Deed headed Warren County. Albert G. Bunkley to Ross
Stephens for $300.00, 2nd Dist., Henry Co. (now Butts), lot #35, surveyed
August 13, 1821, granted February 2, 1822 to John Wilson. Wit: Harmon
Runnels, John Wilson, Thomas Seals, J.P. Page 162.

February 20, 1820. John Hall, John McMichael, Henry Hately, Willis
Jarrell, J.I.C., to Augusten B. Pope for $187.43 the follow-
ing lots Nos. 6, 9, and 12, 4 9/10 acre each and Nos. 29 and 30, in the
town of Jackson. Wit: Abel L. Robinson, Samuel Bellah, J.P. Page 163.

November 14, 1829. Jesse Goodwin to John Hall on acct. promissory note
$55.00 of even date, due November 14, 1830 or before, deeds Lot $156.,
14th Dist., G. M. joining widow Andrews on north, James W. Watkins on
south, if not paid when due, bond void. Wit: James H. Edwards, Henry
Jackson, J.P. Pages 164-165.

May 1, 1829. Reuben Munday of Fayette Co., to Isaac Nolen for $100.00
part of Lot #30, 14th Dist. Monroe (now Butts) 100 a. west half of lot.
Wit: Daniel Kilcrease, Joshua (X) Heflin, C. M. Coody, J.P. Page 166.

December 28, 1820. Hugh W. Ecton of Meriwether Co. to Hugh Goins for
$1800., Lot #60, 14th District Monroe (now Butts). Wit: M. A. Chisholm,
S. M. Adams, C.S.C. Rec. March 8, 1830, Abel L. Robinson, Clk. Deed
headed Meriwether Co. Page 167.

January 26, 1830. Henry Hately to William P. Hill for $400.00, Lot #76,
14th District, Monroe Co. (now Butts). Wit: Abel. Robinson, J. M.
Pearson, J.P. Page 168.

March 1, 1830. John Simmons signs receipt to John Tarpley for $310.00
for a negro girl named Ellen, 14 years old, and warrants title. Wit:
Gideon Tanner. Page 169.

January 5, 1830. Christopher White signs receipt to James R. McCord and
John W. McCord, $250.00, in full payment for negro girl named Betsey,
about 13 years old, and warrants title. Wit: A. L. Robinson, John
Hendrick, J.I.C. Page 169.

January 8, 1830. Charles Bailey, Abel L. Robinson, Hamlin Freeman &
Henry J. Bailey, are bonded to Ordinary's Court for $4,000.00; condition:
Charles Bailey, Adm. of estate John M. D. Taylor, late of this county,

deceased. John McCord, CCO. Page 170.

January 18, 1830. Samuel Bellah, Calvary F. Knight & Henry J. Bailey are bonded to Ordinary's Court for $2,900, condition: Samuel Bellah, gdn. to Richard Knight. John McCord, C.C.O. Page 171.

February 20, 1830. (RS) Leavin Smith & Isaac W. Smith are bonded to Ordinary's Court for $2,000.00, condition: Leavin Smith, Adm. of estate of John Smith, late of Mobile, Alabama, deceased. John McCord, C.C.O. Page 172.

October 20, 1829. Jemima (X) Levsay signs receipt for $200.00 to Thomas Coker in full payment of two negroes: Charlotte, a woman 21 years old; and her boy child. Jordan and warrants same. Wit: Charles R. Waller, J.P. Page 173.

March 22, 1830. William Jones signs receipt to Joel Bailey for $900.00 in full payment for the following property: Negro man George, 20 years old, 17 head of nut cattle, 2 yoke work steers, 40 head of sheep, 3 head horses (2 bay & 1 sorrel, 4, 6, and 8 yrs. old). Condition: William Jones indicted at October S. Court, 1829, for paying. Grand Jury found true bill, and on which a bench warrant was issued Jones was placed in jail and Joel Bailey went on bond for $2000.00. Hence deed of conveyance. If he appears at April court, above contract void. Wit: Charles Ramey, Benjamin Moore. Pages 173-174.

September 1, 1829. Thomas Kinney to Samuel Ridgeway, $225.00, 50 acres land, part of Lot #211, on Cabin Creek, granted to Thomas Kinney by Governor Clark. Wit: Alexander Hale, William Orear, R. R. Kindrick, J.P. Page 174.

December 14, 1829. Abel L. Robinson to Rice Cleveland, 101 3/4 a., 1st District Henry Co. (now Butts) S. half of Lot #91, for $100.00. Wit: Allen Cleveland, Henry Hately, J.I.C. Page 175.

January 20, 1830. Willis Moore to Lewis Moore for $500.00, 1st District Henry Co. (now Butts), half of lot #182, 101¼ a. Wit: Seaborn W. Boales, Benj. F. Tucker, Joseph Key, J.P. Page 176.

November 30, 1829. Armistead Branch appoints Abel L. Robinson, true and lawful attorney to sign his (Branch's) name to a note in Central Bank, Milledgeville, to renew said note, to sign as an endorser on note made by Robert Brown, and discounted in said bank, and on a note made by said attorney for discount in bank, and each endorsed by me. Wit: Charles Bailey, Daniel Tingle. Pages 176-177.

January 15, 1829. John Hendrick, John McMichael and Eli Conger, J.I.C. to Willard Bradley and William Bradley for $50.00, lot of land in town of Jackson, No. 2, Square 6. Wit: Robert W. Harkness, Samuel Bellah, J.P. Page 177.

January 15, 1829. John Hendrick, John McMichael and Eli Conger, J.I.C., Butts Co. to Willard Bradley and William Bradley for $75.00, lot of land, town of Jackson, Lot No. 1, Square No. 6. Wit: Henry Hately, James Brady, J.P. Page 178.

March 30, 1830. Justices of Inferior Court of Butts Co. to Willard & William Bradley for $367.00, 2 lots in town of Jackson, No. 1, in Sq. No. 1, No. 5 in Sq. No. 3. John Hall, J.I.C., Willis Jarrell, J.I.C., John McMichael, J.I.C. Wit: John Tarpley, Samuel Strahan, J.P. Page 178.

January 10, 1830. William H. Andrews for love and affection for Harriet Freeman (minor) daughter of Isham Freeman, gives her the following: one cow, dark red and white. Wit: Abel L. Robinson, Silas Elliott, J.P. Page 180.

March 6, 1830. Augustin B. Pope, to Ermine Case and Eli R. Goodrich (Case & Goodrich) for $25.00, the following lots in town of Jackson, Nos. 6, 9, 12, 4 9/10 ac. each. Wit: O. P. Cheatham, Henry Jackson, J.P. Page 181.

March 29, 1830. Thomas Oglesby signs receipt to John Robinson & Abel L. Robinson for $290.00 for a negro girl named Frankey, ten years of age. Wit: B. F. Tucker, Silas Elliott, J.P. Page 182.

March 29, 1830. John Robinson & Abel L. Robinson, sign receipt to Robert W. Hunter for $200.00 for negro girl Frankey, ten years old. Wit: Willis Moore, Silas Elliott, J.P. Page 182.

December 26, 1828. Abel L. Robinson signs receipt to Lewis Moon for $350.00 for negro boy named Gardner, 12 years old. Wit: Ellis Rogers, Willis Moore. Page 182.

December 25, 1829. Asa Pryor of Morgan Co. to Joseph Wright, for $250.00 Lot #18, 9th District, Henry Co. (now Butts) drawn by William T. Baker & Mary C. Baker, orphans of Daniel Baker. Wit: Maria McMichael, Elijah McMichael, J.P. Page 183.

November 24, 1829. Deed headed Chatham Co., William T. Baker and Mary C. Baker of the city of Savannah, for $100.00, 202½ a., 9th District, Henry Co. (now Butts), Lot #18, orphans of Daniel Baker, deceased. Wit: Thomas Eden, Ben Sheftall, J.P. Page 184.

November 24, 1829. William T. Baker & Mary C. Baker sign receipt for $100 to Asa Prior. Wit: Thomas Eden, Ben Sheftall, J.P. Page 185.

October 30, 1827. William A. Prevatt of Chatham Co. and James Alexander of Bryan Co., for $100.00, 202½ a. for Lot #100, 1st District, Henry Co., drawn by Sarah Womack, widow, granted November 23, 1823. Wit: Mary W. Garbett, William Garbett, J.P.

Dec. 29, 1829. Joseph J. Hambleton of Jones Co. to Samuel Maddox of Monroe Co., for $100, 4th Dist., Monroe Co. (now Butts), Lot #78, grant issued from State. Wit: Ich. McClendon, Charles R. Waller, J.P. Page 186.

September 15, 1829. Neill Strahan to Isaac Nolen for $300.00, 4th Dist., Monroe Co. (now Butts), Lot #24. Wit: Gideon Whitted (Whitehead ?), C. M. Coody, J.P. Page 187.

February 16, 1830. John Hall, John McMichael, Henry Hately, J.I.C., Butts Co. to Abel L. Robinson and John Robinson for $92.00, Lot #4, in Sq. #2, containing 90 ft. on one line and 105 ft. on the other in the town of Jackson. Wit: Henry McCoy, John Hendrick, J.I.C. Page 188.

February 8, 1824. Deed headed Jasper Co. John Harris of Jasper Co. to Henry Hately of Monroe Co. for $250.00, 14th Dist., Monroe Co., Lot #76. Wit: R. Walker, Benj. Barnes, J.P. Page 189.

November 3, 1826. Deed headed Jones Co. William W. Jordan to James Hunt for $162.00, Lot #217, 8th Dist., Henry Co. (now Butts), 202½ a. granted to William W. Jordan. Wit: Samuel Wilson, Joshua Jordan, J.P. Page 190.

July 23, 1822. Deed headed Hall Co. Charles Collins of Hall Co. to Isaac Burson of Warren Co. for $500.00, 4th Dist., Monroe Co., drawn by Charles Collins, Lot #52, surveyed September 22, 1822 by Beverly Allen. Wit: William Gradey, James Johnston, J.P. (Rev. S.) Page 191.

1st Tuesday December, 1829. In obedience to fifas from various courts in favor of Philip Prior vs Jesse Benton and John Ferrell, one in favor of Zechariah Oneal, one in favor of Johnston & Peck, others vs. Jesse Benton, Robert W. Harkness, Sheriff, sold at public outcry Lot #192, 8th Dist., Henry Co. (now Butts), 180 acres property of Jesse Benton, on 1st Tuesday in December 1829, Lazarus Summerlin, highest bidder. $505.00 and deed is made to him. Wit: Abel L. Robinson, Henry Hately. Page 192.

----- -- 1828. (Rev. Soldier). John Wyatt to Rachel Magbie for $200.00, 50 acres, 8th Dist., Henry Co., part of Lot granted to _____. Wit: George L. Thompson, J.P., William J. Rollins, J.P. Page 193

December 29, 1829. Daniel Tingle to Isaac Low for $200.00, W half of

72

Lot #8, 1st Dist., Henry Co. (now Butts), 100 acres. Wit: A. L. Robinson, Henry Hately, J.I.C. Page 194.

January 10, 1829. Royal Burroughs of Madison Co. to John Brown of Butts Co. for $250.00, 1st Dist., Henry Co., (now Butts), Lot #70, granted to Royal Burroughs, December 12, 1825. Wit: Wm. Meroney, Benjamin Brown. Page 195.

January 16, 1829. Benjamin Brown makes affidavit as to signatures before John McMichael, J.I.C. Page 195.

May 26, 1829. John McBride to Ira H. Maddox for $250.00, S half of Lot #165, 8th Dist., Henry Co. (now Butts), 101¼ a. Wit: Michael Summerlin, Henry Summerlin, John Lofton, J.P. Page 196.

August 13, 1829. William B. George of Twiggs Co. to Neill Strahan of Butts Co. for $300.00, 4th Dist., Monroe Co., Lot #24. Wit: S. M. Granberry, James M. Granberry, J.P. Page 197.

September 9, 1829. Jane (X) Reynolds, Thomas P. Reynolds, James Reynolds & William (X) Reynolds to Isaac Nolen, 4th Dist., Monroe Co. (now Butts) 74 acres, part of lot #1, for $150.00. Wit: Thomas Bankston, Richard Nolen. Pages 197-198.

November 17, 1829. L. B. Eubank to George Eubank, Jr., $250.00, 1st Dist., Henry Co., part of Lot #12, 100 acres. Wit: Tho. R. Barker, Henry Hately, J.I.C. Pages 198

January 16, 1830. Samuel McCorkle of Monroe Co. to Abel L. Robinson for $600.00, 1st Dist., Henry Co. (now Butts), Lot #87. Wit: J. W. Melson, John Hall, J.I.C. Page 199.

November 9, 1825. Thomas (X) Hampton to Thomas Runnels, both of Monroe Co. for $500.00, 4th Dist., Monroe Co., 75 acres, part of Lot #1. Wit: Abner Bankston, John Hampton, William W. Bond, J.P. Page 200.

October 5, 1829. James L. Blanton to John Taylor for $500.00, Lot and tenement, town of Jackson, Butts Co., Lot #1, Range #1. Wit: F. A. Cash & A. A. Fisher. Page 201.

February 18, 1830. County of Leon Territory of Florida. A. A. Fisher makes affidavit as to signatures before D. M. Rainey, Clerk and James Hughes, D. C. Page 202.

February 18, 1830. County of Fla., County of Leon. David B. Macomb, presiding Justice of County Court for the Co. and territory mentioned certifies D. M. Rainey when signed the foregoing was Clerk as stated. Page 202.

March 18, 1820. City of Tallahassee. James D. Wescott, who attested the foregoing was presiding justice as aforesaid. James D. Wescott, Jr., Secty. & Actg. Governor of Florida. Page 202.

February 18, 1830. Robert Smith to Wilie B. Ector of Meriwether Co., Exec. in right of wife of William Grant, deceased, his promissory note for $683.21, due January 1, 1830 for $5.00 to Robert Smith, deeds Wilie B. Ector, Exec., 14th Dist., Monroe Co., Lot #61, also negro boy named Lewis, 12 yrs. old in possession of Robert Smith, and given to him by his father-in-law, Joseph Sentell, as further security. Wit: Luke Robinson, John Hall, J.I.C. Pages 203-204.

November 22, 1829. Abel L. Robinson to William A. Burney of Jasper Co. for $150.00, west part of Lot #1, Square #3, 60 ft. front, 120 ft. back, on which the office now occupied by Stark & Pettet, Attorneys at Law stands. Wit: Hamlin Freeman, John Hall, J.I.C. Page 204.

November 18, 1829. George Eubank, Jr. to Littleberry Eubank for $250.00, N half of Lot #21, 4th Dist., Monroe Co. (now Butts) 101¼ a. drawn by Lewis Martin of Jefferson Co. Wit: Tho. R. Barker, E. R. Goodrich, Henry Hately, J.I.C. Pages 205-206.

April 6, 1830. Charles Bailey, Adm. of J. M. D. Taylor, deceased, signs receipt to Henry J. Bailey for $857.00, total $1714, in full payment for following negroes: Leroy, 20 years old; Anthony, 23 years old; Rhoene, 18 years and her child; George, 9 months old; Rose, 16 years old and warrants titles to same. Wit: James H. Hill. Page 207.

April 6, 1830. Henry J. Bailey signs receipt to Charles Bailey for the sum of $1714.00 in full payment for following negroes bought by him at public sale in the town of Jackson, Butts Co. as property of J. M. D. Taylor, deceased. Leroy, a man about 20 years old; Anthony, a man about 25 years old; Rose, a girl about 16 years old; Rhoene, a woman about 18 years old and her infant child; George, about 9 months old and warrants right to same as slaves for lifetime. Wit: David J. Bailey. Page 207.

Nancy Warlick gives to son Jefferson one note for $47.00 dated May 13, 1828, on Solomon Warlick, also an account of twelve or fifteen dollars, amount unascertained, on Solomon Warlick, note and account last in hands of Burrel Jinks for collection for Jefferson Warlick, when he comes of age. Wit: Gales Jinks, Laura (X) Jinks. Page 208.

December 12, 1829. Hugh A. Smith to James Brooks for $44.50 fraction of Lot #91, 14th Dist., Monroe Co., (now Butts) 28 acres. Wit: Elijah McMichael, Jos. C. Dunsieth. Page 208.

July 7, 1828. Jeremiah S. Walker of Jasper Co. to Eleazer Adams of Monroe Co. for $1,000.00, part fraction of Lot #121, 3 acres on Ocmulgee River, adjoining land of F. Ward, near where James Howard once lived, including what is known as Adams Ferry, a cabin where E. Hicks lives now. Wit: Charles Alexander, Hiram Brooks, William Barkley, J.P. Pages 109-210.

March 11, 1830. Deed headed Henry Co. Gideon Matthews of Meriwether Co. to John Duffey of Butts for $900.00, Lot #3, 2nd Dist., Henry Co. (now Butts). Wit: Phoebe Ellis, J. A. Ellis, J.P. Page 210.

March 23, 1830. John Malone and Richardson Mayo give bond to Ordinary's Court for $250.00, condition: John Malone, Sr., Adm. of John Malone, Jr., late of Co., deceased. John McCord, CCO. Pages 211-212.

Melton Bledsoe, Charles Bailey and Samuel R. Nutt are bonded to Ordinary's Court for $4,000.00. Condition: Morton Bledsoe, Admn. of Jane Bailey, late of Henry Co., deceased. Pages 212-213.

This Indenture made April 3rd, eighteen hundred and thirty between Jonathan Reeves of Jasper Co. of the one part and the Baptist Church, called Macedonia of the other part of Butts County, Witnesseth that for and in consideration of the sum of three dollars and twelve and a half cents the receipt whereof is hereby acknowledged hath granted bargained sold and released and delivered and by these presents doth grant bargain sell and release unto the said Macedonia Church forever all that parcel of land containing two and a half acres it being part of Lot #159 in the first district originally Henry now Butts County commencing on the west and of said Lot following the line South sixteen rods to a Black Jack corner East twenty five rods to a pine Stake North sixteen Rods to a pine stake, West twenty-five rods to a pine stake where the first corner commenced on the line running No. 8 South including a passway to the Spring with privileges of water together with all and singular the rights and appeartanances thereof to the only proper use benefit and behoof of the said Macedonia Church forever in fee simple, and the said Jonathan Reeves for himself his heirs and assigns against the Lawful claims of all and every other person of persons whatsoever unto the said Macedonia Church shall and will warrent and forever defend by these presents. In witness, whereof the said Jonathan Reeves hath hereunto set his hand and seal the day and date above written (interlined before Assigned) signed sealed and delivered in the presents of John Copps, Sr., James Carter. Jonathan Reeves (L.S.). Pages 213-214.

Butts Co. Personally came before me James Carter who being duly sworn on oath that he assigned the within deed as a witness and saw John Copps do so likewise and also saw Jonathan Reeves assign the Same for the purpose therein named. Sworn to before me this 23rd April 1830. James Carter (L.S.), Joseph Key, J.P. Page 214.

March 29, 1830. Charles Miller to William Miller for $500.00, 1st District, Henry Co. (now Butts), Lot #164, 202½ ac. Wit: Jesse Goodwin, Henry Jackson, J.P. Pages 214-215.

April 6, 1830. Justices of Inferior Court, B. C., Willis Jarrell, John McMichael, John Hall to Thomas Broadders of Jasper Co., for $236.00, town lot, Jackson, Butts Co., Lot #1, Sq. #2. Wit: J. W. Watkins, Eleazer Mobley, J.P. Pages 215-216.

April 1, 1830. Willard Bradley and William Bradley to Lawrence Gahagan for $100.00 town lot, Jackson, Ga., Lot #5, Sq. #3. Wit: S. P. Burford, James Ray, J.P. Page 217.

July 13, 1829. David Adams signs receipt to Burrell Howell for $500.00, in full payment for lot of land, Henry Co., 1st Dist., Lot #71, drawn by David Adams. Wit: James H. Watson, John D. Montrey, James Spring. Page 218.

August 22, 1829. James H. Watson signs affidavit as to signatures before Thomas Roland, J.P. Page 218.

August 24, 1829. Abel L. Robinson to Lawrence Gahagan for $950.00 for W part of Lot #1, Sq. #3, 55 feet, front; 120 feet back, town of Jackson, Ga. Wit: Benjamin Person, Samuel Strahan, J.P. Page 218.

January 22, 1830. John McBride to John Britton, $325.00, 1st Dist., Henry Co. (now Butts), Lot #34, adjoining land of John Saunders, Higgins, etc. Wit: Amos Goree, George Britton, James Clayton, Jr. Page 220.

February 6, 1830. Amos Goree signs affidavit as to signatures before P. Pane, J.P. Page 221.

May 4, 1830. Joseph Summerlin, Sheriff, on account of foreclosure of mortgage of William A. Calaway against Augustin B. Pope, sells at public outcry lots of land, Nos. 29 and 30, in town of Jackson, belonging to Pope, 5¼ acres each, James R. McCord, highest bidder. $22.00 and makes deed to McCord of same. Wit: Abel L. Robinson, John Lofton, J.P. Page 221.

June 12, 1830. John McMichael, John Hall, Willis Jarrell, J.I.C. to James R. and John W. McCord for $300.00. Lots Nos. 2, 3, 4, each 25 acres. Wit: Steward Lee, Henry Jackson, J.P. Page 222.

July 5, 1830. Joel Wise and John R. Cargile give bond to Ordinary's Court for $4,000.00, Joel Wise, gdn. to Mary Springfield, orphan of Aaron Springfield. John McCord, CCO. Page 223.

July 5, 1830. Morton Bledsoe, Henry J. Bailey and Samuel Strahan are bonded to Ordinary's Court for $2,000.00, Morton Bledsoe, Admm. of estate of Thorogood Bailey, late of Co., dec'd. John McCord, CCO. Page 224.

February 9, 1830. William Stroud to John Lofton, on account promissory note for $73.00, due on or before December 25, 1830. $1.00 paid to Stroud by Lofton, Stroud sells for further security negro woman, Dinah, 23 years old. If note paid by Stroud, security void. Wit: Emanuel Smith, John Hendrick, J.I.C. Pages 225-226.

July 15, 1829. Deed headed Walton Co. Joseph Moss of Walton Co., bound to Henry Summerlin of Butts Co. in sum of $20,000.00. Condition: Joseph Moss and Henry Summerlin, copartners in mercantile business in Butts Co. under firm name of Moss & Summerlin, now dissolved. Summerlin paid Moss sufficient for discharge of all debts of firm and settled with him for his share of profits. If Moss settles all debts then this obligation void. Wit: Richard Butter, J.P., Alford B. Holt. Pages 226-227.

Augusy 8, 1830. Joseph Summerlin, Sheriff of Butts Co., on account of fifas issued from Justice Court in Green Co. by Woodriff & Seymore against O. B. Hopkins, sells Lot $248, 8th Dist. Henry Co. (now Butts) property of Hopkins, sells at public outcry. Joseph Summerlin, A. L. Robinson and R. W. Harkness, highest bidders, $62.68 3/4 and sheriff makes deed to them. Wit: Joseph W. Nichson, George L. Thompson, J.P. Pages 227-228.

July 6, 1830. Joseph Summerlin, Sheriff, on account of fifas from Superior Court, Hancock Co., at instance of J. W. Scott & Huddleston against William Grantham sells at public outcry Lot #78, 1st District, Henry Co. (now Butts) property of William Grantham. Robert W. Harkness, highest bidder, $1.06¼. Wit: John Tarpley, John Hall, J.I.C. Pages 228-229.

February 29, 1830. John R. Cargile to Rosannah Stark & Samuel James H. Stark, the heirs general of Samuel C. Stark, late of Butts Co., deceased, for $300.00 Northwestern quarter Lot #88, 1st Dist., Henry Co. (now Butts), 51 acres. Wit: Lawrence Gahagan, Silas Elliot, J.P. Page 230.

August 28, 1824. John (X) Brinson, Jr. of Butts Co. to William W. Black of Savannah, Chatham Co., $175.00, 1st Dist., Henry Co., Lot #34, granted to John Brinson, Jr., December 29, 1823. Wit: Wm. Hines, Henry P. Jones, J.P. Page 231.

February 9, 1830. John R. Cargile to Lawrence Gahan (Gohagan) for $300.00, 50 acres southwestern quarter Lot #88, 1st District Henry Co. (now Butts). Wit: John Tarpley, Silas Elliott, J.P. Page 232.

October 29, 1829. Deed headed Oglethorpe Co. Dinah Nutt of Oglethorpe Co. to James Anderson of Green Co. for $400.00, 1st District Henry Co. (now Butts) Lot #170, granted to James Otwell. Wit: Henry H. Greer, Charles F. English, Henry Anderson. Pages 232-233.

June 11, 1830. Henry Anderson (Butts Co.) makes affidavit as to signatures before Eleaza Mobley, J.P. Page 233.

July 2, 1827. The Inferior Court of Jasper Co. through application, James Betts and J. C. Gibson, Exec. of Abraham Betts, dec'd. passed an order for sale of undivided estate of deceased (legal notice first appearing in one of the public Gazetts of St. in Georgia Journal for 9 mos. previous to granting of order) same was sold at public outcry in Butts Co., at place of public sales. Henry Summerlin, highest bidder, $250.00. The Execs, 1-28-1830, deed to Henry Summerlin for $250.00, 8th District, Henry Co. (now Butts) Lot #219, granted to Aaron Ham, Powel's District, Burke Co. Wit: J. L. Maddux, R. C. Shorter, J.I.C. Pages 234-235.

January 14, 1829. (Revolutionary Soldier from Pittsylvania Co., Va.). John Miller of Monroe Co. to Eleazar Smith for $300.00, 4th District Monroe Co., (now Butts), Lot #60, lying on waters of Rocky Fork. Wit: Meshach Turner, Abednigo Turner, J.P. Pages 235-236.

June 1, 1830. On account of fifas issued from Justice Court of Jasper Co. at instance of Luke Reed, Luther Gable, Frederick S. Thomas, Pliffs against Stephen D. Beam and others, defendants, Richard Harper, Sheriff, seized Lot of Land, No. 200, 8th District Henry Co. (now Butts) and Joseph Summerlin, Sheriff sold same, when John Lofton and John H. McDaniel were highest bidders, $51.00 and Sheriff makes deed to same. Wit: R. W. Harkness, Joseph Key, J.P. Page 236.

August 3, 1830. On account of fifas issued from Justice Court, Butts Co., at instance of trustees of Jackson Academy against Edward Butler, A. B. Pope and S. Clay, Joseph Summerlin, Shf. seized town lot #4, in Jackson, Sq. #13, 105 ft. square, where on Butler's stable stands, property of Edward Butler and sold same at public outcry. Barnabas Woolbright, highest bidder, $21.18 3/4. Sheriff maked deed to Woolbright. Wit: A. L. Robinson, John Hall, J.I.C. Pages 237-239.

February 16, 1829. Robert C. Beasley of Jasper Co. to Robert W. Hunter of Butts Co., for $500.00, 1st Dist. Henry Co. (now Butts) Lot #180,

granted to Seymor S. Byroms, orphan, now wife of Robert C. Beasley.
Wit: John Hill, Seaborn Jones, J.P.   Pages 239-240.

July 13, 1826.   Jones Co.   Matthew Marshall & Abraham (X) Marshall,
heirs of Ruth Marshal, deceased, to Nehemiah King all of Jones Co. for
$24.00, lot of land on Tussahaw Creek, Lot #238, 2nd Dist., Henry Co.
Wit: Chs. Philips, Robert Lytle, C. W. Alexander, J.P.   Pages 240-241.

September 8, 1829.   Henry Co.   William W. Black of Screven Co. to John
McBride of Butts Co. for $300.00, Lot #34, 1st Dist., Henry Co. (now
Butts).   Wit: Hiram Doss, Britain Adams, Shade C. Russell, J.I.C.
Pages 241-242.

July 30, 1820.   James M. Hairston to James Anderson for $600.00, 2nd
District, Henry Co., Lot #96, 202½ acres.   Wit: Daniel Kimbell, Eldridge
H. Mobley, Eleazer Mobley, J.P.   Page 242.

May 23, 1829.   Henry Hately, John McMichael, John Hall, John Hendrick,
J.I.C. to Lawrence Gahagan, $36.67 for Lot #3, Sq. #24, No. 4 in Sq. #24.
Wit: John Tarpley, A. L. Robinson, Clerk S.C.B.C.   Page 243.

February 20, 1830.   Abel L. Robinson to Rosannah Stark and Samuel James
H. Stark, late of Butts Co., deceased, for $600.00, ½ of Lot #87, 1st
District, Henry Co. cont. 101¼ acres.   Wit: Henry Hately, JIC, John
McMichael, JIC.   Page 244.

February 6, 1830.   William Blalock to Palmer A. Higgins for $11.25, 1st
District Henry Co. (now Butts).   Wit: Joe Saunders, G. T. Speake, J.P.
Page 245.

April 12, 1830.   William Bradley of Coweta Co. in business with Willard
Bradley, firm name W & M Bradley, makes Willard Bradley of Butts Co. his
attorney-in-fact, to deliver to James H. Stark of Butts Co. titles to
the house in Jackson, commonly called Ruder's NE corner Lot #2, Sq. #6.
Wit: Robert C. Mays, L. Gahagan.   Page 246.

April 27, 1830.   Robert C. Mays make affidavit as to signatures before
John Hall, JIC.   Page 246.

April 30, 1830.   Bought by James Marks, 2 negro boys, one named Washington, aged 12 and the other named Willis about 17.   Signed: John R. Cargile.   Wit: Jacob Williams, Jesse Loyal, J.P.   Page 247.

April 22, 1830.   Willard Bradley, atty-in-fact for William Bradley,
acting for himself and Wm. Bradley to James H. Stark for $75.00 lot in
town of Jackson, ground on which stand house, commonly called Reader's
NE corner #2 Lot, Sq. #6, in plan of town.   Wit: James V. Hogg, O. P.
Cheatham, J.P.   Page 248.

April 10, 1830.   John McMichael, John Hall, Willis Jarrell, JIC to James
L. Blanton of Mecklenburg Co., Va. for $100.00 for Lot in town of Jackson,
Lot #1, Sq. #14.   Wit: James H. Stark, Joseph Key, J.P.   Page 249.

James L. Blanton states John Hall had become security for him in bail
warrant in favor of Henry Lee for $16.87 deed to be held by Mrs. Hall as
collateral security.   Wit: J. W. Watkins, John Bullard.   Page 250.

July 23, 1830.   James L. Blanton of Virginia to John Hall, his promissory
note for $150.00 due on or before July and gives deed as security to Lot
#1, Sq. #14, in town of Jackson.   If note with interest paid deed null
and void.   Wit: Willard Bradley, Henry Jackson, J.P.   Page 250.

June 17, 1830.   James L. Blanton of Virginia to John Hall note for $60.00
and as further security, deeds to lot in town of Jackson, Lot #1, Square
#14.   Wit: Aaron Haygood, Henry Jackson, J.P.   Pages 251-252.

March 11, 1830. (Richmond Co.).   Joel Bailey for $5000 has sold to Hurd
& Cook, merchants of the city of Augusta.   John T. Rowland, Merchant of
the town of Macon, and Hosea Webster, merchant of the city of Augusta,
the following negroes: Hannah, a girl 16 years old; Stephen a blacksmith

22 years old; Dick, a man 38 years old; John, a man 25 years old; Jerry, a boy 16 years old; Sawyer, 10 years old; Lucy, a woman 27 years old; Jenny, a woman 20 years old; Becky, a woman 26 years old, and her three children; Grace, a girl 8 years old; Washington, a boy 6 years old; Nance, a child, and 6, not recollected. Condition: Joel Bailey signed promissory note for $2,000 in favor of John T. Rowland, endorsed by Heard & Cook, payable at banks in Milledgeville, Macon, or Augusta, note dated March 11, 1830, due 12 months after date. Wit: Archibald Ramsey, G. W. L. Twiggs. Page 253.

December 12, 1829. Joel Bailey of Butts Co., to John T. Rowland of Bibb Co., Franklin C. Heard and Henry A. Cook, of Richmond Co., to further secure payment of certain sums of money, to John T. Rowland and firm of Heard & Cook for $10.00, deeds fraction of Lot #26, 4th District Monroe Co., 84 acres (granted to Joel Bailey) also Lot #57, 4th District Monroe Co., 202½ acres, granted Asa Langston, also Lot #61, 1st District Henry Co., when granted to Joseph Davis, also Lot #56, 4th District Monroe Co., 202½ acres also Lot #35, 1st District Henry Co., transactions involve another debt of $8000 or more due foregoing by Joel Bailey. Wit: Washington Poe, Thomas J. McCleskey, J.P. Page 254-258.

September 15, 1830. Burwell Howell of Bibb Co. to John Tarpley of Butts Co., for $150.00, Lot #71, 1st District Henry Co. drawn by David Adams, granted July 7, 1829. Wit: John McCord, John Hall, JIC. Page 258-259.

March 11, 1830. Deed headed Richmond Co., Ga. bet. Joel Bailey for $5000.00 to Heard & Cook, Merchants of Augusta, Ga. John T. Rowland, merchant of town of Macon & Hosea Webster, merchant of Augusta, conveys following negroes: Hannah, a girl 16 years old; Stephen, a blacksmith 28 years old; Jeffry, a blacksmith 22 years old; Dick, a man 38 years old; John, a man 25 years old; Jerry, a boy 16 years old; Sawyer, a girl 10 years old; Lucy, a woman 27 years old; Jimimy, a woman 20 years old; Becky, a woman 26 years old, and her two children; Grace, a girl 8 years old; Washington, a boy 6 years old; Nance, a child and 6 others, not recollected. Wit: Archibald Ramsey, G. W. L. Twiggs. Pages 259-260.

September 13, 1830. Archibald Ramsey makes affidavit as to signature before William Shannon, JIC, Richmond Co. Page 260.

October 12, 1830. Charles Bailey, Henry J. Bailey, Richard Bailey and Abel L. Robinson are bonded to Ordinary's Ct., for $7000, Charles Bailey appointed Gdn. to Noah W. Taylor, orphan of George D. Taylor, John McCord, CCO. Page 261.

October 12, 1830. Smith Barron & William (X) Barron are bonded to Ordinary's Ct. for $1400.00. Condition: Smith Barron, Admn. of Estate of John Barron; John McCord, CCO. Pages 261-262.

October 10, 1830. Eli Cooper to James M. Herston for $650.00 for Lot #93, on Indian Creek, 2nd District, Henry Co. (now Butts) granted to Potter E. Posey, grant dated April 13, 1822, place whereon Eli Cooper now lives, adjoining Sterling Kemp. Wit: John Hall, Willis Jarrell, JIC. Pages 262-263.

October 14, 1830. Hamlin Freeman to James H. Stark for $500.00, 2 acres, purchased by Freeman from Augustin B. Pope, whereon Hamlin Freeman now lives. Wit: Henry McCoy, John Hall, JIC. Page 264.

September 23, 1830. Willis Holdefield to Stephen Blisset, 1st District Henry Co., East 1/2 of Lot #76, 101¼ acres. Wit: Robert C. Mays, Samuel R. Nutt, John Hall, JIC. Page 265.

January 2, 1830. Ledferd Edwards to Creed Wise for $135.00, 9th Dist., Henry Co., southwest corner Lot #30, 45 acres. Wit: John S. Sturrice, George P. Speake, J.P. Page 266.

November 4, 1829. John Edwards to Creed Wise for $280.00, 9th District Henry Co. (now Butts) part lot #30, 70 acres. Wit: Pryor Edwards, Patton Wise, George T. Speake, J.P. Page 267.

July 16, 1825. (Oglethorpe Co.). John Beasley, Admn. of Estate of James Williams, deceased, of Oglethorpe Co., is ordered by Court of Ordinary to make title to land to Thomas B. Bailey in compliance with bond given by intestate to Thomas B. Bailey and assigned to Charles Bailey, John Beasley, Admn. for $300.00, 9th District Henry Co., Lot #49, granted to James Williams, May 27, 1825. Wit: John D. Moss, John Hardiman, JIC. Pages 268-269.

September 8, 1830. Zachariah Williams of Jasper Co., to James S. Irby of Jasper Co. for $500.00, 130 acres, part of two lots, east half of Lot #140, 101¼ acres, Lot #117, 39 acres. Wit: A. L. Robinson, John Hall, JIC. Pages 269-270.

February 6, 1830. Richard (X) Langford of Talbot Co., to Robert W. Smith of Butts Co. for $300.00, Lot #59, 14th District Monroe Co., on Big Sandy Creek. Wit: James C. Dunsieth, Elijah McMichael, J.P. Pages 270-271.

January 29, 1830. (Burke Co.) Christian Shultz of Burke Co. to David Higgins for $700.00, Lot #1, 14th District Monroe Co., granted to Andrew Havens of Effingham Co., February 4, 1822, and conveyed to Christian Shultz by Havens on February 28, 1822. Wit: Newton Perkins, Jr., Joab Rowell, J.P. Page 272.

October 23, 1830. Samuel R. Nutt to Stephen Blisset for $250.00, 1st District Henry Co., (now Butts), west half of Lot #76. Wit: A. L. Robinson, Robert Whiter, John Hall, JIC. Page 273.

March 1, 1828. (Emanuel Co.) Matthew Gay of Emanuel Co. to John McMahon of South Carolina, Abbeville District, Lot #14, 1st District Henry Co. (now Butts), 202½ acres, surveyed September 20, 1821. Granted to Charles Miller, conveyed to Matthew Gay on October 23, 1822. Wit: John Gay, Benj. Lanier, J.P. Page 274.

October 6, 1826. James Cannon of Monroe Co. to John Miller for $800.00, 4th Dist. Monroe Co. (now Butts), Lot #60, on waters of Rocky Fork. Wit: John Johnston, Josee Dunn, J.P. Pages 275-276.

July 19, 1830. John McMichael, Willis Jarrell, John Hendrick, John Hall and Charles Bailey, JIC to John W. Williams for $23.00, Lot #31, 1 9/10 acres in town of Jackson. Wit: John Lofton, Joseph Key, J.P. Pages 276-277.

October 6, 1829. On account of fifas from Superior Court, B.C., at instance of Jeremiah Person against Samuel Clay & P. G. Clay, Robert W. Harkness, sheriff, of Butts Co., seized, sold publicly lot of land, Lot #77, 1st District Henry Co. (now Butts) belonging to Samuel Clay and P. G. Clay, David S. Giles, highest bidder, $142.00. Wit: A. L. Robinson, J. M. Person, J.P. Pages 277-278.

July 8, 1830. Drury S. Patterson to Simeon Dering for $175.00, 1st District Henry Co. (now Butts), east half of lot #22, on waters of Sandy Creek. Wit: O. P. Cheatham, Edward Weaver, J.P. Pages 279-280.

October 2, 1830. Deed headed Jasper Co. Robert Brown of Butts Co. to Anthony Dyes of Jasper Co., promissory note for $744.00 due 12 months from date for $10.00 in hand. Brown deeds him negro property as further security: Jery, a negro man 35 years old; Harriet, a negro woman 35 years old; Flora, a negro woman 35 years old; provided above note with interest is not paid when due. Wit: Edward Young Hill, Jesse Loyal, J.P. Page 280.

October 12, 1830. Robert W. Hunter to Alexander Hunter for $500.00, remainder not given. Page 281.

Page 282 is blank.

November 4, 1830. Jesse Goodwin to John Hall, promissory note for $83.00 due on or before December 25, 1831, for foregoing amount, deeds as further security, Lot #156, #612, G.M., joining Widow Andrews on south side, James W. Watkins on north side. Wit: John Bullard, John McMichael, JIC. Pages 283-284.

December 20, 1828. Robert Sharp to Pleasant Potter for $600.00, 9th District Henry Co. (now Butts), part of Lot #52. Wit: William Giles, William Barkley, J.P. Page 284.

November 27, 1830. Casper M. Amos to Seaborn W. Bolls for $120.00, part of Lot #172, 1st District Henry Co. (now Butts), cont. 60 acres. Wit: Lewis Moore, John Hall, JIC. Pages 285-286.

April 6, 1830. On account of fifas from Superior Court, Butts Co., in favor of Bidwell & Casey, Abner Bidwell vs Wm. & Willard Bradley in favor of M. Read, J.S., send from Jasper Superior Court vs Willard Bradley, Jos. Summerlin, Sheriff, seized the mansion house, SW corner public square in town of Jackson, property of William Bradley and Willard Bradley, John Hall, highest bidder, $556.00 and deeds same to Hall. Wit: Jabez Gilbert, R. W. Harkness, George T. Speake, J.P. Pages 286-287.

December 25, 1830. John Hall to Anthony Dyer of Jasper Co., for $1000.00 lot in town of Jackson, Lot #30, Square #1. Wit: James L. Benton, John McMichael, JIC. Page 288.

August 4, 1829. Joseph Carmical of Butts Co. to Joseph E. Carmichael of Monroe Co. for $225.00, Henry Co. (now Butts) on waters of Towaliga River, 100 acres, north half of lot, granted to Justine Crevere February 7, 1822, 2nd District Henry Co., Lot #34, where James Carmichael now lives, adjoining John Sims. Wit: Hugh W. Carmichael, Joseph C. Scott. Page 289.

December 27, 1830. Hugh W. Carmichael makes affidavit as to signatures before Willis Jarrell, JIC. Page 290.

January 3, 1831. John McMichael, John Hendrick, Charles Bailey & Willis Jarrell, JIC, Butts Co., to Richard Bailey for $62.50, Lots #1, 2 in Square #9, in town of Jackson. Wit: William Harper, John Lofton, J.P. Page 289.

January 3, 1831, #2. Alfred Livingston & Robert (X) Grimmet give bond to Ordinary's Ct., for $500., condition: Alfred Livingston, Admn. of Robert Grier, Junior, late of Alabama, deceased. John McCord, CCO. Page 290.

January 3, 1831. Abner Bankston and Stephen Blisset are bonded to Ordinary's Ct., for $1500.00 and Abner Bankston, Gdn. to Angelina, Alston, Abner & John Payne, orphans of William Payne. Wit: John McCord, CCO. Page 291.

January 3, 1831. John Hendrick, John McMichael, John Hall, Willis Jarrell and Charles Bailey, JIC to Grace Beckwith of Morgan Co. for $211., lot in town of Jackson, Lot #3, in Square #3. Wit: Willard Bradley, John Lofton, J.P. Pages 291-192.

January 25, 1830. Samuel Lovejoy signs receipt to John Hendrick for negro boy slave named Jack, 13 years old. Wit: A. L. Robinson, J. W. Melson, Robert Brown. Page 293.

January 17, 1831. John Hendrick, John McMichael, John Hall, Willis Jarrell and Charles Bailey, JIC, to James R. and John W. McCord for $80.00, Nos. 27, 28, 14 acres. Wit: Ellis Rogers, A. L. Robinson. Pages 293-294.

January 18, 1831. A. L. Robinson made affidavit to signatures before Creed Wise, J.P. Page 295.

January 6, 1831. William Glover to James Bones of Richmond Co. for $250.00 for Lot #36, 1st Dist., Henry Co. (now Butts). Wit: R. F. Bush, Robert C. Mays, J. W. Meredith, J.P. Pages 295-296.

November 16, 1830. John Hendrick, John Hall, Charles Bailey, J.I.C. to

John Simmons of Pike Co., for $85.00, lot in town of Jackson, Lot #3, Square #5. Wit: James H. Stark, John Lofton, J.P. Pages 296-297.

August 22, 1830. Ebenezer (X) Smith to Humphrey Gilmore of Morgan Co. for $300., 4th District Monroe Co. (now Butts), Lot #60, drawn by James Cannon. Wit: William Gilmore, S. H. Tomlinson, P. Pay, J.P. Pages 297-298.

January 3, 1831. John McMichael, Charles Bailey, Willis Jarrell, J.I.C. Butts Co., to trustees of Jackson Academy pursuant to Act of Legislature, Lot #15, town of Jackson. Wit: John G. Irby, Clark Hamil, J.P. Page 299.

January 10, 1828. On account of fifas from Justice Court, Butts Co., at instance of Young R. Norris against James Morris, Samuel Clay, late Sheriff of Co. sold lot of land #21, 1st District Monroe Co. (now Butts) property of Morris, Young R. Norris, highest bidder for $26.00, and failed to make deed while in office, and deed being without seal. Joseph Summerlin, Sheriff, January 3, 1831, deeds Norris' the lot by order from Superior Court, October term, 1830. Wit: Charles Bailey, J.I.C., John McMichael, J.I.C. Page 300.

January 3, 1831. John McMichael, John Hendrick, Charles Bailey and Willis Jarrell, JIC's, Butts Co. to Rosannah Stark and Samuel James H. Stark, of State of South Carolina, for $75.00, heirs general of Samuel C. Stark, dec'd., 2 lots in town of Jackson, Lots #3 and #4, in Sq. #8. Wit: William Harper, John Lofton, J.P. Page 301.

October 6, 1829. On account of fifas from Superior Court, Butts Co., at instance of Jeremiah Pierson against Samuel Clay and P. G. Clay, Robert W. Harkness, Sheriff, seized lot of land in town of Jackson, 1½ acres, property of Samuel Clay, sold publicly. Catlett Campbell, highest bidder, $73.00. Wit: H. Williams, John Lofton, J.P. Page 302.

January 27, 1831. James H. Stark to Charles Bailey for $600.00, lot #3, town of Jackson, 2 acres. Wit: Marshal Douglas, J. W. Williams. Page 303.

January 29, 1831. J. W. Williams makes affidavit as to signatures before John Hall, J.I.C. Page 303.

February 3, 1831. William T. Lyon to John Hall four promissory notes, each $73.45¼ due on or before December 23, 1831, for $1.00 to Lyon, he deeds for further security, south half of Lot #7, 1st District Henry Co. (now Butts). If amount $93.81 is paid when due, deed void. Wit: George W. Smith, William G. McMichael, John McMichael, J.I.C. Pages 303-304.

February 1, 1831. Eli Hutto to Mary Ann Hutto, minor, and his niece, for love and affection, gives her following cows and calves: 1 white cow with red head and heifer calf with red sides, and their increase for her special use until she is her own guardian. Wit: A. L. Robinson, John (X) Hutto, Robert Smith, Willis Jarrell, J.I.C. Page 304.

February 1, 1831. John (X) Hutto, Sr. to Hamilton Hutto(N?) and Mary Ann Hutto (minors) heirs of John Hutto, Junior (now in life) for love to his cousin Hamilton Hutto, gives him during his life, one black and white cow and her yearling, black and white, one black sided cow, with white face, two yearlings of the same color, one red and white cow and dun calf with white in face, and yearling black and white, one black and white cow with red and white calf, one black steer, 2 years old, one feather bed and bedstead, one large pot to go to Hamilton at my death-- the cows to go to him at this time. To Mary Ann Hutto: one cow and calf, one bedstead. Wit: A. L. Robinson, Robert Smith, Eli Hutto, Willis Jarrell, J.I.C. Page 305.

January 28, 1831. Robert F. Benton to John Hendrick, promissory note $179.87½ on or before the 29th day of this month, $1.00 from John Hendrick, and Benton makes deed to negro slave boy, Jim, 12 years old. Wit: John C. McDaniel, John Lofton, J.P. Pages 306-307.

81

January 28, 1831. Note recorded with signatures of Robert (X) F. Benton. Wit: John H. McDaniel. Page 307.

May 7, 1830. John Bailey to Benjamin Harrison for $200.00, Lot #93, in 14th District Monroe Co. (now Butts). Wit: Jared Bryant, J. M. Pearson, J.P. Page 308.

July 10, 1830. John M. Pearson makes affidavit as to signatures before A. W. Ferguson, J.P. Page 308.

BUTTS COUNTY EQUITY RECORDS, 1836 - 1845

Pages 1-2: Butts Co., Ga. Inventory and appraisement of estate of Robert Bickerstaff, late of Alabama, dec'd. Sept. 8, 1836. Listed Negroes, good and chattel. Appraisors: Parhan Lindsey, John M. Pearson F. Douglass. Certified by David Smith, J.P. Recorded Sept. 28, 1836.

Page 3: Ga., Butts County, Inv. and Appr. of estate of Ennis Mc-Carty, dec'd made Oct. 7, 1836. One lot of land in Cherokee Co., one gold lot, one pocket book. Appraisors: John Lewis, Thomas Folds, Thomas Foster, John Kendrick. Certified Oct. 7, 1836 by Clark Hamil, J.P. Recorded Oct. 24, 1836.

Pages 4-16: Inv. and Appr. of personal property of Allen McClendon dec'd. sold at public sale Feb. 1, 1836 by William F. Mapp, Admr. Purchasers: Mary S. McClendon, Yelverton Thaxton, Anderson F. Thompson, Erusmus G. Marible, William F. Mapp, Jeremiah M. McClendon, Jordan Compton, John Webb, Young R. Harris, George W. Suttle, Nancy Johnson, Peterson G. Brogdon, Thomas Foster, Thomas J. Ferguson, William Simpson, James H. Campbell, Eli Parks, William M. Graves, Elisha Coker, James Brady, Irwin Stancil, Francis S. Martin, Wiley F. Martin, Isaac Nolen, John Wood, Jeremiah J. M. Mapp, George Jordan, John C. Garrett, Godfrey M. Hartsfield, Bedford H. Darden, David Evans, David Andrews, Pouncy Maxcey, William Blalock, William Jones, James S. Bankston, Charles R. Waller, Edward Weaver, John H. Weaver, Joshua J. Evans, John M. Phillips, James Thurman, James Britton, Green Treadwell, James Carter, Richard Byars, Clayton M. Coody, Samuel W. Thaxton, Archibald Smith, Middleton Hartsfield, William W. Ford, Michael D. Stone, Robert Irwin, John W. Phillips, Isham Freeman, John W. Johnson, Presley Smith, James R. Smith, John Morris, Chany Cawley, Hugh McLin, John H. Moore, James H. Demby, Richard Doggett, Stephen W. Price, Andrew Tennant, Samuel Wilkerson, Oliver McClendon, William J. Bryson, Henry Duke, Washington G. Atkinson, John Harris, William Bartlet, Squire Stilwell, Geo. W. Davis, Abner Bankston, John Goodman, Cornelius Slaton, Ichabod Hood, Burrel Buttrell, Robert A. Griffin, Elijah Phillips, William Akins, Robert Hamilton, Samuel Maddox, Shadrack Kimbrough, Norwell Holloway, John B. Thurman, John N. McCuen, John Bankston, Littlebury Bagwell, Alden Mickleberry, Willis P. Teadly, William Lawrence, Burwell Cannon, James Pye, Carter Hairston, John Whealis, Hughey Wise, Luke Williams, Green Barnett, Joseph Dawson, Franklin Compton, Britton Chapman, William Vaughan, Pendleton Slaughter, William A. Russell, Augustus Wise, George Carlile, Mary Davis, John Price, George Dawkins, James Ransom, George Moor, Nathaniel Goff, James Reynolds, James Neal, Jesse B. Reeves. Signed: Wm. F. Mapp, Admr. Recorded Nov. 12, 1836.

Pages 17-19: Account of sale of perishable property of Robert Bickerstaff late of Alabama. Sept. 9, 1836. Purchasers: Parham Lindsey, E. S. Kirksey, A. R. Bickerstaff, Benj. Harrison, James Pridgeon, Burwell Cannon, John Andrews, John Dingler, Moses Mount, H. Y. Dicken, Robert McGrady, B. H. Darden, Thos. Moore, Creed T. Wise, Robt. T. Dodd, H. P. Slaughter, William Johnson, John Floyd, Walter Andrews, P. B. Bickerstaff, W. W. Williamson, John Higgins, A. F. Thompson, J. Hood, R. Ransom, John Dunlap, John M. Pearson, Robert T. Myrick, A. F. Thompson, James Harkness, Wm. H. Parker, Jason Greer, Ichabod Hood, Alsey Durham, James G. Mayo, Henry Hardin, Benj. Harrison, John F. Preston, William Smith.

Signed: A. R. Bickerstaff, Admr.   Recorded: Nov. 25, 1836.

Pages 19-20. The estate of James M. Rhodes, dec'd. in account with
Josiah Draper year 1836. Sgn: Josiah (X) Draper, Admr. Recorded Nov.
1936.

The estate of Enoch Pearson dec'd. to William H. & John M. Pearson
Exec. Annual return for year 1836. Vouchers paid to Meridith Nelson
for pailing grave, C.C.O., taxes for 1834, Daniel B. Head, Nancy Pearson
in right of her husband Daniel W. Pearson in full, Mary Hill in full,
John M. Pearson in full, John M. Pearson as guardian for Sarah Power in
full, John W. Hill in full, James Pearson in full, William H. Pearson in
full, Wm. H. Pearson as agent for Mary Adair and her children in full,
Wm. H. McKleroy in full, Merideth Nelson in full, William B. Head in full,
William H. Pearson guardian for John McKleroy, minor of James McKleroy,
dec'd. in full, Dawson McKleroy in full, tax for 1835. Signed: John M.
Pearson, Exec. this Nov. 3, 1836. Recorded Nov. 26, 1836.

Page 20: Butts Co., Court of Ordinary, Nov. Term 1836. On application of Polly Camp, Admx. of Sterling Camp, dec'd. and as guardian of
James Camp & Nathan F. Camp, heirs & distributees of sd. Sterling Camp,
court orders Yelverton Thaxton, Clark Hamil, Willis Jarrell & Nathaniel
Anderson or any three be appointed commissioners to divide Negroes and
real estate of sd. Sterling Camp except, land as may be assigned widow
for her dower, into as many parts as there are children. Said widow
made her election to take only her dower out of the real estate and a
child's part of personal estate. Ordered that sd. Polly Camp, Admx. may
sell all perishable estate. Signed: James H. Stark, Atty. for Polly Camp.

Due and legal notice of above order acknowledged and copy waived
Oct. 1, 1836. Signed: John B. McRight in right of my wife Eveline Mc-
Right formerly Eveline Camp. A. H. Daugherty, J.I.C., Ezekiel Walker,
J.I.C., Thomas P. Atkinson, J.I.C. Recorded Nov. 17, 1836.

Page 21: Butts County, Ga. Assignment of land to James Camp one
of minors 152 A. Nathan F. Camp 150 A., Eveline McRight land on east &
northeast of Towaliga River on Dec. 6, 1836. Signed: Clark Hamil, W.
Jarrell, Yelverton Thaxton.

Ga. Butts Co. Assigned to James Camp 4 slaves, Nathan F. Camp 4
slaves, Polly Camp the widow 4 slaves, Eveline Camp 5 negroes. Recorded
Dec. 21, 1836.

Page 22-24: Inventory of part of perishable property of Aristotle
G. Duke, dec'd. sold Dec. 19, 1836. Purchasers: Samuel Hancock, Samuel
P. Burford, Washington G. Atkinson, Wm. Hanes, Ezekiel Walker, John D.
Dodson, John Eideson, Jeremiah Farr. Signed: Charles A. Killgore, Admr.
Recorded Dec. 29, 1836.

Ga. Butts Co., Inventory & App. of estate of William Rey, dec'd.
One lot of land No. 246 Butts Co., Negroes, two lots of land in Cherokee
Co. Appraised Nov. 19, 1836 by Dory (X) Taylor, S. P. Burford, Zacha-
riah (X) O'Nail, Elsey B. Thornton. Certified by Eli Conger, J.P.
Recorded Dec. 29, 1836.

We the undersigned Adms. of estate of William Ray certify that the
whole cotton crop was appraised in inventory without regard to overseers
part. Change from $5000 to $2500. Signed: William G. Ray & C. L. Ray,
Admrs. Recorded Dec. 29, 1836.

Page 24: Ga., Butts Co. Will of Jacob Wise - good health and sound
mind. Item 1: Lend unto my beloved wife Elizabeth Wise all land where
I now reside and everything I have in possession during her life time.
I appoint my three sons Creed T. Wise, Witt C. Wise & Francis Wise Execu-
tors of this Oct. 10, 1832. Signed: Jacob Wise (seal) in presence of
Parham Lindsey, A.L. Robinson, John McCord.

Page 25: In Court of Ordinary Ja. Term 1837. The will of Jacob
Wise was proven by Witt C. Wise, Exec. and appraisement warrant issued
to Parham Lindsey, William McCune, Francis Douglass, Thomas Moor and

Hugh Wise. Signed: John Hall, J.I.C., Ezekiel Walker, J.I.C., Thomas P. Atkinson, J.I.C. Recorded Jan. 2, 1837.

Sale of Negroes belonging to estate of Robert Bickerstaff, dec'd. Jan. 3, 1837 to Creed T. Wise, Clement Moore, Robert G. Duke, A. R. Bickerstaff, Thos. J. Saunders. Signed: A. R. Bickerstaff, Admr. Recorded Jan. 6, 1837.

Pages 26-27: Inv. and app. of estate of Grace B. Reeves, dec'd. List of goods and chattel appraised by E. W. Lane, John Eidson, James Thompson, Joseph Wilson. Certified on Dec. 13, 1836 by John Hendrick, J.P. Recorded Jan. 11, 1837.

Pages 28-31: A list of the sale of perishable property of James Anderson dec'd., Mar. 3, 1836. Purchasers: Mary Anderson, Nathaniel Anderson, David Kimbell, James M. Mangham, William Harper, William Bence, A. L. Robinson, David Anderson, Elisha Coker, Dunkin McVickers, Nancy Blessit, Reason Blessit, Samuel Collins, Thomas McKibben, Dawson Heath, William Nellems, Noah W. Taylor, John Kimbell, Gideon R. Wheeler, Smith Walker, Alden Mickelberry, Henry Bankston, Russell Fish, Josiah Chatham, Benj. Kimbell, John B. Douglass, Ezekiel Gosden, James Terrel, David H. Wall. Certified on Jan. 10, 1837. David Kimbell & John Anderson, Admrs. Recorded Jan. 12, 1827.

Page 31: The estate of Aristotle G. Duke, dec'd. to Charles A. Killgore, Admr. 1836. Pd. tax 1835, necessary items for family. Cr. cotton sold. Signed: Charles A. Killgore, Admr. Recorded Jan. 26, 1837.

Page 32: Annual return of estate of James Harrison to William Harrison, Admr. for year 1836. Pd. Joseph Summerlin, late Sheriff, John McCord, C.C.O., Marion Bartlett for printing. Returned Dec. 31, 1836, William Harrison, Admr. Recorded Jan. 26, 1837.

Estate of minors of James Harrison to William Harrison, guardian for year 1836. Pd. Jeremiah and Tabitha Maxcy for supporting sd. minors (no names listed). Returned Dec. 31, 1836 William Harrison, Guardian. Recorded Jan. 26, 1837.

The estate of William Redman in account with James Carter, Admr. for 1836. Pd. taxes, Mary Redman for boarding and clothing Mary Redman, Martha Redman, William Redman, orphans of William Redman, dec'd., Mary Redman for boarding, clothing and taking care of Elizabeth Redman, mother of William Redman, dec'd. Cr. Rent of land and hireing Negroes. Returned Jan. 23, 1837, James Carter, Admr. Recorded Jan. 26, 1837.

Page 33: Return corrected as to mistake in last item listed. Thomas P. Atkinson, J.I.C., Hugh Wise, J.I.C., Lewis Moore, J.I.C., John McMichael, J.I.C., Reason Blessit, J.I.C. Account of hireing Negroes and renting lands belonging to estate of William Redman for year 1836 to Mary Redman, Negroes & land whereon she lives and plantation lot No. 157 to Daniel Beauchamp. James Carter, Admr. Recorded Jan. 27, 1837.

Annual return on estate of Eli Knight, minor. To C. F. Knight year 1836. Pd. John A. Cuthbert for printing and Yelverton Thaxton for medical services. Return Jan. 3, 1837 C. F. Knight, Guardian. Recorded Jan. 27, 1837.

Page 34: Return of Samuel Bellah, Admr. of estate of William Rhodes, dec'd year 1836. Pd. William Mitchell for tuition for William, Benjamin F., and Josiah Rhodes, heirs of sd. estate. Recorded Jan. 27, 1837.

Return of Samuel Bellah, guardian of Hiram Bellah, Illegitimate. Sold lot No. 123 in Lee now Stewart Co., John McCord, C.C.O., M. Bartlett for printing. Recorded Jan. 27, 1837.

Return of estate of Joel Wise, dec'd. for 1836. Rec'd. of Burwell Cannon, Robt. Coleman, Joseph W. Slaughter, Thomas S. Blann, William Johnson, Barney Wise, Augustus Wise, Hugh Wise, David Madden, Hugh A. Harrelson. Pd. Kellum & Maxey, Hugh A. Harrelson, Wm. Johnson, Thos. G.

Blann for Henry Murry in right of his wife Jane Murry, formerly Jane
Wise, in part; Joseph W. Slaughter for John Murry in right of his wife
Marthw Murry formerly Marthe Wise; William Johnson in right of his wife
Polly Johnson formerly Polly Wise; Hugh Wise, Legacy; Barney Wise for
Patton Wise, Legacy; Barney Wise, Legacy; David Madden, guardian of
Elizabeth Wise; David Madden in right of his wife Mahaley Madden formerly
Mahaley Wise Legacy in part. Augustus Wise in his own right Legacy;
R. F. McGeehee, Clk. of Troup Superior Ct. Returned by Parham Lindsey,
Admr. Jan. 3, 1837. Recorded Jan. 28, 1837.

Page 35-37: An annual return of William F. Mapp, Admr. on estate
of Allen McClendon, dec'd. Paid William M. Leak, Jonathan Adams, Samuel
Snoddy, Isaac B. Williamson, George W. Reeves, Wm. Cunningham, John
Goodman, Ferrel and Ferrel, D. M. Bloodworth, Joseph Campbell, Eggbert
P. Daniel, Nelson Carter, H. H. Higley, William Lynn, Thos. P. Atkinson,
M. D. Garr, James McDowell, Tax 1835, John M. Phillips, Thos. B. Daniel,
Jesse Loyall, Abraham Maddox, Simeon Lovejoy. Credit: Rec'd. from
George Eubanks, John R. McMahan, Dawson Heath, James Morris, John Jones,
Thos. Bearden, Jordan Milam, Edmund Cobb, James Duncan, William Duffy,
William Mebellock, Matthew Orr, William H. Parker, A. F. Thompson, Henry
Vanbibber, William Pryor, Nicholas Purifoy, Jefferson Hicks, William
Hurst, Isaac Parks, Sion R. Bullard, Shurard H. Horn, Dudley Cook, Gillis
Right, Lemon Rogers, Joseph Campbell, John M. Phillips, Wiley Clemmond,
Pouncy Maxcey, Wm. Haden, Arthur Hamilton, Wm. B. Dickerson, Samuel W.
Thaxton, Isaac Hendrick, Jeprtha McClendon, Samuel Andrews, William F.
Mapp, Admr. Recorded Jan. 30, 1837.

Page 37: John E. Jones, guardian for Lavina Thompson. 1836 Paid
to Aquitta Felps Johnson exec. of Hannah Thompson, dec'd. Rec'd. for
sale of 1/5 part of land in Muscogee now Tolbot Co. Debit: Paid physican
bill, J. H. B. River's store, Washington H. Brown for tuition, Bickerstaff & Compton store, W. G. & T. P. Ferrel, Wilson & Maddox, John R.
Dicken. Recorded Jan. 31, 1837.

Page 38: John E. Jones, guardian for Jeremiah Matthews. Paid five
months board, two months board and service rendered, it being the last
illness of sd. ward, expenses of digging grave and making burying clothes,
one pair boots, Samuel Snoddy, Stephen Bailey, E. F. Kirksey for tuition,
Hendrick & Goodman for burying clothes, John W. Williams for coffin.
Recorded Jan. 31, 1837.

John E. Jones, guardian for Jubal Matthews. Paid Stephen Bailey,
E. F. Kirksey for Tuition, 14 months boarding and clothing. Recorded
Jan. 31, 1837.

Page 39. Sale of property of Dennis McCarthy late of Butts Co.,
Dec. 10, 1836 to William Wesley Henderson, David Martin by David Martin,
Admr. Recorded Feb. 3, 1837.

Pages 39-41: Sale of Perishable property of Isaiah Wise, dec'd. on
Nov. 18, 1836 by Riley Wise, Admr. Purchasers: Rosanna Wise, Parham
Lindsey, Elisha G. Kirksey, David Smith, Wm. G. Smith, Barney Wise,
Riley Wise, Robert McGrady, John Marable, R. R. Mayo, Isaac Nelam,
Robert Mayfield, Robert Gilmore, Jacob T. Mayo, George W. Suttle, Eldred
Nixon, Thos. Payne, Amos Gorie, Isaac Nolen, Ichabod Hood, Wm. Higgins,
Washington Hayat, Meredith Nelson, James Maddux, Wm. Echols, Lewis
Bennet, F. Douglass, Joseph Dawson, E. S. Kirksey, Wm. Akin, John Powel,
John Burge, George W. Thomas, John Dawson, Hugh Goin.

List of renting the plantation and hireing Negroes on Dec. 19, 1836
by Admr. to Robert Mayfield, William Vickers. Returned by Riley Wise,
Admr. Recorded Feb. 5, 1837.

Pages 42-43: Account of sale of estate of Jacob Wise, dec'd., Dec.
8, 1836. Sold to Francis M. Wise, Burrell Been, Creed T. Wise, Job
Taylor, William Giles, Jordan Compton, Wm. H. Parker, Hugh Wise. Barna
Wise, Hamilton Stewart, Witt C. Wise, John Murry, John McKelhaney,
Augustus Wise, Jacob T. Mayo, David Johnson, Jeremiah C. Lumsdel, Jesse
Whitley, Elijah Leverett, John Burge, William G. Preston, P. A. Higgins,
William Vickers. Recorded Feb. 6, 1837.

Pages 44-45: Inventory & App. of estate of Jacob Wise, dec'd. Negroes, goods & chattel by appraisors Parham Lindsey, F. Douglass, Hugh Wise. Certified by Samuel K. McLin. Recorded Feb. 7, 1837.

Pages 45-46: Return of estate of Isaiah Wise, dec'd. 1836 by Admr. Paid E. S. Kirksey, Smith Mobley & Lawson, H. Williams, Clement Moore, Charles Bailey, Rosey Wise Legacy in part. Credit: Rec'd for 1836 cotton, from Joseph Dawson, Rosey Wise by Riley Wise, Admr. Recorded Mar. 8, 1837.

Page 46: Estate of Nathan Williams, dec'd. in account with Nathan H. Williams, excr. from probate of will to Dec. 31, 1836. Return No. 1, paid Hand & Barton, P. A. Higgins, James W. Faulkner. Credit: Cash on hand at death, rec'd. of William S. Williams, S. Elliott, Samuel Burford, David Spencer, Roland Williams, N. H. Williams, James W. Faulkner. Returned Jan. 23, 1837 by Nathan H. Williams, Excr. Recorded March 8, 1837.

Page 47: Return No. 2 of estate of Nathan Williams, dec'd. in account with S. W. Price, excr. from probate of will Dec. 31, 1836. To 10 dollars counterfit bills found amongst the money of the dec'd. and charged to me. April 2, paid James H. Stark. Credit: Cash on hand at time of death. Returned Jan. 28, 1837. Recorded Mar. 8, 1837.

A return for 1836 on estate of Robert Bickerstaff dec'd. by Admr. Rec'd. of Barney Wise, Green Owen, Josiah Moore, William Low, William Vann, Guilford Guilder, John Wooten, hire of Negroes. Paid out to Henry Henderson, C.C.O., Taxes, F. Douglass, Dr. Charles Bailey, A. R. Bickerstaff, Admr. Recorded Mar. 9, 1837.

Pages 48-50: Sale of estate of Green B. Reeves, dec'd. taken on Dec. 20, 1836 to George L. Thompson, James Curry, William Wilson, E. W. Lane, E. Hilman, John Goodman, Mary McClendon rent of plantation, Nancy A. Reeves, James Thompson, Nathan H. Williams, Edward W. O'Nail, Henry Barren, William ?inks, Gales Jinks, John Edison, John Hendrick, Wiley Curry, Z. Wyatt, Wm. Wyatt, Wm. Magbee, John Smith, Amos Conger, Robert N. McLin, John Heail, Jasper Reeves, Anthony Gilmore, George M. Head, Josiah Crain, J. W. Evans, E. Walker, James Sumerlin, John Hendrick by George L. Thompson, Admr. Recorded Mar. 9, 1837.

Pages 50-56: Sale of the property of Nathan Williams dec'd. sold on Dec. 6, 1836 to William S. Williams, Agnes R. Evans, John Goodman, C. A. Williams, Perishable property of sd. dec'd. sold on Dec. 7th & 8th, 1836 to Thomas Bailey, C. A. Williams, E. Q. Lane, Stewart Lee, George Suttle, C. Ethrage, Josiah Hardy, Thomas Bailey, Peachy Bledsoe, Samuel Wyatt, Agnes R. Evans, Lemuel Atkinson, Steth H. Goodwyn, Spencer Jinks, Charles Wakefield, John M. Mayo, Henry Duke, Wm. Jinks, N. H. Williams, Griffin McMichael, John McClure, William Simpson, A. R. Evans, J. R. McCord, E. Walker, Palmer Higgins, G. W. Suttle, John Goodman, Robt. Douglass, James Carter, E. Williams, James Thompson, Wm. H. Andrews, Thos. Thomas, James Brown, John McMichael, Silas Elliott, J. B. Mason, J. W. Watkins, Samuel Wyatt, Wm. Henry, Wm. Jinks, Henry Barnes, L. W. Malier, Wm. S. Williams, Ansulum Hull, J. Hardaman, J. J. Mann, James M. Williams, E. Williams, B. H. Darden, S. W. Price, Nancy O. Williams, Isham Freeman. Returned by S. W. Price & Nathan H. Williams, Excrs. Recorded Mar. 10, 1837.

Pages 51-60: Account of sale of personal property of Sterling Camp, dec'd. at public out cry, on Dec. 12, 1836 to Jose Smith, William Bence, Stephen A. Davis, Mary Camp, Nathan Fish, Wm. Cyrus, Phineas Kell, Samuel Price, Thos. Colvin, Samuel Gardner, Samuel Bellah, Wm. Adair, Asa Pane, Calvin Fish, Russel Fish, John Camp, David S. Carr, Moses Rosser, John B. McRight, Daniel B. Ellis, Benjamin Sansing, Furney Hutcheson, Seborn Camp, Joseph Humphris, Thos. D. Johnson, Thos. Davis, Wm. W. Gilman, Jacob Cleveland, Palmer A. Higgins, David Kimbell, Clark Hamil, James Torell, James Draper, Samuel Smith, Wateman Gosden. Returned by Mary Camp, Admrx. Recorded Mar. 13, 1837.

Page 61: Hire of Negroes and rent of land of the estate of Sterling Camp, dec'd. Negroes hired to James Mangham, Wm. Cyrus, W. Jarrell,

Samuel F. Duffey, Russel Fish, Clark Hamil. Land, the Harison place to
Josiah Garrett, barn field to Mary Camp, creek field to Benjamin Kimbrel,
middle field to William Bence. Returned by Mary Camp. Recorded Mar. 3,
1837.

Pages 61-63: Amount of sale of property of Jacob Wise, dec'd. Mar.
22, 1837 to F. M. Wise, W. Hancock, C. T. Wise, Jesse Hodges, J. Tylar,
Augustus Wise, Barney Wise, John Burge, G. W. Barber, Henry Barnes, Hugh
Wise, J. Higgins, M. Matthews, W. C. Wise. Returned by Witt C. Wise,
Exor. Recorded Apr. 12, 1837.

Page 64: Ga. Butts Co., Appraisement of estate of Andrew Gray,
dec'd. by James Hale, James Nolen, Joseph Key. Cash on hand. Certified
by Jesse T. Gunn, J.P. Apr. 15, 1837. Recorded May 3, 1837.

Estate of Samuel C. Stark to James H. Stark, Admr. for year 1836.
Paid Ezekiel Trible in full of his distributive share in right of his
wife, Samuel James H. Stark distributive share in the hands of James H.
Stark, his guardian. Credit: Samuel James H. Stark and E. Trible share
in hire of Negroes. Returned Apr. 9, 1837 by James H. Stark, Admr.
Recorded May 8, 1837.

Page 65: James H. Stark, Admr. of Samuel C. Stark, dec'd. submits
return to Court of Ordinary the following notes & accounts which are in-
solvent or cannot be collected on Heard, Pettit, Mrs. Lindsey, Geo. W.
Martin, John W. Wilson, Andrews, Willis Holifield, Coker, Deason, Foster,
Hamil, Johnathan Bankston, Richard Speake, Barton, Robt. Smith, John
Sheerer, Heard, Childers, Andrew Nutt, Matthew McMichael in part, Gentry,
Hand, A. Ramey, Wray, James Vancey, B. Statnaker, R. Cushman, Rinly,
Thos. B. McCullough, Esq. Elliott, Brooks Foster, A. Milesberry. Return-
ed Apr. 19, 1837 by James H. Stark, Admr. Recorded May 8, 1837.

Page 66: Estate of Samuel James H. Stark in acc't. with James H.
Stark his guardian from date of letter of guardianship to Dec. 31, 1836.
From 1833 to 1836 paid Clerk of Court, amount of wards distributive share
of the estate of Samuel C. Stark dec'd. with interest to Dec. 31, 1836.
Returned Apr. 18, 1837 by James H. Stark, guardian. Recorded May 9, 1837.

Page 66-67: Estate of Sterling Camp in acc't. with Polly Camp
Admx. from letter of administration to Dec. 31, 1836. Return No. 1 -
Cash paid C.C.O., D. J. Bailey, John Hall, Russell Fish, Henry Bankston,
Richard Jones, E. Y. & J. Hill, Attys., John B. McRight, overseer,
Russell Fish for two hats for James and Nathan Camp, Spencer & Mays,
Samuel Collins, John Camp. Credit: Rec'd. from John Camp, Hodges, John
Hairston, Joab Willis, James Willis, Wm. Bishop, Burd Cheek, James &
Stephen Humphries, Wm. W. Gilman, Gideon R. Wheeler. Returned Apr. 18,
1837 by Mary Camp, Admx. Recorded May 10, 1837.

Page 68: Estate of Jamed Anderson to David Kimbell & John Anderson
Admr. for year 1836. Return No. 1 - Paid Myron Bartlett, grant fee on 2
lots drawn by James Anderson, James H. Stark, Atty., Bosdell G. Potter,
1835 taxes, Silas Plunkett. Credit: Rec'd. for amount of sales, rent &
hire to Dec. 26, on note of Matthew Anderson, Russel Fish. Returned Apr.
25, 1837 by David Kimbell & John Anderson, Admrs. Recorded May 11, 1837.

Pages 68-70: Ga. Butts Co., Will of James Jester made Dec. 18,
1836 sound mind but weak in body bequeath and divide all my estate both
real and personal unto my brothers and sisters and mother and friends
namely: Cash to sister Sarah Lofton, William James Lofton, son of John
Lofton, Nancy Hammon, wife of Charles Hammon, William James Hammond, son
of Charles Hammond, Jane D. Mason, wife of Leonard Mason, my mother
Rosann Jester A Negro, my sister Mary Jester land and Negro, to my sister
Mary Jester and brother Henry Jester and brother Benj. Jester and brother
Abner Jester plantation, Negroes and stock. Signed James Jester (seal).
Witnessed by William J. Foster, Penelope (X) Foster, James Ray, J.P. of
Monroe Co. Sworn to and subscribed in open court on Mar. 6, 1837 by
above witnesses.

Butts Inferior Court March Term 1837. The court having notice that
a caveat has been filed against the admission of the same to record and

ordered not to be recorded until a final decision upon caveat aforesaid and the same be ordered to be recorded. Signed: Thomas P. Atkinson, J.I.C., John McMichael, J.I.C., Hugh Wise, J.I.C., Rason Blessit, J.I.C.

At May Term 1837 the will of James Jester ordered to be admitted to record. Recorded May 15, 1837.

Page 71: Ga. Butts Co. Will of William S. Douglass, afflicted in body but sound mind. On June 14, 1837 I constitute my will as follows: After paying my debts equal distribution made between my three little daughters, Narcissa Weakley Douglass, Eugenius Lafayette Douglass and Marcellus Douglass. My stock of goods, house and lot I wish my executors to sell at time best interest of estate. Appoints Thos. Douglass and Francis Douglass, and Robert Pearson of Morgan County my executors. Signed: William G. Douglass in presence of James Campbell, Thomas J. Gresham, Robert G. Duke. Recorded July 7, 1837.

Page 72: Return No. 3 of the estate of William Lee, dec'd. Account with A. H. Daugherty Admr. year 1836. Paid McDaniel & Goodman, Spencer & May, C. B. Lee, A. H. Daughterty, O. P. Cheatham, note on L. B. Eubanks, Ann Russel, A. J. Jackson, W. P. Holefield, T. J. Gresham. Credit: McDaniel & Goodman, Spencer & May, C. B. Lee, A. H. Daugherty, Yelverton Thaxton, T. J. Gresham. Returned by A. H. Daugherty. Recorded July 10, 1837.

Pages 72-73: Sale of land lying in Butts County belonging to estate of Allen McClendon, dec'd. sold first Tues. Oct. 1836 by order of the court to Mary S. McClendon, Yelverton Thaxton, Andrew Tenant, Wm. F. Mapp, Peterson G. Brogden, John Goodman. Sale of land and town property lying in county of Pike sold on first Tues. Nov. 1836 belonging to dec'd. Town lot and store house to F. S. Martin, a tavern to Tilman Leak, stables and lot to John Neal, land to Joanah Foster & E. W. Wells, brickyard lot to John Neal, land to Samuel Mitshel, Wiley E. Mangham, Allen W. Pryor, David Andrews. Sale of land belonging to sd. estate in Jasper Co. sold first Tues. Dec. 1836 by order of court sold to John Wood, James M. Darden, Job Tylor, Andrew W. Brown, James Reynolds, William Hancock, Simeon Dearing, Henry Hardin, W. Kirksey, George Long by William F. Mapp, Admr. Recorded July 13, 1837.

Page 74: The hiring of 40 or more Negroes belonging to the estate of Allen McClendon, dec'd. for year 1837. To Isaac Nolen, Samuel Ridgeway, Drewy S. Petterson, Chany Corley. John W. Phillips, Purifoy Tingle, Wm. F. Mapp, John Carmichael, William McElhenny, Middleton Hartsfield, Zaccus McLeroy, P. G. Brogdon, James Ransom, John Wood, Wiley F. Martin, William H. Adnrews, Mary S. McClendon, Wm. Jones, Moses Mount, A. F. Thompson by Wm. F. Mapp, Admr. Recorded July 13, 1837.

Pages 75-76: Inventory and Appraisement of estate of Wm. H. Johnston dec'd. made Dec. 17, 1836. Listed goods & chattel, Negroes note on John G. Willis & O. J. Willis as furnished by Thos. Hairston Admr. Appraisors: B. F. Ward, H. Williams, Robert W. Smith, Robert McGrady, Arthur Lawson. Certified by David Smith, J.P. Recorded Aug. 22, 1837.

Pages 77-80: Return of sale of personal property of the estate of William H. Johnston, dec'd. sold on 22 & 23 of Dec. 1836 to Francis Johnston, Littleton Johnston, Carter C. Hairston, William H. White, William Simpson, Thos. Hairston, John Shannon, Moses B. Hairston, A. Lawson, John A. Ragland, John C. Parkerson, Martin Holloway, Pollard Payne, Wm. Curtis, Robt. McGrady, Umphrey Gilmore, Robt. Lawson, John Shannon, John Andrews, John W. Hill, Simeon N. G. Waldrup, Robert Pelman, David Smith, David Baggerly, John Walker, Moses Mounts, William Dean, Richard Johnston, Thomas Slaughter, Ichabod Hood, James Pinder, Isaac Maginta, Wm. Simpson, John Lawson, Jacob T. Mayo, Lewis Bennett, Wm. Smith, John G. Willis, C. B. Adams, Pleasant Green, Isaac McGinta by Thomas Hairston, Admr. Recorded Aug. 23, 1837.

Page 80: Return of sales arising from the real estate of William H. Johnston, dec'd. of land and Negroes sold in Jan. 1837. Sold to Benj. F. Ward, Pollard Payne, Henry P. Slaughter, Benjamin Harrison, James H. Stark, Thomas Hairston, Owen J. Willis, David Higgins, Francis Douglass,

Charles C. Hairston, William H. Tanner. Thomas Hairston, Admr. Recorded Sept. 24, 1837.

Page 81: A balance of an annual return of William F. Mapp, Admr. of
Allen McClendon dec'd. for 1836. Vouchers 28-34 paid to Amos Edmund,
Wingate Jackson, H. G. Johnson, Walker & Cobb, D. M. Anderson, J. V.
George. Recorded Sept. 6, 1837.

Estate of James Wooten to John Jones, Admr. for year 1836. Paid
Gordon Guyn, Flanders & Cook, A. F. Thompson, Uriah Napier & Freeman,
service for myself and wife this year. Credit: By cotton sold to William
Beman, J. McMullen. Returned Sept. 1, 1837. Recorded Sept. 6, 1837.

Page 82: Estate of Addison Wooten to John Jones, Guardian from Jan.
1, to Dec. 31, 1836. Paid C. Grimke for tuition. Credit: Rec'd. of
Jesse Wooten, exor. of James Wooten, Sr. dec'd. in part of wards legacy.
Signed John Jones, guardian. Recorded Sept. 6, 1837.

Estate of Seaborn L. Wooten to John Jones, guardian for year 1836.
Rec'd. of Jesse Wooten exor. of James Wooten, Sr., dec'd. in part of
wards legacy. Signed John Jones, guardian. Recorded Sept. 6, 1837.

Estate of Eimeon Wooten, a minor to John Jones, guardian for year
1836. Rec'd. of Jesse Wooten, exor. of James Wooten, Sr., dec'd. in
part of wards legacy. Signed John Jones, guardian. Recorded Sept. 6,
1837.

Pages 83-84: Estate of James Wooten, a minor to John Jones, guard-
ian for year 1836. Credit: Rec'd. of Jesse Wooten, exor. of James Wooten,
Sr. dec'd. estate in part of wards legacy. Signed John Jones, guardian.
Recorded Sept. 7, 1837.

Page 84: The estate of Neill Ferguson, dec'd. in account with A. W.
Ferguson, Admr. up to Mar. 19, 1836. Paid Samuel Snoddy, Moses Mount,
A. Gorey, Joseph Roe, D. B. M. Moore, John M. Pearson, John McCord, A. L.
Robinson, D. J. Bailey, E. S. Kirksey, D. B. Butler, W. H. Crane, Abner
Chapman, Samuel Fulton, Powel & Champion, support of family for year
1836, A. W. Ferguson. Credit: Rec'd. from sale of cotton, H. String-
fellow & A. R. Bickerstaff for corn. Signed A. W. Ferguson, Admr.
Recorded Sept. 8, 1837.

Dr. the estate of Neill Ferguson, dec'd. in account with Alfred W.
Ferguson, Admr. for year 1836. Cash paid Thomas House, James G. Walker,
F. Douglass, 1835 & 1836 taxes, J. C. Patterson, Journal Office, minor
legatee clothing, James G. Walker, legatee, William Jinks, legatee,
Henry M. Duke, legatee, Nathaniel Guyton, legatee. Signed A. W. Ferguson,
Admr. Sept. 4, 1837. Credit: Rec'd. for sale of 2 sides of leather,
barrel of corn sold to H. Duke, 1/2 side of leather. Recorded Sept. 8,
1837.

Pages 85-113: Inv. and App. of estate of William G. Douglass dec'd.
taken on the 5th, 6th, 7th, 8th of July 1837. Listed are all items in
store. Inv. of Notes on Edward Birdsong, Beverly Cooper, J. B. Bateman
& C. H. Simmons, James Wilson, Robert H. Crew & Elisha Crew, Samuel
Smith, Richard Boyd, William Byars, Robert Lawson, Robert W. Smith,
Jackson Mobley, Arthur Lawson, Stephen Mobley, James Hansford, G. G.
White, Thomas Barren, W. W. Gaither, Ferdinand Smith.

Town Lots 1 & 2 in square No. 7 and No. 1 in square No. 8 Land Lot
No. 267, 12th District Houston County, Ga. ...rec'd from notes on C. C.
Gibson, Andrew T. Miller, Jas. Boynton, James Norsworthy... Store ac-
counts on John Saunders, M.D., John Dunlap, Thomas J. Saunders, David J.
Bailey, Bedford H. Darden, Henry Duke, Sr., William T. Jenkins, M.D.,
Elijah S. Gilmore, Rev. Frances Douglass, Mrs. Sarah Jones, Joshiah
Moore, Thompson & Nolen, Frederick Young, Nolen N. Young, Cornelius
Atkinson, Snoddy & Jenkins, John Hutto, Alden Mickelberry, Elizabeth
Jeter, Robert Smith, Robert Gilmore, William Jarrel, Samuel Hendrick,
William Smith, James Bailey, Palmer A. Higgins, Thomas Douglass, Henry
Barnes, John Thompson, Robert B. Saunders, George Byars, Henry P. Duke,
Emanuel S. Smith, Thomas Moore, Samuel Duke, William G. Preston, John

Duffee, Hugh Wise, Daniel R. Ellis, Jarrett Weaver, John R. Williams,
Tucker Higgins, David Brady Moore, Louisa Bagwell, Jesse Hodges, Young R.
Harris, Jesse W. Dunkin, Wiley W. Gaither, William Vickars, dec'd.,
David Phillips, John R. Mahan, Robert Pearman, Esq., Thomas C. Taylor,
Samuel Snoddy, M.D., John Capeheart, Richard Boyd, James A. McCune,
William Akin, John McCune, John Andrews, Walter S. Andrews, Tilman
Higgins, Willis C. Jenkins, Robert McGrady, Wilson Meridith, Miss Sarah
J. Douglass, Mrs. Mary Coleman, Moses H. Brady, Daniel Martin, John W.
Wright, Weekly Duke, John N. Fall, Martha Jenkins, Alexander H. Daugh-
terty, Daniel Osborn, William H. Fare, John M. Pearson, Robert Goen,
John A. Mayhair, James E. Banks, Edmund McDaniel, Pascal H. Jackson,
Jacob T. Mayo, James Byars, E. J. Preston, John Hall, Wm. R. Simpson,
Sterling Jenkins, Wm. Carrouth, Enoch Jarrell, James Jarrell, Wm. H.
Tanner, Austin Clayton & Wm. H. Tanner, William Duffee, George W. Suttle,
Robert Douglass, Mary S. McClendon, Elizabeth McCune, James Carter,
Warren C. Scroggins, Thomas McCibbin, Andrew J. Wilson, Hugh Goen, John
H. Weaver, Jacob Gardner, James Brady, Newton Davis, James Harkness, Sr.,
Meredith Nelson, William McClendon, Hendrick & Goodman, David Kimbal,
Dawson Heath, M.D., Hendrick, Alfred Bankston, Thomas M. Harkness, Hugh
McLin, Stephen W. Price, James H. Campbell, James Cawthon, Isaac Law,
John Phillips, Wm. Carmichael (old man), Burges Cheek, James Wilson,
Henry D. Knight, Wm. Park, James H. Stark, Samuel Nutt, Charles B. Lee,
David W. Maddux, Hampton T. Dicken, James W. Harkness, James C. Dunsieth,
Hubbard Williams, H. B. Hairston, James G. Davis, Nathan H. Williams,
Willis Eidson, Thomas G. Cochran, R. C. Mays, Noah W. Taylor, Lewis
Bennett, Robert P. Coleman, Elisha Coker, Parham Lindsey, Jason Greer,
Robert G. Duke, John S. Irby, Thomas Lacy, James Duke, Hugh W. Carmichael,
John B. Carmichael, Pleasant Potter, Rev. William A. Florence, William
Hogan, William Wilson, William R. Bankston, Jackson Hairston, Joseph
Carmichael, William Harkness, Reason Blessit, James B. Waller, Spencer &
Mays, Micajah McCune, Eli Hutto, John Higgins, James Britton, Saunders
& Low, Lewis Moore, William A. Bledsoe, Squire Stillwell, Moses P. Hay-
nes, P. M. Compton, Isaac Smith, John Smith (near Dublin), William Jinks,
Robert A. Griffin, Arthur Lawson, Elam J. Bankston, John A. Fellers,
Henry Barren, Willis Jarrell, William Simmons, James Curry, John E.
Jones, Russel Fish, Nathaniel G. Waller, William Burford, Absalom Wilson,
Andrew Nutt, John Dawson, Robert Lawson, Messers McCords, James Draper,
Robert Phillips, James Gardner, John L. Hairston, Elijah Twilly, John
Blissit, Samuel P. Burford, William Hobs, McGoodwin, William Harden,
Daniel Beacham, Nathaniel Waller, John C. Morris, Isaac Nolen, Riley
Potter, David Higgins, Ross Collen, Monroe Dicken, Samuel Osborn, Daniel
T. Furgason, David S. Carr, Elizabeth Mays, John B. Reeves, Flemuel
Childers, James Phillips, James Arnold, Samuel Wilkerson, Joseph Camp-
bell, Spencer Jinks, John Anderson, John Carter, William McMichael,
James S. McClure, Alexander Hunter, Hamilton Hutto, Robert Powers, Ben-
jamin Harrison, Randal Right, John W. Williams, William McCune, H. J.
Gilmore, Mrs. Sarah Powers, Ezekiel Walker, Gideon Tanner, William Duke,
Moses B. Hairston, Gustavus Hendrick, William Gilmore.

 Recapitulation: Amt. of store items $5225.76½... Household stuff
in store $953.75... notes & receipts $5015.60½... Store, Accounts
$4922.69... Total $16,117.80 3/4... True appraisement of the estate of
William S. Douglass dec'd. certified this Sept. 22, 1837 by appraisors
Thomas J. Gresham, John Goodman, Robert Douglass. Above certified by
John Greer, J.P. Recorded Oct. 25, 1837.

 Page 114. Account of renting land and hiring Negroes belonging to
estate of Nathan F. Camp, a minor of Sterling Camp dec'd. for 1837. 24
acres to Josiah Garret, 12 acres to Polly Camp, 30 acres to William
Bence, 40 acres to Benj. Kimbell. Negroes hired to Jas. Mangham, Polly
Camp. Returned Oct. 19, 1837 by Mary Camp, guardian. Recorded Oct. 26,
1837.

 Account on estate of James Camp, minor of Sterling Camp, dec'd. for
1837. 40 acres rented to Josiah Garrett. Negroes hired to William
Cyrus, Samuel Duffy, P. A. Higgins, Russel Fish. Returned Oct. 19,
1837 by Mary Camp, guardian. Recorded Oct. 26, 1837.

 Pages 114-115: Butts County, Ga. Will of Henry Lee of sd. county
& state. Sound mind and disposing memory I do hereby make will as

follows: Appoint my sons Edward Lee and Stewart Lee my sole and only
executors... I give to my wife Lillis Lee a Negro woman, bed & furniture,
one cow & calf, a years provisions during her life and at her death to
be sold and equally divided amongst all my children... I give my son
Edward Lee a Negro Benjamin... I give to my son Larkin Lee a Negro Jerry
... I wish balance of my estate sold and equally divided amongst the
balance of my children (none named). Signed on this Aug. 28, 1837
Henry (L) (his mark) Lee... Test: Joseph Key, William Allison, Wade H.
Giles, J.P. Recorded Nov. 9, 1837.

Page 115: Yearly return for 1837 of estate of George M. T. Brock-
man by his guardian Morton Bledsoe. Cash paid Thomas R. Russel for
board & clothing 12 months and schooling, John Goodman, John McCord, John
R. Wilson, Stephen Bailey. Credit: Hire of 4 Negroes to Robert Price,
Thomas R. Russel, Morton Bledsoe. Signed Morton Bledsoe, guardian.
Recorded Nov. 9, 1837.

Page 116: Inv. and Appr. of estate of Henry Lee, dec'd. Negroes,
cotton, cattle, blacksmith tools, farm equipment, household goods, etc.
Certified Nov. 7, 1837 by appraisors William Allison, Matthew Barber,
Josiah Hardy and Wade H. Giles, J.P. Recorded Nov. 21, 1837.

Page 118: Yearly return on estate of Gilliam Preston, dec'd. for
year 1836. Renting land, 22 acres to Sally Preston, 14 acres to E. J.
Preston. Returned by James M. Preston & Elisha J. Preston, Admr. Recorded Dec. 14, 1837.

Annual returns on estate of William Blissit to William Harper,
guardian for 1836. Paid taxes for 1836, Wilson Maddux & Co., Clk. of
Court of Ordinary, John R. Dicken, Henry M. Bankston, taxes for 1835,
P. H. White, physician bill, Spencer & Mays. Credit: Balance due ward
from last return. Returned Dec. 16, 1837 by William Harper, guardian.
Recorded Dec. 20, 1837.

Pages 119-120: The estate of Allen McClendon, dec'd. to William F.
Mapp, Dr. 1837. Paid to Francis Douglass, Thomas P. Atkinson, James Neal
for schooling, Martin & Dodson, J. & J. McBride, John K. Waller, Jesse
Loyal, Nelson Carter, William C. Cleveland, Jefferson Hicks, Tilman
Leak & Co., G. & T. Leak, David Andrews, Henry C. Sills, William Harris,
Eggbert P. Daniel, Daniel R. Read, Grieve & Orm, A. H. Chapel, James
McDowel, Job C. Patterson, John & Sam Bones, William A. Florence, Stovall
& Co., taxes for 1836, Mapp & Hartsfield, John Goodman. Returned by
William F. Mapp, Admr. (no date). Recorded Dec. 21, 1837. Credit: Re-
ceived on notes from Charles Hobbs, William Holloway, Thomas Coker,
Edmund Head, Charles R. Waller, William Pryor, Andrew Tennant, Daniel
Osborn, Peter W. Watton, William B. Dickerson, John Jones, Hiram Lester,
David Montgomery, John Reed, David Madden, Littleton Long, John Akins,
William Akins, John M. Phillips, David Evans, Joseph Campbell, William
Jones, William Hardy, F. S. Martin, Allen Cook, Joseph Centall, Thomas
Coker, Jesse Tolleson, Joel Edwards on execution. Signed William F.
Mapp, Admr. Recorded Dec. 21, 1837.

Pages 121-122: Inv. and Appr. of estate of William Vickers, dec'd.
Listed goods, chattels & Negroes. Certified on Nov. 1, 1837 by apprai-
sors A. R. Bickerstaff, Parham Lindsey, Robert Mayfield and by Wade H.
Giles, J.P. Recorded Dec. 23, 1837.

Pages 123-125: Memorandum of the sale of property of William Vick-
ers dec'd. by Creed T. Wise, Admr. on Nov. 22, 1837. Purchasers: Anna
Vickers, Stephen D. Mayo, James N. Davis, Creed T. Wise, Barna Wise,
Ichabod Hood, Hugh Wise, Robert D. Cannon, A. Bickerstaff, F. M. Wise,
Samuel K. McLin, Wiley Jones, Robert Mayfield, M. Nelson, Anna Wise,
M. F. McCune, S. T. Mayo, L. Bennet, H. W. Gilmore, John Dawson, H. J. W.
Gilmore, R. W. Smith, John D. Mayo, J. T. Mayo, P. Wise, H. Wise, James
Mayo. Signed Creed T. Wise, Admr. Recorded Jan. 8, 1838.

Page 125: No. 1 Annual return of Andrew R. Bickerstaff, guardian
of Robert J. Bickerstaff orphan of Robert Bickerstaff, dec'd. due said
orphan on Jan. 1, 1838, $859., it being part of his distributive share of
the estate of dec'd. Recorded Jan. 8, 1838.

Page 126: The Admr. return for 1837 on estate of Robert Bickerstaff. No. 52, 5th Dist., 1st section sold at publick sale for cash to G. K. Cessnes. No. 1210, 16th Dist., 2nd section sold for cash at publick sale to John Merrit, land rented in Alabama to H. P. Slaughter, land sold in Alabama at publick sale to H. P. Slaughter on credit 1/2 due Dec. 25, 1838, 1/2 due Dec. 25, 1839. Signed A. R. Bickerstaff, Admr. Recorded Jan. 8, 1838.

Pages 126-127: Georgia, Butts Co.... Will of John A. Malone of sd. state & Co. being in sound mind... I do make this my last will & testament. 1st. The whole of my property real and personal be kept together for the use of my wife Martha Malone and my six children, Henry W. Malone, Charles B. Malone, Mary Adraan Malone, Martha Malone, Sarah Malone & Emily Malone and if there is another born which there is a prospect for to share an equal interest in my property with the rest of my children. My property to be under the control of my executors during the widowhood of my wife Martha Malone and in event of her marriage I will that the property be divided as to give my wife an equal share with my children. 2nd. My property managed by executor for the benefit of my wife & children. 3rd. I will that my wife Martha Malone, my friend Thomas Burford & Britton Buttrill be appointed executors of my will and I hereby subscribe my name on April 21, 1837. John A. Malone (Seal). In presence of Isaac Malone, A. F. Thompson, Elizabeth (X) Harrell. Recorded Jan. 16, 1838.

Will probated Oct. 17, 1837 and proven on Jan. 2, 1838 in open court upon the oath of Anderson F. Thompson and Elizabeth Harrell and ordered by John McMichael, J.I.C., Thos. P. Atkinson, J.I.C., Reason Blissit, J.I.C. to be recorded. Recorded Jan. 16, 1838.

Page 127-128: Negroes belonging to estate of Allen McClendon, dec'd. distributed by A. F. Thompson, G. W. Price, W. C. Jenkins on Dec. 26, 1837. Certified by C. M. Coody, J.P. Distribution: 14 in number to Mary McClendon, 14 to William C. McClendon, 11 to Oliver McClendon, 11 to Samuel Snoddy, 13 to Jeremiah McClendon, 13 to Joseph McClendon. Recorded Jan. 16, 1838.

Page 129: Estate of James Anderson to David Kimbell & John Anderson Admrs. for 1837. Return No. 2. Paid: C.C.O., Jas. Anderson, Jr., White & Gresham, William Allison, Spencer & Mays, John Pasham, E. Gasden, Mary Anderson the widow & one of the distributees her share, P. H. White, Wilson Maddux & Co., William Harper, W. S. & T. P. Ferrel, William Bence, A. L. Robinson, Supr. Ct. Fee, John Hall, taxes 1836, Hendrick & Goodman. Recorded Jan. 11, 1838.

Account of sale of Negroes and land of James Anderson, dec'd. Jan. 3, 1836. Lot No. 128, 2nd Dist. sold to William Bence, 50 A. north part of No. 96, sold to Bolyn K. Bankston. Negro man to Samuel Walker. Returned Jan. 1, 1837 by David Kimbell & John Anderson, Admrs. Recorded Jan. 17, 1838.

Page 130: Yearly return on estate of Jacob Wise, dec'd. by Witt C. Wise, excr. for year 1836. Cash paid to S. L. Robinson, James H. Stark, Francis M. Wise, Alfred Shorter, James C. Horton, John McCord, D. L. Duffey, T. C., M. Bartlett, A. H. Chappell, Creed T. Wise. Amount of money received. Cash from Francis M. Wise overseer for cotton sold in Macon. Elizabeth Wise for hogs sold. Recorded Jan. 17, 1838.

The estate of Aristotle Duke to Charles A. Killgore, Admr. Paid Blacksmith account, store account, advertising property. Credit: 3 bales of cotton. Charles A. Killgore, Admr. Recorded Jan. 18, 1838.

Page 131: The yearly return of George L. Thompson, Admr. of estate of Green B. Reeves, dec'd. Paid: John Hendrick, Joseph Summerlin, William G. McMichael, Albert H. Berge, A. H. Daugherty, Samuel Snoddy, James A. McCune, Hendrick & Goodman, John Hail, Robert N. McLin, John Lofton, Absolem Willson, T. G. Bledsoe, William H. Willson, G. Hendrick, William Baker, Wylie Curry, Wylie & T. P. Ferrell, John E. Jones, Tax Collector for 1835 and 1836. Nancy A. Reeves, John R. Dicken, Gustuvas Hendrick, John T. Wooten. Returned by George L. Thompson, Admr.

Recorded Jan. 18, 1838.

Page 132: A return for 1837 on estate of Robert Bickerstaff by
A. R. Bickerstaff, Admr. Paid: Thomas P. Atkinson, Clement Moore,
William S. Smith, Alfred A. Shorter, Lewis Bennet, James L. Maddux, John
Nolen, Hubbard Williams, John F. Preston, tax 1836, for grants for land,
for publication, for crying sale of land, Thomas Moore, Francis Douglass,
J. W. Williams, Robert Lawson, Josiah Moore, A. F. Thompson, William F.
Mapp. Recorded Jan. 18, 1838.

Estate of Daniel McClendon a minor & lunatick in account with John
Goodman, guardian in 1837. Return No. 1 cash paid Clk. of court of
ordinary, Nancy McClendon. Credit: Cash rec'd. of William F. Mapp, Admr.
of Allen McClendon, dec'd. Rec'd. of Nancy McClendon, Admrx. of Wylie
F. McClendon, dec'd. John Goodman, guardian. Recorded Jan. 18, 1838.

Page 133: Return No. 7 on estate of William Redman in account with
James Carter, Admr. 1837. Paid James R. McCord expenses in going to
Richmond County, North Carolina to collect a legacy due estate by Mary
Stanback, J. R. McCord for board of Mary Redman a minor, Mary Redman for
boarding minors Mary Redman, Martha Redman, William Redman and Elizabeth
Redman, mother of dec'd., William A. Florence for tuition for Mary Redman
one of the orphans, M. Bartlett, taxes 1836, Nancy O. Williams, Daniel
Beauchamp. Credit: Renting and hiring of Negroes. Received by hands of
James R. McCord a legacy bequeathed to William Redman now deceased by
Mary Stanback late of Richmond Co., N.C. ($703.35). Nothing rec'd. from
Mary Stanback as was expected for Elizabeth Redman lunatick. Returned
Jan. 1, 1838 James Carter, Admr. Recorded Jan. 19, 1838.

Page 134: Account of hiring Negroes & renting land belonging to
estate of William Redman, dec'd. for year 1837. Negroes hired to Mary
Redman. Land rented to Mary Redman plantation whereon she lives, Daniel
Beauchamp plantation Lot No. 157. Returned Jan. 19, 1838 by James
Carter, Admr. Recorded Jan. 19, 1838.

Pages 134-135: Estate of William H. Johnston in account with Thomas
Hairston, Admr. from Sept. 1836 to Dec. 31, 1837. Return No. 1. Paid:
Littleton Johnston, Robert Lawson, William Watson, Matthew Barnadore,
John Shannon, J. R. & J. W. McCord, John Hall, T. H. B. Rivers, C. H.
Wright, Jesse Loyal. Credit: Rec'd. from sale of land and Negroes, John
G. Willis, O. L. Willis. Returned Dec. 30, 1837 by Thomas Hairston,
Admr. Recorded Jan. 19, 1838.

Page 136: Return of Thomas Douglass & F. Douglass, execs. of
estate of William G. Douglass, dec'd. Amt. of goods sold in 1837. Rec'd.
Bloodworth & Mocks note, sold to Low & Compton, Noah W. Taylor, Robert
B. Saunders, Alden McKelberry, Samuel Snoddy, Thomas Dauglass, Francis
Douglass, Willis C. Jenkins, Martha Jenkins, Tucker Higgins, William &
J. B. Reeves, Sterling Jenkins, Robert & James Pearson, Morton Bledsoe,
Robert G. Duke, Henry Duke, Sarah Jane Douglass, Robert Douglass,
Bedford H. Darden, John Hall, William R. Simpson, James Carter, Bernard
Lee, James H. Campbell, William A. Florence, Spencer & Mays. Returned
Feb. 6, 1838 by Thomas Douglass & F. Douglass Excr. Recorded Feb. 7,
1838.

Pages 137-140: Return of sale of perishable property of estate of
William G. Douglass dec'd. sold Dec. 12, 1837 to highest bidder by
executors Thomas & Francis Douglass on a credit of 12 months. Sold to
Thomas Douglass, Henry Duke, Samuel Snoddy, Francis Douglass, William
Byars, Monroe Dicken, William A. Florence, Robert Douglass, A. Presley,
James Harkness, Sterling T. Higgins, J. W. Camel, James Pierce, William
G. McMichael, Leroy McMichael, Isaac Low (?), E. Thaxton, Joseph Carmic-
hael, John Andrews, M. Woodfin, John McMichael, A. Bankston, Martin D.
Hendrick, W. S. B. Harkness, John B. Reeves, J. S. Ingram, A. L. Robin-
son, Robert Andrews, James Bailey, D. S. Patterson, R. G. Duke, Samuel
Wilkerson, Willis C. Jenkins, John Walker, Thophilus Williams for the
house and lot in town of Jackson, E. S. Kirksey note. Signed Thomas
Douglass & F. Douglass, exrs. Recorded Feb. 8, 1838.

Page 141: Renting of the plantation of Isaiah Wise dec'd. for 12

93

months Jan. 1, 1838 by the Admr. to William Gann and Negro boy Floyd to Rosey Wise. Signed Riley Wise, Admr. Recorded Feb. 9, 1838.

Sale bill No. 2 of the estate of Sterling Camp sold on credit at Jackson Jan. 2, 1838. Slave to William Jinks, slave to Spencer & Mays. Signed Polly Camp, Admx. Recorded Feb. 16, 1838.

Annual return on estate of William Blissit to William Harper, guardian. Paid: White & Gresham acc't., John McCord, Clk. of Ordinary, Amt. due wards estate & interest up to Dec. 31, 1837. Signed William Harper, guardian. Recorded Feb. 16, 1838.

Page 142: Estate of George Blissit to William Harper, guardian. Paid 1835 Geo. W. Lowery, John McCord C.C.O., O. B. William, 1836 James Driskill, Y. Thaxton, Beeks & Clark. 1837 B. H. Martin, McDaniel & Goodman, White & Gresham, Spencer & Mays, William L. Wilson. Returned Jan. 6, 1838 by William Harper, guardian. Recorded Feb. 16, 1838.

Return of estate of Joel Wise, dec'd. by Admr. Rec'd. of Burwell Cannon, John Burge. Paid tax 1836. Returned by Parham Lindsey, Admr. Recorded Feb. 16, 1838.

Page 143-144: Return of estate of Isaiah Wise, dec'd. for 1837 by Admr. Credit: Rec'd. of Washington Hays, F. Douglass, James Smith. Paid to Joseph Dawson, Sr., Jeremiah Pearson, John Saunders, Lewis Benet, James C. Dunsieth, Rosey Wise Legacy, tax for 1836, John McCord. Signed Riley Wise, Admr. Recorded Feb. 19, 1838.

An Inv. & Appr. of estate of Quilla Gilmore, dec'd. on Feb. 15, 1838. Listed goods and chattel. Notes against Riley Potter, Jesse Hodges, Miles Parker, Thomas McClure, Stewart Lee, Benjamin Deason, Emanuel Smith, Samuel McLin, Joseph Key, Hugh Wise, John & James McClure, John McClure, James Bailey. Certified by Appraisors William Allison, Josiah W. Barber, Jesse Jolly & Waid H. Giles, J.P. Recorded Feb. 19, 1838.

Page 145: The estate of James Harrison dec'd. to William Harrison, Admr. Credit: Cash rec'd. from John B. Reeves on note. The orphans of James Harrison dec'd. to William Harrison, guardian Dr. Paid tax 1836, Tabitha Maxey for board, Clk. C.O. Signed William Harrison, guardian. Recorded March 7, 1838.

Jesse Matthews, a minor to John E. Jones, guardian 1836 & 1837 paid James H. Stark for professional service. Signed John E. Jones, guardian. Recorded Mar. 7, 1838.

Jubal Matthews, a minor to John E. Jones, guardian Dr. Paid 1837 & 1838 James H. Stark for professional service, 1836 paid Dr. Stephen Bailey, board & cloathing said minor for 12 months. Signed John E. Jones, guardian. Recorded Mar. 7, 1838.

Page 146: David Smith, guardian of Hugh S. Torbet, a minor, 1837 due minor on settlement. Credit: paid you on settlement. Return Mar. 3, 1838 by David Smith, guardian. Recorded Mar. 8, 1838.

Annual return made by James Draper, guardian for the orphans of James Rhodes, dec'd. for year 1837. Credit: Interest on $250, Samuel Bellah for rent of land for 1837. Paid Jarrell & Duffey for two brown caps for Wm. M. Rhodes and Josiah Rhodes, C.C.O. Signed James Draper, guardian. Recorded Mar. 8, 1838.

Return of Samuel Bellah, Admr. of the estate of William Rhodes, dec'd. for year 1837. Credit: Rent on land which was formerly laid out of the land of sd. estate for the widow dower. Sale of sd. land. Paid C.C.O. M. Bartlett for printing application to sell land. William Mitchel for William R. Rhodes one of the heirs for tuition, Josiah Rhodes one of the heirs for tuition. J. McCord, Harriet C. Rhodes Legatee, John Singleton in right of his wife as a Legatee, James Draper guardian for the heirs of James M. Rhodes, dec'd. former Legatee, Nancy Rhodes widow of James M. Rhodes dec'd. Legatee. Signed Samuel Bellah, Admr.

Recorded Mar. 8, 1838.

Page 147: Ga. Butts Co., Return of Henry Jester temporary Admr. on the estate of James Jester, dec'd. Inv. of present crop made by the Negroes and overseer on the plantation of the above dec'd. this present year 1837. A list of expenses for the plantation and Negroes of James Jester, dec'd. for 1837. Signed Henry Jester, tempo. Admr. Feb. 19, 1838. Recorded Mar. 9, 1838.

Page 148: Ga. Butts Co. An Inv. & Appr. of all the property both real and personal belonging to the estate of George Blessit, dec'd. Cash on hand, note on David Mountcastle and Thomas Foster, security, 101 1/4 A. land lying in the city. Certified by appraisors Robert Andrews, James M. Mangham, James Carmichael and W. Jarrell, J.P. on Feb. 21, 1838. Recorded Mar. 9, 1838.

Ga., Butts Co. - I, Hugh S. Torbet of the county of Monroe & state aforesaid have this day received of my guardian David Smith of the county and state aforesaid the sum of $209.25 in full payment of my legacy of the estate of Francis Torbet late of Fairfield District and state of S. C. Signed Hugh (H) (his mark) Torbet (Seal) on Mar. 11, 1837 in presence of William H. Tanner, Charles Bailey, J.P. Recorded Mar. 9, 1838.

Page 149-151: By William G. Ray & Coleman L. Ray Admrs. A list of the sale of the land & Negroes belonging to the estate of William Ray, dec'd. Sold at Jackson, Butts Co., Dec. 5, 1837. Lot of land No. 145, 1st Dist., Butts Co., to S. W. Langston. Negroes to Daniel Nally, Elizabeth Ray, Henry Youngblood, Samuel S. Scott, James Childs.

A list of perishable property of sd. estate as sold by Admr. to Joseph Wilson, John T. Wooten, John L. Ray, Zachariah Thompson, Francis Miller, John Willard, A. J. Grimmet, D. H. Ellis, C. L. Ray, James Evans, Wm. Stodghill, S. S. Scott, Joseph Wilson, Wm. G. Ray, Robert Grimmet, James S. McKibben, George Gunn, Aaron Onail, Jesse H. Cawthorn, Royal Willard, George Ramsey, Charles Burford, John Betterson, Andrew Stuart, James Childs, William W. Selmon, James Evans, Elizabeth Ray, Adaline Ray, D. H. Ellis, R. B. Tidwell, Robert Crew. Returned Dec. 30, 1837 by Coleman L. Ray, Admr. Recorded Mar. 10, 1838.

Pages 151-153: An Inv. of the personal property of Henry Lee dec'd. sold at publick sale on Dec. 21, 1837 at 12 months credit. Purchasers: Harvy Lee, Henry Barns, William Allison, Burwell P. Key, John Hendrick, Albert A. Watkins, George W. Barber, James Tomlinson, Andrew Hodges, Richard Byars, Samuel Wyett, Josiah W. Barber, Benjamin J. Hardaman, Nathan B. Barnett, Morris Mathis, Thomas J. Giles, widow (no name), Stewart Lee, exor. Recorded Mar. 12, 1838... An inv. of real estate of Henry Lee, dec'd. of Butts County sold at publick sale on Jan. 2, 1838. Negroes purchased by Stewart Lee, Charles Wakefield, Palmer A. Higgins. Recorded Mar. 15, 1838.

Pages 153-154: Account of sale of property of Aquilla Gilmore, dec'd. Apr. 10, 1838. Purchasers: Hugh McLin, William Jolly, Josiah Hardy, Henry Barnes, Jacob Saunders, William Giles, Bedford H. Darden, Mrs. Hardy, Wiley Jones, Elbert Hardy, James Pridgeon, John L. Barnett, Jesse Duncan, George W. Barber, Creed T. Wise. Signed: Josiah Hardy, Admr. Recorded Apr. 16, 1838.

Page 154: A return of hiring of Negroes belonging to Jeremiah P. McClendon for year 1838. 5 to William A. Florence, 1 to Samuel Snoddy, 3 to Wiley F. Martin, 3 to John Wood, 1 to James Britton, Samuel Snoddy, guardian.

Page 155: A return of hiring of Negroes belonging to Joseph F. McClendon minor of Allen McClendon, dec'd. for year 1838. 3 to William F. Mapp, 1 to Pouncy Maxey, 2 to O. H. P. McClendon, 4 to John Mason, 1 to James Buckold, 1 to Chany Cawly. Returned by William F. Mapp, guardian. Recorded Apr. 17, 1838.

A return of hiring Negroes belonging to William C. McClendon minor

95

of Allen McClendon, dec'd. for year 1838. 1 to John Mason, 1 to Pouncy Maxey, 1 to Zacheus McElroy, 2 to John Wood, returned by William F. Mapp, guardian. Recorded Apr. 17, 1838.

Return No. 1 yearly return of Coleman L. Ray, Admr. on estate of William Ray dec'd. Paid vouchers 1-15 to Wiley S. & T. P. Ferrell, W. W. Pearson, John R. Dicken, John Hall, Henry Summerlin, Jesse T. Gunn, Spencer & Mays, James H. Stark, 1837 taxes, Samuel Snoddy, John McCord, C. L. Ray, Henry Summerlin note. Credit: Cash rec'd. from sale of cotton crop for year 1836. Coleman L. Ray Admr. Recorded May 8, 1838.

Page 156: Estate of Simeon Wooten, a minor to John Jones, guardian for year 1837. Paid C.C.O. Credit: Balance of last return, Jesse Wooten exor. of James Wooten, Sr. balance of wards legacy. Returned July 2, 1838 by John Jones, guardian. Recorded July 5, 1838.

Estate of Addison A. Wooten minor to John Jones, guardian for year 1837. Paid: C.C.O., balance due ward Dec. 31, 1837. Credit: Balance due ward as per last return. Rec'd. of Jesse Wooten, exor. of James Wooten, dec'd. balance of wards legacy. Returned July 2, 1838. Recorded July 5, 1838.

Page 157: Estate of Seaborn L. Wooten, a minor to John Jones, guardian. Paid: C.C.O., balance of wards legacy. Credit: Balance of wards legacy from Jesse Wooten, exor. of James Wooten, dec'd. Recorded July 6, 1838.

Estate of James Wooten, a minor to John Jones, guardian. Paid: J. A. Fellows for tuition, C.C.O., balance due ward for 1837. Credit: Rec'd. of Jesse Wooten exor. of James Wooten, Sr. balance of wards legacy. Returned July 2, 1838. Recorded July 6, 1838.

Pages 158-160: Ga. Butts Co. Inv. & Appr. of good and chattel of James Jester, dec'd. on June 15, 1838 also note on Thomas Folds, Henry Vinson, S. W. Thaxton, Clark Hamil, J. McClain, Samuel H. McClain, Wm. McWhorter, James Ray & Solomon Ray, Yelventon Thaxton, Samuel Osborn, Anthony Ivey, Robert Brown, Abraham Gotsen, James Arthur, David Gurgans, Chaney Farrow, John Hornes, William Frazier, Robert Smith & Francis Hall, David L. Bailey, John Galman, Perly Forde. Certified by appraisors Samuel Bellah, Dolphin Lindsey, William J. Foster and Clark Hamil, J.P. Recorded July 10, 1838.

Page 160: An acc't. of sale of the real estate of Charles G. Thaxton, a minor of Charles Thaxton, dec'd. sold at public outcry on Mar. 6, 1838 in the town of Spalding the court house of Murray Co. One lot of land (160 A.) lot No. 174, 9th Dist. 3rd Section of Cherokee survey now Murray Co. purchased by George W. Weaver. Returned May 19, 1838 by Yelventon Thaxton, guardian. Recorded July 11, 1838.

Pages 161-164: Return No. 2 for Estate of Sterling Camp in acc't. with Mary Camp, Admrx. from Jan. 1, 1837 to Feb. 6, 1838. Paid Vouchers No. 15-51 to John B. Douglass, Thomas House, David Kimbell, William Bence, Gideon R. Wheeler, Polly Anderson, R. McDuff, Yelventon Thaxton, Peck & Johnson (note), Anderson & Peck, Moses Roper, John Hall, Russel Fish, Isham Anderson, Thomas P. Atkinson. Myron Bartlett (printer), H. Hately, C.C.O., P. H. White, Hendrick & Goodman, Samuel Snoody, H. B. Hairston, Jno. Blissit, Jno. Tarpley, W. S. & T. P. Ferrell, James Henderson, Wilson Maddux & Co. for plot & grant, taxes 1836, S. Elliott County Surveyor, taxes 1835, C.C.O. Barton Martin. Credit: Balance as per last return, rec'd. on notes of Shadrick Bullock, R. Meeks, Joel Deas, Stephen Humphries, Wm. Adair, Jacob Coker & B. Capes, H. B. Hairston & Jno. L. Hairston, H. Hately, James Henderson, O. C. Cleveland, E. Gosden, cash from Moses Roper, Yelventon Thaxton, sale & hire of 2 Negroes.

The Admx. returns to court evidences of debts as insolvent or uncollectable, to wit: William Bishop, George W. Thomas, William J. Shearer, William Saunders, Isaac Coker, Luke Patrick, James S. Meek, Reuben Bakston, Samuel Benton, Thos. D. Coulter, B. A. Rowland. Returned July 27, 1838 by Mary Camp formerly now Mary Jerrell late Admrs. Recorded Aug. 14, 1838.

Estate of Nathan Camp a minor in account with Mary Camp, guardian 1837 paid William R. Bankston for tuition, C.C.O., Sarah Karnel, board & clothing ward to Feb. 6, 1838 (13 mo.). Balance due minor. Credit: by hire of Negroes & rent of land for 1837. Returned July 27, 1838 by Mary Jarrell formerly Mary Camp. Recorded Aug. 16, 1838.

Annual return to Feb. 6, 1838 of estate of James Camp, a minor of Sterling Camp to Mary Camp, guardian. 1837 paid C.C.O., Moses Rosser, for medical attention, boarding & clothing ward up to Feb. 6, 1838. Credit: hire of Negroes & rent of land for 1837. Balance due minor Feb. 6, 1838. Mary Camp formerly now Mary Jarrell. Returned July 27, 1838. Recorded Aug. 6, 1838.

Account of hiring Negroes & renting land belonging to James Camp & Nathan Camp minors of Sterling Camp. 84 A. rented to Josiah Garret, 30 A. to William Jarrell. Negro hired to Willis Jarrell, Negroes hired to Mary Camp, Russel Fish, John McRight. Returned July 27, 1838 by Mary Camp formerly now Mary Jarrel. Recorded Aug. 16, 1838.

Page 164: Yearly return of George M. T. Brockman, a minor by his guardian Morton Bledsoe for 1837. Cash paid Thomas M. Russell, C.C.O. guardian account. Credit: hire of Negroes to Joseph Bledsoe of Mississippi Morton Bledsoe, Thomas M. Russell. Signed Morton Bledsoe, guardian. Recorded Aug. 16, 1838.

Page 165: Additional return of Polly Jarrell now, formerly Polly Camp Admx. of Sterling Camp. Return to court the following insolvent claims - 2 notes on William Gray & Thomas Gray due Dec. 10, 1831. A Claim for damage on William & Thomas Gray or breaches in convenant in the warranty of a Negro boy named Bob. Returned Sept. 24, 1838 by Polly Jarrell, Admx. Recorded Nov. 7, 1838.

Annual return of estate of James Wooten to John Jones, Admr. for 1837. Paid: Larkin Wilson, Flanders & Cook, Daniel Sanford, Myrick Napier, Rufus R. Graves, James D. Read, physician C.C.O., John R. Dickens, John G. Hill, A. G. & W. P. Fambro, W. G. White, services for self & wife this year. Credit: Balance of last return, cotton sold to F. Cook. Returned Nov. 5, 1838 by John Jones, Admr. Recorded Nov. 7, 1838.

Pages 166-174: A list of the Appr. of Morris Mathis estate. Listed many store items, Pulaski Co., Ga. listed notes on Jeremiah Forehand, John B. Bush, John W. Barkwell, R. W. Barkwell, John James Taylor, William Banbray, Wiley W. Gaither & A. B. Gaither, two accounts on the estate of John Armstrong, John A. Wagner, two notes on Isaac Merchant. Account on John Farecloth, Jackson Collier, Wm. Price, John D. Raney, John Higgins, R. M. Moore, Wm. Parker, Thos. Mills, Alex. Sanders, Alex. Lindsey, L. Tomlinson, Wm. Simpson, G. D. Millen, P. Lindsey, W. A. Westbrooks, Mrs. Gainey, G. Thomas, Miss Martha Bankston, Charles Ross, John Wood, Daniel Kilcrease, R. McCall, Hugh Wise, Emily Kilcrease, Wm. Mullins, P. A. Higgins, T. Dickin, Isaac Bankston, notes on Edward C. Pain, Luke Johnson, John Moore, William Simmons, Peterson G. Brogdon, Moses Mount, S. T. Higgins, Wm. M. Mackee & Susan M. Mackee, William Jones, W. C. Jenkins, James Bailey, Wm. Jones, G. A. Dudley, Joseph Byars, John D. Marable, Isaac Bankston, Richard Barlow, William Mullins, William Davis, G. R. Byars, G. D. Mullins, Coleman Bankston, Robert Myrick, William Simmons, William R. Anderson, Edmund J. Bentley, Henry S. Bankston, Wm. L. C. Read. 1 gold lot No. 893, 14th Dist. 1st Section 40 A in Cherokee Co., 1 golf fraction No. 1188 in 3rd Dist., 4th section, 32 A Cherokee Co. Negroes, list of personal property. Open acc't. on Daniel Aspe, Mrs. Jane Bankston, John B. Marble, William Simmons, Erasmus Marable, Benjamin Harrison, Wm. E. Jones, Doctor Jones, Phillip Thurman, George Wolf, Eli Parks, J. Byour, John Cohorn, Elijah Phillips, Richard N. Wood, Charles Purefoy, Urbin Mounts, Harrel Byars, Dr. Saunders, Hugh Wise, George K. Byars, J. Wood, John Roan, Wm. Higgins, Thomas Douglass, Elijah Preston, W. Jenkins, Mrs. Jenkins, James Bailey, John M. Foster, G. Barber, John W. Harris, Wm. N. Duke, J. W. West, W. Aikin, M. Thurman, Mrs. Thurman, D. Millen, John Idley, Henry Barnwell, Wm. McLane, Wm. C. Derry, Bradford S. Carter, Returned certified Oct. 6, 1838 by appraisors Parham Lindsey, Leonard Roan, Wm. Gilmore and James B. Tomlinson, J.P. Recorded Nov. 19, 1838.

Page 174: An account of the sale of real estate of Dennis McCarty dec'd., sold on first Tuesday in Aug. 1838 at Van Wert in Paulding Co., Ga. 1 lot No. 22 in 17th Dist., 4th Section to George F. Shepherd, 1 lot of land sold on first Tuesday in Nov. 1838, lot No. 33 in 23rd Dist., 3rd section purchased by Walles Warren. Sold at Rome. Returned Dec. 15, 1838 by David Martin, Admr. Recorded Dec. 27, 1838.

Pages 175-176: An Inv. & Appr. of estate of Micajah F. McCune, dec'd. this Dec. 11, 1838. Listed 7 Negroes, 1 lot of land N. 15, 9th Dist. of Butts Co., goods & chattels, notes on Robert W. Hunter, John T. McCune, Littleton L. Burk. Account on Cornelius Atkinson, 1 lot of land No. 124, 2nd section, 13th Dist. Certified on Dec. 11, 1838 by appraisors Nelson Meredith, Creed T. Wise, Jason Greer, Josiah W. Barber, Wade H. Giles, J.P. Recorded Dec. 27, 1838.

Pages 177-179: Memorandom of sale of the property of Micajah F. McCune, dec'd. taken by me William A. McCune, Admr. Dec. 13, 1838. Purchasers: Ward Kesler, Lewis Bennett, Wiley Jones, James Higgins, Jesse Jolly, J. T. Mayo, E. Mayfield, R. R. Mayo, R. T. Mayo, Elbert Hardy, B. Harrison, R. T. Dodd, John McLin, R. B. Saunders, J. McMichael, C. T. Wise, W. A. Florence, T. Maddon, A. Sanders, N. Johnson, John Higgins, H. G. Bennett, E. McCune, T. J. Giles, John Pridgon, E. Hardy, R. McCune, Nancy McCune, Wm. A. McCune, James Pridgon, A. B. White, D. Higgins, E. McDaniel, A. Atkinson, C. Staten, W. J. Head, Hugh Wise, T. J. Giles, John Berry, B. Wise, Mrs. Nancy McCune, James Bailey, Wm. Giles, C. Bailey, W. Floyd, J. Berry, Wm. Higgins, Sr. Signed William A. McCune, Admr. Recorded Dec. 28, 1838.

Page 179: Return of Mrs. Jane Barkley, guardian to minor of John Barkley, dec'd. Paid: J. J. Evans, D. L. Duffey, Delila Roan, Spencer & Mays, James Barkley. Signed: Jane Barkley. Recorded Jan. 3, 1839.

Page 180: Annual return of William F. Mapp, guardian for Joseph F. McClendon for year 1838. Paid Bloodworth & Maxey, O. H. McClendon, Hendrick & Goodman, John McCord, J. A. Fellows. Signed William F. Mapp, guardian. Recorded Jan. 3, 1839.

An annual return of William F. Mapp, guardian of William C. McClendon for year 1838. Paid: William L. Wilson, Robert C. Sanders, O. H. P. McClendon, Hendrick & Goodman, John Goodman, J. R. & J. W. McCord, N. H. Williams. Signed William F. Mapp, guardian. Recorded Jan. 3, 1839.

Page 180: Annual return of William F. Mapp, guardian for Joseph F. McClendon for year 1838. Paid Bloodworth & Maxey, O. H. McClendon, Hendrick & Goodman, John McCord, J. A. Fellows. Signed William F. Mapp, guardian. Recorded Jan. 3, 1839.

An annual return of William F. Mapp guardian of William C. McClendon for year 1838. Paid: William L. Wilson, Robert C. Sanders, O. H. P. McClendon, Hendrick & Goodman, John Goodman, J. R. & J. W. McCord, N. H. Williams. Signed William F. Mapp, guardian. Recorded Jan. 3, 1839.

Return of the sale of real estate of Isaiah Wise, dec'd. 1 lot of land to Robert Mayfield, Negro boy to Rosey Wise. Sold on 1st Tuesday in Jan. 1839 by Riley Wise, Admr. Recorded Jan. 4, 1839.

The estate of Charles G. Thaxton a minor of Charles G. Thaxton dec'd. in account with Yelventon Thaxton guardian from May 19, 1838 to Jan. 7, 1839. Acc't. due said minor after deduction of all credits on a note dated Aug. 10, 1831 due Dec. 25, 1831 payable to Gideon Matthews formerly in the hands of Gideon Matthews the former guardian of said minor. The note has never yet come to my hand the amount due now with interest & principal after deducting all credit is $103.96, Yelventon Thaxton, guardian. Recorded Jan. 8, 1839.

Page 181: The estate of Samuel Johnson, Burwell Johnson, Arnold Johnson, Pickins Johnson, and Pleasant Johnson minors of Arnold Johnson dec'd. in account with Yelventon Thaxton guardian of sd. minors from Oct. 21, 1837 to Jan. 7, 1839 inclusive. By cash on hand rec'd. for sale of lot #100, 6th dist. 4th section of Cherokee County sold in pursuance of an order of the Court of Ordinary of Butts County for $500 sold to John T. Story Sept. 1838. Cash rec'd. for rent of sd. land for 1827-1838. Yelventon Thaxton, guardian. Recorded Jan. 8, 1839.

Annual return of James Harrison to William Harrison, Admnr. from Jan. 1st to Dec. 31st 1838. To amt. charged to me as guardian of Elizabeth Harrison and Thomas Harrison two of the distributees in full of their share $737.56. William Harrison, guardian. Returned Jan. 4, 1839. Recorded Jan. 8, 1839.

Annual return of estate of Elizabeth Harrison and Thomas Harrison, minors of James Harrison in account with Wm. Harrison, guardian from Jan. 1st to Dec. 31st 1838. Paid Jacob Buckhart for boarding and clothing minors for 1838 and part of 1837. Credit: Amt. of distributive share of both minors. Returned Jan. 4, 1839, Wm. Harrison, guardian. Recorded Jan. 8, 1839.

Page 182: Return No. 8. The estate of William Redman, dec'd. in account with James Carter, Admr. from Jan. 1, 1838 to 31st Dec. inclusive. Paid Thos. P. Atkinson, auctioneer, taxes, Mary Redman for boarding and clothing Mary Redman, Martha Redman, Thomas Redman, orphans. Paid same for boarding and clothing and taking care of Elizabeth Redman, mother of William Redman, dec'd. Paid Nancy O. Williams for tuition of Martha and William Redman, two of the minors. Credit: By hire of Negroes for 1838 and sale of land to Mary Redman and H. Gilmore $1843.00. Returned Jan. 3, 1839 by James Carter, Admr.

Account of hiring Negroes belonging to the estate of William Redman, dec'd. for year 1838 to Mary Redman, dec'd. for year 1838 to Mary Redman and Thomas McClure. Sale of land lot #51, 9th dist. originally Henry County sold to Mary Redman for $1000. Lot #157, 1st dist. originally Henry County to Humphrey Gilmore for $528.00. Returned Jan. 3, 1839, James Carter, admr.

Page 183: Return No. 2. Estate of Nathan Williams in acc't. with Stephen W. Price, exor. from Jan. 1st to 31st Dec. 1837. Paid: Burwell Jinks on note, Dr. Samuel Snoddy, J. W. Williams funeral expenses $12.00. John McCord, C.C.O., Zachariah Williams, Thos. P. Atkinson for crying property at sale, Nancy O. Williams, legatee, Wm. S. Williams, John McClure, C. A. Williams, Legatee. John R. Williams, Legatee, W. S. and T. P. Ferrel, Wilson Maddox & Co., Elizabeth Williams, Legatee. Credit: Cash realized on loan of $625.12½ to James Brady. Rec'd. of sales $3582.87½. Returned Jan. 3, 1839 by S. W. Price, Exor. Recorded Jan. 9, 1839.

Page 184: Return on estate of Robert Bickerstaff for 1838. Paid: Robert Coleman, William R. Head, 1837 Taxes, Alsey Durham, paid to following legatees of said Bickerstaff; William R. Head, Alsey Durham, Hugh Wise, Joseph W. Slaughter, Henry P. Slaughter, Creed T. Wise, Pollard B. Bickerstaff, Creed T. Wise as guardian, William R. Head as guardian, retained for myself as guardian, Shadrick McMichael. (Each legatee received $859.00). Notes and executions and insolvent and out of date on Elijah Miles, John Glisson, Harmon Proctor, John Adams, Solomon Touchstone, Joseph W. Slaughter, Alsey Durham, Hugh Wise. Returned by A. R. Bickerstaff, Admr. (no date). Recorded Jan. 9, 1839.

Page 185: Will of James Screws. I James Screws of Butts County, State of Georgia being infirm of body but perfect mind and memory make and ordain this my last will and testament. First of all I give my soul into the hands of Almighty God and that I be buried at the discretion of my executor. I give and dispose of worldly estate in the following manner. First - I give and bequeath at the decease of me and my wife Nancy Screws all the lands, messuages and tennements and everything that I shall possess unto my daughters Mary Evans and her husband, the said Mary Evans and husband taking care of me and my wife Nancy so long as we both shall live. My wife Nancy to control the property so long as she may live and not to convey it to any other person or persons whatever. Secondly - I give unto my son Enoch Screws $5.00 in addition to what I have already given him. Thirdly - I give unto my daughter Elizabeth Thomas $5.00 in addition to what I have already given her. Fourth - I give unto my daughter Sally Webb $5.00 in addition to what I have already given her. Fifthly and lastly - I do make Beverly Evans my only executor. Signed: Feb. 2, 1837. James (X) Screws. Test: Jac Saunders, Thomas J. Saunders, Wade H. Giles, J.P. Recorded Jan. 10, 1839.

Page 186: Return of estate of Isaiah Wise for 1838. Paid: Parham Lindsey, Rosey Wise, Legacy. Credit: Rec'd. of William Gann for rent of land, Rosey Wise for hire of Negroes, William Vickers for iron tools, lot of goats. Returned by Riley Wise, Admnr. Recorded Jan. 10, 1839.

Pages 186-204: A list of the sale of farm property of Morris Mathews dec'd. of Butts County by Morton Bledsoe Admr. October 29, 1838. Sold to James B. Tomlinson, P. G. Brogdon, R. W. Harkness, Stephen Bailley, George Barlow, John Higgins, William R. Anderson, Samuel Snoddy, Wm. L. Wilson, D. J. Bailey, Richard Barlow, Parham Lindsey, P. A. Higgins, G. W. Suttles, A. L. Robinson, Robert Duke, W. Harkness, W. S. B. Harkness, G. Britton, B. F. Ward, A. F. Thompson, J. W. McCord, G. W. Barber, James Byars, John McMichael, E. McDaniel, George A. Dudley, Alex Sanders, W. R. Simpson, L. McMichael, Andrews & McClure, W. C. Jinkins, S. T. Higgins, James Pierce, Moses Mounts, R. McGrady, H. Williams, J. Bankston, J. B. Byars, James Higgins, J. Goodman, Wm. E. Jones, J. M. Mayo, George Byars, B. S. Carter, J. Harkness, Lewis Bennett, Robert Coleman, Elijah Twilly, George K. Byars, J. W. McClendon, J. T. Thaxton, R. Grier, R. Nolen, Widow Mathews, William Tomlinson, James Thurman, Jr., W. L. Wilson, Wm. Byars, James Bougham, R. W. Smith, John Hall, P. Wise, Rufus McCune, J. Cawhorn, J. K. Amos, R. A. Higgins, A. King, Wm. Payne, Jos. C. Parker, W. Mapp, Benj. Roan, Richard Nolen, B. S. Carter, J. Greer, Joel Hardin, Wm. Long, J. W. Roan, Wm. B. Nutt, W. G. McMichael, J. H. Thompson, John Pinkard, M. M. Dicker, James Bond, W. Jones, Ab. Bankston, J. Andrews, Robert McCollom, J. M. Foster, J. Y. Morris, Charles Hobbs, P. M. Compton, R. B. Saunders, John Hood, Elizabeth Thurman, Ben Harrison, R. N. Wood, Jas. Harkness, Sr., Jas. Bailey, G. W. Smith, S. T. Gruson, Wm. Simmons, Ward Keeler, Joseph Wright, Joel B. Byars, Robert Lawson, B. Buttrill, R. McDuffy, Joel Wright, G. B. H. Turner, B. H. Darden, John Coughran, R. W. Anderson, C. M. Coody, James Thurman, John Floyd, B. A. Harden, Leroy McMichael, P. C. Greeson, C. Webb, John C. Morris, Josiah Moore, Walter Andrews, Samuel Wilkerson, Irvin Mounts, F. Stedman, John Woods. Recorded Jan. 11, 1839.

Page 204-214: Indian Springs, Georgia. Jan. 2, 1839. Sale of property (Indian Spring Hotel and furnishings) of Morris Mathews, dec'd. 46 bedsteads and mattress sold to George A. Dudley, M. M. Dickens, W. A. Florence, S. Bailey, Jas. Bougham, C. M. Coody, W. Byars, H. T. Dicken, N. Merida, W. S. B. Harkness, J. Andrews, S. T. Higgins, W. C. Jinkins, J. S. Anderson, James Britton, G. Byars, J. Dennis, J. S. Harkness, R. Barlow, 52 chairs sold to H. T. Dickens, A. J. Kirksey, R. McMahan, Bledsoe. 33 chambers sold to M. Mounce, F. Douglass, piano sold to J. W. McCord. Miscellaneous items sold to S. Snoddy, S. T. Higgins, G. W. Barber, Alex Sanders, John Sanders, H. Williams, Robert Lawson, John Dennis, Griffin McMichael, D. Higgins, S. Bailey, H. N. Byars, A. J. Kirksey, H. T. Dickens, J. Andrews, W. A. Florence, R. Barlow, W. Higgins, O. McClendon, N. W. Taylor, W. Akins, Parham Lindsey, H. Dillon, Thos. P. Ferrel, T. P. Ferrel, Alden Mickelberry, R. Brooks.

Indian Spring Hotel and lot sold to Henry Dillon for $6512.38. Returned by Morton Bledsoe, Admr. Recorded Jan. 24, 1839.

Page 215: Inv. and Appr. of estate of James Crews, dec'd. Jan. 15, 1839. Goods and chattels listed, 70 acres of land. Appraisors: Thomas J. Sanders, Matthew Barber, G. W. Barber. Certified by Wade H. Giles, J.P., Jan. 28, 1839. Recorded Jan. 28, 1839.

Page 216: Return No. 2 - An account of estate of Jeremiah P. McClendon, a minor of Allen McClendon, dec'd. with Samuel Snoddy guardian from Mar. 14, 1838 to June 11, 1839. Rec'd. Sept. 15, 1838 from the administrator of estate of Allen McClendon as part of minors legacy $4000. Paid store account to O. A. P. McClendon for year 1836 and 1837. C.C.O., J. A. Fellows. Recorded Jan. 28, 1839.

Page 217: A return of William F. Mapp, guardian for Oliver H. P.

100

McClendon for 1838. Paid John McCord and O. H.P. McClendon $4000. Jan. 15, 1839, Wm. F. Mapp, Guardian. Recorded Jan. 28, 1839.

An annual return of William F. Mapp, Admr. of estate of Allen McClendon, dec'd. for 1838. Paid John N. McCune, A. L. Robinson, J. A. Fellows, James H. Stark, Samuel Ridgeway, Thomas Wilson, Mary S. McClendon $4000, John McCord 1837 Taxes, Eggbert P. Daniel, Samuel Snoddy, Samuel Snoddy for Jeremiah P. McClendon, $4000. Credit: Rec'd. from Edmund Head, Pouncy Maxcy, William Hardin, William Benson, Peter W. Walton, Jeptha McClendon, John W. Phillips, William Pryor, James Higgins. Jan. 15, 1839 William F. Mapp, Admr. Recorded Jan. 28, 1839.

Page 218: Return of estate of Joel Wise, dec'd. for 1838 by admr. Paid: John McCord C.C.O., 1837 taxes, James H. Stark, Atty., W. R. Bankston for 1835 taxes which voucher was mislaid at the time of making return. Jan. 15, 1839 Parham Lindsey, Admr. Recorded Jan. 28, 1839.

The estate of Macajah F. McCune to William A. McCune admr. 1839. Paid: Stephen Bailey, Elizabeth McCune, John McCord, C.C.O., Clement Moore, taxes 1837. Credit to hire of negroes to Creed T. Wise, C. Atkinson, W. Giles for year 1839. William A. McCune admr. Recorded Jan. 29, 1839.

Pages 218-219: Estate of Nathan Williams in account with N. A. Williams, Exor. from Jan. 1st to Dec. 31, 1837. Paid: John E. Jones, Richard Minter, James M. Williams, Samuel Snoddy, A. Shorter, Powell and Champion, Kellan and Maxey, William S. Williams, Thomas Ferrel, M. Bartlett, for printing, William Allison, G. Simonton, Mary Cargile for wagon ferriage, William S. William for blacksmith work, A. L. Robinson for recording deed, J. A. Cuthbert printer, Aquilla Phelps, William Steel. Credit: Rec'd. of James W. Faulkner, H. B. Stewart. Returned Oct. 29, 1838 Nathan H. Williams, Exor. Recorded Jan. 29, 1839.

Return No. 1 - Estate of William M. Williams to N. H. Williams, Guardian from date of letter of guardianship to Dec. 31, 1837. Paid: John McCord, Elisha F. Kirksey, Wm. Allison, William S. Williams, J. R. Dicken, W. & T. Ferrel, Wilson & Maddox, White & Gresham, A. R. Evans, Thomas C. Taylor, N. O. Williams, John E. Jones, Nathan H. Williams, guardian. Recorded Jan. 29, 1839.

Pages 220-225: Return of Henry Jester, Admr. on the estate of James Jester, dec'd. Cash on hand, cash collected 1837, cotton sold 1837. Inventory of perishable property sold on Nov. 21, 1838 to H. Jester, L. Jester, B. Jester, L. Mason, A. Jester, C. Davis, C. Hamil, H. Duke, A. Woodward, T. Foster, D. Lindsey, J. M. Mason, C. Mason, M. Jester, S. W. Thaxton, T. Connel, G. Hartsfield. Signed: Henry Jester, Admr. Recorded July 31, 1839.

A list of expenses paid against estate of James Jester, dec'd. year 1838. Paid by vouchers #1 - #21 to Toliver Davis for overseeing Negroes of dec'd. for 1838, John McCord, William Gains for making wagon wheels, D. J. Bailey for collection notes on Purley Fourde and John Galmon, Hamilton Hase & Co., Samuel Ridge for insurance of a mule colt, John McCord for recording returns, John Goodman, Childers & Co. for homespun, Charles Hammond for his sons legacy bequeathed to him, Charles Hammond for legacy bequeathed to his wife, L. Duffey for taxes, Mary Jester, Benjamin Jester for Negroes appraised for $2825, Levi Jester a negro girl bequeathed to Rosana Jester in the last will and Testament of James Jester, dec'd., Mary Jester on lot of land and one Negro boy bequeathed to her, Abner Jester five Negroes appraised to $2950. Signed: Henry Jester, Admr. Recorded Jan. 31, 1839.

Inventory and sale of part of Negroes belonging to Jeremiah P. McClendon late of Butts County, dec'd. sold Jan. 1, 1839 by order of Inferior Court of said Co. Negroes bought by William P. Irwin, John Owen, Dawson Heath, Cornelius Slaton. Signed: Samuel Snoddy, guardian. Recorded Jan. 31, 1839.

Memorandom of sale of articles and hiring of Negroes belonging to the estate of Jacob Wise, dec'd. taken by me Witt C. Wise exec. of sd.

estate Dec. 24, 1838. Purchasers: Creed T. Wise, F. M. Wise, Barna Wise, Elizabeth Wise, Anna Vickers, John Wise, Witt C. Wise. Signed: Witt C. Wise Exor. Recorded Mar. 6, 1839.

Page 226: Dr. the estate of Henry Lee, dec'd. of Butts Co. to Stewart Lee executor to Dec. 31, 1838. Paid for sugar and coffee for widow of dec'd., Hendrick and Goodman, Wilson and Maddox, Saunders & Low, M. Bartlett, Nathan B. Barnett, James A. McCune, Simon H. Sanders, Spencer & Mays, Joseph Key, Peyton H. White, Nathan H. Williams, John B. Reeves, D. L. Duffey, Tax Collector, John McCord, Clerk Fee. Signed: Stewart Lee, Exor. Recorded Mar. 6, 1839.

Nancy Rhodes to James Draper guardian for the orphans of James Rhodes, dec'd. Cash paid Nancy Rhodes. Signed: James Draper, guardian. Recorded Mar. 6, 1839.

Annual return of David Martin Adm. of Dennis McCarty dec'd. to Mar. 4, 1839. 1836 cash paid John McCord & M. Bartlett, printer. 1838 cash paid Samuel S. Jack for burial expenses $10, to attention to dec'd. in last illness $80. Signed: David Martin, Admr. Recorded Mar. 6, 1839.

Page 227: Yearly return of William Vickers dec'd. by Creed T. Wise on sd. estate for years 1838 and 1839. Paid to D. L. Duffey, T. C., J. C. Dunsieth, Robert W. Smith, C. W. Brezeal, Barna Wise, John McCord, Simon H. Sanders, H. T. Dicken, Spencer Mays, Clement Moore, W. L. Wilson, William Allison, David Higgins, Robert B. Saunders, James H. Roberts, Lewis Bennett, John Hall, Charles Bailey. Credit: Cash rec'd. of Thomas J. Giles in full Dec. 25, 1838. Signed: Creed T. Wise, Admr. Recorded March 6, 1839.

Page 228: Yearly return on estate of Jacob Wise, dec'd. by Witt C. Wise, Exor. for year 1838. Cash paid to John McCord, C.C.O., Job Tyler, John Saunders, M. Bartlett, printer, D. L. Duffey, T. C., Judson Greer, Samuel K. McLin. Cash pd. for service rendered in going to Milledgeville for sd. estate. Cash paid for shoeing horse to perform the trip to Savannah and to Decatur Co. and to Milledgeville for sd. estate, cash pd. Isaac Russel. Credit: Rec'd. of Creed T. Wise for rent of land 1837, Augustus Wise for rent of land in 1838. Signed: Witt C. Wise, Exor. Recorded Mar. 7, 1839.

Yearly return of my war, Ripley H. Bickerstaff, minor of Robert Bickerstaff, dec'd. for year 1838. Jan. 1, 1838 cash rec'd. of A. R. Bickerstaff, Admr. of sd. dec'd. in part of the legacy.

Yearly return of my ward, William J. Bickerstaff, minor of Robert Bickerstaff, dec'd. for year 1838. Jan. 1, 1838 cash rec'd. of A. R. Bickerstaff, Admr. of sd. dec'd. in part of the legacy. Signed: Creed T. Wise, guardian. Recorded March 11, 1839.

Page 229-230: Inv. and appr. of estate of John N. Smith, dec'd. Listed goods, chattel and credits by appraisors John H. McDaniel, John L. Barnett, Thos. Cook, John Barnes. Certified before Jesse T. Gunn, J.P. Recorded March 12, 1839.

Pages 231-232: Yearly return on estate of Agrilla Gilmore, dec'd. by Josiah Hardy, Admr. for years 1838 and 1839. Cash pd. John McCord, Emanuel Smith, Willis Little, James Baley, William Allison, to Self. D. L. Duffey (?), T. C., James D. Giles, McClure & Beauchamp, Joseph Key, Benjamin Deason, Myron Bartlett, Robert B. Saunders, Thomas McClure, James D. Giles, Low & Compton, T. & J. Saunders, John W. Williams, for coffin, Simon H. Sanders, Spencer & Mays, Hendrick & Goodman, James L. Maddox, Josiah W. Barber, Cash received of Isham Freeman, Willis Holifield, Benj. Deason, Jonathan Carter, John Carter, Riley Potter, Jesse Jolly. S. K. McLin, James Baley, James Pridgeon, M. Parker, Joseph Wright, Edmund Smith, Thomas McClure, John McClure, Benj. Deason, Hugh Wise, Sale of land Lot No. 49 in 9th dist. of Henry now Butts Co. Signed: Josiah Hardy Admr. Recorded Mar. 12, 1839.

Pages 232-233: Ga. Butts Co. Inv. of estate of John A. Malone, dec'd. as follows: premices the widow now lives on, possessions at

Indian Springs, Lot No. 298, 1st & 18th in Cherokee Co., 4 Negroes, goods and chattels, Executors Thomas B. Burford, Britton Buttrill and Martha Malone produced to appraisors Washington G. Atkinson, R. W. Hunter, Burwell (X) Jinks. Certified March 4, 1839 before Washington G. Atkinson, J.P. Recorded April 9, 1839.

Page 234: Account of sale of Negroes and land belonging to the estate of Nathan F. Camp, minor March 1839 sold to Clark Hamil, John Camp, David J. Bailey, Reuben Phillips, Wm. B. Nutt, 123 acres of land to Wm. Jarrell. Signed: William Jarrell, guardian. Recorded Apr. 9, 1839.

Account of sales and Negroes and land belonging to the estate of James Camp, minor March 1839. Sold to R. W. Hunter, Wm. Jarrell, John H. McDaniel, Wm. Bence 5 1/8 acres of land to Wm. Jarrell. Signed: William Jarrell. Recorded April 9, 1839.

Pages 235-237: Account of renting land and hiring Negroes for part of 1839 belonging to the estate of Nathan F. Camp. 10 acres rented to W. Jarrell, Negro hired to Wm. Harrell 2 months, 13 acres land rented to Josiah Garret. The other land not rented. Signed: William Jarrell, guardian. Recorded Apr. 9, 1839.

Account of renting land and hiring of Negroes for part of 1839 belonging to James Camp. Negroes hired to John McRight. Wm. Jarrell. 9 acres of land rented to Josiah Garret, 25 acres to William Jarrell. Signed: William Jarrell, guardian. Recorded Apr. 9, 1839.

Return No. 1 - Estate of James Camp to William Jarrell, guardian from Feb. 7 to Dec. 31, 1838. Paid Spencer & Mays account, Clk. of Ct., boarding and clothing ward to Dec. 31, 1838, Jacob Stokes for medical services. Credit: Interest on sum, hiring Negroes and renting land. Return Apr. 5, 1839 William Jarrell, guardian.

Return No. 1 - Estate of Nathan F. Camp to William Jarrell, guardian from Feb. 7, to Dec. 31, 1838. Paid Clk. of Ct., Spencer & Mays for necessaries, boarding and clothing ward from Feb. 6 to Dec. 31, 1838. Credit: Interest on sum, hiring Negroes and renting land for 1838. Returned Apr. 5, 1838 William Jarrell, guardian. Recorded May 9, 1839.

Return No. 4 - Estate of Sterling Camp to William Jarrell from Feb. 7 to Dec. 31, 1838. Paid John H. McDaniel, James H. Stark, for professional services, A. L. Robinson for recording deed, Stephen Bailey, John Hall, M. Bartlett, for printing, John Camp guardian for Sterling Humphries, Sexton Humphries. These last two items paid on a compromise with the heirs of Humphries on whose estate Sterling Camp was admr. Some of heirs having taken possession of two Negroes which were claimed by said heirs and which the Admx. has not recovered. Credit: By sale of 2 Negroes. Interest on sum that being part of James and Nathan. Signed: William Jarrell, Admr. Returned Apr. 5, 1839. Recorded May 9, 1839.

Page 237: Return No. 1 - Marcelius Douglass. To Thomas & F. Douglass executors of the estate of W. S. Douglass dec'd. Beginning Sept. 19, 1838. Paid William A. Florence for tuition, James Cawthon for board, Anderson F. Thompson, Low & Compton, Cash paid in Macon for one pair of shoes (87½ cents) James R. Brown for cutting coat $.50, Mrs. Polly Ann Anderson for making coat and pantaloons $1.00, Thomas Douglass for 4 months board $20. Signed: Thomas Douglass, Exor. Recorded May 10, 1839.

Page 238: Return No. 1 - Eugenius L. Douglass. To Thomas Douglass & Francis Douglass of the estate of W. S. Douglass dec'd. Beginning Sept. 19, 1838. Cash paid William A. Florence for tuition, James Cawthon for board, Anderson F. Thompson, Low & Compton, cash paid in Macon for one pair shoes, George Thomas for shoes, J. R. Brown for cutting coat, Mrs. Polly Ann Anderson for making coat and pantaloons, Thomas Douglass for 4 months board. Signed: Thomas Douglass, exor. Recorded May 10, 1839.

Return No. 1 - Marcissa Douglass. To Thomas & F. Douglass, Exors. of the estate of William S. Douglass, dec'd. beginning Jan. 2, 1839.

Paid Anderson F. Thompson, Low & Compton, cash paid in Macon for one pair shoes, in Jackson one pair of shoes, Thomas Douglass for 12 months board in 1838. Signed: Thomas Douglass, Exor. Recorded May 10, 1839.

Pages 238-240: Edward W. Lane & Labin Magbee, Exors. of Rachel Magbee, dec'd. in account for year 1837. Paid Dr. Stephen Bailey, Labin Magbee, G. Hendrick, Tax 1835. Clerk. Receipts to be recorded in court. The death of Negro boy Samuel who departed this life Jan. 6, 1835 as lost to the estate $650., James Apperson receipt in full, Tobias Brasel receipt in full in right of his wife Mary Prior formerly, Hiram Magbee receipt and John Lofton receipt in full for his part of sd. estate, William G. Hall lawful attorney for William Prior receipt in full. The land in Paulding Co. we return as no value, it being lot No. 771, 18th district, 3rd section. Returned May 6, 1839. Edward W. Lane & Laban Magbee, Exors. Recorded May 13, 1839.

Ga., Butts Co. In compliance with an order from the Inferior Court July Term 1838. Nov. 26, 1838, We the commissioners make distribution of the estate of James Jester, dec'd. among the legatees of said estate as follows: Henry Jester drew the following Negroes, Yellow Aaron, Daniel, Joseph and Lucy. Mary Jester drew Julius, William, Sillah, Milly, Abner Jester drew Black Sam, Dinah, William, Matilda, Edmund. Abner Jester pays Henry Jester $143.75 and Mary Jester $12.50. Signed: Samuel Bellah and Dolphin Lindsey, Commissioners. Certified before Clark Hamil, J.P. and Robert Mays, J.P. Jan. 7, 1839. Recorded May 13, 1839.

Pages 240-243: A list of appraisements of James Wilson, dec'd. taken Jan. 28, 1839. Listed Negroes, goods and chattel, notes on John R. Wilson, open accounts on Johnson Powell, Moses Rosser, Ney Peugh, 1 lot in town of Jackson 2 acres, 1 lot of land 40 acres No. 324, 2nd dist., 1st section not viewed by the appraisors, 1 lot No. 343, 8th dist., Early Co. 250 acres not viewed. Certified on Jan. 28, 1839 by A. L. Robinson, John Phillips, Morton Bledsoe, John S. Irby Appraisors before John Greer, J.P. Recorded May 14, 1839.

Pages 244-245: Yearly return for 1839 of George L. Thompson Admr. of estate of Green B. Reeves dec'd. Paid John Eidson, Stephen Bailey, John McCord, Peyton H. White, Samuel Snoddy, Travy G. Bledsoe, Tax Collector, William H. Wilson, Bartlett & Willingham, Nancy A. Reeves. Received for rent of land. Returned May 1, 1839 George L. Thompson, Admr. Recorded June 3, 1839.

The estate of W. S. Douglass dec'd. to Thomas & Francis Douglass for the year 1837, 1838, 1839. Paid 1837 John McCord, J. W. Williams, W. H. Snowlinson, Thomas Douglass, Isaac Low, Robert G. Duke, Spencer & Mays, G. W. Suttle (1838), W. C. Jenkins, W. A. Florance, Robert B. Saunders, Alden Mickelberry, M. M. Dicken, Mary Coleman, J. B. Bateman, Robert Pearman, Thomas C. Taylor, John Goodman, D. J. Bailey, John Mc-Cord, S. Rose & Co., Bloodworth & Maxey, James H. Campbell. (1839) J. R. McCord, Spencer & Mays, J. R. Williams, Alpheus Beall, Carran Rogers, Edward Birdsong, William Maxey, A. C. Gibson. Cash paid by Robert Douglass for provisions for family use of the family after death of W. S. Douglass in the year 1837, for books and shoes and other things for use of the family, R. Douglass. Signed: Thomas Douglass, F. Douglass, Exors.

Jackson, Butts Co., July 10, 1837. Thomas & F. Douglass, Exors. to the estate of W. S. Douglass, dec'd. Cash left on hand, sale of lot No. 267, 12th dist. Houston Co. to James Mathews and Thomas Barbel security. Recorded June 3, 1839.

Page 246: Estate of John N. Thompson, minor in account with John Goodman, guardian, 1838 1/3 part per advertising to sell land, 1/3 part for grant to land, 1/3 pd. John McCord, 1/3 part to M. Bartlett, 1/3 part on sale of land Lot 221, 15th dist., 3rd section now Cass Co. Signed: John Goodman, guardian. Recorded June 4, 1839.

Estate of Elmiry E. Thompson minor in account with John Goodman, guardian. 1/3 part account as given above. John Goodman.

Estate of James C. Thompson, minor in account with John Goodman, guardian. 1/3 part account as given above. Signed: John Goodman, guardian. Recorded June 4, 1839.

Pages 247-250: Ga. Butts Co. June 3, 1839. An inventory of the estate of Robert Grimmet, dec'd. of goods and chattel. 18 Negroes, 1 lot of land No. 247, 1st dist. of Henry Co. now Butts Co. 1 lot, 14th dist. of Henry Co. now DeKalb Co. Notes on William M. Grimmet, James Blackstock and Jacob Redwine, Valentine Brock and James L. Brock, A. L. Grimmet, Michael Thompson, John McCane and William Gilbert, Peter Ussery. Certified as true appraisement by Gales Jinks, George L. Thompson, Thos. B. Burford, Appraisors. Sworn before Washington G. Atkinson, J.P. Recorded June 5, 1839.

Pages 250-252: An account of estate of Morris Matthews dec'd. with Morton Bledsoe Admr. to Feb. 9, 1839 (1838) cash on hand at time of decease $1250., cash received as total proceeds of the Indian Springs Hotel $2175., paid cash for chickens, C. M. Coody, W. H. Black, H. Barnwell, Cooly and Robinson, William Woodley, C. D. Howland, W. W. Black, W. C. Derry, John Morris, G. Barlow, John Hall, Geo. Stovall, L. Eckley, C. Slaton, J. McDonald, C. L. Howland, B. S. Carter, S. Mounse, W. Jones, C. Atkinson, A. Bankston, J. Harrison, H. Dillon, James M. Bledsoe, Mrs. Edna Matthews, A. Barber, W. L. Wilson, R. W. Harkness, W. R. Long, J. R. Dicken, M. Bartlett, A. L. Robinson, Ward Keeler, J. W. McCord, C. M. Coody, John McCord, A. F. Thompson, J. Harkness, John Nesbet, S. T. Higgins. Feb. 13, 1839. Recorded July 5, 1839.

Page 252: Daniel McClendon, Dr. to John Goodman, guardian. Paid (1837-1838) Nancy McClendon, John Goodman, Hendrick & Goodman, M. Bartlett for advertising in paper, Bankston & Maddox, John McCord, J. R. & J. W. McCord (1838), John Goodman, Dr. to Daniel McClendon, ¼ part of $281 amt. of sale of land lot No. 74 in 27th dist. Lee now Sumter Co. (1839) Money collected of estate of Allen McClendon. Signed: John Goodman, guardian. Recorded July 6, 1839.

Page 253: The hiring of Negroes belonging to Joseph McClendon for year 1839 to J. M. McClendon, John W. Mason, William F. Mapp, O. H. P. McClendon, Pouncy Maxcy. Signed: W. F. Mapp, guardian. Recorded July 8, 1839.

The hiring of Negroes belonging to William McClendon for year 1839 to John W. Phillips, Jonathon Bull, Thomas Gilphin, William Thaxton, G. W. Thaxton. Signed: William F. Mapp, guardian. Recorded July 8, 1839.

The hiring of Negroes belonging to Jeremiah P. McClendon minor of Allen McClendon late of Butts Co. dec'd. for year 1839 to Isaac Smith, William F. Mapp. Signed: Samuel Snoddy, guardian. Recorded July 8, 1839.

An account return of Samuel Snoddy, guardian for Jeremiah McClendon for 1839. Paid Bartlett and Willingham for advertising sale of Negroes, R. E. C. Bulkley, John McCord. Recorded July 8, 1839.

Page 254: Received of the former guardian of Jeremiah P. McClendon minor of Allen McClendon, dec'd. the following notes and Negroes as the property of said minor it being the entire amount of said minor's estate to wit: Notes on William F. Mapp, Jason Green & F. Douglass, J. E. Jones and A. L. Robinson, James Britton and I. Low. William A. Florence, P. M. Compton, William B. Irvin and Jno. McMichael, S. K. Adams, Dawson Heath, C. Slaton, I. W. Smith, O. H. P. McClendon, William & Richard Nolen. Total $7891.51. Seven Negroes. Returned this July 5, 1839. Signed: O. H. P. McClendon, guardian. Recorded July 10, 1839.

Pages 255-257: List of appraisement of the estate of Robert Andrews, dec'd. 10 Negroes, 8 horses, good and chattels - 432½ acres of land, notes on Walter S. Andrews and John P. McWhorter, Thos. H. Connel, Drewry S. Patterson, Andrews and McClure, Thos. L. Ferguson, Samuel Kendrick, Yelventon Thaxton, Thomas House, total $15,606.35¼. Certified by W. Jarrell, R. Blesset, D. L. Duffey and A. L. Robinson appraisors as true appraisement as exhibited to them by Walter Andrews and John Andrews, Admr. of estate of sd. dec'd. July 18, 1839.

Page 258: Appraisors duties certified by Clark Hamil, J.P. on July 18, 1839. Recorded Aug. 27th, 1839.

Pages 258-260: An account of personal property of John W. Smith dec'd. sold at public outcry on 26th July 1839 on 5 mo. credit to B. P. Key, Washington Mann, Austin G. Smith, Henry Barnes, L. Malear, John H. McDaniel, Joseph Key, J. Freduway, J. Hodges, E. Mann, B. Butral, W. A. Lemmon, E. McDaniel, T. J. Bledsoe, Joseph Higgins, E. Moore, J. T. Gunn, John Barnes, E. S. Mann, William Clark, J. L. Key. Signed: Emanuel S. Smith, Admr. Recorded Sept. 4, 1839.

Page 260: Yearly return on estate of Aquilla Gilmore dec'd. by Josiah Hardy Admr. for year 1838-1839. Cash pd. Thomas P. Atkinson agent for Robert H. McLin, John McCord. Signed: Josiah Hardy Admr. Recorded Sept. 4, 1839.

Estate of Samuel James H. Stark in account of James H. Stark guardian from Jan. 1, 1837 to Dec. 31, 1838. Paid Clerk of Ordinary fees, interest on account for 1837. Balance due ward Dec. 31, 1838 $1035.32. By balance due ward Dec. 31, 1836 as included in former return $905.89½ interest on sum 2 years to Dec. 31, 1838. Returned Aug. 7, 1839. Signed: James H. Stark, guardian. Recorded Sept. 6, 1839.

Page 261: Will of Mary Vincent of Butts County in a low state of health but in my perfect mind and senses do make this will as follows: I do bequeath to my oldest and beloved son Henry Vincent $10; to my second son Nathaniel Vincent $10; to my third son (not named) $10; to fourth son (not named) $10; to my only and beloved daughter Sally Giles the following property viz: 1st all the property or money or claims willed to me by my mother in her lifetime. 2nd, one sorrel mare, four head of cattle and feather bed and clothing and all the money coming to me and some other articles too tedious to mention whereof I have hereunto set my hand and seal this 24th day June 1839. Mary (X) Vincent. Signed in presence of James G. Mayo, William Vincent, Samuel K. McLin, J.P. Recorded Sept. 6, 1839.

Page 262: Yearly return on estate of William Ray dec'd. by William G. Ray Admr. for years 1838 and 1839. Cash pd. Thomas Valentine, Sr., D. L. McJunkins & Co. Hendrick & Goodman, Moil M. Tedwell, John T. Wooten, Henry Harris, John Hail, Francis Miller, Clerk of Superior Court of Henry Co. for costs, Tax Collector 1838. John McCord, J. R. & J. W. McCord for articles for the use of the family by C. L. Ray and W. G. Ray. To each of the following legatees $360.00 H. Youngblood, S. S. Scott, R. Y. Ray, Aron Onail, W. H. Ray, W. H. Miller, Elizabeth Ray, Daniel H. Ellis, J. L. Ray, C. L. Ray. Signed: William G. Ray, Admr. Recorded Sept. 7, 1839.

Page 263: Return on court case in Henry Co. about a Negro girl belonging to estate of William Ray dec'd. being claimed by W. H. Miller. The Admr. William G. Ray & C. L. Ray returns that Spring term 1839 Henry Co. Jury's verdict was that William H. Miller had his choice to hold Negro by paying $550. Miller took an appeal. A compromise of suit was that Miller take Negro at the value set by jury. Signed Sept. 2, 1839 William G. Ray Admr. Recorded Sept. 7, 1839.

Estate of James Wooten a minor to John Jones guardian from Jan. 1 to Dec. 31, 1839. Paid Clerk of Ordinary, C. Grinkle for tuition Knott & Pope for necessaries, ½ of services and expenses in going four trips to Spart on business and returning ($8.00). Balance due ward $527.54. Credit: By balance due ward as per last return and interest thereon. Returned Sept. 7, 1839 John Jones, guardian. Recorded Sept. 9, 1839.

Page 264: Estate of Addison A. Wooten to John Jones guardian from Jan. 1 to Dec. 31, 1838. Paid Charles Grinkle for tuition, Clerk of Court for ½ expences of 4 trips to Sparta. Balance due ward Dec. 31, 1838. Returned Aug. 7, 1838 John Jones, guardian. Recorded Sept. 9, 1830.

Estate of Seaborn L. Wooten a minor to John Jones guardian from Jan. 1 to Dec. 31, 1838. Paid John A. Fellows for tuition, Clerk of Court

106

for ¼ expences to Sparta four times and returning. Balance due ward Dec. 31, 1838. Returned Aug. 7, 1838 John Jones guardian. Recorded Sept. 9, 1839.

Estate of Simeon Wooten to John Jones guardian Jan. 1 to Dec. 31, 1838. (Same report as above).

Page 265: Estate of James Wooten to John Jones, Admr. from Jan. 1 to Dec. 31, 1838. Paid Smith & Jones for necessaries, N. Bellamy, A. W. Martin, Bardwell Phillips blacksmith, John Higgins blacksmith, Gorden & Gwyn, William Holloway blacksmith, Myrick Napier and Freeman, John R. Dicken, O. H. P. McClendon, Richard P. Smith, services self and wife this year. Balance due estate Dec. 31, 1838. Credit: Balance due estate as per last return and interest thereon Dec. 31, 1838. Crop of 1838, 6 bags of cotton sold to James Richardson. Returned Aug. 7, 1839 John Jones Admr. Recorded Sept. 9, 1839. Examined and approved by a committee of the grand jury Sept. term 1839.

Pages 266-271: Account of the sale of perishable property of James Wilson dec'd. sold Feb. 6, 1839. Purchasers: John R. Wilson, Stephen Bailey, A. L. Robinson, William Buttrill, Britton Buttrill, John McCord, John S. Irby, Alfred King, Pleasant M. Compton, R. W. Harkness, J. H. Stark, W. S. B. Harkness, E. Walker, Leroy McMichael, John McMichael, John Phillips, John Greer, Burrell Jinks, James Harkness, Jr., William Jarrell, J. R. McCord, Jacob Sanders, William R. Bankston, Nathan H. Williams, Samuel R. Nutt, Henry Duke, James Filder, J. H. Stark, Perkins Cook, James Boughan, Henry Barron, J. M. Fielder, Richard McDuff, Thos. C. Taylor, Alden Mickelberry, James Harkness, Sr., B. G. Potter, Jas. A. McCune, James Phillips, Reuben Phillips. Returned Sept. 23, 1839 by J. H. Stark and J. W. McCord Admr. Recorded Oct. 3, 1839.

Page 271: Rec'd. of William Harper guardian of William S. Blessit minor of Elisha Blessit dec'd. Jan. 1, 1838. Signed: Reason Blessit guardian. Recorded Oct. 3, 1839.

Annual return of Reason Blissit guardian of William S. Blissit. Paid W. R. Bankston, D. L. Duffy, tax collector, Isham Anderson, W. L. Wilson & Co., Willis Jarrell, J. McCord C.C.O. Signed: Reason Blissit. Recorded Nov. 7, 1839.

An inventory of land sold Sept. 3, 1839 in McDonough, Henry County belonging to Nathan F. Camp and James Camp orphans of Sterling Camp dec'd. 149 acres part of lot No. 93, 2nd dist. Henry Co. sold as the property of James Camp to William Jarrell for $600. 70 acres part of lot No. 93 and 68 acres 2nd dist. Henry Co. as the property of Nathan F. Camp to William Jarrell for $250. Signed William Jarrell, guardian. Recorded Nov. 7, 1839.

Pages 272-273: Estate of Elizabeth and Martha Anderson minor to Mary Anderson guardian from date of guardianship to 31st Dec. 1838. Paid Clerk of Court of Ordinary fees, Isham Anderson for tuition. Balance due minors Dec. 31st 1838 $863.85. Credit: Received of John Anderson and David Kimbill, Admrs. of James Anderson. Returned Oct. 9, 1839. Signed: Mary (X) Anderson guardian. Recorded Dec. 6, 1839.

Inventory and appraisement of property of John Barkley, dec'd. six Negroes put in lots for the purpose of division. Two to John H. Barkley, one to Jane Barkley, widow, one to Elizabeth Ann Barkley. Appraised Dec. 26, 1839 and distributed by R. W. Harkness, John B. Harkness, W. S. B. Harkness, W. B. Nutt, S. R. Nutt. Certified by W. G. McMichael, J.P. Recorded Jan. 2, 1840.

Pages 273-274: We the referrees appointed by the court of Ordinary of Monroe County to divide Negroes belonging to estate of James Wooten dec'd. have divided the Negroes this Dec. 27, 1839. John Jones distributive share 4 negroes, James Wooten 3 negroes, Simon Wooten 3 negroes, Addison Wooten 3 negroes, Seaborn Wooten 3 negroes, each distributive share $1445. Referrees William F. Mapp, James B. Tomlinson, Thomas Douglass, C. M. Coody, J.P. Recorded Jan. 2, 1840.

Page 274: We the commissioners appointed by the Inferior of Butts County to appraise and divide Negroes belonging to estate of Robert Andrews dec'd. have divided in the following order: Sarah Andrews, Jr. drew Lewis, Sarah Andrews, Sr. drew Rachel &, child Manervy, John Andrews drew Caroline, W. S. Andrews drew Berney, William Woodward drew Manoah, Martha Andrews drew Sam, William Andrews drew Jeff, Given under our hand this Jan. 1, 1840. Appraisors Morton Bledsoe, Reason Blissit, John Goodman. Certified by Clark Hamil, J.P. Recorded Jan. 3, 1840.

Page 275: Commissioners appointed by Court of Ordinary of Butts Co. to divide the estate of M. F. McCune, dec'd. made the following division. To Nancy McCune, widow of dec'd. Negroes Jessey, Eliza, Caroline and Ben valued $2431. To Cornelius M. McCune a minor of dec'd. Negroes Sarah, Clem, Mary and Sarah Ann valued at $2431. Certified by commissioners Jason Greer, F. Douglass, Richard M. Stewart, Charles Bailey on Dec. 26, 1839. Certified to above by Charles Bailey, J.P. Recorded Jan. 9, 1840.

Pages 276-280: Inventory of sale of goods and chattel sold of the estate of Robert Grimmett dec'd. to William Holbrook, Harry Blackman, John H. Cash, A. J. Grimmitt, N. Mangum, James Blackstock, Stephen Mitchell, N. Mitchell, Peter Mitchell, A. Malcomson, Daniel Ferguson, H. Peacock, James Mangum, Alexander Ratterll, James Robberts, Harry B. Man, Jacob T. Cain, William Ferguson, L. Peacock, James Dickens, David Smith, Jethro Baker, John Redwine, A. Mimms, S. Lovejoy, Green Thornton, Z. Clark. Signed: James H. Grimmitt Admr. Recorded Jan. 10, 1840.

Memorandom of sale of personal property of Robert Grimmitt of Butts Co. taken Jan. 1, 1840. Purchasers: Thomas L. Grimmitt, A. J. Grimmitt, Thomas B. Burford, Mary Grimmitt, T. G. Bledsoe, Elizabeth Grimmitt, William Grimmitt, Hiram Ramsey, Edward Onail, James H. Grimmitt, Labon Magbee, Sarah Stewart, James Noles, Samuel S. Hunter, J. V. McBride, Wiley Curry, Zachariah Thompson, T. Harris, G. M. Head, David Campbell, W. G. Atkinson, Mary May. Signed: J. H. Grimmitt, Admr. Recorded Jan. 11, 1840.

An inventory of real estate of Robert Grimmitt, dec'd. sold on Jan. 7, 1840 by James H. Grimmitt, Admr. Purchasers: A. J. Grimmitt, T. L. Grimmitt, Hiram Ramsey, William Grimmitt, Mary May, George E. Hodge, Calvery F. Knight, J. H. Grammitt, Mary Grammitt, John Mackelroy, Elizabeth Grimmitt, T. P. Atkinson. Signed: James H. Grimmitt, Admr. Recorded Jan. 11, 1840.

Return of Charles Hammond guardian for William J. Hammond minor. Received of Henry Jester, Admr. of estate of James Jester for sd. William on Nov. 6, 1838 $300 principal and $36.40 interest. Paid John McCord, Clerk. Balance on hand. Recorded Jan. 24, 1840.

Pages 281-282: Return No. 1 - Estate of James Wilson, dec'd. in acct. with James H. Stark and John W. McCord, Admrs. from date of letter of admr. to Dec. 31, 1839. Paid: Low & Compton, Ruth McDuff, Shff on fifa in favor of William Allison vs. James Wilson in part, P. M. Compton on note, John Greer, John McMichael, McCune and Taylor, M. Bartlett Printer, John McCord, Thomas C. Taylor, B. Butrill, J. R. and J. W. McCord, Jane Tyson, Stephen Bailey, John R. Wilson, John Hall, Bankston & Maddox, Robert White, Spencer & Mays, John Greer, J.P., Moses Rosser vs. A. L. Wilson and James Wilson. Credit: Cash rec'd of John H. Wilson and James Wilson by sale of perishable property by hiring Negroes 1839. Returned Jan. 1, 1840 by James H. Stark and John W. McCord, Admr. Recorded Jan. 27, 1840.

Page 282: Return No. 3 - Estate of Nathan Williams in account with S. W. Price from Jan. 1, 1838 to Dec. 31st. Paid: James M. Williams Legatee, William S. Williams on order from Marcus E. Carter Legatee, William S. Williams Legatee, Nathan H. Williams guardian for his minor brother William Williams, Nancy O. Williams Legatee, Nathan H. Williams Legatee, Elizabeth Williams Legatee, Elizabeth Williams guardian for her two minor daughters Martha T. and Mary Ann Williams Legatees, John McCord Clerk. Credit: Balance due estate as per last return and interest. Signed: S. W. Price, Exor. Returned Dec. 9, 1839. Recorded Jan. 27, 1840.

Page 283: Estate of James Anderson to Mary Anderson guardian from date of letters to final settlement. Paid Clerk of Ordinary, paid your distributive share in full. Credit: Rec'd. of John Anderson and David Kimbell, Admrs. of James Anderson $310.06½. Returned Oct. 9, 1839 by Mary (X) Anderson, late guardian. Recorded Jan. 27, 1840.

Yearly return on estate of James Screws, dec'd. by Beverly Evans Exor. for 1839. Cash paid to John McCord, Thomas J. Walker, John W. Williams for making coffin ($4.00), Isham Anderson, tax collector. Signed: Beverly Evans Executor. Recorded Jan. 27, 1840.

Return on estate of Isaiah Wise dec'd. for 1839. Rec'd. of Creed T. Wise for the estate of William Vickers dec'd, Rasmur Marable, Robert Mayfield. Paid John McCord, Bartlett and Willingham for advertising. Recorded Jan. 27, 1840. Returned Jan. 2, 1840 by Riley Wise, Admr.

Page 284: Annual return of estate of Samuel James H. Stark in account with James H. Stark guardian from Jan. 1 to Dec. 31, 1839. Paid John S. Ingram for services and expenses in going to South Carolina in order to remove the slaves of ward to the state of Georgia after the death of the Carolina guardian $43.25, C.C.O. fees. Balance due ward Dec. 3, 1839 $1063.09½. Credit by balance due ward. Returned Jan. 2, 1840 James H. Stark guardian. Recorded Jan. 28, 1840.

The estate of John N. Smith in account with Emanuel Smith, Admr. Dr. to furnishing 8 bu. corn to feed the stock of hogs belonging to the estate, keeping & feeding horse of estate, taking care and feeding stock seven months to wintering 5 head of cattle, E. Man for crying property at sale, A. G. Smith on account, for five days in going to Morgan County to obtain stray cattle of the dec'd. and finding calf and horse. Signed: Emanuel S. Smith, Admr. Recorded Jan. 28, 1840.

Page 285: Return No. 9 - The estate of William Redman dec'd. in account with James Carter Admr. from Jan. 1 to Dec. 31, 1839. Paid Mary Redman for boarding and clothing of Mary Redman, Martha Redman, and William Redman, orphans of William Redman, dec'd. and Elizabeth Redman, mother of dec'd., Nancy O. Williams, S. H. Sanders, J. R. and J. W. McCord, Expenses and services in going to Randolph and Early counties to sell land of estate. Credit: Hire of Negroes for 1839, for account of sale of lands in 1839. Returned Jan. 13, 1840 by James Carter, Admr. Recorded Jan. 29, 1840.

Account of hiring Negroes belonging to Estate of William Redman, dec'd. for year 1839. Mary Redman hired Stepney, Wiley, Alsey, Dafney, Agnes, Esther for $285. Returned 13 Jan. 1840. James Carter, Admr. Recorded 29 Jan. 1840.

Terms of selling land in Randolph and Early Counties belonging to estate of William Redman, dec'd. late of Butts Co. A credit to Dec. 1st, 1840, notes with two approved securities. Blakely, Early County 1 Oct. 1839. James Carter, Admr. Lot No. 118, 18th Dist. Harris, not sold; Lot No. 202, 28th Dist., Early County to James Buchannon for $100; Lot No. 245, 10th Dist. of formerly Lee now Randolph to Reuben Jones for $800.06½ on above terms. James Carter, Admr. Recorded 29 Jan. 1840.

Pages 286-287: Georgia, Butts Co. - I, Frances Johnston of sd. County am firmly bound unto Moses B. Hairston of Butts Co. for sum of $17,883.36½ for true payment of which will be faithfully done. Sealed and dated this...day of Sept. 1839.

Conditions that whereas the sd. Moses B. Hairston acting as Admr. de bonis non of the estate of William H. Johnston, dec'd. has this day delivered into my hands all the goods, chattels rights and credit that were remaining in his hands as Admr. consisting of money and notes, to be disposed of by me as guardian of orphans of sd. William H. Hairston and as my distributive part of sd. estate. If sd. Moses B. Hairston as Admr. shall be sued in any court I shall be made liable to cost on account of sd. estate.

Georgia, Butts Co. - In person came Robert Brown this day before me,

Stephen Bailey, a J.P. in sd. Co. and saith he was present at the settlement of the estate of William H. Hairston, Admr. and Frances Johnston
then in life but now deceased. That Moses B. Hairston paid over to
Frances Johnston the amount due her which she admitted to be in full all
due her. That sd. Frances Johnston then instructed this deponent to
write a receipt and she would sign. The deponent wrote the within intended as a receipt and a refunding bond, and sd. Frances Johnston departed this life before deponent had opportunity to submit it to her for
her signature. Signed: Robert Brown. Sworn before Stephen Bailey, J.P.
6 Jan. 1840.

Estate of William H. Hairston to Moses B. Hairston, Admr. de bonis
non. 1839 pd. Frances Johnston the widow of intestate in her own right
and a guardian for her two children, William and Monroe Johnston in full,
$17,883.36. Returned 13 Jan. 1840. Moses B. Hairston, Admr. Recorded
30 Jan. 1840.

Page 288: Account of sale of the slaves and one town lot of estate
of James Wilson, dec'd. sold on 7th Jan. 1840 for ½ cash the balance due
in full 25th Dec. 1840. Moses sold to John R. Wilson for $1100; Alfred
to John Hendrick for $625; Dave to John Hendrick for $752; Harriett and
two children to James H. Stark for $1050; Anna to James H. Stark for
$351; Dan to James H. Stark for $401; Lafayette, a girl, to Samuel Ridgeway for $736. Lot in Jackson to R. C. Mays for $159. Total: $5174.
Returned 17 Jan. 1840 by James H. Stark and John W. McCord, Admrs.
Recorded 30 Jan. 1840.

The hiring of Negroes belonging to Jeremiah P. McClendon for year
1840 to O. H. P. McClendon, Wm. F. Mapp, Jas. B. Hanson. Signed: O. H.
P. McClendon, guardian. Recorded 30 Jan. 1840.

Butts Court of Ordinary, Jan. Term 1840. On application of James H.
Stark and John W. McCord, Admrs. of estate of James Wilson, dec'd.
Court ordered that David Spencer, Robert C. Mays, John Goodman, Ward
Keeler and David J. Bailey or any three be appointed commissioners to
divide the estate of sd. James Wilson subject to distribution (as con-
taining the advancement made to each distributee by James Wilson in his
life time) into as many parts as there are distributees. John McMichael,
J.I.C., G. H. Darden, J.I.C., Thos. P. Atkinson, J.I.C.

Page 289: We consent to passage of within order. James H. Stark,
guardian for James Wilson, John Phillips, John R. Wilson, A. J. Wilson.
Recorded 14 Jan. 1840.

Georgia, Butts County: In person came David Spencer, John Goodman
and Ward Keeler this day before me, John McMichael, J.I.C. and swore they
made distribution of the estate of James Wilson to the best of their
understanding. Sworn 21 Jan. 1840 by above names. Recorded 1 Feb. 1840.

James H. Stark and John W. McCord, Admrs. of estate of James Wilson
report to commissioners notes due and several dollars which will be subject to distribution as soon as outstanding debts are paid. 21 Jan. 1840.
Recorded 1 Feb. 1840.

Page 290: Georgia, Butts County. Distribution of estate of James
Wilson by Commissioners. Found amount paid in advance to each distribu-
tee by sd. James Wilson in his life time. Therefore addition assigned
by commissioners to each as followers: John R. Wilson $493.30; Eliza
Ann Phillips, wife of John Phillips $553.94; Andrew J. Wilson $450.83;
James H. Stark, guardian for James Wilson $501.91. Signed: 21 Jan. 1840
David Spencer, John Goodman, Ward Keeler, Commissioners. Recorded 1 Feb.
1840.

Georgia, Newton County: Court of Ordinary, March Term 1839. I,
William D. Luckie, D.C.C.O. certify that Alfred Brewer has given bond
as guardian of David Lewis Coleman, Francis Harris Coleman and David Ann
Dorothy Coleman, orphans of David Coleman in term of law. May 11, 1839.
Recorded Feb. 4, 1840. Butts Co., Ga.

Page 291-293: An inventory of estate of Robert W. Hunter, dec'd.

of Butts Co., Ga. On 4th Nov. 1839 by appraisors appointed by the court and presented Nov. 19, 1839 to Alexander Hunter, Sr., Admr. Notes on A. Hunter, Robert Martin, Samuel S. Hunter, John W. Trotter, Reuben Phillips, John L. Coleman. Lots of land No. 108, No. 109, No. 114, 18 Negroes, cattle; goods and chattels appraised for $18,824.35 1/4. Signed: James Harkness, James Brownlee, John S. Irby, Appraisors. Recorded Feb. 4, 1840.

Page 293: Return of the sale of Negro property of the estate of John H. Smith, dec'd. at public outcry on 7th Jan. 1840 in the town of Jackson. Negroes purchased by Stephen Nolen, Emanuel S. Smith, Admr. Recorded Feb. 8, 1840.

Pages 294-298: Account of sale of personal property of Robert Andrews dec'd. and sold at public outcry in Butts Co. on 27 Nov. 1839. Purchasers: Sarah Andrews, Thomas H. Connell, Wm. Thaxton, Aaron Woodward, W. J. Lewis, Joseph Carmichael, H. W. Carmichael, O. R. Jenkins, A. Bankston, Stephen Bailey, Thos. Folds, G. C. Thaxton, Wm. McClendon, S. F. Duffey, Thos. McKibbin, Henry Stormant, S. Collins, D. L. Duffey, Dawson Heath, J. R. McMahan, P. G. B. Brogdon, John Andrews, Willis Jarrell, William Jarrell, J. B. Carmichael, D. S. Patterson, Clark Hamil, Theophilus Williams, W. A. Florence, S. W. Thaxton, J. H. Weever, W. B. Nutt, J. T. Thaxton, Nancy Blissit, John Nixon, Wm. Connell, T. J. Ferguson, Thos. Foster, D. Thompson, Wm. Andrews, N. W. Peters, T. J. Campbell, Walter S. Andrews, Richard Stillwell, David Evans, Y. Thaxton, Jas. Brady. Signed: John Andrews & W. G. Andrews, Admrs. Recorded 5 Mar. 1840.

Page 298: Georgia, Butts Co. We, Thomas H. Connell and Margaret Connell formerly Margaret Andrews, John B. Carmichael and Mary Carmichael formerly Mary Andrews, Walter S. Andrews, John Andrews, William Andrews, Nancy Andrews and Martha Andrews, Sarah Andrews children and the legal representatives of sd. Robert Andrews agree to divide beds, bedstead, and furniture of sd. Robert Andrews equally. Signed: Thomas H. Connell, Margaret (X) Connell, John B. Carmichael, Mary Ann (X) Carmichael, Wm. Woodward, Sarah (X) Andrews, W. S. Andrews, John Andrews, guardian for William Andrews, Martha Andrews and Sarah Andrews, minors. Recorded 5 March 1840.

Page 299: Return of A. R. Bickerstaff, Admr. of estate of Robert Bickerstaff, dec'd. Jan. 1839 paid to the legatees as per vouchers 1-7 to William R. Head, Alsey Durham, Hugh Wise, Joseph W. Slaughter, Henry P. Slaughter, Creed T. Wise, Pollard B. Bickerstaff, for self and guardian for Robert, one of the legatees of sd. estate.

Jan. 1840 - Paid as per vouchers 8-15 to Alsey Durham, Henry P. Slaughter, Pollard B. Bickerstaff, William J. Bigerstaff, Creed T. Wise, Hugh Wise, Joseph W. Slaughter for self and guardian for Robert, one of the legatees. Signed: A. R. Bickerstaff, Admr. Recorded 5 Mar. 1840.

Returned by A. R. Bickerstaff as guardian for Robert J. Bickerstaff for Jan. 1, 1839 to Jan. 31, 1840. Recorded 5 Mar. 1840.

Page 300: Estate of N. Williams in account with N. H. Williams, Exor. to 31 Dec. 1838 inclusive. Feb. 20, 1837, paid Marcus E. Carter in right of his wife Legacy; John Sanders, C. A. Williams, A. R. Evans, Marcus E. Carter, J. W. Falkner. Returned 6 Feb. 1840 by N. H. Williams, Exor.

Return #2 on estate of Wm. M. Williams to N. H. Williams, guardian Jan. 1 to Dec. 31, 1838. Received a legacy. Dr. Jan. 15, 1838, pd. Thomas Douglass, Exor. of estate of Wm. Douglass, dec'd. Balance due minor. Returned Feb. 6, 1840, N. H. Williams, guardian. Recorded Mar. 6, 1840.

Return #3 on Estate of Wm. M. Williams to N. H. Williams, guardian from Jan. 1st to Dec. 31, 1839. Balance due minor. Returned Feb. 6, 1840. Recorded Mar. 6, 1840.

Page 301: Yearly return on estate of Jacob Wise, dec'd. by Witt C.

Wise, Exor. 1839. Paid John McCord, C.C.O., Isham Anderson, Simon H. Sanders, Hugh Wise. Cash received of Wm. A. McCune for 30 acres of land, Samuel R. McLin for lot of land lying in Early County it being sold legally to highest bidder $6.75. Signed: Witt C. Wise, Exor. Recorded 30 Mar. 1840.

Page 301-302: Georgia, Butts Co. Return of Henry Jester, Admr. of estate of James Jester, dec'd. for year 1839. A list of receipts from the legatees. Paid Benjamin Jester, Abner Jester, Mary Jester, William Foster in right of his wife Mary Foster. Henry Jester, Admr. A list of insolvent notes chargeable against the estate of James Jester on Bailey Hold, Chaney Farrow, Samuel Osborn, Francis Hall, William Frazier, David Gurganes, John Homes, Abraham Goldin. Returned Feb. 26, 1840, Henry Jester, Admr. Recorded Mar. 31, 1840.

Page 303: Return of estate of Joel Wise, dec'd. for 1839. Paid 1838 taxes, John McCord for recording return, John Wise Legacy in part ($772.26). Returned Jan. 15, 1840, Parham Lindsey, Admr. Recorded Apr. 1, 1840.

The estate of Henry Lee, dec'd. Dec. 31, 1839, Stewart Lee, Exor. Paid Miles Parker, J. R. & J. W. McCord, 1838 taxes, Samuel Snoddy, John McClure, A. L. Robinson, James H. Stark. Recorded Apr. 1, 1840.

Pages 303-304: An annual return of William F. Mapp, Admr. of Allen McClendon, dec'd. for year 1839. Paid A. L. Robinson, Wright & Co., James H. Stark, A. W. Pryor, Pryor and Martin, 1838 taxes, S. T. Bailey, John McCord, T. Leak; Cr.; Eli Parks, Nicholas Purifoy, Jeptha McClendon, Peter W. Welton, William Pryor, Raney and Raney. William F. Mapp, Admr. Recorded 2 Apr. 1840.

Return of William F. Mapp, guardian for William McClendon for 1839. Paid 1838 taxes, Thomas C. Taylor, Bloodworth and Maxey, John McCord, O. H. P. McClendon. Recorded Apr. 3, 1840.

Return of William F. Mapp, guardian for Joseph F. McClendon for 1839. Paid A. F. Thompson, Bloodworth and Maxey, Low and Compton, 1838 taxes, John McCord, O. H. P. McClendon. Recorded Apr. 3, 1840.

Page 305: Annual return of Jane Barkley, guardian for minors of John Barkley, dec'd. Paid Samuel Snoddy, 1838 taxes. Recorded Apr. 4, 1840.

Third return on estate of Dan El McClendon, Idiot. Paid: Nancy McClendon, John McCord, Goodman and Andrews. John Goodman, guardian. Recorded Apr. 4, 1840.

1840. Second return on estate of Almira E. Thompson, minor, Feb. 26. Paid Goodman & Andrews, John Goodman, guardian. Recorded Apr. 4, 1840.

Morton Bledsoe, guardian to the estate of Geo. M. T. Brockman. Jan. 1838 to hire of three Negroes belonging to sd. minor to Joseph Bledsoe, Thomas R. Russell, Morton Bledsoe. Recorded Apr. 5, 1840.

Page 306: Return of T. & F. Douglass, exors. of estate of Wm. S. Douglass, dec'd., 1839 Pd.: D. L. Bailey, John McCord, J. Anderson, D. L. Bailey for Reese & Bell, Henry Duke. Returned by Thomas Douglass, Exor. Recorded Apr. 6, 1840.

Return for Narcissa Douglass, minor of William S. Douglass. Pd. John McCord, Low & Compton, W. A. Florence, T. Douglass. Thomas Douglass Exor. Recorded 6 Apr. 1840.

Return for Eugenious L. Douglass, minor of William S. Douglass. Pd. Ann Anderson, S. P. McCary, T. C. Taylor, S. T. Higgins, W. A. Florence, J. McCord, Lew & Compton, to board 1839. Thomas Douglass, Exor. Recorded 6 Apr. 1840.

Page 307: Return for Marcellus Douglass, minor of William S.

Douglass. Pd. (same as above). Thomas Douglass, Exor. Recorded Apr. 6, 1840.

Pages 307-308: Estate of Micajah F. McCune, dec'd. in account with William McCune, Admr. from 15 Jan. 1830 to 2 Mar. 1840. Pd. Thos. P. Atkinson, taxes, Meredith Nelson, Low & Compton, Heard & Hungerford, Samuel R. McLin, John Saunders, James A. McCune, J. R. & J. W. McCord, Charles Bailey, James D. Giles, A. F. Thompson, H. T. Dickens, P. G. Brogdon, Anna Byars, Thos. J. Sanders, N. H. Williams, Robert W. Smith, Robert T. Dodd, John Hall, R. B. Saunders, Spencer & Mays, John Andrews, John Higgins, Cornelius Atkinson as guardian of Nancy McCune, Heard & Hungerford, Cornelius Atkinson, John Hendrick, William A. McCune, Admr. Cr: Land sold in Butts Co., note on Cornelius Atkinson. Signed: William A. McCune, Admr. Recorded 6 Apr. 1840.

Pages 308-311: Dec. 23, 1839. Memorandom of sale of property of Robert W. Hunter, dec'd. taken by Alexander Hunter, Admr. Articles sold to Britton Buttrill, Margaret Hunter, James Harkness, Stephen Bailey, A. Hunter, Jr., John E. Jones, B. F. Tucker, Thomas Harkness, Willis Jarrell, Thos. P. Atkinson, Alex. Hunter, Sr., R. W. Harkness, Mrs. Hunter, Hardman Duke, Henry Duke, James A. McCune, John Goodman, David Berry, Y. R. Norris, Clark Hamil, J. B. Harkness, James Brownlee, Bailey & Harkness, John Greer, Robert Phillips, Edmund McDaniel, William Harkness, Lewis Moore, James S. Irby, A. L. Robinson, Doctor Hunter, Y. R. Norris, A. Hunter, Admr. Recorded Apr. 8, 1840.

Page 311: Inventory and appraisement of estate Mary Vincent, dec'd. Mar. 14, 1840. Goods and Chattels and Negro man, valued at $798. Appraisors: James G. Mayo, Stewart Lee, Samuel R. McLin. Recorded 9 Apr. 1840.

Page 312: Appraisement of estate of James L. Compton, late of Butts Co. Cash on hand $19.25; 160 acres Lot of land not visited by appraisers. Notes on John Hall, John Andrews, William Maddux. 5 notes on S. W. Booles and William A. Beeks indorsed by James Beal; J. M. & M. T. Simmons indorsed by T. C. Taylor. Personal property: Silver leaver watch $45; 8 Vol. Robins Ancient History; The Texas Revolution $2; Walkers Dictionary $.50; 1 Letter writer $.25; 1 Vol. Gilslap $.25; 1 Vol. Lucanies $.25; 1 pencil book $.37½; 12 Nos. Casket $1; 1 frame for pictures $1; 1 watch Seal $4; 1 flute $2. Certified on 4th April 1840 by appraisors Robert Mays, James B. Brown, J. R. McCord and John Hendrick, J.I.C. Recorded 9th April 1840.

Pages 313-315: Annual return of Morton Bledsoe, Admr. of Morris Matthews, dec'd. to March 1840 from 13th Feb. 1839. Pd. P. M. Compton, E. W. R. R. Graves, J. B. Byars, W. H. Roberts, L. L. Barer, C. Bailey, J. W. Watkins, W. B. Parker, J. H. Clearshaw, J. H. & W. Ellis, W. Smith, D. Earp, John Dawson, J. Anderson, T. C. Gwen, M. Mounce, Spencer & Mays, S. T. Higgins, C. M. Coody, B. S. Carter, C. G. Webb, G. D. Millen, B. F. Ward, A. F. Thompson, J. McCord, Parham Lindsey, Richard Barlow, Edna A. Matthews, J. H. Stark, George R. Byars, P. A. Higgins, W. E. Jones, James Byars, Geo. A. Dudley, Martha Bankston, S. Snoddy, W. R. Anderson, W. C. Jenkins, H. Williams, Y. Haynes, W. Simmons, John Higgins, J. Roberts, J. Hood, J. Cawhorr, H. Barnwell, J. R. & J. W. McCord, Andrews & McClure, A. F. Thompson, Robert Nelson & Co., P. Thurman, J. S. Bankston, D. J. Bailey, John Hall. Cr.: Received from H. Dillon, Levi Eckley, R. Mays, Ben Harrison, John Hall, Sale of 40 acres lot of land to R. Findley; B. W. Chapman collected from J. Pinkard, John V. Berry, P. A. Higgins, P. Thurman. Returned by Morton Bledsoe, Admr. Recorded 11th May, 1840.

Pages 315-316: Annual return of O. H. P. McClendon, guardian for Jeremiah P. McClendon from date of letters to 16 March 1814. Vouchers 1-14 paid to Stephen Bailey, 1838 taxes, Loe & Compton, Smith & Roan, O. H. P. McClendon, Goodman & Andresa, John McCord, W. A. Florence, R. Barlow, A. F. Thompson, J. B. Colbert & Co., John L. Jones. Returned by O. H. P. McClendon, guardian. Recorded 13 May 1840.

Page 316: Yearly return of balance for my ward Ripley H. Bickerstaff Received cash Jan. 21, 1840 from A. R. Bickerstaff, Admr. of estate of

Robert Nickerstaff, dec'd. Balance in full. Signed: Creed T. Wise, guardian. Recorded 13 May 1840.

Pages 316-317: Yearly return on estate of William Vickers, dec'd. by Creed T. Wise, Admr. for part of 1839 and ending in 1840. Pd. Robert Mayfield, Hendrick & Goodman, Benjamin Harrison, Isham Anderson, T.C., Beathlem & Hare, Francis & Thomas Douglass, John McCord, C.C.O., Thomas J. Sanders, Thoms P. Atkinson, Witt C. Wise, Riley Wise, Hugh Wise. For hire of Negroes in 1838 and 1839. Cash received from Anna Vickers, Thomas J. Giles, Pollard Bickerstaff, Green Moody, Barna Wise. Signed: Creed T. Wise, Admr. Recorded 15 May 1840.

Inventory & appraisement of property belonging to estate of David Phillips, dec'd. One horse, saddle, and watch $93.00. Certified 2 Mar. 1840 by appraisers James Bougham, James Brownlee, James W. Harkness and signed James W. Harkness, J.P. Recorded 15 May 1840.

Pages 318-320: Inventory and appraisement of estate of John Tarpley, dec'd. Lots of land No. 71, 202½ acres; No. 91, 202½ acres $2000. 1 lot 490 acres in Appling Co. and 1 lot 40 acres in Cherokee Co. not viewed. 4 Negroes: Notes on James J. Tarpley, E. W. Reynolds, W. H. Lyons and John Berry & P. A. Higgins, Matthew Allen, William Harmon, Jr., William Harmon, Sr., William B. Smith, W. H. Lyons and James Liles. Received from Stephen Bailey for 2 notes on Jonathan Carter and Jesse Jolly, James Wilson, James E. Buntyn, execution on Jonathan Carter and Ebenezar Carter. Goods and chattels. Certified on May 2, 1840 by appraisers J. R. McCord, Pleasant M. Glass, Ward Keeler and Stephen Bailey, J.P. Recorded 4 June 1840.

Page 321: Estate of James Anderson to David Kimbell and John Anderson, Admrs. from 1st Jan. to 31st Dec. 1838. Return No. 3 1838 pd. Mary Anderson, guardian for James, Elizabeth and Martha Anderson; Mary Anderson balance in full her share; David Anderson one of distributees his share in full; Nathan Anderson his share in full; David Kimbell his share in full; John Anderson and Isham Anderson in full. Returned 21 May 1840 by David Kimbell, Admr. Recorded 5 June 1840.

Annual return estate of Elizabeth and Martha Anderson, minors to Mary Anderson, guardian from 1st Jan. to 31st Dec. 1839. Pd. David Evans for shoes; James D. Giles, J. R. & J. W. McCord, Spencer and Mays, Robert B. Saunders for necessaries. Credit: Balance due wards as per last return. Returned 28th May 1840 by Mary (X) Anderson, guardian. Recorded 5 June 1849.

Pages 322-324: Return on estate of Sterling Camp, dec'd. to William Jarrell, Admr. from 1st Jan. to 31st Dec. 1839. Paid John B. McRight one of distributees; to guardian William Jarrell for James Camp and Nathan F. Camp distributees. Retained for my wife a distributee. Credit: Received from notes on E. Hill, Jail Dear. Reuben Payne, James R. Smith, 12 months interest on share of two distributees not included in return for 1838. Returned 14 May 1840. William Jarrell, Admr. Recorded 6 June 1840.

Return No. 2 on estate of Nathan F. Camp, minor of Sterling Camp in account with William Jarrell, guardian for year 1839. Paid: D. L. Duffey for 1837 taxes; Spencer & Mays; J. R. & J. W. McCord, Alexander McMahan and Willis Jarrell for tuition, 1838 taxes, Samuel K. McLin, Bartlett and Willingham, boarding ward for 1839 ($50). Cr: hiring and renting land and Negroes, sale of land in Henry Co. Returned 14 May 1840 by William Jarrell, guardian. Recorded 10 June 1840.

Return No. 2 on estate of James Camp, minor of S. Camp in account with William Jarrell, guardian for 1839. (Same as above).

Page 324: Estate of John A. Malone, dec'd. to Martha Malone, Executrix and Britton Buttrill, Executor. Paid 1839 Vouchers 1-15 to J. R. & J. W. McCord Store, James M. Fielder, W. G. Atkinson, A. H. Daugherty, Thomas Ragland, Compton & Bowles, James R. Wilson, Burwell Jinks, E. Walker, Thos. B. Burford, Spencer & Mays, Tax 1838, Britton Buttrill, Smith & Roan. Cash received for crop of cotton, rent for

house at Indian Springs, Brandy made and sold, beef sold.   Recorded 7th
July 1840.

Page 325:   Inventory and appraisement of estate of Peter McFarlin,
late of Butts Co.   Goods and chattels, 100 acres land in Bibb Co. not
viewed by appraisors.   Certified July 8, 1840 by appraisers J. R. McCord,
O. H. P. McClendon, William Y. Lyons and William F. Mapp, J.P.   Recorded
16 July 1840.

Page 325-331:   Georgia, Troup County - Inventory and appraisement
of property of Daniel Curry, dec'd. 101¼ acres of land, goods and
chattels.   Certified by appraisors as a true appraisement as produced by
Aggy Curry on Jan. 5, 1837.   Signed: B. Edmundson, Wiley L. Edmundson,
Thomas Tatom, William E. Mercer, appraisors and James McLain, J.P.
Recorded Apr. 17, 1837.

Account of sale of property of Daniel Curry dec'd. sold at public
sale 11 Jan. 1837.   Buyers: Aggy Curry, Tilmon Taylor, George Nickleson,
Thomas Christopher, Sheriff Brewster, Green Caudle, Burwell Smith,
Thomas Tatom, Jeff Lukers, Charles Timmons, Wiley Edmundson, George
Whitehead, James Cannon, William S. Edmundson, Jefferson Vickers, Daniel
McLark, George Forrester, James Cook, John Burk, rent of plantation to
Elijah Hallox, Harris Parish, Bryant Edmundson, George Whitaker, Simpson
Russell, Ignatius Russell.   Wit: Robert Booth, March 6, 1837.   Signed:
Aggy (X) Curry, Admx.   Recorded Apr. 18, 1837.

Aggy Curry, Admx. to estate of Daniel Curry, dec'd.   Return for
1837 & 1838.   Hire of Negroes and sale of 101¼ acres of land in 4th
Dist. of Troup Co., Ga. sold by order of court before Courthouse door in
LaGrange 1st Tues. in Jan. 1838.

Contra - Amt. paid printers, N. N. Howell, Amos Shaw, David Christo-
pher, certified by Aggy (X) Curry, 20th Dec. 1838 before Wiley Wilson,
C.C.O.   Examined by January Term of Court 1839.   John Traylor, J.I.C.
Recorded Jan. 22, 1839.

Pages 331-332:   Georgia, Butts County, I, William H. Smith of Butts
County being weak in body and sound mind make this my last will and
testament.   Item 1 - My debts paid.   Item 2 - Sale of properties (named)
to buy a small bit of land and two cheap farm horses such as will be
sufficient to carry on small farm for the support of wife and wife to
have balance of perishable property.   Item 3 - All money arising from
sale above buying of small farm kept as belonging to estate and used for
wife.   Item 4 - My son Joseph to be boarded and sent to school one year
and tuition paid.   Item 5 - Son Simon boarded and sent to school for 18
months and tuition paid.   Item 6 - At death or marriage of wife all
property sold at the highest bidder and final distribution made.   If wife
should marry she be given a child's part.   Item 7 - My eldest, James
Smith and my daughter Verlinda Wallace and my son William B. Smith and
my son Ebenezar Smith orphans, and my son Elijah Smith and my daughter
Martha Smith and my daughter Kissiah Dawson, and my son Joseph Smith and
my daughter Elizabeth Smith and my son Simon all be considered by my
executors as legal heirs of my estate and an equal division made between
them except my son William Smith and the orphans of my son Ebenezar.
My son William Smith has had $70 which I hold notes for, that amount is
to be taken out of his part and also Ebenezar Smith orphans there is $75 to be taken out of their part as their father
was given him in his life time.   Also a deduction of $12 each out of the
part of my three married daughters parts for a bed that I gave each of
them.   Verlinda Wallace and Martha Smith and Kissiah Dawson these deduc-
tions made and then division made.   Item 8 - Son Elijah Smith and Riley
Wise and John M. Pearson be my executors this 6th Aug. 1836.   Signed:
William H. (X) Smith.   Test: Humphrey Gilmore, Stephen (X) Bailey, James
(X) Bentley.   Recorded Sept. 8, 1840.

Pages 333-337:   Memorandom of sale of property of James Wooten,
dec'd. taken by John Jones, Admr. 8 Jan. 1840.   Purchasers: John Jones,
Theophilus Williams, John Hutchenson, N. W. Newman, James Wooten, John
Blesset, Stephen T. Biggers, William McClendon, A. A. Wooten, Daniel
Tingle, Pollard Payne, T. Williams, Eli Parks, A. F. Thompson, H. B.

Wilson, William Simpson, John W. Phillips, R. C. Smith, Thomas Payne, William H. White, James Sales, C. M. Sutter, S. Wooten, Thos. P. Atkinson, Oliver McClendon, A. B. White, J. Y. Morris, Jefferson Smith. Returned 4 Sept. 1840 by John Jones, Admr. Recorded 18 Sept. 1840. Examined and approved by a committee of Sept. Term Grand Jury 1840, Robert B. Saunders, David Evans, Josiah W. Barber, John L. Barnett, Robert P. Coleman.

Pages 338-339: Return of Sale of perishable property belonging to Estate of Peter McFarlin sold in Butts Co. 27 Aug. 1840 by Admr. Purchasers: A. Shockley, T. Williams, G. Tredwell, John Andrews, P. M. Compton, D. Elder, C. Ross, J. W. Watkins, R. Mays, J. Aycock, D. J. Bailey, A. L. Robinson, R. H. McCollum, J. F. McCollum, J. Blessit, J. Bearden, Willis Jenkins, T. Williams, D. Heath. Signed: Robert Mays, Admr. Recorded 28 Sept. 1840.

Page 339: Yearly return on estate of William Ray, dec'd. by William G. Ray, Admr. Sept. 1839 to Sept. 1840. Paid John Betterton, Peter Warren, C.C.O. Legatees as follows: Elizabeth Ray, W. H. Miller, Aaron Onail, D. H. Ellis, W. H. Ray, R. Y. Ray, J. L. Ray, S. S. Scott. For publishing sale to J. Sturgis. Signed: William G. Ray, Admr. Recorded 29 Sept. 1840.

Page 340: Sale of Cherokee Land sold as part of real estate of William Ray late of Butts Co. sold by Admrs. Sold: 1 Lot No. 724, 4th Dist., 1st Section formerly Cherokee now Forsyth sold to Wade H. Ray for $600; 1 Lot No. 887, 18th Dist., 2nd Section formerly Cherokee now Campbell sold to Joseph Summerlin for $7.37½. Signed: William G. Ray, Admr. Recorded Sept. 29, 1840.

Sale of perishable property of David Phillips, Dec'd. Oct. 6, 1840. Purchasers: Robert White, William B. Nutt, Henry S. Mays, William R. Simpson, James R. McCord, Toliver Madden, W. R. Bankston, John Greer, John Phillips, Jr. Signed: John Phillips, Admr. Recorded 14 Oct. 1840.

Inventory and sale of personal property of estate of Robert Andrews, dec'd. sold in town of Jackson 1st Dec. 1840. Sold to Cornelius Slaten 1 thrasher and fan; W. G. Andresa 1 cotton gin; J. B. Carmichael 282½ acres of land ($1,132.00). Signed: John Andrews, Admr. Recorded 9th Dec. 1840.

Pages 341-342: Court - Nov. term 1840 ordered that Gustavus Hendrick, Washington G. Atkinson, Abel L. Robinson, Britton Buttrill and John McMichael, Esqrs. or any three are appointed commissioners to divide Negroes belonging to estate of Robert W. Hinter, dec'd. into as many shares as there are distributees. B. H. Darden, J.I.C., Thomas P. Atkinson, J.I.C., John Hendrick, J.I.C.

Ga., Butts Co., Personally appeared before me Gustavus Hendrick, Washington G. Atkinson and John McMichael, commissioners named in above order and saith that they to the best of their judgement appraised and let off to each of the distributees of the estate of Robert W. Hunter, dec'd. Nov. 28, 1840. Signed by above commissioners before Thomas P. Atkinson, J.I.C.

The appraisement and division on Nov. 28, 1840 of Negroes belonging to estate of Robert W. Hunter, dec'd. Listed are names of 18 Negroes valued at $9500. This amount divided into three equal shares. Each Legatee received $3166 2/3. Mrs. Margaret Hunter received 6 Negroes ($300), Lydia Isabella Hunter received 6 Negroes ($3265), Sarah Ann Hunter received 6 Negroes ($3285), Mrs. Hunter's Negroes falls short $166 2/3 of equal share so Isabella pays $98 1/3 and Sarah Ann pays $68 1/3 to Mrs. Hunter. Signed by above commissioners and recorded Dec. 12, 1840.

Butts Co. Court Sept. Term 1840. Ordered by court that Matthew Gaston be appointed Admr. of the estate of Daniel Curry dec'd. in right of his wife Aggy Curry on his filing in this office an exemplification of all her actins and doings as Admrx. on the estate of said Daniel Curry and on giving bond and secruity for $4000 and further ordered that

William G. McMichael, Ezekiel Walker, Henry Barren, William Curry and
Edward W. Lane Esqr. be appointed commissioners to divide the estate of
Daniel Curry subject to distribution into two parts equally and to
assign one share to Aggy Gaston, late widow of Daniel Curry and other
share to Harriet Ann Curry the only child of Daniel. Signed: John
Hendrick, J.I.C., David M. Nutt, J.I.C., Thos. P. Atkinson, J.I.C.

Page 343: We certify that we have valued a Negro boy belonging to
the above estate as $650 the only property submitted to us and assigned
same by Lot to Matthew Gaston Sept. 26, 1840. E. W. Lane, William Curry,
E. Walker, Commissioners. Sworn before D. M. Nutt, J.I.C. Recorded
Dec. 16, 1840.

Account of Sale of Land of the Estate of Robert Grimmett, dec'd.
Feb. 1840. 1 Lot of land in DeKalb Co. sold to A. J. Grimmet, J. H.
Grimmet, Admr. Returned 28 Dec. 1840. Recorded Dec. 29, 1840.

James H. Grimmet, Admr. of Robert Grimmet returns Hochpot accounts
not returned on account of advancement made by Robert Grimmet in his life
time to the following children, James H. Grimmet, George E. Hodge,
William M. Grimmet, Mary May, Thomas L. Grimmet. Returned Dec. 29,
1840 by J. H. Grimmet, Admr. Recorded Dec. 29, 1840.

Page 344: Dec. 2, 1840 - Charles A. Killgore, Admr. of A. G. Duke
dec'd. Received $880.65 on due bill and $1508 on note - it being a distribution share in full for within named minors (to wit) Ann Duke, Polly
Duke, Coatsworth Duke, William Duke, Elizabeth Duke, Aristotle Duke
making $2388.65 rec'd. by me as guardian for said minors. Eli Conger,
guardian. Recorded Jan. 4, 1841.

Rec'd. of Charles A. Killgore, Admr. of my father Aristotle Duke,
dec'd. the sum of $397.52 in full my distributive share of the estate
of said dec'd. this 2nd Dec. 1840. Signed: Charles P. Duke. Recorded
4 Jan. 1841.

Others received their distributive share as follows: John Duke received $397.52; Sarah (X) Duke received $356.80; William E. Jones received $397.52.

Page 345: Georgia, Harris County - I, James Barr, D.C.C.O. of said
Co. certify that Joel T. Crawford of said Co. was this day, Dec. 14,
1840, appointed guardian for the person and property of Sarah Jane and
Lydia Issabella Hunter, orphans of Robert W. Hunter by said court and
given bond and security. Signed: James Barr, D.C.C.O. Recorded Butts
Co., Ga. Jan. 6, 1841.

Received of Alexander Hunter, Admr. of Robert W. Hunter, dec'd. 12
Negroes belonging to Sarah Jane and Lydia Isabella Hunter, orphans of
said dec'd. Signed: Joel T. Crawford, guardian. Rec'd. of Alexander
Hunter, Admr. of the estate of Robert Hunter, dec'd. 7 Negroes and
$166 2/3 in full my distributive share of the Negro property of said
estate. Nov. 28, 1840. Signed: Margaret Hunter. Recorded 6 Jan. 1841.

Yearly return of the hire of the Negroes and the rent of land of
Robert W. Hunter, dec'd. for the year 1840 by me Alexander Hunter, Admr.
Negroes to Thomas P. Atkinson, Spencer and Mays, Margaret Hunter, Mrs.
Hunter, Clark Hamil, Jack Williams, Samuel S. Hunter. To Margaret Hunter
50 acres of land, for rent of land to Stephen Bailey, Bailey & Robinson,
W. Cathan, James Brownlee & Irby, John G. Irby. Signed: A. Hunter, Admr.
Recorded 7 Jan. 1841.

Pages 346-347: Ga., Butts Co., Sept. 8, 1840. A list of the
appraisement of estate of William H. Smith, dec'd. Goods and chattles.
Notes on James Smith, Hugh H. Heard, David Rowe, Joseph Smith, Green
Smith, William B. Smith. Certified 8 Sept. 1840 by appraisors Richard
M. Stewart, William Gilmore, Hugh H. Heard and J. B. Tomlinson, J.P.
Recorded 7 Jan. 1841.

Pages 348-349: Memorandom of sale of perishable property of the
estate of Aristotle Duke dec'd. taken by me 30 Nov. 1840, Charles A.

Killgore, Admr. Purchasers: Eli Conger pr. Mr. Dicken, J. B. Orr,
Washington G. Atkinson, Royal Willard, Jesse H. Cothern, William E.
Jones, Benjamin H. Hull, Sarah Duke, William Irvine, George W. Thomas,
Seaborn M. Tidwell, James A. McCune, Lewis Moore, B. F. Hull, Willis
Holifield, William Cothern, Amos Conger, Thomas Burford. Sale of real
estate No. 2, lot of land to widow's dower excepted land and 5 Negroes.
Signed: Charles A. Killgore, Admr. Recorded 7 Jan. 1841.

Page 350: Estate of Aristotle G. Duke to Charles A. Killgore, Admr.
for year 1838. Store account, schooling, blacksmith, pd. E. Jones, John
Jinks, John McCord, Samuel P. Burford. CR: Sale of cotton. Signed:
Charles Killgore, Admr. Recorded 8 Jan. 1841.

The estate of A. G. Duke to C. A. Killgore for year 1839. Pd: A. H.
Daugherty, J. P. Williams, J. Hardy, William Jinks, W. G. Atkinson for
tax, G. Hendrick, coffee, shoes, S. Bailey, J. McCord, D. Taylor. Cr:
Sold six bales of cotton. Signed: Charles A. Killgore, Admr. Recorded
8 Jan. 1841.

Page 351: Yearly return on estate of Aristotle G. Duke, dec'd. for
year 1840 by Charles A. Killgore, Admr. Paid Charles P. Duke, Joseph
Godard, J. J. Chaiffin, J. P. Williams, Bailey & Hunter, Jinks & Forrest-
er, John Jinks, Harry G. Lee, Edward W. O'Nail, Washington G. Atkinson,
J. C. Williamson, T. C., Scott & Carhart, Spencer & Mays, Thos. P.
Atkinson, Samuel P. Burford, William Jones, John McCord. Credit: Cash
for cotton sold in Macon, Hannah Cooksey for board ($5.00). Signed:
Charles Killgore, Admr. Recorded Jan. 9, 1841.

Return No. 2 - Jan. Term 1841 - Return of Charles Hammond, guardian
of William J. Hammond, minor. Balance on hand and interest. Signed:
Charles Hammond, guardian. Recorded Jan. 9, 1841.

Page 352: Annual return of George L. Thompson, Admr. of estate of
Green B. Reeves, dec'd. up to date. Dec. 20, 1836 - Amount of sale bill
of perishable property $1137.88½ rent of land, sale of land ($500). Paid
in 1st and 2nd return, Nancy A. Reeves, taxes for 1838 and 1839, John
McCord. Signed: George L. Thompson, Admr. Recorded 12 Jan. 1841.

Sale of perishable property of James L. Compton dec'd. Sold 7
July 1840 on credit until 18 Nov. next. Purchasers: P. M. Compton,
Robert Douglass, S. H. Sanders. Signed: P. M. Compton, Admr. Recorded
14 Jan. 1841.

Page 353: Account of sale of real estate of Peter McFarlin, dec'd.
by Robert Mays, Admr. to order of court at Macon, Bibb Co. before court
doors Jan. 5, 1841, 101¼ acres, 13th Dist. originally Monroe now Bibb
Co. sold to Robert McInvale for $430. Returned 16 Jan. 1841 by Robert
Mays, Admr. Recorded Jan. 16, 1841.

Return No. 10 - Estate of William Redman, dec'd. in account with
James Carter, Admr. from Jan. 1, to Dec. 31, 1840. Paid William A.
Florence, taxes 1839. Goodman & Andrews, James M. Fielder, John W.
Williams, Mary Redman, J. R. & J. W. McCord. Cr: Hiring of Negroes for
year 1840. Returned 11 Jan. 1841. Signed: James Carter, Admr. Recorded
4 Feb. 1841.

Page 354: Account of hiring of 7 Negroes to Mary Redman for year
1840. James Carter, Admr. Recorded 4 Feb. 1841.

Page 354: Account of hiring 7 Negroes to Mary Redman for year 1840.
James Carter, Admr. Recorded 4 Feb. 1841.

Annual return of O. H. P. McClendon, guardian for Jeremiah P. Mc-
Clendon from 4 Mar. 1840 to 4 Jan. 1841. Pd. Fielder & McClure, Bloods-
worth and Maxey, 1839 taxes, James B. Hanson, Catherine Brewer, John L.
Jones, C. F. Newton, P. M. Compton, Spencer & Mays, John McCord, O. H. P.
McClendon guardian. Recorded 5 Feb. 1841.

Annual return of Eli Knight, minor with Calvary F. Knight, guardian.
1840 - Pd.: 8 months board for ward. Signed: C. F. Knight, guardian.

118

Recorded 5 Feb. 1841.

Return on estate of Robert Bickerstaff, dec'd. by Admr. for 1840. Pd: William R. Head, A. R. Bickerstaff, Admr. Recorded 5 Feb. 1841.

Pages 355-356: Yearly return on estate of Robert H. Hunter, dec'd. by Alexander Hunter, Admr. for year 1840. Cash paid Joshua Patrick, Isham Anderson, T.C., Reuben Phillips, James Harkness, Stephen Bailey, Alexander Hunter, Jr., William Jarrell, John Duffey, B. F. Tucker, J. B. Harkness, M. Bartlett, John Hendrick, John McCord, Jabez Gilbert, R. P. Mayo, T.C., Spencer & Mays, Samuel B. Hunter, James H. Stark, P. M. Compton, John R. Wilson, Theophilus Williams, James A. McCune, John Mc-Michael, Booles & Compton, Bankston & Maddux, Thos. P. Atkinson, Margaret Hunter, Robert White. Cash received from Samuel S. Hunter, R. Phillips, J. S. Irby, Robert Martin, John W. Troter. Signed: A. Hunter, Admr. Recorded 5 Feb. 1841.

Pages 356-358: Annual return of estate of Robert Grimmet from date of letter of Admr. to 31 Dec. 1840. Paid Vouchers 1-34 to Thomas L. Grimmet, John E. Sewell, Hearn & Redwine, Thomas Smith for funeral expenses $8.00, J. P. Williams, Travy G. Bledsoe, Frances Miller, E. W. Perry, Thos. B. Burford, N. & J. Hornsby, Elizabeth Grimmet, William Gilbert, James Roberts, Thos. P. Atkinson, Allen N. Young. To distributees George Hodge, Mary Grimmet, A. J. Grimmet, T. L. Grimmet, Hiram Ramsey, Nathaniel May, Elizabeth Grimmet, James Stewart, A. J. Grimmet, guardian for Robert Grimmet a distributee, retained out of the assets in part my distributive share, Hiram Ramsey in full his share, Mary Grimmet in full her share, A. J. Grimmet in full his share, A. J. Grimmet, guardian for Robert Grimmet in full his share, Thomas L. Grimmet in full his share. 1840 - Credit: Amount of sales rendered, notes on William M. Grimmet, James Blackstack & J. Redwine, V. Brock and James Brock, A. J. Grimmet, Michael Thompson and J. Rape, John McCord & W. Gilbert, Peter Ussery. Returned 1st Jan. 1841 by J. H. Gimmet, Admr. Recorded 6 Feb. 1841.

Page 358: Martin B. Bowles, Lunatic to G. Hendrick, guardian. 1840 paid William Stroud for shoes, taxes, Hendrick & Goodman. Cash paid your son per order, sundries. Signed: Gustavus Hendrick, guardian. Recorded 6 Feb. 1841.

Page 359: Estate of James Screws, dec'd. to Beverly Evans, Exrs. Paid: taxes 1839, John T. Wells for a Legacy, C.C.O. Signed: Beverly Evans, Exr. Recorded 8 Feb. 1841.

Estate of Mary Vincent, dec'd. Paid Wade H. Giles, Admr. will annexed. Dec. 1839 - paid legacy to Nathaniel Vincent, Powel P. Vincent, Thomas Vincent, Henry Vincent, John W. Williams for making coffin. Wade H. Giles, Admr. with will annexed. Recorded 8 Feb. 1841.

Return No 1 - The estate of Richard Smith to Josiah W. Barber, guardian 1840 paid: G. W. Thomas for boarding and clothing for 1839 - 1840, 1838 credit: Amt. purchased at sale of dec'd. by widow, amt. rec'd. from Jas. W. Watkins, J. Higgins, Isaac Smith, Jeptha Smith. Signed: Josiah W. Barber, guardian. Recorded 8 Feb. 1841.

Pages 360-361: Return No. 2 - Estate of James Wilson in account with James H. Stark and John W. McCord from 1st Jan. to 31st Dec. 1840. Paid by vouchers 29-66 to James Lyles, Andrew & McClure, William Jones, Smith and Roan, John Hall, James M. Bledsoe, John Hendrick, James H. Stark, 1838 taxes, Ney Pugh. Paid distributees share in part to John Phillips, John R. Wilson, A. J. Wilson, James H. Stark, guardian for James Wilson minor. Paid Charles Bailey on note, Samuel Snoddy, Mark & Flournoy, John Phillips, S. H. Sanders, John McCord, S. W. Price, Eli Conger, James H. Stark, taxes 1839, Stephen Bailey, David J. Bailey, James H. Stark guardian for James Wilson in part of his share, John R. Wilson, A. J. Wilson in part of his share, John Phillips in right of his wife in part of his share. Credit: Sale of Negroes and Lot in Jackson ($2587.10) Rec'd. of Hugh B. Stewart, interest from John Phillips, Mary Anderson, John R. Wilson, James M. Simmons, A. Mickelberry. Returned 19 Jan. 1841 by James H. Stark & John W. McCord Admrs. Recorded 9 Feb.1841.

119

Return of estate of Isaiah Wise, dec'd. for year 1840. Paid John McCord for recording return, Rosey Wise, Legacy in part. Riley Wise, Admr. Recorded 10 Feb. 1841.

Page 362: Return on estate of Martha Anderson, minor in account with Mary Anderson, guardian from Jan. 1 to Dec. 31, 1840. Paid Spencer & Mays, David Evans, P. M. Compton, J. R. & J. W. McCord, McCune & Taylor, Bankston and Maddux, Goodman and Andrews. Returned 29 Jan. 1841 by Mary (X) Anderson, guardian. Recorded 10 Feb. 1841.

Return on estate of Samuel James H. Stark in account with James H. Stark, guardian from Jan. 1 to Dec. 31, 1840. Balance due ward Dec. 31, 1840. Cr: Interest on cash. James H. Stark, guardian. Returned 16 Jan. 1841. Recorded 10 Feb. 1841.

Page 363: Return of Yelventon Thaxton, guardian for minor of Arnold Johnson from 1838 to Feb. 1, 1841. Paid J. Carmichael, John McCord for plat and grant and postage, expences for travelling ten days to Walker Co., Ga. to sell land of minors ($13.18 3/4), ten days for services and horse to travel to sell land of minors ($10.00), fees for selling land, D. L. Bailey, Samuel Johnson his legacy of the estate ($106.00). Yelventon Thaxton, guardian. Recorded Feb. 11, 1841.

Return of the estate of Joel Wise, dec'd. for year 1840. Paid: J. McCord, C.C.O., A. H. Chappell, Ed A. Broddis. Returned 11 Jan. 1841.

Pages 363-364: Inventory and appraisement of estate of William Burford, dec'd. Lot of land No. 215 deceased residence, 1 Lot in Cherokee Co. 160 acres No. 66, 12th Dist., 2nd Section; 11 Negroes, good and chattels. Certified by appraisors William S. Bivins, Lewis Moore, Alfred H. King, 18 Nov. 1840 and John Greer, J.P. Recorded 17 Feb. 1841.

Page 365: Georgia, Butts Co. - I consent that the Inferior Court of Butts Co. shall grant an order to divide the estate of William Redman, dec'd. amongst the distributees of sd. William Redman. Signed: Mary (X) Redman. Jan. 11, 1841. I likewise consent and waive the notice Jan. 11, 1841. James Carter, guardian for Mary C. Redman, Martha Redman & W. T. C. Redman.

Butts Co. Court of Ordinary Feb. Term 1841 - It appearing to the court that notice for the purpose of obtaining the following order has been waived by the parties in interest - that a portion of estate of William Redman, dec'd. is still unsold and undistributed by Admr. - that a considerable portion of estate has been converted into cash by him and remains undistributed because several of distributees have not had any legal representation and the growing unequality of the expences of each of the distributees is continually becoming greater and may lead to confusion on a final settlement. It is ordered by the court that John McCord, Sr., John Goodman, John Hendrick, William B. McMichael and Abel L. Robinson or any three be hereby appointed to divide so much of the estate of William Redman as had been converted into money by the Admr. after deducting the disturdements of each, into four parts equally and they they assign one part to Mary Redman, the widow of said dec'd., one part of James Carter, guardian for Mary C. Redman, one part to James Carter, guardian for Martha Redman, and one part to James Carter, guardian for William T. C. Redman. Recorded Feb. 23, 1841.

Page 366: Ga., Butts Co. - The undersign commissioners appointed by court of said county to divide so much of estate of William Redman, dec'd. reported that they have discharged their duty. They find on Feb. 1, 1841 on hand of James Carter a balance of $5151.42 and distribute to James Carter, guardian for Mary C. Redman her share $1037.44½, for Martha Redman her share $1200.87½, for William T. B. Redman his share $1218.92½. To Mrs. Mary Redman, widow of dec'd. $1694.17½. Signed: Feb. 3, 1841 - John McCord, John Goodman, John Hendrick, W. G. McMichael, A. L. Robinson, Commissioners. Certified by Thomas P. Atkinson, J.I.C. Recorded 23 Feb. 1841.

Page 367: Yearly return on estate of Jacob Wise, dec'd. by Witt C. Wise exor. Feb. 27, 1841 cash paid John McCord, C.C.O., A. L. Robinson,

Goodman and Andrews, S. H. Sanders, David J. Bailey. Recorded 2 Mar. 1841.

Jan. 1, 1841. Return of hire of Negroes belonging to estate of Jacob Wise, dec'd. by Witt C. Wise, exor. to Job Tylor and Augustus Wise. Recorded 2 Mar. 1841.

Rec'd. 24 Dec. 1840 of Witt C. Wise, five Negroes hitherto secured to us by convenant with the heirs of Jacob Wise, dec'd., also our respective share due us from the estate of said Jacob Wise. Signed: Job Tylor, Augustus (X) Wise, Judith Wise, exor. of William Hancock, dec'd., Creed T. Wise, Admr. on estate of William Vickers, dec'd. Recorded 2 Mar. 1841.

Page 368: Dec. 19, 1839. Rec'd. of Witt C. Wise the exor. of the estate of Jacob Wise, dec'd. $367 in cash, it being in part or in full my legacy which is coming from said estate at the death of my wife's mother, Elizabeth Wise, who was the wife of said Jacob Wise, dec'd. It is understood by the executor Witt C. Wise and myself if on division of the property that if the sum failed to amount to the sum of $367 that I will refund to Witt C. Wise as executor the amount due from me as one of the legatees. Signed: Barna Wise. Recorded Mar. 2, 1841.

Annual return on estate of Elizabeth Anderson, a minor to Mary Anderson, guardian from Jan. 1 to Dec. 31, 1840. Paid Spencer & Mays, McCune and Taylor, Bankston and Maddux, David Evans, P. M. Compton, Goodman & Andrews, John McCord, C.C.O. Paid James P. Middlebrooks, husband of ward in full. Returned Jan. 9, 1841 by Mary (X) Anderson, guardian. Recorded 3 Mar. 1841.

Page 369: Yearly return on estate of Robert W. Hunter, dec'd. by Alexander Hunter, Admr. Feb. 21, 1841. Paid Lewis Moore, Alexander Hunter, Thomas House, J. P. Williams, John Hall, John McCord, Thomas C. Taylor, Asa Buttrill, Goodman and Andrews, A. L. Robinson, Spencer & Mays, James W. Harkness, M. Barber, S. H. Sanders, William F. Mapp, B. F. Tucker, Edward Pane. Credit: Rec'd. from Edward Pane, Atty., James Oliver. Signed: A. Hunter, Admr. Recorded Mar. 3, 1841.

Pages 370-371: Estate of Robert Andrews, dec'd. in account with John Andrews and Walter S. Andrews, Admr. 1841 - Credit: Cash received from J. Garret, Y. G. Malone, D. Lindsey, B. V. Hamil, R. Fish, A. Woodward. Paid: 1838 taxes, S. Bailey, Y. Thaxton, John R. Dicken, J. Carmichael, B. V. Hamil, Goodman & Andrews, Taxes 1839, John W. McCord, Bankston & Maddux, J. R. & J. W. McCord, Low & Compton, A. Woodard, Thomas House, Jarrell & Duffey, Walter S. and John Andrews, W. J. Lewis. Signed: John Andrews and W. S. Andrews. Recorded 4 Mar. 1841.

Page 371: Estate of James L. Compton, dec'd. to P. M. Compton, Admr. From date of letter to 26 Feb. 1841. Paid Vouchers 1-18 to Joshua Patrick, John Hall, Spencer & Mays, Goodman & Andrews, Bankston & Maddux, Stephen Bailey, William Irvine, John McCord, R. P. May, taxes, James M. Fielder, Alden Mickleberry, Stephen T. Biggers, Bailey & Hunter, Low & Compton, John Sanders. Signed: P. M. Compton, Admr. Recorded 4 Mar. 1841.

Page 372: Narcissa Douglass to Thomas Douglass, exor. on estate of W. S. Douglass, dec'd. Cash paid year 1840 to D. Kelley, P. M. Compton, Martha Jinkins, C. F. Newton, one year board. Signed: Thomas Douglass, Exr. Recorded 4 Mar. 1841.

Yearly return on estate of Macajah F. McCune, dec'd. by William A. McCune, Admr., Mar. 1, 1841, cash paid Jesse McClendon, R. P. Mann, T.C., David Higgins. Recorded Mar. 4, 1841.

Yearly return made by me for my ward Cornelius M. McCune, William A. McCune, guardian. Cash paid Nancy McCune, John McCord. For year 1840 the hiring of the Negroes of my ward Cornelius M. McCune to William Giles and Thomas J. Giles. Signed: William McCune, guardian. Recorded Mar. 4, 1841.

Page 373: Annual return of William F. Mapp, Admr. of Allen McClendon, dec'd. for year 1840. Rec'd. on notes from Thomas J. Ferguson, Arthur Hamilton, Jesse Tolleson, Raney & Raney, Anderson Brown, Jeptha McClendon, Caswell Purifoy. Paid J. H. Stark, J. H. Shivers, Jacob Martin, A. L. Robinson, Jesse Loyall, Hugh A. Smith, William L. Conant. Returning to Samuel Snoddy, guardian for J. P. McClendon $5775.00 Negro property. Returning to Samuel Snoddy Negro property $6375.00. Returning to Mary S. McClendon $6025.00 Negro property. Signed: William F. Mapp, Admr. Recorded Mar. 5, 1841.

A return of William F. Mapp, guardian for William McClendon for year 1840. Paid William McClendon $5278.80. Returning to William McClendon Negro property for $5825.00. Signed: William F. Mapp, guardian. Recorded Mar. 5, 1841.

Pages 374-375: Received of William F. Mapp as guardian Negroes amounting to $6025, they being my distributive share of Negroes belonging to estate of Allen McClendon, dec'd. this 25 Feb. 1841. Signed: O. H. P. McClendon. Recorded Mar. 5, 1841.

Inventory of perishable property of John Tarpley, dec'd. sold at house of dec'd. on 12 Nov. 1840 to highest bidder. Bought by Mary Tarpley, W. A. Florence, T. Ragland, John McMichael, A. H. Daugherty, Martin Smith, James J. Tarpley, G. W. Barber, Elizabeth Tarpley, John H. Thompson, W. H. Roberts, W. G. McMichael, Samuel Smith, Henry S. Mays, Geo. W. Thomas, R. T. Mays, Ward Keeler. Signed: W. A. Florence. Recorded 9 Mar. 1841.

Pages 376-377: Inventory of sale of land and Negroes of John Tarpley, dec'd. sold at court house door in town of Jackson on 5th Jan. 1841. 91½ acres off of Lot No. 71 it being east half of Lot on which John Tarpley died purchased by John Goodman; 101¼ acres of Lot No. 91, north half where James J. Tarpley now lives purchased by John Goodman; 101¼ acres south half of Lot 91 on which E. W. Reynolds now lives purchased by John Goodman; 4 Negroes. Signed: W. A. Florence, Admr. Recorded 10 Mar. 1841.

The estate of John Tarpley to William A. Florence, Admr. Vouchers paid to Dr. Bailey, James Britton, J. R. & J. W. McCord, P. M. Compton, John McCord, E. Walker, S. H. Sanders, Printers, J. B. Thurman, J. R. Wilson, Spencer & Mays, Snoddy, J. M. Fielder, Goodman & Andrews, J. M. & J. B. Thurman, G. W. Thomas, W. A. Florence School, W. R. Simpson Smith. Credit: Hire of Negroes, sale of 781 lbs. cotton, E. W. Reynolds note, part on execution of Johnathan & Ebenezar Carter. Signed: W. A. Florence, Admr. Recorded 10 Mar. 1841. Examined and approved by us a committee of Grand Jury 18th Mar. 1841. Signed: O. H. P. McClendon, D. L. Patterson, J. M. Mangham.

Page 377: Jan. 5, 1840. Rented to John B. Carmichael 40 acres due Dec. 25, 1840. Rented to James Mangham 1st Mar. 1840 1 ps land. Signed John Andrews, Admr. Recorded. Apr. 6, 1841.

Pages 377-378: An inventory of property of Aaron Onail, dec'd. Lot of land No. 2461, Goods and chattels. Appraised Apr. 2, 1841 by George L. Thompson, Hiram Ramsey, William H. Wilson. Certified Apr. 2, 1841 by Nathan C. Williamson, J.P. Recorded Apr. 8, 1841.

Page 378-380: Appraisement of property of Willia C. Jenkins, dec'd. held on 31st Mar. 1841. 12 Negroes, goods and chattels. Note on Bartholonew Still, William T. Jenkins, Accounts against H. Dillon, Theaphelus Williams, Jerry Neal, James Morris, Washington Phillips, John White, William T. L. Lyons, Daniel Kelsey, Russell Brooks, James Thurman, William Johnson, John Anderson, 1 lot of land Lot No. ? in Randolph Co. Total value $13,073.51. Appraised on Mar. 31, 1841 by A. F. Thompson, John Coughran, Bartholonew Still. Certified by C. M. Coody, J.P. Recorded Apr. 9, 1841.

Pages 381-382: Butts County Court of Ordinary March term 1841. Ordered that Gustavus Hendrick, John W. McCord, Robert C. Mays, Ward Keeler and Stephen Bailey be appointed commissioners to divide the estate of Robert Andrews of said county dec'd. Signed: T. Walthall, J.I.C., Edmund McDaniel, J.I.C., E. W. Lowe, J.I.C., Thos. P. Atkinson, J.I.C.

Above commissioners took oath on Apr. 7, 1841 to make division of estate of Robert Andrews, dec'd. among the legatees. Signed: Stephen Bailey, J.P.

Results of their labour that aggragate amount of estate is $9740.64; widow (Sarah Andrews) having received her dower was not allowed by any part of the proceeds of land and a child's part of balance of said estate and that the distributive share of each legatee except the widow is $1096.38 3/9. It then appears paid to widow, Mrs. Sarah Andrews, J. B. Carmichael, John Andrews, Thomas H. Connel, W. J. Woodward, Martha Andrews, William Andrews, Sarah Andrews, Walter S. Andrews pays estate $63.51 6/9. Each received a Negro. Submitted Apr. 7, 1841 by commissioners J. W. McCord, Robert Mays, Ward Keeler, Gustavus Hendrick. Recorded Apr. 13, 1841.

Page 382: Return No. 4. Estate of Nathan Williams in account for year 1839 with S. W. Price, Exr. Paid Elizabeth Williams, guardian for her two minor daughters Martha T. and Mary Ann Williams. Returned Dec. 31, 1840 by S. W. Price, Exor. Recorded May 6, 1841.

Thomas Douglass, Exr. on estate of William S. Douglass, dec'd. for Marcellus Douglass 1840. Paid to John McCord, C. Campbell, D. Kelsey, Goodman and Andrews, P. M. Compton, G. A. Dudley, C. F. Newton & Co., one year board ($75). Signed: Thomas Douglass, Exor. Recorded May 7, 1841.

Page 383: Thomas Douglass, exor on estate of W. S. Douglass for Eugenius Douglass for 1840. Paid John McCord, D. Kelsey, Goodman & Andrews, C. Campbell, Jackly Dudley, C. F. Newton, one year board ($75). Signed: Thomas Douglass, Exor. Recorded May 7, 1841.

Return No. 4 - Estate of Nathan Williams in account with Nathan H. Williams exor. up to Dec. 31, 1840. Vouchers paid to Legatees James M. Williams, Nancy O. Williams, John R. Williams, Marcus E. Carter, C. A. Williams, William S. Williams, Elizabeth Williams. Return Apr. 12, 1841. Signed: N. H. Williams, Exor. Recorded May 8, 1841.

Page 384: Return No. 4 Estate of William M. Williams to N. H. Williams, guardian from Jan. 1st to Dec. 31, 1840. Paid John McCord, C.C.O. Cr: Interest on $570.57½. Signed: N. H. Williams, guardian. Recorded May 13, 1841.

Return No. 5 - Estate of James Camp in account with William Jarrell guardian for year 1840. Paid Goodman & Mays, taxes 1839. To boarding and making clothes and washing and mending for ward 12 months 1840. Balance due ward Dec. 31, 1840 $5334.18. Credit: Balance and interest for 1840. Returned Apr. 23, 1841. Signed: William Jarrell, guardian. Recorded May 18, 1841.

Return No. 3 - Estate of Nathan F. Camp, a minor of Sterling Camp in account with William Jarrell guardian for year 1840. Paid C.C.O., 1839 taxes, Henry Farrer for tuition and making clothes for ward for 12 months 1840. Balance due ward Dec. 31, 1840 $4917.94. Returned Apr. 23, 1841. Signed: William Jarrell, guardian. Recorded May 19, 1841.

Page 385: Return No. 6 - Estate of Sterling Camp in account with William Jarrell, Admr. for 1840. Paid 1838 and 1839 taxes. Credit: Interest realized for year 1840. Returned Apr. 23, 1841 William Jarrell, Admr. Recorded May 20, 1841.

Annual return of Creed T. Wise, Admr. of William Vickers dec'd. Paid: C.C.O., 1839 taxes, George D. Millen, Joseph Fielder school accounts. Returned May 2, 1841. Creed T. Wise, Admr. Recorded May 20, 1841.

Page 386: Yearly return on estate of William Ray dec'd. by me, William G. Ray, Admr. from Sept. 1840 to May 1841 which will show a full

and final settlement with all the Legatees of said estate. Cash paid
Aaron Onail, W. H. Miller, Elizabeth Ray, D. H. Ellis, C. L. Ray, S. S.
Scott, R. Y. Ray, W. H. Ray, H. Youngblood. Signed: William G. Ray,
Admr. Recorded May 20, 1841.

A return for year 1841 by Eli Conger guardian of the minors of
Aristotle G. Duke dec'd. Jan. 4, 1841. Paid notes to Charles Bailey,
Charles A. Killgore, W. G. Atkinson, James A. McCune, William Cathern,
Y. Orr, Thos. B. Burford, George W. Thomas. Received the above notes
in cash from Charles A. Killgore, Admr. on the estate of A. G. Duke,
dec'd. for the named minors of said dec'd. Martha Ann Duke, Polly
Duke, Coatsworth Duke, Elizabeth Duke, Aristotle Duke and William Duke.
Signed: Eli Conger, guardian. Recorded July 14, 1841.

Pages 387-388: Georgia, Butts County. I, Levi Jester being aged
and weak in body but sound of mind do make this my last will and testament as follows: 1st: I bequeath to my beloved wife Rosanna all ready
money I may have at my death and if overplush at her death it is to be
equally divided between my daughter Mary Jester and my three sons Henry,
Benjamin and Abner Jester and if a lack it to be made up by the said
Mary, Henry, Benjamin and Abner. 2nd: To my daughter Sarah Lofton, wife
of John Lofton one Negro woman and son and her increase and one dollar.
3rd: To my daughter Nancy Hammond, wife of Charles Hammond one Negro
girl and her increase and one dollar. 4th: To my daughter Mary Jester
11 Negroes (named) also household goods (names). 5th: To son Henry
Jester 6 Negroes (named) also my interest in my law suit in Morgan
Superior Court against George W. Tuggle, Admr. of the estate of David
Davis. 6th: To son Benjamin Jester 6 Negroes (named). 7th: To son
Abner Jester 6 Negroes (named). 8th: To granddaughter Jain Mason, wife
of Lenerd Mason one Negro girl Leeanner. 9th: To two sons Henry & Benjamin Jester one Negro woman and all household & kitchen furniture, Blacksmith bench & plantation tools, all my thrashing machines and fans,
waggons, horses and all other livestock, all crops gathered and ungather-
ed. 10th: Appoint my son Henry Jester my executor. Signed and sealed
June 15, 1839. Levi Jester (Seal). Wit: Clark Hamil, Samuel Bellah,
Dolphin Lindsey, Thomas Folds. Recorded July 14, 1841.

Pages 388-389: Return of Robert Mays, Admr. of estate of Peter
McFarlin, dec'd. 1840. Return No. 1 - June 19, 1840. Voucher paid
Joshua Patrick, J. W. Watkins, John Coughran, Macon Telegraph, John Mc-
Cord. 1841 paid Poe & Nesbit & Sheriff of Bibb Co., Robert McInvale,
McInvale & McFarlin, James McFarlin, A. L. Robinson, Spencer & Mays,
T.C., Jinks & Forrester, S. W. Booles. Returned Apr. 17, 1841 by Robert
Mays, Admr. Recorded July 15, 1841.

Pages 389-390: Account of sale of land devised by will of James
Wooten by John Jones, Admr. Mar. 1840 at Jackson - 300 acres sold to
James Wooten, 202½ acres to Addison L. Wooten. Returned July 5, 1841 by
John Jones, Admr. Recorded July 15, 1841.

Estate of James Wooten to John Jones, Admr. from July 1st 1839 to
Dec. 31, 1840. Paid: Thos. P. Atkinson auctioneer, C.C.O., A. Bellamy,
for necessaries, R. C. Smith, blacksmith, Hardiman Graybill Co., C.
Shark, Elias Beall & Co., Daniel Sanford, Fort & Clopton, Alexander &
Sale, Isaac Winship, Flanders & Cook, Pressley Smith, Samuel Snoddy
medical bills, service as overseer for 1839. Credit: Interest on balance
for 2 years, by sale of cotton to Wm. P. Rowland and R. T. Green, sale
of perishable property, sale of land. Returned July 5, 1841 by John
Jones, Admr. Recorded July 15, 1841.

Page 390: Estate of Simeon Wooten to John Jones, guardian from
Jan. 1, 1839 to Dec. 31, 1840. Paid Jane Bledsoe taylor bill, Margaret
Shivers for board, Daniel Kelsey, A. B. Phillips, Alva B. White, Richard
Bumley, E. B. Stow taylor, C.C.O., J. S. Hoggaham for tuition, Martha E.
Jones, taylor bill, 2 months board 1840. Credit: Balance due ward Dec.
31, 1838. Interest thereon 2 years, one slave hired 1840 to John Jones.
Returned July 5, 1841, John Jones, guardian. Recorded July 16, 1841.

Page 391: Estate of Seaborn Wooten, minor to John Jones, guardian
from Jan. 1, 1839 to Dec. 31, 1840. Paid: J. P. S. Ingraham for tuition,

A. B. Phillips, Bell & Bumley, R. Bumley, Jane Bledsoe taylor, Margaret Shivers for boarding. Credit: Balance due ward Dec. 31, 1839. Interest thereon for 2 years, hire of Negro to Alvenus White 1840. Returned July 5, 1841, John Johns, guardian. Recorded July 19, 1841.

Estate of James Wooten a minor to John Jones, guardian from Jan. 1, 1839 to Dec. 31, 1840. Paid Alexander & Sale, C.C.O. Credit: Balance due ward and interest. Returned July 5, 1841 John Jones, guardian. Recorded July 19, 1841.

Estate of Addison A. Wooten a minor to John Jones, guardian from Jan. 1, 1839 to Dec. 31, 1840. Paid: C.C.O. Credit: Balance due ward with interest. Hire of Negroes to N. Newman and William Gilmore. John Jones, guardian. Recorded July 19, 1840.

Page 392: Estate of Daniel Curry in account with Matthew Gaston, Admr. to Dec. 31, 1841. Paid: C.C.O. for one final return recording. Transferred to Matthew Gaston, guardian for Harriett Ann Curry. By balance returned as in the hands of Aggy Curry, Admrx. on Jan. 1, 1839. Interest for 2 years on sum, hire of slave to William Wooten 1839 and Matthew Gaston 1840. Amount left for distribution between two distributees Dec. 31, 1840. Returned May 18, 1841. Matthew Gaston, Admr. Recorded July 19, 1841.

Estate of Harriett Ann Curry to Matthew Gaston guardian up to Dec. 31, 1840. Balance due ward transferred from my hands as Admr. into my hands as guardian due Dec. 31, 1840. Returned Mar. 18, 1841. Matthew Gaston guardian. Recorded July 19, 1841.

Pages 393-395: Butts County, Georgia. Inventory & appraisement of estate of Levi Jester late of said county dec'd. 29 Negroes (named) goods and chattels listed. Notes on Willis Case, accounts against Richard Stillwell, Dolphin Lindsey, execution against George W. Tuggle, Admr. of David Davis Estate ($2356). Appraisors: Samuel F. Diffey, Clark Hamil, Dolphin Lindsey. Certified by Samuel Bellah, J.P. Recorded July 20, 1841.

Page 395-396: Sale of perishable property of Aaron Onail by the Admr. July 23, 1841. Buyers: John Hail, E. W. Onail, Frances Onail, William S. Bevens, D. H. Ellis, Josiah Crain, Joseph Scott, Wiley Curry, George L. Thompson, Frances Miller. Signed: E. W. Onail, Admr. Recorded Aug. 3, 1841.

Page 396: Ga., Butts Co. Indenture made by and between C.C.O. of one part and Robert McMahan of the same place & other part. The said C.C.O. hath this day by the consent of all parties concerned bound and put as an apprentice to the said Robert McMahan an illigitimate John Bankston to learn the art or mystery of Farming and to serve from the day of date during the full term of twenty years all which time has said master he shall faithfully obey, he shall do no damage to his said master, nor see it done by others without giving him notice, he shall not contract matrimony within said term, nor absent himself by day or night from his said masters service without his leave and his master shall teach and instruct said apprentice in the trade and mystery of farming and provide said apprentice sufficient meat, drink, apparel, and lodging and all other things fitting for an apprentice during the said time, education required by the act of the legislature in each case made and provided. Wit: Turman Walthall, J.I.C., Sept. 6, 1841. Signed: John McCord, C.C.O. Recorded Sept. 8, 1841.

Page 397: Yearly return of George L. Thompson Admr. of the estate of Green B. Reeves dec'd. Paid: Thomas B. Burford, Nancy A. Reeves, John McCord. Signed: Aug. 30, 1841. G. L. Thompson, Admr. Recorded Sept. 22, 1841.

Georgia, Butts County - Aug. 7, 1841. I Joseph Wilson of County & State aforesaid being of sound mind but feeble in bodily health do make this my last will and testament and revoke all others I may have made. I will 1st: All my just debts paid. 2nd: All estate real and personal to my beloved wife Sally Wilson during her natural life to be managed and controlled by her according to her discretion and at her death to go to my beloved son William H. Wilson. 3rd: To daughter Christian Foster $5.00. 4th: Appoint my beloved wife Sally Wilson and my son William H. Wilson my executors. Given under my hand the day and year first above written. Signed: Joseph Wilson (Seal). Wit: Nathan C. Williamson, George L. Thompson, John Hendrick. Recorded Sept. 22, 1841.

Page 398: Will of William Burford. This Aug. 8, 1834, I, William Burford of County of Butts, State of Georgia do make this my last will and testament. As to the property God gave me I give as follows: To Green Fuller and Susanna Fuller $5.00. 2nd: To Alfred Fuller and the heirs of Agness Fuller $5.00 in full of their Legacies. 3rd: All the balance of the estate after debts and funeral expenses paid to my three sons to the equally divided amongst them and each of them to take care of three Negro women I have set free, Thomas B. Burford, John B. Burford & Samuel P. B. Burford and lastly I appoint Thomas B. Burford, John B. Burford and Samuel P. B. Burford executors. Signed: William (X) Burford (Seal). Wit: Eli Conger, J.P., Gales Jinks, Willis Holifield. Recorded Nov. 22, 1841.

Pages 398-399: Estate of John A. Malone to Britton Buttrill, Exor. Paid 1840-1841 J. P. Williams, Jinks & Forrister, W. G. Atkinson, Bankston & Maddux, John McCord, C.C.O., A. H. Daughterty, S. T. Higgins, J. R. Willson, Tax 1841, E. & R. R. Graves, H. S. Lee, J. R. McCord, Britton Buttrill, John McClure. Credit: Cotton crop 1840. Rent on house & lot at Mineral Springs. Signed: Britton Buttrill, Exor. Recorded Nov. 22, 1841.

Pages 399-400: Inv. & Appr. of estate of Joseph Willson dec'd. by William H. Willson Exor. Listed goods and chattels. Also 1 Lot Land No. 248, 8th Dist. Henry County, Ga. Note on William Boiles. Appraised Nov. 2, 1841 by John Hendrick, George L. Thompson, Josiah Crain. Certified by Nathan C. Williamson, J.P., Nov. 23, 1841. Recorded 23rd Nov. 1841.

Page 400: Butts Court of Ordinary Nov. Adj. Term 1841. Ordered by Court that John Hendrick, William Allison, Henry Barnes, Jesse Jolly and Thomas McClure be appointed to divide slaves of William Redman, dec'd. into as many parts as there are distributees by lot or otherwise to them shall seem proper & to assign to each distributee or their guardian one of said shares. Signed: E. W. Lane, J.I.C., Thos. P. Atkinson, J.I.C., E. McDaniel, J.I.C. Recorded Nov. 15, 1841.

Pages 400-401: The following distribution made by lot (to wit). To John McMichael, guardian for Levi McMichael, husband of Mary C. McMichael formerly Mary C. Redman the following named (to wit) 3 Negroes (named) plus $210 paid to equalize shares; to James Carter guardian for Martha Redman 2 Negroes (named) plus $40 to equalize share; to James Carter guardian for William T. C. Redman 2 Negroes (named) plus $80 to equalize shares; to Mrs. Mary Redman one Negro man (named) plus $90 to equalize share. Signed: Dec. 9, 1841 by commissioners John Hendrix, William Allison, Henry Barnes, Thomas McClure, Jesse Jolly. Certified by W. G. McMichael, J.P. Recorded Dec. 14, 1841.

Pages 401-402: Sale of Estate of William H. Smith, dec'd. on Dec. 15, 1841. Goods and chattels sold to John Morris, William Tomlinson, Joseph Smith, Austin Cleaton, Hubbard Williams, A. H. Addcock, James Bentley, Richard Nolen, Wm. Payne, Simon Smith, Joseph Higgins, Henry Payne, Pollard Payne, R. M. Stewart, John Dawson, Thos. Bailey, J. C. Dunsieth, Lewis Bennett. Returned Dec. 31, 1841 by Elijah Smith, Exor. Recorded Jan. 5, 1842.

Page 402: Sale of Estate of Aaron Onail dec'd. One tract of land in Butts County, No. not recollected, sold Dec. 7, 1841 to William H. Wilson for $525.00. Edward W. Onail, Admr. Recorded Jan. 17, 1842.

Page 403: Return No. 3 Jan. Term 1842. Return of Charles Hammond guardian for William J. Hammond, minor. Balance on hand with interest for 1841. Paid Clerk for recording return. Balance on hand. Signed: Charles Hammond, guardian. Recorded Jan. 17, 1842.

Estate of Robert Grimmet in account with James H. Grimmet, Admr. from Jan. 1st to Dec. 31, 1841. Paid William Grimmett his distributive share of estate, Elizabeth Grimmet her share, James Stewart his share, George E. Hodge his share, Clerk of Court. Credit: Balance due estate per last return, Apr. 19, 1839, Cash on hand belonging to dec'd. at time of his death omitted in inventory and former return. Interest. Returned Jan. 1, 1842 by J. H. Grimmet, Admr. Recorded Jan. 17, 1842.

Page 404: Annual return of O. H. P. McClendon guardian for Jeremiah McClendon from Feb. 25, 1841 to Jan. 3, 1842. Vouchers paid Taxes for 1841, T. Williams, D. Kelsey, W. McClendon, O. H. P. McClendon, Bloodworth & Co., J. McCord. Credit by hire of Negroes for 1842. Signed: O. H. P. McClendon, guardian. Recorded Jan. 17, 1842.

Annual return of O. H. P. McClendon guardian for Jeremiah McClendon for hire of Negroes to O. H. P. McClendon, Seth K. Adams, A. F. Thompson, T. J. Ferguson. Recorded Jan. 17, 1842.

Pages 404-408: Return No. 11. Estate of William Redman, dec'd. on account with James Carter Admr. from Jan. 1 to 31st Dec. 1841. Transferred into hands of James Carter guardian the share assigned to Mary C. Redman, Martha Redman, William T. C. Redman by commissioners appointed to divide the estate. Paid Mary Redman, widow of dec'd. her share. Paid tax collector. Editors, C.C.O. Credit: By hire of slaves for 1841. Returned Jan. 10, 1842, James Carter, Admr. Recorded Jan. 18, 1842.

Annual return of estate of Mary C. Redman, minor for 1841. Paid C.C.O., tax collector, Lofton & Stodghill, John W. Williams, C. F. Newton & Co., Mary Redman, Goodman & Andrews, John McMichael guardian for Levi McMichael who married the ward. Credit: Wards distributive share assigned by commissioners, Cash received of William Cliett of Columbia Co., Ga. ($2787.44½), interest. Returned Jan. 1, 1842 by James Carter former guardian of Mary C. Redman now Mary C. McMichael. Recorded Jan. 19, 1842.

Annual return of Martha Redman, minor in account with James Carter guardian from date of letter of guardianship to Dec. 31, 1841. Paid C.C.O., tax collector, D. H. Moncrief, Mary Redman. Credit: Ward share of estate of William Redman, dec'd. Returned Jan. 10, 1842. Recorded Jan. 19, 1842.

Annual return of William T. C. Redman, minor in account with James Carter guardian from letter of guardianship to Dec. 31, 1841. Paid C.C.O., Mary Redman, tax collector. Credit: Ward's share in estate. Returned Jan. 10, 1842. Recorded Jan. 19, 1842.

Account of hiring of Negroes belonging to estate of William Redman, dec'd. To Mary Redman 8 Negroes. Returned Jan. 10, 1842 by James Carter, Admr. Recorded Jan. 20, 1842.

Page 408: Return No. 1 - James R. McCord guardian to Sarah Watts orphan of Jubal Watts dec'd. for year 1841. Credit: Amount received from C. N. Daniel, Exor. of estate of Jubal Watts, dec'd. in following notes and cash. Notes on Elijah Ballard endorsed by Jackson Bowles, Richard Asbury, Sr. and Richard V. Asbury. Paid W. C. Dawson, W. A. Florence, John W. McCord, James R. McCord, C.C.O. Signed: J. R. McCord, guardian. Recorded Jan. 20, 1842.

Pages 409-410: Return No. 1 of James R. McCord guardian to Jubal Watts orphan of Jubal Watts, dec'd. for year 1841. Credit: Amount received in cash and notes from C. N. Daniel Exor. of Jubal Watts, dec'd. Notes on Richard V. Asbury and Richard Asbury. Paid William C. Dawson, W. A. Florence, John W. McCord, James R. McCord, C.C.O. Signed: J. R. McCord, guardian. Recorded Jan. 20, 1842.

Ordered by the Court that John McMichael, Robert W. Harkness and Joseph Godard be appointed commissioners to divide estate of Jubal Watts dec'd. between Sarah & Jubal Watts orphans of said dec'd. Signed: G. Hendrick, J.I.C., Edmund McDaniel, J.I.C., E. W. Lane, J.I.C.

To the Court of Ordinary - We the commissioners appointed apportioned to Sarah Watts $1424.67 her share of said estate. To Jubal Watts $1457.39 his share. Signed by above commissioners.

Ga., Butts Co. - Sworn by commissioners that the division of said estate is just and true according to the showing to us by James R. McCord guardian of said orphans. Signed: Robert W. Harkness, John McMichael, Joseph Godard. Sworn Jan. 10, 1842 before G. Hendrick, J.I.C. Recorded Jan. 20, 1842.

Pages 410-412: Account of sale of property of the estate of William Burford, dec'd. Sold Dec. 3, 1840 to Thos. B. Burford, Bedford H. Darden, Samuel P. Burford, James Bledsoe, John Lofton, Jackson Grimmet, Alexander Craig, John W. McCord, Valentine Brock, Samuel Walker, E. M. Conger, Mark M. Powell, Lewis Moore, James Daniel, A. H. Daugherty, George W. Thomas, Ward Keeler, Griffin C. McMichael, George M. Head, Burwell Jinks, Wm. G. Bivens, Edward Onail, Amos A. Conger, John Duffey, John B. Burford, James H. Stark, Elizabeth Burford, Thomas Grimmet, John B. Burford, Jr. Signed: Thomas B. Burford, Exor. Recorded Jan. 21, 1842.

Pages 412-414: Georgia, Butts Co. John McCorc, C.C.O. authorized Robert Grier, Thomas Grimmet, Richard Shepard, A. S. Grier & Geo. Forister to appraise goods and chattels of William Stroud dec'd. as produced by Barsheba Stroud the Temporary Admx. Signed: John McCord, C.C.O., Jan. 17, 1842. List of appraisement of estate of William Stroud dec'd. this Jan. 28, 1842. 630 acres of land $2530.00, 12 Negroes, goods and chattels listed total value $7038.00. Signed by appraisors Richard Shepard, T. L. Grimmet, Algernon S. Grier. Certified by Larkin B. Mason, J.P. Recorded Feb. 1, 1842.

Page 414: Butts Co. Know that I Joel Baker attorney for Stephen H. Baker in right of his wife Edna A. Baker formerly Edna A. Matthews all of the State of S. C., Chesterfield District are held and firmly bound to Morton Bledsoe his heirs, executors, Admr. and Assigns in the sum of $200 for the payment of which I bond myself, my heirs, Exor., Admr., etc. sealed this Jan. 30, 1842. The condition of the above obligation is that the said Morton Bledsoe, Admr. on the estate of Morris Matthews late of said County has this day paid to Joel Baker as guardian for James M. Matthews a minor of said dec'd., and as attorney for Stephen M. Matthews a minor of said dec'd., and as attorney for Stephen H. Baker and his wife Edna A. Baker, the sum of $905.50 as the legacy due said minor and the said Edna A. from the estate of said dec'd. Now if Joel Baker refund and pay to Morton Bledsoe any sum that may be recovered from him as Admr. at any time together with costs and all expenses that may be incurred by said Morton for collecting these sums from said Baker if he is required to be at trouble and expense in demanding the same - then the above bond to be void. Signed: Joel Baker attorney for Stephen M. Baker and Edna A. Baker, guardian for James M. Matthew, minor of Morris Matthew, dec'd. Recorded Feb. 1, 1842.

Page 415: Yearly return by Eli Conger, guardian for following orphans and minors of A. G. Duke, dec'd. for year 1841. For orphans Martha Ann Duke, Mary Duke, Coatsworth Duke, Elizabeth Duke, William Duke, Aristotle Duke for each to J. R. McCord, Tucker and Compton, Harva S. Lee, Sarah Duke for board of said orphans and Commission for collecting $1200 for orphans, C.C.O. for recording bond and letter of guardianship for six children. Signed: Eli Conger, guardian. Recorded Mar. 8, 1842.

Page 416: Yearly return of George L. Thompson, Admr. of estate Green B. Reeves, dec'd. Paid Nancy A. Reeves, John McCord. Signed: March 5, 1842, George L. Thompson, Admr. Recorded Mar. 8, 1842.

Return No. 2 - Of the estate of John H. Thompson. Paid John H. Thompson, John McCord, C.C.O. Signed: John Goodman, guardian. Recorded Mar. 8, 1842.

Return No. 3 - Of Estate of Elmirey E. Thompson 1842. Cash paid ward Apr. 3, 1840, Obadiah Johnson, husband of above, John McCord, C.C.O.

Signed: John Goodman, guardian. Recorded Mar. 8, 1842.

Page 417: Return No. 4 on Estate of Daniel McClendon from Jan. 1, 1840 to Jan. 1, 1842. Paid Nancy McClendon, J. R. & J. W. McCord, Goodman & Andrews, Bailey & Hunter, cash paid ward by guardian. Signed: John Goodman, guardian. Recorded Mar. 8, 1842.

Return No. 2 of Josiah W. Barber, guardian for 1841 on estate of Richard Smith, orphan of Richard Smith, dec'd. Paid C.C.O. for recording return. Credit: Cash on hand. Amt. received from J. W. Wilkins. Signed: Josiah W. Barber. Recorded Mar. 9, 1842.

Annual return of estate of Martha Anderson, minor in account with Mary Anderson, guardian for 1841. Paid C.C.O. amount due ward. Credit: Interest. Returned Feb. 15, 1842 by Mary (X) Anderson, guardian. Recorded Mar. 9, 1842.

Page 418: Return of Morton Bledsoe, guardian to George M. T. Brockman, for 1840-1841. Paid Thos. R. Russell for board, clothing and tuition. M. Bledsoe for boarding and clothing a Negro girl. Credit: Hire of Negroes for 1840. Signed: Morton Bledsoe, guardian. Recorded Mar. 10, 1842.

Return for estate of George M. T. Brockman, minor for year 1840-1841. Hire of Negroes to James Bledsoe, Thos. R. Russell. Signed: Morton Bledsoe, guardian. Recorded Mar. 10, 1842.

Page 419: Yearly return of Jane Barkley for the minors of John Barkley, dec'd. for 1841. Paid W. A. Florence & H. G. Lee for tuition of John H. Barkley, my ward, Lofton & Stodghill, Tax Collector. Credit: For hire of Negroes to Jane Barkley, guardian. Signed: Jane Barkley, guardian. Recorded Mar. 10, 1842.

Received of Jane Barkley, guardian for my wife, formerly Jane A. Barkley a Negro woman and her child which is in full of my distributive share of the estate of John Barkley, dec'd. this July 17, 1841. John Robertson (Seal). Wit: S. R. Nutt, A. B. Bostwick, J.P. Recorded Mar. 10, 1842.

Page 420: Received of Jane Barkley, guardian for myself Elizabeth A. Barkley, a Negro girl and $100 in cash in full my distributive share of estate of John Barkley, dec'd. this March 4, 1842. Elizabeth A. (X) Barkley (Seal). Wit: Robert W. Harkness, W. G. McMichael, J.P. Recorded Mar. 10, 1842.

Georgia, Butts Co. Return of Henry Jester, Exor. of last will and testament of Levi Jester, dec'd. for year 1841 as follows: Received from William J. Foster for six Negroes and furniture, Abner Jester for seven Negroes, Benjamin Jester for seven Negroes, stock and furniture, Leonard Mason for one Negro, tax receipt. Returned Mar. 1, 1842 by Henry Jester, Exor. Recorded Mar. 10, 1842.

Page 421: Estate of Robert Andrews, dec'd. in account with John & Walter S. Andrews, Admrs. from Jan. 8, 1841 to Mar. 3, 1842. Paid Thomas Bagby (Printers), William J. Foster, D. J. Bailey, A. L. Robinson, Thomas W. Connel, John Andrews, S. K. McLin, Jarrell & Duffey, John McCord, Sarah Andrews, John B. Carmichael, William J. Woodward, William Andrews. Signed: John Andrews, Admr. Recorded Mar. 14, 1842.

Estate of Martha Andrews, minor of Robert Andrews, decd. in account with John Andrews, guardian to Mar. 3, 1842. Paid William A. Florence, tuition, Bailey & Hunter, G. W. Thomas, Goodman & Andrews, Jesse Loyall, J. R. McCord, Joshua Patrick, Sarah Andrews, R. P. Mayo, tax collector. Credit: Cash received by hire of Negroes. Recorded Mar. 14, 1842.

Page 422: Estate of Sarah Andrews, minor of Robert Andrews, dec'd. in account with John Andrews, guardian. Paid H. H. Farrer for tuition, Goodman & Andrews, Spencer & Mays, W. Jarrell, Jarrell & Duffey, R. P. Mayo tax collector. Credit: Cash received. Recorded Mar. 14, 1842.

Pages 422-425: Account of sale of personal property of Willis C.
Jenkins, dec'd. Dec. 1, 1841. Buyers: Asa Buttrill, Lewis Ethridge,
Henry Duke, Sr., R. McCollum, G. C. McMichael, S. S. Jenkins, Joel Byars,
J. Goodman, P. Jenkins, E. Jarrell, William Johnson, Wm. Thaxton, John
Cochran, Robert McMahan, J. Y. Morris, Jordan Morris, Thos. J. Sanders,
David S. Waller, Daniel Arp, Martha Jenkins, B. Still, Wm. F. Morris,
David Elder, Ward Thaxton, S. H. Sanders, H. Dillen, Robert Byars, Wiley
Edmundson, Wm. R. Simpson, F. Douglass, R. Mays, Russell Brooks, Wm. A.
Elder, Dr. Jenkins. Signed: Sterling S. Jenkins, Admr. Recorded Mar.
15, 1842. Examined and approved by us a committee of the Grand Jury
Mar. 23, 1842. Asa Buttrill and Lewis Moore.

Pages 425-426: Georgia, Butts Co. Will of I. William Stroud, of
said Co. being weak in body but sound mind and memory do make this my
last will and testament as follows: Item 1 - I bequeath to my beloved
wife Bathsheba Stroud during her life as widowhood tract of land whereon
I reside 202½ acres; also 300 acres adjoining also 101¼ acres all in
same settlement; also 13 Negroes together with all household furniture
and all stock. Item 2 - to Jesse Mercer husband of my daughter Emily
$5. Item 3 - To Jane Mercer daughter of Jesse and Emily Mercer at my
wife death or marriage the said slaves (4 named) horse and saddle and
$175. Item 4 - To daughter Matilda Mays 8 Negroes (named) and 637 3/4
acres whereon I now reside, stock also all other property belonging at
death or end of my wife widowhood, none of the estate to be removed out
of the county of Butts but to be controlled and managed by my executor
Alexander H. Daugherty and Bathsheba Stroud. A man named Abram to belong
to my wife during her life or widowhood then said slave to be set free
and Alexander Daugherty to be his guardian. Signed: William (X) Stroud
(Seal). Witnessed this Aug. 4, 1839 by George W. Thomas, John V. Berry,
Samuel R. Nutt. Recorded Mar. 30, 1842.

Page 427: Ga., Butts Co. Personally came before us Bradford H.
Darden and David M. Nutt acting J.I.C. for John V. Berry, George W.
Thomas and Samuel R. Nutt on oath said they upon request of William
Stroud they signed said will in presence of said William Stroud acknow-
ledged at the time that this was his last will and testament and believe
William Stroud was of sound mind. Sworn July 15, 1840 before B. H. Dar-
den, J.I.C., David M. Nutt, J.I.C. Recorded Mar. 30, 1842.

We, the Jury find in favor of will. Edmund McDaniel, Foreman.
Return of the sale of 50 acres of land belonging to Estate of William
Vickers, dec'd. It being part of Lot No. 48, 14th Dist. of originally
Monroe now Butts Co. sold 1st Tues. Dec. 1841 to Thomas P. Atkinson.
Signed: Creed T. Wise, Admr. Recorded Apr. 8, 1842.

Page 428: Yearly return on estate of William Vickers, dec'd. by
Creed T. Wise, Admr. 1840-1841. Cash paid A. B. Forsyth, Robert P.
Mayo, T.D., Witt C. Wise, Augustus Cargile for tuition of Elizabeth
Vickers and Howard Vickers, John McCord. 1840 cash rec'd. for hire of
Negroes from Witt C. Wise, Pollard Bickerstaff, Ichabod Hood for rent of
land. 1841 Hire of Negroes to Joseph Slaughter, Benjamin J. Johnson,
Samuel W. Andrews for rent of land. Signed: Creed T. Wise, Admr. Re-
corded May 6, 1842.

Return of Thomas Douglass and Francis Douglass, Exors. of estate of
William S. Douglass, dec'd. for 1841. Cash paid Abel L. Robinson, David
J. Bailey, James H. Stark, Robert Mayo, John McCord, Samuel Bellah, W. R.
Bankston, Wiley W. Gaithers, H. B. Hairston. Hire of Negro woman of
estate by Thomas Douglass. Signed: Thomas Douglass, Exor. Recorded 13th
May 1842.

Page 433: Return on estate of Robert W. Hunter dec'd. by Alexander
Hunter, Admr. for balance of year 1841 up to June 24, 1842. Cash paid
Britton Buttrill, Spencer & Mays, Robert Mays, James M. Fielder, P. M.
Compton, Margaret Hunter, S. H. Sanders, Henry Summerlin, John McCord
C.C.O., Thomas Bagly, R. P. Mayo, D. J. Bailey, Attorney. Rent of land
to D. J. Bailey. Signed by A. Hunter, Admr. Recorded July 15, 1842.

Sale of 311½ acres of land of Robert W. Hunter, dec'd. to John B.
Harkness, 115 acres to William Willingham at public outcry. Alexander

Hunter, Admr. Recorded July 15, 1842.

Yearly return on estate of James Screws up to 27th June 1842. Cash paid John McCord, C.C.O., Robert P. Mayo, T.C. by Beverly Evans, Exor. Recorded July 15, 1842.

Page 434: Estate of Harriet Ann Curry in account with Matthew Gaston guardian up to Dec. 31, 1841. Paid for clothing and boarding ward for 1841. C.C.O. Credit: Balance due ward and interest. Matthew Gaston, guardian. Recorded July 15, 1842.

Yearly return for Sarah E. Beavers, Harriet A. Beavers, and Eliza L. Beavers by Sterling T. Higgins, guardian for year 1840-1841. Paid John C. Rees D.C.C.O., John M. Daniel for pailing in grave of Silas M. Beavers, dec'd., W. A. Florence 1840 tuition for Sarah E. Beavers, D. H. Moncrief 1841 tuition for Sarah E. Beavers, D. H. Moncrief 1841 tuition for Harriet E. Beavers and Eliza L. Beavers. Retained for the boarding of Sarah E., Harriet A., and Eliza L. Beavers. Hire of Negroes 1840-1841. Signed by S. T. Higgins, guardian. Recorded July 15, 1842.

Page 435: Inv. & appr. of estate of Jesse Ball, dec'd. as produced by Thomas Lacy Admr. June 29, 1842. Slaves (4). Notes on James Brady and Samuel Wilkerson, Jas. H. Campbell and H. B. Mays, John Andrews, Dawson Heath and S. W. Price. D. S. Patterson & J. H. Stark, J. H. Stark and J. R. McCord and J. W. McCord. 152½ acres of land in Jasper Co., Ga. a part of Lot No. 118, 15th Dist. of originally Baldwin Co. not seen by us. F. G. Bledsoe, James H. Campbell, P. M. Compton, John Andrews, appraisors. Certified by G. Hendrick June 29, 1842. Recorded July 21, 1842.

Pages 435-438: Inv. & appr. of estate of Robert Humber dec'd. Negroes (9) Goods and chattels listed, 1 cotton gin. Notes on Monroe Railroad Bank, J. H. Davis, D. B. M. Moore, J. Hood, Hugh Goin, John L. Anderson, John Winn, W. W. Vaughan, W. J. Bickerstaff, John L. Cole. Certified by appraisors H. Williams, Lewis Bennett, William S. Smith, Robert (X) Thornton sworn and subscribed before Charles Bailey July 26, 1842. Recorded Aug. 1, 1842.

Page 438: Estate of Levi McMichael in account with John McMichael, guardian to Aug. 1842. Paid William Willingham for Negro woman and child, J. R. McCord, ward in person balance in full ($2106.90) 1841. Credit: Received of James Carter former guardian for Mary Redman. Interest realized, Returned Sept. 5, 1842 by John McMichael, guardian. Recorded Sept. 8, 1842.

Page 439-440: A list of appraisement of estate of Richardson Mayo, dec'd. this Sept. 16, 1842. Negroes (6), 202½ acres, Lot No. 32, 9th Dist. originally Henry, now Butts, 1/3 lot of land No. not known adjoining George W. Barber, Goods and chattels. Lot of land No. 259, 10th Dist. Appling Co. not visited by appraisors, notes on John Deavours, Enoch Powell and Jacob Henderson, Mary Cargile, Thomas J. Snaders, Hugh Wise. Certified on Sept. 16, 1842 by appraisors S. T. Higgins, Merideth Nelson, A. L. Robinson and W. G. McMichael, J.P. Recorded Sept. 24, 1842.

Page 441: Return for Rachel Gray, J. A. Gray and William Gray orphans of James Gray, dec'd. 1838 paid to Elizabeth Gray guardian, tuition for Rachel Gray (1838), Johnson A. Gray (1838), William & J. A. Gray (1839). Clothing furnished Rachael Gray (1838-1839), William Gray (1840-1841), Rachael Gray (1841), J. A. Gray (1840). Returned July 8, 1842 by Elizabeth Gray, guardian. Certified Aug. 10, 1842 by Turman Wallthall, J.I.C. Recorded Nov. 8, 1842.

Yearly return of Thomas Burford, Exor. of William Burford, dec'd. for 1842. Paid D. J. Bailey, Jas. H. Stark, Spencer & Mays, John Goodman, J. R. & J. W. McCord, J. P. Williams, William Jinks, P. M. Compton, J. R. Wilson, Bailey & Hunter. Signed: Thomas B. Burford, Exor. Recorded Nov. 8, 1842.

Page 442: Return No. 2 - 1841. Estate of John Tarpley, dec'd. to

131

W. A. Florence, Admr. Paid George Barber, James J. Tarpley, J. R. & J. W. McCord, B. H. Harper, Mary Tarpley, W. A. Florence, guardian, Clerk and Sheriff, Samuel R. McLin, R. P. Mayo for taxes, Stephen Bailey, John McCord, C.C.O. Signed: W. A. Florence, Admr. Recorded Nov. 9, 1842.

1841 - W. A. Florence, guardian for Joannah E. Tarpley, minor of John Tarpley, dec'd. To said minor legacy of said estate. Return No. 1 - Paid J. R. McCord, J. W. McCord, Mary Tarpley, Spencer & Mays. Signed: W. A. Florence, guardian. Recorded Nov. 9, 1842.

Page 443: 1841 - W. A. Florence, guardian for John Tarpley, minor of John Tarpley, dec'd. To said minor Legacy of said estate. Return No. 1 - Paid W. A. Florence, Thompson & Thomas, J. W. and J. R. McCord, Spencer & Mays, Mary Tarpley, William Irvins. Signed: W. A. Florence, guardian. Recorded Nov. 9, 1842.

1841 - W. A. Florence, guardian for Matthew Tarpley, minor of John Tarpley, dec'd. to said minor his legacy of said estate. Return No. 1 - Paid W. A. Florence, J. W. & J. R. McCord, Thomas & Thompson. Signed: W. A. Florence. Recorded Nov. 9, 1842.

Pages 443-444: 1841 - W. A. Florence, guardian for David T. Tarpley, minor of John Tarpley, dec'd. to said minor his legacy of said estate. Return No. 1 paid W. A. Florence, William Irvine, J. R. & J. W. McCord, Spencer & Mays taxes. Signed: W. A. Florence, guardian. Recorded Nov. 9, 1842.

Page 444: Inv. & appr. of property of estate of Samuel B. King, dec'd., lot of land, 40 acres No. 1039, 12th Dist., 1st Section Cherokee Co., Ga., not viewed. Certified by appraisors A. Hunter, Samuel P. Burford, Lewis Moore before John Greer, J.P. Recorded Nov. 12, 1842.

Return of estate of Isaiah Wise, dec'd. by Riley Wise, admr. Collected of Robert Mayfield, Riley Wise, Admr. Recorded Jan. 2. 1843.

Page 445: Appraisement of estate of Clifford Woodruff dec'd., 1 Negro man. Appraisors J. R. McCord, Robert Mays, John Goodman, A. L. Robinson certified before Edward Weaver, J.P. Recorded Jan. 11, 1842.

Georgia, Butts Co. Will of Young R. Norris - I Young R. Norris of state and county aforesaid do make publick and declare this my last will and testament. Item 1 - My debts paid. Item 2 - Give to my nephew James M. Norris $75 paid in three notes I hold against Willis Holyfield and a sorrel horse. Item 3 - Give to my beloved wife Martha Norris and son William David Norris jointly, balance of estate and when son becomes of age equally divided between them. Item 4 - Appoint Stephen W. Price, Exor. Affix seal Oct. 17, 1842. Young R. Norris (Seal) in presence of Simon H. Sanders, S. W. Price, David Berry.

Page 446: Jan. Term Court of Ordinary 1843. S. W. Price & S. H. Saunders swear they saw Young R. Norris sign will. Sworn before Edmund McDaniel, J.I.C., Turman Walthall, J.I.C., Thos. P. Atkinson, J.I.C. who ordered that will be admitted to record. Recorded Jan. 12, 1843.

Page 447: Annual return of Joel Wise dec'd. by Parham Lindsey, Admr. for 1841-1842. Paid James H. Stark, Joseph W. Slawter (Slaughter) part John Murry's wife Martha's legacy, William Johnson in right of wife Polly Wise formerly his distributive share. Charles Bailey, William Akin, A. L. Robinson. Thomas Bland, Barna Wise. Signed: Parham Lindsey, Admr. of Joel Wise dec'd. Recorded Jan. 13, 1843.

Page 448: Estate of Robert Grimmet in account with James H. Grimmet Admr. from Jan. 1, 1842 to present. Final Return - paid in full their share to Nathaniel May, H. Ramsey, Elizabeth Grimmet, George E. Hodge, Thomas L. Grimmet, James Stewart, A. J. Grimmet, guardian for Robert Grimmet, A. J. Grimmett, Mary Grimmet, William Grimmet. Retained balance of my share. Credit: Balance due estate as last return. Signed: J. H. Grammit, Admr.

State of Georgia, Troup County. On Dec. 17, 1842 James H. Grimmet

swore before Thomas Wyatt, J.P. in and for said County to be a true
return. Signed: J. H. Grimmit Admr. Recorded Jan. 13, 1843.

Return No. 4 - Jan. Term 1843 Return of Charles Hammond guardian
of William J. Hammond minor. Balance and interest for year 1842.
Charles Hammond, guardian. Recorded Jan. 14, 1843.

Page 449: Yearly return of Josiah W. Barber for 1842 for my ward
Richard Smith. Paid for board in 1842, remaining on hand amount. Josiah
W. Barber, guardian. Recorded Jan. 14, 1843.

Estate of Eli Knight to Calvery F. Knight guardian. 1841 and 1842
paid ward in person. Returned Oct. 8, 1842 C. F. Knight late guardian.

The State of Alabama, Talapoosa Co. In person came Calvary F.
Knight, this Dec. 27, 1842 and swore that above return is true. Signed:
C. F. Knight before William Henry Price, J.P. Recorded Jan. 16, 1843.

Page 450: Estate of Henry Lee dec'd. to Charles Wakefield guardian
for Lillis Lee 1842. To corn, coffee, medicine, 1 pair shoes for Negro
woman. C. Wakefield, guardian. Recorded Jan. 16, 1843.

Return of William F. Mapp Admr. of Allen McClendon dec'd. for 1841,
1842. Paid taxes 1841 and 1842, R. A. and D. Reed on note, J. R. Martin,
John McCord. Credit: Cash received on Purifoy note and Jesse Tolleson
note, F. S. Martin notes in Pike Superior Court who brought up an account
against estate admitted by court, received of J. R. Martin. Signed:
William F. Mapp Admr. Recorded Jan. 17, 1843.

Page 451: Return of William F. Mapp guardian of Joseph F. McClendon
for 1842. Paid J. F. McClendon. Recorded Jan. 17, 1843.

Received of William F. Mapp my guardian 13 Negroes they being my
distribution share of Negroes belonging to estate of Allen McClendon
dec'd. This Nov. 21, 1842. Signed: J. F. McClendon.

Pages 451-452: Georgia, Butts Co. Will of George K. Byars. I
George K. Byars of said state and county being of advanced age make this
my last will and testament hereby revoking and annulling all others made
by me. Item 1 - My body buried in decent and christian like manner.
Item 2 - Just debt paid. Item 3 - I give to my beloved wife Anna with
whom I have lived with forty years all property I now possess and my
sons Benjamin and Harrel N. and James M. Byars received an equal portion
with those who have already drawn property and paid to them as they become
of age. The above mentioned property to belong to wife Anna during her
natural life (to wit) on lot of land which I now live on also all household furniture, horses and mules, stock, farming utensils. I desire to
be equally divided among my children that may survive my beloved wife
Anna at her death. I appoint Joel B. and Richard G. Byars executors
this Dec. 30, 1842. Signed: George K. Byars (Seal) before Isaac Smith,
Geo. W. Byars, Cintha (X) McMahan, Robert (X) McMahan. Butts County
Court of Ordinary Jan. Term 1843. In open Court Jan. 23, 1843 the will
approved and ordered recorded. Recorded Jan. 26, 1843.

Page 453: Inv. and Appr. of estate of Micajah Ferrell dec'd., 1
lot of land 40 acres No. 1089, 12th Dist., 1st Section of formerly
Cherokee now Lumpkin Co. Sworn as a true appraisement of goods and
chattel of estate of Micajah Farrell by John Hendrick, John McMichael,
S. P. Burford, John Goodman, appraisors before W. G. McMichael, J.P. on
Dec. 20, 1842. Recorded Feb. 6, 1843.

Yearly return on estate of Robert W. Hunter dec'd. by Alexander
Hunter, Admr. from June 24, 1842 to Feb. 25, 1843. Paid Joel Crawford
guardian for Lydia Isabella Hunter and Sarah Jane Hunter minors, Lewis
Moore, R. P. Mayo for taxes, services rendered in traveling on business
for estate. Credit: Rec'd. in note from Robert Martin, 21 acres land
rented to S. Bailey. Returned by A. Hunter, Admr. Recorded Mar. 9, 1843.

Page 454: Annual Return No. 2, 1842. Estate of Martha Redman
minor in account with James Carter guardian for 1842. Paid C. F. Newton,

Caleb Jennings, tax collector, C.C.O., N. R. Trammel, Mary Redman, James R. McCord. Hire of Negroes for 1842. Returned Feb. 9, 1843, James Carter, guardian. Recorded Mar. 9, 1843.

Page 455: Account of hiring Negroes belonging to Martha Redman, William T. C. Redman orphans of William Redman dec'd. for year 1842. Recorded Mar. 9, 1843.

Annual Return No. 2 - Estate of William T. C. Redman minor in account with James Carter, guardian for 1842. Paid Henry Barnes, N. R. Trammel, Tax collector, Mary Redman, J. R. McCord. Hire of Negroes for 1842. Returned Feb. 9, 1843. James Carter, guardian. Recorded Mar. 11, 1843.

Page 456: Return No. 12 - 1842 Estate of William Redman dec'd. in account with James Carter Admr. Paid Boman and Perkins, C.C.O., tax collector, Mary Redman for maintaining Elizabeth Redman. Credit: Rec'd. of Mary Redman her part, ¼ for maintaining Elizabeth Redman, Levi Mc-Michael his part for the same purpose, James Carter guardian for William T. C. Redman for same purpose. James Carter for Martha Redman her part for same purpose. Returned Feb. 9, 1843. James Carter, Admr. Recorded Mar. 13, 1843.

Page 457: Return of Thomas Douglass Exor. of estate of William S. Douglass dec'd. for 1841. Paid out for Eugenius L. Douglass one of the minors to John McCord, W. A. Florence, P. M. Compton, board for 1842. Paid W. L. Crawford, Jesse B. Ray, Simeon D. McClendon, Sarah Ann Shurby, J. B. Smith, board, hire of Negroes for 1843. Recorded Mar. 13, 1843.

Return of Thomas Douglass and Francis Douglass Exors. of estate of William S. Douglass dec'd. for year 1841. Cash paid for Mercelus Douglass minor of William S. Douglass to W. A. Florence tuition, John McCord, board to Thomas Douglass, Tucker and Compton. Thomas Douglass, Exor. Recorded Mar. 14, 1843.

Page 458: Marcelus Douglass expenses for 1842. Paid William L. Crawford, Simeon McClendon, Jesse B. Ray, Sarah Ann Shurby, board. Thomas Douglas, Exor. Recorded Mar. 14, 1843.

Return for Narcissa Douglass minor of William S. Douglass. Paid Tucker and Compton, John McCord, W. A. Florence for tuition, board to Thomas Douglass. Signed: Thomas Douglass, Exor. Recorded Mar. 14, 1843.

Return No. 5 - Estate of William M. Williams to Nathan H. Williams guardian for 1840. Balance due ward with interest. N. H. Williams, guardian. Recorded Mar. 15, 1843.

Page 459: Annual return on estate of Martha Anderson minor in account with Mary Anderson, guardian for 1842. Paid taxes for ward, Isham Anderson, Hungerford & Co., Spencer & Mays. Returned Feb. 3, 1843 by Mary (X) Anderson, guardian. Recorded Mar. 15, 1843.

Annual return of O. H. P. McClendon guardian for Jeremiah P. McClendon for 1842. Paid L. Goddard, Tucker and Compton, C. F. Newton and Co., Rebecca McClendon, J. F. McClendon, Daniel Kelsey, 1842 taxes, Daniel Sanford, John McCord. Signed: O. H. P. McClendor guardian for Jeremiah P. McClendon for hire of Negroes to Tilman Lewis, A. F. Thompson, J. Mason, O. H. P. McClendon. Recorded Mar. 15, 1843.

Page 460: No. 2 yearly return of James R. McCord guardian of Sarah Watts and Jubal Watts minors for 1842. Paid L. Robinson, taxes 1842, Caleb Jennings, J. R. & J. W. McCord, C.C.O. of Greene Co., Ga. Signed: J. R. McCord, guardian. Recorded Mar. 16, 1843.

Page 461: Return No. 1 - Yearly return of John Goodman and James R. McCord, Admrs. on estate of Richardson Mayo dec'd. Credit: Sale of cotton in Macon, order on T. J. Sanders, bill on Mary Cargile, paid J. R. McCord note, C.C.O. of Butts Co., Margaret Mayo, John M. Mayo, J. W. Mc-Cord. Recorded Mar. 16, 1843.

Georgia, Butts Co. - Rec'd. of Morton Bledsoe Admr. of estate of
Morris Matthews dec'd. in full due Edna A. Baker late wife of said deceased and James M. Matthews minor of said dec'd. his part and portion
due the said Edna A. Baker formerly wife of said dec'd. and her husband
in right of his wife Stephen H. Baker this Jan. 29, 1842. Signed: Joel
Baker guardian for James M. Matthews minor of Morris Matthews dec'd. and
attorney in part for Stephen Baker in right of his wife Edna A. Baker
late wife of Morris Matthews, dec'd. of said Co. Recorded Mar. 16, 1843.

Pages 462-464: Inv. & Appr. of goods and chattel of George R.
Byars dec'd. 8 Negroes, goods and chattel. Notes on Thos. S. Rice, A.
Bomer, Joel B. and Richard G. Byars, Exor. Certified by William Byars,
Eli Buckner, Alfred McWatkins, appraisors and Thos. P. Saunders, J.P.
Recorded Mar. 27, 1843.

Pages 464-466: Will of Elizabeth C. Dennis. Georgia, Butts County.
I, Elizabeth C. Dennis weak in body but sound mind wishing to dispose of
my worldly affairs in the following way: (to wit) 1st - My body buried in
a Christian manner. Item 1 - All just debts paid by executor. Item 2 -
I give to my four sisters Martha Norris, Julia M. Price, Mary Bledsoe,
Harriet Harkness and my nephew John J. D. Berry three Negroes (named)
and stock. Three Negroes, one each to go in possession of sisters Martha, Julia and Mary and remain until a division on fair and equitable
terms. My stock as above named equally divided amongst them. My four
sisters to get my bed clothing except such things hereafter named. Also
I give my sisters my kitchen things to be equally divided also all my
affairs about my "dary" to go to my sisters equally including knives,
forks, spoons and except eleven silver spoons. I also give my sisters
all my corn, fodder, oats, cotton, bacon and all things about my Smoke-
house, also my geese, ducks and c. Item 3 - I give my sister Mary
Bledsoe my trunk, and all wearing apparel including my gold ring, saddle,
bridle. Item 4 - I give to my sister Harriet Harkness my carpet. Item
5 - I desire my executor to make up to my three other sisters the value
of carpet to make them equal with sister Harriet. Item 6 - I give my
nephew John J. D. Berry $100 to make him equal with four sisters. Item
7 - I give to my two nieces and nephew Mary Ann M. Bledsoe next bed
and furniture, to Martha E. Price next bed and furniture, to John J. D.
Berry a pine bed and furniture. Item 8 - I give my beloved brother John
V. Berry and my dear old father all the demands I have against Brother
John to be equally divided. Item 9 - I give Thomas J. Townsend tract of
land I live on also 200 acres land joining John Greer, 2 mules and 2
horses also plows, hoes and waggon, also my Beaureau, large folding
table, desk and book case and all my sitting chairs and clock, three bed
and furniture, two Negroes Rachael and Clark provided Thomas J. pays
Dennis L. Townsend $500. If Thomas J. refuses to pay $500 to Dennis L.
then Negroes go to Dennis L. Item 10 - I give to John Dennis the son
of Isaac Dennis my gold watch and chain. Item 11 - I give to William
Armstrong, John Armstrong, James Armstrong, and also Sarah and Nancy
sisters of the above Armstrong, who is married and I do not know their
husbands names and their heirs, Negroes Sarah, Eli, and Leroy, Sarah
and Leroy to be sold in Butts County and money divided equally. Also my
carriage and harness including money notes and whole residue of my estate
except things as hereafter excepted to be equally divided amongst them
and heirs. Item 12 - I give to John Greer, Cagey and notes I have on
John Greer and David Greer with understanding that Greer is to see to the
support of my old Negro woman Cagey during her life time. Also allow
John Greer to retain in his hand $1000 to be used in settling up my es-
tate and maintaining my old Negro. If any of $1000 left after expenses
paid them John Greer is to divide equally among Armstrong Family. Item
13 - I give Nancy L. Greer my Loom and everything pertaining to it. I
Charge John Greer as sole executor and in the event of failure of Greer
I charge Britton Buttrill with execution. Declared my last will and
testament. Signed: E. C. Dennis (Seal). Test: A. L. Robinson, S. H.
Saunders, Sarah Hudson.

I certify that foregoing will was wrote in the day and signed by
testator in presence of the witnesses and admitted to be dated at the
time of signing. 26th day of April 1843 Wednesday. I also certify that
I wrote the will and am one of the witnesses. A. L. Robinson.

135

Butts Court of Ordinary May Term 1843. The last will and testament of Elizabeth C. Dennis was exhibited for probate. Ordered to be recorded and letter testament are issued to John Greer the exor. Ordered warrant of appraisement issued to Lewis Moore, James W. Harkness, John S. Irby, Asa Buttrill and William G. McMichael. Signed by J.I.C. Turman Walthall, G. Hendrick, S. H. Saunders, Thos. P. Atkinson.

Page 467: John Greer swears in open court May 8, 1843 that he will execute will and make inventory. Recorded May 11, 1843.

Pages 467-470: Georgia, Butts Co. Inventory of good and chattel, land and tenements of Y. R. Norris Dec'd. appraised on Jan. 18, 1843. Listed goods and chattel and notes made payable to Y. R. Norris signed by S. B. Milner and Enoch Jarrel, T. & C. D. Quenn, William Thaxton, A. L. Robinson, C. Hamil, Bradford Carter, Matthew Gaston and William Curry, Thos. M. Harkness, J. F. Boyd and Isaac Low, James Boughan, Willis Holyfield, Jesse Boles and Y. G. Malone, S. W. Price. Accounts on John Tillery. Collection of notes on Thos. Beardin and Wm. F. Mapp and John H. Moore. Notes on James Morris, David Berry. Certified by appraisors; James Brady, David Greer, J. R. McMahan and Samuel Bellah, J.P. on Jan. 18, 1843. Recorded May 11, 1843.

Pages 470-472: Annual return on estate of James Wooten to John Jones, Admr. from Dec. 31, 1840 to Dec. 31, 1842. Paid printer for advertising and distributed out of sale of land to John Jones, guardian for James Wooten, Addison L. Wooten, Seaborn Wooten, Simeon Wooten. Retained to self in right of my wife of sale, James Wooten. Distributed to John Jones guardian for James Wooten, A. L. Wooten, Seaborn Wooten, Simeon Wooten. Returned by John Jones, Admr. Apr. 5, 1843. Recorded May 13, 1843.

Page 472: Ordered by court that Willis Jarrel, Eli Conger, John McMichael, John Hendrick and John W. McCord be appointed commissioners to make a final distribution of the estate of Robert Andrews remaining in hands of Admrs. Signed: Turman J.I.C., S. H. Saunders, J.I.C., Thos. P. Atkinson, J.I.C., G. Hendrick, J.I.C.

Georgia, Butts Co. - We do swear to abide by order of court. Signed: May 17th, 1843 by John Andrews, W. G. Andrews, T. H. Connel, John B. Carmichael, William J. Woodward. Sworn before above commissioners.

Page 473: The undersigned commissioners met and after a careful examination of remaining amount in hands of the Admr. of said estate report they found the sum of $87.03 1/8 subject to distribution after deducting a bill of $20 on Chatahoochee Railroad and Banking Co. which amount is made up of following items: a horse, rent on 12½ acres rented by Mrs. Sarah Andrews which after paying bills divided among distributees. Given to each $9.67; to Mrs. Sarah Andrews, J. B. Carmichael, Thomas H. Connell, W. J. Woodward, Martha Andrews, William Andrews, Miss Sarah Andrews, John Andrews, Walter S. Andrews. Given under our hand May 17, 1843. Signed: John Hendrick, W. Jarrell, John McMichael, Eli Conger, J. W. McCord, Arbitrators. Recorded May 18, 1843.

Return No. 8 - Estate of Sterling Camp in account with William Jarrell Admr. for 1842. Balance due estate. Returned Apr. 18, 1843 by William Jarrell Admr. Recorded May 19, 1843.

Page 474: Return No. 5 - Estate of Nathan F. Camp account with William Jarrell guardian for 1842. Paid J. C. Garrett a witness in case of William Jarrell guardian for N. F. Camp vs. D. J. Bailey and others, Thos. P. Atkinson a witness in case, Johnson Jones and Co., Spencer & Mays, Hungerford & Co., Willis Jarrell for tutition, Sarah Andrews for boarding ward. Signed: William Jarrell, guardian. Recorded May 19, 1843.

Page 475: Return No. 5 - Estate of James Camp with William Jarrell guardian for 1842. Paid for necessaries, Willis Jarrell tuition; Sarah Andrews for boarding ward. Returned by William Jarrell guardian Apr. 18, 1843. Recorded May 19, 1843.

Annual return of Creed T. Wise, Admr. of estate of William Vickers, dec'd. Hire of Negroes in 1842 to Creed T. Wise, F. M. Wise, B. Johnson. Taxes, Joseph H. Fielder for tuition. Signed: Creed T. Wise. Recorded May 20, 1843.

Page 476: Yearly return for ward Cornelius McCune by William McCune, guardian. Paid for necessaries, Robert Mays, S. H. Saunders, Georgia W. Thomas; taxes, John McCord. Hire of Negro boy to C. Slaton, woman and two children to Mary Anderson. Recorded May 20, 1843.

Received of William A. McCune, Admr. of Micajah F. McCune dec'd. $3022.10 the distributive share of Nancy McCune of said estate in part this June 2, 1840. Signed: Cornelius Atkinson. Recorded May 20, 1843.

Received of William McCune, Admr. of Micajah F. McCune dec'd. four Negroes, goods (named) value at $2727.75. Paid $294.35 Cornelius Atkinson for her daughter Nancy McCune before my marriage for which said amount was for her benefit during widowhood, making in all paid by Admr. $3022.10 to Cornelius Atkinson dated June 2, 1840. The same being distributive share of my wife Nancy McCune in part of said estate to this date. Signed: Robert Mays. Recorded May 20, 1843.

Page 477: Estate of Harriet Ann Curry in account with Matthew Gaston guardian up to Dec. 31, 1842. Paid for boarding and clothing. Recorded May 25, 1843.

Pages 477-478: Yearly return for my wards the orphans of A. G. Duke dec'd. for year 1842. Eli Conger, guardian. Paid for Martha Ann Duke for necessaries, taxes (part) Sarah Duke for board. Paid for Mary Duke orphan necessaries; H. S. Lee for tuition, her part on taxes; Sarah Duke for board. Paid for Coatsworth Duke orphan for necessaries, part on taxes. Sarah Duke for board. Paid for Elizabeth Duke orphan; H. S. Lee for tuition, part on taxes, Sarah Duke for board. Paid for William Duke orphan, necessaries, taxes, Sarah Duke for board. Paid Aristotle Duke orphan necessaries, taxes; Sarah Duke for board. Paid lawyer fee, postage on letters to Wilkes Co., cash paid V. Brock for going to Wilkes Co. for money to 6 days service man and horse. Signed: Eli Conger, guardian. Recorded May 25, 1843.

Page 479: Return to be added to Inventory of the Appraisement of estate of Clifford Woodruff, Jr., dec'd. not viewed by appraisors. One note on hand on Benjamin Woodruff for $125 bearing interest from Dec. 25, 1842 to Feb. 1843. Samuel Bellah, Admr. Recorded June 21, 1843.

You, Asa Buttreill, Lewis Moore, John S. Irby and James W. Harkness do swear that you will make a true appraisement of all goods and chattels of Elizabeth C. Dennis dec'd. and return same certified unto the said John Greer, Exor. Signed by above appraisors and sworn on May 9, 1843 before W. G. McMichael, J.P.

Pages 479-482: A list of appr. of estate of Elizabeth C. Dennis dec'd. taken May 9, 1843. Listed 300 acres land in Butts and Henry Counties, 9 Negroes, goods and chattel listed. Notes on J. A. Callis, Thos. M. Harkness, John Andrews, John and Isaac Dennis, S. W. Price, John V. Berry, Samuel Walker & J. P. Williams, David Greer, John Greer and A. L. Robinson, S. W. Price, James M. Bledsoe, E. W. and J. Dennis, A. A. Conger, E. Conger, Charles Bailey and Stephen Bailey, S. H. Saunders and T. G. Bledsoe, Mortgages on James Brady, Young G. Malone. Money found in hand of deceased at her death in specia (in Central Bank Bill, Chattachochy Rail Road and Banking Co., old Macon Bank bills), cash rec'd. from sale of cotton. Account on John Goodman. Certified by appraisors Asa Buttrill, James W. Harkness, Lewis Moore, John S. Irby on May 9, 1843. Recorded July 14, 1843.

Page 483: Butts County of Ordinary Nov. Term 1843, ordered that Jason Greer, Cornelius Atkinson, Charles Bailey, Parham Lindsey and Richard Barlow are hereby appointed commissioners to divide the Negroes belonging to estate of Willia C. Jenkins dec'd. into as many shares as there are distributees. Signed: G. Hendrick, J.I.C., Edmund McDaniel, J.I.C., E. W. Lane, J.I.C.

137

Ga., Butts Co. Certified Nov. 7, 1842 by John McCord, C.C.O. that above is a true extract from minutes of said court.

Ga., Butts Co. By virtue of an order from Inferior Court of said County directed us to make distribution of estate of late Willis C. Jenkins dec'd. among distributees of said estate. We ascertain that there were five distributees (to wit) Penelope Jenkins, widow, John T. Jenkins, William F. Jenkins, Simeon C. Jenkins, Willia C. Jenkins, sons and minor children of said Willis C. Jenkins dec'd. The shares were No. 1-5 and assigned to the distributees in following manner (to wit) the names of distributees were written on a piece of paper and placed in a hat, the numbers were written on a piece of paper and put into another hat, the hats were both well shaken, a name and number was then drawn from each hat as follows: No. 1 - Simeon C. Jenkins drew three negroes and a child (named). No. 2 - Willis C. Jenkins, 3 Negroes and a child (named). No. 3 - Penelope Jenkins, widow, 3 Negroes (named). No. 4 - John T. Jenkins 3 Negroes (named). No. 5 - William F. Jenkins 3 Negroes (named). No. 1 and No. 4 - pays No. 2 and No. 3 $19.00 each. No. 1 & No. 4 pays No. 5 $24.00. Signed: Nov. 24, 1842 by Parham Lindsey, Richard Barlow, Charles Bailey, commissioners. Recorded July 14, 1843.

Page 484: Annual return of Morton Bledsoe guardian to George M. T. Brockman for 1842. Hire of Negroes to James M. Bledsoe, Morton Bledsoe, Thos. R. Russell. Paid Thos. R. Russell for boarding and clothing George M. T. Brockman. Morton Bledsoe, guardian. Recorded July 15, 1843.

Closing return of Almiria E. Thompson, now Almiria E. Johnson. Paid Obadiah Johnson. John Goodman, guardian. Recorded July 15, 1843.

Return No. 5 of Daniel McLendon 1843. Paid Nancy McClendon, C. F. Newton, Goodman & Andrews, J. R. and J. W. McCord. John Goodman, guardian. Recorded July 18, 1843.

Page 485: Return of Emanuel Smith to the C.C.O. of Butts County on estate of John N. Smith dec'd. July 3, 1843. Paid N. Smith, John McCord, David J. Bailey, J. W. Williams, John Lofton, Bartlett & Willingham; taxes Jesse Laden. Emanuel G. Smith, Admr. Recorded July 18, 1843.

Annual return of executors on estate of John A. Malone dec'd. 1842-1843. Paid Lofton & Stodghill, Lewis Moore, Spencer & Mays, Tucker & Compton, Britton Buttrill, Henry S. Lee, Goodman & Andrews note; Bailey & Andrews note. By Thomas B. Burford one of executors. Recorded July 18, 1843.

Pages 486-487: Butts Co., Ga. - The petition of the undersigned shewth that they are joint owners of following slaves (4 named) and received by petitioners under will of Elizabeth C. Dennis, late of said county and are on hand undivided and that each petitioner may have and enjoy his or her part of slaves. Petition commissioners to act under oath prescribed by law. James Berry by his guardian, David Berry, Martha Norris, James Bledsoe, Thomas B. Harkness, S. W. Price.

Butts Court of Ordinary July Term 1843 - On hearing petition ordered that Lewis Moore, W. G. McMichael, John S. Irby, James W. Harkness, Asa Buttrill are appointed commissioners to divide said slaves among petitioners according to law. G. Hendrick, J.I.C., Edmund McDaniel, J.I.C., S. H. Saunders, J.I.C.

Georgia, Butts Co. - Commissioners assigned slaves as noted in will. Petitioners consented to division and settled in full with each other. July 18, 1843. Signed by petitioners. Recorded July 18, 1843.

Pages 487-488: Georgia, Butts Co. - Will of John Edison. I, John Edison being of sound mind make this my last will and testament. Item 1 - My body buried in Christian manner. Item 2 - Just debts paid. Item 3 - To my beloved wife Mary Edison with whom I have lived 22 years all real and personal estate for use of supporting and educating my children, with all that is appertaining to the land which is joining to Samuel P. Burford and others whereon I now live. Item 4 - When youngest

daughter Frances Maries or arrive to age 21 that equal division of all
my estate take place and my beloved wife Mary, my sons William T. Edison
and James Edison, my daughters Harriet, Anna, Sarah A., Elizabeth,
Nancy, Mary and Frances to receive each an equal share of my estate.
Item 5 - Constitute my friend William Curry and Matthew Gaston executors
of my last will and testament this April 20, 1843. John (X) Edison
(Seal). In presence of John McMichael, Wylie Ferrell, Morton Bledsoe,
W. G. McMichael, J.P.

Butts Court of Ordinary July Term 1843 - John McMichael, Wylie
Ferrell, W. G. McMichael came and swore in open court July 11, 1843 that
they saw John Edison sign will. Will having been proven by three witnesses and oath of executors. Same be admitted to record G. Hendrick,
J.I.C., Edmund McDaniel, J.I.C., S. H. Saunders, J.I.C. Recorded July
18, 1843.

Page 489: Georgia, Butts Co. - Will of Nancy McClendon. I, Nancy
McClendon being sick in body but sound mind make this my last will and
testament. I leave the whole of my estate to my son Daniel McClendon
to be vested in and managed by John Goodman his guardian for use of
supporting said Daniel as long as he shall live and at death of Daniel
after paying all debts and my funeral expenses, if any left to be divided
equally among all my children, share and share alike. I appoint John
Goodman guardian of said Daniel McClendon and executor of this my will.
Signed: Nancy (X) McClendon June 1, 1843 in presence of A. L. Robinson,
J. H. Stark, John Hendrick, John McCord.

Butts Court of Ordinary July Term 1843 - James H. Stark, John Mc-
Cord and Abel L. Robinson came and swore it a true will. Will proven
and ordered recorded by Edmund McDaniel, J.I.C., S. H. Saunders, J.I.C.,
G. Hendrick, J.I.C. July 11, 1843. Recorded July 19, 1843.

Page 490: List of appraisement of estate of Nancy McClendon, dec'd.
Listed goods and chattel and 2 Negroes. Certified by appraisors J. R.
McCord, A. L. Robinson, Russell (X) Brooks and G. H. Hendrick, J.P.
July 25, 1843. Recorded July 28, 1843.

Page 491: Inv. of property of John Edison, dec'd. made July 25,
1843. Goods and chattel listed. 226 3/4 acres land. Certified July
25, 1843 by Henry Barron, James A. McCune, S. T. Burford appraisors as
goods and chattels produced by Matthew Gaston and William Curry executors
and W. G. McMichael, J.P. Recorded July 28, 1843.

Pages 492-493: Sale bill of property of estate of Elizabeth C.
Dennis, dec'd. July 20, 1843. Buyers: Thomas Townsend, Stephen Bailey,
John Goodman, John Duffey, Asa Buttrill, John B. Harkness, Britton
Buttrill, John S. Irby, Thomas W. Harkness, John Andrews, Lewis Moore,
Robert W. Harkness, John Greer, James M. Bledsoe, John Greer, Executor.
Recorded Aug. 29, 1843.

Page 493: Annual return William F. Mapp, Admr. of Allen McClendon
dec'd. for 1842. Paid Joshua Hill, James H. Stark. Credit: Received of
Arthur Hamilton, Andrew Tenant, William Hardy. William F. Mapp, Admr.
Recorded Sept. 6, 1843.

Pages 494-495: Dec. 31, 1842 - W. A. Florence guardian of John Tarpley minor of John Tarpley, dec'd. To said minor his legacy. Return No.
2 - To W. A. Florence guardian of said minor. Recorded Sept. 6, 1843.

Dec. 31, 1842 - W. A. Florence guardian for Matthew Tarpley, minor
of John Tarpley, dec'd. To minor his legacy. Return No. 2 - To W. A.
Florence for guardian of said minor. Recorded Sept. 6, 1843.

Dec. 31, 1843 - Return No. 2 - W. A. Florence for Joannah E. Tapley,
minor of John Tarpley dec'd. To said minor her legacy to W. A. Florence
guardian for said minor. Recorded Sept. 6, 1843.

Page 496: Aug. 5, 1843 - List of sale of property sold by Thos. P.
and Washington G. Atkinson, Exors. of estate of Arthur C. Atkinson dec'd.
in accordance with will of said dec'd. of all property the wife of said

139

Arthur C. Atkinson died in possession of and also money on hand of the said Elizabeth Atkinson dec'd. Buyers: W. G. Atkinson, Thos. P. Atkinson, J. C. Garrett, Samuel Hancock. Signed: Thomas P. Atkinson and Washington G. Atkinson, Exors. Recorded Oct. 10, 1843.

Page 496: Return of Robert Mays, Admr. of estate of Peter McFarlin, dec'd. from April 29, 1842 to Nov. 1, 1843. Paid F. Douglass, J. R. & J. W. McCord, S. W. Price, S. Rose and Co., Nat Waller, John McCord. Robert Mays, Admr. Recorded Nov. 24, 1843.

Page 497: Return of estate (no name given) - Amount money expended and paid out by Admr. since last return to Court of Ordinary. Paid: H. Dillon, R. Coleman, A. F. Thompson, M. Bartlett, S. Rose & Co., J. W. and W. A. Jones, C. Campbell, Craft & Lewis, John C. Girtman, Grive & Orme, B. W. Bracewell, J. S. Anderson, J. Higgins, Spencer & Mays, G. W. Thomas, W. H. Bullock, J. W. Williams, Georgia Constitutionallist Office, J. Caruthers, J. G. Jewell & Co., Rawls King & Co., E. J. Preston, J. McCord, S. Bailey, D. J. Bailey, E. A. Matthews, M. Bledsoe for 41 days riding to various places in state at $3.00 per day.

Jan. 29, 1842 - Paid Joel Baker guardian for James M. Matthews, minor of Morris Matthews dec'd. and attorney for Steven Baker in right of his wife Edna A. Baker, late wife of Morris Matthew dec'd. Paid Michael Johnson, Morton Bledsoe, Admr. Recorded Nov. 24, 1843.

Page 498: Received by Admr. since last return $125 from Joseph Carruthers Dec. 18, 1841 for lot of land in 21st Dist. of County of Pulaski containing 202½ acres known in plan as Lot No. 393. $19.37½ from William Naiper. Robert Mays, Admr. Recorded Nov. 24, 1843.

Estate of James L. Compton dec'd. to P. M. Compton, Feb. 26, 1841 to Apr. 25, 1842. Paid A. B. Forsyth, J. R. Brown, Jacob Martin, John N. Mangham, John McCord, F. J. Childers, J. Andrews, 1843 taxes; 1842 taxes, James A. and F. S. Welch, expenses to Gilmer Co. and back to sell lot of land. Credit: By sale of land in Gilmer Co., Ga. $7.00. P. M. Compton, Admr. Recorded Nov. 24, 1843.

Return of sale of one lot of land belonging to estate of James L. Compton dec'd. lying in Gilmer County. Lot No. 31, 11th Dist., Section 2 sold first Tues. in July 1843. Bought by John L. Reid for $7.00. P. M. Compton, Admr. Recorded Nov. 24, 1843.

Pages 498-499: Georgia, Butts County - Will of Nelson Meridith. I, Nelson Meridith of county and state aforesaid being of low health but sound mind do make this my last will and testament in the following manner. 1st - I give to my beloved wife Mahala Meridith all land whereon I now live in said county together with 3 Negroes (named) all (goods and chattel named) during her life or widowhood. At her death or entermarriage all above property sold and equally divided between all my children (viz) William H. Meridith, Nancy Louiza M. Meridith, Elizabeth M. Meridith. 2nd - I appoint my wife Mahala Meridith and my son James A. Meridith executors of my will. Signed this Oct. 19, 1843. Nelson Meridith (Seal) in presence of William Gregory, William A. McCune, Alexander Sanders. Recorded Nov. 24, 1843.

Georgia, Butts Co. - Adjourned Court of Ordinary Nov. Term 1843. Will proven in court on oath of William Gregory, William A. McCune and Alexander Sanders. Ordered recorded this Nov. 20, 1843 by Turman Walthall, J.I.C., Edmund McDaniel, J.I.C., Thos. P. Atkinson, J.I.C.

Pages 500-502: Georgia, Henry Co. - Will of John S. Ingram. I, John S. Ingram being weak in body but sound mind and memory do make this my last will and testament in form following: 1st - My body buried in plain and decent manner. Item 2nd - I desire after making of present crop my plantation and following slaves (2 named) be sold and just debts and funeral expenses paid and slaves as best can be spared hired out for next year. The surplus fund remaining my executors purchase a suitable residence and plantation for support of my wife and children. Item 3rd - I bequeath to my wife's oldest son Jefferson Warlick when of age $50. Item 4th - I bequeath whole residue of estate to be managed and worked

for use and support of beloved wife Nancy Ingram and my children, William
Burwel Ingram, John Spiers Ingram, Nancy Elizabeth Ingram, James Madi-
son Ingram. Item 5th - In event my wife marries again, I desire an
equal division of estate between wife and children. Lastly appoint
Nancy Ingram, John Greer and James H. Stark, executors and executrix.
Signed: John S. Ingram (Seal) June 28, 1843 in presence of James King,
Alfred J. Grimmet, Alfred King. Recorded Nov. 25, 1843.

Will - proven in Henry Co., Ga. in open court and inventory and
appraisement made. James H. Callaway, J.I.C. Sept. 4, 1843. Verified
Sept. 5, 1843 by John H. Low, C.C.O., Henry Co., Ga. Recorded in Butts
County, Ga. Nov. 25, 1843 by John McCord, C.C.O.

Page 502: List of property sold Sept. 12, 1843 of John Edison
dec'd. Buyers: Charles Wakefield, John McMichael, Griffin C. McMichael,
A. A. Wadkins, Asa Bruttrill, Jeremiah Far, John Harkness, Edward Onail,
James A. McCune, Washington Atkinson, William Curry, Exor. Recorded Nov.
27, 1843.

Ga., Meriweather County - Received of N. H. Williams $659.58 in
full legacy bequeathed Nathan Williams late of Butts Co. dec'd. whereas
his legal executors and N. H. Williams were my legal guardian. Signed:
W. M. Williams Sept. 13, 1843. Wit: Bosdell G. Potter. Recorded Nov.
28, 1843.

Pages 503-505: List of sale and hiring of slaves of the estate of
Richardson Mayo dec'd. sold Nov. 2, 1842. Purchasers: Lucy Mayo, John
Mayo, Vincent T. Thompson, Elisha Mayfield, John McCord, G. W. Barber,
Wm. Irvine, C. Billings, Jacob T. Mayo, Margaret Mayo, Dawson McKleroy,
David Higgins, J. M. Thurman, John W. Hill, E. J. Preston, Spencer &
Mays, John Saunders, Griffin C. McMichael, Joseph Higgins, Wm. A. Elder,
S. H. Saunders, Wm. Harris, Thomas Moore, G. W. Thomas, Hugh Heard, Lewis
Bennett, Robert Smith, Ichabod Hood, James Harkness. Goodman & McCord,
Admr. Recorded Jan. 6, 1844.

Rent of land belonging to estate of Richardson Mayo dec'd. for 1843.
To G. W. Barber place near Iron Springs, J. T. Mayo where he lives, E. J.
Preston where he lives, Margaret Mayo where she lives, Lucy Mayo where
she lives. Goodman & McCord, Admr. Recorded Jan. 5, 1844.

Hire of Negroes of estate of Richardson Mayo dec'd. from Feb. 1,
1843 to April 1, 1843 to G. W. Barber, James G. Mayo, David Higgins, Z.
Faulkner, J. B. Byars, Goodman & McCord, Admrs. Recorded Jan. 15, 1844.

Sale of Negroes of estate of Richardson Mayo, dec'd. sold 1st Tues.
Apr. 1843 to James S. Mayo, David Higgins, Joel B. Byars, Samuel Duffey,
William Jones. Goodman & McCord, Admr. Recorded Jan. 15, 1844.

Page 506: Sale of land belonging to estate of Richardson Mayo
dec'd. sold Oct. 1843. Place near Iron Spring to Thomas J. Giles, E. J.
Preston, Lucy Mayo where each lives, Dawson McKleroy where Margaret Mayo
did live. Goodman & McCord, Admrs. Recorded Jan. 15, 1844.

Yearly return on estate of Robert W. Hunter dec'd. by Alexander
Hunter, Admr. from Feb. 25, 1843 to Jan. 2, 1844. Paid John W. Williams,
John McCord C.C.O., Robert Mayo tax collector, Thos. B. Burford, Joel J.
Crawford, guardian to Lyddia Isabella Hunter, Sarah Jane Hunter. Cash
received on note of Robert Martin and James W. Harkness, rent of land.
A. Hunter, Admr. Recorded Jan. 22, 1844.

Page 507: Yearly return 1843 of George L. Thompson, Admr. of estate
of Green B. Reeves, dec'd. Paid Nancy A. Reeves. George L. Thompson,
Admr. Recorded Jan. 22, 1844.

Return No. 5 - Jan. Term 1844. Charles Hammond, guardian of
William J. Hammond, minor. Balance on hand. Paid taxes. Charles Hammond, guardian. Recorded Jan. 22, 1844.

Estate of Henry Lee dec'd. to Charles Wakefield 1843. To maintain
Lillis Lee, widow. Charles Wakefield guardian for Lillis Lee. Recorded

Jan. 22, 1844.

Pages 507-510:   An annual return of William F. Mapp, Admr. on
estate of Allen McClendon dec'd. for 1843.   Rec'd. notes from Jeptha
McClendon, Caswell Purifoy, Andrew Tenant, for forty acres land in
Cherokee County. Paid D. L. Bailey interest on said commissions, Jesse
Loyall, Freeman McClendon, Jeremiah McClendon, Wm. M. Fincher. William
F. Mapp, Admr. Recorded Jan. 23, 1844.

Annual return of William F. Mapp guardian to O. H. P. McClendon,
William McClendon, Joseph F. McClendon. Paid interest 1843 on commissions for each. William F. Mapp, guardian. Recorded Jan. 23, 1844.

Page 510:   Annual return of Thomas B. Burford Exec. of William Burford dec'd. 1843.   Paid John B. Burford, Samuel P. Burford, R. P. Mayo
tax collector, Alfred Fuller, S. W. Booles, Thos. B. Burford, Exor.
Recorded Jan. 23, 1844.

Pages 510-511:   Yearly return of estate of Willis C. Jenkins, dec'd.
to Sterling S. Jenkins, Admr. 1841.   Paid Dr. Bailey & Hunter, Dr.
Charles Bailey, C. F. Newton & Co., F. C. McKinley & Co., 1841 taxes,
John Ball, Hubbard Williams, John White, Martha Jenkins; John Dawson for
shoes; Daniel Kelsey for tuition; J. Bartlett, Parham Lindsey, Simeon D.
McClendon, John S. Anderson, R. P. Mayo tax collector. Credit: Sale of
cotton ($1204.42½). Cash paid Grif Lynch, James Hoard, Jefferson Adams,
John Anderson, Martha S. Butts, A. C. Scott, Thomas Ragland, Sterling S.
Jenkins, Admr. Recorded Jan. 24, 1844.

Pages 511-513:   A list of appr. of estate of John S. Ingram dec'd.
of Henry County, Ga. taken Dec. 19, 1843.   150 acres where dec'd. lives,
one lot No. 79, 5th Dist., 2nd Sec T., 160 acres not viewed by appraisors,
14 Negroes, goods and chattel, notes on John R. Humphries, William S.
Bivens. Certified by Britton Buttrill, William S. Bivens, Lewis Moore,
Alfred J. Grimmet and John Greer, J.P. Recorded Jan. 24, 1844.

Page 514:   Sale bill on estate of John S. Ingram dec'd. sold Jan.
2, 1844 to Jacob Rape, Josiah Newman, Elijah Phillips, Wm. G. Becket.
John Greer, Exor. Recorded Jan. 24, 1844.

Annual return of Elijah Smith Exor. of William H. Smith dec'd.
Paid Hannah Smith, widow of dec'd., Hubbard Williams, C. F. Newton & Co.,
J. C. Dunsieth, C. Moore, A. W. Adcock, Robert Mayfield, R. W. Smith,
W. Tomlinson, John McCord, C.C.O., S. B. Smith, Elijah Smith, Exor.
Recorded Jan. 25, 1844.

Pages 514-515:   Second annual return of Goodman & McCord, Admr. on
estate of Richardson Mayo dec'd. Paid Mary McLure, P. M. Compton, Jacob
T. Mayo, James Britton, H. Williams, Mack Goodwyn, Goodwyn & Carter,
Richard R. Mayo, Sr., Thos. J. Saunders, C. F. Newton & Co., V. T. Thomp-
son, Dawson McKleroy, Thos. P. Atkinson, John Saunders, Jas. H. Stark,
S. H. Saunders, R. P. Mayo, T. C., R. G. Byars. Dawson McKleroy guardian.
Elisha J. Preston, Jacob T. Mayo, Lucy Mayo, Received from rent of land
and hire of Negroes, J. T. Mayo, sale of perishable property. J. R. Mc-
Cord & John Goodman, Admrs. Recorded Feb. 6, 1844.

Page 516:   Annual return of Jas. R. McCord guardian for Sarah Watts
& Jubal Watts to Dec. 31, 1843. Paid Augustus Cargile, J. R. & J. W.
McCord, C. Hungerford & Co., taxes 1843, A. L. Hammond, J. R. McCord,
guardian. Recorded Feb. 7, 1844.

Pages 517-518:   Estate of James Wooten to John Jones guardian
(1830-1841). Interest realized on commissions in 1843. Returned by
John Jones guardian Jan. 12, 1844. Recorded Feb. 7, 1844.

Pages 518-519:   Recapitulation in part of estate of Martha Ann Duke
in account with Eli Conger from last return to Jan. 18, 1844. Interest
realized, collecting note on Charles A. Killgore. Paid taxes, C. Hungerford & Co.; Sarah Duke for board; Leroy Betterton. Credit: Received of
C. A. Killgore Admr. of A. G. Duke. Interest for 1841-1843. Returned
Jan. 19, 1844 by Eli Conger, guardian. Recorded Feb. 7, 1844.

142

Page 519:   First annual return of Dawson McKleroy guardian of
orphans Stephen D. Mayo dec'd.   Paid C.C.O.   Dawson (X) McKleroy,
guardian.   Recorded Feb. 7, 1844.

Return of Wm. Harrison guardian to Elizabeth & Thos. Harrison,
orphans of James Harrison dec'd. for the year 1839-1843.   Paid J. Buckhart for boarding, clothing & schooling orphans for years 1839-1843;
taxes 1839, 1842, 1843.   William Harrison, guardian.   Recorded 7 Feb.
1844.

Pages 520-521:   Estate of Elizabeth C. Dennis dec'd. in account with
John Greer Exor. from death of testator until Dec. 31, 1843.   Paid 1843
Spencer Jinks, Joshua Patrick, 1843 taxes; Macon Telegraph for advertis-
ing sale of two Negroes and perishable property; James Brady, John W.
McCord, A. L. Robinson, Goodman & Andrews, J. P. Williams, James Childs,
Wyatt Rose, free person of colour, Rebecca Moore, postage and expenses.
Credit: Cash in Central Bank bills, rec'd. from Thos. M. Harkness, James
Brady, sale of perishable property, Samuel Hancock, Amos A. Conger, A. L.
Robinson, John Goodman.   Sale of two slaves.   Returned Jan. 20, 1844.
John Greer, Exor.   Recorded Feb. 8, 1844.

Pages 521-523:   Return No. 13 - Estate of William Redman dec'd. in
account with James Carter, Admr. for 1843.   Paid A. Cargile, taxes; Mary
McClure, Larkin D. Lee, Burney & Newton, Mary Redman.   Credit: Received
of Levi McMichael part of expenses to the maintenance and burial of
Elizabeth Redman.   Returned for part of same to Mary Redman, Martha Redman and Wm. T. C. Redman.   Returned Jan. 27, 1844 by James Carter, Admr.
Recorded Feb. 8, 1844.

Annual Return No. 3 - Estate of Martha Redman & William T. C. Redman, minor in account with James Carter, guardian for 1843.   Returned
Jan. 27, 1844 by James Carter, guardian.   Recorded Feb. 8, 1844.

Pages 523-524:   No. 3 Yearly return of W. A. Florence, guardian for
John Tarpley, Matthew Tarpley, Joannah Tarpley, minors for year 1843.
Amount due minors with interest.   W. A. Florence, guardian to estate.
Recorded Feb. 11, 1844.

Page 524:   Yearly return by Josiah Barber, guardian for Richard
Smith, minor of Richard Smith dec'd. for 1843.   Balance due minor with
interest.   Paid for boarding and clothing said minor.   Josiah Barber,
guardian.   Recorded Mar. 6, 1844.

Page 525:   Estate of Aaron Onail dec'd. to Edward W. Onail, Admr.
1842.   Paid B. F. Hull, J. A. McCune, T. G. Bledsoe, D. H. Ellis, W. G.
Ray, S. W. Langston, J. R. & J. W. McCord, Lofton & Stodghill, J. P.
Williams, R. J. Harper, Josiah Crain, James J. Summerlin, J. Goddard, J.
Betterton, J. B. Orr, Frances Miller.   Credit: Sale of cotton.   Edward W.
Onail, Admr.   Recorded Mar. 6, 1844.

An annual return of O. H. P. McClendon, guardian for Jeremiah P.
McClendon for hire of Negroes in 1844 to O. H. P. McClendon, Amos Edmonds,
Isaac Smith.   O. H. P. McClendon, guardian.   Recorded Mar. 6, 1844.

Page 526:   Annual return of O. H. P. McClendon guardian for Jeremiah
P. McClendon.   Paid 1843 taxes, J. L. Banning, McClendon & Lawson, Bell
Kelton, Burney & Newton, John McCord, C.C.O.   O. H. P. McClendon, guar-
dian.   Recorded Mar. 6, 1844.

Yearly return of Samuel Bellah, Admr. of estate of Clifford Woodruff
dec'd.   Recieved of Benjamin Woodruff on note.   Paid John McCord, Macon,
Ga. Telegraph, 1843 taxes.   Samuel Bellah, Admr.   Recorded Mar. 7, 1844.

An account of sale of personal property of Clifford Woodruff dec'd.
Sold Aug. 1, 1843 to Dolphin Lindsey.   Hired Negro for 7 mo.   Samuel
Bellah, Admr.   Recorded Mar. 7, 1844.

Page 527:   Yearly return of my ward the orphans of A. G. Duke dec'd.
for year 1843 by Eli Conger, guardian.   For Mary Duke, Coatsworth Duke,
Elizabeth Duke, William Duke, orphans paid for necessaries; Sarah Duke

for board; taxes. Returned by Eli Conger, guardian. Recorded Mar. 7, 1844.

Pages 528-529: Appr. of property of estate of Nelson Meridith dec'd. Lot of land No. 17, 9th Dist. originally Henry County, now Butts; 3 Negroes; goods and chattel; notes on Fleming Childers and T. G. Bledsoe; order to pay from A. G. to S. H. Sanders. Certified on Nov. 23, 1843 by Alexander Sanders, Thomas G. Giles, William A. McCune, William Gregory, Jason Greer, Appraisors. Recorded Mar. 8, 1844.

Page 530: Butts County, Ga. We the undersigned being Legatees of John Mason dec'd. certify that each have received our part of estate of said John Mason from Mary Mason. Signed: Richard S. Mason, Churchill Mason, Nancy (X) Wray, John Fargason, Sarah (X) Mason, Larkin B. Mason, John W. Mason, Leonard Mason. Test: Nathan P. Lee, Turman Walthall, J.I.C. Witnesses and signed Mar. 19, 1844. Examined and approved by committee March Term 1844, W. G. McMichael, T. Williams, D. Evans. Recorded Mar. 20, 1844.

Pages 530-538: List of an Appr. of estate of John Saunders dec'd. Mar. 7, 1844. Listed are 37 Negroes (named), Lot No. 63, 1st Dist. originally Henry, now Butts, Lot No. 62, 1st Dist. originally Henry, now Butts; Lot No. 66, 1st Dist. originally Henry, now Butts County; Lot No. 34, 1st Dist. originally Henry, now Butts; Lot No. 31 (140) 1st Dist. originally Henry, now Butts; Interest in fraction No. 34, goods and chattel listed, Medical account due estate of John Saunders on Mrs. Elizabeth McCune, Young R. Norris (deceased), John L. Andrews, Sr., Thos. P. Atkinson, Thos. Moore, Mrs. E. C. Dennis (deceased), Thos. Harkness, J. R. Deason, E. Preston, Mr. Dodd Nelson (deceased), Thompson Floyd, John Morris, John Hall, Alex Saunders, Sundry individuals good and bad out of date. Notes on John McClure, H. H. Byars, Elisha Preston, William Higgins, John R. Dyer. Certified by S. T. Higgins, William A. McCune, Thos. J. Giles, appraisors and Thomas J. Saunders, J.P. this April 13, 1844. Cash on hand at death of John Saunders dec'd. which was Dec. 10, 1843 $500. Nancy Saunders, Admrx. Recorded Apr. 24, 1844.

Page 538: Estate of Harriet Ann Curry account with Matthew Gaston guardian up to Dec. 31, 1843. Paid wards taxes 1843. Levi McMichael for tuition. Credit: Balance and interest. Matthew Gaston, guardian. Recorded May 13, 1844.

Page 539: Estate of William Vickers in account with Creed T. Wise, Admr. for 1843. Paid J. H. Fielder tuition for Howard Vickers, Prudy Vickers, Jacob Vickers, R. P. Mayo for 1843 taxes. Credit: Hire of Negroes for 1843. Creed T. Wise, Admr. Recorded May 13, 1844.

Yearly return of Morgon Bledsoe, guardian on estate of George M. T. Brockman for 1843. To hire of three Negroes. Paid Thos. R. Russell for boarding, clothing and schooling for 1843. Morton Bledsoe, guardian. Recorded May 15, 1844.

Estate of Simeon Wooten to John Jones, guardian. Paid 1841 and 1842 taxes; C. F. Newton & Co., Martha E. Jones, A. M. D. McElroy for tuition; paid James Wooten the orphan due him on division of Negroes, 1841-1842 Board of self and horse, 1842, paid Martha E. Jones. Balance due ward. Returned Apr. 5, 1843 by John Jones, guardian. Recorded May 16, 1844.

Pages 540-543: Estate of Addison A. Wooten & Seaborn L. Wooten to John Jones, guardian. 1831-1833 commissions on disbursement these years. Interest 1833-1843. Board 1841-1842, William J. Head. Credit: Balance due ward. Returned Jan. 12, 1844. Recorded May 17, 1844.

Page 543: Annual return of O. H. P. McClendon, guardian for Jeremiah P. McClendon from Mar. 4 to May 10, 1844. Paid J. F. McClendon, F. McClendon, Maxey and Bloodworth. O. H. P. McClendon, guardian. Recorded June 10, 1844.

Return of John F. Preston, guardian to Thomas J. Preston, orpahns of Gilliam Preston dec'd.; amount rec'd. from Elisha J. Preston, one of Admrs. of Gilliam Preston dec'd. John F. Preston, guardian. Recorded

June 10, 1844.

Page 544: Yearly return by Willis Holifield for Christopher H. Holifield my ward for 1843. Paid C. Hungerford & Co., John McCord, C. M. Coody for tuition, Driskew & Maddux, for service rendered going to Monticello attending to business for minor two days; paid J. P. in Monticello for writing and qualifying me to affidavit commission on $32.50 charged against me. Credit: For hire of Negro girl to Wm. R. Bankston for 1843. Willis Holifield, guardian. Recorded June 10, 1844.

Pages 544-545: Return of Sterling S. Jenkins, Admr. of estate of Willis C. Jenkins for 1843-1844. Paid Burney & Newton, John McCord, taxes; Martha Butts, Richard Garrett & G. Hill, P. M. Compton; notes on S. S. Jenkins, Willis C. Jenkins. Sterling S. Jenkins, Admr. Recorded July 6, 1844.

Page 545: Estate of Samuel H. Stark in account with James H. Stark, guardian. Balance due ward with interest thereon. Returned June 21, 1844 with the remark that I have several receipts for taxes and returns, etc. which I claim the right of charging to estate within my next return. Recorded July 9, 1844.

Thomas Douglass to estate of William S. Douglass for hire of Negro for 1843. Thomas Douglass, Executor of estate of Williams. Douglass paid John McCord, Joseph W. Lawrence, Thos. Douglass, Exor. Recorded July 6, 1844.

Page 546: Three returns of Thomas Douglass, Exor. of William S. Douglass for 1843. Paid John McCord, H. A. Wilcox, S. P. Meril, Jesse B. Key & Co., Thomas S. Graves, Stow & Starr; board for 1843; E. McDonald for Narcissa Douglass. Thomas Douglass, Exor. Recorded July 6, 1844.

Page 547: Return of Frances Douglass Exor. of William S. Douglass for 1843. Paid J. M. Hoard, R. P. Mayo, P. Threatt, R. F. Douglass, F. Douglass, Exor. Recorded July 9, 1844.

This is to certify that I received of Alois P. Davis, Admr. of Lewis C. Davis $100 in Spring of 1835, $200 in Feb. 1837 by virtue as power of attorney made me by W. S. Douglass guardian of Sarah J. Douglass and that after the return of each collection paid said sum to William S. Douglass, guardian as aforesaid.

Georgia, Morgan County. Personally came to me Elijah E. Jones, J.I.C., Robert Douglass and saith that the facts stated are true. Sworn before me this Mar. 12, 1843. Elijah E. Jones, J.I.C., Robert Douglass. Recorded July 1, 1844. Butts Co., Ga. John McCord, C.C.O.

Received of Frances Douglass, Exor. of estate of Wm. S. Douglass $485.30 as legacy coming to Sarah Jane Douglass the right of my wife, July 1, 1844. Signed: Robert F. Douglass. Recorded July 10, 1844.

Pages 547-548: Return No. 9 - Estate of Sterling Camp in account with William Jarrell, Admr. from July 1 to Dec. 31, 1843. Paid R. P. Mayo for 1842 taxes, C.C.O. Balance due ward. Returned May 19, 1844, William Jarrell, Admr. Recorded July 10, 1844.

Page 548: Estate of Nathan F. Camp and James Camp in account with William Jarrell, guardian Jan. 1 to Dec. 31, 1843. Return No. 6. Paid Abner Hammond for tuition; C. Hungerford for necessaries; R. P. Mayo for taxes; James H. Stark, Atty. at Law for services, William Jarrell vs. D. J. Bailey; boarding and clothing ward for 1843. Balance due ward. June 19, 1844. William Jarrell, guardian. Recorded July 1, 1844.

Page 549: Estate of Micajah F. McCune dec'd. to William A. McCune, Admr. Paid Harrison & Moore, Moses Lee, execution on Littleton L. Burke. Returned June 20, 1844. William A. McCune, Admr. Recorded July 11, 1844.

Yearly return for my ward, Cornelius M. McCune for 1843. Paid Robert Mays, Nancy Saunders, taxes; Spencer & Mays, Driskill & Maddux, Burney & Newton, John McCord commission on Negro hire. Credit: Hire of

William McCune, guardian. Recorded July 12, 1844.

Pages 550-552: Georgia, Butts Co. Will of James H. Campbell. I, James H. Campbell being weak in body but sound mind make this my last will and testament. Item 1 - Body intered in decent and christian manner. Item 2 - Just debts paid. Item 3 - I desire my wife Permelia D. Campbell take charge of all property and sell plantation where I now live and purchase a place near some good Academy for purpose of education my children. Item 4 - Desire Executrix and Executor sell ½ lot of land I have joining Samuel Clark in Butts County and a Negro woman. Item 5 - Desire balance of estate kept together for purpose of raising and educating my children. As children arrive at mature age or marry each shall have 3/4 of their portion of estate. In event my wife dies before youngest child arrives at mature age such child to receive equal to older children. Item 6 - That my beloved wife to have equal portion during life time. Item 7 - Portion belonging to daughter Celestia Antonet and Ophelia Elizabet Glenn be given to them in such a manner it cannot be squandered by their husbands provided they do marry - my wife to be their trustee. Item 8 - That my step mother-in-law Jane J. Lane to have decent support during her life time. Lastly appoint Joel B. Mabry and Permelia D. Campbell Exor. and Exerx. of will. Signed this Mar. 3, 1844, James H. Campbell (Seal) in presence of John Goodman, J. R. McCord, Humphrey Gilmore, J. W. McCord.

Page 553: Annual return of estate of Martha Andrews, minor of Robert Andrews dec'd. John Andrews, guardian 1842. Hire of Negroes, paid Sarah Andrews, Jesse Loyall, 1842 taxes; Hungerford & Co., Driskill & Maddux, C. F. Newton and Co. Recorded Sept. 5, 1844.

Return of estate of Sarah Andrews, minor of Robert Andrews dec'd. by John Andrews, guardian. Paid David Evens, Spencer & Mays, 1842 taxes; Abner Hammond. Recorded Sept. 5, 1844.

Annual return of Yelventon Thaxton guardian for minors of estate of Arnold Johnson dec'd. Paid Arnold Johnson & Burwell Johnson. Legatees of said estate, A. Hammond tuition for P. P. Johnson. Recorded Sept. 6, 1844.

Pages 554-558: Inventory & appr. of estate of Abner Bankston dec'd. Listed 17 Negroes. Good and chattels as produced by John Goodman & Jas. R. McCord, Admr. of estate. Certified by Parham Lindsey, William J. Head, Richard Barlow, Appraisors and Thos. J. Saunders, J.P. Recorded Sept. 11, 1844.

List of notes found in possession of Abner Bankston dec'd. on Daniel Earp, Eli Parks, A. B. Payne, Philip L. Bode, James S. Morris, Elisha J. Preston, James Bailey, Stephen Bailey, Jordan Morris, Thomas J. Stone, R. N. Wood, John Goodman and J. R. McCord, Admr. Recorded Sept. 11, 1844.

Pumpkintown, Ga. June 26, 1844. Appr. of property of Abner Bankston dec'd. in Randolph County. Goods and chattels, 5 Negroes as produced by John Goodman and J. R. McCord, Admr. June 16, 1844. Certified by Mastin Hendrick, Leroy Jenkins, McKeen Cook, Appraisors and Mastin D. Hendrick, J.P. Recorded Sept. 11, 1844.

Pages 558-559: Inv. & Appr. of goods and chattels of James E. Bankston dec'd. on June 15, 1844. Certified by R. Blissit, Nathaniel Anderson, J. T. Kimbell appraisors and Briton Buttrill, J.P. Recorded Sept. 12, 1844.

Pages 559-561: Sept. 3, 1844. Appraisement of estate of Nancy Higgins dec'd. One lot of land and 4 Negroes, other goods and chattel. Certified by Parham Lindsey, William McCune, Thomas J. Giles, appraisors and Thos. J. Saunders, J.P. Recorded Oct. 15, 1844.

Pages 562-564: Inv. and Appr. of estate of James H. Campbell dec'd. Sept. 28, 1844. Goods and chattels, 15 Negroes, notes on Dawson B. Lane, William H. C. Lane, William Irvine, Drewery S. Patterson, C. C. Hodges, Drewery C. Cox, Robert W. Slough, 202½ acres of land, 100 acres of land.

Certified by O. H. P. McClendon, Thos. Lacy, Drewery S. Patterson and Seth K. Adams, J.P. Recorded Nov. 13, 1844.

Pages 564-565: George, Campbell Co. We the undersigned are held and bound unto Justices of Inferior Court of said County for sum of $4000 which we bind ourselves this Sept. 14, 1844. Condition is that if Thos. B. Burford temporary Admr. of good and chattel of Richard H. Darnall dec'd. makes a true inventory of estate of said deceased and shall deliver and pay to such persons as are entitled and same proved before court and executors obtain a certificate then this obligation to be void. Signed: Thos. B. Burford, D. Darnall, Christopher C. Morris, John Terry, Wm. Yates. Certified by R. C. Brewer, C.C.O. Recorded Butts County, Nov. 13, 1844.

Page 565: Georgia, Campbell Co. Thos. B. Burford, C. C. Morris, J. A. Smith made bond for estate of Richard H. Darnall dec'd. Nov. 9, 1844. Certified by R. C. Beavers C.C.O. Recorded Butts Co. Nov. 13, 1844.

Pages 566-572: Georgia, Campbell Co. At May Term Court 1844 Thos. B. Burford shows he made bond to J.I.C. in Butts Co. for true performance as Admr. of estate of Richard H. Darnall dec'd. The said Burford applies to court for order to have a full copy of all estate of said Richard Darnall dec'd. and that he have to leave to remove same to Butts Co. and granted that he remove effect of said estate and all returns for the future to the Courts of Butts Co. this May 6, 1844. Wade White, David B. Smith, Thos. Camp, Justices of Inferior Court. True extract certified by R. C. Beavers, C.C.O. Recorded Butts Co. Nov. 13, 1844.

Copy of Inventory of estate of Richard H. Darnall dec'd. Goods and chattel. Notes on A. W. Davis, Solomon Barfield, A. Barfield, Joel Foster, T. J. & A. S. Foster, Job Smith, Jas. Carroll, H. K. Smith, C. C. Morris. Certified by appraisors John B. Smith, John A. Smith, C. C. Morris, Moses M. Smith and Elijah Hammond, J.P. Nov. 15, 1844. Recorded Nov. 15, 1844, Butts County, Ga.

Pages 573-1581: Inventory & Appr. of property of Burwell Jinks dec'd. this Nov. 26, 1844. Goods and chattel listed with 800½ acres of land and 21 Negroes. Certified by James A. McCune, Lewis Moore, Samuel P. Burford, appraisors and W. G. McMichael, J.P. Recorded Jan. 16, 1845.

Property of estate of Burwell Jinks dec'd. sold to highest bidder Dec. 11, 1844. Buyers: E. W. Onail, James Baughan, James Chiles, John McMichael, S. P. Burford, Samuel Collins, William Irvine, A. A. Conger, Nancy Ingram, W. S. B. Harkness, Abner Nolen, Griffin C. McMichael, Wm. S. Blissit, Edmund McDaniel, H. S. Lee, Israel Pricket, Samuel Bucket, Rebecca Moore, Alfred A. King, H. S. Mays, Larkin D. Lee, John Duffey, Walter Andrews, J. R. McCord, John S. Irby, John J. Chafin, James A. Mc-Cune, Wm. B. Nutt, James King, Wm. B. Carter, Henry Malone, J. W. Doss, Jane Barkley, John Goodman, Samuel Collins, Dory Taylor, Moses Rosser, Jefferson Warlick, James Findley, Henry Barron, Minton Jinks, John Dor-ton, L. B. Johnson, H. S. Kee, Samuel Wakefield, Isaac Bishop, C. B. Malone, Augustus Cargile, Eli M. Conger, Martha Slaton. Gales Jinks, Admr. Recorded Jan. 17, 1845.

Page 581: Appr. of estate of Reuben Phillips dec'd. taken Dec. 14, 1844. Goods and Chattels. Notes on John Phillips, William Phillips. Certified by appraisors James Boughan, James Brownlee, W. S. Andrews and Thomas J. Giles, J.P. Recorded Jan. 18, 1845.

Pages 582-583: List of property sold by Robert White, Admr. or Reuben Phillips dec'd. on 20th & 21st day of Dec. 1844. Purchasers: Martha Phillips, William Greer, James Brownlee, Jason Greer, John Phil-lips, Arnold Johnson, Walter S. Andrews, Sackville Lynch, John Phillips, Sr., William Phillips, William S. Blissit. Robert White, Admr. Record-ed Jan. 18, 1845.

Pages 583-585: Georgia, Butts Co. Will of John Greer. I, John Greer of said county being of sound mind make this my last will and testament in form following. Item 1 - I desire my just debts and funeral

147

expenses paid and every article and thing embraced in last will of Elizabeth C. Dennis dec'd. be performed and carried out according to will of
deceased. Item 2 - I charge my son David Greer with $150 given by me to
him and he receive nothing further out of my estate until all my other
children shall receive like sum. Item 3 - I bequeath my whole estate to
my executors that it remain for support of my wife and children until
children come of age (or marry if girls) that each receive in money and
property then give what she can spare graduating the Legacies equally.
Estate remain whole during life or widowhood of wife, if in event of her
marriage or death estate be equally divided between her and all my
children, deducting what my son David has received from his part. Item
4 - Immediately after my death son Samuel have my sorrel filley for $60.
Item 5 - My children above mentioned are David Greer, Nancy Greer, Mary
Greer, Samuel Greer, Jane Greer, Johnston Greer, Sarah Ann Greer, Thomas
H. Greer, John S. Greer, Elizabeth L. Greer all of whom shall be made
equal when final division shall take place. Item 6 - Appoint my beloved
wife Elizabeth Greer and my son David Greer exorx. & exor. this Dec. 11,
1844. Signed: John Greer. Wit: Thos. B. Burford, Charles T. Burford,
James H. Stark. Proven in open Court Jan. Term 1845. Recorded Jan.
20, 1845.

Page 585: Return No. 6. Jan. Term 1845. Charles Hammond, guardian
of William J. Hammond. Balance on hand from return 1844. Recorded Jan.
21, 1845.

Pages 585-586: Estate of Martha Andrews now Martha Kimbell to Mary
Anderson, guardian from Dec. 31, 1842. Paid 1843 Spencer & Mays for
necessaries, John McCord C.C.O., Joshua Patrick, 1841 paid James Childs,
1844 paid James G. Kimbell who married ward. Returned Nov. 15, 1844 by
Mary (X) Anderson, guardian. Recorded Jan. 21, 1845.

Page 586: Estate of Joseph Wilson dec'd. to William H. Wilson Exor.
1842-1844, paid notes to Lofton & Stodghill, Travy G. Bledsoe, Joseph
Goddard, Stephen Bailey, Goodman & Andrews with interest. William H.
Wilson, exor. Recorded Jan. 21, 1845.

Page 587: Estate of William H. Smith, dec'd. to Elijah Smith,
Executor 1841-1844. Paid Hannah Smith, widow of dec'd. Feb. 25, 1841-
1844; Crayton and Mathew. Elijah Smith, Executor. Recorded Jan. 21,
1845.

Yearly return on Estate of Robert W. Hunter for 1844 by Alexander
Hunter, Admr. Jan. 1, 1845. Paid Joel T. L. Crawford, guardian for L.
J. Hunter, John H. McDaniel, John M. Mayo for taxes. Credit: Rec'd. on
note of Samuel H. Hunter, A. Hunter, Admr. Recorded Jan. 22, 1845.

Pages 588-589: Yearly return No. 4 of W. A. Florence, guardian for
John Tarpley, Matthew Tarpley, Joanna E. Tarpley for 1844. Balance due
minors Dec. 31, 1843 with interest, deduct expenditures. W. A. Florence,
guardian. Recorded Jan. 23, 1845.

Pages 589-590: Return of Martha Malone, Executrix of John A. Malone,
dec'd. Paid Lewis Moore, H. S. Lee, 1844 taxes, boarding and clothing
Martha Malone, Emily Malone and my support for year 1844; Mack Goodwyn,
John McClure, Stephen Baily, John W. McCord, advertising land. Martha
Malone, executrix. Recorded Jan. 23, 1845.

Pages 590-591: Annual return of O. H. P. McClendon, guardian for
Jeremiah McClendon from May 10, 1844 to Jan. 13, 1845. Paid 1844 taxes;
George W. Thomas, Andrew & Little, Isaac W. Smith, H. Clark, David
Andrews. Recorded Jan. 23, 1845.

Pages 591-592: Biennial Return No. 1 - Estate of John Saunders in
account with Nancy Saunders, Admr. to Dec. 31, 1844. Paid George Tenant
for service; Goodman & McCord, C. Hungerford & Co., Burney & Newton,
Smith & Maddux, John H. Ellis, J. Winship, Reece & Swanson, J. Hall, S.
K. McLin, J. S. Anderson, Thomas J. Giles, H. Fitsh, John Simmons, George
W. Lane, A. E. Edgeworth, Will Irvine, J. J. Jones, Will M. Roberts,
Thos. Collins, G. W. Woodruff, E. B. Weed, John Mayo, Alex Saunders,
Mack Goodwyn, G. McLargre, J. Johnson, J. C. Pearson, H. H. Hurd.

Credit: Rec'd. from J. R. Dyer, John Hall, John Greer, S. W. Price, J. Winship, John Goodman, Wm. Gregory, Dawson Mickelroy. Returned Jan. 13, 1845 by Nancy Saunders, Admr. Recorded Jan. 24, 1845.

Pages 592-593: Return of Thomas Douglass, Executor of William S. Douglass, dec'd. for 1844 for Eugenius Douglass, Marcellus Douglass, Narcissa Douglass for year 1844. Paid for necessaries and board. Thomas Douglass, Exor. Recorded Jan. 24, 1845.

Page 593: Yearly return on estate of Richard H. Darnell dec'd. for 1844 for Thomas B. Burford, Admr. Paid Thomas Mackey, Benjamin Camp, C. C. Morris, M. M. Smith, A. A. Camp, A. Austell, R. P. Ramsey, D. Darnell, A. R. Richardson. Recorded Jan. 29, 1845.

Page 594: Return of Samuel Bellah, Admr. of estate of Clifford Woodruff, dec'd. for 1844. Received of Benjamin Woodruff and Dolphin Lindsey. Paid Larkin Woodruff, Malinda Woodruff, now Malinda Martin, Reuben L. Bellah, Elizabeth Woodruff, W. S. Carr. Samuel Bellah, Admr. to going to Oglethorpe settlement with the Executors of estate of Clifford Woodruff, Sr., dec'd. Signed: Samuel Bellah, Admr. Recorded Jan. 29, 1845.

Return of David Berry, guardian of John J. D. Berry estate 1844. Rec'd. from estate of Elizabeth C. Dennis. Paid C.C.O, David Berry, guardian. Recorded Jan. 29, 1845.

Pages 594-597: Inventory and appraisement of estate of Cornelius Slaten dec'd. taken Jan. 16, 1845 by appraisers John McMichael, James Brady, James W. Harkness, and Thomas M. Harkness. Listed goods and chattel. Certified by W. G. McMichael, J.P. Recorded Feb. 1, 1845.

Pages 597-600: Court of Ordinary of Morgan Co., Ga. granted letter of Administration to Harriet B. Beavers on estate of Silas M. Beavers, dec'd. of said Co. Inv. & Appr. of estate of Silas M. Beavers. Listed goods and chattel. Appraisors Wm. H. Clark, Josiah Dennis, Thos. B. Cheeny, Peter Campbell. Certified by William Lewis, J.P. Examined and approved Feb. 22, 1836. Recorded June 9, 1836. (Recorded in Butts Co. in 1845 record).

Sale of estate of Silas M. Beavers Jan. 8, 1836. Purchased by Robert Duke, H. B. Bevers, Henry Clark, D. Davis, Harriet B. Beavers, Charles Addison, H. Harper, J. Nelson, D. Pattilo, J. Daniel, Henry Duke. Harriet M. Beavers appeared in Open Court of Morgan Co., Ga. and saith it is a true return of sale on Mar. 4, 1836. Test: John W. Porter, C.C. O. Recorded in Butts Co., Ga. Feb. 5, 1845.

Pages 600-606: Inventory of sale of perishable property of Cornelius Slaten, dec'd. Jan. 27-28, 1845. Purchased by Willis Wilkins, C. Lunceford, Martha Slaten, Stephen Bailey, R. L. Lunceford, Joseph C. Little, Asa Buttrill, W. S. B. Harkness, W. Irvine, David Kimbell, Thos. M. Harkness, Y. G. Malone, W. A. Elder, S. Collins, S. Wilkerson, J. Gilbert, J. McMichael, J. Goodman, T. M. Harkness, D. S. Carr, D. T. Evens, A. A. Conger, J. B. Harkness, J. Riggs, G. C. McMichael, J. Boughan, D. J. Bailey, O. H. P. McClendon, S. H. Saunders, A. Cargile, T. Connell, W. Faukner, D. Death, Levi McMichael, S. Lynch, C. Lunceford, H. Duke, R. L. Crawford. Hire of Negroes and rent of land. Signed: J. R. & J. W. McCord, Admrs. Recorded Feb. 7, 1845.

Pages 607-608: Inventory of sale of perishable property of James E. Bankston dec'd. Nov. 9, 1844. Purchased by Elizabeth Bankston, James R. Bankston, Wm. S. Blissit, Samuel Collins, M. H. Jackson, Wm. Coker, David Kimbell, Wm. R. Bankston, David Anderson, Reason Blissit, P. H. Jackson. Signed: Wm. R. Bankston, Admr. Recorded Feb. 10, 1845.

Page 608: Yearly return 1845 of George L. Thompson, Admr. of Green B. Reeves, dec'd. Paid Nancy A. Reeves. Returned Jan. 6, 1845 by Geo. L. Thompson, Admr. Recorded Mar. 5, 1845.

Return of Emanuel Smith, Admr. of John H. Smith dec'd. Paid Jesse Ladden, Joseph Key for Jesse Ledden, John McCord. Returned Mar. 3, 1845.

149

Emanuel Smith, Admr. Recorded Mar. 5, 1845.

Pages 609-610: Yearly return for year 1842 and 1843 by Sterling T. Higgins for my wards, the minor of Silas M. Beavers dec'd. to viz: Sarah E. Beavers, Harriet A. Beavers, and Eliza L. Beavers. Paid boarding and clothing for 1842 and 1843. Returned Jan. 6, 1845 by S. T. Higgins, guardian. Recorded Mar. 5, 1845.

Yearly return by S. T. Higgins for wards for year 1844 (to wit) Sarah E. Beavers, Harriet A. Beavers and Eliza L. Beavers paid Robt. T. Mayo taxes, John M. Mayo taxes; Joseph H. Fielder tuition. 1844 clothing and boarding Harriet A. Beavers and Eliza L. Beavers. Returned Jan. 6, 1845. Recorded Mar. 6, 1845.

Page 610: Annual return of William T. Mapp, guardian for O. H. P. McClendon for 1844. Paid balance in valuation in Negro property. John McCord, C.C.O. Returned Mar. 3, 1845. Recorded Mar. 6, 1845.

COLUMBIA COUNTY, GEORGIA, WILLS BOOK H, 1803-1821

20 April 1803: I, Joseph Allen being unwell but of tolerable mind and memory. I give to my son John T. Allen one negro man Robie. I give to my dtr. Smith one negro man Aaron. I give to my son James Allen one negro man George. I give to my son Joseph Allen one negro man Reuben now with John T. also one horse or eighty Dollars. I give to my wife my land where I now live, and what not already given during her life time. I give to my son Frances two thirds of my land where I now live, the other third to my dtr. Sally after the death of their mother. If either should die before they come of age, the whole to the survivor. I give unto my dtrs. Alice, Anne, Susanna, Elizabeth, Harriet, Sally and my son Francis all the rest of my estate or increase to be divided equally between them...I appoint my three sons John, James & Joseph Allen my executors...Sgn. Joseph Allen...As I have made a mistake in giving to my son Joseph or Reuben. I have scratch out Jack and interlines Reuben, then comes my dtr. Charlotte portion which is Jack now with John T. also one horse or $80...Dated 20 April 1803...Sgn. Joseph Allen...Recd. 19 Dec. 1803. NO witnesses. Proved on oath of Anderson Crawford, being duly sworn saith that he was acquainted with the hand writing of Joseph Allen the decd. and has no doubt to be his last will. Sgn. A. Crawford. Dated 19 Dec. 1804. Pages 1-2.

This day the 19 Dec. 1804, John, James & Joseph Allen were sworn as executors of Joseph Allen, decd. last will according to law, to make a true and perfect inventory of the goods and chattels, rights and credit. To return to this office in three months of the date hereof. Sgn. John Foster, Esq. Page 3.

20 Feb. 1804: I, Richard Neal being of sound mind & memory, first all my just debts & funeral charges to be paid. I give unto my beloved wife Elizabeth Neal, one bay mare and one feather bed. I bequeath negro girl Milly unto my chn. To wit, Mary and one child yet unborn to be equally divided & her increase, to them & their heirs, if no heirs, then to my brother Bassel Neal, and his heirs, but my wife to have said property as long as she remains my widow. I appoint my brother Bassel Neal my executor. My will is that the cow & calf that came with my wife, one should go to her and for her disposal. Wit: James Wood, Elias Welborn. Signed: Richard Neal. Proved & recorded on the 19 Dec. 1804. A. Crawford, Clk. Pages 4-5.

Bassel Neal was sworn as executor of the above will, he to make a true & perfect inventory of the goods & chattels and credits and exhibit the same to the Clerk of Court within three months. Sgn. John Foster, Esq. This 19 Dec. 1804. Page 6.

12 Oct. 1804. I, George Ray, being low in body but of sound mind

150

& memory. I appoint Benjamin Ray & John Ray my executors. I give unto
my wife Catharine for her use during her widowhood all stock of hogs,
cattle and household furniture, with 50 acres of land whereon my house
now stands, agreeable to an agreement made between myself & Lazarus
Langston for the other part of the tract to which the said 50 acres belong, at my wife marriage or death which ever may first take place. I
will that the said 50 acres of land with the personal property be equally
divided between my son George & my little dtr. yet unnamed, the chn. of
Catharine. I give unto my son George & dtr. unnamed $100 each. The
rest of my property both real & personal to be divided as, after payment
of my just debts, one ninth part to my son Benjamin, John & William Ray
each. Also one ninth part to my son-in-laws John Stith, William Ansley,
Coonrod Wall, William Stanford each and the chn. of James Wright by my
dtr. Mary. One part divided between the heirs of my dtr. Sarah Hill
that she hath or may have. Wit: David Langston, Robert Lazenby & Edward
Forbes. Proved and recorded in open Court, the 19 Dec. 1804. Pages 7-8.

Benjamin & John Ray was sworn as executors of the above will. They
to make a true & perfect inventory of goods & chattels and credits and
exhibit the same to the Clerk of Court in three months. Sgn. John
Foster, Esq. This 19 Dec. 1804. Page 9.

24 Sep. 1800: I Isaac Skinner, being of sound mind & memory, First
I desire my debts & dues to be paid by my executors. I give unto my beloved wife Jane Skinner all my property both real & personal, during
her natural life, if she should remarry, from that time she to have a
child part only. That is to say all my property to be divided amongst
my wife Jane, Haney, John, Elizabeth, Richard, Howard, Jane & Thomas
Hiram Abelh Skinner. I will that my wife Jane be my executor. Wit:
John Foster, Charles Barham & Jas. Foster. Sgn. Isaac (X) Skinner.
Proved & recorded 4 Jan. 1805. Pages 10-11.

4 Jan. 1805: The will of Isaac Skinner was proved by Col. John
Foster, Charles Barham & Jas. Foster. Before A. Crawford, Clk. Jane
Skinner was sworn as executor. She to make a true inventory of all
goods & chattels and exhibit the same to the Clerk Office in three
months. Sgn. John Foster, Esq. Pages 12-13.

14 Nov. 1804: I, John Jones, of King & Queen County, Virginia.
Being very sick & weak in body. I leave all my estate both real & personal to my wife, Nancy Jones, until my son William come of age provided
she remain my widow, but in case of her intermarriage before Son William
come of age. I leave her during her natural life negro woman Lydda also
negro named Hannah and their increase, also $300 in money. I leave to
my son William a negro between the ages 15 yrs. to twenty five yrs. also
a horse, saddle & bridle, the value of $100. I give to my son John
Jones a negro between the age of 15 yrs. & twenty five yrs. also one
horse, saddle & bridle, the value of $100. I appoint my brother, William
Jones, of the State of Georgia and William Bates of Virginia to be my
executors. Wit: Dan Ritchy, Major Eubanks & Richd. Eubanks. Sgn. John
Jones. Proved on oath of the names Witnesses on this 7 Jan. 1805.
A. Crawford, Clk. Recd. 9 Jan. 1805. Pages 14-16.

Page 17 is blank.

(No date on will). I, Abram Gibson, being in good health & sound
mind. First, I will that my crop of cotton, two horses, Buck & Jack, my
wagon & gear, carpenter & cooper tools, my grit stone be sold on credit
of six months, with the money in hand and book accounts be applied to
the payment of my debts and the remainder divided between my two dtrs.
Sarah & Tarresa and my wife Elizabeth Gibson. I give to my wife Elizabeth my negro named March. I give to my dtr. Sarah my negro named Dawl
& her increase, one bed & furniture also one horse called Sweper. I
give to my wife, Elizabeth Gibson, all the land I hold in North Carolina,
household & kitchen furniture, all tools & stock of every kind except
what I have given to my dtrs. I appoint Dexter Gibson, wife Elizabeth
Gibson & Shadrach Gibson as executors. Wit: E. Bowdre, James Harris &
Larkin (X) Tally. Sgn. Abram Gibson. Proved on oath of Edmond Bowdre,
who saw James Harris sign his name & Larkin Tally make his mark. This
7 Jan. 1805. Sgn. A. Crawford. Recd. 9 Jan. 1805. Pages 18-19.

151

7 Jan. 1805: Dexter Gibson was sworn as executor of the above will, he to make a true & just inventory of all goods and chattels and exhibit the same into the Clerks Office within three months. Sgn. John Foster, Esq. Page 20.

20 Oct. 1804: I, Thomas Jones, being weak and low in body, but of sound mind & memory. Have heretofore given by deed of gift to my sons, Thomas & William Jones, 350 acres of land on Ogeukee River in full of their part of my est. also to my sons, Robert & Elias Jones, 300 acres on Sandy Run in full of their part of my est. I give to my sons Randol & James Jones the land whereon I now live to be divided between them, also my waggon & gear & tools. I desire my executors in three months after my decease to pay my dtr. Jeremalem Willoughby $200, also the same time & amount to my son William Jones his heirs & assigns. Randol & James to have a good riding horse when of full age. My household & kitchen furniture and stock except what is mentioned to be divided among my dtrs. Sarah, Mary & Ann. I desire that my five youngest chn. be keep together on my place and supported until full age, namely, Randol, Sarah, Mary, James & Ann. When my youngest child come of age, I desire my executor to sell my negroes and money divided among the children named. I appoint my sons, Thomas & Randol, my executors. Wit: A. Crawford, Abram Gibson, James Martin. Sgn. Thos. Jones. Proved on oath of James Martin & Anderson Crawford in open Court. 2 Feb. 1805. Recd. 11 Feb. 1805. Pages 21-23.

2 Feb. 1805: Thomas & Randol Jones was sworn as executors to the will of Thomas Jones, decd. To make a true & perfect inventory of all goods & chattels of the decease and exhibit the same in three months in the Clerk Office this 2 Feb. 1805. John Foster, Esq. Page 24.

6 Dec. 1803: I, Jesse Rice, being weak of body but of sound mind & memory. I give to my beloved wife Susanna Rice 150 acres of land whereon I now live and the whole of my property as long as she remains a widow. If wife remarry, she to have one third part, the remainder to be divided between my three children, as they marry or come of age. Should my wife be with child now, it to have an equal share with the others. Whereas I & Robert Reeds hath been on a trade or swap of negroes, my executors to carry through as they see proper. I appoint my wife Susanna Executrix & friend William Jones, Junior & Anderson Crawford and Joseph Allen my executors. Wit: T. S. Allen, Lucy Jones, Wm. (X) Thompson. Sgn. Jesse Rice. Pages 25-26.

N. B. The statement that my wife to have the whole of my estate, is only while the children are minors or unmarried. When they marry or are of age an equally division between my chn. Wit: J. S. Allen, Lucy Jones, Wm (X) Thompson. Sgn. Jesse Rice. Proved on oath of John T. Allen and Lucy Jones in open Court this 23 Feb. 1805. Sgn. A. Crawford, Clk. This 23 Feb. 1805; Susanna Rice was sworn as executrix of the will of Jesse Rice. To make a true & perfect inventory of the goods & chattels of the decease and exhibit the same in the Clerk Office in three months. Signed, John Foster, Esq. this 23 Feb. 1805. Recd. 8 March 1805. Pages 27-28.

15 Oct. 1804: I, Shadrack Roberts, being low in body but sound mind. I give unto my beloved wife Delley Roberts, one third of the astate of Joseph Catlege. To my beloved dtr. Pations Roberts, I give one bed & furniture & one pot. To my son David Roberts, one horse colt, also to my sons Joseph & Absolam one horse each the value of David's. Also my son John Roberts and the son or daughter my wife is now pregnant with, each to have an equal share, to be paid by the other sons & daughters. To my dtr. Fanny Roberts, one bed & furniture an equal part of my astate when she come of age. To my dtr., Genny Roberts, one bed & furniture, an equal part of the astate when she comes of age. I appoint Isaac Willingham & Benj. Williams my executors. Wit: Minor Mead, John Willingham. Sgn. Shadrack Robert. Page 29.

Will proved on oath of Minor Mead & John Willingham in open Court this 23 Feb. 1805. Sgn. A. Crawford, Clk. This 23 Feb. 1805 came Isaac Willingham and Benj. Williams and being sworn as executors of the late Shadrack Roberts Will. To make a true and perfect inventory of the goods & chattels and exhibit the same in the Clerk Office in three months. Signed John Foster, Esq. this 23 Feb. 1805. Recd. 8 March 1805. Pages 30-31.

30 Oct. 1795: I, John Griffin, being weak in body but of perfect mind & memory. I leave to my brother, Roland Griffin, six negroes to wit: Ben, Anthony, Pat, Elice, Benard & Abigail & one feather bed & furniture & all my household & kitchen Furniture & tool of all kinds. To my brother, Isham Griffin, I leave the sum of 1 shilling, to my sister, Diana Clarke, I leave the sum of 1 shilling. To my brother, Thomas Williams Murrell, I give the following negroes, Kate, Aggy, Frankey, and Poladore & young Pat & my mare Nancy Hunton bridle & riding saddle, and my land containing 225 acres known as the Buck Pond tract I wish to be sold and all the negroes continue to be hired out until all debts are paid. I appoint James Sims & Roland Griffin and John Shackleford my executors. Wit: Jeremiah Day, Richard (X) Downs & Sally Shackleford. Sgn. John Griffin. Proved on oath of Richard Downs the 16 Jan. 1804, before A. Crawford, Clk. Recd. 1 June 1805. Pages 32-33.

1 Jan. 1805: I, Joseph Roberts, being very sick and weak in body. I give unto my son James Roberts during his life and after his death to his wife, Patty Roberts, during her life all the tract of land containing 100 acres, lying on the South side of the North fork of Keg Creek, the land on which my son now lives on. After his & her death, I give the said tract of land to my grand-son, Eli Roberts, forever. I give unto my sons, George & Josiah Roberts, the remainder of my real estate to be divided between them. Also I give to George, negro boy Jack & girl Mary, two feather beds and furniture. I give to my son Josiah a negro boy Peter & girl Nell, with two beds & furniture. I give to my dtr., Elizabeth Blanchard, a negro boy Daniel. I give to my loving wife, Faith Roberts, during her life time or widowhood a negro woman Winny, and after her death to my son George. I give to my son Richard Roberts $50 in money. I give to my son Wiley Roberts a negro girl named Suk & her increase with one feather bed. I give to my son John Roberts $10 in money. I give to my dtrs. Ann Culbreath & Jude Mims $1 each. I give two stills, one set blacksmith tools & the remainder of my household property to my sons, George & Josiah Roberts, to be divided between them. I appoint my sons George & Josiah Roberts my executors. Wit: Danl. Ritchy, Uriah Blanchard & James S. Johns. Sgn. Joseph (X) Roberts. Pages 33-35.

Joseph Roberts will was proved on oath of Daniel Ritchy & Uriah Blanchard in open Court this 1 June 1805. Before A. Crawford. George and Josiah Roberts was sworn as executors of the above will, to make a true & perfect inventory of all goods & chattels and exhibit the same before the Clerk in three months. This 1 June 1805. Sgn. John Foster, Esq. Reg. 1 June 1805. Pages 36-37.

23 Oct. 1804: I, Daniel McNeil, Senr. Being weak in body but of sound mind & Memory. First I give to my son, Daniel McNeil, one tract of land in Green County on Richland Creek, containing 287½ acres, one pot rack & no more. I give to my beloved wife, Sarah McNeil, all the balance of my estate both real & personal during her natural life, & after her death to be divided as follows: I give to my son, Jesse McNeil, the sum of $214.25, to my dtr. Sarah Reeve(s) the sum of $214.25. I give to my dtr. Ann Lastly (Lashly), the sum of $214.25. I give to my dtr. Aimey Youngblood, $214.25. I give to my dtr. Mary Robeson, $214.25. The sum of $214.25 be divided between my grand-children as follows: Stephen Hoge, William Hoge, Solomon Hoge, Jacob Hoge, Casandia Hoge, Polly Hoge, and the sum of $214.25 be divided between my grand chn. John Youngblood, Daniel Youngblood, Anna Youngblood and Caty Youngblood. Should any property remain, it shall be divided among the said children and grand children. Also I will that my grand chn., Samuel McNair, John McNair and Anna McDonald shall share equal in the last division of property. I appoint Jesse McNeil & John Reeve sole executors. Wit: William Drane, Wiley Olive, W. Drane. Sgn. Daniel McNeil. Proved on oath of William Drane, Wiley Olive & Walter Drane, Esq. this 18 Jun. 1805. A. Crawford, Clk. This 18 Jun. 1805 John Reeve was sworn as executor to make a true and perfect inventory of the goods & chattels and exhibit the same before the Clerk within three months. Signed, John Foster, Esq.

Reg. 18 June 1805. Pages 38-41.

4 Aug. 1805: I, John FitzGarrald, being sick in body, but sound
mind & memory. I give unto my wife, Ann, during her natural life or
widowhood the whole of my estate both real & personal. After her death
or marriage of my wife, I give unto my children (except my sons John &
Silas) the whole of my personal estate to be divided amongst them as
they come of age. I give to my sons John & Silas the 100 acres of land
whereon I now live, with any lots that I may draw in the lottery. Sons
to have their legacey at the age of 18, the dtrs. at the age of 16.
Executors to provide for the two youngest, Silas & Sarah, until they can
care for themselves. I appoint my wife, Ann, executrix & son John,
Executor. Wit: Peter Crawford, James Caldwell, James (X) Thompson. Sgn.
John FitzGarrald. Proved on oath of Peter Crawford, James Caldwell &
James Thompson in open Court this 16 Dec. 1805. A. Crawford, Clk.
This 16 Dec. 1805 Ann FitzGarrald was sworn as executor, and to make a
true & perfect inventory of the goods & chattels of said John FitzGarrald
decd. and exhibit the same at the Clerk of Court Office in three months.
Signed John Foster, Esq. Reg. 16 Dec. 1805. Pages 42-45.

19 Aug. 1799: I, Hugh McGee, being weak in body, but of sound mind
& memory. I give to my beloved wife, Catharine, all my property to be
at her disposal during widowhood, at her death to be equally divided between my two chn., Julia & Thomas, but if she marries I desire that she
to have one third and the children the other two thirds. I appoint my
wife, Catharine, executrix and Hugh Blair executor. Wit: Henry Hampton,
John Ayres, Thos. White. Sgn. Hugh McGee. Proved on oath of Thomas
White, Esq. and John Ayers. This 16 Dec. 1805. A. Crawford, Clk. Pages
46-47.

(The will of Thomas Meriwether written on this page by mistake. It
is in the proper place on page 134. JEW). Page 48.

18 March 1805: I, Joseph Ray, being weak in body but of sound mind
& memory. I lend unto my beloved wife, Nancey Ray, during her natural
life the following negroes, Allen Jarratt, Fanny and two children and
the residue of my negroes (Ben, Nancey and child excepted). I lend to
her during widowhood. I give unto my son, John Ray, (exclusive of the
$550 already given), my negroes Ben, Nancey and child, with two horses,
one now in his possession now, the other I bought of Robert Skelton, also
the sum of $500 cash. I give to my dtr. Nancy Ray the following negroes,
Isbel & two children, Lucy and her increase, one good feather bed &
furniture and $1500 in cash. I give to my four sons, Joseph, James,
William & Henry all my land to be equally divided between them. Reserving the use of the plantation on the lower side of the creek with the
mill & distillery for my wife use & funds in raising the chn. Also to
each of the four named sons to have $1500 in cash when they come of age,
also one good bed & furniture each. I give to my son-in-law Henry West
who married my dtr., Sally, now decease the sum of $2000 to be paid in
two yrs. I appoint my wife executrix & Henry West & Thomas Hemphill
executors. Wit: James Ray, John Avera, Jeremiah Smith, James McCorkle.
Sgn. Jos. Ray. Proved on oath of James Ray & Jeremiah Smith this 17
Dec. 1805. A. Crawford, Clk. This 17 Dec. 1805. Nancey Ray & Henry
West was sworn as executors of the above will, to make a true & perfect
inventory of the goods & chattels of the deceased and exhibit the same
before the Clerk of Court within three months. Signed, John Foster,
Esq. Reg. 17 Dec. 1805. Pages 49-53.

29 March 1805: I, Charles Denham, being weak in body but sound in
mind & memory. To my son, James Denham, I give the fee simple right to
my plantation & the tools, two horses, four good cows & calves also negro
Sylvia and her two chn. Jack & Alex, also two beds & cloathing & all
kitchen furniture. I give to my dtr., Nancey Gilpin, the negroes Sam &
Rose. To my son, Charley Denham, I give negro Dennis. To my son,
Nathaniel, I give negro Sam. To my dtr., Susannah, I give negro Sambo.
As to my dtr., Elizabeth Seukey, & her husband, they have had a good portion out of my estate, I now leave them two silver dollars. The remainder of my personal property to be sold and to give to my dtr., Juanna
Ingleman, the sum of $500, if there is any overplus, it to be given to
my son James Denham. I appoint John Gartreth & James Ray my executors,

154

also to be guardian to my son, James Denham, until he come of age. Wit:
Wm. Beekham, Thos. W. Merrell, Danl. Duffey. Sgn. Chas. (X) Denham.
Proved on oath of William Beekham & Daniel Duffey this 18 June 1805.
A. Crawford, Clk. This 17 Dec. 1805. John Gartreth & James Ray was
sworn as executors to the above will, to make a true & perfect inventory
of the goods & chattels of the decease and exhibit the same in the Clerk
of Court Office within three months. Sgn. John Foster, Esq. Reg. 17
Dec. 1805. Pages 54-57.

11 Sept. 1805: I, Benjamin Rees, being sick & weak in body but of
a sound mind & memory. I give to my son, Richa Rees, $100 to be paid
one year after my decease. I give unto my dtr., Martha Bull, negro girl
Cate. I give to my son, Jeremiah Rees, negro boy Dick. I give unto my
dtr., Ephatha Rees, negro girl Nelly. I give to my dtr., Sarah Rees,
negro girl Milla. I give to my son, Tallifero Rees, negro girl Derry.
I give to my son, James Rees, negro boy Jordin. I give to my son, Tolbert Rees, negro boy Jamy. I give to my son, Albert Rees, negro boy
John. I give to my beloved wife, Sarah Rees, one third of all my remaining property both real & personal. I desire my executors to lay out
five 100 acres lots for each of my son to wit: Richa, Jeremiah, Toli-
ferro, Tolbert, Albert, this land can not be sold or desposed of in any
manner until the youngest come of the age of 21 yrs. Then an equal
division to be made. I appoint my wife, Sarah Bull & Adam
Jones my executors. Wit: Thomas White, Wylie Davis & Mathew Murray this
7 Jan. 1806, before A. Crawford, Clk. This 7 Jan. 1806, Sarah Rees,
Jesse Bull & Adam Jones was sworn as executors of the above will, to
make a true & perfect inventory of all goods & chattels of the decease
and exhibit the same before the Clerk within three months. Signed, J.
Appling, Judge. Rdg. 6 Jan. 1806. Pages 58-61.

11 Feb. 1805: I, Hannah Crute, being sick & weak in body but of
perfect mind & memory. I give unto my dtr., Caty D. Jennings, $200. I
give unto my dtr., Rebekah, negro woman named Cook, also $150 now due
me for the lease of my land in Virginia to be collected and delivered
unto dtr., Rebekeh Foster. I give unto my dtr., Morning Womack, all and
every part & parcel of my estate both real & personal. I appoint my two
friends Edmond Womack (my son-in-law), and Thomas Barron of Lincoln Co.,
Ga. my sole executors. Wit: Thomas Hogan, Mary Hogan. Sgn. Hannah (X)
Crute. Proved on oath of Thomas & Mary Hogan this 13 Jan. 1806. Before
A. Crawford. This 13 Jan. 1806. Edmond Womack was sworn as executor of
the above will, to make a true & perfect inventory of the goods &
chattels of the decease, and exhibit the same before the Clerk of Court
within three months. Signed, J. Appling, Esq. Reg. 13 Jan. 1806.
Pages 62-65.

11 July 1805: I, Charles Nelson, being low in body but of sound
mind & memory. I appoint beloved wife, Lydda Nelson, and John Langston
my lawful executors. I give to my wife, Lydda Nelson, all & every part
of my estate during her life or widowhood, consisting of two horses,
lands, cattle, hogs & household & kitchen furniture, after her entermarriage or death, that my estate to be divided among my children: Polly,
Jesse, John, Jane & Elizabeth Nelson. Wit: John Langston, William Hand
& Henry Hand. Sgn. Charles Nelson. Reg. 13 Jan. 1806. Page 65.

28 June 1805: I, William Winfrey, Being of sound mind & memory.
First, I will that my just debts and funeral charges be paid. I give
unto my son, Hill Winfrey, four negroes, Edmond, Daniel, Fibby & her
child, also one half of the tract of land whereon I now live. I give
unto my son Reuben Winfrey four negroes, Tom, Joe, Sally & Sam and the
other half of the land whereon I now live. I give unto my two sons,
Hill & Reuben Winfrey four negroes, Judah, Amey, Rachel & Mariah in
trust for my dtr., Elizabeth Pearcey, and if she die with out heir, then
the negroes to belong to my two sons named above. I give to my grand
daughter, Ann Winfrey, $600 to be put into two negroes, if she should
die with out heir then the money or negroes to belong to my three chn.
I appoint my sons, Hill & Reuben Winfrey, my executors. Wit: James Wood,
Abraham Franklin, W. J. Stevens. Sgn. William Winfrey. Proved on oath
of James Wood & William J. Stevens this 5 May 1806. A. Crawford. This
5 May 1806 Reuben Winfrey was sworn as executor of the above will, to
make a true and perfect inventory of the goods & chattels of the decease

155

and exhibit the same before the Clerk of Court within three months of this date. Sgn. Thos. Cobb, Justice. Reg. 8 May 1806. Pages 66-70.

17 March 1806: I, Isaac Lowe, being sick & weak but of perfect mind & memory. I give unto my beloved wife, Elizabeth, negro woman Delcy & her issue, also negro boy Moses, one girl named Nelly, one brown mare & riding chair, two feather beds & furniture, saddle & bridle during her natural life, then to be divided amongst my children. I also give unto my wife negroes, Charley, Nancey, Maria, Betty, Dicey, Peter, Lillie, Jack, Guy, Nedd & Thos. the last five is for the raising & educating my children. I give to my wife during her natural life the tract of land whereon I now live with 50 acres adj. I give unto my son, Curtis Lowe, 100 acres of land original granted to Richard Jones, also one feather bed & furniture. I give unto my son, Isaac Lowe, 100 acres of land, being part of the land granted unto John Stubbs, decd. adj. land of Daniel Vaughan, also one horse colt & one feather bed & furniture. I give unto my sons, David Walker Lowe & George Lowe, a tract of land containing 116 acres grain & one saw mill, originally granted to John Stubbs, decd. adj. lands of Saton & Johnston to be equally divided between them when they come of age, also one horse, saddle & bridle, one feather bed & furniture each when of age. I give to my dtr., Sarah, one negro, one horse, saddle & bridle, feather bed & furniture, an equal portion, at the death of my wife. I give unto my dtr., Elizabeth, a young negro, one horse, saddle & bridle, bed & furniture, with an equal portion at the death of my wife. I give unto my dtr., Esther, a young negro, one horse, saddle, bridle, feather bed & furniture, an equal portion at the death of my wife. I give unto my dtr., Martha Slayton Lowe, one young negro, one horse, saddle & bridle, one feather bed & furniture with an equal portion of the personal property at my wife's death. I give unto my dtr., Rebecca R. Lowe, one young negro, one horse, saddle & bridle, one feather bed & furniture, an equal portion of the personal property at the death of my wife. I give to my dtr., Matilda, one young negro, one horse, saddle & bridle, one feather bed & furniture, an equal portion of the personal property at the death of my wife. I will that my dtr., Polly Slaton, be placed on an equal footing with the rest of my dtrs. before mentioned. I appoint my wife Elizabeth executrix and son Curtis Lowe executor. Wit: Moses Jackson, Thomas White, Katharine White. Sgn. Isaac Lowe. Proved on oath of Thomas & Katherine White. This 5 May 1806. This 5 May 1806, Elizabeth Lowe & Curtis Lowe was sworn as executors of the above will, to make a true & perfect inventory of the goods & chattels and exhibit the same before the Clerk of Court within three months. Signed, Thomas Cobb, Justice. Reg. 8 May 1806. Pages 71-75.

3 March 1806: I, John McCarthy, being very weak in body, but perfect mind & memory. I give to my loveing wife, Mary McCarthy, the land whereon I now live, so long as she remains a widow then to be divided between my two sons, Rhesha & James. Likewise I give to my wife all farming tools, waggons, household furniture, to be divided between my two sons at my wife's marriage or death. I also give to my wife all stock after giving my dtr., Keziah, one red cow & calf, to my dtr., Salome, one speckled cow & calf, to my grand daughter, Linna Wiley, one black heifer. I appoint my wife, Mary McCarthy & Thomas Johnson as executors. Wit: Winnefred (X) Johnson, William Harris. Signed John McCarthy. Proved on oath of William Harris, this 5 May 1806. Sgn. A. Crawford, Clk. This 5 May 1806, Mary McCarthy & Thomas Johnston was sworn as executors of the above will, to make a true & perfect inventory of the goods & chattels and exhibit the same before the Clerk of Court within three months. Sgn. Thomas Cobb, Judge. Reg. 8 May 1806. Pages 76-79.

6 Nov. 1775: I, Benjamin Horn of the Provence of Georgia, being very sick and weak of body, but of perfect mind & memory. I give to my beloved wife my lands and mill and all the negroes belonging to me, also my horses, hogs, cattle and every personal belonging to me. To my son, Benjamin Horn, I give one shilling sterling, also after my wife's death the whole of my estate to be sold & divided equally among my grandchildren as aforesaid mentioned. I appoint this subscriber to my executors. Wit: Edward (C) Weathers & John Anderson. Sgn. Benjamin (B) Horn. Before his excellency Archibald Bullock, Esq., President and Commander

in Chief of said Provence and Ordinary of the same. Personally appeared
Edward Weathers, planter and John Anderson a school master, both of St.
George Parish, was sworn, and saith that they saw Benjamin Horn sign,
seal and publish his last will & testament. And they were qualified as
executors. Given under my hand this 12 Dec. 1776. Signed, Arch. Bullock. A true copy taken from the record in Book A fol. 269-270. Signed
James Whitefield, Secy. Reg. 7 July 1806. Pages 80-82.

3 May 1810(?): I, Dixon Perryman, being weak of body but of sound
mind & memory. First I desire all my just debts be paid. I desire all
my personal property to remain in the hands of my wife, Rebecca Perryman, during her widowhood or my children are under the lawful age. I
desire my executors to divide my real estate in an equitable manner between my children or in such a way that they think most proper. Likewise, all my moveable property such as notes, accounts, negroes, household furniture, and cattle also be equally divided accordingly. I wish
my friends Anderson Crawford, Daniel Marshall, David Stanford & my
brother, Elisha Perryman, my executors. Wit: Col. John Appling, W. Ware,
Rachel Perryman. Sgn. D. Perryman. Proved on oath of W. Ware & Elisha
Perryman, this 7 July 1806. A. Crawford, Clk. This 7 July 1806, David
Stanford & Elisha Perryman was sworn as executors to the above will, to
make a true & perfect inventory of all the goods & chattels of the decease and exhibit the same before the Clerk of Court within three months
of this date. Sgn. John Foster, Justice. Reg. 11 --- 1806. Pages 83-
86.

24 Sept. 1805: I, Stephen Stanford, being in a low state of health
but of sound mind & memory. I appoint John Bayne & my beloved wife,
Nancey Stanford, my executors. I give unto Nancey, my beloved wife,
during her natural life all my lands, cattle, furniture & crops in the
field. I give to my son Josep(h) Stanford one dollar. I give to my
dtr., Patty Howell, one dollar. I give to my son, William Stanford, all
my land at my wife's death or marriage, except 100 (acres) to be divided
amongst the children that Nancey brought to me. Wit: Polly Mathew,
Polly Owens, John Bayn. Sgn. Stephen (X) Stanford. Proved on oath of
Polly Mathew & Polly Brown (formerly Polly Owens) this 7 July 1806.
This 7 July 1806, Nancey Stanford was sworn as executor of the above
will, to make a true & perfect inventory of the goods & chattels of the
decease and exhibit the same before the Clerk of Court within three
months. Sgn. John Foster, Esq. Reg. 11 July 1806. Pages 87-90.

27 Aug. 1802: I, Rebecca Smith, being frail in body but of sound
mind & memory. I give unto Rebecca Flint, the dtr. of Thomas Flint, a
negro woman called Doll, also my riding saddle and wearing apparel. I
give unto Sarah Flint, the dtr. of Thomas Flint, one negro named Pat. I
give unto Thomas H. Flint, negroes, Harry, Alek, Philly, also all my
feather beds & furniture and household furniture, also 200 acres of land
bought from Hezekiah Jones and any other land I may have at my death.
I give unto John Flint the son of Thomas H. Flint, negro girl Easter. I
give unto William Flint the son of Thomas Flint, negro girl Cate. I
give unto James, Thomas & Aquilla Flint, the three youngest sons of
Thomas H. Flint, the money now due me for the rent, about $80 to be
equally divided between them. I give unto Thomas H. Flint all my stock
of every kind. I appoint Thomas H. Flint my executor. Wit: A. Crawford,
William Young, Peter (X) Young. Sgn. Rebekah Smith. Proved on oath of
Anderson Crawford & William Young this 7 July 1806. Sgn. John Foster,
J.I.C. This 7 July 1806, Thomas H. Flint was sworn as executor of the
above will, to make a true inventory of the goods & chattels of the
decease and exhibit the same before the Clerk of Court within three
months. Sgn. John Foster, Judge. Reg. 11 July 1806. Pages 90-94.

29 April 1806: I, Edward Sanders, being weak in body but of sound
mind & memory. I desire all my outstanding debts due me to be collected
and to pay any which I may owe at my death. I give unto my wife, Betsey
Sanders, during her natural life & no longer, a tract of land lying in
Wilkerson County, containing 202½ acres, known as lot #18, at my wife's
death I give the same unto my child, Caroline Matilda Sanders, also in
the same manner a tract of land lying in the first district of Baldwin
County, of 101¼ acres, known as lot #352, I also give unto my child,
Caroline Matilda Sanders the other half of the above lot #352, also one

157

feather bed and furniture, three cows & two calves which I have at
father-in-law W. Ingram. I give unto my wife, Betsey, my two horses,
my riding chair, one feather bed & furniture and the remainder of my
personal estate. I appoint my wife, Betsey Sanders, Edmond Blunt and
Jesse Sanders Junr. my executors. Wit: Jesse Sanders, N. Sanders, & P.
Sanders. Sgn. Edward Sanders. Proved on oath of Jesse Sanders, Philip
Sanders, & Nancey Sanders. This 7 July 1806. This 7 July 1806, Edmond
Blunt & Jesse Sanders, Junr., was sworn as executors of the above will,
to make a true inventory of the goods & chattels of the decease and
exhibit the same before the Clerk of Court within three months. Signed,
John Foster, Judge. Reg. 12 July 1806. Pages 94-98.

18 Jan. 1806: I, Betty Tyler, being weak in body but of sound mind
& memory. First, if I owe any debts, I desire they be paid. I give
unto my niece, Lucy Blackwell, a negro woman Fanny and her child Celia.
I give to my niece, Betty Blackwell, a negro man Gerald (by trade a
carpenter), a woman Sall and her chn., Ben, Phill, Cyrus & Page, also my
feather bed & furniture, my chest of drawers, & trunks. I give to my
niece, Alice Blackwell, a negro man named Fielding. I give to my niece,
Sally Blackwell, my negro boy named Willis & negro woman Daphne. I desire
after my death, my house wench Dinah shall belong to my sister, Sally
Blackwell, or to either or my nieces. I give to my sister, Sally Blackwell, my negro man Phill, also to my niece, Betty Blackwell, my riding
chair. I appoint John Tyler Allen & Marshall Kieth my executors. Wit:
Ann Stanton, William Bryant, & J. L. Allen. Sgn. Betty Tyler. Proved
3 Nov. 1806, and this day was sworn John Tyler Allen & Marshall Kieth as
executors of the above will, to make a true inventory of the goods &
chattels of the decease and exhibit the same before the Clerk of Court
within three months. Signed Thos. Cobb, Judge. Reg. 5 Nov. 1806.
Pages 98-101.

17 Dec. 1806: I, William Dunivan, am very sick and poorly but in
perfect mind & memory. Do appoint Harberd Dunivan & Notley Whitenmoe
my executors. To my son, Harband Dunivan, I give one shilling, having
received his part. I give Claricey Roberts one shilling, she having
received her part. I give to Elizabeth Bradberry one shilling. I give
to dtr., Polly, one feather bed & furniture, also one loom & gun, one
spinning wheel. I give to my son, Man Dunivan, to have all the rest of
my estate both personal & moveable after the death of Mary Dunivan, his
mother. Wit: Mandrake (X) Rukerton & Joseph Downs. Sgn. William (X)
Dunivan. Proved on oath of Marendrake Rukerton & Joseph Downs this 5
Jan. 1807. Pages 102-103.

Page 104 is blank.

19 July 1805: I, Hickerson Cosby, of Wilkes County, Ga. being in a low
state of health, but of a sound mind & memory. Whereas I have purchased
a tract of land in Columbia Co. from John North, and made a partical
payment, I desire my executors to sell my negro woman Eve for the purpose
of making payment. After my just debts are paid I desire that the ballance of the property be used to support the wife & children. After the
death of my wife I desire that my estate both real & personal be equally
divided between my children. I appoint my friend, John Wingfield, Robert
Harris and Peter B. Terrill and my son, Garland Cosby, my executors.
Wit: David Terrell & Sanders Stallings. Sgn. Hick-- Cosby. Proved on
oath of Sanders Stallings this 5 Jan. 1807. A. Crawford. This 5 Jan.
1807, Garland Hickerson (?) (Cosby), was sworn as executor of the above
will, to make a true inventory of the goods & chattels of the decease
and exhibit the same before the Clerk of Court within three months.
Signed, John Foster, Judge. Reg. 8 Jan. 1807. Pages 120-123.

14 Jan. 1806: I, William Miles, being in an advanced stage of life
but of sound mind & memory. I give to my beloved wife, Mary Miles, the
sum of $500, also during her natural life, negro woman called Cate & her
dtr. Rose, also household furniture and one third part of the plantation
whereon I now reside and one third part of the stock of horses, cattle,
hogs, & sheep. At the death of my wife, executors to make application
to the Legislature of this State for the emancipation of the following
negroes, Quammony, Peter & Cate. I give to my friend, Peter Watson, &
his heirs the tract of land whereon I now reside, containing near 400

acres, bound by lands of Prudence W. Nrun, Thomas Shorts & Aaron Parks, but not to be considered his until the death of my wife. I also give to Peter Watson, negroes Dave, Jem, Allen, & Hannah after my decease, and also negro girl Rose after the death of my wife, likewise negro Delcy. I give to my half nephew by the mother side James Mappin, son of John Mappin one negro boy named Isam, one feather bed & furniture, one cow & calf & no more. I give to Peter Watson the remaining two thirds of the stock, wagon & gear, household & kitchen furniture. I give to my negroes Quammony, Peter & Cate at the time of emancipation a tract of land supposed to be 40 acres, and it shall be the duty of my friend Peter Watson to furnish them with one cow & calf, one club axe, two weeding hoes, one horse of $50 value, one small plough, also 20 bushels of corn, 150 pounds of meat, the land to be considered the property of Peter & Cate, during their natural life & no longer; the lands joining Shields & John Moore near where an old school house used to stand. I appoint Aaron Parks & Thomas White executors. Wit: Mauldon Amos, Jesse Bull & Danl. Massingal. Sgn. William Miles. Proved on oath of Mauldon Amos, Jesse Bull & Daniel Massingall, this 4 May 1807. Sgn. A. Crawford, Clk. This 4 May 1807. Thomas White was sworn as executor of the above will of the above will of the decease, to make a true inventory of the goods & chattels and exhibit the same before the Clerk of Court within three months. (Not signed). Reg. this 5 May 1807. Pages 108-112.

2 Jan. 1807: Noncupative will of Winnefred Jenkins. "Personally appeared before me Martha Collins wife of William Collins, Senr. and after being duly sworn, deposeth and saith that on Sunday last this deponant was sent for to attend on the dying moments of the widow of the late Col. James Jenkins deceased but after some short time the widow recovered so that she lived several days but as soon as she Mrs. Jenkins could talk she then told this deponant how she wish a part of the property divided (JE), one brown cow to James Reed's wife and children to make beef so Elizabeth Dentinack the warp & felling for one habit Pattern. (?) To Margaret McGill one new black bonnet, to this deponant one old black bonnet and wear it for the sake of the deceased. To Joshua and Hightower Thorn all her household and kitchen furniture to be equally divided between them. To the children of Prestly Thorn $50 to be appropriated to the education of the said children under the direction of her brother Hightower and this deponant further saith that she has attended on Mrs. Jenkins till her death which took place this day and never heard the decease say any thing to her contrary. Sworn to before this 2 Jan. 1807. Signed Martha Collins, before James Simms, J.P." Pages 112-113.

17 May 1807: I, Anthony Garnett, being very sick & weak but of sound mind and memory. I give to my beloved wife Rebecah all my personal estate during her life, after paying my just debts. I give to all my children an equal part of my estate after the death of my wife. I appoint John Eubanks & Asa Doggett my executors. Wit: Gerard Morris, Thos. Jones, Richard Eubanks. Sgn. Anthony (X) Garnett. Proved on oath of Gerard Morris, Thomas Jones, Richard Eubanks. This 6 July 1807. Sgn. A. Crawford, Clk. This 6 July 1807 John Eubanks and Asa Doggett was sworn as executors of the above will, to make a true inventory of the goods & chattels of the decease and exhibit the same before the Clerk of Court within three months. Signed, Jno. Foster, Judge. Reg. 7 July 1807. Pages 114-116.

14 May 1807: I, Amos Sessoms, being weak in body but of sound mind and memory. I will & desire my executors to sell 10 head of cattle for the support of my wife Mary Sessoms & three dtrs. to wit: Dolly, Caty & Nancy Sessoms and to pay the fee should I be drawn in the land lottery. The ballance of my property to remain for my wife Mary's support during her natural life, then to be sold and the money equally divided between my three dtrs. I appoint Walter Maddox and Archer Avary my executors. Wit: Garner Doggett, Walter Maddox, Harriet T. Lamkin & Elizabeth Lamkin. Amos (X) Sessoms. Proved on oath of Walter Maddox & Garner Doggett, this 6 July 1807. Sgn. A. Crawford. This 6 July 1807, Walter Maddox and Archer Avary was sworn as executors of the above will, to make a true inventory of the goods & chattels of the decease and exhibit the same before the Clerk of Court within three months. Sgn. John Foster, Judge. Reg. 7 July 1807. Pages 117-119.

159

11 Aug. 1807: I, Levi Marshall, give unto my wife the house &
land I now live on, Beginning at Timothy Pittman's land, up Keoka Creek
to Daniel Marshall's land to Green Brier then down creek to John Marshall's mill, I reserve 3 acres opposite his mill for his use, during my
wife's life time, then to my son Levi. I give to my son Joseph Marshall
the land I bought of Col. Few containing 400 acres. In case Levi should
die before full age, then his land to become the property of Joseph. I
give unto my two youngest dtrs. Elisa & Emely the tract of land lying on
the other side the mill, in case either should die, the other shall have
the property when of full age. I give to my two dtrs. Sally & Polly
Crawford the tract of land whereon Robert Bartee now lives containing
333 acres to be divided between them. I give unto Nathan Crawford the
lot of land I drew in the last lottery. I give unto Polly Crawford
negroes, Bill & Nanee, Dave, Nance, Milly & Jinny, the value of $1550.
I give unto my son Joseph, negroes Jinny, Charlotte, Abraham, Harry,
Natt, Dick the value of $1550. I give unto my wife during her life,
negroes, Cate, Dick, Nick, Pherby, & Dicey the value of $1450. At her
death to be the property of my son Levi. I give to my dtr. Sally, negroes Hannah, Rachel, Lewis, Aggy, & Little Will the value of $1450. I
give unto my dtr. negroes, Monday, Nance, Natt, Louisa the value of $1400.
I give unto my dtr. Emely, negroes, John, Beck, Charly, & Candis at the
value of $1400. I desire that my son Joseph and the other children as
they come of age to have a horse, 4 cows, one bed & furniture. I appoint my wife & my son Joseph, Doc. Nathan Crawford and my brother Daniel
Marshall my executors. Wit: William Booke, Mike Smalley, James Leeke.
Sgn. Levi Marshall. Proved on oath of William Books, Michael Smalley &
James Leeks, this 7 Sept. 1807. A. Crawford, Clk. This 7 Sept. 1807.
Sarah Marshall, Joseph Marshall, Nathan Crawford & Daniel Marshall was
sworn as executors to the above will, to make a true inventory of the
goods & chattels of the decease, and exhibit the same before the Clerk
of Court Office within three months. Signed, John Foster, Judge. Reg.
8 Sept. 1807. Pages 120-123.

20 Nov. 1807: Walter Dranes will. Baldwin County, Ga. I, Being
weak in body, but of perfect mind & memory. First I desire that my just
debts to be paid. I desire that all my estate both real & personal to
be equally divided between my beloved wife Allethe Drane and my six
children to wit: Cassander, Anna, Betsey, Walter, Polly and Efey to
share alike. I appoint my brother William Drane, & brother-in-law Benjamin Leigh my executors. Wit: Hugh Blair, Jr., B. Williams, & John
Foster. Sgn. W. Drane. Proved on oath of Hugh Blair, Junr., Benjamin
Williams & John Foster. They saw Walter Drane, Esq. sign his last will.
This 4 Jan. 1808. Signed A. Crawford. This 4 Jan. 1808. William
Drane was sworn as executor to the above will. To make a true inventory
of the goods & chattels of the decease, and exhibit the same before the
Clerk of Court within three months. Sgn. John Foster, Judge. Recd. 5
Jan. 1808. Pages 124-126.

7 Aug. 1807: I, David Harris, being of sound mind & memory. I
desire that my just debts to be paid and that my son John Harris is to
be my sole executor. I give unto my beloved wife, Mary Harris, all the
property both real & personal during her natural life or widowhood. I
will that my grand-son, David Harris, son of John Harris when he arrive
at lawfull age one negro called Phil, in case of David's death before
full age the property to belong to son, John Harris. I desire that my
grand-son, Williamson Speers, to have one feather bed & furniture when
he comes of age, in case of his death the property to belong to his
sister, Drusilla, which is in their possession. I give one feather bed
to my grand-dtr., Mariah Bowder, on her coming of age or marriage. I
will that my son Edward Harris have one certificate for 640 acres due of
the State to Z. Franklin and I have given Benjamin Bledsoe the husband
of my dtr. Sarah, also Samuel Bowder the husband of my dtr. Polly, who
have receive amply property out of my estate. In case my wife marry
again, she to have a negro woman named Candace a reasonable part of the
household & kitchen furniture & stock, at her death to be the property
of my son John. I give to my grand-son Richmond Bledsoe one feather bed
& furniture when he is of full age, in case he should die before, it to
be the property of his brother Giles Bledsoe. Wit: Wm. Colvard, Levi
Pearre, & Joshua (X) Vaughn. Sgn. D. Harris. Proved on oath of William
Colvard, Levi Pearre & Joshua Vaughn, this 4 Jan. 1808. A. Crawford.

This 4 Jan. 1808. John Harris was sworn as executor of the above will, to make a true inventory of the goods & chattels of the decease and exhibit the same before the Clerk of Court within three months. Signed, A. Appling, Judge. Reg. 6 Jan. 1808. Pages 127-130.

22 Oct. 1807: I, Ervin Brown, being at this time of a sound mind & memory. I give the part of my father's estate belonging to me to John Brown, Joseph Brown, Henry Brown, Nancey & Patsey Brown my brothers & sister to be equally divided between them. I give my mare & wearing apparel to my beloved friend & half-brother Allen Warren. I wish & desire that the money due me, to wit: one note on William Calhoun of Abbeville Dist., S.C. for $100 placed in the hands of John Bowies for collection, one note on Wyate Logan for $7 in the hands of Sidwell Bacon of S.C. for collection, two notes on John Bowie, Jr., of S.C. for $85 & for $22 in the hands of said Bacon for collection, to pay my just debts. Any money left to be divided between my brothers & sisters afore mentioned. I appoint my friend Allen Warren & brother John Brown my executors. Wit: John Todd, John Bradberry & Elizabeth I. Todd. Sgn. Ervin Brown. Proved on oath of John Todd & John Bradberry this 4 Jan. 1808. A. Crawford, Clk. This 4 Jan. 1808, John Brown was sworn as executor to the above will, to make a true inventory of the goods & chattels of the decease, and exhibit the same before the Clerk of Court within three months. Signed, John Foster, Judge. Reg. 7 Jan. 1808. Pages 131-133.

7 Aug. 1807: I, Thomas Meriwether, do make this my last will and testament. I give to Micah Evans at present living with me for the good she has rendered to me two thousand dollars. I give to my brother Nicholas Meriwether whom I likewise appoint my sole executor, and all my lands, mesuages & tenements with all my slaves, stock of every kind, household furniture, money on hand, all debts, dues and demands. Wit: Archer Avary, James Boyd & Asa Avary. Sgn. Thos. Meriwether. Proved on oath of Archer Avary & Asa Avary, this 2 May 1808. A. Crawford. This 2 May 1808. Nicholas Meriwether was sworn as executor of the above will, to make a true inventory of the goods & chattels of the decease and exhibit the same before the Clerk of Court within three months. Signed, John Foster, Judge. Reg. this 3 May 1808. Pages 134-136.

17 Feb. 1808: I, Abner Sims, being of sound mind & memory. First I desire that my just debts to be paid, in order to do this, it is my desire my executors to sell my crop of cotton that I may possess at my death. I desire that the 400 acres of land on the Augchee River in Warren County, joining McKinley and 202½ acres in the third district of Baldwin County, #204, granted in my name, to be sold and the money for the use of my wife & children as my executors think best. The rest and residue of my property I give to my wife during her life time or widowhood, then to be equally divided amongst all my children. I appoint my wife Mary Penn Sims executrix, and my friend Charles T. Beall & Peter Crawford my executors. Wit: Man Sims, Thomas Parker & Eliza Hanson. Sgn. Abner Sims. Proved on oath of Thomas Parker in open Court 4 July 1808. This 4 July 1808 Charles Beall was sworn as executor of the above will, to make a true inventory of the goods & chattels of the decease and exhibit the same before the Clerk of Court within three months. Signed, John Foster, Judge. Recd. 11 July 1808. Pages 137-140.

11 May 1808: I, John Treel, being sick & weak in body but of sound mind & memory. I give to my dtr., Mary Hicks, one negro boy named Bob now in her possession, also $200. I give to my son, Lewis Treel, one wagon and my rifle gun. I give to my dtr., Elizabeth, one negro boy named Ostin also during her natural life 101½ acres of land, being one half of lot #33, lying in the 14 district of Baldwin County, to her & her heirs forever. Also one mare & colt, 13 head of cattle, one feather bed & furniture, 6 head sheep, 6 head of hogs, 20 geese. I give to my dtr. Keziah Roberts $50. I give unto my dtr. Ann Ellis $14. I give to my dtr., Winnifred Martin, 101½ acres being the other half of #33 lying in the 14 district of Baldwin County, to her & her heirs forever, also $25. I give to the heirs of my deceased son John Treel $1. I give to my beloved wife negroes, Volentine, Rose, Dick, Claey, and I do give all and every part of my estate not given to my beloved wife during her natural life then to be divided amongst the above named children. I appoint my wife Elizabeth Treel my executrix & friend Hugh Blair, Esq.

161

& my grandson John Hicks executors. Wit: Waters Dunn, John Culbreath,
& J. Few. Sgn. John (X) Treel. Proved on oath of Walter Dunn & John
Culbreath this 4 July 1808. Sgn. A. Crawford. This 4 July, Elizabeth
Treel & John Hicks was sworn as executors of the above will, to make a
true inventory of the goods & chattels of the decease, and exhibit the
same before the Clerk of Court within three months. Signed, John Foster,
Judge. Recd. 10 July 1808. Pages 140-143.

9 Nov. 1807: I, Waters Dunn, Senr. being of sound mind & memory.
I lend unto my beloved wife, Winny, the tract of land whereon I now live
during her widowhood. I give to my two youngest children, Alfred Jefferson & Elbert Baldwin Dunn, the priviledge of liveing on the place &
their negroes until each are of full age, also they are to have the tract
of land given unto my wife at marriage or death, to be divided as, beginning at the persimmon corner on the line between said land & James
Reed near my gate, land to be divided into equal parts, with my son
Elbert Baldwin Dunn to have my brick house. I give to my sons, Waters
& George Washington Dunn, the tract of land whereon Waters now live, to
be divided between them, with Waters to have the part whereon he now
lives. I give to my dtr., Elizabeth, all that tract of land I drew,
lying in the 5th district of Baldwin County. All other land I wish to be
sold and the money used for my wife & children. I give unto my wife,
Winny, negroes, Polly & her chn. Cicero, Ralph & William. I give unto
my dtr., Elizabeth, negroes, Patty & her chn., Charlotte, Henry & Peter
with boy Sam. I give unto my son, George, negroes, Jacob, Hannah, Dice
& her child Simon. I give to my son, Alfred, negroes, Harriett & her
chn. Milley & John. I give to my son, Elbert, negroes, Winney & her
three chn. Dick, Robin & Tom. My wife to have first choice of bed &
furniture and each of the children to have likewise. I appoint my wife
executrix & my sons, Waters & George at the age of eighteen my executors.
Wit: John Briscoe, Catharine Briscoe, Geo. A. Brown. Sgn. Waters Dunn.
Proved on oath of John & Catharine Briscoe, this 1 Aug. 1808. A. Crawford. This 1 Aug. 1808. Winney Dunn & Waters Dunn was sworn as executors to the above, to make a true inventory of the goods & chattels of
the decease and exhibit the same before the Clerk of Court within three
months. Signed, John Foster, Judge. Reg. 4 Aug. 1808. Pages 144-148.

12 May 1808: I, John Eubanks, First I give unto my loving wife,
Rebecah Eubanks, six negroes, Batty & her three chn., Letty, Isaac &
Dice & Joe & Isham, also six hundred dollars in cash, and one bay gilden.
I give unto my son, William Eubanks, all my land & premises whereon I
now live, also 9 negroes, Harry, Cate, & her seven chn. Hal, Clary, Rachel,
Lucy, Peter, Alce & Mary. I appoint my wife Rebecah Eubanks, & my
brother, Richard Eubanks, and William Jones my executors. Wit: Jesse
Roberts, Major Eubanks, John Germany, Junr. Sgn. John Eubanks. Proved
in open Court on oath of Major Eubanks the 5 Sept. 1808. In the Court
of Ordinary, John Germany, Senr. & Jesse Roberts testified to the contents of the above probate made by Major Eubanks. Sworn in open Court
this 7 Nov. 1808. A. Crawford, Clk. This 7 Nov. 1808, Richard Eubanks
& William Jones was sworn as executors to the above will, to make a
true inventory of the goods & chattels of the decease and exhibit the
same before the Clerk of Court within three months. Signed, John Foster,
Judge. A. Crawford. Reg. 7 Nov. 1808. Pages 149-151.

28 Oct. 1808. I, John Ramsey, give unto my beloved wife, Mary
Ramsey, 203½ acres of land where I now live, also 5 negroes, Old Peter,
George, Tiller, Susan & Suky, one waggon & team, also one mare called
Poll, also all cattle of hoggs, Sheep, household & kitchen furniture
during her natural life or widowhood. In the event of either death or
intermarriage the property to belong to my son, Isaac Ramsey, except
what household furniture she thinks proper to divide among the rest of
the children. I give unto my dtr., Martha Ramsey, 300 acres of land
lying on the waters of Kiokels, originally granted to Isaac Ramsey, Senr.
and known as the race tract also 200 acres of pine land granted to myself
lying between the heads of Reedy & Deep creeks, also 7 negroes, Sam &
his wife Else, and her 2 chn. Edmund & Johnston, Old Sal, Sidney & Joshua.
I give unto Samuel Ramsey 358 acres, lying on Little Keokee, being part
of a 600 acres grant given unto Randal Ramsey, joining lands of Williamson Wynne & Isaac Ramsey, also 8 negroes, Abraham & his wife Sal & their
3 chn. Hannah, Hager & Austin, Beverly Lewis & Nance, also one sorrel

162

horse, one rifle gun. I give to my son, Isaac Ramsey, 300 acres of land,
lying on Little Keokee, one hundred acres granted unto James Graves, the
other 200 acres being part of a 600 acres tract granted unto Randal
Ramsey, joining Balis & John Culbreath also seven negroes, Big Peter,
Jerry, Gilbert, Tom, Willey, Lucy and her child Bibb also one filley,
and a shot gun. I will & desire that four head of horses, 30 bales of
cotton now on hand and all the present crop of cotton and all outstanding debts to be applied to the payment of my just debts. I appoint my
wife Mary Ramsey executrix & John Culbreath and Isaac Ramsey executors.
Wit: Isham Baylis, Eleanor Ramsey & Elisha Ryan. Sgn. John Ramsey.
Proved on oath of Isham Baylis, Eleanor Ramsey & Elisha Ryan, in open
Court this 6 Feb. 1809. This 6 March 1809. Mary Ramsey & John Culbreath
was sworn as executors to the above will, to make a true inventory of
the goods & chattels of the decease, and exhibit the same before the
Clerk of Court within three months. Signed: John Foster, Judge. Reg.
6 Feb. 1809. Pages 163-166.

24 July 1805: I, Ambrose Jones, give unto my son, Richard Jones,
110 acres of land in the County of Green, lying on Hills Creek, joining
Samuel & Nathaniel Hix when surveyed, to be taken off the upper end of
the original bounty, and to include the Gum spring. To make him equal
with my son Thomas Jones & dtr. Sarah H. Avery. I also give to son
Richard one negro named Lewis, one feather bed & furniture, one horse,
bridle & saddle, and $30 at marriage or age of 21 yrs. old. I give to
my son Gabriel Jones one negro. I give to my dtr., Catharine E. Jones,
one negro named Samuel, one feather bed & furniture, one horse, bridle &
saddle and $30 at her marriage or age of 21 yrs. old. The rest of my
estate I leave to my beloved wife, Mary Jones. Notwithstanding my three
youngest chn. to wit: Ambrose, Gabriel & Catharine Jones shall be supported and schooled from the est. At the death of my wife, I give the
rest of my estate to my chn. to share alike, that is Richard, Thomas
Jones & Sarah H. Avery, Ambrose, Gabriel, and Catharine Jones. I appoint
my wife Mary, Richard, Thomas Jones & Archer Avery to be executors and
to be guardians of my minor children. Wit: John Walton, Philip Tinsley
& James Walton. Sgn. Ambrose Jones. Proved on oath of James Walton on
the 2 June 1809 also Phillip Tinsley on the 6 March 1809. On the 9 March
Mary, Richard and Thomas Jones was named executors to make a true & perfect inventory of the goods & chattels, and exhibit the same within
three months before the Clerk of Court. Signed John Foster, O.C.C.
Signed A. Crawford, Clk. Reg. 4 April 1809. Pages 156-158.

7 March 1809: I, John Marshall, son of Revd. D. Marshall, being low
in health, but in possession of reason, memory and power of mind. I
wish the servants, horses, stock & tools to be keep together until the
present crop is made. I wish that Jude & her two chn. Mary & Elender
with all she may have & William be put in possession of my dtr., Merrian
Morriss, on the first day January next to serve her for five years from
said date then Jude and the other named servants to be set free. In like
manner my negroes David & Andrew to serve my dtr., Sarah Jones, the same
time & manner then to be free. My servants Charles and Herculus to be
hired out for five years from January next and then set free. I wish all
debts due me in bonds, notes, and book accounts be collected and part of
my horses, cattle, hoggs be sold and discharge my just debts. I wish my
household & kitchen furniture remain in hands of my two dtrs., Merrean
& Sarah, until the heirs of my dtrs. Elizabeth & Eunice, come of age,
then equally divided amongst all, that is chn. of Elizabeth one fourth
part, Dtr. Eunice son have one fourth part, Merrian chn. to have one
fourth part, Sarah chn. to have one fourth part. I will that the 100
acres that my dtr. Elizabeth lived on & died be rented and the profit be
given to her chn. for their raising & schooling. I wish my two dtrs.
Merrian & Sarah take possession of the remaining land, horses, mill &
fields and that no destruction of tember or clearing of land be made.
As or when the heirs come of age an equal division be made. To this I
appoint my two son-in-laws Thomas Jones & G. Morris my active executors,
also I appoint my three brothers A. Marshall, S. Marshall & J. Marshall
to council and advise and execute with equal power this will. Wit: D.
Marshall, Joseph Marshall & Samuel (X) Marshall. Sgn. John Marshall.
Proved on oath of Daniel, Joseph & Samuel Marshall, this 3 April 1809.
The same date Daniel, Samuel & Thomas Marshall and Thomas Jones with G.
Morris was appointed executors, to make a true and perfect inventory of

the goods & chattels of the decease and exhibit the same before the
Clerk within three months. Signed, J. Foster. Reg. 5 Apr. 1809. Pages
159-163.

2 March 1809: I, John Benning, being weak in body but of sound
mind & memory. I give unto my son, Joseph Benning, negroes Bob, Ned,
Charles and Jenny, also a tract of land purchased from Herbert Avary. I
give to my son Thomas Benning the land whereon I now live lying above
my Spring Branch, joining Mr. Normond's line & Yancy Sander's land, also
negroes, Sam, Jacob, Abram, Sire, Hannah, Ben & Fary. I give to my son
Pleasant the other part of the above land, with negroes, Tom, Harry,
Hannah & Phill. I give to my dtr., Elizabeth Fur, negroes, Patt, Nancy,
Polydore, Patrick & Agg. I give to my dtr., Rowanna, negroes, Big Bob,
Mage, Daniel, Bird, Lucy, Grace, & Lucy Jr. also Mary. I give to my dtr.
Susannah, negroes Ailsey, Lewis, Milly & Sisley. I give unto my dtr.,
Martha D., negroes Marlin, Winny, George, Jacob Ann, Theny, Ureley &
Isaac. I give unto my dtr., Sally C. Benning, negroes, Ned, Doll, Venus,
Rachel, Patt, Nicy, Cumberland and Carey. I give to my dtr. Nancy
negroes, Ephraim, Adam, Molly, Peter, Sawney, Moses, Hampton & Phillis.
I give unto my dtrs. Rowanna, Martha D., Sally C. and Nancy Benning one
feather bed & furniture. I give unto my grandson Thomas P. Thompson one
negro named Terry. I give unto my granddaughter Lucinda Thompson $300
to be paid when she come the age of 21 yrs. old or marry. All the residue of my estate to be divided among my sons, Joseph, Thomas & Pleasant
& dtrs., Rowanna, Martha, Sally & Nancy. I appoint my son Pleasant
Benning my executor. Wit: F. Doyal, Jacob Martin, Charles Jennings &
Thomas M. White. Signed John Benning. Proved on oath of Charles Jennings
& Thomas M. White this 3 April 1809. This same day Pleasant Benning was
granted to be executor, to make a true & perfect inventory of the goods
& chattels and exhibit the same before the Clerk of Court within three
months. Signed John Foster. Reg. 7 April 1809. Pages 163-166.

(No date). I, James Allen, being sick but of sound mind & memory.
I give unto my beloved wife Elizabeth all my estate both real & personal,
in her possession or otherwise during her natural life. In case my wife
have issue in nine months, then the property to be equal divided between
my wife & the child. My desire is that all the property that came my
wife father estate or will receive be at my wife disposal. At my wife's
death the estate to be divided equally amongst my father's children or
their heirs. I appoint my wife Elizabeth Allen executrix and Armstear
White of Virginia my executor. Wit: Thomas Tyler, Ann T. Allen, Peggy
Tyler. Signed: James Allen. Proved on oath of Thomas Taylor, Ann T.
Allen & Peggy Tyler. This 6 Nov. 1809. This day Elizabeth Allen qualified as executor, to make a true inventory of the goods & chattels within three months and exhibit the same in the Clerk Office. Signed Thad.
Beale. Reg. 8 Nov. 1809. Pages 167-169.

(No date on will). I, James Simms, being sick in body, but of
sound mind & memory. I appoint Christian Nature Simms and Jared Pounds
my executors. First 250 acres of land joining Ramsey & Marshall, also
100 acres, joining Pullen and Oneal and all my crop of cotton to pay my
just debts. I leave my son Brittian Simms 50 acres of land lying in
Richmond County and 37 acres joining Polk & Jones and 23 acres joining
Marshall also 5 acres whereon my house now stands, also one rifle gun &
a musket. This 18 July 1809. Wit: J. Foster, Allen Lovelace, Eleanor
Lovelace. Signed Jas. Simms. Proved on oath of Allen Lovelace & Eleanor Lovelace. This 6 Nov. 1809. This day Christian Nature Simms &
Jared Pounds qualified as executors, to make a true inventory within
three months and exhibits the same in the Clerk Office. Signed Thad.
Beale. Reg. 8 Nov. 1809. Pages 170-172.

27 July 1809. I, Nicholas Merewether, being of perfect mind and
memory. I give unto Mirah Evans, a woman of colour the following property, all my land that I possesse, hold or claim, all household & kitchen furniture, horses, cattle, hogs, corn, fodder, one road waggon, one
riding chair, farming tools also sixteen negroes with their increase,
viz. Stephen, Lucy, Jane, Ned, Frank, Jacob, Mercar, Isaac, Rachel,
Nelly, Frank, Betty, Caps, Polly, Arthur and Betty his wife. I give
to Thomas & William Merewether the priveledge of fishing at my fishing
landing two days each in every week during every season. I give unto

Thomas Merewether, negroes Bath & Isbel. To Jane Merewether, I give
negroes, Jacob & Delpha. To Matilda Merewether I give negroes Bill and
Sally. The residue of my property to be divided amongst the following
persons whom I do make and ordain my just and lawful heirs, viz: Thomas
M. White, Melinda White, Nicholas M. White, Clem White the present chn.
of my sister Mary White. Also Thomas Merewether, Jane Merewether,
Francis Merewether, Matilda Merewether, William Merewether, and Robert
Merewether the present chn. of William Merewether. I give to my sister
Mary Whit $10 to be drawn from each of the above named heirs annually
by my executor and by him placed to her during her natural life. I
appoint Thomas Merewether one of the above named heirs as my lawfull
executor and we pay all my lawfull debts if any there be. Wit: Archer
Avery, Wm. Merewether, Jesse Roberts, Washington Germany. Proved on
oath of Archer Avary & Jesse Roberts and Washington Germany. This 6
Nov. 1809. This same day Thomas Merewether was qualified as executor to
make a true inventory of the goods & chattels and exhibit the same in
the Clerk Office within three months. Sgn. Thad. Beale, Judge. Reg. 8
Nov. 1809. Pages 173-176.

(No date on will). I, John Appling, being weak of body. It is my
will that my estate be keep together until my just debts are paid, after
that my whole estate real & personal I wish to be equally divided between
my wife, Elenor, my son, Daniel, & dtr., Rebekah, share and share alike.
I appoint Peter Crawford, Esq. & Doctor Nathan Crawford my executors.
Wit: Elizabeth Wynne, Chas. Goodwin, H. Hampton. Sgn. John Appling, JP.
(His X Mark). Proved on oath of Elizabeth Wynn, that she saw John
Appling, Esq. sign his name to the above writing. She also saw Charles
Goodwin & Henry Hampton, Esq. sign their named to the above. This 6 Nov.
1809. On the 4th Dec. 1809 Henry Hampton, Esq. proved the contents of
the affadavit of E. Wynne to be true & just. On the 4 Dec. 1809 Nathan
Crawford was qualified as executor of the above will, to make a true
inventory of the goods & chattels and exhibit the same before the Clerk
of Court within three months. Signed, Thos. Cobb, Justice of the Peace.
Reg. 4 Dec. 1809. Pages 177-179.

18 Sept. 1808: I, Thomas H. Flint, being of sound mind, memory and
understanding. After my just debts are paid, I will that my loving wife,
Jane Flint, be possessed with all my estate both real & personal during
her natural life or widowhood. Should she again marry the est. to be
divided according to law. Then to my youngest dtr. Elizabeth Flint the
sum of $150. I give unto my youngest sons James Thomas & Aquella Flint
the sum of $339 to be equally divided among them. The remainder of my
est. to be divided among six of my chn. to wit: William James Thomas,
Sarah, Aquella, & Elizabeth Flint. (comma as in film). I appoint my
wife, Jane & son William Flint my executrix & executor. Wit: John
Gartrete, Samuel Fuller, and Isham Fuller. Signed: Thomas H. Flint.
Proved on oath of John Gartrete, Samuel Fuller & Isham Fuller this 1
Jan. 1810. This day Jane Flent qualified as executor to make a true &
perfect inventory of the goods & chattels and exhibit the same before
the Clerk of Court within three months. Signed John Foster, Judge. Reg.
Jan. 9, 1810. Pages 180-183.

14 Nov. 1809: I, William Hunt, being weak in body, but of sound
mind and memory. First I desire that all my just debts be paid. It is
my will that my beloved wife, Jannet Hunt, shall possess my whole estate
both real & personal during her natural life, she to have my land,
negroes, stock of all kind. Negroes named Jude & Jenny. At my wife's
death the property shall become the bona fide property of Henry Hunt &
Constance Hunt the chn. of my brother Thomas Hunt and to be held by them,
share & share alike. If either should die the property shall belong to
the other. In case both should die the property shall belong to Thomas
White, William White chn. of Thomas White, Senr. I appoint my wife
Executrix & my friend & neighbors James Ray, Esq. & James Lovelace
executors. Wit: William Buckham, William Stapler, James Stapler &
Cyntha (X) Roberson. Signed: William Hunt. Proved on oath of William
Buckham, William Stapler, Cyntha Roberson this 1 Jan. 1810. This day
Jannet Hunt, Executrix & James Ray, Esq. & James Lovelace qualified as
executors, to make a true inventory of the goods & chattels and exhibit
the same before the Clerk of Court within three months. Signed John
Foster, Judge. Reg. 9 Jan. 1810. Pages 183-186.

18 Dec. 1809. I, Eli Wheat, being sick in body but of sound mind & memory. First I lend two negroes men named Will & Hannibel also negroes Polly & her child called Presky and their increase, with one bay horse & one bay mare to my father & mother during their natural life. When my father dies the negro man Will to go to my brother Wesley Wheat and said Wesley to pay to my brother Iled (?) Wheat half the value of said negro. Also after the death of my father & mother the other named negroes to go to my brother, Harvey, he paying the heirs of my sister, Rebecah Oneal. I give to my friend Rev. Jona Randle of Green County my time piece watch. I appoint my brother Wesley Wheat & James Wray, Esq., my executors. Wit: Robert Walton, Junr., Francis Gouldman, William Downing, Senr. Signed, Eli Wheat. Proved on oath of Robert Walton, Junr. & William Downing, Senr. This 7 May 1810. This day Wesley Wheat & James Ray qualified as executors, to make a true inventory of the goods & chattels and exhibit the same before the Clerk of Court within three months. Signed, Thomas Cobb, Judge. Reg. May 9, 1810. Pages 187-189.

1 April 1809. I, Beverly Lowe, First I desire my just debts to be paid. I give to my beloved son, Obadiah Lowe $30, I give unto my daughter-in-law, Judith Lowe, wife of Obadiah Lowe $400 in the place of a negro I had intended for her. I will that my wife, Obedience Lowe, shall have her maintainance from my estate during her natural life, also one negro girl to wait on her. It is my desire that my three faithfull servants to wit: George, Eady & Nancey be emancipated and made free. Executors shall petition the State of Georgia for their freedom, also that George shall have use of my carpenter tools and Nancey Taytor to have the use of one loom & gear, one spinnerwheel, one pair of cards, one bed & furniture and one blue chest. I give unto my grand-daughter, Elizabeth Culbreath, dtr. of James Culbreath two negro girls to wit: Nell and Phily. I give unto my dtr., Susannah Culbreath $30. I give unto my son-in-law, Angus Martin $1.00. I give unto my grand-children, that is to say the legitimate children of my dtr. Susannah Culbreath & the legitimate chn. of my son, Obadiah Lowe, that they may have at the death of my wife, all my estate both real & personal. To share and share alike. I appoint my son Obadiah Lowe, son-in-law James Culbreath and James Foster my executors. Wit: Jno. Germany, James Oats, James Foster. Signed Beverly Lowe. Proved on oath of John Germany & John Foster this 7 May 1810. This day Obadiah Lowe, James Culbreath & John Foster was qualified as executors to make a true inventory of the goods & chattels and exhibit the same before the Clerk of Court within three months. Sgn. Thomas Cobb. Reg. 9 May 1810. Pages 189-192.

17 Oct. 1809. I, Ninion B. Magruder, being weak in body, but of sound mind and memory. I give unto my beloved wife, Rebekah, all my real and personal estate during her natural life, and the collection of all notes now in my possession and after her death. I give to my son, Samuel Magruder, a tract of land on the East side of Haw branch, joining Bowders, up said branch to his own line, I also give him a negro boy named Dick. I give to my daughter, Eleanor Beale, hereto before her share of my estate, I therefore give her nothing more. I give to my dtr. Altetha Drane, one negro named Rachel. I give unto my dtr., Cassander Drane, one negro named Alse. I give to my dtr., Margaret Sims, one negro man named Berans. I give unto my dtr., Elizabeth Magruder, one negro named George & one negro girl named Nancey, one feather bed & furniture, one horse, bridle & saddle. Should my dtr. Elizabeth die without issue, the said property to revert to Althetha Drane, Margaret Sims & Mary Leigh, Cassander Drane, Samuel Magruder and William Magruder. I give to my son William Magruder called James. I give unto my dtr., Mary Leigh, one negro named Simon, I give unto Rebekah Robertson's three children, James, Mary & Leavel Nobly $600 to be divided between them and to herself $50. I give unto my dtr., Susannah Silvers, $800 after the decease of my wife. The rest of my property of negroes & land to be sold and the money divided among Altetha Drane, Margaret Sims, Elizabeth Magruder, William Magruder, Cassander Drane equally. I appoint my son, William Magruder and Benjamin Leigh my executors. Wit: R. Y. Langston, Lewis Gardner, Richard (X) Miles. Signed Ninian B. Magruder. Proved on oath of Reuben Y. Langston & Richard Miles. This 7 May 1810. This day William Magruder qualified as executor, to make a true inventory of the goods & chattels and exhibit the same before the Clerk of Court

166

within three months. Signed, Honor. --------, Judge. Test. A. Crawford,
Dlk. Reg. 9 May 1810. Pages 193-195.

2 June 1809. I, William Shields, being weak in body but of sound
memory. First after paying my just debts, I give unto my beloved wife
the plantation whereon I now live also one other tract adjoining the same
of 84 acres, both to be a total of 184 acres. For her support. Also my
beloved wife, Mary Sheils, all my house hold, stock, except one horse
colt, and saddle, one cow & yearling, mentioned hereafter, all family
utensils, also one negro wench named Jude. The above named property to
be used by my wife for her use & raising and education her children to
wit: Robert & Susan. Should Mary Shields die before her children become
of age, the executors to set aside enough for the property suffecunt for
the purpose. After Mary Shields death the property to be divided as,
100 acres to be given to my son, John Shields, also $100 to be given to
my dtr., Hannah Shields, also $100 to be give to my dtr., Beddy Shields,
also $100 given to my son, Robert Shields, also $100 to be given to my
dtr., Susan Shields. I give to my son, Robert Shields one colt & saddle
& one cow & yearling. After which I desire the ballance of my estate to
be equally divided among all my heirs. I appoint my beloved wife, Mary
Shields, & my son, James Shields, my executors. Wit: Samuel (X) Crabb,
William Hunt, Andrew Sterges. Signed, William Shields. Proved on oath
of Andrew Sterges & Samuel Crabb this 7 May 1810. This day Mary Shields
& James Shields was named as executors, to make a true inventory of the
goods & chattels and exhibit the same before the Clerk of Court within
three months. Signed, Thos. Cobb, Judge. Reg. 9 May 1810. Pages 196-
198.

14 Jan. 1810. I, Lewis Gardner, being weak in body, but of sound
mind & memory. My will is that my land whereon I now live of 132 acres
& 200 acres in Bullock County on Ogechee River, one negro named Milly &
child Cena and my negro named Joe to be sold and discharged my debts.
I desire that my negro boy named Tom, all household & kitchen furniture,
stock, tools to be enjoyed by my wife Mary. I desire that my negro girl
Rachel & boy named Simon, one jewel watch be possessed by my dtr., Eliza
Brown, she to receive the same at marriage or of full age, also one
feather bed & furniture. I desire that my dtr. have the whole at my
wife's death. In the final distribution of my brother, William Gardner's
est. the interest for myself & Jesse Gardner to be paid over to my wife
& dtr. Eliza Brown Gardner. I appoint my wife Mary Gardner executrix &
Anderson Crawford my executors. Wit: Samuel Magruder, E. Bowdrie,
Hezekiah Magruder. Signed, Lewis Gardner. Proved on oath of Samuel
Magruder & E. Bowdrie. This 7 May 1810. This day Mary Gardner qualified
as executrix, to make a true inventory of the goods & chattels and
exhibit the same before the Clerk of Court within three months. Signed
Thos. Cobb, Judge. Reg. 12 May 1810. Pages 199-202.

11 March 1810. I, Major Eubank, first I give unto my beloved wife,
Easter Eubank, all my land on the West side of the road leading from
Grinasser Mill on Little River to Augusta, also three negroes named James,
York & Easter, two horses & waggon, two feather beds & furniture, two
cows and calves, two sows & pigs, one half of my tools during her natural
life, at her death, I give my land lying on the West side of the road to
my two youngest sons, Thomas & Major Eubank. I give unto my two oldest
sons, Reuben & James Eubank, all my land lying on the East side of the
road. I give unto my four dtrs. Fanny Lyon, Rhoda Eubank, Elizabeth
Jamison & Milly Eubank $400 each to be paid in money. Personal property
to be divided among all my children. I appoint my son-in-law, John Lyon
& my sons, Reuben & James Eubank, my executors. Wit: William Jones, John
Gray & Richard Eubank. Signed, Major Eubank. Proved on oath of William
Jones, John Gray & Richard Eubank. This 2 July 1810. This day Reuben &
James Eubank was qualified as executors, to make a true inventory of the
goods & chattels and exhibit the same before the Clerk of Court within
three months. Signed, John Foster, Judge. Reg. 5 July 1810. Pages
202-205.

17 Dec. 1808: I, Isaac Ramsey, being sick & weak of body, but of
sound mind & memory. First I desire my just debts to be paid. I give
unto my beloved daughter, Elenor Frazer Ramsey, the tract of land whereon I now live containing 250 acres, also one tract of land in Jefferson

167

Co. on Brier Creek containing 200 acres, known as the Polk Tract. Also
the negroes Luke, Flora, Saura, Simon, Genna, Tom, James, Nancy, Sarah
& Hiott. Also one half of the noted studhorse Galeteen, also one half
of the negro Charles a blacksmith, with all stock, cattle, horses, hogs,
sheep. I lastly appoint my sole executors (no names given). The date
is given, but no witnesses or signed or record of probate. Written
above will. Reg. 8 Jan. 1811. Pages 206-207.

15 Feb. 1811. I, John Moore, desire that my just debts discharged
as usual. I leave to my eldest son, Isaac Dennis, one dollar in cash.
I leave to my eldest son, James Moore, one dollar. I leave to my son-
in-law, George McKinze, living in the State of Ohio, $100 note on Asa
Cloer living that State. I give to my son-in-law, Erick Johnson, $50
cash. I leave to my son-in-law, John Perriman, $50 in cash, also one
bed & furniture and some pewter after the death of my brother, Richard
Moore, also two chairs, one table & a trunk. I leave to my son, John
Moore, $50 in cash, also one bay horse, bow collar. I leave to my son,
Hiram Moore, $1 in cash. I leave to my grand-son, John Moore, Junr. one
lot of land in the 16th district of Wilkerson County, containing 202½
acres. Lott #99 lying on falling Creek. I leave another tract lying
in Columbia Co. on the South side of Uptons Creek containing 140 acres,
to be rented out until it can be sold for cash. Also a lot of land
containing 202½ acres, lying in 21st district of Wilkerson on waters of
Beaver Dam to be sold for cash. An equal distribution of the money
between George McKinze, Erick Jackson & John Moore and John Perriman.
I leave to my wife all my rights, interest, or claims on the estate
David Baldwin, deceased, to hers & her heirs forever. I appoint Joseph
Miller & Owen Baldwin my executors. Wit: T. Wiley, Wm. Wiley, Silas
Mote. Signed John Moore. Proved on oath of Taylor Wiley, William Wiley
& Silas Mote. This 1 July 1811. This day Joseph Miller & Owen Baldwin
qualified as executor, to make a true inventory & exhibit the same before
the Clerk of Court within three months. Signed John Foster, Jdg. Reg.
9 July 1811. Pages 208-210.

7 Feb. 1810. I, Henry Hand, Senr., being weak in body but of sound
& perfect mind. First I desire all my debts be paid. I give my loving
wife, Sarah Hand, the house whereon I now live with all the furniture,
lands, cattle, hogs during her life. After her death to my son-in-law,
Jacob Newberry, all but one cow & calf, to be given to my granddaughter,
Janmia Nelson. I give unto Robert Hand 5 shillings. I give unto my son,
Henry Hand, 5 shillings. I give unto my son, John Hand, 5 shillings. I
give unto my son-in-law, James Nelson, 5 shillings. I give unto my son-
in-law Levy Newberry, 5 shillings. I give unto my dtr., Lidy Nelson, 5
shillings and every part of my estate to Jabeck Newberry. I appoint my
wife, Sarah Hand, Executrix. Wit: Moses Spevey, Rebecca Spevey, Taphley
Spevey. Signed, Henry (X) Hand. Proved on oath of Moses & Taphley
Spevey & Rebecca Owne late Spevey. This 2 Sept. 1811. (Executrix not
sworn). Pages 211-212.

21 Aug. 1809. I, Ignatius Few, being of sound mind & memory. I
wish my just debts to be paid. Both my real & personal est. to be
divided equally among my chn. William, Ignatius, Lavinia, Leonidas,
Alfred, Laduska and Camillus. My son, William, being of full age, I
request he receive my Pomona plantation on which he now lives of 900
acres, granted to me, also a tract of 85 acres surveyed by Henry Candler.
This tract was sold by the sheriff of Wilkes Co. for a debt due by Henry
Chandler & paid off by me. Also 500 bushels of corn, all fodder left on
the land by William Slatter. Also Pompey & his wife Becke & their child.
Peter & his wife Lucy & their children, Alick & Clary, negro man named
Hampton which he sold to Samuel Devereaux, also Moses who died in his
possession. Also negro named Solomon, one bed & furniture he bought of
his mother, & all furniture that was in the house when he took possession. One waggon I bought of William Lee, also black mare, a sorel
horse, a bay mare bought of James Russell, all tools, cattle belonging
to the Pomona plantation. Be it understood that 50 acres of the 900
acres has been sold to John Dyoort & conveyed to him, being where Mrs.
Few now lives, also 32 acres sold out of the same tract to Mr. Thomas
Faunlain for repairs of Permona House to be 4 chains wide and 80 chains
long. My will is that my son Ignatus Few when he arrives at full age
receive my Mount Carmel plantation, the 350 acres originally granted to

168

Thomas Weekly, the 41 acres tract granted to my father and conveyed to me, the 400 grant to me, including Cobham, the 200 acres tract including the race path, granted to me, and the 773 acres in the name of William Smith. Also negroes to wit: Harry, Jude and her three chn. Dick, Lylla, Peter, four good ploughs, horses now on the property, one waggon four gears, with tools. Also four cows & calves, ten sheep, one bed & furniture, one large walnut table, one mahogany tea table & six chairs. It is my request that Mary Frail alias Hicks with my children Lavinia, Leonidas, Alfred, Laduska, Camillus and Crassus which last child was ommitted above, also a child that Mary Frails alias Hicks is now supposed to be pregnant with, should it be born and live to maturity to draw an equal share of my estate with my other children. They shall live at Mount Carmel plantation until my son, Ignatius, is of age. When my dtr., Lavinia, arrives at the age of 16 yrs. old I give unto her two fifths of a tract of land granted to William Candler deceased. Tract called for 1150 acres, sold by the Sheriff of Washington Co. bought by me, she to have all profits from the fisheries & ferry on the Oconee. Also I give her Bob & his wife Betty & their three chn. Sam & his wife Sylvia & their two children. Also Tilla & her child, a yellow girl named Carmelia now at William Fews. One black horse, two bay horses with gears, 7 cows & calves, two beds & furniture I bought of Benjamin Scott, all stock at the plantation opposite Milledgeville, books, set of tea china, one round mahogany tea table, one walnut dining table. She to have her support until she is sixteen yrs. of age. I give to my son, Leonidas, 1760 acres on Walnut Fork of Broad River granted to me, joining a 3,900 acre tract surveyed by John Templeton of Franklin Co., also two thirds of a tract in said County containing 1000 acres surveyed for the heirs of Greenberry Lee & conveyed by John & William Lee, also a bond for the title for two thirds of a tract of 287½ acres granted to Cornelius Mc-Cardle to be conveyed to me by John & William Lee. Also I give my son, Leonidas, negroes, Betty & Cyrus & their five children, Elinon, Rachel, Mary, Anderson & Susan. Also Cud, Joe, Moses, Dick, also 4 good work horses with gears, also 4 cows & calves, 10 head sheep, two sows & pigs, one bed & furniture. He is to have three years of schooling by a strict teacher and then three years apprintice schooling by a strict teacher and then three years apprintice trade. I give unto my son, Alfred, 3,000 acres in the County of Franklin, granted to me. Lying on the Walnut Fork of Broad River, joining the land given to Leonidas and surveyed by John Thompson. Also Fan & her six chn. Edie, Milly, Elmina, Ned, Fann & Wilson also Dick's two sons, Emanual & Avington, 4 work horses, 4 cows & calves, 10 head sheep, 2 sows & pigs & some tools, one feather bed & furniture. He to be put in school to acquire a good English education including book keeping, then to be put as an apprentice to a merchant until he is eighteen, then put in some merchantile house until he is 21 yrs. of age. Then my executors shall furnish him with $2000 at 1% interest for one year. I give to my son, Camillus, a tract of 287½ acres of land lying in Washington County in the name of Lewis Davis, also another tract in the same County of 287½ acres granted to Ezekiel Miller both tracts joining, with some land on the River banks. Also 400 acres of pine land, joining the above tracts, granted to John Colves, also 250 acres joining the above granted to Eli Cummins. Also two thirds of a tract of 287½ acres lying in Washington Co. on Oconee River near the mouth of Buffalo granted to George Wainwright & he sold to John Lee I have a bond on Lee to make title. Also one tract of 287½ acres lying on the Main Buffalo, granted to John Sutton and conveyed to me. Also Negroes, Betty, Hamilton & their four chn. Daniel, Maria, Limus & Simon also Alex, Lucinda, Peter, Delce, & Lucy the last two the chn. of Rachel. Also 4 good work horses, four cows & calves & 10 head sheep, 2 sows & pigs & farming tools for the hands. One feather bed & furniture. My son Camillus to be sent to school when at proper age for a good English education, then as an apprentice, trade to be choosen by my executors. I give unto my dtr., Lodoiska, 100 acres of land in Columbus County lying on both sides Germanies's Creek, granted to John Benntt who sold to Edward Telfair who sold to Thomas Few who sold to me with the mill, gin & store house, also I desire my executors to purchase another 100 acres joining said mill tract from Thomas Few on the East side. Also 100 acres on the North side from James Ross. Also two thirds of 400 acre tract near the head of the North Fork Little River in Oglethorpe, joining Geoffry Early granted to Greenberry Lee & conveyed to John & William Lee, land now in suit. I have a bond on it. Also negroes Sal, her chn. Nelly

169

& Polly, Bess, Tim, Nat, Cinda bought of John Garvin, Matilda, Hannah,
2 good work horses, 4 cows & calves, ten head of sheep, one feather bed
& furniture with a set of tea china, a walnut dining table, one looking
glass. She to have a good English education at a day school or convenent or boarding school. I give unto my son, Crassus, 925 acres of land
on both sides of Rocky Confort in Warren County, granted to me, where I
have a grist & saw mill and a cotton machine. Also 40 acres opposite
the mills granted to George Upton and conveyed to William Few, Senr.,
Deceased, title of both now in my possession. Also 5 hundred acres
lying about three miles below said tract granted to Gray & he conveyed
to me. Also 500 acres in Warren County on the waters of Joy Creek,
granted to Benjamin Few, and sold by the Sheriff of Columbia County.
Also 1,000 acres in Warren County on Foits Creek, joining Thompson
Miller, granted to John Hollingshead. Also 200 acres in Warren Co. on
Sweet water Creek, granted to John McDuffey. Also negroes: Rose, & her
son, also Flora, Jack, Daphne, Isaac, Mark, York. One good work horse,
4 cows & calves, 10 head of sheep, 2 sows & pigs, one feather bed &
furniture as a suit against Davison for 200 acres of the 925 acre tract
he obtained. My son Crassus shall have equal in land from the estate.
When my son Crassus arrives at proper age, my executors shall put him in
a day school in convenent in not a boarding school until he has a good
English Education. If he should discover a capacity for the purpose of
studing and practizing Physie that he be put with some respectable prac-
tioner in the healing art. I give unto Mary Frail alas Hicks 150 acres
of land whereon John Lee formerly lived on Germanies Creek, granted to
William Tanner & conveyed to me, conveyed to me by Benjamin Few, and
from B. Few to William Few, Senr. decd. Also negroes, August, Rachel
his wife & their 2 chn. Plato & Winney, the negroes & land to be her
property during her natural life or that she stay single. Also 2 good
horses, 2 cows & calves, 5 head sheep, 2 sows & pigs, 2 feather beds &
furniture, including one bought by her, 6 chairs, a walnut dining table,
1 set common tea ware, 1 doz. earthen plates, and one oven. The child
she Mary Frails alias Hicks is now supposed to be pregnant with should
it arrive to the age of maturity, shall at her dec. or marriage be entitled to all the property. Be it understood that the whole to be under
care of my executors and to be considered as hers' married or single
while she remains in the County. Also the said child to share an equal
share of my estate, including what is left to Mary Frail alias Hicks at
her decease. Said child to have an equal English education. I also
desire that my library of books be equally divided among my chn. My
executors to make distribution of them as the chn. arrive at proper age
to read & understand them. My executors may work, use the said negroes,
stock, tools on any plantation or tract of land they may think best for
the family or estate, until a child comes of age. Having married a Miss
Mary Candler now called Mary Few and living many years with her a mutual
separation having taken place. I paid her up her dower with her own
consent   taking   her full and voluntary relinguishment and receit
the probate of which is recorded in the Clerk office of Columbia County.
I therefor consider Mary Few has no claim or interest on my estate,
except the $60 per annum to be paid to her during her natural life or
widowhood. Whereas my daughter Elizabeth who married William Devereause
and whose decease has been long since leaving no living issue. The property given to my deceased dtr. to be keep by her husband as when she
was alive. I have given to William Devereaux (?) one fifth part of a
1150 acre tract of land on the big bend of Oconee River oposite Milledgeville, said land relinquished to me by John Candler and conveyed unto
William Devereux, now in his possession, which I have declared to be the
whole of my dearest dtr. share. (the following are persons named in land
conveyance or suit in Court) John Binder of Clark Co., Thomas Curry,
Richard Early, Hope Hull, Richard Nalls, Uriah Humphrey, John Coleman,
William Thompson, John Howard of Augusta, Archibald Martin, Phelps &
Howard, Henry Candler, Thomas Scoggins in Oglethorpe County, Daniel
Elam, Peter Crawford, Freeman Walker, Rhoda Earley, William Hamilton,
Thomas W. Cobb. I appoint my son William Few, son Ignatius Few, my
nephew, Doctor William Lee, my friend & attorney Archibald Martin & my
old friend Thomas White. Wit: William Hunt, Thomas Hunt, John Clark,
William Rousseall. Signed I. Few. Codicil....This 4 Dec. 1809. This
codicil to correct some things not made in the last will & testament
made the 21st Aug. 1809. I wish my sons Leonidas, Alfred & Cammillus
to receive their legacies when they arrive at the age of 21 years of age.

my two dtrs. Lavinia & Laduska to receive their legacies when they
arrive at 16 yrs. of age. The said Levinia, Leonidas, Alfred, Loduska,
Cammilles & Crassus was on the 29 November 1809 by an act of the legislature and approved by the Governor on the 1 Dec. 1809, changed from
Hicks to Few as will appear by said act which said children I acknowledge to be legal heirs to my estate with my other children. I do hereby revoke the appointment of my son Igantius as executor in my will,
there is one of that branch of my family as executor. As all of the
children of my other branch minors, I have removed my son and placed my
friend Doctor George Archer Brown my executor. Wit: John Clark, Wm.
Scott, Thomas Hunt. Signed I. Few. Proved on oath of William Roussell,
Thomas Hunt & John Clark this 8 March 1811. (William Hunt is decd.)
This day William Few was qualified as executor, to make a true inventory
of the goods & chattels and exhibit the same before the Clerk of Court
within three months. Signed J. W. Goode, Judge. Recd. 9 Nov. 1811.
Pages 213-237.

15 July 1811. I, Jacob Stalling, being weak in body, but of sound
mind & memory. First I will that my just debts be paid from those that
are indebted to me. It is my will that my beloved wife, Edy Stallings,
have all my estate, both real & personal during her natural life and
after her decease, I will that my two sons, Joseph and Isaac Stallings,
shall have the 190 acres of land whereon I now live, equally divided
between them and the balance of my property to be equally divided between
William, Edy, James, Sarah, & Polly Stallings. I appoint my wife Edy
my executor. Wit: Patrick Dougherty, Edw. Ross, William Winfrey.
Signed Jacob Stallings. Proved on Patrick Dougherty, Edward Ross,
William Winfrey, this 4 Nov. 1811. This day Edy Stalling was qualified
as executor, to make a true inventory of the goods & chattels and exhibit the same before Clerk of Court within three months. Signed John
Foster. Reg. 9 Nov. 1811.

19 Aug. 1811. I, Charles Clayton, knowing that my great & final
change is about to take place. First I desire my just debts to be paid.
I lend to my beloved wife, Hannah Clayton, one third part of the tract
of land whereon I now live, four negroes, Phill, Billy, Kefsa & Nan, one
riding chair & mare called Jolly, 2 cows & calves, 10 head of hogs, one
bed & furniture, one chest called hers, glass ware & setting chairs, one
fourth of the kitchen furniture, the waggon & gun, cotton house & gin,
during her natural life or widowhood. I give unto my beloved chn. Nancy,
Eliza & Mary Ann Clayton all the property that I have lent unto my wife
during her life or widowhood, to be equally divided between them. I give
unto my beloved chn. above named all the rest of my property both real &
personal after the payment of my just debts. I desire my estate to be
keep in the hands of my executors unto my chn. come of age or marry. I
appoint Samuel Clayton, Asa Doggett, and John Foster my executors. Wit:
Collier Foster, Hardy Foster, Elizabeth Foster, John Foster. Signed
Charles Clayton. Proved on oath of Collier Foster, Hardy Foster & John
Foster this 10 Feb. 1812. This day Samuel Clayton, Asa Doggett & John
Foster was qualified as executors, to make a true inventory of the goods
& chattels and exhibit the same before the Clerk of Court within three
months. Signed Thomas Cobb. Reg. 13 Feb. 1812. Pages 240-243.

18 Jan. 1812. I, William Merewether, being of sound mind & memory.
I give unto my dtr., Jane Benning, the wife of Joseph Benning, Frances
Merewether, and Marshall Mims, my son-in-law, the following tract of
land known as the Hogan tract containing 109 acres to be equally divided
by appraisment amongest the three above named. I give unto my sons
William & Robert Merewether all the residue of my real estate to be
equally divided between them by appraisment when Robert arrives at the
age of 21 yrs. of age. I give unto Francis Merewether the following
negroes, Nanny, Peter, Betty & Melvina. I give unto my son William,
negroes, Judy, Little Sam, Franky, & Little Buky. I give unto my son
Robert, negroes, Little Dinah, Henry, Betsey & Allen. I give unto
Joseph Benning my son-in-law $10. I give unto my dtr., Francis, and my
sons, William and Robert, all my household & kitchen furniture, with the
stock to be divided between my sons when Robert comes of age. After
paying my just debts, all crops now in the barns, or growing to be used
for support of Francis, William & Robert which now lives with me. When
chn. are of age a division to be made to Thomas Merewether. I appoint

171

my son William Merewether & Archer Avary my executors. Wit: Thomas
Lyon, Jeremiah Larkin, Robert Foster. Signed Wm. Merewether, Senr.
Proved on oath of Thomas Lyon & Jeremiah Lamkin this 3 March 1812. Reg.
18 Mar. 1812. (Executors not qualified in will book). Pages 244-246.

28 June 1808. I, William Bealle, Senr. being weak in body, but of
sound and perfect mind & memory. It is my will that all my just debts
be paid. I give unto my beloved wife, Nancy Bealle, the whole of my
estate both real & personal during her natural life. I give unto my son,
John Bealle, one negro named Bridget, with her present & future increase,
He has her in his possession now and at the death of my wife I give him
negro boy named Lewis. I give unto my dtr., Elizabeth Yarbrough, negro
woman named Trrey, she is now in her possession. After the death of my
wife another negro named Alice. I give unto my son Hezekiah Bealle negro
woman named Keziah. After the death of my wife he to have negro named
Peter. I give unto my dtr., Ann Finny, one negro woman named Henny, her
oldest girl Phillis I give unto Patsey Finny the dtr. of said Ann Finny,
which is now in possession of Benjamin Finny. After the death of my
wife I give Ann a negro boy named Henry. I give unto my son William
Penn Bealle, after the death of my wife negroes Ben & Solomon. I give
unto my dtr., Mary Sims, after the death of my wife, negroes, Uleadon,
Jesse, Sarah Subrine. I give unto my son Charles T. Bealle after the
death of my wife 426 acres of land whereon I now live, also the land
bought of Joshua Grinage, where my son lately lived. Also having paid
George W. Nime for the land my son William now lives on. Also all stock
& household furniture, also negroes, Tom, Vinns, Jencey, Dilsey, Jerry,
Nancey, Lucy & Bobb. I appoint my wife Nancy Bealle my executrix, & my
son Charles T. Bealle executor. Wit: Jonathan Cliett, Mary Ann Crawford,
Peter Crawford. Signed William Bealle. Proved on oath of Peter Crawford & Jonathan Cliett this 7 Sept. 1812. This day Nancy Bealle and
Charles F. Bealle was qualified as executors, to make a true inventory
of the goods & chattels and exhibit the same before the Clerk of Court
within three months. Signed John Foster, Judge. Reg. 16 Sept. 1812.
Pages 247-250.

16 June 1810. I, William Bukham, being now of sound mind & memory.
First I desire my just debts to be paid. I give the tract of land whereon I now live, containing 300 acres, also the tract I bought from Denham
to my beloved wife, Catharene Bukham, during her life time. Then to my
grand-son, Thomas W. Cobb & his heirs, provided the said Thos. W. Cobb
shall within twelve months after my wife death decease by written instrument exonerate William Cobb, deceased his heirs executors & admnr. and
Lewis Cobb his heirs executors & admr. of and from the purchase of land
to be made for him, pursuant to the will of John Cobb, Decd. the father
of said William, Thomas and Lewis, in case of the death of said Thomas
W. Cobb his executor or admnr. fail or refuse to make such exonerating
written instrument within the limited time after my wife decease, the
said land to be equally divided between my great grandson, William Bukham
Cobb, & my grandsons, Thomas & Lewis Cobb. If the said Thomas Cobb shall
during my life time make such exonerating instrument & deliver the same
to me or shall within 12 months after my wife's death, deliver the same
to the Clerk's office of this County there to be recorded, the same shall
comply with my will. I give unto Thomas W. Cobb negroes, Patrick, Tamar
& her two chn. Chandis & Charles. I give unto my granddaughter, Catharine E. Cobb negroes, Pallas & Such, Rachel. I give unto my grandson,
Alfred Ellis, negroes, Sol & Sally. I give unto my grandson, Simpson
Ellis, the son of Charles G. Ellis & my dtr. a negro boy named Peter. I
give unto my grandson, G. E. Bukham Ellis, negro named Bob to be hired
out, and the money put on interest until said grandson comes of age. I
give to my great grandson, William Bukham Cobb, a negro named Phil, said
negro to stay with my executor Thomas W. Cobb until great grandson arrives
at full age, also a horse & saddle. In case of death said property to
belong to Thomas W. Cobb. I give unto, Great Granddaughter, Adeline
Cobb, dtr. of Grandson, Thomas W. Cobb, negroes Betsey & Leach. I give
unto Polly W. Cobb, the wife of Grandson, Thomas W. Cobb, my gray mare
called Jane. I appoint my wife executrix & Thomas W. Cobb my grandson
my executor. Wit: James Lovlace, Patr. Dougharty, Jas. Staple, Jno. B.
Minor. Whereas since making my will my grandson Simpson Ellis mentioned
in the 6th section has deceased, whereby the negro boy Peter given to
him has become a lapsed legacy & since his death I have sold & disposed

172

of said negro Peter for an old negro wench named Sarah, I therefor make
this a codicil to my last will & testament to annulling the said 6th
section of my will. Also I desire that the negro woman, mentioned shall
be given unto my Grandson G. E. Bukham Ellis named in the 7th section of
my last will, in like manner, in every respect as the negro boy Bob.
This bequeath is made to him because Sarah is the mother of said boy Bob.
This 18 Jan. 1812. Wit: Joseph J. Moore. Signed Wm. Bukham. Proved on
oath of James Stapler & Patrick Dougherty, this 2 Nov. 1812. James
Welch came into Court, being sworn saith that he saw William Bukham sign
the within codicil to his last will & heard him request Maj. Joseph J.
Moore to subscribe it, that is the reason why this deponant did not sign
as a witness was that being an inhabitant of the State of Kentucky he
would not be present when it would be necessary to prove, and this deponant understands that Maj. Joseph J. Moore now lives in Oglethorpe
County, so he thinks proper for him to sign said codicil in his own hand
writing. Signed James Welch. This 2 Nov. 1812, Thomas W. Cobb was
qualified as executor, to make a true inventory of the goods & chattels
and exhibit the same before the Clerk of Court within three months.
Signed John Foster. Reg. 5 Nov. 1812. Pages 250-256.

7 Oct. 1812. I, Daniel Sturges, being of advanced age and enjoyment of full understanding have thought proper to make this my last will.
As my possessions are but small & my wife being but one year younger
than myself, I, therefor, give unto my wife, Eleanor, all my estate both
real & personal. I have already given to my other chn. what I think
equitable & my son John has continued to live with me since he come of
age & assist me in the management of my affairs. I, therefor, give unto
my son John what may be left at the decease of his mother. Should John
die without issue, then the estate to be divided between the chn. of my
son Daniel by his first wife & the chn. of my son Robert. I appoint my
wife and my son John my executors. Wit: Elias Lazenby, John Briscoe,
Junr., John Briscoe, the elder. Proved on oath of Elias Lazenby & John
Briscoe, Junr., this 2 Nov. 1812. This day John Sturges was qualified
as executor, to make a true inventory of the goods & chattels & exhibit
the same before Clerk of Court within three months. Signed John Foster,
Judge. Reg. 6 Nov. 1812. Pages 257-259.

2 June 1810. I, John Hand, being sick and weak in body yet of
sound mind & memory. First I give unto my wife, Margaret Hand, the whole
of my real & personal property during her life or widowhood, if she lives
single and then to equally divided between my chn. Sarah, Aberaham, John,
William, Mary, Rebea, Rody, Henry & Thomas. I appoint my wife, Margaret
Hand, my executor. Wit: Moses Spivey, John (X) Durden & Joab (X) Spivey.
Signed John (X) Hand. Proved on oath of John Durden & Joab Spivey, this
2 Nov. 1812. This day Margaret Hand was qualified as executor, to make
a true inventory of the goods & chattels and exhibit the same before the
Clerk of Court within three months. Signed John Foster, Judge. Reg. 6
Nov. 1812. Pages 259-261.

7 Dec. 1812. In the Court of Ordinary. Ordered that letter of
testamentry issued to William Merewether named executor in the last will
of William Merewether decd. said reg. on page 244. This day William
Merewether qualified as executor to William Merewether will, to make a
true inventory of the goods & chattels, and exhibit the same before the
Clerk of Court within three months. Signed John Foster.

8 Feb. 1812. I, Anthony Cooper, (Mill wright) being of sound mind
& memory and in good health. First I desire all my just debts or dues
be paid. I give unto my son Joseph Cooper, .25 cents. I give unto my
two chn. Rebeckah & John Cooper, the chn. I had by my last wife, one
tract of land on the Savannah River that I bought from Thomas Jones,
granted to Quinsten Bobler, and all real & personal property that I may
have or possess at death. I desire my estate to remain in the hands of
my executors until my said minor children come of age, then to share &
share alike. I appoint Robert Frazure & John Foster my executors. Wit:
Robert Frazor, John Walton & John Foster. Signed Anthony Cooper. Proved
on oath of Robert Frazure, John Walton & John Foster this 7 Dec. 1812.
This day John Foster & Robert Frazure qualified as executors, to make a
true inventory of the goods & chattels & exhibit the same before the
Clerk of Court within three months. Signed Thomas Cobb, Judge. (a second

173

date on the probate record. 2nd. Nov. 1812. JEW). Reg. 8 Dec. 1812.
Pages 263-266.

5 Sept. 1789. I, Daniel Wolecon, of Richmond County. I give unto
my Grandson Daniel Wood all that lot of land on Broad Street in the town
of Augusta, known as Lot #26, being the same whereon John Meals, Esq.
now keeps the treasury office. Also a tract of 200 on Little River I
bought from Huke Middleton, also one tract on Savage Creek, joining
Doctor James Sanders. I give unto my Grandson Jeremiah Wood a lot of
land, of one acre near the public ferry in the town of Augusta, known as
lot #1, also all that tract of land on Greenbrier Creek in Richmond
County formerly William Mansory, containing 450 acres, with 12½ acres
joining which was granted to me. I give unto my Granddaughter Honor Cox
three negroes or as much money to purchase them, & four cows & calves.
I give unto Lucy Tutt formerly the wife of my decd. son Daniel and to
her child 5 shillings each. I give unto my Granddaughter Mary Wool Ł 300
which is to be paid by the Hon. George Walton for 2 lots on Ellis Street,
known as lots 50 & 51. In case the said George Walton or his heirs
should not comply with the contract made with me, then the said lotts to
be the property of my Granddaughter Mary Wood. I give unto my Grandson
Joseph Wood a negro or the amount of money to buy one from the land in
Carolina, as an heir at law to his father Isaac Wood, I consider to be
equal to his brothers or sisters. I give unto my beloved wife Mary her
living from the land whereon we now live called Sandbar during her life.
I desire my executors pay my just debts & funeral charges maintainance
of my wife & grandchn. named Wood while under age. After my wife's
death, I give the Sandbar tract of land, also 100 acres of land bought
from Bugg & all other real estate unto my Grandson John Wood & Granddaughters Martha, Nelly, Marg & Elizabeth Wood. I appoint my Grandson
Joseph Wood & friend Samuel Scott my executors. (There are two articles
or paragraphs too blurred to read, they deal with some slaves. JEW).
Wit: Jno. (X) Holt, Seaborn Jones, N. H. Bugg. Signed Daniel (X) Wolecon. Richmond County. Proved on oath of Hobson Bugg & Seaborn Jones.
This 10 Sept. 1789. Clerk Office, Court of Ordinary. "I certify that
the forgoing is a correct copy taken from the records in this office of
the last will and testament of Daniel Wolecon, Decd." This 23 Nov. 1810.
Isaac Herbert, Clerk. Reg. 8 Jan. 1813. Pages 266-271.

3 May 1813. I, Hugh Blair, being weak of body but of sound mind &
memory. First I desire my just debts to be paid. I give unto my beloved
wife Mary two beds & furniture, two horses, with the whole of the real
estate that my wife was entitled to from the estate of Greenberry Lee,
Esq. decd. All the residue of my est. both real & personal together
with the undivided moirty of my father's real & personal, I give unto my
beloved chn. William & Ann, to share & share alike, I desire my estate
to be divided when my son come of full age. I desire my executors to be
the guardians of the person & the property of my said chn. my executors
may sell some stock, and what land lying outside of the County of Columbia to pay my debts, if any is left, it to be used for the family. I
appoint my friend Anderson Crawford, Edmond Bowdire, Samuel Bowdire &
David W. Crawford, and Peter Crawford executors. Wit: Thos. A. Hamilton,
John Wyne, Uriah Blanchard, and Jose. Marshall. Signed, Hugh Blair.
Proved on oath of John Wyne, Thomas N. Hamilton & Uriah Blanchard, this
5 July 1813. This day Peter Crawford & Edmund Bowdier was qualified as
executors, to make a true inventory of the goods & chattels and exhibit
the same before the Clerk of Court within three months. Signed John
Foster, Judge. Reg. 7 July 1813. Pages 271-274.

13 May 1813. I, Francis Shepperd Beall, being sick in body but of
sound mind & memory. First I desire my just debts to be paid. I give
unto my brother Augustus Beall one negro man named Bill or Will forever.
I give unto my beloved mother Jane Beall the ballance of my estate both
real & personal during her natural life. At her decease I give unto my
sister Martha Tennason Beall, negroes, Abram, Ailsey & Matdigon for ever.
I give unto Thomas Beall, Reason D. Beall, William L. Beall, John S.
Beall & Charles T. Beall, my brothers, after the death of my mother, all
the balance of my property, not give unto my sister. I appoint & desire
my mother Jane and my brother Thomas Beall be my executors. Wit: John
Foster, Harwood Roberts & James S. Walton. Signed, Francis S. Beall.
Proved on oath of John Foster & Harwood Roberts this 6 July 1813. This

day Thomas Beall was qualified as executor, to make a true inventory of the goods & chattels and exhibit the same before the Clerk of Court within three months. Signed John Foster, Judge. Reg. 7 July 1813. Pages 274-277.

16 April 1813. I, Robert Shaw, Senr. being weak and low but of sound mind & memory. I give unto my son, Charles Shaw that tract of land whereon he now lives, of about 60 acres, being part of the Smith & Bryant's survey, lying on Uclree, to be divided from my other lands by a fence now standing near Rocky Mount Meeting House, also five negroes, Violet & her four chn. Simon, Somersat, Aaron & Linder. I give unto my son James Shaw three negroes, Mary & her two chn. Richard & Jacob. I give unto my son Robert Shaw the land whereon I now live, including all my land on the East side of the Uclree Creek it being part of survey to Roda Mercer & W. Tindill, crossing the said creek at or near the tan trough, through a field that James Shaw cleared some years ago, to an old brick kiln, near Mrs. Gringes field, to Peter Zachery's corner, to Smith line near the school house, containing about 300 acres, also 4 negroes, Aggy, Peter, Cleb & Peggy. I give George Magruder my late son-in-law one dollar in full of all demands he may have against my est. on account of intermarriage with my late daughter Eleanor now deceased. The residue of my estate to be divided among my sons Charles, James & Robert Shaw, share & share alike. I appoint Charles, James & Robert Shaw, Jr. my executors. Wit: A. Crawford, Joseph Day & I. Gilpin. Signed, Robert Shaw. Proved on oath of Joseph Day & Ignatius Gilpin this 5 July 1813. (Executors not qualified, JEW). Pages 277-279.

27 Sept. 1811. I, Charles Crawford, Senr. being in good health & of sound mind & memory. I give unto my wife Jane Crawford during her natural life all my lands that I occupy in Columbia County on the West side of Dyars Creek, also all household & kitchen furniture, all live-stock, and six negroes of her choice. I leave to my Grandson Joel Barnett one negro called Sarah, also I give said grandson $200 for a tract of land I had contemplated giving to my dtr. but did not make title before her death. I desire my negroes not given be keep together in families and to be divided among my ch. in the final settlement. That is Anderson Crawford, Mary Ann Crawford, Nathan Crawford & Joel Crawford. My son John Crawford children to have his share as if he was alive. My son William Crawford children to have his share as if he was alive. I desire the property that my wife may hold at her death to be divided among my chn. above named. I appoint my sons Anderson, Nathan, Peter and Joel Crawford my executors. Wit: Thomas Parker, Leonard Smith, William Underwood. Signed, Charles Crawford. Proved on oath of Thomas Parker, William Underwood & Leonard Smith this 3 Jan. 1814. This day Anderson Crawford, Peter Crawford & Nathan Crawford was qualified as executors, to make a true inventory of the goods & chattels and exhibit the same before the Clerk of Court within three months. Signed John Foster, Judge. Reg. 4 Jan. 1814. Pages 279-283.

20 Dec. 1812. I, George Dent, being by accident placed in a precarious situation do while my memory is sound and rational, faculties unclouded do make this my last will & testament. First my legal debts & legacies paid. I give unto my wife Ann M. Dent one fifth part of the remaining property both real & personal. I give unto my son James T. Dent my riding horse & the following personal property, Betty, Roderick, Clole, Mira, Laura, Albert, Allen he is to have control after my death, charging him to remember that he is to use every exertion to liberate them agreebly to my will now expressed. Betty when her dtr. Mira arrives to the age of 18. All males at the age of 21, & females the age of 18 yrs. I give unto my son George Columbus Dent two fifths of what ever property left after debts & legacies are paid. I give unto my son Dennis Dent two fifths of what property left debts & legacies are paid. I give to my dtr. Sarah M. Tindall .25¢ for reasons she will duly appreciate. I give unto Dapline Hornsby one negro boy named Kelly, also one cow & calf, one feather bed with common furniture. I desire that no division be made until my son Dennis come of age, except the legacies to James T. Dent & Dapline Hornsby. I appoint my son James T. Dent, Dennis Dent with my brother Thomas M. Dent, & my nephew John Dent joint executors. Wit: Thos. M. Dent, Samuel Neilson & James (X) Parnell. Signed G. Dent. Proved on oath of Thomas M. Dent & Samuel Neilson this 3 Jan. 1814. This

175

day Marshall Dent (?) was qualified as executor, to make a true inventory of the goods & chattels and exhibit the same before the Clerk of Court within three months. Signed John Foster, Judge. Reg. 6 Jan. 1814. (Another date given, 7 Feb. 1814. JEW). Pages 283-286.

21 Jan. 1814. I, James Tinsley, being at this time soarly afflicted and diseased in body, but of sound mind & memory. I give unto my beloved wife Lucey two negroes, named Sally & Joe, also Peter & Rachel. Two horses, six cows & calves, about 20 head of hogs, my sheep, all household & kitchen furniture & tools during her life time or widowhood. I desire my chn. to stay with their mother or mother-in-law to be supported & educated from the plantation. At my wife marriage or death, I desire my land whereon I now live be sold, and the money divided equally among my chn. Philip, William, John, Abram, Nancey, Ann, Sally and a child to be born. Other property not to be sold, and the money divided among my chn. Philip, Polly, James, Nancey, William, John, Abram, Betsey Ann, Sally & one to be born. My son Philip having already receive some property, not to receive part of the last sale. After the death of my wife I give unto my young chn. Polly, one negro named Rachel, also a moiety of 200½ acres tract of land lying in Wilkinson Co. I give unto my son James negro Dick, also a moiety of the tract of land in Wilkinson Co. I give unto my son William negro named Charles, one feather bed & furniture. I give unto my dtr. Nancey, negro named Mariah, one feather bed & her property called hers, one speckled mare. I give unto my son John, negro named Sopha also Peg's colt, one feather bed & furniture. I give unto my son, Abram, one negro named Peter, also the speckled mare's colt, one feather bed & furniture. I give unto my dtr. Betsey Ann, negro named Mary, one feather bed & furniture. I give unto my dtr. Sally one negro named Matilda, one feather bed & furniture. I give unto the child yet to be born, one negro named Lewis, one feather bed & furniture whereas my sister Sarah Wofford is living on the same tract of land, that I now live on, I desire she may remain and can cultivate up to 40 acres until the property is sold according to the first page of this will. I appoint my son Philip Tinsley, David Maxwell Crawford & Augustus Crawford executors. Wit: Pleasant Tindell, Thos. Wilkins, Jonathan Tindell, William Tindell. Signed James Tinsley. NB. As my family having two sets of chn. to prevent discord among them, my will is that should any one or more of either set die without issue, the legacies to such deceased shall go to & be divided amongst the children of their mother's side. Also the negro Lewis I bought of William Tyrey be sold by my executors, and the money to pay off the ballance I owe him & the surplus to be divided between my eldest set of chn. Proved on oath of Pleasant Tindell, Thomas Wilkins, Jonathan Tindell & William Tindell this 7 Feb. 1814. This day Philip Tinsley was qualified as executor, to make a true inventory of the goods & chattels and exhibit the same before the Clerk of Court within three months. Signed John Foster, Judge. Reg. 7 Feb. 1814. Pages 301-303.

13 Feb. 1814. I, Robert George, being weak in body, but of sound mind & memory. First I desire all my just debts to be paid from my personal estate. I give unto my brother Jordan George, two notes of $2,000 each given by Daniel Low to William Low & one $500 note given by Grimes Nicholson to Greenwood, also one note of $40 given by Charles Hanes to him & his heirs forever, subject to a deduction in the hands of my executor of $1,000 to raise a fund for the support of my brother James George. I give my brother James George the sum of $1,000 to be vested in bank stock & the proceeds annually drawn and paid to the support of my brother James George. I give unto my beloved Fanny Carr & her son Thomas Low one tract of land lying in Richmond County, containing 200 acres whereon Booker Tindal formally lived, known as the Bay Spring. I give unto Dr. Cleghorn my cream colored horse, harness & sulkey. My two colts & eight head of cattle to be sold. I appoint Col. Thomas Carr my executor. Wit: Samuel Ramsey, John J. Bealle, Nancy Beale & Polly N. Ramsey. Signed Robert George. Proved on oath of Samuel Ramsey, John J. Beale, Polly N. Ramsey this 7 March 1814. This day Thomas Carr was qualified as executor, to make a true inventory of the goods & chattels and exhibit the same before the Clerk of Court within three months. Signed, John Foster, Judge. Reg. 10 March 1814. Pages 292-294.

1 Feb. 1814. I, William Zachry, being at this time somewhat in-

disposed but of sound mind & memory. After paying my just debts. I
lend my wife, Nancy Zachry, during her natural life my land whereon I
now live, also 50 acres, over the Uehee Creek near the Grove Meeting
House, all household & kitchen furniture, my stock, tools & five negroes,
George, Philis, Hannah, Bob, Bridget & Jane also ten shares in the
Augusta Bank, said stock to be under controul of my executors. My wife
is intrusted with raising and educating my four youngest children. Being
possessed with several tracts of land & 4 negroes named China, Lewis,
Jim & Polly, some cotton and some ready money. I desire my executor to
sell the land & cotton and add the sum to the ready money. After my
decease divide the same between my wife Nanch & chn. I appoint my wife
Nancy executirx & my son-in-law Jesse Albritain, and James Yarbough, son
of William Zachry executors. Wit: Littleton Yarbough, James Blackstone,
Mary (X) Golyghty. Signed, Wm. Zachry. Proved on oath of Littleton
Yarbrough & James Blackstone this 7 March 1814. This day Nancy Zachry,
Jesse Albritain, James Yarbrough, & William Zachry was qualified as
executors, to make an inventory of the goods & chattels and exhibit the
same before the Clerk of Court within three months. Signed, John
Foster, Judge. Reg. 11 March 1814. Pages 295-298.

23 Oct. 1807. I, John Germany, being of perfect mind & memory but
weak in body. I give unto my chn. herein named William, Mary Miller,
John, Ellender, Joseph, Samuel, Robert, Washington, James & Benjamin
Germany the following negroes to wit: Sam, Old Sarry, Poll, Young Sarry,
Susannah, Charly, Cate to be divided among them. I also give unto
Ellender, Washington & Benjamin each a feather bed & furniture, and unto
my son Benjamin my ring which I now wear. The rest of my household &
kitchen furniture to be divided among the above named chn. share & share
alike. I give unto my dtr. Sarah Garrett $20 to purchase a mourning
suit at my death, as I have already given unto Eli Garrett which I confirm to them forever. I give unto my said chn. first named, all my
farming tools, stock, of every kind. I desire that Philis an old negro
shall be free at my death, and she may choose which of my chn. she will
live with, should she become helpless, she is to be maintained during
her life. I appoint my sons, John, Robert & Benjamin Germany my executors. Wit: Hugh Blair, Junr., Joseph G. Blunt & Samuel Oneal. Signed
John Germany. Joseph Blunt, came into open Court and swore he saw Hugh
Blair, Junr. at the home of John Germany, Senr. He understood that he
had made the will for said Germany, and that he signed as a witness,
this 4 July 1814. Signed Joseph G. Blunt. William Jones & James Luke,
Esqs. being sworn, they said they was sure of handwriting of John Germany the elder & Hugh Blair Junr. now deceased. This 4 July 1814. Reg.
6 July 1814. (This will is repeated on pages 304-306. In this record,
all real estate to be divided among his chn.). Pages 299-301.

8 Feb. 1818. I, Charles Finnell, being in perfect sence & memory.
I lend to my beloved wife Nancey Finnell all my estate both real & personal, for her use & benefit to herself & my sons Leroy & Ugeane, for
maintaining & education until they are at the age of 21 yrs. old. Then
I give unto my dtr. Hiturah Vasser $5. I give to my son Skilton $5. &
no more, then my estate both real & personal be equally divided between
my wife & my sons Collins, Leroy & Ugeane & my dtr. Francy Sanders and
my dtr. & Granddaughter Nancy Prudeson Gathrell & Verlenda Vasy. I
appoint my son Collins & Reuben Sanders my executors. Wit: Robert Jones,
John Parks, Adam Guest. Signed Charles Finnell. Proved on oath of
Robert Johns this 4 July 1814. This day Collin Finnell & Reuben Sanders
was qualified as executor, to make a true inventory of the goods &
chattels and exhibit the same before the Clerk of Court within three
months. Signed, John Foster, Judge. Reg. 6 July 1814. Pages 301-303.

3 June 1813. I, Charles Porter, being of sound mind & memory.
First, I give to my wife Elizabeth during her natural life one third
part of my property both real & personal. I give unto my son George
Nicholas Porter $1. I give unto the child or children of my son George
150 acres of land, lying on Little River, joining Samuel Goode & others,
granted to me, also negro Sinthea, to remain in the hands of my executors in trust for their use. I give unto my dtr. Gracy Mathews one
negro named Kitty & her child Daphney. I give unto my dtr. Sally Porter
Rees one negro named Reuben now in her possession. I give unto my dtr.
Brunett Simpson one negro named Nancy & her child Sarah. I give unto my

four sons viz Stanton my natural born son commonly called Stanton Porter, Fayette, Charles Hansford, and Bradford Porter an equal part of my remaining land as they come of age, and from the profit of the estate I desire my son Bradford to have a good English education, and at my wife's death all my property, after paying my just debts to be equally divided amongst said chn. George N. Porter excepted. I appoint Stanton Porter, Capt. David Simpson & Peter Crawford and Anderson Crawford, Esq. my executors. Wit: Taylor Wiley, Julius Seay & B. Porter. Signed, Chas. Porter. Proved on oath of Taylor Wyly, Julius Seay & Benj. Porter, this 5 Sept. 1814. This day Stanton Porter was qualified as executor, to make a true inventory of the goods & chattels and exhibit the same before the Clerk of Court within three months. Signed, John Foster, Judge. Reg. 14 Sept. 1814. Pages 304-306.

31 Aug. 1814. I, Lewis Hobbs, being weak in body but of perfect mind & memory. I lend unto my parents John & Sarah Hobbs my plantation in this county during their natural life also one bed & furniture. I have deposited with Pleasant Tindal the sum of $150 to be appropriated to the use of my father & mother as my executors may direct. I have given unto Pleasant Tindal the sum of $25. for the service rendered. I give unto William Tindal my nephew my watch. I give unto my niece, Salley Tindal, my horse on condition that my mother is to have use of said horse whenever she may call for him. I give unto my nephew, Lewis Hobbs, one two year old heifer. I give unto my nephew, Thomas Lewis Tindal, one bed & furniture after the death of my mother. After the doctor bills & funeral expenses are paid, the remainder of my property to be equally divided between my brother William Hobbs & my sister Polly Tindal also my land after the death of my father & mother to be sold and the proceeds divided between my brother & sister. I appoint William Hobbs & Pleasant Tindal my executors. Wit: Abda Christian, Patrick (X) Gordan & Wm. Tindal. Signed Lewis Hobbs. Proved on oath of Patrick Gordan & William Tindal this 7 Nov. 1814. This day Pleasant Tindal & William Hobbs was qualified as executors, to make a true inventory of the goods & chattels and exhibit the same before the Clerk of Court within three months. Signed, William Jones, Judge. Reg. 7 Nov. 1814. Pages 310-312.

26 Feb. 1812. I, John Collier, being perfect health of body and mind. I give unto my son, William, three negroes named Harry, Sillar, and Jesse also a tract of land containing 54 acres lying on the lower end of Germanys Island. I also give unto my son Edward when he come of age the same amount from the estate. The remainder of the estate to be left in the hand of my legal wife Sarah Collier until her death, then to be divided between my sons William & Edwards. Wit: Marshall Keith, Aron Aldridge & John Crawford. Signed, John Collier. Codicil...I, John Collier, appoint my sons William & Edward Collier my executor. This 29 Feb. 1812. Wit: Marshall Keith, John Crawford & Aron Aldridge. Signed John Collier. Proved on oath of John Crawford & Aron Aldridge, this 7 Nov. 1814. This day William Collier & Edward Collier was qualified as executors, to make true inventory of the goods & chattels and exhibit the same before the Clerk of Court within three months. Signed William Jones, Judge. Reg. 8 Nov. 1814. Pages 313-316.

11 April 1805. I, Thomas Wroe, it is my desire that after my just debts & funeral expenses are paid, that my son Thomas Wroe, Junr. should have all the property which I may die possessed of every nature & kind, on condition & charges as may here after made in this will. It is my wish that my son Tom should pay unto my dtr. Nancy Monroe $500 within 2 years after my decease. He may rent or sell any negro he inherits from me. Also if my son does not come to this State to live he shall not inherit the negroes, Samuel, Ned or Jack. I wish that my executor hire then out for say Samuel for six yrs., Ned for seven yrs., & Jack for eight yrs. then at that time to be liberated, provided my son should not come to this State to live. Should the negroes be hired out the money to be equally divided between my son Thomas & dtr. Nancy. I wish my negro Judy to be liberated for life. I appoint my son Thomas Wroe & Marshall Keith as executors. Wit: Joshua Pharoah & Bennett Burroughs. Signed, Thos. Wroe. Proved on oath of Joshua Pharoah & Bennett Burroughs this 2 Jan. 1815. This day Marshall Keith was qualified as executor, to make a true inventory of the goods & chattels and exhibit the same before

the Clerk of Court within three months. Signed, Wm. Magruder, Judge.
Reg. 3 Jan. 1815. Pages 316-319.

19 Aug. 1812. I, Littleton Yarbrough, being sick in body, but of
sound mind & memory. First I desire my debts to be paid. I give unto
my beloved wife Elizabeth negroes, Creasy, Abram, Charles, she may dispose of them as she think proper. The rest of my property I lend to my
wife during her natural life, at her death I desire my negro man named
Frank to be sold and the money divided between my sons William & James
Yarbrough. I desire my executors to sell all my lands & from the proceeds, I give unto dtr. Patsey Harden $300, the ballance with the stock
to be equally divided among all my chn. Also after the death of my
wife, all tools, household & kitchen furniture shall be sold and the
money divided equally amongst my five youngest chn. Bealle, Elizabeth,
Thomas H., John W., & Rebecca Yarbrough. I also give unto my son Bealle
a negro named Cleartoll & her increase. I give unto my dtr. Elizabeth a
negro named Phillis & her increase. I give unto my Thomas H. negro
named Solomon. I give unto my son John W. a negro named Venus & her
increase. I give unto my dtr. Rebecca, negroes Isham & Esther & her increase. My desire is that the legacy left us by the last will of William
Bealle, decd. shall be sold & the money divided equally among my five
youngest chn. I appoint my wife Elizabeth Executrix, & my son William
Yarbrough & my friend Anderson Crawford my executors. Wit: John Barker,
Charles T. Bealle, & Peter Crawford. Signed, Lttn. Yarbrough. Codicil..
Since making of my last will & testament my dtr. Elizabeth has inter-
married with James Walton & I have given to them a negro named Phillis
that I had given to Elizabeth, I now give unto my son John W. forever.
This 11th Oct. 1814. Wit: Peter Crawford & Charles T. Bealle. Signed
Littleton (X) Yarbrough. Proved on oath of Peter Crawford & Charles T.
Bealle this 2nd Jan. 1818. This day Elizabeth & William Yarbrough was
qualified as executors, to make a true inventory and exhibit the same
before the Clerk of Court within three months. Signed John Foster,
Judge. Reg. 2 Jan. 1815. Pages 319-323.

15 Feb. 1815. I, John Culbreath, being weak in body but of sound
mind & memory. First I give unto my beloved wife Nancy Culbreath the
tract of land bought from Morris, joined by lands of Tankerley & Wool-
fork during her natural life, also negroes, Ben, Rose & Mary my mare
also the filly known as Nance, my stock of hogs, four cows & calves, four
head of sheep, some farming tools, all the kitchen furniture, also to
have an equal share of the household furniture. I give unto my son
Thomas the land on Sullivans Creek with the mill, with my family have the
right to grinding or he may keep it toll free. I also give him negroes,
George, Tenar, Easter & Jude, also an equal share of the horses & other
stock with the other chn. I give unto my son John, 85 acres of land on
the corner near Zachery McDaniels, also negroes, Bob, Jude & her child
Dina, also the stud horse, an equal share of meat, stock & household
stuff. I give unto my son West, negroes, Jesse, Young Sara & Louis an
equal share of my stock & furniture not willed, also an equal share of
the land not willed. I give unto my dtr. Lucy, negroes Charlotte, Nelson,
& Clary, with an equal share of the stock & furniture not willed and a
colt. I give unto my son James McNeal Culbreath, negroes, Henry, Ralph
& Stephen with an equal share of my stock, furniture & land not willed.
I give unto my son Patrick Culbreath, negroes, Dick, Allen & Nell, With
an equal share of my stock, furniture & land not willed. I desire my
wife to keep the young childrens property until they come of age and
should my dtr. Mary give up her property. I desire my just debts to be
paid by my heirs equally. I appoint my wife executrix & my son Thomas
Culbreath and John Avery as executors. Wit: Wm. B. Tankersley, James
Blanchard, James Roberts. Signed John Culbreath. Proved on oath of
William B. Tankersley, James Blanchard & James Roberts this 6 March 1815.
This day Thomas Culbreath was qualified as executor, to make a true
inventory of the goods & chattels and exhibit the same before the Clerk
of Court within three months. Signed, (name blurred out. JEW). Reg. 11
March 1815. Pages 324-327.

23 Oct. 1814. I, James Reed, being weak in body but of sound mind
& memory. It is my will & desire that all my just debts be paid. I
will unto my beloved wife Jane Reed all my estate both real & personal
during her natural life. I give unto my dtr. Jane Reed one trunk and all

her wearing apparel, one feather bed & bed clothing, two cows & calves, one sow & pigs, one negro boy named Reason. I give unto my dtr. Gracy Reed one trunk and all her wearing appearel, one good feather bed & bed clothing, two cows & calves, one sow & pigs, one negro girl called Lydia. I give unto my dtr. Elizabeth Luke $200. in cash. I give unto my dtr. Mary Luke $200. in cash. I will & desire that the residue of my property shall be equally divided between my chn. eight in number and my Granddaughter Martha Pullen, it is my desire that James Luke shall receive the part allotted to my named granddaughter, to be kept by him for her use & benefit while she lives unmarried. I appoint my beloved wife Jane Reed sole executrix. Wit: George Roberts, John Culbreath, Junr., Juriah Harriss. Signed James (X) Reed. Proved on oath of George Roberts, John Culbreath, Junr., Juriah Harris this 6 March 1815. This day Jane Reed was qualified as executrix, to make a true inventory of the goods & chattels and exhibit the same before the Clerk of Court within three months. Signed, John Foster. Reg. 11 Mar. 1815. Pages 328-330.

7 Jan. 1814. (Non cupative will). I, Stephen Beard, being sick in body but of sound & desposing mind & memory, doth at this time feel very ill. Do say at this time. I possess in fee simple and in my own rights, two negroes, named Daniel & Flora, with other property & in case I should (die) of my present illiness it is my will that the said slaves Daniel & Flora should go to my two brothers, Matthew Beard & John Beard also the remainder of my small estate, after payment of my just debts. On the 25th April 1815, personally appeared before me (John Culbreath) and made oath that Stephen Beard, late of this County was ill at his house and died there on the seventh evening of February 1814. In the morning prior to his decease said Stephen Beard expressed a desire to make his will in the presence of John Culbreath, Doctor George Cleghorn & Timothy Pittman. Dr. Cleghorn asked decedent who he wish to leave his property to (?). He said to his two brothers Mathew & John Beard. The Dr. said he would watch for Col. Foster as he passed the Court, and would call him in to make the will. He the Stephen Beard stated that he wish no part of his property to go to Joseph Marshall & wife. Col. Foster could not come to the home where said Beard was at that time because of the Court, but when he did return to the house Beard had just expired. Signed John Culbreath, George Cleghorn & Timothy Pittman. On the 25th April 1815 came Timothy Pittman, Esq. & made oath that some four or five months prior to the death of Stephen Beard and at sundry other times told the said Timothy Pittman that if he did die in this State, he desired that his two brothers should have his little estate, and that Joseph Marshall and his wife should have none of it. And he was present when Capt. Culbreath heard said Beard express his wish. Signed Timothy Pittman. Before, Allen Lovelace, JP., Personally appeared before me, Matthews Beard and made oath Stephen Beard of Columbia Co. State of Ga. was his elder brother, and he came from the State of Virginia, County of Accamac. He had left his home as soon as he could, after receiving a letter from John Colbreath & Nicholas Ware, Esqs. A British squardon was less than 30 miles from his door, and he had fear for his family. He had left Virginia by sail in May and arrived in Columbis County the 14 or 16th day of March. Sworn to this 25 April 1815. Signed, M. Beard. Signed Allen Lovelace, J.P. Pages 345-350.

5 March 1813. I, William Sims, Senr., being weak in body but of sound mind & memory. First I will my just debts to be paid. I give unto my son Mann Sims $1. I give unto my dtr. Ann Hendly Cowen $1. I give unto my dtr. Peggy Hanson $1. I give unto my son Lenny Sims $1. I give unto my executor the rest & residue of my real & personal estate during the life time of my dtr. Aggy Sims in trust as, the whole of my estate to be keep together during the life time of my dtr. Aggy and the profit shall be for her support, and if any surplus if any to be applied to the estate. It is my will that my daughter-in-law Mary Penn Sims shall have the care & direction of my dtr. At my dtr. Aggy's death, I give the tract of land of 150 acres unto my Grandson William Sims son of Abner Sims, & if he should die without child, the land to belong to the next oldest son of Abner Sims. The rest of my estate to belong to my Daughter-in-law Mary P. Sims the widow of Abner Sims. I appoint my friend John W. Smith & Peter Crawford my executors. Wit: Thomas Parker, J. B. Smith, Charles T. Bealle. Signed William Sims, Senr. Proved on oath of Charles T. Bealle & Thomas Parker this 1 May 1815. This day

Peter Crawford & John W. Smith was qualified as executors, to make a true inventory of the goods & chattels and exhibit the same before the Clerk of Court within three months. Signed John Foster. Reg. 3 May 1815. Pages 335-338.

19 April 1815. I, Mary Stone, being weak in body but of sound mind & memory. First I give unto Daniel & Robert Sturgess my nephews & chn. of my brother Robert one square of land in Putnam County on waters of Rooty Creek, containing 202½ acres, one feather bed & furniture, negroes, Simion, Ben, Harry, Tone & Livisia to be equally divided between them when they come of age. I give unto my niece Mariah Sturgess, the dtr. of my brother Daniel one negro named Nell & her increase, one feather bed & furniture, when she comes of age or marry. The residue of my property, horses, cattle etc. to be equally divided between my brother John & my nephew Benjamin H. Sturgess by valuation or public sale. I appoint my brother John Sturgess & my sister-in-law Susan Strugess. Wit: George Miller, Jesse Winfrey, A. Crawford. Signed Mary Stone. Proved on oath of Anderson Crawford & Jesse Wingrey this 1 May 1815. This day John Sturgess was qualified as executor, to make a true inventory of the goods & chattels and exhibit the same before the Clerk of Court, within three months. Signed John Foster, Judge. Reg. 3 May 1815. Pages 388-341.

13 April 1814. I, Eleanor Germany, being weak in body but of sound mind & memory. I give unto my son Thomas Germany, negroes, Cate & a child named Dianah. I also give daughter Clauisa Germany, negroes, Arva & Pink. I also wish the legacy that is coming from my father's estate to go to pay my just debts. I wish the balance to be divided between my two chn. They are to divide what property is left at home. I appoint James Luke, Esq. my executor. Wit: Joseph Manhall & J. Wynn & Samuel Germany. Signed, Eleanor (X) Germany. Proved on oath of Joseph Manshall & Samuel Germany this 1 May 1815. (Executor not qualified, JEW). Reg. 3 May 1815. Pages 341-342.

6 May 1814. I, George Columbus Dent, being of sound mind, memory & understanding. All my just debts must be paid out of the estate. The rest to be divided into three equal parts, one part to my brother James T. Dent to hold in trust for the use of my sister Sarah M. Fendall & her chn. I give one third part to my brother James T. Dent. I give unto Dapleue Hornby and her heirs forever. I appoint my brother James T. Dent & cousin John Dent executors. Wit: Samuel Neilson, William Glasscock, & Isaac Authony. Signed, Geo. C. Dent. Proved on oath of William Glasscock & Samuel Neilson. 1 May 1815. Reg. 3 May 1815. (Executors not qualified, JEW). Pages 343-345.

24 Oct. 1815. I, Jesse Winfrey, being low weak in body but of sound mind & memory. First I desire my wife Francis A. remain on the plantation whereon I now live during her natural or widowhood or the youngest child come of age. The profit over the support of the family to be put on interest. If my executors think best, they may rent or sell part of the estate for the support of the family, Mrs. Winfrey to have negro Lucy & her child. I desire my executors sell 400 acres of land in Warren County, also my negro man Hannibal a blacksmith, to be hired out and money put on interest. I desire my dtrs. Martha & Nancy be after my death put in boarding female school for two years. I give unto my dtr. Frances, 335 acres of land in Columbia Co., the land I bought of the est. of N. H. Collins, my sorrel horse & saddle, one feather bed & furniture, four negroes, Betty & her two chn. & Jim. I give unto my son Benjamin 600 acres whereon I now live after the death or marriage of his mother, also negro man named Daniel & after my death the negro named Phil. I give unto my dtr. Martha 200 acres of land on Town Creek in Hancock Co. & 550 acres lying in Edgefield Dist. SC. two negroes Mary & her child, one feather bed & furniture, one horse & saddle. I give unto my dtr. Nancey 900 acres in Effingham Co. granted to William Gardner, three negroes Jinny & her two chn., one feather bed & furniture, one horse & saddle. I give unto my Grandson Jonathan Winfrey Wood two small negroes, named, Susan & Elvey. Having gone through the legatees, except my Grandson Robert W. Walker whose mother was my dtr. Julia now decd. was the wife of Adam Walker, now decd. received three negroes, named Nancey, Sam, & Harry, now there are six in number, negroes having been lent to my decd.

181

dtr. I wish they to be delivered to my grandson when he come of age.
The residue of my estate to be divided equally among my chn. Sarah, Banjamin, Francis, Nancey & Martha. I appoint my wife Francis A. Winfrey
my executrix & my son Banjamin Winfrey, Jonathan Wood & James Walker and
my friend Peter Crawford, Esq. Wit: A. Crawford, Isaac Vaughan & James
Yarbrough. Signed: Jesse Winfrey. Proved on oath of Anderson Crawford
& Isaac Vaughan this 6 Nov. 1815. This day Jonathan Wood, James Walker
& Peter Crawford was qualified as executors, to make a true inventory
of the goods & chattels and exhibit the same before the Clerk of Court
within three months. Signed, William Jones, Judge. Reg. 11 Nov. 1815.
Pages 345-350.

10 Oct. 1814. I, Mary Davis, being of sound mind & memory. First
I will that my just debts & dues that I may owe to be paid. I lend unto
my daughter-in-law, Elenor Davis, two negroes during her natural life or
widowhood. Negroes named Edenborough & Sarah, then unto the chn. of my
late son, Blauford Davis, to share & share alike. I lend unto my son,
Vachel Davis, & his wife Mary two negroes named, Cassae & John during
their natural life then to their chn. I lend to my son, Thomas Lemar
Davis, two negroes, named Charles & Jerry during their natural life, then
unto his child or children. I give unto my Grandson, Alexander H.
Allison, one negro called Silvey & her child named Monday & one boy named
Herculeas, during his natural life, except his mother Martha Cooper,
should after becoming a widow the use of said negroes, then at her death.
Said Alexander H. Allison to have compleat controll of said negroes. I
give unto my Granddaughter, Mary Justic, one negro named Little Dinah
during her natural life. I give unto my Granddaughters, Ann Lamar &
Cassuder Lamar, one negro named Nelson, said negro to be hired out for
four years, or when the oldest marry, each of them to share in the hire
& share in the value of said negro. I give unto my Granddaughters,
Gassicvay Davis, Sarah Williams, Mary Hill, Sarah Carmichael $200 to be
raised from my estate & to share & share alike. I give unto my daughter-
in-law, Elener Davis, one riding chair & harness & chair horse to be
hers forever I desire that negro Old Dinah to live with the family, under
the care & direction of my executors. The residue of the estate to be
sold to pay debts & the legacies named. I appoint my son, Vachel Davis,
Thomas Lamar Davis & Grandson Alexander H. Allison, my executors. Wit:
Jno. Foster, Collier Foster, Robert S. Foster. Signed Mary (X) Davis.
Proved on oath of John Foster & Collier Foster this 6 Nov. 1815. This
day Thomas Lamar Davis & Alexander H. Allison was sworn as executors to
make a true inventory of the goods & chattels and exhibit the same before
the Clerk of Court within three months. Signed William Jones, Judge.
Reg. 20, ----- 1815. Pages 350-354.

3 June 1813. I, Thomas Sampler, by trade a stone mason, being in
perfect health & of sound memory. I give unto my sons, Robert & Jeremiah Sampler, all my estate, both real & personal, by paying the legacies herein described and all my just debts. I give unto my beloved wife,
Trecy Sampler, all the property she has got from her father's estate or
may here after get. Also she to have her support out of my estate during
her life or widowhood. I give unto my dtr. Mary Price Davis the sum of
$50. I give to my dtr. Targ Sampler, the sum of $200, also she may live
with my sons, R. & J. Sampler, while she remains single & acts agreeable,
also I give her the spinning machine, wheel, and loom. I give unto my
dtr., Sarah Samplers, while she remains as she now is, blind, and con-
tinues under the protection of her brothers & her mother or either of
her sisters, a sufficient and decent support out of the estate. I give
unto my sons, Samuel, Johnson & Wm. Sampler, the sum of $50 each. The
legacies of the girls to be paid at my death. For the boys to be paid
when they are of full age. In case any child should die without issue,
the share shall go to Sally. I give except the young bay mare to myself,
also five acres of land joining Mr. F. M. Hunt, including a spring, for
my wife & daughters should they want to build a house, also Robert &
Jeremiah shall give their brothers a good schooling, and learn them a
trade of blacksmith, busness, or wheelwright. I do appoint my sons,
Robert & Jeremiah Sampler, executors. Wit: Jno. Embree & Adam Scott.
Signed Thomas (X) Sampler. Proved on oath of John Emery & Adam Scott
this 2 Jan. 1815. Reg. March -- 1816. (Executors qualified on P. 369).
Pages 355-358.

22 Oct. 1807. I, John Bell, being very sick and weak in body, but
of perfect mind & memory. First I give unto Hugh Bell my son, 12 head
of cattle, two horses, twelve head of hogs, four beds & furniture & all
household & kitchen furniture. I give unto John Bell my son one dollar.
It is my wish for my wife Marry to have the use of the property her lifetime. Wit: No. Whitcomb, John Partridge. Signed, John (X) Bell, Senr.
Proved on oath of Notley Whitcombe this 4 March 1816. (No executor
named or qualified). Pages 358-359.

3 Oct. 1807. Loveless Savidge, being weak in body, but of sound
mind & memory. It is my will & desire that all my just debts should be
paid. I give unto my son, James & his heirs, one bay mare called Janus'
mare, one sorrel stud named Little John, also a colt, 120 acres of land
except the mill & seat, joining Johathan Wood, surveyed & platted &
known as James's land, lying between Timothy Barham & Zachariah Garnetts
land, and to take possession at my death. I give unto Timothy Barham
the tract of land whereon he now lives, discribed, joining lands of
Timothy Barham, Zachariah Garnett's, Jacks Corner, Quaker Road, William
Walton survey, Savage's Creek. I give unto my wife, Elizabeth, one
negro woman named Grace, to be disposed of at her pleasure. I give the
rest & residue of my estate unto my wife, Elizabeth, both real & personal
during her natural life, except two tracts of land excepted. I give
unto my wife the mill & seat lying on James' land, and the following
negroes, Peter, Frederick, Sam, Chloe, Vilet, Judy, Lewis, and Milly,
also one negro named China & her child named Judy, loanded to & now in
possession of Barnett Whittington, also one negro girl loanded to & now
in possession of Alexander Allison, also one negro boy loanded to & now
in possession of Zachariah Savedge, named Wally. After the death of my
wife the property to be divided as, James to have the mill & seat with
his own land & negroes Peter & Frederick. Zachariah to have one moity
of 180 acres of land adjoining his own, negroes, Sam & Wally. To dtr.,
Sarah Whittington, two negroes, China & her child Judy. To dtr., Susannah Garnett, one tract or part of a tract of land joining Zachariah
Garnett, lying on the South of his land, also negro girl named Judy. To
Lucy Allison the tract of land whereon I now live (quantity not known),
one negro girl named Charlotte. To dtr., Elizabeth Foster, I give $350
to be raised from the est. after the death of my wife. To my three
grandchildren, the dtrs. of my son Robert, I give $50 to be raised from
the estate after the death of my wife. It is my will that the following
property should be set aside for a fund to pay the legacies & debts that
may be due, all stock of every kind, tools, household & kitchen furniture,
the increase of the negroes, also negroes Lewis, Chloe & Milly & two
tracts of land in Richmond County, one on Rae's Creek of 200 acres, also
530 acres on Batles' Creek both tracts granted to me in my name. If any
money is left over to be divided amongst sons, James & Zachariah & dtrs.
Susannah Garnett & Rebecca Barham, share & share alike. I give unto my
Granddaughter, Eliza Maria Savage, dtr. of my son Asa, one moiety of 180
acres of land, the other moiety to belong to my Grandson Zachariah Savage
forever. My departed friend Humphrey Walls conveyed to me part of a lot
known as Fox's Lot fronting on Ellis Street & containing one fourth of an
acre for a Baptist Church, & benfit of the Red's Creek church in particular. I therefor give all my rights, titles & interest in said lot in
the city of Augusta. I appoint my wife Elizabeth Executrix, with my sons,
James & Zachariah Savage and Alexander Allison my executors. Wit: Archd.
Adam, Archd. H. Adam, Jonathan Cliett, Peter Crawford. Signed Loveless
Savage. Codicil...This codicil to be made part of my last will & testament made the 3 Oct. 1807. In liue of two negroes, Peter, now dead &
Fred that I did give unto my son James, I now give him, negroes Sam that
was given unto son, Zachariah, and negro named Lewis which was to be part
of my estate & sold. I give unto my son, Zachariah, negro named Fred.
I give unto my dtr., Rebecca Brasham, $350 to be paid after the death of
my wife. Having sold the moiety of the 180 acres of land, given unto my
Granddaughter, Eliza Maria Savidge, the dtr. of my son Asa, in liew
thereof I give her $50. Wit: Peter Crawford, Joseph Daley, Notley Whit-
cumbe. Signed, Lovelace Savidge. Proved on oath of Peter Crawford &
Jonathan Cliett. (Here the testator is Rev. Lovelace Savidge). This 4
March 1816. This day Elizabeth, James & Zachariah Saviage and Alexander
Allison was qualified as executors, to make a true inventory of the
goods & chattels and exhibit the same before the Clerk of Court within
three monghs. Signed, John Foster. Pages 360-368.

183

2 Jan. 1816. The Judge of the Court of Ordinary did this day qualified Robert & Jeremiah Sampler named in the last will of Thomas Sampler, Senr. as executors, to make a true inventory of the goods & chattels, and exhibit the same before the Clerk of Court within three months. Signed, John Foster, Judge. Page 369.

17 Feb. 1816. I, Richard Harrison, the elder, being sick & weak in body but of sound mind & memory. First I give unto my beloved wife, Betty Harrison, the sum of $600 & a negro woman named Sarah to wait on her, also two feather beds & furniture, one horse, saddle & bridle, her choice of the horse and to remain on the plantation while she is my widow. I also give unto my wife one trunk, one chest & her choice of a table, if the negro woman, Sarah, should outlive my wife, said negro to belong to my son-in-law John Embree, and the remainder of the property given to my wife, at her death to be divided equally between my sons, Richard & James Harrison. I give to my son-in-law, Adam Jones, one negro named Patience & one named Jin, also one bay filly three years old in trust for his son Richard Jones. I give to my son Perryman Nuplicrd Harrison, one negro man named Surry & one woman named Amy, also one girl named Vilet, in trust for his son Dick Franklin Harrison, also 202½ acres of land in Old Wilkerson of Little Sandy Creek. I give to my son, Tyrrel Cook Harrison, one negro man named Joe & a girl named Harrot, also one negro named Franky in trust for his son Dick Harrison. I also give to my Grandson, Sullivan Harrison, one negro named George & one boy named Nathan in trust for Mat Richard Tyrrel Harrison until he shall be able to act for himself. I give to my son, Gadwell Reines Harrison, 287½ acres in Washington County white ponds joining Sandersville, one feather bed & furniture he now has, one young sorrel horse, one negro man named Daniel & negro woman named Mariah, one cow & calf, one sow & 7 pigs. I give to my son, Richard Harrison, one half of the land where I now reside containing 347 acres, also one negro named Suckey & one negro boy named Arthur, also half of the stock of horses, cattle, sheep & hogs. I give unto my son, James Harrison, the other half of the land whereon I now reside, containing 347 acres to be divided between them, each to have share, also one negro woman named Sylvia & child Sam also Peg & her child Sopley, one waggon & gear, one still. I give unto my son-in-law, John Embree, one negro named John. Should it please God to take me hence that a division of my estate both real & personal be made on the first day Jan. 1817. I appoint my son Terrel Cook Harrison and John Embree my son-in-law executors. Having omitted in the proper place, My son Dinwiddie Harrison I give him a negro man named Peter. Wit: Aquilla Howard, E. Short & Thomas White. Signed, Richard Harrison. Proved on oath of Aquilla Howard & Thomas White this 2 Sept. 1816. This day Tyrrel Cook Harrison & John Embree was qualified as executors, to make a true inventory of the goods & chattels and exhibit the same before the Clerk of Court within three months. Signed, John Foster. Pages 370-374.

13 Dec. 1812. I, John Richardson, being of sound mind & memory. I give unto my beloved wife, Rosanna Richardson, during her natural life all the property which I may die possessed, except as hereafter excepted. After the decease of my wife, I give unto my dtr., Mary Ann Richardson, & her issue all the property which may come to my wife after my death. Should she die without issue then the property to belong to my son, James Richardson, I also give unto my son, James Richardson, the land I drew lying in the County of Wilkinson, that is lot #52 in the 4th district, being the same whereon James now lives, I also leave him my stock, household & kitchen furniture. Should James die without issue, the property given to him to be divided among my other children & their heirs. I give unto my son, John, one cow & calf, should he call for it. I appoint my wife. Rossanna. & mv dtr., Mary Ann Richardson & Marshall Keith my executors. Wit: Burnel Burrough, Joseph (X) Overton & Marshall Keith. Signed, John Richardson. Proved on oath of Marshall Keith this 8 Oct. 1816. This day, Rossanna & Mary Ann Richardson was qualified as executors, to make a true inventory of the goods & chattels and exhibit the same before the Clerk of Court within three months. Signed, John Foster, Judge. Reg. 20 Dec. 1816. Pages 374-377.

27 Jan. 1814. The LWT of Richard Moore. I being in perfect reason of mind & memory. First after my just debts & funeral charges are paid. I will unto Richard Baldwin one sorrel mare now in possesskon, also three

184

head of cattle now in possession of Peter Ryon, also one cow in posse-
sion of William Low, also my notes, bridle & saddle, all furniture be-
longing to my bed, all money now in my possession. I do hereby appoint
Owen Baldwin my executor. Wit: Jno. B. Fleming, Wm. Wiley, Elizabeth
Wiley. Signed, Richard (X) Moore. Proved on oath of William & Elizabeth
Wiley this 2 Dec. 1816. Recd. 10 Dec. 1816. (Executor not qualified).
Pages 378-379.

18 April 1816. I, Isaac Dubose, being of sound mind & memory. I
desire that the whole of my estate to remain in possession of my wife,
Sarah Dubose, during her natural life. I give unto my dtr., Martha, all
my library for her own use, also her own bead steads, bed & furniture,
also 4 negroes & their increase, to wit. Beuah, Abner, Anthony & Betty.
After the payment of my just debts, I give the rest of my estate to my
other chn. to wit. Clemenet, Elizabeth, Hannah, Fra---y (blurred), David
and Ann to be equally divided between them, after the death of my wife
Sarah. I appoint my wife Sarah Dubose executrix & George Bullock executor. Wit: Benjamin Sims, William P. Dearmond & Thomas C. Russell.
Signed, Isaac Dubose. Proved on oath of Thomas Russell this 4 Nov. 1816.
This day Sarah Dubose & George Bullock was qualified as executors, to
make a true inventory of the goods & chattels and exhibit the same before
the Clerk of Court within three months. Signed, Wm. Jones, Judge. Recd.
20 Dec. 1816. Pages 380-383.

11 Nov. 1815. I, Samuel Sullivan, being in a low state of health
but of sound mind & memory. Do appoint my brother, Obadiah Sullivan &
James Gregory of this State & County my executors. I desire my just
debts to be paid. Then I wish an equal distribution between my chn. to
wit. James Madison Sullivan & Arabel Sullivan my only heirs. Wit: John
Cartledge, & Mark (X) Sullivan. Signed, Samuel Sullivan. Proved on
oath of John Cartledge this 8 Oct. 1816. (then) In open court on the 27
Jan. 1817 Mark Sullivan made his oath to the above will. On the 27 Jan.
1817 Obadiah Sullivan & James Gregory was qualified as executors, to make
a true inventory of the goods & chattels and exhibit the same before the
Clerk of Court within three months. Signed John Foster. Reg. 17 Feb.
1817. Pages 383-385.

1 March 1817. I, William L. Beale, being of sound mind & memory.
I give unto my beloved wife, Maryann Beale, during her natural life, four
negroes named, Pompey, Mary, Mariah & Frank all my household & kitchen
furniture, one fourth part of my stock of every kind, also the use of my
plantation whereon I now live until my son Charles Simmons Beale come to
the age of twenty one yrs. of age. I give unto my son Charles S. Beale,
one negro man named David, also one third part of my stock of every kind,
after my wife has taken her share or one fourth part. I give unto my
son, Augustus Beale, one negro man named Henry, also one third part of
my stock of every kind, after my wife has taken her share. I give unto
my son, William, one negro girl named Orry, also one third part of my
stock of every kind, after my wife has her share. The rest of my estate
both real & personal to be sold for the benfit of the estate. I appoint
my wife Maryann Beale & William Jones executors. Wit: Jas. Toole, Junr.,
John Gray, Asa Avary. Signed Wm. L. Beale. Proved on oath of John Gray
& Asa Avary this 3 March 1817. This day William Jones was qualified as
executor, to make a true inventory of the goods & chattels and exhibit
the same before the Clerk of Court within three months. Signed, John
Foster, Judge. Reg. 4 March 1817.

26 Nov. 1816. I, Edward Oneale, being of perfect sound mind & memory, but far advanced in years. I give unto my beloved wife, Rebecca,
4 negroes, to wit. Cate, Jinny, Roben & Nick, also my waggon horses,
stock of all kind, all household & kitchen furniture during her natural
life, then to be equally distributed among her four children to wit.
July, Polly, Bazil & Edward. I give unto dtr. July, negroes, John, Lill
& Daphney. I give unto my dtr. Polly, negroes, Clary, Meal & Solomon.
I give unto my son Bazil, negroes, Bigg, Isaac & Squire. I give unto my
son Edward, negroes, Ben & Little Isaac. I give unto my dtr. Jane Luke,
.25¢. I give unto my son, Samuel .25¢. I give unto my dtr., Kazziah
Stanford, .25¢. I give unto my Grandson, son of Samuel Germany & Fanny
Washington Germany .25¢. I give unto my dtr., Elizabeth Eubanks, .25¢.
I give unto my dtr., Susannah Oneale, .25¢. I give unto my dtr. Peggy

185

Oneale, .25¢. The rest of my estate to pay my just debts & then equally
divided among my chn. July, Polly, Bazzel & Edward. I appoint my wife,
Rebecca Oneals, executrix & Solomon Marshall & Harvey Wheat my executors.
Wit: Allen Lovelace, Eleanor Lovelace, John Barron. Signed, Edward
Oneale. Proved on oath of John Barron, Allen Lovelace & Harvey Wheat
this 5 May 1817. This day Harvey Wheat was qualified as executor, to
make a true inventory of the goods & chattels and exhibit the same before
the Clerk of Court within three months. Signed, John Foster, Judge.
Recd. 8 July 1817. Pages 389-394.

   3 Aug. 1816. I, Josiah G. Telfair, being of sound mind do make
this my last will & testament. I give unto my dear mother, Sarah Telfair
all debts due me, either upon bond, notes or open accounts, to be collected by my executor. Also $1,000 to be paid out of my crop at my
plantation in Columbia County. I also give unto my mother, Sarah Telfair
$600 annually during her natural life, this legacy to be paid by my
brothers, Thomas & Alexander Telfair, as I have given the said brothers
a certain portion of my estate for this purpose. I give unto my brother,
Thomas, all my plantation in Columbia County, containing about 1000 acres,
being in three tracts, one tract of 150 acres granted to Benjamin Upton,
another tract of 300 acres granted to John Cobb, another tract of the
ballance granted to Howard & Few. I give unto my brother Thomas all my
rights, titles & interest in a lot on the bay in the city of Savannah,
on which my mother & family now lives. Known as lot #13. I give unto
my brother Thomas, all my rights, titles, & interest in a plantation
lying in Chatham County, which was devised to my deceased uncle, Barack
Gibbons, to my mother, Sarah Telfair, during her natural and after her
death to his nephews, Josiah G. Telfair, Thomas Telfair, Alexander Telfair & Noble W. Jones. I give my brother, Thomas Telfair, the following
negroes, Caesar, Ned, Joe, Lemerick, Moses, Watty, Pamela, Marcus, Binah,
Phebe, Davie, Delia, Little Davie, George, Saltage, Bella, Joshua, Lewis,
Alick, Charlotte, Sophy, Little York, Jim, Little Joe, Nanny, York, Oera,
Peter & Phebe, also the rest & residue of my estate in Columbia County.
I give unto my brother, Alexander Telfair, all my plantation in Jefferson
County containing 1500 acres, being a moiety of two tracts of land,
granted to Habersham, to him & his heirs forever, also the following
negroes, Nanny & her child named Charles May, Maurice, Judy, Jeffery,
Tom, Doll, August, September, Toney, Peggy & her child, Jenny, Rose,
Hetty, Sally, Quamina, Jenny, Dilsy, Prescilla, Cussia, Roderick & Amy.
Also all the rest & residue of my estate in Jefferson County. I give
unto my brothers Thomas & Alexander Telfair all rights, claims or interest in a lot in the city of Savannah known as lot #14 & West of Bull
Street, which was devised to our uncle and he gave to our mother Sarah
Telfair and at her death to his nephews. I give unto my sisters, Mary
Telfair, Sarah G. Haig and Margaret Telfair, all the rest & residue of
my real estate, & all rights, titles & claims in the estate of my decd.
father, Edward Telfair, & decd. uncle, William Gibbons, and under a
marriage settlement of my mother Sarah, subject to the payment of the
debts of my father's estate. I appoint Thomas and Alexander Telfair my
brothers to be executors. Wit: William Upton, Jared Pounds, Thomas W.
Murrel. Signed, John G. Telfair. Proved on oath of Jared Pounds &
Thomas W. Murrel this 5 May 1817. This day Thomas Telfair was qualified
as executor, to make a true inventory of the goods & chattels and exhibit
the same before the Clerk of Court within three months. Signed John
Foster, Judge. Reg. 9 July 1817. Pages 395-403.

   15 Jan. 1813. I, John Avery, (Avary) I do declare this to be my
last will & testament. I make no further provision for my dtr., Martha
Welborn, inasmuch as she has heretofore received her proportion. I give
unto my dtr., Elizabeth M. Smith, one negro girl named Anne & her increase. I give unto my son, Harbert Avery, one negro girl named Sal & her
increase. I give unto my dtr., Milly Farrar, one negro girl named Rachel & her increase. I give unto my son, Archer Avery, all & the whole
of my real estate, also one negro girl named Eliza & her increase. I
give unto my son, Asa Avery, one negro man named Bob also the sum of
$600, if not paid before my death, then within six months after my death
out of my estate. I give unto my son, John Avery, one negro boy named
Nelson. The aforesaid negroes has been delivered to the legatees. The
residue of my estate to be sold & the money from the sale divided among
my four sons. I appoint my son Archer Avery & my friend Anderson Crawford

my executors. Wit: John Gartrell, William P. Beale & Walter Jones. Signed John Avary. Proved on oath of Walter Jones & Wm. P. Beale this 7 July 1817. This day Archer Avery was qualified as executor, to make a true inventory of the goods & chattels and exhibit the same before the Clerk of Court within three months. Signed, A. Crawford, Clk. Reg. 9 July 1817. Pages 423-425.

8 July 1816. I, Sarah Marshall, dtr. of Levi Marshall, decd. do make this my last will & testament. I give unto my brother, Levi Marshall, one cow & calf. I give unto my mother a negro girl named Hannah, during her life time and at death to be equally divided between my sisters Eliza & Emily Marshall. I request my negro Lewis to be sold, and the money to buy another negro, such as my executors think best, and the negro so bought to be part of my estate. I give unto my sisters the negro so bought by my executors in room of Lewis, with one boy named Bill, one wench named Rachael, also 250 acres of land joining Doctor Crawford & Richard Eubanks, to be equally divided when Eliza shall come of age. I give unto my sister Eliza one bed & furniture, the debts due me, with the balance of my part of the estate of Daniel Marshall, dec'd. to be applied to paying my debts and what's over, I give to my mother. I appoint my mother & my brother, Joseph Marshall executors. Wit: William Booker, Thomas Jones, Gerald Morris, Wm. D. Wilkins. Signed Sarah Marshall. Proved on oath of William Booker & Thomas Jones this 7 July 1817. This day Sarah Marshall was qualified as executor, to make a true inventory of the goods & chattels and exhibit the same before Clerk of Court within three months. Signed, John Foster, Judge. Reg. 10 July 1817. Pages 407-410.

18 Sept. 1815. I, Peter Overbay, being weak in body but of sound mind & memory. First I will that all my just debts be paid. I give unto my beloved wife, Susannah, during her natural life, all my estate for the purpose of raising & educating my children, viz: William, Samuel & Benjamin, except the old negro man named Ishamael who is to have plot of land to till for himself & to be under the direction of my wife, and he is not to be put under any other person. I give unto my son, William, a negro woman named Aggy. I give unto my son, Samuel, a negro called Edinburgh. I give unto my son, Benjamin, a negro woman named Peggy. I desire that all my real & personal estate be equally divided after the death of my wife. I desire that all the money that is owing to me should be collected for the support of my wife & children. I appoint Robert Walton & Jacob Smith my executors. Wit: Moses Ivy, James (X) Muller & Rebekah (X) Melton. Signed Peter (X) Overbay. Proved on oath of Moses Ivy & James Muller this 7 July 1817. This day Robert Walton was qualified as executor, to make a true inventory of the goods & chattels and exhibit the same before the Clerk of Court within three months. Signed, John Foster, Judge. Reg. 10 July 1817. Pages 411-417.

6 Sept. 1815. I, James Hamilton, being of sound mind & memory. I give unto my son-in-law, Samuel W. Goode, Esq. one negro named Harry & his wife Charlotte. I give unto my son, Thomas N. Hamilton, my Kioke tract of land & the following negroes, Peter, Leah, Jim & Peggy. I give unto my brother, Alexander Hamilton, of the State of Ohio, all my Ohio land containing about 1000 acres in trust for the benfit of my brothers & sisters who now resides in the Kingdom of Ireland. I give unto my son, James Hamilton, all the rest of my real & personal property. I appoint my sons Thomas N. & James Hamilton & my friend Peter Crawford executors. Wit: A. Crawford, R. Johns & P. Crawford. Signed, James Hamilton. Proved on oath of Robert Crawford & Robert Johns this 1 Sept. 1817. This day Thomas N. Hamilton was qualified as executor, to make a true inventory of the goods & chattels and exhibit the same before the Clerk of Court within three months. Signed, (not signed). Reg. 17 Nov. 1817. Pages 418-420.

21 Aug. 1817. I, Joseph Marshall, Junr. being sick abed but of sound judgement. I give unto my beloved wife the land whereon I now live during her widowhood also Betty to her during her life time and then to my two children, Sarah & Peter, and her part of Beardn estate. I give unto my son Peter the house where I now live and the land (225 acres) and Sarah Francis the ballance and the negroes to be divided when Sarah becomes of age, to wit. Jerry, Harry, Mat, Dick, Charlotte, Old

187

Abram and Young Abram, two small ones, Milly & Jeny. Executors, Sarah
Marshall, Doctor Nathan Crawford and Lewis Marshall when become of age.
Signed, Joseph Marshall. Wit: James Cartledge, Junr., Joseph Marshall,
Senr., John (X) Reed. I do leave my two children to my mother (to wit)
Sarah and Peter, and also for my negroes to work on the place to pay for
the land. Signed, Joseph Marshall. Proved on oath of James Cartledge,
Junr., John Reed & Joseph Marshall, Senr. this 1 Sept. 1817. This day
Nathan Crawford & Sarah Marshall was qualified as executors, to make a
true inventory of the goods & chattels and exhibit the same before the
Clerk of Court within three months. Not signed. Reg. 17 Nov. 1817.
Pages 420-422.

6 Sept. 1817. I, Joseph Marshall, Senr. the son of the Rev. Daniel
Marshall, being low in body but of sound mind & judgement. To be buried
in my own grave yard. I wish all my just debts to be paid. I give unto
my beloved wife a comfortable support during her widowhood, life time or
till my youngest child come of age. I give unto my dtr., Mary Murray,
in addition to the negroes already given, viz. Janrey, Fariny, Melinda,
Moses & Winny. Also 100 acres of land that I bought from E. Perryman,
the tract whereon Mr. A. Appling now lives, also 100 acres lying on
Scotts Road, purchased at Sheriff's sale, the property of Zach McDaniel,
in both cases the 100 acres is not warrented but taken as more or less.
The ballance of my property to be keep together until the youngest child
comes of age, the chn. to be schooled & raised in a christian like manner. I give unto Revd. A. Marshall $20 to be paid 1 Jan. 1818. I give
to the Baptist unicorporated church at the Keokee $10 per year for ten
years. When my youngest child comes of age a division of my estate to
be made between my four youngest chn. to wit. Joseph, Huldah, Saluda &
Oneel Plesder Marshall. I appoint Ann Marshall, Jabez P. Marshall &
Marshal Pitman. Wit: Edward Cater, Martha Marshall & Jabal P. Marshall.
Signed, Joseph Marshall. Proved on oath of Edward Cater, Martha Marshall
& Jubal P. Marshall this 1 Dec. 1817. This day Ann Marshall and Jabez
P. Marshall was qualified as executors, to make a true inventory of the
goods & chattels and exhibit the same before the Clerk of Court within
three months. Not signed. Pages 423-425.

7 June 1817. I, James Savidge, being sick in body but of sound
mind & memory. First I desire that my just debts to be paid. I give
unto my beloved wife Elizabeth Savidge, during her natural life, one
third of my real & personal estate. I give unto my natural son, John,
whom I call John Savidge and his sister, Rebecca Savidge, my dtr. the
ballance of my estate both real & personal, to them each to share & share
alike. The chn. property to remain in the hand of the executors until
one of them marry or come of age. Also the legacy given to my wife at
her death shall be divided between the two children. I appoint my wife,
Elizabeth Savidge, James Foster & Timothy T. Barham my executors. Wit:
Timothy T. Barham, Joseph (X) Jones, Jas. Foster & Susannah (X) Garrett.
Signed, James Savidge. Proved on oath of Joseph Jones & John Foster
this 5 Jan. 1818. This day Elizabeth Savidge was qualified as executor,
to make a true inventory of the goods & chattels and exhibit the same
before the Clerk of Court within three months. Not signed. Reg. 24 Jan.
1818. Pages 426-429.

5 Nov. 1817. I, Josiah McGee, being in perfect health & my sound
mind and memory. I appoint Jona. Stanford my executor and my wife,
Judath McGee, my executrix. I give unto my step-son-in-law, Milba McGee
$2. I give to my son, Levin McGee, $2. I give to my son-in-law, James
Dunn, $2. I give to my son-in-law, Daniel Burgen, $2. I give unto my
wife Judeth McGee, and my dtr., Mary Ann McGee, and the child my wife
may have in nine months, all my land which I hold and whereon I now live,
with all stock of horses, cattle, hogs & sheep, household & kitchen
furniture. In case my wife should not bring an heir in nine months, my
son, John McGee, shall have one third of the mentioned property or $2,
in cash. Wit: William Stanford, Nancy (X) Stanford & Jnos. Stanford,
JP. Signed, Josiah McGee. Proved on oath of William, Nancy and Jona.
Stanford this 4 May 1818. This day Jona. Stanford and Judiah McGee was
qualified as executors, to make a true inventory of the goods & chattels
and exhibit the same before the Clerk of Court within three months.
Signed, John Foster. Reg. 31 July 1818. Pages 430-431.

27 Feb. 1818. I, Reuben Wilborn, being low in health weak in body
but of sound mind & memory. I desire that my just debts be paid. I give
unto my beloved wife, Susanah Wilborn all my estate both real & personal
to be held & possessed by her during her natural life, then to decend to
my beloved Step son, Samuel Clark Rice, to be held, owned & possessed by
him forever. I appoint my wife, Susanah, my executrix. Wit: S. W. Gibson, J. W. Gibson & W. Wilkins. Signed, Reuben Wilborn. Proved on oath
of Williams Wilkins and Shadrick W. Gibson this 6 July 1818. No executor qualified. Reg. 1 Aug. 1818. Pages 432-433.

23 March 1818. I, Isaac Winfrey, being unwell but of sound mind &
memory. I will that all my just debts be paid. I give unto my son,
Samuel Winfrey, $20 in addition to what I have already given him. I
give unto my dtr., Elizabeth Wellborn, the following negroes, Charlotte
& her child named Isham, Arch, Austin & Chloa, this being all I intend
for her to have. I give unto my dtr., Sarah Hampton Davie, negroes, John,
Sylvia, Mary & her child named Henry. I give unto my son, Reuben Winfrey,
negroes, Princes, Minor & Katy. I give unto my son, John Winfrey,
negroes, Abraham, Neal & Sarah. I give unto my dtr., Juda Seay, negroes,
Parrot & Chloe & her child Sam. I give unto my son, Henry Winfrey,
negroes, Hall, Peter & Lydia. I give unto my dtr. Mildred Winfrey,
negroes, Jerry, Flora & Charity. I give unto my dtr., Jane Winfrey,
negroes, Ceaser, Wilson & Mary. I give unto my dtr. Cyntha Winfrey, negroes
Bob, George & Nancey. I give unto my beloved wife, Sarah Winfrey during
her natural life, negroes, Jeffery, Hector, George, Titus, Abraham,
Letly, Fanny, Phillis, Lovey & Betty, also one tract of land of 460 acres
whereon I now live, also 202½ acres lying in Wilkinson County, known as
lot #219 in the nineth district, also all stock of horses, cattle, sheep,
hogs, farming tools, household & kitchen furniture during her natural
life. At my wife's death I give the property she has to my chn. to wit:
Samuel, Winfrey, Sarah Davie, Reubin & John Winfrey, Juda Seay, Henry,
Mildred, Jane, Cyntha Ann Winfrey. The last four named chn. each to have
a horse & saddle paid from the estate when they come of age, the value
of $125. I appoint my son, Reuben Winfrey & son-in-law, Randolph Davie,
my executors. Wit: William Barnett, John (X) Perryman, Lyddia (X)
Beall. Signed, Isaac Winfrey. Proved on oath of William Barnett & Ea-
dith Beale this 6 July 1818. This day Reuben Winfrey & Randolph Davie
was qualified as executors, to make a true inventory of the goods &
chattels and exhibit the same before the Clerk of Court within three
months. Signed, John Foster, Judge. Reg. 1 Aug. 1818. Pages 434-439.

1 April 1818. I, William Walton, being weak in body but of sound
mind and memory. First I desire my just debts to be paid. I give unto
my dtr., Blanchy Wood, negroes China, Cyrus, Mary & Henry, which she now
has in her possession. I give unto my son, William Fairfax Walton, one
negro, named Polydore. I give unto my son, Jesse Sims Walton, one negro
named Daniel. I give unto my dtr., Frances George Walton, negroes,
Little Sally, Moses, Ket & Mariah. I give unto my beloved wife during
her natural life the tract of land whereon I now live, with the rest &
residue of my personal estate. After the death of my wife, I desire that
the tract of land whereon I now live to be divided equally between my
sons, William & Jesse Walton. Also I desire that my dtr., Frances G. to
have negro girl named Tabby. Also I desire that negroes, Lucy, Betty,
Tow, Isbel, Young Lucy, Matilda, Banister, Old Sally, Nancey, Lewis,
Mansfield, Hannah, Baalaw, Elvia, Wally, Dick & Vandy should be equally
divided among my four chn. share & share alike. The rest & residue of
my estate to be equally divided amongst my three youngest chn. I appoint
my wife, Sarah Walton, my executrix and my son, William F. Walton, executor. Wit: Martha I. Cleghorn, Benjamin Berry, A. Jennings & Peter Crawford. Signed, Wm. Walton. Proved on oath of Benjamin Berry, Anderson
Jennings and Peter Crawford this 7 Sept. 1818. This day Sarah Walton was
qualified as executor, to make true inventory of the goods & chattels
and exhibit the same before the Clerk of Court within three months. Not
signed. Reg. 22 March 1819. Pages 440-443.

25 May 1818. I, John Ray, being in perfect sence & memory. First
I desire my just debts to be paid. I give unto my beloved wife, Betsey,
the plantation and land whereon I now live, with household & kitchen
furniture, tools, all stock of horses, cattle, hogs & sheep, also negroes
Garrett, Ben, Nance, Meriah & her child Polly, "Peter when he is returned

189

from a mortgage and all other property" for the use & benfit of Betsey
& my chn. to wit: Sally, Phebe, Lewis, Joseph C. & Nancy M. I appoint
my friend, Jeremiah Griffin & my wife, Betsey Ray, my executors. Wit:
Robert Johns, Phebe (X) Seay, David Seay. Signed, John (X) Ray. Proved
on oath of Robert Johns & David Seay this 7 Sept. 1818. This day Jeremiah Griffin & Elizabeth Ray was qualified as executors, to make a true
inventory of the goods & chattels and exhibit the same before the Clerk
of Court within three months. Not signed. Reg. 24 March 1819. Pages
443-445.

    11 June 1817. I, James Savidge, being sick of body but of sound
mind & memory. First I will & desire that my just debts to be paid. I
give unto my beloved wife, Elizabeth Savidge, during her natural life,
one third part of my real & personal estate. I give unto my natural son,
John, whom I call John Savidge and his sister, Rebecca Savidge, my dtr.
the ballance of my estate, both real & personal to them & theirs heirs
forever, share & share alike. I desire that my chn. property to remain
in the hands of my executors until one of them come of age or marry.
After the death of my wife the property left to her, to be divided between my two chn. equally. I appoint my wife, Elizabeth Savidge, James
Foster & Timothy T. Barham as my executors. Wit: Timothy T. Barham,
Joseph (X) Jones, Jas. Foster, Susannah (X) Garrett. Signed, James
Savidge. Proved on oath of Joseph Jones, and John Foster this 5 Jan.
1818. This day Elizabeth Savidge was qualified as executor, to make a
true inventory of the goods & chattels and exhibit the same before the
Clerk of Court within three months. Not signed. Reg. 24 March 1819.
(This seem to be the same will as on pages 426-429). Pages 445-448.

    2 June 1818. I, Barnett Whittington, being weak in body but of
sound mind & memory. I desire that my just debts to be paid by my executor. I give unto my beloved wife, Sarah, one negro named China, to be
disposed of at her death in any way she think proper. I also give unto
my wife one negro girl named Gadess during her natural life. I give
unto my dtr., Elizabeth Barham, one negro girl named Rhoda. I give unto
my son, Ephriam, one negro named Amos & $100 to be raised out of the est.
I give unto my dtr., Mariah, one negro girl named Philis and $200 to be
raised out of my est. I desire that the land whereon I now live be sold
and after paying my debts, another tract of land to be bought for my
wife & chn. to live on during my wife's natural life, then to be divided
equally among my children. I appoint my wife, Sarah, executrix & Arthur
Foster executor. Wit: Alex. H. Allison, Hugh Patrick & David Cooper.
Signed, Barnett Whittington. Proved on oath of Alex H. Allison, Hugh
Patrick & David Cooper this 7 Sept. 1818. This day Sarah Whittington &
Arthur Foster was qualified as executors, to make a true inventory of the
goods & chattels and exhibit the same before Clerk of Court within three
months. Not signed. Reg. 25 March 1819. Pages 449-451.

    13 Dec. 1818. I, William Few, I give the whole of my property both
real & personal to be equally divided share & share alike between my beloved wife, Hannah, and my children, Ignatius, William, Emilus, Paullus,
Eliza, Frances & Amelia. Also my share of my father's estate such as
now due to me, shall be equally divided between my wife and my children
share & share alike. I desire that my estate be kept together by my
executors until all my just debts are paid, should my wife remarry she
to have her divided share of my estate and of the estate debts. The
said children to receive their share when they are of full age. They
are to have a good education in law or physic for the sons and female
education for the dtrs. The chn. are not to be placed in the hands of
guardians, but to be under the direction of my executors. I appoint my
brother Ignatius Few, My friend Doctor Clement Billingslea and my brother
by marriage George Hardwick, Esq. my executors. Wit: M. A. Caudler, R.
Gerald & J. A. Caudler. Signed, Will Few. Proved on oath of Mark A.
Caudler, Randal Gerold & Joseph A. Caulder this 1 March 1819. This day
Ignatius A. Few was qualified as executor, to make a true inventory of
the goods & chattels and exhibit the same before the Clerk of Court
within three months. Not signed. Reg. 26 March 1819. Pages 452-456.

    Same will as on pages 423-425. Joseph Marshall, Senr. Pages 457-
460.

22 Sept. 1817. I, Ann T. Johnson, being weak in body but sound in mind & memory. I give all my estate both real & personal to my son Mones Johnson, but in case of his death before he marries or is of age, it is my desire that the estate be equally divided between my brothers & sisters. I desire that my negro Cloe be sold to whom soever owneth her mother at the valuation of two disinterested men. I desire my friend & Brother Edward Woodin have a bed, pair of sheets and counterpin. I appoint my friend, Peter Crawford, my executor. Wit: J. T. Allen, Wm. Yarbrough, Sarah Allen. Signed, Ann T. Johnson. Proved on oath of Francis T. Allen, Wm. Yarbrough, and Sarah Allen this 5 April 1819. (Executor not qualified). Pages 461-462.

7 April 1819. I, Dorsey Howard, being weak of body but perfect mind & memory. I give unto my wife, Fanny Howard, my now dwelling plantation and the land adjoining, containing 144 acres, being part of a tract granted unto Henry Wright joining James Mapp, Peter Watson & Aquilla Howard and 50 acres I bought at sheriff sale of Thomas Howard land, joining the old negro man by the name of Fitus, all my horses, cattle stock, household & kitchen furniture during her widowhood, if she should remarry, she is to have one fourth part of my estate. With the rest equally divided among my chn. to wit: Ruthy Whitaker Howard, Mary Ann Howard, Dorsey Howard, Junr. Wit: William Mullen, Thomas Souncers, William Scott, JP. Signed, Dorsey Howard. Proved on oath of William Mullen & Thomas Souncers & William Scott, Junr., this 5 July 1819. Reg. 11 Sept. 1819. (No executor named in will). Pages 462-465.

24 Jan. 1811. I, Farlton Fleming Keith, of Fauquier County, Virginia, being in sound health of body. I desire my just debts to be paid. Then I give my estate unto my wife during her widowhood, if she should remarry then she to have only a third part. Also having no child or children, the ballance of my estate to be divided between my brothers, James, Peter Grant & Isham Keith, and after my wife death her part of my estate to be divided between my brothers. What ever my wife may have given her, it shall be at her disposial. I appoint my father-in-law Mr. William Stone & Mr. Mumford Marshall my executors. Wit: Caleb Rodger, James Rodgers, John Weedon. In Court of Ordinary, this 5 July 1819. Marshall Keith appearing with the will of Farlton F. Keith, decd. being sworn, saith he saw John Meedon put his own name to said will. Sworn in open Court. Sgn. Marshall. Reg. 11 Sep. 1819. Pages 464-465.

21 Oct. 1815. I, Aquilla Howard, being weak in body but of sound mind & memory. I wish my just debts & funeral charges be paid. I give unto my wife Elizabeth Howard all my estate both real & personal which I may possess at my decease, during her natural life and at her death. I give unto my brother, John Howard, all the estate which may remain both real & personal. I appoint my brother, John Howard and Mark Price Davis the executors. Wit: P. B. Short, Jas. Mappin & Mark Price Davis. Signed, Aquilla Howard. Proved on oath of Peter B. Short, James Mappin & Mark P. Davis this 6 Sept. 1819. This day John Howard & Mark P. Davis was qualified as executor, to make a true inventory of the goods & chattels and exhibit the same before the Clerk of Court within three months. Signed, John Foster, Judge. Reg. 11 Jan. 1820. Pages 466-468.

6 March 1817. I, Perry Graves, being sick & weak in body, but of perfect mind & memory. First I give unto my Sister, Cloe Graves, all my personal estate of negroes, horses or anything else. I give unto my sister, Cloe Graves, all the land whereon I now live on the Big Kioka Creek containing 553½ acres, also 830 acres & one third in Warren County, being part of a five thousand acres run for Humphrey Graves, and 202½ acres in Wilkinson County which I drew, which I give unto the chn. of my brother George Graves. I give unto the chn. of my decd. sister, Cassandre Pearre, viz: 173 acres in Columbia Co. on Head Stull Creek, also 100 acres in Burke Co. being part of 600 acres run for Geo. Kirkland. Also 150 acres in Wilkes Co. on Broad River, being part of 750 acres run in the name of Robertson. Also 143 3/4 acres in Jackson County, being part of a tract run for Thomas Graves. The last three tracts being part of which I received from Humphrey Graves Est. I appoint my sister Cloe Graves and my brother George Graves as executors. Wit: John W. Walton, Wm. P. Bealle & Stephen (X) Frederick. Signed, Perry Graves. Proved on oath of William P. Bealle this 1 Nov. 1819. This day Cloe Graves and

George Graves was qualified as executors, to make a true inventory of
the goods & chattels and exhibit the same before the Clerk of Court
within three months. Not signed. Reg. 11 Jan. 1820. Pages 468-471.

12 Oct. 1819. I, Jesse Albritton, being at this time in a low state
of health but of sound mind & memory. After paying my just debts, I
advise my executors to sell the land and purchase another tract for my
wife, Martha Albritton, & family to live on or she may desire to divide
the property among herself & the chn. Tomil, Ausil, Melton, Nancy Lee &
Matilda. Should my wife desire to live on the land that a division is
to be made after her death among the chn. I desire my personal estate
be divided when the children come of age or marriage. I appoint my
friend William Zachery, and James Yarbrough my executors. Wit: Betsey
Ann Beale, James Albritton & Amos Albritton. Signed, Jesse Albritton.
Proved on oath of James Albritton & Amos Albritton this 1 Nov. 1819.
This day William Zachery & James Yarbrough was qualified as executor, to
make a true inventory of the goods & chattels and exhibit the same before
the Clerk of Court within three months. Signed, John Foster. Reg. 1
Feb. 1820. Pages 471-473.

No date on will. I, Elias Lazenby, being in a low state of health
but of sound mind & memory. First that my three children that are
married to keep all the property that I have given heretofore as their
part of my est. The three dtrs. & one granddaughter that lives with me
to have all the property that I may possess, to be equally divided between them at any time they may think best for all, they are, Nancey,
Daborah & Martha Lazenby and Martha Martin. My executor may sell as
much as they think it will take to pay my just debts. Any money over to
be used for the last named girls. I appoint my friend Shadrick W. Gibson and my dtrs. Nancey & Martha Lazenby my executors. Wit: Robert
Martin, J. Sturges & Francis Martin. Signed, Elias Lazenby. Proved on
oath of Robert Martin and John Sturges this 6 Sept. 1819. This day
Shadriek W. Gibson, Nancey & Martha Lazenby was qualified as executor,
to make a true inventory of the goods & chattels and exhibit the same
before the Clerk of Court within three months. Signed, John Foster,
Judge. Reg. 17 Jan. 1820. Pages 474-476.

26 Aug. 1819. I, Matthew Killingsworth, being weak in body but of
sound mind & memory. After my just debts are paid out of the est. I
give unto my beloved wife, Liza Killingsworth, my plantation and the
whole of my property to be & remain in the same situation until her
death. After my wife decease, I give unto my son, Freeman Killingsworth,
my land whereon I now live, with one cow & calf he may choose at that
time. One bed & furniture known as his bed at this time, one still &
utensils. I give unto my son, John Killingsworth, one negro woman named
Dinah forever. I give to my son, Daniel Killingsworth, one negro man
named George forever. I give unto my dtr., Susannah Kindrick, one negro
girl named Jenny forever. I give unto my dtr., Sarah Bosworth, one
negro girl named Chaney forever. I leave my negro boy named Jack to be
divided between my dtrs., Susannah & Sarah. I give all my stock of
horses, cattle, hogs, sheep & household & kitchen furniture to be equally
divided among my chn. John, Daniel, Susannah & Sarah. I appoint John,
Daniel & Freeman Killingsworth my executors. Wit: Philip Tinsley, Mason
A. Tinsley & Sol. Hoge. Signed, Mat. Killingsworth. Proved on oath of
Philip & Mason A. Tinsley and Solomon Hoge 1 Nov. 1819. This day Daniel
& Freeman Killingsworth was qualified as executor, to make a true inven-
tory of the goods & chattels and exhibit the same before the Clerk of
Court within three months. Not signed. Reg. 17 Jan. 1820. Pages 476-
478.

5 Jan. 1819. I, Ann McFarland, a relict of James McFarland, decd.
being weak & low in body & in an advanced period of life, but of perfect
mind & memory. I give unto my son, John McFarland, & his heirs one negro
woman named Charlotte & her four children named, Linny, Mima, Kizia &
Sampson, also Issabel & her two chn. named Alfred & Jim. Also one negro
boy named Thomas. Also the money when collected due me from Andrew
Shephard for which I have a judgement in Wilkes Superior Court. I give
unto my grand son, Alexander McDonald, the sum of $100. I give unto my
grandson, Stephen Coleman, the sum of $100. I give unto my negro girl
Heina one feather bed & furniture. All horses, cattle stock of every

kind & house hold & kitchen furniture to be desposed of as my executor
see or think best. I appoint my son, John McFarland, my executor. Wit:
Thomas White, Robert Wiseman, Senr. Proved on oath of Thomas White &
Robert Wiseman this 14 Sept. 1819. This day John McFarland was qualified as executor, to make a true inventory of the goods & chattels and
exhibit the same before the Clerk of Court within three months. Not
signed. Reg. 18 Jan. 1820. Pages 479-481.

19 July 1819. I, Abraham Marshall, a minister of the gospel, and
pastor of the Baptist Church at the Keokee, and son of the Reverend
Daniel Marshall & his wife, Martha, late of this county. Being sick &
weak in body but of perfect mind & memory. My just debts to be paid out
of my present crop. My tract of land containing 575 acres lying on the
Oconee River to be sold and the money applied to the payment of my debts
& my negro Liddy & her child may be sold for the same purpose. I give
unto my son, Jabez Plaeidy Marshall, one half of my estate both real &
personal. I give unto my son, Jubel Orion Marshall, one half of my est.
both real & personal. After my death the land on Keokee to be divided
by the creek, or letting the creek be the line between the North tract
& the South tract. The negroes to be divided in families and no child
taken from the family under the age of ten yrs. The ballance of the
estate as stock of cattle, horses, hogs, & sheep with household & kitchen furniture, books, cash, debts, tools to be divided between my sons.
The eight negroes I lent to my son Jabez to be returned to the estate
and divided with the whole. I appoint my sons, Jabez Pleidy Marshall &
Jubel Orion Marshall, my executors. Wit: John Boyd, Marshall Pittman
& Priscilla Pittman. Signed, A. Marshall. Proved on oath of Marshall
Pittman & Priscilla Pittman this 14 Sept. 1819. This day Jabez P.
Marshall & Jubel O. Marshall was qualified as executor, to make a true
inventory of the goods & chattels and exhibit the same before the Clerk
of Court within three months. Not signed. Reg. 19 Jan. 1820. Pages
482-485.

11 June 1818. I, Jonathan Tindell, being of sound mind & memory.
I give unto my beloved wife, Betsey Tindell, negroes, Stephen & Aggy
forever. I give unto my dtr., Nancey M. Kindrick, one negro girl called
Darcas. I give unto my dtr., Sally C. Tindell, one negro girl called
Nelly. I give unto my dtr., Anna T. Tindell, one negro girl called
Linney. I give unto my son, Henry W. Tindell, one negro boy called Dave.
I give unto my son, Robert H. Tindell, one negro called Doctor. I de-
sire that my whole estate both real & personal to remain in common, for
the benfit & support of my wife & family. I desire the chn. to have
their share at marriage or at the age of twenty one yrs. I appoint my
wife, Betsey Tindell, & my friend, John Franklin Bennett, my executors.
Wit: P. Tindell, Hillory Simmons & John B. Tindell. Signed, Jonathan
Tindell. Proved on oath of Pleasant Tindell this 1 Nov. 1819. Executors not qualified. Reg. 19 Jan. 1820. Pages 486-487.

13 May 1815. I, Mary Smith, being of sound mind & memory. I wish
that the child of my son, Hugh B. Smith, by the name of Mary Ann to own
& possess in her own right the first negro child that may be born of
either Letty or Liddey have such issue or either of them. I will to my
dtr., Tabitha Prater, to have five dollars, and should she have a child
either male of female such child to have, own or possess the second
child that may be born of either of my negro girls. I wish my son,
Hugh B. Smith, $5. All the residue of my estate I give unto my son,
John Smith. I appoint my son, John Smith, my executor. Wit: John (X)
Prescott, Joseph H. Carmichael, Wm. Wilkins. Signed, Mary (X) Smith.
Proved on oath of John Prescott, William Wilkins & Joseph W. Carmichael
this 1 May 1820. Pages 488-489.

5 Sept. 1820. I, John Langston, being low in body but of sound
mind & memory. First I will that all my just debts be paid. I give
unto my son, James Langston, 150 acres of land whereon Mackling Sills
now lives. I give unto my son, John Langston, the tract of land whereon he now lives containing 100 acres. I give unto my son, Elvey Langston, 180 acres of land forever, whereon Robert Mills now lives, on
condition the said Elvey does not marry Amanda Adams. I will unto him
150 acres of land adjoining the former place, but in case he the said
Elvey Langston does marry Amanda Adams, I give the last named place

called Kiths old place to my son Isaac Langston. I also give one bay
mare called Doctor to my son Elvey Langston. I give unto my wife,
Rebecca Langston, all the rest of my land, except my draw in the land
lottery during her natural life or widowhood, at her marriage or death
to my son Isaac. Also personal property of one bay mare, 6 cows &
calves, 15 head of hogs, 3 beds & furniture, all kitchen furniture. I
give my son, Isaac, one filly, saddle & my desk. I give unto my dtr.
Mary Willson, $100 in notes. I give unto my dtr., Martha Shanklin,
$100 to be paid in notes. I appoint my wife, Rebecca & my son, John
Langston, my executor. Wit: Robert Lazenby, William Stanford & Michael
(X) Flinn. Signed, John Langston. Proved on oath of Robert Lazenby,
William Stanford & Michael Flinn this 6 Nov. 1820. This day Rebecca &
John Langston was qualified as executors, to make a true inventory of
the goods & chattels and exhibit the same before the Clerk of Court
within three months. Not signed. Reg. 17 Nov. 1820. Pages 490-493.

20 Aug. 1819. I, James Willson, being weak in body but of sound
mind & memory. I desire my just debts to be paid out of my estate. I
give unto my wife, Mary Willson, all my estate both real & personal &
possessed by her to educate & support my children confortably and at the
close of her natural life the property to be equally divided among the
chn. to wit: John, Rebecca, Elias, Anderson, James, Madison, Elizabeth,
and David Walker Willson, when any arrive at full age. I appoint my
friend Robert Lazenby & David Willson and John Langston, Junr. my executors. Wit: John Hannon, David Cooper & John G. Davis. Signed, James
(X) Willson. Proved on oath of John Hannon, David Cooper & John G.
Davis this 13 March 1820. This day John Langston, Junr. was qualified
as executor, to make a true inventory of the goods & chattels and exhibit
the same before the Clerk of Court within three months. Not signed.
Reg. 18 Nov. 1820. Pages 493-496.

EMANUEL COUNTY GEORGIA MARRIAGES

INDEX, BOOK A, 1817-1860

GROOM	BRIDE	DATE MARRIED	PAGE
Anderson, Joel	Dobey Powell	July 24, 1842	7
Anderson, John	Lucinda Yeomans	March 31, 1853	40
Anderson, John D. G.	Louisa Yeomans	March 3, 1853	44
Anderson, John L.	Julia Ann Meadows	Feb. 24, 1857	61
Anderson, Joseph C.	Mary Tison	May 16, 1844	13-A
Atkison, Alexander W.	Elizabeth H. Tims	Jan. 2, 1840	13-A
Barnes, James H.	Elizabeth W. Flanders	April 24, 1842	7
Barwick, William W.	Wineford Odum	Sept. 17, 1840	2
Basemore, John	Eliza Ann Yeomans	Dec. 31, 1850	31
Bass, Wests (?)	Elizabeth Rose	Oct. 9, 1844	13-A
Baughtrite, Daniel	Eady Briant	Nov. 8, 1849	31
Baughtrite, Reuben	Demaris Rich	Dec. 9, 1851	34
Beacham, Lewis	Martha H. Knight	June 1, 1842	7
Beasley, Asa	Sarah Rhiner	June 23, 1853	45
Beasley, Elbert	Martha Meeks	---- 4, 1841	1
Beasley, John	Mary Hall	Jan. 22, 1852	35
Beasley, William	Elizabeth Rhynor	March 7, 1850	30
Bedgood, John	Phada Elis	Mch. 3, 1837 & Oct. 18, 1840	4
Bell, David	Margaret Lanner	March 4, 1844	12
Bennett, Thomas	Elizabeth Ann Oglesby	Sept. 12, 1850	30
Bennett, John	Margaret Roberts	Dec. 28, 1851	37
Benton, Adam	Matilda Rinor	March 11, 1852	36
Bird, Adam	Nancy Deakle	Jan. 5, 1844	12
Bird, Jackson	Elizabeth Edenfield	June 21, 1845	15-B
Bird, Jefferson	Jane E. Stubbs	Nov. 25, 1842	12
Bird, Mathew	Elizabeth McCollough	Jan. 12, 1840	1

194

GROOM	BRIDE	DATE MARRIED	PAGE
Bird, William	Amanda Bird	Aug. 25, 1845	15-A
Bird, William	Sarah Ann Phillips	July 18, 1845	15
Bishop, Alfred	Mary Lennup	Aug. 20, 1845	14
Bishop, William	Susan Hall	May 6, 1849	24
Bishop, John	Mary Wallace	Oct. 30, 1856	55
Black, John	Milly Ann Fennell	Aug. 21, 1857	60
Blunt, Daniel	Mary Parsons	Jan. 27, 1850	28
Boatright, Reuben	Julia Ann Sconyers	Jan. 6, 1850	27
Boatright, William	Tabitha or Telitha Bryant	Dec. 4, 1853	47
Boyt, Elijah	Elizabeth Martin	Dec. 28, 1856	57
Brady, Joshua	Saday Scon(y)ers	April 9, 1846	17
Brinson, Alexander	Anna A. Kent	Nov. 6, 1851	34
Brinson, Isaac	------------	Nov. 30, 1850	43
Brinson, Jesse A.	Mary Ann Durdan	May 11, 1851	33
Brinson, Noah M.	Elizabeth Durdon	Jan. 11, 1849	23
Brown, James	Rachel Coleman	April 21, 1842	8
Brown, Jesse	Mary Deckle	April 16, 1848	20
Brown, John T.	-----------	August 11, 1857	59
Brown, Sam	Nancy Dekle	Sept. 25, 1845	14
Bunn, Mathew	Margaret Waley	Sept. 23, 1847	19
Burk, Hugh L.	Elizabeth A. Lewis	Nov. 21, 1853	47
Burt, John T.	Maryann Baughtright	Oct. --, 1841	3
Burt, William B.	Mary Oglesby	Dec. 27, 1852	43
Campbell, Iley	Elizabeth Grant	May 29, 1848	21
Canneday, Solomon	Martha Cowart	April 17, 1849	24
Cannady, Solomon	Elizabeth Edenfield	Dec. 27, 1854	50
Chambers, Henry	Mary Mason	June 1, 1842	7
Clark, William	Elizure Faircloth	Oct. 6, 1840	2
Clements, Jesse	Margaret Smith	Oct. 27, 1844	14-A
Clements, Mortimer	Falima Mires (Mikus)	Jan. 28, 1844	12
Cobb, Britian	Mariann Brown	April 4, 1847	18
Coleman, Alfred	Mary E. Brinson	Feb. 5, 1852	36
Coleman, Elias	Mary Ann Sutton	Oct. 14, 1849	25
Coleman, Elisha	Wina Douglass	Nov. 28, 1841	41
Coleman, Elisha S.	Ruby Ann Sutton	Aug. 9, 1846	17
Coelman, Jeremiah	Nancy Hester Ann Thompson	Nov. 4, 1841	3
Coleman, Welcome	Sarah J. Sconyers	Dec. 21, 1856	55
Coleman, Welcom	Sabria Stevens	March 14, 1850	28
Coleman, William	Sarah Sutton	April 22, 1841	1
Cowart, A. L.	Nancy A. Barwick	Feb. 22, 1855	50
Cowart, Nathan E.	Mable Cobb	April 17, 1845	15
Cromer, Jerry	Rachel Bishop	April 4, 1853	40
Curl, Elijah	Mary Williams	Sept. 28, 1857	63
Curl, Reuben	Mary J. Thompson	April 1, 1847	18
Daley, Thomas	Miriam Moore	June 1, 1851	32
Davis, George C.	Matilda Price	March 31, 1857	60
Davis, James	Nancy Powell	May 5, 1852	44
Davis, James A.	Alley Williams	Feb. 4, 1857	62
Davis, John R.	Mary Norris	Dec. 8, 1854	49
Davis, Lewis	Mary Anderson	Nov. 12, 1845	15-A
Davis, William G.	Dicey Williams	Jan. 13, 1853	41
Davis, William J.	Philena Edenfield	Oct. 17, 1854	52
Deakle, John	May Muse	April 19, 1846	15-B
Dealy, John	Eady Ann Gilbert	Jan. 24, 1855	62
Denden, Simeon	Susanah Barwick	March 17, 1842	6
Dicks, John H.	Elizabeth Wilks	May 24, 1857	58
Douglass, William R.	Eliza Anderson	May 3, 1854	47
Dudley, James	Susannah Strange	Dec. 28, 1848	19
Durden, Albert N.	Eliza (Elezea) Brinson	Jan. 22, 1851	34
Durdon, Elimason	Rocksann Rountree	Nov. 6, 1846	17
Durden, John	Jincy Kennady	Jan. 6, 1853	44
Durden, Nathan N.	Belida Kea	May 10, 1857	59
Durden, Rowan W.	---------	Dec. 21, 1852	42
Durdon, William	Delilah Hutcherson	Dec. 3, 1848	22

GROOM	BRIDE	DATE MARRIED	PAGE
Edenfield, David J.	Eliza Jane Kennedy	June 16, 1857	58
Edenfield, Eli	Elizabeth Wiggins	March 27, 1856	53
Edenfield, Ephraim H.	Sarah Ann Kennedy	June 21, 1857	59
Edenfield, James	Agiah Oliver	July 11, 1850	29
Edenfield, James	Lucrecia Coleman	Sept. 9, 1852	38
Edenfield, James A.	Mary Cannaday	Jan. 8, 1852	36
Edenfield, James H.	L. V. Coleman	April 9, 1853	42
Edenfield, John	Narcissa Canaday	March 26, 1848	20
Edenfield, Richmond	Elizabeth Davis	March 16, 1848	21
Edenfield, William D. or H.	Lenna or Susan Cannay (Cannaday)	Feb. 8, 1844	11
Faircloth, Enoch J.	Rachael Hays	Sept. 25, 1856	55
Faircloth, George Washington	Sarah Dugers	Aug. 30, 1846	16
Farrow, Jesse P.	Mary Spence	Dec. 4, 1853	--
Fennell, Cullen	Dorian Wiggans	Dec. 17, 1847	25
Fennell, Nathan	Catharine I. Donaldson	Sept. 14, 1857	61
Flanders, Alexander C.	Rachel Moxley	April 7, 1856	31
Flanders, Barnabas	Susan Williams	June 4, 1848	22
Flanders, Francis T. or Y.	Anna Adams	Nov. 15, 1846	14
Flanders, Frederick W.	Bathsheba Winfred Drake	Aug. 22, 1850	29
Flanders, Jordan	Sarah Thompson (2nd wife)	March 6, 1817	2
Flanders, Jordan	Mary J. Daniel	Jan. 12, 1834	2
Flanders, Joseph S.	Sarah Hall	Aug. 31, 1853	46
Flanders, Richard B.	Jane S. Konyers	July 11, 1841	4
Flanders, William A.	Kitsy Hall	Feb. 27, 1853	41
Flanders, William J.	Winnefred Hawl (Hall)	Oct. 17, 1850	30
Fortner, Michel J.	Axey Bedgood	Feb. 23, 1840	4
Foskin, Allen M.	Juliann Tison	July 19, 1854	47
Foster, Richard	Winny Meeks	May 14, 1848	23
Fulford, Owen	Susan Wilson	June 13, 1849	24
Gay, Batt	Edy Bland	Feb. 13, 1845	13
Gay, Michael	Ann May Clifton	Sept. 7, 1847	15-B
Gilams(?), Clarence	Maunday Wilkes	Feb. 9, 1846	17
Gillis, Andrew J.	Elizabeth Ricks	June 21, 1855	52
Gornto, Benjamin	Jane Stokes	Oct. 4, 1849	27
Gornto, Nathan	Mrs. Mary Rowland	Jan. 17, 1850	27
Green, Daniel	Mahally Hall	Oct. 22, 1843	15-B
Greenway, Berryan	Martha Melverna Santford	Aug. 2, 1840	4
Grimes, Daniel	Mahalley Hall	Oct. 22, 1843	10
Groom, Thomas	Holley J. Nunn	May 25, 1850	29

(A note is beside the above, probably placed there by a researcher, that the name is Green and not Groom)

Gross, Edward	Lucretia Lane	Jan. 3, 1856	53
Hackle, Talbert	Sarah McKinsey	Sept. 1, 1856	54
Hall, Daniel E.	Catharine E. Love	Dec. 31, 1854	50
Hall, Henry	Elizabeth Bishop	April 16, 1857	57
Hall, Isaac B.	Penelopy Brinson	March 30, 1851	38
Hall, Jackson	Nancy Jewell	Dec. 26, 1839	35
Hall, James	Avy Brown	Nov. 16, 1848	22
Hall, James	Jane R. Drew	March 10, 1850	29
Hall, John N.	Margaret Rich	Sept. 11, 1854	49
Hall, Joseph	Lewisinda Hall	Dec. 9, 1849	26
Hall, Juniper	Sarah Folkes	July 31, 1851	33
Hall, Lyman	Elizabeth Durdan	Nov. 28, 1849	28
Hall, Thomas	Martha Flanders	Jan. 25, 1857	56
Hall, Travis	Martha Mores	March 30, 1848	21
Hall, William	Sarah Rawles	Feb. 23, 1851	31
Hall, William	Elizabeth Jane Hall	July 2, 1857	59
Hall, Willis	Clarky Fennell	Sept. 10, 1857	60

GROOM	BRIDE	DATE MARRIED	PAGE
Hamblett (Hambleton)			
Irwin	Mary Ann Davis	Feb. 7, 1852	36
Hart, Amos	Melberry Ann Durden	Nov. 21, 1841	6
Hart, Jesse	Pheraby Rountree	Sept. 21, 1842	8
Hart, Joseph	Siprey (Liprey)?	July 16, 1844	14
Hays, Gary (or Hare)	May Cooksey	Aug. 22, 1846	15-B
Heckel, John	Hetty Green	April 28, 1853	45
Hendrix, William	Mary A. Rigdan	Dec. 26, 1848	22
Herington, Manning	Lucretia Philips	Nov. 6, 1851	45
Herrington, Ephraim	Sarah Ann Arlin	Aug. 25, 1844	15
Hickes, William P.	Elizabeth Jane Outlaw	Sept. 1, 1850	31
Higdon, Robert	Temperance Price	Nov. 2, 1826	2
Higdon, Robert	Emillia Griffis	Jan. 12, 1837	1
Hightower, James	Francy Meek	June 12, 1842	10
Hightower, John	Drewcilla May	Dec. 9, 1849	27
Holton, Isaac	Jane Brinson	Jan. 16, 1851	31
Hook, Jacob	Katharine Hutcherson	Sept. 16, 1849	25
Hooks, Allen	Susan Johnson	April 6, 1856	54
Hooks, Hardy	Hulacy Hutchinson	June 7, 1857	62
Hooks, John	Elizabeth Nunn	Feb. 12, 1854	48
Hoskey, Standly M.	Charlott C. Branby	Dec. 23, 1851	35
Hutcherson, James	Lucreicy Tucker	March 25, 1849	23
Hutcherson, John J.			
(G.)	Treacy Hightower	Oct. 5, 1851	33
Hutcherson, William	Elizabeth Meeks	Sept. 23, 1849	24
Hutcherson, Enoch	Zelpha Meek	Dec. 25, 1842	8
Hutcherson, John	Nancy Fulfort(d)	March 21, 1844	12
Hutcheson, Lewis	Penny Jane Miller	May 6, 1855	52
Hutchinson, Andrew E.	Bethany M. Youngblood	Feb. 1, 1857	55
Hutchison, Ira	Milley Beasley	Dec. 24, 1848	18
Jenkins, Edman E.	Georgiann Dailey	April 11, 1852	37
Jewel, William	Sarah Ann Marshall	Aug. 1, 1850	30
Johns, Griffith	Lucinda Corbin	July 24, 1854	47
Johnson, Benjamin W.	Beneator Shearward	April 16, 1850	29
Johnson, C.	Margaret Rowell	Sept. 8, 1842	9
Johnson, Elias	Sarah Meakes	June 27, 1844	13-A
Johnson, Finny	Sarah Wiggins	May 3, 1840	6
Johnson, Henry	Elizabeth Heath	March 20, 1851	35
Johnson, Henry	Fatima Williams	Dec. --, 1848	23
Johnson, James W.	Seneth Love	March 20, 1851	33
Johnson, John D.	Mary Aarons	Dec. 13, 1855	52
Johnson, Kinard	May Bishop (Burlap)	Dec. 24, 1846	13
Johnson, Mearddy	Mary Kent	Jan. 23, 1842	6
Johnston, Daniel	Elizabeth Ogleby	June 14, 1849	27
Johnston, Emanuel B.	Rebecca Ann McLendon	June 7, 1850	28
Jones, James	May Scarborough	June 26, 1845	15
Kea, Bennett	Caroline Barwick	June 6, 1857	58
Keal, William B.	Mary Ann Rowell	Sept. 19, 1857	63
Kemp, Henry	Fadey Sumner	Jan. 18, 1844	11
Kemp, John	Elizabeth Sumner	March 14, 1847	18
Kemp(e), Joshua	Jane Warren	April 17, 1851	32
Kemp(e), Kinchen	Susannah Sconyers	Oct. 23, 1848	28
Kendrick, M. N.	Moselle Lewis	July 17, 1855	52
Keet, Henry	Exa Bowin	April 7, 1845	15
Kennedy, J. B.	Abigal Wiggens	Sept. 17, 1848	21
Kerby, Hiram	Lohoiry Nunn	Sept. 30, 1855	--
Kercy, John B.	Sariann S. Burris	Nov. 22, 1848	23
Kersey, John D.	Mary Ann Binns	May 11, 1852	36
Kersey, Solomon	Kenrietta Woods	May 1, 1852	39
Key, Westly (Wesley?)	Ann Kitchens	Dec. 22, 1844	14-A
Key, Wiley	MaryAnn Purling Mason	Sept. 16, 1841	3
Kirkland, Abraham L.	Rachel R. Coleman	July 24, 1856	54
Kirkland, E. L.	Eliza T. Coleman	Jan. 20, 1854	46
Kirkwood, Cylis	Lennah Bird	Aug. 27, 1843	12
Kitchens, James	Katherine Thompson	Jan. 20, 1853	46
Kite, Green	Anna Price	Nov. 16, 1851	45

GROOM	BRIDE	DATE MARRIED	PAGE
Kite, Shadrick	Milly Norris	April 18, 1841	4
Kite, William	Rebecca Thomas	Jan. 13, 1850	26
Lane, John C. C.	Lewsindah Johnson	Oct. 17, 1849	27
Lane, W. W.	E---- Pree	Feb. 8, 1845	14
Langford, George	Elizabeth P. Darby	Jan. 8, 1850	26
Law, Benjamin L.	Mary Ann Johnson	Dec. 20, 1841	7
Law, Thomas	Julia Barnes	Sept. 7, 1843	11
Lewis, Joshua K.	Elizabeth Sconyers	Aug. 25, 1857	62
Lewis, Zachariah	George Ann Bennett	Oct. 28, 1849	27
Linnear, Guy	Wiliby Bard	Feb. 18, 1846	15-B
Love, James	Mary Logue	Feb. 17, 1857	56
Manor, Emory	Mary Phillips	March 6, 1856	58
MARKS & BRANDS (See Sneed & Scott)		63-64	
Martin, James	Elizabeth Phillips	April 14, 1857	58
Mason, Madison H.	Mary Ann F. Ellington	April 18, 1848	20
Mason, Robert	Harriet Mims	Oct. 15, 1851	33
McArthy, Peter J.	Assenath Glass (?)	Oct. 15, 1846	13
McDonald, A. J.	Eley Farlmer or Forkner	Jan. 10, 1843	9
McGrath, James	Katharine Tools	Aug. 11, 1857	60
McLeemon, John	Elizabeth Lamb	March 22, 1853	40
McLemon, Ira T.	Phrabey (Boredict) or Barwick	Feb. 22, 1842	5
McLendon, John	Elizabeth Lamb	March 22, 1852	37
McLeod, D.	Amanda E. Smith	Oct. 2, 1843	10
McLeod, Neill	Mary Griffis	April 25, 1841	3
Meekan, Allen T.	Abigal Crawford	Dec. 21, 1845	14
Meekes, Jonah	Appy Townsen	May 6, 1847	18
Milber, William B.	Elizar Hunter	Oxt. 28, 1847	19
Miller, William	Lydia Cowart	April 24, 1849	26
Mims, John	Catharine Flanders	Sept. 24, 1848	22
Mixon, Mikel	Mary Fennel	April 4, 1849	45
Moore, Augustus M.	Jerushia Lee	Dec. 15, 1854	49
Moore, Dempsey	Mary Ann Thompson	March 20, 1851	32
Moore, Drewry S.	Mary Youmans	Feb. 1, 1844	11
Moore, John	Sarah J. Jenkins	Oct. 19, 1851	33
Moore, Mannen	Mary Rowland	April 20, 1847	18
Moore, Martin B.	Sarah Minnis	Aug. 15, 1851	3
Moore, Simeon	Dicy Hall	Feb. 1, 1855	50
Moore, Thomas	Cintha Ornea Trapnal	June 18, 1848	21
Moore, William	Lydia Riner	Nov. 17, 1853	48
Moore, William	Mary Matilda Waters	April 27, 1851	32
Mosely, Elbert	Elnar Mosely	Jan. 16, 1846	16
Mosely, E. W.	Polly A. Monroe	May 14, 1854	46
Moxley, Benjamin A.	Sarah Moxley	Sept. 12, 1850	30
Nasworthy, George Washington	Juliann Abigal Swain	Jan. 13, 1850	25
Neal, John W.	Elizabeth Marsh	March 9, 1851	34
Neil, John	Martha Ann Douglass	Dec. 21, 1848	23
Newton, Phillip	Ann Roberts	Nov. 27, 1843	11
Noble, John	Elizabeth Edenfield	April 8, 1841	1
Noris, Isaac	Elizabeth Powell	July 29, 1847	19
Norris, Jordan	Judy Ann Huffman	Sept. 7, 1853	44
Norsworthy, Willy	Permealey Swain	Feb. 28, 1847	18
Nunes, Philip H.	Elizabeth Watts	Feb. 11, 1855	62
Nunn, Joshua	Elizabeth Snider	Jan. 10, 1856	63
Odom (written Otom), John	Deoda (Noland) or Rowland	May 2, 1844	13-A
Oglesby, Seaborn	Sarah Drew	June 14, 1849	26
Oustreeter, Henry	Mary Cowart	July 4, 1843	10
Oustreeter, Mathew	Martha Ann Sutton	Nov. 2, 1843	10
Outlaw, Charles C.	Eliza Ann Tennell	July 21, 1842	8
Outlaw, Morgan	Roxann M. C. Snell	July 22, 1847	19
Outlaw, William L.	Martha Davis	Dec. 19, 1854	51

GROOM	BRIDE	DATE MARRIED	PAGE
Overstreet, James	Sarah Hall	June 5, 1842	7
Page, Thomas T.	Charity Whitfield	Feb. 15, 1849	24
Paul, Ancel S.	Margaret Swain	Oct. 29, 1848	22
Perkins, Staring B.	Mary B. Wiggins	Jan. 26, 1854	--
Phillips, Daniel	Lucinda Yeomans	Feb. 1, 1852	37
Phillips, Daniel	Lucinda Yeomans	Feb. 1, 1853	39
Phillips, Ephraim D.	Arminda Phillips	Feb. 17, 1857	57
Phillips, Robert	Mary Sillivent	Dec. 23, 1847	20
Phillips, Ryal B.	Nancy Phillips	Feb. 4, 1844	11
Powell, Aden	Ann Whitfield	Dec. 19, 1839	35
Powell, Bretten	Alfa Martin	Dec. 11, 1842	9
Powell, Calvin	Sarena D. Wise	July 2, 1845	15-A
Powell, Lamar	Moatia Ross	Dec. 22, 1844	14-A
Powell, Stephen	Caroline Price	March 31, 1857	60
Price, Alfred	Margaret Greenaway	July 8, 1856	61
Price, Berry	Elizabeth Fennel	Oct. 15, 1848	24
Price, Clement	Mary Ann Wheeler	Feb. 6, 1853	41
Price, Henry P.	Martha Cannaday	Aug. 26, 1852	38
Price, Henry P.	Martha Cannady	Aug. 26, 1853	43
Price, J. H.	Marianna Flanders	Feb. 13, 1853	41
Price, Wiley Small	Mary Begood	Aug. 15, 1854	49
Pritchard, C. B.	---------	Feb. 2, 1853	42
Pritchet, Ashley	Elzear Coleman	April 2, 1850	28
Proctor, Augustus D.	Lucinda Lewis	Sept. 25, 1856	55
Proctor, (Johnston), Robert	Martha Faircloth	April 21, 1844	13-A
Proctor, Thomas	Elizabeth Wood	Feb. 19, 1846	13,17
Prur, George	Martha Price	May 4, 1846	17
Rhiner, John B.	Sarah Hutcherson	March 31, 1853	45
Rich, Joab	Kisiah Parrot	Nov. 7 or 1,1841	4
Rich, Joseph A.	Latha A. Davis	Dec. 15, 1850	30
Rich, Stephen	Sarah Coleman	March 14, 1852	37
Rich, Steven	Sarah F. Coleman	March 14, 1852	40
Rich, William J.	Susan Truett	March 20, 1856	53
Richardson, Samuel	Lavinah Faircloth	April 4, 1847	18
Ricks, John	Martha Durden	May 3, 1855	51
Ricks, Warren W.	Lucy Ann Barwick	Dec. 25, 1855	57
Riner, Amos	Rebecca Beasley	April 2, 1857	57
Riner, Wilson	Sarah Rountree	Jan. 9, 1845	14-A
Ross, James	Jane Wiggens	Dec. 24, 1839	35
Roundtree, Allen	Elizabeth Burnett	April 25, 1850	34
Roundtree, John	Elizabeth Cowart	Oct. 7, 1847	19
Roundtree, William	Manny Johnson	Nov. 30, 1848	22
Rountree, George	Milhan A.R.W.M. Lewis(?)	Oct. 14, 1852	38
Rountree, M. M.	Harriett Burnett	July 12, 1853	48
Rowell, John	Exeline Williams	Apr. 19, 1849	24
Rowland, James S.	Dacus Susan Johnson	Nov. 23, 1856	56
Santford, J. Y. or G.	Nancy Paul	May 19, 1841	4
Saultur, William	Mary Wilkes	Jan. 16, 1848	20
Scott, Henry	Martha Hall	July 22, 1845	15-A
Sconyeares, Isaac	Zilpha Braddy	Sept. 1, 1847	19
Sconyers, John	Cicty Kempe	Nov. 13, 1851	33
Scarborough, Silas	Katharin Bird	May 9, 1847	18
Scarborough, William	Elizabeth Briant	Dec. 1, 1853	47
Scott, Jesse	Martha Lamb	Sept. 3, 1843	11
Scott, Jesse See MARKS & BRANDS			64
Seasley, Burrell (Beasley ?)	Mary Hall	Aug. 28, 1856	55
Sharp, Cammel	Jane Bullard	Sept. 3, 1856	61
Sharpe, Lewis T.	Matilda L. Philip	Dec. 15, 1847	19
Sherad, Benjamin	Mary Powell	Oct. 16, 1842	9
Sherrard, Benjamin Jr.	Lean Lawrence	Jan. 1, 1857	56
Sherrard, Joseph L.	Eliza J. Crump	Feb. 19, 1856	53
Sherrod, William G.	Edith Spence	Jan. 29, 1854	48
Slaughter, Riley	Martha Matilda Parson	April 28, 1850	28

199

GROOM	BRIDE	DATE MARRIED	PAGE
Smith, Benjamin D.	Doriann L. Rountree	Oct. 13, 1853	46
Smith, Chales (Charles?) T.	Nancy Burnett	Oct. 3, 1854	48
Smith, George	Margaret Mosely	Feb. 12, 1857	56
Smith, John	Mary Tison	Feb. 6, 1845	13
Smith, John	Milly Andrews	Feb. 21, 1849	23
Smith, John G.	Mary Tison	Feb. 6, 1846	17
Smith, Joseph C.	Elizabeth Mason	Jan. 15, 1857	57
Smith, Lawson	Lucia Douglass	Dec. 31, 1854	49
Smith, Whit R.	Rachel Maryann Flanders	March 20, 1842	6
Smith, Zachariah	Sophia P. Burnett	Nov. 14, 1854	50
Sneed Family See MARKS & BRANDS			63-64
Spence, Green B.	Amanda McGar	Oct. 26, 1854	50
Spence, John A.	Sarah Roberts	Dec. 18, 1855	53
Spence, Matthew	Mary Drew	Nov. 24, 1850	30
Spivey, Jasper	Mary H. Kea	Dec. 9, 1849	26
Stephens, William	Elizabeth Prissilla Green	Nov. 25, 1847	19
Stephens, William	Susan L. Brinson	--- 2, 1852 (?)	--
Stevens, William	Susan L. Brinson	Dec. 2, 1852	39
Stone, Henry Holcombe	Melvina Wiggins	July 14, 1854	47
Stone, Henry H.	Nancy Aycock	Sept. 3, 1856	54
Strange, Mitchell	Mary McLeod	Feb. 10, 1848	21
Stroud, James	Sabra Drew	March 19, 1846	13
Stroud, John	Susan Drew	Dec. 23, 1850	31
Stroud, Thomas	Martha Rich	Nov. 18, 1849	26
Stuart, John or Jake W.	Frances Bolling	Feb. 28, 1845	16
Stuart, Nathan	Harriett Hester	July 13, 1851	32
Sulivant, Astabb	Elizabeth Wilkes	Dec. 30, 1847	20
Sumner, Alexander C.	Sarah Jan Kitchens	Jan. 14, 1840	3
Sumner, Bird L.	Lucinda Rountree	Oct. 26, 1843	10
Sumner, Daniel T.	Delila Key	Aug. 27, 1843	9
Sumner, David	Ruth Sumner	Oct. 25, 1849	25
Sumner, Jethro	Elizabeth McGarr	April 6, 1854	49
Sumner, John C. Jr.	Nancy Douglass	March 25, 1841	1
Sumner, Robert	Jane Bedgood	Sept. 13, 1849	25
Sumner, William	Nancy Rountree	Feb. 6, 1845	14-A
Sutton, James E.	Merendy Hully Ann Martin	Feb. --, 1850	29
Sutton, Jordan	Martha Warren	Dec. 7, 1840	6
Swain, Eldred	Laduska Douglass	Sept. 13, 1857	63
Swain, William	Huldy Price	April 21, 1854	46
Tapley, James M.	Martha Norris	Feb. 15, 1855	51
Tapley, John C.	Mary Ann Durdan	June 19, 1851	32
Tapley, T.	L. J. Rountree	March 2, 1853	42
Tapley, William L.	Louisa M. Durdan	Apr. 10, 1851	32
Thigpen, William G.	Delila Clemans	Aug. 17, 1856	54
Thomas, John	Mary Heath	Nov. 30, 1853	47
Thomas, Manen	Sariann Neel	Oct. 24, 1848	20
Thompson, Allen	Katharine Kitchens	Dec. 27, 1849	26
Thompson, John N.	Arrena R. Kea (Key)	Feb. 3, 1848	20
Thompson, Reuben J.	Martha Daniel	Feb. 2, 1842	5
Tison, Daniel	Maryann Joan Neal	Jan. 6, 1846	15-A
Tison, Daniel P.	Martha Shepard	Oct. 13, 1853	51
Tison (Tyson), John	Martha Tyson	--- --, 1845	16
Tison, Noah	Barbera Anderson	April 24, 1848	25
Topseck, Jesse	Nancy Ann Marsh	June 5, 1851	34
Townsend, Isaac N.	Tabitha Page	Sept. 25, 1856	62
Townsend, Silas	Eliza Kin(g)	Sept. 3, 1846	16
Trapnal, Algearne	Nancy Kenady	Jan. 4, 1849	22
Truett, Edward J.	Elizabeth J. Kirkland	Aug. 5, 1857	63
Turner, John L.	Mary Anderson	Sept. 3, 1844	13-A
Turner, John L.	Arminda J. Sutton	June 14, 1857	59
Walker, James W.	Kisiah Outlaw	June 10, 1849	29
Wallace, James S.	Martha Boatright	April 23, 1855	51
Walters, Joseph	Margaret Nabb	March 7, 1853	44

GROOM	BRIDE	DATE MARRIED	PAGE
Warnock, Jesse K.	Jane Martin	April 8, 1849	24
Warren, James	Mary Van Coarsey	Feb. 4, 1844	14-A
Warren, Moses	Elizabeth Cobb	Oct. 12, 1853	48
Waters, Gabriel	Irene Yeomans	Dec. 13 or 17,1852	39
Waters, Joseph	Margaret Nabb	March 7, 1852	32
Watts, Joseph	Ami (Ann) Massey	March 1, 1846	16
Webb, Alford G.	Rebecca Rowel	Sept. 28, 1854	49
Webb, Elias G.	Mary Rowell	Jan. 5, 1843	9
Webb, James A.	Elizabeth M. Rowel	April 2, 1854	48
Webb, Kinchen J.	Selah Tison	Jan. 3, 1850	27
Webb, Levi	Elizabeth Powell	Dec. 21, 1841	5
Webb, William A.	Mariann Beasley	Feb. 13, 1851	33
Wheeler, Charles	Sarah Meadows	Dec. 31, 1851	35
Whitfield, Samuel	Sarah Anders	June 29, 1848	22
Wheeler, Shadrack	Mary T. Gunn	Oct. 24, 1852	37
Wheeler, Shadrack	Mary Givens (?)	--- --, 1852	39
Whitfield, Robert	Jane Townsen	July 29, 1849	35
Wiggens, Amos W.	Mary Outlaw	April 10, 1856	61
Wiggins, Pleasant	Martha Ann Wiggins	Nov. 21, 1841	6
Wilkes, James	Elizabeth Causey	April 11, 1850	29
Wilkes, John	Elizabeth Johns	June 26, 1851	32
Williams, Rubin M.	Sintha Edenfield	June 28, 1842	8
Williamson, Mathew	Mary Fountain	June 14, 1841	2
Williamson, Samuel	Elezear Williamson	Nov. 16, 1851	34
Williamson, Schley	Permelia Boyt	July 13, 1856	54
Willis, Reuben	Nancy Moris	April 6, 1848	21
Wilson, James	Susan Meek	Nov. 24, 1839	35
Wilson, John B.	Lydia Tison	May 31, 1857	59
Woods, John L.	Jamima Flanders	Jan. 13, 1850	30
Yeomans, Ephraim	Tempa Ann Sutton	April 4, 1850	29
Teomans, James	Sarah Bazemore	Sept. 20, 1849	24
Yeomans, John	Martha Warren	Jan. 31, 1856	53
Yeomans, Jordan S.	Selina V. Trapnall	May 5, 1853	51
Yeomans, Solomon	Elizear Ann Barwick	April 15, 1849	23

BOOK B 1856-1879

Alexander, Alfred T.	Cary Chance	Dec. 7, 1876	329
Almond, E. G.	Laura Woods	Oct. 23, 1867	176
Allmand, Elzea	Jane Moxley	Feb. 24, 1869	220
Anderson, Calvin	Mary Ann Johns	June 24, 1860	66
Anderson, John L.	Julia Ann Meadows	Feb. 24, 1857	4
Anderson, Swain M.	Ellender Sutton	Sept. 19, 1865	111
Anderson, Uriah	Charlotte Davis	March 9, 1859	47
Andrews, Columbus	Emma Willice	May 8, 1870	259
Andrews, Garnett W.	Eliza Womack	April 6, 1869	243
Andrews, George	Fannie Boles	June 23, 1878	345
Andrew(s), William	Jane Deal	April 13, 1869	212
Atkinson, William	M. A. Williamson	Jan. 7, 1876	294
Baker, Basel (Col.)	Amy Williamson	April 26, 1869	238
Barber, John	Martha Edenfield	May 19, 1878	311
Barwick, Berry	Mary Rountree	Jan. 3, 1875	279
Barwick, George J.	Jane Rountree	Nov. 16, 1865	118
Barwick, James	Delila Kea	Jan. 14, 1858	19
Barwick, Lucian	Elizabeth Tapley	July 12, 1879	363
Beal, E. J.	Nancy Lane	July 24, 1866	184
Beasley, Elijah (Elias)	Elizabeth Price	Oct. 22, 1868	203
Beasley, John	Mary Ann Hutcherson	Nov. 24, 1861	81
Beasley, William A.	Kisier Hutcherson	Nov. 22, 1861	81
Beaufort, Richard	Sallie Clark	Jan. 6, 1867	145
Belcher, Benjamin B.	Amanda Cross	Jan. 9, 1866	122
Bell, J. P.	M. A. B. Johnson	July 28, 1864	103
Bell, Matthew	Vianna Kemp	Oct. 20, 1869	226

201

GROOM	BRIDE	DATE MARRIED	PAGE
Belle, William	Sallie Jones	March 24, 1878	230
Bennett, Aaron	Elizabeth Johnson	Feb. 21, 1858	26
Bennett, Benjamin L.	Anna Roberts	March 12, 1865	139
Belt, C. T.	Ela I. Innman	Jan. 5, 1871	269
Bennett, Charles	Matilda Green	Aug. 6, 1879	370
Bell, Green	Sallie Sumer	Jan. 27, 1870	207
Bennett, Isaac	Clarisa Wiggins	Aug. 8, 1866	157
Bennett, Lovel J.	Mary Ann Johnson	Oct. 28, 1866	146
Bibb, Joseph M.	Margaret R. Thompson	Sept. 3, 1865	96
(Someone has added a note that the name Bibb should be Webb)			
Bird, John T.	Louvenia Parrish	April 9, 1868	202
Bird, Louis	Ann Oliff	Oct. 4, 1866	186
Bird, Melton	Marietta Johnson	May 31, 1866	183
Bird, Robert	Eliza McLeod	April 17, 1870	221
Bishop, Allen M.	Susan Warnock	Aug. 18, 1879	351
Bishop, Berryan W.	Anna Dunford	Dec. 23, 1874	277
Bishop, Henry	Ophela Dye	Feb. 27, 1870	251
Bishop, J. F.	Elizzie Cowart	Dec. 23, 1877	321
Bishop, James	Ozena Barwick	Feb. 5, 1871	267
Bishop, Mathew	Martha E. Pritchard	Jan. 24, 1858	17
Bishop, William E.	Eliza Ward	Oct. 2, 1869	205
Black (Block), John	Milly Ann Fennell	Aug. 21, 1857	1
Blount, O. P.	Nancy M. Phillips	July 24, 1870	280
Boatright, John	Adaline Melvina Pierce	April 17, 1859	36
Boatright, John	Nancy Deal	Sept. 10, 1877	305
Boyd, Henry	Adaline Edenfield	July 30, 1868	213
Boyd, Stephen	Emily Virginia Reece	Nov. 7, 1858	33
Boyt, James	Elizabeth Junes	May 4, 1868	226
Boyt, James E.	Lucretia Edenfield	Feb. 6, 1866	129
Boyt (Bout), James E.	Lucretia Edenfield	Feb. 6, 1866	144
Bouyt, W. H.	Betty Edenfield	June 7, 1868	198
Brady, Oliver B.	Martha Turner	June 24, 1866	149
Branch, Baelum	Darcus Williams	May 27, 1878	346
Brantley, James M.	Nancy Smith	Sept. 23, 1858	29
Briant, Needham W.	Roxey Ann Wiggins	March 1, 1860	51
Brinson, David M.	Jinnie M. Redding	Dec. 31, 1868	223
Brinson, John S.	Catharine Gregory	Dec. 16, 1866	157
Brinson, Matthew	Elizabeth Wilks	May 10, 1860	61
Brinson, Mathew S.	Sarah A. Rountree	Oct. (Nov.) 26, 1857	16
Brown, Andrew	Lohamia Whitehead	May 30, 1867	169
Brown, G. E.	Tilda Coleman	May 4, 1868	187
Brown, Green (Col.)	Drucilla Bird (Col.)	June 10, 1877	303
Brown, Henry L.	Saphronia Johnson	Dec. 9, 1869	219
Brown, J. E.	Prunelea Everett	Dec. 19, 1867	179
Brown, James B.	Nancy Warren	Aug. 20, 1856	18
Brown, John	Amanda Lennear	Nov. 12, 1867	185
Brown, John T.	Martha A. Overstreet	Aug. 11, 1857	7
Brown, Matthew L.	Mary Jane Cowart	Dec. 18, 1860	67
Brown, L. E.	Viannah Yeomans	May 26, 1870	223
Brown, Robert (Col.)	Susan Brown (Col.)	March 21, 1878	344
Brown, William E.	Luvena E. Coleman	Jan. 7, 1869	238
Brown, William J.	Nancy Cowart	Aug. 11, 1870	236
Bryant, Gus	Levena Grubbs	Oct. 23, 1865	183
Bryant, Lewis	Omelia Herd	Nov. 15, 1872	275
Bullard, Ashley	Zelpha Grant	June 25, 1867	167
Burris, Alfred	Susannah Grant	July 4, 1858	27
Burton, Robert	Laura Sutton	Jan. 27, 1867	147
Burton, Robert	Mary J. Johnson	July 16, 1870	246
Camel, Eli	Sarah Dunigen	March 27, 1868	189
Camp, Josephus	Phrony Brown	Jan. 9, 1870	209
Corbin, Nelson	Nancy Williamson	Aug. 22, 1868	211
Carpenter, Leroy	Eliza A. J. Snipes	July 23, 1877	298
Carter, Ben	Emeline Collins	Dec. 13, 1874	288
Casey, Thomas	Martha Strange	June 28, 1874	301
Cannady, John	Alice Sumner	May 10, 1878	326
Cannady, John W.	Elender Jones	Oct. 20, 1870	255

GROOM	BRIDE	DATE MARRIED	PAGE
Cannadey, William	Elizabeth J. Sumner	April 1, 1865	113
Cannady, William	C. Branch	Jan. 6, 1878	320
Chance, Calvin	Katy Doth	Aug. 30, 1874	288
Chance, Colonel	Rachel Johnson	April 25, 1869	217
Chance, William C.	Lucinda Brown	March 14, 1867	159 & 161
Christian, Theophilus	Harriet Outlaw	Sept. 28, 1857	16
Clark, James A.	Saleta A. Miller	Dec. 16, 1858	32
Clayton, L. R.	Lou McBride	Nov. 3, 1878	340
Clark, Lucius	Oliff Wiggins	July 5, 1878	313
Coleman, A. H.	Mary Warnock	Jan. 21, 1878	314
Coleman, Andrew	Emeline Roberts	Sept. 4, 1868	217
Coleman, B. F.	Lizzie Wiggins	Jan. 2, 1878	322
Coleman, C.	Mary Bishop	Jan. 31, 1866	150
Coleman, Cord	Aurend (?) Cross	March 18, 1879	368
Coleman, Charles	Caroline Trull	Feb. 24, 1866	128
Coleman, Charles M. (Of Johnson Co.)	Colsey D. McBride	Sept. 22, 1865	130
Coleman, F. J.	S. M. Johnson	Dec. 6, 1877	336
Coleman, George (Col.)	Ann McLeod (Col.)	April 23, 1870	242
Coleman, Isaac	L. Murphree	Nov. 12, 1866	184
Coleman, Isaac	Patience McKinnie	May 15, 1869	257
Coleman, James	Winny Youngblood	Feb. 13, 1858	19
Coleman, James	Melvina Collens	Sept. 12, 1861	79
Coleman, James E.	Sarah M. Brinson	Oct. 22, 1865	126
Coleman, James E.	Lavina Lanier	May 26, 1870	224
Coleman, Jeremiah	Mary Ann Beasley	April 9, 1863	93 & 105
Coleman, Jeremiah H.	Gracy Jane Johns	Nov. 20, 1859	42&45
Coleman, L. B.	Martha D. Bronson	Dec. 2, 1866	151
Coleman, Malcum C.	Armenda J. Turner	May 8, 1867	165
Coleman, Milton	----------	Jan. 31, 1865	130
Coleman, Welcomb L.	George Ann Scott	June 17, 1858	20
Coleman, William A.	America Griffis	May 4, 1873	276
Collins, Perry	Lavina Kirkland	June 28, 1855	24
Cooksey, Thomas B.	Eliza Anderson	June 6, 1860	64
Cooner, Jasper	Mary McLane	Jan. 18, 1863	92
Cooner, Jasper	Mary C. McLane	Jan. 18, 1863	102
Coppock, Sampson	Elis Sherod	Dec. 19, 1867	169
Coppock, Toby (Col.)	Lizzie Bird	Nov. 14, 1877	335
Corbin, Nelson	Nancy Williamson	Aug. 22, 1868	211
Corbin, Wellington	Jane Coleman	Sept. 22, 1864	109
Coursey, Howell	Elizabeth Parker	Jan. 7, 1871	261
Coursey, William P.	Sallie E. Flanders	May 15, 1877	297
Cowart, Curtis	Emily A. Proctor	Jan. 21, 1864	99
Cowart, George (Freedman)	Louisa Deamond (Freedwoman)	Dec. 27, 1866	156
Cowart, Hezekiah P.	Nancy J. Daniels	Apr. 16, 1870	222
Cowart, Isaiah	Anny Jones	Jan. 19, 1862	86
Cowart, James J.	Sarah Ann Kirkland	March 2, 1862	80
Cowart, David C.	Mary Ann Dunford	Nov. 15, 1860	67
Cowart, Joseph W.	Sallie J. Overstreet	April 5, 1867	164
Cowart, William D.	Lucinda Smith	Oct. 29, 1861	82
Cowart, Zack	Mary Overstreet	Nov. 30, 1865	177
Cross, Allen (Col.)	Savannah Pane (Col.)	Dec. 30, 1878	338
Cross, Isaac	Julia A. Spence	Jan. 30, 1870	253
Cross, James	Laura Green	March 1, 1868	216
Cross, Nathan	Betsey Moore	Dec. 16, 1869	210
Curl, Elijah	Mary Williams	Sept. 28, 1857	7
Curl, Kinchen	Mary H. Hays	Dec. 7, 1866	143
Curl, Matthew Jr.	Masouri Ann Youngblood	Jan. 6, 1861	73
Curl, Peter	Pheraba Hays	Jan. 12, 1871	265
Dallis, George	Rachel Farmer	May 3, 1867	196
Daniels, Freeman	Elizabeth Banks	Aug. 30, 1864	177
Daniel, Hambleton G.	Letishia Horn	March 1, 1863	108
Daniell, Hambleton G.	Letishia Horn	March 1, 1863	92
Darden, Berrien W.	Elizabeth J. Rountree	March 2, 1859	43

203

GROOM	BRIDE	DATE MARRIED	PAGE
Daughtry, James	Elizabeth Sutton	June 12, 1859	44
Davis, David	Sarah Strange	Aug. 29, 1859	49
Davis, George C.	Matilda Price	March 31, 1857	9
Davis, James A.	Alley Williams	Feb. 4, 1857	6
Davis, John J.	Sophia B. DeLoach	Dec. 4, 1878	354
Davis, Josiah	Sarah T. Cannedy	Dec. 20, 1867	182
Davis, Louis J.	Mary J. M. -----	Feb. 22, 1867	164
Davis, Matthias M.	Mary McLane	Aug. 7, 1864	98
Davis, William	Senio Smith	Nov. 3, 1859	45
Davis, William	Senia Smith	Nov. 3, 1859	41
Deal, James	Elizabeth Reid	Dec. 9, 1868	214
Deal, James	Mrs. Elizabeth Grimes	June 17, 1869	221
Deckle, Beryan	Molen Mercer	Jan. 9, 1867	173
Deakle, G. W.	Susan Lanier	Jan. 1, 1868	178
Dekle, Monda	Nancy Dekle	Jan. 13, 1871	266
Dekle, Peter (Col.)	Sarah Berrian	March 11, 1869	228
Derisco, J. E.	Susan E. Newman	April 7, 1878	313
Dickey, Joseph W.	Liney E. Davis	March 12, 1868	203
Dickerson, Stephen	Nancy Atkinson	Nov. 28, 1860	68&69
Dickerson, W. R.	Calcia N. Edenfield	June 17, 1877	305
Douglass, David	Nancy M. Kea	Jan. 5, 1858	17
Drake, N. J.	Sal Heart	Dec. 8, 1867	175
Drake, Tourner	Eliza Jones	Dec. 27, 1870	252
Drake, William L.	Rachel L. Oglesby	Sept. 20, 1864	105
Drew, J. D.	Sally Martin	Nov. 11, 1869	206
Drew, Thomas	Martha Ann Bennett	Oct. 13, 1859	54
Dunford, James A.	Anna E. Dye	Mch. 15, 1871	263
Durden, Albert	Polly Coleman	Oct. 17, 1874	283
Durden, Aljareon	Milly Moor	Jan. 18, 1866	122
Durden, August G.	Dicy Herington	Sept. 7, 1879	369
Durden, Dennis J.	Marethy Lanier	Jan. 17, 1875	284
Durden, Denis S.	Mary A. E. Hooks	Dec. 12, 1867	194
Durden, F. J.	A. E. Stevens	Jan. 6, 1878	325
Durden, George D.	India Sherrod	June 30, 1878	353
Durden, Jack (Freedman)	Rachael Phillips (Freedwoman)	Dec. 1, 1866	158
Durden, John G.	Martha Hall	Aug. 12, 1860	59
Durden, Lott	Sarah Flaunders	Oct. 4, 1866	196
Durden, Robert	Silva Chance	Apr. 3, 1873	273
Durden, Rowan	Susan Moore	May 2, 1869	213
Durden, William R.	Ellen Lanier	Mch. 20, 1873	275
Edenfield, Andrew J.	Jincy Kemp	Apr. 9, 1866	137
Edenfield, David J.	Eliza Jane Kennedy	June 16, 1857	8
Edenfield, Ephraim	Sarah Ann Kennedy	June 21, 1857	8
Edenfield, George W.	Sarah Woods	Apr. 5, 1866	125
Edenfield, Ephram	Jane Kimbrell	Jan. 6, 1867	172
Edenfield, James W.	Sarah E. Boyt	May 24, 1868	232
Edenfield, L. H.	Susan M. (E.) Morgan	Oct. 25, 1879	309
Edenfield, Manord	Lucinda Wiggins	Sept. 12, 1868	212
Edenfield, Thomas	Zoah Collins	Jan. 10, 1860	49
Edenfield, Thomas	Sarah Waters	Aug. 13, 1879	351
Faircloth, Alex	Jane Corbin	Dec. 26, 1869	233
Faircloth, Andrew	Tempy Corban	May 12, 1869	229
Faircloth, Charles	Mary J. Daniels	June 13, 1869	234
Fairclott, (sic) Chesly	Lucy Boatright	Jan. 13, 1867	146
Faircloth, Elly	Fannie Boatright	July 1, 1878	315
Faircloth, G. N.	G. McKinsy	Oct. 12, 1876	334
Faircloth, James	Rosa Ann Murry	Aug. 16, 1860	63
Faircloth, John R.	E. L. Coleman	Mch. 1, 1879	364
Farmer, E. F.	Catharine Deriso	Feb. 9, 1873	275
Fendley, Malachia F.	Susannah Warnuck	June 26, 1853	22
Fennel, Nathan	Catharine T. Dallison	Sept. 14, 1856	3
Fields, Charles	Margaret Durden	Oct. 21, 1867	190
Fields, J. W.	Rosa N. Smith	Dec. 5, 1879	334
Findley, Leander	Lucy Jones	July 6, 1878	361

GROOM	BRIDE	DATE MARRIED	PAGE
Finity, James P.	George Ann Lewis	Nov. 24, 1870	232
Flanders, Alexander C.	Delila Hays	Sept. 15, 1878	312
Flanders, John R.	Emma Black	Nov. 12, 1862	91
Flanders, Joseph P.	Celia E. Brantley	Apr. 22, 1877	297
Flanders, Paul F.	Louisa Hall	Aug. 12, 1860	62
Flanders, Richard B.	Julia Ann Coleman	May 3, 1858	20
Flanders, William J.	Nancy Webb	Oct. 5, 1870	249
Flanders, William T.	Mary Sumner	Mch. 14, 1877	293
G----, Lewis T.	Elinner Hall	May 4, 1878	355
Gay, Calvin C.	Elizabeth Anderson	Sept. 30, 1858	29
Gay, George (Col.)	T. Mincy	Oct. 9, 1879	367
Gay, Mathew	Susannah Johnson	Dec. 6, 1859	42
Gay, Mathew	Susannah Johnson	Dec. 15, 1859	52
Geiger, John C.	Minnie Beacham	Sept. 8, 1879	369
Gillis, Augus A.	Mary Barwick	Jan. 2, 1879	337
Gillis, Mathew	Nancy Wilks	Oct. 26, 1867	194
Gillis, N. C.	M. C. Ricks	Mch. 9, 1871	276
Gillis, Sandy	Jane Wilks	Oct. 26, 1867	195
Gillis, Thomas	Rhoda Thigpen	July 10, 1869	270
Glisson, Robert (Col.)	Hetty Coleman	Feb. 8, 1868	272
Grant, Thomas	Lila Love	Feb. 7, 1879	366
Grant, William G.	Catharine Beasly	July 1, 1860	56
Gray, Isham	Melviny Brow-n	Dec. 25, 1866	147
Green, Daniel A.	Mary J. Bethea	July 2, 1859	37
Green, E. L.	A. M. Brown	Jan. 21, 1864	100
Green, Felix (Col.)	Lina Miller	July 3, 1879	357
Green, Thomas	Avy Green	June 17, 1870	246
Green, William	Elizabeth Anderson	Oct. 30, 1869	206
Green, William	America Bird	Nov. 5, 1874	291
Griffin, Benjamin E.	Nancy Hooks	July 7, 1859	36
Griffin, T. W.	Elizabeth Dickerson	July 26, 1877	300
Griffis, William S.	Christian Durden	Sept. 20, 1860	59
Grimes, William	Elizabeth Deal	Feb. 13, 1861	72
Goss, John M.	Elizabeth Nuem	Feb. 4, 1866	124
Guay (sic), Charlton	Marth(a) Newton	Mch. 7, 1867	171
Hall, Daniel G.	Mary Jane Darden	Nov. 26, 1857	21
Hall, Evans	Winnie Cross	Nov. 3, 1869	205
Hall, Henry H.	Sarah Rich	Apr. 4, 1860	56-7
Hall, Henry T.	Maranda Rogers	May 15, 1870	260
Hall, Isaac	Eliza Durden	Dec. 9, 1867	160
Hall, J. W.	R. C. D. Rodgers	Nov. 12, 1878	342
Hall, John	Harriett Hays	July 20, 1879	362
Hall, Junaper	Martha C. Durden	Dec. 7, 1865	123
Hall, M. H.	Mary C. Kitchens	Sept. 18, 1879	370
Hall, William	Fanny Dudly	June 13, 1867	150
Hall, William	Catharine Grant	Feb. 9, 1873	275
Hall, Willis	Clarky Fennell	Sept. 10, 1857	1
Ham, Green B.	Eliza Johns	Feb. 1, 1871	270
Hammett, Walter	Fannie Blackmon	Feb. 16, 1877	332
Hanberry, Hesekiah	Elizabeth Curl	Mch. 26, 1866	154
Handberry, James	Lucy Curl	Aug. 29, 1870	230
Handbury, Soloman	Lucky Handbury	Dec. 14, 1869	210
Harel, Edward (or Horel)	Jane Thigpen	Nov. 24, 1866	156
Harris, Luke	Jane Williams	Dec. 20, 1877	327
Hart, Berry	Emma Mulling	Oct. 27, 1868	227
Hart, Henry	Henrietta Glison	Mch. 26, 1870	215
Hays, Garry Jr.	Nancy Smith	Jan. 12, 1871	250
Hays, James	Delilah Rich	Oct. 3, 1858	35
Hayes, John	Sarah Flanders	Oct. 8, 1865	119
Hays, Marshall	Phereba Brady	Oct. 14, 1865	144
Helton (Hetton), J.T.	L. Gay	Jan. 23, 1879	230
Hendrix, Marida	Mary Durden	Apr. 15, 1869	228
Hendrix, Robery	Nancy Parish	Sept. 11, 1870	225
Hendricks, Wiley	Sarah Williams	Feb. 28, 1864	107
Hendry, J. W.	Adaline Nunn	July 28, 1878	318

GROOM	BRIDE	DATE MARRIED	PAGE
Henry, J. T.	Laura Henry	Aug. 26, 1877	304
Herald, W. R.	Winniford Barwick	Jan. 1, 1878	349
Herington, Berian	Mollie Nevils	Dec. 15, 1878	337
Herrington, John	Sarah Ann Watts	Dec. 25, 1861	78
Herrington, John C.	Liza Yeomans	Aug. 25, 1878	360
Hines, Allen (Col.)	Ann Parish	July 29, 1866	240
Holland, Josiah	Jane L. Sutton	Jan. 22, 1871	262
Holloway, Adam	Hanna Eason	Nov. 7, 1878	367
Hollaway, Perry	Angie Bird (Col.)	June 17, 1877	303
Holloway, Perry	Mauda Franklin	Feb. 9, 1879	355
Holmes, John	Nellie Gray	Mch. 10, 1867	163
Holmes, M.	Mary Overstreet	Dec. 6, 1877	231
Holton, Daniel	Martha Brinson	May 30, 1860	65
Holton, F. J.	S. Darby	Jan. 28, 1879	343
Holton, G. J.	Q. H. Collins	June 9, 1878	340
Holton, Isaac	Christun Daely	Mch. 3, 1866	159
Holton, Isaac B.	Christianner Darly	Mch. 1, 1866	135
Holton, William S.	Sarah Jane Hart	Oct. 8, 1864	103
Holton, William S.	Mary Ann Moor	Jan. 21, 1866	---

(Note: someone has added a note beside the bride's name:
Widow, "Polly" Ann Thompson)

Hooks, Ephraim	Martha J. Smith	Sept. 16, 1860	60
Hooks, Hardy	Hulday Hutchinson	June 7, 1857	11
Hooks, J. W.	Mary Andy Anderson	Aug. 9, 1860	63
Hooks, Jack	Lou Anderson	Dec. 26, 1877	324
Hooks, Michael	Mary Burt (Bart)	Dec. 22, 1859	46
House, Benjamin L.	Sarah M. L. G. Redding	July 21, 1859	38
Howard, Jack	Nancy Austin	Sept. 24, 1870	237
Howell, Thomas	Lindy Canady	Dec. 4, 1873	278
Hutcheson, Henry E.	E. A. J. Odam	Dec. 13, 1860	70
Hutcherson, James	Sophia Johnson	Feb. 1, 1868	181
Hutchinson, John P.	Mary C. Hall	Feb. 23, 1879	363
James, Calvin	Sarah Oglesby	Jan. 30, 1868	201
Jenkins, Charlie J.	Nannie McLeod	July 14, 1874	290
Jenkins, Charles J.	Mary E. McLeod	Jan. 17, 1877	300
Jenkins, Charles J.	Rosa Scriven	Sept. 8, 1878	316
Jenkins, Henry (Col.)	Nancy Brown	Apr. 27, 1879	357
Johns, Andrew J.	Serene Barwick	Oct. 13, 1878	339
Johns, James	Letta Huckley	Aug. 20, 1878	329
Johnson, Thomas (Col.)	Jane Brown (Col.)	Mch. 24, 1878	345
Johns, William R.	Susan J. Guay	May 27, 1869	209
Johnson, Benjamin	Eliza Lewis	Feb. 16, 1860	66
Johnson, Beny	Sarah Griffin	Apr. 1, 1869	203
Johnson, Colonel	Rachel Chance	Apr. 25, 1869	217
Johnson, Daniel W.	Eliza Sherrod	Apr. 30, 1865	106
Johnson, Francis	Roxy Ann Miller	Dec. 26, 1866	153
Johnson, Isham	Elizabeth Lane	Dec. 21, 1857	14
Johnson, Jack	Emeline Laney	Sept. 1, 1867	182
Johnson, James	Lucy Buch	Jan. 10, 1874	279
Johnson, Lebon	Elarrinda Bernett	Dec. 26, 1868	264
Johnson, Lewis	Savannah J. Lewis	Sept. 11, 1870	237
Johnson, Samuel	Mary Hooks	Dec. 26, 1869	250
Johnson, Thomas (Col.)	Jane Brown (Col.)	Mch. 24, 1878	345
Johnson, William R.	Susan J. Gay	May 27, 1869	208
Jones, Ben	Dicy Daniel	Feb. 3, 1878	326
Jones, John F.	Drucila Wallace	May 3, 1879	368
Jones, Seaborn A.	Lucy W. O. Johnson	May 11, 1864	110
Johnson, John	Susan Johnson	Oct. 1, 1865	120
Jones, Thomas	Lilly Ann Clark	Feb. 18, 1867	150
Jones, William	Susan Deakle	Sept. 13, 1860	90
Kea, James	Ann Akin	Aug. 26, 1869	233
Kea, Warren W.	Francis D. Flanders	Sept. 25, 1859	40
Keal, William B.	Mary Ann Rowell	Sept. 19, 1857	10
Kelly, Edward	Adeline Pierce	Dec. 2, 1866	152
Kemp, A. C.	Eddy Hall	Feb. 11, 1871	267

GROOM	BRIDE	DATE MARRIED	PAGE
Kennedy, J. D.	Mil. Morgan	July 26, 1867	176
Kemp, John	Sophronia Kemp	June 14, 1874	287
Kemp, John A.	Zilpha Rountree	Dec. 24, 1846	22
Kemp, John S.	Mary Turner	Jan. 9, 1867	149
Kemp, William A.	Phrona Coleman	Dec. 9, 1869	226
Kennedy, Gideon H.	Casanda Griffis	Dec. 30, 1838	41
Kennedy, Gideon H.	Elizabeth Cheatain	Oct. 22, 1865	115
Kennedy, Henry A.	Martha A. Edenfield	Jan. 23, 1859	35
Kennedy, John P.	Lizzie C. Snell	Oct. 25, 1865	115
Kent, Augustus	M. Rountree	Dec. 27, 1877	327
Kibbee, Thomas H.	Julia A. Rountree	Apr. 19, 1866	134
Kimbrell, William	Mary Bell	Apr. 27, 1861	74
Kimsey, J. L.	Martha Woods	Dec. 17, 1877	364
Kirkland, Alfred	Julia Deckle	Oct. 26, 1866	174
Kirkland, E. L.	Agie Spann	Aug. 19, 1877	306
Kirkland, H. C. C.	Hannah L. Churchill	Feb. 28, 1871	220
Kirkland, Henry T.	Mary Lamb	Jan. 3, 1861	71
Kirkland, Isaac	Georgian Prescott (Col.)	Dec. 2, 1877	320
Kerkland (Kirkland), Richard	Martha Deckle	Jan. 10, 1867	173
Kirkland, Thomas B.	Elizabeth Coleman	Oct. 8, 1857	12
Kitchens, Gaston A.	Nancy E. Thompson	Feb. 16, 1860	51
Kitchens, John W.	Martha A. A. Sconyers	Sept. 11, 1879	358
Kitchens, Joseph H.	Rutha Sumner	Apr. 13, 1860	55
Knight, H. L.	Lucretia Herrington	Jan. 1, 1865	131
Kuhn, N. W.	Martha N. Rhodes	July 25, 1867	166
Lamb, E. J.	A. Alldy	Jan. 13, 1878	328
Lane, Edward E.	Virginia Drake	Jan. 7, 1861	71
Lamb, Eli	Susannah Kelly	Sept. 19, 1864	102
Lamb, George	Seasy Anderson	July 17, 1866	152
Lamb, Henry	Nancy Powell	July 13, 1862	83
Lamb, Isaac D. G.	Matilda A. Quincy	Dec. 7, 1865	120
Lamb, John	Nelly Joiner	Dec. 8, 1863	129
Lamb, John A.	Martha P. Green	Apr. 4, 1861	87
Lane, B. L.	Kate Brinson	Dec. 22, 1877	365
Lane, Bob	Mandy Cross	Feb. 7, 1878	318
Lane, Joseph	Mariah Johnson	May 1, 1870	231
Lane, Willis (Col.)	Hattie Coleman (c)	Oct. 13, 1878	311
Lanier, Lewis F.	Mary Ann Low	Jan. 2, 1860	44
Lanier, Thomas	Delengist Coleman	Jan. 25, 1869	211
Lanier, William	Rebecca Cannady	Mch. 20, 1869	242
Laurence, J. D.	Nancy Sherrod	Apr. 16, 1867	163
Lenzy, Wesley	Elizabeth Thompson	Jan. 28, 1866	126
Lewis, Amaseah	Julia Ann Kulcher	Dec. 28, 1865	127
Lewis, Amariah	Julia Ann Keelin	Dec. 28, 1865	142
Lewis, C. E.	E. Hanbury	Aug. 13, 1867	181
Lewis, Daniel	Louvenia A. Johnson	Mch. 15, 1868	202
Lee, General W.	Elizabeth Ann Brown	July 21, 1863	139
Lee, George W.	Adelia M. Johnson	June 8, 1865	174
Lewis, James	Sarah Lane	Nov. 19, 1865	121
Lewis, Joshua K.	Elizabeth S. Conyers	Aug. 25, 1857	10
Lewis, Malachi	Elizabeth Newton	Apr. 12, 1866	140
Lewis, Obadiah	Elizabeth Walea	Feb. 20, 1861	73
Lewis, Thomas M.	Nancy McLeod	Dec. 21, 1859	33
Lewis, Thomas M.	Emeline Moring	Apr. 14, 1865	111
Love, Calop	Needy Tapley	Sept. 7, 1859	40
Low, William Daniel	Mary Jane Kea	Aug. 5, 1866	136
Marshall, William H.	Missouri A. Crump	Oct. 27, 1867	207
Martin, Isaac W.	Julia Ann Collens	Feb. 8, 1866	125
Martin, John	Isebella Newton	Sept. 14, 1865	116
Martin, John Rufus	Mrs. Martha Priscilla Lamb	Oct. 1, 1863	95
Martin, Nelson W.	Lucy Cowart	June 22, 1864	111
Martin, Reubin	Jane Ann Cavenah	Dec. 23, 1858	34
McBride, J. R.	Adeline McGar	July 10, 1870	227
McCay, William	Georgia A. Gordy	Sept. 14, 1865	118

GROOM	BRIDE	DATE MARRIED	PAGE
McColough, J. E.	Mary Edenfield	June 8, 1878	342
McDonald, Reed	Vina Green (Col.)	Nov. 9, 1877	341
McGar, George W.	Sallie Kennedy	Dec. 8, 1868	203
McGrath, James	Katharine Tool	Aug. 11, 1857	11
McGruder, Green (Col.)	Mary Johnson	June 30, 1868	239
McGruder, J. A.	Susan A. M. Lewis	July 24, 1861	77
McKenzie, John	Sarah L. Moore	Oct. 19, 1864	98
McKinner, William	Violet Kea	May 15, 1870	260
McKinsey, William E.	McLary Francis Dasher	May 26, 1870	248
McLane, John	Mary C. Edenfield	June 7, 1860	58
McLean, John	Susan Curl	Jan. 3, 1858	14
McLean, William	Mary Fendly	Aug. 9, 1863	94
McLemore, Lawson A.	Bettie C. Moore	May 13, 1877	294
McLeod, Abraham (Col.)	Zeny Gay (Col.)	Sept. 13, 1877	304
McLeod, Allen	Hetty Glisson	Nov. 28, 1870	252
McLeod, Charles (Col.)	Katy McLeod	Mch. 10, 1871	265
McLeod, George W.	Mattie S. Pugsley	June 2, 1868	257
McLeod, Phillip	Hager Bird	Dec. 13, 1877	321
McLeod, Sam Jr.	Eliza Bird	Dec. 3, 1877	319
McLeod, William	Eliza Williams	No date	273
Meeks, William R.	Sallie Williams	Feb. 26, 1871	256
Mercer, Joe (Col.)	Edy Bird (Col.)	May 2, 1878	325
Mercer, Malakiah	Nancy Warren	Jan. 30, 1859	30
Mercer, Soloman	Anna Eliza Collens	Dec. 22, 1864	80
Miller, Joe (Col.)	Clara Moring (Col.)	Mch. 12, 1878	308
Miller, Joe (Col.)	Clarra Moring (Col.)	Mch. 14, 1878	350
Miller, Joel	Amanda Melvina Hutcherson	Aug. 1, 1861	87
Minsey, Dennis (Col.)	Lucy Howell	Jan. 26, 1871	269
Mires, Seaborn F.	Mary E. Lawson	Feb. 26, 1866	133
Mondy, Willis	Lucretia Hostello	Feb. 3, 1874	280
Monro, Donald	Catharine Johnson	Nov. 20, 1860	84
Montgomery, Joseph C.	Mrs. Margum Phillips	Feb. 21, 1877	293
Moon, John F.	Lou Tapley	Sept. 24, 1874	281
Moore, A. L.	Elizabeth Collins	July 24, 1879	359
Moore, F. D.	Martha Hall	Oct. 6, 1867	185
Moore, James	J. M. Lane	Oct. 20, 1877	352
Moore, James B.	Nannie Anderson	May 5, 1870	271
Moore, John	Sarah Deriso	Nov. 15, 1860	76
Moore, John A.	Sarah A. Howell	Dec. 23, 1866	148
Moore, Lewis H.	Martha Rhyner	Feb. 15, 1871	266
Moore, Seaborn S.	Rachael Hooks	Oct. 17, 1877	353
Moot, Andrew	Deby Spencer	July 16, 1865	117
Morgan, Jesse C.	Nancy Lourana Moore	Feb. 23, 1860	54
Moring, Andrew	Celia Cain	Jan. 30, 1870	253
Moring, Joel J.	Jane Barwick	June 24, 1860	58
Moring, P. B.	Mollie E. Camp	Nov. 5, 1874	286
Moring, Thomas	Frances Wig	Aug. 18, 1869	204
Moring, W. T.	M. A. E. Edenfield	Dec. 20, 1874	286
Morris, Albert	Mariah Phillips	June 5, 1874	282
Morris, Harper (Col.)	Mary Green (Col.)	Apr. 22, 1878	339
Mosley, Ashley I.	Missouri Gordon	Feb. 20, 1873	274
Mosley, Champion	Patsey Williamson	June 4, 1868	200
Mosely, Clement T.	Mary C. Collens	May 8, 1865	124
Moseley, W. S.	Mary Findly	Mch. 10, 1878	317
Mosley, William	Ema Eliza Brady	June 17, 1861	74
Mosley, William W.	Cassie Williamson	Nov. 25, 1868	218
Moxley, Henry M.	Lucindy Coleman	Jan. 24, 1878	324
Moxley, J. T.	Martha E. Hall	Jan. 9, 1869	229
Moxley, John H.	Elizabeth J. Kea	Jan. 26, 1862	78
Moxley (Maxey), Joseph	Eliza Weese	June 18, 1868	200
Moxley, Joseph	Catharine Lamb	Jan. 5, 1875	277
Murphey, Michael	Elizabeth Acock	Jan. 11, 1866	121
Murphy, Michell	Elizabeth Aycock	Jan. 11, 1866	132
Murphy (Murphree), William	Mahalin Kent	Jan. 6, 1867	145
Murry, Benjamin E.	Sarah A. Hollinsworth	Oct. 8, 1867	258
Murrey, Jasper	Ellen Cooner	Oct. 5, 1862	89
Murrey, Jasper	Ellen Cooner	Oct. 5, 1862	100

GROOM	BRIDE	DATE MARRIED	PAGE
Newton, Benjamin F.	Elizabeth Bennett	Feb. 6, 1867	153
Newton, J. C.	Winnie Gay	June 2, 1869	241
Newton, James B.	Susan L. Lane	Jan. 22, 1860	53
Neel, James L.	Louisa Jane Carr	Oct. 13, 1858	30
Nuton (Newton),	Lucinda Turner	Aug. 17, 1861	76
Phillip D.			
Nunas, Phillip H.	Elizabeth Watts	Feb. 11, 1855	15
O'Brien, William	Martha Lindler	Dec. 24, 1878	350
Odom, Bennett W.	Mary Watts	May 22, 1870	235
Odom, Scott	Harriet Jordan (Col.)	Dec. 19, 1869	247
Oglesby, Allen E.	Louiza Stephens	Mch. 18, 1869	216
Oglesby, Benjamin S.	Margaret Wiggins	Mc. 12, 1865	141
Oglesby, Daniel	Frances Bishop	May 30, 1870	258
Oglesby, Jack	Mary Pierce	Oct. 12, 1870	231
Oglesby, James H. W.	Rockey Johnson	Sept. 8, 1870	264
Oglesby, John W.	Martha A. Cowart	July 24, 1860	90
Oglesby, John W.	Elizabeth Roberts	Sept. 7, 1862	91
Oglesby, John W.	Cyntha Aron	Feb. 15, 1864	107
Oglesby, William	Margaret Gay	Oct. 1, 1865	119
Olds, Alex (Col.)	Amy Pierce (Col.)	Aug. 10, 1877	306
Oliff, Benjamin	Anna Lanier	Dec. 22, 1859	85
Oliff, Benjamin	Missori Kennedy	Jan. 27, 1871	268
Oliff, Matthew	Anna Cowart	Apr. 30, 1863	108
Oliver, Mark	Martha Edenfield	Feb. 24, 1859	31
Outlaw, William D.	Nancy E. Johnson	Nov. 13, 1857	15
Overstreet, Henry	Nancy E. Sumner	Dec. 15, 1870	254
Overstreet, John	Adison L. Kennedy	July 7, 1870	248
Overstreet, Matthew	Nancy Hargrove	Mch. 3, 1870	224
Parker, William H.	Sarah Roberts	Sept. 4, 1878	348
Parks, David (Col.)	Lydia Murphy (Col.)	June 24, 1877	298
Parrish, Hezakiah	Rachael Daughtry	Dec. 17, 1855	24
Parrish, P.	M. Cowart	Dec. 7, 1867	186
Parish, Solomon	Ellen Rountree	Jan. 20, 1878	317
Peebles, C. C.	V. Hooks	Oct. 17, 1871	333
Perkins, Alexander	Jennie Hudson	Sept. 15, 1878	310
Perry, Fabuis (Col.)	Sallie (Nancy) Coppock	Apr. 27, 1879	356
Perry, J. C.	Mary Reid	Dec. 8, 1870	256
Perry, Peter	Jane Kennedy	Apr. 5, 1866	136
Phillips, Anthony			
(Executor of Will of John Warnock)		June 17, 1863	93
Phillips, Francis M.	Miss H. J. Warnock	June 17, 1863	93
Phillips, Frances M.	Henrietta Jane Warnock	June 17, 1863	112
Phillips, Isaac	Minty Phillips	Dec. 3, 1877	341
Phillips, J. J.	Jane Turner	Nov. 23, 1876	328
Phillips, Jacob	Lane Phillips	Dec. 20, 1866	191
Phillips, James	Elizabeth W. Norris	Feb. 21, 1864	110
Phillips, John D.	Dicy A. Williamson	Jan. 15, 1865	113
Phillips, John G.	M. Willis	Dec. 15, 1867	197
Phillips, Joseph	Rosabell Ferguson	June 27, 1867	187
Phillips, Moses	Betty Phillips	Dec. 18, 1866	191
Phillips, Sherrod	Cornelia Youngblood	Aug. 12, 1877	299
Phillips, Wilder	Elizabeth Phillips	July 1, 1858	27
Phillips, William C.	Elizabeth Williamson	Mch. 11, 1858	26
Pierce (Purse), Charles	Hannah Boles	Dec. 3, 1868	204
Pierce, George	Annie Boatright	June 5, 1869	234
Pool, Turner	Margaret E. Brinson	Aug. 24, 1859	62
Powell, Ashley	Mary Ann Swain	May 26, 1859	37
Powell, Britian D.	Elizabeth Lane	Dec. 20, 1857	13
Powell, Stephen	Caroline Price	Mch. 31, 1857	9
Price, Alphord	Margaret Greenaway	July 8, 1856	2
Price, John F.	Lou Hall	July 15, 1877	299
Phillips, Ephraim B.	Eliza Fendly	Aug. 16, 1863	94
Pritchard, L. J.	Martha Fountain	Nov. 12, 1863	95
Pritchard, Marcus	Laney Sutton	Jan. 27, 1859	39
Proctor, Adeson E.	Rachel V. Bishop	Jan. 29, 1864	111
Proctor, George W.	Susan Martin	Jan. 11, 1862	104

GROOM	BRIDE	DATE MARRIED	PAGE
Proctor, Jones	Malidda Grimes	June 20, 1866	151
Proctor, William A.	Martha A. Brown	Jan. 30, 1867	154
Pugsley, Jacob P.	Mary E. Mobley	Dec. 19, 1867	168
Rains, Mitchael	Rachel Lee	June 9, 1867	166
Ratford (Radford), Anderson	Tempy Rhiner	Feb. 13, 1870	253-A
Ratchford, M. N.	L. Coleman	Mch. 25, 1868	179
Ray, Levy	Laura Harris (Harrel)	June 23, 1867	165
Reid, James R.	Mary W. Lanier	Nov. 2, 1868	204
Reinhart, George	Dicy Wallace	Apr. 24, 1870	244
Rheyner, Wash (Col.)	Margaret Meeks	Mch. 18, 1867	161
Rhiner, Joseph A.	Elizabeth V. Tyson	Nov. 18, 1869	235
Rich, Daniel E.	Mary M. Moore	Jan. 18, 1871	222
Rich, Joseph A.	Frances Delila Kea	Nov. 2, 1865	123
Rich, Martin V.	Mary Emalene Plunket	Mch. 14, 1864	99
Rich, William J.	June Peebles	Nov. 25, 1878	333
Richardson, E. J.	L. V. Rich	Sept. 8, 1878	231
Ricks, Jacobs (Freedman)	Margaret Barwick (Freedwoman)	Dec. 24, 1866	155
Ricks, Lyman D.	Elizabeth P. Cole	Nov. 23, 1858	34
Ricks, Richard W.	Eliza Ann Need	Sept. 27, 1859	50
Ricks, William G.	Amanda Cale (Cole)	Sept. 14, 1858	28
Ricks, William G.	Matilda Ricks	Oct. 28, 1866	160
Riner, Lawson	Katharine Odom	Dec. 31, 1857	13
Riner, William	Adalene Meaks (Meeks)	Aug. 28, 1860	69
Riner, William	Adaline Meeks	Aug. 28, 1860	60
Roberts, James M.	Sally P. Durden	Jan. 3, 1875	282
Roberts, John	Betsy McLeod	Oct. 14, 1874	290
Roberts, Thomas	Ellen Boller	Mch. 26, 1869	241
Roberts, Thor	Eliza Barber	Jan. 26, 1874	289
Roberts, W. L.	Maryan Adams	Oct. 18, 1874	289
Roden, Vanburen	Nancy Lambert	Mch. 11, 1860	53
Rogers, Luke W.	Sallie Wiggins	Dec. 9, 1870	255
Rountree, Benjamin (c)	Tener Durden	Mch. 18, 1870	272
Rountree, George C.	Delila Beasley	Oct. 18, 1874	284
Rountree, James	Lavinia McLane	Oct. 10, 1866	137
Rountree, Joshua W.	Mahala H. Durden	Apr. 20, 1871	262
Rountree, Joshua W.	Dora M. Sumner	Apr. 4, 1871	253-A
Rountree, K.	Sarah Dekle	Jan. 5, 1879	354
Rountree, Robert	Riela Brinson	Dec. 13, 1874	291
Rountree, W. P.	Laura A. Coleman	Jan. 13, 1870	244
Rountree, William	Caroline Dekle	Sept. 8, 1856	25
Rowel, Henry G.	Nancy Meaks	Sept. 12, 1860	72
Rowell, John F.	Addley Hall	June 14, 1874	292
Rowland, Williamson	Vina Douglass	Jan. 18, 1859	31
Sample(s), Calop L.	Rachael Brown	Dec. 29, 1860	43
Sample(s), Peter	Jane Prescott	Dec. 27, 1866	150
Scarboro, G. W.	Mrs. Mary Tutt	Mch. 21, 1877	302
Scarborough, Samuel E.	Susanah P. Janes	Aug. 13, 1858	28
Sconyers, J. E.	Celia Pritchard	Dec. 22, 1878	359
Scott, Daniel Z.	Rachel Coleman	Feb. 13, 1878	348
Scott, George L.	Sarah A. Stroud	June 13, 1869	271
Scott, Thomas	Nancy G. Flanders	Apr. 27, 1862	82
Screws, Zachariah	Elis Kersey	June 25, 1867	168
Semore (freeman)	Sooky (freewoman)	Aug. 31, 1866	172
Sharp, Cambell	Jane Bullard	Sept. 3, 1856	2
Sheart, George (of Montgomery Co.)	Mary Wilks	Jan. 31, 1864	--
Sherrod, Benjamin	Mary Broxton	July 28, 1870	230
Sherrod, G.	Adalen Roberts	Mch. 3, 1867	162
Sherrod, John W.	Elvira Roberts	Sept. 20, 1874	287
Skinner, J. T.	Sarah M. Skinner	Jan. 5, 1879	360
Skinner, Zachariah	Eliza Ann E. Hicks	June 22, 1859	38
Smith, Daniel	Nancy Odom	Oct. 7, 1869	208
Smith, David H.	Mary Ann Abiella Hooks	Sept. 30, 1860	64
Smith, E. P.	Christian Griffity	Jan. 18, 1863	112

210

GROOM	BRIDE	DATE MARRIED	PAGE
Smith, Henry	Abigail Clifton	Jan. 31, 1871	263
Smith, John T.	Sarah Meeks	Feb. 16, 1870	245
Smith, Tony (Col.)	Anna Deekle	July 7, 1867	170
Smith, White R.	Ann E. Mulling	Aug. 1, 1867	167
Stanford, H.	Patsey Johnson	Mch. 15, 1868	180
Stapleton, William	Lucy Farrill	Dec. 9, 1878	336
Stapleton, William J.	Ludcay (Ludicey) Lane	July 7, 1863	104
Stephens, B. F.	M. J. Murdock	Jan. 2, 1879	362
Stephens, J. F.	Rebecca McDaniel	Aug. 26, 1878	312
Stevens, William	Nancy M. Durden	June 18, 1856	18
Stewart, Berrian	Jane Hauberry	Apr. 21, 1878	347
Trapnell, Perry	M. L. Rountree	Mch. 20, 1879	352
Trewitt, Laurence	Sallie Flanders	Mch. 12, 1868	180
Truett, David	Susan Lafayett Collens	Jan. 3, 1864	101
Truett, Edward J.	Elizabeth J. Kirkland	Aug. 5, 1857	5
Turner, A. L.	D. J. Sutton	Feb. 19, 1873	283
Turner, Absolem	Jane Coleman	June 27, 1861	77
Turner, Gabrel	Marthy L. Edenfield	Nov. 7, 1872	285
Turner, William H.	Ann Lamb	July 25, 1859	39
Turner, William H.	Ann Lamb	July 25, 1859	46
Turner, William H.	Martha J. Lamb	Dec. 26, 1867	243
Tucker, William J.	Jency Rountree	Dec. 5, 1868	215
Tye, Samuel (Col.)	Emma Rivers (Col.)	May 31, 1879	361
Walea, Thomas	Rachel Sherrod	July 9, 1865	116
Walea, William W.	Eliza Oglesbey	Jan. 28, 1866	135
Wall, J. N.	Elizabeth Williams	Feb. 1, 1870	245
Warnock, J. F.	Malissa Herrington	May 31, 1877	295
Warnock, John (Adm. of Estate of Simeon Warnock)		June 17, 1863	93
Warnock(h), Simeon, Estate of		June 17, 1863	93
Warren, Davis	Sarah Oliver	Apr. 13, 1877	296
Warren, Eleayar	Jane Hendley	May 5, 1857	---
Warren, Francis M.	Winforee Green	Dec. 14, 1865	171
Warren, Henry G.	Mary R. Mosley	June 26, 1862	88
Warren, James	Margaret F. Dasher	Apr. 6, 1873	274
Warren, James J.	Susan E. Martin	Feb. 5, 1866	128
Warren, James J.	Susan E. Martin	Feb. 8, 1866	142
Warren, Jasper	Lucinda Brady	Jan. 15, 1867	151
Warren, Moses	Martha Nabb	Sept. 24, 1860	68
Warren, Moses	Martha Nabb	Oct. 7, 1860	70
Warren, William	Susan E. Watson	Nov. 15, 1867	175
Watkins, Elisha	Sarah Spence	May 29, 1870	259
Watson, George	Emily Green	Jan. 3, 1868	218
Watson, James	Martha Lamiosen	June 1, 1866	170
Watson, Solomon (Col.)	Elizabeth McGregor (c)	Jan. 22, 1878	308
Watson, Solomon (c)	Elizabeth McGregor	Jan. 22, 1878	344
Watson, William	Anna Sutton	July 20, 1879	356
Weay, James M.	Ellin Wells	Dec. 23, 1866	178
Webb, Levi E.	Elizabeth Odom	Jan. 20, 1859	32
Webb, William A. (of Johnson Co.)	Adella Beasley	Apr. 5, 1877	295
Welch, Henry	Sarah Lanier	Dec. 30, 1861	86
Wells, George D.	Mollie F. Inman	Mch. 21, 1871	261
White, Peter	Easter Wilson	May 29, 1868	199
Whitehead, Frank	Hettie McLeod	Dec. 20, 1877	323
Whitehead, William	Teina Brown	Jan. 11, 1868	201
Wiggens, Amos W.	Mary Outlaw	Apr. 10, 1856	3
Wiggins, Daniel W.	Marietta Kent	Apr. 17, 1870	236
Wiggins, J. M.	Luda Aldmond	Aug. 24, 1879	366
Wiggins, Jesse A.	Amanda Bennett	Jan. 11, 1866	131
Wiggins, John C.	Martha G. Wiggins	Oct. 9, 1870	264
Wiggins, John E.	Caroline Lane	Jan. 29, 1860	52
Wiggins, Joseph	America V. Oglesby	Feb. 16, 1862	79
Wiggins, Josiah	Susan M. Oglesby	Nov. 29, 1857	25
Wiggins, Lige	Amanda Brown	July 8, 1866	151
Wikstoom, Charles	Kate Hall	Sept. 25, 1877	335
Wikstrom, Charley W.	Kate Hall	Sept. 25, 1877	307

GROOM	BRIDE	DATE MARRIED	PAGE
Wiley, Edward	Harriet Huffin	Dec. 18, 1866	143
Wilks, Elias	Mirum Fendly	Jan. 8, 1865	117
Wilks, Israel	Martha Phillips	Dec. 26, 1866	190
Wilks, Jordan B.	Nancy Morris	Apr. 27, 1862	101
Wilks, Peter	Elizabeth Mosely	Nov. 15, 1857	6
Wilkes, Wiley	Milly Holton	Mch. 30, 1871	281
Wilkinson, Mingo (Col.)	Caty Dekle (Col.)	Dec. 25, 1877	315
Williams, James	Elis Edenfield	July 15, 1866	148
Williams, John	Oliff Rufer	Apr. 26, 1870	247
Williams, Phillip	Matel Danes	Mch. 23, 1867	162
Williams, R. W.	Mary Edenfield	Aug. 15, 1874	285
Williams, William P.	Malinda Powell	Dec. 9, 1857	48
Williamson, A. J.	Lucy An Phillips	Sept. 22, 1867	198
Williamson, Charles (c)	Rachel Chance (c)	Jan. 12, 1879	310
Williamson, D. S.	F. H. Williamson	June 2, 1878	314
Williamson, James R.	Elizabeth Barwick	Sept. 4, 1861	75
Williamson, John A.	Decy Phillips	Feb. 4, 1867	195
Williamson, John G.	Dicy Phillips	May 27, 1860	65
Williamson, Nlicious L.	Mary Ann Trapnell	Nov. 20, 1865	140
Willis, Reuben	Margaret G. Gillis	June 13, 1867	197
Wilson, John B.	Lydia Tison	May 31, 1857	5
Wilson, Sam (Col.)	Nancy Coppock	Jan. 17, 1878	322
Wise, Charles (Col.)	Lou Rountree (Col.)	Feb. 20, 1879	332
Withers, John	Isabell Rich	Mch. 2, 1864	109
Woods, Archibald	Easter Maxley	Feb. 3, 1864	106
Wood, Joseph	Sarah Ann Noble(s)	July 3, 1860	57
Woods, Peter J.	George Ann Lively	July 13, 1864	141
Woods, William J.	Malinda Tapley	Sept. 6, 1865	97
Yeomans, Alberene	Cassa Kennedy	June 17, 1877	302
Yeomans, James B.	Susan A. Dougherty	Mch. 13, 1879	358
Yeomans, Jordan S.	Sipper Warren	June 3, 1877	296
Yeomans, Nathaniel	Mary Ann Edenfield	May 30, 1868	199
York (a freeman)	Rachel (a freewoman)	Oct. 13, 1866	138
Youmans, E. L.	F. E. Herington	Oct. 20, 1878	343
Youman, John E.	Agnis Youngblood	Mch. 2, 1879	309
Youngblood, Auday J.	Lucinda Moor	Apr. 29, 1866	132

NOTE: "Col" & "c" means they were "Persons of Color". Often the Clerk recorded the same marriage more than once in his book.

EMANUEL COUNTY, GEORGIA-TAX DIGEST, 1841

(?)District
(The first 55 names missing)

1. Marshall Hart
2. James Martin
3. Joseph Anderson
4. William Edenfield
5. Stephen Youmans
6. James Griffin
7. Jesse Edenfield
8. William Edenfield
9. John Noble
10. Dempsey Phillips
11. Royal B. Phillips
12. James Edenfield
13. Alford Moore
14. William S. Mosely
15. C. T. Mosely, Trustee for William S. Mosely
16. Stephen Phillips

59th District

1. Allen Rountree
2. Jorden Sutton
3. Dennis Durden
4. Allen Linear
5. Moses Warren
6. Reuben Williams
7. Nathan Roberts
8. William Durden
9. John Rountree
10. T. Lott
11. George Dekle
12. Berrien Daughtery
13. William Durden
14. Simeon Durden
15. Abner Sutton
16. William Coleman
17. Eleazer L. Cowart
18. Hiram Jones
19. ---- Braddy
20. Hezekiah Parish
21. William Jones
22. Thomas Jones
23. Ezekiel Clifton
24. Ezekiel Parish

25. Augustus M. Cowart
26. Live Patrick
27. William Turner
28. Thomas Casey
29. Elijah Casey
30. Ephraim G. Willis
31. Jackson Bird
32. Farthy Bird
33. Allen Proctor

34. John Proctor
35. Stephen Cowart
36. William Deal
37. William Proctor
38. Needham Bryan
39. Curtis Cobb
40. Jeremiah Grimes
41. Henry Brown
42. William Smith

43. Jesse Brown
44. Mary Marsh
45. Samuel Kenneda
46. Martha Cowart
47. Right Casey
48. Arelza Anderson
49. Albert Neil
50. Nathan Barwick,Trustee for Lott Barwick

49th District

1. John Johnson
2. James J. Cowart
3. Edward Lane
4. Henry Johnson
5. William Johnson
6. Thomas Kent
7. Lewis Bird
8. Jepthah Purvis
9. Daniel Kent
10. John Bennett
11. Elizabeth Bennet
12. Benjamin Bennet
13. Johann Barns
14. Stephen Lewis
15. John Hendley
16. Abraham Hendley
17. William Johnson
18. Abraham Gay
19. Adam Wilcher
20. John Wiggins, Sr.
21. Nathaniel Cowart
22. John Wiggins, Jr.
23. William Lewis

24. Thomas Davis
25. Margaret Wiggins
26. John Clifton
27. William Johnson,Trus. fro Sebirn Johnson
28. William Arons
29. George W. Clifton
30. Sebern Cowart
31. Benjamin L. Newton
32. John Newton
33. Benjamin L. Lane
34. William Miller
35. William Martin, Jr.
36. William Martin, Sr.
37. John Martin
38. Nathan Johnson
39. John Lane, orphan
40. Gideon Kennedy
41. Right Hendley
42. Henry J. Parish
43. Burrel Linear
44. James R. Miller
45. James R. Miller

46. Sarah Miller
47. James Williams
48. William Davis
49. John H. Cowart
50. Mathew Buie
51. John Buie
52. Mary Buie
53. Charles Miller
54. James Oglesby
55. Lewis Beacham
56. John Oglesby
57. Allen Oglesby
58. Bird L. Newton
59. James Oglesby, Jr.
60. William Martin, Trus. for Dorcas Clark
61. Lewis Gay
62. Mathew Gay
63. Daniel J. Proctor
64. Phillip Newton

57th District

1. James Brown
2. William Stephens
3. William Bishop
4. Rachael Coleman
5. Rowan Johnson
6. Lucy Coleman
7. William Burt
8. John Burt
9. George McKinsey
10. William Hall
11. Elijah Trapnell
12. John G. Hull
13. Thomas Drew
14. Thomas Drew, Trus. for James Ruis, free person of color
15. Wilson Drew
16. Henry S. Brown
17. Samuel Green
18. John Overstreet
19. John Overstreet,Guardian for Matthew & Henry Overstreet
20. John C. Crump, Trus. for Mary Lewis
21. A. L. Kirkland
22. Daniel Green (57 slaves)

23. Edward McGar
24. Edward McGar, guard. for orphans of John Hackle
25. Edward McGar, guard. for William Jones, man of color
26. Edward McGar, trus. for Owen McGar
27. Jesse Martin
28. Enoch Farmer
29. Eli Roberts
30. Eli Roberts, Trus. for Tabitha Roberts
31. Lindsey Coleman
32. Mathew Lamb
33. David Coleman
34. Josiah Drew
35. Josiah Drew, Trus. for Allen Torance
36. Severn Wala
37. Severn Wala, Trus. for Ann Lessey
38. Lindsey Coleman
39. R. A. Love
40. Patrick Hall
41. Sarah McCollough
42. William G. Sherrod

43. John Sherrod
44. Littleton Spence
45. Juniper Hall
46. Juniper Hall, Trustee for Robert Hall
47. William Rawls
48. Button Scott
49. James Brown, agent for est. of Henry Brown
50. Zacchus Eavens
51. James Jenkins
52. Elisha Coleman
53. Samuel Richardson
54. Rufus Knight
55. Jeremiah Spence
56. John Love
57. Thomas Mikel
58. Anthony Sapp
59. William Davis
60. William B. Nabb
61. Griffin Mercer
62. Thomas J. Bird
63. Sebern Collins
64. William B. Miller

53rd District

1. David Edenfield
2. David Edenfield, Jr.
3. Garry (?) Hays
4. Jesse Moore
5. Jorden Flanders
6. A. W. Adkinson
7. William M. Archer
8. John G. Pollette
9. Elisha Coleman, Jr.
10. Samuel Strange
11. Ashley E. Wiggins
12. N. D. McLeod
13. Henry Durden
14. William Godfrey
15. Levie Drew
16. Allen Meck
17. John C. Sumner
18. John C. Sumner, agent
19. Wilson J. Keene, trustee
20. John Coleman
21. Jonathon Hooks
22. Manning Moore
23. James Kitchens
24. William Cannady
25. Bartly Sconers
26. Joshua Rountree
27. Henry Durden, trustee
28. William Rowel
29. Asa Thompson
30. Elizabeth Williams
31. Daniel E. Rich
32. W. R. Smith
33. Robert Thompson
34. Robert Thompson, trustee
35. Elisha Coleman
36. John R. Flanders
37. John R. Flanders, trustee
38. Spencer Key
39. James Stroud
40. James Faircloth, trustee for James & William Gaircloth
41. Henry Rowel
42. John Deal
43. Reuben Boatright
44. Alexander C. Sumner
45. J.L.B. Faircloth
46. Mathew Curl, Jr.
47. John A. Kemp
48. John A. Kemp, trustee for John & Rebeckah Durden
49. Alexander C. Sumner, trustee
50. Wilson J. Kierce (?)
51. Bird L. Sumner
52. Benjamin E. Brinson
53. Benjamin E. Brinson, guardian
54. James R. Nunn
55. James R. Nunn, guardian for James Dudley Deal
56. Furney Deal
57. Charles Coleman
58. Charles Coleman, parent for Jeremiah Coleman
59. Reuben Thompson
60. John Sconers

55th District

1. James Meadows
2. Samuel Grenway
3. David Davis
4. James M. Tapley
5. James M. Tapley, trus. for Sarah Tapley
6. James Price
7. Loyd Price
8. Shadrack Kite
9. Jeremiah W.P. Stevens
10. James Overstreet
11. William Williamson
12. Sampson Powel
13. Sampson Powel, trus. for Elias Powel
14. Sampson Powel, trus. for Calvin Powel
15. Mitchel Fortner
16. Linear Powell
17. Isaac Norris
18. Bennett Yeates
19. Lewis Davis
20. Silas Powel
21. Andrew G. Sorenson (?)
22. Miles Whitfield
23. Joseph Brantley
24. William Norris
25. Darling Swain
26. Darling Swain, trustee for Allen Paul
27. James J. Black
28. William Roland
29. William Roland, trustee for Andrew J. Snider
30. Richard Sumner
31. William Riner
32. William Riner, trustee for John Riner

395th DISTRICT

1. Richard G. Casey
2. Thomas Jones
3. Lemuel Love
4. Lemuel Love, trustee for Katharine Tison
5. Sion Key
6. Eleazer Durden
7. William Durden
8. Nathan Barwick
9. John D. Gillis
10. John D. Gillis, trustee for Sarah Mimms
11. John Wilks
11. Stephen Wood
12. John Smith
13. Reason Hampton
14. John Hall
15. Malcom Wilks
16. Nathan Barwick
17. Warren Key
18. William Thigpen
19. Travis Hall
20. Burrel Key
21. Mary Sulvant (?)
22. Riley Watts

214

Deed Book B follows Deed Book 2 on microfilm. For abstracts of Deed
Book 1 and 2, see Some Georgia County Records, Vol. 2 (Easley SC: Southern Historical Press, 1977) pp. 162-311.

Page 1.   5 Mar. 1792. Newman Pounds and Julius Sanders to Elisha
            Hern, both parties of Greene Co., for Ł150, 200 acres granted
31 Aug. 1785, which grant we now deliver. s/ Julius Sanders, Newman (X)
Pounds. Wit: Ben. Welch, Wm. Hearne, Levin Smith. Proved by Levin
Smith....(rest of deed cut off).

Page 2.   3 Jul. 1790. Thomas Napier and Cloe his wife of Richmond
            Co. to Isaac Stocks of Greene Co. for Ł100, 450 acres on
waters of Town Creek, beginning at Carmichall's pine, to Corzart's line,
Alison's line, Panil's line. s/ Th. Napier. Wit: Thos. B. Scott, JP,
H. Hampton, John Cook. Rec. 13 Mar. 1793. Wm. Daniell, Clerk.

Page 3.   10 Feb. 1790. William Ayres (Attorney for Roger Brooks,
            Bearing date 2 Aug. 1778) of Wilkes Co. to Nathan Clay of
Greene Co. for Ł5 GA money, 240 acres formerly bounded N by Carr, S by
the Academy land, SW by Simons, granted by his honor George Handly, Esq.
26 Jun. 1780. s/ Wm. Ayres, Attorney for Roger Brooks. Wit: Robert
Walton, Eliza. (X) Walton, Edmd. Samuell. Proved by Robert Walton before
Henry Ware 9 Apr. 1790. Rec. 13 Mar. 1793.

Page 4.   19 Mar. 1793. I, Robert McAlpin of Greene Co. stand indebt-
            ed to Tyre Clements of same for Ł200 sterling, to be null
and void if the said McAlpin disclaims an instrument of writing signed
by Tyre Clements 21 Dec. last past, wherein the said Clements mortgaged
the tract of land whereon he then lived, and other things excepting a
negro wench named Patt, and the said Clements totally exonorated therefrom. s/ R. McAlpin. Wit: E. Lyman, JP, Wm. Daniell. Rec. 8 Apr.
1793. J.

Page 5.   1 Apr. 1793. Thomas Heard of Georgia to Enoch Hedges of
            Virginia for Ł75, 204 acres in Greene Co. on waters of Oconee
in the Reserve. s/ Thos. Heard. Wit: E. Lyman, JP, John Wallace. Rec.
25 Apr. 1793.

Page 6.   25 May 1792. Robert Shipley of Franklin Co. to Bithiah
            Alexander of Greene Co. for Ł80 sterling of GA, 60 acres on
the Oconee opposite the mouth of Richland Cr. on a branch of said Oconee
River. Part of a tract of 295 acres granted to the said Robert Shipley,
beginning at the upper end of the Island, it being an island in the Oconee River. s/ Robert Shipley. Wit: Wm. Horton, Thos. Butler, John
Smith, Saml. Alexander. Rec. 9 May 1793.

Page 7.   10 Mar. 1789. Exum Oneil of Greene Co. to Demsey Jordan of
            same for Ł50, 250 acres on South Fork of Ogeechee R. bounded
E by Henry Peaks, S by Thomas Criddile & Francis Poythryss, W by Julius
Alford, N by Benjamin Fauver, being the land where the said Demsey Jor-
dan now lives and granted to said Oneill 11 Nov. 1788. s/ Exum (X)
Oneil. Wit: Benja. Whitfield, Thos. Credille. Proved by Benja. Whit-
field before Wm. Greer JP, 18 Mar. 1793. Rec. 11 May 1793.

Page 8.   6 Mar. 1793. Curby Whatley and Ann his wife of Wilkes Co.
            to William Fain of Greene Co. for Ł50, 110 acres on waters of
Rush Cr. adj. William Burford, Cornelius Batchelor. s/ Curby () Whatley,
Anna Whatley. Wit: John A. Miller, Lucy (X) Whatley. Proved by John A.
Miller 7 May 1793 before Wm. Cochran JP. Rec. 18 May 1793.

Page 9.   9 Feb. 1793. William Burford and Judith his wife of Greene
            Co. to Curby Whatley of the county aforesaid for Ł50 sterl.
of GA, 170 acres on waters of Town Creek and ___ ? ___ Creek adj. John
Adam Miller, Samuel Thornton, land belonging to the Revd. Silas Mercer,
Clements land, William Burford. s/ Wm. Burford Jnr., Judan ( ) Burford.
Wit: Jas. Daniell, Wm. Fain, Cornelius Batchelor. Proved by William
Fain 27 Feb. 1793 before Wm. Greer, JP. Rec. 18 May 1793.

Page 10.   15 Jan. 1793.   Thomas Daniell of Greene Co. to Adam Hayes for
             50 pds. sterling, 154 acres on the S side Oconee R. in the
Reserve, adj. land granted to Thomas Daniell on the S and Easley's land
on the N. s/ Thomas Daniell. Wit: Wm. Daniell, Saml. Coleman. Proved
by Wm. Daniell 21 May 1793 before E. Lyman, JP. Rec. 23 May 1793.

Page 11.   3 Jul. 1793.   Buckner Harris of Wilkes Co. to William Daniell
             of Greene for Ł5, 750 acres in Franklin Co. on waters of the
Appalachee River, surveyed in my own name and the name of the aforesaid
William Daniell. It is to be understood that the said Buckner Harris
is not to be accountable in case the aforesaid land should have been
previously surveyed for any other person or lye out of the present boundary line. s/ Buckner Harris. Wit: George Sheffield, Betsey Earley.
Proved by George Sheffield 4 Jul. 1793 before Peyton Smieth, J.P. Rec.
5 Jul. 1793.

Page 12.   17 Jun. 1788.   Robert Harper and Mary his wife of Wilkes Co.
             to William Glass of same for Ł75, 300 acres on the waters of
Fulsoms Cr. in Greene Co. s/ Robert Harper, Mary ( ) Harper. Wit:
Zachariah Glass, John Harper. Witnessed and acknowledged before L. (?)
Harper, JP. 17 Jun. 1788: Rec'd. of Wm. Glass the consideration money
within mentioned. s/ Robert Harper Senr. Rec. 6 Jul. 1793.

Page 13.   17 Jan. 1793.   William Glass and Sarah his wife of Greene Co.
             to William Battle of same for Ł75, 200 acres on Fulsoms Cr.
beginning at a water oak where Lamars Trail crosses said Creek, to
Shivers pine to Buckhorn Cr. s/ Wm. Glass, Sarah (X) Glass. Wit: Matt
Rabun JP, Drury Cook, Aner (his mark - not shown) Atkinson. Rec. 7 Jul.
1793.

Page 14.   2 Nov. 1792.   Joshua Martin Senr. and Mary his wife of
             Wilkes Co. to Robin Hobbs of Greene Co. for Ł70 Sterling,
144 acres on the headwaters of Town Cr. where the said Martin formerly
lived, bounded E by the Wilkes Co. line, S by Samuel Thornton, W by unknown, N by Robert Beasley. s/ Joshua Martin, Mary (X) Martin. Wit: Wm.
Cockran (?) JP. Rec. 8 Jul. 1793.

Page 15.   5 Aug. 1789.   William Thompson and Sarah his wife of Washing-
             ton Co. to Daniel Bankston of same for Ł60 sterling, 234
acres in Greene Co. bounded NE by Ogechee River, S by James Beasley &
Joel Banckston, NW by James Runer (?), granted 1 May 1789. s/ William
Thompson, Sarah (X) Thompson. Wit: Barton Hannon. Proved before Benja.
Thompson JP. Rec. 8 Jul. 1793.

Page 16.   4 Dec. 1789.   Edward Wilbourn and Matthus (?) his wife of
             Wilkes Co. to Thomas Wilbourn Junr. of county aforesaid, for
Ł50, 230 acres on waters of Greenbrier Cr. s/ Edward Wilborn, Mathus
(X) Wilborn. Wit: Thomas Wilborn, B. Netherland. Proved before Thos.
Wootten JP. Rec. in Wilkes Co. Book GG folio 126-127, 1 Jan. 1790. Rec.
Greene Co., 9 Jul. 1793.

Page 17.   20 Jan. 1793.   Walton Harris of Greene Co. to Vinson Greer
             of Wilkes Co. for Ł50 GA money, 287½ acres in Greene Co.,
originally granted to Benjamin Davis 16 Sep. 1784 and conveyed to said
Walton Harris, bounded S by Englins land, E by Johnson, N by Academy land,
on the waters of Fishing Creek. s/ Walton Harris. Wit: John Gritman,
William Grigsby. Proved before Wm. Greer, JP. Rec. 12 Jul. 1793.

Page 18.   4 Sep. 1792.   Samuel Cranford of Greene Co. to Moses Going
             of Wilkes Co. for Ł100 sterl., 100 acres on the waters of
Ogeechee adj. Jacob Banckston, Fitzjarrell, and Davis. s/ Samuel Cran-
ford. Wit: Isaac Bankston, James Langford, Ethd. Wood, JP. Rec. 13
Jul. 1793.

Page 19.   16 Jun. 1792.   George Phillips of Greene Co. to Stephen Eavns
             of same for Ł20 sterl., 150 acres on the waters of Shoulder-
bone granted to the said George Phillips 9 Feb. 1792. s/ Geo. Phillips.
Wit: ___?___ Rutledge, Abner Evans. Ack. before E. Clyma (?) JP. Rec.
14 Jul. 1793.

216

Page 20.   28 Feb. 1793.   Moses Parker of Greene Co. to George Hill of
            same for Ł50 sterl., 72 acres on Richland Cr. adj. Talbot,
Parker. s/ Moses Parker, Susannah (X) Parker. Wit: G. W. Foster, JP.
Rec. 15 Jul. 1793.

Page 21.   17 Nov. 1792.   William Fluker of Wilkes Co. to Phillip
            Blasengame of Greene for Ł 100 sterl., 170 acres where Blasen-
game now lives adj. George Wagoner. Part of a tract granted to said
Fluker who sold part of the tract to Joseph Lemon. The creek between
Lemon and Blassingame is to be the line. Land was granted 12 Oct. 1785.
s/ William Fluker. Wit: Isaac Fluker, Benjamin Blasengame. Proved before William Greer, JP. Rec. 16 Jul. 1793.

Page 22.   17 Oct. 1792.   Richard Jones and Nancy his wife of Greene Co.
            to John Chappell of same for Ł50 sterl., 106½ (?) acres on
Richland Cr., bounded N & W by Kimbrough, S by Spradling, E by Thompson.
(Further into deed it states to John Chappell and his wife Nanney.) s/
Richard (X) Jones, Nancy (X) Jones. Wit: John Chappell Junr., Joseph
Chappell. Proved by John Chappell Junr. before James Adams, JP, 13 Mar.
1793. Rec. 17 Jul. 1793.

Pages 23-24. 28 Jul. 1792. Joshua Wilborn and Elizabeth his wife of
            Wilkes Co. to Thomas Welborn Junr. of same for Ł34 sterl.,
191 (?) acres in the Continental Reserve in the fork of the Oconee &
Appalachee Rivers on both sides of Greenbrier Cr. bounded by Whatley,
Curtis Wilborn, Edward Wilborn and Greer's (?) land. Granted to said
Joshua Wilborn 12 Jul. 1790 (?). s/ Joshua Wilborn, Elizabeth (X) Wil-
born. Wit: J. Abernathie, Catherine Dodd. Proved before Thomas Wootten,
JP. Rec. 18 Jul. 1793.

Page 24.   7 Mar. 1792.   Abraham Smith of Greene Co. to Joshua Martin
            of Georgia for Ł20 sterl., 144 acres bounded S by Samuel
Thornton, NE by Wilkes Co. line, NW by Harbeys (?) land; granted to said
Abraham Smith 2 Mar. 1791. s/ Abraham Smith. Wit: Anderson Comer, JP.
Winney Smith relinquished her dower the same day. Rec. 18 Jul. 1793.

Page 25.   7 Jul. 1791.   John Gill of Greene Co. to Benjamin Whitfield
            of same for Ł100, 100 acres, bounded SW by Powells Cr., SE
by Nathan Jones, NE by Ajonadab Read and by Benj. Whitfield's land,
being the land where said Gill now lives; granted to Ezekiel Slaughter
5 Oct. 1785. s/ John Gill. Wit: Robt. Bryan, (unreadable), Wm. Cochran,
JP. Rec. 19 Jul. 1793.

Page 26.   21 May 1792.   James Ward of Greene Co. to Moses Going of
            Wilkes for Ł100, 238 acres on waters of the Ogeechee in
Greene and Washington Counties adj. SE the lands of Brewer, NW by Banks-
ton and on the other side by William Mattock. s/ James Ward. Wit: Moses
Lewas, Samuel Cranford. Proved before Ethd. Wood, JP. Rec. 20 Jul. 1793.

Page 27.   25 May 1792.   Robert Shipley of Franklin Co. to Samuel Alex-
            ander of Wilkes Co. for Ł80 sterl. GA money, 237 acres on the
Oconee River near the mouth of Richland Creek and branch of said Oconee,
including sundry islands in said Oconee River. s/ Robert Shipley. Wit:
William Horton, Thos. Butler, John Smith. Rec. 21 Jul. 1793.

Page 28.   13 Nov. 1792.   Charles Burke of Wilkes Co. to Benjamin Posey
            of Greene Co. for Ł120, 622 acres on waters of Shoulderbone
Cr. s/ Charles Burk. Wit: David Love, Phillip Tigner. Proved 7 Jun.
1793 before David Love, JP. Rec. 21 Jul. 1793.

Page 29.   23 Feb. 1792.   Jonathan Williams and Anna his wife of Greene
            Co. to Robert Cook for Ł30 sterl., 116½ acres on waters of
Richland Cr. bounded N and W by Cimbrous land, S by Spradling, E by
Thompson. s/ Jonathan Williams. Wit: John Kimbrough, Thomas Kimbrough.
Proved by Thos. Kimbrough before Geo. Reid, JP, 22 Jul. 1793. Rec. 22
Jul. 1793.

Page 30.   16 May 1792.   Robert Cook and Elizabeth his wife of Greene
            Co. to Richard Jones and Nancy his wife of same for Ł40
sterl., 116½ acres on Richland Cr. bounded N & W by Kimbrough's land, S

217

by Spradlings, E by Thompson. s/ Robt. (X) Cook, Eliz. (X) Cook. Wit:
Charles Cessna, JP. Rec. 31 Jul. 1793.

Page 31.   30 Dec. 1790. I Daniel Bevers of Greene Co. appoint my
            friend Daniel Burford of same as my attorney to obtain a
title for a certain tract of land on Buck Cr. or otherwise to settle the
same with Stephen Heard who has given me a bond for the said land. s/
Daniel Bevers. Wit: Wm. Daniell, Wm. Cochran, JP. Rec. 4 Sep. 1793.

Pages 31-32.   17 Aug. 1792. William Daniell of Greene Co. to Obediah
               Belcher for Ł10 sterl., 150 acres on the Beaverdam fork of
Richland Cr. adj. lines of the said William Daniell, granted to the said
Daniell 1 Dec. 1786. s/ Wm. Daniell. Wit: R. C. Royston, Wm. Cochran,
JP., William Anderson. Rec. 4 Sep. 1793.

Pages 32-34.   28 May 1792. Thomas Grace and Sarah his wife of Greene Co.
               to Jonathan Hosea of same for Ł20 GA money, 20 (?) acres,
part of a tract granted to Josiah Carter and part of another tract granted to Robert Flournoy, both on the waters of Hooppoll Cr. and on Turkey
branch of said creek, including the house and plantation where the said
Hosea now lives. s/ Thomas Grace, Sarah (X) Grace. Wit: Josiah Dennis,
Robert Waddington, Mathew Raburn, JP. Rec. 10 Oct. 1793.

Pages 34-35.   26 Nov. 1791. William Maddux, Senr. and Betey his wife of
               Greene Co. to George Cotten of same for Ł100, 60 acres
adj. Leven Ellis, John Lamar, Thomas Lamar. s/ Wm. Maddux, Betey Maddux.
Wit: Benjamin Maddux. Rec. Oct. 1793.

Pages 36-37.   6 Jul. 1793. Headed Greene Co. Jeremiah Bonner of Wash-
               ington Co. to William Battle of the county above written,
for four thousand weight of tobacco, 344 acres on waters of Town Cr.,
part in Washington and part in Greene, adj. said Bonner's line, including the upper Big Spring. s/ Jeremiah Bonner. Wit: Robt. McGinty, John
Ragan, JP. Rec. Oct. 1793.

Pages 37-38.   6 Jul. 1793. Abraham Redick and Hannah his wife of Greene
               Co. to Isaac Evans of same for Ł50 sterl., 75 acres being
part of a thousand acres annexed to a grant in Alexander Redick's own
name, on Fulsoms Cr. adj. Benjamin Evans. s/ Abraham (X) Redick, Hannah
(X) Redick. Wit: Agrippa Atkinson, John Greer. Rec. Oct. 1793.

Pages 39-40.   19 Nov. 1792. Zachariah Glass and Nancy his wife of Greene
               Co. to Jonas Shivers of same for Ł165 sterl., 200 acres on
the waters of Hoop pole Creek. s/ Zachariah Glass, Nancy (X) Glass.
Wit: William Rabun, William Speir. Rec. Oct. 1793.

Pages 40-41.   11 Jul. 1793. John Lamar of Greene Co. to George Cotten
               of same for Ł13, 13 acres adj. said Cotten and Col. Thos.
Lamar. s/ John Lamar. Wit: Jas. Harvey, JP. Rec. Oct. 1793.

Pages 41-43.   19 Aug. 1786. John Garrott of Augusta, Richmond Co., GA,
               Gentleman, and Catharine his wife to John Cook of the same
place, taylor, for Ł50 GA money, 290 acres in Greene Co. bounded NW by
Whatley's land, NW by Cawley and Fitzpatrick, SE by Greer, SW by Sanford
& Fitzpatrick. s/ John Garrett. Wit: Will. Stith, Seaborn Jones. Certified by Wm. Stith, Judge, 13 Sep. 1793.

Pages 43-45.   20 Dec. 1791. Joshua Houghton & Nancy his wife of Greene
               Co. to Joshua Roberts for Ł25 GA money, 167 acres on
waters of Richland Cr. s/ Joshua Houghton, Nancy Houghton. Wit: Wm.
Houghton, Reubin Edwards, Wm. Cochran, JP. "NB: This recorded in folio
59. Wm. Daniell, Clk." Rec. November 1793.

Pages 45-46.   28 Sep. 1792. Seymore Catching of Western Territory South
               of Ohio, G. C., to Samuel Atkinson of Wilkes Co. for Ł100
Ga money, 287½ acres on both sides of Sandy Creek. s/ Saymer Catching.
Wit: D. Roberts, Mary Roberts. Proved by Daniel Roberts 17 Nov. 1792
before A. Bedell. Rec. 18 Nov. 1793.

Pages 46-47.   25 Dec. 1792. William Daniell of Greene Co. to James Nesbit

of same for Ł30, 300 acres on Beaverdam of Richland Cr. adj. Obadiah
Belcher, Tyler's line, Joel Mayberry. s/ Wm. Daniell. Wit: R. C. Royston, John Sanders, John Armor, JP. Rec. 28 Dec. 1793.

Pages 47-48. 1 Dec. 1791. John Reed to Isaac Stocks of Greene Co. for
        L-100 GA money, 245 acres granted the said John Reed, sur-
veyed by Micajah Williamson, D.S., adj. James Stewart on S side, W by
Cribbs. s/ John Read. Wit: Thomas Espey, JP, Isaac Williams. Rec. 30
Nov. 1793.

Pages 48-49. 4 Mar. 1793. Tunstal Roan and Milley his wife of Greene
        Co. to Nathan Jones of same for Ł100 GA money, 200 acres
in Greene Co., formerly Wilkes adj. Micajah Williamson at the time of
original survey, originally granted Micajah Williamson in 1784 and released and made over to said Roan 4 Feb. 1789. s/ Tunstall Roan, Milley
(X) Roan. Wit: Hen. Graybill, JP., William Jackson. Rec. 9 Jan. 1794.

Page 50. 29 Nov. 1793. James Thompson Senr. of Greene Co. to James
        Thompson Junr. of same for Ł70 sterling, 187½ acres on
waters of Fishing Cr. bounded N by said Thompson Senr., W by William
Greer, S by Triplet & Stephens, E by John Thompson; granted to Lewis
Crain 12 Oct. 1785. s/ James Thompson. Wit: Thomas Hall. Ack. 24 Dec.
1793 before Wm. Greer, JP. Rec. 27 Jan. 1794.

Pages 51-52. 3 Apr. 1790. John Maynor (Mainer) and Kesiah his wife of
        Wilkes Co. to Benjamin Whitfield of Greene, for Ł100 sterl-
ing, 200 acres on waters of Powells Creek adj. Alford, being the land
where said Whitfield now lives. Purchased by said Mainer of Nathan
Jones, said land granted to Jones 13 Oct. 1785. s/ John Maynor, Kezia
(X) Maynor. Wit: Robert Bryan, Ebenezer (X) Starnes. Proved by Robert
Bryan 16 Sep. 1793 before Abraham Womack, JP. Rec. 10 Feb. 1794.

Page 53. 16 Feb. 1793. Curby Whatley and Ann his wife of Wilkes Co.
        to Cornelius Batchelor of Greene, for Ł25 sterling, 100
acres on waters of Rushy Creek adj. Battle, Clements, William Burford.
s/ Curby ( ) Whatley, Anna Whatley. Wit: Reuben DeJernatt, JP, John
Armor. Rec. 17 Feb. 1794.

Pages 54-55. 26 Nov. 1791. William Maddux Senr. and Betsey his wife of
        Greene Co. to George Cotten of same for Ł100, 60 acres
adj. Leven Ellis, John Lamar, Thomas Lamar. s/ William (X) Maddux, Betsy
(X) Maddux. Wit: Benja. Maddux, Elisha Harris, John Twitty. Proved by
Benjamin Maddux 5 Oct. 1793 before Roberd Thomas, JP. Rec. 19 Feb. 1794.

Pages 55-56. 6 Jul. 1793. Jeremiah Bonner of Washington Co. to William
        Battle of Greene, for 4000 pds. tobacco, 344 acres on
waters of Town Cr. part in Washington and part in Greene Co. adj. said
Bonner, including the upper big spring. s/ Jeremiah Bonner. Wit: Robt.
McGinty, John Ragan, JP. Rec. 20 Feb. 1794.

Page 57. 4 Dec. 1788. Curtis Welborn and Mary his wife of Wilkes
        Co. to Elijah Welborn of the county aforesaid for Ł50
Specie, 287½ acres on the Oconee River. s/ Curtis Welborn, Mary Welborn.
Wit: Thomas Welborn, Holman Freeman, JP. Rec. 10 Mar. 1794.

Page 58. 9 Jul. 1791. James Thompson of Greene Co. to John Thomp-
        son, son of said James Thompson of same, for Ł50 sterling,
land (no acreage listed) on Fishing Cr. beginning at the S side of the
Academy land; part of a Bounty of aforesaid Thompson's land. s/ James
Thompson. Wit: James Thompson, Samuel Thompson. Rec. 27 Mar. 1794.

Page 59. 20 Dec. 1791. Joshua Houghton & Nancy his wife of Greene
        Co. to Joshua Roberds (Roberts) for Ł25 GA money, 167
acres on waters of Writchland Cr. s/ Joshua Houghton, Nancy Houghton.
Wit: Wm. Houghton, Reuben Edwards, Wm. Cochran, JP. Rec. 1 Apr. 1794.

Page 60. 11 Jul. 1793. John Lamar of Greene Co. to George Cotten
        of same for Ł13, 13 acres lying between said Cotten's
line and Col. Thomas Lamars and said John Lamar's line. s/ John Lamar.
Wit: Jas. Harvey, JP, Jas. Bynum. Rec. 19 Jun. 1894.

Page 61.   16 Jun. 1794.   Elizabeth Huitt of Greene Co. to William
              Huitt of same for L10 Specie, one cow and yearling, one
featherbed & furniture, chest, table, 2 bedsteads, chairs, dutch oven,
pots, dishes, washtub and every other species of property I now possess.
s/ Elizabeth (X) Huitt. Wit: Wiliam Daniell, Jno. Meador. Proved by
Wm. Daniell 16 Jun. 1794 before G. W. Foster, JP. Rec. 20 Jun. 1794.

Page 62.   6 Jan. 1787.   Joshua Houghton of Greene Co. to Adam Hayes
              of same for L50 GA money, 200 acres bounded by William
Burfit on W and E by William Daniell, on the South fork of Beaverdam of
Richland Cr. s/ Joshua Houghton, Nancy Houghton. Wit: R. FPatrick,
Patrick Hayes. Proved by Reane FzPatrick 14 Jan. 1794 before Geo. Reid,
JP. Rec. 21 Jun. 1794.

Page 63.   10 Apr. 1793. Mitchel Burford and Nancy his wife of
              Greene Co. to William West of same for L150 sterling, 250
acres on waters of Richland Cr. adj. a post oak corner of Daniel Burford's
old survey which is now the corner of William Melton's land, to an ash
corner of William Daniell. Originally granted to Jacob Dennis 30 Sep.
1784 containing 287½ acres. s/ Mitchel Burford, Nancy (X) Burford. Wit:
Solomon Burford, Ellis West. Proved by the witnesses 26 Apr. 1793 before
Tho. Houghton. Rec. 23 Jun. 1794.

Page 64.   5 Jun. 1790.   William Greer and Sarah his wife of Greene
              Co. to Thomas Stephenson of same for L70, 287½ acres on
waters of Ogeeche. s/ Wm. Greer, Sarah Greer. Wit: Wm. Cochran, Adam
Hayes, Tho. Baldwin, JP. Rec. 23 Jun. 1794.

Page 65.   22 Nov. 1792. Lambeth Hopkins of Greene Co. to Richard
              Copland of Wilkes for L340 sterling, 230 acres on S side
Oconee River and on Roes (Rose?) Creek, granted to Lachlan Phinney 22
Jul. 1785. s/ Lambeth Hopkins, Prissiler Hopkins. Wit: Thomas Duke,
Chas. Smith, Joseph Lumpkin. Proved before Jno. Lumpkin, J.P.W.C. (JP
Wilkes Co.). Rec. 23 Jun. 1794.

Page 66.   6 Jul. 1793.   Abraham Reddick and Hannah his wife of Greene
              Co. to Isaac Evans of same for L50 sterling, 75 acres, part
of 1000 acres granted to Abraham Reddick. On Fulsoms Cr. adj. Benjamin
Evans. s/ Abraham (X) Reddick, Hannah Reddick. Wit: Agrippa Atkinson,
John Greer. Proved 13 Jul. 1793 by Agrippa Atkinson before Matthew
Rabun, JP. Rec. 24 Jun. 1794.

Page 67.   28 Sep. 1790. Jacob Dansby and Catereen his wife of
              Wilkes Co. to Stephen Edwards of the county aforesaid for
L100 sterling, 170 acres on Shoulderbone Cr. granted the said Jacob
Dansby 10 Jan. 1787. s/ Jacob (X) Dansbay, Catereen (X) Dansbay. Wit:
Andrew Hamilton, William Cureton, Wm. Lancaster. Proved 26 Oct. 1793 by
Andrew Hamilton before Jas. Adams, JP. Rec. 27 Jun. 1794.

Page 68.   19 Nov. 1792. Zachariah Glass and Nancy his wife of Greene
              Co. to Jonas Shivers of same for L165 sterling, 200 acres
on waters of hoop Pole Cr. s/ Zachariah Glass, Nancy (X) Glass. Wit:
Wm. Rabun, Wm. Speir. Proved 11 Sep. 1793 by the witnesses before
Matthew Rabun, JP. Rec. 27 Jun. 1794.

Page 69.   20 Jul. 1793. Abraham Redick of Greene Co. to Zeal Milsted
              of same for L50 GA money, 102 acres on branches of Fulsoms
Cr. s/ Abraham (X) Reddick. Wit: Isaac Evans, John Greer. Proved by
Isaac Evans 20 Jul. 1793 before Matthew Rabun, JP. Rec. 30 Jun. 1794.

Page 70.   13 Nov. 1792. John Swepson of Greene Co. to Littleton
              Mapp of same for L100 sterling, 300 acres near the head of
the South Fork of Powell's Creek and on the head of Jacksons fork of
Shoulderbone, bounded NW by Wall, NE by Cain, SE by Williamson; granted
to John Swepson 22 Jul. 1789. s/ John Swepson. Wit: John Mapp, Jacob
Cain, B. Jeffries. Proved by John Mapp 18 Mar. 1794 before R. DeJernatt,
JP. Rec. 30 Jun. 1794.

Page 71.   7 Aug. 1793.   Joseph Howard of Greene Co. to William
              Beauchamp of same for L50 Ga money, 191 acres on N side

220

Rocky Cr. adj. said Howard's line.   s/ Joseph (I) Howard.   Wit: Jesse
Sanford, JP.   Rec. 9 Jul. 1794.

Page 72.   7 Jul. 1794.   I, Thomas Carleton of Greene Co., Executor
                to the LW&T of William Kennedy of Greene Co., deceased,
appoint Charles Thompson, Gent., of Hanover Co. VA my attorney in fact
for the purpose of claiming on my behalf all the property of said deceased in the state of VA, and to examine the claims of every kind existing
in said state against the said William Kennedy dec'd. s/ Thos. Carleton,
Exor.   Ack. 8 Jul. 1794 before Tho. Houghton, JP., David Peeples. Rec.
9 Jul. 1794.

Page 73.   1 Aug. 1789.   William Wilson of Greene Co. to Robert
                Maison of same for Ł65 sterling, 270 acres on waters of
Oakconee River it being part of a parcel of 670 acres granted to Charles
Cessna 19 Aug. 1788, conveyed by Cessa to Wilson.   Adj. lines of Perry,
Gresham's or Williamson's.   s/ William Wilson.   Wit: Jno. Cissna, Robert
Cissna.   Not proven.   Rec. 15 Jul. 1794.

(The following is evidently a loose paper in the deed book).   No date.
Ordered that George W. Foster, Nathan (Westfield?), & Ambrose Hutchinson
be appointed to divide the negroes belonging to the estate of George
Barsh late of South Carolina, dec'd, between William S. Talley in right
of his wife Eugenia I. Talley formerly Eugenia I. Barsh orphan of the
said George, pursuant to the laws of South Carolina, with William Talley
getting one third, and Anne C. Barsh two thirds.

Page 74.   3 Jun. 1794.   John Cessna, Sheriff of Greene Co. to William
                Daniell Esq. Clerk of Greene Co. by virtue of an execution
out of Inferior Court of Greene Co. on the date aforesaid, did expose to
sale a tract taken as the property of George Williams containing 575
acres on the Beaverdam waters of Richland Cr. bounded by Col. Porter &
others, granted to said Williams 4 Feb. 1786.   William Daniell was the
highest bidder at 35 pounds 10 shillings sterling.   s/ Jno. Cessna, Shff.
Wit: G. W. Foster, JP, Hugh Spratt.   Rec. 25 Jul. 1794.

Page 75.   10 Jul. 1793.   Eustace Daniell of Greene Co. to Patrick
                Hayes of same for Ł200 sterling, 210 acres on W side of
Oconee River in the Reserve.   s/ Eustace Daniell, Sarah (X) Daniell.
Wit: Henry Carleton, Tho. Houghton, JP.   Sarah Daniell relinquishes
dower 10 Jul. 1794 before Tho. Houghton, JP.   Rec. 11 Feb. 1795.

Page 76.   7 Apr. 1794.   Thomas Daniell and Sarah his wife to Eustace
                Daniell, all of Greene Co. for Ł25 sterling, 220 acres on
the S side Oconee River adj. Adam Hayes and McIntosh's line on the river.
s/ Thomas Daniell, Sarah (X) Daniell.   Wit: Betsey Daniell, Wm. Cochran,
JP.   Rec. 12 Feb. 1795.

Page 77.   1 Mar. 1792.   Received by Mr. Ellis West and Mr. William
                West in full of all claims or demands of me to that portion
of the Estate of Francis West dec'd. that fell to me by heirship from
said Estate.   I do relinquish, sell and make over the same unto the
aforesaid Ellis West and William West for full compensation received by
me.   s/ Tyre (X) Clements.   Wit: Wm. Daniell, Solomon Burford, Wm. Burford Junr.   Proved by William Daniell 18 Feb. 1795 before Robt. McAlpin
JP.   Rec. 18 Feb. 1795.

Page 77.   4 Feb. 1794.   Bouth Fitzpatrick of Greene Co. to Eustace
                Daniell of same for Ł10 sterling, 38½ acres on waters of
the Oconee River in the Reserve, part of a tract surveyed for the aforesaid Bouth, adj. lines of McIntosh and Thomas Daniell.   s/ Bouth Fitzpatrick.   Wit: Tho. Baldwin, JP, Edm. (?) Daniell.   Rec. 18 Feb. 1795.

Page 78.   ___ Feb. 1793.   John McElroy and wife Magy of Wilkes Co. to
                Joseph Cd. Thrasher for Ł500 sterling, 230 acres granted
to said McElroy 30 Nov. 1784.   s/ John McElroy, Magy McElroy.   Wit: Job
Bird, Duncan Cammorron, Wm. McElroy.   Proved by Dunkin Cammran who also
Jacob Bird sign 9 Oct. 1794 before William Greer, JP.   Rec. 20 Feb. 1795.

Page 79.   16 Jan. 1793.   William Fitzpatrick of Green Co. to Joseph

221

C. Thrasher of same for Ł50, 185 acres on the Oconee
River. s/ W. FPatrick. Wit: Davis Gresham, Saml. Flenniken, Richd.
Thrasher, Wm. Greer, JP. Rec. 5 Mar. 1795.

Page 80.   19 Apr. 1794. Thomas P. Wagnon of Oglethorpe Co. to
                William Merit of Warren Co. for Ł400 sterling, 409 acres on
S fork of Ogeechee bounded E by John (King?), W by Dawson, S by John
Bostwick. Part of 1,150 acres originally granted to Benjamin Few and
conveyed by said Few to Robert Middleton, from Middleton to Littleberry
Bostwick, from Bostwick to John P. Wagnon, from Wagnon to said Thomas P.
Wagnon. s/ Thomas Wagnon. Wit: Jno. Powers, Edmd. Daniell, JP. Rec.
8 May 1795.

Page 81.   5 Apr. 1794. William Daniell and Mary his wife of Green
                Co. to Miles Bevers of Wilkes Co. for Ł35 Sterl., 170 a.
on waters of Beaverdam of Richland Cr. adj. lines of Houghton & Mayberry.
Part of a tract originally granted to William Daniell. s/ Wm. Daniell,
Mary K. Daniell. Wit: Ann (X) Hodges, Wm. Cockran, JP. Rec. 9 May 1795.

Page 82.   16 Feb. 1794. James Adams and Mary his wife of Hancock Co.
                to Thomas Grimes of Greene Co. for Ł105, 200 ac., formerly
in Wilkes Co. but now in Greene, on the S fork of Ogeechee R., bounded
all sides by vacant land, granted said James Adams 20 Sep. 1784. s/
James Adams, Mary Adams. Wit: David Adams, Alexr. Reid, JP. Rec. 29
Jul. 1795.

Page 83.   19 May 1794. Ezekiel E. Park to James Rutledge (no resi-
                dence given) for Ł50, 250 ac. in the Greene & Wilkes Co. on
N fork of Ogeechee R., bounded N by Abram Landers (Sanders?) & Nathaniel
Howell, E by Joseph Carson, S by Samuel Harriss and vacant land on all
other parts at time of surveying. s/ E. Park. Wit: William Watts, Saml.
Reed. Proved by Wm. Watts. Rec. 11 Aug. 1795.

Page 84.   Headed Oglethorpe Co. 25 Jan. 1795. Howell Tatum of
                county aforesaid to Malekiah Stallings of Greene for Ł70
Sterl., 287½ a. on Richland Cr. s/ Howell Tatum, Henneriar (?) Tatum.
Wit: Wm. Ragsdall, John (X) Booker, Jas. Nisbit, JP. Rec. 11 Aug. 1795.

Page 85.   18 Jun. 1795. Andrew Barnes of Greene Co. to James Leg-
                gitt of Co. aforesaid for Ł35 sterl., 287½ a. on waters
of Shoulderbone & Beaverdam, bounded W by Isaac Gaskins land and all
other sides by Barnes land. s/ Andw. Burns. Wit: Joseph Skinner, John
Armor, JP. Rec. 13 Aug. 1795.

Page 86.   27 Nov. 1794. Gilbert Cribbs of Oglethorpe Co. to Gideon
                Harrison of Greene, for Ł100, 100 a. on Beaverdam
of Oconee adj. the creek, Cribbs line. s/ Gilbert Cribbs. Wit: Jothn.
Williams, John Robinett, Joseph Harris. Proved by Jonathan Williams Jun.
1795 before Saml. Thornton, JP. Rec. 13 Aug. 1795.

Page 87.   27 Nov. 1794. Gideon Harrison of Greene Co. to Ann Hodges
                of same for Ł50 sterl., 100 a. beginning at a maple by the
creek, to Thompson's line; including the land and plantation where the
said Gideon Harrison now resides. s/ Gideon Harrison. Wit: Joseph Carmichall, Eustace Daniell. Ack. 12 Dec. 1794 before Tho. Houghton, JP.
Rec. 13 Aug. 1795.

Page 88.   30 Aug. 1786. William Baldwin and Betsy his wife of
                Wilkes Co. to William Kimbrough of county aforesaid, for
Ł100 (?) specie, 345 a. on Beaverdam Cr. in Washington Co. (now Greene)
bounded E by land of Wm. Kimbrough, granted to the said Baldwin 20 Jan.
1785. s/ William Baldwin, Elisabeth (X) Baldwin. Wit: Sanders Walker,
Thomas Deay, Elijah Cooper, JP. Rec. 13 Aug. 1795.

Page 89.   19 Apr. 1794. Thomas P. Wagnon of Oglethorpe Co. to
                William Merit of Warren Co. for Ł400 Sterl., 409 a., part
of 1150 a. orig. granted to Benjamin Few and conveyed by said Few to
Robert Middleton, from Middleton to Littleberry Bostick, from L. Bostick
to John P. Wagnon, from John P. Wagnon to said Thomas P. Wagnon. Land
is on the S fork of Ogeechee bounded E by land of John King, W by Dawson,

222

S by John Bostick. s/ Thomas Wagnon. Wit: Jno. Powers, Edmd. Daniell,
JP. Rec. 14 Aug. 1795.

Page 90.   21 Aug. 1794. Joseph Spradling to Reuben Smith for Ƚ100,
              287½ a. adj. Bolden's line. s/ Joseph ( ) Spradling. Wit:
David Love, JP, Jno. Mapp. Rec. 14 Aug. 1795.

Pages 91-92. 8 Apr. 1793. William Houghton & Betsey his wife of Greene
              Co. to Leonard Burford for Ƚ57 GA money, 230 a. on waters
of Oconee R., beginning on the W side of Oconee R. and adj. land of Smith,
Ware and Allison. s/ Wm. Houghton, Betsey Houghton. Wit: Stephen
Sunter (?), Jos. Houghton, Junr. Proved by Stephen Sunter 14 Jan. 1794
before Wm. Cockran, JP. Rec. 14 Aug. 1795.

Pages 92-93. (Blank) 1791. Littleberry Bostick of Wilkes Co. to John
              Peter Wagnon of Augusta, GA, for Ƚ300 GA money, 600 ac. on
S fork of Ogeechee, bounded E by land of John King and W by George Daw-
son, being part of 1150 a. orig. granted to Benjamin Few, from Few to
Robert Middleton and the said 600 a. from Middleton to said Bostick. s/
L. Bery Bostick. Wit: James Mitchell, Z. Beal, JP. Rec. 14 Aug. 1795.

Pages 94-95. 5 Sept. 1793. Isaac Stocks and Catron his wife of Greene
              Co. to John Heard of same for Ƚ100 sterl., 245 a. on
Beaverdam of Richland Cr., granted to John Reed and bounded S by James
Stewart, W by Crebs. s/ Isaac Stocks, Catron Stocks. Wit: Thos. Heard,
JP, Abraham Heard. Rec. 15 Aug. 1795.

Pages 95-96. 1 Nov. 1792. Peter Kelley and his wife Jenney of Greene
              Co. to Dunkin Cammron of same for Ƚ100 sterl., 135 a.
beginning at a line between Alexander Awtrey & Peter Kelley, being orig.
in Washington Co. granted to William Phillips in 1785. s/ Peter Kelley,
Jenney Kelley. Wit: Richard Thrasher, Joseph Clarkson, Abel Pennington.
Rec. 15 Aug. 1795.

Page 96.   7 Jan. 1794. John Brown & Polley his wife of Hancock Co.
              to Samuel Barnett of Greene for Ƚ50 sterl., 200 ac. on
waters of Ogeechee & Richland Cr., surveyed for Wilkes Co. but now in
Greene. Granted the said John Brown 22 Mar. 1785. s/ John Brown, Polley
Brown. Wit: Wm. Melton, Daniel Brown. Proved by Wm. Melton 15 Feb.
1794 before Robt. McAlpin, JP. Rec. 20 Aug. 1795.

Pages 97-98. 27 May 1790. Charles Cessna of Greene Co. to William
              Wilson of same for Ƚ5 sterl., 670 a. on waters of Richland
Cr. and Oconee R. adj. James Sanders, Perry, Ogletree. "P.S. The Intent
of the above conveyance is not to compel the above bound Charles Cessna
to make a right to said Wm. Willson in case any older or prior right
should come forward to take the above mentioned lands and that said
Cessna is only to give it from him his heirs & assigns all other persons
excepted." s/ Chas. Cessna. Wit: John Cessna Senr., Jno. Cessna, Junr.,
Saml. Cessna. Ack. by Charles Cessna 2 Sep. 1795 before R. DeJernatte,
JP. Rec. 22 Sep. 1795.

Pages 98-99. 20 Apr. 1793. William Phillips of Greene Co. to the Revd.
              Thomas Daniell of same for Ƚ30 specie, 100 a. being the
lower part of a grant of 200 a. to said Phillips. On waters of S fork
of Ogeechee R. s/ Wm. Phillips. Wit: Aron (X) Livingston, Thos. Baldwin, JP. Rec. 22 Sep. 1795.

Pages 99-100. 3 June 1790. Samuel Hough and Sarah his wife to James
              Wilson of Ƚ20, 200 a. in Greene Co. s/ Sam ( ) Hough,
Sarah (X) Hough. Wit: Wm. Allison, Zach. Ranfroe, Samson Ranfrow. Proved by Wm. Allison before Tho. Carleton, JP. Rec. 22 Sep. 1795.

Page 101.   15 Nov. 1793. Tyre Clements & Elizabeth his wife of Greene
              Co. to Lewis Wiggins of same for Ƚ50 sterl., 16½ a. on
waters of the Rushy Fork of Richland Cr., adj. the old tract that said
Clements sold to Wiggins. s/ Tyre (X) Clements, Elizabeth (X) Clements.
Wit: Wm. Patrick, Chas. Daniell. Proved 18 Mar. 1794 by Charles Daniell
before Tho. Hughton, JP. Rec. 23 Mar. 1795.

Page 102.   4 May 1795.   Abraham Heard, Tax Collector of Greene Co. to
             Thomas Daniell of Greene Co. & Wm. Vason of Wilkes, land
exposed to public sale, the property of John Brewer, Trustee for James
Danaly, for Tax due on said land for the year 1793. 460 a. on waters of
Apalachee, adj. Websters land. Highest bidders were the said Daniell
and Vason at Ł4.1.0. s/ Abraham Heard. Wit: G. W. Foster, JP, Peyton
Smith. Rec. 23 Sep. 1795.

Page 103.   27 May 1791.   Ezekiel Slaughter of Greene Co. to John Gill
             of same for Ł50, 100 a. on Powell's Cr. adj. Ajonadab Reed,
Nathan Jones, George Roan, James Alford & Benjamin Whitfield, being the
land whereon said Gill now lives. s/ Ezekiel Slaughter. Wit: Tho.
Bonner, Whitmill Bonner, John Simmons. Proved by Thomas Bonner 16 Jul.
1795 before Robt. McAlpin, JP. Rec. 23 Sep. 1795.

Page 104.   7 Dec. 1793.   Benjamin Posey of Greene Co. to John Smith
             of same, for Ł50, 155¼ a. on waters of Shoulderbone, adj.
Joseph Young and the Cool spring branch. s/ Benjamin Posey. Wit:
Reuben Smith, Robt. Howson Mapp, Tho. Baldwin, JP. Rec. 27 Sep. 1795.

Page 105.   19 Sep. 1795.   William Heard of Greene Co. to John Malone
             of Oglethorpe for Ł50 sterl., 191 a. adj. lines of Battle,
West, Daniell, Townsend; granted 1 Dec. 1786. s/ William Heard. Wit:
Wm. Daniell, Stephen Heard. Proved by Wm. Daniell 19 Sep. 1795 before
R. DeJernatte, JP. Rec. 27 Sep. 1795.

Page 106.   3 May 1793.   William Allison of Greene Co. to Richard
             Knight of same for Ł40 sterl., 143 3/4 a. on the Rocky
fork of Shoulderbone adj. Love's line. s/ William Allison. Wit: Jno.
Cartwright, Jos. Cartwright, Peter Cartwright. Sworn before Jas. Nisbit,
JP. Rec. 25 Sep. 1795.

Page 107.   4 May 1795.   Abraham Heard, Tax Collector of Greene Co. to
             William Vason of Wilkes Co., William Daniell and Thomas
Daniel both of Greene Co., land of John Collins exposed to public sale
for tax arrears due in 1794. 230 a. adj. Clement Nash. The above men
were the highest bidders at Ł21.05.02. s/ Abraham Heard, T.C.G.C. Wit:
G. W. Foster, JP, Peyton Smith. Rec. 28 Sep. 1795.

Page 108.   1 Apr. 1795.   John Adam Miller of Pendleton Co., SC to
             John Pierce of Greene Co., for Ł100 sterl., 240 a. on Town
Creek, below the waggon ford. s/ John Adam Miller. Wit: Wm. Daniell,
Mary K. Daniell. Proved by Wm. Daniell 14 J(not visible) 1795, before
Sm. Houghton, JP. Rec. 28 Sep. 1795.

Pages 109-110. 12 Dec. 1792. Nicholas Long, Junr. of Wilkes Co. to
             William Daniell of Greene, for Ł10 GA money, 45 a. on
waters of Richland Cr., beginning on said Daniell's old survey and
Mitchell Burford's line; part of an old survey granted to Reason Bowie.
s/ N. Long. Wit: Stephen Heard, David Fowler. Proved by Stephen Heard
26 Jun. 1795 before Wm. Cockran, JP. Rec. 20 Mar. 1796.

Separate notation on slip of paper: J. P. Wagnon esq. to Mr. Tho.
Wagnon, deed, 600 acres. N. Long Jr. to Wm. Daniell, Deed 45 acres.
Gilbert Cribs to Ann Hodges, deed 212 (?) acres. Wm. Daniell to pay the
above.

Pages 110-111. 16 Aug. 1792. John Kimbrough and his wife Mary to Jo-
             nathan Jackson for Ł40, 130 a. being part of the tract
that John Kimbrough now lives on. s/ John ( ) Kimbrough, Mary ( ) Kimbrough. Wit: Joseph White, Shadrack Kimbrough. Proved by Joseph White
10 Jul. 1794 before Thomas Houghton. Notation: The Wife not present to
be privately examined. Rec. 24 Mar. 1796.

Pages 111-112. 6 Apr. 1791. John Peter Wagnon of Augusta, Esq., to
             Thomas Wagnon of said place, for Ł300 GA money, 600 a.
on S fork Ogeechee bounded E by John King, W by John Dawson; part of
1140 a. orig. granted to Benjamin Few, conveyed from Few to Robert Midleton and said 600 a. from Middleton to Littleberry Bostwick and Bostwick
to John Peter Wagnon. s/ John Peter Wagnon. Wit: Jno. Scott, Edm. Blan-

ton, George Poythress. Proved by Jno. Epes (?) Scott 19 Apr. 1791 before A. Bidell. Rebecca Wagnon, wife of John Peter Wagnon, relinquished her dower 29 Apr. before A. Bidel. Rec. 24 Mar. 1796.

Pages 112-113. 27 Jul. 1794. Gilbert Cribs and Margaret Cribs his wife of Greene Co. to Joseph Harris of same for Ł100 GA money, 200 ac. Gaither, the creek, Gilbert Crib. s/ Gilbert Cribs, Margaret Cribs. Wit: Tho. Carleton, Ezekiel Robinett, John Robinett. Ack. before Tho. Carleton, JP. Rec. 20 Apr. 1796.

Pages 113-114. 12 Sep. 1794. William Melton and Lucy his wife of Greene Co. to Thomas Carleton of same for Ł150 GA money, 300 a. on both sides Beaverdam Cr. whereon the said William Melton once (?) lived, adj. Willson's line, being the land that the said Melton had of Wiliam Daniell. s/ Wm. Melton, Lucy (X) Melton. Wit: Robert Melton, John Heard. Proved before A. Grisham, JP, 14 Mar. 1797. Rec. 14 Mar. 1797.

Page 114. "Doctor Thomas Owens Mark is a Crop & over keel in each--" Rec. 20 June 1799. Tho. Carleton, Clk.

Page 115. 11 May 1796. Whereas I John F. Gardiner of Greene Co. am seized in fee, in and to 60,000 a. in Franklin Co. on the Oconee R. surveyed in my name, I appoint my friend William White of Augusta, Richmond Co., my attorney to sell and dispose of the aforesaid tract. s/ John F. Gardiner. Wit: Jacob Finley, Thomas Baldwin, JP. Rec. 12 May 1796.

Pages 116-117. 19 Mar. 1793. William Melton & Lucy his wife of Greene Co. to Joshua Willson of same for Ł50, 100 a. on Beaverdam of Richland Cr. bounded NE by John Davidson, NW by George Lambert, SW by Thomas Carleton, SE by W (?) Beavers land. s/ William Melton. Wit: Geo. W. Foster, JP, Robert McAlpin, JP. Rec. 1 Sep. 1796.

Pages 117-118. 15 Sep. 1796. Robert Burns of Jefferson Co. to Wm. Hightower of Greene for Ł40, 287½ a. on waters of Shoulderbone, bounded N by Thomas Wyatt, S by Kennon. s/ Rt. Burns. Wit: Jno. Oslin, Jo. Huchingson. Proved by John Osling 15 Sep. 1796 before A. Gresham, JP. Rec. 15 Sep. 1796.

Page 119. 2 Jun. 1794. William Kimbrough & Rebecca his wife of Greene Co. to Richd. Lewis of same for Ł100 sterl., 137 3/4 a. on waters of Richland Cr., being part of a tract purchased by Kimbrough from Micajah Williamson Senr. adj. Wm. Baldwin and a path leading from land of John Bush to Wm. Kimbrough Senr. which lines were agreed upon by said Kimbrough and Thomas Connell. s/ William Kimbrough, Rebeccah (X) Kimbrough. Wit: Wm. Baldwin. Ack. before Jno. Smith, JP. Rec. 14 Sep. 1796.

Page 120. 8 Aug. 1796. Isaac Phillips of Greene Co. to Joshua Willson of same for $300, 100 a. on Sandy Cr. at the mouth of Robert Sorrell's spring branch, down the creek to Uriah Greer's line. s/ Isaac Phillips. Wit: Tho. Carleton, G. Rentfrow. Proved by Tho. Carleton before Jo. Carmichael, JP. Rec. 21 Sep. 1796.

Page 121. 24 Sep. 1796. Gilbert Cribs of Greene Co. to Anne Hodges of same for $100, 21½ a. on Beaverdam of Richland Cr., bounded on two sides by Jackson's land on the creek and Daniell's land on the other side. s/ Gilbert Cribs. Wit: Tho. Carleton, Wm. Daniell. Proved by Tho. Carleton 8 Nov. 1796 before A. Grisham, JP. Rec. 9 Nov. 1796.

Page 122. 15 Aug. 1793. Joshua Roberts & Sarah his wife of Greene Co. to George Rentfroe of same for Ł100, 167 a. on Beaverdam of Richland Cr., where said Roberts now lives. s/ Joshua Roberts, Sarah Roberts. Wit: Tho. Carleton, Geo. W. Foster, JP, Thomas Hoff (?), Zachariah Rentfroe. Rec. 9 Jan. 1797.

Pages 123-124. 27 Jul. 1794. Gilbert Cribs & Margaret his wife of Greene Co. to Joseph Harris of same for Ł100 GA money,

225

200 a. beginning at Gather's corner, and down the creek to said Crib's line. s/ Gilbert Cribs, Margaret Cribs. Wit: Tho. Carleton, JP, Ezekiel Robinet. Rec. 12 Jan. 1797.

Page 128.   19 Oct. 1796. Sally Smith of Greene Co. appoints William Jenkins of Rockingham Co. NC power of attorney to sell 100 acres on Pig River in Franklin Co., VA, formerly the property of Thomas Smith dec'd. and decreed by him in his Will to be sold for the use of his heirs. s/ Sally Smith. Wit: David Grisham, Judge Inf. Court G.C. Rec. 19 Oct. 1796.

Pages 126-127.   30 Dec. 1786. Nathaniel Ragin of Wilkes Co. to Hugh Jones of the county aforesaid for £50 GA money, 160 a. adj. Wm. Kimbrough's corner, Baldwin, John Kimbrough. s/ Nathanile Ragin. Wit: Zack. Cox, Nancy Ray. Ack. before A. Burroughs, JP of Wilkes Co., 25 Apr. 1796. Rec. 16 Jan. 1797.

Pages 128-129.   9 Jan. 1797. George Rentfroe & Anne his wife of Greene Co. to Humphrey Gilmore of same for $300, 168 a. on Beaverdam of Richland Cr. adj. Meadors, Wm. Daniell. s/ George (X) Rentfroe, Anne (X) Rentfrow. Wit: Tho. Carleton, Zachariah Rentfroe. Proved by Tho. Carleton 6 Feb. 1797 before John Armor, JP. Rec. 6 Feb. 1797.

Pages 129-130.   17 Jan. 1797. Joshua Willson & Lucy his wife of Greene Co. to Sampson Rentfrow of same for $200, 100 acres on Beaverdam of Richland Cr. bounded E by Jno. Davidson, NW by George Lambert, SW by Thos. Carleton, SE by land that William Melton sold to Isaac Moore. s/ Joshua Willson, Lucy Willson. Wit: Tho. Carleton, Booker Jeffries. Proved 6 Feb. 1797 before John Armor, JP. Rec. 7 Feb. 1797.

Page 131.   10 Jun. 1796. Charles Burk to John Smith for $400, a Negro boy named Molida and a girl Siller, about 12 years old each. s/ Charles Burk. Wit: Robert Astin, James Nisbet, JP.

Page 131.   18 Mar. 1797. Moody Burt of SC appoint my trusty friend Aaron Neill power of attorney to conduct business in a tract of land in the possession of Elijah Cooper & David McMichael which I have obtained a Judgement for in the Superior Court of Greene Co. March Term 1797. s/ Moody Burt. Wit: James Cooper, Joseph Cook. Rec. 20 Mar. 1797.

Pages 132-133.   7 Aug. 1793. William Milton of Greene Co. to John Davidson of same for £45, 164 a. on Beaverdam of Richland Cr. granted to Leonard Benfo____(?), bounded N by James Daniell, W by Joshua Willsin, S by James Shackleford, E by Robert Porter. s/ Wm. Mitin. Wit: Robert Mitin, Josiah Allin. Proved by Robert Miten 14 Mar. 1797 before A. Grisham, JP. Rec. 14 Mar. 1797.

Pages 133-134.   10 Sep. 1796. Davis Gresham of Greene Co. to Archerbald Gresham of same for $400, 212 a. on waters of the Oconey R., beginning on said Gresham's spring branch, to lines of Karr, Pannell, Flanikin. s/ Davis Gresham. Wit: James Ware, Wm. Greer, JP. Rec. 16 Mar. 1797.

Page 135.   15 Apr. 1795. William Daniell of Greene Co. to George Rentfrow of same for £3, 19½ a. on waters of Beaverdam of Richland Cr. adj. Meadors & said Daniell. s/ Wm. Daniell. Wit: John Heard, Saml. Holloway. Ack. 7 Apr. 1797 before Wm. Grier A.J., Tho. Carleton. Rec. 8 Apr. 1797.

Pages 136-137.   14 Sep. 1796. Ezekiel Offutt of Warren Co. to Shadrack Rozer of Louisville, GA for £10 GA money, 382 a. bounded NW by William Thomas, NE by Barnard Heard, SW by John Kendall. s/ Ezekiel Offutt. Wit: John Mourland, Clayburn Rozer. Proved by Clayburn Rozer 9 Nov. 1796 before John Barron, JP in Jefferson Co. Rec. 16 Jun. 1797.

Pages 137-138.   21 Nov. 1796. Shadrach Rozer of Louisville, Jefferson

Co., to John Mapp of Hancock Co. for $300, 303 a. bounded by William Thompson, Barney Heard, Hogg, Kinmons. (See preceding deed). s/ Shadrack Rozer. Wit: John Wilkinson, Tho. Hill, Hack Walker. Sworn before Isaac McClendon, JP. Rec. 16 Jun. 1797.

Page 139.   10 Nov. 1796. William Fitzpatrick & Joseph Fitzpatrick of Greene Co. to Moses Herring of same for Ł100, 121 a. on waters of Fishing Cr. adj. Lewis Jinkins, Davis Gresham & Joseph Fitzpatrick. s/ Wm. Fitzpatrick, Jos. Fitzpatrick. Wit: Davis Gresham, JP, Augustin Harris. Rec. 19 Jun. 1797. (Plat is drawn).

Pages 140-141.   27 Nov. 1795. Rene Fitzpatrick of Greene Co. to Joseph Hubbard of NC for Ł25, 100 a. adj. Thomas Houghton on a branch that John Reid built his Cabbin on, to a dividing line for part of said tract sold unto Saml. Parker; orig. granted to William Smith for 200 acres. s/ Rene Fitzpatrick. Wit: Saml. Holloway, Isham Holloway, Tho. Carlton. Proved by Tho. Carlton before A. Porter, JP. Rec. 19 Jun. 1797.

Pages 141-142.   7 Feb. 1797. John Armor of Greene Co. to Joseph Hubburd of same for $300, 100 a. on Beaverdam fork of Richland Cr. s/ John Armor. Wit: Humphrey Gilmore, Joseph Jones, Davis Gresham, JP. Rec. 19 Jun. 1797.

Pages 143-144.   14 Mar. 1797. Rene Fitzpatrick of Greene Co. to Samuel Parker of same for $130, 100 a. on waters of Beaverdam fork of Richland Cr. adj. lines of Daniell, Thomas Houghton, the branch that John Reed built his cabbin on; orig. gr. to William Smith for 200 acres. s/ Rene Fitzpatrick. Wit: Moses Parker, John Armor, JP. Rec. 11 Jan. 1798.

Page 145.   16 Jan. 1798. I do hereby disannull & revoke all Power of Attorney by me made unto Aaron Neel. s/ Moody Burt. Wit: Tho. Carleton, Clk.

Page 145.   18 Jan. 1798. Thomas Hyde of Greene Co. appoint George Craighead Esqr., atty. at Law in Lunenburg Co. VA my attorney in fact for the purpose of claiming on my behalf & in my name as guardian for the person & property of Robert Hyde & Elizabeth Hyde, orphans of James Hyde dec'd., all the monies due me and them from Robert Hyde of NC. s/ Thomas Hyde. Wit: Jno. Armor, JP, Jno. Harrison. Ack. by Thomas Hyde 18 Jan. 1798. Rec. 18 Jan. 1798.

Pages 146-147.   3 Feb. 1796. Joseph Harris of Greene Co. to Wiley Bozman of same for $500, 200 a. adj. Gaither, Gilbert Cribs. s/ Joseph Harris. Wit: Tho. Carleton. Proved by Carleton 27 Jan. 1798 before John Armor, JP. Rec. 27 Jan. 1798.

Pages 148-149.   21 Feb. 1798. Henry Chambers of Greene Co. to William Slaughter of same for $232, 58 a. on Richland Cr., part of a tract formerly granted to Fredrick Rennolds 17 Aug. 1785; bounded W by Chambers, S by Kimbrough. s/ Henry Chambers. Wit: John Slaughter, Wm. Hill, Tho. Snow, Isaac McClendon, JP.

Pages 149-150.   1 Feb. 1798. Henry Chambers of Greene Co. to John Kimbrough of same for $54, 13 6/10 a. on waters of Richland Cr., formerly granted to Frederick Runnells 17 Aug. 1785; bounded W by Chambers, N by Jones, E by Kimbrough. s/ Henry Chambers. Wit: John Slaughter, Wm. Hill, Tho. Snow, Isaac McClendon. Rec. 15 Mar. 1798.

Pages 151-152.   22 Apr. 1797. William Kimbrough Senr. & Mary his wife of Greene Co. to John Kimbrough of same for $50, 39 6/10 a. s/ William (W) Kimbrough, Mary (M) Kimbrough. Wit: Wm. Slaughter, John McMichael, Isaac McClendon, JP. Rec. 15 Mar. 1798.

Pages 152-153.   22 Apr. 1797. William Kimbrough Jr. & Rebecca his wife of Greene Co. to John Kimbrough of same for $50, 41 a. adj. said John Kimbrough. s/ Wm. Kimbrough, Rebeckah (X) Kimbrough. Wit: Wiliam Slaughter, John McMichael, Isaac McClendon, JP. Rec. 15 Mar. 1798.

Pages 154-155.   29 Jun. 1796.   Joshua Houghton & Nancy his wife of
            Greene Co. to Jesse Heard of same for $400, 97 a. on the
Beaverdam Creek.   s/ Joshua Houghton, Nancy Houghton.   Wit: Saml. Holloway, John Heard, John Armor, JP.

Pages 155-157.   29 Jan. 1798.   Medy Bozman of Greene Co. to John Ellis
            of same for $500, 200 a. adj. Gaither's corner, the
creek, Gilbert Cribs.   s/ Medy Bozman.   Wit: Tho. Carleton, Tho. Ellis.
Proved by Tho. Carleton 5 Feb. 1798 before Chs. Cessna, JP.   (Note:
There is no page 156.)

Pages 158-159.   29 Jun. 1796.   Joshua Houghton & Nancy his wife of
            Greene Co. to John Heard of same for $400, 71 a. on
Beaverdam of Richland Cr.   s/ Joshua Houghton, Nancy Houghton.   Wit:
Saml. Holloway, Jesse Heard, Jas. Nisbet, JP.   Rec. 19 Mar. 1798.

Pages 159-160.   Deed that was recorded on pages 154-155 and marked out.

Pages 161-162.   23 Aug. 1796.   William Melton of Greene Co. to John
            Heard of same for $200, 500 a. in Franklin Co. on Wolf
Cr.; part of a tract containing 920 a. first granted to Lewis Bullard 13
Oct. 1785.   s/ Wm. Melton.   Wit: Skelton Standifer, Eliz. (X) Standifer.
Proved by Skelton Standifer before Thos. Carleton, Clk.   Rec. 10 Jan.
1798.

Pages 163-164.   30 Jun. 1798.   William Fitzpatrick & Richd. Bradley to
            Miles Beavers, all of Greene Co. for $300, 230 a. adj.
lands of Ellison, Mathews & Moreland, on the waters of Ellison's Cr. in
the reserve fork of Oconee and Appalachee.   s/ Wm. Fitzpatrick, Rd.
Bradley.   Wit: Isaac Stewart, Robert Stewart.   Proved by Robert Stewart
12 Jul. 1798 before A. Gresham, JP.   Rec. 12 July 1798.   Tho. Carleton,
Clk.

Pages 164-165.   30 Jan. 1796.   Abram Heard, tax collector of Greene Co.
            to Skelton Standifer of same; whereon A. Heard on 4 May
last posted notification of sale of property of John Ross, cont. 100 a.
in Oglethorpe Co., formerly Greene, on waters of Big Creek adj. Alexr.
Reed & others; the said Standifer was highest bidder at Ł3.14.0.   s/ A.
Heard, T.C.G.C.   Wit: Wm. Cochran, John Armor, JP.   Rec. 10 Jun. 1798.

Page 166.   29 Jun. 1796.   Joshua Houghton & Nancy his wife of Greene
            Co. to Samuel Holloway of same for Ł50 GA money, 83 a. on
waters of Beaverdam Creek.   s/ Joshua Houghton, Nancy Houghton.   Wit:
John Heard, Jesse Heard, John Armor, JP.   Rec. 11 Oct. 1798.

Page 167.   25 May 1795.   David Adams and Betsey his wife of Hancock
            Co. to John Chappell of said county for Ł20, 116½ acres on
waters of Richland Cr. bounded N & W by Kimbrough, S by Spradling & E
by Thompson.   s/ David Adams, Betsey (X) Adams.   Wit: Robt. Hill, Jonath.
Adams, James Adams, JP.   Rec. 15 Sep. 1798.

Page 168.   1 Dec. 1784.   John McGill of Ninety Six Dist. SC to George
            Dardin of Wilkes Co. GA, Bond of Ł500 sterling to make
good and lawful right to a Bounty Warrant sold by said McGill to Dardin.
s/ John (R) McGill.   Wit: F. R. Le Roy (?) Duerrgual (?).   6 Jun 1785,
Bond assigned by Geo. Dardin to Wm. Tombs.   s/ Geo. Dardin.   Wit: Alexr.
Brown, Benj. Catchins.   Rec. 13 Nov. 1798.

Page 169.   12 Nov. 1798.   William Cribs of Jackson Co. to Thomas
            Elliss of Greene, for $200, 70 a. on one of the Beaverdams
of Richland Cr. adj. lines of Leonard Burford, Smith, and the upper part
of the tract that John Elliss purchased of Mede (?) Bozman and being the
land that the said <u>Thos</u>. Elliss now lives on.   s/ Wm. Cribs.   Wit: Tho.
Hyde, Tho. Carleton, JP.   Rec. 23 Dec. 1798.

Page 170.   16(?) Mar. 1799.   Joseph Phillips of Greene Co. to Adam
            Carson for $350, a Negro girl named Hanah, age 20, healthy
and sound.   s/ Jos. Phillips.   Wit: Js. Coleman, Wm. Greer, A. J.
Rec. 18 Mar. 1799.

Page 171.   1 Apr. 1799.   Richard Parker Senr. of Greene Co. to my son
                Richard Parker Junr., for love and affection and $10, four
Negroes Cader, Judah, James & Jency; also one tract of land which I now
live on, 516 a. on Powells Cr., part in Greene Co. and part in Hancock
Co. adj. land of John Cain, James Alford & John Johnston; together with
the dwelling house thereon, the furniture contained therein, also the
stock and mark of all kinds together with my substance of every kind not
parted from to my other children before this date. s/ Richd. Parker.
Wit: Reubin Slaughter, Jno. C. Mason, Tho. Baldwin, JP. Rec. 6 Apr.
1799.

Page 172.   17 Apr. 1799.   I, George W. Foster of Greene Co., appoint
                William A. Whitlock of Virginia my lawful attorney to ask
demand receipt from Burwell Jackson of Kentucky for 100 acres, the one
half of a Bounty Warrant delivered to said Jackson for 200 acres which
said B. Jackson was to survey and carry through the different offices
for the one half. I authorize my attorney to make use of all lawful
means to obtain the same, and to sell the land. s/ Geo. W. Foster. Wit:
John Armor, JP. Rec. 22 Apr. 1799.

Page 173.   20 Apr. 1799.   John Powers Senr. do freely grant and give
                to my son John Powers, one Negro fellow named Sam. s/ John
Powers Senr. Wit: William Powers. "N.B. Please to have these few lines
recorded in your office." s/ John Powers Senr. Proved by Wm. Powers 20
May 1799. Rec. 20 May 1799.

Page 173.   22 Dec. 1797.   I have this day sold and delivered to
                Isaac McClendon Esq. one Negro woman named Edy and her two
children Lucy & Jinney. s/ Tho. Carleton. Wit: Davis Harrison. Rec.
14 Jun. 1799.

Page 174.   6 Jul. 1799.   Elizabeth Melton of Greene Co. to my daughter
                Elizabeth Melton of same for love and good will, a Negro
woman named Amelia now in Nansemond Co., VA, and in the possession of
Josiah Reddick of same county, being the Negro that my father Abraham
Spencer (?) gave me some years ago before my marriage with Thos. Holloway now deceased, & willed by the said Holloway to me. s/ Elizabeth
Melton. Ack. same day before A. Gresham, JP, and Jos. Armor, JP. Rec.
8 Jul. 1799.

Page 175.   21 Jul. 1799.   Received of Burkit Deane $430 in full pay-
                ment for a man slave named Archer. s/ Henry Carleton, John
Cox, Ellison Ellis. Wit: William Tillmon, Tho. Castelen Jr. (?). Rec.
23 Jul. 1799.

Page 175.   Joseph Peeple's mark is a Crop in the left ear and a slit
                in the right ear. Rec. 9 Jul. 1800.

Pages 176-177. 1 Jan. 1791. Thomas Daniell & Sarah his wife of Greene
                Co. to William Daniell of same for Ł50 Specie, 295 a. on
Richland Cr. adj. Wheeler, lands surveyed by Nicholas Long, Dennis' old
survey. Daniel Burford's line. Part of two grants, one to Wm. Baldwin
for 287½ a., and one to Thomas Daniell aforesaid for 36 a. adj. the first
grant mentioned. s/ Thomas Daniell, Sarah ( ) Daniell. Wit: Chs.
Daniell, Betsey Daniell.

Pages 178-179. 30 Jan. 1792. Robert Smith of Washington Co. to William
                Daniell of Greene for Ł25, 100 a. on S Fork of Ogechee,
beginning on Alexander's line where it crosses the said fork, to Wheat-
ley's line, to Glenn's fence. Part of a tract of 500 a. granted to John
Oneal 18 Jan. 1786. s/ Robert Smith. Wit: Richd. C. Roysten, Elijah
Wyatt. Proved by Elijah Wyatt 27 Jun. 1795 before Samul. Thornton, JP.
Rec. 23 Dec. 1799.

Pages 180-181. 27 Mar. 1797. Headed Greene Co. Robert Melton to Nathan
                Jones for $600, 145 a. on the Beaverdam Fork of Richland
Cr. adj. lines of Ramsey, Kennedy, John Robernett. s/ Robt. Melton,
Eliz. (X) Melton. Wit: Fields Kennedy, Dorothy (X) Reynolds. Proved by
Fields Kennedy 6 Jan. 1800 before Tho. Carleton, Clk. Rec. 6 Jan. 1800.

Page 182.   29 Dec. 1798.   Davis Gresham as agent of the University, of Greene Co. to Nathan Jones of same for $200, lot #12 in the town of Greenesborough, 180 ft. in length and 120 ft. in breadth, being the lot where Mordecai Baldwin now resides.   s/ Davis Gresham. Wit: Jno. Armor, JP.   Rec. 4 Jan. 1800.

Pages 183-184.   13 Aug. 1798.   John Nisbet of Iredell Co. NC to James Nisbet of Greene Co. GA for $1,000, 300 a. on N fork Ogechee River bounded N by Henry Hunt and all other sides vacant at time of survey, formerly Wilkes Co. now Greene, granted to Zachariah Phillips 15 Dec. 1784.   s/ John Nisbet.   Wit: Jesse McKinne Pope, Chrisr. Houston. Proved by Houston 20 Dec. 1799, before Wm. Greer, JP.   Rec. 3 Mar. 1800.

Pages 185-186.   18 Jan. 1800.   John Whitlock to my niece Sarah M. Whit-lock daughter of my brother Josiah Whitlock, for $5.00 and real love and affection, a Negro girl named Tiller, already in her possession.   To Mary Whitlock, dau. of said Josiah Whitlock, a Negro girl named Phillis; if Mary dies without heirs, Phillis is to go to Mary's brothers and sisters.   Also $5.00 and a Negro woman named Sall and her son Abraham to the rest of Josiah Whitlock's children, and also all the personal property that my said brother is now possessed with at his and his wife's death, but should his wife Mary Whitlock be the long-est liver and marry again then the aforementioned property to be divided among the living children except Sarah and Mary.   I bind myself and heirs in the penalty of Ten (?) thousand dollars not to revoke this my deed of gift as I have received full satisfaction for the forementioned property and do this day put the said property in the full possession of said Josiash Whitlock.   s/ John Whitlock.   Wit: Hen. Carleton, George W. Foster, James Johnston.   Proved by Foster & Johnston 21 Jan. 1800 before A. Gresham, JP.   Recorded same day.

Page 187.   12 Apr. 1799.   Robert Melton of Greene Co. to Alexander Hall of same for $400, a Negro woman and child named Lucy & Jane, sound and healthy.   s/ Robt. Melton.   Wit: Hugh Hall.   Rec. 9 Jan. 1800.

Pages 187-188.   25 Nov. 1799.   Ambrose Edwards & William Edwards of Greene Co. to Alexr. Hall of same for $350, a Negro boy named King, about 12 years old, sound and healthy.   s/ Ambrose (X) Edwards, Wm. Edwards.   Wit: Malachi Stalling.   Rec. 9 Jan. 1800.

Pages 188-189.   27 Mar. 1799.   Mark Phillips of Greene Co. to Demcy Hood of same for (no consideration given), 185 a. in the re-served land between the Oconee and Appalachee, on the Appalachee River. s/ Mark (P) Phillips.   Wit: Obediah Mayfield, Bartley Morland.   Proved by Obediah Mayfield 6 Nov. 1799 before Curtis Welborn, JP.   Rec. 10 Mar. 1800.

Pages 190-191.   -- --- 1800.   Richard Asbury & Elizabeth his wife to Simon Morris of Greene Co. for $850, 230 a. adj. lines of Wilborn, Greene, a branch, and Daniell.   s/ Richd. Asbury, Eliz. Asbury.   Wit: Hen. Carleton, Edmd. Daniell, Redmon Thornton, JP.   Rec. 10 Mar. 1800.

Pages 191-192.   12 Nov. 1799.   Lucy Whatley of Greene Co. to Redmon Thornton of same for $140, 70 a. on the S fork of Little River, adj. Hunt, Thornton, & Fluker.   s/ Lucy Whatley.   Wit: Wm. Gibony, Saml. Cunningham Jr. (?), O. Porter, JP.   Rec. 10 Mar. 1800.

Pages 193-194.   3 Feb. 1800.   Alexr. Reddock, adm. of estate of William Reddock Senr. late of Hancock Co., deceased, to Richard Vandeford of Jackson Co.; whereas the said William Reddock Senr. having in his lifetime sold a tract of land herein described but having depart-ed this life before making lawful title, the Court has ordered the title be made to Richd. Vandeford agreeable to the tenor of a bond given by the said Intestate to the said Vandeford.   For the sum of $1,000, do sell 200 a. adj. land bounded S by John Lynn, all other sides vacant at time of survey, granted to said Wm. Reddock dec'd., on Beaverdam Creek. s/ Alexr. Reddock.   Wit: Thomas ( ) Bonner, Hirum ( ) Moore.

Page 195.   13 Nov. 1799.   Mary Williams of Greene Co. for the good
             will and esteem which I have for my loving children Marga-
ret Williams, Patsey Williams & John Williams of the county aforesaid,
three Negro slaves named Tom, Grace & Jobe her child. The said Negroes
to continue in the possession of Mary Williams during her natural life,
then to be divided equally. s/ Mary (X) Williams. Wit: Saml. Harper,
JP. Rec. 17 Mar. 1800.

Page 196.   24 Dec. 1798.   Wm. Daniell & Mary Kemp Daniell his wife to
             Saml. Parker for $20, 37½ a. on waters of Beaverdam of
Richland Cr. adj. Doctor Nisbet, Jonas Meder, Humphrey Gilmore, said
Parker. s/ Wm. Daniell, Mary K. Daniell. Wit: Humphrey Gilmore, Reuben
Edwards. Proved by Gilmore 11 Mar. 1800 before Tho. Carleton, Clk. Rec.
same day.

Pages 197-198.   14 Mar. 1798.   John Robernett of Greene Co. to Nathan
             Jones of same for $28, 9½ a. & 2 chains on waters of
Beaverdam of Richland Cr. adj. said Jones and the fork of Beaverdam;
part of a tract of 487½ a. formerly granted to Wm. Evans 27 Jun. 1786
and conveyed to said Robernett. s/ John Robernett. Wit: Tho. Carleton,
Clk. & JP, Exof., Charles Daniell. (Plat included). Rec. 5 Jan. 1800.

Page 199.   3 Feb. 1798.   I, Joseph Hubbard of Greene Co. am firmly
             bound to my sons Saml. Hubbard & Davis Hubbard of same, in
the sum of $500. If the said Joseph Hubbard do give his said sons free
and peaceable possession of 100 a. of land and building whereon he now
lives, the whole tract to be to them and no other so long as the said
Joseph Hubbard lives. s/ Joseph Hubbard. Wit: Jno. Armour, Hum. Gilmore.
Proved by Jno. Armour 22 Apr. 1800 before Tho. Carleton, Clk. Rec. same
day.

Pages 200-201.   16 Feb. 1798.   John Lester (Lister?) of Greene Co. to
             Joseph Jackson of same for $93, 62 a. on the waters of
the Big Beaverdam, part of a survey the said Jno. Lester now lives on
that was granted to Jno. Cessna. s/ Jno. Lister. Wit: Daniel Beauchamp,
Abner Biddle. Proved by Beauchamp 21 Apr. 1800 before Tho. Carleton,
Clk. Rec. same day. (Plat included.)

Pages 202-203.   4 Jun. 1796.   John Dunn of Greene Co. to Joseph Jackson
             of same for $40, 31½ a. on waters of Big Beaverdam bound-
ed E by the said Jackson and W by the said Dunn. s/ John Dunn. Wit:
Jno. (?) Lister, Geo. Lister. Proved by Geo. Lister 21 Apr. 1800 before
Tho. Carleton, Clk. Rec. same day.

Pages 204-205.   26 Sep. 1794 (?).   Thomas Cribs of Greene Co. to Joseph
             Jackson of same for ₤200 GA money, 373 a. bounded SE by
John Dunn, S by Moses Shelbey, E by Charles Cessna, NE by Harrison (?), E
by Gideon Harrison, SE by Johnson N by Johnson, SW by John Dunn. s/
Thos. ( ) Cribs. Wit: Tho. Carleton, Gilbert Cribs, John Dunn, John
Bidell. Proved by Tho. Carleton 21 Apr. 1800 before Jo. Phillips, JP.
Rec. 21 Apr. 1800.

Pages 205-206.   8 May 1800.   Andrew Borland of Hancock Co. to Jacob Butts
             of Greene for $2,000, 633 a. beginning at Phillips' stake
corner on the Appalachee. s/ Andrew Borland. Wit: Jno. Wm. Devereux,
JP, Leon Abercrombie. Rec. 13 May 1800.

Page 207.   29 Nov. 1799.   Wm. Greer, Surveyor of Greene Co., certifies
             that he resurveyed a tract of land for Jacob Butts on the
Appalatchee River orig. granted to Andw. Borland for 412 a. but on re-
survey find it to contain 633 acres. s/ Wm. Greer, S.G.C. Chain Carriers:
John Thompson, Willis Newton. (Plat shows the land adjoins Wilborn. Also
lists name of Arthur Foster). Rec. 13 May 1800.

Page 208.   19 Aug. 1799.   John Sorrill of Greene Co. to Ellis West for
             $330, a Negro girl named Lucy. s/ John Sorrill. Wit: Wm.
Browning, JP, Douglas Watson. Rec. 11 Jun. 1800.

Page 207.   20 Aug. 1799.   Ellis West of Greene Co. to my sister Eliza-
             beth Clements for natural love and affection, a Negro girl

231

named Lucy. At Elizabeth's death, Lucy to be apportioned to Elizabeth's
children. s/ Ellis West. Wit: J. Clower, Wm. Browning, JP. Rec. 11
Jun. 1800.

Page 208.   Headed Greenesborough, 23 May 1799. Rec'd. of Ellis West
               $220 for a Negro boy Harry about 8 years old. s/ Wm.
Ballard. Wit: Jno. Cox (?), Danl. Sanford. Proved by Danl. Sanford 10
Jun. 1800 before Wm. Browning, JP. Rec. 11 Jun. 1800.

Page 210.   -- --- 1800. Richd. Asbury & Elizabeth his wife to Thomas
               Lyne of Greene Co. for $800, 200 a. on Sherrill's Cr. adj.
Tuggle & Danniell. s/ Richd. Asbury, Betsy Asbury. Wit: Hen. Carleton,
Edmd. Daniell. Ack. before Redmond Thornton, JP, 22 Feb. 1800. Rec. 10
Jun. 1800.

Pages 211-212. 13 Jul. 1799. Robert Beavers of Greene Co. to Skelton
                Standefer of same for $190, 133½ a. on waters of South
Fork of Little River, bounded NW by Joshua Martin, SW by Wm. Richards, E
by Joel Newsome. s/ Robert Beavers, Jane Beavers. Wit: Henry English,
JP, Wm. Greer, JP. Rec. 11 Jun. 1800.

Pages 212-213. 26 Jun. 1800. Benj. Fitzpatrick of Greene Co. GA appoint
                Patrick Nappier of Fluvannah Co., VA my lawful atty. to
make good title in my name to 200 a. in Fluvannah Co. on the headwaters
of Cary Creek adj. lands of Ben. Woodson, Hezekiah Stone, John Manley &
Dunkin McLauchlin (?). s/ Bena. Fitzpatrick. Ack. before Alexr. King,
JP, Tho. Crawford, JP. Rec. 26 Jun. 1800.

Pages 213-214. 5 Jul. 1800. James Cooper of Greene Co. to Henry Sanford
                of same for $78.62½, part of lot #13 in Greensborough, it
being that part whereon his house now stands adj. Wm. Houghton, being 22
ft. on Main St. and 26 ft. back. s/James Cooper. Wit: Jmgm. (?) Monnox
(?) (Monroe?), O. Porter, JP. Betsey Cooper, wife of James. rel. dower
same day. s/ Betsey Cooper. Rec. 5 Jul. 1800.

Pages 215-216. 9 Apr. 1799. William Fitzpatrick to John Hood, both of
                Greene Co. for $200, 100 a. in the Reserve Fork adj.
Buchannan, Collins & Walker. s/ W. FPatrick. Wit: Wyley Martin, Jos.
Jno. (?) Martin, Joshua Hogatha (?). Proved by Wyley Martin 9 Nov. 1799
before Jno. Sims (?), JP. Rec. 24 Jul. 1800.

Page 217.   5 Aug. 1799. Aaron Livingston of Greene Co. to John Reid
               of same for $300, 162 a. on the waters of the South Fork
of Ogeechee, being the upper part of a survey of 500 a. granted to Isaac
Jackson. s/ Aaron (X) Livingston. No witnesses.

Pages 218-219. 24 Mar. 1799. Robert Barnes of Hancock Co. and William
                Caldwell of Greene to David Davis of the county last
mentioned, for $200, 143 3/4 acres on waters of Shoulderbone Creek, where
the said Davis now lives, bounded W by James Davis dec'd., S by Journickin (?), E by Jerry (?) Baker, N by Moore, the road that leads from
Greenesborough by Chamber's mill on Shoulderbone. s/ Robt. Burns, Wm.
Caldwell. Wit: John Davis, James Burns. Proved by John Davis 5 Jul 1800
before James McDonald, JP.

Pages 219-221. 4 Jul. 1800. William Shaw of Greene Co. to Thomas Adams
                of same for $400, 190 a. on waters of Beaverdam of Rich-
land Cr. adj. James W. Daniel & Nott Whaley, Phillips, Gilbert Shaw. s/
Wm. Shaw. Ack. before Tho. Carleton, Clk. Rec. 4 Jul. 1800.

Pages 221-223. 19 Feb. 1798. Lodowick Tuggle of Ogle. Co. to Thomas
                Tuggle of the county afsd. for ₤75, 162 a. in Ogle. Co.
on the South Fork of Little River adj. Wilkerson, crossing the river.
s/ Lodowick Tuggle. Wit: Robt. Tuggle, Sally (X) Tuggle, Eunice (X).
Proved by Robert Tuggle & Eunice Tuggle, who also saw Miss Sally Tuggle
sign, 23 Oct. 179- before DF (?) Roberts, JP. Rec. 16 Aug. 1800.

Page 223.   22 June 1792. Received of James Stean 19 Shillings 3
               pence in full of all accompts due debts and demands from
the beginning of the world to this day...s/ Ramond (X) (no last name).

Rec. 25 Sep. 1800.

Page 223.   8 Nov. 1793. Received of James Stean the just sum of 20
               pounds, 19 shillings & 4 pence for my part of my father
Christopher Stean's estate and 20 pounds for my part of my Father's land
in full of all demands due. s/ Levan (?) (X) Stean. "Witness to the
assignment Coss." Rec. 25 Sep. 1800.

Pages 224-225. 9 Sep. 1800. Andrew Burnes of the town of Louisville to
               William Hightower of Greene Co. for $500, 287½ a. on
waters of Shoulderbone Cr. bounded SE by Wm. Hightower, E by Wyatt, W
by Reuben Smith, NW by James Legett. s/ (unreadable signature.) Wit:
D. Davis, Keeth Rutledge. Ack. before Robert Grier, JP, 9 Sep. 1800.
Rec. 10 Sep. 1800.

Page 226.   20 Mar. 1800. John Jinkins of Greene Co. to Abel Hargerty
               of same for $130, 50 a. on the waters of Greenbrier in the
fork of the Oconee & Appalachee Rivers adj. Matthews line. s/ John (X)
Jenkins. Wit: Benja. Sims, John Sims, JP. Rec. 10 Sep. 1800.

Pages 227-228. Headed Lincoln Co. 21 Oct. 1800. Ann Bennett, John Ben-
               nett, Jacob Bennett, William Bennett, Tho. Howard &
Joseph Harriss, all of Lincoln Co., heirs and representatives of John
Bennett, dec'd., to Henry Carleton of Greene for $60, all that tract or
bounty of land, 230 a. in the fork of Oconee and Appalatchee, which said
bountyland was surveyed 5 Jul. 1784 by Reuben DeJernett Esq., deputy
surveyor for Francis Tennelle Esq. on a Continental Warrant in the name
of the heirs of Clement Nash, Joseph Landan (?) and unknown land. Signed by above names. Wit: Wm. Dowsing, JP, William Kelly (?). Rec. 23
Oct. 1800.

Page 228.   Charles Williams' mark is a crop and two slits in the right
               ear & a half moon under the left. Rec. 12 Mar. 1800.

Page 229. 6 Dec. 1800. Henry Carleton of Greene Co. to Samuel Henderson
               of same for $170, 7 acres whereon he now lives lying in
the Reserve fork of the Oconee and Applachee adj. Abel Hagarty's line
where it crosses the main road. Matthew's line, up a branch. s/ Henry
Carleton. Wit: Jno. Houghton. Rec. 6 Dec. 1800.

Pages 230-231. 6 Dec. 1800. Henry Carleton of Greene Co. to Wiliam
               Heagerty of same for $350, 140 a. in the Reserve fork of
the Oconee and Appalachee rivers adj. land of Butler, Gilliam, Stovall,
Henderson, the main road. s/ Henry Carleton. Wit: James H. Nickolson,
Tho. Carleton, Clk. Rec. 6 Dec. 1800.

Pages 231-232. 23 Apr. 1800. Duncan Cameron & Molly his wife of Ogle.
               Co. to James Turner of Greene for $1590, 318 a. on the
SW side of the Oconee River, beginning on the bank of the river, and adj.
lands of Thrasher Fambrer & Robert Thompson. s/ Duncan ( ) Cameron,
Molly (X) Cameron. Wit: Robert Sorrill, Greene Sorrill, Anderson (X)
Fambrough, Richd. Copelin, JP. Rec. 12 Sep. 1800.

Page 233. 4 Dec. 1798. Hiram Holt, Sheriff of Hancock Co. to John Mc-
               Michael of Greene; whereas an Execution issued against the
property of Robert Middleton & William Owsley in favor of John McKinzey
and the same being levied on a bounty of land of 287½ acres as the property of said Middleton & Owsley, on the waters of Richland Cr., granted
to George Wyche, was purchased at public sale by said McMichael for $25.
s/ Hines Holt. Wit: Chs. Abercrombie, A. Comer, J.I.C. Rec. 10 Aug.
1800.

Page 234.   18 Jan. 1799. Sary Murphy, for divers good causes, to
               Elizabeth Murphy, 1 cow and feather bed & furniture. To
Bartholomew Murphy one cow and calf. s/ Sally (+) Murphey. Wit: Jos.
White, Little B. Gresham, JP. Rec. 23 Jan. 1801.

Pages 235-236. 10 Feb. 1801. Margarett Allan, widow of Greene Co. to
               Willm. & Jane Allan, son & daughter to said Margarett,
for natural love and affection and for their better maintenance, all the

right, title and interest in land that said Margaret may be entitled to
by the death of her husband William Allen, by dower, child's part, or
otherwise, in Franklin Co. on Curry's Creek in the reserve. s/ Margarett
(X) Allen. Wit: Saml. Harper, JP, John Strozier. Rec. 13 Feb. 1801.

Pages 236-237. 15 Sep. 1799. Davis Gresham as agent for the Trustees
of the Univ. of Georgia, to James Cooper of Greene Co.
for £8 Sterling or $34.29, lot #25 in the town of Greensborough on
Broad St., King St. and an alley, 180 ft. by 120 ft. s/ Davis Gresham.
Wit: John Harrison, Little B. Gresham, JP. Rec. 15 Feb. 1801.

Page 238. 6 Mar. 1800. Pleasant Hardwick to Jacob Kittwell (?) for
£80 VA money, a Negro girl named Rachel, about 15 years
old. s/ Pleasant Hardwick. Wit: Tho. Barnett, Wm. Spiller (?), John
Worsham. Rec. 10 Dec. 1800.

Page 238. 6 Mar. 1800. Pleasant Hardwick to Jacob Kittwell for £80
VA money, a Negro woman named Silvey about 18 years of age.
s/ Pleasant Hardwick. Wit: Thos. Barnett, John Worsham. Rec. 10 Dec.
1800.

Page 239. 6 Jan. 1801. William Allen of Greene Co. to my loving
wife Sarah Allen for love and good will, Negroes Jane,
Elisha and Amey with their increase, half of my stock of cattle, horses
and hogs with all my household furniture consisting of all my beds and
furniture, desk, four riding chair (?), reserving unto myself the use of
the property as long as I live. s/ William Allen. Wit: George Slaughter, Joseph (‡) Spradling. Rec. 14 Mar. 1801.

Pages 240-241. 10 Jan. 1800. Wm. Burford of Greene Co. to Saml. Black
of same for $108, 150 a. on waters of Beaverdam of Rich-
land Cr. adj. Barron (?), Porter & Shaw. (Plat also shows Baldwin as
adj. land.) s/ Wm. Burford. Wit: Wm. Phillips, Little B. Gresham, JP.
(Plat included.) Rec. 2 Apr. 1801.

Pages 242-243. 14 May 1801. Richard Walden of Greene Co. in consideration of the inconvience of conducting my affairs in
Halifax Co. VA, appoint my friends Lewis Walden & William Walden, residents of Halifax Co. in the fork of the Dan and Staunton Rivers, my
attys. to dispose of my two tracts of land in said county adjoining each
other near the fork of the Dan and Staunton Rivers, on the waters and
both sides of Grassey Cr. which I formerly bought of Joseph Ligon and
John Dismukes, each then of the said Co. & state. No signature. Rec.
14 May 1801.

Pages 244-245. 28 May 1797. William Baldwin of Greene Co. to John Mc-
Michael for (no consideration given), 87½ acres on waters
of Richland Cr. bounded S by Baldwin. s/ William Baldwin. Wit: Edwd.
Hawthron, Isaac McClendon, JP. Rec. 10 Aug. 1800.

Pages 246-247. 24 Mar. 1799. Robert Burns of Hancock Co. and Wm. Cald-
well of Greene, to Jane Davis & David Davis, admrs. of
estate of James Davis, dec'd., of the county last above mentioned, for
$200, 143 3/4 acres where said Jane Davis now lives on waters of Shoul-
derbone Cr. bounded N by Moore, W by Smith, SW by Jonican, E by David
Davis, the road that leads from Chambers' Mills on Shoulderbone to
Greensboro. s/ Robt. Burns, Wm. Caldwell. Wit: John Davis, James Burns.
Proved by John Davis 5 Jul. 1800 before James McDonald, JP. Rec. 10
Mar. 1801.

Page 248. 11 Feb. 1801. I do hereby warrant and defend title to a
certain Negro boy named Tom about 13 years of age which I
sold Salley Peeples for $300. s/ James Emerson. Wit: Garland Maxcey.
Rec. 5 Dec. 1801.

Page 249. 1 Jan. 1802. John Cox to Daniel Robertson for $1800, 7
Negroes: man Stafford about 18 or 19 years old, woman Cloe
and her 2 children Dilsey & Moriah, woman Dolley and her two children
Lucy and Ben. s/ John Cox. Wit: Tho. Carleton, JP Exof., Saml. Sharp.
Rec. 2 Jan. 1802.

Page 250.   4 Apr. 1797. Caty Boner of Greene Co. to Saml. Harper for
             5 shillings, five Negroes: woman Nell and her four youngest
children. s/ Cary Boner. Wit: Charles Boner. Proved by Charles Boner
16 Jan. 1802 before Tho. Carleton, JP Exof. Rec. same day.

Page 251.   14 Jan. 1802. Little Bury Bostwick and Lucy Williamson
             Bostwick his wife of Greene Co. to David Jackson of same
for $300, a female Negro slave named Hannah.   s/ Little Bury (X) Bost-
wick, Lucy W. Bostwick. Wit: N. Jernigan Jr., Nathan Bostwick. Rec. 3
Feb. 1802.

MARRIAGE RECORDS OF GREENE COUNTY, GEORGIA (1787-1875)

Aaron, Edward S. & Martha Ann Mullins - 6/25/1860 (Jas. M. Kelly)
Aaron, Geo. W. & Mary Susan Taylor - 9/6/1860
Aaron, Thos. B. & Martha J. Mitchell - 11/2/1858 (J. H. Bragg)
Abel, Wm. A. & Eliza Reid - 1/24/1839 (Jas. W. Godkin)
Abercrombie, Anderson & Sydney Grimes - 2/24/1819 (Lovick Pierce)
Acree, James M. & Sarah Smith - 12/1/1841
Adair, Robert & Babsy (?) Reid - 8/28/1800
Adair, Virgil J. & Mary F. Crawford - 3/26/1868 (Thos. P. Sanford)
Adams, John & Patsey Johnson - 3/5/1804
Adams, Wm. & Rachel Sweeney - 11/2/1820
Adams, Wm. E. & Sallie E. Copelan - 11/18/1874 (W. R. Johnson)
Aderhold, John H. P. & Anna N. Arnold - 6/5/1866 (Hart C. Peck, D. M.)
Adkins, Booker & Adaline Tuggle - 7/6/1832 (John Armstrong)
Adkins, Joseph & Mary Lanford - 10/1/1818 (Thos. Stokes)
Aikens, Wm. & Betsy Ann Grigsby - 1/25/1821 (O. Porter)
Akers, John & Rebecca Turner - 12/4/1827 (Wm. Bryan)
Akers, Samuel & Nancy Robins - 2/28/1828 (Wm. Bryan)
Akin, Edmond & Sarah Ann Veazey - 10/13/1830 (John Harris)
Akins, Elijah & Eliza Ball - 2/7/1822 (John Harris)
Akins, Henry T. & Eliza J. Daniel - 2/28/1864 (Wm. A. Overton)
Akins, James & Nancy Ivey - 3/17/1800
Akins, James & Betsey Cooper - 3/4/1818
Akins, Joseph & Mary Rea - 4/23/1818 (Lemuel Green)
Akins, Wm. A. & Elizabeth Andrews - 10/2/1836 (W. D. Murden)
Aldridge, Samuel R. & Sarah Ann Furlow - 8/27/1836 (Cobb M. Key, M.G.)
Alfriend, Benjamin & Margaret Simonton - 10/7/1837 (Jno. G. Holtzclaw)
Alfriend, Benjamin C. & Eliza J. Smith - 12/22/1863 (John W. McCrary,Mg.)
Alfriend, Edward W. & Mary E. Dunn - 1/4/1841 (F. R. Golding)
Alfriend, Wm. L. & Sarah Frances Dunn - 2/22/1842 (ditto)
Alford, Bertus & Mary Boone - 10/1/1801 (W. Stocks)
Alford, Briton & Betsey Brassel - 3/19/1805 (Thos. Crawford)
Alford, Chinchez & Deany Wooten - 1/18/1806
Albritton, Ansel M. & Evaline J. Macon - 1/20/1856 (T. D. Martin, Mg.)
Alexander, Rimardo B. & Harriett C. Dolvin - 9/12/1843 (Wesley P. Arnold)
Alexander, Joseph K. & Patience T. Alfriend - 12/19/1844 (John Howell)
Alford, Julius & Eliza Cook - 3/14/1821 (Lovick Pierce)
Alford, Lodowich & Judith Jackson - 5/16/1798
Alford, Wm. H. & Georgianna J. Mullins - 1/5/1858 (T. D. Martin, M. g.)
Alford, Zadock & Perrin Sherrill - 11/3/1814 (Evans Myrick)
Allen, Benj. W. & Martha J. Barnhart - 8/15/1860 (J. H. Kilpatrick)
Allen, Dickson E. & Nancy C. Jackson - 6/7/1859 (L. B. Caldwell)
Allen, E. M. & Eliza Catherine Part - 8/5/1847 (Francis Bowman)
Allen, James & Sultana Broadway - 8/2/1824
Allen, John & Eliza Carleton - 3/20/1805
Allen, John & Polly Jackson - 1/31/1828 (Joshua Cannon)
Allen, J. H. & Missouria A. Hooks - 12/21/1869 (L. B. Caldwell)
Allen, Josiah & Rachel Coldough - 11/18/1824
Allen, Pleasant Josiah & Martha Pyran - 6/11/1832 (Thos. W. Grimes)
Allen, Stephen & Martha Pyran - 8/14/1830
Allen, W. A. & Martha A. Jackson - 1/2/1872 (L. B. Caldwell)
Allen, Wiley & Penelope Powers - 4/19/1821 (Francis Cummins)

235

Allison, Reuben & Louisiana King - 7/7/1836 (Geo. F. Pierce)
Allison, Wm. & Martha Price - 6/4/1822 (Robert Booth)
Alliston, Wm. P. & Martha A. Walton - 4/16/1848 (Hinton Crawford)
Allred, Wm. & Jane Park - 2/13/1825 (John Webb)
Allred, Wm. & Sarah F. Rowland - 5/23/1865 (Jefferson Wright)
Alston, Willis & Eliza Howard - 12/18/1828 (Lovick Pierce)
Alvis, Ashley & Catherine McIntosh - 9/16/1825 (John Dawson)
Ammons, Richard & Rebecca Watson - 12/9/1830 (George Hall)
Amoss, George M. & Patience A. Smith - 9/2/1865
Atkinson, James C. & Theodosia Wray - 9/13/1857 (John H. M. Barton)
Atkinson, John & Sally Moreland - 3/18/1800
Atkinson, Lazarus & Elizabeth Echols - 7/11/1837 (Ephraim Bruce)
Atkinson, Nathan & Polly Parker - 5/28/1813 (Robt. Rea)
Atkinson, Nathan L. & Frances B. Slaughter - 11/28/1834
Atkinson, Thomas & Mary Merrett - 10/27/1842 (H. H. Laurence)
Atkinson, Thomas L. B. & Elizabeth A. Bagley - 3/2/1848 (Jas. B. Nickel-
son)
Aubrey, Lewis & Dinah Harris - 6/24/1802
Autrey, Jacob & Isabella McClane - 5/20/1829
Autrey, O. P. & Georgia Sanford - 1/6/1870 (Phillip Robinson)
Avery, Joseph & Mary S. Haynes - 4/9/1874 (John O'Neal)
Awtrey, John & Martha Moore - 1/20/1820 (Malachi Murden)
Awtrey, Reynolds & Martha Carr - 2/9/1820 (Jas. Brockman)
Axson, Samuel E. & Margaret J. Hoyt - 11/23/1858 (N. Hoyt, M.g.)

Babb, Wm. & Susanna Heard - 1/19/1796
Bachelor, Archibald & Lucy Ann Mallory - 12/22/1831 (Thos. W. Grimes)
Bachelor, Con. & (not shown) - 5/8/1768
Bachelor, Richard & Ella Seay - 9/14/1869 (Phillip Robinson)
Bagby, Chas. L. & Amanda M. Strange - 2/9/1865 (J. A. Preston, M.g.)
Bagby, Geo. E. R. & Georgia A. P. Bowden - 4/27/1868 (Jas. W. Godwin)
Bailey, Nathaniel & Armietta Wms - 7/22/1849 (J. F. Findley)
Bailey, Samuel Armstrong & Rebecca F. Lloyd - 5/19/1831 (Lovell Pierce)
Bailey, Simon & Faithey Parker - 12/14/1806 (B. Maddox)
Baker, Christopher & Nancy Daniel - 12/20/1805
Baker, Jonathan & Mary Stallings - 10/29/1818 (Thos. Riley)
Baker, Silas & Mary M. Walker - 12/29/1830 (S. M. Wathall)
Baker, Wm. & Nancy Wms. - 9/24/1805
Baker, Wm. & Rebkah Howell - 7/12/1807 (Jas. Holt)
Baldwin, Benj. & Catherine Watson - 1/4/1802
Baldwin, Chas. & Susannah Love - 8/22/1839 (Hinton Crawford, M.g.)
Baldwin, David & Eliza Owens - 2/3/1804
Baldwin, James & Eliza White - 3/13/1804
Baldwin, Joseph H. & Harriet E. Edmondson - 7/28/1837 (Jas. Moore)
Baldwin, Robt. & Sarah Boning - 12/22/1788
Baldwin, Samuel & Nancy Wms - 2/7/1833 (B. M. Sanders)
Baldwin, Thos. B. & Anne E. Skidmore - 2/14/1837 (Vincent Thornton)
Baldwin, Frances I. Morris - 12/10/1840 (James Jones)
Ballard, Geo. & Peggy Armour - 11/9/1801
Ballard, John & Nancy McLain - 6/8/1807 (Wm. Greer)
Ballard, Wm. & Nancy King - 9/22/1802
Barber, Richard J. & Ann Nicholson - 10/29/1840 (B. M. Saunders)
Barefield, Arthur & Sally Freeman - 10/12/1804
Barfield, Sampson & Mary Bell - 4/1/1847
Barker, James & Elizabeth Finch - 4/25/1841 (Jas. W. Godkin)
Barksdale, Green B. & Celia Connell - 10/24/1839
Barkwell, Julius & Ruth Harper - 11/20/1818 (Jack Lumpkin)
Barnes, Asa & Mary Ann Mapp - 9/27/1849 (L. C. Peek)
Barnes, Asa & Martha Mapp - 1/13/1853 (W. W. Moore)
Barnes, Joshua & Caroline Ledbetter - 11/28/1865 (H. C. Peek, O. M.)
Barnes, Samuel & Elizabeth Barnhart - 5/25/1789
Barnes, Wm. H. & Martha Ann McMillian - 8/5/1841 (R. F. Griffin)
Barnett, John & Sally Sorrell - 10/8/1802
Barnett, John & Mary Willis - 11/8/1827 (Edward Maxey)
Barnett, Wm. & Betsey Johnson - 8/29/1804
Barnhart, Bruce & Christopher Smith - 6/12/1816 (Thos. Snow)
Barnhart, Leroy & Sarah Parker - 4/15/1842 (Jas. Moore)
Barnhart, Seaborn R. & Talula E. Alford - 12/19/1875 (J. I. Dolvin)
Barnwell, Alexander & Catherine Watts - 12/28/1819 (Thos. Stocks)
Barnwell, Benj. F. & Elizabeth Ann Parrott - 7/3/1866 (P. B. Robinson)

Barnwell, Henry & Maria Powers - 1/31/1822
Barnwell, Henry & Delila Booles - 7/16/1822 (Thos. Stocks)
Barnwell, Jesse S. & Rachel Nelson(?) - 10/6/1858 (Jas. L. Tarwater)
Barr, Oliver & Margaret Freeman - 12/10/1873
Barrett, John & Luraney Lewis - 2/1/1831 (Butt? L. Cato)
Barron, Thos. & Sally Clay - 3/12/1805
Barrow, Cyrus B. & Frances E. Wms. - 4/19/1851 (Hinton Crawford)
Barry, M. M. & Lucretia Cook - 7/4/1851 (J. W. Godkin)
Bartlett, Abner & Mary Chewning - 1/22/1807 (W. McGiboney)
Barton, Thompson & Sarah Daniel - 11/18/1860 (J. W. Godkin)
Bass, James A. & Caroline McMillian - 2/21/1849 (L. B. Jackson)
Batchelor, Jesse & Sarah A. Grant - 12/11/1856 (Jas. L. Lawrence)
Bates, Robert & Patsey Campbell - 7/13/1821 (John Harris)
Bates, John & Elizabeth Alford - 11/26/1818 (Thos. Snow)
Bates, Nathaniel & Nancy Channell - 4/2/1827 (Absolem Baugh)
Bates, Wm. & Nancy Parker - 11/4/1827 (John Harris)
Battle, John & Elizabeth Atkinson - 12/22/1819 (Francis West)
Bauchcum, Aaron & Mary Camp - 10/9/1864 (Wm. G. Chapman, M.G.)
Baugh, Abram & Rietley Colley? - 7/18/1852 (B. Rowland)
Baugh, Jas. E. & Ada R. Smith - 5/9/1865
Baugh, Richard Henry & Marcaline A. Gresham - 5/12/1858 (F.F. Reynold)
Baughcum, Aaron & Martha Holder - 3/22/1866 (Ezekiel L. Wms.)
Baughcum, Pinckney & Susan Jane Connel - 11/17/1864 (Wm. H. Chapman, M.G.)
Baughcum, W. W. & Anna Clifton - 12/20/1871
Baxley, Aaron & Nancy Howell - 1/4/1805
Baxter, Wm. & Sarah E. Oslin? - 1/5/1847 (H. H. Lawrence)
Baynon, Watkins & Ann Barnett - 1/10/1825
Bays, Joseph & Edith Broadaway - 7/27/1823 (Nicholas Lewis)
Bearden, Richard & Elizabeth Patrick - 10/31/1829
Bearding, Arthur & Rebekah McClendon - 12/13/1795
Beards, Washington & Nancy Phillips - 12/28/1808 (Thos. Crawford)
Beasley, Hiram & Lewanse Duberry - 2/1/1851
Beasley, Wm. & Nancy English - 6/5/1805
Beasley, Wm. & Mary Forrester - 12/4/1845 (E. S. Hunter)
Beasley, Wm. & Rachel Robinitte - 9/23/1794
Beasley, ----- & Anna Watson - 1801
Beatie, John & Anna Todd - 12/22/1822 (Lovick Pierce)
Beavers, Daniel & Nancy Pursy - 11/19/1799
Beavers, Nathan & Sally Blurton - 4/3/1805
Beck, T. J. & Mary L. King - 12/16/1869 (H. H. Tucker)
Beckom, John & Ruth Biddle - 1/11/1816 (Archibald Watts)
Bedell, John & Susan Perdee - 3/18/1828 (R. L. Dickinson)
Bedell, Micajah & Ann Smith - 10/14/1831 (Vincent R. Thornton)
Beeman, Henry & Carolyn Myrick - 2/15/1823 (Nathan Beeman, M.G.)
Beeman, Samuel H. & Frances Julia Ann Cone - 1/25/1831 (T. W. Grimes)
Begnon?, Cassmere J. & Mary Z. Johnson - 3/16/1871 (Philip Robinson)
Beland, James & Easter McElroy - 2/2/1806
Bell, A. H. & Missouri Stephen - 12/23/1873 (W. A. Partee)
Bell, James & Sophia Woodham - 1/28/1812 (Robert Rea)
Bell, James & Virginia Ward - 9/18/1859 (R. B. Kelly)
Bell, Jarard & Rody Smith - 12/9/1811 (W. Johnson)
Bell, John & Mary Beasley - 3/1839 (John Harris, M. G.)
Bell, Kendall & Nancy Allen - 1/9/1856 (G. H. Thompson)
Bell, Nathaniel & Elizabeth Weeks - 9/8/1787
Bell, Pierce & Margaret Daniel - 12/24/1846 (R. F. Griffin)
Bell, Wm. & Elizabeth Hopkins - 12/20/1821
Bellah, Jas. W. & Elizabeth G. McKowan - 2/27/1845 (Hinton Crawford)
Benedict, John C. & Susan Bates - 1/27/1850 (Jas. T. Findley)
Benham, Lyman & Sarah King - 11/24/1818 (W. Cone)
Bennett, Chas. & Cynthia Carter - 5/28/1854 (B. Rowland)
Bennett, Elias L. & Emaliza L. Harper - 9/14/1863 (E. A. Burgess)
Bennett, James & Laura Dobbs - 1/3/1855 (B. Rowland)
Bennett, Jas. A. & Tabitha C. Brazzell - 10/4/1859 (Homer Hembree)
Bennett, Reuben & Jane Lindsay - 11/18/1819
Bennett, Reuben & Sarah Forrester - 10/26/1848 (E. S. Hunter, M. G.)
Bennett, Riley W. & Louisa Cosby - 4/3/1864 (A. W. Rowland)
Bennett, Wm. & Peggy Hogg - 4/23/1804
Bent, John & Mary Bugby - 12/1838
Berger, Seaborn & Josephine Wood - 12/6/1870 (W. C. Birchmore)
Berry, Carey W. & Mary J. Tuggle - 5/21/1868 (Wm. A. Overton)

237

Berry, Chas. S. & Mary E. Booles - 5/7/1861 (Vincent Thornton)
Beshell, Hezakiah G. & Elizabeth Fambro - 12-24-1844 (Jas. F. Findley)
Bessent, Abraham W. & Lucinda E. Wright - 4/22/1866 (A. W. Rowland)
Bethune, Lauchlin & Allatha Greer - 9/4/1802
Bethune, Lauchlin & Sally Fitzpatrick - 4/8/1815 (Jas. Martin)
Bethune, Wm. M. & Elizabeth S. Hester - 6/28/1826
Bettie, Wm. H. & Elizabeth C. Grimes - 3/14/1865 (M. W. Arnold, M.G.)
Bickers, Benj. F. & Cordelia E. Colclough - 12/4/1860
Bickers, Joseph & Elizabeth Stewart - 5/26/1818
Bickers, Lewis & Nancy Cartwright - 2/8/1795
Bickers, Wm. & Nancy Ivy - 1/2/1834 (Thos. Stocks)
Bickers, Wm. C. & Almira Sophronia Arnold - 10/14/1858 (L. B. Jackson)
Biddly, Macajah & Lavinia Sherrel - 12/15/1819 (Wm. Cone)
Billups, Thos. & Elizabeth Victory - 1/30/1823 (Lovick Pierce)
Bird, Jos. & Lucretia Watson - 12/11/1828 (Jas. Park)
Bird, Michael & Susannah Lewis - 10/11/1818 (Robt. Booth)
Bishop, Asa & Nancy Garrett - 2/5/1809 (Geo. Stovall)
Bishop, J. J. & Amelia Red - 2/19/1847 (Peter Whelan, Priest)
Bishop, Lafyaette & Martha C. Hix - 11/3/1867 (Wm. H. Thrasher)
Bishop, Wilson S. & Panthea T. Thompson - 4/30/1833 (H. Pendergrass, M.G.)
Bice, Chas. & Malissa Wms. - 10/15/1854 (W. S. Porter)
Black, Carwell B. & Sarah Ann Smith - 4/24/1834 (Caleb W. Kay, M. G.)
Black, Geo. & Mary Ralls - 2/16/1840 (Francis Bowman)
Blair, Thos. & Polly Wall - 12/23/1795
Blankenship, John & Mahalla Caldwell - 12/24/1833 (Jas. Moore)
Blankes, Demsey & Mary A. Hill - 1/11/1818 (Robt. Rea)
Blanks, Wm. & Narcissa Young - 11/8/1819 (Jas. Riley)
Blanton, W. M. & Julia Thompson - 11/6/1840
Blassingame, Jas. T. & Evaline C. Greer - 9/25/1834 (T. W. Grimes)
Bledsoe, Aaron & Nancy Stokes - 7/30/1808 (Wm. Browning)
Bledsoe, John & Elizabeth Autrey - 12/28/1820 (L. B. Johnson)
Bledsoe, Joseph & Elizabeth Greer - 12/20/1819 (Jas. Brockman)
Bledsoe, Wm. & Pamely Ann Booth - 10/21/1823 (John W. G. Greer)
Blitch, Jos. L. & Martha A. Busby - 10/5/1863 (N. M. Crawford, M. G.)
Blount, Whitfield L. & Della Whitehead - 3/5/1876 (R. L. Burgess)
Blythe, Leroy & Betsey Caroline Wars - 4/7/1829 (Wm. Bryan)
Blythe, Jos. L. & Martha A. Beasley - 10/5/1863 (N. M. Crawford, M. G.)
Blythe, James & Doly Credille - 9/15/1806
Blythe, Wm. H. & Betheney Ward - 7/26/1832 (J. P. Leverett)
Boggs, Samuel & Polly Kent - 12/11/1793
Boles, Jackson & Betsey Lindsey - 1/8/1812 (Lemuel Green)
Boles, Turner & Frances Greene Robertson - 10/25/1823
Boling, John S. & Anne W. Nancy - 2/7/1833 (Abraham Yates)
Bones, John H. & Peggy Burns - 6/22/1796
Bookes, Samuel & Elizabeth Stokeley - 11/28/1799
Booles, Allen & Averyela Broach - 12/12/1815 (Lauchlin Bethune)
Booles, Bevan & Charity Yewen - 1/8/1828 (Abraham Yeats)
Booles, Jackson & Nancy Brooks - 11/16/1845 (Jeremiah Lindsay)
Booles, Jeremiah & Sarah Malon - 1/5/1846 (Samuel Ely)
Booles, John & Mary Bennett - 11/12/1822 (John Bools)
Booles, John A. & Rebecca Hackney - 9/13/1849 (E. S. Hunter)
Booles, Wm. T. & Martha Wms. - 11/14/1837 (B. M. Sanders)
Booles, Willoughby & Sarah Ann Wilson - 8/4/1836 (V. R. Thornton)
Boon, Alfred C. & Martha Ann Barnhart - 8/29/1833 (Jas. Moore)
Boon, Francis M. & Harriett A. Greene - 8/12/1834 (Abraham Perkins)
Boon, Jesse & Sarah Hicks - 4/5/1824
Boon, Sion & Gilly Hawkins - 11/26/1804
Boon, ----- & ----- - 12/5/1844 (E. S. Crummer)
Boone, Allen R. & Marietta R. Hightower - 3/9/1867 (Wm. Bryan, M. G.)
Boon, Benj. & Betsey Alford - 4/22/1810 (Isaac Cook)
Boone, Benj. & Dorothy Fay - 5/28/1824
Boone, David L. & Mary Christopher - 1/28/1841 (V. R. Thornton)
Boone, John D. & Mary Hood - 12/2/1858 (Carlos W. Stephens)
Boone, Warren J. & Rebecca Runnells - 12/2/1841 (E. S. Hunter)
Booth, Beverly & Sarah Ansley - 7/29/1819 (Robt. Booth)
Borqust, Robt. & Phoebe Fuller - 7/12/1821 (Abraham Teater)
Bostwick, Nathan & Lucy Burk - 11/17/1819 (Wm. Cone)
Bostwick, Wm. & Jane Smith - 3/6/1823 (John Harris)
Boswell, Reuben B. & Narcissa A. Mayo - 12/16/1869 (W. A. Overton)
Boswell, Wm. J. & Josephine Malone - 6/11/1862 (H. H. Tucker, M. G.)

238

Bowden, Elliott C. & Frances Heard - 9/22/1842 (Jas. Jones, M. G.)
Bowden, Geo. Thomas & Cynthia W. Shirlin - 11/15/1846 (Wm. Bryan)
Bowden, Richard & Martha Cartwright - 2/6/1848 (Isaac Williams)
Bowden, Robt. C. & Elizabeth Jackson - 1/25/1844 (J. W. Godkin)
Bowden, Robt. C. & Frances L. Arnold - 11/20/1856 (J. P. Duncan, M. G.)
Bowden, Wm. & Pamelia Bell - 8/9/1820
Bowden, Wm. & Sarah Jones - 10/30/1833
Bowden, Wm. & Mary Brock - 12/22/1844 (E. S. Hunter)
Bowen, T. J. & Lurana H. Davis - 5/31/1853 (Chas. M. Irwin, M. G.)
Bowles, Henry & Lucinda Bowles - 8/4/1835 (Jesse H. Watson)
Bowles, Henry & Mary Farmer - 9/22/1872 (W. A. Moore)
Bowles, Jesse & Sally Anderson - 3/24/1802
Bowles, Jesse B. & Jane Bennett - 8/26/1833
Bowles, John & Sally (Blassingame?) Blasigame - 3/8/1800 ?
Bowles, Littleberry & Cena Cochram - 8/29/1833 (Nathan Hobbs)
Bowles, Thos. & Acintha Cothrine - 4/1/1819 (Wm. Tuggle)
Bowles, Wm. & Jincey Wade - 12/18/1805
Bowles, Wm. H. & Nancy H. Cartwright - 8/19/1875 (A. J. S. Jackson)
Bowles, Wm. V. & Margaret M. Dennis - 21/10/1863 (V. R. Thornton)
Boyce, Geo. & Jimmy Greer - 8/17/1803
Boyce, ----- & Polly Davis - 4/23/1805
Boykin, Leroy H. & Laura E. Hunter - 2/3/1859 (T. J. Bowen, M. G.)
Bozeman, James & Margaret Shelton - 2/20/1820 (Lovick Pierce)
Brack, Wm. H. & Nancy Crossley - 3/12/1871 (N. M. Jones)
Braddy, John & Aseneth Wright - 1/7/1847 (Hinton Crawford)
Braddy, Jos. E. & Mary E. Turner - 12/2/1869 (C. D. Mitchell)
Bradley, Chas. A. & Emaline Harris - 7/7/1859 (Chas. W. Launis)
Bradley, Harrelson & Agnes Rice - 10/19/1799
Bradley, John & Rachel Wester - 8/6/1802
Bradshaw, Asa & Polly Carrol - 6/30/1803
Bradshaw, Elijah & Sarah Frances Coffield - 11/16/1873 (W. A. Porter)
Bradshaw, Erastus & Elizabeth Findley - 2/27/1838 (J. L. M. Porter)
Bradshaw, George & Dulsey McCain - 11/20/1838
Bradshaw, Asa & Rhoda C. Askew - 6/13/1862 (John W. Godkin)
Bradshaw, Wm. & Susan Bridges - 3/19/1872 (Rev. J. S. Potter)
Bradshaw, Wm. & Letia Sheilds - 12/30/1873 (W. A. Partee)
Bragg, Matthew & Anne Cheney - 1/6/1804
Bragg, Thos. & Lovina Lunceford - 12/28/1797
Branch, John & Sarah Broughton - 1/21/1830 (Odiel? Sherwood)
Branch, Robt. M. & Margaret S. Wier - 5/31/1854? (W. A. Florence)
Branch, Wm. H. H. & Sarah Margaret Robinson - 12/6/1864 (N. M. Crawford)
Brassel, James & Sally Davis - 4/16/1805
Braswell, Isom & Mary Morris - 4/6/1806
Brewer, David & Polly Parker - 4/21/1804
Brewer, Geo. Washington & Julia Priscilla Bruec - 12/25/1872 (N.M.Johnson)
Brewer, Henry & Lukey Mitchell - 8/31/1800
Brewer, Wiley & Mary Clements - 4/4/1854 (Benj. Merritt)
Brewer, Wm. & Polly Harper - 11/11/1799
Brewer, Wm. & Polly Moore - 12/2/1810 (Arthur Foster)
Briant, John & Mary Copeland - 3/4/1830
Brice, Alfred & Martha Wms. - 12/11/1845 (Ephraim Bruce)
Bridges, Ezekiel & Frances Slaughter - 10/14/1845 (J. C. Lucas)
Bridges, Ezekiel J. & Elizabeth T. Smith - 6/24/1849 (Wm. Bryan)
Bridges, Hardy & Nancy Copelan - 12/17/1822 (Henry Slaughter)
Bridges, James & Susan Copelan - 10/27/1831 (Lewis Parker)
Bridges, James & Nancy Rowland - 8/30/1827 (E. Tally)
Bridges, John J. C. & Mary Ann Credille - 2/5/1852 (Hardy Bridge)
Bridges, Robert C. & Eliz. F. Copelan - 6/6/1850 (Hardy Bridge)
Bridges, Wm. & A. H. Copelan - 5/12/1850 (John Copelan)
Brimberry, Matthais & Betsey Hinton - 4/10/1827
Briscoe, John & Elizabeth Dunn - 4/22/1858 (Jno. W. Reid, M. G.)
Briscoe, Lucius M. & Ann Catherine Strozier - 5/10/1850
Briscoe, Thos. & Sarah F. Cheney - 7/14/1851 (Dabney Jones)
Britain, Henry & Louisa Booker - 9/6/1825
Britain, Wm. & Nancy Farris - 1/25/1852 (H. C. Peck?, M. G.)
Broach, Alexander & Nancy Durham - 12/18/1836 (Jno. G. Holtzclaw)
Broach, James & Lucinda Yeats - 10/28/1824
Broach, J. E. & Sally Lankford - 11/12/1874 (John T. Dolvin)
Broach, Wm. & Polly Sherrill - 12/24/1811 (Wm. Cone)
Broach, Wm. H. & Margaret Davidson - 6/30/1872 (John R. Young)

Broddus, Thos. & Agnes Fielder - 12/4/1798
Brockman, Moses & Penelope Bunch - 10/17/1819 (Lemuel Greene)
Brook, Jas. & Julia Reynolds - 2/17/1834 (Nathan Hobbs)
Brook, Jas. E. & Eliza Ann Johnson - 5/20/1844 (J. M. Davidson)
Brook, John T. & Clestia M. Sayers - 1/5/1857 (Thos. Callahan)
Brook, John S. & Nancy A. Reynolds - 8/1/1860
Brooks, Archibald D. & Frances D. Turnell - 10/28/1850 (H. C. Peck)
Brooks, Archibald & Mrs. Lucy A. Cremer - 12/1/1859 (Hart C. Peck)
Brooks, Augustus G. & Emeline F. Ellis - 10/20/1843 (W. C. Veazey)
Brooks, Covington & Nancy Walker - 5/30/1833 (J. P. Leverett)
Brooks, Jesse & Elizabeth Watts - 8/15/1823
Brooks, Peter R. & Francina Creddile - 1/1/1843 (R. F. Griffin)
Brooks, Thomas & Polly Jackson - 3/26/1815 (John Riley)
Brooks, Wilson L. & Julia Fart? - 1/10/1860 (T. J. Bowen)
Broome, Alpheus & Josephine Anderson - 10/8/1868 (C. A. Mitchell)
Broome, Lucius & Eliz. Irby - 4/3/1860 (Wm. A. Corry)
Broox, Henry & Sarah Broox - 11/20/1824
Broughton, Edward & Sarah Ann Lackey - 1/7/1829
Broughton, Edward & Essey Broughton - 5/22/1838 (Thos. Stocks)
Broughton, John R. & Ganett L. Broughton - 5/8/1833 (Geo. Heard)
Broughton, John T. & Anne Amelia Perkins - 8/26/1843 (Francis Bowman)
Brown, Benj. & Nancy Newby - 2/25/1815 (Gilly Moore)
Brown, Benj. F. & Tennese King - 11/19/1833 (Thos. W. Grimes)
Brown, Burwell & Fanny Brown - 6/6/1798
Brown, Chas. & Amanda Bennett - 11/14/1869 (Philip Clements)
Brown, Daniel & Adeline Wilson - 10/10/1858 (Jas. Davidson)
Brown, Ezekiel & Elizabeth Merritt - 12/15/1803
Brown, Ezekiel & Emily Greene - 12/1/1825
Brown, Ezekiel & Hannah Oslin - 8/2/1827 (E. Talley)
Brown, Jas. L. & Julia Martin - 12/19/1843 (P. H. Mell)
Brown, Jesse F. & Lillie B. McElroy - 5/18/1865
Brown, John & Burchet Baxter - 5/2/1814 (B. L. Hulme, M. G.)
Brown, Thos. & Mary Foster - 11/4/1829
Brown, Thos. & Eliza A. Merritt - 1/21/1858 (John R. Young, M. G.)
Brown, Wm. & Mary E. Littleton - 4/2/1854 (J. R. Hall)
Browning, Daniel & Nancy Sorrell - 7/12/1808 (Wm. Browning)
Browning, Nathan P. & Eunice Haralson - 7/27/1815 (Thos. Stokes)
Bruce, Abner W. & Rebecca Bridges - 1/16/1843 (Francis Colley?)
Bruce, Anderson & Mary A. Ward - 12/30/1847 (H. H. Lawrence)
Bruce, Benj. F. & Martha A. Allen - 12/17/1871 (L. D. Caldwell)
Bruce, Edward D. & Mrs. Patience F. Clifton - 12/19/1865 (W. H. Blythe)
Bruce, Ephraim M. & Sarah M. Moon - 4/13/1852 (A. A. V. Carroll)
Bruce, Henry C. & Mattie L. Chapman - 5/12/1872 (W. H. Blythe)
Bruce, James & Ella Richards - 5/2/1816 (Walker Lewis)
Bruce, Jas. & Mrs. Mary A. Bridges - 9/13/1866 (Jas. Moon)
Bruce, Jas. & Sarah Ransom - 10/13/1833 (W. H. Blythe)
Bruce, Jas. R. & Jane E. Lucas - 12/19/1844 (Francis S. Colley)
Bruce, Jas. S. & Mary Lewis - 12/12/1844 (Ephraim Bruce)
Bruce, Joel & Charlotte L. Lewis - 1/20/1835 (Ephraim Bruce)
Bruce, John & Tempsy Sayers - 8/28/1827 (Jno. Armstrong)
Bruce, Jonathan & Martha Shell - 6/2/1844 (Ephraim Bruce)
Bruce, Seaborn M. & Catherine Cruse - 12/7/1847 (F. S. Colley)
Bruce, Turnell & Martha Thigpen - 5/16/1852 (B. Rowland)
Bruce, Wilson & Allah Gatlin - 12/17/1829 (J. P. Leveritt)
Brunt, Jas. & Elizabeth Caldwell - 7/31/1834 (Ephraim Bruce)
Brunt, John & Patience Rowland - 1/5/1825
Brunt, Williby & Nancy Caldwell - 8/31/1836 (Ephraim Bruce)
Bryan, Asbury & Mary Ann Tarpley Ward - 1/19/1826 (T. W. Slaughter, J.P.)
Bryan, Jas. & Mary Ann Clark - 11/18/1830 (W. M. Bryan)
Bryan, Jas. P. & Lucinda Oliver - 2/13/1868 (W. M. Bryan, M. G.)
Bryan, Jesse M. & Mary Ann Oliver - 6/12/1868 (Alex H. Smith)
Bryan, Littleton J. & Martha Bryan - 5/17/1855 (Wm. Bryan)
Bryan, Nathan & Mary Ann Griggs - 7/4/1837 (Ephraim Bruce)
Bryan, Richard & Sarah Ann Oliver - 10/20/1836 (Ephraim Bruce)
Bryan, Thos. M. & Sallie F. Morris - 11/14/1866 (Wm. A. Overton)
Bryan, Wm. & Martha Tarpley - 1/21/1840 (Jas. Jones)
Bryan, Wm. & Elizabeth Langford - 12/16/1841
Bryan, Wm. & Sarah Rapley - 6/28/1855 (J. P. Duncan, M. G.)
Bryan, Wm. J. & Elizabeth Smith -   (Wm. Bryan)
Bryant, Chas. J. & Nancy L. Simmons - 12/20/1875 (H. C. Peck)

Bryant, John O. & Patsey Gentry - 4/10/1836 (B. Rowland)
Bryant, Russell - Sydney Martin - 12/22/1824
Bryant, Whit & Laura Moore - 2/25/1875 (J. S. Calloway)
Byce, Wm. C. & Emeline R. Coffield - 12/21/1874
Bynum, Jas. R. & Lucy A. A. Houghton - 7/1/1852 (W. A. Corry)
Byrd, Wm. & Mary Hudson - 6/6/1825
Bickning, -----
Bucking, Peter & Sarah Furlow - 3/26/1820 (Wm. Cone)
Buckner, David & Betsey Findley - 5/8/1802
Bugg, Hampton C. & Martha Moore - 4/24/1845 (I. Gleen, M. G.)
Bugg, Hampton & Sarah Moore - 11/9/1847 (Hinton Crawford)
Bugg, Wm. B. & Mary C. Wheeler - 5/16/1867 (A. Nelson, M. G.)
Bunkley, Howell & Ruth Newsome - 10/5/1841 (V. R. Thornton)
Bunn, Aldredge & Catherine Palmer - 3/22/1831 (Ephraim Bruce)
Burdile, Robt & Margaret Hays - 7/25/1827 (Wm. Wingfield)
Burford, John & Edna Jackson - 1/5/1815 (Jno. Browning)
Burford, John E. & Mary A. Bryan - 8/19/1875 (A. J. S. Jackson)
Burford, Leonard & Polly Smith - 5/12/1795
Burge, Wm. & Milley Thompson - 1/29/1833 (Jas. A. Park)
Burger, Noah & Mary Jane Coffield - 1/22/1874 (W. A. Porter)
Burgess, A. C. & Frances E. Freeman - 9/6/1870 (W. A. Colclough)
Burgess, Edward A. & Augusta E. Fambrough - 1/11/1859 (W. A. Partee)
Burgess, Jas. D. & Satira J. Fambrough - 12/22/1857 (L. R. L. Jennings)
Burgess, Jonathan & Nancy Cone - 9/18/1818 (Thos. Stocks)
Burgess, Robt. L. & Emma E. Fambrough - 12/9/1866 (Jno. R. Young, M.G.)
Burgess, Thos. L. & Martha Wade - 10/11/1840 (I. M. Wilson)
Burgess, Wm. & Adaline Stephens - 10/8/1867 (E. A. Burgess)
Burgens, Wm. & Emaline Vurger - 12/18/1873 (W. A. Partee)
Burk, Columbus? & Elizabeth Foster - 5/16/1850 (H. Crawford)
Burk, Jas. & Martha A. Wynn - 10/1/1847
Burk, Seaborn & Elizabeth Adair - 5/2/1847
Burke, Chas. I. & Caroline Jenkins - 11/1/1823 (Thos. Johnson)
Burke, Jas. & Martha A. King - 1/28/1844 (J. W. Godkin)
Burke, Valerious A. & Elizabeth Arnold - 3/24/1856
Burnett, David S. & Agnes S. Fool? - 4/22/1875 (P. H. McWhorter)
Burns, Owens & Nancy Horn - 7/29/1826
Burns, Robt. & Elizabeth Greene - 1/9/1806
Burrough, James & Betsey Weathers - 5/18/1803
Burt, Dr. H. L. & Penelope Simonton - 7/16/1845 (Francis Bowman)
Burton, Wm. & Martha Robertson - 7/20/1826
Busby, John E. & Adaline M. O'Neal - 6/9/1864 (L. D. Caldwell)
Bush, John & Win. Alford - 8/22/1787
Bush, John & Nancy King - 3/27/1804
Bush, John L. & Mary A. Ashe - 3/2/1874 (Henry Newton)
Bush, John T. & Mary C. Stewart - 11/4/1875 (L. D. Caldwell)
Buss, Wm. & Betsey Maddox - 4/19/1810 (Jno. Cox)
Bussey, Jas. & Elizabeth Lake - 12/21/1814 (C. Maddox)
Butler, Edward & Fannie Garrett - 4/9/1788
Butler, John T. & Adaline Wray - 2/11/1869 (E. A. Burgess)
Butler, John W. & Elizabeth Hubbard - 3/15/1824
Butlord, Wm. & Elizabeth Dilder? - 11/10/1805

Cagle, Alexr. & Amanda Wright - 11/23/1847
Cain, Thos. L. & Mary R. Swan - 9/4/1833 (Jas. Moore)
Caldwell, Augustus G. & Frances Jernigan - 8/9/1849 (Wm. A. Corry)
Caldwell, Early & Jane Peck? - 3/31/1844 (R. H. Mapp)
Caldwell, Early J. & Nancy Jarrell - 3/27/1848 (Wm. A. Corry)
Caldwell, Elisha & Susan King - 11/27/1873 (J. H. Kilpatrick)
Caldwell, James & Nelly Shockley - 5/29/1814 (W. M. McGiboney)
Caldwell, Jonathan E. & Martha Ann Peck - 8/9/1860 (W. W. Moore)
Caldwell, Joshua & Mary Tippet - 6/3/1830 (Jno. Harris)
Caldwell, Joshua A. & Eliza Ann Wright - 1/19/1865 (W. A. Partee)
Caldwell, Littleton & Cynthia McHargue - 9/4/1825 (Jno. Harris)
Caldwell, Littleton D. & Mary C. McLelan? - 11/16/1856 (J. A. Wms.)
Caldwell, Miles & Mary Ann Caldwell - 3/2/1832 (Wooten O'Neal)
Caldwell, Wm. & Polly Parker - 10/28/1805
Caldwell, Wm. & Polly Woodward - 11/1/1820 (Wm. McGiboney)
Caldwell, Wm. H. & Sarah F. Andrews - 7/1/1869 (L. D. Caldwell)
Calhoun, Londa & Lucy Webb - 8/4/1831 (Geo. Hall)
Callahan, Andrew & Alice Higgins - 12/1/1838 (C. D. Kinnebrew)

Callahan, Edward & Mary Stevens - 12/20/1815 (Francis Cummins)
Callahan, Henry & Rhoda A. Credille - 12/6/1849 (J. M. Kelly)
Callahan, Jas. W. & Susan P. Brooks - 11/2/1869 (L. M. Dickey, M. G.)
Callahan, John & Ann Stephenson - 10/25/1794
Callahan, Wm. & Elizabeth Wilson - 3/20/1821 (Jack Lumpkin)
Callahan, Wm. & Francies Hall - 12/18/1845 (J. W. Godkin)
Callaway, Lemuel L. & Anna Josephine Mullins - 12/23/1863 (Nathan
   Crawford, M. G.)
Callaway, Lewis & Mary Hunter - 11/1/1824
Callaway, Willis B. & Margarite A. Willis - 1/1/1845 (Thos. Stocks)
Callaway, R. S. & Sarah Ann Callaway - 1/22/1846 (P. H. Mell)
Callaway, Wm. & Harriet A. Boone - 6/15/1851 (S. G. Hillyer)
Callaway, Wm. R. & Rhoda Ann Cheney - 1/17/1838 (Reuben Owen, M. G.)
Calway, Night & Mary Connell - 12/31/1799
Cameron, Henry C. & Mary E. Ware - 2/28/1872
Campbell, James & Scintha Hill - 7/18/1807 (Claborn Maddox)
Campbell, Obediah & Luria Norris - 4/17/1825
Campbell, Samuel & Charity Edwards - 5/28/1801
Cato, Wm. & Ariadne? Kinney - 6/14/1863 (E. S. Wms)
Cato, Wyche & Patsey Peoples - 1/26/1803
Catrehead, John & Phebe Foster - 12/2/1807 (Wm. Johnson)
Causey, Philips & Sarah Laws - 9/3/1822 (Wm. Wingfield)
Cawthon, John W. & Mary A. E. Barnhardt - 12/1/1858 (Geo. O. Clark)
Cauthon, J. W. & Nannie Barnhardt - 12/17/1868 (J. J. Jones)
Chafin, Thos. & Sarah G. Taylor - 12/27/1824
Chambers, John Finch & Emily Adaline Hall - 3/7/1835 (Jas. H. Taylor)
Chamberlain, Elliott R. & Mary K. Watson - 4/10/1854 (Sam'l K. Talmadge)
Champion, Henry W. & Lucinda P. King - 9/9/1852 (T. W. Wilkes, M. G.)
Champion, Jas. D. & Mary S. Jones - 5/19/1864 (N. M. Crawford)
Champion, Jesse & Louisa Jackson - 11/8/1827 (Wm. Austin)
Champion, Jesse W. & Mary V. Champion - 7/20/1870 (R. A. Johnson, M. G.)
Chandler, Daniel B. & Georgia A. Moss - 4/5?/1866 (Jas. Davidson)
Chandler, Walton & Martha Hamilton - 8/27/1845 (W. A. Florence, M. G.)
Channel, Isham & Nancy Howell - 5/2/1830 (T. Wright)
Channell, Littleton & Sally Skinner - 11/29/1804
Channell, Littleton & Nancy Tolver - 3/24/1832 (John Copeland)
Channell, Michael & Tebathy? Marchman - 5/16/1831 (Butt L. Cato)
Channell, Michael & Sarah Westbrooks - 7/18/1833
Channell, Thos. & Eliz. Montgomery - 1/17/1835
Channell, Wm. & Eliz. Wilson - 9/19/1826 (Butt L. Cato)
Channell, Wm. H. & Georgia Ruark - 1/21/1868 (John C. Merritt)
Chapman, John M. & Martha Crews - 1/1/1838 (Ephraim Bruce)
Chapman, John M. & Sarah E. Jones - 5/27/1855 (Benj. Merritt)
Chapman, John & Sarah Ann Everett - 2/12/1860 (Jas. W. Wragg)
Chapman, Miles & Margaret Harper - 3/4/1864?
Chapman, Randle & Eliz. Tally - 7/23/1822 (Stephen Hightower)
Chapman, Randol & Nancy Perkins - 5/30/1833 (J. P. Leaverette)
Chapman, Thos. & Catherine Bruce - 5/25/1848 (Ephraim Bruce)
Chapman, Wm. M. & Sarah C. Lewis - 12/14/1837
Chapman, Wm. M. & Jeanette Norris - 5/10/1857 (Hart C. Peck)
Chapman, Wm. & Amanda Allen - 9/30/1859 (R. B. Kelly)
Chappell, John & Anne Forrester - 4/12/1820 (Wm. Cone)
Chappell, Robt. & Martha Frances Quill - 1/8/1854 (W. A. Florence)
Chatman, Miles & Mary C. Wiggins - 3/1/1868 (A. H. Smith)
Cheatman, Lovera B. & Emma A. Printup - 6/15/1875 (E. W. Spur?)
Cheek, Asbell & Eliz. R. Bennett - 1/6/1848 (Wm. F. Gaston)
Cheney, Enoch R. & Sarah H. English - 10/5/1852 (P. H. Mell, M. G.)
Cheney, John F. & Martha E. Wilson - 1/8/1867
Cheney, Wm. O. & Mary F. English - 4/7/1857 (J. R. Young)
Chester, Francis & Ann G. Neal - 1/17/1832 (Raleigh Green)
Cheves, Adoniram? J. & Anna M. Sanford - 12/15/1863 (N. M. Crawford)
Cheves, Greef? & Betsey Parker - 11/8/1808 (Wm. McGiboney)
Cheves, Joseph & Mary E. Stubblefield - 10/15/1846 (Wm. I. Parks)
Chew, John & Ann Montford - 12/15/1814 (Thos. Stocks)
Chew, Thos. J. & Mary Jane Fountain - 12/9/1852 (Jas. M. Kelly)
Chewning, Wm. I. & Parmelia Adams - 2/28/1826
Chonn?, Chas. C. & Sarah E. Strozier - 12/5/1867
Christopher, Henry & Mary Bugg - 12/22/1872 (B. P. Taylor)
Christopher, Seaborn & Allie Mayhan - 8/22/1822 (Robt. Newsome)
Christopher, Wm. & Nancy Parker - 12/29/1829 (John Copeland)

242

Christopher, Wm. H. & Martha H. Johnson - 12/4/1868
Chriswell, John & Martha J. Norris - 4/22/1866 (Wm. Champion, M. G.)
Chriswell, Wm. & Nancy Bennett - 8/22/1866 (E. T. Wms.)
Clark, Arthur & Agnes Hall - 7/18/1799
Clark, Benj. & Mary L. Woodward - 10/28/1847 (H. Crawford)
Clark, Jas. & Sally Robinson - 10/26/1810 (Robt. Rea)
Clark, J. S. & Betsey Prince - 8/2/1803
Clark, Wm. J. & Martha A. Lawrence - 2/16/1847
Clark, Francis A. & Sarah E. West - 12/16/1875 (C. C. Davison)
Clarke, Wm. & Frances Penny - 12/20/1827 (E. Talley)
Clay, Samuel & Eliz. Fitzpatrick - 2/7/1803
Clayton, Phillips & Lenora Harper - 5/2/1837 (Geo. F. Pierce)
Clemance, Ellis & Martha Merritt - 12/7/1871 (W. H. Wright)
Clements, Aaron & Hannah Clements - 6/20/1796
Clements, Anderson & Lucy Burford - 12/19/1834 (Francis West)
Clements, Anderson & Eliza Rhodes - 12/11/1862 (Jas. M. Kelly)
Clements, Franklin & Loueza Channell - 10/30/1868 (Jno. E. Merritt)
Clements, Jesse & Jane Rhodes - 9/24/1851
Clements, Peyton & Polly Ward - 12/1/1808 (Francis P. Marlin)
Clements, Peyton & Mary Tyler - 9/2/1824
Clements, Peyton & Eliz. Wright - 1/16/1845 (Ephraim Bruce)
Clements, Phillips & Eliz. Howell - 10/8/1803
Clements, Phillip & Sarah Blythe - 10/5/1841
Clements, Wm. B. & Malissa Jackson - 2/5/1867 (Wm. Bryan)
Clepbon, Daniel & Eliza Ledbetter - 7/4/1826
Cleveland, Larkin & Sally Buchanan - 9/16/1802
Clifton, Alanson & Nancy Marchman - 3/4/1847 (R. L. Clifton)
Clifton, Chas. & Winney Kinney - 1/10/1849 (W. T. Gaston)
Clifton, John R. & Sarah Ruark - 1/20/1873 (L. D. Caldwell)
Clifton, Wm. & Martha Watson - 10/13/1824
Clifton, Wm. & Patience Kinney - 1/27/1848 (W. F. Gaston)
Coats, Jas. & Eliz. Laws - 8/31/1831 (Matthew Wingfield)
Cobb, John & Mary Grimes - 12/2/1819 (F. Cummins, M. G.)
Cochran, Jas. M. & Eliz. Hutchinson - 2/8/1853 (J. W. Yarborough)
Cochran, John & Peggy Dorough - 11/10/1803
Cochran, Samuel & Sally Furlow - 3/23/1802
Cochran, Samuel & Judith Gentry - 9/26/1841 (J. M. Wilson)
Cochran, John & Martha Bridges - 1/22/1852 (L. B. Jackson)
Cocraft, Jas. & Caroline B. Lewis - 11/9/1833 (Wm. S. Parks, M. G.)
Cof__, Lewis C. & Eliz. Mills - 5/15/1842 (Jas. Davidson)
Cogen, Jacob H. & Harriett Cook - 1/15/1837 (Jas. Moore)
Colbert, Fred K. & Tempy Powers - 1/31/1816 (Archibald Watts)
Colcough, John M. & Fannie J. Boswell - 2/15/1874 (Henry Newton)
Colcough, Wm. A. & Matilda J. Moore? - 11/12/1854 (W. H. C. Cone)
Cole, Thos. & Eliz. Talley - 8/12/1801
Coleman, Daniel & Clavendia A. R. Randle - 1/7/1824 (Adiel Sherwood)
Coleman, Samuel & Sally Evans - 7/4/1805
Coleman, Thos. & Jane Trimble - 4/2/1805
Coley, John & Eliza Ann Swan - 6/1/1835
Coley, John C. & Catherine Marchman - 12/1/1837
Coley, John & Catherine Bruce? - 1/24/1867 or 9 (W. H. Blythe)
Coley, Wm. & Mary Bivins Wood - 1/13/1828 (J. P. Leveritt)
Collier, Edwin & Henrietta Brown - 7/7/1829 (Jas. Asgood Andrew)
Collier, Jas. & Frances Brown - 6/14/1820 (David White)
Collier, Thos. & Mary Wms. - 1/9/1811 (Josiah Randle)
Collier, Wmnsn? & Sarah Denson - 11/27/1822 (John W. Grier)
Collins, Jas. & Rebecca Carr - 12/21/1826 (Jos. Wright)
Collins, Jones & Sophronia Wright - 5/3/1818 (John Wilson)
Collins, Richard & Eliz. M. Parker - 1/23/1859 (J. M. Kelly)
Collins, Nathaniel & Eliz. Coleman - 11/25/1818 (John Wilson)
Colon, Jas. & Eliz. P. Furlow - 1/22/1825
Colwell, Edward & Polly Payne - 9/22/1812 (Elias Bell)
Condon, Wm. D. & Anna A. Statham - 3/21/1856 (Francis Bowman)
Cone, Ezekiel & Margaret Bethune - 1/25/1810 (W. McGiboney)
Cone, Francis & Jane W. Cook - 1/8/1829 (Francis Cummins)
Cone, Jas. T. & Martha A. Boon - 12/23/1833 (Elijah E. Jones)
Cone, Rich. & Patsey Perkins - 10/29/1794
Cone, Robt. & Barby Ann Kinnewbrew - 9/20/1872 (N. R. Peck)
Conine, Richd. & Patsey Boon - 4/20/1804
Conine, Wm. & Eliza Swindall - 12/26/1839 (Hinton Crawford)

243

Conley, S. W. & Mary F. Cochran - 12/4/1873 (P. H. McWhorter)
Connell, David & Nancy Hammond - 10/28/1849 (John C. Merritt)
Connell, Hartwell & Sarah Ann Kinney - 2/18/1865 (E. S. Wms.)
Connell, John & Sarah Awsby - 1/30/1801
Conner, Abel C. & Maria D. Hightower - 9/28/1843 (Ephraim Bruce)
Conner, Burill & Lucinda Ivey - 2/16/1848 (L. B. Jackson)
Cook, Emory & Nancy Keaton - 10/19/1819 (Walder Lewis)
Cook, Jas. & Eliz. Ransom - 9/11/1808 (Francis Ross, M. G.)
Cook, Jasper T. & Henrietta Porter - 6/25/1874 (John R. Young)
Cook, John & Lucy McCain - 1/16/1823 (Geo. Watkins)
Cook, John R. & Cornlia Sayer - 2/11/1873 (H. C. Peck)
Cook, Joseph & Anne Curtis - 10/11/1818 (Hinton Crawford)
Cook, Joshua & Mary Figgs - 3/15/1831 (Ephraim Bruce)
Cook, Joshua & Martha Bruce - 8/4/1831 (Ephraim Bruce)
Cook, Thos. & Eliz. Stone - 11/30/1809 (H. Ransom)
Cook, Thos. & Mary Colquitt - 8/25/1819 (Lovick Pierce)
Cook, Wm. & Frances Ann Walker - 10/17/1844 (E. R. Thornton)
Cooper, Amos & Gedida Bradshaw - 1/21/1821 (Davy Perrill)
Cooper, Thos. B. & Corrie A. Stow - 5/20/1856 (P. H. Mell)
Cooper, Wm. & Betsey Rhodes - 12/20/1811 (Wm. Jones)
Copelan, A. H. & A. M. Maddox - 4/8/1875 (John T. Dolvin)
Copelan, Daniel E. & Eliz. J. Lundy - 2/27/1873 (John D. Copelan)
Copelan, Elias D. & Judy Sanders - 7/21/1834
Copelan, John & Eliz. Wood - 12/22/1822 (Stephen Hightower)
Copelan, John & Nancy Wms. - 5/17/1827 (John Harris)
Copelan, John B. & Annie V. Copelan - 12/1 or 7/1867 (Philip B. Robinson)
Copelan, John D. & Sarah E. Wynn - 11/3/1865 (Thos. F. Pierce)
Copelan, Major & Adeline Alfriend - 12/29/1782 (John T. Dolvin)
Copelan, Miles G. & Ellen J. O'Rear - 3/14/1867 (Wm. Bryan, M. G.)
Copelan, Obidiah & Sarah R. Credille - 12/16/1830 (W. Alexander)
Copelan, Obidiah G. & Sarah Eliz. Lundy - 1/21/1864 (Wm. Bryan)
Copelan, Obidiah G. & Mary J. Lundy - 10/10/1867 (Wm. H. Blythe)
Copelan, Rowan & Parmelia Winslett - 12/4/1872 (J. W. Godkin)
Copelan, Thos. M. & Mary A. E. Walker - 4/30/1848 (W. F. Gordon)
Copelan, Wiley R. & Antionette W. Downing - 1/17/1871 (J. H. Kilpatrick)
Copeland, Alexr. & Julia A. Tuggle - 4/18/1837 (Vincent R. Thornton)
Copeland, Archibald H. & Agathy Ledbetter - 5/1/1826
Copeland, Coalson & Martha Richards - 7/1/1826
Copeland, Jasper & Mary E. Furlow - 11/28/1831 (A. Hutchinson)
Copeland, N. & Patience C. Zachery - 2/15/1872 (Geo. W. Yarbrough)
Copeland, John & Betsey Ann Credille - 3/27/1828 (Wm. Bryan)
Copeland, Peter & Mary Tuggle - 11/24/1825
Copeland, Wm. & Nancy Tally - 1/2/1816 (Thos. M. Bush)
Copeland, Wm. Jr. & Mary Dunn - 12/15/1839 (Wm. Tuggle)
Copeland, Wm. D. & Eliz. D. Hailes - 1/20/1859 (Geo. C. Clarke)
Core, Richd. & Eliza Mead - 3/12/1808 (Peter Early)
Corry, Daniel & Addie Forrester - 1/3/1830 (Robt. Newsom)
Corry, G. T. & Jane E. Harris - 11/24/1852 (Thos. Stocks)
Corry, Jas. Thos. & Irwia Rhodes - 12/15/1872 (Henry Newton)
Corry, John & Eliz. Carter - 11/22/1822
Corry, John A. & Mary A. Reynolds - 5/12/1864 (P. A. Houston, M. G.)
Corry, Wm. A. & Martha M. Brinley - 5/19/1838
Cochrum, Thos. & Lottie Brown - 3/17/1868 (Jas. W. Godkin)
Cotton, Henry & Maria Jenkins - 5/28/1825
Cowles, Samuel & Judith Harroway - 4/11/1820 (Lovick Pierce?)
Cox, Jas. M. & Sarah A. Rawls - 5/4/1852 (V. R. Thornton)
Cox, John T. & Sarah T. Houghton - 4/29/1847 (E. S. Hunter)
Crabb, Benj. R. & Fannie A. Bryan - 8/6/1861 (Albert Gray)
Craft, Hugh & Eliza Collier - 9/9/1830 (Francis Cummins)
Crane, Wm. H. & Henrietta W. Statham - 5/31/1859 (R. A. Houston, M. G.)
Crawford, Bennett & Nancy Crawford - 12/6/1808 (Isaac Cook)
Crawford, Titus? & Nancy Powers - 5/8/1814 (A. Bledsoe)
Crawford, Geo. & Louisa Burk - 8/12/1847 (J. F. Billingslea)
Crawford, Jas. Thos. & Beatrice H. Rosser - 11/24/1853 (Hinton Crawford)
Crawford, Jas. & Harriett C. Ballard - 9/13/1855
Crawford, Jas. Thos. & S. E. R. Peeples - 12/18/1855 (Hinton Crawford)
Crawford, Josiah H. & Mary Howze - 12/20/1855
Crawford, Nowell & Jane Finley - 12/1/1829 (John Park)
Crawford, Wm. & Nancy Hemphill - 10/27/1801
Crawford, Wm. H. & Harriett L. McGivier - 7/25/1867 (Thos. F. Safford)

Credille, Cullen S. & Jane Phillips - 12/19/1833 (H. Crawford)
Credille, Gray & Polly Smith - 9/27/1804
Credille, Henry & Sarah Smith - 10/27/1804
Credille, Henry R. & Sarah P. Jones - 1/20/1839 (John Copelan)
Credille, Jesse & Sarah Shackley - 4/15/1819 (Wm. McGiboney)
Credille, Reuben A. & Mary A. Hines - 11/27/1852 (Wm. Owen)
Credille, Wm. & Lina Smith - 12/22/1814 (Jas. Baldwin)
Credille, Wm. G. & Mary Ann Smith - 12/11/1845 (Wm. Bryan)
Credille, Wm. H. & Fannie L. Blythe - 1/31/1865
Credille, Wm. S. & Mary Rosser - 9/15/1842 (Wm. Arnold)
Crenshaw, Wm. H. & M. R. Newsom - 5/6/1873 (Henry Newton)
Crenshaw, Wm. L. & Mary A. Craddock - 12/14/1844
Crittenden, Isaac & Tolitha E. Tolbert - 12/20/1865 (Lorengo D. Carlton)
Crockett, Augustus C. & Harriett A. Skidmore - 11/1/1855 (G.L. McChuskey)
Cross, Fethershaux? & Mary Tucker - 4/13/1820 (Wm. Cone)
Crosky?, C. M. & Mary Veazey - 1/28/1847 (Jas. Jones)
Crosky, Columbus M. & Annie Luck? - 4/25/1871 (J. M. Loury, M. G.)
Crosky, Edward & Parmelia Linch - 12/1/1840 (Reuben B. Armer?)
Crosky, Edward & Harriett Drake - 11/19/1842 (John Howell)
Crossley, Edward ---
Crossley, Edwin & Nancy Wright - 6/24/1824
Crossley, Josiah & Rena Channell - 4/30/1843 (Reuben Armor)
Crossley, Lemuel & Sally Shipp - 12/14/1821 (Thos. Whaley)
Crossley, Wiley A. & Cynthia A. E. Leslie - 10/10/1859 (W. G. Johnson)
Crouch, Jos. & Eliz. Joiner - 12/20/1821 (Thos. Riley)
Crow, Stephen & Rebecca Kinnie - 12/30/1870
Crow, Stephen & Rebecca Kinney - 8/20/1871 (Rev. J. S. Patton)
Crowser, Richd. P. & Lucy Ann Thompson - 5/17/1843 (John L. Oliver)
Crowley, Thos. & Lurania R. Ward - 3/5/1828 (Roger Dickinson)
Crutchfield, Geo. & Martha Matilda Moore - 11/18/1836 (Wm. Cone)
Crutchfield, John & Jinney W. Jelk - 1/9/1806
Crutchfield, John & Jane E. Stephen - 10/27/1842 (E. Sparks Hunter)
Crutchfield, John W. & Alice J. Harris - 4/13/1871 (J. M. Loury, M. G.)
Crutchfield, Robt. F. & Martha J. Turnell - 9/28/1866 (I. A. Wms.)
Culbertson, David & Lucy Wilkinson - 12/24/1818 (John Browning)
Culbertson, David & Sarah Stovall - 6/15/1819 (L. Bethune)
Culberson, Jeremiah F. & Nancy Macon - 3/27/1827 (Jas. Culberson)
Culberson, Wm. B. & Margaret Carter - 8/6/1852 (J. F. Findley)
Culp, Peter & Martha Bennett - 9/20/1835 (John I. Holtzclaw)
Culver, Alfred & Arena Credille - 12/22/1842 (R. F. Griffin)
Culver, Geo. P. & Emma P. Arnold - 3/19/1872 (Jas. L. Pierce)
Culber, John P. & Martha F. Strozier - 12/23/1871 (J. H. Kilpatrick)
Culver, Joshua I. & Mary Figgs - 6/20/1843 (E. P. Jarrell)
Cumbie, Peter & Lucinda Wms - 2/6/1853 (Ephraim Bruce)
Cunningham, Cornelius & Sarah Eliz. Cessend - 7/8/1844
Cunningham, Thos. T. & Jane Fereba Gastin - 10/6/1831 (Jas. Anderson)
Cunningham, Wm. & Ann Eliza Early - 7/15/1830 (H. Reed)
Cunningham, Wm. H. & Ella F. Knowles - 11/30/1873 (J. Knowles)
Cureton, Wm. & Margaret Crawl - 11/4/1789
Curry, James & Mary Forrester - 10/7/1828 (Robt. Newsome)
Curry, Wm. H. & Sarah E. Wright - 5/1/1864 (Robt. Newsome)
Curtis, Johnson & Isabella Smith - 5/3/1815 (Francis Cummins)
Curtis, Robt. & Margaret Taylor - 1/30/1811
Curtis, Robt. & Sarah Johnson - 1/27/1820 (Wm. Cone)
Curtis, Wm. & Sarah Grier - 1/10/1821
Curtwright, John & Isena? Warde - 1/7/1833 (Thos. W. Grimes)
Curtwright, Samuel & Barbara Howell - 3/4/1827 (Jas. Woodham)

Dale, Archibald Buchanan & Margaret Ritchie - 10/24/1832
Daniel, Chas. S. & Adeline Jones - 4/8/1852 (W. A. Corry)
Daniel, Chas. W. & Eliz. Ann Jenkins - 12/22/1835
Daniel, Cordial & Ann Eliza Watts - 4/17/1824
Daniel, Dana B. & Julia F. Hunter - 2/16/1865 (J. A. Preston, M. G.)
Daniel, Denton & Saddy Jones - 2/10/1806
Daniel, Henry F. & Martha S. Moore - 8/1/1832
Daniel, Ira A. M. & Rebecca I. Walker - 8/20/1835 (Wm. Choice)
Daniel, James & Eca Woodham - 12/7/1819 (Jas. Holt)
Daniel, James & Grezil Clements - 12/21/1789
Daniel, John & Polly Fuller - 6/11/1808 (Thos. Crawford)
Daniel, John & Mary McLain - 1/31/1822 (John Leftwich)

Daniel, Oliver P. & Fanny M. Clark - 6/13/1848 (Francis Bowman)
Daniel, Oliver? T. & Jane Victoria Cone - 11/3/1858 (Samuel K. Talmadge)
Daniel, Samuel B. & Mary E. Morgan - 1/12/1843 (John Reid, M. G.)
Daniel, Wm. & Mary King - 3/9/1789
Daniel, Wm. & Adaline Moore - 11/15/1827 (Francis Cummins)
Daniel, Wm. & Sarah J. Watts - 12/20/1853 (John Scott)
Daniel, Wm. & Rebecca A. House - 12/7/1856 (N. M. Crawford)
Daniel, Wm. T. & Letitia M. Branch - 1/4/1859 (John W. Reid, M. G.)
Danley, Wm. L. & Lucy G. Shaffer - 1/19/1866
Darnell, Zachariah & Jenny Hopkins - 10/20/1811 (O. Porter)
Darrocott, Wm. & Sally Beckley - 10/17/1804
Davant, Jas. & Rebecca F. Matthews - 3/26/1843 (B. M. Sanders)
Davant, P. E. & Hortense Moore - 1/8/1856 (N. M. Crawford, M. G.)
Davant, Samuel & Agnes Ledbetter - 3/15/1824 (Wm. Rowland)
Davant, Wm. F. & Anna Cocraft - 10/28/1856 (J. P. Duncan)
Davenport, Burkett & Sophia Park - 5/12/1824
Davenport, Henry & Eliz. Hubbard - 3/9/1824
Davies, John O. & Mary Jane Eden - 10/29/1854 (G. H. Thompson)
Davies, Wm. & Nancy Rutledge - 2/28/1801
Davies, Wm. (Capt.) & Susannah Barnett - 10/31/1808
Davis, Aaron L. B. & Elizabeth Hancock - 8/9/1853
Davis, Abner & Eliz. Parish - 12/11/1817 (Thos. Rhodes)
Davis, Augustus B. & Francis L. Saggus - 12/9/1873 (Henry Newton)
Davis, C. A. & A. B. Surft - 2/27/1849 (P. H. Mell)
Davis, David & Rebecha Woodwin - 5/11/1809 (Wm. McGiboney)
Davis, Geo. C. & Emma J. Reynolds - 1/16/1875 (Henry Newton)
Davis, John & Eliz. Downey - 3/11/1830 (Jas. Burton)
Davis, John W. & Lizzie Bass - 12/4/1873 (W. H. Chapman)
Davis, Leroy W. & Martha O'Neal - 12/11/1855 (H. D. Murden)
Davis, Martin & Frances Harper - 12/4/1806 (Thos. Crawford)
Davis, Reuben & Eliz. Glaze - 2/23/1847 (Wm. Bryan)
Davis, Reynolds & Catherine Tuggle - 12/20/1823
Davis, Thos. & Patsey Woodwin - 5/18/1801
Davis, Thos. W. & Adaline H. Jackson - 12/25/1859 (T. J. Bowen)
Davis, Wm. & Hannah Cochran - 2/9/1802
Davis, Wm. G. & M. A. E. Grant - 11/15/1863
Davis, Wm. L. & Eliz. Forte Foster - 3/15/1863 (J. M. Stillwell)
Davis, Wm. M. & Va. A. Ely - 8/29/1860 (Jas. H. Kilpatrick)
Davis, Wm. S. & Ann S. Kimbro - 10/27/1853 (J. W. Yarbrough)
Davison, Jas. & Rebecca F. Matthews - 3/26/1843 (B. M. Sanders)
Davison, Jas. & Ella M. Duke - 12/8/1872 (W. A. Overton, M. G.)
Davison, Jas. M. & Mary Ann Southerland - 1/14/1833 (Abram Yeats)
Davison, Jas. M. & Margaret Moore - 7/6/1852 (J. Findley)
Davison, Reuben & Eliz. Wilson Jones - 2/18/1841 (V. R. Thornton)
Davison, Robt. E. & Hattie Armstrong - 12/22/1875 (P. H. Mell, M. G.)
Dawsey, Daniel & Unity Copelan - 11/13/1808 (F. T. Martin)
Dawson, Geo. Jnr. & Sarah Branch - 6/17/1818 (Lovick Pierce)
Dawson, Geo. W. & Mary D. Riley - 3/21/1839 (Thos. Stacks)
Dawson, Jas. I. & Missouri S. Martin - 8/5/1847 (J. L. Dagg)
Dawson, Wm. Crosby & Henrietta Wingfield - 1/28/1819 (Lovick Pierce)
Dawson, John T. & Betsey A. Park - 9/20/1865 (Wm. C. Bass, M. G.)
Day, John & Frances Harris - 4/30/1848 (R. B. Kelly)
Day, Wiley & Sarah Jane Gaston - 10/15/1850 (Jas. M. Kelly)
DeFour, Wm. & Mary Jane House - 1/2/1848 (Wm. F. Gaston)
DeFur, Jos. & Martha Ray - 3/30/1856 (B. Rowland)
DeJarnett, Reuben & Nancy Reid - 12/26/1795
DeLaney, Drury W. & Laura Elliott - 7/16/1857 (Littleton D. Caldwell)
Dennard, Jarred & Emma H. Macon - 1/26/1858
Denning, Geo. A. & Sarah G. Tunison - 2/4/1863 (R. A. Houston, M. G.)
Dennis, Geo. W. & Sarah Ann Jackson - 11/21/1865 (Lorengo D. Carlton)
Devaney, John Thos. & Emily Harris - 4/20/1857 (Daniel Owens)
Devaney, Wm. & Mary Ann Palmer - 11/10/1871 (J. H. Kilpatrick)
Devant, Jas. M. & Celina Cocroft - 11/5/1860 (J. J. Wallace, M. G.)
Deviney, Thos. & Tempy Riley - 12/4/1821 (A. Hutchinson)
Dick, Wm. & Polly Price - 1/3/1811 (H. Gatlin)
Dickins, Tillman & Sarah Jane Pickett - 4/3/1852 (Hart. C. Peek)
Dickerson, Wm. & Eliz. Credille - 11/5/1819
Dickerson, Francis & Eliz. Garrett - 11/9/1826 (A. H. Scott)
Dickerson, John T. & Ella Lindsay - 5/3/1869 (Wm. A. Overton)
Dickerson, Roger & Catherine Daniel - 2/11/1825

Dickerson, Wm. & Cornelis David - 6/22/1859
Dicks, Geo. & Nancy Elton - 4/8/1800
Dillard, Geo. & Martha Wall - 7/29/1822 (Lovick Pierce)
Dillon, John & Lethea Thigpen - 4/16/1848 (W. F. Gaston)
Dix, John W. K. & Sarah Eliz. Martin - 7/23/1851 (P. H. Mell, M. G.)
Dixon, David & Martha Aubrey - 3/10/1788
Dixon, Hugh & (Reb) Reckah Alford - 10/3/1807 (Geo. Stovall)
Dixon, Joel & Nancy Watson - 1/10/1820? (O. Porter)
Doble, Joshua M. & Ellen V. Wilson - 2/16/1869 (P. H. Mell, M. G.)
Dolvin, Jas. & Peggy Anne McHargue - 12/18/1823 (Thos. Johnson)
Dolvin, Jas. & Nancy Boone - 2/7/1821 (Wm. Cone)
Dolvin, Jas. & Be McMillan - 12/7/1835 (John H. Steele?)
Dolvin, Jas. H. & Sarah E. E. Turnell - 6/17/1856 (I. A. Wms.)
Dolvin, Wm. B. & Sarah C. Boswell - 2/8/1855 (J. W. Reed)
Dooley, L. J. & Martha W. Smith - 11/11/1852 (Wm. Bryan)
Dossey, John & Nancy Smith - 1/25/1815 (Jas. Baldwin)
Dosta, Jonathan & Amanda Edge - 8/27/1854 (Absalom Rhodes)
Dosta, Wm. T. & Sarah E. Hale - 1/8/1852 (Hamer Kendel)
Doughter, Wm. & Martha Norsworthy - 9/3/1803 (Jesse Lacey)
Dowell, Jas. W. & Eliz. Carson - 12/19/1790
Downing, Thos. & Adaline Galtin? - 12/28/1826 (Gatlin)
Downs, Wm. A. & Mary A. Moore - 12/18/1856 (Wm. Wms.)
Drake, Jas. W. & Caroline F. Boswell - 2/6/1837 (V. R. Thornton)
Drake, Jas. V. & Mrs. Sarah A. Callaway - 9/6/1856
Drake, John & Ellen Baugh - 12/7/1869 (W. C. Birchmore)
Drake, Patrick Henry & Martha Billbrath? - 4/24/1826 (Gilbreath)
Drake, Thos. R. & Laura R. Carlton - 2/23/1864 (W. R. Foote, M. G.)
Duke, Green & Ann Robinson - 8/5/1830 (Francis West)
Duke, Isham & Eliz. Sherrill - 10/1/1806
Duke. Robt. & Patty Halloway - 2/19/1800
Dunaway, John & Eliz. Maybay - 9/20/1821 (Francis West)
Duncan, Daniel & Paty Johnson - 12/7/1806 (Thos. Crawford)
Duncan, Daniel & Millie Wms. - 1/16/1844 (Thos. Stacks)
Duncan, Jas. & Sally S. ----- - 7/22/1805
Dunn, Hiram & Letitia Grier - 2/5/1821
Dunn, Ishmael & Martha Darlington - 1/8/1833 (J. P. Leveritt)
Dunn, Wm. & Anne Thompson - 12/5/1788
Dupree, Jas. & Susan Jones - 2/6/1872 (N. M. Jones, M. G.)
Dupree, Jas. M. & Jane Shedd - 12/7/1867 (Columbus Heard)
Durham, Abram & Eliz. Durham - 2/4/1845 (Samuel Ely)
Durham, Columbus & Catherine Reynolds - 12/5/1871
Durham, Geo. W. & Hattie M. Hendon - 12/18/1859 (J. M. Stillwell)
Durham, Henry H. & Fannie C. Edwards - 6/27/1865 (Jno. R. Young, M. G.)
Durham, Jas. & Rebeccah Norris - 8/10/1837 (John G. Holtzclaw)
Durham, J. D. & Cordelia West - 5/20/1875 (John S. Callaway)
Durham, John C. & Sarah Bowles - 11/17/1831 (Augustine Evans)
Durham, Jonathan D. & Eliza Ann Parham - 1/31/1867 (Wm. Britain, M. G.)
Durham, Jos. V. & Hartie? A. Tool? - 4/22/1875 (P. H. McWhorter)
Durham, Samuel D. & Rebecca Armstrong - 7/5/1835 (Jack Lumpkin)
Durham, Samuel D. & Alzira E. Watson - 1/24/1839 (B. M. Saunders)
Durham, Samuel D. & Henrietta Morgan - 12/12/1858 (P. H. Mell)
Durham, Samuel J. & Nancy Harris - 10/9/1866 (E. B. Moody)
Durham, Silas & Alvina Booles - 12/4/1827
Durham, Wm. & Reba Reynolds - 1/5/1805
Durham, Wm. J. & Va. A. Moss - 11/27/1866 (P. H. Mell)
Durat, Aldolphus F. & Henrietta W. Crane - 2/28/1861 (R. W. Houston)
Duval, Ezekiel & Luriah Hunt - 7/3/1838 (Jas. M. Godkin)
Dyer, John & Frances Pendergrass - 12/7/1817 (Hinton Crawford)

Eades, W---- & Lucy E. Heath - Sept. 2, 1860 (Hart Peek)
Easley, Clement & Frances Terrell - Jan. 8, 1819 (A. Gresham)
Early, Jeremiah & Eliza. Cunningham - Oct. 15, 1806 (Thomas Crawford)
Early, Seaborn & Nancy Porter - Nov. 8, 1819
Easlin, James M. & Sara Anne Turner - Oct. 20, 1841 (Ephriam -----)
Eason, Thomas T. & Mary A. Hightower - Aug. 2, 1857 (Joseph R. -----)
Echols, Robert & Polly Freeman - April 22, 1824
Echols, Silas M. & Sarah C. Hammonds - Jan. 4, 1838 (Vincent R. -----)
Edmonds, Reuben B. & Miriam Kennedy - Dec. 21, 1837 (Nathan -----)
Edmonds, Wm. & Frances G. Greer - Oct. 19, 1856 (Wm. English)
Edmondson, Augustus & Mary Ann Jones - June 26, 1842 (N. M. Lu-----)

247

Edmondson, John & Martha Freeman - April 8, 1859 (Geo. A. Math-----)
Edmondson, Joseph & Rebecca Ann Wilson - Dec. 29, 1846 (W. H. Con-----)
Edmundson, James & Elizabeth Humphrey - March 28, 1817 (James Greer)
Edwards, Ambrose & Betsey Kimbrough - May 12, 1807 (Wm. Johnson)
Edwards, Ethelbred & Julie Ogletree - Dec. 9, 1823
Edwards, Gresham & Emily Armstrong - Oct. 23, 1840
Edwards, Jacob & Matilda Acre - Dec. 14, 1815 (Thomas Lyne)
Edwards, John & Susan McBride - Dec. 23, 1848
Edwards, Leroy & Polly Allen - Jan. 8, 1824 (Chesley Bristow)
Edwards, Pitman R. & Elizabeth I. Malone - Aug. 24, 1845 (R. L. McWhorter)
Edwards, Thomas & Angeline Chain - Dec. 18, 1848
Eidson, Ellis & Celia Fuller - July 12, 1821 (Abraham Teates)
Eidson, John R. & Mary Harris - Dec. 23, 1835 (John Wilson)
Eidson, Thomas & Mary Hodges - Dec. 5, 1827
Eidson, Willis & Mary Richardson - Aug. 30, 1840 (James M. Porter)
Elder, John & Susan Barnett - Nov. 25, 1823
Elder, Wm. H. & Catherine Jackson - June 23, 1806
Eley, Samuel & Sarah Brooks - Feb. 13, 1828 (Sylvanus Gibson, M. G.)
Eley, Wilborn & Mary Newsom - June 3, 1829
Ellington, Enoch & Nancy C. Blankenship - Feb. 12, 1816 (R. Baugh)
Ellington, Hekekiah & Lucy A. G. Green - Jan. 5, 1809 (Francis Ross, M.G.)
Ellington, Richard & Eliza White - Dec. 24, 1825
Elliott, Benj. & Elizabeth Williams - Dec. 27, 1860 (John O'Neal)
Elliott, David & Dionia Findley - Nov. 6, 1818 (L. Bethune)
Elliott, George & Mary Malone - Oct. 7, 1819 (Wm. Cone)
Ellis, James H. & Lucienda Hendricks - June 29, 1843 (J. W. Godkin)
Ellis, John W. & Elizabeth Ellerbee - Dec. 9, 1847 (J. J. Loudermilk)
Ellis, Mathew & Martha McHargue - July 8, 1819 (Thomas Johnson)
Elmore, John Wm. & Martha Sims - August 30, 1824
Elmore, Matthew & Lucy Tait - September 15, 1824
Ely, James J., Jr. & Menlo Rucker - Nov. 15, 1873
Ely, John & Frances Jernigan - Jan. 12, 1843 (James Jones, M. G.)
English, Henry & Nancy Middleton - May 10, 1807 (J. Mapp)
English, James N. & Sallie M. Greer - Oct. 17, 1865 (John B. Young)
English, J. H. & Elijah Holtzclaw - Dec. 18, 1855 (P. H. Mell)
English, John & Ann Holtzclaw - Jan. 2, 1847
English, John H. & Mary V. Beazley - Nov. 26, 1868 (Wm. A. Overton?)
English, Stephen & Martha Cheney - Dec. 13, 1849 (Enoch Callaway)
English, Wm. & Mary Durham - Nov. 28?, 1851? (B. L. Word)
Epps, Alexander & Louisa Hunter - June 10, 1869 (W. H. Bri__berry)
Epps, Alexander W. & Melissa Jane Butler - June 6, 1868
Epps, Chesley & Elizabeth T. Mitchell - March 4, 1858 (J. H. Wragg)
Epps, Wm. C. & Emaline Barnes - Dec. 27, 1868 (E. A. Burgess)
Epps, Wm. & Amanda Roberts - Oct. 9, 1825 (R. A. Credelle)
Errick, Charles C. & Martha Ann Elizabeth Williams - March 26, 1866
  (Johnson)
Espry, Robert & Mary Barnette - Sept. 21, 1799
Ethridge, Henry C. & Sarah E. Sharp - Aug. 5, 1868 (H. H. Tucker)
Evans, Arden & Elizabeth Carmichael - Jan. 15, 1805
Evans, Ardin B. C. & Josephine McMichael - Sept. 15, 1842 (James McK---)
Evans, Benj. T. & Emma F. Littleton - Feb. 7, 1867 (A. J. S. Jackson?)
Evans, Elijah & Polly Pee--- - Dec. 24, 1811 (Malachi Murden?)
Evans, Nicholas H. & Catherine C. White - Nov. 16, 1860 (T. R. Swanson)
Evans, Winston & Elizabeth Jackson - May 14, 1823 (John Park)
Evans, Winston & Sarah Park - July 3, 1827 (Julius Alford)
Ezell, Henry Clay & Olive M. Arnold - Jan. 14, 1869 (Hart C. P----)
Ezell, James M. & Martha H. Arnold - Feb. 9, 1865 (Hart C. Peek)
Ezell, James M. & Frances L. Bowden - Oct. 28, 1870

Floyd, George F. & Maranda Copeland - June 15, 1833 (Wm. Bryan)
Floyd, John & Ruth Grimes - Jan. 29, 1833 (A. Hutcheson)
Fluker, John C. & Mary Ann Culbreth - Oct. 12, 1837 (John B. Ca----)
Fluker, Jesse M. & Julia Holtzclaw - Feb. 14, 1872 (W. A. Overton)
Fluker, Oscar S. & Mollie Sanford - Jan. 12, 1869 (Philip H. Robinson)
Folis, Turner P. & Nell Ledbetter - June 3, 1802
Folly, Wm. & Elizabeth Ellis - March 9, 1816 (C. Maddox)
Force, Albert W. & Irene Howell - Dec. 22, 1870 (Homer Hendee, M. G.)
Force, Benjamin W. & Julia Ann Harper - Oct. 21, 1841 (F. R. Golding)
Ford, John S. & Sarah Ann May - April 14, 1840 (John G. Holtzclaw)
Ford, Wm. & Sarah Wyatt - April 27, 1852 (B. Rowland)

Ford, Wm. & Virginia Bennett - April 21, 1853 (B. Rowland)
Ford, Wm. & Winnie Thigpen - Sept. 30, 1855 (B. Rowland)
Forrest, James N. & Sarah Chapple - Jan. 30, 1864 (M. W. Arnold, M. G.)
Forrester, Gresham & Jane Waddell - March 14, 1831
Forrester, Jesse M. & Sarah Ann Mitchell - Dec. 17, 1840 (V.R. Thornton)
Forrester, Joel & Sarah Tatum - Oct. 24, 1799
Forrester, Joel & Elizabeth Newsom - Sept. 26, 1833 (Jesse H. Watson?)
Forrester, Redman & Martha E. Holtzclaw - June 19, 1858
Forrester, Wm. & Sarah Hunt - March 5, 1804
Forrester, Wm. & Nancy Payne - May 9, 1822 (Robert Newsom)
Forrester, William & Polly Boles - Jan. 9, 1812 (Lemuel Greene)
Foster, Anderson & Sally Bellingsby - Nov. 29, 1801
Fort, Feruch S. & Lena Chambers - July 8, 1835 (James H. Taylor)
Foster, Arthur & Elizabeth Glenn - Feb. 12, 1790
Foster, Arthur & Harriet Crawford - Oct. 15, 1819 (Thomas Stocks)
Foster, Arthur R. & Mrs. Harriet T. Leverett - Nov. --, 1874 (Albert Gray)
Foster, James F. & Matilda Houghton - June 18, 1815 (Lovick Pierce)
Foster, John & Nancey Mallory - Nov. 3, 1808 (Wm. Johnston)
Foster, Joseph & Charlotte Daniel - Jan. 13, 1819 (Wm. Robinson)
Foster, Robert & Nancy Ellis - July 18, 1833 (Hartwell H. Laurence)
Foster, Robert M. & Nancy Watts - June 22, 1852 (Vincent R. Thornton)
Foster, Samuel & Jane Watkins - March 13, 1827
Foster, Seaborn & Clementine P. Simmons - Aug. 8, 1842 (Ephriam Bruce)
Foster, Thomas T. & Mary Higginbothams - May 14, 1851 (S. I. Pinkerton)
Foster, Wm. & Mary Talley - Sept. 10, 1833 (H. H. Lawrence)
F------, Elias G. & Rachel A. Duncan - May 15, 1859 (Reuben Kelly)
Frogier, John V. & Martha Irby - Nov. 18, 1841 (John Howell)
Freeman, Beasley & Polly Cummins - Aug. 2, 1840 (J. M. Wilson)
Freeman, George A. & Catherine S. Edmonds - Dec. 23, 1858 (James Davison)
Freeman, James & Anny Thurmon - Dec. 19, 1822 (Abraham Teak?)
Freeman, John G. & Martha J. Durham - Oct. 7, 1852 (Wm. Tuggle)
Freeman, Valentine & Nancy Legett - March 20, 1805
Freeman, Zacharia & Margaret Findley - July 3, 1842 (John H. Zuber?)
French, Lewis & Julia Ann Newton - Apr. 10, 1823 (Hugh Smith, M. G.)
Fretwell, Micajah H. & Jane L. Harper - Nov. 11, 1804
Fuller, Elijah & Elizabeth Bogger - Oct. 25, 1811 (A. Veagey)
Fuller, David & Lucy Bedford - Jan. 19, 1817 (Wm. Cone)
Fuller, Elijah & Nancy Bowles - Jan. 31, 1825
Fuller, Frederick C. & Julia M. Nickelson - June 20, 1860 (Homer Hend---,
    M. G.)
Fuller, Greene & Susanna Burford - March 18, 1811 (A. Vezgey)
Fuller, Jesse & Polly Jackson - Nov. 25, 1807 (Wm. Browning)
Fuller, Simon & Nancy Hall - Jan. 4, 1842 (James Hutchinson)
Fuller, Wm. S. & Celea White - Dec. 13, 1836 (James Moore)
Fulwood, John Thomas & Rebecca Lamar - Sept. 30, 1846 (B. M. San----)
Furlough, Charles & Elizabeth Tucker - Feb. 1, 1820
Furlow, David & Sally Dawson - March 20, 1804
Furlow, Geo. W. & Lucy J. Dickins - Nov. 21, 1850 (J. T. Billingslea)
Furlow, James & Peggy Pugne? - Feb. 5, 1803
Furlow, James T. & Sarah Ann Hutchinson - Feb. 28, 1839 (Wm. L. S----)
Furlow, Osborn & Sarah Anne Brinckley - Jan. 14, 1831 (Wm. Cone)
Futral, Benjamin & Nancy Smith - Oct. 17, 1811 (Robert Rea)
Fambrough, James & Elizabeth Lewood - Dec. 10, 1854 (W. A. Partee)
Fambrough, Jesse M. & Delilah Jane Freeman - Jan. 24, 1856 (W. A. P----)
Fambrough, Thomas M. & Jane Freeman - Nov. 30, 1840 (James Por----)
Fambrough, Wm. & Sally Bradshaw - March 10, 1814
Fambrough, Zachariah & Elizabeth Jane Jackson - Sept. 10, 1830 (James
    M. Po-----)
Fannin, Isham & Peggy Porter - Sept. 1, 1809 (Samuel Harper)
Fannin, Jepthah & Catherine Porter - May 10, 1814 (Jack Lampkin)
Fannin, Wm. & Nancy Pierce - Jan. 13, 1800
Fannin, Wm. & Catherine Martin - Jan. 18, 1807 (J. Mapp)
Farmer, Wm. Thomas & Mary Jane Bowles - Dec. 22, 1871 (Wm. A. Overton)
Farrar, Wm. J. & Louisa Bailey - June 11, 1848 (T. M. Fambrough)
Farris, James & Nancy Aurena Bennett - June 26, 1856 (Isaac R. Hall)
Farrow, Nathaniel & Jane Williams - Dec. 8, 1850 (Joseph W. Drennan)
Fassett, Early P. & Martha Brunt - Sept. 29, 1842 (Robert F. Griffin)
Farwater, James L. & Mary Ann Hall - Oct. 9, 1840 (Wm. I. Heard)
Fauch, Jonas & Polly Daniell - Oct. 20, 1793
Faulkner, Zachariah & Sarah A. D. Thompson - Dec. 2, 1866

Fauntheroy, Geo. L. & Aphiah F. B. Todd? - Nov. 10, 1831 (Lovick Pierce,
    M. G.)
Fay, Frank & Dorothy Hicks - Jan. 25, 1821 (Francis Cummins)
Fears, Ezekiel -- & Alisey Stringfellow - June 9, 1803
Fears, James P. & Elizabeth Bowden - Dec. 13, 1864 (N. M. Arnold, M. G.)
Fears, Jesse W. & Mary E. Perkins - Sept. 6, 1864 (E. W. Warren, M. G.)
Ferril, Archelaus & Sally Parker - Aug. 28, 1797
Few, Joseph & Fanny Fields - July 23, 1804
Fields, Joseph W. & Emily Foster - July 24, 1851 (M. G. Foster)
Fields, Lewis & Eliza Fetten? - Dec. 27, 1827 (Francis Cummins)
Fields, Thomas & Sally Kilgore - Dec. 19, 1791
Fillingham, Counsel & Nancy Williams - Aug. 29, 1814 (Archibald Walls?)
Fillingham, Henry C. & Angeline C. O'Neal - Dec. 14, 1865 (L.C. Caldwell)
Fillingham, Jarvis W. & Nancy A. Veazey - Dec. 14, 1843 (John L. Veazey)
Fillingham, Jarvis W. & Eliza Stanley - Dec. 14, 1868 (L. D. Caldwell)
Finch, George W. & Martha Ann Pierce - Oct. 22, 1837 (Nathan Hobbs)
Finch, John E. & Almira Moody - Nov. 12, 1840 (James Davidson)
Finch, John E. & Mary R. A. Patrick - Dec. 12, 1866 (Lucius C. Broome)
Finch, Wm. & Elizabeth Stallings - Aug. 25, 1831 (George Hall)
Finley, John & Mary Ray - May 3, 1804
Finley, Leroy I. & Hannah Woodham - Jan. 23, 1840 (John Hutchinson)
Finley, Norwood H. & Cynthia Caldwell - Jan. 1, 1835 (Abraham Jenkins)
Finley, Robert & Jane Finley - Nov. 26, 1802
Finley, Robert & Lucendia Finley - Aug. 18, 1803
Finley, Thomas & Anna Waggmer - Nov. 9, 1833
Finley, Thomas & Nancy Gregory - Aug. 3, 1846 (W. D. Maddox)
Finley, Thomas L. & C. A. Crawford - Aug. 19, 1869 (W. R. Fo----)
Finley, Wm. & Polly Sharpe - June 29, 1805
Fisher, Joseph & Mrs. Georgia Ann White - May 10, 1865
Fitzgerald Bird & Eliz. B. Springer - Dec. 20, 1825
Fitzpatrick, Joseph & Ruth Hodge - July 12, 1823 (Hinton Crawford)
Fitzpatrick, Rene & Polly Watts - Jan. 15, 1816 (Jack Lumpkin)
Fitzsimmons, Henry & Elmira Burk - April 22, 1819
Flanagan, Edward & Frances R. Moose - Sept. 4, 1864 (Ezekell S. W-----)
Flanagan, Wm. & Marietta Holder - Feb. 10, 1867 (E. S. Williams)
Fleetwood, Littleberry & Tillitha J. Evans - Oct. 15, 1857 (L.B. Jackson)
Fleetwood, William & Mary Ann Jackson - April 17, 1832 (J. P. Lucrett)
Fleming, William & Delila Kennedy - July 31, 1836 (Jos. H. McWhorter)
Flint, William T. & Lella W. Moore - Feb. 18, 1874 (J. H. Kilpatrick)
Florence, Frank S. L. & Sarah Eldeces Winfield - April 17, 1860 (A. Gray)
Florence, Wm. A. & Betsey Ann Park - June 7, 1859 (Geo. C. Clarke)
Flourney, Gibson & Huldy Williams - Sept. 8, 1802
Flow, Coleman & Elizabeth Coleman - Feb. 23, 1809

Gafford, Thomas & Polly Whatley - May 1, 1801
Gavert?, John Mathews & Delacy? Hughes - Aug. 22, 1844
Gailsfield, Thomas & Polly Tarby - Feb. 28, 1801
Gann, John & Susan Johnson - Jan. 5, 1856 (B. Rowland)
Gann, Marion & Sarah Z. Wright - Jan. 29, 1852 (Alfred L. W-----)
Gann, Samuel & Mary Hambrion? - April 24, 1788
Gantt, Eli & Elijah Dunn - June 28, 1856 (J. W. Reid, M. G.)
Gardner, Samuel & Sarah E. H. Bowles - Dec. 7, 1869
Gardner, S. A. & Selina S. Durham - Dec. 8, 1870 (W. R. Wilson)
Garlington, James & Martha Colquitt - July 17, 1820 (Wm. Tally, M. G.)
Garlington, Thomas C. & Elizabeth Edmonds - Dec. 10, 1835 (V.R. Thornton)
Garner, John J. & Mary Cumbree?? - Feb. 14, 1856 (B. Rowland)
Garner, Thomas & Martha Webb - Sept. 6, 1821 (Thomas Riley)
Garner, Wm. & Elizabeth Webb - Jan. 28, 1819 (Thomas Riley)
Garner, Wm. B. & Elizabeth Cheek - July 29, 1855 (B. Rowland)
Garrad, Wm. W. & Mary M. Urquhart - Aug. 4, 1840
Garret, John & Jean Greer - April 4, 1816 (Miller Hunter)
Garrett, Thomas B. & Betsey Ann Cole - Dec. 17, 1818 (John Park)
Garrett, John & Anny Cob? - June 24, 1818 (L. Bethune)
Garrett, Robert & Mary Hale - Oct. 5, 1818
Gartrelle, John O. & Mary A. W. Randle - Dec. 19, 1848 (L. G. Hillyer)
Gartrelle?, Wm. J. & Eliza. A. Scott - Dec. 30, 1849 (Hinton Crawford)
Gastin, Alexander & Sally Garner - Dec. 9, 1802
Gaston, John & Martha Blanks - Jan. 8, 1826
Gaston, Matthew & Rebeckah Harden - Dec. 13, 1793
Gaston, Matthew & Phereba Brown - April 11, 1827

Gaston, William & Louisa A. Fos---t - March 16, 1839 (Robert F. Griffin)
Gaston, William & Sarah Matthews - Jan. 19, 1843 (B. F. Griffin)
Gaston, William & Mary Ann Wilson - Aug. 2, 1849 (J. M. Kelly)
Gatewood, Phillip & Sarah Colquitt? - Oct. 7, 1821 (C. Maddox)
Gatlin, Alpheus & Mariah Gatlin - May 1, 1826
Gatlin, Churchwell & Patsey Moore - May 1, 1802
Gatlin, Lemuel M. & Elizabeth H. Jackson - Mar. 8, 1829 (Ephraim Bruce)
Gatlin, Major & Darkes? Gatlin - Sept. 21, 1808 (S. Gatlin)
Gatlin, Radford & Elizabeth Daniel - June 5, 1818
Gaylord, Giles & Ferreby Jones - Jan. 26, 1811 (Arthur Foster)
Gentry, Burgess & Polly Parrish - March 29, 1825
Gentry, John D. & Nancy Copelan - April 25, 1850 (Wm. Bryan)
Gentry, Seaborn & Malinda Shirley - Aug. 6, 1839
Gentry, Samuel & Cynthia Connell - Feb. 1, 1820 (Wm. McGiboney)
Gentry, Wm. & Mary Gilmer - Oct. 17, 1848 (W. T. Gaston)
Gentry, Wm. H. & Laura Tunnell - Dec. 28, 1871 (R. P. Perdue, M. G.)
George, John R. & Lucy C. Anderson - Feb. 1, 1859 (Geo. C. Clarke)
George, William & Elizabeth Grimes - Oct. 10, 1821 (Thomas Johnson)
Gerdine?, George Augustus L. J. & Anne Fleming Cadwright - Dec. 20, 1871
Germany, John & Elizabeth Brown - March 7, 1806
Gettathews, George & Cassandra Wells - Feb. 5, 1816 (N. Lewis)
Gibbs, Miles & Martha Shepherd - Oct. 3, 1803
Gibbs, Thomas & Nancy Maddox - June 2, 1819 (Thomas Johnson)
Gibbs, Thomas & Julia Cornelia Ralls - May 26, 1842 (W. M. I. Hard)
Gibson, Henry A. & Sarah A. Jones - Nov. 10, 1862? (B. M. Sanders)
Gibson, Isaiah & Lydia White - Nov. 24, 1804
Gibson, Isaiah & Lydia White - Sept. 1, 1808 (Thomas Carle----)
Gibson, Thomas C. & Clementine J. Reid? - Nov. 23, 1868? (J. M. Dickey)
Gilbrea--, Daniel & Martha Gwinn - Aug. 26, 1819 (Wm. McGiboney)
Gilbert, Robert & Eliza Turner - July 8, 1831 (J. P. Leverest?)
Giles, Thomas & Mary Whatley - Jan. 7, 1804
Giles, William & Nancy Da--iel? - April 11, 1805
Gillen, John & Jane Caldwell - May 4, 1834 (James M. D----)
Gillen, Samuel I. & Margaret J. --reen--- - Dec. 21, 1875 (M.M. Landrum,
   M. G.)
Gilmer, Joseph & Susan Du---- - Feb. 13, 1853 (W. H. Blythe)
Gilmore, John & Betsey Cartwright - Jan. 8, 1802
Gilding, Charles & Ann H. G. Green - April 17, 1854 (S. G. Hillyer)
Glass, B. & Sally White - Aug. 20, 1808
Glass, Elias & Sally Wilson - Nov. 26, 1804
Glass, James & Penny Pace - June 25, 1805
Glass, Jonathan & Milly Fuller - June 22, 1814 (John Browning)
Glass, William & Mary Baker - Oct. 7, 1799
Glass, Z., Jr. & Sally Wilson - Dec. 18, 1799
Glawson?, Eli & Mary Ann Divine - Oct. 15, 1849 (R. F. Griff)
Gla---, Samuel & Elizabeth Gl----om - July 27, 1848 (W. F. Gas----)
Gla---, Hyram & Nancy Lassiter - Sept. 24, 1804
Glover?, L. L. & Ramelia N. Wheeler - July 27, 1873
Gooch, Nathan & Polly Jenkins - Aug. 19, 1819 (L. Bethune)
Good----, David W. & Lucretia C. Littleton - Dec. 15, 1859 (James W.
   Godkin)
Gore, Thomas & Mary Alford - Nov. 26, 1818 (Thomas Snow)
Gorley, Jonathan & Mary Beckom - March 31, 1825
Gouger, Stephen & Julia Veazey - Nov. 4, 1819
Graham, Joseph & Nancy Catchings - Dec. 18, 1803
Graham, Joseph & Winney Gooch - Dec. 20, 1808 (John Dingler)
Grant, Allen & Mary Ann Barnhart - Jan. 4, 1855 (W. J. Hanley)
Grant, Cullan E. & Robelia? H. Bales? - Dec. 8, 1850 (Daniel Hightower)
Grant, Daniel & Lucy Crutchfield - June 20, 1810 (Josia Randle)
Grant, James & Eliza Wright - Jan. 4, 1848 (James Moore)
Grant, James T. & Frances Hester - July 4, 1872 (J. H. Kilpatrick)
Grant, John G. & Sarah F. Coley - Dec. 10, 1861 (Joseph R. Parker)
Grant, John C. & Texana Howell - Oct. 14, 1870
Grant, Joseph & Eliza T. Grant - May 16, 1851 (Daniel Hightower)
Grant, J. T. & Mary S. Chew? - April 6, 1841 (Thomas Stocks)
Grant, Thomas & Mary --? Baird - Jan. 4, 1826 (Lovick Pierce, M. G.)
Grant, Wm. S. & Nancy R. Lundy - Oct. 10, 1847 (Francis Bowman)
Graves, Joseph & Mary Shorter - Feb. 12, 1822 (James Woodberry)
Grav--, Young W. & Martha E. Holtzclaw - Nov. 12, 1852
Gray, Archibald & Cynthia Arnold - Jan. 29, 1807 (Robt. M. Cunningham)

251

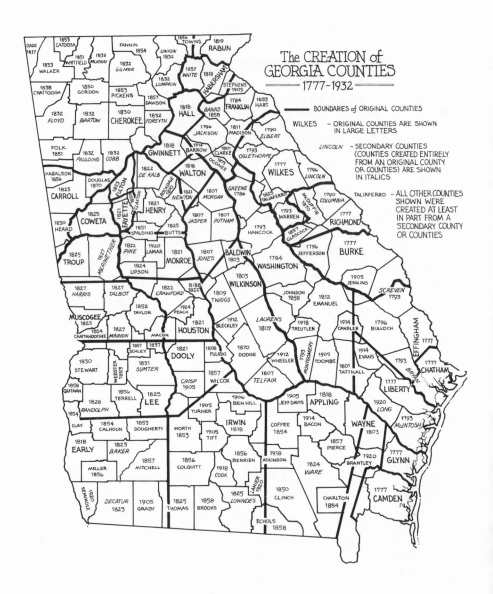

The CREATION of
GEORGIA COUNTIES
1777-1932

── BOUNDARIES of ORIGINAL COUNTIES

WILKES – ORIGINAL COUNTIES ARE SHOWN
IN LARGE LETTERS

LINCOLN – SECONDARY COUNTIES
(COUNTIES CREATED ENTIRELY
FROM AN ORIGINAL COUNTY
OR COUNTIES) ARE SHOWN
IN ITALICS

TALIAFERRO – ALL OTHER COUNTIES
SHOWN WERE
CREATED AT LEAST
IN PART FROM A
SECONDARY COUNTY
OR COUNTIES

Greene, Argustus F. & Amanda Jane Robertson - Jan. 27, 1840
Greene, Benjamin F. & Susan Amorette Greene - Nov. 24, 1846 (Francis
  Bowman)
Greene, Farnafald? & Ruth Dawson - July 8, 1818 (Lovick Pierce)
Greene, James H. & Ann Rad---- - Jan. 27, 1853 (J. R. Hall)
Greene, James H. & Permelia D. Criswell - Oct. 2, 1864 (E. S. Wms.)
Greene, John & Patsey Curtis - May 20, 1821 (Wm. Moore)
Greene, Joseph & Tabitha Whatley - Dec. 14, 1804
Greene, Lemuel & Nancy Merritt - Oct. 22, 1806 (Jesse Lacey)
Greene, Lemuel & Eliza Palmer - May 6, 1824 (Jack Lumpkin)
Greene, Lemuel & Sarah Clements - Feb. 22, 1842
Greene, Lemuel H. & Frances King - Aug. 21, 1843 (John W. Reid)
Greene, Lemuel & Pharebee Jane Hall - Aug. 4, 1850 (James M. Kelly)
Greene, Walter & Nancy W. Maddox - Jan. 4, 1825
Greene, Wm. & Frances Tucker - July 3, 1822 (Robert Newsome)
Greenwood, Thomas & Nancey Mitchell - Apr. 25, 1805
Greenwood, Thomas & Lenora Ann Mounger - Mar. 9, 1819 (Lovick ------)
Greenwood, Thomas E. & Emaline D. Baird - Mar. 31, 1833 (T. P. C. -----)
Greer, Aquila & Thena? Yates - Aug. 11, 1814 (Thomas Johnson)
Greer, Aquilla & Sarah Sayers - Nov. 29, 1826 (Abraham Yates)
Greer, Archibald & Elizabeth King - June 10, 1828 (Wm. Cone)
Greer, David & Sarah Greer - Dec. 19, 1822 (Jeremiah Ragan?)
Greer, D. L. & Annie Durham - Nov. --, 1873?
Greer, Henry & Nancy Hoobes? - May 12, 1818
Greer, Henry F. & Ann A. Ragan - Dec. 4, 1800 (Jack Lumpkin)
Greer, Henry & Polly Nichols - Mar. 2, 1845 (Robt. McWhorter)
Greer, Isaac & Ione Harp? - Mar. 25, 1800
Greer, James & Pansey Merritt - Feb. 3, 1802
Greer, John & Elizabeth Greer - Apr. 1, 1805
Greer, John & Emma Crawford - Mar. 20, 1822 (Thomas Stocks)
Greer, John & Emily Talbot - June 23, 1830 (W. B. Barnett)
Greer, John & Jane Pinkard - June 24, 1823 (A. B. Longstreet)
Greer, Richard & Lucy Greer - Nov. 5, 1824
Greer, Robert & Carolina McCoy - Jan. 21, 1822
Greer, Thomas G. & Catherine Stephens - Dec. 20, 1831 (Wmson Bir---)
Greer, Thomas L. & Elizabeth White - June 16, 1831 (Wm. Bird)
Greer, William & Delilah Haynes - Jan. 15, 1794
Gregory, Benj. F. & Ann C. Ray - Dec. 18, 1856 (John W. M. Barnes?)
Gresham, Albert & Mary Wells - May 10, 1827 (Jacob King----)
Gresham, Albert W. & Emma E. Lindsey - Jan. 9, 1866 (R. A. H-----)
Gresham, John H. & Susan E. Phymes - Jan. 26, 1865 (H. H. Fitzpatrick)
Gresham, Sterling A. & Sarah F. Stokes - June 5, 184? (Frances Bowman)
Gresham, Y----- & Henson Harrison - June 10, 1803
Gresham, Young Felix & Sarah Jane Baugh - June 15, 18-- (F.F. Reynolds)
Griffin, John A. & Ann L. Scudder? - May 4, 1871 (C. W. Lane, M. G.)
Griffin, Walter & Rosina Willis - June 18, 1846 (Francis Bowman)
Griffith, Nathan & Judith Booles? - Nov. 3, 1828
Griffey, John & Frances Rainey - Dec. 19, 1825
Griffin, Andrew J. & Adaline Sanders - Dec. 30, 1835 (John F. Hallyer?)
Griffin, Matthew & Harriett Carrell - Jan. 6, 1824
Griffin, Robert & Susanna Brooks - Sept. 8, 1824
Griffith, Jedekiah & Jane Johnson - June 20, 1848 (T. D. Martin, M. G.)
Griffith, Thomas & Becky Akind? - Nov. 17, 1824
Griffith, Wm. P. & Sarah A. Wilson - Dec. 21, 1856 (J. G. Holtzclaw)
Griffith, Wm. V. & Martha L. Dickson - Dec. 16, 1860 (J. M. St----well)
Grimes, Henry & Mary W. King - Feb. 24, 1831 (Frances Cunnins)
Grimes, James & Lucinda King - Jan. 29, 1833 (James H. Taylor)
Grimes, Jesse & Rhoda Bates - Oct. 2, 1832 (Dickerson Jones)
Grimes, Joseph & Eliza. Cunningham - Oct. 21, 1824
Grimes, Joseph & Harriett Bouden - Dec. 11, 1833 (Wm. Park, M. G.)
Grimes, R. M. & Leila M. Jernigan - Feb. 10, 1870 (C. P. Beeman)
Grimes, Robert M. & Lucy M. Jernigan - Apr. --, 1874
Grimes, Sterling F. & Sarah Bowdre - May 5, 1841
Grimes, Thomas & Frances Meriwether - June 29, 1843 (Francis Bowman)
Grimes, Thomas W. & Anne Coleman - Jan. 11, 1844 (Otis Smith)
Grimes, Wm. P. & Martha A. Sayers - Jan. 28, 1858 (C. W. Launis?)
Grimmett, Robert & ----- - July 10, 1788
Guill, Wm. B. & Virginia Moody - March 26, 1856 (John B. Holtzclaw)
Greene, Isaac N. & Nancy Corry - Oct. 26, 1831 (C. T. Beeman)
G-----, Wm. M. & Sarah Harper - Sept. 2, 1870

G----, John L. & Mary Wright - Dec. 1, 1838 (James M. Porter)
Gwynn, Thomas & Emily Crossley - Apr. 12, 1846 (L. B. Jackson)

Hackney, John & Nancy Musgrove - Oct. 25, 1815 (Evan Myrick)
Hackney, Samuel & Cornelia C. Dorsey - Nov. 1, 1868 (James Davison)
Hackney, Wm. & Patsey Barker - Oct. 5, 1818
Hagaby, Joshua & Sally W----- - Feb. 11, 1801
Hagerty, Abel & Anna Backhannon - Dec. 30, 1803
Hailes, Henry J. & Margaret Findley - Apr. 29, 1852 (J. T. F-----)
Hailes, John T. & Amanda A. Hall - Jan. 30, 1868 (Wm. Bryan)
Hailey, James A. & Mary E. Crenshaw - Apr. 20, 1852 (John R. Young)
Haisten?, James & Margaret Cartwright - Aug. 12, 1819 (John Harris)
Hall, Dickson & Priscilla Baugh - Nov. 3, 1818
Hall, Edihugh & Elizabeth Kelly - Sept. 21, 1818
Hall, George & Malinda Dunn - May 5, 1822 (Thomas Riley)
Hall, George & Nancy Slaughter - Apr. 17, 1824
Hall, Hugh & Sally Hall - Mar. 2, 1803
Hall, Hugh & Mary Brown - Nov. 10, 1824
Hall, Hugh A. & Susan Ann Jackson - Aug. 17, 1848 (L. B. Jackson)
Hall, Isaac R. & Sarah E. Hall - May 14, 1863 (L. B. Jackson)
Hall, James D. & Sarah Pyron - Oct. 15, 1861 (Hinton Crawford)
Hall, James F. & Missouri A. Corry - Feb. 26, 1857 (J. S. K. A-----)
Hall, John & Polly Little - Aug. 27, 1811 (Josiah Rand----)
Hall, John & Nancy E. Leverett - Mar. 17, 1834 (A. Hutch----)
Hall, John L. & Emma A. Zimmerman - Nov. 5, 1863 (R. A. House)
Hall, Josiah T. & Elizabeth Taylor - Oct. 3, 1855 (W. H. C. Co----)
Hall, Samuel & Nancy Smith - Feb. 26, 1806
Hall, Samuel & Nancy Malone - Feb. 7, 1840 (Jas. C----)
Hall, Vincent S. & Mary E. Hall - Sept. 3, 1872 (W. ------)
Hall, Young & Mariah Ann Howell - Sept. 7, 1825 (Thos. -----)
Hames A. Baker & Macon Hester - Sept. 21, 1871 (W. R. Foote)
Hammett, James & Elizabeth Brooker - June 13, 1816 (Geo. O-----)
Hammond, Robert & Lovy? Hines - April 5, 1810 (Robert Re-----)
Hammond, Wm. & Mary Johnson - April 2, 1816? (Francis Cummins)
Hammond, Wm. & Nancy Clark - Sept. 22, 1835 (J. P. Leverett)
Hancock, George & Elizabeth O'Neal - Nov. 7, 1847 (John W. Reed?)
Hancock, George P. & Nannie E. Stewart - Oct. 29, 1874 (C.H. Strickland)
Hancock, Henry L. & Katherine Elizabeth Stewart - July 14, 1864 (John
  O'Neal)
Hancock, Henry W. & Elva Emma Saggus - Mar. 26, 1874 (W. A. Overton)
Hancock, James A. & Mattie Simpson - May 23, 1872 (Henry Newton)
Hand, Richard & Unity Medley (Uny) - June 25, 1842
Haralson, Braddy B. & Martha Ann Chambers - Dec. 21, 1848 (W. H. C. Cone)
Haralson, Hugh & Caroline M. Lewis - Nov. 27, 1828 (Lovick Pierce)
Haralson, Jesse B. & Elizabeth R. Conyers - Mar. 22, 1827 (James Culber-
  son)
Haralson, Kinchin? L. & Jane W. Lewis - Feb. 28, 1833 (Sam J. Cassels)
Haralson, Vincent & Lucy English - Jan. 10, 1809 (Wm. Greer)
Harbin, James T. & Fanny Pitman - Dec. 24, 1872 (H. C. Peek)
Harden, Henry & Mary Ann Watson - Mar. 17, 1829 (Ephriam Bruce?)
Hardin, James & Matilda Richards - Mar. 27, 1821 (John Harris)
Hardwick, James & Violet Elder - May 10, 1806
Hardy, W. J. & Hannah Rimes - Dec. 10, 1804
Harg--, Alex & Gressy Bonow? - Nov. 28, 1796
Hargroover, Sanford & Frances Bickers? - Apr. 27, 1833 (Lovick Pierce,
  M. G.)
Harlbert, Roswell & Frances Ella Davis - July 11, 1871
Harlow, James B. & Ella Geer - Feb. 16, 1874
Harp, Samuel & J. Clames? - Sept. 23, 1810 (W. Johnson)
Harp, William & Polly Brewer - Dec. 23, 1799
Harper, Allen & Lucy Smith - Feb. 28, 1801
Harper, Axamins & E. Ward - Jan. 3, 1805
Harper, George A. & Sophy J. Perkins - May 6, 1858 (J. M. Wragg)
Harren, James H. & Rosamond A. Caldwell - Jan. 1, 1837 (T. W. Grimes?)
Harris, Benjamin & Susan Pyron - Nov. --, 1829
Harris, Charles & Tabitha Gibbs - Dec. 20, 1820 (Lovick Pierce)
Harris, Charles F. & Rachel James - Dec. 7, 1831 (Joshua Cannon)
Harris, Elios & Nancy W. Hudson - May 10, 1800
Harris, Henry C. & Mary H. Taylor - June 16, 1848 (John B. Chappell)
Harris, James & Lucretia Jones - Nov. 10, 1817 (Francis Cummins)

Harris, James & Abigail Fambrough - July 5, 1833 (John H. Ray)
Harris, Jesse & Rachael Pendleton - Jan. 12, 1789
Harris, Jesse & Louisa Ra----- - Dec. 1, 1838?
Harris, John & Betsey Wilkinson - Mar. 19, 1816 (Robert Rea)
Harris, John & Henrietta Jackson - Apr. 29, 1846 (Francis Cowman)
Harris, John M. & Olive Stevens - June 10, 1819 (Thomas Johnson)
Harris, John T. & Frances C. Leslie - Feb. 1, 1852 (Hart C. Peek)
Harris, J. P. & Mary Elizabeth Allen - Jan. 6, 1878 (J. F. H-----)
Harris, Myles G. & Lucy Elizabeth S--y--- - Apr. 2, 1845 (Francis Bowman)
Harris, Nathaniel N. & Ellen N. Victory - Dec. 14, 1826 (Lovick Pierce,
   M. G.)
Harris, Robert & Mary Freeman - July 13, 1818 (Jesse Mercer)
Harris, Robert L. & Susan L. Head - Aug. 3, 1875 (F. G. Hughes)
Harris, Capt. S. B. & Patience Williams - Dec. 9, 1794
Harris, Seaborn & Polly Shaw - Dec. 19, 1823
Harris, Singleton & Maria Acree - Dec. 23, 1822 (Horatio A. B. Nunally)
Harris, Thomas McCall & Margaret Baldwin - Aug. 27, 1804
Harris, Thomas & Sarah Hall - Aug. 8, 1829 (Geo. Hall)
Harris, Thomas & Elizabeth Bunkley - Apr. 12, 1836 (Wm. Cone)
Harris, Thomas & Catherine Baldwin - Mar. 3, 1840 (James Jones)
Harris, Thomas & Burget Ann Burford - July 22, 1852
Harris, Wm. & Hannah Hogg - Aug. 23, 1787
Harris, Wm. & Matilda Blanks - Oct. 5, 1818
Harris, Wm. & Chrisaline Bruce - Feb. 19, 1846 (H. Lawrence)
Harris, Wm. L. M. & Sementha D. Johnson - Dec. 3, 1850 (P. H. Mell, M.G.)
Harris, Wm. L. U. & Sarah F. Johnson - Oct. 13, 1856
Harrison, Benjamin & Jane Matthews - Dec. 11, 1814 (Thomas Stocks?)
Harrison, James & Mary Harrison - July 31, 1801
Harrison, Jane W. & Elender? T. Evans - Feb. 10, 1831 (Leveritt V. Dee?)
Harrison, Robert & Isabel Pattils - May 6, 1821 (Wm. Tally)
Harrup, James & Ridley Harrup - Aug. 14, 1816 (Arch McCoy)
Harrup, Warren & Angeline T. Taylor - Feb. 11, 1849 (L. B. Jackson)
Hart, Isaac & Polly Merritt - Sept. 20, 1855 (W. W. Moore)
Hart, John S. & Martha J. Leverett - Sept. 10, 1857 (W. W. Moore)
Hart, Thomas & Ann Barnett - Jan. 18, 1810 (Clayborn Maddox)
Hart, Wm. M. & Mary E. Nave? - Jan. 12, 1869 (Philip H. Robinson)
Harvell, Daniel & Mary C-----1 - Nov. 11, 1801
Harvill, Thomas & Mary Chatham - Sept. 4, 1818 (Lovick Pierce)
Harwell, James M. & Sarah Lou Smith Moore - Apr. 14, 1857 (G. Bright, M.G)
Harwell, Wm. & Polly Hobbs - Mar. 21, 1816 (John Browning)
Hatchett, John & Eliza Tuggle - Dec. 18, 1820 (Lemuel Greene)
Hatton, Thomas & Nancey Lacey - Mar. 15, 1810 (Wm. Cone)
Hawke, John & Mary Head - Jan. 4, 1806 (Matthew Winfield)
Hawke, Peter & Polly Roberts - Jan. 4, 1806
Hayes, Ezekial & Rebecca Shelton - May 2, 1874
Hayes, Robert & Susan Beckham - May 2, 1820 (Lovick Pierce)
Hayes, Wm. & Polly Head - Oct. 26, 1801
Haynes, Jasper & Elizabeth Armstrong - Jan. 15, 1846 (S. G. Hillyer?)
Haynes, John & Elizabeth McKnight - Sept. 3, 1829 (Robert Newsom)
Haynes, Parmen---- & Mary Anne Tuggle - Oct. 10, 1843 (P. H. Mell, M.G.)
Haynes, Robert & Elizabeth Reid - May 16, 1825
Hays, Howard & Sarah A. V. Walker - Apr. 19, 1853 (J. W. Yarbrough)
Hays, Wm. & Nell Luckey - Mar. 29, 1805
Hazel, John & Leonard Levine - Aug. 4, 1816 (Thomas Bush)
Hazlett, Wilson & Nancy Mullins - Sept. 14, 1873 (D. H. Moncrief)
Heard, Franklin & Anne Bozeman - Feb. 22, 1820
Heard, James T. & Amorette Green? - July 5, 1866 (Philip B. Robinson)
Heard, John & Nancy Wallis - Jan. 26, 1805
Heard, John T. & Margaret F. Mitchell - Jan. 12?, 1860 (H.H. Tucker, MG)
Heard, Stephen I. & Lucy S. Foster - Nov. 30, 1840
Heard, Thomas & Ann Richards - Jan. 7, 1830 (Peter Johnson)
Heard, Woodrow & Polly Peoples - May 29, 1805
Heard, W. T. & Lula W. Moore - Nov. 9, 1875 (J. K. Kilpatrick)
Heard, Clem Freena & Martha L. Hester - Oct. 31, 1858 (John Calvin
   Johnson)
Hearn, Wm. T. & Betsey Ann Armor - May 22, 1867 (John W. Talley)
Heath, Matthew & Elizabeth Clements - Nov. 28, 1831 (Ephriam Bruce)
Heath, Rylan & Ann Gilbert - Apr. 26, 1808 (C. Maddox)
Heck, Thomas & Elizabeth Sturdivant - Aug. 17, 1818 (Wm. Cone)
Hedge, Whitfield & Elizabeth Greene - Dec. 10, 1817 (Wm. Cone)

Heflin, James & Sarah Winn - Feb. 19, 1802
Heflin, James & Nancy Thurmon - Dec. 30, 1805
Heflin, James & Nancy Thurman - Dec. 31, 1806 (Wm. Browning)
Hemphill, Hiram & Jane Moore - Dec. 22, 1840 (Francis Bowman)
Hemphill, Thompson & Rhoda Baggett - Jan. 21, 1808 (John Dingler?, M.G.)
Hemphill, Wm. & Nancy Hughes - Oct. 10, 1800?
Hendel, Homer & Frances King - June 1, 1847 (Francis Cowma--)
Henderson, Joseph M. & Emma H. J. Dawson - Feb. 18, 1864 (P.H. Mell, MG)
Hendricks, James M. & Frances V. Pollard - Dec. 28, 1865 (Wm. R. Wilson)
Hendry, C. M. & L. A. Blackman - Jan. 5, 1873 (W. A. Moore)
Henry, Thomas Wyatt & Mary Francis Cunningham - Jan. 13, 1852
Henson, Louden & Nancy Robinson - Nov. 8, 1829 (John Chew)
Hermon, Wm. & Betsey R. N--lton - Nov. 10, 1802
Hern, Wm. & Peggy Haynes - Sept. 4, 1825 (James Culberson)
Hern, Zabad & Lydia Rumsey - July 21, 1818
Hester, Francis & Mary Ann McCowen, - Aug. --, 1837
Hester, Robert A. & Roxanah Martin - July 6, 1837 (John Hender---)
Hester, Simeon & Ann Elizabeth Tuggle - Nov. 27, 1866 (Wm. A. -----)
Harmon, Hete? & Elizabeth West - Sept. 9, 1819 (Robert Borth?)
Hewston, John & Nancey Harris - Dec. 17, 1807 (Geo. Stovall)
Hickey, Wm. & Mary Connell - Sept. 12, 1844 (J. J. Howell)
Hiear?, Cornelius & Amanda Fisher - Mar. 25, 1873 (Jas. W. Godkin)
Higginbotham, Riley N. & Martha Little - Mar. 8, 1868 (Jas. H. McWhorter)
Hightower, Daniel & Betse-- Johnson - May 24, 1801
Hightower, Daniel Lee & Mary A. Credille - May 19, 1843 (Wesley Arnold,
  M. G.)
Hightower, Elisha & Polly ---lling - Dec. 31, 1816 (Gilly Moore)
Hightower, Jacob & Nancy Culbert - Feb. 18, 1799
Hightower, Matthew & Mary Copeland - Oct. 2, 1821 (H. G. Slaughter)
Hightower, Oscar T. & Mary R. Tunnison - Jan. 13, 1870 (Albert Gray, MG)
Hightower, Pressly & Polly Ann Woodson - Sept. 3, 1805
Hightower, Stephen & Sally Coplan - Dec. 21, 1815 (Gilly Moore)
Hightower, Thomas & Minny Credille? - Dec. 18, 1838 (Hinton Crawford)
Hightower, Wm. & -------- - Dec. 10, 1807 (J. Mapp)
Hightower, Wm. & Nancy Parrott - Aug. 29, 1838
Hill, Abner R. & Mary Ann Fitzpatrick - Apr. 27, 1844 (E. S. Hunter)
Hill, James & Christian Laseter - Sept. 15, 1806
Hill, James & Elizabeth Smith - Mar. 14, 1825 (Horatio Nunnally)
Hill, James & Lucy Baldwin - Jan. 10, 1830 (S. W. Michael)
Hill, Joseph & Henrietta W. Dawson - July 11, 1849 (Francis Bowman)
Hill, Robert & Elvina Bledsoe - Oct. 2, 1825 (Jack Lumpkin)
Hill, Wm. & Lucy Purdue - June 14, 1820 (Lovick Pierce)
Hill, Wm. G. & Ella F. Poulain - Apr. 25, 1861 (R. A. Houston)
Hillsman, Jeffre E. & Martha Alexander - Sept. 12, 1841 (John Howell)
Hillsman, Micaph? & Nancy Barnett - July 15, 1823
Hillyer, S. G. & Elizabeth T. Dagg - May 12, 1846 (P. H. Mell)
Hines, Nathaniel & Martha Lewis - July 26, 1815 (Walker Lewis)
Hines, Nathaniel & Elizabeth Lewis - Sept. 16, 1824
Hines, Sabury R. & Susan Anderson - Sept. 29, 1850 (Wm. Bryan)
Hinton, L. H. & Nancy L. Broom - July 5, 1852 (W. W. Moore)
Hitchcock, Samuel Ch---er & Lou---- Marion Walker - Dec. 21, 1851
  (Francis Bowman)
Hixon, E. C. & Ezenomia? A. Thornton - June 22, 1865 (John R. Young)
Hix, Ephriam & Edith Lucas - Oct. 25, 1804
Hobbs, Isham & Martha Lankford - May 6, 1821 (Abraham Yates)
Hobbs, James & Jurasha Adkinson - Sept. 27, 1810 (Thomas Stocks)
Hobbs, Joseph & Peggy Summerland - Jan. 25, 1807 (Jon Cox)
Hobbs, Nathan & Mary Lankeford - Nov. 16, 1812 (Ebenezer Torrence)
Hodge, Alston & Phaney Barker - Nov. 9, 1827
Hodge, Alston & Mary Jane Dunson - Feb. 25, 1841 (E. P. Jarrell)
Hodge, James & Louisa Coleman - Oct. 31, 1820 (Geo. Watkins)
Hodges, James & Polly Price - July 23, 1818
Hodges, John Jr. & Ruthey Hodges - Mar. 26, 1818 (L. Bethune)
Hogg, Henky? T. & Sarah Ann Burgess - Sept. 4, 1851 (James Geer)
Hogg, Hugh & Margaret Ray - Feb. 8, 1818
Hogg, Isaac & Mary Caldwell - Oct. 20, 1833 (Nathan Hobbs)
Hogg, John & Susan Johnson - Jan. 20, 1825
Hogg, Mathew & Lucy Reed - Aug. 11, 1807 (J. Mapp)
Hogg, Wm. & Mary Forrester - Dec. 22, 1835 (V. R. Thornton)
Hogg, Wm. D. & Nancy Ann Johnson - Sept. 4, 1845 (W. H. C. Cone)

256

Hodnette, James & Sarah Greer - Nov. 2, 1820 (James Brockman)
Holcomb, H. L. & L. A. Devereaux - Nov. 23, 1845 (I. W. Simmons)
Holland, Harrison & Elizabeth Rowland - Dec. 2, 1802
Holland, Tobias & Mary A. Watson - Aug. 10, 1872 (J. H. Kilpatrick)
Holland, Thomas & Elizabeth Wall - Sept. 24, 1821 (Hermon Mercer)
Holliday, John & Kittey Colleman - Apr. 20, 1809 (Josias Randle)
Holliday, Wm. & Elizabeth Neel - Aug. 13, 1789
Holloway, David & Pelee? Hardeys? - Dec. 15, 1807 (O. Porter)
Holmes, Geo. P. & Mary Jane Swindall - Aug. 25, 1831 (Wm. Rowland)
Holns, John & Nancy East - Oct. 17, 1807 (A. Gresham)
Holt, David S. & S. Catherine Godkin - Aug. 26, 1847 (Francis Bowman)
Holt, Robert & Emily Moore - Dec. 15, 1829 (Thomas Darley)
Holt, Thomas & Charity Slaughter - Apr. 27, 1830 (J. P. Leverett)
Holtzclaw, John G. & Lucy M. Newcome - Dec. 14, 1825
Horn, Edward & Sally Butler - Feb. 9, 1810 (Ben Crawford)
Horn, John & Elizabeth Allen - Sept. 10, 1828 (Joshua Cannon)
Horn, Preston A. & Mary Ann Purdue - Sept. 30, 1835 (Geo. Heard)
Horton, James W. & Georgianna A. Hart - Feb. 12, 1852 (Alfred T. Mann)
House, John H. & Armania H. Medley - Aug. 14, 1840 (J. M. Wilson)
House, John & Mary Bell - Nov. 17, 1849
House, Lion S. & Elizabeth Shirley - Mar. 8, 1842 (I. M. Wilson)
Houghton, Alex & Tabitha Cheatham - Nov. 19, 1799
Houghton, Alexander & Rebecca Finley - May 15, 1815 (John Arm-----)
Houghton, Henry W. & Martha Ann Rebecca Dolvin - Apr. 4, 1837 (W.R.H.
    Moseley)
Houghton, James & Sarah Burke - Aug. 11, 1788
Houghton, James & Lourena Thornton - Dec. 19, 1822 (Lovick Pierce)
Houghton, James R. & Ophelia T. Gentry - Dec. 18, 1866 (Thos. F. Pierce)
Houghton, Josiah & Elizabeth Crawford - Nov. 26, 1804
Houghton, Matthew & Elizabeth King - Dec. 12, 1827 (Wm. Cone)
Houghton, Seaborn & Ann Newsom - Feb. 21, 1823 (Abraham Yeates)
Houghton, Wm. & Elizabeth Burke - Mar. 3, 1788
Houghton, Wm. M. & Mary S. Smith - Jan. 18, 1842 (James Jones, M. G.)
Howard, James & Nancy Wells - Aug. 24, 1822 (Abraham Yeats)
Howell, Allen & S. Thompson - Aug. 19, 1805
Howell, Alonzo & Annett Parrott - Jan. 18, 1860
Howell, Clark & Margaret A. Park - Mar. 26, 1863 (W. J. Cotter, M. G.)
Howell, Daniel & Mary Oslin - Apr. 7, 1824
Howell, David & Mrs. Bettie A. Florence - Nov. 21, 1865? (R.A. Houston,
    M. G.)
Howell, Matthew C. & Sarah M. Simonton - Mar. 31, 1831 (C. P. Beeman)
Howell, Nathaniel & Elizabeth Wagner - Mar. 27, 1804
Howell, Wm. J. & Anne Jernigan - Nov. 21, 1871 (J. H. Kilpatrick)
Howell, Wyly & Sally Wiggins - Nov. 9, 1803
Hubbard, Andrew Jackson & Elizabeth Gatlin - Sept. 29, 1836 (James W.
    Godkin)
Hubbard, Augustus & Martha Jones - Mar. 9, 1847 (N. M. Crawford)
Hubbard, James & Sarah Tippett - Jan. 5, 1826
Hubbard, Larkin & Elizabeth Yates - Nov. 11, 1830 (John Armstrong)
Hubbard, Thomas & Sarah Jackson - Oct. 25, 1831 (Benj. F. Martin)
Hubbard, Wm. H. & Irene Jackson - June 5, 1826
Huckaby, James & Mary Griffin - Feb. 18, 1828
Hudson, Garrett & Polly Parker - Apr. 5, 1802
Hudson, John & Martha Patrick - Mar. 15, 1807 (Adam Hays)
Hudson, Thomas & Elizabeth Patrick - Oct. 25, 1810 (Jon. Heard)
Hudson, Ward & Jimmy Haynes - Feb. 19, 1805
Huff, John & Malinda Martin - Dec. 25, 1818 (Thomas Riley)
Huff, Ralph & Polly Palmore - Dec. 4, 1817
Hughes, John & Nancy Holloway - Jan. 22, 1800
Hughes, John & Alis? Dixon - Dec. 15, 1803
Hughes, John & Francis Bryant - Dec. 2, 1855 (B. Rowland)
Hughes, Wm. M. & Mary A. Cant - May 31, 1864 (J. F. Zimmerman)
Hughey, Thomas & Sam. B. Fielder - Jan. 24, 1827
Humphries, Neil? M. & Frances E. Rainwater - Oct. 23, 1870 (J.H.K-----)
Hunnicutt, Matthew R. & Martha L. McGraw - Oct. 20, 1850 (A. L. -----)
Hunt, Anderson & Archy Tyler - Sept. 29, 1818 (L. Bethune)
Hunt, George & Susannah Ware - Feb. 22, 1816 (Wm. Cone)
Hunt, James & Agnes Hunt - Mar. 8, 1800
Hunt, James T. & Rebecca May - Oct. 23, 1834 (Nathan Hobbs)
Hunt, John & Elizabeth Sorrell - ----- 4, 1807

257

Hunt, Timothy & Letitia Mayfield - Nov. 26, 1815 (James Martin)
Hunter, Edward & Sarah Dans - Oct. 19, 1820 (John Harris)
Hunter, Elisha C. & Ann E. Rally - Oct. 4, 1836 (Thomas Stocks)
Hunter, Henry M. & Ann J. King - Dec. 10, 1833 (James Donnelly)
Hunter, Phillip & Mary Jackson - Apr. 6, 1806 (Jesse Lacey)
Hunter, Samuel & Charity Whatley - Feb. 7, 1800
Hunter, Wm. A. & Sophronia A. Heard - Apr. 8, 1826
Hunter, Wm. C. & Lucinda Bowles - Aug. 4, 1835
Hunter, Wm. C. & Elizabeth Scoggins - Oct. 9, 1837
Hurlbert, Roswell & Casandria Corlew - Sept. 20, 1812 (J. W. Godkin)
Hurlbert, Roswell & Eliza Hamilton - Apr. 29, 1828 (J. P. Leverette)
Hurt, George & Lucy Wilkins - Dec. 25, 1827 (Abraham Yeats)
Hutcheson, Albert M. & Henrietta L. Champion - Nov. 27, 1866 (B.F. Bre--)
Hutcheson, John & Evelina A. Greene - May --, 1831? (J. N. Gheen)
Hutchinson, Albert S. & Harriett A. Lawrence - Nov. 28, 1839
Hutchinson, Ambrose & Rachel Robins - Mar. 30, 1815 (John Turner)
Hutchinson, Charles R. & Mary Kimbrough - Oct. 23, 1856 (J. P. Duncan,MG)
Hutchinson, James & Jane Walker - Dec. 22, 1829 (J. P. Leveritt)
Hutchinson, Richard & Harriett Turlow - (no date) (Thomas Stocks)
Hutchinson, Seaborn L. & Martha J. Champion - June 2, 1859 (J.H. Kilpatrick)

Idson, John & Mary Corry - Oct. 25, 1821 (Robert Booth)
Ingram, Abraham & Nancy Greer - Feb. 28, 1801
Ingram, James G. & Rebecca McGibony - Oct. 6, 1859 (Jos. R. Parker)
Irby, Abraham & Tabitha Evans - Dec. 6, 1821 (Wm. Robertson)
Irby, Eli & Mary A. Tunnell - Feb. 27, 1850 (W. A. Corry)
Irby, Elisha & Elizabeth Satterwhite - July 17, 1842 (E. P. Jarrell)
Irby, Thomas F. & Martha M. Peek - Nov. 15, 1849 (J. J. Loudermilk)
Irving, Carnell & Catherine E. Keith - Dec. 5, 1855 (J. P. Duncan)
Irwin, James & Amanda Nisbet - Mar. 8, 1816 (Francis Cummins)
Ivey, Jerrey & Fanny Williams - Apr. 4, 1801
Ivey, John & Nancy Evans - Feb. 27, 1823 (John Harris)
Ivy, James & Lucinda Rowland - Oct. 4, 1838 (Robert T. Griffin)
Ivy, Jeremiah & Milly Shockley - Aug. 27, 1811 (W. McGibony)
Ivy, Jordan & Polly Smith - Dec. 8, 1817
Ivy, Jordan & Patience Woods - Mar. 29, 1827 (Wm. L. Austin)
Ivy, Josiah & Patience Williams - Aug. 11, 1803

Jacks, John W. & Anna Carson - Dec. 11, 1873 (C. H. Strickland)
Jackson, Aldridge & Celia Pendergrass - Apr. 15, 1824
Jackson, Alexander J. S. & Sarah F. Hudson - Dec. 4, 1860
Jackson, Alfred & Martha Wright - Mar. 31, 1844 (J. J. Howell)
Jackson, Alfred H. & Julia E. Parrott - Oct. 10, 1850 (W. W. Moore)
Jackson, Allen & Elizabeth Short - Nov. 15, 1830 (Lewis Pyron)
Jackson, Andrew F. & Adaline M. O'Neal - Apr. 4, 1867 (L. D. Caldwell)
Jackson, Arthur M. & Sarah Elizabeth Hester - Feb. 12, 1867 (J.C.Johnson)
Jackson, Daniel & Sally Bowan - Jan. 15, 1805
Jackson, Daniel & Mary Phillips - Nov. 20, 1806 (Thomas Crawford)
Jackson, Daniel & Cassandra Maddox - Jan. 14, 1823 (Thomas Stanley, MG)
Jackson, David & Rachel Lewis - Nov. 30, 1796
Jackson, David & Elizabeth Beckers - Aug. 2, 1824
Jackson, Edmond & Abbe Jackson - Dec. 23, 1806 (O. Porter)
Jackson, Edmund & Sally Shaw - Dec. 19, 1823
Jackson, Floyd & Mary Fambrough - (no date)
Jackson, George A. & Fanny V. Baker - May 29, 1866 (J. W. Tall----)
Jackson, Henry & Delilah Gorden - Dec. 20, 1809 (Wm. Watson)
Jackson, Isaac & Elizabeth Perkins - Jan. 25, 1821 (Jr. Roberts)
Jackson, Isaac & Lousa Caldwell - July 12, 1825 (John Harris)
Jackson, Isaac M. & Sarah F. Smith - Sept. 13, 1866 (Hart C. Peek, M.G.)
Jackson, Israel & Amy W. Callahan - Dec. 21, 1845 (S. G. Hillyer)
Jackson, Jacob & Patsey Simes - Nov. 19, 1807 (Frances S. Martin)
Jackson, James & Mary Underwood - Dec. 2, 1827 (Wm. Cone)
Jackson, James & Nancy Lewis - Apr. 10, 1828 (John Harris)
Jackson, James & Electra Ann Bird - Apr. 2, 1846 (Wm. Parks)
Jackson, James A. & Martha Fullingham - Nov. 27, 1856 (Wm. T. Merritt)
Jackson, James W. & Catherine M. Butler? - Feb. 5, 1840 (Francis Bowman)
Jackson, James W. & Martha Ann Broom - Sept. 9, 1852 (Daniel Hightower)
Jackson, Job & Mary Heart - Oct. 7, 1819 (John Harris)
Jackson, John & Jane Richards - Apr. 15, 1800

Jackson, John & Mary Webb - Feb. 18, 1818 (Thomas Riley)
Jackson, John E. & Martha Ann Eliza Dans - Apr. 16, 1833 (Albert R. ----)
Jackson, John E. & Julia A. Hudson - Jan. 1, 1862
Jackson, John H. & Eliza J. Moore - Nov. 2, 1872 (J. H. Kilpatrick)
Jackson, John S. & Artimissa Hall - July 6, 1856 (L. R. L. Jennings)
Jackson, John S. & Alice A. Jones - Mar. 2, 1865
Jackson, Jesse W. & Julia C. Tunnell - Mar. 15, 1863 (W. G. John----)
Jackson, Littleberry & Patience Harris - July 4, 1827
Jackson, Luther R. & Frances Parmelia Ivy - Jan. 11, 1840 (Thomas Stocks)
Jackson, Luther R. & Emma A. Carlton - May 11, 1875 (F. G. Hughes, M.G.)
Jackson, Mark & Elizabeth R. Pyron - Dec. 17, 1828 (Joshua Cannon)
Jackson, Martin & Rachael Martindale - Sept. 13, 1826
Jackson, Martin & Frances Hendricks - Oct. 11, 1832 (Wm. Moncrief)
Jackson, Martin & Mary E. Harris - Apr. 19, 1853 (A. L. Willis)
Jackson, Moody & Patience T. Bishop - Sept. 9, 1833 (Thos. W. Grimes)
Jackson, Peter & Mary Lindall - Mar. 16, 1796?
Jackson, R. H. & Mary E. Hall - Jan. 14, 1847 (L. B. Jackson)
Jackson, Robert B. & Lilly V. Jones - Dec. 13, 1874 (J. H. Kilpatrick)
Jackson, Robert Hausen & Mary M. Ely - Mar. 12, 1844 (J. J. Howell)
Jackson, Roling & Susannah Richards - Sept. 20, 1807 (J. Mapp)
Jackson, Stephen & Jimmy Brooks - July 9, 1805
Jackson, Thomas & Pearly Bullwood - Aug. 28, 1807 (John Robertson)
Jackson, Thomas & Mary Smith - Dec. 5, 1826
Jackson, Wm. & Holly Harwell - Mar. 9, 1816 (John Browning)
Jackson, Wm. & Martha Foster - Mar. 23, 1830 (J. P. Leveritt)
Jackson, Wm. N. & June Daniel - Nov. 26, 182?
Jackson, Wm. T. & Mary A. E. Brooks - Feb. 23, 1869 (J. M. Dickey)
James, Henry & Mary Grier - Mar. 7, 1825
James, John & Priscilla Greer - Jan. 9, 1823 (Jeremiah Ragan)
James, Thomas G. & Elizabeth P. Sanford - July 26, 1839 (Shales G. Hillyer)
James, Williamson & Rachel Martindale - Oct. 6, 1828
James, Thomas & Malinda West - Jan. 30, 1821 (Jesse Mercer)
James, Thomas G. & Elizabeth P. Sanford - July 28, 1839 (S.H. Hillyer,MG)
Jarrell (Giles), Jacob & Miller Chandler - Dec. 28, 1820 (Francis West)
Jarrell, Jacob & Frances Williams - May 8, 1828 (Francis West)
Jarrell, Redden & Elizabeth Johnson - July 15, 1836 (James Moore)
Jarrell, Willis & Mary Campbell - Dec. 27, 1818 (Thomas Snow)
Jarrell, Ruben & Ann Gentry - Dec. 24, 1868 (J. H. Kilpatrick)
Jefferson, Francis M. & Elizabeth Chappell - Nov. 17, 1859 (Geo. C.
  Clarke)
Jefferson, Wm. M. & Mary Chappell - Oct. 15, 1857 (G. Bright, M.G.)
Jeffrey, Thomas & Elizabeth Morris - Dec. 23, 1803
Jeffries, Wm. & Nancy Tuggle - Oct. 24, 1806 (Jesse Lacey)
Jenkins, Elijah & Amy Daniel - Feb. 13, 1797
Jenkins, Harmond & Julia Ann Simpkins - Apr. 16, 1834
Jenkins, James R. & Milly Gresham - Apr. 19, 1807 (Wm. Browning)
Jenkins, James & Betsey Duncan - July 5, 1810 (Bennett Crawford)
Jenkins, James A. T. & Francis B. Sanders - Oct. 5, 1838 (James W. Godkin)
Jenkins, John & Meron L. Hobbs - Sept. 13, 1845
Jenkins, Jesse & Anne Martin - Feb. 24, 1805
Jenkins, Mass? & Opheleb? E. Jenkins - Oct. 28, 1875 (Philip Robinson)
Jenkins, Pleasant C. & Harriett A. Daniel - Nov. 9, 1831 (Wm. Jones)
Jenkins, Robert & Sarah B. Johnson - Apr. 3, 1806 (Thos. Crawford)
Jenkins, Waites & Jane H. McHargue - May 25, 1843 (John W. Ru----)
Jennings, Giles & Mary Hague - Jan. 11, 1820 (Lemuel Greene)
Jennings, Henry & Elizabeth J. McWhorter - Feb. 13, 1866 (J. M. Stilwell,
  M. G.)
Jernigan, Albert & Lucy Perkins - Dec. 23, 1822
Jernigan, Albert & Henrietta M. Shaffer - Jan. 14, 1867 (A. Gray, M. G.)
Jernigan, Albert A. & Rebecca A. Parrolt? - Oct. 15, 1850 (L. C. Peek)
Jernigan, Hardy E. & Margaret A. Alexander - Dec. 2, 1862 (Hart C. Peek,
  M. G.)
Jernigan, John E. & Margaret Rankin - Dec. 9, 1830 (Francis Cummins)
Jernigan, John R. & Sideria D. Mann - Feb. 2, 1868 (C.A. Mitchell, M.G.)
Jernigan, Petolemy & Sarah Jarrell - Jan. 8, 1822 (James Woodberry)
Jernigan, Seaborn J. & Eveline B. Williams - Mar. 13, 1838
Jeter, Samuel & Winney Cone - Oct. 1, 1822 (Anderson Ray, M. G.)
Jeter, Wm. P. & Lou Anna McCarty - Nov. 25, 1872 (W. A. Overton)
Jett, Francis & Elizabeth Lee - July 26, 1818 (C. Para, M. G.)
Jewell, James Jr. & Eliza C. Colcough - Dec. 1, 1859 (John G. Holtzclaw)

259

Jones, Andrew J. & Ellen A. Johnson - Jan. 15, 1866
Jones, B. F. & M. E. O'Neal - Jan. 15, 1874
Jones, Charles P. & Mary V. Overton - Dec. 17, 1873 (J.H. Kilpatrick)
Jones, Dickinson & Martha Harris - Oct. 28, 1829 (Francis Cummins)
Jones, Hezekiah & Hulda Simmons - Jan. 10, 1857 (Ephriam Bruce)
Jones, Hezekiah & Nancy L. Norris - June 14, 1866 (W. M. Chapman)
Jones, Isaac & Temperance Akins - Jan. 22, 1825
Jones, James A. & Mary A. Price - Jan. 5, 1875 (L. D. Caldwell)
Jones, James & Elvey Rowland - Jan. 6, 1802
Jones, James & Sally Harper - Sept. 14, 1810 (H. Davenport)
Jones, James J. & Louisa M. Hightower - Oct. 28, 18-7 (John C. Lucas)
Jones, John & Emily W. Sims - Oct. 7, 1847
Jones, John & Mrs. Martha Bruce - May 8, 1857 (A. L. Willis)
Jones, John P. & Sarah A. Veazey - Sept. 12, 1849 (Wm. A. Corry)
Jones, Joseph & Sarah Heard - Dec. 18, 1791
Jones, Joseph & Penelope S. Pullen - Jan. 29, 1824
Jones, Joseph A. & Lucy M. Manley - May 30, 1843 (James F. Findley)
Jones, L. N. & Adalade Jackson - Dec. 18, 1853 (I. A. Williams)
Jones, Nathan & Sarah Jett - June 21, 1818 (Lovick Pierce)
Jones, Nicholas M. & Emeline Veazey - Dec. 8, 1847 (J. J. Loudermilk)
Jones, Nicholas M. & Marita? Jackson - Oct. 26, 1851 (Hart C. Peek, MG)
Jones, Robert & Harriett Macon - Oct. 6, 1825 (Lovick Pierce)
Jones, Robert & Sarah Conyers - Feb. 22, 1827 (James Culberson)
Jones, Robert S. & Julia Amanda Peek - Jan. 15, 1841 (James Jones)
Jones, Robert W. & Pharabe? Cunningham - Mar. 25, 1841 (Reuben Armor)
Jones, Russell & Mary Tuggles - Nov. 25, 1801
Jones, Sanders & Virginia Stewart - Feb. 2, 1875
Jones, Starling W. & Martha Swinney - Apr. 29, 1847 (Hinton Crawford)
Jones, Thomas & Emily West - Jan. 17, 1828 (Jonathan Davis)
Jones, Thomas & Matilda Marie Caldwell - June 8, 1831 (Peter C. Johnson)
Jones, Thomas D. & Mary D. Harper - June 12, 1808 (I. Porter)
Jones, Wiley & Sarah Ball - Apr. 15, 1821 (Thomas Slaughter)
Jones, Wm. & Emelia Paterson - Jan. 5, 1808 (A. Hayes?)
Jones, Wm. & Rebecca Baldwin - July 19, 1832 (A. Perkins)
Jones, W. T. & Sallie Wilson - Nov. 13, 1872
Jones, Zachariah & Sarah R. Morris - Nov. 12, 1831 (J. P. Leveritt)
Johnson, Allen & Nelle Finley - June 12, 1820
Johnson, Allen & Elizabeth Eidson - July 2, 1843 (James P. Findley)
Johnson, Amos & Priscilla Marchman - Nov. 9, 1843 (Ephriam Bruce)
Johnson, Amos & Catherine Moon - Nov. 6, 1860
Johnson, Barnard & Sally Taylor - Dec. 1, 1814 (Francis Cummins)
Johnson, Frederick & Patience Knowles - Nov. 9, 1809 (Wm. Johnson)
Johnson, George W. & Sarah H. V. Bickers - July 21, 1859 (L.B. Jackson)
Johnson, Gilbert & Susan Smallwood - June 29, 1850 (I. A. Wms.)
Johnson, James T. & Corcyra E. Matthews - Aug. 9, 1838 (Francis Bowman)
Johnson, James & Liza Harrison - Dec. 13, 1817 (Lovick Pierce)
Johnson, James W. & Mary Anne Franklin - Oct. 4, 1864 (G.G. Norman, MG)
Johnson, James W. & Sarah J. Rankin - June 17, 1875 (Henry Newton)
Johnson, Jesse & Nancy Johnson - Feb. 20, 1816 (Francis Cummins)
Johnson, Jesse & Lucy Barnett - Nov. 14, 1817
Johnson, John & Anne Butt - Jan. 25, 1802
Johnson, John & Prudence Farley - Sept. 4, 1804
Johnson, John & Nancy Williams - Nov. 26, 1815 (Alex Johnson)
Johnson, John & Joice Fears - May 24, 1823
Johnson, John & Martha Smith - Dec. 18, 1845 (Wm. Bryan)
Johnson, John & Cornelia J. Ledbetter - Nov. 25, 1856 (Geo. C. Clarke)
Johnson, John & Corrinne C. Moore - Jan. 18, 1866 (J. H. Kilpatrick)
Johnson, John R. & Mary Ann Briscoe - Jan. 25, 1831 (Abraham Jenkins)
Johnson, John S. & Caroline E. Hogg - Jan. 3, 1854 (Wm. English)
Johnson, Kinchen & Matilda McGiboney - Dec. 28, 1856 (Wm. W. Moore)
Johnson, Laban Scott & Susannah Walker - Oct. 7, 1830 (J. P. Leveritt)
Johnson, Leonidas B. & Mary A. Raden - Dec. 22, 1857 (T. D. Martin)
Johnson, Littleberry & Mary Robinson - July 27, 1819 (Robt. Booth)
Johnson, O. B. & Martha E. McLaurin - Mar. 31, 1869 (J. J. Brantley)
Johnson, Peter & Clairssa Bedell? - May 18, 1820 (Thomas Johnson)
Johnson, Peter G. & Susan Bedell? - May 18, 1835 (Thomas W. Grimes)
Johnson, Robert & Nancy Dolvin - Mar. 4, 1800?
Johnson, Robert G. & Eleanor Johnson - Nov. 23, 1838 (Thomas W. Grimes)
Johnson, Samuel & Patsey Hightower - Sept. 11, 1804
Johnson, Silvester A. & Louisa Underwood - Dec. 10, 1874 (H. C. Peek)

Johnson, Terry & Rebecca Fleming - Dec. 1, 1839 (C. D. Kennebrew)
Johnson, Thomas & Terza. Greene - June 21, 1818 (Thomas Johnson)
Johnson, Thomas & Nancy Tippett - Dec. 25, 1825 (E. Talley, J. R.)
Johnson, Wm. & Martha Ann Hall - Oct. 1, 1846 (V. R. Thornton)
Johnson, Wm. B. & Mary P. Brown - Apr. 20, 1864 (R. A. Houston, MG)
Johnson, Wm. Daniel & Manissa R. Channell - Jan. 13, 1870
Johnson, Wm. H. & Martha English - Dec. 22, 1859 (R. A. Houston)
Johnson, W. G. & Mary Statham - Apr. 26, 1844 (Francis Cummins)
Johnson, W. T. & Mattie J. Fillingim - Feb. 28, 1871 (H. C. Peek, MG)
Joiner, Henry & Elizabeth Taylor - July 20, 1828 (George Hall)
Johnston, Geo. & Tabitha Johnston - July 13, 1808 (Thomas Crawford)
Jordan, Edward & Nancy Moore - Mar. 5, 1807 (W. McGiboney)
Jordan, Zachariah & Betsey Reed? - July 7, 1819 (Wm. McGiboney)
Jourdan, Elijah & Cynthia King - Apr. 13, 1814 (Isaac Moore)
June, John Houghton & Mary McDowell - Nov. 23, 1824
Kearney, Richard B. & Elizabeth Cuchanan - Mar. 29, 1827 (James Blasin-
   game)
Keaton, James K. P. & Dora Copeland - Sept. 12, 1867 (H.H. Tucker, MG)
Keller, David C. & Mary E. Carlton - Feb. 22, 1855 (J. P. Duncan, M. G.)
Kelley, James & Polly Wade - Dec. 20, 1808 (James Holt)
Kelley, Reuben B. & Bellina Linch - Dec. 20, 1840 (Matthew Olivia?)
Kelly, Charles & Betsey Wiley - Oct. 17, 1810 (James Holt)
Kelly, Hugh P. & Margaret S. Young - Apr. 18, 1848 (W. H. Cone)
Kelly, James M. & Holly Ann Sayers - Nov. 10, 1836 (A. Hutcheson)
Kendall, Thomas K. & Mary Mapp - July 15, 1841 (John I. Howell)
Kendall, Thomas & Asenith W. Mapp - Feb. 20, 1843 (John Howell)
Kendrick, Robert & Elizabeth Park - Mar. 30, 1823
Kennebrew, C. D. & Nancy J. Wilson - Jan. 22, 1849
Kennebrew, Marcus B. & Julia M. Edmondson - May 9, 1862 (John R. Young,
   M. G.)
Kennedy, James & Sarah Eidson - Mar. 5, 1846 (T. D. Martin)
Kennedy, John & Agnes Sanders - Apr. 28, 1804
Kennedy, John & Sally Price - July 6, 1808 (Wm. Browning)
Kennedy, John E. & Mary Ann McCarty - Feb. 21, 1869 (H. H. Tucker)
Kenney, James & Vernecey Baughcum - Apr. 1, 1866 (Wm. Chapman)
Kenny, Jesse & Polly Smith - Sept. 17, 1816 (Robert Rea)
Kenny, Joshia & Catherine Langston - Nov. 25, 1789
Kenney, Seaborn & Jane H. Clifton - Apr. 26, 1837 (Lemuel T. Crossley)
Keough, Wm. L. & Josephine Echols - Apr. 26, 1870 (Thomas F. Pierce, MG)
Kicker, Wm. G. & Elizabeth S. Lee - Dec. 12, 1841 (Wm. C. Veazey)
Kicklighter, Spencer C. & Mary M. Jean - Jan. 30, 1873 (H. C. Peek)
Kilgoar, Wm. & A. Higginbotham - Dec. 19, 1791
Killpatrick, James H. & Cornelia Hall - May 9, 1856 (H. C. Peek)
Kimball, David & Susannah Anderson - June 23, 1827 (Miller? Bledsoe)
Kimbro, Isaac & Bessie Anne Hall - Aug. 3, 1851 (L. R. L. Jennings)
Kimbrough, Alexander & Sarah A. Smith - Dec. 8, 1870
Kimbrough, Asbury & Eliza Rowland - Dec. 13, 1838 (James W. Godkin)
Kimbrough, Augustus L. & Mary A. E. Champion - Dec. 10, 1860 (Jas. H.
   Kilpatrick)
Kimbrough, Bradley & martha Wingfield - Feb. 4 or 9, 1820
Kimbrough, Bradley & Lucinda Clark - June 22, 1830 (Wm. Bryan)
Kimbrough, Jesse & Sarah E. Creddile - Aug. 24, 1848 (W. T. Gaston)
Kimbrough, John & Esther Winslett - Dec. 12, 1815 (Gilly Moore)
Kimbrough, John P. & Mary A. Copelan - Jan. 7, 1875 (W. H. Blythe, M. G.)
Kimbrough, Locket M. & Mary E. Credille - Apr. 15, 1862
Kimbrough, Stephen T. & Agathy N. Peek - Aug. 31, 1837 (L. O. Peek, M.G.)
Kimbrough, Thomas & Sally Stallings - June 27, 1806
Kimbrough, Wm. & Mary Rowland - Apr. 28, 18--?
Kimbrough, Wm. A. & Emma M. Simpkins - June 4, 1875 (J. Knowles)
Kimbrough, Wm. G. & Sarah H. Credille - Aug. 8, 1848 (W. T. Gaston)
King, Charles M. & Josephine Gray - Oct. 7, 1874
King, Drury & Elizabeth Taylor - July 2, 1823 (Thomas Johnson)
King, Drury & Martha Taylor - Apr. 11, 1830 (S. M. Michael)
King, Edwin D. & Nancy Hunter - May 10, 1814 (Jack Lampkin)
King, Elisha & Margaret Champion - Aug. 12, 1832 (J. P. Leveritt)
King, Ezekiel & Lorena McGee - Dec. 8, 1842 (James McKenzie)
King, Henry & Caroline Greenwood - Jan. 29, 1846 (J. O. Andrew)
King, Hugh Moore & Virginia C. Todd - Nov. 20, 1852
King, James & Fanny Perkins - June 6, 1798
King, James & Elizabeth Moore - Sept. 6, 1825 (Francis Cummins)

King, James R. & Susan F. Wright - Nov. 5, 1867 (Thos. F. Pierce)
King, James William & Nancy Jane Swindall - Oct. 4, 1843 (R.F. Griffin)
King, James W. & Frances B. Slaughter - Sept. 11, 1843
King, Jesse & Sarah L. Rankin - Feb. 18, 1837 (Thomas Stocks)
King, John Jr. & Patsey Lacey - Feb. 16, 1796
King, John & Irene P. Moore - Feb. 20, 1866 (J. W. Talley, M. G.)
King, Joseph & Elizabeth Cone - Mar. 5, 1816 (Wm. Cone)
King, Joseph & Sarah Ballard - Jan. 4, 1831 (A. Perkins)
King, Ulysses B. & Celest C. Swinney - May 11, 1857
King, Wm. & Elizabeth Davis - May 6, 1822 (John Harris)
King, Dr. Wm. & Margaret Barnett - May 1, 1834 (Wm. Cone)
King, Wm. C. & Martha Wright - June 23, 1835 (James Moore)
Kinman, John & Elizabeth Lewis - Aug. 22, 1804
Kinmore, Robert & Eliza Catherine Tribble - Feb. 29, 1844 (I.M. Wilson)
Kinney, James & Mary Ann Clifton - Dec. 29, 1846
Kinney, James & Jemiah J. Compton - Jan. 9, 1849 (W. T. Gaston)
Kinney, Wm. R. & Martha A. E. Ruark - Dec. 5, 1865 (W. H. Blythe, M. G.)
Kinnion, James & Sally Williams - Jan. 15, 1805
Kirk, John & Barsheba Tyler - Aug. 14, 1826 (L. Bethune)
Klotz?, John & Maria Clark - no date
Knight, Coffield & Edey Murphey - June 23, 1802
Knight, Joel & Elizabeth Pollard - Nov. 21, 1815 (Edwin D. King)
Knight, Robert B. & Kitty Bailey - July 21, 1802
Knowles, Benjamin & Joanna Thomas - Nov. 9, 1820 (Wm. McGiboney)
Knowles, Brittain & Rebecca Ransom - Aug. 12, 1826
Knowles, Edmond & Christian Thomas - Feb. 24, 1820 (Wm. McGiboney)
Knowles, Isaac & Mary H. Owen - Mar. 25, 1824
Knowles, James Jr. & Amy Read? - Jan. 3, 1806 (W. M. Johnson)
Knowles, James & Anna Thomas - Apr. 25, 1821
Knowles, James & Lucy Thomas - Feb. 9, 1823 (Thomas Slaughter)
Knowles, John & Martha Grubbs - Oct. 2, 1855 (B. H. Thompson)
Knowles, Pretty & Patsey Greer - Aug. 3, 1802
Knowles, Richard P. & Dell Martin - May 13, 1801
Knowles, Thomas & Matilda McGiboney - Nov. 11, 1819 (Wm. Cone)
Knowles, Thomas B. & Adaline Wheatt - Nov. 4, 1833 (Ephriam ------)
Koch, Henry I. & Lucy Borach - Jan. 14, 1846 (J. M. Davison)

Laffold, Seaborn & Julia Heard - Jan. 6, 1818 (E. Torrence)
Lambkin, Wm. & Eleanor Fambrough - July 4, 1841 (I. M. Wilson)
Lancaster, Samuel & Rebecca Bowden - Sept. 17, 1822 (Whitman Hill)
Landrum, Alsey L. & Margaret Ari---- - Aug. 29, 1833 (John W. Cox)
Landrum, James N. & Sarah M. Underwood - Dec. 5, 1840 (E. S. Hunter)
Langford, James M. & Caroline B. Hobbs - Dec. 1, 1844 (Jeremiah Lindsey)
Lanier, Manson E. & Elizabeth Fitzpatrick - Dec. 31, 1838
Lankford, Daniel Jr. & Betsy Tolly - Apr. 25, 1833 (Alvin Perkins)
Lankford, James C. & Mary A. Wilson - Jan. 5, 1868 (Lucuis C. Broome)
Lankford, Robert & Elizabeth C. Burton - Jan. 4, 1842 (P. W. Farabee)
Lankford, Robert C. & Elizabeth Bennett - Mar. 4, 1860 (Thomas B. Cooper)
Lankford, Willis J. & Mildred A. S. Black - Aug. 28, 1856 (John G. Holtz-
   claw)
Landsdale, Wm. S. & Lizzie Zimmerman - Oct. 23, 1855 (J. P. Duncan, MG)
Lasley, David & Patience Winfield - Apr. 24, 1832 (J. P. Leveritt)
Lassiter, Brown & Anne Stewart - Jan. 1, 1802
Lassiter, Elisha & Nancy Baker - Jan. 1, 1802
Lassiter, Jesse & Dype? McClendon - Jan. 28, 1806
Lassiter, John & Nancey Griffen - Dec. 10, 1804
Laurence E. C. & C. W. Hubbard - Jan. 18, 1844 (B. M. Sanders)
Laurence, Hartwell & Elizabeth Wingfield - Aug. 28, 1821 (Wm. Tally)
Laurence, John & Harriett Ward - Feb. 27, 1823 (W. H. Sledge)
Laurence, Orson & Arabella Allen - Feb. 2, 1823 (A. Hutchinson)
Lawrence, Enoch C. & Mary H. Daniel - Jan. 30, 1837 (V. R. Thornton)
Lawrence, James & Ginney Lawson - May 2, 1795
Lawrence, James & Mary Simonton - Mar. 29, 1810 (Wm. McGiboney)
Lawrence, Thomas & Polly Moreland - Oct. 15, 1796
Laws, Bennett & Sarah Thornton - Jan. 20, 1836 (John T. Holtzclaw)
Laws, Isarn & Rhody Chhings - July 21, 1806 (A. Hays)
Lawson, John T. & Matilda Broach - Jan. 2, 1849 (E. S. Hunter)
Lawson, Shelton & Polly Bird - Dec. 11, 1818 (Philemon Ogletree)
Layers, Wm. & Rachael Ward - Feb. 22, 1816 (Gilly Moore)
Leach, John B. & Caroline Nash - Mar. 14, 1858 (James M. Kelly)

Leach, John W. & Bertha Lynch - May 22, 1873 (W. H. Blythe)
Ledbetter, James & Rebecca Furge - Jan. 11, 1849 (W. T. Gaston)
Ledbetter, James C. & Irena C. Coffield - Oct. 5, 1875 (W. H. Blythe)
Ledbetter, Littleberry & Sarah Ann Kinney - Aug. 26, 1842 (Reuben Armor)
Ledbetter, Malden S. & Patience Smith - Jan. 28, 1841 (Ephriam Bruce)
Ledbetter, Wm. T. & Sallie Callahan - Jan. 9, 1875 (Joel F. Thornton)
Lee, Charles & Elizabeth Broughton - Oct. 21, 1828 (James Park)
Lee, Elijah & Malinda Phillips - Dec. 13, 1821 (Jo or Jr. Fitzpatrick)
Lee, James & Elizabeth Phillips - Aug. 31, 1814 (Lemuel Greene)
Lee, Nathan & Olivia Heard - Dec. 20, 1824
Lee, Wm. & Sarah West - Dec. 31, 1817 (Walter Lewis)
Leftwich, John & Mary Brooker - Feb. 20, 1822 (Hermon Mercer)
Leonard, Irbane & Rebakah Collier - Feb. 2, 1815 (Thomas Stocks)
Leonard, Coleman & Eliza Johnson Ledbetter - Sept. 1, 1837
Leonard, Wm. & Penelope Massingale - Aug. 13, 1829 (Wm. Bryan)
LeRabour, B. A. & E. E. Heard - Nov. 20, 1853 (J. W. Yarborough)
Leslie, Julius W. & Mary F. Ashley - Nov. 25, 1858 (W. G. Johnson)
Lester, Benj. & Betsey Hill - April 22, 1801
Lester, Josiah & Leleta Johnson - Aug. 30, 1818 (Isom Goss)
Letbetter, Washington & Lucy Bostwick - June 21, 1801
Leverett, Francis M. & Susan Cartwright - May 28, 1836 (Thomas Stocks)
Leverett, George & Delila Cook - Dec. 8, 1831 (Ephriam Bruce)
Leverett, Joel & Mary Bishop - Nov. 18, 1827 (John Harris)
Leverett, Wm. & Nancy Woodham - May 27, 1837 (Robert F. Griffin)
Leveritt, L. D. & Hattie Pennington - May 23, 1870
Lewis, Cyphas & Sarah Ellis - Nov. 14, 1834 (James Moore)
Lewis, Cephas & Emily Chambers - Jan. 30, 1843 (James Moore)
Lewis, Curtis & Jane Collier - Mar. 13, 1826 (N. H. Harris, M. G.)
Lewis, Fields & Hannah Hall - Sept. 6, 1796
Lewis, Frisman & Aseneth Connell - Feb. 26, 1831 (J. P. Leverett)
Lewis, Gabriel & Mary Hightower - Feb. 7, 1828 (R. White)
Lewis, George & Charlotte Baugh - Mar. 6, 1820
Lewis, Henry & Nancy Edwards - Jan. 1, 1807 (J. Holt)
Lewis, Ira & Lourina Cook - Jan. 3, 1820
Lewis, John & Jenny Moore - Aug. 17, 1819 (John Turner)
Lewis, Miles W. Jr. & Amorette? C. Champion - Oct. 20, 1873 (Albert
   Gray, M. G.)
Lewis, Richard & Susannah Hightower - Feb. 23, 1802
Lewis, Theophilus & Rebecca Ship - May 31, 1827 (John Harris)
Lewis, Thomas S. & Leah Williams - Nov. 9, 1852 (Benj. Marritt)
Lewis, Thomas W. S. & Margaret Sullivan - Dec. --, 1838 (James Moore)
Lewis, Walker & Polly Graham - June 1, 1798
Lewis, Wm. & Mary Woods - Dec. 1, 1818
Lewis, Wm. & Temperance Lewis - July 6, 1820 (R. White)
Lewis, Wm. & Sarah Cartwright - June 21, 1827 (Nat. Harris)
Lewis, Wm. & Margaret Beasley - Jan. 4, 1861
Lewis, Wm. Jr. & Mary T. Moody - Oct. 27, 1853 (Wm. T. Doster?)
Lewis, Wm. W. & Priscilla Marchman - Apr. 4, 1856
Legon, John & Sarah Barker - Feb. 29, 1816 (Geo. Owen)
Legon, Thomas & Betsey C. Daniel - May 20 or 30, 1805 (A. Gresham)
Lely?, John E. & Malinda Bryan - Jan. 22, 1841 (Reuben B. Arnold)
Linch, Elihue & Nancy Kinney - Sept. 25, 1842 (Reuben Armor)
Linch, James C. & Martha A. F. Bryan - Jan. 16, 1866 (C. R. Hutcheson)
Linch, Wm. & Lucienda Bryan - Dec. 27, 1869
Lindsey, Clabourn & Nancey Therman - Jan. 8, 1812 (Lemuel Greene)
Lindsey, Jeremiah & Julian Edmondson - May 18, 1837 (W.R.N. Mosely, MG)
Lindsey, John & Nancey Houghton - Nov. 21, 1817 (Lovick Pierce)
Lindsey, Wm. & Mary Whitaker - Aug. 4, 1840 (James M. Davidson)
Lindsey, Wm. T. & Mrs. Martha B---ns - Oct. 13, 1870 (W. A. Overton)
Linton, Alexander & Jean Daniel - Nov. 21, 1811 (Jesse Mercer)
Linton, Samuel D. & Mary Cunningham - Aug. 21, 1847 (Francis Bowman)
Linton, Wm. & Martha Inorans Grimes - Aug. 5, 1847 (Francis Bowman)
L-----, Edwin & Melaney Martin - Feb. 28, 1826
Little, Anderson & Sarah Ann Gwill? - Nov. 22, 1846 (P. H. Mell)
Little, Charles E. & Winnie F. Copelan - Feb. 22, 1870 (J.M. Lowney?,MG)
Little, James F. & Martha J. Seals - Sept. 5, 1860 (H. H. Tucker)
Little, John W. & Mary Mason - Dec. 5, 1875 (W. T. Foster)
Little, Walter G. & Mary E. Gresham - Dec. 17, 1874 (Henry Newton?)
Little, Wm. & Mary A. Callahan - Aug. 15, 1867 (Philip Robinson)
Littlejohn, Thomas & Elizabeth Hall - Nov. 11, 1804

Livingstone, Aaron & Respy? Ship? - Mar. 8, 1821 (Wm. McGiboney)
Locke, Josiah & Sarah Johnson - Sept. 21, 1841 (Wooten O'Neal)
Lofton, Van & Rebakah Walls - Jan. 27, 1795
Love, David & Elizabeth King - Apr. 12, 1810 (Wm. McGiboney)
Love, Henry Chappel & Rebecca S. Houghton - Mar. 3, 1836 (J.W.F. Pierce)
Lovett, Robert W. & Marietta A. Smith - Oct. 24, 1865 (Albert Gray, MG)
Lowrey, Benjamin & Mary Hogg - Apr. 20, 1790
Loyd, Alfred & Jemima? Connell - July 3, 1818
Loyd, James T. & Lorena H. Brook - Aug. 17, 1862 (W. R. Wilson)
Lucas, John & Elizabeth Kimbrough - Dec. 11, 1845 (Francis Cally)
Luck---, Wm. F. & Frances Delaney Sayers - Apr. 19, 1853 (T. D. Martin)
Ludwig?, L---- Kohl & Nancy Susan Kennedy - Nov. 11, 1853
Luke, David & Elizabeth Scoggins - Aug. 28, 1837
Lumpkin, Edmund & Lucy Dillard - May 24, 1825
Lumpkin, James & Mary E. Porter - Oct. 24, 1850 (J. W. Godkin)
Lumpkin, James & Mary E. Porter - Oct. 24, 1850 (J. W. Godkin)
Lumpkin, Leroy & Elizabeth Bryan - Jan. 16, 1848 (James Findley)
Lumpkin, Wm. & Rebekah Moon - Mar. 14, 1816 (L. Bethune)
Lumpkin, Wm. & Elizabeth Bowden - June 30, 1818 (Lovick Pierce)
Lundy, Alexander S. & Matilda M. Lee - Feb. 22, 1870 (J. M. Lowney)
Lundy, Archibald P. & Martha Jane Grimes - Apr. 20, 1854 (Hinton Crawford)
Lundy, Lewis W. & Jane K. Turner - July 19, 1832 (Lewis Parker)
Lundy, Wm. C. D. & Martha C. Parrott - Mar. 16, 1869 (Wm. Bryant, M. G.)
Lupo, James M. & Elizabeth Bowden - Sept. 19, 1848 (J. W. Godkin)
Lyle, Charles V. & Francis S. E. Parker - Jan. 25, 1854 (J. S. Key, M. G.)
Lynch, Edlow & Elizabeth Thomas - Sept. 21, 1820

Mabry, Alfred 7 Sarah Curry - Dec. 30, 1826
Mabry, Hinchia & Lynnea Stallings - Oct. 20, 1818 (Thomas Riley)
Mabry, John & Elizabeth Irby - Jan. 3, 1821 (W. Robertson)
Mabry, Thomas & Sarah Irby - Jan. 8, 1824 (Thomas Johnson)
Maddox, Clayborn & Betsey Weaver - September 4, 1818
Maddox, Wm. J---- & Elizabeth W. Tally - Dec. 1835 (James Moore)
Maddox, John D. & Nancy F. Fisher - June 3?, 1870
Maddox, Joe C. & Sarah Morrow - Dec. 31, 1788
Maddox, Joseph D. & Eliza Copelan - Nov. --, 1875 (W. H. Wright)
Maddox, Robert T. & Margaret S. Mahaffey - Jan. 1, 1854 (J. R. Hall)
Maddox, Wm. D. & Elizabeth E. Davenport - Dec. 26, 18-6 (Thomas W. Grimes)
Mague, Laban & Rebekah Whatley - Jan. 4 or 9, 1806
Maisey, Wm. & Sarah ---- Randle - May 20, 1869? (Thos. F. -----)
Mallory, Irvin & Caroline ----rd - May 30, 1833 (W---- Bryan)
Mallory, John & Nancy Brown - Oct. 8, 1813 (Robert Mapp)
Mallory, Joseph & Elizabeth Mitchell - Jan. 13, 1818? (E. Torrence)
Mallory, Rollin D. & M. J. Dagg - July 28, 1853 (B. D. Mallory)
Mallory, Thomas & Patsey Moore - Aug. 21, 1818
Malone, Drury & Elizabeth Delouch - Oct. 18, 1829 (Geo. Hall)
Malone, John & Susannah Boring - Nov. 10, 18-- (A. Gresham)
Malone, John & Harriett ----- - Oct. 16, 1834 (John Hillyer, M. I.)
Malone, John & Margaret Jane Bowles - ---. 24?, 1836? (John Holtzclaw)
Malone, Thompson & Laura Wms. - Nov. 5, 1839 (B. M. Sanders)
Malone, Washington & Frances Deloach - Sept. 6, 1839 (Geo. Hall)
Malone, Wm. B. & Lucy Hicks - Nov. 21, 1823
Malone, Young & Mary Price - Dec. 18?, 1829 (Wm. James)
Manley, Wm. & M. F. Garner - Oct. 24, 1845
Mann, David & Polly Nelson - Jan. 15, 1818 (Geo. Dillard)
Mann, Jesse & Annie Nelson - Jan. 15, 1818 (Geo. Dillard)
Mann, Joseph B. & Saphrone Channell - July 10, 1853 (B. Rowland)
Manning, Michael & Elizabeth Watson - Dec. 18, 1824
Mapp, Al---- & Susan Copelan - Sept. 25, 1847 (Francis Bowman)
Mapp, Archibald P. & Rebecca Lundy - Dec. 10, 1874 (J. H. Kilpatrick)
Mapp, E. J. & Antoinette Snelling - Sept. 30, 1872
Mapp, R. Hanson & Hannah Jackson - Sept. 27, 1794
Mapp, Henry S. & Ha---- Howell - Feb. 8, 1864 (J. H. Kilpatrick)
Mapp, James H. & Sarah Jane Moore - Sept. 22, 1857 (Wm. W. Moore)
Mapp, James H. & A--t-- Howell - Nov. 22, 1859 (James Kilpatrick)
Mapp, James & Mary Wright - Nov. 25, 1800 (John W. Harris)
Mapp, J. F. & Elizabeth D. Chapman - Dec. 22, 1870 (J. R. Parker)
Mapp, Littleton & Lucretia McGiboney - July 23, 1818 (John Harris)
Mapp, Moore & Lucy R. Jetter - Feb. 6, 1822 (Lovick Pierce, M. G.)
Mapp, Robert H. & ----- Taylor - Nov. 12, 1857 (W. W. Moore)

Mapp, Robert H. & Teresa Pittmen - June 5, 1859 (Carlos W. Stephens)
Mapp, Wm. & Marietta J----- - Oct. 20, 1846? (Wm. I. Parks)
Mapp, Wm. B. & Mattie J. Mathews - Nov. 27, 1875 (W. H. Blythe)
Mapp, Wm. J. & Patience C. Alexander - Dec. 8, 1859 (J. H. Kilpatrick)
Marable, Augustus & Mary W. Hester - June 17, 1842 (Hinton Crawford)
Marable, Champion & Julia A. Wagnon? - Aug. 19, 1866 (L. D. Carlton)
Marable, John & Elizabeth Shelton - Nov. 24, 1803
Marable, John & Fanny Lawson - Dec. 13, 1804
Marchman, Cicero S. & Margaret Watson - Sept. 18, 1842 (Thomas Stocks)
Marchman, James & Emily Bruce - Dec. 26, 1843 (Fra--- S. Coley?)
Marchman, John M. & Virginia Barnhart - Aug. 23, 1857 (James J. Laurence)
Marchman, Levi & Adaline Montgomery - Jan. 26, 1831 (Ephriam Bruce)
Marchman, Nathan & Sarah Ranson - Dec. 10, 1835 (Ephriam Bruce)
Marchman, Risdon & Martha Johnson - Mar. 5, 1848 (James Moore)
Mark, Samuel & Susannah Brewer - May 31, 1805
Markwalter, Martin & Mary Ann E. Winter - Mar. 10, 1864 (J. W. Godkin)
Martin, Archabal ---- & Nancy Houghton - Dec. 17, 1803
Martin, Bally G. & Eliza Jane Boon - Jan. 19, 1864 (J. R. Parker)
Martin, Elijah & Jane McDoal - Nov. 18, 1819 (John Harris)
Martin, Francis & Betish McClendon - Dec. 29, 1807 (J. Mapp)
Martin, John & Amanda E. McCarty - Mar. 27, 1873 (W. A. Overton)
Martin, Joseph John & Polly Jenkins - Jan. 3, 1800
Martin, Robert & Betsey Jones - Apr. 6, 1802
Martin, Robert & Edna Sanford - May 10, 1820 (Lovick Pierce)
Martin, Thomas D. & Sarah A. M. Northern - Dec. 21, 1843 (P. H. Mell)
Martin, Wm. & Jane Copeland - Nov. 27, 1828
Martin, Wm. M. & Julia E. Nickelson - July 2, 1835 (G. A. Chappell, M.G.)
Martin, Zadah & Peggy Robertson - Nov. 9, 1802
Martindale, Westley & Elizabeth Southerland - Dec. 1, 1838 (Nathan Hobbs)
Mason, Charles B. & Sarah M. Carson - Nov. 6, 1867 (Philip B. Robinson)
Mason, Edwin & Amanda Grimes - Nov. 1, 1821 (Lovick Pierce)
Mason, Wiley & Martha Cunningham - Oct. 21, 1824
Massey, James & Nancy Miller - Aug. 9, 1818
Massey, John W. & Mattie J. Harris - Dec. 23, 1875 (R. L. Burgess)
Massingale, John & Polly Moore - May 30, 1826
Massingale, Jordan & Mary Prince - July 8, 1830 (Wm. Bryan)
Massingale, Nathan & Cynthia Jarrel - Dec. 27, 1821 (A. Hutcheson)
Masters, James & Martha O'Neal - Sept. 4, 1851 (Joseph W. Drennan)
Mathews, Charles L. & Lucy Early - Jan. 31, 1807
Mathews, Charles L. & Emeline T. Strain - Sept. 15, 1831 (Lovick Pierce)
Mathews, James T. & Martha Ann Kimbrough - Dec. 3, 1842 (R. F. Griffen)
Maull, James & Rebecca Alford - June 18, 1829
Maxey, Barnabus A. & Sarah F. Powell - Dec. 4, 1867 (M. M. Landrum, M.G.)
Maxey, Booze & Sarah Landman - Dec. 21, 1823 (J. Ragan)
Maxey, Jeremiah & Jane Finley - Aug. 3, 1830
Maxey, George W. & Virginia E. Burgess - Dec. 13, 1866 (E. A. Burgess)
Maxey, Joseph W. & Mary Peek - Dec. 15, 1825
Maxey, Wm. & ----- DeGraffenreid - June 9, 1815 (A. S. Johnson)
May, Isaac & Sarah Shelton - June 15, 1820 (Thomas Johnson)
May, John & Emily Jackson - Dec. 31, 1850 (Hart C. Peek)
May, Major W. & Rebecca Hunt - Dec. 30, 1828 (James Park)
May, Thomas & Mary McLane - Oct. 1, 1828 (Robert Newsom)
Mays, Wm. & Elizabeth Gentry - May 1, 1831 (Nathan Hobbs)
Mayne, James P. & Emma B. Stovall - Apr. 24, 1866 (John Calvin Johnson)
McAlpin, Andrew & Nancy Hubbard - Dec. 13, 1827 (Alex. McAlpins)
McCain, Robert Patrick & Nancy Dickson - May 29, 1835
McCall, James P. & Claud M. Weaver - Dec. 15, 1868 (Luther M. Smith)
McCarthur, James & Elizabeth Harriett Mabry - Aug. 10, 1837 (John Wilson)
McCarty, Walker & Rosa Landrum - Feb. 9, 1874
McCarty, Wm. & Marion L. Jenkins - July 8, 1860 (Wm. A. Colclough)
McClain, Bennett & Jariah Freeman - Sept. 9, 1828
McClain, Elisha & Nancy Wyatt - Aug. 5, 1852 (B. Rowland)
McClain, Elijah & Rosa Ray - Aug. 1, 1822 (Abraham Yeats)
McClain, John & Mary Williams - Sept. 19, 1822 (Abraham Yeats)
McClellon?, James & Sarah Sturdivant - Jan. 16, 1825
McClendon, Jeremiah & Elizabeth Sheffel - Dec. 23, 1795
McClendon, Marvel & Phebe Williams - Nov. 24, 1803
McCluskey, Thomas & Julia Ann Dillard - June 14, 1820 (Lovick Pierce)
McCommon, James H. & Helen Mary Geer - Nov. 3, 1864 (John R. Young, MG)
McCowen, John W. & Ann Perkins - Sept. 11, 1817 (Robert Gilbert)

McCoy, Ewell & Rebecca Boone - Jan. 25, 1821 (Wm. Cone)
McCoy, John & Lucy Fitzpatrick - Feb. 18, 1823 (John Park)
McCrary, John W. & Elizabeth Anderson - Aug. 11, 1853 (J. W. Yarborough)
McCrea, Wiley B. & Laura A. McWhorter - Jan. 5, 1871? (J. C. Calvin)
McDonald, Daniel & Susan A. Bridges - Apr. 11, 1858 (T. J. Bowen)
McDonald, Marion & Sarah Alfriend - Feb. 7, 1851 (L. C. Peek)
McGan, Wm. Henry & Rachel Copeland - Sept. 1, 1835
McGiboney, Wm. R. & Lodusca? Irby - Sept. 1, 1865 (J. R. Parker)
McGray, Richard T. & Mary Ann Warner - June 2, 1850 (J. W. Drennan)
McGruder, Bryan & Martha Bryan - Nov. 23, 1838 (Thos. W. --rimes)
McGuire, A. & Patsey Aldmon - Nov. 10, 1818
McGuire, Thomas & Peggy Hays - Apr. 22, 1795
McGuire, ----- & Peggy Hays - Apr. 22, 1795
McGuire, James & Polly George - May 9, 1795
McHargus, Wm. T. & Julia A. F. Hendericks - June 29, 1843 (James W. God-
kin)
McHenry, James H. & Sarah G. Poullain - May 30, 1843 (Francis Bowman)
McIntosle?, David & Polly Dawson - Dec. 29, 1795
McIntosh, Jesse & June Cartwright - June 19, 1802
McKenzie, Josephus & Nancy A. E. Mays - Mar. 15, 1866 (James Davison)
McKinley C. & Antionette Wingfield - Jan. 12, 1832 (Francis Cummins)
McKnight, John & Susan Drake - July 28, 1842 (Wm. Manley)
McLain, James & Nancy Ward - Oct. 9, 1859 (J. M. Kelly)
McLain, Samuel & Adaline Landrum - Apr. 15, 1841 (Hardy Bridges)
McLaughlin, Owen A. & Almarine C. Cheney - Dec. 25, 1851 (Enoch Calloway?)
McMahan, Noel & Mary Jane Morgan - Mar. 21, 1861 (W. R. Wilson)
McMahan, Wm. I. & Henrietta Higgins - Jan. 12, 1838
McMichael, Charles & Polly Carmichael - Oct. 17, 1807 (James Holt)
McMichael, David & Sally Kimbro - Feb. 20, 1789
McMichael, Samuel & Dicey Winslett - Jan. 17, 1808 (W. M. Johnson)
McMichael, Seaborn & Elizabeth Riley - Feb. 17, 1824
McMillan, Eli & Candis Richards - June 25, 1822 (Wm. Wingfield)
McMillan, Micajah & Mary Harrison - May 18, 1828 (A. Ray, M. G.)
McMullen?, David & Hannah Pickard - Dec. 19, 1803
McMurray, James & Agnes Curtis - Feb. 21, 1821 (Francis Cummins)
McWhorter, Beeman C. & Elizabeth Barnhart - Dec. 18, 1873 (W. A. Overton)
McWhorter, Frederick & Elizabeth A. Johnson - Dec. 28, 1841 (N.H. Hill)
McWhorter, John & N. H. Hall - Dec. 18, 1855 (T. B. Martin, M. G.)
McWhorter, Robert & Nancy W. Jones - Nov. 2, 1843 (B. M. Sanders)
McWhorter, Robert & N. Pope Thurmond - Feb. 22, 1849 (P. H. Mell)
McWhorter, Robert L. & Mary E. Boyd - Apr. 20, 1875 (C. H. Strickland)
McWhorter, Wm. H. & Adaline Edmondson - Oct. 26, 1837 (Jack Lumpkin, MG)
McWhorter, Wm. H. & Mary E. Cheney - Nov. 14, 1865 (P. H. Mell, MG)
McWhorter, Wm. P. & Sarah J. Crawford - July 21, 1857 (P. H. Mell, MG)
Meadows, Benjamin & Nancy Parker - Dec. 17, 1805 (B. Maddox)
Meaddows, Benjamin & Nancy Parker - Dec. 20, 1805
Meadows, Wm. & Jean Meadows - June 29, 1815 (Malichi Murden)
Mealer, John W. & Minnie Brooks - Jan. 5, 1871 (W. R. Wilson)
Means, Francis M. & E. Louisa Crutchfield - Nov. 22, 1866 (A. Kearns)
Meddows, Benjamin & Nancy Parker - Oct. 12, 1805
Meddows, Alexander & Mary A. Morgan - Feb. 11, 1875 (C. H. Strickland)
Medlin, Andrew H. & Mary Sherley - April 13, 1845 (James T. Findley)
Meeks, Albert H. & Naomi Brooks - Sept. 12, 1872 (James Griffen)
Melborn, Levi T. & Roxana Bethune - April 15, 1824
Melton, James K. & Louisa H. Clements - July 13, 1864 (L. B. Jackson)
Melton, Robert & Patsey Boon - Oct. 10, 1804
Melton, Wm. Allen & Nancy Haynes - Jan. 25, 1807 (Wm. Greer)
Merritt, Allen & Mary Sherling? - Mar. 5, 1873 (W. H. Wright)
Merritt, Benj. & Susan M. Heath - Dec. 19, 1850 (James Billingslea)
Merritt, James & Nancy Williams - Mar. 18, 1875 (W. H. Wright)
Meredith, James & Harriett A. M. Fleetwood - Aug. 13, 1843 (John Robins)
Merritt, Franklin & Cornelia C. Stewart - Aug. 31, 1865 (John C. Merritt)
Merritt, Henry & Jackann Crawford - Dec. 7, 1818
Merritt, James & Sarah Sidwell - Dec. 12, 1867 or 9 (James W. Godkins)
Merritt, John & Lucy Clements - Apr. 30, 1844 (H. H. Laurence)
Merritt, John C. & Lousa F. Crawford - July 15, 1849 (James W. Godkin)
Merritt, Lovett & Sarah Gatlin - Feb. 8, 1820 (John Harris)
Merritt, Lovett & Mary O'Rear - Sept. 25, 1837 (Ephriam Bruce)
Merritt, Stephen & Susan C. O'Neal - Feb. 11, 1868 (L. D. Caldwell)
Merritt, Thomas & Patsey Roland - Feb. 28, 1815 (Robert Rea)

Merritt, Thomas & Caroline A. Heath - Spr. 26, 1855 (L. C. Peek)
Merritt, Wm. & Nancy J. Burk - Aug. 22, 1854 (W. A. Florence, M.G.)
Merritt, Wm. & Sarah V. Ledbetter - Oct. 29, 1865 (Wm. Bryan, M. G.)
Merriwether, Francis & Sarah Watts - Nov. 3, 1818 (Lovick Pierce)
Merriwether, James & Fanny Bradshaw - Feb. 27, 1814
Metcalf, Edward & Ephronia M. Dawson - May 22, 1851 (Francis Bowman)
Michael, Thomas J. & Almeda T. Johnson - Sept. 2, 1853 (W. A. Par---)
Middlebrooks, Zara B. & Marita E. Maddox - Oct. 14, 185- (J. M. St--, MG)
Middleton, Wm. & Nancy Lumpkin - Nov. 29, 1814 (John Browning)
Miller, Charley & Isabella Kennedy - Aug. 30, 1804
Miller, John & Elizabeth Bird - Mar. 21, 1822
Miller, John A. & Sarah Jane Smith - May 19, 1836
Miller, Parker C. & Marita Anne Caldwell - Sept. 13, 1843 (Wooten O'Neal)
Miller, Thomas S. & Mary Jane Jackson - Nov. 18, 1853 (E.L. Whatley, MG)
Milligan, James & Elizabeth Cessna - Aug. 19, 1788
Mills, Henry & Elizabeth Lindsey - Jan. 21, 1849 (Newell Lumpkin)
Milner, Obadiah & Precilla Meddows - Jan. 4, 1806
Miner, Hermon & Elizabeth Andrews - Sept. 3, 1802
Mirnner?, Wm. & Cynthia Young - May 21, 1816 (Walker Lewis)
Mitchell, Cicero A. & Elmira C. Smith - May 23, 1858 (O. L. Smith, M. G.)
Mitchell, Edward & Essy Terzeach? - Feb. 1, 1821 (Lovick Pierce)
Mitchell, Isaac & Parizade Love - Jan. 19, 1819 (Lovick Pierce)
Mitchell, John & Elizabeth Catchings - Dec. 27, 1868 (James W. Godkin)
Mitchell, Joshua M. & Valeria T. Randle - Oct. 17, 1867 (Francis S. ----)
Mitchell, Reuben S. & Elizabeth Forrester - July 9, 1843 (E. S. Hunter)
Mitchell, Sterling & Betsey Brewer - Aug. 31, 1800
Mize, Anderson & Sally Wood - Apr. 24, 1810
Mize, Jo & Jemima Wyatt - Sept. 7, 1804
Moncrief, David & Nancy Price - Apr. 22, 1830 (Jack Lumpkin)
Moncrief, Isaac & Nancy Kecker - Dec. 30, 1819 (A. Hutchenson)
Moncrief, Marshall & Elizabeth Bolles - Dec. 18, 1845 (Samuel Ely)
Moncrief, Thomas I. & Mary Ann Roberson - Aug. 20, 1833 (Thomas Stocks)
Moncrief, Wm. & Nancy Booles - Sept. 6, 1849 (J. D. Williams)
Monk, Tearson B. & Martha Watts - Dec. --, 1838 (Vincent R. Thornton)
Montfort, Alexander & Elizabeth B. Smith - Nov. 25, 1852 (J.W. Yarbrough)
Montfort, John & Nancy Curry - Mar. 22, 1810 (C. Maddox)
Montfort, John C. & Elizabeth H. Quill - Nov. 26, 1850 (J. W. Godkin)
Montfort, Oscar L. & Margaret A. Hillsman - Dec. 16, 1858 (M. H. Hubbard)
Montfort, Wm. & Matilda Jane Patrick - Jan. 3, 1822 (James Dunn)
Montgomery, James M. & Margaret Culp - Jan. 14, 1836 (John G. Holtzclaw)
Montgomery, Wm. & Chloe Lewis - June 25, 1870
Moody, Elias B. & Susan Brook - Sept. 14, 1845 (Samuel Ely)
Moody, Elias B. & Sarah E. Durham - Oct. 11, 1863 (W. R. Wilson)
Moody, George & Eliza Velvin - Feb. 21, 1833 (Wm. H. Price)
Moody, George W. & Emeline Moody - Dec. 28, 1835 (Wm. H. Price)
Moody, Greene & Betsey Dove - Aug. 10, 1816 (Vincent Lanford)
Moody, Henry & Frances Patrick - Apr. 19, 1855 (J. M. Davison)
Moody, James A. & Elizabeth F. Brook - Mar. 13, 1836 (John G. Holtzclaw)
Moody, James A. & Mary Elizabeth Adkins - May 10, 1860 (Wm. R. Wilson)
Moody, James A. & Sarah Jane Mays - Jan. 22, 1865 (James Davison)
Moody, John & Nancy Velvin - Dec. 23, 1817 (Hinton Crawford)
Moody, John C. & Rebecca Robertson - Oct. 8, 1850 (James W. Godkin)
Moody, L----- B. & Mrs. Catherine S. Freeman - Sept. 28, 1865(James Denson?)
Moody, Waldman & Georgia Ann Moore - July 24, 1864 (Alfred L. Willis?)
Moon, Causby & Louisa Melton - Dec. 22, 1868 (Joseph R. Parker)
Moon, Franklin H. & Sarah Crawford - Jan. 5, 1869
Moon, George W. & Phobe J. Johnson - Mar. 25, 1866 (John O'Neal)
Moon, George W. & Electrian Wright - Nov. 20, 1866 (John C. Merritt)
Moon, Wm. L. & Priscilla Bruce - Jan. 2, 1852 (D. Hightower)
Moor, David & Sally Aubrey - Oct. 20, 1807 (Wm. Greer)
Moor, Isaac & Nancy Wyatt - Oct. 5, 1807 (J. Mapp)
Moor, Young & Rebekah Aubrey - Oct. 16, 1807 (Wm. Greer)
Moore, Anderson C. & Georgia A. Howell - May 4, 1868 (J.H. Kilpatrick)
Moore, Asbury Green & Sarah Jane Caldwell - Dec. 23, 1855 (H. C. Peek)
Moore, Bertam & Mattie Ely - Dec. 18, 1873 (J. H. Kilpatrick)
Moore, Curtis & Agnes Smith - Sept. 14, 1789
Moore, David C. & Sarah Ann Greer - Dec. 24, 1857 (James H. Wragg)
Moore, Freeling H. & Sarah H. Crawford - Jan. 7, 1869 (W. R. Foste?)
Moore, George & Maria Wright - June 9, 1822 (Stephen Hightower)

Moore, George & Jincey Atkinson - Jan. 14, 1847 (James Rowland)
Moore, George & Lucy Wilson - Aug. 24, 1856 (J. F. Wright)
Moore, George W. & Margaret E. Hogg - Nov. 16, 1872 (John R. Young)
Moore, Gillis & Betsey Cooper - Dec. 22, 1798
Moore, Henry H. & Mrs. Martha W. Dooly - Oct. 10, 1865 (W. H. Blythe)
Moore, Hiram & Elizabeth I. Turner - Feb. 18, 1847 (Ephriam Bruce)
Moore, Isaac & Mrs. Bethena Wilson - July 2, 1855 (W. W. Moore)
Moore, Isaac D. & Mary Jane Howell - Jan. 15, 1852 (D. Hightower)
Moore, Isaac J. & Elizabeth Caldwell - June 23, 1848
Moore, Jackson & Nancy Stevens - July 7, 1821 (Chesley Bristoe?)
Moore, James & Bethine Jordan - Dec. 14, 1818
Moore, James M. & Eliza Ann Wilson - Feb. 2, 1837 (W. D. Coudrey?)
Moore, Jeremiah & Martha Gilbert - Apr. 6, 1830 (W. B. Barnett)
Moore, Jesse I. & Frances A. Mapp - Jan. 28, 1844 (J. J. Howell)
Moore, John & Elizabeth Hammond - Mar. 19, 1800
Moore, John & Cordelia Ann Lumpkin - Sept. 14, 1837 (W. R. M. Moseley)
Moore, John B. & Marian B. McHenry - June 11, 1872 (C. W. Lane)
Moore, John C. & Rebecca A. Wagnon - Jan. 22, 1857 (H. H. Parks, M. G.)
Moore, J. D. & Mary Ely - Nov. 4, 1869 (J. H. Kilpatrick)
Moore, Joseph & Matilda Goss - Jan. 18, 1810 (Wm. McGiboney)
Mitchell, Reuben S. & Elizabeth Forrester - (?)
Moore, Osborn & Latha Brake - Dec. 18, 1873 (J. H. Kilpatrick)
Moore, Oscar D. & Mattie Newsom - Dec. 22, 1874 (J. H. Kilpatrick)
Moore, Ransom & Mary Ann Hudgens - Dec. 29, 1819 (John Myrick)
Moore, Samuel & Lucy Ward - Jan. 16, 1821 (Spencer Moore)
Moore, Spencer & Luky Grimes - Sept. 24, 1801
Moore (or Brown), Wm. & Mary Wood - Mar. 4, 1821 (H. G. Slaughter)
Moore, Wm. & Jedidah Perkins - Dec. 5, 1822 (John Harris)
Moore, Wm. & Sydney Connell - Jan. 25, 1828 (John Harris)
Moore, Wm. & Jane Monfort - Dec. 12, 1831
Moore, Wm. & Frances Rea - Apr. 25, 1844 (Francis Bowman)
Moore, Wm. & Nancy Atkinson - Dec. 9, 1847 (J. J. Loudermilk)
Moore, Wm. B. & Mary Ann Creddelle - May 20, 1858 (W. G. Johnson)
Moore, Wm. H. & Margary Veazey - Mar. 15, 1844 (E. P. Jarrell)
Moore, J. W. & E. C. Park - Apr. 26, 1871 (Geo. W. Yarborough)
Moran, Basil & Nancy Harvey - Mar. 2, 1789
Moreland, James M. & Elizabeth F. Bridges - Dec. 29, 1853 (L.E. Culver,MG)
Moreland, James M. & Pheraby Wagnon - Dec. 15, 1870 (L. D. Caldwell)
Morgan, Adrain S. & Annie M. Spencer - Dec. 20, 1865 (H. H. Tucker, MG)
Morgan, Adrain S. & Amanda E. King - Dec. 25, 1867 (J. J. Brantley)
Morgan, Drury Chipsom & Priscilla Southerland - Dec. 8, 1836 (Nathan
    Hobbs)
Morgan, Enoch C. & Mary S. Johnson - July 30, 1850 (P. H. Mell)
Morgan, Thomas H. & Elizabeth D. Strozier - Nov. 21, 1852 (P. H. Mell)
Morgan, Wm. & Temperance Coleman - Aug. 19, 1819 (Lovick Pierce)
Morgan, Wm. & Caroline Wittick - Apr. 29, 1830 (James A. Andrews)
Morgan, W. H. & Mary Mounger - May 13, 1830 (Lovick Pierce)
Morrel, Simeon & Marial Harris - Dec. 10, 1818 (Robert Moore)
Morris, Andrew Jackson & Mary Jane Andrews - Dec. 28, 1854 (Hart C. Peek)
Morris, George & Frances Morris - June 3, 1824 (Malichi Murdow?)
Morris, Lemon & Patsey Colclough - Oct. 10, 1816 (Thomas Legue)
Morrison, Isaac & Rebecca Montfort - Mar. 23, 1837 (J. W. Godkin)
Morrison, Wm. J. & Elizabeth J. Chew - Jan. 18, 1842 (James W. Godkin)
Morrow, Hugh E. & Ellen Mathew - June 26, 1839 (Francis Bowman)
Moseley, Benjamin & Mary Ann Calloway - Dec. 14, 1847 (Geo. F. Pierce)
Moseley, John A. & Eliza Ann Johnston - Jan. 8, 1839 (John W. Wilson)
Moseley, Lewis & Rebekah Jones - Oct. 12, 1809 (John Turner)
Moss, Carson F. & Sarah F. Wheeler - Mar. 9, 1873 (W. A. Overton)
Moss, Henry & Jane Nance - Feb. 26, 1843 (Samuel Ely)
Moss, Peter M. & Emma Jernigan - Dec. 12, 1867 (J. H. Kilpatrick)
Motte, Levi S. & Sarah V. Chambers - May 15, 1866 (Ezekiel S. Wms.)
Mulkey, James & Betsey Dawson - June 25, 1807 (Claborn Maddox)
Mullins, Charles & Georgia Ann Andrews - Dec. 16, 1869 (W.A. Overton, MG)
Mullins, John & Julia Ann Williams - Sept. 2, 1836 (B. M. Sanders)
Mullins, Julius S. & Rosey Marcay - Dec. 17, 1803
Mullins, Thomas K. & Permelia H. Brockman - Dec. 9, 1830 (John Chew)
Murden, Henning D. & Cornelia F. Pinkston - Apr. 12, 1837 (J.G. Gilbert)
Murden, Malicia & Nancy Asbury - Jan. 16, 1806
Murden, Redmond & Sarah A. Mitchell - Mar. 16, 1864 (H. H. Tucker)
Murphey, Andrew & Sydney White - Dec. 14, 1829 (John Chew)

Murphey, John & Polly Lake - Dec. 19, 1811 (Clayborn Maddox)
Murrah, James & Ann Windale - Mar. 5, 1821 (John Beattie)
Murray, George & Eliza Ann Glazier - July 19, 1846 (T. M. Famborough)

Nazery, Henry & Polly Springer - Oct. 3, 1801
Neal, Alder & Sally Cochran - Jan. 13, 1811 (Hinton Crawford)
Neal, Geo. W. & Eliza W. Edmondson - July 12, 1850 (P. H. Mell)
Neal, Robert & Alice Burnett - Dec. 26, 1872 (B. P. Taylor)
Neely, John F. & Mary Ann Cone - May 30, 1850 (John T. Cox)
Nelms, Oliver & Mary Shorter - Dec. 8, 1819
Nelms, Samuel & Sally Holland - Dec. 28, 1815 (Geo. Owens)
Nelms, Thomas & Nancey Gillman - Feb. 13, 1805 (H. Gatlin)
Nelms, Thomas & Polly Worrell - Feb. 10, 1819 (Moore Robert)
Nelms, Thomas & Mary E. Haddaway - Feb. 22, 1870
Nelson, Abrams & Elizabeth Ellis - Dec. 23, 1799
Nelson, Geo. W. & Mary N. White - Sept. 3, 1833
Nelson, John B. & Sophia Roberts - Oct. 21, 1818 (Jesse Mercer)
Nelson, John W. & Mary Fenn - Dec. 29, 1874 (L. D. Caldwell)
Nelson, Joseph F. & Mary M. Parker - Jan. 8, 1845 (James Moore)
Nelson, Perry & Martha McGaughey - Nov. 7, 1821
Nesbit, Dr. James & Penelope Cooper? - July 30, 1794
Newell, Wm. & Priscilla Jones - Jan. 24, 1822 (Walker Lewis)
Newsom, David A. & Mrs. Maggie W. Carlton - Feb. 9, 1869 (Philip Robinson)
Newsom, Joseph N. & Addie Lewis - Nov. 24, 1874 (John W. Swa---)
Newsom, Robert & Nancey Asbery - Sept. 29, 1808 (Peter Joyner)
Newsom, Wm. J. & Elizabeth W. Haley - Jan. 11, 1871 (P. H. Mell, MG)
Newton, Elijah & Betsey Collier - May 14, 1822 (Lovick Pierce)
Newton, Wm. & Betsey Dorough - Jan. 3, 1804
Nichols, Thomas & Emmaline Wiggins - Dec. 29, 1858 (R. B. Kelly)
Nichelson, Geo. W. & Eliza C. Bridges - May 12, 1859 (Jefferson F. Wright)
Nichelson, Archibald & Sally Robinson - Sept. 27, 1846 (Abner R. Hill)
Nickelson, George & Nancy Jackson - July 22, 1823 (Wm. Greer, M. G.)
Nickelson, Henry Clay & Harriett M. Poullain - June 14, 1866 (Geo. -----)
Nickelson, Oscar E. & Martha C. Maddox - Nov. 30, 1865 (V.A. Bell, M.G.)
Nickelson, Samuel & Sarah A. Williams - Feb. 5, 1860 (John R. Young)
Nickelson, Wm. & Susan Williams - Nov. 2, 1828 (Jack Lumpkin)
Nickelson, Wm. & Elizabeth Atkinson - Aug. 24, 1862 (Wiley G. Johnson)
Nickelson, Wm. B. & Louisa C. Mullins - Jan. 30, 1866 (V. A. Bell, M.G.)
Nicks, Henry & Emily Bradley - Oct. 8, 1865 (Jefferson F. Wright)
Norris, Jacob & Liney Wood - Nov. 23, 1819
Norris, James & Sally Patrick - July 23, 1800
Norsworthy, Frederick & Mary Alford - July 18, 1821
Northington, James & Sally Houghton - Sept. 26, 1814 (Evans Myrick)
Norton, Charles C. & Anne M. Foster - June 3, 1844 (Wm. Arnold)
Norwood, James M. & Mary A. Maddox - July 8, 1835 (James Moore)
Norwood, Wm. & Mary F. Luckey - Jan. 26, 1836 (James Moore)
Nowell, Robert & Martha Moncrief - Dec. 3, 1839 (B. M. Sanders)
Nunn, C. W. & Mattie Battle - Nov. 23, 1873 (W. A. Overton)
Nunn, F. L. & S. E. Moody - Apr. 22, 1874 (James A. Thornton)
Nunn, John B. & Mary A. Moody - Feb. 28, 1875 (James M. Griffin)

O/Conner, John & Nancy Braswell - June 28, 1822
Oglesby, Thomas & Mary Alford - Oct. 7, 1818 (L. Bethune)
Ogletree, Samuel T. & Martha J. Williamson - Dec. 8, 1866
Ogletree, Samuel T. & Margaret A. Underwood - July 4, 1867 (Hart C. Peek)
Ogletree, Wm. D. & Sarah C. Underwood - Dec. 18, 1866 (Hart C. Peek)
O'Keefe, Daniel & Ann Walch - June 21, 1865 (P. J. Kirby)
O'Keefe, D. C. & Sarah Branch - May 7, 1851 (L. G. Hillyer)
O'Kelley, Patrick & Nancy Reed - Jan. 6, 1843 (Lemuel Greene)
Olcott, John & Emmelin Moody - Dec. 11, 1848 (Thomas Stocks)
Oliphant, Aaron P. & Emily M. Wright - Oct. 24, 1843 (Francis S. -----)
Oliver, Alexander & Mary Dren---n - Nov. 15, 1846 (R. F. Griff)
Oliver, Andrew & Mary Dority - Oct. 13, 1819
Oliver, Charles C. & Julia Frances Caldwell - Sept. 27, 1857 (Hart C.Peek)
Oliver, Columbus C. & May-- Flornoy Bowden - Nov. 28, 1868
Oliver, John & Nancy Cartwright - Apr. 3, 1823 (Thomas Johnson)
Oliver, John G. & Mary H. Cartwright - May 26, 1831 (John N. Harris)
Oliver, Milus W. & Maggie Heard - Dec. 3, 1874 (J. M. Loury)
Oliver, Thomas A. & Julia F. Heard - Nov. 29, 1855 (Hinton Crawford)
Oliver, Wm. & Jane Cartwright - Jan. 5, 1845 (John L. Veazey)

Oliver, Wm. I. & Cena Bryan - Mar. 20, 1845 (Ephriam Bruce)
O'Neal, Alexander S. & Malissa Ann Daniel - Nov. 12, 1872 (H. C. Peek)
O'Neal, Alfred & Martha King - Oct. 17, 1868
O'Neal, Augustus & Georgia A. U. Stewart - Dec. 12, 1843 (H.F. Bunkley?)
O'Neal, Daniel H. & M. Fannie Johnson - Dec. 16, 1874 (Hart C. Peek)
O'Neal, Edward & Elizabeth Roberts - Oct. 2, 1799
O'Neal, Hampton & Charlotte I. Peek - Feb. 19, 1834 (James Moore)
O'Neal, Ha---- & Elizabeth Colclough - Dec. 17, 1819 (Malichi Murden)
O'Neal, Harrison & Jane Wms. - Oct. 9, 1860 (L. D. Caldwell)
O'Neal, James & Julia Ann Rhodes - July 8, 1849 (J. T. Findley)
O'Neal, John & E---sah Caldwell - Oct. 10, 1839 (James Moon)
O'Neal, John & Charlotte Hancock - Oct. 25, 1841 (James Moore)
O'Neal, Joshua & Sarah Jane Davis - Oct. 14, 1852
O'Neal, Wm. H. & Fanny Irby - Dec. 23, 1874 (Hart C. Peek)
O'Neal, Williamson & Rebeccah Holland - Dec. 9, 1823 (Malichi Murden)
O'Neal, Wooten & Mary Stevens - Jan. 27, 1820 (Francis Cummins)
O'R-ss, Benj. & Elizabeth Cook - May 27, 1819 (Wm. McGiboney)
O'R---, Josiah & Lucinda Lewis - Nov. 30, 1824
O'Rear, Osburn & Lucisss? Lewis - Dec. 27, 1829 (Dacheus Wright)
O'Rear, Robert & Sally Knight - Nov. 30, 1807 (Wm. McGiboney)
Orr, Wm. & Jane Harris - Feb. 10, 1820 (Lovick Pierce)
Osborn, Wm. T. & Florida Wray - Sept. 14, 1863 (L. R. L. Jennings)
Ostin, John & Rachel Anderson - Dec. 16, 1819
Overton, Gilchrist & Harriet R. Morris - Nov. 29, 1821 (Charles Baldwin)
Overton, M. C. & M. A. Caldwell - Dec. 19, 1871
Overton, Simeon W. & Emma Jones - Jan. 20, 1874 (A. A. Fluker)
Owen, Phillman & Betsey Fluker - Mar. 1, 1803
Owen, John & Nancy Woods - Dec. 5, 1822 (Henry Slaughter)
Owen, Wm. & Elizabeth Ann Crawford - Oct. 18, 1825
Owen, Wm. & Emily Durham - Dec. 9, 1852 (John R. Young)
Owens, Charles & Mary Kirkendall - May 26, 1861 (E. S. Williams)
Owens, Charles W. & Sarah M. Wiggins - Feb. 2, 1868 (W. M. Chapman, M.G.)
Owens, Daniel & Louisa Hendricks - Feb. 10, 1847 (R. F. Griffen)
Owens, Daniel & Carolina Marsh - Apr. 26, 1857 (Wm. Hudson)
Owens, Jefferson & Josephine Marsh - Apr. 23, 1854 (B. Rowland)
Owens, Morefield & Martha Parker - Aug. 30, 1821 (A. H. Scott)

Pace, Barnabus & Patsey Harris - Mar. 12, 1807 (Thomas Crawford)
Palmore, Francis & Ann Simmons - Sept. 21, 1840
Palmore, James & Nancey Foster - July 11, 1816 (Wm. Armor)
Palmore, James & Cressa Moore - Nov. 29, 1846 (Ephriam Bruce)
Palmore, James & Lucy A. V. Devaney - Aug. 17, 1860 (Jefferson F. Wright)
Palmer, James M. & Sarah A. M. Jackson - Oct. 23, 1847
Palmer, John C. & Abbigail B. Littleton - Mar. 16, 1859 (James W. Godkin)
Palmer, Landon & Eliza Coleman - Mar. 7, 1821 (Lovick Pierce)
Palmer, Wm. W. & Lorena Adkinson - Feb. 14, 1833 (J. P. Leverett)
Panton, Abner & Rebekah Barnhardt - Nov. 28, 1802 (Thomas Crawford)
Parham, Darling P. & Eliza Ann Tarpley - Jan. 19, 1842 (Vincent R. Thornton)
Park, Columbus M. & Mary Ann W. Armor - Aug. 7, 1838 (Robert F. Griffin)
Park, Ezekial E. P. & Frances A. Redd - Apr. 11, 1833 (A. M. Sanders)
Park, Hugh H. & Anna S. Mays - Jan. 21, 1874 (W. A. Overton)
Park, James B. & Missouri Billingslea - Feb. 22, 1848 (Hinton Crawford)
Park, James L. & Harriet F. Cunningham - Aug. 23, 1820 (Lovick Pierce)
Park, Richard & Catherine Musgrove - Oct. 7, 1804
Park, Richard S. & Nancy T. Walker - July 15, 1841 (Reuben Arnold)
Park, Thomas & Eliza Billingslea - Feb. 12, 1825
Park, Wm. J. & Mrs. Emily A. Carlton - Oct. 6, 1857 (B. H. Overby, M.G.)
Parker, Aaron & Mary Williams - Feb. 27, 1801
Parker, Asa J. & Susan M. A. Bat--- - Dec. 20, 1849 (W. W. Moore)
Parker, Austin & Esther Williams - July 10, 1828 (Reuben White)
Parker, David & Lydia Radmore - June 30, 1803
Parker, Edwin & Rebecca Astin - Jan. 11, 1846 (James Moore)
Parker, Emanuel & Polly Austin - Jan. 30, 1807 (B. Maddox)
Parker, James B. & Virginia W. Sayers - Apr. 1, 1867
Parker, J. F. & Sarah Jane Jackson - Jan. 18, 1849 (L. B. Jackson)
Parker, Lewis & Martha H. Turner - Jan. 6, 1825 (Thos. W. Slaughter)
Parker, Robert F. & Patima Simmons - July 25, 1833 (J. P. Leveritt)
Parker, Wm. & Eunice Nelson - Feb. 21, 1818
Parks, Wm. M. & Elizabeth Bradshaw - June 23, 1864 (John F. Zuber)

Parmentree, Jason & Catherine Heard - Sept. 21, 1799
Parrott, Asberry L. & Lavinia R. Smith - Dec. 9, 1875 (W. H. Blythe)
Parrott, Asbury L. & Fanny Turner - Oct. 12, 1869 (W. H. Blythe)
Parrott, Benjamin & Patience Johnson - July 28, 1828 (John Wood)
Parrott, Benjamin & Nancy Williams - Feb. 14, 1838 (J. P. Leverett)
Parrott, Curtis & Sarah K. Rowland - Dec. 30, 1833
Parrott, Henry & Patsey Dolvin - Feb. 13, 1812 (Wm. Cone)
Parrott, James & Amy King - Oct. 16, 1804
Parrott, James & Matilda Harris - Feb. 2, 1840 (Reuben B. Armor)
Parrott, Obadiah & Elizabeth Horn - Mar. 22, 1822 (Robert Booth)
Partee, Walter A. & Elizabeth Carr - Feb. 10, 1826
Paschel, Samuel D. & Georgia E. Hutcherson - Dec. 7, 1854 (---- Winchel)
Pate, Edward & Mary Fitzpatrick - Oct. 15, 1819 (Rich Gilbert)
Patrick, Benj. B. & Adaline Maddox - Mar. 1833 (John M. Cox)
Patrick, Charles L. & Amanda J. Sidwell - Sept. 10, 1858 (Wm. J. Parks)
Patrick, Constantine & Polly Perkins - Jan. 9, 1797
Patrick, Josiah & Bethsheba Phillips - Dec. 30, 1801
Patrick, Lucius & Sarah C. Jarrell - Jan. 21, 1869 (Joe R. Parker)
Patrick, Robert & Kitty Curry - Apr. 26, 1796
Patrick, Samuel Jr. & Mary E. Lewis - Apr. 26, 1875 (C. C. Davison)
Patridge, Charles & Mary Lankford - Oct. 27, 1874 (John T. Dolvin)
Partridge, Thomas & Elizabeth Loyd - Dec. 22, 1868 (E. B. Mosely)
Patterson, John & Susan Pryor - Nov. 25, 1817 (Wm. Watson)
Patterson, John G. & Ann Smith - May 5, 1850 (Joseph W. Drennon)
Patterson, Wm. H. & Fannie C. Williams - June 20, 1858 (J.H. Kilpatrick)
Patterson, Wm. P. & Martha A. Moody - Sept. 3, 1840 (Robt. Talfree)
Pattillo, Charles & Amelia Holt - Dec. 7, 1820 (Samuel Cowles)
Pattillo, Henry A. & Henrietta H. Hall - June 20, 1866 (V. A. Bell, MG)
Pattillo, James & Elizabeth Jeter - Jan. 11, 1810 (Wm. Giboney)
Pattillo, John & Polly Winifield - Feb. 20, 1816 (Robert Rea)
Pattillo, Samuel & Fanney Hall - Apr. 14, 1795
Paulson, Neil & Rebeccah Cochran - Apr. 16, 1819 (John Myrick)
Peak, Leonard & Jane Barnhardt - July 8, 1832 (James M. Norwood)
Peck, Hart C. & Elizabeth C. Brooks - Jan. 27, 1829
Peek, Archibald P. & Emily Robinson - Feb. 1, 1866 (Henry C. Weaver)
Peek, John C. & Jane Adeline Michael - Mar. 18, 1830 (Wm. Bryan)
Peek, John C. & Frances Bryan - Aug. 15, 1838 (Reuben Arnold?)
Peek, Leonard & Sarah Patrick - Dec. 7, 1841 (James Davidson)
Peek, Leonard & Sarah Patrick - May 14, 1846 (James W. Godkins)
Peek, Littleberry & Elizabeth Williams - Mar. 15, 1824
Peek, Micajah L. & Judah Ann A. Johnson - Dec. 24, 1833 (Wm. Bryan)
Peek, Robert & Emily J. L. Trippe - Feb. 22, 1833 (Wm. Bryant)
Peek, Simon T. & Elizabeth Jones - Jan. 14, 1845 (M. F. Baker)
Peek, Singleton & Louisa Moody - Dec. 28, 1843 (J. M. Davison)
Peek, Wm. C. & Martha C. Bell - Dec. 29, 1874
Peek, Wm. J. & Viney J. Porter - Jan. 7, 1875 (John R. Young)
Peek, Wm. T. & Amanda Colley - Oct. 30, 1874 (J. R. Parker)
Peeler, Anderson J. & Malinda Cook - Jan. 1, 1826 (E. Talley)
Peeler, Anthony & Mary Williams - Dec. 2, 1827 (Wm. Austin)
Peeler, Berry & Emily McClellan - Dec. 30, 1829 (Wm. Bryan)
Peeler, Jacob & Sally Martin - Nov. 24, 1814 (Thomas Riley)
Peevy, Allen & Elizabeth Hightower - Mar. 7, 1815 (Thomas Bush)
Pendergrass, Jesse & Polly Devaney - Sept. 5, 1830 (Peter Johnson)
Penn, Moss & Penny Bird - June 25, 1804
Penn, Wm. S. & Eliza White - Dec. 16, 1834 (George Heard)
Pennington, James & Martha Crawford - Oct. 2, 1845 (Thadeus Pennington)
Pembleton, Joshua & Jane Griffen - Sept. 20, 1805
Peoples, Benj. & Mary Watts - Nov. 4, 1824
Peoples, Dudley & Matilda Park - Oct. 6, 1819
Peoples, Hubbard & Elizabeth Heard - Jan. 15, 1795
Peppin, Noah & Betsey Rowland - Dec. 18, 1825
Peppin, Noah & Emma Patrick - Nov. 12, 1868
Perdue, Daniel & Houghton ---- - Nov. 7, 1815 (West Harris)
Perdue, Daniel & Mary S. Finley - Nov. 7, 1839 (Hinton Crawford)
Perdue, George & Sarah Johnson - Aug. 1836
Perdue, James H. & Elizabeth Billingslea - Nov. 26, 1857 (G. Bright)
Perdue, John & Dimny? Hunt - Sept. 24, 1839 (P. C. Johnson)
Perdue, L. Crawford & Ella Carey - Jan. 13, 1870 (J. M. Dickery)
Perdue, Thomas & Peggy Gaston - Dec. 10, 1807 (C. Maddox)
Perkins, Absalom & Frances A. Moore - Oct. 29, 1870

Perkins, Albert & Mary C. Braddy - Oct. 21, 1847
Perkins, Ezekell & Sally English - Feb. 1, 1810 (Wm. Greer)
Perkins, Hamilton & Emma Lewis - Apr. 23, 1871 (J. M. Lowry, M. G.)
Perkins, James H. & Mary E. Gresham - Nov. 10, 1867 (J. M. Springer, M.G.)
Perkins, James I. & Frances W. Terrell? - Jan. 14, 1838 (Vincent R.
  Thornton)
Perkins, John & Nancy Ransom - Dec. 30, 1819 (John Harris)
Perkins, Nichols & Cecile? Jackson - Dec. 9, 1834 (Albert Jackson)
Perkins, Nicholas & Mary Dixon - Dec. 7, 1850
Perkins, Robert & Sarah B. Johnson - Mar. 4, 1806 or 01
Perkins, Wm. & Polly Harp - Jan. 30, 1805
Perkins, Wm. & Nancy Davis - Jan. 28, 1816 (L. Bethune)
Perman?, Wm. & Maria J. E. Merritt - May 2, 1867 (A. H. Smith)
Perry, Dickerson & Eliza McMillan - Feb. 23, 1825
Perry, Robert H. & Lucy A. Stone - Mar. 25, 1875 (James W. Godkin)
Peteat, Wm. E. & Mary Ann Brown - Nov. 18, 1869 (J. M. Dickey, M.G.)
Peters, John & Sally Haynes - Feb. 1, 1807 (Wm. Greer)
Peterson, Josiah S. & Matilda Manley - June 6, 1844 (J. N. Glenn?)
Petty, Wm. H. & Mattie D. Fambrough - Dec. 15, 1870 (Malone M. Landrum)
Peurifoy, Jackson B. & Virginia A. Hutchinson - Dec. 18, 1851 (Wm. Bryan)
Peurifoy, McCarroll & Phebe Anderson - Oct. 31, 1865 (John W. McCrory?)
Pharr, Ephraim & Mary Mathews - Apr. 12, 1819
Phelps, Augustus B. & Sabrina Brown - Apr. 27, 1861 (R. A. Houston)
Phelps, Henry & Rebecca H. Bowden? - June 16, 1842 (N. H. Hill)
Phelps, Jackson & Rebecca Hobbs - Apr. 1, 1840 (John G. Holtzclaw)
Philemon, Edmundson & Nancy McGee - Dec. 21, 1815 (Lemuel Greene)
Phillips, Abner & Ann B. Burford - Jan. 3, 1853 (Ephriam Bruce)
Phillips, Daniel & Parthenia Vaughn - Apr. 26, 1835 (Wm. Rowland)
Phillips, Elbert & Charlotte Howell - Sept. 25, 1810 (James Holt)
Phillips, Elijah & Tabitha Walker - Sept. 29, 1805
Phillips, Hardy & Rebekah Veazey - Oct. 23, 1814 (Archibald Watts)
Phillips, Henry & Eliza Fuller - Feb. 2, 1831 (Thomas Grimes)
Phillips, Jackson & Daney Connell - Dec. 23, 1873 (W. A. Porter or Partee)
Phillips, Jesse & Betsey Martin - Dec. 27, 1821 (W. W. Moore)
Phillips, Jonathon & Betsy Howell - Jan. 24, 1800)
Phillips, Thomas E. & Cary Ann Connell - Dec. 22, 1870 (Rev. J.S. Pa----)
Phliips, Zacharih & Mary Ann Richards - July 18, 1850 (E. S. Hunter?)
Phillups, Lancelot & Martha Ann R. Mapp - June 22, 1852 (J.F. Billingslea)
Pierce, Bartley & Betsey Gilmore - Feb. 3, 1802
Pierce, Edmund & Lou--- Took? - Sept. 16, 1818 (W. Cone)
Pierce, John & Margaret Moon - Apr. 13, 1790
Pierce, Lagerous & Mary Smith - Feb. 4, 1803
Pierce, Lovick & Ann Martin Foster - Sept. 27, 1809? (Josias Randle?)
Pierce, Matthew & Nancy Bates - Oct. 30, 1836 (James Moore)
Pierce, Wiley M. & Sarah E. Wright - Aug. --, 1863 (Eugenius L. King)
Pierce, Wyly & Rebekah Harrell - Sept. 28, 1806 (Henry English)
Pilgrim, Green & Nancy Ann Bryan - Aug. 26, 1--- (David R. E-----)
Pimm, Joseph & Martha A. Paynter - Feb. 19, 186- (R. A. Houston, M. G.)
Pinthart, John & Judith Jett - Dec. 17, 1807 (Geo. Tuggle)
Pioer?, Wm. & Jane McMichael - Dec. 18, 1805
Piper, Zadick & Amy Bearden - Feb. 8, 1805
Pitman, Joel L. & Ohenaley Emaline Peek - Jan. 30, 1853 (Hart C. Peek)
Polsy, Bennett & Nancy Griffin - Mar. 21, 1796
Pollard, Brittian C. & Sarah E. Benham - Nov. 24, 1834 (Vincent R. Thorn-
  ton)
Pollard, Frederick & Mary Wright - Sept. 23, 1819 (John Harris)
Pollard, James & Louisa King - Nov. 22, 1824
Pollard, Josiah & Susan L. Goodman - Nov. 20, 1866
Pollard, Stephen & Anna Willson - July 2-, 1818 (John Harris)
Ponsonbry, George & Catherine Howe - July 6, 1803
Pool, Gilmon & Janey Patrick - July 3, 1807 (Clabourn Maddox)
Poole, John & Martha Stovall - March 15, 1840 (Thomas Stocks)
Pope, John Hardeman & Demarias Carter Hubbard - Oct. 15, 1850 (M.M. Craw-
  ford)
Pope, Littleberry & Martha A. Cockram - Dec. 15, 1865
Pope, Willson & Nancy Rowland - Dec. 8, 1818 (James Riley)
Porter, David O. & Elizabeth Anne Mays - Nov. 27, 1855 (Wm. English)
Porter, John & Mary Chesser - Nov. 28, 1799
Porter, Robert & Mrs. Willis Thompson - Aug. 21, 1856 (J. G. Holtzclaw)
Potter, Charles & Sarah F. Worthy - Feb. 13, 1868 (E. H. Burgess)

272

Potter, Geo. Washington & Mary Thurmond - Jan. 11, 1855 (W.A.P. -----)
Potts, Wm. & Isabel Simons - Oct. 25, 1788
Poullain, Feliz - Evaline H. Foster - Nov. 11, 1841 (Geo. Pierce)
Poullain, Thomas N. & Mildred P. Sanford - Dec. 4, 1873 (C.H. Strickland)
Powers, Allinus & Eugenia A. Stewart - Feb. 16, 1872
Powers, Isaac & Mary Louisa Stovall - Nov. 22, 1839 (John Harris)
Powers, John & Elizabeth Palmore - Nov. 8, 1829 (Butt L. Ca---)
Powers, Wm. & Nancy Houghton - Aug. 9, 1804
Pratt, James & Susan Wellmaker - Aug. 3, 1857 (Larkin? R. Sisson?)
Pratt, Thomas S. & Lillian H. Logan - Oct. 11, 1853 (Robt. Logan)
Preston, James A. & Cornelia C. Davis - Mar. 1, 1860 (T. J. Bowen)
Price, Adam A. & Emily Frances Jones - Dec. 28, 1854 (V. R. Thornton)
Price, Enoch N. & Nancy Colley - Dec. 1, 1859 (A. A. Junigan?)
Price, Ephrum & Elizabeth Sayer - Aug. 28, 1828 (Robt. Booth)
Price, Hamsford & Mary Cook - Dec. 21, 1828 (Ephriam Bruce)
Price, James T. & Mary B. Jones - July 30, 1854 (I. A. Williams)
Price, Theophilus A. & Mary A. Clifton - Jan. 16, 1868 (W. H. Blythe)
Price, Wm. E. & Alvina Anne Burkes - Jan. 28, 1842 (Geo. Lumpkin)
Pridges, Laurence (Alonzo) G. & Susan Rhodes - Feb. 1, 1855 (W.W. Partee?)
P----st, Miles M. & Emma Bennett - Dec. 9, 1875 (R. A. Credelle)
Primrose, James & Sarah Moore - Nov. 19, 1822 (Wm. Winfield)
Prince, George & Patsey Lawrence - Dec. 27, 1807? (W. M. Johnson)
Prince, John & Nancy Clark - Nov. 1, 1805
Prior, Harden M. & Nancy Montfort - Nov. 3, 1836 (Thomas Stocks)
Pritchell, James & Winney Cone - Sept. 14, 1831 (Benj. F. Martin)
Prudden, Sydney C. & Isabella Simonton - Mar. 30, 1843 (Francis Bowman)
Pryer, Jackson & Sarah Waggoner - July 7, 1844 (I. N. Wilson)
Pryor, Allen & Elizabeth Ca--- - Sept. 18, 1799
Pryor, Marlow & Mary Armor - Sept. 12, 1816 (Lovick Pierce)
Puckell, John & Tabitha Richards - Oct. 3, 1811 (Wm. McGiboney)
Pugh, Berry & Martha J. Vine - Jan. 7, 1874 (W. A. Partee)
Pugh, James & Anna Vine - Feb. 12, 1874 (W. A. Partee?)
Pullen, Sanford & Susannah Pullen - Jan. 10, 1828 (John Harris)
Purdee, George & Sarah Johnson - June 17, 1840
Purdee, John & Dimmy? Hunt - Sept. 24, 1839 (P. C. Johnson, J.P.)
Purdell, John Thomas & Sarah Frances Nunn - July 12, 1869 (Wm. K. -----)
Purdue, John T. & Eliza F. Smith - Nov. 26, 1843 (James W. Godkin)
Purks, Wm. & Sarah E. M. King - June 25, 1857 (Wm. M. Crumby, M. G.)
Pyron, Charles & Nancy Pyron - Mar. 20, 1827 (Joshua Cannon)

Quinn, Charles & Dilly Houghton - Feb. 6, 1801
Quinn, John C. & Frances E. Branch - Nov. 11, 1854

Raburn, Mathew & Hannah Walls - Nov. 11, 1802
Raden, John & Nancy Curry - Oct. 6, 1814 (John Browning)
Raden, J. N. & Anita A. M. Dixon - Jan. 28, 1855 (B. E. Spencer)
Radin, George & Elizabeth Ray - Jan. 22, 1829 (Elijah Holtzclaw)
Ragan, Ibzan & Caroline Perkins - Feb. 15, 1841 (V. R. Thornton)
Ragan, John & Susanna Battle - Dec. 21, 1789
Ragan, Moses & Martha Newsom - May 25, 1847 (V. R. Thornton)
Ragard, John & Maria Harper - June 9, 1814 (O. Porter)
Rainey, Etheldred & Elizabeth Amanda Johnson - Mar. 10, 1840 (B.M. San--)
Rainey, John H. & Mattie Lunsford - Aug. 31, 1811 (John R. Young)
Rainey, Wm. J. & Ella V. Sanford - Nov. 19, 1868 (J. M. Dickey, M. G.)
Rainwater, Charles A. & Cornelia J. Veazey - Apr. 6, 1875 (J.H. Kilpatrick)
Rainwater, Joseph H. & Letitia Williams - Dec. 28, 1875 (N.M. Jones, MG)
Rainwater, Lacy D. & Dorothy Bell - Sept. 5, 1846 (R. F. Griffin)
Rainwater, W. T. & Asthenath Wright - June 16, 1856 (Greene Thompson)
Ralls, Hector & Nancy Atkinson - Dec. 22, 1814 (John Browning)
Ralls, James H. & Sarah Newsom - May 14, 1846 (E. S. Hunter)
Randall, Thomas W. & Mirium Hunter - Oct. 3, 1831 (Thomas Stokes)
Randle, Augustus Henry & Emily Reid Asbury - July 27, 1836 (V.R. Thornton)
Randle, James G. & Sally Coleman - Jan. 26, 1808 (Peter Early)
Randle, J. W. & Avarilla Boatsman - Nov. 20, 1870 (W. R. Wilson)
Randle, Thomas & Elizabeth E. Sanford - Feb. 2, 1830
Randle, Wm. C. & Mary S. Hartes? - Nov. 5, 1835 (G. A. Chappell)
Rankin, Adam W. & Sarah Burke - June 11, 1828 (Wm. Cone)
Rankin, David & Mary Moore - Jan. 27, 1823
Rankin, James R. & Eliza A. Irby - May 13, 1837 (Peter C. Johnson)
Ransom, Joseph & Patsey Carrel - June 26, 1818 (Wm. McGiboney?)

273

Ransom, Robert & Polly Ransom - July 26, 1807 (Francis Ross)
Ransom, Thomas H. & Mrs. Nancy Price - Apr. 23, 1871 (J. M. Lowry)
Ray, Andrew & Nancy Barker - Jan. 12, 1828
Ray, Benjamin & Elizabeth Bennett - Dec. 29, 1822 (John Bowles)
Ray, Benjamin & Sarah E. Lanham - Apr. 6, 1848 (T. M. Fambrough)
Ray, David & Elizabeth Jackson - Sept. 18, 1827 (Joshua Cannon)
Ray, Emanuel & Martha James - Jan. 29, 1822 (J. A. Leftwich?)
Ray, Isaac & Elizabeth Sayers - Feb. 19, 1825
Ray, John H. & Sarah Ann Barksdale - Aug. 23, 1852 (B. Rowland)
Ray, John T. & Nannie S. Watts - Nov. 26, 1868
Ray, Nimrod & Polly Mays? - Mar. 22, 1825
Ray, Shadrach E. & Delia A. Smith - Sept. 11, 1860 (Wm. Bryon)
Ray, Wm. & Mary Orr - Nov. 13, 1807 (Wm. Greer)
Ray, Wm. & Susannah Burk - July 5, 1830
Ray, Wm. & Mary Kennedy - Nov. 17, 1836 (Nathan Hobbs)
Rea, Benj. F. & Laura Gresham - July 13, 1847 (Francis Bowman)
Rea, Robert & Jane Smith - Aug. 26, 1818
Rea, Robert & Nancy Akins - Dec. 27, 1821 (O. Porter)
Read, James & Rhoda Brown - Nov. 26, 1804
Redd, Albert G. & Henrietta E. Daniel - Apr. 25, 1849 (Francis Bowman)
Redd, James & Mary Lewis - May 27, 1830 (Iovick? Pierce)
Reddin, James & Elizabeth Bledsoe - Oct. 9, 1816 (John Browning)
Reddin, James & Polly Nickleson - Apr. 30, 1818 (John Myrick)
Redding, Thomas & Mary Brockman - June 25, 1825
Redmond, John & Frances Aaron - Aug. 6, 1871 (W. C. Birchmore)
Reed, Freeman & Nancy Ray - Dec. 10, 1835 (Wm. H. Pr-----)
Reed, James & Ann Bickers - Feb. 6, 1842 (Thomas Stocks?)
Reed, Robert N. & Julia K. Brown - June 15, 1865 (P. H. Mell, M. G.)
Reed, Wm. & Nancy Jarrell - Feb. 6, 1828 (Hermon Mercer)
Reed, Zachariah? & Ginney Adams - Mar. 3, 1789
Reece, Charles & Lucy Merriwether - Apr. 15, 1830 (M. Reed)
Reece, Drury & Phi----- Phillips - June 11, 1849
Reeves, J. I. & Elizabeth M. Hodge - July 24, 1840
Reed, Felix C. & Sallie C. Lightfoot - Oct. 15, 1863 (J.M. Kilpatrick)
Reid, Reuben & Polly Alford - Dec. 15, 1788
Reid, Wm. T. & Mary A. E. Kendall - Apr. 28, 1859 (C. W. Key)
Reid, Zachariah & Polly Lawrence - Jan. 14, 1790
Reynolds, James & Lucretia Perkins - Dec. 27, 1840 (David Dansel?)
Reynolds, James & Eliza Wright - Mar. 25, 1856 (J. A. Duncan)
Reynolds, James H. & Emily J. Stewart - Nov. 12, 1867 (W. R. Wilson)
Reynolds, John & Cynthia S. Reynolds - Jan. 3, 1858 (T. Callahan)
Reynolds, John & Martha J. Freeman - Sept. 5, 1875 (John S. Callaway)
Reynolds, John C. & Emma Moody - Dec. 31, 1868 (Wm. A. Overton)
Reynolds, Levy & Metsey? Moore - Oct. 15, 1811 (Arthur Foster)
Reynolds, Mordecai J. & Ann A. Tuggle - May 29, 1858
Reynolds, Mordicia J. & Electra A. Durham - Sept. 5, 1865 (Wm. R. Wilson)
Reynolds, Wm. E. & Lizzie A. Newton - July 20, 1875 (Henry Newton)
Reid, Brice & Sarah Tanner - Feb. 15, 1821 (John Harris)
Rhimes, Wm. & May Anderson - Sept. 18, 1821 (Francis West)
Rhodes, A. S. W. & Sarah Smith - Dec. 8, 1841 (Ephriam Bruce)
Rhodes, Henry & Rebecah Day - Sept. 16 or 6, 1823
Rhodes, Henry & Eliza ----- - Dec. 17, 1850
Rhodes, Johnson & Martha Patter? - Apr. 2, 1855 (I. R. Hall)
Rhodes, Johnson R. & Caroline Horton - Jan. 4, 1868 (R. B. Kelly)
Rhodes, Martin V. & Elizabeth Finley - Apr. 25, 1841? (S. M. Wilson)
Rhodes, Thomas & Frances Gresham - Oct. 29, 1817 (Jesse Mercer)
Rhodes, Wiley & Margaret Mitchell - Dec. 17, 1840 (V. R. Thornton)
Rhodes, Wiley A. T. & Elizabeth Ann Patterson - Oct. 5, 1840 (S.G.Jenkins)
Rhodes, Wm. & Milly Evans - Dec. 10, 1820 (Mallichi? Murden)
Rhodes, Wm. C. & Mary F. Gordon - Nov. 15, 1868 (James Davison)
Richards, Azaria & Letila? Woods - Oct. 3, 1820
Richards, Calvus? & Myrtus Thornton - Aug. 12, 1873 (W. A. Ocerton)
Richards, Pickerel & Hannah Beardin - Nov. 30, 1799
Richards, Tirah & Lucy B--1--- - Dec. 17, 181-? (John Harris)
Richards, Wm. A. & Savannah W. Ledbetter - Sept. 9, 1851 (John C. Merritt)
Richards, Willis & Elizabeth Irby - Dec. 29, 1846 (I. A. Williams)
Richardson, James & Betsey Kineman - July 1, 1807 (John Mapp)
Richardson, Robert & Nancy Carter - Jan. 2, 1831 (Butt L. Cato)
Richter, Charles W. J. & Mary L. Hunter - Sept. 12, 1866 (P.B. Robinson)
Rights, John & Rebeccah Panton - Nov. 6, 1804

Riley, Henry N. & Lavina Bell - May 14, 1851
Riley, James G. & Mary F. Brunt - June 8, 1843 (R. G. Griffin)
Riley, James G. & Sarah Ann Sims Woodward - Mar. 19, 1845 (Hinton
   Crawford)
Riley, Joseph & Betsey Smith - Apr. 2, 1811 (Robert Rea)
Riley, Thomas & Sally Hill - Jan. 10, 1808 (Geo. Smith)
Riley, Thomas P. & Linnie Armor? - Oct. 18, 1870 (J. M. Dickey)
Riley, Wm. M. & Louisa Ann Mallory - Jan. 8, 1835 (James Anderson)
Rissel, Wm. & ----- McCullough - June 29, 1799
Road, Benjamin & Sally Whitlock - Mar. 27, 1803
Roarks, Joel & Emily Wright - Nov. 28, 1845 (Ephriam Bruce)
Robarts, David & Eliza Green Robarts - Dec. 20, 1818 (A. Gresham)
Roberts, Andrew & Susan Bennett - June 21, 1856
Roberts, Frederick & Martha Lewis - Nov. 12, 1826 (Abraham Baugh)
Roberts, Jr. & Clarey Goode - Sept. 5, 1804
Roberts, John & Polly Melton - June 24, 1803
Roberts, Richard & Sally Baker - Sept. 13, 1804
Roberts, R. F. G. & Nancy Meredith - May 10, 1846 (J. B. Chappel)
Roberts, Wm. & Frankey Samson - Dec. 30, 1801
Roberts, Wm. B. & Emily Greer - Dec. 22, 1842 (Hinton Crawford)
Robertson, Jesse & Mary Irby - Mar. 6, 1820
Robertson, John & Jennett Evans - Apr. 13, 1832 (John Park)
Robertson, Wilkes & Polly Coleman - Dec. 13, 1804 (Thomas Crawford)
Robertson, Wm. & Anny Stringfellow - Feb. 4, 1818 (O. Porter)
Robertson, Z. & Susannah Bridges - Jan. 2, 1800
Robins, Albert M. & Dianah D. Walker - Apr. 5, 1859 (L. B. Jackson)
Robins, James R. & S. M. Wilkins - Apr. 29, 1873 (E. Heist, M. G.)
Robins, John & Elizabeth Stoutamire - July 22, 1827 (Wm. Aston)
Robins, Thomas S. & Sarah A. Avery - Oct. 17, 1850 (James M. Kelley?)
Robins, Wm. & Sarah Williams - Oct. 23, 1827 (Nat Harris)
Robinson, Benj. & Narcisa Harris - Nov. 14, 1815 (Thomas Lyne)
Robinson, Benj. & Martha Cochran - Aug. 11, 1868 (A. J. S. Jackson)
Robinson, Benj. & S. M. Bruce - Aug. 15, 1871 (W. H. Wright)
Robinson, James & Eliza Kicker - Aug. 3, 1826 (Reuben White)
Robinson, John Pope & Sarah Williams - Apr. 8, 1828 (E. Tally)
Robinson, John Pope & Julia Pearman - Jan. 9, 1873 (John P. Wagnon?)
Robinson, Joseph & Martha Ellis - Aug. 25, 1836 (Wm. L. Pullen)
Robinson, Joseph W. & Caroline B. Smith - Oct. 12, 1841 (F. R. Golding)
Robinson, Lewellin & Amelia Coleman - June 24, 1819 (Lovick Pierce)
Robinson, Phillip? B. & Mrs. Nancy T. Sweet - Oct. 26, 1858 (Wm. J. Parks)
Robinson, Milford & Francina Parker - Dec. 29, 1830 (Mathew Winifield?)
Robinson, Thomas W. & Mary E. Park - June 25, 1861 (Albert Gray)
Robinson, Wm. H. & Malinda Patrick - Oct. 17, 1866 (Lorenzo D. Carlton)
Robinson, Wm. H. & Henrietta Bruce - Apr. 16, 1872 (John Dolvin)
Rodgers, Andrew J. & Mary J. Owen - Dec. 24, 1872 (John D. Cleveland)
Rogers, Joel B. & Lizzy Jones - Feb. 22, 1872 (John D. Copeland)
Rogers, John & Mary Kizerk - Jan. 23, 1802
Rose, Wm. & Frankey Burch - June 13, 1804
Ross, Samuel & Polly McCombs - Feb. 23, 1815 (John Armor)
Roum, Charles & Adelaid? King - Feb. 22, 1847 (J. F. Billinglea)
Rounsevall?, Robert & Grace Finley - Dec. 20, 1821 (Francis Cummins)
Rouzel, Hiram & Emaliza Wms. - Mar. 21, 1840 (John G. Holtzclaw)
Rowland, Charles R. & Mattie Ledbetter - Aug. 26, 1875 (W. R. Blythe)
Rowland, Barksdale & Elizabeth Parrott - Oct. 1, 1837 (Lemuel T. Crossley)
Rowland, David R. & Cornelia Smith - Dec. 22, 1868 (W. H. Blythe, M.G.)
Rowland, James & Emily Jackson - May 7, 1824
Rowland, James & Julia F. Hutcherson - Arp. 22, 1842 (James Godkin)
Rowland, John & Harriett Stines - Jan. 8, 1854 (B. Rowland)
Rowland, John G. & Sarah Virginia Cutwright - Dec. 1, 1857 (Wm. J. Park)
Rowland, John J. & C. L. Hutcheson - Nov. 15, 1849
Rowland, Jordan & Sally Swan - May 17, 1797
Rowland, Jordan & Lucinda Wright - July 12, 1829 (Wm. Bryan)
Rowland, Wiley & Elizabeth Akers - Oct. 12, 1826 (Jacob Riley)
Rowland, Wm. & Mary Jackson - Jan. 26, 1829 (John Harris)
Rowland, Wm. Sr.? & Winnie R. Newton - Feb. 23, 1862 (W. J. Cotter, M.G.)
Rowland, Wm. A. & Sallie M. Hudson - Dec. 13, 1859 (O. L. Smith)
Rowland, Wm. D. & Sarah F. R. Bryan - Nov. 2, 1855 (Wm. Bryan)
Royston, John & Polly Cuna - Jan. 6, 1803
Rozier, Wm. & Rhoda C. Drennon - Jan. 23, 1852 (J. T. Finley)
Ruarks, Joel J. & Mrs. Mary F. Hooks - July 11, 1858 (L. B. Jackson)

Rummey, James E. & Mary E. Hendrey - Jan. 2, 1868 (L. D. Carlton)
Rumiel, Greenberry & Polly Jones - Mar. 2, 1805
Rundles, James & Amy Wilson - Sept. 20, 1819
Russell, Ignatious & Eleanor Kimbrough - July 20, 1801
Russell, Samuel H. & Elizabeth Parrott - Jan. 12, 1826 (Benj. Gilders---)
Rutland, Wiley & Pamelia Chewnings? - Jan. 2, 1819
Ryan, Haynes S. & Mary M. Roberts - Sept. 8, 1836 (James Moore)
Rye, Joseph & Betsey Wilson - July 10, 1790
Ryles, James G. & Mary E. Jones - Jan. 13, 1852 (B. M. Sanders)

Sams, James & Adeline Wright - Oct. 2, 1828
Samson, Robert & Polly Mosely - June 29, 1805
Samson, Wm. & Delphy Clay - June 27, 1806
Sanders, Al---- & Elizabeth Newberry - Feb. 27, 1805
Sanders, George & Sarah Clarke - May 29, 1824
Sanders, George & Polly Jones - Jan. 28, 1825
Sanders, James & Polly Hall - June 13, 1805
Sanders, James Ragan & Cornelia M. Jones - Jan. 4, 1842 (B.M. Sanders)
Sanders, John I. & Cordelia E. Hard (Hart) - July 4, 1833 (Thomas -----)
Sanders, Thomas L. & Parmelia White - Feb. 19, 1852 (F. W. Pri----)
Sanders, Wm. & Elizabeth Jenkins - Dec. 15, 1835 (Thomas Stocks)
Sanders, Zadock & Holly Sayers - Dec. 12, 1819 (Reuben White)
Sanderson, Geo. W. & Eugenia H. Sayers - Mar. 30, 1866 (R. C. Peek)
Sanford, Ben & Jimmy Armor - Aug. 11, 1805
Sanford, Henry & Susan Ann Smith - Apr. 2, 1840 (Thomas -----)
Sanford, Shelton P. & Maria F. Dickerman - July 30, 1840 (Otis Smith)
Sanford, Wm. & Polly Harris - Mar. 11, 1805
Sanford, Wm. & Sally B. Darnel - July 3, 1814 (Nicholas Lewis)
Sankey, Dr. John T. & Anna Daniel - 1801
Sankey, Richard D. & Mary M. Watts - May 4, 1854 (S. G. Hillyer)
Sankey, Dr. Richard T. & Frances Love - Oct. 20, 1831 (J. N. G-----)
Sankey, M. D. & Margaret Daniel - Mar. 2, 1824
Sapp, Richard H. & Sarah M. Killam - Aug. 24, 1852 (N. M. Crawford)
Sargeant, John C. & Nancy Anne Bruce - Feb. 15, 1852 (B. Rowland)
Saxon, Lewis W. & Eliza Parnell - Oct. 8, 1867 (E. A. Burgess)
Sayers, David & Elizabeth Robinson - Sept. 15, 1804
Sayers, James M. & Delana Richards - Nov. 24, 1825
Sayers, James M. & Nancy A. Lucky - Jan. 8, 1835 (James Moore)
Sayers, John S. & Frances Price - Mar. 3, 1834 (G. W. West)
Sayers, Joshua L. & Permelia Ansley - Nov. 18, 1834 (James F. Hillyer)
Scamper, Daniel & Polly Finley - Apr. 1, 1803
Scoggins, John & Mary Ann Nelms - Apr. 15, 1829 (Robt. Burdell)
Scoggins, John I. & Mary Forrester - Dec. 14, 1826
Scott, James N. & Mary J. Bowles - Dec. 12, 1856
Scott, John I. & Ann B. Cartwright - Sept. 2, 1834 (Thomas W. Grimes)
Scott, Pulaskie? S. & Charity N. Grimes - May 1, 1838 (Francis Bowman)
Scudder, Samuel C. & Eunice Safford - Nov. 13, 1848 (H. Safford)
Seals, Henry & Angelina Carrel - Nov. 3, 1827
Seals, John H. & Mary E. Sanders - Oct. 1, 1857 (Wm. Wms.)
Self, James E. & Artemi--- Jordan - Sept. 8, 1850 (Daniel Hightower)
Self, Wm. & Matilda Knowles - Mar. 11, 1828 (Wm. Austin)
Sessions, Jeremiah M. & Sarah E. Porter - Nov. 5, 1856 (W. H. C. Cone)
Seymore, Evabon & Lucy E. M. Wingfield - Apr. 10, 1822 (Francis Cummins)
Seymour, Henry C. & Anne Cornelia Wingfield - Apr. 20, 1841
Shackelford, Charles & Rebecca Elizabeth Huntor? - Oct. 5, 1836
   (Jonathan Davis)
Shackelford, Josephus & Cordelia Stowe - Apr. 18, 1855 (L.R.L. James)
Shackelford, Lloyd & Ida J. Mitchell - Jan. 20, 1869 (J. J. Brantley)
Shannon, Wm. & Margaret Nickelson - Oct. 1, 1820 (Lovick Pierce)
Sharkley, Silas & Dor---- Tait - Dec. 23, 1818
Sharp, Benj. & Martha Jackson - Jan. 25, 1843 (B. M. Sanders)
Sharp, John & Sally Peeples - June 12, 1801
Sharp, Martial & Matilda McGuire - Nov. 30, 1819
Sharp, Richard & Polly Guinn - May 11, 1815 (Wm. McGiboney)
Sharp, Robert & Lucinda Newell - Feb. 15, 1818 (Thomas Johnson)
Shaw, Creytin & Caroline Barnes - Aug. 7, 1870 (W. C. Birchmore)
Shaw, James E. & Josephine M. Davis - Dec. 13, 1868 (Wm. A. Overton)
Shaw, John & Della Finley - Nov. 18, 1818 (L. Bethune)
Shaw, Samuel & Emma Rae - Dec. 28, 1869 (James W. Godkin)
Sheats, Benojah? & Mary Ann Richardson - July 23, 1838 (Thomas Grimes)

Shed, Prelow & Nancy Nichols - Mar. 20, 1861
Shed, Wm. & Amanda M. Parks - July 4, 1860 (R. B. Kelly)
Shell, Reuben R. & Jane Lucas - Jan. 2, 1843
Shell, T. I. & Clarissa Bruce - Dec. 9, 1846 (L. A. Williams)
Shelton, Geo. W. & Mary Ann Morris - Oct. 5, 1858 (J. H. Wragg)
Shelton, John L. & Rebecca A. Sidwell - Dec. 8, 1864 (James W. Godkins)
Sheridan, Dennis & Polly Riley - May 24, 1815 (Robert Rea)
Sheridan, R. W. & Lucinenda Shell - Mar. 7, 1852 (B. Rowland)
Sherley, Richmond & Delila Blythe - June 10, 1820 (Wm. McGiboney)
Sherrill, Littleberry & Elizabeth Bedell - Mar. 9, 1825
Sherwood, Adial & Ann Early - May 18, 1821
Shey, Samuel & Mary B. Crawford - Sept. 3, 1846 (Wm. I. Parks, M. G.)
Shields, Wm. & Catherine Cone - Aug. 25, 1801
Shipp, John H. & Elizabeth O'Neal - Dec. 27, 1866 (John C. M-----)
Shipp, Lemuel & Elizabeth Peak - July 18, 1844 (James Moore)
Shipp, Stephen & Luciena? Irby - May 15, 1834 (James Moore)
Shirling, James N. & Martha Ann Peek - Sept. 12, 1841 (Ephriam Bruce)
Shirling, Rabun W. & Mary Ann Gaston - Dec. 29, 1846 (R. F. -----)
Shirling, Richard & Rebecca W. Lewis - Aug. 3, 1855 (Wm. Bryan)
Shirling, Richard & Nancy Lewis - July 6, 1858 (Wm. Bryan)
Shivers, Thomas J. & Sarah Ann Martin - Feb. 25, 1836 (Geo. Pierce)
Shockley, Benj. & Patsy Gatlin - Dec. 28, 1819
Shropshire, James H. & Sally Henly - Dec. 17, 1805
Shropshire, ----- & Elizabeth Booles - Dec. 1, 1822 (Wm. Greer)
Shropshire, Wesley & Nancy Swanson - Jan. 5, 1826
Shy, Wm. H. & Eliza May Bowden - Nov. 23, 1868
Sidwell, John & Sallie E. Bruce - June 10, 1866 (L. C. Broome)
Signaw, Thomas & Betsey Daniell - May 30, 1805
Silvey, Hinton C. & Sarah Jane Holder - Nov. 8, 1864
Simmons, Charles & Polly Parker - Nov. 20, 1793
Simmons, Charles & Nancy Little - Dec. 25, 1836 (Mathew Oliver)
Simmons, Frank M. & Mary S---- - Dec. 20, 1860 (J. M. Kelly)
Simmons, Franklin & Susan Channell - July 23, 1856
Simmons, Henry S. & Aseneth Parker - June 15, 1833 (J. P. Leveritt)
Simmons, Jack & Polly Leonard - Aug. 7, 1821 (H. G. Slaughter)
Simmons, Simeon & Nancy Parrott - Dec. 30, 1828
Simmons, Stephens & Matilda Leonard - July 31, 1823 (T. W. Slaughter)
Simms, Frederick & Sally Baine - Apr. 3, 1804
Simonton, Ezekiel & Sophia Greer - Jan. 17, 1816 (Wm. Cone)
Simonton, Joel & Sarah Powers - Sept. 7, 1814 (A. Watts)
Simonton, John A. & Catherine A. Jossey? - Oct. 18, 1843 (W.D. Martin,MG)
Simonton, Thomas & Rebecca Potts - Mar. 14, 1787
Simpson, Wm. H. & Sarah J. Hancock - Dec. 29, 1865? (L. D. Carlton)
Sims, A. F. & Lavinia Williams - Apr. 1, 1855 (J. F. Thrasher, Jr.)
Sims, John M. & Beheathalon? Grisby? - Nov. 29, 1824
Sims, Wm. & Falbra Richards - June 26, 1822
Sinclair, Wm. F. M. & Camilla J. Rowles - Feb. 27, 1868
Singleton, Joseph & Mary Ann Terrell - Jan. 4, 1825
Skidmore, Crosley S. & Eliza W. Smith - May 21, 1843 (V. R. Thornton)
Sladen?, Arthur & Frances Evans - Jan. 29, 1825
Slaughter, George & Susannah Copeland - Oct. 8, 1818
Slaughter, Henry G. & Elizabeth Kimbrough - Dec. 14 or 4, 1815 (Gilly Moore)
Slaughter, John & Elizabeth Sayers - Nov. 8, 1803
Slaughter, John & Temperance Harris - Sept. 27, 1827 (Francis Cummins)
Slaughter, Raney S. & Nancy L. Credille - Nov. 22, 1838 (Nathan Oliver)
Slaughter, Reubin & Polly Lawson - Aug. 19, 1789
Slaughter, Thomas & Nancy Lewis - Dec. 7, 1815 (Walker Lewis)
Slaughter, Wm. & Nancy Kimbrough - Dec. 16, 1796
Smallwood, James & Mary O'Neal - Dec. 8, 1850
Smith, Alexander & Elizabeth L. Blythe - Dec. 12, 1833 (Wm. Bryan)
Smith, Alexander H. & Sallie F. Swann - Jan. 18, 1871 (Thos. F. Pierce)
Smith, Azariah & Celestia Brooks - Jan. 5, 1871 (L. D. Caldwell)
Smith, Burgess & Elvia? Carlton - June 3, 1875 (Clement A. -----)
Smith, Daniel N. & Sophronia Ann Channel - Apr. 25, 1848 (W. F. -----)
Smith, Ebenezer & Cynthia Lewis - Mar. 12, 1818 (John Harris)
Smith, George N. & Sarah C. Bryan - Sept. 16, 1873 (James L. Pierce)
Smith, George W. & Leonora McCummons? - Jan. 19, 1864 (John R. Young)
Smith, Hillard A. & Mary E. F. Tarpley - Dec. 18, 1866 (J. F. Wright)
Smith, Isaac & Eliza Moore - Aug. 28, 1806 (A. Harp)

Smith, Isaac & Mary Martin - Jan. 28, 1819 (Reuben White)
Smith, Isaac & Elizabeth Keely? - July 28, 1852 (A. L. Willis)
Smith, Isaac F. & Susan A. Phelps - Jan. 31, 1867 (Thomas J. Peek)
Smith, Isaac H. & Eliza Ruark - Sept. 11, 1866 (Wm. Bryan)
Smith, Isaac H. & Amanda M. Smith - Feb. 11, 1873 (N. M. Jones)
Smith, James & Rebecca Winfield - Oct. 4, 1824
Smith, James & Jane E. Houghton - Dec. 19, 1833 (C. T. Beeman)
Smith, James Jr. & Patience Atkinson - July 31, 1842 (H. H. Lawrence)
Smith, James & Mary Anderson - June 1, 1845 (R. F. Griffi--)
Smith, James & M. Fredonia Smith - Nov. 30, 1868
Smith, James C. & Fredonia Credille - Dec. 8, 1868 (W. H. Blythe)
Smith, James D. & Mary Jane Oliver - July 31, 1866 (L. O. Carlton)
Smith, James H. & Anna L. J. Hendry - Jan. 22, 1874 (W. A. Overton)
Smith, James H. & Mattie N. Moreland - Dec. 16, 1875 (L. D. Caldwell)
Smith, James R. & Edna Cheek? - Nov. 26, 1850 (James M. -----)
Smith, James W. & Caroline M. Swindell - Oct. 14, 1852 (J. W. -----)
Smith, Jediah? & Flora Williams - Sept. 5, 1822 (John Harris)
Smith, Jeremiah & Mary Peters - Oct. 4, 1818 (John Wilson)
Smith, Joel & Frances McLellan - May 6, 1847 (Wm. Bryan)
Smith, John & Milly Hightower - Feb. 15, 1810 (W. McGiboney)
Smith, John & Harriet Park - Apr. 1, 1812
Smith, John & Elizabeth Catherine Oliver - Mar. 14, 1839 (Ephriam Bruce)
Smith, John & Martha A. Miller - Dec. 14, 1843 (Francis Bowman)
Smith, John F. & Mary A. Hargrove - June 1, 1858 (L.R.L. Jennings)
Smith, Nathan & Fanny Smith - Mar. 30, 1815? (Robert Rea)
Smith, Nathaniel & Elizabeth Hutson - Nov. 24, 1808 (Henry English)
Smith, Reddick & Polly Hall - Dec. 20, 1811 (A. Veazey)
Smith, Reddick & Mary Clarke - Jan. 11, 1816 (Robert Rea)
Smith, Reuben C. & Sarah Kimbrough - Nov. 21, 1836
Smith, Richard A. & Susan R. Smith - Oct. 9, 1860 (A. Gray, M. G.)
Smith, Thomas & Anna Peters - Nov. 21, 1817 (John Williams)
Smith, Thomas & Patience Smith - Apr. 22, 1847 (James W. Godkin)
Smith, Thomas H. & Emily A. P---due - Nov. 19, 1840 (James Jones)
Smith, Wm. & Betsey Holland - Feb. 6, 1802
Smith, Wm. C. & Lavinia A. Swinney - Jan. 25, 1859 (W. J. Parks, M. G.)
Smith, Wm. G. & Patience Smith - Mar. 6, 1845 (Wm. Bryan)
Smith, Wm. T. & Susan M. E. Armor - June 26, 1866 (A. Gray, M. G.)
Smity, Young & Rebekah Channel - Dec. 28, 1814 (James Baldwin)
Smith, Youngest & Elizabeth Smith - Apr. 18, 1816 (Thomas Snow?)
Sneed, Wm. & Caroline Scoggins - Nov. 24, 1836 (Nathan Hobbs)
Snow, John P. & Susannah Smith - Jan. 24, 1819 (Osborne Rogers)
Snow, Samuel G. & Polly Copeland - Dec. 18, 1807 (J. Holt)
Sorrell, George & Sally Cameron - Nov. 16, 1799
Sorrow, Joseph C. & Sarah E. Allen - Feb. 2, 1869 (John C. Merritt)
Sorrow, Nicholas & Sidney E. A. Nickelson - Sept. 2, 1866 (J. F. Wright)
Southall, Hallman & Nancy Green - Jan. 21, 1819
Southerland, John & Sally Hobbs - Apr. 17, 1808 (Henry English)
Sparks, James & Susan Meadows - May 8, 1815 (Malichi Murden)
Sparks, Thomas H. & Ann Linton - Feb. 20, 1845
Spencer, John & Fanny Whatley - Nov. 17, 1804
Spencer, Levi & Rebecca DeLoach - Nov. 25, 1822
Spinks, Henry N. & Anna E. Miller - Apr. 24, 1861 (R. A. Houston)
Spivey, Francis M. & Irene Saxon - Oct. 6, 1859 (J. M. Kelly)
Spivey, Wm. & Amey Batchelor - Oct. 10, 1831 (Geo. Hall?)
Spivey, Wm. H. & Effie J. Armor - Feb. 25, 1874 (A. Gray, M. G.)
Spradling, James & Sally McMurray - Jan. 7, 1805
Spradling, Wm. & Hannah McMurray - Feb. 15, 1804
Spurlock, John & Judith Blackmon - Nov. 26, 1815 (Alex. Johnson)
Stack, Henry H. & Eliza Reynolds - Dec. 24, 1865 (Thos. -----)
Stallings, John E. & Mary Bass - Mar. 11, 1819 (O. Porter)
Stallings, Moses & Mary Mabry - Jan. 8, 1827
Stallings, Wilson & Susanna Smith - July 14, 1822 (H. P. Mabry)
Standifer, Jesse & Elizabeth Houghton - Nov. 19, 1799
Stanford, George & Indiana Treadway - Nov. 25, 1874 (Hart C. Peek)
Stanley, Isaac & Nancy Hough - Jan. 1, 1802
Stanley, Thomas & Margaret A. E. Oliver - Mar. 26, 1857 (Hart C. Peek)
Stanley, Wm. T. & Martha A. Irby - Aug. 3, 1856 (I. J. Beck)
Stanley, James & Amy Ellis - June 27, 1806
Sta--min, Newell & Elizabeth Tally - Mar. 15, 1821 (John Beattie)
Stapp, Stephen & Sarah Curry - Sept. 15, 1825 (Robert Booth)

Starr, Elijah & Hannah Townsend - Apr. 15, 1805
Statham, Memory & Malissa Campbell - July 28, 1826
Steele, Alexander & Polly Harper - June 8, 1804
Still, Archibald & Sarah Sanders - June 7, 1855 (B. Rowland)
Stephens, Henry & Matilda Stephens - May 20, 1839 (W. L. Strain)
Stephens, Jesse & Mary Jane Irby - Nov. 22, 1842 (James Moore)
Stephens, John & Charlotte Bragg - Nov. 23, 1841 (James Moore)
Stephens, Silas & Illisa? Rankin - Aug. 18, 1842 (F. R. Golding, M.G.)
Stephens, Walter & Sarah Ann Oneal - May 27, 1840 (James Moore)
Stephens, Wm. & Henrietta Ogletree - Aug. 2, 1825 (Horatio Nunnelly)
Stephenson, Thomas & Sarah Roun---val-- - Aug. 18, 1818 (---- Harris)
Sterling, Jenkins I. & Sevener? Ann Borders - June 4, 1833 (Reuben
   Thornton)
Stevens, Edmund & Mary Goss - Feb. 4, 1810 (W. McGiboney)
Stevens, John & Patsey Parker - Dec. 26, 1803
Stevens, John & Mary Christopher - Nov. 30, 1854 (Daniel Hightower)
Stevens, Rollins W. & Mary A. Greene - Dec. 18, 1860 or 61 (Albert Gray,
   M. G.)
Stevenson, Stephen W. & Mary J. Jenkins - Nov. 14, 1835
Stewart, Frederick & Margaret Nelson - Dec. 30, 1847 (James Moore)
Stewart, George & E. Augusta Weaver - Mar. 10, 1859 (W. J. Parks, M. G.)
Stewart, Wm. D. & Martha Ann Stovall - Aug. 14, 1845 (Hinton Crawford)
Stillman, Samuel & Nancy R. Harris - Dec. 22, 1829 (Thomas Sanford)
Sti---son, Wm. & Elizabeth Anderson - Oct. 25, 1824
Sticker, Solomon & Mary Bays - June 18, 1822 (Chesley Bristow)
Stocks, John & Nancy Fitzpatrick - May 14, 1800
Stocks, Thomas & Frances A. Davis - Nov. 26, 1848 (P. H. Mell)
Stocks, John G. & Anna M. Matthews - Dec. 14, 1856 (John P. Duncan, MG)
Stone, John T. & Mary Anne Daniels - Nov. 7, 1850 (James W. Godkin)
Stone, Hardy & Jenny Blankenship - June 19, 1815 (W. McGiboney)
Stone, John W. & Effie L. Carson - Oct. 26, 1865 (R. A. Houston)
Stovall, John & Martha M. Pryor - Dec. 22, 1830 (John Park, J. P.)
Stovall, Littleberry & Mary Buchannon - June 14, 1818 (L. Bethune)
Stovall, Powhattan & Temperance Bishop - Nov. 15, 1824
Stovall, Powhattan & Sarah Ann Crawford - Nov. 14, 1827
Stovall, Wm. H. & Sallie K. Bunkley - Oct. 29, 1874 (J. H. Kilpatrick)
Strain, W. W. & Sally Spruce - Oct. 28, 1799
Strange, James W. & Margaret McLellan - Aug. 25, 1864 (R. A. -----, M.G.)
Strickland, James K. & Susan E. Rhymes - Apr. 9, 1864
Strickland, C. C. O. & M. G. A. Chandler - Feb. 4, 1872 (W. T. Foster)
Stroud, John & Sarah Phillips - Oct. 13, 1787
Strozier, Reuben I. & Mary W. Wright - Dec. 13, 1846 (W. J. Park)
Stubblefield, Gustavus? & Eliza Perry - Apr. 3, 1828 (Wm. Winfield)
Sturdivant, Geo. W. & Frances Z. Y. Nelson - Feb. 16, 1854 (Daniel High--)
Sturgis, Charles M. & Martha C. Thor---ton - Apr. 14, 1868 (Wm.A.Overton)
Swain, John & Mary Whitlock - Oct. 16, 1831
Swann, George & Elizabeth Baker - Dec. 21, 1819
Swann, John & Elizabeth Musgrove - Dec. 22, 1819
Swann, John W. & Lucy P. Jernigan - Apr. 20, 1848 (W. H. Evans)
Swann, Joseph & Anne Surnden - May 17, 1804
Swanson, Graves & Sally C. Brown - Dec. 8, 1808 (Geo. Tuggle)
Swanson, Graves & Nancy Wilkinson - Mar. 18, 1819 (John Browning)
Sweet, James F. & Nancy J. Park - Jan. 18, 1854 (N. M. Crawford)
Swindall, Daniel & Eunice Ward - Mar. 6, 1828 (Wm. Bryan)
Swindell, Thomas & Mary Curtwright - June 17, 1837
Swindle, Thomas & Levinia Curtwright - Aug. 7, 1832 (Samuel Curt-----)
Swinney, Henry & Martha Lasseter - Dec. 21, 1819 (John Park)
Swinney, Jothram & Nancy McIntosh - Nov. 5, 1827 (Thomas Grimes)
Swinney, Marcus & Dianah Jackson - Feb. 17, 1824
Swinney, Wm. & Peggy Moore - Feb. 20, 1819

Talbot, James & Sarah Ann Phillips - Nov. 26, 1829 (J. W. Gleen?)
Talley, Wm. L. S. & Nancy R. Smith - Sept. 6, 1838 (James W. Godkin)
Tally, Elkanah & Sarah Anderson - Feb. 1, 1821 (John Simmons)
Tally, Nathan & Catherine Sayer - Jan. 22, 1819 (D. L. McBride)
Tally, Nathan & Martha Travis - Feb. 6, 1851 (Hinton Crawford)
Tally, Thomas & Lucy Tippett - Nov. 12, 1822 (George Watkins)
Tanner, Floyd & Judith Tanner - Nov. 1, 1810 (Robert Rea)
Tanner, Jesse & Martha Ware - Feb. 27, 1820 (A. Hutchinson)
Tappan, A. B. & Anne A. Wright - Feb. 21, 1854 (Daniel Hightower)

Tappan, Alexander & Adalaine Wright - Dec. 8, 1850 (J. C. Simmons)
Tappan, Randolph & Eliza Ely - Mar. 22, 1861 (A. Gray, M. G.)
Tappan, Samuel W. & Cornelia Merrits - Jan. 16, 1873 (J. L. Pierce)
Tarpley, Archibald & Ann Lee - Oct. 24, 1811 (Thomas Stocks)
Tarpley, Archibald & Nancy M. Tunnell - July 18, 1866 (John W. Talley)
Tarpley, Augustus & Genette Broughton - Oct. 19, 1843 (B. M. Sanders)
Tarpley, John & Jane Bowden - Feb. 21, 1839 (Hinton Crawford)
Tarpley, John L. & Mary F. Bryan - Sept. 30, 1861
Tarwater, James S. & Rebecca Phelps - Nov. 20, 1847 (B. M. Sanders)
Tattum, Joel & Polly Price - Nov. 9, 1808 (Stephen Gatlin)
Taylor, Abraham & Elizabeth Peeler - May 17, 1818 (James Hall)
Taylor, Archibald E. & Eliza Head - Oct. 26, 1831 (Matthew Winifield)
Taylor, Archibald & Martha Dean - Aug. 20, 1844 (Matthew Winifield)
Taylor, Brantly & Ellen Smith - Sept. 29 or 20, 1870 (W. C. Birchmore)
Taylor, Henry & Mary Ann Houghton - Aug. 1, 1822 (Lovick Pierce)
Taylor, James & Charity Howard - Dec. 8, 1831 (Thomas J. Park)
Taylor, John & Martha Kirkley - Mar. 6, 1853 (J. R. Hall)
Taylor, John & Susan Herron - Feb. 11, 1866 (Wm. M. Chapman)
Taylor, Rudolph & Nancy Andrew - Dec. 22, 1874 (J. H. Kilpatrick, M.G.)
Taylor, Samuel S. & Esther E. Williams - Dec. 20, 1855 (T.R. Morgan, MG)
Taylor, Seaborn H. & Fatina Smith - May 8, 1865
Taylor, Semion & Elizabeth Ann Carr - Jan. 5, 1832 (A. Perkins)
Taylor, Thomas & Sarah Maddox - Sept. 29, 1819 (Thomas Johnson)
Templer, Stuart & Frances Fitzpatrick - Nov. 30, 1799
Terry, Wm. & Prudy Wester - July 4, 1804
Thaxton, Daniel & Mary English - June 27, 1875 (James M. Griffen)
Thaxton, James & Polly Lindsey - Sept. 21, 1825 (John Hatchett)
Thaxton, James N. & Sarah N. Nash - Jan. 2, 1862
Thaxton, Jermiah & Mary Boales - Dec. 29, 1836 (John G. Holtzclaw)
Thaxton, Nathaniel & Susan Lindsey - Sept. 28, 1815 (Lemuel Greene)
Thaxton, Simon & Nancy Lindsey - Jan. 15, 1823 (Robert Newsom)
Thomas, James H. & Avarilla Harper - Nov. 19, 1850 (Thomas Scott)
Thomas, John & Caroline M. Gregory - Nov. 1, 1823
Thomas, John & Sarah Ann Hunter - Dec. 4, 1827 (Rev. Anderson Ray)
Thomas, John I. & Claudia F. McKinley - Aug. 25, 1853 (Nathan Hoyt)
Thomas, Seth & Ruthy Ashley Furlow - Dec. 19, 1826 (David Terrell)
Thomas, Wm. & Polly Richardson - Dec. 21, 1789
Thomas, Wm. & Susan E. Burks - July 28, 1831 (Thomas W. Grimes)
Thomas, Wm. & Lucy Ann Harper - July 27, 1858 (J. H. Wragg)
Thompson, George & Rebecca Greene - Nov. 5, 1837 (John G. Holtzclaw)
Thompson, Henry B. & Mrs. Mary J. Seals - Nov. 9, 1865
Thompson, Hiram & Emily Evans - Nov. 10, 1835 (Mathew Winifield)
Thompson, James & Eliza Jane Horn - Aug. 17, 1814 (Nicholas Lewis)
Thompson, James & Christian Collocan - Feb. 4, 1818 (O. Porter)
Thompson, James & Elizabeth Penny - Oct. 20, 1820 (A. Hutchinson)
Thompson, Jeremiah & Elizabeth Edmundson - Sept. 9, 1828 (James Park)
Thompson, John & Nancy Cony--- - Dec. 20, 1821 (Jack Lumpkin)
Thompson, Joseph & Nancy Greer - Dec. 20, 1827 (Isaac Brockman)
Thompson, Joseph M. & Nancy B. Lucas - July 15, 1841 (H. Bridges)
Thompson, Matthew & Lydia Goldsby - Oct. 8, 1803
Thompson, Moody & Elizabeth Thompson - Jan. 31, 1824
Thompson, Moses & Matilda Ray - Nov. 4, 1828 (John Armstrong)
Thompson, Richard M. & Martha Hubbard - May 6, 1834 (Thos. B. Thompson)
Thompson, Samuel & Polly Lumsden? - Feb. 22, 1805
Thompson, Thomas & Mary Murrah - Dec. 14, 1819 (A. Hutchinson)
Thompson, Thomas & Susanna Woodward - Jan. 28, 1844 (I. M. Wilson)
Thompson, Thomas B. & Margaret Finley - Jan. 4, 1841
Thompson, Thomas H. & Elizabeth Lucas - Dec. 24, 1846 (A.G. Hutchinson)
Thompson, Wm. & Mary Patrick - Nov. 30, 1799
Thompson, Wm. A. & Mary Genett Safford - May 11, 1852 (Francis Bow----)
Thompson, Wm. F. & Sarah Elizabeth Jones - Oct. 2, 1839 (Francis S. Colley?)
Thornbury?, Wm. & Sarah Bryan - July 27, 1827
Thornton, Henry C. & Laura Beasley - May 20, 1861
Thornton, Jesse & Mary Holtzclaw - Apr. 27, 1847 (V. R. Thornton)
Thornton, Jesse M. & Mrs. Catherine D. Dickinson - Aug. 6, 1861
Thornton, Joe F. & Annie Foster Pierce - Jan. 19, 1871 (Geo.W.Yarbrough)
Thornton, Otis S. & Elizabeth Heard - Sept. 5, 1865 (John R. Young, MG)
Thornton, Richard & Elizabeth B. Eley - Mar. 25, 1828
Townsing, Anderson C. & Betsey Ann Barnet - Jan. 24, 1809

Townson, Wm. & Betsey Shropshire - May 21, 1807 (Geo. Tuggle)
Treadway, Elijah & Rachael Sweeney - Dec. 3, 1820 (John Parks)
Tribble, John & Nancy A. Anderson - Mar. 28, 1845
Trip, James M. & Rhoda H. Rowland - Dec. 11 or 17, 1835 (A. Hutcheson)
Truit, John & Ellivia Besbit - Jan. 26, 1804
Tucker, Jeremiah & Alice Hunt - Jan. 10, 1818
Tucker, Jeremiah & Tabatha Houghton - Dec. 2, 1821 (Robert Newsom)
Tucker, John & Mary Daniel - Dec. 31, 1818 (Thomas Stocks)
Tucker, ----heart & Judith Hall - Apr. 10, 1808 (Geo. Tuggle)
Tuggle, Augustus See? & Sarah Ann Haynes - Dec. 3, 1840 (Neville Lumpkin)
Tuggle, Augustus W. & Martha Brimberry - Jan. 21, 1868 (Wm. A. Overton)
Tuggle, E. B. & M. E. Bledsoe - Nov. 29, 1869 (W. A. Overton, M. G.)
Tuggle, G. H. & Dora Overton - July 7, 1872 (Henry Newton, M. G.)
Tuggle, Hollard? & Nancy Henley - Dec. 7, 1815
Tuggle, Leonard & Nancy Henley - Dec. 7, 1815 (Thomas Lyne)
Tuggle, Littleberry & Mary Ann McWhorter - Dec. 19, 1837 (Jack Lumpkin, M. G.)
Tunnel?, Jesse W. & Martha A. Heard - Sept. 6, 1857 (I. J. Beck, M. G.)
Tunnison, Wm. C. & Sallie E. Comer - Oct. 23, 1874 (Albert Gray)
Thornton, Samuel & Margaret Reid - Mar. 6, 1823 (Herman Mercer)
Thornton, Vincent & Phereba Lynes? - July 28, 1827 (Jonathan Davis)
Thornton, Wm. R. & Zymonia? - Dec. 27, 1859
Thrasher, Alexander B. & Mary Ann Smith - Aug. 17, 1851 (Wm. Bryan)
Thrasher, Early W. & Martha S. Oliver - Sept. 24, 1854 (Hart C. Peek)
Thrasher, John F. & Mary A. Rowland - Apr. 4, 1850 (Hinton Crawford)
Tigner, Hope H. & Liza Ann Gleen - Jan. 13, 1819 (Lovick Pierce)
Tigner, Philip & Nancy Hall - Feb. 1, 1794
Tiller, Martin & Temperance Newsom - Jan. 20, 1853 (V. R. Thornton)
Tindal, W. & Martha Harris - Dec. 21, 1789
Tippett, Frederick & Nancy Hubbard - Nov. 27, 1821 (A. N. Scott)
Tippett, John & Matilda Cartwright - June 2, 1836 (James W. Godkin)
Tippett, Wm. & Fathex Wilkerson - Nov. 22, 1825 (John Harris)
Tippin?, Noah & Lucy Lindsey - Feb. 3, 1833 (Thomas W. Grimes)
Todd, John H. & Eliza F. King - Feb. 17, 1827
Torbert, Benj. F. & Mary E. Bacone? - Dec. 5, 1871 (W. D. Atkinson, M.G.)
Torbert, John I. & Mary A. Jones - May 31, 1864 (P.M.W. Arnold, M. G.)
Torbert, Samuel A. & Jane E. Walker - Apr. 14, 1870 (Philip Robinson)
Torrence, Ebenezer & Louisa Beard - Jan. 19, 1830 (Lovick Pierce)
Torrence, John & Mary Bledsoe - July 8, 1859 (Lovick Pierce)
Touchstone, Wm. & Georgia Stevens - May 11, 1871 (W. C. Birchmore)
Towns, Benj. & Mahala Hunter - Apr. 6, 1823 (Herman Mercer)
Towns, Drury & Ann Sankey - Oct. 17, 1814
Towns, Drury & Sarah Watson - Feb. 9, 1828 (Augustine Greene)
Towns, John W. & Elizabeth Lyne - Dec. 30, 1824
Townsend, Duncan C. & Lenora Clayton - May 23, 1872 (R. W. B. El-----)
Turner, A. & Jenny Ransome - Mar. 15, 1806
Turner, Boswell & Virtuous Love - June 8, 1801
Turner, David & Francine Veazey - Mar. 16, 1791
Turner, David & Nancy Credille - Jan. 12, 1830 (Wm. Bryan)
Turner, Eli & Rebekah Baker - Feb. 13, 1816 (Wm. Cone)
Turner, Henry C. & Louisa J. O'R--- - Sept. 8, 1859 (A. A. Jernigan)
Turner, James & Elizabeth Cox - Sept. 8, 1811 (A. Gresham)
Turner, James W. & Mary Jane Grimes - Mar. 19, 1839 (M. P. Purifoy)
Turner, Jarrell L. & Rebecca Slaughter - July 5, 1855 (Wm. Bryan)
Turner, John & Lorenor Dawson - Dec. 1, 1824
Turner, Reuben T. & Phebe Ann Bishop - May 29, 1835 (James W. Godkin)
Turner, S. S. & Penelope F. Fatlin - Oct. 4, 1855 (J. M. Kelly)
Turner, Thomas & Lurana Credille - Dec. 5, 1833 (C. D. Teurnfog?)
Tutt, George C. & Annie McDaniel - Sept. 15, 1873 (James L. Pierce)
Tyler, Alexander & Martha Catchings - Feb. 4, 1822 (Wm. Winfield)
Tyler, Robert & Mary E. Crutchfield - Nov. 1, 1865 (S. J. Pinkerton)
Tyler, Willis & Sallie Jackson - Sept. 3, 1819

Umphrey, Erastus? & Matilda Olephant - Dec. 21, 1834 (Joseph Robert)
Underwood, Benj. F. & Elizabeth Veazy - Jan. 14, 1845 (Wooten O'Neale)
Underwood, Daniel & Nancy Fillinggame - July 19, 1832 (V. R. Thornton)
Underwood, George C. & Mary Veazey - Aug. 17, 1851 (I. A. Williams)
Underwood, Jesse H. & Melvina Jackson - Dec. 9, 1875 (N. M. Jones)
Underwood, Miles P. & Sarah McLelland - Mar. 5, 1834 (V. R. Thornton)

Van Trieau, Constantine & Louise Jane Peek - May 20, 1852 (H. C. Peek)
Van Valkinburg, Alonza Wandison? & Catherine Park - Oct. 27, 1829 (H.
  Peek?)
Varner, Joseph W. & Martha E. Durham - Oct. 28, 1867 (P. H. Mell, M.G.)
Vason, John & Rebecca Newton - May 21, 1803
Vaughn, Isaac & Adaline M. Harris - July 13, 1865 (Jefferson F. Wright)
Vaughn, Wyatt & Eliza Parker - Jan. 30, 1845 (E.C.I.B. Thomas)
Veal, James H. & Matilda Underwood - Jan. 27, 1842 (John L. Veazey)
Veazey, Albert A. & Frances Gresham - Mar. 30, 1841 (Francis Bowman)
Veazey, Allanson E. & Mariah McGiboney - Mar. 8, 1827 (Absalom Baugh)
Veazey, Eli A. & Mary A. Jackson - Oct. 14, 1851 (I. A. Williams)
Veazy, Eli A. & Josephine A. Jackson - July 28, 1868 (Hart C. Peek)
Veazy, Ezekiel & Jean Parker - Aug. 21, 1814 (Wm. McGiboney)
Veazy, James & Polly Morris - Dec. 12, 1811 (Jesse Mercer)
Veazy, James? & Ruth Veazey - Mar. 28, 1816 (Wm. Cone)
Veazy, James? & Sarah Aikens - Feb. 13, 1823 (John Harris)
Veazy, John & Permelia Veazey - Nov. 8, 1825 (John Harris)
Veazy, Timothy & Martha Phillips - Oct. 25, 1821 (Thomas Johnson)
Veazy, Wm. C. & Mary Ann Lucas - Dec. 5, 1840 (John ---ey?)
Veazy, Wm. D. & Emaline Oliver - Mar. 7, 1861 (H. C. Peek)
Veazy, Wm. D. & Mary E. Jackson - May 30, 1871 (W. A. Overton)
Veazey, Wm. I. & Tranquilla C. Parrott - Sept. 11, 1853 (W. H. Blythe)
Velvin, Thomas & Nancy Coleman - Dec. 8, 1810 (Robert Dale)
Venable, Robert A. & Mildred A. Stovall - Jan. 7, 1873 (D. W. Elder, MG)
Vincent, Charles A. & Susan A. Williams - Apr. 17, 1851 (Richard Lane,MG)
Vincent, Sanford Jr. & Ann Broughton - Nov. 14, 1822 (A. H. Scott)
Vincent, Wm. & Nancy Simonton - Sept. 18, 1823 (Wm. McGiboney)
Vought, J. L. & Adaline Walker - Apr. 26, 1848 (James Rowland)

Waddell, Marshall & Jane Payne - Jan. 13, 1825
Waddle, Isaac W. & Sarah R. Daniell - Sept. 14, 1831 (Nathan Hoyt, M.G.)
Wade, James & Mary Elizabeth Thompson - June 26, 1840 (B. M. Sanders)
Wade, John & Aggie Peek - Dec. 28, 1787
Wade, John & Anny Cook - May 31, 1822 (Wm. Moore)
Wade, Joshua & Nancy Tucker - Feb. 2?, 1820 (Wm. Cone)
Waggoner, Thomas & Mary Ann Laurence - Dec. 13, 1846 (O. M. Fambrough)
Waggoner, Wm. & Elizabeth Finley - Nov. 12, 1818 (L. Bethune)
Wagnon, Daniel M. & Martha M. Swindell - Dec. 11, 1834 (A. Hut-----)
Wagnon, Eugenius N. & Mary E. Gantt - Jan. 23, 1866 (John W. -----)
Wagnon, Geo. H. & Susan F. Ruarks - Mar. 21, 1861 (Hinton Crawford)
Wagnon, John P. & Mary J. Moore - Dec. 1, 1848 (V. R. Thornton)
Wagnon, Joshua H. & Emily Southerland - Aug. 21, 1845 (Thomas H. D-----)
Wagnon, Pittman M. & Frances A. Leveritt - Feb. 1, 1866 (Lounza? D. ----)
Wagnon, Thomas & Harriett Houghton - Oct. 15, 181- (Lovick Pierce)
Wagnon, Wm. S. & Marita? M. McLellan - July 5, 1860 (Hart C. Peek)
Walden, Smith & Elizabeth Whatley - Jan. 28, 1806
Walden, Towner & Susannah Greer - Nov. 26, 1804
Walker, Andrew & Polly Graham - Oct. 28, 1801
Walker, Edwin I. & Josephine Alexander - Dec. 10, 1868 (Thomas F. Pierce)
Walker, Edwin I. & Mary Lenora Fleetwood - Sept. 8, 1874 or 14 (J.L.Pierce)
Walker, Henry & Vicey Phillips - May 19, 1800
Walker, Henry & Mary Ann Hutcherson - Apr. 24, 1828 (U. Ray)
Walker, James T. & Ruthy A. Phillips - Oct. 31, 1849 (R. F. Griffen)
Walker, John & Elizabeth Talley - May 10, 1805
Walker, John & Betsey Murphey - May 4, 1807? (James Holt)
Walker, John & Elizabeth Brown - Mar. 13, 1823 (Lovick Pierce)
Walker, John E. & Mary E. Gaston - Oct. 12, 1847 (J. L. Rowland)
Walker, Johnson & Sarah Swindall - Nov. 30, 1815 (Wm. Cone)
Walker, Mena? M. & Marita Anne Hardeman - Oct. 12, 1855 (B. R. Elder)
Walker, Robert & Frances A. E. Walker - Feb. 26, 1846 (R. C. Smith)
Walker, Samuel R. & Falby? - Dec. 5, 1840 (E. P. Jarrell)
Walker, Wm. & Elizabeth Wynn - Apr. 24, 1788
Walker, Wm. & Nancy Connell - Jan. 26, 1803
Walker, Wm. H. & Mary L.? Fillingin? - Jan. 9, 1872 (Hart C. Peek)
Walker, Wm. & Martha I. Colquitt - Jan. 8, 1833 (J. P. Leveritt)
Walker, Z. I. & Fanny Ely - Dec. 18, 1873 (J. H. Kilpatrick)
Walker, Wm. I. & Anne E. Tuggle - Dec. 23, 1856 (I. D. Martin, M.G.)
Wall, Frank & Catherine W. Culloche? - May 22, 1789
Wall, Richard W. & Elizabeth Gilbert - Dec. 23, 1830 (Augustine Greene?)
Wallace, Aaron B. & Elizabeth Wallace - Dec. 18, 1860 (Elisha Elliott)

Wallace, Augustus & Rebecca Shell - Nov. 3, 1831 (J. P. Leverett)
Wallace, Bartley & Susan Ann Parker - Sept. 29, 1836 (James Moore)
Wallace, B. G. & Alice Cofer? - Jan. 16, 187- (Henry Newton)
Wallace, Woolford & Martha Ann Crosley - Oct. 11, 1849 (Ephriam Bruce)
Waller, Benj. B. & Louisa Turner - Jan. 20, 1870 (W. H. Blythe, M.G.)
Waller, James & Susan J. Epps - Apr. 8, 1849 (R. F. Griffen)
Waller, Thomas & Rachael Blackman - Mar. 20, 1850 (J. W. Drennan)
Waller, Wm. & Sidney W. Tunnell - Apr. 9, 1867 (J. R. Young, M. G.)
Walls, Jubal & Nancy Forrester - Sept. 16, 1828 (Robt. Newsom)
Ward, Austin & Sarah Staples - Nov. 21, 1852 (J. T. F---ley)
Ward, Eneas & Altetha? Winfield - Jan. 29, 1828 (Wm. Bryan)
Ward, Enos Wesley & Elizabeth Smith - Sept. 25, 1825
Ward, Enos W. & Mary Rowlin - July 14, 1831 (Wm. Rowland)
Ward, Enos W. & Lorisa Rowland - Aug. 13, 1836 (A. Hutcheson)
Ward, George & Frances C. Perdue - Mar. 10, 1857 (J. S. K. Axson)
Ward, James S. & Milly Harp - Feb. 17, 1824 (Butts L. Cato?)
Ward, John & Carey Fambrough - Feb. 14, 1828 (Joshua Cannon)
Ward, Joseph S. & Sarah Ann Bryant - Sept. 18, 1839
Ward, Richard & Urethea White - Mar. 10, 1825
Ward, Stephen & Jane Wood - Apr. 6, 1802
Ward, Stephen & Jane Davis - Feb. 13, 1822 (Lovick Pierce)
Ward, Wiley & Atheria L. R. Snow - Dec. 13, 1824
Ware, Edward H. & Mrs. Harriet M. Nichelson - Nov. 27, 1873 (E.W. Speer)
Ware, Henry C. & Harriet Rainey - Dec. 19, 1839 (Francis Bowman)
Ware, Hudson & Elizabeth Farrell - Oct. 27, 1821
Ware, James & Elizabeth Walker - Nov. 24, 1787
Ware, John & Patsy Peeler - Aug. 13, 1819 (Thomas Riley)
Ware, Robert & Martha Norris - May 23, 1821 (Thomas Riley)
Ware, Thomas & Phoebe Peeler - June 2, 1818 (Geo. Dillard)
Ware, Wm. & Susan Perkins - Nov. 29, 1825
Warner, Robert & Betsey Sims - Mar. 5, 1804
Warner, Wm. & Ann Watson - Jan. 31, 1825
Warren, Geo. W. & Emily Swindalle - Oct. 27, 1838 (Robert I. Griffen)
Warren, James R. & Burnetta Caldwell - May 18, 1834 (James Moore)
Warren, Slady & Elizabeth Johnson - Aug. 17, 1820 (John I. -----)
Washam, John & Sally Studman - Oct. 30, 1806 (Isaac McClendon)
Waters, Arthur & Sally Sherrill - Dec. 16, 1799
Waters, Isaac & Elizabeth Fitzpatrick - Mar. 17, 1809 (Wm. Johnson)
Waters, Matthew & ----- Stringfellow - Jan. 27, 1824
Waters, James W. & C. C. Gustavious - Jan. 8, 1787
Watkins, George & Polly Early - Dec. 26, 1801
Watkins, John & Elizabeth Atkinson - Sept. 18, 1816 (Robert Rea)
Watkins, Josiah & Dicey Sropshur? - July 31, 1805
Watkins, Wm. & Polly Kennedy - Oct. 31, 1811 (Wm. McGiboney)
Watson, Andrew Jackson & Louisa Jane English - Nov. 26, 1840
Watson, Briant & Priscilla Perkins - Dec. 27, 1827 (John Harris)
Watson, Douglas C. & Elba N. Stovall - Nov. 1, 1832 (I. W. Grimes)
Watson, Elias & Arean M. Lillan - Dec. 11, 1829 (John Harris)
Watson, Jesse & Amanda Jones - Mar. 21, 1847 (V. R. Thornton)
Watson, John & Minerva Mabry - Aug. 12, 1829 (George Hall)
Watson, John A. & Eliza Copeland - May 10, 1833 (L. P. Leverett)
Watson, Marcus L. & Emily Houghton - July 20, 1854 (S. G. Halyer)
Watson, Nicholas A. & Mary Harris - Apr. 1, 1852 (Hart C. Peek)
Watson, Solomon & Nancy Akins - Dec. 18, 1823
Watson, Wm. & Abagail Brewer - Mar. 5, 1806
Watson, Wm. & Sarah Williams - Dec. 18, 1824
Watson, Wm. B. & Lavinia Catchings - Dec. 5, 1871 (-----. L. Lupe)
Watts, Hampton & Amanda Davenport - Jan. 14, 1825
Watts, Hardy K. & Martha Bunch - Dec. 10, 1834 (Bennet A. Ely)
Watts, Harrison & Mary Daniel - Nov. 2, 1824
Watts, Harrison H. & Jane Forrester - Jan. 12, 1834 (Bennett Hellamer?)
Watts, Holton & Selattia Smith - July 22, 1805
Watts, Jacoby & Elizabeth Harrison - Feb. 24, 1804
Watts, John R. & Elizabeth I. Asbury - Sept. 23, 1833 (Bennett Hellimer?)
Watts, Joseph & Eliza Jenkins - July 30, 1818 (John W-----)
Watts, Lillte? B. & Nancy Whatley - Feb. 21, 1801
Watts, Presley & Abbey Andrews - July 20, 1808 (John Cox)
Watts, Richard & Martha Watts - Oct. 27, 1839 (C. D. Kennebrew)
Watts, Richard N. & Mary S. Watts - May 30, 1837 (V. R. Thornton)
Watts, Wm. & Nancy Williams - Sept. 21, 1845 (E. S. Hunter)

Watts, Wm. H. & Patsey Roberts - Feb. 17, 1804
Watts, Wm. H. & Mary Robinson - Dec. 10, 1828
Weatherly, John S. & Rhoda Cheney - Mar. 18, 1861 (P. H. Mell)
Weatherly, Wm. & Frances Smith - Nov. 28, 1818
Weathers, Jesse & Unity Johnson - July 18, 1815 (Robert Rea)
Weathers, John & Polly Kelley - Nov. 17, 1808 (James Holt)
Weaver, Francis & Priscilla Ely - Apr. 15, 1847 (John Harris)
Weaver, James M. & Jane Amanda Harris - Dec. 28, 1847 (S. G. Hillyer)
Weaver, John & Elizabeth Harrelson - Feb. 6?, 1812 (A. Veazey)
Weaver, Wm. M. & Margaret Nickelson - Mar. 14, 1860 (G. F. Pierce)
Weaver, Wm. & Caroline M. Mango - Apr. 8, 1824 (Lovick Pierce)
Webb, John & Jane Fambrough - Aug. 10, 1859 (James H. Wragg)
Webb, John G. & Lucy Clarke - Feb. 28, 1827
Webb, Robert & Polly Sorrell - Feb. 10, 1812 (Thomas Rhodes)
Weeks, Samuel & Anne Jackson - Sept. 5, 1788
Welborn, Wm. & Martha Elizabeth Sanders - Oct. 12, 1842
Welborn, Jonathan & Rebekah Williams - May 18, 1806 (John Robinson)
Welbourn, Jeremiah & Polly Morris - Dec. 13, 1824 (Geo. Johnson)
Welburn, James & Mary Elizabeth Harris - Apr. 12, 1832 (R.I. Dickerson?)
Wells, George & Polly Moore - Feb. 27, 1823 (Lovick Pierce)
Wells, John & Emily F. Booles - May 15, 1826
West, Edward & Elizabeth Copelan - Aug. 18, 1801
West, Elijah & Matilda Sorrell - Feb. 4, 1808 (Wm. Browning)
West, George & Matilda Prio-- - Nov. 4, 1830 (Jonathan Davis)
West, J. I. & C. T. Horton - Dec. 24, 1872 (J. I. Wood)
West, Reuben S. & Margaret Hogg - Oct. 27, 1842 (N. M. Lumpkin)
West, Thomas J. & Matilda Asbury - Nov. 25, 1841 (W. H. Stocks)
West, Warren & Betsey Whaley - Feb. 4, 1803
West, Wm. & Sarah Butts - Aug. 22, 1827
West, Wm. E. & Lizzie Moncrief - Nov. 7, 1875 (John R. Young)
West, Wm. M. & Harriett Brooks - Dec. 17, 1844 (Samuel Ely)
Westbrooks, Allin & Frances Huff - Oct. 20, 1818
Westbrooks, Thomas & Aley Ball - Dec. 7, 1819
Westbrooks, Wm. & Susanna Lee - Feb. 5, 1816 (Richard Baugh)
Wester, Edward & Elizabeth Yancey - Nov. 17, 1804
Wester, John & Anne Wester - Jan. 20, 1803
Whaley, Burwell & Polly Whitlock - Mar. 14, 1803
Whaley, Edward & Elizabeth Caldwell - Aug. 20, 1803
Whaley, James & Nancy Lake - Oct. 11, 1803
Whaley, Thomas & Mary Smith - Oct. 21, 1828 (Jos. Roberts, M. G.)
Whatley, Floyd & Alsay Hunt - Dec. 16, 1823 (Robt. Newsome)
Whatley, John & Polly Blanks - June 24, 1803
Whatley, John & Patsey Bowles - Jan. 28, 1806
Whatley, Michael & Elizabeth Peoples - Aug. 26, 1799
Whatley, Robert & Polly Swann - July 10, 1808 (Geo. Tuggle)
Whatley, Thomas W. & Julia Davis - Nov. 8, 1853 (E. L. Whatley, M. G.)
Whatley, Wyatt & Elizabeth Wright - Jan. 11, 1800
Whealy, John & Mary Porter - Mar. 17, 1789
Wheat, Jonathan & Mary Ann Horn? - Nov. 29, 1838 (Thomas Stock)
Wheat, Jonathan & Eilizabeth Merritt - Jan. 21, 1847 (R. F. Griffen)
Wheeler, Hardy & Hannah Rimes - June 12, 1806 (J. Mapp)
Wheelas, Joab & Jane Spradling - Aug. 20, 1807 (James Hall)
Wheeler, Avery & Rebeccah Cunningham - Oct. 10, 1804
Wheeler, Elijah & Elizabeth Jackson - Aug. 25, 1800
Wheeler, Laurence F. & Mary Anne Watkins - Dec. 16, 1841 (N. H. Hill)
Wheelous, Wm. & Arry Fambrough - Jan. 16, 1859 (W. A. Par-----)
Whetsone?, John A. & Ann C. Banks - Jan. 8, 1827
Whitaker, Wm. & Mrs. L. D. Florence? - Mar. 20, 1873 (W. A. Florence)
White, Andrew & Mary Smith - Dec. 10, 1803
White, Coleman & Ann Allen - Aug. 29, 1821 (A. Hutcheson)
White, David M. & Nancy Woodard - Dec. 6, 1842 (John L. Veazey)
White, D. A. & Rebecca Reynolds - Dec. 24, 1848 (W. H. C. Cone)
White, Edmund & Sarah Rea - Apr. 19, 1827 (John Armstrong)
White, James I. & Sarah Tolly - July 23, 1823 (John N. Harvey)
White, James & Caroline Gatlin - Jan. 26, 1837 (James W. Godkin)
White, John & Lucy Jones - Nov. 24, 1803
White, Reuben & Nancy Hines - Jan. 5, 1802
White, Samuel & Sarah Nelson - June 20, 1822 (Thomas Johnson)
White, Wiley M. & Mary S. Moore - Nov. 28, 1833 (Geo. Heard)
White, Wm. & Anna Maddox - Apr. 24, 1806 (Ewing Morrow)

White, Wm. H. & Jane S. McIntyre - Dec. 9, 1823 (Francis Cummins)
White, Wm. H. & Permelia Baldwin - June 27, 1826
White, Wm. & Georgia Anna Daniel - Oct. 2, 1863 (James W. Godkin)
Whitehead, John W. & Inez English - Dec. 22, 1874 (W. A. Cheney)
Whitely, Richard Henry & Margaret Eliza Divine - Nov. 29, 1849 (Wm.Bryan)
Whiteside, Andrew J. & Mary Ann Greer - May 12, 1848
Whitfield, Ivy I. & Susan P. Ramsey - Nov. 3, 1850 (J. T. Findley)
Whitfield, James A. & Mary E. Shipp - Dec. 13, 1866 (Hart C. Peek)
Whitlaw, James H. & Anna A. Broach - Dec. 25, 1859 (James Davison)
Whitlock, Wm. A. & Louisa Emily Johnson - Apr. 3, ---- (V. R. Thornton)
Wiggins, Benj. ç Sara Ann Rhodes - Feb. 28, 1845
Wiggins, John & Nancy Hall - June 28, 1815 (John Browning)
Wiggins, Whittenton & Nancy Atkins - Nov. 29, 1830
Wiggins, Wm. & Sarah Laurence - Feb. 20, 1789
Wilford, Walter & Nancy Hester - Mar. 22, 1802
Wilkerson, Dempsey & Lydia Bishop - Jan. 21, 180- (Thomas Crawford)
Wilkins, John & Cynthia Lanier - Jan. 16, 1816 (John Armor)
Wilkins, John & Lucy Thompson - May 4, 1820 (Geo. Watkins)
Wilkinson, Abner & Ami Mathew - Dec. --, 1803
Wilkinson, Henry & Maria Towers - Sept. 17, 1823 (Francis Cummins)
Wilks, John A. & Rebecca Jackson - Dec. 19, 1852 (J. I. Findley)
Williams, Albert & Julia Ann Linch - Feb. 13, 1866 (Jefferson F. Wright)
Williams, Anderson & Martha Lancastor? - Dec. 17, 1835 (James W. Godkin)
Williams, Benj. & Anna B. Billingslea - Feb. 18, 1868 (James L. Pierce)
Williams, Crawford & Mahala Frances Wade - Dec. 18, 1839 (James M. -----)
Williams, David & Elizabeth Scott - Sept. 17, 1850
Williams, Ed. G. & Kate M. Pierce - Jan. 19, 1871 (George W. Pierce)
Williams, Elisha & Mary Phillips - Oct. 21, 1827 (Abraham Yeates)
Williams, Ezekiel & Cynthia Swann - Dec. 17, 1818
Williams, Ezekiel S. & Emma L. Parrott - Jan. 10, 1867 (Wm. Bryan)
Williams, Francis Key & S. A. McLellan - Apr. 13, 1856 (H. C. Peek)
Williams, Frederick H. & Nancy Daniels - Jan. 8, 1815 (Jesse Mercer)
Williams, Henry P. & Mildred J. P. Burk - Oct. 18, 1865 (N. M. Crawford)
Williams, Henry P. & Eliza J. Alfriend - Dec. 18, 1873 (N. H. Blythe)
Williams, Isaac & Emily Atkinson - Feb. 7, 1836 (A. Hutcheson)
Williams, Isaac & Almira A. Bowden - Apr. 28, 1842 (James Jones, M.G.)
Williams, Isaac & Ella Dora Bruce - Dec. 31, 1869 (W. H. Blythe, M. G.)
Williams, Isaac & Sarah Andrews - Jan. 30, 1869
Williams, James & Susan A. Copelan - Oct. 24, 1847 (John C. Lucas)
Williams, James B. & Nancy V. Terrell - Apr. 6, 1841 (V. R. Thornton)
Williams, James D. & Matilda Goodroe - Sept. 10, 1871 (Rev. J. S. Patten)
Williams, Jesse & Elizabeth McMichael - June 4, 1826
Williams, Jo & Polly Boon - Nov. 26, 1804
Williams, John & Anne Wade - Nov. 10, 1788
Williams, John & Delpha Watkins - Nov. 21, 1803
Williams, Jonathan & Rebeccah Williams - May 18, 1808 (John Roberson)
Williams, Joseph & Mary Boon - June 10, 1804 (Thomas Crawford)
Williams, Littleberry & Amanda Cato - May 1, 1827
Williams, Orrin & Rebekah Stephens - Aug. 19, 1808 (Stephen Gatlin)
Williams, Patrick & Ariam Ingram - Nov. 15, 1837 (Thomas I. Park)
Williams, Peter & Lucinda Park - Feb. 3, 1818 (Lovick Pierce)
Williams, Pleasant & Harriet Perkins - June 5, 1856 (B. R. Elder)
Williams, Poleman? & Nancy May - May 7, 1846 (E. S. Hunter)
Williams, Richard S. & Emma J. West - Mar. 5, 1860 (Thomas B. Cooper)
Williams, Robert & Rebekah Whatley - Jan. 9, 1800
Williams, Robert B. & Georgia Ann Fisher - Sept. 23, 1869 (James W.Godkin)
Williams, James & Nancy Dingler - May 1, 1827 (E. Tally)
Williams, Thomas & Edney Scroggins - June 12, 1822 (Robert Newsome)
Williams, Wm. & Elizabeth Atkinson - Apr. 9, 1829 (Wm. Bryan)
Williams, Wm. & Louisa R. Parrott - Aug. 8, 1847 (Ephriam Bruce)
Williams, Wm. A. Jr. & Martha A. Robinson - Jan. 22, 1854 (J. R. Hall)
Williams, Wm. B. & Susan Ann M. Bruce - Feb. 25, 1868 (Joseph R. Parker)
Williams, Wm. N. & Nancy Baldwin - Jan. 11, 1843 (Thomas Stocks)
Williams, Wm. T. J. & Rhod----? Ann Crossley - Dec. 30, 1860 (J.M. Kelly)
Williams, Willis & Jane F. Booles - Feb. 17, 1848 (B. M. Sanders)
Williams, Wilson & Sarah Kimbrough - July 8, 1820
Willey, James H. & Julia Foster - Apr. 29, 1841 (Geo. Pierce)
Willis, Alfred L. & Florida C. Duncan - June 2, 1856? (J. P. Duncan)
Willis, Eugene L. & Serapta A. Hackney - Jan. 29, 1865 (J. R. Young)
Willis, James & Margaret Ann Chew - Feb. 13, 1834 (Thomas Stocks)

285

Willis, London & Priscilla Thompson - May 27, 1815 (Sol. Lockett)
Willis, Louden & Sarah D. Ferrell - Sept. 30, 1819 (Jesse Mercer)
Willis, Richard & Sarah Foster - Jan. 25, 1848 (Thomas Stocks)
Willis, Robert & Lucy Baugh - June 13, 1820 (Lovick Pierce)
Willis, Washington & Susan Martin - Nov. 14, 1825
Willoughby, Wm. R. & Sarah N. Ray - Oct. 21, 1856 (John W. M. -----)
Willson, James & Phebe White - June 2, 1789
Willson, Joshua & Comfort Knowles - Apr. 8, 1807 (W. M. Johnson)
Willson, Larkin & Polly Cab----- - Dec. 22, 1808 or 03
Wilson, A. A. & Ann Hailes - Jan. 6, 1876 (John I. Dolvin?)
Wilson, George S. & Mary F. Lankford - Jan. 8, 1874 (John F. Dolvin)
Wilson, James & Nancy Heard - Jan. 4, 1821
Wilson, James & Mary Ann McAuly - Nov. 26, 1835
Wilson, James L. & Emma Lankford - May 22, 1870 (W. A. Colclough)
Wilson, Jesse P. & Cornelia C. Wright - Oct. 30, 1860 (Homer Handee?)
Wilson, John L. & Mary Jane Harris - Aug. 21, 1839
Wilson, John M. & Mrs. Talisha J. Jackson - Sept. 10, 1874 (J.L.Pierce,MG)
Wilson, John R. & Martha A. Gentry? - Jan. 12, 1858 (W. W. Moore)
Wilson, John I. & Naomi Gilmer - Mar. 7, 1853 (B. Rowland)
Wilson, Joseph P. & Caroline L. Whitstone - June 3, 1862 (P.H. Mell, MG)
Wilson, Lewis & Eliza I. Kittell - Feb. 9, 1841 (Thomas Stocks)
Wilson, P. F. & Julia Ann Fambro - Dec. 29, 1844 (John Zuber?)
Wilson, Samuel G. & Sarah N. Poullain - Jan. 6, 1875 (G. F. Pierce, MG)
Wilson, Thomas B. & Ellen A. Durham - Sept. 8, 1872 (W. A. Overton)
Wilson, Wm. & Elizabeth Jones - Jan. or Jun. 6, 1789
Wilson, Wm. & Arenath Pullen - Mar. 1, 1825
Wilson, Wm. & Mrs. Caroline Durke - Mar. 3, 1859 (Geo. C. Clarke)
Wilson, Wm. A. & Mary? I. Lankford - Jan. 2, 1869 or 67 (Lucuis C. Broome)
Wilson, Wm. W.? & Lucy Perkins - Aug. 6, 1834 (James Moore)
Wilson, Willis & Carrie F. Morris? - June 20, 1875 (James A. Thornton)
Winfield, James & Frances Duncan - July 20, 1826
Winfield, James & Mary Gooch - May 18, 1828 (Robt. Burdell)
Winfield, James & Claudia Jackson - Feb. 7, 1856 (N. M. Crawford)
Winfield, John & Barsheba Wade - Dec. 21, 1817 (Lauchlien? Bethune)
Winfield, Matthew & Rebecca Wade - Nov. 26, 1828 (Robt. Burdell)
Wingfield, Alfred & Frances Cunningham - Oct. 1, 1845 (Francis Bowman)
Wingfield, Junius? A. & Mary I. Mosely - Nov. 9, 1836 (I. M. Grimes)
Winfrey, H. L. & Lydia L. Greer - Sept. 13, 1868 (P. H. Mell, M. G.)
Winn, J. H. & Nettie V. Smith - Nov. 22, 1870 (John M. Loury?)
Winn, Thomas & Nancy Greer - Dec. 23, 1819 (James Brockman)
Winn, Thomas E. & Sophia I. Park - Dec. 13, 1865 (Thomas F. Pierce)
Winningham, Jarrett & Lukey Woods - July 18, 1801
Winslett, I. I. & Mary A. E. Bickers - Aug. 31, 1851 (A. In. N. Vandivere)
Winslett, Jonathan & Gelly? D. Bagley - June 11, 1818 (R. White)
Winslett, L. B. & Mary N. Copelan - Dec. 14, 1871 (James W. Godkin)
Winslett, Richard & Perethene? Bagley - Mar. 5, 1815 (Thomas Bush)
Winslett, Wm. & Elizabeth Harp - Sept. 14, 1799
Winslett, Wm. & Peggy Woods - June 13, 1801
Winslett, Wm. & Eliza B. Copelan - May 3, 1831 (Thomas W. Grimes)
Winter, Albert H. & Dora Tunnell - Feb. 26, 1874 (Albert Gray)
Winter, D. Henry & Nancy Carlton - Dec. 15, 1850 (James M. Davison)
Winter, D. Henry & Lucy Ann Grier - Oct. 16, 1859 (James Davison)
Wirsley?, John & Sarah Hammons - June 13, 1807 (J. Bethune)
Womack, Mancey? & Sarah Rogers - Sept. 11, 1790
Wood, Aristorchus & Fanney Newton - Jan. 14, 1799
Wood, Elial & Martha Bunn? - June 21, 1827 (E. Talley)
Wood, Ethelred & Dicey Bagby - June 10, 1790
Wood, James & Irabellah Patrick - Feb. 8, 1802
Wood, John & Sally Reid - Apr. 2, 1807 (Adam Hays)
Wood, John & Elizabeth Saxon - May 30, 1854 (A. L. Willis)
Wood, John C. & Nancy F. Greene - June 3, 1856 (J. S. R. Axon)
Wood, John Henry & Harriett C. B. Crawford - May 4, 1854 (J.W. Yarborough)
Wood, Richard & Tabitha Glass - Apr. 21, 1790
Wood, Taylor & Mary Burger - Dec. 5, 1872 (W. A. Partee)
Wood, Thomas & Polly Hill - Mar. 28, 1810 (W. Johnson)
Wood, Wm. T. & Ugenia J. Talley - Oct. 18, 1838 (Robt. F. Griffen)
Woodall, Jamie & Beckey Watson - May 15, 1801
Woodall, June Martin & Polly Lacey - June 18, 1803
Woodall, Michael & Betsey Bird - Aug. 11, 179-
Woodard, Jonathan & Elizabeth Brunt - Jan. 16, 1825

Woodjin?, Wm. G. & Helen James - July 21, 1860
Woodham, Everett & Harriett Phillips - Jan. 25, 1821 (Lovick Pierce)
Woodham, James & Peggy Peek - Apr. 21, 1814 (John Turner)
Woodham, John E. & Miriam J. Callahan - Mar. 31, 1859 (Wm. Bryan)
Woods, Cyrus & Frances Pinkard - June 24, 1823 (Aug. B. Longstreet?)
Woods, Matthew & Myrum Woods - Jan. 19, 1826 (Wm. L. Asten? J-----)
Wooten, James & Elizabeth Laurence - Apr. 6, 1789
Wooten, John & Polly Beavers - June 22, 1801
Worthy, Zachariah P. & Emily Caldwell - May 9, 1839 (James M. -----)
Wray, Pleasant J. & Mrs. Rebecca Bagly - Nov. 10, 1864 (W. A. Par-----)
Wray, Sylvanus & Mrs. Rebeccah Ogle----- - Dec. 20, 1864 (W. A. -----)
Wray, Wm. T. & Mrs. Martha G. Edmondson - Dec. 20, 1864 (W. A. -----)
Wright, Christopher C. & Rebecca B. Moore - May 13, 1838 (James N. -----)
Wright, Jacob T. & Eliza W. Few - May 7, 1838 (James M. Porter)
Wright, James A. & Scott Branch - Oct. 23, 1873 (W. H. LaP-----)
Wright, James Osborn & Alice E. Reynolds - June 24, 1866 (I. F. ------)
Wright, Jefferson & Louisa Kimbrough - Apr. 29, 1849 (J. C. -----)
Wright, John & Nancy Jones - Dec. 18, 1804
Wright, John & Celia Rowland - Jan. 11, 1825 (E. Tally)
Wright, John & Frances Bowden - Nov. 23, 1868
Wright, John E. & Sarah H. Bickers - Apr. 9, 1839 (Thomas S-----)
Wright, John W. & Sarah Lewis - May 31, 1855 (J. S. Williams)
Wright, Joseph & Mary Ann Stark - Dec. 11, 1817 (John Browning?)
Wright, J. F. & L. A. Burk - Oct. 29, 1846 (Wm. I. Parks)
Wright, Loren-- D. & Mary Lewis - Jan. 11, 1866 (J. F. Wright)
Wright, Nathaniel & Eliza M. Robson - Jan. 12, 1852 (A. L. Willis, J.R.)
Wright, Redock T. & Merium Mabry - Nov. 16, 1832 or 82? (T. W. Grimes)
Wright, Reuben & Jane Hays - July 3, 1827 (Robt. W. Bardell)
Wright, Reuben & Mary Conner - Dec. 4, 1828 (Anderson Ray, M. G.)
Wright, Robert & Margaret Bledsoe - May 31, 1808 (Wm. Browning)
Wright, Samuel & Frances Julian Perkins - Dec. 1, 1835 (Wesley Arnold)
Wright, Thomas & Nancy Tucker - Feb. 14, 1823
Wright, Wiley & Sarah Lewis - Apr. 28, 1821 (Robt. Flourney)
Wright, Wm. & Rhoda Cummins? - Jan. 11, 1816 (C. Maddox)
Wright, Wm. & Maria Brunt - Oct. 12, 1831 (L. P. Leveritt)
Wright, Wm. & Hannah Orr - June 7, 1844 (James Moore)
Wright, Wm. & Susan Mapp - Aug. 13, 1844 (J. J. Howell)
Wright, Wm. & Eleanor Johnson - Apr. 17, 1846 or 41 (J. W. Godkin)
Wright, Wm. H. & Sarah Isadore Colclough - Dec. 22, 1858 (L. B. Jackson)
Wright, Willis & Sarah I. Kitterall - Dec. 9, 1833 (A. Hutcheson)
Wright, Zacheus & Asentha Lewis - Nov. 19, 1820 (John Harris)
Wynn, John & Martha H. Smith - Jan. 27, 1842 (J. W. Godkin)
Wynn, R. I. & Sarah M. Rawls - Jan. 28, 1841 (J. W. Godkin)
Wyman, Samuel H. & Mary E. Sidwell - May 29, 1856

HANCOCK COUNTY GA. WILLS AND ESTATES VOL. AA

Volume AA follows Volume A. in the series of Wills and Estate
Records 1794-1804, Vols. A-AAAA and B. Volume A was concluded in Issue
#52-53.

Pages 1-2.   Inventory and Appraisement of the Estate of John Waller
                  dec'd. dated 7 June 1798. Nathan Melvin, Exr.   Total
amount $88.22½. Signed by Pr. Boyle, John (+) Castleberry, Allen Whatley.
Vouchers paid, notes and proven accounts: Thos. Methvin (?), Joshua
Bishop, John Castlebury. Account of sales registered in Book 6, p. 58.

Pages 3-4.   Appraisement of the personal property of Hart Champion,
                  late of Hancock Co., dec'd. Negroes listed: woman Mil-
ley, girl Beck, girl Chany. Total value $1218.25. Dated 24 Jan. 1798.
Signed by Jesse Pope, Wm. Alford, Jonas Shivers. Matt Rabon, Adm.

Page 5.   Account of Sales of part of the property of Hart Champion
                  dec'd. as sold 24 Jan. 1798. Buyers: Benjamin Waller,
Edwd. Turner, William Mangrum, Joseph Maddox, Needham Jernagan, Thomas
Melvin, J. Williams, John Champion, Butler Turner, Robert Gilmore,

287

Shildrake Brown, Thomas Williams.

Pages 5-6.   Accounts current of Hart Champion, dec'd. (No date).
                  Interest collected of: Shildrak Brown, Needham Jernagan,
William Biggins, Wilie Abercrombie. Signed: Chas. Abercrombie, Matt
Rabun, admrs. Accounts dated 1803: Interest rec'd of William Mangham,
S. Waller, Willie Abercrombie.

                  Received 14 Apr. 1809 of Matthew Rabun and Charles
Abercrombie, admrs. of Hart Champion dec'd., the whole estate both real
and personal which is subject to equal division among us the undersigned
subscribers: Henry Champion for himself and guardian for Peggy Champion,
Eli Champion, Patsey Champion and Elias Champion, orphans; Lucy Champion,
Alexander Champion, Jesse Champion, John Champion, John Comer Peck Junr.,
Elizabeth Champion. Wit: Thos. Cooper, R. Moore, Junr. Reg. 25 May
1813.

                  Sale of part of property of Hart Champion dec'd: 1807
and 1808: Buyers: Asa Islands, William Thornton.

Pages 7-9.   Appraisement of the Estate of John Cook Senr. late of
                  Hancock Co. dec'd. as produced to the appraisers by John
Harbirt, John Cook Junr. and Phillip Cook, admrs., 6 Jul. 1798. Negroes
listed: man Arthur, woman Joan, man Peter, girl Edith, boy Arthur, man
Vol, woman Jinny, girl Fanny, boy Anthony, girl Esther, man Frank, man
Sam, woman Hannah & girl child Nancy, boy March, boy Jacob, man Joe,
woman Nan & boy child Jim, girl Salley, boy Dick. Interesting books and
hymn books listed. Total value: $7103.73. Signed: James Horton, Theo-
dosius Turk, John Ragan, appraisers.

Pages 10-13.   Account of the Sales of part of property of John Cook
                  dec'd., 31 Dec. 1798. Buyers: John Edmondson, Charles
McDonald, Thomas Spencer, Nathaniel Waller, Gayle Lewis, Robert Williams,
Joseph Montgomery, John Cook, Jas. M. Montgomery, James Ross, John Har-
birt, Dixon Harp, Solomon Oliver, Finny Dismukes, Joseph Dennis, Charles
Miller, James Fail, Stephen Waller, Henry Trippe, Mordecai Jacob, Greene
Williamson, Joseph Cox, Josiah Montgomery, (John?) Turk, Solomon Thorn-
ton, Matthew Kinchen, George P. Dykes, Solomon Butts, John Humphries,
John Edmondson, Abraham Smith, William Parker Junr., Samuel Parker, Henry
Low, Solomon Mangrum, John Smith, Thomas Dent, Matthew Durham, Jeremiah
Walker, Elisha Waller, Samuel Williamson, Benjamin Hutchinson, Joe (Cooks
Negro), Sam (Cook's Negro), Benjamin Bolt, William Brown, Thomas Glenn,
Isham Smith, Caleb Oliver, John Gholson, Robert Montgomery, Osborn
Brewer, Moses Marshall, William Horton, James Horton, Miss Gracy Cook,
Seth Kennedy, Joseph Denson, Benjamin Jacobs. Amount: $1339.31, carried
to page 63 in Book AA.

Page 14.   Account of Sales of the Estate of Martin Hammond, late
                  dec'd., 31 Mar. 1798. Buyers: Jas. Turner, Susannah
Hammond, Isaac Ellis. Amount: $177.68. Susannah Hamond and Jas. Turner,
admrs. Debts paid out: Anderson Comer, Butler Turner, Saml. Barron.

Page 14. (Second page 14.) Account of sale of personal property of Ben-
                  jamin Shipp, dec'd. No date. Buyers: James Perry,
David Ship, John Spear, Jesse Ashlock, Wm. Hardwick, Daniel Mitchell,
Robert Knight, Chas. Sturdivant, Wm. Stith Junr., Benj. Colding. Total:
$132.68. Matt Rabon, Exor.

Pages 15 and 16 blank.

Page 17.   Account of vouchers of the Estate of Wm. Wright dec'd.
                  brot to this office by Wm. Wright Junr., admr., 21 Sep.
1798. One note of hand Wm. Wright against estate of Wm. Wright dec'd.
for $147.00.

Pages 18-19.   Will of John Sledge of Hancock Co., dated 14 Apr. 1798.
                  To my son Nathaniel Sledge a Negro fellow named Harry,
a horse, etc. To daughter Jane Jackson a girl Doll, and furniture. `To
son Hartwell Sledge, a Negro Little Harry, a horse, etc. To son Mins
Sledge, a Negro Patt, horse, etc. To son John Sledge a Negro Martin,

horse, etc. To daughter Rebecca Southall, a Negro Lucey, furniture, etc.
To son Shirley Sledge, half of the tract of land where I now live join-
ing Clark, Wheeles, Crocket & Rogers on the West side of the survey join-
ing Rogers & Clark, also a Negro Absom, a horse, etc. To son Collin
Sledge, the other remaining half of the land where I now live, and two
Negroes Squire & Deadon, a horse, etc. To daughter Amey Sledge, a Negro
Nancy and furniture. To daughter Martha Sledge a Negro Suck and a boy
Joe, and furntiure. Exors: sons Nathaniel, Mins and John Sledge. Sign-
ed: John (+) Sledge. Wit: John Coulter, William Waller, Cornelius Clark.
Proved by John Coulter 11 Oct. 1798.

Pages 20-21 blank.

Pages 22-23.   Will of Mark Stroud of Hancock Co., weak in body, dated
                7 Jun. 1798. To my beloved wife Martha Stroud, during
her natural life, all my estate both within doors and without. My wife
shall raise and support my children upon the incomes of my Estate. After
my wife's death or marriage, my Estate to be divided equally between my
Eight children William, Levi, Eli, Mary, Sarah, Alban, Orion and Tillatha
Stroud. Exors: Jonathan Melton and Isaac Crow. Signed: Mark Stroud.
Wit: George Norsworthy, John Stroud. Proved by George Norsworthy 5 Nov.
1798.

Pages 24-26 blank.

Pages 27-29.   Will of Robert Wilson, very sick and weak in body, dated
                12 Oct. 1798. To my wife Susannah and children all the
profits that may arise from my land until the youngest comes to a lawful
age and then to be disposed of as follows: the whole of my land to be
given to my son James Wilson, and if the child my wife is pregnant with
should be a man child he is to be named Robert, and when Robert comes to
21 years, is to get half the land. But if the unborn child is a girl,
all the land to go to James. If James or the unborn child should die,
land is to go to daughter Betsey. Exors: my worthy friends Charles
Abercrombie and Andrew Boreland. Signed: Robert (X) Wilson. Wit: John
Brown, John C. Slocumb, William Reaves. Proved by Brown and Slocumb 4
Dec. 1798.

Page 30.   Appraisement of Estate of William Reddock Senr., dec'd.,
                8 Nov. 1798. Negroes listed: Duke, Diner, Esther, Jin,
Nell, Cintha. Total: $2569.47. George Thompson, Zachry Booth, appraise-
rs.

Page 31 blank.

Pages 32-35.   Account sale of the Estate of William Reddock late of
                this county, dec'd., as sold 9 Nov. 1798. Buyers: Mary
Reddock, William R. Reddock, John Reddock, Alexander Reddock, David Red-
dock, John Booth, Robert Montgomery, Seth Canady, John Downs, George
Thompson, John Brown, Daniel Dikes, Thomas Tayler, Joshua Scurlock, John
Humphreys, Jacob Collins, Thomas Messe, Obedier Moses, Levinah Bruster,
Wm. Weeks, Prater Fuguay, Wm. McKinzey, Wm. Mogin, Simon Goslin, Joel
McClendon.

                Book Accounts: Wm. R. Reddock, Lewis Page, W. D. (?)
Masson (?), Charles Hutson, George Greyer, Joseph Morran, Leaven Moore,
Benjamin McInvail (?), Allen Burton, Wm. Morgan, Robert McGinty, James
Bonner, Samuel Beekin, Charles Burk, John Mays, Robert Sheats, Augustin
Williams, Samuel Moore, Richard Banderford, Solomon Beekin.

Page 36:   3 Jan. 1799. Rec'd. of William Hardwick Junr. an Exor.
                of James Daniell dec'd. 25 Negroes, stock of every kind
and all my legacy that was willed to me by said James Daniell dec'd.
Also $667. Signed: Levi Daniell.

                3 Jan. 1799. Rec'd. of William Hardwick, as above, 4
Negroes given me and 21 Negroes lent me by said James Daniell dec'd.,
and stock of all kinds, also beds and furniture, etc. Signed: Nancy
Daniell.

18 Apr. 1803. We have received of William Hardwick, surviving Executor of James Daniel dec'd. a note of hand on James Taylor willed by James Daniel to his wife Nancy Daniel now Nancy Barrow, dated 28 May 1793, for L242 19 shillings sterling. Signed: James Barrow, Nancy Barrow.

Pages 37-39. Accounts of James Daniell, late of Hancock Co. dec'd. Inventory and Appraisal of part of the Estate, as shown to us by Levi Daniell and Wm. Hardwick, Exors. Total $254.20. Signed: John Harbirt, Stephen Horton, John Ragan, appraisers. Dated 24 Aug. 1798.

A list of Notes of Hand belonging to Estate of James Daniell, dec'd: Note on James Taylor dated 28 May 1793 for L242 19 sh. sterl = $1036.94. Note on Dudley Curry dated 2 Apr. 1794 for $128.57. Book account on Matthew Kinchen. Cash rec'd. of Levi Daniell, Thomas Harbirt, Mary Parker. Dated 2 Jan. 1799, signed: Levi Daniell, Wm. Hardwick, Exors.

Sale 22 Nov. 1798 of the property left out of the will of James Daniell dec'd. Buyers: Nancy Daniell bought a negro girl Jinny; Levi Daniell.

Proved accounts against the estate: Levi Daniell, J. Hamill, Wm. Jones, Dr. Robert Hendrick. John Harbirt and Robert McGinty, Exors. of Levi Daniell, dec'd. Dated 26 May 1799.

Pages 40-41. Estate of Thomas Cooper, dec'd. 7 Jan. 1799. Vouchers registered: Jas. Nesbits (legatee); H. Holt; Jas. Cooper, guardian for Micajah Cooper, minor; Wm. Stith; Augustin Thos & Joseph Stovall & Augustin Thomas of Virginia to collect the legacy of John Waller a legatee of Thomas Cooper dec'd lodged in my office by the Exors. of said Estate 7 Jan. 1799; Martin Martin's receipt for costs of Wm. Lawson agaist T. Cooper Exr.; J. C. Walton's receipt for fees in the above suit; Henry Graybill; Micajah Cooper; Randolph Rutland; S. Abercrombie. Received of Moses Going for the Estate: $132.39.

5 Oct. 1801, an account of money paid out; $27 each to Thos. Lancaster, George Hamilton, Jas. Nesbit, John Weeks, Micajah Cooper, Jos. Cooper. $30 to John Cooper. John Matthews, $8.00, Myles Green 1.75, Andrew Baxter's note $19.36. Thomas Cooper, Exor.

Pages 42-44. Account of the Estate of Jas. Adams dec'd. returned 10 Jan. 1799 by Jon Adams Acting Executor. Paid Wm. Allen; Jean McGaughey, Legatee, receipt for a negro girl as lent in the will of the dec'd; Robert Harper, Robt. Chambers; Esther Mills.

January 1800: Paid for land for Jas. Adams; to John Ragan for resurving a tract of land; J. Comer, Moses Wiley, Jonathan Adams, Robert Hill, Jas. Adams.

Sale of part of the Estate of Jas. Adams dec'd. 10 Apr. 1798. Buyers: Planners Shores, Jonathan Adams, Wm. Adams, Wm. Walker, Isaac Moreland, Jno. Brewer, Mary Adams, David Adams.

List of items allowed for the widow's moity, including a Negro boy named Sam. Total $673.00. Signed by Mary Adams as having rec'd. articles.

Page 45 blank.

Pages 46-47. Inventory and Appraisement of goods and chattels of John Sledge dec'd. as shown to us by his executors, 13 Nov. 1798. Negroes listed: man Harry, man Dedan, boy Martin, boy Squire, boy Harry, boy Joe, girl Nance, woman Patt, girl Sook, boy Abram, women Judy & Cloey, woman Sealey, boy Sam. Notes of hand: Samuel Maddox; Theodorick Pike & Wm. Ballard; Edwd. Olms & Lemuel Clifton; Edwin Clifton & L. (?) Clifton. Order unpaid: Dabney Cawthon. Receipts on Jno. Southall, Hartwell Sledge, John Sledge, Shirley Sledge. Signed: David Dickson, John Coulter, Jon Adams, appraisers. 31 Dec. 1798.

Page 48.   List of vouchers and receipts of legatees and others of
                  the Estate of John Sledge dec'd. 7 Jan. 1800. Receipts:
John Southall, legatee; James C. Adams; C. Clark for Negro girl Nance &
feather bed; Jas. Adams for Negro woman Sook and 1 mare; Shurley Sledge
for Negro boy Abram & 133¾ acres land, woman Jude, etc.; Frederick Ashfield, John Dewbery; Hartwell Sledge, legatee; Benj. Jackson, legatee;
James Adams, legatee. Accounts: Robert Clark, Tabitha Clark, Mins
Sledge, J. Comer, Saml. Maddox, Sterling Catoe, Reuben Foreman, Christopher Williams, George Smith, Wm. Pike, Jeremiah Nelson, Isham Whellis,
Robert Hill. John Sledge, Exor. Carried to page 64 for want of room.

Pages 49-51.   Accounts of the Estate of Hubbard Dykes, dec'd. Apprai-
                  sal: Certified 7 Nov. 1798 for total of $225.95. Signed:
Wm. Hamilton, Jesse Grigg, John Griggs. Reg. 29 Jan. 1799.

                  Sale bill dated 1 Dec. 1798. Buyers: Jno. C. Peek,
Robert Tucker, Wm. Cox, J. Comer Peek, John Griggs.

                  Proved accounts: Benja. Anderson, Samuel Hall, John
Freeman, William Ewing, Timothy W. Rossiter, Reese & Co., Samuel Enabery,
Jos? Bonner, Jas. Thweatt, William Maddox, James Huddleston, Cain Ray.
Notes: William Ewing, William Clowers. No date. John C. Peek, Adm.

Page 52.   A list of book accounts belonging to the Estate of John
                  Brewer Senr. dec'd. 21 Sep. 1798. Names: Bartlett Sims,
Wm. Cureton, Mrs. Rivers, John Brodnax, Andrew Reed, Hugh Hall, Joseph
Adcock, Wm. Harper, Charles Jones, James Thweatt, John Jack, John Rivers,
Andrew Boreland, Stephen Evans, Turner Hunt, Judkins Hunt, Joseph White.
Appraisers: Absalom Harris, Turner Hunt, Andrew Jeter. Total: $607.42½.
John Brewer, Exor. Recorded 26 Mar. 1799.

Pages 53-54.   Inventory and Appraisement of Estate of John Brewer Senr.
                  dec'd. 15 Nov. 1798. Included 6 Negroes (not named) at
$500 each, also Mary & Patience, $500; Sampson & Lucy, $500; Martha &
Ben, $300; Jinney, $300; Judy, $200. Total appraisal: $6110.43. Same
appraisers as above. Reg. 1 Feb. 1799.

Pages 55-56.   Account of sales of Estate of John Brewer, dec'd., 17
                  Nov. 1798. Buyers: Sterling Cato, George Roper, Jno.
Brewer, Wm. Wilson, Jehu Smith, Thomas Jack, Hamblin West, Noe Dodridge,
James Dickson, Daniel Low, Joseph Adcock, George Whitehead, Charles Ivey,
James Greene, John Lewis Senr., Joseph Chambers, Robert Hill, Saml. Reed
for Alex. Reed, Reuben Westmoreland, John Foster, Reubin Foreman, Maning
Harrup, Moses Wiley, James Ross, Anderson Harwell, Turner Hunt, Robert
Mitchell, Wm. Flournoy, Owen Davis, John White, Alexander Reid. Also
Negroes Polley, Henry & Jinney bought articles.

Pages 57-58.   Account of the sales of the Estate of John Brewer Senr.
                  dec'd. as sold 24 Nov. 1798. Names in addition to those
listed in previous sale: Green Cato, Alexr. Dunn, John McCoy, Joseph
Westmoreland, Myles Greene, Wm. Trippe, James Oneal Junr., Isaac More-
land, Zachariah Williamson, John H. Lett, Elisha Copeland, Robert Clark,
Nathaniel Hendrick, Jnothan. Adams, Reuben Herndon, Wm. Adams, Benjamin
Woodrooff, Stephen Wright, William Ross, Jeremiah Thrower, Isham Lett,
Jeremiah Moore, Hugh Comer, Cornelius Clark, Hugh Montgomery, Jno. Swin-
ney, Tulley Choice, Allen Cook, Francis Lewis Jr.

Pages 59-60.   Returns of Exors. of Abraham Womack, dec'd., of Bonds,
                  Notes & Proven Accounts, 23 Feb. 1799. Notes of hand:
Shearward Womack, Francis Coleman. Proven Accounts: Doctor Jno. Deyam-
pert, John Hester, Matthew Jones, Jno. Rogers, Haden Prior, Wm. Veasey,
James Allford, David Womack, Estate of Partrick Hayes. Legatees: David
Womack, Wm. Stone, Clemt. Glenn, Francis Coleman. Reg. 27 Feb. 1799.

Pages 61-62.   Will of John Hunt of Hancock Co., dated 13 Jan. 1799.
                  To my well beloved wife Rebekah Hunt I lend the planta-
tion where I now live with all tools, houses and furniture and a Negro
girl Sary. To son Henry Hunt $5.00. To sons Thomas Hunt and Daniel Hunt
a 300 acre tract of land on the Ohopy (sic) to be equally divided between
them lying in Washington County. To my daughter Letty I bequeath the

291

negro girl I lent to my wife. To son Michael C. Hunt the land I lent to my wife at either her marriage or death. To Daniel Hunt, Thomas Hunt and Curtis Hunt, $5 each. "In a low state of Health." Signed: John (H) Hunt. Wit: Richard Grimsley, James Thompson. Proved by Richard Grimsley 1 Mar. 1799.

Page 63 blank.

Page 64.   Account of money paid out of estate of John Sledge dec'd.
                Brot from page 48. Proven Accounts: Mims Sledge, John Sledge, Nathaniel Sledge, Shurley Sledge. C. Clark's rec't. for Negro woman Cealey. Receipts in full against said Estate: C. Clark, S. Sledge, James Adams, Rebekah Clark. No date.

                Sales of part of the estate as sold 22 Dec. 1798. Buyers: John Sledge, Francis Martin, Robert Clark, John Sledge.

                An account of money received of the estate of Nathaniel Sledge dec'd. in favour of this estate is $95.88.

Pages 65-67.   Will of Archibald Smith Senr. of Hancock Co., dated 22 Feb. 1799. "Weak in body." To my son Jehu Smith a Negro boy Daniel. To son Archibald Smith a Negro boy Sam. To daughter Nancy Thompson a Negro girl Ester. To daughter Judith Sharp a Negro woman Milley and her child Jinney, $80 in cash and 100 acres of land whereon she now lives. To my daughter Salley Smith a Negro woman Obey and her child Abram and a girl child called Millen. To son George W. Smith all the tract of land where I now live, that is unsold and unwilled; also six negroes Cesar, Israel, Rose, Simon, Huffy and Will; also stock, tools, furniture and $100 cash for the purpose of saving a bounty of land South of the Oconee when obtained. My wife Mary Smith is to hold in her possession the land, Negroes, tools and every part of the property that I have willed to my son George W. Smith during her widowhood, and that she raise, board and educate him to age 21 and then she to take 1/3 of the property and give him 2/3. At her death or marriage he is to have her third. Exors: wife Mary Smith and sons Jehu and Archibald Smith. Wit: James Davis, Ishmail Davis, M. Greene. Proved 9 Mar. 1799 by James & Ishmail Davis.

Pages 68-70.   Appraisement of Estate of Archibald Smith, Senr., dec'd.
                4 Apr. 1799. Negroes listed: man Cesar, old woman Moll, woman Milley and child Millen, child Jinney, woman Rose, woman Ibbey & boy child Abram, man Israel, boy Sam, boy Kuffey, boy Simon, boy Daniel, boy Will, woman Ester. Appraisers: Robt. Moreland, Britain Roger, Alexr. Reed. Additional appraisal 1 Jul. 1799 included notes on Jno. Jackson, Anderson Harwell, Jas. Grace, Daniel Milson. "Carried to page 74."

Pages 71-72.   Inventory and appraisement of Estate of Mark Stroud late dec'd., 19 Nov. 1798. Book accounts: Richard Strawther, John Holcomb, Joel Holcomb, Matthew Hubbard, Daniel Davison, Matthew Dennis, Eli Townsend, James Strawther, Aaron Oins (?), Benjamin Gagood (?), Aaron Parker. Appraisers: Aaron Parker, Isham Humpry, Benja. Hagood. Reg. 26 Mar. 1799.

Page 73 blank.

Page 74.   Part of the Estate of Archibald Smith Senr. dec'd. returned by Exors. 25 Oct. 1799. Due bill on Andrew Bourland, notes on Jehu Smith and Dr. Richd. Lee. Proven accounts paid out: Daniel Milson, John E. Smith (printer), Ishmael Davis, Joel Rees, David Clements, Wm. Sharp, James Grace, Dr. R. H. Lee, Doctor Timothy Reseter (?), Joshua Turner, Jehu Smith, Archibald Smith. Legatees: John Thompson, Jehu Smith, Wm. Sharp, Salley Smith.

Pages 75-76.   Money paid to the legatees of John Brewer, dec'd., returned by John Brewer, Acting Executor, 12 Apr. 1799.
Paid to Alexander Read and George Roper for their part of Negroes, $3000.

                Proven accounts: George Smith, Jno. Adams, Jno. Freeman,

J. Hunt for making a coffin, Robert Hill, J. Comer, Noel Doddridge, John Brewer's expenses in going on business to Virginia.

May 6, 1799: Paid Andrew Boreland. 7 Feb. 1798, paid Jas. Thweatt for smith's work. 27 Aug. 1800, paid to Wm. Stith (attorney) for advice. John Brewer Junr's account paid.

Return dated 7 Jan. 1800 by Jno. Brewer Junr., administrator of said dec'd.: Received of John Newson (?) (Norfolk), £28.14.3 Virginia money. Received of Andrew Boreland, Joseph Adcock, Noah Dodridge, Lockette Mitchell for D. Watters (?), Jas. Thweatt & Co.

Pages 77-78. Inventory of property of Edward Moore, dec'd. dated 11 Aug. 1799. Appraisers: Loyd Kelly, Drury Cook, Reubin Jones. Total: $641.81. Money paid out as of 28 Feb. 1801: Proper Horten, Mark Gonden, Jordan Lacy, Ezekiel Smith, Jonathan Davis, Edward Moore Junior, Donaghey & Love, James M. Burton, John Hobson, Robert Abercrombie, Aron Owen, Will Keeling.

Pages 79-80. Will of Thomas Harbirt of Hancock Co., weak of body, dated 2 Apr. 1799. To my sons John, George & Thomas Harbirt 226 acres lying on Town Creek and also 16 Negroes: Peter, Cloe, Jack, Hannah, Vilet, Jacob, Bob, Hal, Sam, Reuben, Chaney, Ellis, Big Sam, Siller, Peter, Salley, to be equally divided between them. To my grand daughter Alice Wright Harbirt $400 when she comes of age, and if she dies without heirs, the money to be given to my grandson Hardy Harbirt son of John Harbirt when he comes of age. To my son-in-law Burrell Cook $2.00. Exors: John Harbirt, George Harbirt & Thomas Harbirt. Signed: Thomas Harbirt. Wit: Levi Daniell, Joseph Denson, Hubert Reynolds. Proved 27 May 1799 by Levi Daniell and Joseph Denson.

Pages 81-82. Inventory and Appraisement of the Estate of Thomas Harbirt dec'd. returned by the acting Executor, John Harbirt, 1 Jun. 1799. Negroes named: Jacob, girl Siller, man Jack, man Bob, boy Reubin, man Peter, woman Violet, woman Chloe, girl Chaney, boy Hall, boy Sam, boy Ellis, woman Hannah & young girl child Charlotte, man Sam, boy Peter. Total: $4506.26. Appraisers: John Humphries, Levi Daniell, Mat Kinchin.

Pages 83-84. Account of Sales of part of Estate of Thomas Harbirt dec'd., 21 and 23 Dec. 1799. Buyers: Daniel Dikes, John Harbirt, Henry Low, Stephen Dikes, Josiah Dennis, Hardy Smith, Thomas Spencer, William Horton, Matthias Dennis, Jno. Ragan, Elisha Ellis, Demcy Justus, George Harbirt, Abraham Peavy, Green Williamson, John Reed, Geo. Parker Dikes, Wm. Fairchild, Wm. Vines, John Smith, James Scarlett, John Winslet, John Gray, Robert Williams, Solomon Smith, Jephthah Strickland, Nathaniel Waller, Wm. Ryan, Louisa Bruster, Elijah Moore, Thomas Lamar, John Cook, Thomas Dent, Elijah Hearn, Joseph Hambrick, Thomas S. Harbirt, Wm. Spencer, George Dawkins, John Edmondson, Leonard Gordy. Certified by John Harbirt, George Harbirt, Exors.

Pages 85-86. Sales of the property of John Waller dec'd. sold by Nathan Melvin, Exor., 14 Jul. 1798. Buyers: Edward Turner, Shadrack Taylor, Wylie Hillard, Benjamin Waller, Abraham Betts, Thomas Methvin, Joshua Bishop, Robert Parham, Allen Whatley, John Castleberry, Ephraim Salmonds, Nathan Methvin, Jeremiah Castlebury, Samuel Betts, Joshua Maddox, James Turner, Thomas Williams, Eliza Collins, Robert Parham, George Collins, John Kelley. Total: $87.56. Reg. 6 Jun. 1799.

Page 88. A Schedule of all the Negroes with their increase now in life (except one Negro man Sanco sold by James Barrow) that were lent by the last Will and Testament of James Daniell dec'd. to his widow and relict Nancy Daniel, afterwards Nancy Barrow, wife of James Barrow, during her natural life: Old Tom, Zouer (?), Old Rachel, Charlotte, Hester, Flander, Acre, Daphney, George, Moriah, Hictor, Biner, Dover, Caty, Peter, Pompy, Peggy, Ned, Ellinney, Billy, Moriah, Levin, Becky, Bob, Rachel, Hector, Sam, Sally, Sucky, Driver, Jupiter, Bob, Ellick, Pompy, Flander. Signed: James Barrow, 12 March 1814. Wit: Jacob Cobb, Garland Hardwick.

Pages 89-90.   Inventory of the Estate of George Vest dec'd. 28 Mar.
                1799. Total $944.22. Appraisers: A. Comer, Michael
Maddox, Jas. Comer. Mary Vest, Adm., Saml. Barron, Adm. Reg. 17 Jun.
1799.

Page 91.   Book Accounts of Estate of George Vest, dec'd. Saml.
                Brady, Morton Gray, Jonathan McKissack, Osborn Brewer,
Reubin Blankinship, Saml. Standfield, John McGuirt, Allen Cook, James
Murphey, Jesse Clements, Abraham Reddock, Edmund Bradbury, Wm. Brown,
Thomas Stephens, Jas. Christopher, Jas. Lamar, Frederick Rose, Anderson
Comer, Jas. Garrett, Jas. Yarbrough, Robert Hill, Meyr. David Adams,
Reubin Westmoreland, Jeremiah Spiller, Jos. Westmoreland, Benja. Wills,
Richd. Fretwell, Jno. Huckaby, Annie Hudgins, Tully Choice, Pleasant
Rose, Thomas McKissack, John McGaughey, Robert Winn (?), Jas. Cooper,
John Duke, Thomas Brady, John McKissack, Archbd. (?) Traylor, John Hud-
mon, Hubert Brown, Hezekiah Blankenship, Francis Dannelly, Elisha Ellis,
Lew Tucker, Penelope Jordan, Saml. Gilbert, Phillip Clements, Wm. John-
son, Wm. Evans. Total $121.11. Returned 15 Jun. 1799 by Mary Vest,
admx. & Saml. Barron, Admr.

Page 92.   Account of sales of property of George Vest dec'd., 11
                Apr. 1799. Buyers: Mary Vest, Saml. Barron, Anderson
Comer, Archbd. Trayler, Richd. Hamblin, Jno. McGaughey, Reubin Blankin-
ship, Robert Finch, Saml. Halley, Thornton Hudgins, Edmund Butler, Green
Williamson, Morten Gray, Chas. Sturdivant, James Yarbrough, John Barren,
Saml. Pruet, Wm. Brown.

Page 93.   Account of Stock made use of for the orphans of George
                Vest, dec'd., 1799. To clothing 6 children - $24.00.

Page 94 blank.

Pages 95-96.   Will of Edward Price, late of the neighborhood of
                Philadelphia, now of Fort Wilkinson in the Creek Nation,
dated 14 Jan. 1799. To Sarah the daughter of Susannah Baker of Philadelphia, reputed to be my natural child, and to the male child of Rachel
the daughter of Thomas Giles late of Buffeloe Settlement Hancock County
(interlined) said child was named ____?____ by the ___?___ ___?___ ___?___
King of the Cussetah. My whole estate to be equally divided between the
two children, reserving for the support of the mothers of the said two
children. Exors: Mr. John Wilson of the Bank of the U. States Account-
ant, my Brother Joseph Price of Montgomery Co. Pa., and my friend Richard
Tunis, Merchant of Philadelphia. Signed: Edwd. Price. Wit: Matthew
Hopkins, Wm. Carson. Proved by the witnesses 2 Sep. 1799.

Pages 97-98 blank.

Pages 99-101.   Will of William Mapp of Hancock Co., Gentleman, weak in
                body, dated 14 May 1799. I give to the care of my father
and loving brother Howsin Mapp $2000 that is in the hands of Julius
Allford and Robertus Love when the Negroes are sold to be distributed
among my brothers and sisters after my just debts are paid and for my
brother Howsan to have $50 for his trouble. To my loving brother Jere-
miah one negro named Sam for ten years and then the said Negro to be set
free; also one horse called Yankee and saddle. I give unto my loving
brother one watch likewise. Exors: father Littleton Mapp Senr. and
Howson Mapp. Signed: Wm. Mapp. Wit: Elam Ward, Anne Ward. Proved 2
Sep. 1799 in open court by Elam Ward.

Pages 102-104. Inventory and Appraisement of Estate of James Cathell
                late dec'd. 20 Sep. 1799. Negro man George, girl Flora,
other items. Total $1559.24. Appraisers: Jesse Talbot, John Miles,
Samuel Slaughter. Jean Cathell and Archbd. Smith, adm.

                Sale of Estate 14 Nov. 1799, the whole amt. $370.17, the
particulars of which sale is deposited in the office. The other sales
are registered in Book D, page 83.

                Vouchers showing money paid out: Aaron McKenzie, Charles
Abercrombie, Martin Martin, Hubard Ferrel, Samuel Slaughter, Wm. Burns,

Isaac Downs, Charles Hutson, Jonathan Hosea, Thomas Farley, John Minor, Josiah Dennis, John Minor, Exr. of Wm. Minor dec'd.

Pages 105-108.   Inventory and Appraisal of Estate of Thomas Cooper dec'd. 3 Jul. 1799. Total $220.51 3/4. Will Dent, Risdon Moore, R. Moore Junr., Jesse Connell, Appraisers. Returned 30 Sep. 1799 by Patsey Cooper, admx. and Obadiah Richardson, Admr.

Sale of estate: buyers not listed.

Cash received which was due the estate of Thomas Cooper dec'd., from Joshua Low, Wm. Lawson Junr., Ralph Lowe, Elijah George, Saml. Dent.

Money paid out: Stephen Kirk.

Page 109.   Will of William Buckner, in a low state of body, dated 12 Mar. 1799. My executors to sell my land if they think best. To my beloved wife Tabitha Buckner I lend the rest of my Estate during her widowhood to raise my children and give them such schooling as the nature of the case will admit, and if my children should not be treated as well after my wife's marriage as before, my executors should take the said lent estate together with my children out of her hands, and an equal distribution be made of the same between all my then surviving children. Exors: loving brother Joel Buckner and loving uncle John Brown. Signed: William (X) Buckner. Wit: Richard Respess, James Morris, John Gay. Proved 7 Oct. 1799.

Pages 110-112.   Inventory and Appraisement of estate of William Buckner dec'd. 17 Oct. 1799. Total $435.75. No appraisers listed. Moneys paid out: Doctor T. W. Rosseter, Appleton Rosseter, Polley Lockey, D. McLean (?), Lewis Barnes, Peter Grammar, Myles Green. Cash paid Jas. Rush one of the heirs of said Buckner in right of his wife, $20.59.

List of sales 15 Jan. 1805. Buyers: Elisha Self, Henry Darnall, James Rush, John Grammar, Henry Brown, Singleton Holt, Geo. Maddox, Tabitha Self, John Gay, Isham Reese. 101 acres of land sold to Henry Denslie (?) 3 Aug. 1807.

Pages 113-115. Will of William Washington, of weak and frail body. Whereas I have before given to my children in possession the chiefest part of my estate, and as providence hath provided that a small estate hath fallen into my hands, which is my desire that it shall descend as follows: To my son John Washington one book, title Concordance and no more. To my son Ephraim Washington 9 shillings sterling & no more. To my children John, Ephraim, Mary and Sarah my Bible and all the remaining part of my books to be equally divided among them. My executors to receive into their possession the remaining part of my estate consisting of stock and one tract of land of 200 acres whereon I now live on Logdam Creek in Hancock Co., out of which property and the profits arising therefrom I do desire them to give my son William Washington a comfortable maintainance in decent clothing, washing and lodging, his being an Idiot, and he shall not be put to any labor at all. After his death, my executors to deliver it up to my grandson Washington Rose or to his heirs. Exors: Myles Greene, Britain Rogers, William Hurt. Dated 25 Jan. 1796. And whereas a certain tract of land has fallen to me as heir of Etheldred Washington, who served as a fifer in the Continental Line in North Carolina, containing 500 acres, it being one half of a tract of 1000 acres, granted as aforesaid in Davidson County, on Parsons Creek, a branch of Red River, that empties in on the South side of said Creek, about four miles from the mouth, as further described in said platt. Said land to be sold by my executors and the money equally divided between my grandsons Ephraim Rose, John Rose, and Pleas (torn) White, son of Sarah White. I acknowledge that this is an essential part of my will, dated 12 Aug. 1799. Signed: Wm. Washington. Wit: Pleasant Rose, Mary Rose, Martha Powell. Proved by Pleasant Rose 15 Oct. 1799, and Britain Rogers and Wm. Hurt qualified as exors.

14 Jan. 1812. Rec'd. of William Hurt & Briton Rogers

295

Exors. of William Washington dec'd., his son William Washington's estate
which was left him by his father in his will for his maintenance consisting of one tract of land containing 200 acres adjoining Warren & Thweatt,
also one note for $20. Signed: Howell Rose, Guardian for Wm. Washington.
Wit: Jno. Lucas.

Pages 116-118.   Inventory and appraisement of Estate of William Washing-
                 ton dec'd. 2 Nov. 1799. Notes and Book accounts: Fredk.
Rose, Mr. Rutledge, John Murphy, Reuben Blankinship, Jethro Jackson,
John Lewis, Joseph Bridges, Reuben Westmoreland, Thomas Henson, Jno.
Scott, Fredk. Rose Junr., Rawleigh Greene, Quinny Powell, Sarah Murphy.
Total $384.07. Rawleigh Greene, Jesse Warren, John Sturdivant, apprai-
sers.

                 Further appraisement and sale carried to page 164.
Vouchers: Quinny Powell, Henry Jackson, Stephen Stephens, M. Greene's
rec't. for clothes for Wm. Washington; Pleasant Rose, Ephraim Rose,
Roundtree Taylor, Archibald Taylor.

Pages 119-121.   Inventory of Estate of John Cook Senr. dec'd. produced
                 by the administrators and appraised by John Ragan, Theo-
dosius Turk and James Horton Esquires. Negroes named: Man Arthur, woman
Joan, man Peter, girl Edith, boy Arthur, man Vol, woman Jinny, girl Fanny,
man Anthony, girl Ester, man Frank, man Sam, woman Hannah & child Nancy,
boy March, boy Jacob, man Joe, woman Nan & her child Jin, girl Salley,
boy Dick. Other items including books. No total given. Dated 6 Jul.
1798.

Page 122.   Account of moneys paid out of the Estate of William
                 Buckner dec'd. by Jno. Brown, Exor. 27 Jan. 1810, paid
James Rush in full of his part of said Estate as per his receipt.

                 Received 7 Feb. 1816 of Samuel Evins (?) adm. of Joel
Buckner dec'd. who was Exr. of William Buckner dec'd. the sum of $38.84,
the balance in full of my distributive share of said William Buckner's
estate. Signed: Lester Buckner. Rec. 14 Oct. 1816.

Pages 123-125.   Will of Willis Whatley, weak in body, dated 1 May 1799.
                 I lend to my well beloved wife Catheron Whatley my land
whereon I now live, also four negroes Jacob, Captin, Easter and Fain,
also cattle, household goods, etc., to remain in my wife's possession if
she should live until my youngest son Willis Whatley arrives to 21 years
of age; but if said Willis should die, the property to remain in my
wife's hands no longer than my next youngest heir comes of age - then to
be equally divided between my wife Catheron Whatley and my heirs, Shurley Whatley, Greene Whatley, Ornan Whatley, Gennit Whatley and Willis
Whatley. I leave my land in the fork of the Oconey and Appalacha on
Green Brier Creek in Greene County to be sold by my executors, the money
from this to be put out on interest until my daughter Nancy Whatley comes
of age, then I give one third part of money to my daughter Nancy Whatley,
and one Negro girl named Edy, and the other two thirds to be equally
divided between my five sons Shurley, Green, Ornan, Gennit & Willis
Whatley. Exors: brother Michael Whatley and son Shurley Whatley. Signed: Willis Whatley. Wit: Job Tison, Zerob. Williamson, Sarah (+) Basor.
Proven in Open Court by Zerob. Williamson & Sarah Basor and ordered to
be recorded 6 Jan. 1800. Michael Whatley qualified Executor.

Pages 125-127.   Inventory and appraisement of the Estate of Willis
                 Whatley dec'd. taken 7 Jan. 1800. Negroes named: man
Jacob,   man Captain, woman Ester, girl Fain, girl Edith. Total
value $2511.87½. Appraisers: John Hamilton Senr., Bryon Stonum, Zerob.
Williamson.

                 Moneys paid out of estate for proven accounts: Charles
Hutson, James Comer, John T. Sankey, John Brown, John Lucas, John Hamilton, James Thweatt. A note given by said Willis Whatley to Jas. Cooper.
John McArthur's receipt for $79 being his part of land willed to his wife
on Greenbrier Creek in Greene County. No date. Total paid out: $155.54.

Page 128.   Buckner Estate. Rec'd. 8 Apr. 1817 from Samuel Ewing,

admr. on estate of Joel Buckner dec'd. who was Exr. of
the LW&T of William Buckner dec'd. $173.04 in full of my legacy or dis-
tributive share of the estate of my father, the said William Buckner,
dec'd. Signed: Morris Buckner. Wit: James H. Jones. Rec. 14 Aug. 1817.

Received Feb. 1818 from Samuel Ewing admr. of Joel
Buckner dec'd. who was Exr. of William Buckner dec'd. $170.30 in full of
my distributive share of the estate of my father the said William Buckner dec'd. Signed: Richmond Buckner.

Page 129 blank.

Pages 130-131. William Mapp Estate. Inventory and appraisement of the
estate of William Mapp, dec'd. 10 Sep. 1799. Negroes
named: Hannah & child Patt, Sybba and child Cornelius, George, Jack,
Sophia, Isaac, Sambo for ten years. Silver watch also listed. No total.
Appraisers: Boling Hall, Hines Holt, Thomas Hill, Taylor Nelson.

Account of sales of the estate - no buyers listed. No
date. Total: $2107.69. Robert H. Mapp, Qualified Executor.

Receipts returned by Robert H. Mapp, Exor., 6 Nov. 1809:
John Mapp's receipt dated 21 Aug. 1801; Reuben Smith, 1 Sep. 1804; Henry
Jackson, 1 Sep. 1804; Littleton Mapp, 1 Sep. 1804; John Smith, 1 Sep.
1804; Robert Aslen, 1 Sep. 1804; Jeremiah Mapp, 24 Dec. 1804; Nancy Mapp,
28 Nov. 1804; James Mapp, 27 Feb. 1809.

Pages 132-137. Jesse Clark Estate. Inventory and appraisement of the
Estate of Jesse Clark dec'd. 28 Oct. 1799. Many yards
of fabric, apparell, etc. listed. He was evidently a merchant. Total:
$4034.45. Negro listed: boy Stephen. Appraisers: Obadiah Richardson,
John Weeks, James Bynum.

Pages 138-141. Account of the Sales of the Estate of Jesse Clark dec'd.
20 Nov. 1799. Buyers: Samuel Dent, William Sutton,
John Harvey, Peter Dent, John Cooper, Isaac Carter, Joseph Henry, William
Maddux, James Christopher, Ramsom Harwill, Robert Owsley, George Weather-
by, Thomas Weeks, Thomas Scott, Epaphroditus Drake, George Lewis, William
Thomas, Isaac Ellis, Micajah Godwin, William Davenport, Hillery Phillips,
David Christopher, John Holcomb, William Lord, John Tankersley, Robert
Holt, John Weeks, Benjamin Jones, Stephen Daniel, Thomas Breedlove,
Nathan Daniel, C. Kelly, Joshua Breattan (?), James Crowder, Henry Jer-
nigan, Joseph Bryan, Edward Flowers, Seth Tatum, Benjamin Gilbert,
William Johnson, Robert Gilmore, Thomas Johnson, William Maddux, Joseph
Maddux, Joseph Mason, Gabl. Richardson, John S. Williams, John Pope,
Edmund Butler Junr., Thomas W. Coxan, William Lancaster, William Owsley,
Thomas Cates, Oba. Richardson, Jonathan Pearson, Theophilus Thomas,
George Mifflin, Risdon Moore Junr., Richard Ship, Moses Powell, Mary
Langston, James Bynum, James Harvey, Robert Sims, Wythe Whatley, Evan
Harvey, Barthl. T. Dowdle, Thomas Clark, Joseph Cooper Junr., Leonard
Maddux, David D. Smith, Joshua Askey, John Jones, Barthl. Walker, William
Clark. Signed: William Clark, Admr.

Account of expenses in managing the estate of Jesse
Clark dec'd.: Proven accounts and services: James McIntosh, Henry Gra-
bill, Jas. Harvey, Hines Holt, Thomas Patten, Mrs. Cooper, Moses Powell,
Jos. Madux, J. Lacey, Jas. Hester, Jesse Ellis, James Beach, Jacob Goar,
Wm. Owsley, D. Christopher (?), Uriah Askey. Amount carried to Book
AAAA, page 24.

Pages 142-143. Will of Allen Jones, weak in body, dated 4 Aug. 1799.
All my property is to remain in the hands of my beloved
wife (not named) till my youngest child comes of age, with the exception
that my horse creatures be sold, except my bay mare. When youngest
child comes of age, then to be divided between my children and my wife.
My wife to be sole executor with my loving friends Alexander King and
John Jones as overseers of my will according to my true intent and
meaning without waste or extravagancy. Signed: Allen Jones. Wit: John
Wilson, William Lancaster, Benjamin Jones. Proved by the witnesses in
Open Court 16 Jan. 1800.

Pages 144-145. Inventory and appraisement of Estate of Allen Jones, dec'd., 22 Jan. 1800. Negroes named: man Peter, girl Charlotte. Also a bay mare Fly and Sorrel mare Diamond. Appraisers: Samuel Hart (?), Edmund Butler Junr., William Lancaster. Sales of the Estate of Allen Jones dec'd., 22 Jan. 1800. Buyers: Augustin Potter, Alexr. King, William Googer, William Lancaster, Thos. Lancaster, Saml. Lancaster, Daniel Wilson.

Account of moneys paid out of estate of Allen Jones, dec'd. as returned by Mary Ann Jones, Extrx. (These names marked through with marginal notation that they were entered in the first line returned by Extrx. (?): John Hester, John Burch.) March 1803, paid Britain Jones, Daniel Wilson & Alexr. King notes.

Pages 146-147 blank.

Pages 148-149. Will of Charles Moore dated 1 Apr. 1799. To my son Risdon Moore (Moore scratched through) my riding horse and also an obligation on George Wells Foster, same on Nathan Bostick and same on John Pollard. To my son Jonathan the unconveyed part of a tract of land lying in Greene Co., being originally granted to Samuel Jack for 520 acres, two cows and yearlings one of which is in the possession of Levi Benson. Also cloth for a suit of clothes now in my possession. To my grandson William Moore son of Risdon one tract of land in Greene Co. on waters of Stewards Creek originally granted to Thomas Reeves for 287½ acres. Also an obligation on John Kimbro for $137.50 to be lodged in his father's hands for the express purpose of schooling my said grandson William Moore. Exors: sons Risdon and Jonathan. Signed: Chas. Moore. Wit: Will Dent, Z. Middleton. Proven in Open Court by the witnesses and ordered to be recorded 16 Jan. 1800.

Pages 150-152. Inventory and appraisement of Estate of Charles Moore Dec'd. made 17 May 1800. Articles included 1 Silver Watch with a pinch back case and 1 Silver Set stock buckle. Total $169.31¼. Appraisers: Will Dent, Isaac Benson, Z. Middleton. Estate sale 17 May 1800. Buyers: Jonathan Moore, Risdon Moore Senr., William Dent, James Waller, Obadiah Richardson, James Randle, Risdon Moore, Zachary Middleton, Benjamin Gilbert, Thomas Shockley, Robert Gilbert, John Henderson. Certified by Risdon Moore Junr., Adm. One horse rec'd. of John Pollard for Estate - $113.00.

Pages 153-154. Will of Robert Bryant, weak in body and very sick, dated 12 Apr. 1799. To my beloved wife Sarah Bryant two negroes Dina and Pegg. I lend to my wife during her widowhood my plantation, tools, stock, furniture, etc., or as much as necessary to raise and support my children. The parts that can be spared may be sold and put to interest or laid out in young Negroes. The rest of my Negroes not given to my wife to be kept together and as my children come of age I allow them to get an equal division of all but the land. When youngest child comes of age, my land to be sold and money divided among my children. Or land may be sold at the marriage or decease of my wife. Exors: wife Sarah Bryant, and Ajonadab Reed, Dred Wilder and Tunstal Roan my joint executors in trust to see my will executed. Signed: Robert Bryan. Wit: Wm. Phillips, Saml. Hart, Solomon Stapp. Proven in Open Court by Samuel Hart and Solomon Stapp 16 Jan. 1800.

Pages 155-158. Inventory and appraisement of the personal estate of Robert Bryan dec'd., 11 Feb. 1800. Negroes named: woman Dinah, woman Peg, girl Amey, boy Jerry, girl Judy, Richard, girl Polley. Total: $2350.22. Appraisers: Shearward Womack, Wm. McLellan, Saml. Hart. Salley Bryan, Exrx.

Sale of estate of Robert Bryan dec'd., 4 Dec. 1800. Buyers: Richard Reynolds, John Henderson, Benjamin Whitefield, Augustin Potter, John Wilson, Jesse Bell, David Chuning, Michael Gilbert, William Johnston, Thomas Sparks, Samuel Hart, Geo. West, Edmd. Butler, Elijah George, Warren West, David Patillo, John Jackson, John Lee, Samuel Chuning, Ezekiel Veasey, Tunstel Roan, Thomas Sparks, Josephus Love, Peter Byrd, John Rudisill, Daniel Wilson, Joshua Stevins, Will Lawson, Martin Gilbert, Elijah Stevens, Will Hodges, Epaphroditus Drake, Ajonadab Read,

Wilborne Dickerson, Reubin Read.

Pages 159-161. Will of Richard Cureton, Senr., in perfect health, dated
11 Mar. 1797. To my son Richard Cureton, a Negro boy
named Jupeter. To my daughter Mary Palmer, a Negro boy named Adam. To
my daughter Jean Cureton, a Negro girl named Dorcas. To my daughter
Rebekah Conner, a Negro girl named Amy. To my daughter Winnefred Cureton a Negro girl named Rachel. To my son John Cureton a Negro boy named
Jacob. To my son Rezon Cureton a tract of land of 200 acres in Hancock
Co. on Dry Creek, waters of Ogeechee River, whereon I now live, and improvements thereon. To my son Robert Cureton a Negro wench named Rachel
together with her increase after this date. To my daughter Hannah Cureton a Negro girl named Sukee. To my dearly beloved wife Martha Cureton
all my lands, cattle, horses, goods and chattels that are not otherwise
mentioned or bequeathed in this will, during her life or widowhood, and
at her marriage or death the said cattle, horses etc. should be divided
equally between my said son and daughter Robert and Hannah. To my son
William Cureton a Negro man named Jame. To my son Bolin Cureton a Negro
girl named Mourning. Exors: sons William and Bolin. Signed: Richard
(R his mark) Cureton. Wit: Henry Townsend, JP, Elizabeth Warthen, D.
McLean, James Wilson, Edward Castleberry. Legally proven in Open Court
and ordered to be recorded 16 Jan. 1800.

Pages 162-163 blank.

Page 164.   Additional Appraisement of the Estate of William Washington dec'd. 23 Oct. 1802. Three horses valued at $255.00.
Appraisers: John Rivers, Henry Jackson, John Sturdivant.

                An account of sales in addition to the former sale made
23 Oct. 1802. Buyers: Ephraim Rose, Frederick Rose, Josiah Simons.
Exors: Wm. Hurt and Britain Rogers.

Page 165.   Will of Ephraim Bowings, in a low state of health, dated
29 Jan. 1800. To my beloved wife Mary Boings (sic) all
my lands and other property. She is to pay my mother Elizabeth Boings
$50 within twelve months after my death if she should live to enjoy it.
Signed: Ephraim Bowen. Wit: Thomas Lamar, Joseph (‡ his mark) Howard,
__becca (+ her mark) Hawkins. Proven in Open Court and ordered to be
recorded 25 Feb. 1800.

Pages 166-168. Inventory and appraisement of the personal estate of
Ephraim Bowings, dec'd. 18 Apr. 1800. Total: $368.50.
Appraisers: Thomas Lamar, Joseph Howard, Daniel Hunt.

                Account of moneys paid out: Proven account of Thomas
Lamar, Elizabeth Bowings for one horse in lieu of $50, Jacob Levert (?),
John Reddock.

Page 169.   Received this 7 Feb. 1814 from Henry Hurt and Joel Hurt,
admrs. of the estate of William Hurt dec'd. $62.91½ it
being the full amount of my proportion of a certain tract of land lying
in the State of Tennessee and left to be sold in will by my grandfather
Washington and the money to be divided equally between Ephraim Rose,
John Rose and Pleasant White, rec'd. by me a guardian for Pleasant White.
Signed: Howell Rose, Guardian. Test: Thos. W. Baxter (?).

Pages 170-173. Inventory and Appraisement of the personal estate of
Hosea Bradford late dec'd. as appraised 19 Apr. 1800.
Total: $220.75. Appraisers: Geo. Williams, Wm. Hill, Wm. Williams.
Robert Rivers, qualified, adm.

                Account of sales as sold 10 Feb. 1800. Buyers: Sabry
Bradford, Peter Mahone, Samuel Halley, William Hill, Malone Mullins,
William Barron, Henry Greene, Thomas Spencer, Francis Lawson, Jacob
Pruet, Brice Miller (bought a tomahawk), John Bond, Gideon Bond, John
Greyor, Thomas Owsley. Signed: Robert Rivers, Adm. Total: $285.25.

                Money paid out: Barbary Bradford's receipt for $139.20;
to James Pruet for hunting up the cattle of said estate, Robert Rivers

proven acct.

Page 174 blank.

Page 175.   An Inventory and Appraisement of the estate of Isham
             Thompson dec'd. 3 Mar. 1800. Notes: John Michael, James
Lucas, Hugh Hall, Edmond Corley. Total: $812.81. Appraisers: James
Lucas, John Burch, Jerard Burch. Edmond Corley, Adm. Account of sales
carried to Book AAAA, page 23.

BOOK AAA

Page 1.   Will of John Respess, dated 1 Mar. 1800. "Being reduced
             by a long serious of afflictions to a very weak state of
body." To my beloved wife Nancy Respess all my property both real and
personal during her natural life as a donation for her kind services and
tenderness towards me, which I hope she may enjoy without interruption
from any person. At the death of my wife I give to my nephew, Thomas
Respess, my land on the head of North fort Creek, deeded to me by Esqr.
John Hamilton. At the death of my brother Richard is to take my
Negro man Tom Punch into his care and keep him while he lives. To my
niece Polly Lockey my Negro girl called Rose, and my will and desire is
for my niece Polley Lockey to hire out said Rose for two years and pay
the hire to my Executors to be put to interest for my niece Polley Respess Lockey, till she comes of age or marries. At the death of my wife,
all remaining property not before given, to be sold and the money equally
divided between all my brothers and sisters children and grand children
that is now in this state except Thomas Respess, Polley Lockey and Polley
Respess Lockey whose legacies are already given, provided nevertheless
that there be any among them that are objects of pity and charity, my
will and desire in that case is that they should be relieved out of said
money as far as my executors may think right in the sight of God. Exors:
dearly beloved wife Nancy Respess, and trusty and well beloved brethren
and friends, Richard Respess Senr., John Henderson and Jesse McKinne
Pope. Signed: John Respess. Wit: John Purify, James Lockey. No date
of probate.

Pages 3-5.   Inventory and appraisement of estate of John Respess
              late dec'd. 22 Sep. 1800. Negroes listed: girl Rose,
man Tom. Total: $666.25. Appraisors: Lewis Barnes, Isham Rees, John
Brown. Richd. Respess Senr., John Henderson, Exors.

             Account of sales, 18 Oct. 1800. Buyers: John Crowder,
Casy Askew, Thomas C. Spencer, Joseph Hartley, Nicholas Lamb, James Rees,
Stephen Daniell, James Shakelford, James Gray, Frederick Echols, Jesse
Blaky, Robert Hartley, Widow Respess, Myles Greene, John Purify, William
Griggs, John Gay, Richard Respess. Books sold by name were Miltons
Paradise Regained, Psalm Books, Boston's Fourfold State, ditto Sermons,
Answer to Pain, Memorandum Book. Total: $143.34.

Pages 6-7 blank.

Pages 8-12.   Inventory and Appraisement of the Estate of Henry Dunn
              dec'd. 30 Jan. 1800. Total: $959.52. Appraisors: Loyd
Kelley, John Parker Senr., Joseph Howell. John Hicks, adm.

             Sale, 6 Feb. 1800. Buyers: Benjamin Oliver, Joseph
Howell, Nancy Dunn, James Wood, David Potter, Benjamin Humphrey, Robert
Butler, Allen Dorman, Jesse Butler, James Miller, Bud Fulsome, John Lary,
William Pritchett, John Hix, Alexander Steel, Richard Castleberry,
Hezekiah Howell, Cecil Camp, John Parker Senr., Loyd Kelly, Isaac Edmund-
son, James Miller. Total: $551.22.

             Account of moneys paid out, returned by John Hicks, adm.
Proven accounts: Jeremiah Lary, Hinchier Lary, Danby Lary, Nancy Dunn.

             Received 16 Aug. 1806 of John Hicks, adm. of estate of
Henry Dunn dec'd., my wife's third part in full of said estate being
$256.97. Signed: Willie Hillard. Wit: Wm. Rabun.

Received 16 Aug. 1806 of John Hicks, adm., the full amount of said estate belonging to Henry Dunn's three orphans namely William Dunn, Henry Dunn and Susanna Dunn amounting to $367.24. Signed: Willie Hillard, Guardian. Wit: Wm. Rabun.

Received 13 Aug. 1804 of John Hicks adm. of Henry Dunn dec'd. the full amount of my wife's legacy being one of the heirs of said deceased, amounting to $128.48. Signed: William Eavns. Wit: Wm. Rabun.

1824.   The above receipts registered by order of Court 3 Apr.

Pages 13-18.   Inventory and appraisement of the Estate of John Shakelford Senr. late dec'd. made 29 Sep. 1800. Negroes named: Old Tim, Hannah, Abrahm, Peter, Thony, Old Sarah, Sam, Dave, Bill, Ole Poe (?), Lucy, Silvy, George. Total: $6544.16. Appraisers: Jeremiah Moore, James Bishop, Brice Gaither. Administrators: Francis Shakelford, James Shakelford.

An account of money paid out, returned 27 Feb. 1802 by James Shakelford, adm. Receipts: John Shakelford for Nancy Shakelford, Betsy Shakelford, Polley Shakelford, John Shakelford for Fanny Shakelford, John and Francis Shakelford for Edmond Shakelford, Francis Lawson's receipt for Negroes, Ann Shakelford, John Shakelford's Relinquishment.

Page 19 blank.

Pages 20-23.   Will of William Lawson of Hancock Co. To my beloved wife Jane during her natural life, the plantation whereon I now live, negroes Daniel, Dick, Lett & Rachel, household furniture, stock etc., and after the death of my wife the personal part of the property to be equally divided between my sons Thomas, Mounford, Dudley & David. I have already given my son Francis a tract of land whereon he did formerly live, and which he sold unto Dr. Joshua Lacy. I give to my son Francis after the death of my wife, a negro fellow called Jack. To my son William Lawson the tract of land whereon he now lives containing 218 acres, also a negro man named Bartlett and woman named Hannah, furniture, stock, horse, etc. After the death of my wife, the plantation whereon I now live including the Mill be equally divided between my two sons Thomas and David. I also give my son Thomas a Negro man named Abraham and one named Neil, furniture, horse, etc. To my son Mountford a tract of land whereon my son John did live, negroes David and Hannah, furniture, horse, etc. To my son Dudley one bounty of land to be purchased by my executors, horse, etc. To my son David the half of the plantation whereon I now live, two negroes Mill and Sutton, horse, etc. Whereas I have given unto the heirs of my son John Lawson by deed of gift one negro winch and other matters that may appear by the said deed, I also give the heirs of my said son John ten shillings and no more. To my daughter Sarah Thomas a Negro man named Pompey and woman Beck, a mare, saddle, furniture etc. which she has already received. To my daughter Mary Slaughter a Negro boy named Dick and girl Nan, mare, saddle, etc. To my daughter Jane Lawrence a Negro man Harry, a girl Stace (?), horse, etc. To my daughter Margaret Bullock a Negro man James and girl Rachel, horse, etc. Exors: well beloved wife Jane, son Francis Lawson and Reubin Slaughter. Dated 30 Apr. 1799. Signed: W. Lawson. Wit: Will Dent, James Barnes, Robert Newsom. Proved 25 Oct. 1800 in Open Court in Hancock Co. by Barnes & Newsom. Jane Lawson and Francis Lawson qualified as Executors.

Pages 24-26.   Inventory and Appraisement of the Estate of Wm. Lawson Dec'd., 18 Dec. 1800. Negroes named: man Will, boy Sutton, boy Jack, boy Abraham, boy Neal, boy David, woman Mill & child Doll, woman Rachel, girl Hannah, old woman Lett. One note of hand on Samuel Yarbrough. Total $4821.29. Appraisers: Risdon Moore, Andw. Baxter, Jno. Bailey.

Items sold 15 Jan. 1801: Buyers: Robert Ransom, Benjamin Woodruff, Samuel Dent.

Pages 28-32.   Inventory and Appraisement of the Property of John
                Swinney Dec'd 3 Mar. 1800. Negroes named: man Dick,
woman Patt, man Phill, man Handy, man Bob, woman Mill, woman Ginney,
woman Rose, woman Charity, boy Harry, boy Ben, girl Sary, girl Dicy,
girl Luce, boy Joe, boy Isaac, woman Esther, girl Beck, woman Ann, girl
Benir, boy Ned. Total: $6757.58. Appraisers: Alexander Reid, Andw.
Baxter, Thads. Holt. Notes on Mr. Moore, Jas. Bishop Jr., Thadeus Holt,
Jesse Clark, Thomas Low. 658 acres land, 287½ acres Washinton Co., 400
acres Camden Co. not appraised. Total $2209.36. Administrators: Nathl.
Robertson, Rosey Swinney. Dated 25 Oct. 1800.

            Account of money paid out: Receipts from Jeremiah Moore,
Ransom Swinney, James Bishop, Jeremiah Moore (guardian) receipt for money
rec'd. for Dudley Swinney, Rosey Swinney as guardian for Wilson Swinney,
John Freeman, Jesse Baker, John Shakelford, Myles Greene (clerk), J.
Dudley Swinney, Clerk's receipt for cost in a suit admrs. of John Swin-
ney vs. Freeman Lewis, B. Hall, J. Nelson, John B. Devereux, Theophilus
Thomas, Lea Abercombie, Wm. Ware, Henry Gaines, Hamblin Lewis, Septimus
Weatherly, Sterling Howard, Jas. Thweatt, David Clements, John Lucas,
Thads. Holt, Martin Martin, Nathaniel Robertson, Doctr. Bird.

Pages 33-36.   Papers of the estate of Axiom O'Neal dec'd. as brought
                from the Clerk of Ordinary's office in Greene Co. and
ordered to be recorded in this office. Appraisement: Negroes named:
Venus, Pegg, Hannah, boy Cary. Total: Ⱡ458.0.5. Inventory of Notes and
Open Accounts: Names listed: Lewis Barnes, Jno. Alford, Moses Wiley,
Turner & Hall, Richd. Mills, Thomas Spencer, Nathaniel Culver, James
Brazewell, John Jack, William Biggins, Stephen Evans, Phillip Pritchett,
John Griggs, Alexander Dunn, David Dixon, Edmund Oneal, John Butler,
Stephen Powell, Saml. Brazell, Wooten Oneal, John Whitehurst, Jesse
Grigg, Hannah Smith, Cader Powell, Lewis Bandy. (These were evidently
store accounts.) Total amount of estate: Ⱡ525.6.3 3/6. Reg. 28 Jul.
1794, Wm. Phillips, R.P. Greene Co., Clerk's Office: The foregoing are
a true copy of the Estate now on record in my office - 12 May 1800. Tho.
Carleton, CCGC.

            Vouchers of Estate of Axiom Oneal Dec'd. Paid: Jno.
McCullock for Schooling, M. Hammer, Jas. Thweatt, Boreland Mitchell,
George Hargraves, Isaac Moreland for schooling, Jno. White, Jno. Butler,
Nathan Oneal, Edmund Oneal, Wm. Farrell, Edmd. Moore for schooling,
Richard Holmes, Thomas Morriss for boarding & schooling orphans of Axiom
Oneal. Date of last entry: 1797.

Pages 37-41.   Will of Levi Daniell of Hancock Co., dated 8 Dec. 1800,
                in a low state of health. To my beloved wife Martha
during her natural life, 150 acres land including the dwelling house and
premises whereon I now live on Island Creek, to be laid off on a square
adjoining a dividing line that may be hereafter run between my Stepmother
Nancy Daniell and myself agreeable to my father's will, and to adjoin
the lands of John Harbirt. I also lend to my wife Negroes Abby, Ivey,
Lucy, March, Sam, Friday, George, Flora the younger, and Maggy. After
my wife's death the land and negroes to be equally divided between my
three children hereinafter named. To my son James Daniell 100 acres on
Island Creek adj. the land lent to my wife and adj. Robert Carr & John
Ragan. Also to James the use and profits of one half of a tract of land
in Washington Co. as I am interested in same by the will of my father
James Daniell Dec'd. Also to son James the following Negroes: Will, Rose,
Sampson, Aleck, Moses, Bill, Hannah, Milley and Molley. To my daughter
Catherine Daniell one half of the remainder of the lands that I own on
the waters of Island and Rockey Creek. Also the following Negroes: Cato,
Flora the elder, Toby, July, Simon, Harriot, Cynthia & John. To my
daughter Juliett all the remaining part of my lands on waters of Island
or Rockey Creek on a division with my daughter Catharine, be there 100
acres. Also to Juliett the following Negroes: Joe, Nan, Armor, Jack,
Abram, Sue, Davy, Ben, Siller, Tom, & Dinah. All the lands lent to my
Stepmother Nancy Daniell by my father's will adj. the lands whereon I
now live which falls to me as my Stepmother's decease to be divided among
my three children. Exors: trusty friend Robert McGinty, Senior and John
Harbirt. Signed: Levi Daniell. Wit: John Lamar, Stephen Horton, Philip
Cook. Proved in Open Court and ordered recorded 5 Jan. 1801. Nominated

Executors qualified. M. Greene, CCO.

Pages 41-47.   Inventory and Appraisement of estate of Levi Daniell
                 Dec'd. as returned by John Harbirt and Robert McGinty,
Exors. 30 Jan. 1801. Negroes named are the same as named in will. Inventory was extensive and included several religious books. Total:
$10,157.62½. Appraisers: Thos. Lamar, Henry Low, Lazr. Battle. A List
of Notes and Accounts belonging to the Estate for want of room here is
carried to Book AAA, p. 73. Money paid out: Elijah Bivins, John Comer
for L. Abercrombie (tax), Stephen Horton, Robt. Hendrick & Matthew
Howell, Jas. Pinkston, John Knight, Bird B. Tindall, Joseph Baker, Nancy
Daniell's Rect. for her part of a Machine and division of stock, Duncan
McLean, D. Clements, Joseph McGinty, "cash paid expenses of a negroe
hunting a beast," Clements & Reynolds, Martha Daniell, Nathan Cook,
Solomon Mangham, Clement Moore, Lazarus Battle. Cash received 1801-1802:
Samuel Hulley for John Wilson, David Clements, Drury Jackson, Phillip
Cook, Isham Brooks, John Armstrong, Henry Green, Matthew Durham for John
Hamblen, Abraham Miles, Samuel Parker, Francis Stubbs, Abraham Miles.

Pages 48-49.   Will of Dorothy Adamson of Hancock Co., sick of body,
                 dated 12 Nov. 1794. To my daughter Mary all my bedding
and wearing apparel. The rest of my property to be sold and equally
divided between Anner McDonald, Elizabeth McDonald, Alexander McDonald,
and Charles James McDonald, children of my daughter Mary and Charles Mc-
Donald. Exors: daughter Mary and her husband Charles McDonald. Signed:
Dorothy Adamson. Wit: Catherine McDonald, Charles (X) McThay (?), P.
Boyle, JP. Proved by Peter Boyle, Esq. 5 Jan. 1801.

           Account of sales of the estate of Dorothy Adamson Dec'd.
made 12 Nov. 1808: Negroes: Woman Charlott, boy Jack, Abraham, Isaac.
Books including Bunyans Works 6 Vols. Total sales $1050.75, all purchas-
ed by Alex. McDonald. Signed: Charles McDonald, Acting Executor.

Pages 50-51 blank.

Pages 52-55.   Will of Christopher Williams of Hancock Co., dated 21
                 Sep. 1800. To my two sons Joseph Williams and William
Williams one bounty of land to be equally divided between them, a cow &
calf each. To my beloved daughter Margate Williams one Sorrel mare,
saddle & bridle. Joseph Williams may have a colt from the sorrel mare.
Also other items to Margate. To my daughter Elizabeth Williams a bay
mare, saddle, bridle & other items. My son William Williams is to have
one colt from the bay mare. To my daughter Easter Williams one young
horse worth $80 to be purchased out of my estate for her, & other items.
To my daughter Rachel Barnheart $10. To my three youngest daughters
Sarah Williams, Mary Williams & Bethania Williams, a cow and a calf each.
To my dear and beloved wife Margate Williams all the remainder of my
estate during her natural life or widowhood, after which it is to go to
my three youngest daughters Sarah, Mary & Bethania Williams. Exors: wife
Margate and Robert Clark, Cornelius Clark and William Clark. Signed:
Christopher Williams. Wit: Jeremiah (X) Thrower, Benjamin (X) Laster,
Wm. Clark. Proved in Open Court 5 Jan. 1801, and Robert Clark and Mar-
garet Williams qualified as Exors.

Pages 55-58.   Inventory, Appraisement & Sales of the Estate of Christo-
                 pher Williams, Dec'd. No Negroes listed. Notes of hand:
Joseph White, Thomas Heath. Accounts against David Adams & Phillip
Barronhart. Total: $1167.87. Appraisers: Nathl. Sledge, Jno. Sledge,
Jno. Adams.

           Account of vouchers of money paid out, returned 1 Jun.
1801: Ransom Mitchell (Legatee), Phillip Barnhart (Legatee), George Sims'
receipt for his wife's legacy in full, Greene Sims' receipt for his wife's
legacy in full (p. 58), J. Nelson's proven account, receipt given by Geo.
Sims, guardian for Joseph & William Williams' part of the estate.

           Sale of Personal estate as sold 27 Nov. 1802: Buyers:
Jeremiah Thrower, Philip Barnheart, Colson Heath, Hardy Wheelis, Greene
Sims, Judkins Hunt, David Adams, James Rollins, Kinchen Carter, Daniel
Low, John Bridges.

Pages 59-62.   Inventory, Appraisement & Sales of Estate of John
                Southall, dec'd. Negroes named: girls Lucy, Sall &
Agge. Notes: Jas. Adams, John V. Patillo. Total: $320.00. Appraisers:
Jon. Adams, Robert Clrk, Wm. Clark. Adm: Nathl. Sledge, Rebekah South-
all. No date. Additional appraisment carried to Book AAAA, p. 18.

                Account of sales as sold 18 Oct. 1800. Buyers: Robert
Hill, Jas. Adams, Thomas Conner, Noah Doddridge, Rebeckah Southall,
Nathaniel Sledge, John Bridges, Shurly Sledge, James Bridges, Peyton
Sledge, Nathan Morgan, John Gilleon, Robert Clark, John Wallace, Joshua
Mitchell, William Sutton, John Sledge, Joseph Bridges, John Rymes,
William Wallace, William Clark, Drury Chaves, John V. Patillo, Asa
Sutton. Vouchers Registered in Book AAAA, p. 87.

Pages 63-71.   Sale of the Estate of John Cook, dec'd., brought from
                page 13 in Book AA. Buyers: John Cook, John Gholson,
John Harbirt, Michael Maddox, Seth Kennedy, Joseph Montgomery, Isaac
King, John Edmondson, Herbert Brown, Robert Finch, Mordecai Jacobs,
Moses Marshall, John Gray, Benjamin Wallis, William Vaughan, Matthew
Hawkins, John Hamlin, Jacob Collins, Richard Hamlin, Robert Williams,
Jeremiah Walker, William Butler, William Wynn, Matthew Kinchen, Miss
Gracy Cook, Michael Maddox, Thomas Glenn, Mrs. Sarah Cook, Malone Mullins,
Henry Trippe, Stephen Waller, John Smith, Joseph Montgomery, Benjamin
Bolt, Jonathan Johns, James Horton, Charles Miller, Charles McDonald,
Joseph Denson, Elisha Waller, Jeremiah Spiller, John Humphries, Solomon
Thornton, Henry Low, Isaac King, Joseph Cox, Thomas Lamar, Miss Patience
Cook, Caleb Bazer, Simon Brewer, Stephen Horton. Total $2159.78½. John
Harbirt, Philip Cook, John Cook, Admrs.

                Account of the hire of Negroes: John Cook hired Arthur,
Joan & little boy Arthur.   John Harbirg hired Joe, Nan & 4 children.
John Hudman hired Sam, Hannah & 2 children; also Anthony. Jonathan Johns
hired Fanny.   Charles McDonald hired Vol & Jinny. Mathew Durham hired
Frank.   Samuel Halley hired Peter. Thomas Glenn hired Esther. John
Winslet hired Edith.

                2 Jan. 1799, Rent of the Plantation of deceased for said
year: John Gray, Robert Williams, Joseph Denson, William Butler, Howell
Brewer, John Cook.

                Hire of Negroes and Rent of Plantation for the year 1800:
John Cook - 3 negroes Arthur, Joan & boy Arthur; William Bird - 5 Negroes
Sam, Hannah & 3 children; William Hutchinson 5 negroes Joe, Nan & 3
children; John Cook 2 Negroes Vol & Jinny; Lazarus Battle, Fanny; Abner
Abercrombie, Edith; Stephen Waller, Frank; Charles McDonald, Peter;
John Cook, Anthony. Rent of land: Peter McFarlin, John Gray, Robert
Williams, James Horton, John Cook.

                Another list of Negroes hired and land rented has many
of same names.

                Another sale dated 10 Jun. 1799. Names of buyers not
listed previously: Peter Flournoy, William Blakey, Solomon Mangham,
Stephen Williams, William Ingram, Samuel Felps, Morton Gray, John Murphy.

Page 72.   1 Feb. 1817. Estate of Christopher Williams, Robert
                Clark and Margarett Thrower, Exors. Receipt of John
Kindrick for Mary Williams, now Mary Kindricks, for part of the estate
of said dec'd. in full. Signed: John Kindrick.

                18 Feb. 1817. Received of Robert Clark & Margaret
Thrower, Exors. $135 in full of my part of the Estate of said deceased.
Signed: Sally Williams. Wit: William Williams.

Pages 74-76.   Inventory and appraisement of Personal Estate of Jesse
                Boran Dec'd. made 8 Sep. 1803. Total: $508.87½. Andw.
Baxter, Eli Harris, Jon Adams, appraisers.

                "The account in favour of this estate against the estate
of Alexander Reid is incorrect as appears by vouchers filed that the

account ought to have been only $117.31½ instead of $406.00 as it stands stated in the inventory altered by order of court. Myles Green, Clk."

Sale of the Estate of Jesse Boran dec'd. dated 15 Oct. 1803. Buyers: Nancy Boran, Eli Harris, Peyton Sledge, Stephen Durdan, John Hearn, Samuel Ferguson, Robert Mills, Abram Laurence, James Adams, Eli Mash (?), Abraham Lawrence, adm.

Money paid out: Abm. Lawrence, Eli Harris, Shadrack Bowe, Myles Greene, Robert Mills, John Hearn, Charles Simmons, Mrs. Nancy Boran, Jonathan Clower.

Monies Rec'd: Andrew Baxter, Payton Sledge, Robert Clark, Eli Marsh, Samuel Ferguson, Abraham Laurence, Eli Harris.

BOOK AAAA

Pages 2-3.   Will of John Swint of Hancock Co., dated 12 Jan. 1801, in a low state of health. To my dearly beloved wife Elizabeth all my property during her widowhood except one horse which I gave my dearly beloved son John, when he is 21, the family is to have use of the horse until then. My wife is to give to my children that is not grown such property as she can spare as they come of age. If my wife should die or marry before the children grow up, there shall be an equal distribution of the property between John, Edmond, Frederick, James, William, Joseph & Saml., all my children. Exors: James Bonner & Jos. Green. Signed: John Swint. Wit: (unreadable), Abr. Boreland. Proved in Open Court 28 Mar. 1801.

Pages 3-4.   Inventory and Appraisement of the Estate of John Swint dec'd. 25 Feb. 1802. Total $413.25.

Book Accounts: Stephen Jackson, Wilder Newman, Charles Allen, Daniel Hogins.

Pages 6-9.   Inventory and appraisement of the Estate of Richard Lockhart Dec'd. 14 Nov. 1800. Negroes named: men Charles & Stiff, women Phebe & Silvey, girl Juda, boys Ransom & Peter. Some items: 1 Northward Still contents 40 gallons, set of surveying instruments. Total: $3291.43 3/4. Appraisers: Jesse Pope, Reubin Jones, Jonas Shivers. Admrs: Mary Lockhart, Collin Pope, Wm. Rabun.

Account of Sales: Buyers: Wm. Owsley, Jefry Barksdale, William Battle Esq., Thomas King, William Turner, Collin Pope, James Miller, Jonas Shivers, John Pope, Jesse Allen, Jesse Pope, M. Middlebrooks, Hardy Hawkins.

Account of moneys paid out: Jonas Shivers, Thompson Bird, Appleton Rossiter, Temple Lee, Charity Low, Thomas Grace, Collin Pope, all proven accounts. Cash collected on note of Saml. Betts 2 Jul. 1810.

"The administrators of the Estate of Richard Lockheart dec'd. returned a receipt in full for all the real and personal property belonging to said Estate signed by John Benton, Guardian for the orphans and Legatees, dated 7 Jan. 1811."

Pages 10-13.   Inventory, Appraisement & Sales of the Estate of Byre Bynum dec'd. made 4 Feb. 1801. Total: $6.38 3/4. Wm. Rabun, W. Hardwick, Joseph Grant, appraisers.

Sale. Buyers: David Henry, Wm. Hardwick, Wm. Spikes, Levi Spikes, Willis Shivers, Richd. Ship, John Reid, Joel Holcomb, Wm. Battle, Jas. Tomlin, David Dixon, Shadrack Roe, Wm. Biggins, Joseph Grant, Betsy Byrum, David D. Smith, Robt. Wood. Wm. Spikes, Adm.

Pages 14-16.   Inventory & Appraisement of the Estate of Dorothy Adamson dec'd. made 31 Jan. 1801. Negroes listed: woman Charlotte, boys Jack, Abram & Isaac. Thirty-five books listed by name, including religious works and Arabian Nights. Appraisers: John Harbit,

John Cook, John Ragan. Exor: Charles McDonald.

Page 18.   Estate of John Southall dec'd., articles omitted in the
                 former appraisement of same. Robert Clark, Jon. Adams,
Wm. Clark, appraisers.

                 "Acct. belonging to the estate of John Southall dec'd.
from the estate of John Sledge Dec'd. 10 Aug. 1802. $6.66. Signed:
Rebekah (X) Clark, adm."

Pages 19-22.   Inventory, Appraisement & Sale of the Estate of Basdel
                 Foster dec'd. Negroes listed: woman Lott, boys Jim &
Abram, girl Amy. Total: $1001.50. Shad. Roe, Dav. Henry, Jon Adams,
appraisers.

                 Sale 14 Feb. 1801. Buyers: James Hill, John Bridges,
Robert Middlebrooks, John Foster, Thomas Smith, John Brewer, Wm. Clower,
David Henry, Thomas Willcoxan, Wm. Rimes, Nicholas Booty, Asa Sutton,
Salley Foster, Jonathan Adams, Stephen Durdan, Stephen Henry, Joseph
Middlebrooks, James Clark, Robert Clark, James Reid, Colson Heath, Robert
Hill. Balance of sale carried to page 129.

                 Money paid out. Proven accounts: Nathaniel Sledge, John
Smith, Hardin Ives, Thomas Wilcoxen, David Henry, Robert Hill, Jeremiah
Nelson's Doctor bill, Robert Clark. Salley Foster's receipt for her
proportion of said dec'd - $269.00. Receipt of W. D. Lane, $12.00.

Page 20.   Account sales of the Estate of Isham Thompson dec'd.
                 sold 3 Mar. 1800. Items sold: One mare, wearing apparel,
one pair saddle bags. An account of moneys paid out, Vouchers returned
by Edmond Corley, admr. Jesse Thompson's receipt in full for his account
and legacy (no amount given); Benjamin Thompson, legatee, $42.50; Rebekah
Jones, legatee, receipt in full (no amount); Gideon Thompson, legatee,
in full for his part, $35.00; John Sherman's account for schooling,
$6.25; Edmond Corley's proven Account, $81.00; Tolefer (?) & Doughty;
Doctor Lee; Susanah McIntosh recpt. for $30, John Thompson's order to
Jno. Michael.

Page 24.   Jesse Clark, dec'd. An account of moneys paid out.
                 Vouchers: Samuel Maddux, Joshua Shropshire, Jamison
Andrews, Jesse Connell, William Owsley, legatee, $136.71; James Harvey,
legatee, $140; David Christopher, legatee, $83; Jas. Christopher recpt.
$42; David Christopher recpt. $20.65; Thomas Clark, legatee, $202; John
Jones as per due bill, $260.59; James Harvey, legatee, $16; D. D. Smith's
acct. John Myrick's due bill; Wm. Owsley's bill for goods; Wm. Pallsey
Cooper & O. Richardson's note.

Pages 26-27.   Will of Tunstall Roan of Hancock Co., planter, sick of
                 body, dated 25 Sep. 1800. To my beloved wife Milley,
six negroes Isaac, Hethy, Harriot, Nutt, Biller & Squire, and my plantation whereon I now live with all stock, crop, etc. as long as she lives.
At her death all to be divided equally amongst my beloved children James
Roan, George Roan and Nancy George, with Nancy having $200 more than an
equal share. Exors: wife Milley, James & George Roan and Elijah George.
s/ Tunstall Roan. Wit: John Wilson, Ajonadab Read, John Bates. Proved
in Open Court 1 Jun. 1801 by Ajonadab Read & John Wilson.

Pages 28-29.   Inventory & Appraisement of Estate of Tunstall Roan,
                 dec'd. returned by Milley Roan and George Roan, Exors.
14 Aug. 1801. Negroes named: man Isaac, women Hetty & Nutty, girls
Heicenty (?) & Sindyrilla, boy Squire. Total appraisal $1960.25.
Ajonadab Reed, Benja. Whitefield, James Alford & John Wilson, appraisers.

Pages 32-36.   Inventory, Appraisement & Sales of the estate of Francis
                 Dannelly, dec'd. 11 Apr. 1801. Debts to the estate:
Hardy Smith, Ducan McLean, Richard Hamlin. Appraisers: John Rivers,
Tully Choice, Lewis Parker. Administrators: Arthur Dannelly, George
Stephens. Buyers at Sale: Elizabeth Dannelly, James McKissack, James
McCormack, Jesse Clements, George Stephens, William Simmons, Samuel Brady,
Thomas Bradford, Thomas Stephens, John Rivers, Arthur Fail, Lew Tucker,

Henry Jackson, Jane Dannelly, Elizabeth Dannelly Junr. Old Debts collected since: James Somer, Richard Hamlin, Edward Hatcher. "An account of the moneys paid out & collected stands in page 149."

Pages 37-39.   Inventory & Appraisement of estate of Albright Averat, dec'd. 6 Jan. 1801. Negroes named: man Catoe, woman Salley and two children, woman Silvy. Appraisers: William Cureton, Thomas Dickson, Wm. Gilliland. Buyers at sale 8 & 9 Jan. 1810: Arch. Averatt bought 1 negro woman and 2 children Frank & Stephen, and man Cato; Patty Griffin bought the negro winch named Silvy. Other buyers: John Averat, Zach Bickim (?), Wm. Worthen, Wm. Averat Junr., Richard Worthen, Joshua Jacobs, Arthur Herring, Robert McCook, Benjamin Averat, Jno. Caudle, Bolin Curenton, Shadk. Taylor, John Averat Junr., Wm. Pritchit, Jas. Wadsworth, Edward Denton, John Graves, Sterling Ammons, Patty Griffin, Joseph Jacobs, James Page, William Averat Senr., Jno. Brown, Sanders Herring, Thos. Dixon, David Averat, Assa Jordon. Total sales, bonds and notes $2035.98. Exors: wife Sarah and son John. s/ Isham Huckabee. Wit: Mitchel Morriss, Drury Cook. No date of probate.

Page 41.   Estate of Robert Bryan deceased. Money paid out 1799: Benjamin Whitefield & wife, Thomas Ryding, Doctor R. H. Lee, Joshua Lacy, Nicholas Thomas. 1800: D. Septimus Weatherby, James Alford, Michael Collins, schoolmaster. To the support & maintenance of seven white children from 1 May 1800 to 1 Jan. 1801 at $3 each per month; two negroes ditto at $1.50 per month. Widows dower on $540.37 being the amount of sale of property not particularly willed. Cash due and received from John Read $50. "The Return of expenditures for 1801 of the above estate carried to page 80 for want of room here."

Page 42.   Inventory & Appraisement of estate of Benjamin Waller late deceased 30 Jan. 1801. Total $35.12. Appraisers: William Alford, James Waller Senr., Littleton Carter. Stephen Waller, adm., qualified.

Pages 43-45.   Will of Daniel Johnson Low of Hancock Co., weak in body, dated 17 Mar. 1800. To my beloved wife Elizabeth, negroes Dick, Alse, Nell, Lucy, Salley, Nan & little Dick; also household & kitchen furniture, mares and colts during her life or widowhood. To my son William Low, 5 shillings sterling and no more, to him & his heirs forever. To my grandson Daniel Low the remainder of my negroes, Ben, Vilet, Jefry, Daniel, Suck, Poll & Forest, and any outstanding debts due me. After the death or marriage of my wife Elizabeth, my grandson Daniel Low is to have all the property that I have lent to my wife. Exor: grandson Daniel Low. s/ Daniel Johnson Low. Wit: John Foster, Reuben Foreman, John Damron. Proved in Open Court 2 Sept. 1801.

Pages 46-47.   Will of Joshua Kenny of Hancock Co., dated 14 Jun. 1801. "In a weak and low state of bodily health and expect drawing near the close of life." Four of my horses and wagon should be sold for the payment of my debts. To my beloved wife Catherine, choice of any two of my horses, all stock of every kind, household furniture. I also lend to her the land where I now live until the child she is now pregnant with arrives at lawful age to whom I give and bequeath it, but should the child not live to lawful age, I give it to my son Anderson when he becomes 21 years old. My negro woman Nan should be sold at the descretion of my executors and the proceeds used to the purchase of smaller ones which I give and bequeath unto my son Anderson and daughter Nanny equally. To my daughter Betsy my negro girl Juda. Exors: beloved wife Catherine and friends Obadiah Richardson & Joseph Bryan. s/ Joshua (X) Kenney. Wit: Nathan Daniel, Samuel (X) Parsons. Proved in Open Court 2 Sep. 1801.

Page 48.   Inventory & Appraisement of goods & chattels of Daniel Johnson Low dec'd. 30 Nov. 1801. Negroes named: Dick, Alsa, Lucy, Ned, Vilet, Ben, Sall, Suke, Nan, Moll, Dick, Forest, Alsa. Total $3366.12. s/ Daniel Low, qualified Exor.; Appraisers Stephen Evans, Robert Hill, David Adams.

Pages 49-51 blank.

Pages 52-53.   Inventory, Appraisement & Sales of estate of Thomas
                 Lyon, deceased, 11 Apr. 1801. Notes & Accounts against
Jas. Comer, Malica (?) Brantly (?). Total appraisement $249.27. Buyers
at sale: Joshua Askey, William Thornton, William Purify, Jesse Blakey,
John T. Spencer, William Griggs, Arrington Purify, David Blakey, William
Blakey, Hubbard, James Arter, Casey Askey, Joseph Bullock, Hubard
Ferrell, Stephen Daniell, John Whitehurst, Charles Hurt, Betsey Lyons.
William Griggs, Adm. "Further account of the above estate is found in
page 130."

Page 54.   Will of Isham Huckebey of Hancock Co., dated 28 May 1801.
                 To my beloved wife Sarah Huckabee all my estate real &
personal, except what is hereafter excepted, during her natural life,
and after her death what remains to be equally divided between my eight
children: Mary Faner, John, Nancy, Kesiah, Jeremiah, James, Josiah &
Betsey Huckabee. Also to my son John Huckabee, one horse called Herod,
a saddle, bridle, cow, calf & yearling. Exors: wife Sarah and son John.
s/ Isham Huckabee. Wit: Mitchel Morriss, Drury Cook. No date of probate.

Pages 55-56.   Inventory & Appraisement of estate of Isham Huckeby dec'd.
                 as returned by Sarah Huckeby & John Huckeby Exors. 22
Oct. 1801. Total $824.37. s/ Drury Cook, Mitchell Morris, Loyd Kelley,
JP, appraisers.

Page 57 is blank.

Page 58.   Account of sales, part of the estate of Thomas Fail,
                 dec'd. Buyers: James Fail, Francis Fail, Thomas Fail.
"the balance of sale in BB 206."

Page 59.   Account of sales, part of the property of estate of
                 Axiom Oneal dec'd. sold 12 May 1800. One bounty of land
287½ acres $979.10; one negro boy named Simon, $180.50. No buyers listed.

Pages 60-61.   Inventory, appraisement, & sales of the estate of Edward
                 Worsham, dec'd. Appraisal 7 Apr. 1801. Total $539.23.
s/ John C. Mason, Robert S. Ransom, Tayor Nelson, appraisers. Reubin
Slaughter, adm. Sales 14 Apr. 1801. Buyers: Reubin Slaughter, Samuel
Butler, John C. Mason, Buckner Duke, William Lawson, Joseph Heginbotham,
Tayler Nelson.

Page 62.   Inventory & Appraisement of estate of Elisha Ellis, dec'd.
                 14 May 1801. "Total carried over" $153.31; evidently
incomplete; no appraisers named.

Pages 63-64 missing; possibly skipped over during microfilming.

Page 65.   Account of moneys paid out of estate of Henry Dunn,
                 dec'd. (Marked out; no other entry.)

Page 66.   Inventory & Appraisement of estate of Joseph Dawdle,
                 dec'd. 5 Nov. 1801. Total $94.80; no appraisers or
administrator named.

Page 67 blank.

Pages 68-69.   Will of John Castleberry, dated 21 Apr. 1801, in a low
                 state of health. To my beloved wife Mary Ann my house
and plantation, stock, household furniture, etc. during her natural life.
To my beloved son James Castleberry my house and plantation after the
death of my wife. My wife may dispose of the furniture and stock as she
pleases at her death; if she thinks it advantageous to sell the house
and plantation I authorize my executors or any two of them to do so and
buy a tract of land of equal value and convey the same to my son James.
Exors: wife Mary Ann, Joab Durham, Allen Gay. s/ John (X) Castleberry.
Wit: P. Boyle, Benja. Thompson, Jeremiah Castleberry. Proved by Peter
Boyle 30 Jan. 1802.

Page 70.   Inventory and Appraisement of estate of John Castleberry
                 dec'd. 6 Mar. 1802. Total $350.25. s/ Peter Boyle,

308

Francis Lewis Senr., John Buckner, Edmond Beard, appraisers. s/ Mary
Ann Castleberry, Joab Durham, Allen Gay, exors.

Pages 71-72 blank.

Pages 73-76.   Estate of Levi Daniel, dec'd. A list of notes of hand
                and open accounts: John Humphries, Drury Jackson, Andrew
Boreland & Lazarus Battle, Robert Williams, Henry Bond, Hardy Smith,
John Armstrong, John Reed, John Ragan, William Hardage. A list of notes
of hand belonging the one half to the estate of Levi Daniell dec'd. and
the other half to Nancy Daniell: John Humphries, William Weeks, William
Smith, Drury Andrews & Francis Strother, Caleb Bazer & Wm. Bazer, Fran-
cis Stubbs, Lewis Underwood & Robert Rivers. Book accounts belonging
half to said deceased and half to Nancy Daniell: John Bond, William
Butler, Reubin Blankinship, Francis Lawson, John Greer, Joseph Benson,
John Dorse, John Hamlin, Matthew Kinchen, Nathaniel Mullins, Henry Green,
William Burgay & George Gray, Thomas Spencer, James Yarbrough Senr., John
McVay, Charles Sturdivant, John Waller, William Hill, Francis Stubbs,
John Cohoon, Abraham Fairchild, Ellington Morgan, Jeremiah Culverhouse,
William Spencer, John R. Gregory, Solomon Mangham, Benjamin Jacob, James
Scarlet, Elijah Hearn, Chas. McDonald, David Ticed (?), ----- Harrod,
Peter Mehone, Jonathan Godwin, Samuel Parker, Alexander Lyall, Henry
Lowe, Isham Brooks. s/ Robert McGinty, John Harbirt, Exors. 19 Jan.
1802.

                Account of cash received (mostly for bushels of corn)
dated 1804-1807: Haddaway, Wm. Rhodes, Benja. Parker, Dr. Berry Chapman,
Gates, Maffet, Wm. Fenly, Scott & Thomas, Saml. Files, Jos. McGinty,
John Robinson, John Jones, Geo. Simpson, Isaac Chapman, Robt. McGinty,
Charles Rhodes, Henry Rogers, Danl. Gafford, Abrim Miles. Total
$2043.25.

Pages 77-78.   Account of moneys paid out of estate of Levi Daniel dec'd.
                by Robert McGinty, Exor. 1801: Paid Stephen Horton's
proved account, William Horton's ditto. 1802: Lewis Parker for boarding
& schooling Jesse Oston in the preceding year and 1802. 1803: paid
Collector of the direct Washington tax. 1805: Paid Jas. Barrow on final
settlement being a balance due the legacy of James Taylor's heirs in
James Daniel's estate - $404.67. 1806: Paid D. Doyle, P. Cook, J. W.
Devereux, Wm. Monk, Z. Wade, Ellender Coleman, Richard G. Brown, Saml.
Buffington, Gachet & Stubbs, G. Simpson, Wm. Grayer, Freeman Lewis, Saml.
S. Steele, John Brown, Thos. Miles, B. Hubert, Isaiah Chapman, Doctr.
Wendorweddle for attention. 1807: George Simpson, B. Hall, John Robin-
son, Thad. Holt, Z. Lamar, John Neaves, William Jones, John Scott, A.
Bryson, Jas. Thweatt, John Ursery, Benjamin Thompson, Jacob Barrow.
"For further returns see Book E, page 126."

Page 79 blank.

Page 80.   Estate & Orphans of Robert Bryan dec'd. To Benja. White-
                field for the year 1801. Maintenance of 7 white children
1 year at $2.50 a month, 2 small negroes at $1.50 a month, 1 fine hat
for Betsey, John and Robert. Paid Doctor Weatherby for attendence and
medicine, Paid Henry Ransom for 5 months schooling, paid Amos Brantley's
account, John Wilson for teaching 3 children 10 months, Brown & Co.
Merchants in Augusta. A return of the hire of the negroes at one year's
credit, 5 Dec. 1801: 1 girl Judy to Benjamin Whitefield, boy Jery to
Henry Long, girl Amey to John Goode, small boy Dick to Jesse Bell, small
girl Polley. "Further accts. as above carried to page 124." s/ Dread
Wilder. Exor: Sarah Whitefield, Exrx.

Pages 81-82.   Inventory & Appraisement of estate of Charles Waller,
                dec'd 11 Apr. 1801. Total $240.62. John Bond Senr.,
Gideon Bond, William (X) Brooks, appraisers. Accounts due: John Hutson,
Turner Lamonson (?), Charles Owsley, Lewis Underwood, William Brooks,
John Hammack, ----- Burge, ----- Andrews, Burwel Yarbrough, Abraham
Reddick, Ellington Morgan, Thomas Owsley, Brice Miller, Sarah White,
Lewis Underwood Senr., Jacob Pruit, Frances Lawson & Licor (?), Joshua
Kenny. Total $88.80. Joseph Waller, Adm.

Pages 83-86.   Account of sales of the estate of Charles Waller, dec'd.
                sold 5 June. 1801. Buyers: Alexander Sample, Weldon
Owsley, Joseph Waller, Rachel Waller, Josiah Dennis, Jacob Pruit, Benja-
min Bolt, Nathaniel Halley, Peter Mahone, Leonard Cranford, Stephen
Waller, John Smith, Thomas Owlsey, Ellington Morgan, Littleberry Patillo,
James Pruit, William Barron, David Collum, Francis Lawson, Samuel Halley,
Barbara Bradford, James Yarbrough, Henry Greene, John Grear, William
Emberson, William Waller. Money paid out in proven accounts: Joseph
Waller, Henry Gaither, John Humphries, Simon Day, Nathl. Mullins, James
Pritchett, Isaiah Parker, John McLemore. 15 Dec. 1815: Received of
Joseph Waller Senr. Adm. of Charles Waller dec'd., $216.06 in full for
all demands against him in the capacity of administrator, I say received
by me the only surviving heir of said dec'd. s/ William Waller. Wit:
James C. Humphries, Nathl. Waller.

Page 87.   John Southall, dec'd. Money paid out, returned Feb.
                1806, proven accounts and notes: John Gillion, Robert
Hills, Thompson Bird, Mins Sledge, John Bridges, Jas. Arrington, Jonathan
Clower, Sterling Gardner, William Clark, Nathaniel Sledge.   Total $234.14.

Pages 88-89.   Inventory & Appraisement of estate of Thursby Brown,
                dec'd. 6 Mar. 1802. One note of hand given to Isham
Huckaby by Benjamin Oliver & Loyd Kelley, One ditto given to ditto by
Jas. Wilson & Lemuel Davidson, One ditto given to ditto by Willoby Fann
& Temple Lea, note given by Jacob Owen and Larkin Turner, notes by Anne
Thompson & Jesse Thompson, Job Taylor & James Miller, Drury Cook &
Benjamin Cook, Lemuel Davidson & Benjamin Cook. s/ Wm. Chandler, Loyd
Kelly, Drury Cook, appraisers. Sarah Huckaby, Admx. Monies paid out:
Milly Brown, legatee, $52.39; Aaron Brown, ditto, $61.24; Moses Brown,
ditto, $61.24.

Page 90.   Inventory & Appraisement of estate of Sarah Brown, dec'd
                23 Apr. 1802. Total $64.06. s/ Isaac Fann, Adm., W. M.
Chandler, Drury Cook, Loyd Kelley, appraisers. 15 Jun. 1802, Buyers at
sale: Isaac Fann bought most, Isaac Evans, Richard Huckeby.

Pages 91-92.   Inventory & Appraisement of estate of William Pride,
                dec'd. 8 Feb. 1802. Some items: 1 chest of carpenters
& house joiners tools at $100, 1 British musket at $5.00. Total $267.50.
s/ Wm. Reese, adm., John Hamilton, Henry Mitchell, Jno. Crowder, appraisers. Sales, 6 Mar. 1802. Buyers: Balaam Wallace, Duke Hamilton,
Thomas Carrell, John Stone, Henry Mitchell, John Hamilton, Robert Pollard,
William Reese, Edmd. Abercrombie, John Gay, James Gary (?), Philip Jackson, Parham Buckner, John Lewis, John Freeman. "Vouchers showing moneys
paid out of the Estate are entered in Book B, page 203."

Pages 93-96.   Appraisement of the estate of Jonathan Johns 12 Jun.
                1802. Included were 1 Negro woman and 3 children, 1
Negro man (none were named). Total $1648.76. s/ Anthony Butts, Admr.,
Geo. Gray, Geo. Williams, William Hill, appraisers. Account of sales:
no buyers listed.

Page 97 blank.

Pages 98-99.   Will of Ephraim Moore of Hancock Co., in a very weak and
                low state of body, dated 16 Jul. 1801. To my beloved
wife Nancy Moore the land where I now live, during her natural life, to
belong to her and her heirs forever. To my son William a tract of land
lying on Mountplier Road containing 300 acres. The above tract of 300
acres to belong to my wife during her widowhood or until my son William
becomes of age. Also to son William a Negro boy called Will. To my son
Neubil a Negro boy Pomp. My son Neubil to be bound as an apprentice to
Thomas Taylor provided he will endeavor to learn him the house carpenter's trade. To my daughter Tabith one negro girl Jincy. To my son
Levin and a child my wife is now pregnant with, all the increase of a
Negro woman called Clo, from the present date. To my beloved wife Nancy
a Negro woman called Clo. s/ Ephraim Moore. Wit: Aaron Benston, William
Yarbrough. N.B. I appoint Thomas Lamar to be joint executor with my
wife Nancy. No date of probate.

310

Pages 100-102.   Inventory and Appraisement of estate of Ephraim Moore
                 dec'd. 8 May 1802. Negroes named: man Pompey, age 32;
man Will, age 19; woman Cloe, age 25; girl Jenny, age 1. Total $2382.88.
s/ William Bivins, Arthur Dannelly, Levin Moore, appraisers. Nancy
Moore, Thomas Lamar, Exors.

Pages 103-104.   Inventory and Appraisement of estate of Robert Pikard
                 dec'd. 10 Jul. 1802. Notes due: William Gay, Thompson
Bird, Jesse Williams. Account of Jno. Wallace. s/ Joel Patterson, James
Wood, Job Taylor, appraisers. Jonathan Davis, Adm. Purchaser at sale
14 Aug. 1802: Micajah Pickard. Money paid out: Doctor Thompson Bird's
account, Joel Patterson for funeral expenses, note to Jonathan Davis,
note to William Mangham.

Pages 105-108.   Inventory and Appraisement of estate of Nathaniel Sledge,
                 late deceased, 29 Oct. 1802. Negroes named: woman Lydda,
boy Leven, child Jinny, girl Ede, boy Bob, boy Sam, boy Dave, woman
Ibby, woman Nance, man Harry. Book accounts: Daniel Low, Robert Clark
Junr., Robert Mitchell, Drury Chaves, Thomas Thrower, Phillip Barron-
heart, Nicholas Booty, Joseph Johnson, John Slaughter, William Glass,
Bailiff Loven, Thomas Ingram, George Richards, Marget Williams, John
Chapell Junr., John Bishop, William Giles, Abner Evans, Absalom Harris,
William Raybun, John Foster, John Garner, Richard Whatley, Edward Woodom,
James Tarrentine, Lewis Leget, Thomas Brawdis (?), Edward Brown, Widow
White, Daniel Kelley, William Newberry, James Rolland, David Rosser,
George Sims, Waller Hamilton, John Bishop, Nathaniel Howell, Archibald
McCoy, James Adams, Mins Sledge, James Adams, Jonathan Clower, George
Clower Senr., Isaac Motley, William Adams, John Chapell Senr., Richard
Smith, Stephen Durden, Chappell Heath, Collen Sledge. Notes of hand:
Abner Wheeler, Jonathan Clower, Zachariah Glass, William McGauhey, James
Cooper. Total $4777.70. "One Note on Jas. Adams which was thro' error
returned as the property of John Sledge dec'd." s/ Jon. Adams, David
Adams, Stephen Evans.

Pages 109-115.   Account of Sales, estate of Nathaniel Sledge dec'd. 4
                 Jan. 1803. Buyers: Widow Sledge, John Sledge, Isham Let,
Peyton Sledge, Chappell Sledge, William Walker, Cornelius Clark, Jehu
Smith, John Thweatt, James Adams, Robert Hill, James McGaughey, Hiram
Whatley, John Chappell Junr., Phillip Barronheart, William Sutton, David
Walker, John Foster, Philemon Foster, Daniel Whatley, Benjamin Chappell,
Henry Harris, John Bishop, Jonathan Adams, Joseph Chappell, William
Adams, Elisha Whatley, Shurley Sledge, James Foster, Robert Clark, James
Sutton, Nancy Sledge, William Glass. Money paid out: Henry Carlton,
Thomas Wilcoxon, Chapel Heath, L. Abercrombie, Martin Martin, Jonathan
Clower, Robert Hill, J. Nelson, Myles Green, Mrs. Elizabeth Sledge ac-
count against the heirs for goods furnished. "Mrs. Sledge, Henry Harris,
and Benja. Chappell, admrs. (?) of Joseph Chappell and John Sledge who
were admrs. of Nathaniel Sledge dec'd. returned Chappell Sledge's rect.
in full for said Estate 5 Sep. 1808." A list of notes returned on the
appraisement of the estate of Joseph Chappell dec'd. through an error
belonging to the Estate of Nathaniel Sledge, dec'd: James McGaughey,
John Chappell, Jesse Maddox, Jehu Smith, John Sledge, Benjamin Chappell.
Certified 7 Sep. 1807 by Henry Harris, Benja. Chappell, admrs.

Pages 116-120.   Inventory, Appraisement & Sales of the personal estate
                 of James Davidson, dec'd. 8 May 1802. Total appraisement
$799.02. s/ Drury Cook, Abner Atkinson, John Latimer, appraisers.
Aquila Davidson, Loyd Kelley, admrs. Buyers at sale, 29 May 1803: Ben-
jamin Oliver, Aquilla Davidson, Lemuel Davidson, Robert Hicks, Martin
Pruitt, John Latimer, Loyd Kelley, Isaac Evans, William Barefield, John
Parker, Matthew Humphrey, Arnold Kelley, William Seales, Solomon Barfield,
John Davidson, Benjamin Cook, Benjamin Humphrey, Hezekiah Howell, Mrs.
Kelley, Francis Maxfield, Andrew Stewart, Abi Kelley, Samuel Barron.
Money paid out: Jonathan Davis.

HANCOCK COUNTY CIVIL WAR SOLDIERS

The following two rosters were found in an old box in a room on the third
floor of the Hancock County courthouse and were returned to the box after
copying. The roster of the second company is particularly interesting
because it shows where the soldiers were living after the war. For more
information on these and other soldiers, see the massive Civil War hold-
ings at the Georgia Department of Archives and History. For Hancock
County soldiers, see Volume one of Elizabeth Wiley Smith, The History of
Hancock County, Ga. (Washington, Ga.: Wilkes Publishing Co., 1974.)

The Maunscripts Section, Georgia Department of Archives and History,
also has a collection of Civil War letters written from Hancock County
soldiers to the clerk of the Superior Court, usually requesting that he
look after their families. These letters are in the Judge James Thomas
Papers, AC 80-058. The soldiers included are:

Alfriend (?), E. W. 1861
Attaway, James W. 1861
Barksdale, Alfred 1861
Berry, G. J. 1865
Boston, John 1861
Brooke, J. F. 1861
Brown, Turner F. 1861
Buchanan, R. 1861
Bush, R. W. 1861
Butts, M. H. 1861
Cain, E. 1861
Cheeky, Mary 1861
Cullen, A. A. 1861
Culver, H. C. 1861
Daniel, Thomas M. 1861
Dawson, E. G. 1861
Dawson, J. C. 1861
Echols, Peter 1861
Ester, J. B. 1861
Foster, A. G. 1861
Hardwick, Thomas 1861
Hart, W. P. 1861
Heath, Peterson 1861
Holliday, John 1861
Hood, G. R. 1806
Howell, C. W. 1861
Hudson, William 1861
Johnson, Hershel V. 1861
Johnson, R. W. 1861
Latimer, J. B. 1861

Latimer, Mark 1861
Latimer, Thomas H. 1861
Lumpkin, Jos. Henry 1861
McCall, Jacob 1861
Medlock, J. M. 1806
Mitchell, Thomas 1862
Osborn, Lou 1861
Redmond, D. 1860
Rocker, Herbert 1861
Rogers, H. 1860
Sayres, William H. 1860-62
Smith, Rabun (?) 1860
Starnes, E. (?) 1861
Stephens, Alexander H. 1861
Stephens, Linton 1861
Thomas, G. E. 1861
Thomas, Thomas W. 1861
Thompson, Charles 1861
Trice, E. 1861
Turner, Thomas M. 1861
Voullard, E. A. 1861
Warthen, George W. 1861
Warthen, W. Richard 1861
Wartzfelder, E. 1861
Wasden, Joseph 1860-61
Watts, Naucie (?) 1861
Whittle, L. H. 1861
Willet, J. E. 1861
Wright, A. P. 1861

Roster of Company J, 49th Georgia Volunteers (Hancock County). The
Pierce Guards was organized at Sparta, Ga. on March the 4th (?) 1862 and
left Sparta for Camp Davis on March the 10th 1862 with the following
names (officers & men to wit):

1. Lane, A. J. Capt.
2. Laurence, Jas. J. 1st Lt.
3. Lamar, Lavasim L. 2nd Lt.
4. Amons, William 3rd Lt.
5. Medlock, Chas. Ordley. Sgt.
6. Haynes, D. S. 2nd Sgt.
7. Latimore, Alf 3rd Sgt.
8. Brown, Gaston 4th Sgt.
9. Jones, P. T. 1st Corpel.
   Killed at Wilderness
10. Hill, Joe 2nd Corpel; lost
11. Deas, Jos. A. 3rd Corpel.
    Killed at Wilderness 5-6-64
12. Allen, John W. Pvt.
13. Allen, Jasper N. Pvt.
14. Allen, Thos. J. Pvt.
15. Akin, Frank Pvt.

    Killed at Wilderness May 6-64
16. Baugh, Jos. C. Pvt.
17. Barnes, John Pvt.
    Killed at Wilderness
18. Bonner, William Pvt.
19. Babcock, Jos. B. Pvt.
20. Birdsong, Albert H. Pvt.
21. Burnett, Frank Pvt.
22. Burnley, Joe C. Pvt.
23. Brantley, Wm. D. Pvt.
24. Brantley, W. Henry Pvt. - killed
25. Brantley, Wm. Pvt.
26. Brooks, Lee Pvt. - killed
27. Beckem, Cambell Pvt.
28. Beckem, William Pvt.
29. Alfriend, Dr. H. L. Pvt.
30. Costello, Jos. Pvt.

312

31. Cain, John Pvt. - lost
32. Callwell, Charles Pvt.
33. Callwell, John Pvt.
34. Crosley, W. H. Pvt.
35. Carr, William Pvt.
36. Christian, John Pvt.
37. (blank)
38. Dunn, Thos. J. Pvt.
39. Dunn, Dock Pvt.
40. Dunn, Jos. M. Pvt.
41. Dickens, R. Lee Pvt.
    Killed at Wilderness
42. Deas, Wm. A. Pvt.
43. Duggan, Jay W. Pvt.
44. Dupree, David D. Pvt.
    killed
45. Frasier, Wm. F. Pvt. killed
46. Garrett, Thomas Pvt.
47. Griffeth, John T. Pvt.
48. Grimes, John Pvt.
49. Green, Wm. H. Pvt.
50. Hitchcock, David Pvt.
51. Hutchens, Charles Pvt.
52. Hutchens, Wm. E. Pvt.
53. Humphrey, D. F. Pvt.
54. Humphrey, Chas. Pvt.
55. Hyman, John J. Pvt.
56. (blank)
57. Johns, John M. Pvt.
58. Jackson, Jas. R. Pvt.
59. Johnson, J. Dick Pvt.
60. Johnson, Jack Pvt.
61. Jenkins, George Pvt.
62. Knold, Wm. T. Pvt.
63. Kitchens, Terel Pvt.
64. Latimore, Ed Pvt.
65. Latimore, Thos. H. Pvt.
66. Lattimore, James H. Pvt.
67. Long, Jackson Pvt.
68. Long, Larkin Pvt.
    Killed at Seven Pines

69. Little, James Pvt.
70. Little, John Pvt.
71. Latimore, John Pvt.
72. Lewis, Ples Pvt.
73. Moore, James W. Pvt.
74. Mullally, Wm. T. Pvt. - killed
75. McCook, Wm. Pvt.
76. McCook, Alf Pvt.
77. McCray, Jasper Pvt.
78. Moat, Freeman Pvt.
79. Moat, Joe Pvt.
80. Pearson, Jerry C. Pvt.
81. Parker, Joe Pvt.
82. Pool, Peter Pvt. - lost
83. Pool, Fred B. Pvt.
84. Pool, Hardy Pvt.
85. Pound, Ed F. Pvt.
86. Powell, Dr. T. O. Pvt.
87. Rodgers, John Pvt.
88. Rodgers, Dock Pvt. - killed
89. Rodgers, Joseph Pvt.
    Killed at Wilderness
90. Rodgers, Rufus Pvt.
91. Rainwater, Thed. W. Pvt.
92. Rainwater, Aloy C. Pvt.
93. Rainwater, Vergal
    Killed at Wilderness
94. Rachels, Pleasant W. Pvt.
95. Reynolds, Hardy Pvt.
96. Roose, John A. Pvt.
97. Smith, James P. Pvt.
98. Stevens, Roland W. Pvt.
99. Skrine, Charles Pvt.
100. Thomas, James Pvt.
101. Waller, Ben Pvt.
102. Whitehead, Wm. S. Pvt.
103. Wheeler, Eligar Pvt.
104. Wine, William Pvt.
105. Youngblood Pvt.
106. Lee, Frank Pvt.

Roster of Company K, 15th Georgia Regiment (Hancock County).
Officers Men at Camp Walker, Aug. 29, 1861.
Capt. T. H. Latimer - living near Milledgeville, Ga.
1st Lt. J. L. Culver - living at Culverton.
2nd Lt. Mark Latimer - living in Texas.
3rd Lt. D. Connell - living at Culverton.
Corp. G. W. Warthen
Corp. (?) J. D. Ferrill - killed by sharp shooters in 1864 between
    Spotsylvania C. H. and Richmond.

Mess No. 1

John Laughlin - killed in battle at Gettysburg.
Wm. Dickson Sr. - died in 18
Wm. Dickson Jr. - living in Hancock
Henry B. Pinkston - living in Hancock
J. D. Redfern
Andrew Redfern - living in Washington Co.
H. B. Seals - killed in battle at Sharpsburg.
W. D. Seals - living near Powelton.
W. H. Hardwick - made Lt. in 1864 - killed in battle at Gettysburg.
Wm. A. Thomas
Joseph F. Deas - living in Leesburg.
David Warthen - living in Hancock.

Mess No. 2

Corp. A. S. Bass - living at Devereaux.

313

Com. G. B. Medlock - killed in battle at Fort Harrison, on the James.
Sergt. C. M. Medlock - died in 18.
Corp. G. C. Middlebrooks - discharged in 1861; joined cavalry - killed in Mississippi.
Lucius A. Moore - living at Sharon, Ga.
Geo. L. Waller - killed at Fort Harrison on the James.
Asst. Com. R. A. Beall - living in Glasscock.
Sergt. G. P. Culver - made Lt. in 1863; killed in battle at the Wilderness.
Corp. B. C. Culver - living at Culverton.
G. W. Nelson - killed in 1864 between Spotsylvania C. H. and Richmond.
J. W. Nelson.

Mess No. 3

G. W. Dudley - died of brainfever at Front Royal Hospital, Jan. 23rd 1862.
J. M. White
J. I. Mason - living in Sparta.
Joseph D. Mason - died of typhoid fever in Bird Island Hospital, Richmond, December 5, 1861.
Thos. M. Mason - killed in battle at Sharpsburg.
G. P. Dunn - died of pneumonia at Chanborays Hospital, March 10, 1862.
A. F. Dunn - living near Culverton.
J. F. Hawkins
Charles Rocker - living near Culverton.
James Barnes - living in Augusta.
Robt. W. Jones - died at 2nd Ga. Hospital, Richmond, June 15, 1862.

Mess No. 4

O. Serg. J. A. P. Robson - living in Linton.
R. G. Stone - living in Linton.
Pat. F. Cheek - killed in battle at the Wilderness.
Wm. F. Robison - living.
Winfield Robison - living in Washington Co.
Ivy W. Duggen - living in Linton.
James A. Ray - living in Washington Co.
Wm. A. Ray - living in Washington Co.
H. Mat. Hooks - living in Washington Co.
G. L. Hooks - died at home, soon after war, of Typhoid fever.
Green R. Peeler - died in camp near Centerville, Dec. 3rd, 1861, Typhoid, pneumonia.
E. Wade Simpson - killed on post, below Richmond in 1864.

Mess No. 5

Wm. S. Neel - living.
John H. Neel - living.
Sgt. Maj. (?) A. D. Sharpe - died soon after the war.
J. H. Sharpe - died since the war.
J. (?) A. Scott
R. L. Dickens - died at 2nd Ga. Hospital, Richmond, July 7, 1862.
A. B. Parrott - died since the war.
Sgt. Hamlin Lewis - living.
A. E. Curran - lost at the Wilderness; perhaps killed.
Mont. Harrison - killed in battle at Gettysburg.

Mess No. 6

Chas. H. Eubank - died since the war.
Joseph C. Dickson - killed in battle at Gettysburg.
Q. L. Dickson - killed at the battle of Chickamauga.
W. T. Warthen - captured at Gettysburg; died at Fortress Monroe in 1865.
W. J. Lovett - died at 3rd Ga. Hospital, Richamond, Nov. 21, 1861.
J. Lovett
J. R. Parnell
John Powers - died of brain fever at Front Royal Hosp. Feb. 13, 1862.
John Wheelin - died since the war, in Sandersville, Nov. 3, 1869.
Joseph Flury - living in Hancock.

314

John Layfield - died of typhoid fever at Camp Walker, Sep. 1861.
Dawson McCook
John Rachels - sent to Richmond very sick, May 31, 1863, never heard
  from, no doubt died.
Cicero Broome - wounded at Malvern Hill, body not found, considered dead.

Mess No. 7

John Yarborough
Lewis Brantly - died.
James Brantly - living in Hancock.
D. S. Reynolds - sent to Richmond very sick, Apr. 16, 1862; never heard
  from - dead.
Jas. R. Reynolds - living in Atlanta.
James Jones
Levi Cove (Cone?) - died at Chimboraya Hosp., Oct. 25, 1861.
James Black - died of typhoid fever at 1st Ga. Hosp., Richmond, Sep. 1861.
John Barnes - discharged, joined 57th Ga., died near close of war.
James Cheek
John Cheek

Came later to K.

Thomas Beaman - killed in 2nd Manassas battle.

Everard H. Culver - killed in battle at Gettysburg July 2d 1863.
Oscar D. Scott - died in 1885.
George Bass - captured at Gettysburg, and died in prison.
Jas. T. Middlebrooks - living in Hancock.
Martin Parker - killed in battle at the Wilderness.
Owen Alford - killed in battle at Garnetts Farm, June 27, 1862.
Simon D. Bass - living in Hancock.
James E. Medlock - living in Virginia (dead).

Note: This book is a transcription of the original.

Pages 1-5.   Dated 26 Jan. 1802. LW&T of David Clements of
                    Hancock Co., weak and sick. I ordain that all the
cotton and my stock of goods remaining in land, at my stores in Sparta
and on Island Creek be sold by my executors. (Part of will evidently
missing at this point). ...To him and his heirs forever, but as he is
now subject to epileptic fits and at times incapable of transacting
business or taking charge of his property, none of the property I have
bequeathed him should be at his disposal to be sold without the consent
of my executors, who during the minority of my son Stephen are to be his
guardians, and when Stephen reaches age 21, he shall take the guardianship of my son John during his epileptic illness or other deplorable ma-
lady. To my son Stephen Clements all the tract of land which I purchased
from the Rev. Mr. Skelby adj. the town of Sparta, 200 acres with the improvements thereon, one half of my lot with improvements in Sparta, my
lot on the hill No. 111 in the town of Montpelier, two Negroes Harry and
Keziah, two horses, six Winsor chairs, feather bed & furniture, and $500
cash. As the guardianship of his brother John is to be committed to him
at age 21, it is my desire that if my said son John...(part of will
missing)....The cotton machine thereon erected, one and a half acre of
land adj. the same which I purchased of John Watkins, three Negroes
Aleck, Willie & Levi, one workhorse, feather bed & furniture, six Windsor
chairs, $500 cash. To my daughter Sarah L. Dowman (?) the tract of land
which I purchased of Benjamin Anderson, on the Sparta & Georgetown Road
cont. 162½ acres, two Negroes Rachel & Stafford, cows, my bay mare, &
two feather beds & furniture now in her possession. To my daughter Eliza
Clements my lot No. 200 in the town of Montpelier, three Negroes Aber-
deedn, Lewis and Kate, six Windsor chairs, a dining walnut table, feather
bed & furniture, one of my large trunks, my pine chest, and $700 cash.
To my daughter Betsy North Clements my lot No. 205 in the town of Montpelier, two Negroes Chloe and Toney, one of my walnut dining tables, my
walnut desk, one of my large trunks, feather bed & furniture, $700 cash.
And if so much should remain after paying the foregoing legacies, I give
the sum of $250 for building and erecting a meeting house or school
house near or in the town of Sparta, to encourage religion or literature
only. I lend unto my present clerk, James (?) Jones the use of my store
house on Island Creek to be used & occupied by him until my son David
shall come of age. My books are to be equally divided among my children.
The meeting house I have given money to build should be built on one
acre in the corner of the tract I have given my son Stephen, adj. the
present grave yard. It is my desire that my mother and my sister live
with and be supported out of the legacy left my son John, and if they
survive him, they are to live with my son Stephen. Exors: my friends the
Rev. Robert M. Cunningham and the Rev. Myles Greene, whom I also appoint
guardians for my children now under age. s/ David Clements. Wit: John
Wm. Devereux, Martin Martin, Francis Maxwell, James H. Jones. Proved in
Hancock Co. by Devereux, Maxwell & Jones, no date.

Pages 6-7.   LW&T dated 5 Sep. 1802. Samuel Halley of Hancock
                    Co., weak in body. I lend to my beloved wife Grace
Halley my whole estate during her life or widowhood, or until my youngest
child William Halley reaches age 21, at which time all my property that
remains (after my three children are raised and reasonably educated in
the English language) shall be sold by my executors and equally divided
between my wife (should she continue to be my widow) and my three
children John Halley, Elizabeth Emerson Halley & William Halley. My
brother's son Samuel Halley shall have a cow and calf out of my estate.
Exors: beloved brother Nathaniel Halley and friends Robert Rivers and
George Stephens. s/ Samuel Halley. Wit: John Rivers, Peter Hutchingson,
Stephen (X) Stephens. Reg. 3 Feb. 1803. Proved by the three witnesses.
(Note that the inventory carried to page 42.)

Pages 8-10.   LW&T, 25 May 1802. George Norsworthy of Hancock
                    Co., sick and weak. I lend to my beloved wife Sal-
ley during her life or widowhood the use of the land and the plantation
where I now live, and five Negroes Luke, Diner, Amey, Milley and Jesse,
furniture, stock and working tools. To my son Frederick Norsworthy,

after the marriage or death of my wife, the land and plantation where I
now live. To my three children Frederick, Salley & Betsey Norsworthy,
Negroes Robert, Cloey, Viney, Chaney, Winney, Rhoda, Hanner, Adston (?),
Will, David, Lyda, to remain in possession of my wife until either of my
children reach 21 or marry. My executors are to judge when my children
have a sufficient education. If none of my children or wife survive, the
whole of my estate should be for the support of the pore, and also the
Gospel. Executors: Myles Greene, William Rabon and Jonas Shivers. s/
George Norsworthy. Wit: Matt Rabon, John Cartwright, Andrew Stewart.
Proved by Matt Rabun and John Cartwright 25 Dec. 1802. (Note that the
Inventory, sale, etc. Registered in B 4th (?), page 184-186.)

Pages 11-13.   LW&T dated 27 Apr. 1801. Edmond Butler of Hancock
                      Co., in a tolerable state of health. I lend to my
dearly beloved wife Mary the plantation where I now live, with the mansion house, household furniture, livestock, tools, and Negroes: man
Frank, woman Fanny, boys Arthur and Jack, and girl Martha. After my
wife's death, the land, 262½ acres, is to be divided between my well beloved sons John, William & Harry. To my well beloved son Edmond, 87½
acres including the plantation whereon he now lives, and a Negro girl
Sarah. To my well beloved son John, a Negro girl Sukey. To my well beloved son William, a Negro boy Moses. To my well beloved son Harry, a
Negro boy Adam. To my well beloved son in law, Benjamin Gilbert, the sum
of one dollar. To Samuel, Edmond, Polley, Patsey, & John Gilbert, my
beloved grandchildren, $625 to be equally divided amongst them. To my
well beloved grand daughter Fanny Gilbert, a Negro girl named Mary. The
two last mentioned legacies to be paid after their grandmother's death.
Executors: sons Edmond & John Butler, and Randolph Rutland, my well beloved friend. s/ Edmond (X) Butler. Wit: Hen. Graybill, James Harvey,
R. Rutland. Proved by the three witnesses, no date. (Note that the
Inventory and Appraisal of the foregoing property registered on page 53.)

Pages 14-18.   Estate of Elijah Freeney, late of Hancock Co.,
                      dated 22 Oct. 1802. Inventory and Appraisement in-
                      cludes two black and white counterpains, and one
blue and white counterpain, many dishes of various kinds, and stock.
Negroes: Cudjoe, George, woman Hannah & child, girls Febe, Leah, Mat,
Filis; men Isac, George, Lever (?), Spencer; boy Samuel. Furniture,
tools, tablecloths, towels, loom, Bible, Testament, Prayer Book, musket.
An obligation on Thomas Freeney of Sussex Co., Delaware for Ł97, 12
shillings, dated 19 Nov. 1798. Judgement against R. Middleton; Notes
against Wm. Bonner (?) (Berrice?), J. Gholson, J. Waller, J. Doden (?),
due in 1801 and 1802. Whole amount: $6448.53¼ . Appraisers: Peter
McFarlin, Theo Turk, John Cook. Administratix: Nancy Freeney.

Pages 19-24.   LW&T dated 12 Dec. 1802. John Brewer of Hancock
                      Co. My dearly beloved wife Polley Brewer is to
keep all my Negroes, house and household furniture, some stock, horses,
etc. for the support of my said wife and my children Betsey, Bethis,
Maria & Nancy Brewer until they are of age or marry, and then to receive
an equal part of my estate with my wife. At my wife's death my estate
is to be returned to my children. Exors: wife Polley, Andrew Jeter and
Francis Lewis. s/ John Brewer. Wit: James Hunt, Jon Adams. Proved by
Jonathan Adams & James Hunt 15 Jan. 1803, and Andrew Jeter & Francis
Lewis Junr. qualified as Executors.

                      Inventory dated 19 Feb. 1803 included five geldings,
fillies, mares, 1 black horse Jack, 1 sorrel filley Flimnass (?), ½ bay
gelding, wagon & gear, 2 stills and 20 tubs, shot gun, pair of pistol &
holsters, 10 Negroes Gloucester, Hampton, Warren, Patt & Ben, Tener,
Polley & Patience, Sarah, furniture, 1 "bofat," 3 books, etc.   5064
lbs. seed cotton, 2462 lbs. tobacco. One Judgement on land W. Boreland;
Accounts on Eli Harris, William Low, Walter Hasselton, Henry Jackson,
William Adams, Moses Wilie (?), Esq. Whole amount: $5746.44½. s/ David
Rosser, David Adams, Samuel Harris, appraisers. s/ Andrew Jeter, Francis
Lewis, Exors.

                      Sale of John Brewer JN dated Dec. 1803. Buyers:
William Thomas, Wilkins Jackson, William Low, John Trippe, John Lewis,
Abner Lockett, Polley Brewer, Dudley Hargroves, William Reese, James

McGehe, Noah Doddridge, William P. Downman, John Smith, James Hall, Walter Hamilton, Thomas Simmons. Dec. 1804, 300 acres land sold for $2300.

The following is crossed out and stated as entered in Book E, folio 24: Monies paid out: Mary Adams, Jonathan Clower, Alexander Reid, Abram Lawrence, Joshua Lacy, Thomas Hudson, Gale Lewis.

Pages 25-30.   LW&T dated -- ----, 1802. James Randle of Hancock Co., sick and weak. To my dearly beloved wife Rosanna the tract of land containing 368 acres, which takes in 34 acres I bought of Henry Long, and 34 acres I bought of T. Cooper; eight negroes Roger, Caterine, Vilet, George, Charles, Roger, Sue (?), Mary and her increase, and Fann. Also the house I now live in, furniture, stock, etc. during her life and widowhood. The labor of the said Negroes to go to raise and school my young children until they come of age, and after the death of my wife, the negro Mary and her increase to be equally divided between my three youngest sons, Washington, Peter & Edmond, and the rest of the Negroes and property lent to her to be sold and equally divided among all my children. To my well beloved son John Randle 100 acres of land where he now lives for which he was to have given me $500, but hath only paid $200; the said land adjoins Henry Long, Wm. Johnston, Birom & Robert Sims land. I also give him Ben and Jum (?) a Negro fellow & woman, sows, pigs, bed, and a great coat all which he has already received. To my well beloved son William Randle $1000 in lieu of 3 Negroes which I gave to him named John, Agge and Doll. Also $300 as an equivalent for what I gave my other sons in land, also horse, bridle and saddle, great coat, etc. To my well beloved son James Graves Randle 50 acres, part of the tract bought of Cooper adj. Henry Long; 3 Negroes John, Agge and Sarah, a mare bridle & saddle, great coat, etc. To my well beloved son William (sic) Randle 50 acres adj. James Randle, 2 Negroes Robert and Amy and her increase, a colt bridle & saddle, the colt to be fed and raised until it is three years old upon my corn and fodder; etc. To my well beloved son Washington Randle 3 Negroes Hall, Dice and Beck, etc. when he comes of age. To my well beloved son Peter Randle 3 Negroes Bob, Solomon & Doll, etc. when he comes of age. To my well beloved son Edmond Randle three Negroes Julius, Daniel and Letty, etc. when he comes of age. Executors: wife Rosanna and sons John, William, James Graves Randle & William Randle. s/ James Randle. Wit: Hen. Graybill, Joseph Barksdale, William Skelley, Jonathan Moore.

Appraisement, dated 13 Aug. 1803. Some items: 1 curtain bedstead & furniture, 1 trunnel (sic) bed, 4 other beds, 3 spinning wheels, 3 old negroes Roger, Catoe & Vilet, fellows George, Charles, Roger, Robin; boys Bob, Hall, Julius, Daniel, Solomon; girls Dicey, Dolley; woman & child Mary & Letty; ditto Amey & Beck, girl Fanny. Notes and accounts: Dr. Lee, Mark More, Wm. Johnson, dec'd., Jas. Holliday, Henry Garrett, Henry Long, Edmond Butler, dec'd., John Randle, James Moore, Robert Sims, James Byrom, Wm. Randle, Beverly Randle dec'd., McAlister in Greene county. No total. s/ Henry Long, Jas. Barksdale, Jas. Lucas, Appraisers. Signed by all executors named.

Receipts given by the Legatees, returned to court 5 Feb. 1810: William Randle signed 2 Jun. 1806 for $1300 and the other items left him. Wit: J. G. Randle. J. G. Randle signed 2 Jun. 1806 for items left him. Wit: William Randle. Willis Randle signed 2 Jul. 1806 for Negroes Robin, Amy, etc. Wit: J. G. Randle. W. Randle signed for Catoe, Dicey & Beck, etc. on 7 Jan. 1809, witness Willis Randle. J. G. Randle signed, as Exor., for Negroes Ben, Jenny & Lew, 50 acres, etc., 5 Feb. 1810.

Pages 31-34 blank.

Pages 35-41.   David Clements, dec'd. Account of Sale of part of the estate, 25 Nov. 1802. Buyers: Gale Lewis, William Downman, Robert Hutching, Brice Gaither, Howell A. (?) (faded), Joseph Turner Senr., John Clements, Stephen Clements, James Shackleford, Wiette Collier, Jesse Connell, John Wilson, John Walls, John Brewer.

Sale, 27 Nov. 1802, at Island Creek: John Cook,

318

Thomas Stephens (rent of cabbin where John Turk lived), Henry Caigle, John Knight, Francis Gray, Elisha Waller, Myles Greene, Solomon Smith, Hubert Reynolds, Robert Williams, Charles Miller, John Duke, Samuel Guery (?), John Oliver, James Fail, Solomon Oliver, Frederick Lipham, James Crane, Leonard Bowman, John Dowdle, Jesse Smith, John Gregory, John McAlister, Jonathan Day, Elizabeth Godwin, Nancy Freeney, Joseph McGinty, John Gray, Thomas (blank) (to rent plantation), George Walker, John Felps. Over 50 gallons of brandy was sold. Total sale: $1287.

Page 38.   A state of Negroes hired 1 Jan. 1803, belonging to
                    the heirs: Lewis & Ben by Wm. Downman; security
James H. Jones. Ellick by James Hall; sec. Henry Mitchell. Willie by
John Buckner; sec. John Brome (?). Harry by John Thweatt; sec. Francis
Lewis Sen. Toney by John Brome; sec. John Buckner. Aberdeen by Edmd.
Beard; sec. Benjamin Hill. ----- & children by John Clements; sec.
John Freeman. Thompson Bird rented the plantation and dwelling house
adj. Sparta. Negroes hired 2 Jan. 1804 until 25 Dec. next: Tony & Lewis
by Wm. Downman; sec. M. Armstrong. Willie by John Buckner; sec. John
Brown (?). Chloe & Len by John Clements. Aberdeen by A. Steward; sec.
Isaac Hill. Ellick by James Hall; sec. Bird Ferrill. Ben by Stephen
Clements; sec. John Freeman. Parterick rented the plantation on Island
Cr. for the year 1804. s/ M. Greene, Exr.

Page 39.   Negroes hired 1 Jan. - 25 Dec. 1805. Chloe & Lem by
                    John Clements. Lewis by Wm. Downman; James Wood,
sec. Toney by Philip Turner; S. Devereux, sec. Willie, Ellick, Aberdeen
& Benn by Stephen Clements; Henry Darnell, sec. Cato by Henry Moss.
Plantation on Island Cr. rented to C. Patrick.

Page 40.   Monies paid out 1802-1803: Herbert Reynolds for
                    overseeing: Jesse Veasey, J. & B. Sanford, H. A.
Reese, F. Fears, Wm. Downman, James Wood, John E. Dawson, Joel Patterson,
Capt. James Bishop, Ann Holomon, Ed Bazer, Samuel Ewing, Job Ricon (?),
John Reed, Van Swearingen, Benj. Thompson, Bryan Butler, Jonathan Davis,
Rt. Oliver, James Taylor, James Lucas, Rt. Hill, David Smith, John Stone,
Wm. Bazer, Thos. Carrell, Benj. Cook, John Ragan, Natt Waller, James
Pinckston, Gale Lewis, John Dowdle, Thos. Mason, Wm. Montgomery, Benj.
Evans. (Continued in Book C, p. 164.)

Pages 42-43.   Inventory and Appraisement of Samuel Halley dec'd.,
                    2 Dec. 1802. Negro lad Dick, girl Charity. Unbrel-
la, silver watch, etc. Notes on Thomas Breedlove, Thomas Spencer, Matthew Kinchen, Wilson Owsley, Richard Strother. Due bill on John Knight.
Open account on Peter Mahone, Matthew Durham. Appraisers: William
Williams, George Williams, Peter F. Flournoy. 28 Feb. 1805: Gracey
Halley returned voucher of moneys received by her in favour of the estate
of Samuel Halley dec'd. Moneys paid out: Thos. Glascock, John Vest,
William Spencer, John Knight, William Kelly, John Barron, William Hutchinson, John Ragan, James Yarbrough, Wm. (blank).

Pages 44-45.   Dated 11 Oct. 1799. LW&T of Samuel Wilson of Han-
                    cock Co., in a reasonable state of health. To my
son Samuel Wilson the upper end of the tract of land I now live on, and
the other half to my grandson Levi Wilson. To my beloved wife Ann Wilson two cows & calves, one bed and furniture during her natural life or
widowhood, then to go to her daughter Ruth Burnass. To my daughter Ruth
Burnass one mare & colt and citchen furniture except one big pot for
Sarah Buchannon. The rest of my property if any to be divided between
my beloved sons Robert Wilson & Samuel Wilson, and my son Samuel to
furnish my wife Ann Wilson with 200 wt. of pork and 15 bushels of corn a
year as long as she seeth cause to stay by the same. My money to be
equally divided among my children. Exor: beloved son in law Robert
Buckhannon. s/ Samuel (X) Wilson. Wit: John Boyer, John Wilson, Robert
Buckhannan.

Pages 48-49.   Dated 4 Jan. 1801. LW&T of Gilliam Fox of Brunswick
                    Co., Va. in perfect health. To my brother John
Wynne one half of my estate real & personal. To Har-----(sic) son of
Green Wynne the remainder of my estate. Exor: friend Green Wynne. s/
Gilliam Fox. Wit: John Drummond Junr., Jno. Nicholson, William Betty.

Proved in Brunswick Co., Va. and executor qualified in Hancock Co. and will ordered recorded 6 Apr. 1803.

Page 49.   Inventory & Appraisement, 7 May 1803. Total inven-
                           tory: 1 saddle, 1 blanket, 1 screw auger, 1 whip.
Total $14.00. Obadiah Richardson, Isaac Benson, Hugh Hall, appraisers.
Account of sale 7 May 1803: Purchasers: John Turner, Green Wynne, Moses
---ston, Lewis ---ly. Total $14.75.

Page 50 - blank.

Pages 51-52.   Dated 12 Feb. 1803. LW&T of John Goldson. It is
                           my will that my son Anthony do -- and possess five
Negroes -----, Stepheny, Moll, Jerry, -----, and all land and improvements....with all my .... and intent of .... children .... and it is my
what my .... received from me at the time of our marriage, in said division, at the same time reserving my lands to be equally divided amongst
my three sons Anthony, Egleston & Jackey. Exors: son Anthony and John
Cook esq. s/ John (X) Goldson. Wit: Joseph Young, Jno. Gibney. Proved
by the witnesses 6 Apr. 1806. Inventory entered page 72.

Pages 53-55.   Edmund Butler dec'd. Inventory & Appraisement, no
                           date. Negro man Frank, woman Fanny, children Mary
& Martha, boys Arthur, Jack, Moses, Adam; girls Sarah & Suck. 1 lot of
books, 1 bed & furniture, 1 bed and bedstead, 3 bedsteads & furniture,
inspected tobacco, etc. Total $4474.07. Henry Graybill, Risdon Moore,
Robert Sims, appraisers.

Page 55.   Estate of Edmund Butler Junr. dec'd., Fanny Butler,
                           Adm. Term 1804, 1 Jan. (Rest of page blank.)

Pages 56-60.   Dated 26 Jan. 1803, Inventory & Appraisement of
                           estate of Nathaniel Parham dec'd., appraised by
William John, Greenberry Pinkston & William Gilliland. Notes on Edmond
Beard, Abel Johnston, Elisha Roberts, John Nielay, James Parham, John
Woodyar (sic), Lewis Parham, John Henry, James Walker, Richard Cary (?).
Total appraisal $862.50. Tanzy Parham, Benj. Th-----, Admrs.

          Sale 15 Mar. 1803. Buyers: Tanzy Parham, Thompson
Bird, John Hall, Arthur Herring, John Lewis, Archibald -----, William
Cain, William Grantham, Thomas Gray, Overoff Jordan.

          Moneys paid out: John Buckner, Isaac Dennis, Joab
Durham, Claburn Sanders for shoes; B. Thompson, Rountree & Taylor.

          3 Aug. 1807, sale of 120 acres to Oliver Skinner
for $261.50.

          11 Jan. 1816, Rebeckah Parham received her legacy
of $242.00 from Benjamin Thompson, Admr. Wit: ----- Nichols.

          18 Nov. 1819, John Parham received his legacy. Wit:
T. A. Smith.

          20 Apr. 1819, Received of Benj. Thompson his pro-
missory note to John Wilson as guardian of Polly & Tanizey Parham, for
$242, being their full legacy from Nathl. Parham dec'd. s/ William
Stubs (?) for John Wilson.

          Moneys paid out: ---- Turner, ----- Henry, -----
Myles Green, P. Turner & son, Henry Rhodes, Lucas & Butts (1811); Joel
Crawford Junr. (1812), Jonathan Nichols (1816).

Pages 62-64.   Will of Ephraim Barnes, dated 16 Jan. 1803. Weak
                           in body yet perfect in mind and understanding. To
my son Abel one horse, bridle & saddle. To my son Jesse one mare,
bridle & saddle; to my daughter Jilpah one feather bed & furniture. To
sons Abel & Jesse feather beds & furniture. To my daughter Sarah Wells
5 shillings sterling. To my daughter Patty Dickerson's daughter Elizabeth Barnes one cow & calf. (blank spaces in recorded will) during ...

widowhood...remaining of estate children except Sarah Wells and give to her no more than five shillings as before mentioned. I appoint Absolom Barnes & Lewis Brandy executors this 16 January 1803. s/ Ephraim (X) Barnes. Wit: N. Dixon, Wenburn Dickinson, Amos Daniel. Proved in open court by all witnesses and ordered recorded (no date). M. Green, Clk.

2 Apr. 1803, Inventory & Appraisement includes looking glass and household furniture, farm equipment, 1000 lbs. bacon, 1 stud colt, 17 hogs, blacksmith's tools, 17 geese, 1 still, 9 head cattle. Total: $778.75. Sworn appraisers: Singleton Holt, Thomas Cates, Marshal Smith. s/ Absalom Barnes, Extr.

Pages 65-71.   Benjamin Harris, dec'd.   Inventory and Appraisement made 22 Jan. 1803 (pp. 65-66). Hogs, horses, farm equipment, spinning wheel, looking glass & Bible, 3 counterpanes & rug, etc. One Negro girl Ginney, Negro fellow Hark; accounts on William Walker, James Elerson, Joel Rees, Daniel Neeves, Henry Tripp, Littleton Rees. Total: $1696.25. Appraisers: John Sledge, Wm. Walker, David Walker. Henry Harris, Adm.

Sale of Estate (pp. 67-70). Buyers: Sterling Catoe, Michael Blocker, John Alford, Jesse Lyons, John Rymes (?), Asa Sutton, David Evans, Joseph Middlebrooks, Robert Hill, Absalom Harris, Turner, Polly Harris, Samuel -----, David Ro---, Daniel Orear, William Walker, Wm. Sutton, Wyche Catoe, Asa Alexander, Ezekiel Wilkeson, Green Cato, Saml. Mattox, Henry Harris, David Rosser, Abner Evans, Francis Jeter, David Walker, Turner Hunt, Edmond Knoles, Matthew Hogg, Thomas Simmons, Richard Smith, Nicholas Booty, Cader Carter, Henry Porch, William West, John Fanning. Total: $1729.93. An account of Absalom Harris mentioned.

Page 71.   Moneys paid out from proven accounts, etc. Steges estate, H. Lewis (tax for 1802), A. Torry, Jonathan Clower, John E. Smith, Joseph Turner, D. L. Rayn, Wyche Catoe, Thomas Simmons, James Thweat, Jeremiah Nelson, John Lucas, Henry Trippe, Thompson Bird, Myles Green, Robert Hill, Absalom Harris, Dudley Hargroves. John E. Smith receipt for Mrs. Polley Harris's receipt for her half of the estate. Notation that the following, which is crossed out, is entered in Guardian Book A, folio 45: 1813, Oct. 14. Paid Wm. E. Adams for board & clothing Eliza R. Harris, orphan of sd. dec'd. for 1812, $35.00. Cash paid Myles Greene 37½ cents.

Pages 72-77.   John Gholstone, dec'd. Inventory & Appraisement, 11 May 1803. (pp. 72-76). Farm equipment, furniture, dishes, 2 looking glasses, 1 Bible and hymn book, rocking cradle. Girl Mary, Negro men Suton, Stephen & Samuel; boy Jerry. Notes and Accounts: Jn. Kinchen, note on Alexander Gordon dated 1793, John Cook, Joseph Pollard, James Crain, Daniel Powell, Joseph Wheat, Thomas Carter, Elizabeth Freeney, Nancy Freeney, Robert Thornton, Thomas Methrin, Gillah (?) Freeny, Abs. Boreland, Stephen Waller, Elisha Waller, Saml. Gilbert. Total: $3023.81½. Appraisers: H. M. Comer, H. Reynolds, Theodo. Turk, Peter McFarlin. John Cook, Esq., cert. of qualification of appraisers. Also mentions property of deceased in hands of Anthony Gholston, Samuel Gilbert, William Kinchen. Anthony Gholston, Exr.

Account of sales of part of estate, 8 Oct. 1803. Buyers: Thomas Glenn, John Cook, Mordicai Jacob, Thomas Melvin, Anthony Gholston.

Moneys paid out: Gillah Freeney, A. Miles, Mary Kinchen, William -----, Jazarus B---tte, Elizabeth -----, Badget & Harton, Jonathan Day, Stephen Waller. Note & Interest: Hardy Cain, Thomas Methiers, Deveraux & Co., Elizabeth Grunbie, Samuel Gilbert, John Johnston, Stephen Waller, Archibald Devereux, Wm. Kinchen. Paid to: Wm. McFarlin, John Cook, admr. of John Cook Senr. dec'd., Est. of David Clements dec'd., George Simpson, Edmond Godwin, Rountree & Tayor, James Horton, Solomon Mangham.

Pages 78-81.   Emanuel Merit, dec'd., Will, dated 17 February 1803. (pp. 78-79). Emanuel Merit of Hancock Co., very sick and weak. To John Howell, son of Hezekiah Howell, 1 cow. To Peggy

Howell, dau. of Hezekiah Howell, 1 cow, 1 feather bed & bolster. To
Hiram Howell, 1 heffer yearling. To James Howell, 1 heffer yearling.
To Carrie Jacks a chest, pot & dishes. To Hezekiah Howell aleaven
dollars in the hands of Absalom Biddle or his executors, and to Rachel
Howell seven & twenty dollars in the hands of John Davison. To Hezekiah
Howell a $20 note on James Humphys, & three $20 notes in the hands of
John Parker Jr. on a certain Barnhart, and to Rachel Howell $5 on Francis
Griffis. Exors: Hezekiah Howell & Rachel Howell his wife. s/ Emanuel
Merit. Wit: Loyd Kelley, John Atkison, Jeremiah (X) Lary. Proved in
Open Court, no date.

Inventory and Appraisement 2 July 1803. (p. 80).
Notes on Francis Griffis, John Davidson, Absalom Bidle. Total: $196.25.
Appraisers: Jeremiah Lary, John Andrews, Demcey Griffis. Exr: Hezekiah
Howell & Rachell Howell.

Account of Sales, Jan. 1804. (p. 81). Buyers:
Hezekiah Howell, Wilie Hilliard, Joseph Howell, Micajah White.

Pages 82-84.   James Hogg Senr., dec'd. Will (pp. 82-83), dated
                    4 Apr. 1803. James Hogg Senr. of Hancock Co., sick
& weak. To my son James Hogg my riding horse & saddle, my rifle gun,
$200 and my feather bed and furniture. To grandson John Justice my
Negro woman Barbary and Negro girl Fanny. To my two grand daughters
Salley Conner & Liddier Montgomery my Negro girl Jenny. To my friend
Samuel Parsons my Negro boy Tom. To my grandson Stephen Justice, $100.
To my gr. dau. Elizabeth Jordan, wife of Radford Jordan $50. To my
two gr. sons James & William Hogg all the remainder of my estate real &
personal not heretofore devised. Exors: friends Obadiah Richardson &
Samuel Parsons, and I revoke all other wills by me made. s/ James (X)
Hogg. Wit: Thomas B. Todd, William (+) Twilley, James Marchman. Proved
in Open Court,no date.

Inventory & Appraisement (p. 84). Negroes: boy Tom,
girls Jinney & Fanny, woman Barbary. Total: $1120. Appraisers: Henry
Dixon, Thos. Greene, James Waller.

Pages 85-87 are blank.

Pages 88-93.   William Bishop, dec'd. Will (pp. 88-90) dated 3
                    Mar. 1803. William Bishop of Hancock Co., weak in
body. To my well beloved wife Jane Bishop my whole estate both real and
personal: my land, four Negroes Jo, Fillis, Tom & Clabun; all my stock,
furniture, working tools and all that has not been mentioned, during her
natural life on condition that she is not to sell, barter, dispose of
nor remove any part of the property above mentioned off of the plantation whereon I now live, during her life without the consent of my executors. At the death of my wife, my land and all other property to be
sold at a credit of 12 months except the four Negroes and 2 feather beds
& furniture; those are to be appraised and together with what my other
property sells for, it should be divided as follows: To my son William
Bishop, ¼ of my estate including the Negro boy Clabon. To my daughter
Rebecca Langford, ¼ of my estate including the Negro boy Tom. To my
daughter Dorcas Fussell, ¼ of my estate. To my two gr.daus. Betsey &
Polley, daughters of my dau. Nancy Kilgore, ¼ of my estate including the
two feather beds to be equally divided between them. To my dau. Nancy
Killgore $25. I annul and disavow all wills heretofore made by me; this
and no other in my LW&T. Exors: William Hardwick & Jonas Shivers. s/
William (X) Bishop. Wit: Lewis Moss, William Bynamm, John Killgore.
Proved in Open Court, no date.

Inventory & Appraisal (pp. 90-91). Negro man Joseph,
woman Phillis, boys Tom & Clabun. Farm animals & equipment & household
furniture. Note given by Charles Kilgore payable 1 Dec. next for $39.
Cash, $11. No total. s/ Wm. Rabun, Lewis Moss, Temple Lee, appraisers.

Money paid out (p. 92), no date. Henry Jones'
note, $50. M. Greene's fees, $4.80. (p. 93) Received of Charles Kilgore on note of hand, $39.00.

Pages 93-95.   Estate of John Gholston, dec'd., Account of Sales
5 March 1812.   Buyers: Cary Curry; Alex Reddick;
Littleton Beauchamp bought Negro man Sutton; Anthony Gholston (also
Gholson) bought several items including the Negro man Stephen and two
small Negro girls, not named; Robert Hill; John Perdue; George Perdue;
Wm. Arnold; Joshua H. Perdue; Jon. H. Perdue; John B. Perdue; Marshall
Smith; Jonathan Thomas; Isaac Moseley; William Perdue; Eggleston Gholson
bought Negro man Jerry; Jas. H. Perdue bought the Negro man Sam. Total
sales: $2198.68¼. s/ Anthony Gholson, Exr.

Pages 96-97.   Will of James Lucas of Hancock Co., dated 19 Jan.
1803. "in a low state of health and finding my end
of life approaching." All the property I die possessed of, real and
personal, to continue in the hands of my Executors until my eldest son
John is age 21, execpt property hereafter mentioned. From 100 to 300
acres including the Will--- Hard--- be sold at the discretion of the
exors. for the payment of my debts. We------- both real and personal
after my son, John Lucas comes of age to be equally divided between my
wife and children, except my wife is to have a Negro wench Lucy over her
share. The property which my daus. Elizabeth --- Mildren Lucas may
possess to be to them and the heirs of their body lawfully begotten. My
sons to be kept at school until they have enough education. Exors: my
beloved wife, my brother John Lucas and --- Mitchell; also William
Bunkley. s/ James Lucas. Wit: ---son Bird, ---- Brown, ---- Porter, Jr.

A court order with many words missing mentions
children Walter, Mildred Lucas, Elizabeth Lucas, John Lucas. s/ John
Lucas, Guardian.

Pages 98-99.   John Gholson, dec'd. 7 May 1812. Received of
Anthony Gholson Exor. estate John Gholson dec'd.
all my legacy in full (signature and some words missing). Wit: Joshua
H. Perdue, 18 Nov. 1815, Eggleston Gholson received his legacy. s/
Eggleston Gholson. Wit: William Beauchamp. Nov. 1814, S. ----------
received a legacy. Wit: Wm. Butler. 8 Dec. 1815, ------Harper received
legacy -------- wife from said estate --- hundred & fifty seven dollars.
s/ W------. Wit: Stephen Arnall. 8 Dec. 1815, William Arnall received
his legacy of $257.37½. s/ William Arnall. Wit: Stephen Arnall. 8 Dec.
1815, William Arnall, guardian of ----- Gholson, received two hundred ---
seven 39½ cents. 8 Dec. 1815, William Arnall, guardian of ----- Chatham
---- received $257.39½. --- 29, 1817, William Arnall, guardian of
Sinthe Gholson, received $257.39½.

Pages 100-101 are blank.

Pages 102-104.   Elizabeth Walker of Hancock Co., dec'd. Will, pp.
102-103, dated 11 --- 1799, recorded 29 Oct. 1803.
Many words missing. David Walker, Fanny ---- ----- & Elizabeth Grant,
---- Negroes Isom, Ned, ---- to have Ned, ------ to have Rose ----
equally divided amongst the above legatees ----- Fanny Silman, Mary -----
----- Grant or their heirs ----- other property of ----- be equally divi-
ded ----- children or their heirs ----- Fanny Silman, Mary ----- -----
John H. Walker, William Walker. Exors: David Walker & Wiliam Silman.
s/ Elizabeth (X) Walker. Proved in Open Court by two of the witnesses
John Coulter & David Walker and recorded 29 Oct. 1803.

Appraisement of Estate (p. 103). Rose is old & in-
firm & of no value; note on Wm. Walker, Negroes Isham & Nell. Total
$1214.62½. s/ Andrew Baxters, ----- Evans, Sterling Cato.

Sale (p. 104). Buyers: William Walker, James
Shackleford, Nicholas Booty, ----- Middlebrooks, Walker plantation, Henry
Walker, David Walker, James Finch, John Walker, William West, Michael
Seawell, Elizabeth Farmer 1 counterpin, Stephen -----, James Lyon.

Money paid out per vouchers in office this 20 Feb.
1805: William Coventon $237.50 & $27.00, Myles Green, Joseph Grizard,
D. L. Ryan, John H. Walker $15.71½, William Walker $30.00, Hamlin Lewis,
William Silman $56.50 & $25.00, Elizabeth Grant $250.50 & $30.00, David
Walker $237.50 & $30.00; 2 gallons of brandy for the use of the estate $3.

Pages 106-111.   Freeman Allen of Hancock County, dec'd. Will,
                      pp. 106-107, dated 19 July 18--, proved and recorded
(no date). In a low state of health. To my beloved wife Jane Allen,
100 acres of land and plantation whereon I now live, with all improvements and appertancies, hereunto belonging, A Negro boy named Phil,
furniture, hogs, cattle, sheep and plantation tools, out of which she is
to raise, support and educate my children until they marry or arrive at
lawful age, to her and her heirs forever. The land and plantation that
I bought of James Simmons containing 196 acres together with a Negro
man named Dick to be sold at publick sale by my executors, and after my
debts are paid, the balance to be divided among my children as they come
of age or marry. Exors: wife Jane and friend James Bullard. s/ Freeman
Allen. Wit: Wooton Oneal, John Bush.

                      pp. 108-9, Inventory and Appraisement dated 11 Nov.
1803. Among articles named were 4 feather beds and furniture, several
books, looking glass, Negro man Dick $450, man Phil $500. Total not
given. s/ Collier Alford, John Rogers, Wooten Oneal, appraisers. Sworn
before Benj. Wh------. p. 109, Account of sales: only items named were
196 acres land and one negro fellow, amounts apparently torn or worn.
Moneys paid out to John Bush & Nancy King, no amount given. p. 111,
moneys paid out (no date) to James Whatley, Doctor L. Weatherby, Doctor
Roberts, Thomas Harris, Sherward Womack, William Thetford, William
Stephens, Nathaniel Stephens, Leonard Peak, Isaac Robertson acct., George
Grumbels, John Williams, Daniel Wagnon (?), Myles Greene, Robert M.
Cunningham, James Bullard act., Mr. Fletcher. July 2nd, Britton Williams
James Whaley, Willis Roberts, Archibald Martin. 1812 March 2, James
Ballard; James Whaley, Guardian $30.50.

Pages 112-113.   John Pinkson (Pinkston) of Hancock Co., deceased.
                      Will dated 10 (15?) May 179-, proved 29 Oct. 1803.
Sick of body. To my beloved son Greenbury, all my plantation where I
now live cont. five hundred seven---- acres - ------ and their heirs and
assigns forever ------- divided in the following manner. Gr----- 87½
acres where he now lives ----- ---- containing the old ----- my well
beloved wife Mary. To my beloved sons James and John all that tract of
287½ acres lying between the waters of Buffaloe, together with the -----
thereon erected, as tenants in common, and not as joint tenents. To my
beloved wife Mary during her life, all that part of my lands whereon I
now live containing the part allotted for my son Henry after her death,
including the houses, orchards and plantations thereunto belonging, with
all the stock of horses, cattle, sheep, hogs, etc., household furniture,
implements of husbandry, on condition that on the marriage of any and
every of my children who yet remain single, secure out of the above
devise towards preparing them for housekeeping in kind and value with
those who are married have received. Also to my wife during her life
Negroes ----- Harry, Aggy & Batchell. At the death of my wife, all
property is to go to my four sons and ----- Stacy. Exors: My three sons
Greenbury, James and -----). s/ John Pinkston. Wit: ------. (Many words
lost in this transcription).

Pages 114-118.   Michael Dickson, deceased. Will, pp. 114-116, dated
                      27 Aug. 1803, proved (no date). Weak in body. I
lend to my beloved wife M----- Dickson 100 acres beginning on a dogwood
corner ----- Harrel's line ----- until twenty fif-- ----- ----- her
death. Also lend her a bay mare named ----- until she has a colt ---
piece. ----- David, and one supposed to be ----- and each to suck until
they are nine minths old, and then to remain the property of my wife
forever so continue the rent of Hanner and Jude, hers during her natural
life. I also lend to my wife one Negro boy called James, until my son
Curry becomes age 21. I also give her a chestnut sorrel mare, and all
the stock of cattle that was formerly hers before I married her, half
the stock of hogs by quantity, plantation tools, household and kitchen
furniture, bedding and drye cattle excepted. Also a feather bed and
furniture. To my five oldest children John, Benjamin, William, Thomas
and Curry $500 each to be received as they come of age. If my son
William see cause to take my Negro fellow Harry at the sum of $425 if
----- the said Negro to be sold in Washington County when my son William
becomes of age. If my son Curry sees cause to take my Negro fellow James
at the sum of ----- when he arrives at age 21 -----, ----- ----- Dickson

and my sons Benjamin, John, William, Thomas & Curry a feather bed &
furniture. My sons Cyrus & David a feather bed & furniture when they
come of age. Also to Cyrus & David and the child supposed to be unborn,
$500 as they come of age or marry. My land in Green to remain unsold
and the Island on the Altamaha, all other lands to be sold the land in
Green and the Island not to be sold until David comes of age. The stud
horse to be sold in Washington Co. next August. ----- to be sold in
1809 in August. The remainder part of my hogs, cows, sheep, goats and
part of my crop to be sold this fawl. I also give half my crop of corn
fodder to my wife. I also order that my wife's claim of this land where
she now liveth is to be sold and laid out in a negroe to help school and
raise the children. Exors: sons John Dickson and ----- ----- -----
-----. s/ Michael Dickson, Martha (her (blank) mark) Dickson. Wit:
John Womack, John -----, Sh----- Womack.

                    p. 117, Inventory taken 3 Dec. 1803 by Shearward
Womack, Wallar Brown, and Reuben Read; sworn before Benj. Whitfield, JP.
Much of the inventory is missing, but some items were 1124 lbs. tobacco
at 3.75 per pound, 41 gallons peach brandy, 60 lbs. iron, 1 set candle
molds, 2 stills.

                    p. 118, Sale of part of the estate, 3 Dec. 1803.
Purchasers: Samuel Chewning; Waller Brown; John Rules (?); David Womack;
Benjamin Varington (?) 1 bee hive; Samuel -----; John Dickson, hire of
Negro girl; Shear Read; Benjamin -----; Joseph Womack; John Cooper;
Robert -----; Bird Brazz; James Alford; Francis Coleman, 37 gal. brandy
$37.25.

                    p. 119, additional return. Notes on George Prince,
John Rogers, William Price.

Page 120.   Will of Jacob Dickinson, dated -- Aug. 1799, proved
                    (no date). Much of this will is missing. Weak of
body. To beloved wife Judah Dickinson. To my son ----- (missing); to
my son Henry Dickinson. To Knudson (Kundson?) W. -----. (Missing) ----
in the state of ----- (Missing) ----- my son Jo-----. s/ Jacob Dickinson. No witnesses given.

Pages 121-124 are blank.

Page 125.   William King, dec'd. Sale of personal property,
                    no date. Buyers: The Widow, Jeremiah Baxter,
William Blake, James Arthur, Hubbard Ferrill, Beatrix Thompson (many
items), John Michael. (Account is unfinished.)

Pages 126-129.   Jeremiah L. (S?) Thompson, dec'd. Inventory pp.
                    126-127, taken Oct. 1803; A Negro boy Solomon $375,
boy Peter $200. (Much of list is missing.) Total $1131.65. s/ James
Harvey, Thos. Cooper, ----- Graybill, appraisers.

                    Pp. 128-129, Account of sale (continued; first part
missing.) Buyers: ----- Thompson, Richard Long, Charles Grass, Samuel
Lord, Isaac Holland, Benjamin Henry, Daniel Mitchell, Ebeneezer Doughty,
Samuel Blankenship. Total $878. s/ John Michael, Adm.

                    p. 129, Monies paid out: ----- Shivers, Holliday,
Henry, Brown, Lucas, Thompson Bird, Birch, Carley, Stephen Jones, John
Michael, Daniel Mitchell, Needham Jernigan. Monies received: Amt. sales
9 Apr. 1804, $878.41; Richardson & Benson, $70.

Pages 130-131.   Will of Peter Coffee of Hancock Co., dated 18 Oct.
                    1803, proved (no date, but faint date of 28 Jan.
1804 is seen at the end of the will.) Sick and weak of body. (Many
words missing.) To ---- --- Betsey Daniel, to my ---- ---- Nancy Hurd,
to my ---- ---- Susannah Randol. To my ---- dau. Sally Harris one Negro
fellow named Pool, one Negro ---- Nase (?), and $300. To my son John
Coffee $2,000, two men named Daniel & Jack, a boy Harry, one bed &
furniture, one filly got by fox hunter. To my wife Salley Coffee the
balance of the property until one of my four youngest children, viz.
Joshua Coffee, Polly Coffee, Sinthy Coffee or Patsy Coffee marry or

settle in the world, they shall have a portion then equal to what the
other children had when married. After they all have an equal share,
and after ----- ---- dies, the remainder to be divided among the four
children. All my real and personal property should be kept together for
the use and support of my wife and young children. Exors: Abraham H--d
(Hurd?) and William Harris. s/ Peter Coffee. Wit: Tamerlan (?) Jones,
Robert Pogue. P.S. After my son John Coffee becomes of age he may become one of my Executors if he thinks best. (Notation that ----- recorded in page 194.)

Pages 133-136 are blank.

Page 137.   Will of Ezekiel Wilkinson of Hancock Co., dated 19
               Dec. 1803, proved (no date). Weak in body. To
----- Wilkinson all my -----. Also, to Peasley (?) Taylor my mother also
my brother John Wilkinson and Milla Wilkinson, ---- J--- Wilkinson and
Anne Wilkinson and William and Stephen Wilkinson with my mother -----
and brothers and sister and ----- ---- within mentioned for the rest of
my property equally to be divided ------. Exor: Starling -----. s/
Ezekiel Wilkinson. Wit: Wyche Cato, James Wilkinson, Green Cato.

Pages 138-139 are blank.

Pages 140-145.   Jonathan Miller of Hancock Co., dec'd. Will, pp.
                    140-142, dated -- Dec. ----, proved and recorded
(no date). Weak and feeble in body. To my wife Mary Miller during her
life all the plantation and land joining it on which I now live, live-
stock and farm utensils to support the family as usual, but if she sees
best to sell the plantation and land aforesaid she may, but price of the
land must be applied for the ----- of other land to be disposed of as
hereafter mentioned. Also to wife Mary all my household furniture during
her life. To my son Lewis Miller, one negroe named Caesar to have after
my wife's death, a tract of land of about 700 acres in Washington Co.,
one lot of land at Mont---, $350 in cash and half of a soldiers bounty
warrant. To my son Francis ----- 96 acres in ----- County, 200 acres on
Washington Co., and one half of a soldiers bounty warrant. To my son
----- Miller one negroe named Murriber (?), one negro woman named Sarah,
after my wife's decease and one filly. Directly after my death -----
reserve that he shall pay out of his part of the estate unto my son
Francis Miller in lieu of the negro woman over and above what is left
above to said Francis $350 the negro woman lives to come into his posses-
sion, otherwise he is not to pay for her. To my son Jonathan Miller one
negro man Toney, one half the ----- ----- land above mentioned after my
wife's death -----. (Many words missing here.) To my daughter ----
---- out of my outstand---- ---- Anne and my daughter ---- each and one
bed ----- each. Whatever ready money ---- is not disposed of -----
-----ted and divided among ----- Francis, William and ----- -----..
equally divided among my four sons and five daughters and all the stock
that remains after my wife's death shall be divided amongst all my daughters, and all horses, farming utensils and tools to belong to the two
boys William & Jonathan. Exors: trusty friends ----- ----- and my son
-----. s/ Jonathan Miller. Wit: John Brown, Nathan Veal, George Trawick.

                    pp. 143-145, Inventory, no date, many words missing.
Negroes Mumber $500, Toney $550, Cesar $450, woman Sara $370, child
Cindy $25. No total. s/ John Brown, George Trawick, Francis Trawick,
James Gary, Appraisers. ----- Boyle, ----- Miller, ----- Miller, Exors.
Additional accounts carried to Book C, page 48.

Pages 147-148.   John McCaskill, dec'd. Inventory and Appraisement
                    14 Jan. ----. s/ by Andrew Baxter, Samuel Harris
& Henry Turner, sworn appraisers. 1 saddle, 5 saddle bags, bridle, old
ring, 1 ----- Arithmetic, handkerchiefs, cravat, many clothing items, 1
set platting instruments, 1 bell. Sale, 29 July 1803, no buyers listed.
Items: Spotted velvet overalls, cassemere, homespun and white overalls,
swansdown vest, nankeen overalls, hose, stockings, shoes, etc., -----
surveying, 1 case instruments. Many words missing. No total.

Page 150 is blank

Pages 151-153.   John Pinkston, dec. Inventory & Appraisement dated
                  11 Nov. 180-. Prices, apparently for 11 Negroes
listed, but only Ben $450, Rachel $300, & Sarah $40 named. Livestock,
crops and farm equipment listed. Total: $4072.37½. Most words missing
from other accounts.

Pages 154-157.   Peter Bird, dec'd. Inv. & App. 15 --- 1803. Negroes
                  named: man Mingo $370, woman Betty $100, girl Edney
$50, girl Lydda $175, boy David $175. Farm equipment; many words miss-
ing. Certified by Isaac Battle. s/ Solomon Jorden, Jno. Champion, Jno.
Veazey, Appraisers. Sale of personal property, many words missing.
Some buyers: Auston Potter, Warren West. Certified by Penelope Bird,
Admr. "A list of monies paid out is registered in Book C, page ---."

                  Account of sales 7 Dec. 18--. Buyers: A. Rawls, 2
negroes, not named; Jas. Bird, 3 negroes, not named; A. Hodge, Henry
Turner, J. Morgan, Solomon Jordan, ----- Burck, ----- Bird, ----- Battle,
Jno. Champion, Randolph Bullard.

Pages 158-162.   Levi Lancaster of Hancock Co., dec'd. Will, pp.
                  158-159, dated 18 Dec. 1803, proved (no date). In
a weak and low condition and to all human expectations near the close of
life. To my beloved wife Ann Lancaster 1 feather bed & furniture, the
debt due me from Mark--- G----- all the debts due me for Tay-----, the
debt due me from Tap----- for tobacco sold him. The ----- to the family
of negroes we now have in possession (to wit) Abigail and her issue
agreeable to an -------- by Benjamin Jones my ----- relative thereto
(many words missing). Also (to my wife) during her natural life the
plantation where I now live , furniture, etc. ----- to my son Thomas
Lancaster the sum of one ----- to be collected out of debts owed me,
also one half of a Soldiers Bounty Warrant. To my daughter Nancy Harvey
one half of a Soldiers Bounty Warrant. To my three grandchildren -----
Am Weeks, Elizabeth Weeks and Nancy Weeks, $2 each. The land I own in
partnership with Joseph Bryan on the Oconee River to be sold as soon as
thought best. (Many words missing) Thomas -----. Exors: beloved wife
Ann Lancaster, son Thomas Lancaster and Joseph Bryan. s/ Levi Lancaster.
Wit: Josia Askey, Ann Bryan.

                  pp. 160-162, Inventory, no date. The first page
lists household goods. At bottom of page: "The above articles from the
first calculation amounting to $158.55 are kept by Mrs. Lancaster agree-
able to the will." Other items: walnut desk, dictionary, Methodist
Magazine, Pamphlets, Methodist Minister, 1 Watts Hyms, 1 sett money seals,
crockery, farm produce. s/ James Bishop, Simon Holt, John Bailey,
appraisers. Signed by Joseph Bryan at the request of appraisers. "Amt.
of monies received & monies paid out carried to Book C, page 318."

Pages 163-167.   Job Tison, dec'd. Inventory dated 29 Dec. 1803.
                  Negroes named: Lucy $250, Rachel $400, Aggey $400,
Edey $325, Philip $450, Wil---- $450, Isaac $450, Joel $450, Ne--- $300,
Dinah $250, Aaron $225, M----- $200, Fi----- $75, Br----- $150, Mary
$150. Several counterpins, bolsters, curtains, quilts, nice furniture
and dishes, dictionary, Church Bible, books, farm equipment and animals.
Book Accounts: Bryant Butler, Henderson Collier, Thos. Carrell, Joel
McClendon, William Thornton. Total not given, but over $6201.60. s/ D.
Henderson, Andrew -----, Zorl -----, appraisers. Sworn before Jno.
Crowder, JP, 30 Jan. 1804. Note that vouchers showing money paid out
registered on page 261.

Pages 168-169.   Michael Gilbert, dec'd. Inventory; appraisers
                  sworn before Robert Holt, Esq., no date. Negroes
named: men Jim $500, Harry $500, Tom $350; woman Chaney & child $460;
women Tilla $280, Fanny $350; girl Vilett $200; boy Lewis $200. Furniture, books, farm tools and stock mentioned. Total not given but over
$3062.50. s/ Wm. C. Barksdale, John Dudley, John Kelley, appraisers.

Pages 170-172 are blank.

Pages 173-176.   William Johnston, dec'd. Sale dated 29 Oct. ----.
                  Buyers: ----- Barksdale bought Negro wench Delilah

327

& child $461; ---- Johnston bought fellow Tom $420 and wench Dicey $321;
---- Garrett bought Charlotte $200, ---- Johnston bought boy Frank for
Rebecca $88, Reuben for John $183, and ---- for Malcum $175. Rebeckah
Johnston bought most items including a Bible and a roan colt & saddle
for John; Collier Barksdale, William Lancaster, Nathan Smith, John Ran-
dle, John ----, James ----, Wilbourn Dickinson, John Butler, William
Garrett, Jonathan Hagety, Thomas Johnston. Appraisers names are miss-
ing. Note that vouchers of this estate entered in page 264.

Pages 177-179.   Benjamin Orare, dec'd. Will (p. 177) dated 13 Nov.
                       1803, proved no date. To my beloved wife Mariam
Orare during her widowhood my two negroes Tobe & Jane, and on her marri-
age, to be ---- ---- all their increase, twelve ----- credit, to the
highest bidder and the money to be put on interest till the three child-
ren come of age then to be equally divided between them, my daughter
Lizer, my son William and my daughter Sileatia. Exors: wife Miriam and
Jesse Brantley & William Loyd. s/ Benjamin (X) Orare. Wit: J. Goare,
John Kelley, Daniel Orare.

                       Inventory & Appraisement dated 29 Feb. ----. Neg-
roes named: boy Tobe $450, girl Jane $330. Furniture, stock & farm
equipment. Total not given but over $1235.29. s/ J. Goare, Nicholas
Dixon, Irby Hudson, appraisers. Sworn before ---- Dent, JP. Miriam
Orare, Extrx.

                       Monies paid out, no date: Doct. Bird, Wm. Horton,
Jno. Dudley, Doct. Nelson, Myles Greene, Benjamin Williams, Wm. Hudson,
Andrew Baxter, Woodlef Scott, Robert Mitchell, Rees & Beal, A. Barnes,
Printer, Philip Sims, Benj. Woodruff. No total.

Pages 180-183.   William ----- (Hutson?) dec'd., dated 29 Dec. 1803.
                       Furniture, farm equipment & animals; Negro boy
named Gloster $400; notes on Solomon Thornton, Jesse Hewby, Robert Par-
ham. Total not given.

                       Sales of William Hutson, dec'd., -- Jan. 1804.
Buyers: Hubert Brown, William Hudson, Alexander Greene, Robert Moreland,
Solomon Thornton, Alexander ditto (Thornton?), John Brantley, Robert
Simmons, Joseph Harper, Robert Parham, Ephraim West, Gale Lewis, James
Rose, Jonathan ----, John Rivers, William Hutson, G---- Thweatt, John
Dickson, ---- Sturdivant, Allen Hudson, James Simmons, Myles Greene.
Total not given.

Page 184 is blank.

Pages 185-186.   Ezekiel Wilkinson, dec'd. Inventory & Appraisement
                       dated 4 Feb. 1804. Notes on: William Martin, John
Alford, Warsham Easley, Alexander Reid, dec'd., Wyche Cato, John Wilkinson, Asa Alexander, Samuel Ferguson; due bill on Samuel Wins--; Open
accounts on Mgr. D. Adams, Lucy Reid, Wm. Kimbroe, dec'd. Gelding $135,
saddle & saddle bags, History of ---- Parks Travels, 1 plated spur, 1
umbrella, set of carpenters tools $50, 1 gold ring. (That was the com-
plete inventory listed.) Total $1205.85. s/ Greene Cato, James Wooten,
Benjamin Parrott, Appraisers. Sterling Cato, Exr.

                       Account of Sales dated 27 ---, 1804. Buyers:
Philip Cato, Eli Harris, Anderson Middlebrooks, Sterling Cato, Thomas
Wilkinson. Total $177.25. Received one receipt of John Wilkinson in full
for the above estate signed by said John Wilkinson attorney for the
legatees.

Page 187 is blank.

Pages 188-193.   James Fail, dec'd. Inventory & Appraisement (pp.
                       188-189) dated 9 Feb. 1804. Negroes named: woman
Judith $385, girl Priscilla $225. Furniture & farm tools and animals.
Note on Cecil Kimbroe; open accounts against Phillip Spillers, Leonard
Bowman. Total $1103.31. s/ William Williams, Peter F. Floynoy, William
Floynoy, appraisers. Chloe Fail, Malone Mullins, Admrs.

328

Sale of personal estate 18 Feb. 1804. Buyers:
Jesse Mallet, Isaac Simmons, Peter F. Floynoy, Wm. Tankersley, Francis
Gray, Adam Butt, William Perry, John Gray, Nathl. Halley, Arthur Fail,
Malone Mullins, Briton -----, Christopher Bustain, Matthew Durham, Gar-
rett Hudman, Wm. Walker, Sal Foster, Hardy Cain, James Horton, James
Williams, Thomas Glenn, Robert Tankersley, Go. Gray, John Oliver, Charles
McDonald, Robert Rivers, John Thompson, Fredk. Lipman, Chloe Fail, Jas.
Greene, Joseph Wheat, Hardy Cain. Total $1074.94. s/ Chloe Fail, Malone
Mullins, Admrs.

Monies paid out 12 Dec. 1806. (Only large amts.
listed here.) Jos. Wheat $106.66, Jno. Oliver $85.26, Wm. Anders (?)
for B. Harper, Richd. Clark, Wm. B. Tankersley $97, Wm. Downman, Elisha
Spiller $227, Isaac Simmons, John Little, John Cooke, Danl. Orgood, Thos.
Fail, Gracy Fail, Jos. Wheat for H. Wheat, Bagget & Horton, Jas. Williams,
Hardy Cain, Peter McFarlan, Wm. Ryan for Janth Day, David Kelley Junr.,
M. Greey Clerk, Dennis L. Ryan.

Pages 194-197.   Peter Coffee, dec'd. Inventory & Appraisal made 6
                        Feb. 1804. Negroes named: men Fill $500, Bob $500,
Lewis $500; boy Daniel $500, man Dan $100, boys Jacob $300, Charles
$225, Guy $175, David $150, Isaac $175, Abednego $150; women Anna $250,
Lucy $300, Fanny $400, Sarah $375. 5 feather beds, 20 chairs, walnut
tables & desk, 1 "beaufat" & furniture, 6 trunks, books, stock, 7 bee
hives, cotton machean. Notes on E. Thomas, John McAlister, Micajah
Little, John Low, Thomas Jones, Samuel Alexander, Loyd & Randle, Bullard
& Oneal, Wm. & S. Willson, ---- Coffee, James Alston. Book accounts
against John Rhymes, Peter Bird dec'd., John Wilson, Thomas Collins,
Waller Brown, Micajah Little, Noah Kelcy, Jas. Alford. Judgement against
Wm. Hodge. Note on Estate of Chas. Daniell. Total $9454.29 3/4. One
negro girl purchased for the Estate since, about 8 yrs. old. s/ Tamer-
lane Jones, James Lawrence, Benjamin Whitfield, appraisers. Monies paid
out: Shearward Wammack, William Russell, Myles Greene, Wm. Thetford,
---- Abercrombie, Peter Wright, William Lee, James & Collier Alford.

Page 199.   Willis Jones, dec'd. Inventory & Appraisement dated
                        21 Apr. 1804. Negro woman Violet $325; note on
Morgan Rutland; notes on Kno. Rhymie totaling $265; 1 saddle, bridle &
blanket, 1 silver watch, 1 pr. pistols & holsters, 1 pr. plated spurs,
Cash T. Jones $550, 1 umbrella, 1 trunk. (That is complete inventory.)
No total given. s/ Jno. Coffee, Sherrard Womack, Jesse White, appraisers.

Page 201.   William Sanders, dec'd. Inventory & Appraisement
                        dated 16 Apr. 1804. 2 feather beds, 2 chairs, 2
chests, few dishes & pots, cotton spinning wheel. Total $76.37½. s/
Daniel Low, Ralph Low, David Adams, appraisers. Mrs. Elizabeth Sanders
& Jas. B. Fannin, Admrs.

Page 202.   William Roach, William Coulter, & John Sergeants,
                        dec'd. Inventory, no date. "The sworn Appraisers
certify that there appears to be due from United States to the Estates
of the persons hereafter mentioned, the several sums annexed to their
names (viz) William Roach $13.04, William Coulter $11.28, John Sergeants
$33.84." s/ Jonn Holsted, W. Hall, Samuel Tinsley, Appraisers. -----,
Admr.

Page 203.   William Pride, dec'd. Vouchers showing money paid
                        out returned per William Reese, Admr. Accounts and
notes: Thompson Bird, estate of Jno. Swinney, Simeon Loomis, Timothy
Rosseter, Lewis Moss, David Pinkerton, John Whitehurst, Melby McGee,
James Evans, John Lucas, Daniel Wells, William Hardage, Edwd. B. Broad-
nax, Thos. Johnston for ----- Clements due bill. Moneys received from
Duke Hamilton, Philip Jackson, John Lewis, Jas. Hall.

Page 204.   Isham Westmoreland, dec'd. Inventory & Appraise-
                        ment dated 7 Feb. 1804. Bed, weavers loom, iron
pot, dishes, womans saddle. Total $35.75. s/ John Sturdivant, Jesse
Warren, Thomas Stembridge, appraisers. Elizabeth Westmoreland, Admr.

Page 205.   Truitt Collins, dec'd. Moneys paid out, no date:

329

B. Cook, Samuel Betts, Abraham Betts, George Collins, Jonathan Davis, Abner Atkerson, Doctor J. Lacy, Thompson Bird, Samuel Betts receipt for Maugham & Rollin note. No total.

Pages 206-208. Thomas Fail, dec'd. Sale dated 15 Jul. 1800. Buyers: Phillip Spiller bought Negro girl Silvey for $355; James Fail bought Negro woman Juda for $410; Mary Vaugn bought Negro girl Hannah for $301; Thomas Fail bought Negro George for $230; Francis Fail bought 1 girl child Siller for $80; John Wallace; Samuel Halley; Robert Rivers; Thomas Spencer; William Kinchen; James Boswell; William Newsom; Esom Franklin; John Cook; Wm. Horton; Arthur Fail. Total $1567.75. Money paid out: note of hand to Philip Spillers.

Pages 209-213. Joshua Ellis of Hancock Co., dec'd. Will (pp. 209-211) dated 6 Jan. 1804, proved (no date). In a low state of health. To beloved son James Ellis, 65 acres to be laid out on the lower side toward the mouth of Shoulder Bone Creek, from James Davis' line to said Shoulder Bone to run square with the line of the original survey on said lower end, including the place whereon he now lives. To beloved son Stephen Ellis 70 acres to be laid off adj. his brother James land, from one end to the other, including his house and spring whereon he now lives. To my beloved wife Abigail Ellis all the tract where I now live (that I have not before herein given away) including the plantation and houses of every kind, furniture, etc., during her natural life. After her death that land should be evenly divided between my two youngest sons; my youngest Elisha to have the part including my houses, and Joshua to have the upper part adj. William Hunt's land. To my daughter Sarah Mattocks $30 cash. Other items including furniture to sons Joshua & Elisha. At my wife'd death all items lent her to be divided among all my children, except my shop and blacksmiths tools which I give to my four sons equally. Exors: sons Stephen & James Ellis. s/ Joshua Ellis. Wit: William Hunt, Joel Hunt.

Inventory & Appraisement dated 23 June 1804. Much farm equipment, furniture, pewter dishes, etc. Notes and open accounts: James Bynam, Micajah Middlebrooks, Jesse Mattock, Jesse Ellis, John Vison, Isaac Ellis, Jos. Burges, William Low dec'd. Total $1042.10. s/ William Hurt, Jehu Smith, Jas. Davis, Danl. Low, appraisers.

Sale (pp. 213-214) dated 4 Aug. 1804. Buyers: George Huff, Charles Bradley, Joshua Ellis, Jesse Ellis, John Comer, Levi Ellis, Philip Barnheart, Allen Hudson, Stephen Ellis, James Ellis, Judkins Hunt Senr., Jethro Jackson, William Wallace, John White, James Ross, Noah Dodridge.

Monies paid out: Elijah Trewett, Stephen Ellis, Elisha Boyce, Ishmael David, Alexander Reede, John Broadnax, Dr. Bird.

The Georgia Department of Archives and History has brought in numerous collections of loose county records that otherwise might have remained inaccessible to the public or even destroyed. One of the largest of these collections is the loose county records of Jasper County. Reproduced below is the Georgia Archives' inventory of loose Jasper County wills in Record Group 179-2-4. These wills are open to use by the public at the Georgia Archives.

The Georgia Archives must be encouraged to bring in the loose records that remain in old courthouses across the state. You can help in this effort by writing to Secretary of State, Max Clelland, State Capitol, Atlanta, Ga., 30334.

Aaron, Mitchel, 1881
Adams, James, 1857
Aken, James, 1871
Akins, Samuel S., 1851
Akins, Thomas, 1853
Alexander, Jane, 1822
Allen, Harris, 1854
Allen, Samuel, 1857
Allen, Susan, 1854
Allen, William, 1858
Armstrong, William, 1834
Avant, Henry, 1873
Avery, Samuel, 1883

Bailey, William H., 1855
Bailey, Williamson, 1857
Ballard, Mrs. W. E., 1903
Banks, Benjamin W., 1857
Banks, John C., 1861
Banks, Josiah C., 1859
Banks, Mary, 1859
Banks, Nancy, 1857
Barnes, Nancy, 1861
Barnett, Nathaniel, 1824
Bartlett, Eugene S., 1879
Bartlett, George T., 1885
Bartlett, Mary, 1851
Baynes, Elbert W., 1886
Baynes, John H., 1842
Benton, Abba, 1852
Binford, E. A., 1906
Blackwell, Samuel H., 1894
Bogan, John, 1868
Borum, George, 1823
Bowden, Nancey, 1853
Boyd, Richard, 1822
Brandon, John, 1859
Bridges, Bennett R., 1865
Broddus, Thomas, 1854
Byars, Obadiah, 1875

Campbell, Richard, 1851
Carter, Temperance, 1849
Chapman, Asa W. F., 1851
Cheek, William, 1868
Clark, Allen, 1884
Clark, George, 1846
Clark, Gilbert, 1885
Clark, John, 1861
Clark, Leama, 1907
Clay, Martha, 1851
Comer, Mary B., 1867
Comer, Thomas J., 1865
Compton, Jordan, 1863

Compton, Pleasant, 1822
Cornwell, George W., 1861
Couch, N. H., 1905
Couch, Nancy, 1884
Cox, Sarah, 1834
Cox, Wiley J., 1833
Crawford, Andrew, 1876
Crawman, Mary, 1843
Cross, John, 1823
Cunard, John, 1869
Cunard, John, Jr., 1861
Cunard, Jumina, 1872
Curry, Thompson, 1857

Daniel, Isaac, 1856
Digby, Berry T., 1879
Doggett, John, 1813
Doster, James C., 1863
Downs, John, 1817
Dozier, Abner C., 1869
Dozier, Adaline B., 1888
Driskell, Julia G., 1882
Dunn, William G., 1886
Dyer, Anthony, 1849

Edmonds, Rachel, 1824
Edwards, Reuben, 1864
Ellis, Henry, 1881
Ellis, Radford, 1811

Faulkner, John, 1861
Faulkner, Maston, 1849
Fears, Ailsey, 1859
Fish, Calvin, 1861
Fish, Emily B., 1871
Franklin, John Carter, 1877
Freeman, Cynthia A., 1879
Freeman, Floyd, 1905
Freeman, James, 1848
Freeman, Josiah, 1824
Freeman, Mary C., 1865

Gay, Sherrod H., 1859
Geiger, Elizabeth, 1853
Geiger, Harman H., 1868
Glover, Eli, Sr., 1858
Goode, James Henderson, 1857
Goode, Jesse, 1833
Goode, John C., 1862
Goolsby, Carden, 1882
Goolsby, Cincinnatus L., 1890
Goolsby, Jacob, 1862
Goolsby, William, 1872
Gordon, Louise, 1855

Gregory, Lewis, 1824
Grier, Thomas, 1849

Hardman, Alphonso, 1864
Hardwick, Charity, 1886
Hartsfield, Middleton, 1851
Hawk, Henry, 1903
Henderson, Charles, 1885
Henderson, James, 1856
Henderson, Samuel, 1850
Hines, James, 1845
Hodge, D. R., 1879
Holloway, Dabney P., 1879
Holloway, Jesse, 1822
Horton, Elisha, 1853
Houghton, Josiah
Howard, J. B., 1897
Howard, J. B., 1897
Howard, Stephen, 1860
Hunter, Alexander A., 1864
Hunter, James T., 1860

Jackson, Pleasant, 1860
Jenkins, Francis, 1862
Jenkins, William, 1864
Johnston, James M., 1851
Johnston, John, 1844
Johnston, Martha M., 1875
Johnston, Thomas, 1844
Jones, David C., 1864
Jones, William, 1850
Jordan, Fleming, Sr., 1864
Jordan, Reuben, 1857

Keene, Ann T., 1852
Kelly, John R., 1878
Kelly, John W., 1875
Kennedy, Jane, 1823
Key, B. P., 1870
King, Dolly, 1849
Kitchens, Charles, 1864

Lane, William D., 1882
Langston, John E., 1862
Lawrence, Leroy, 1864
Lawrence, William, 1846
Lazenby, Mary A., 1886
Leverett, Martha Caroline, 1905
Long, George, 1858
Lowry, Ann, 1858
Lowry, Elizabeth, 1869
Lunsford, Leonard L., 1823
Lynch, Jarrett, 1863

Macon, Martha Williamson, 1809
Maddux, John, 1870
Maddux, John C., 1859
Maddux, William D., 1898
Malone, Anna B., 1888
Massey, Enos, 1880
Maxey, William, 1873
Meriwether, David, 1866
Meriwether, Sallie A., 1905
Minter, Jeremiah P., 1863
Mitchell, Richard, 1818
Montgomery, James N., 1866
Moreland, Frances, 1833
Morris, Benjamin F., 1859
Morris, Sarah M., 1884
Moseley, Henry, 1822

McClendon, Isaac, 1821
McClendon, Stephen W., 1857
McDowell, Daniel, 1860
McGlaughlin, James, 1889
McKee, John F. M., 1849
McKissack, Thomas, 1888
McMichael, Elijah H. L., 1863
McMichael, Shadrach, 1861
McMury, John, 1829

Newton, Aristarchus, 1869
Nolan, Elizabeth C., 1902

Oxford, Washington, 1891

Parker, Urania Elizabeth, 1853
Pearson, Jeremiah, 1855
Penn, Joseph, 1863
Penn, Martha A., 1883
Penn, Thomas R., 1906
Perkins, Moses, 1816
Peurifoy, Avaline, 1882
Peurifoy, B. W., 1896
Phelps, Aquilla, 1853
Phillips, Lewis, 1847
Phillips, Mary E., 1866
Phillis, Wiley, 1869
Porter, Matilda M., 1857
Post, Samuel, 1840
Pou, John T., 1880
Powell, A. L., 1892
Powell, Evan H., 1857
Powell, Rachel, 1879
Preston, William H., 1863
Price, Mary, 1858
Pye, James, 1854
Pye, Jordan, 1856
Pye, Theophilus, 1868

Ragland, Mary R., 1893
Ratcliff, Moses, 1837
Reese, Cuthbert, 1853
Reid, Samuel, 1836
Reid, William A., no date
Rivers, Benjamin, 1866
Robey, Nathan, 1826
Robey, Timothy, 1825
Robinson, William C., 1857
Roby, Williamson, 1834
Rogers, Dred, 1820
Ross, William, 1857

Satterwhite, Dawson, 1854
Shaw, John, 1868
Shepherd, Eleazer W., 1863
Shepherd, Sarah, 1862
Showers, Paschal, 1879
Shropshire, James W., 1866
Shropshire, Olivia J., 1873
Shy, Seaborn J., 1858
Smith, Abraham H., 1887
Smith, Charles S., 1856
Smith, David, 1865
Smith, Henry T., 1854
Smith, Henry T., 1906
Smith, John 1826
Smith, John W. A., 1887
Smith, William G., 1863
Speairs, Caleb W., 1879
Spearman, G. T., 1868

Spearman, John, 1862
Spearman, Martha, 1883
Spears, Columbus A., 1863
Spears, Creed A., 1864
Spears, John, 1855
Spears, William H., 1881
Speights, James, 1872
Standifer, Archibald, 1867
Stanley, Martin, 1823

Talmadge, Stephen C., 1873
Taylor, Leonard, 1812
Thomas, William 1907
Thomason, Thomas, 1850
Thompson, Henry, 1817
Toland, Michael M., 1857
Tompkins, Lucy Ann, 1849
Towns, John G., 1823
Traylor, Champion T., 1817
Traylor, Thomas, 1811
Tuggle, Elizabeth, 1854
Tuggle, William J. L., 1864
Turk, John, 1875
Turner, S. W., Sr., 1896

Vaughn, Stephen, H., 1864

Wade, Benjamin, 1824
Waits, Benjamin, 1839
Waits, Leroy, 1863
Waldrep, Leecil J., 1883
Walker, Hackey, 1853
Walker, Henry, 1874
Ware, Henry, 1822
Watters, John C., 1854
Watters, Robert P., 1859
West, Andrew, 1851
White, Ann H., 1856
White, John, 1824
Whitfield, Matthew, 1864
Wilkins, Drury, 1834
Williams, James M., 1887
Wilson, Arkillis, 1831
Wilson, Joseph, 1822
Wilson, Rachael, 1879
Wooten, Elizabeth, 1828
Wyatt, Mary Ann, 1904
Wyatt, Thomas, 1853

Yancy, Lewis D., 1843
Yancy, Nancy, 1887

LOOSE JASPER COUNTY ESTATE PAPERS 1809-1907

The Georgia Department of Archives and History has brought in several collections of loose early Georgia county records. These collections are cleaned up, organized, inventoried, and made available to researchers at the Georgia Archives. For many collections, this process has been their rescue, saving them from the dump, attics, basements, etc.

Reproduced below is the Archives' inventory of its loose Jasper County estate papers, Record Group 179-2-3. The Archives also has several other large collections of Jasper County records in Record Group 179.

The Georgia Archives needs to be encouraged to save other collections of loose records that still remain in various courthouses. To support cause, write to Secretary of State, Max Clelland, State Capitol, Atlanta, Ga., 30334.

Aaron, James C.
Aaron, John L.
Aaron, John M.
Aaron, Mitchel
Abbott, Ezekiel
Adams, David L.
Adams, Elizabeth L.
Adams, George W.
Adams, James
Adams, Jonathan
Adams, Jonathan
Adams, Meridith
Aiken, Charles P.
Aiken, John C.
Aikens, James
Akens, Daniel
Akins, Samuel S.
Akins, Thomas
Alexander, Abden
Alexander, Adam
Alexander, Eliza
Alexander, George

Alexander, Robert J.
Allen, David
Allen, Harris
Allen, John
Allen, Macon
Allen, Phoebe
Allen, Robert A.
Allen, Samuel
Allen, W. W.
Allen, William
Ambrose, Warren
Anderson, S. M.
Anderson, Samuel
Andrews, Davis R.
Andrews, Greene
Andrews, Robert
Annis, Emerson B.
Annis, Martha G.
Anthony, James
Antony, Milton
Appling, Otho H.
Armor, James

Armstrong, William
Arnold, William W.
Arrington, Elizabeth
Ashurst, Josiah T.
Askew, William
Atcheson, James A.
Avant, Henry
Averett, James
Avery, Asa G.
Avery, Herbert
Avery, Rose Ann
Avery, Samuel
Avery, William

Bailey, William H.
Bailey, Williamson
Baldwin, John
Baldwin, Marcus A.
Ballard, W. E.
Banks, Benjamin W.
Banks, Charles
Banks, Christopher C.

Banks, Dunstan
Baks, Eaton
Banks, James
Banks, John C.
Banks, John T.
Banks, Josiah C.
Barbee, Joseph
Barclay, Leroy P.
Barclay, William
Barkley, William
Barnes, Nancy
Barnett, Elijah F.
Barnett, Eliza
Barnett, Nathaniel
Barnwell, Elizabeth A.
Barr, Harriett N.
Barr, William J.
Barron, Andrew J.
Bartlett, Abner
Bartett, Eugene S.
Barlett, George T.
Bartlett, Mary
Bartlett, Samuel Eugene
Bass, Micthel
Bass, William A.
Baynes, Alfred J.
Baynes, Elbert W.
Baynes, Gene
Baynes, John H.
Baynes, Sarah Elizabeth
Baysden, Mary
Beach, James
Beal, Elizabeth
Beall, James D.
Beasley, Robert C.
Beasley, Stephen W.
Beckwith, W. B.
Beckwith, William S.
Belcher, Green B.
Belcher, Isham S.
Belcher, Obadiah R.
Belcher, William D.
Bell, John
Bender, John S.
Benson, James M.
Benton, Abba
Benton, James
Benton, Jeremiah
Benton, John
Benton, Lucian
Benton, Otis M.
Benton, Sarah J.
Berner, William R.
Berry, A. T.
Berry, Anderson
Betts, Abraham
Binford, Cicero S.
Benford, Henry W.
Binford, Joseph T.
Binford, Josephine S.
Binns, Burwell
Birdsong, Benajah
Blackwell, J. H.
Blackwell, Samuel H.
Blackwell, Samuel S.
Blizzard, Henry
Boount, John
Blount, Susan
Bogan, John
Bond, William S.

Bonner, Whitmill
Boon, Exum
Boon, Jacob
Boram, George
Boram, John
Boswell, Henry
Bowden, Amanda M.
Bowden, Nancy
Boyd, Samuel
Boykin, Francis
Boykin, Jesse W.
Boykin, William P.
Boynton, Stewart
Bozeman, Samuel
Bradford, Edmund
Brady, Thomas
Brandon, James
Brandon, John
Brantley, Green D.
Branum, Harris
Brazil, Samuel
Brazil, William
Brazwell, Aaron
Breedlove, Ann
Brewer, Elisha W.
Bridges, Bennett
Bridges, Wiseman
Briers, John
Britt, Willis
Broddus, Edward A.
Broddus, Edward S.
Broddus, Thomas
Brooks, Iverson S.
Brooks, James, Sr.
Brooks, Russell
Brooks, William
Broughton, Belitha
Broughton, Charles
Brown, Bartlett
Brown, Edward
Brown, George A.
Brown, James
Brown, Jeremiah
Brown, John W.
Brown, Josiah
Brown, Robert
Brown, Russel J.
Brown, Sucky
Bryant, Artemus
Bryant, John
Buchanan, Benjamin
Buchannan, Alexander N.
Buchannon, James, Sr.
Buchannon, John
Buis, John
Bullard, James, Sr.
Bullard, Wiley
Bullard, William
Burney, Charles C.
Burney, J. H.
Burney, John W., Sr.
Burney, Tom
Butler, Thomas
Butts, Samuel
Byars, Obadiah
Byrom, John
Byrom, Seymore S.

Caldwell, William D.
Callaway, James C.

Callaway, John
Callaway, Joshua
Calvert, Susan E.
Campbell, Charles EFW
Campbell, Charles G.
Campbell, Cooley
Campbell, Dorcas
Campbell, James L.
Campbell, Jarrett
Campbell, Richard
Campbell, Richard S.
Campbell, William C.
Cardel, John C.
Cardell, Peter
Carden, James
Cardin, William
Cargile, Charles
Cargile, John
Cargile, Thomas
Carlisle, Mary
Carmichael, John
Carter, Kissiah
Carter, Landon
Carter, Richard
Case, Wiley J.
Castellow, John B.Sr.
Castleberry, Thomas
Catchings, Elbert G.
Chaffin, Beverly
Chaffin, John T.
Champion, Moses
Chapman, Abner
Chapman, Asa W. F.
Chapman, Edmond
Chapman, John
Cheek, John W.
Cheek, LaFayette
Cheek, William
Cheney, William R.
Cherry, Jesse
Childs, Henry
Childs, Jack
Clark, Emily
Clark, Francis A.
Clark, George W.
Clark, Gilbert
Clark, John
Clark, Joseph
Clark, Joshua
Clark, Joshua R.
Clark, Lindsey
Clark, Thomas
Clark, Thomas
Clay, Hezekiah
Clay, James C.
Clay, Jesse, Sr.
Clay, Martha S.
Cleckley, Jacob
Clements, Allen
Clements, Peyton
Coats, James
Cochran, Cheadle
Cochran, John
Cochran, Jubil
Cole, Elizabeth L.
Cole, Rene
Cole, William
Collier, John
Collier, William
Colquit, John Terry

334

Comer, Lydia
Comer, Mary B.
Comer, Thomas J.
Compton, John W.
Compton, Jordan
Compton, Pleasant
Compton, Polly Ann
Conner, John W.
Cook, Benjamin W.
Cook, John W.
Cornwell, Elijah
Cornwell, George W.
Cornwell, Gibson H.
Cornwell, Obadiah
Cornwell, William D.
Couch, Moses
Couch, N. H.
Couch, Nancy
Cousins, Thomas
Cox, Jesse
Cox, Wiley J.
Crain, Spencer, Sr.
Crall, James
Crawford, Andrew
Crawford, Samuel
Crawman, Mary
Creagh, Thomas B.
Crenshaw, Jarrell
Cross, George
Cross, John
Crow, Elisha
Crow, John M.
Culbertson, Samuel
Cunard, John
Cunard, Jumina
Curry, John
Curry, Thompson
Cuthbert, Alfred

Dabney, Anderson
Dabney, Hannah
Daniel, Alexander
Daniel, Isaac
Daniel, John W.
Daniel, Levi
Daniel, Moses
Daniel, Thomas
Dannielly, Nancy
Darden, James M.
Darden, John
Darden, John B.
Davidson, John, Sr.
Davidson, Robert
Davis, Thomas
Dawkins, George
Dawkins, Partheny
Deadwilder, Eva
Deal, William
Deane, Nathaniel
Deane, Thomas
Dennis, Jesse
Dickinson, Henry A.
Digby, Benjamin
Digby, Berry T.
Digby, John
Digby, John B.
Dillard, John A.
Dillard, Thomas
Dillon, John
Dingler, William

Dismukes, Martha D.
Dodson, Elijah
Doggett, Garner
Doggett, John
Dorsett, Palemon W.
Doster, James C.
Doster, James W.
Dougherty, William
Downs, S. P.
Downs, Skelly
Dozier, Abner C.
Dozier, George R.
Dozier, Woody
Driskell, James B.
Driskell, John
Driskell, Julia G.
Duke, Isham
Duncan, Thomas
Dunn, Albert G.
Dunn, Gatewood
Dunn, William G.
Durden, Stephen J.
Dyer, Anthony
Dyer, John P.

Echols, Elizabeth
Edmonds, Rachel
Edmondson, Benjamin C.
Edmondson, Crawford
Edmondson, Samuel
Edwards, Herbert
Edwards, James
Edwards, Joel J.
Edwards, John
Edwards, Reuben
Edwards, Robert S.
Edwards, William J.
Egnew, William
Elder, Edward A.
Elder, Susan
Elder, Turner
Ellis, Henry
Ellis, James
Ellis, John B.
Ellis, Radford
English, Augustus
Epps, Joseph
Eubanks, Magers
Evans, Henry W.
Evans, Jesse, Sr.
Evans, Josiah J.
Ezell, Braxton R.
Ezell, John
Ezell, Robert

Farley, John
Farrar, William G.
Faulkner, James Hilton
Faulkner, John
Faulkner, Maston
Faulkner, Zachariah
Favors, Joseph C.
Fears, Alsea
Fears, Benjamin Franklin
Fears, Ezekial
Fears, William Q.
Fears, Wyly
Featherston, Richard
Fincher, Leonard C.
Fish, Calvin

Fish, Nathan
Fitzpatrick, Bouth
Fitzpartick, William
Fitzsimmons, Emma
Flemister, Ellender G.
Flemister, James C.
Florence, A. S.
Flournoy, Josiah
Flournoy, Samuel A.
Flournoy, William F.
Folds, Charles J.
Folds, Grandason
Folds, Jacob
Folds, John
Ford, Washington
Foreman, Jacob
Franklin, John C.
Frazier, Andrew
Freeman, Bailey
Freeman, Benjamin B.
Freeman, Daniel
Freeman, George
Freeman, Hartwell WB
Freeman, Hopson
Freeman, Isaac H.
Freeman, James
Freeman, Josiah
Funderburk, William A.

Gallman, John C.
Gallman, John C.
Gardner, Ethelred
Garland, John
Garrett, Blunty
Garrett, George S.
Gaston, Catharine
Gaston, Nancy A.
Gaston, P. F.
Gaston, Thomas
Gay, Sherrod H.
Geiger, Elizabeth
Geiger, Harmon H.
Geiger, Randal H.
Geiger, Washington
George, James
Gholston, Anthony
Gibson, John C.
Gilstrap, John B.
Glenn, Thornton I.
Glover, Eli
Glover, Eli S.
Glover, Henry S. Sr.
Glover, John
Glover, John E.
Goggins, Madison
Good, Sterling
Good, Theophilus
Goode, James H.
Goode, Jesse
Goode, John C.
Goode, William
Goodman, Barney
Goolsby, Cardin
Goolsby, Cincinattus L.
Goolsby, Dennis
Goolsby, Jacob
Goolsby, James B.
Goolsby, John, Sr.
Goolsby, Levi
Goolsby, Wade B.

Goolsby, William
Gordon, Charles P.
Gordon, Louisa
Gordon, Mary D.
Gordon, Thomas A.
Grace, John
Graham, James
Grant, Samuel
Grant, Thomas
Graves, Lewis
Gray, A. T.
Green, Pleasant
Green, William, Sr.
Greene, Burwell
Greer, Aaron
Greer, Abraham
Greer, Crawford H. Sr.
Greer, Hattie
Greer, Jefferson
Greer, John R.
Greer, Robert S.
Greer, Thomas L.
Gregory, Lewis
Gregory, Matthew
Grier, Aaron W.
Griggs, John J.
Grimmett, James T.
Grimmett, Sarah E.
Grimmett, William
Grinnell, Benjamin
Grinnell, Charles
Gross, John
Grubbs, Elisha C.
Grubbs, Wiley B.
Guinn, Franklin
Gunn, Gabriel

Hadley, Thomas
Hairston, Moses B.
Hairston, Thomas
Hale, Josey
Hall, James N.
Hall, John
Hamilton, Thomas P.
Hamilton, Winney
Hammel, G. A.
Hancock, William
Hardman, Alphonzo
Hardin, John S.
Hardin, Silas M.
Hardwick, William
Hardy, Benajah
Hardy, Cornelius
Hardy, William P.
Harral, James
Harris, David
Harris, Isham
Harris, John
Harris, Mary
Harrison, Epthpatha
Harrison, Henry
Hartsfield, Middleton
Harvey, Zepheniah
Harwell, Mason
Hatcher, Uriah
Hawk, Seaborn J.
Hawkins, John W.
Hay, Edmond
Hay, Stephen
Hay, Washington

Hay, William T.
Hays, Rebecca
Heath, Richard
Henderson, Charles
Henderson, Frankie
Henderson, Isaac W.
Henderson, James
Henderson, Jane L.
Henderson, John
Henderson, Joseph
Henderson, Samuel
Henderson, William
Henly, Abijah
Hester, William
Hicks, John
Hicks, John J.
Hicks, Joseph
Higginbotham, Jacob
Higginbotham, Joseph
Higginbotham, Robert
Hill, Isaac
Hill, James
Hill, Lawrence
Hill, Theophilus
Hill, William
Hines, Elias
Hines, James, Sr.
Hines, John
Hitchcock, Matthew
Hitchcock, William
Hobson, Christopher
Hobson, John
Hodge, Duke R.
Hodge, James
Hodge, William
Hodnett, Benjamin
Holifield, Polly
Holifield, Wiley
Holland, Henry J.
Holland, J. L.
Holland, James W.
Holland, Jonas H.Sr.
Holland, Lawson S.
Holland, Levinia
Holland, Lewis C.
Holland, Margarett
Holland, Mary A.
Holland, William T.
Holloway, Alsey
Holloway, Dabney P.
Holloway, Elizabeth
Holloway, Isam
Holloway, James M.
Holloway, Jesse
Holloway, Samuel
Holsenbeck, Alfred
Holsey, George
Hood, Wiley
Hooks, John W.
Hooten, James
Horton, Elisha
Horton, James
Horton, Mary Jane
Horton, Seaborn R.
Houghton, Josiah
Howard, James B.
Howard, Samuel
Howard, Stephen
Hubbard, Samuel
Huff, Clayton W.

Huff, Ralph
Huff, Thomas
Hungerford, Anson, Jr.
Hunt, James
Hunt, Jesse
Hunt, W. H.
Hunter, Henry
Hunter, James T.
Hunter, S. A.
Hunter, I. P.
Hurt, William
Huson, David
Hutchings, Richard S.
Hutchison, M. H.
Hutchison, Thomas L.

Ivey, Lot
Ivy, Henry
Ivy, Robert W.
Ivy, Wenney

Jackson, Eliza
Jackson, Isaac
Jackson, John
Jackson, Pleasant
Jackson, Thomas
Jeffries, B. S.
Jeffries, Colbert
Jeffries, Cordial D.
Jeffries, Georgia Ann
Jeffries, Thomas
Jeffries, William R.
Jenkins, Cyrus R.
Jenkins, Francis
Jenkins, John H.
Jenkins, William
Jewett, Martha
Johns, Thomas
Johnson, Alexander
Johnson, Alfred
Johnson, Annis T.
Johnson, Felix
Johnson, Haney
Johnson, James M.
Johnson, John
Johnson, Snellen
Johnson, Thomas M.
Johnson, Walter
Johnson, William, Sr.
Johnston, Martha M.
Johnston, Nathan
Johnston, Thomas
Johnston, William A.
Johnston, William H.
Jones, David C.
Jones, Edward
Jones, Joseph
Jones, Mary
Jones, Vincent
Jones, William, Sr.
Jones, William L.
Jordan, Benjamin
Jordan, Bill
Jordan, Fleming, Sr.
Jordan, Jack
Jordan, Reuben, Sr.
Jordan, Spencer
Jordan, Sterling
Jordan, Thomas H.
Jordan, William P., Sr.

Keeling, William
Keene, Ann T.
Keene, Benjamin F.
Dello, Samuel B.
Kelly, Allen
Kelly, Daniel
Kelly, Eaton S.
Kelly, Jane E.
Kelly, Jarrett B.
Kelly, John C.
Kelly, John H. Sr.
Kelly, John R.
Kelly, John W.
Kelly, Mary
Kelly, Seaborn C.
Kendrick, Shadrack
Kendrix, Angie
Kennedy, David
Key, B. P.
Key, Mary G.
Kilby, William
Kilgore, William
Kimball, Benjamin
Kimble, David
Kinard, Francis M.
Kinard, John H.
Kinebrew, Shadrack
King, B. G.
King, Cattel
King, Dolly
King, John Mitchel
King, Mitchel
King, Richard D.
King, William
Kirby, David D.
Kitchens, Charles
Knight, John Sr.

Lacey, Philemon
Landrum, Thomas
Lane, Augustus W.
Lane, Davis
Lane, John T.
Lane, L. A.
Lane, William D.
Langston, David M.
Langston, Isaac L.
Langston, Jefferson F.
Langston, John E.
Lanier, William
Lasetter, Elisha
Lawrence, James
Lawrence, Leroy
Lawrence, Seaborn
Lawrence, William Sr.
Lawrence, William Jr.
Laws, Martin
Lawson, David
Lawson, Mary
Lawson, Sarah A.
Lawson, William
Layson, C. C. Sr.
Lazenby, Ellender
Lacenby, John
Lazenby, William
Ledbetter, Henry
Lee, William
Leggett, C. R.
Letson, Robert
Leverett, Jesse

Leverett, William C.
Lewis, James B.
Lewis, Mary Ann
Lewis, Phillip
Lindsey, John L.
Lindsey, Samuel
Littlejohn, Thomas
Lloyd, Edmund
Lockwood, James
Long, George
Lovejoy, Colman B.
Lovejoy, Eleazer
Lovejoy, John D.
Lovejoy, Pleasant P.
Lowery, Ann
Lowery, Kirby D.
Lowry, Elizabeth
Loyall, Jesse
Loyd, Thomas Jr.
Lucas, John
Luckie, William F.
Lumpkin, John
Lumpkin, Mary
Lumsden, Jeremiah
Lunsford, Leonard L.
Lynch, Jarrett
Lyon, John

Macon, Nathaniel G.
Maddux, John
Maddux, William D.
Malay, James
Malone, Allen M.
Malone, Annie B.
Malone, Cader
Malone, Floyd
Malone, Francis
Malone, Frank Sr.
Malone, Jarrel
Malone, Jarrett
Malone, Jeptha
Malone, Mary Lucy
Malone, Sherod
Malone, W. B.
Malone, William
Mapp, Jeremiah
Marks, James K.
Martin, Hugh M.
Mashburn, Jefferson
Massey, Enos
Mathews, Jefferson
Maxey, Garland
Maxey, William
Mayberry, Adam P.
Mays, Abney
Medford, George
Medlock, George
Melton, Timothy
Mercer, William
Meriwether, Charles
Meriwether, David Sr.
Meriwether, George M.
Meriwether, Lula
Meriwether, Matilda A.
Meriwether, Sallie A.
Messer, William
Middlebrooks, Joseph A.
Millen, George D.
Millen, Henry
Millen, John

Miller, Daniel
Miller, William
Minter, F. B.
Minter, Jeremiah P.
Minter, Joe
Minter, John W.
Minter, Richard
Minter, Robert J.
Minter, Thomas C.
Minter, William S.
Miser, Joseph
Mitchel, Daniel
Mitchell, Richard
Mize, James
Mobley, Stephen
Montgomery, Benjamin H.
Montgomery, David
Montgomery, James H.
Moore, Augustus C.
Moore, Hiram
Moore, John
Moore, Palatine
Moreland, Francis
Moreland, John
Moreland, Thomas
Morgan, Charles
Morgan, Milton
Morgan, Stokley
Morgan, William J.
Morris, Benjamin F.
Morris, John G.
Morris, Sarah M.
Morris, Stephen
Morris, William
Mosely, Henry
Mosely, W. R.
Moses, John
Moss, Archibald
Moss, Susannah C.
Moye, Thomas W.
Mygatt, George
Myles, William H.

McAfee, Greene
McAfee, Robert
McBean, Henry L.
McClelland, David
McClendon, Ethelred
McClendon, Isaac
McClendon, Joel
McClendon, Jonathan
McClendon, Moses J.
McClendon, Stephen W.
McClendon, Washington
McClendon, Wiley F.
McCormack, James
McCune, Thomas B.
McDaniel, George F.
McDaniel, Jacob
McDonald, William A.
McDowell, Daniel
McDowell, James M.
McDowell, John M.
McDowell, Mary Ann
McDowell, Michael A.
McDowell, William
McElhenney, G. W.
McElhenney, John
McElhenney, Vincent H.
McEncroe, William

337

McGahee, Benjamin
McGehee, Edward
McKee, Lewis W.
McKemie, James
McKemie, John
McKinley, Lula
McKissack, Duncan
McKissack, John
McKissack, Thomas
McKissack, William T.
McLaughlin, James
McLemore, Catherine
McLendon, Francis M.
McLeroy, James
McMichael, David
McMichael, Elijah
McMichael, Elijah H.L.
McMichael, Greene L.
McMichael, James
McMichael, John L.
McMichael, Shadrack
McMichael, William
McMichael, William T.
McMichael, Zachariah
McMurin, John
McMurry, John
McNeil, Daniel F.

Nall, Nathan
Newby, John
Newton, Aris
Newton, Julia
Newton, Lucien B.
Newton, Mark L.
Newton, Martha B.
Newton, Mary F.
Newton, O. H. P.
Newton, Oliver H.
Newton, Willis
Nichols, Jeff
Noles, Elinor
Noles, J. H.
Noles, John W.
Noles, William D.

Odoms, Mrs. S. E.
Odum, Winburn
Organ, Matthew
Orr, Allen
Osborne, William
Owens, Jacob
Owens, Stewart
Owens, Susannah C.
Oxford, James W.
Oxford, R. L.
Ozborn, James

Paine, Thomas
Parham, Polly
Parker, Ann Eliza
Parker, Isaac L.
Parker, Lewis S.
Parker, William C.
Parks, John B.
Parks, William
Parnell, John
Parrot, Henry
Paschall, Samuel
Patterson, Jesse
Payne, John

Peacock, Daniel
Peacock, John
Peacock, William
Pearson, Austin
Pearson, Jeremiah
Pearson, John W.
Pearson, Reese
Peddy, Wiley
Peeler, Anthony
Pelot, S. C.
Penn, Joseph
Penn, Martha A.
Penn, Stephen A.
Penn, William
Penn, William C.
Pennington, Thomas
Pennington, William B.
Penson, James
Perkins, David A.
Perkins, Moses
Perkins, Paul
Perry, Elvira
Perry, James
Perry, William
Persons, Benjamin
Peurifoy, Arrington
Peurifoy, Avoline
Peurifoy, B. W.
Peurifoy, McCarroll
Peurifoy, Silas M.
Phelps, Aquilla, Sr.
Phelps, Aquilla, Jr.
Phelps, Washington
Phillips, Augustus C.
Phillips, Bryant G.
Phillips, Hillery
Phillips, Isaac
Phillips, John B. M.
Phillips, Lewis
Phillips, Mary E.
Phillips, Richard
Phillips, Wiley H.
Phillips, William L.
Phinizee, William
Pinchard, James
Piper, Thomas L.
Pitts, John D.
Pitts, Joseph A.
Pitts, Nester
Pitts, Permelia
Platt, George
Plummer, Samuel
Polk, Charles E.
Polk, Joshua F.
Pollard, Richard
Pon, John T.
Pon, Taylor
Poole, Abram
Poole, Thomas
Pope, Annie J.
Pope, John C.
Pope, Josiah
Pope, Miller W.
Pope, William K.
Porter, Catharine
Porter, Elizabeth
Porter, Matilda M.
Porter, William
Portwood, Catherine
Post, Samuel

Potter, Adam C.
Potter, Pleasant
Potts, Stephen
Powell, Allie Laura
Powell, Evan H.
Powell, John G.
Powell, Moses
Powell, Whit
Powell, William R.
Preston, Charles T.
Preston, William H. Jr.
Price, Edward
Price, John
Price, Robert
Pritchett, Alfred M.
Pritchett, T. J.
Pritchett, William H.
Puckett, Martin
Purkins, Daniel
Pye, Bartheny
Pye, Griffin L.
Pye, Harmon W.
Pye, James
Pye, Jordan
Pye, Thadeus
Pye, Theophilus
Pye, Thomas W.

Radcliff, Moses
Radden, David
Ragan, Asa
Ragland, Pettus
Rainey, Matthew
Rainey, Nathaniel H.
Rainey, William
Ramey, Absalom
Ramey, Allice
Ramey, Clarissa
Ramey, Daniel M.
Ramey, Elizabeth P.
Reddick, George
Reddick, Henry
Reese, Cuthbert
Reeves, Joel A.
Reeves, Joseph
Reid, Samuel
Reid, Virgil
Reid, William A.
Repass, Churchwell
Rhodes, Samuel P.
Richardson, George
Richey, Edward J.
Ricketts, Richard S.
Ridley, Archibald B.
Rivers, Benjamin
Rivers, Fred
Rivers, James
Robert, Lawrence Wood
Roberts, Bartholomew G.
Roberts, Daniel
Roberts, James H.
Roberts, Sarah
Robertson, Isaac E.
Robertson, John
Robey, Eliza Jane
Robinson, Cornelius
Robinson, James F.
Robinson, James T.
Robinson, Jerry
Robinson, John

Robinson, Thomas
Robinson, William C.
Roby, Milledge
Roby, Nathan
Roby, Thomas L.
Roby, Timothy
Roby, Walter L.
Roby, Williamson B.
Rodgers, James H.
Rogers, Enoch
Rogers, Robert
Ross, William
Rowe, John C.
Russel, David
Ryan, Lewis

Sanders, Ephraim P.
Sansom, Richard
Satterwhite, Dawson
Seymore, John R.
Seymore, Martha
Shard, Cornelius
Sharman, James
Sharp, James
Sharpe, William
Shaw, John
Shaw, Watson
Sheffeld, Barnabee
Shepherd, Abraham
Shepherd, Eleazer W.
Shepherd, William L.
Shepherd, Winburn R.
Shipp, Gustavus V.
Shockley, George W.
Shorter, Oliver
Showers, Elridge
Showers, Paschal
Shropshire, James E.
Shropshire, James W.
Shropshire, Mrs. M. G.
Shy, Frank
Shy, Peyton
Shy, Samuel
Shy, Seaborn J.
Siler, William D. Sr.
Simmons, Sanders W.
Simms, Richard S.
Simonton, Gilbraith
Simpson, John
Simpson, John J.
Sistrunk, Samuel
Slaughter, Andrew G.
Slaughter, Elizabeth T.
Slaughter, Henry
Slaughter, John B.
Slaughter, Nathan T.
Slaughter, Sarah
Slaughter, Thomas K.
Sluder, John
Smart, Elisha
Smart, Francis B.
Smith, Abraham H.
Smith, Alexander
Smith, Andrew
Smith, Charles L.
Smith, David
Smith, Edgar T.
Smith, Edward B.
Smith, Fanny
Smith, Francis

Smith, Harrison J.
Smith, Henry T.
Smith, Jacob E.
Smith, Jeff
Smith, Jesse
Smith, Jesse H.
Smith, John H.
Smith, John T.
Smith, John W. A.
Smith, Lucy B.
Smith, Mattie A.
Smith, Richard B.
Smith, Rolin
Smith, Samuel R. Sr.
Smith, Thomas
Smith, Thomas J.
Smith, Thomas R.
Smith, Thomas W.
Smith, William G.
Smith, William H.
Smith, Wyatt R.
Smith, Zachariah A.
Smith, Zipporah A.
Spear, Harry
Spearman, Gabriel T.
Spearman, John F.
Spears, Augustus
Spears, Columbus A.
Spears, Creed E.
Spears, Eaton
Spears, James T.
Spears, Jesse
Spears, John
Spears, John Wesley
Spears, Joshua B.
Spears, Josiah C.
Spears, Sidney
Spears, Thomas J.
Spears, William
Spears, William H.
Speights, James
Spence, Paul
Spencer, Jesse M.
Standifer, Archibald
Stanford, Joel
Stanford, Jordan
Steel, Francis M. W.
Steel, William F. M.
Stevens, Tucker I.
Stewart, Francis M.
Stewart, James
Stokes, Ignatius
Stokes, William B.
Stone, John W.
Stone, Mahala Ann
Strickland, Solomon Sr.
Stringfellow, George W.
Stringfellow, James
Stubbs, James Sr.
Swanson, F. M.

Talmadge, John
Talmadge, John H.
Talmadge, Stephen C.
Taylor, Francis N.
Taylor, Leonard
Taylor, William H.
Teddars, C. M.
Tedders, Samuel
Terrell, Thomas

Thomas, William
Thomason, Jackson C.
Thomason, Thomas
Thompson, Alexander
Thompson, Hannah
Thompson, Jacob M.
Thompson, James
Thompson, Jeremiah
Thompson, Robert M.
Thompson, Sallie
Thurman, Phillip
Thurman, Phillip
Thurmond, Fountain M.
Tillman, John
Tillman, Phoebe
Tindill, Jonathan
Toland, Michael M.
Toland, Sally
Toland, Samuel
Tomlinson, John D.
Tompkins, Lucy Ann
Towns, John G.
Towns, John T. C.
Traylor, Champion T.
Traylor, William H.
Trippe, William
Truit, Riley
Truitt, John
Trussell, Charles H.
Tucker, Allen
Tucker, Sarah
Tuggle, Elizabeth
Tuggle, Junie A.
Tuggle, Robert
Tuggle, William J. L.
Tuggle, William R.
Tuggle, Willie
Turk, John
Turk, Jonathan
Turk, William C.
Turner, John G.
Turner, Thomas M.
Turner, Toliver A.
Turney, P. F.
Tyler, Francis M.
Tyler, Job
Tyler, John
Tyler, Marcus H.
Tyler, Samuel B.
Tyner, R. John
Tyson, Henry F.

Urquhart, Alexander
Urquhart, Mary V.

Vardeman, William
Varner, William
Vaughn, Benjamin T.
Vaughn, James M.
Vaughn, Stephen H.
Vaughn, Thomas J.
Vaughn, William
Vickers, Elijah

Wade, Benjamin
Wade, Elizabeth L.
Wade, H.
Wade, James
Wade, Mary A. E.
Wagner, Sampson

339

Wagoner, Hiram
Waits, Alexander
Waits, Amy
Waits, Benjamin
Waits, John
Waldrep, Leecel
Waldrop, Delphia A.
Waldrop, Johnson
Waldrop, Solomon
Walker, Hackey
Walker, Henry
Walker, James
Walker, Magers
Walker, Moses
Walker, William W.
Walthall, Edward
Walton, Bluford M.
Walton, Henry B.
Walton, Hiram
Walton, Robert J.
Wammack, James
Wammack, Williamson L.B.
Ward, James D. S.
Ward, John E.
Ware, Henry
Ware, Joseph H.
Warren, Bray
Warren, Edmond
Warren, Edward
Waters, Robert P.
Watkins, Alexander
Watson, James
Watters, Jane
Watters, John C.
Watters, Mary C.
Weathersbee, Owen
Webb, Annie J.
Webb, Eliza
Webb, James
Webb, P. A.
Webb, Thomas P.
Weights, John

Weldon, Andrew
Weldon, Isaac
Weldon, Mary
Wellborn, William T.
West, J. A. J.
Wethersbee, Charlott M.
Whatley, Willis
Whitaker, John P.
White, Ann H.
White, John
White, Joseph
White, Lucius
White, Nehemiah B.
White, Samuel
White, Thomas
Whitfield, John B.
Whitfield, Matthew
   (2 folders)
Whitfield, Matthew C.
Wiggins, Wade
Wilburn, Herman H.
Wilburn, Leonidas C.
Wilder, Dred
Wilder, Isaac
Wilkerson, Harmon
Wilkins, Drury
Wilkins, William
Willard, Roswell
Williams, Alfred
Williams, Augustus L.
Williams, Francis M.
Williams, James M.
Williams, N. M.
Williams, Thomas R.
Williams, William L.Sr.
Williams, Zachariah
Williamson, Isaac
Williangham, William
Willis, Arthur
Willsi, Jonathon
Willson, George
Willson, James E.

Willson, John
Wilson, A. J.
Wilson, Adell S.
Wilson, Arkillis
Wilson, Elijah
Wilson, George J.
Wilson, Jenkins
Wilson, Joseph A.
Wilson, Rachael
Wilson, Sarah
Wilson, Thomas S.
Wilson, William S.
Wimbush, Mary Jane
Wise, Barney
Wise, Isaiah
Wise, James C.
Wise, Patton
Wiseners, Thomas
Wolfe, William
Wood, John
Wooten, Elizabeth
Wooten, James
Wright, George W.
Wright, Thomas
Wyatt, G. W.
Wyatt, Mary A. F.
Wyatt, Thomas
Wyatt, William H.
Wynens, Elisha S.
Wynn, William

Yancey, Lewis D.
Yancey, Nancy
Yancey, Sarah
Yancey, Ellender
Yancy, Layton
Yates, James
Young, Ernest L.

Zachary, Abner S.

JASPER COUNTY GEORGIA DEED BOOK 2

Pages 1-2.   6 Oct. 1808. Headed Oglethorpe Co. Morgan
                    Griffith of the county aforesaid to William Spears
of same for $400, 202½ acres drawn by said Griffith in the late land
lottery, Dist. #19, lot 223, then in Baldwin County. Signed: Morgan
Griffith. Wit: Wm. Lumpkin, Benjamin Gill. Proved by Benjamin Gill 25
Jan. 1809 before A. McEwen, JP, in Oglethorpe Co. Rec. 25 Nov. 1809.

Pages 2-3.   25 Sep. 1809. Samuel Henderson of Randolph Co.
                    to James Buckannan of same for $200, lot #1 in
18th Dist. supposed to be 50 acres, lying on the South & East side of
Murder Creek, bordering the district line. Signed: Samuel Henderson.
Wit: Patton Wise, Thomas Gaston, David Neil, JP. Rec. 25 Nov. 1809.

Pages 3-5.   26 Oct. 1808. Jesse Thomas of Bulloch Co. to
                    Timothy B. Humpherville, planter, of Scriven Co.
for $200, 202½ acres, lot #130 in 18th Dist. Baldwin now Randolph Co.
and drawn by said Thomas in the late Land Lottery, bounded by lots 133,
135 and the 16th Dist. line. Signed: Jesse Thomas. Eit: William Lucas,
John Marchment. Proved by John Marchment 25 Nov. 1808 before Lewis
Lanier in Scriven Co. Rec. 25 Nov. 1809.

Pages 6-7.   18 Jan. 1808.   John Pearce Senior of Jackson Co.
                          to Whitmell Bonner of Morgan, for $550, 202½
acres in 14th Dist., lot #15, drawn by said Pearce in the land lottery.
Signed: John Pearce.   Wit: William Selmon Senr., William ( ) his mark
Self, H. Selman Junr (?) (Senr?).   Proved by one of the witnesses 25
Nov. 1809 before Jos. Heard, JP.   Rec. 25 Nov. 1809.

Pages 7-8.   8 Jun. 1808.   Nicholas Williams, Sheriff of
                          Warren County to Turner Passons.   In obedience
to a writ of fiere facias issued out of the Justices Court in Warren Co.
at the suit of Bill & Dent & Mathew Parram, Wyat Bonner constable did
lately seize the tract of land herein described, as the property of the
said Mathew Parham...lot was publicly advertised in Warren Co. and
Turner Passons was highest bidder at $103.   Lot #199, 16th Dist. Randolph
on waters of Murder Creek, 202½ acres.   Signed: N. Williams, Sheriff.
Wit: E. Thomas, Thos. Battle.   Proved by Thomas Battle in Warren Co. 17
Nov. 1808 before Isaac Ball, JP.   Rec. 29 Nov. 1809.

Pages 8-11.   23 Nov. 1809.   Headed Jackson Co.   Obadiah Light
                          as attorney in fact for Benjamin Phips, by power
of attorney dated 14 Nov. Inst., to Morin(g) Moore for $1000, lot #63 in
13th Dist. formerly Baldwin Co., 202½ acres, drawn and granted to said
Benjamin Phips, the said Phips being a resident of Jackson Co. at the
time of drawing.   Signed: Obadiah (X) his mark Light, as attorney in fact
for Benjamin Phips.   Wit: Nancy Harris, Wilie Harris, B. Harris JIC.
Rec. 30 Nov. 1809.

Pages 11-12.   17 Dec. 1808.   Headed Clark Co.   Allan Kelly of
                          the County aforesaid to David Meriwether of same
for $200, lot #101 in the 18th Dist., formerly Baldwin Co.   Signed: Allen
Kelly.   Wit: Abner Banckston, James Meriwether.   Rec. 2 Dec. 1809.

Pages 12-13.   29 Dec. 1808.   Andrew Russel of Hancock Co. to
                          Robert Chambers of Jones Co. for $500, lot #116
in 17th Dist., formerly Baldwin Co. now Randolph.   Bounded by lots #15,
125, 117, 95.   Signed: Andrew Russel.   Wit: Smith Waller, Jonathan
Waller, Nathl. Waller, JP.   Rec. 2 Dec. 1809.

Pages 13-14.   21 Dec. 1807.   Henry Tripp of Hancock Co. to John
                          Tripp for $1000, lot #175 in 15th Dist. Baldwin
Co., bounded by lots #186 & 176, containing 202½ acres.   Signed: Henry
Trippe.   Wit: Nathan Sanders, John Whitehurst, Wm. Mitchell.   Proved by
John Whitehurst & William Mitchell 23 Dec. 1807 before William Barnes,
JP, in Hancock Co.   Rec. 2 Dec. 1809.

Pages 14-15.   6 Nov. 1807.   William McClesky of Jackson Co. to
                          Henry Trippe Senr. of Hancock Co. for $1000, lot
#175 in 15th Dist. Baldwin Co., 202½ acres.   Signed: Wm. McCleskey.   Wit:
D. McLean, Thos. Wagnon Junr.   Proved by Thomas Wagnon 24 Nov. 1807 before William Barnes JP, in Hancock Co.   Rec. 4 Dec. 1809.

Pages 16-17.   22 Jan. 1808.   Dennis Laurence Lyon of Barnets
                          Dist., Hancock Co. to Samuel Harrill of Warren
Co. for $800, lot #147 in 13th Dist. Baldwin Co. on waters of Cedar Creek
bounded by lots #148, 142, 146 & 174, drawn by said Ryan in the late
Land Lottery.   Signed: Dennis L. Ryon.   Wit: Hardy (X) Raines (?),
Thomas Heath.   Proved by Thomas Heath 7 May 1808 before M. Hubert J), in
Warren Co.   Rec. 4 Dec. 1809.

Pages 18-19.   2 Jan. 1809.   Grief Carril of Greene Co. to Kysiah
                          Sandrous of Randolph for $500, 202½ acres drawn
by William Davis of Burke Co., lot #145 in 14th Dist. Randolph Co. adj.
lots #144 & 146 and on the waters of Murder Creek.   Signed: Grief Carriel.
Wit: John D. Carriel, Joseph Waddaill, James Crawley.   Ack. by Grief
Carriel 7 Jan. 1809 before Thos. Broaddus, JP, in Randolph Co.   Rec. 10
Dec. 1809.

Pages 19-20.   20 Jan. 1809.   Headed Jones Co.   Stephen Kirk of
                          the county aforesaid to Isaac Foreman of Edgefield
Dist. SC, for $1000, lot #37 in the 13th Dist. Baldwin Co., 202½ acres,

341

granted to Jesse Blackwell 19 Dec. 1807, bounded by lots #36, 28, 33 & 60. Signed: Stephen Kirk, Anney ( ) Kirk. Wit: Harrison Cabiness, George (G) Cabaness, Jesse (X) Ivey. Proved by Harrison Cabaniss 4 Feb. 1809 before Adam Carson, J.I.C., in Jones Co. Rec. 11 Dec. 1809.

Pages 20-22.   7 Nov. 1809. William Lyon of Richmond Co. and Mary his wife to Moses Powell of Hancock Co. for $1000, lot #21 (Dist. not mentioned), bounded by lots #12, 20, 22 & 44. Signed: William Lyon, Mary Lyon. Wit: Peter Donaldson, Wm. G. Sturgis, Tho. C. Russell, JP. Mary Lyon relinquished her dower 7 Nov. 1809 before Tho. C. Russell, JP, in Richmond Co. Rec. 11 Dec. 1809.

Page 23.   21 Dec. 1808. William Wilkins and John Wilkins of Elbert Co. to William Hollamon of Randolph Co. for $1000, lot #174 in the 15th Dist. Baldwin, now Randolph, drawn by William Wilkins. Signed: William (X) Wilkins, John (X) Wilkins. Wit: Thos. Cook, JP, Elijah Buckley, John Butler. Rec. 13 Dec. 1809.

Page 24.   8 Aug. 1809. William Hollomon of Randolph Co. to Thomas Holloman of same for $1000, lot #174 in the 15th Dist., drawn by William Wilkins in the late land lottery. Signed: William Holliman. Wit: Bryant Lee, Braswell (X) Overstreet. Rec. 13 Dec. 1809.

Pages 25-26.   11 Nov. 1809. Thomas Holliman of Randolph Co. to Thomas Greer of Greene Co. for $850, lot #174 in the 15th Dist. Randolph, drawn by William Wilkins in the land lottery, containing 202½ acres. Signed: Thomas Hollomon. Wit: Cullen Alford, Collin Wooten, George Tillery. Ack. by Thomas Holliman 11 Nov. 1809 before Wm. Stephens in Greene Co. Rec. 13 Dec. 1809.

Pages 26-27.   14 Jan. 1809. William Kenner (Keener) of Wilkinson Co. to William H. Pearson of Putnam Co. for $500, lot #16 in the 15th Dist. on waters of Murder Creek, granted to William Wyatt 3 Dec. 1807, surveyed 25 Nov. 1806, bounded by Dist. #14, and lots #15, 17, & 45. Signed: William Keener Senr., Jno. Keener. Wit: Elizabeth ( ) Averitt, B. McCullers, JP. Rec. 16 Dec. 1809.

Pages 28-29.   5 Nov. 1808. John Bearden of Putnam Co. to Ichabod Reeves of Wilkes Co. for $500, lot #13 in 16th Dist. Randolph Co., 202½ acres, bounded by lots #12, 14, & 18, and Dist. #14. Signed: John ( ) Bearden. Wit: Malichi Reeves, James Thomson, John Rowland. Rec. 28 Dec. 1809.

Pages 29-30.   11 Dec. 1807. Headed Burke Co. Robert Balflower of the county aforesaid to Capt. Moses Mulkey of same for $20, lot #26 in the 17th Dist. Baldwin Co., bounded by lots #5, 25, 35, 27. Signed: Robert Balflower. Wit: Abel Lively, James Godby, Jno. Royal, JP. Rec. 29 Dec. 1809.

Pages 30-32.   15 Nov. 1809. Headed Burke County. Moses Mulkey to Daniel Miller for $50, lot #26 in the 17th Dist. formerly Baldwin, now Randolph Co., containing 202½ acres. Signed: Moses Mulkey. Wit: James Godby, J. K. Gregory, Jno. Royal, JP. Rec. 29 Dec. 1809.

Pages 33-34.   16 Dec. 1809. Zachery Estis of Randolph Co. to Thomas Pool of Spartanburg Dist. SC for $600, lot 120 (?) in 17th Dist. Randolph Co. on waters of Falling Creek, bounded by lots #119, 121, 91 and the 13th Dist. line. Signed: Zachery Estis. Wit: Henry B. Cabaniss, Benj. Edmondson. No recording date.

Pages 34-35.   19 Mar. 1808. Robert Finley to Henry Stringfellow both of Greene Co., for $300, lot #113 in 17th Dist. Randolph Co., containing 202½ acres, bounded by lots #128 & 198, drawn by me in the late land lottery. Signed: Robert Findley. Wit: 0. Porter, JIC, John Anderson. Rec. 30 Dec. 1809.

Pages 35-36.   25 Nov. 1809. John Brown of Camden Co. to Bouth Fitzpartrick of Randolph Co. for $100, lot #161 in the 12th Dist., drawn by Mills Drewry at Camden Co. Signed: John Brown. Wit: D. M. Coy, Mary (X) Swagzens (?). Rec. 30 Dec. 1809.

Pages 36-37.   4 Nov. 1809. Thomas Lightfoot to David White for $175, lot #172 (122?) in 16th Dist. Baldwin, now Randolph Co. Signed: Thos. Lightfoot. Wit: T. W. Harris, Henry Walker. Rec. 1 Jan. 1810.

Pages 37-38.   5 Mar. 1808. Willis Deans of Randolph Co. to Briant Rushing of Clarke Co. for $300, 101¼ acres on the waters of Barr (?) Cr., lot #38 in 18th Dist., formerly Baldwin Co., now Randolph, adj. Knight's line. Signed: Willis (X) Deans. Wit: Gilbert Gay, Balde Alford, John Knight. Proved by John Knight 6 Dec. 1809 before Alexandr. McKey, JP. Rec. 1 Jan. 1810.

Pages 39-40.   5 Mar. 1808. Willis Deans of Randolph Co. to Elisha Knight for $300, half of lot #38 in 18th Dist. on waters of Bear Creek, adj. lot fraction #59, lot #39, containing 101¼ acres. Signed: Willis (X) Deanes. Wit: Gilbert Gay, Balde Alford, John Knight. Proved by John Knight 6 Dec. 1809 before Alexander McKey, JP, in Randolph Co. Rec. 1 Jan. 1810.

Pages 41-42.   7 Nov. 1809. Charles Crawford, John Martin, John Cargill & Solomon Strickland, commissioners for Randolph Co. to Charles Cargill of the County aforesaid, for $200, lot #31 in the town of Monticello, containing 200 feet square. Signed by above men. No witnesses. Rec. January 1810.

Pages 42-43.   7 Mar. 1808. Hardy Duke of Greene Co. to Micajah Stenson of Randolph for $350, 202½ acres in 19th Dist., lot #280, Randolph Co., on waters of Murder Creek adj. lots #271, 281, 297. Signed: Hardy (X) Duke. Wit: Robert (X) Hobbs, Geo. Tuggle, JP. Rec. 2 Jan. 1810.

Pages 43-45.   19 Jan. 1809. Ann Lumpkin (widow of Joseph) of Oglethorpe Co. to Joseph Wallace of Newberry Co. SC, for $300, 202½ acres in 13th Dist. Baldwin Co. now Randolph, lot #115. Signed: Anne (X) Lumkin, widow of Joseph. Wit: James Beland, Benjamin Beland. Proved by Benjamin Beland 23 Aug. 1809 before John Moon, JIC, in Oglethorpe Co. Rec. 2 Jan. 1810.

Pages 46-47.   25 Dec. 1809. William Pace, Senr., late of Clarke Co. to John Hicks of Randolph Co. for $440, lot #177 in 13th Dist. Baldwin, now Randolph, granted to said William Pace 8 Jan. 1808. Signed: William Pace. *Wit: John Harris, Richard Bird, Jas. Hitchcock, JP. *Assigned by re Robert H. Higenbotham, said William Pace's lawful agent and attorney. Rec. 2 Jan. 1810.

Pages 47-49.   1 Oct. 1809. James Crawley to William Cook, both of Randolph Co. for $253.50, lot #45 in the 15th Dist. containing 202½ acres. The condition of the above bargain & sale is whereas the said James Crawley is indebted to the said William Cook in the sum of $250.50 by nine several notes bearing even date with these presents (notes are itemized), if James Crawley pays his debts the above sale of property to be void. Signed: James Crawley. Wit: Benjamin Edmondson, Charles Crawford, JIC. Rec. 2 Jan. 1810.

Pages 49-50.   22 Oct. 1808. John Kelly of Randolph Co. to William Kelly of same for $75, lot #279 in the 19th Dist. Baldwin, it being granted to said Hays, containing 50 acres adj. Micajah Stinson's Spring Branch on the waters of Murder Creek. Signed: John Kelly. Wit: Benj. Kitchins, Francis (X) Morgan, Johnson Strong, JP. Rec. 3 Jan. 1810.

Pages 51-52.   27 Oct. 1808. William Kelly of Randolph Co. to Micajah Stinson of same for $6, 3 acres in the 19th Dist. beginning at John Kelly's and Micajah Stinson's corner #279 & 280. Signed: William (X) Kelly. Wit: Joshua Baker, Jonathan Nichols, Johnson Strong, JP. Rec. 3 Jan. 1810.

Pages 53-54.   17 Mar. 1808.   Thomas Stowers of Franklin Co. to
                      Flemming Jordan of said County aforesaid for $150,
202½ acres in the 13th Dist. Baldwin Co., lot #69. Signed: Thomas (X)
Stowers. Wit: Hundley Vaughan, John Jordan, W. Christian, JP. Rec. 3
Jan. 1810.

Pages 54-55.   Headed Oglethorpe Co. 2 Dec. 1809. James Thomson
                      "of the county and state" to James Farley of
Randolph Co., lot #24 in 18th Dist., 202½ acres, granted 5 Apr. 1808,
for $600. Signed: James Thompson. Wit: John Evans, John Thompson.
Proved by John Evans 1 Jan. 1810 before Alexr. Markey JP, in Randolph Co.
Rec. 3 Jan. 1810.

Pages 56-57.   28 Dec. 1807. James Young of Franklin Co. to Abr.
                      *Bonner of Clarke for $500, 202½ acres in 12th
Dist., lot #162, bounded by lots #121, 191, 163 & 159, drawn by James
Young & granted him 17 Dec. 1807. Signed: James Young. Wit: Jacob
Milsaps, Arnold Adkinson. Rec. 3 Jan. 1810. *Also listed as Allen
Bonner.

Pages 57-59.   12 Sep. 1808. Neily McCoy of Putnam Co. to Jacob
                      Brassel of Randolph for $100, half of lot #1 in
15th Dist. Baldwin Co. now Randolph, the line to be drawn so that Jacob
Brassel will take a certain spring in his half of the lot and shall join
the 16th Dist. and the other half & join lot #2. Signed: Neily McCoy.
Wit: Richard (X) Braswell, Richard Odam. Proved by the witnesses 11 Mar.
1809. Rec. 3 Jan. 1810.

Pages 59-61.   4 Nov. 1809. Thomas Lightfoot to David White for
                      $175, lot #172 in the 16th Dist. Randolph Co.
Signed: Thos. Lightfoot. Wit: T. W. Harris, Henry Walker. Proved by
Thomas W. Harris before Isaac McClendon, JIC, 2 Jan. 1810 in Randolph
Co. Rec. 4 Jan. 1810.

Pages 61-62.   28 Dec. 1809. Griffin Mizel of Bullock Co. to
                      Chrles Cargill of Randolph for $625, lot #89 in
16th Dist. Randolph Co., drawn by Joshua Hodges of Bullock Co. Signed:
Griffin Mizell. Wit: F. S. Martin, Jonathan Philips, JP, Charles Crawford, JIC. Rec. 4 Jan. 1810.

Pages 62-64.   9 Nov. 1809. Reuben Radford of Morgan Co. to
                      Joseph Crocket of Randolph Co. for $250, ¼ part of
lot #84 in the 16th Dist. of Randolph Co. containing 50½ acres, being
the SW corner of said lot, bounded by lots #85, 67, & 84. Signed: Reuben (RR) Radford. Wit: Ewel McCoy, Levy McCoy, John McCoy JP. Elizabeth
Radford, wife of Reuben, relinquished her dower 20 Nov. 1809 before the
above witnesses in Morgan County. Signed: Betsy ( ) Radford. Rec. 4
Jan. 1810.

Pages 65-67.   16 Dec. 1809. Zachary Estis of Randolph Co. to
                      Thomas Pool of Spartanburg, SC, for $600, Lot #
120 in the 17th Dist., bounded by lots #119, 121, 91 and the 13th Dist.
line, on waters of Falling Creek. Signed: Zachery Estis. Wit: Henry B.
Cabinass, Benjamin Edmondson. Proved by Benjamin Edmondson 4 Jan. 1810
before Jno. Cargill, JIC. Rec. 4 Jan. 1810.

Pages 67-68.   5 Nov. 1808. Headed Baldwin Co. James Rhodes of
                      the county aforesaid to James Jackson of Jones Co. for $300, 202½ acres
in the 16th Dist. Randolph, lot #63. Signed: Jas. Rhodes. Wit: William
McDade, Nathan Williams. Rec. 5 Jan. 1810.

Pages 69-70.   3 Nov. 1809. Zacheus Philips Esquire, Sheriff of
                      Randolph Co. to David Adams of Hancock Co. for
$5, by virtue of an order issued out of Magistrates Court of Greene Co.
dated 24 Feb. 1808 wherein Jared Bell was plaintiff and John Tindil defendant, sells to David Adams lot #184 in the 17th Dist. Randolph Co.,
and David Adams by Isaack McClendon was the highest bidder at $5.00.
Signed: Zacheus Phillips, Sheff. Wit: P (?) Fitzpatrick, Henry Walker,
Jno. Martin, JIC. Rec. 5 Jan. 1810.

Pages 71-72.   5 Jul. 1809. James Spradling of Randolph Co. to
                       James Buchannan of same for $312, 100 acres of lot
#2 in the 18th Dist., on the S side of Murder Creek adj. lot 23, Jacob
Finly's line, Isaac Lang*, & Samuel Henderson. Signed: James (X)
Spradling. Wit: Wm. McCane, John McMurray, Ann (X) Thompson. Rec. 5
Jan. 1810. *Isaac Lary?

Pages 72-73.   17 Dec. 1808. William Barber of Camden Co. to
                       Stephen Pilcher of Wayne Co. for $100 sterling
money of this state, lot #30 in the 6th Dist. of Baldwin Co., now the
county of Jones. Signed: William Barber. Wit: William Knight, JP,
Edward Pilcher. Rec. 5 Jan. 1810.

Page 74.   17 Feb. 1809. Jonathan Phillips of Randolph Co.
                       to William Spurlin of same for $300, lot #182 in
the 17th Dist. Randolph Co. surveyed 4 Apr. 1807 by Edmond B. Jenkins
District Survey. Signed: Jonathan Phillips. Wit: Selby Hearne, Wm.
Hearne Junr. Proved by William Hearne 12 Dec. 1809 before Robt. Richards,
JP, in Randolph Co. Rec. 5 Jan. 1810.

Page 75.   17 Oct. 1808. Charles Jent of Clark Co. to Jesse
                       Clay of Greene for $300, lot #109 in the 13th
Dist. Randolph Co. adj. lots #110, 115, 108 & 84. Signed: Charles Jent.
Wit: William (X) Preston (?), Hiram Hays, Sherwood Strong, JP. Rec. 6
Jan. 1810.

Page 76.   23 Dec. 1809. Burell Bowen of Randolph Co. to
                       James Wyatt of same for $400, lot #138 in the 19th
Dist. Randolph. Signed: Burell Brown (also Brown in the body of the
deed). Wit: Jas. Wood, Thos. Thiloson (?), Jas. Heard JP. Rec. 8 Jan.
1810.

Pages 77-78.   1 Feb. 1808. Headed Morgan County. Samuel Bras-
                       well Senior of Morgan Co. to Radford Ellis of
Oglethorpe Co. for $185, lot #110 in the 19th Dist. Randolph, granted to
Samuel Braswell Senior 28 Jan. 1808, bounded by lots #109, 111, 139,
in the 15th Dist. Signed: Samuel Braswell. Wit: Mary (X) Foster, Jno.
Foster JP. Rec. 8 Jan. 1810.

Page 79.   29 Dec. 1807. Arthur Herring and his wife Milly
                       of Hancock Co. to Darby Lary of same for $500,
lot #63 in the 18th Dist. Baldwin Co. drawn by Milly Harwell of Hancock
Co., Shivers Dist., surveyed 29 Jan. 1807 by John D. Ferrell (?).
Signed: Arthur Herring, Milly (X) Herring. Wit: Isaac Hill Senr.,
Alexander Nelson, Zachariah (X) Harrell, Thomas (?) JP. Rec. 8 Jan. 1810.

Page 80.   21 Oct. 1808. Darby Lary of Hancock Co. to Jesse
                       Mallet of same for $500, lot #63 in the 18th Dist.
granted to Milly Harell 31 Oct. 1807. Signed: Darby (X) Lary. Wit:
William John, John Turner JP. Rec. 8 Jan. 1810.

Pages 81-82.   12 Oct. 1809. Headed Wilkes Co. Elijah Smythe*
                       of Wilkes to Phillip Thurman of Edgefield Co., SC,
for $600, lot #88 in the 13th Dist. Baldwin Co. Signed: Elijah (X)
Smith, Lesa Smith. Wit: John Wilson, John Spene (?). Ack. before
Archie Simpson, JP. Rec. 10 Jan. 1810. *& Lese his wife.

Pages 82-83.   17 Oct. 1809. John Martin, Solomon Strickland &
                       John Cargill, commissioners of Randolph Co. to
Bolin Smith of said county for $330, lot #8 adj. the public square in
Monticello, containing ½ acre. Signed by above men. Wit: Solomon Gross,
David Brown, JP. Rec. 11 Jan. 1810.

Pages 83-84.   1 Mar. 1809. Benjamin Cleveland of Franklin Co.
                       to Jeremiah Smith of Baldwin Co. for $700, lot
#53 in the 14th Dist. Randolph Co. Signed: Benj. Cleveland. Wit: B.
Smith, Stephen Durdin. Proved by Bolin Smith 11 Jan. 1810 before John
Martin in Randolph Co. Rec. 11 Jan. 1810.

Pages 84-87.   29 Feb. 1808. Benjamin Smith of Randolph Co. to

345

John Speer of same for $312, lot #248 in the 19th
Dist., surveyed 12 Jan. 1807 by William Mitchell. Signed: Benjamin (X)
Smith, Polly (X) Smith. Wit: Jno. Martin, JIC, Joshua (?). Rec. 13
Jan. 1810.

Page 87-88. 25 Mar. 1807. Having received payment in full
for two Negroes, Dine & Sam her child, I warrant
& defend the title of said Negroes to Henry Slater. Signed: Wm. Hill
(?). Wit: Wm. McMichael. Richd. Carter & Z. Michael swore that they
were acquainted with Wm. McCichael's handwriting and believed that he
assigned the same as a witness. Signed: R. Carter, Zack. McMichael. 13
Jan. 1810. G. Hardwick, JP. Rec. 15 Jan. 1810.

Pages 88-89. 21 Oct. 1809. William Cook to James Crawley,
both of Randolph Co. for $400, lot #75 in the
15th Dist. Signed: William Cook. Wit: Benjamin Edmondson, Charles
Crawford, JIC. Rec. 19 Jan. 1810.

Pages 89-91. 23 Dec. 1808. William E. Barnes of Richmond Co.
to William Cook of Washington Co. for $210, lot
#75 in the 15th Dist. Baldwin Co. Signed: William E. Barnes. Wit: H.
McC. (as written), John Wilson, JIC. Rec. 19 Jan. 1810.

Pages 91-92. 21 Oct. 1809. Riley Truit of Warren Co., Kentucky
appoint my trusty friend Benjamin Read of Hancock
Co. GA my lawful attorney to conduct any business and make title to a
tract of land in Greene Co. Signed: Riley Truit. Wit: Thos. Credille,
Richd. B. Fletcher, JP. Rec. 19 Jan. 1810.

Pages 92-93. 6 Feb. 1809. Simon Johnson of Jones Co. to Isaac
McClendon of Greene for $60, 32½ acres being his
own and his brother Benjamin Johnston's proportionable part of a tract
of land drawn by Jeremiah Johnson deceased, Lot #22 in 16th Dist. Baldwin, now Randolph, surveyed by Hugh McDonald 14 May 1807, bounded by lots
#21, 9, 23, 39. Signed: Simon ( ) Johnston. Wit: Joel McClendon, JP,
William (X) Procter, Joseph Parmer. Rec. 20 Jan. 1810.

Pages 94-95. 25 Oct. 1809. Benjamin Phips of Smith Co. TN to
Isiah Phips of Randolph Co. GA for $500, lot #63
in the 13th Dist. Randolph, drawn and granted to said Benjamin Phips 7
Dec. 1807. Signed: Benjamin (X) Phips. Wit: William Goode, Jno. Cargill JIC. Rec. 22 Jan. 1810.

Pages 96-97. 1809. Robert Hall, Senior of Elbert Co. to
William Gaar of the county aforesaid, for $170,
lot #156 in the 17th Dist. Randolph Co. Signed: Robert Hall Senr. Wit:
Williamson Clark, Samuel Jenkins, Patsy (X) Clark. Proved by Samuel
Jenkins 19 Jan. 1810 before John Carroll, JP in Elbert Co. Rec. 25 Jan.
1810.

Pages 97-98. 13 Nov. 1809. Robert Chambers of Jones Co. to
Christopher Dreadwilder of Randolph Co. for $500,
lot #116 in 17th Dist. Randolph Co., granted to Andrew Russell 14 Dec.
last. Signed: Robert Chambers. Wit: Henry Pope, Jesse (?). Rec. 26
Jan. 1810.

Pages 98-100. 5 Jul. 1809. Absalom Bryant of Glynn Co. to
William Collins of Wayne Co. for $250, a lot
drawn by Temperance Bryant in the late land lottery - Temperance was of
the first district of Wayne Co. The lot drawn was lot #195 in the 19th
Dist. Baldwin Co., adj. lots #168, 194, 196 & the 15th Dist. line.
Signed: Absolom Bryant*. Wit: Henry (X) Summerlin, Allen B. Powell,
JICWC. *Mary (X) Bryant. Rec. 27 Jan. 1810.

Pages 101-102. 8 Jan. 1808. Fuller & Temple Tullis appoint my
truly beloved friend Jones Temple our lawful
attorney in our names to view and look out for the late land lottery &
as we have sold to Jones Temple do empower him to subscribe our names to
each tract the above John Tullis named to the tract in the 16th Dist.,
lot #124 (?) and the said Temple Tullis to the tract in Baldwin Co. the

346

20th (?) Dist., #28, to a deed warrantee in fee simple that we have this day made for $442 (?). Signed: John Tullis, Temple Tullis. Wit: Lewis Lanier, Anderson (X) Williams. Signature certified by Lewis Lanier, JP, in Scriven Co. 16 Dec. 1809. Rec. 27 Jan. 1810. (Note: extremely difficult to read.)

Pages 102-104.   1 Jun. 1808. Jethro Mobly of Randolph Co. to
                    Abel Pennington of same; the said Jethro Mobly by virtue of a deed of conveyance made to me by Jones Temple as attorney for John Tullis for a lot of land drawn by said Tullis in the last land lottery, the grant dated 8 Feb. 1808, in the 16 Dist. Randolph, lot #194, adj. lots #147 (?), 195, 197 & 192. Jethro Mobley conveys one half of the above mentioned lot to Abel Pennington. Signed: Jethro Mobly. Wit: Isaac Kendall, Joshua (X) Reeves, Joshua Callaway. Rec. 29 Jan. 1810.

Pages 104-105.   4 Jan. 1810. Elizabeth Stewart of Clarke Co. to
                    John Chisolm of said county, for $425, lot #77 in the 15th Dist. Randolph. Signed: Elizabeth (X) Stewart. Wit: Reuben Stevens, Jepthah ( ) Stewart, Joseph Herndon. Proved by Joseph Herndon 27 Dec. 1810 before Wm. Stroud, JP. Rec. 29 Jan. 1811.

Pages 106-108.   1 Feb. 1808. John Freeman, Senior of Hancock Co.
                    to Thomas P. Hamilton of same for $1000, lot #40 in the 14th Dist. Baldwin Co. on Camp Creek, drawn by said Freeman & granted 8 Dec. 1807. Signed: John Freeman. Wit: D. Hamilton, (?) Turner, John Turner JP. Rec. 29 Jan. 1810.

Pages 108-109.   24 Dec. 1808. John Kimbrew & Allen Stokes both
                    of Randolph Co. witnesseth that said Kimbrew doth lease a certain part of lot #66 in the 16th Dist. of said County from him for the term of four years, and the said Stokes in consideration of said Stokes clearing and leasing 15 acres of said land under a good ten said fence. . . Signed: John ( ) Kimbrew, Allen (X) Stokes. Rec. 29 Jan. 1810.

Pages 109-110.   27 Jan. 1810. Wilie Roberts to David Conden both
                    of Randolph Co. for $210, lot #184 in the 19th Dist. containing 101¼ acres. Adj. lots #185, 179, 183. Said lot was granted to Richard Hudspeth and deeded to said Roberts. Signed: Wilie Roberts. Wit: David Allen, Elisha Night, Chas. Cargill, JP. Rec. 29 Jan. 1810.

Pages 110-111.   2 Mar. 1809. William Person of Randolph Co. to
                    Levy Benston of Clarke Co. for $250, 100 acres, part of lot #100 in the 19th District, drawn by Henry (Husk?) and deeded from him to Caleb Touchstone and from said Calop to William Person. Beginning at a stake on Little River. Signed: William Person. Wit: James (X) Lovvorn (?), John Stroud, JP. Rec. 29 Jan. 1810.

Pages 112-113.   27 Feb. 1809. Samuel Lovejoy to Simeon Lane both
                    of Randolph Co. for $300, 101¼ acres, half of lot #201 in the 19th Dist. of Randolph Co. on waters of Murder Creek, surveyed 19 Jan. 1807 by William Mitchell. Signed: Samuel Lovejoy. Wit: Samuel Lane, Adam Mabry, Matilda Lane. Proved by Samuel Lane 27 Jan. 1810 before Johnson Strong, JP. Rec. 29 Jan. 1810.

Pages 115-117.   27 Jan. 1810. Green McAfee to Robert McAfee of
                    Randolph Co. for $175, lot #123 in the 16th Dist. on White Oak Creek, waters of Murder Creek, containing 52 acres, adj. lots #122, 148, 124. Signed: Greene McAfee. Wit: A. MaFee (?), Edward McGehee, Charles Crawford, JIC. Rec. 29 Jan. 1810.

Pages 117-118.   18 Dec. 1809. Arthur Lott, William Lott Junr. &
                    Thomas Watts to Wiley Burge of Hancock Co. for $1000, land (lot # not given) in the 19th Dist., Randolph Co., adj. lots #152, 154, 180 & 156. Signed: Arthur Lott, William Lott, Thomas Watts. Wit: Epps Brown, Wm. Deveraux, JP. Rec. 29 Jan. 1810.

Pages 119-120.   9 Jan. 1810. Jarrot Campbell to Thomas W. Harris
                    for $500, half of lot #11, in the 14th Dist.

Randolph, whereas Jacob B. Warbington now lives. Adj. lot #10. Contains 101¼ acres. Signed: Jariot Campbell. Wit: William Cook, Benjamin Edmondson. Proved by William Cook 30 Jan. 1810 before Johnson Strong, JP, in Randolph Co. Rec. 30 Jan. 1810.

Pages 121-122.   23 Oct. 1807. Headed Oglethorpe Co. William Birk Senr. to George Cross for $100, lot #71 in the 16th Dist. and adj. lots #72, 80, 50, & 70. Signed: William (X) Burk. Wit: Hope Hull, David Stephens, John (X) Burk. Proved by David Stephens 31 Oct. 1807 before B. McKigney, JP of Clarke Co. Rec. 30 Jan. 1810.

Pages 122-123.   6 Feb. 1809. Burton Steen of Randolph Co. to Aaron Moore of same for $500, 101¼ acres, half of lot #27 in the 13th Dist. Randolph Co., surveyed 25 Dec. 1806 and granted to John Lanier 2 Nov. 1807 and conveyed by said Lanier to Lewis Smith. Signed: Burton (X) Steen. Wit: Richd. Carter, JP, Edmund Foreman. Rec. 31 Jan. 1810.

Pages 124-126.   10 Jan. 1810. Charles Payne of Franklin Co. to Richard Bird (?) of Randolph Co. for $500, lot #86 in the 13th Dist. Randolph Co. granted to Harris Brannan 5 Oct. 1808. Signed: Charles Payne. Wit: John Reid, Richard Bird Junr., Ranson Whatley. Proved by John Reid before G. Hardwick JP. 13 Jan. 1810 in Randolph Co. Rec. 1 Feb. 1810.

Pages 126-128.   9 Jan. 1808. Jarrot Wright & Tabitha his wife of Greene Co. to Benjamin Fitzpatrick of the county aforesaid, for $500, lot #12 in the 15th Dist. Randolph Co., bounded by District line 16 & lots #13, 19, 11. Signed: Jarrot Wright, Tabitha (X) Wright. Wit: John Roach, O. Belcher, Alexander F. Patrick. Ack. 9 Jan. 1808 before Jesse Lary (?) JP, John Bethune, JP. Rec. 1 Feb. 1810.

Pages 128-129.   5 Jan. 1809. Presley Ingram of Baldwin Co. to John Lang of Putnam Co. for $500, 202½ acres in 16th Dist., lot #151. s/ Prestly Ingram. Wit: Wm. Williams, Barnes Holoway, JIC. Rec. 6 Feb. 1810.

Pages 129-131.   28 Mar. 1809. Jacob B. Warbington & Ellender his wife of Randolph Co. to Joseph Campbell and John Campbell of same for $100, one half of lot #11 in 14th Dist., drawn and granted to Jarrot Campbell, 100 3/4 acres on the NW side of said land. s/ Jacob (X) B. Warbington, Ellender B. Warbington. Wit: Jonathan Smith, Ellemander Warbington, Bennedick Jetton (?). Proved by Bennedick (X) Jetton 8 Feb. 1810 before Charles Cargill, JP. Rec. 8 Feb. 1810.

Pages 132-133.   13 May 1808. Giles Tompkins of Putnam Co. to John H. Marks of Elbert Co. for $800, lot #153 in 16th Dist. Baldwin Co., cont. 202½ acres. s/ Giles Tompkins. Wit: Benjn. Whitfield, Jared Bell. Rec. 8 Feb. 1810.

Pages 133-134.   7 Oct. 1808. Polly Connelly of Franklin Co., Christians Dist., to John H. Marks of Elbert Co. for $1000, lot #148 in 16th Dist. Baldwin Co., now Randolph, cont. 202½ acres. s/ Polly Connelly. Wit: Thomas Jones, David Erving, JP. Rec. 8 Feb. 1810.

Pages 135-136.   10 Nov. 1808. Peter Thomas, Esquire of Laurens Co. to John H. Marks of Elbert Co. for $500, lot #96 in 16th Dist. Baldwin, now Randolph Co., drawn by & granted to Solomon Mercer of Montgomery Co. 7 Nov. 1807. s/ Peter Thomas. Wit: Ben Chaires (?), Allen Daniel JP. Rec. 8 Feb. 1810.

Pages 137-138.   6 Feb. 1808. George Hall of Jackson Co. to John H. Whatley Jr. of Baldwin Co. for $20, lot #206 in 12th Dist. Baldwin, cont. 202½ acres, granted to said Hall 13 Nov. 1807, reg. in Book 12 Baldwin Fol. 33, 30 Nov. 1807. s/ George Hall. Wit: Jas. Huie, JP, Robt. Huie. Rec. 10 Feb. 1810.

Pages 138-140.   9 Feb. 1810. Samuel Mays of Randolph Co. to

348

John H. Whatley of same for $250, part of lot #101 in 13th Dist. Baldwin, now Randolph Co., granted to George Pritchett, supposed to contain 68 acres. On the waters of Cedar Cr. beginning at a (Per)Simmon Corner on Benjamin Bennits & Mays corner, Kennans (?) line. s/ Samuel Mays. Wit: John A. Carter, Richard Carter, JP. Rec. 10 Feb. 1810.

Pages 140-141.   2 Feb. 1810. Benjamin Bennett of Randolph Co. to John H. Whatley of same, for $55, part of lot #100 in 13th Dist. Baldwin, adj. Bennetts Spring Branch, Hilson's line; cont. 10 acres, 52 rods. s/ Benjamin Bennet. Wit: John Carter, Richd. Carter. Rec. 10 Feb. 1810.

Pages 141-143.   25 Sep. 1809. Thomas Jenkins Senr. of Bedford Co. TN to Chapley Ross Welborn of Franklin Co. for $500, 202½ acres, lot #95 in 11th Dist. Baldwin, adj. lots 94, 116, 96 & 86. Granted said Thomas Jenkins Senr. 26 Sep. 1808. s/ Thos. Jenkins Senr. Wit: Johnson Welborn, Sarah Wellborn, Larkin Barton. Proved in Wilkes Co. by Johnson Wilborn 8 Feb. 1810 before Holman Freeman, JIC. Rec. 12 Feb. 1810.

Pages 143-145.   1 Jun. 1809. Benjamin Chaires (?) of Baldwin Co. to Anthony Porter of same for $700, lot #10, drawn in the land lottery by Thomas Turner of Tarver's Dist., Jefferson Co., and conveyed to said Benjamin Chaires 20 Aug. 1808. s/ Ben Chairs. Wit: B. Terrell, Am. Devereux, JIC.

Pages 145-147.   20 Aug. 1808. Headed Jefferson Co. Thomas Turner of Jefferson Co. to Benjamin Chairs of Baldwin Co. for $400, lot #10 in 16th Dist. Baldwin, now Randolph Co. drawn by said Thomas Turner in the late land lottery. s/ Thomas (T) Turner. Wit: R. G. Haslip, Walter Robinson, JIC.

Pages 147-147.   5 Feb. 1810. Richard Barber of Washington Co. to William Barber of Randolph Co. for $5, one half of lot #194 in 19th Dist., bounded by lot #69. s/ Richard (X) Barber. Wit: Bennet Ferrell (?), J. W. Devereux, JP. Rec. 6 Feb. 1810.

Pages 147-148.   5 Feb. 1810. Richard Barber of Washington Co. to George Daniel of Randolph Co. for $5, one half of lot #194 in 19th Dist., lying on the SW side of said lot bounded by lot #197. s/ Richard (X) Barber. Wit: Bennet Ferrell, J. W. Devereux, JP. Rec. 16 Feb. 1810.

Pages 149-150.   19 Jan. 1809. Headed Oglethorpe Co. Asa Atkins of Oglethorpe Co. to Abrim Bankston of Morgan Co., 202½ acres in Baldwin Co. now Randolph on Irvins fork of Wins (?) Cr., drawn and granted to the said Atkins 3 Dec. 1808. Lot #73 in the 17th Dist. s/ A. Atkins. Wit: Jos. Rogers Junior, Jehu (Ragin?), Henry C. (?) Dawson. Proved by Jonathan Rogers Junior in Oglethorpe Co. before F. (?) Billingslea, JP, 26 Jul. 1809. Rec. 16 Feb. 1810.

Pages 151-153.   23 Jan. 1808. Lewis Hall of Tattnall Co. to James Beaty of Washington Co. for $200, lot #51 in 17th Dist. Baldwin, granted to Lewis Hall 9 Jan. 1808. s/ Lewis (X) Hall. Wit: David Foreman, William Williams, JP. Rec. 16 Feb. 1810.

Page 153.   17 Feb. 1810. Henry Graybill of Randolph Co. appoints Benjamin Peterson of Northampton Co. NC as attorney in fact to act for me concerning the estate of Arthur Gregory late of Northhampton Co. dec'd., which descends to my wife Mary Graybill, formerly Mary Gregory as one of the heirs and legatees of said Arthur Gregory dec'd. s/ Henry Graybill. Wit: (unreadable), Charles Crawford, JIC.

Page 154.   8 Dec. 1809. I, Minor W. P. Johnson of Randolph Co. have this day sold and delivered to Henry Walker a certain negro girl named Silvey for $350. s/ Minor W. P. Johnson. Rec. 17 Feb. 1810.

Pages 154-157.   25 Oct. 1809. We Burton Rucker and Alexander
                        McDonald both of Elbert Co. do by these presents
enter into partnership to carry on the tanery and currying business in
Randolph Co. near Monticello for the full term of three years from and
next after the first day January next on the following principles: I
the said Burton Rucker on my part engage and obligate myself to be well
acquainted with the tanery and currying business and have a perfect
knowledge of tanning and currying leather. And the said Alexander
McDonald on his part engages that he will during the full term of three
years work in the yard and also find a negro lad of about fifteen years
of age to work with him. The said Burton Rucker on his part promises to
instruct the said Alexander McDonald and the said Negro boy in the tanery
business as soon and with as much care as possible. The land on which
they settle is to be paid at their mutual expense, and titles obtained
in both their names. And whereas the said Burton Rucker has a family
wherein the cooking, washing, mending, and attention in sickness of both
the said Burton Rucker and Alexander McDonald and the negro aforesaid,
and such hirelings or hands as may be employed about the business of the
said yard is to be done at the expenses of the said family as to provision firewood, etc. is to be mutual only that said Alexander McDonald
pays yearly $7 to the said B. Rucker who individually finds a negro
woman or girl to assist in doing the washing and cooking as aforesaid...
s/ Burton Rucker, Alex. McDonald. Wit: E. Sims, Ez. Alexander. Rec.
19 Feb. 1810.

Pages 158-159.   5 Mar. 1808. Matthew Rabun of Hancock Co. to
                        Thomas Harris of Oglethorpe Co. for $200, land on
the waters of Heard Cr. in the late acquired territory, lot #17 in the
17th Dist., surveyed by Edmund B. Jenkins and bounded by lots #18, 14,
16 and 44; 202½ acres granted to the said Matthew Rabun 30 Nov. 1807.
s/ Matthew Rabun. Wit: Lewis Moss, John Davenport, T. Crowder, JP.
Rec. 19 Feb. 1810.

Pages 159-161.   26 Dec. 1809. Headed Burke Co. Gilbert Neyland
                        of Burke Co., planter, to Isaac Melton of Jones
Co., planter, for $100, lot #65 in the 18th Dist. Baldwin Co., drawn by
Gilbert Neyland in the lottery. s/ G. Neyland. Wit: Edmund Pior, David
Bedingfield, Samuel Davis.   Burke Co.: Edmund Pior and Samuel Davis
both of the county aforesaid swore that they saw Gilbert Neyland sign
and deliver the within deed to Samuel Davis for the use of Isaac Melton,
and that they were witnesses to the same, 27 Dec. 1809 before Lewis
Emanuel JP. Rec. 19 Feb. 1810.

Pages 161-163.   15 Mar. 1809. Jacob Moore of Randolph Co. to
                        Joshua Reeves of same for $200, lot #224 in 16th
Dist. on Murder Cr., 202½ acres adjoining the 15th Dist. s/ Jacob (X)
Moore. Wit: James Buchanan, Jane (X) Buchanan. Proved by James Buchan-
an 19 Feb. 1810 before Gbt. Bardin, JP. Rec. 19 Feb. 1810.

Pages 163-166.   7 Jan. 1808. Headed Bulloch Co. James Newman
                        Junr., planter, of Bulloch Co. to David Lastinger
of same, planter, for $20, 202½ acres, lot #56 in the 15th Dist. Baldwin
Co. adj. lots #55, 65, 57 and 35. Granted to said James Newman 25 Nov.
1807. s/ James Newman, Mourning Newman. Wit: George (X) Lastinger,
W. H. Reding JP. Mourning Newman, wife of James, relinquished her dower
7 Jan. 1808 before W. H. Reding JP. Rec. 20 Feb. 1810.

Pages 167-169.   10 Feb. 1809. James McGuynes of Jackson Co. to
                        Williamson Roby and Thomas Wilborn of Putnam Co.
for $300, lot #42 in 15th Dist. Baldwin Co., bounded by lots #43, 41,
19 and 49. s/ James (X) McGuynes. Wit: Thomas Willson, William Norman.
Mrs. Elizabeth McGuinnes, wife of James, relinquished her dower in
Franklin Co. before Geo. Christian, JP, 27 Jan. 1810. Rec. 20 Feb. 1810.

Pages 169-170.   25 Nov. 1809. Absolem Hendrick of Elbert Co. to
                        Minor W. S. (?) Johnston of Randolph Co. for $700,
lot #60 in 16th Dist., Baldwin Co. on waters of Wolf Cr., 202½ acres
adj. Dist. #13 and lots 61, 59, and 31. s/ Absolem Hendrick. Wit: Ann
Woods, H. Strickland. Proved by Henry Strickland 20 Feb. 1810 before
Charles Crawford, JIC.

Pages 171-173.   28 Jun. 1809 (?). Headed Bulloch Co. David
                        Lastinger of Bulloch Co. to Andrew Lastinger of
same for $100, 202½ acres, lot #56 in 15th Dist., granted to James New-
man Jr. 25 Nov. 1807. s/ David (X) Lastinger, Dinah (X) Lastinger.
Wit: John Griner (?), W. H. Reding, JP. Rec. 21 Feb. 1810.

Page 173.   28 Aug. 1809. Susannah Powel of Randolph Co. to
                        Samuel Heard of same for $394, a Negro woman
named Delilah about 18 years of age. s/ Susannah (X) Powel. Wit: John
Armstrong, Junr., Zacheus Powel. Rec. 21 Feb. 1810.

Pages 174-175.   25 Jul. 1809. Headed Randolph Co.   Wm. Marrable
                        of Oglethorpe Co. to John Reid of the county
aforesaid for $500, lot #64 in the 13th Dist. Randolph Co., granted the
said Marrable 2 Jan. 1809. s/ Wm. Marrable. Wit: John Alexander Carter,
Richd. Carter JP. Rec. 21 Feb. 1810.

Pages 175-176.   25 Oct. 1809. James Ponder of Oglethorpe Co. to
                        William Allen of Orange Co. NC, for $500, lot
#112 in 15th Dist., bounded by lots #111, 113. Granted the said Ponder
25 Nov. 1807. s/ James Ponder. Wit: Robinson Hendon, Johnston Hendon,
Jno. Luckie JP. Rec. 22 Feb. 1810.

Pages 177-178.   20 Feb. 1810. Charles Crawford, John Martin,
                        John Cargill and Solomon Strickland, Commissioners
for Randolph Co. to Absalom Hammill of same, for $199, lot #11 in the
town of Monticello, 100 feet in front and 150 feet in back. s/ Jno.
Martin, JIC, Jno. Cargil, JIC, Solomon Strickland, JIC, ----- (?) -----
McLendon (?) JIC. Wit: Robt. Stewart, Richd. Carter. Rec. 24 Feb. 1810.

Pages 179-180.   7 Nov. 1809. Whereas Baxter Pool late of Rich-
                        mond Co. deceased did oblige himself to make good
title to William Lyon of said state & county for a tract of land lying
in the 14th Dist., lot #21 in Baldwin Co., and whereas said Pool died
intestate before making title, the Court has ordered the administrators
of said Pool to make good title for the land. Therefore, William G.
Sturges and Anne his wife late Anne Pool and wife of said Baxter Pool of
the county aforesaid, to William Lyon of same, for $250, lot #21 in
Baldwin Co. at time of grant, bounded by lots 12, 20, 22 and 24. s/ Wm.
G. Sturges, Ann W. Sturges. Wit: Peter Donaldson, Thos. C. Russell, JP.
Ann Sturges relinquished her dower in Richmond Co. 7 Nov. 1809 before
Thos. C. Russell, JP. Rec. 28 Feb. 1810.

Pages 183-184.   24 Feb. 1810. Isaac McLendon to Daniel Miller
                        both of Randolph Co. for $100, 50 acres, part of
lot #6 in the 17 Dist. Baldwin now Randolph Co., bounded by lots #7 and
25 where Isaac Jackson now lives on both sides to be of equal distance
from the corner. s/ Isaac McLendon. Wit: Reuben Saffold, Isaac Jackson,
Jno. Cargill. Rec. 28 Feb. 1810.

Page 185.   24 Feb. 1810. Daniel Miller to Isaac Jackson,
                        both of Randolph Co. for $400, 202½ acres in the
16th Dist., lot #44, bounded by lots #45, 47, 43 and 17. s/ Daniel
Miller. Wit: Michael Whatley, Francis S. Martin, Isaac McLendon, JIC.
Rec. 28 Feb. 1810.

Page 186.   24 Feb. 1810. Sanders Crawley of Randolph Co.
                        appoint my well beloved friend James Courtnay my
lawful attorney to take and receive titles to certain tract of land
known as #71 in the 12th Dist. drawn by John Cash in the late land
lottery. s/ Sanders ( ) Crawley. Wit: John Bender, Robt. Richard, JP.
Rec. 2 Mar. 1810.

Pages 181-182.   (Second set of these numbers). 30 Oct. 1807.
                        Headed Jackson Co. Thomas Elliot to Thomas Hyde,
both of the county aforesaid, for $250, lot #129 in the 15th Dist.,
Baldwin Co. s/ Thos. (X) Elliot. Wit: Jos. Phillips, Walter Ellis, A.
Scott. Proved by A. Scott in Jackson Co. 8 Sep. 1809 before David P.
Mcrary, JP. Rec. 5 Mar. 1810.

Pages 182-184.   (Second set of these numbers.)   12 Aug. 1808.
                         Headed Warren Co. Lilath Farr of Warren Co. to
Jacob Watson of Putnam Co. for $70, lot #5 in the 13th Dist. Baldwin,
bounded by lots 4 and 6; granted to Lilath Farr. s/ Lilath (X) Farr.
Wit: William Smith, Nathaniel Thompson. Proved by William Smith in
Putnam Co. before Benj. Hill, JP, 1 Apr. 1809. Rec. 6 Mar. 1810.

Pages 184-185.   (Second set of these numbers.)   6 Mar. 1810.
                         Stephen Duke of Randolph Co. for the natural love
and affection which I have for my beloved children Joseph Duke and Moses
Duke begotten by Sarah Webb, give to the said Joseph and Moses Duke,
three negroes: man Frank, woman Hannah, and child Dick, cows, horses,
hogs, blacksmiths tools, wagon, rifle, etc. I appoint Sarah Webb the
mother of the aforesaid children as Trustee in behalf of said children
to keep in her possession the aforesaid goods until it shall be lawful
to deliver the said personal estate to the children Joseph Duke and
Moses Duke. s/ Stephen Duke. Wit: James Woodruff. Rec. 6 Mar. 1810.

Pages 186-187.   6 Mar. 1810. Edwin Sturdivant and John Lockhart
                         as guardian for Lucy Sturdivant of Lincoln Co. to
Richard Carter of Randolph Co. for $220, lot #67 in the 13th Dist.
Randolph, granted 15 Dec. 1808. Bounded by lots #94, 66, 62 & 68. s/
Edwin Sturdivant, John Lockhart. Wit: H. Walker, D. McCoy JP. Rec. 10
Mar. 1810.

Pages 187-189.   3 Feb. 1810. Thomas Cox and Martha his wife of
                         Franklin Co. to Josiah Burgess of the county
aforesaid for $800, lot #87 in the 17th Dist., Randolph Co. bounded by
lots #88, 64, 86 and 94. s/ Thomas (X) Cox, Martha (X) Cox. Wit:
George Turman, Jno. Mullin, JP. Martha relinquished dower the same day.
Rec. 10 Mar. 1810.

Pages 190-191.   5 Mar. 1810. John Cargile, John Martin, Solomon
                         Strickland, Isaac McClendon and Charles Crawford,
Commissioners for the town of Monticello, to Nathan Williams of Randolph
Co. for $325, lot #42 in the town of Monticello, 200 feet square. s/
Solomon Strickland, Jno. Cargile, Isaac McLendon, Jno. Martin. Wit: Jno.
Armstrong, Jesse Johnson, James McLeroy, JP. Rec. 21 Mar. 1810.

Pages 192-193.   13 Oct. 1809. Martha Dale of Jones Co. to Judkins
                         Hunt of Hancock Co. for $800, lot #204 in 13th
Dist. Randolph Co. on Cedar Cr. adj. lots #204, 205, 203, 186 & 213.
s/ Martha Dale. Wit: Saml. Dale, Hubd. Bonner. Proved by Samuel Dale
in Jones Co. before Daniel Gafford, JP, 13 Oct. 1809. Rec. 15 Mar. 1810.

Pages 193-194.   2 Mar. 1810. Gabriel Freeman of Columbia Co. to
                         Isaac McKelroy of Randolph Co. for $1000, lot
#20 in 17th Dist. Randolph adj. lots #19, 11, 21 & 41. s/ Gabriel Free-
man. Wit: William McKennon, James McElroy, JP. Rec. 16 Mar. 1810.

Pages 194-196.   6 Mar. 1810. William Hammett, William Phillips
                         and Jane Phillips, adm. of Isaac Phillips, dec'd.,
to William Scott, all of the county aforesaid (sic) for $100, lot #137
in 17th Dist. Randolph on waters of the Ocmulgee River. s/ Jane Phillips,
William Phillips, William Hammett. Wit: J. (?) Evans, Junr., Isaac
McClendon JIC. Rec. 13 Mar. 1810.

Pages 196-197.   6 Jun. 1808. Wylie Sims of Oglethorpe Co. to
                         Bailey Freeman of Greene Co. for $300, 202½ acres
granted to said Sims 12 May 1808; no lot # or District given. s/ Wyley
Sims. Wit: see page 200.

Pages 198-199.   9 Nov. 1808. Jonathan Phillips of Randolph Co.
                         to John McLemore of Hancock Co. for $1100, lot
#82 in 14th Dist. Randolph Co., surveyed 14 Jan. 1807. s/ Jonathan
Phillips. Wit: Adam Glazier, J. Evans Junr. Proved by Adam Glazier 18
Mar. 1810 who also saw Jesse Evans, Junior witness before Chas. Cargill,
JP. Rec. 21 Mar. 1810.

Page 200.   Continuation of deed from page 197: Wit: Berry

Y. (?) Bridges, Richd. Bailey. Mary (X) Sims,
wife of Wyley, relinquished her dower 10 Mar. 1809 before Jno. Luckie in
Oglethorpe Co.   Rec. 17 Mar. 1810.

Pages 201-202.   4 Feb. 1810. Young Beckham of Washington Co. to
                        Benjamin Lasiter of Randolph Co. for $500, lot
#34 in the 12th Dist. Randolph Co. adj. lots #33, 31, 35, 63. s/ Young
Beckham. Wit: Abner Durham, John Bender, JP. Rec. 20 Mar. 1810.

Pages 202-204.   5 Mar. 1810. William Hammett, William Phillips
                        & Jane Phillips adm. of Isaac Phillips dec'd. to
William Scott, all of Randolph Co. for $35, 3½ acres of lot #161 in the
17th Dist. Randolph. s/ Jane Phillips, William Phillips, William
Hammett. Wit: Isaac McLendon JIC, Phillips Fitzpatrick. Rec. 20 Mar.
1810.

Pages 204-205.   22 Nov. 1808. Charles Cargile of Randolph Co. to
                        Isaac Welding of same for $375, lot #64 in 12th
Dist. Baldwin Co., adj. lots #33, and on the district line; drawn by
Shugar Williams & granted 28 Mar. 1808. s/ Charles Cargile. Wit:
William Germany, James Cargile, John Cargile, JIC. Rec. 20 Mar. 1810.

Pages 205-206.   11 Oct. 1809. Batson Bullock of Wilkinson Co. to
                        John Cashin of Richmond Co. for $800, lot #164 in
the 16th Dist. Baldwin Co., adj. lots #163, 165, 167, 37. s/ Batson
Bullock. Wit: Benjn. (X) Everitt, John Bivin, William Bivins, JP. Rec.
21 Mar. 1810.

Pages 207-208.   4 Jul. 1809. John Martin, John Cargile & Solomon
                        Stricklin, Commissioners of the town of Monticello
to Richard Hands, all of Randolph Co., for $205, lot #57 in the town of
Monticello. s/ by above commissioners. Wit: Thomas W. Harris, Thos.
Broaddus, JP. Rec. 23 Mar. 1810.

Pages 208-210.   22 Feb. 1810. James Strawn of Randolph Co. to
                        Moses Daniel of Wilkes Co. for $500, lot #112 in
16th Dist. Randolph Co. on waters of Shoal Cr., granted to Rebecca Wood
(W) (sic), adj. lots #99, 111, 129, 113. s/ James Strawn, Martha (X)
Strawn. Wit: John Collier, Thos. Hooks. Proved by John Collier, who
attested to signatures of James Strawn and Martha his wife, 23 Feb. 1810
before Gbt. Barden, JP. Rec. 23 Mar. 1810.

Pages 210-211.   1 Aug. 1809. James Rogers of Randolph Co. to
                        George Rogers of same for $550, lot #136 in the
18th Dist. Randolph Co. s/ James Rogers. Wit: Wm. Crawford, Samuel (X)
Crawford, Solomon Strickland, JIC. Rec. 29 Mar. 1810.

Page 212.   17 Dec. 1807. Wilie Pope of Washington Co. to
                        Richard Head of same for $400, lot #25 in 19th
Dist. Baldwin Co. on waters of Falling Cr.; 202½ acres. s/ Wylie Pope.
Wit: Joa (?) Atkins, Neill Urquhart. Proved by Atkins 16 Jun. 1808.
Rec. 30 Mar. 1810.

Page 213.   29 Sep. 1809. Enoch Foster of Washington Co. to
                        Joseph White of Randolph Co. for $758, 202½ acres,
lot #56 in 13th Dist. s/ Enoch Foster. Wit: Rebekah Peddy, Ezekiel
Harris. Proved by Ezekiel Harris before Thomas White, JIC, of Jones Co.,
17 Jan. 1810. Rec. 30 Mar. 1810.

Page 214.   20 Jan. 1809. Headed Bulloch Co. William Prid-
                        gen of Bulloch Co. to Luke Pridgen, planter, of
same for $300, 202½ acres, lot #56 in the 13th Dist. Baldwin Co. s/
William Pridgen. Wit: Benjamin Lanier, Charles McCall, JP.

Page 215.   1 Jan. 1810. By an order from the Court of
                        Ordinary authorizing a sale on the 9th Dec. last
on the herein described tract of land when Joseph White of Randolph Co.
became the purchaser at the price of $1275, sold by the guardians of the
orphans of Alexander King, dec'd. Land is 202½ acres, lot #43 in 13th
Dist. s/ Rodrick Leonard; J. C. Fuller (?), agnt.; Thos. Sparks, gard.;

Alex King, gard.; Wm. Smith, gard. Wit: Thomas Wynne (?), Thos. Pinck-
ard, MMC (?) Giboney (?), JP. Rec. 30 Mar. 1810.

Page 216.   16 Feb. 1809. Headed Washington Co. Luke Prigin
                         of Bulloch Co. to Enoch Forbes of county afore-
said for $400, 202½ acres, lot #56 in 13th Dist. formerly Baldwin. s/
Luke Pridgin. Wit: Ellis Burney, Wesley Forbes. Proved by Wesley Forbes before H. Favor, JP, 13 Sep. 1809. Rec. 31 Mar. 1810.

Page 217.   20 Jan. 1810. Isabel Harris of Greene Co. to
                         Obadiah Belcher of Randolph Co. for $400, lot #87
in 15th Dist., bounded by lots 88, 94, 80, & 64, on the waters of Camp
Cr.; granted to said Isabel Harris 20 Dec. 1808. s/ Isabel (X) Hariss.
Wit: Robert Osteen, Motten (?) Gilbert, John Armor, JP. Rec. 3 Apr.
1810. H. Walker, Clk.

Page 218.   6 Apr. 1810. John Lang Senr. to Robert Lang, both
                         of Randolph Co. (no consideration stated), all
that part of lot #151 in 17th Dist. which lies S of a creek running
through said lot, now supposed to contain 80 a. s/ John Lang. Wit:
Jeremiah Pearson, Allen McLendon, Charles Crawford, JIC. Rec. 6 Mar.
1810.

Page 219.   7 Apr. 1810. Johnson Strong of Randolph Co.
                         appoints Charles Crawford my lawful attorney to
take out my grant to lot #275 in the 1st Dist. of Wayne Co. and to dispose of the same. s/ Johnson Strong. Wit: James Woodruff, Charles
Crawford, JIC. Rec. 10 Apr. 1810.

Pages 219-220.   11 Apr. 1810. Nathan Fish (?) to James Phillips
                         of Randolph Co. for $500, lot #108 in 16th Dist.
Randolph Co. s/ Nathan Fish. Wit: Nathan Philips, Joseph Lang, Isaac
McLendon, JIC. Rec. 19 Apr. 1810.

Pages 221-222.   Headed Chatham Co. Dated at Savannah 3 Apr. 1808.
                         Joseph King, Margaret King, John Lewis & Susan
M. Lewis to Mr. Nathan Fish of Randolph Co. for $500, lot #108 in 16th
Dist. Randolph Co. s/ Joseph King, Margaret King, John Lewis, Susan M.
Lewis. Wit: William King, James Bolton. Proved by William King 4 Apr.
1810 before W. Fobbis (?) JP. Rec. 20 Apr. 1810.

Pages 222-223.   28 Dec. 1807. Darcas Harper of Clarke Co. to
                         Everet Harper of the county aforesaid for $400,
lot #28 in 15th Dist. Baldwin Co., drawn by said Darcas Harper, adj.
lots #27 & 29. s/ Darcas (X) his mark Harper. Wit: Jourdon (?) Baker,
William Edwards, William Dyson, JP. Rec. 21 Apr. 1810.

Pages 224-225.   5 Oct. 1809. William Balinger of Elbert Co. to
                         Voluntine Mooney of Morgan Co. for $555, 202½
acres in Randolph Co. on the S fork of Little R., drawn in the late
land lottery by William Smithwick of Elbert Co. in Keelings Dist. Lot
#178 in 15th Dist. bounded N by lot 183, SW by #179, SE by #153, NE by
#177. Gr. to Wm. Smithwick 21 Nov. 1807. s/ William Ballenger. Wit:
Charles Sorrels (?), Elisha Johnson, Allen Daniel, JP. Rec. 23 Apr.
1810.

Pages 226-227.   22 Feb. 1810. Arthur Williams of Co. aforesaid
                         (no county mentioned) to William Penn (?) of same
for $300, 202½ a., lot #72 in 16th Dist. s/ Arthur Williams. Wit:
William W. Kennon, Robert Leverett, Isaac McClendon, JIC. Rec. 21 Apr.
1810.

Pages 227-228.   27 Jan. 1808. William Smithwick to William
                         Balinger, both of Elbert Co., for $400, 202½ a.
in Baldwin Co. on S fork of Little R. in 15th Dist., lot #178; bounded
by lots 183, 179, 153, 177; granted to Wm. Smithwick 21 Nov. 1807. s/
William Smithwick. Wit: Abraham Brown, David Ballanger, B. Pace.
Elizabeth Smithwick relinquished her dower before Barnabas Pace, JP of
Elbert Co., 27 Jan. 1810. s/ Elizabeth (X) Smithwick. Rec. 24 Apr. 1810.

Page 228.   25 Apr. 1810. Richard Holms to Gabriel Johnson
                   for $300, a Negro boy named Larry about 17 years
of age. s/ Richard Holms. Wit: Harry Walker, Clk. Rec. 25 Apr. 1810.

Pages 229-230.   1 May 1810. Phillip Fitzpatrick Esq., Sheriff
                        of Randolph Co. to William Mitchell of same for
$55, by virtue of an execution issued out of McIntosh Co. 6 Nov. 1807,
wherein William Goodson was plaintiff and James Oberry defendant, lot
#21 in 15th Dist. Randolph Co. sold at public outcry and said Mitchell
was highest bidder. s/ P. Fitzpatrick, Sheriff. Wit: Harison Young,
James Moore, Isaac McLendon, JIC. Rec. 1 May 1810.

Pages 230-231.   1 May 1810. John MCoy of Warren Co. to Nathan
                        Chafin of Randolph for $300, lot #149 in 16th
Dist. Randolph Co. s/ John MCoy. Wit: B. C. Edmondson, Jarrel Beasley,
D. MCoy, JP. Rec. 2 Mar. 1810.

Pages 232-233.   23 Nov. 1808. Henry Walker of Randolph Co. to
                        Joseph W. Jones of same for $300, 202½ a., lot
#69 in 12th Dist. Randolph Co. s/ H. Walker. Wit: J. Evans Junr.,
Charles Murrah (?). Rec. 2 May 1810.

Pages 233-234.   20 Apr. 1810. Robert Lang of Randolph Co. to
                        John Lang Junr. of same for $200, 202½ a., lot
#152 in 17th Dist. Randolph Co. s/ Robert Lang. Wit: Milner Echols,
John Lang. Proved by John Lang Senr. 27 Apr. 1810 before Peters (?)
Richards, JP. Rec. 2 May 1810.

Pages 234-236.   1 Mar. 1810. William Hammett & William Phillips,
                        admrs. and Jane Phillips Admx. of Isaac Phillips,
dec'd., of Randolph Co. to William Scott of same, for (blank) dollars,
all that fraction or parcel of land, lot #160 in 17th Dist., bounded on
one side by the Ockmulgee River. s/ Jean Phillips, William Phillips,
William Hammett. Wit: Isaac McClendon, JIC, Phillips Fitzpatrick. Rec.
3 May 1810.

Pages 237-238.   4 Feb. 1809. Headed Greene Co. Jesse Clay of
                        Greene Co. to James Hines of same for $200, a
half tract of land containing 101¼ a., lot #109 in 13th Dist. Randolph
Co., bounded S by lot #84 adj. Jesse Clay by a new marked line. s/Jesse
Clay. Wit: Samuel Clay (Senr.?), Samuel Clay Junr., Alston T. (?)
Greene. Ack. by Jesse Clay 25 Nov. 1809 before Lemuel Green (?) JP in
Greene Co. Rec. 4 May 1810.

Page 239 is blank.

Pages 240-241.   5 Jan. 1809. Jourdan Smyth of Washington Co. to
                        John Wright of Greene for $200, lot #127 in 12th
Dist. Baldwin, drawn by said J. Smyth. s/ Jordan Smith. Wit: Simon
Smyth, Stephen Wright. Proved by Stephen Wright 23 Feb. 1810 before Wm.
Gibony, JP. Rec. 7 May 1810.

Pages 242-243.   4 May 1810. Nathan Williams of Randolph Co. to
                        William Beasley of Oglethrope Co. for $500, lot
#57 in 13th Dist. Randolph Co., 202½ a. on waters of Falling Cr. and
bounded by lots 56, 72, 58, 40. s/ Nathan Williams. Wit: Henery Walker,
B. C. Edmondson, Johnson Strong, JP. Rec. 7 May 1810.

Page 244.   22 Aug. 1808. Robert Moore of Randolph Co. to
                   the members of the Baptist Church at Cedar Creek
in Randolph Co. for $50, 2 a., part of lot #151 in 13th Dist., including
half the Spring lying on the S side of the branch on his spring lies (?)
that now uses including also the high iminence (?) SE of the spring for
the purpose of the Social and publick worship of GOD. s/ Robert Moore.
Wit: Jacob Tomlin, James Bowden (?), Nathan Williams, JP. Rec. 8 May
1810.

Page 245.   "Brot from book K Folio 228." 9 Apr. 1810.
                   William Allen Ack. the above deed. Wit: John
McRagan (?), D. McCoy, JP. Rec. 8 May 1810.

Pages 245-244 (sic).   5 Jan. 1810.   Phillips Fitzpartick Esqr., Sheriff
                        of Randolph Co. to Jesse Evans of same for $19,
by virtue of a Execution issued out of Superior Court of Liberty Co.
dated 25 Jan. 1808 whereas Olovir (?) Sturgis is plaintiff & William
Lambright defendant.   Lot #138 in 18th Dist. Randolph Co. on waters of
Hardy Cr., sold at public sale and Evans was highest bidder.   s/ P.
Fitzpatrick.   Wit: Z. Philips, Will Lee, G. Hardwick, JP.   Rec. 10 May
1810.

Pages 244-245 (sic).   Headed Greene Co. 2 Apr. 1808.   I, Hatty McMichael
                        grant & confirm unto Eady Steedman one red sow &
her increase, for the good will & love I have for said Eady Steedman.
s/ Heaty ( ) McMichael.   Wit: John ( ) Kimbrow.   Pro. 10 May 1810.

Page 245.   7 Mar. 1808.   I, David McMichal, for the good
                        will & Love I have for Eady Steedman, one red cow
and her increase.   s/ Heaty (sic) (X) McMichaall.   Wit: John ( ) Kimbrow.
Rec. 10 May 1810.

Pages 246-247.   Headed Morgan Co. 26 Dec. 1808.   Thomas Campbell
                        & Anna his wife of Putnam Co. to William Messer
of Morgan Co. for $125; lot #283 in 19 Dist. Randolph Co., 202½ a.   s/
Thomas (X) Campbell, Anna (X) Campbell.   Wit: Elijah Gilmer, James
Spers (?), Barbary (X) Carpenter.   Proved by Elijah Gilmer who also saw
James Spiers & Barbara Carpenter sign; 11 Feb. 1809 before Robert Shaw,
JP in Morgan Co.   Rec. 10 May 1810.

Pages 247-248.   25 Dec. 1808.   Thomas Steedman of Randolph Co.
                        for natural love & affection to my Granddaughter
Nancy Worsham, one cow and a white calf marked with a crop & a slit in
the left ear and a half crop in the right ear.   Also one feather bed.
s/ Thomas (X) Steedman.   Wit: James Woodruff.   Rec. 16 May 1810.

Pages 248-249.   27 Dec. 1809.   George Hudspeth & Anny his wife of
                        Oglethorpe Co. to John B. Parks of Randolph for
$600, lot #222 in 19th Dist. Randolph Co., bounded NW by #197, SW by
221, SE by 225, NE by 223.   s/ G. Hudspeth, Any (X) Hudspeth.   Wit: Wm.
T. Morgon, Thomas Duke JP.   Rec. 15 May 1810.

Page 250.   15 Mar. 1810.   John Lasseter to Samuel Maddox
                        Junr. for $200, lot #159 in 12th Dist. Randolph
Co.   s/ John Lasseter.   Wit: John Payne, John Binder JP.   Rec. 19 May
1810.

Pages 250-252.   15 Apr. 1809.   James Armstrong of Warren Co. to
                        James Duckworth of the said county for $100, lot
#65 in 17 Dist. Randolph Co. on the waters of West's Cr. cont. 202½ a.
granted to James Armstrong 21 Oct. 1807; bounded by lots #64, 56, 66,
86.   s/ Joseph Armstrong.   Wit: Randol Duckworth, Levi Stanford, Samuel
(X) Wilson.   Proved before John Hardiway in Warren Co. by Randol Duckworth 15 May 1810, who saw Joseph Armstrong duly sign.   Rec. 23 May 1810.

Pages 253-254.   -- Jan. 1808.   William Townsen of Bulloch Co.,
                        planter, and Mary his wife to Alexander Lane Senr.
of the county aforesaid for $300, lot #138 in 16th Dist. Baldwin Co.,
202½ a. bounded by lots 139, 163, 137, 133, granted to said Townsen 14
Jan. 1808.   s/ William Townsend, Mary (X) Townsend.   Wit: John Lane,
Claborn Denmark.   Ack. by William Townsend 1 Feb. 1809 before D. K.
Zachery JP in Putnam Co.   Rec. 23 May 1810.

Pages 255-256.   1 Jan. 1810.   John Robertson of Randolph Co. to
                        Samuel Henderson of Morgan Co. for $200, lot 254
in 19th Dist., 202½ a. adj. lots 245, 255, 271.   s/ John Robison.   Wit:
Jordan Baker, Charles (X) Whaley.   Pro. 21 Apr. 1810 before Jos. Heard
JP.   Rec. 25 May 1810.

Pages 256-257.   23 Dec. 1809.   Alexander Smith of Washington Co.
                        to John Rushing of Warren Co. for $500, lot 131 in
17th Dist. Randolph, 202½ a. bounded by lots 130 & 132.   s/ Alexander
Smith.   Wit: Joel Rushin, John Rushing Junr.   Proved by Joel Rushin who

also saw John Rushing Junr. sign. Rec. 28 May 1810.

Pages 258-259. 8 Dec. 1809. Bouth W. Fitzpatrick of Randolph Co. to Phillips Fitzpatrick of same for $500, lot #161 in 12th Dist. Randolph; 202½ a. s/ B. Fitzpatrick. Wit: Henry Walker, Eli Glover, Johnson Strong JP. Rec. 27 May 1810.

Pages 258-260. 26 Aug. 1809. Headed Wilkes Co. James, William, and Elizabeth Smith heirs of David Smith dec'd. of Wilkes Co. to Samuel (Lemuel?) Wooten & George Hughs both of Wilkes Co. for $600, lot 139 in 17th Dist. Randolph, 202½ a. s/ James (X) Smith, William (X) Smith, Elibeth (X) Smith. Wit: Theodrick Stubblefield, John H. Maloroy, John Peterson (?), Thos. Smith, Phillips Thurman. Proved by Theodrick Stubblefield before Boling Anthony JP, in Wilkes Co. 14 May 1810 and Thomas Smith before Thos. Evans in Wilkes Co. 17 May 1810. Rec. 27 May 1810.

Pages 260-261. 28 Apr. 1810. Bersheba Kelly & Jacob Kelly of Clarke Co. to William Johnson of Randolph for $150, lot 119 in 17th Dist. Randolph Co. s/ Jacob Kelly, Beersheby Kelly. Wit: Patton Wise, Polley Wise. Proved by Patton Wise before Isaac McClendon JP, 28 May 1810 in Randolph Co. Rec. 28 May 1810.

Pages 261-262. 29 May 1810. George Lumpkin of Randolph Co. to Polly Lumkin & Drucilla Lumkin of same, for the sum of $325, lot 130 in 16th Dist. Randolph Co., granted to Elijah Dyer and bounded by lots 141, 131, 111, 129. s/ George Lumkin. Wit: John Collier, Moses Daniel, Walter Lumkin. Proved by John Collier before Isaac McClendon 30 May 1810. Rec. 30 May 1810.

Pages 264-265. Headed Mississippi Teritory, Baldwin Co. 25 Oct. 1809. John Cash, late of Washington Co. GA, Collins Dist., to Joseph Pulosky Kenedy of the territory & county aforesaid, for $500, 202½ a., lot #71 in 12th Dist. Baldwin Co., drawn by the said John Cash in the late land lottery. s/ John Cash. Wit: Tho. Davis, James (X) Sims. Ack. by John Cash before William H. Hargrove, J. Quorum in Baldwin Co. MS, 7 Apr. 1810. John Johnston, Chief Justice of Baldwin Co. MS, certified that Hargrove was a Justice of the Quorum, 18 Apr. 1810. Rec. 3 May 1810.

Page 265. 23 May 1810. Received of Henry Walker $200 in full for a Negro boy named Peter about 6 years old. s/ Jonathan Phillips. Wit: B. C. Edmonson. Rec. 15 Jun. 1810.

Pages 265-266. 20 Nov. 1811 (?). Received of Mrs. Mary Yancy $380 in full for a Negro woman named Martha and her son Sisero (?) now in her arms. s/ Henry Carleton. Wit: S. Hemphill, Allen Stewart. Ack. before Jno. H. Whatley JP. Rec. 4 Jun. 1810.

Page 266. 29 Nov. 1802. Received of Polly Yancey by the hand of William Foster $100 in full for a Negro man named Gundy. s/ Robert C. (X) Day. Wit: Thos. Harkins, J. Leager. Ack. by William (X) Foster 5 Jun. 1810 (?) before Chs. Cargill, JP. Rec. 4 Jun. 1810.

Pages 267-268. 18 Jan. 1810. Hamilton McCain of Putnam Co. to Robert Grier Junr. for $265 (?), lot #110 in 15th Dist. Randolph; adj. lots 109, 131, 111, 101. s/ Hamilton McCain. Wit: Robert Grier Senr., James Gatlin, Aaron Grier. Proved 31 Mar. 1810 by James Gatlin & Aaron Grier before John Riley, JP. Rec. 4 Jun. 1810.

Pages 268-270. Headed Chatham Co. 30 Mar. 1810. James Goven, guardian for Nancy Addington to Ezekiel Fears for $250, lot #39 in 17th Dist. Baldwin Co. s/ James Goven, guardian. Wit: A. Pemberton JP, Wm. Howe (?), Joseph Parker. Rec. 12 Jun. 1810.

Pages 271-272. 13 Jul. 1808. Robert Stewart of Jackson Co. to Joel Moody of Randolph for $500, lot #120 in the 16th Dist., 202½ a., surveyed by Hugh McDonald, Surveyor. s/ Robert Stewart. Wit: James Woods, Jno. Martin, JP. Rec. 12 Jun. 1810.

Page 272-273.　　　　　　7 Feb. 1809.　Thomas Lightfoot of Hancock Co. to
　　　　　　　　　　　Micajah Rogers of Randolph for $700, lot #80 in
17th Dist. Randolph, drawn by Celia Perkins of Burke Co.　s/ Thos.
Lightfoot.　Wit: Wm. Head, Jas. Grace.　Proved by James Grace 14 Jun.
1810 before Robt. Germany JP.　Rec. 14 Jun. 1810.

Pages 273-274.　　　　　　3 Oct. 1808.　Richard Ricks of Wilkinson Co. to
　　　　　　　　　　　John Knight of Baldwin Co. for $500, lot #88 in
the 13th Dist., 202½ a.　s/ Richard (R) Ricks.　Wit: B. (?) Hubert, W.
Watson JP.　Rec. 26 Jun. 1810.

Pages 275-276.　　　　　　2 Jan. 1808.　Adam Pool of Jackson Co. to Hugh
　　　　　　　　　　　Harriel (Harwell written over) of Wilkes Co. for
$300, lot #17 in 14th Dist. Baldwin Co., bounded N by the 16th Dist.
line, W by lot 16, S by 18, E by 48.　s/ Adam Pool.　Wit: Malichi Reeves,
James Holmes, Jno. Raiton (?) JP.　Rec. 20 Jun. 1810.

Pages 276-277.　　　　　　30 Jan. 1809.　Gottleib Schnneider of Effingham
　　　　　　　　　　　Co. to Robert Owen of Oglethorpe Co. for $200,
lot #153 in 15th Dist. Randolph Co., 202½ a., drawn by said Schneider &
granted 5 Dec. 1807.　s/ Godleib Schneider.　Wit: Jno. G. Walsingham,
Jacob Guann (?), Jacob Owen.　Proved by Jacob Owen 5 Jun. 1810 before
Jona. (?) Cargill JIC.　Rec. 26 Jun. 1810.

Pages 278-279.　　　　　　Headed Baldwin Co. 9 Oct. 1808.　Benja. Jones of
　　　　　　　　　　　Washington Co. to George Stephens of Putnam Co.
for $500, lot #38 in 13th Dist. Randolph Co., 202½ a. on the waters of
Falling Cr., bounded by lots #27, 39, 59, 37.　s/ Benjamin Jones.　Wit:
J. H. Posey, John Matthews JP.　Rec. 1 Jul. 1810.

Pages 279-281.　　　　　　12 Sep. 1808.　Diana Hilson of Warren Co. to
　　　　　　　　　　　William Simmons for $300, lot #119 in 13th Dist.
Baldwin Co., 202½ a. on waters of Cedar Cr., granted the said Diana
Hilson 2 Feb. 1808; bounded by lots 120, 106, 181, 138.　s/ Diana (X)
Hilson.　Wit: Jos. Phillips, Robert Dickens.　Proved by Joseph Phillips
4 Nov. 1808 before John Hatcher, JP, in Warren Co.　Rec. 2 Jul. 1810.

Page 281-282.　　　　　　16 Dec. 1807.　Burwell Tompkins of Washington Co.
　　　　　　　　　　　to John Armstrong of Baldwin Co. for $556, lot
#151 in 16th Dist. Baldwin Co. on waters of Murder (?) Cr., 202½ a. adj.
lots 150, 152, 130 & Dist. 14.　s/ Burwell Tompkins.　Wit: Michael
Harvey, William B. Peek.　Proved by William B. Peek 26 May 1810 before
William D. Lane, JP.　Rec. 10 Jul. 1810.

Page 283.　　　　　　18 Jan. 1810.　Simon Jones of Burke Co. to Andrew
　　　　　　　　　　　Weldon of Columbia Co. for $400, lot #31 in the
13th Dist., 202½ a. on waters of Falling Cr.　s/ Simon Jones.　Wit: Jos.
Tankersley JP, Austin Wallace (?) JP.　Rec. 10 Jul. 1810.

Pages 285-287.　　　　　　Headed Hancock Co. 13 Jan. 1810.　James Reed of
　　　　　　　　　　　Hancock Co. to Charles Webb of Randolph Co. for
$600, lot #201 in 16th Dist. Baldwin Co., 202½ a. adj. lots 190, 200,
220, 202.　s/ James Read, Rebeckah (X) Read.　Wit: Edmond Read, R. B.
Fletcher JP.　Rebeca Read, wife of James, rel. her dower in Randolph Co.
30 Jan. 1810 before R. B. Fletcher, JP.　Rec. 6 Jul. 1810.

Page 288.　　　　　　9 Jul. 1810.　Phillips Fitzpatrick of Randolph Co.
　　　　　　　　　　　to Scynthia Steedman, Spinster daughter of Thomas
Steedman for love & affection, a sorrel gelding now in possession of
Thomas Steedman.　s/ Phillips FPatrick.　Wit: Thomas W. Harris.　Rec. 9
Jul. 1810.

Page 289.　　　　　　Headed Morgan County 16 June 1808.　Reuben
　　　　　　　　　　　Lockete to George Hearne of Randolph Co. for $300,
lot #65 in 13th Dist. Baldwin Co. at time of survey, 202½ a.　s/ Reuben
Lockett.　Wit: John Reid, James Dismukes.　Proved by John Reid in Randolph Co. 2 Jul. 1810 before Richard Carter, JP.　Rec. 10 Jul. 1810.

Pages 290-291.　　　　　　30 Jan. 1808.　David Sims, attorney in fact of
　　　　　　　　　　　John Dyer, by virtue of a lottery drawn at the

358

town of -----ville, to James Glenn Sims and William Sims, for $10, all
interest and claim to lot #107 in 18th Dist. Randolph, which lot hath
lately been drawn in the said lottery in the name of the said John (in
Clarke Co.). s/ John Dyer by D. Sims, atty. Wit: Edw. Moore, Jno.
Smith R.H., T. W. (?) Fannin. Proved by J. H. (?) Fannin 9 July 1810
before Thomas Simons, J.P. in Jones Co. Rec. 10 Jul. 1810.

Page 292.   Headed Columbia Co. 3 Mar. 1810. James Roberts
                             of said Co. to John Bender of Randolph Co. for
$100, 202½ a., lot #121 in 17th Dist., joining lots 120 & 122, and #1
in the 12th Dist., drawn by said Roberts in the last land lottery. s/
James Roberts. Wit: Andrew Wildon, John Lampkin, JP. Rec. 10 Jul.
1810 by B. C. Edmondson for H. Walker, Clk.

Page 293.   3 Jul. 1810. John Cargill, John Martin, Solomon
                             Strickland, Isaac McLendon and Charles Crawford,
commissioners of the town of Monticello to John Cashin and Eli Glover of
Randolph Co. for $100, lot #62 in Monticello, 300 ft. in back and 200 ft.
in front. Signed by all but Cargill. Wit: Stokely Morgan, Timothy
Freeman, Charles Crawford, JIC. Rec. 10 Jul. 1810.

Pages 294-295.   3 Jul. 1810. John Cargill, John Martin, Solomon
                             Strickland, Isaac McClendon and Charles Crawford,
commissioners of the town of Monticello to John Cashin and Eli Glover of
Randolph Co. for $222.50, the South part of lot #9 adj. lot #8 on the
South, cont. 150 ft. in back by 50 ft. in front. Signed by all but
Cargill. Wit: Timothy Freeman, Stokely Morgan, Charles Crawford, JIC.
Rec. 10 Jul. 1810.

Pages 295-296.   22 Feb. 1810. Philip Stroud to John Love (?)
                             (Low?) for $200, lot #204 in 17th Dist. Baldwin,
now Randolph Co. s/ Philip Stroud. Wit: T. (?) W. Hains (?) (Harris?),
J. Evans, Junr. Rec. 11 Jul. 1810.

Pages 296-297.   16 Feb. 1808. Christian Pope of Wilkes Co. to
                             John Pugh of Georgia for $300, lot #2 in 17th
Dist., drawn by said Pope of Welborns Dist. of Wilkes Co., cont. 202½
a. s/ Christian (X) Pope, Susannah (X) Pope. Wit: Shelton Wellborn,
JP, Francis Gartrell, JP. Rec. 11 Jul. 1810.

Page 298.   1 Sep. 1809. Reuben Radford of Morgan Co. to
                             Richard Holmes of Randolph Co. for $700, 151 2/3
a., it being 3/4 of a lot of land in 16th Dist. Baldwin, now Randolph,
lot #84, adj. lots 97, 83, 67 & 85. s/ Reuben (X) Radford. Wit: Jeremiah Pearsons, Edmd. W. Taylor, John McCoy JP. Rec. 12 Jul. 1810.

Pages 299-301.   18 Jul. 1810. Minor W. S. Johnson & Hannah his
                             wife of Randolph Co. to Wekem (Welcome) Parks of
Oglethorpe Co. for $1,000, 202½ a., lot #60 in the 16th Dist., adj. lots
61, 31, 59 and the 13th Dist., on waters of Wolf Cr. s/ Minor W. S.
Johnson, Hannah Johnson. Wit: Wm. T. Morton, Chs. Cargile, JP. Rec. 18
Jul. 1810.

Page 301.   18 Jul. 1810. Charles Kannon to Richard Garner
                             for $400, a Negro woman, age 15, named Esther.
s/ C. Kennon. Wit: Robt. Robey. Rec. 19 Jul. 1810.

Pages 302-303.   Headed Hancock Co. 4 Apr. 1810. Stephen Evans
                             Senr. of Hancock Co. to John Evans of Randolph Co.
for $10, 202½ a., lot #49 in 17th Dist. s/ Stephen Evans. Wit: Jacbin
(?) Evans, Stephen Farley. Proved by Jabin Evans 13 Jul. 1810 before
Jas. Cooper, JP in Hancock Co. Rec. 19 Jul. 1810.

Pages 303-304.   27 Jan. 1810. James Martain of Bryan Co., Abraham
                             Giger, Felix Geiger, Elijah Martin and Stephen
Reigs of Bullock Co. to John Hendrick of Wilkes Co., lot #58 in 12th
Dist., adj. lots 39, 59, 91 (?), 57 on Falling Creek. s/ James Martin,
Abraham (X) Giger, Felix (X) Giger, Elijah Martin, Stephen (X) Reigs.
Wit: Dempsey Stanaland, W. W. Reading (?) JP. Rec. 20 Jul. 1810.

Page 308.   30 Jan. 1807. Whereas I have sold the chances of
                               my draws in the present land lottery to Ephraim
Ellis and am about to remove away, I appoint Joseph Baker my lawful atty.
that if my land should be drawn in my name he may take out my grant or
grants and execute title to Ellis. s/ Jonathan Day. Wit: Margit Baker,
Robert Flournoy, JP. Rec. 23 Jul. 1810.

Pages 308-309.   7 May 1808. Joseph Baker of Baldwin Co., atty.
                               in fact for Jonathan Day to Ephraim Ellis of
Jones Co. for $30, (see preceding P. of A.) 202½ a. in 14th Dist., lot
#110, adj. lots 115, 111, 109, 83. s/ Jos. Baker. Wit: Saml. Parker,
John Miles (?), JP. Rec. 23 Jul. 1810.

Page 304.   27 Jun. 1810. Joseph Hubbard of Randolph Co. to
                               Isham Holaway, for the natural love and affection
I do have for Isham Holaway and for divers other good causes and consi-
derations to wit $100, two feather beds & furniture, six head of cattle,
and all my house furniture. s/ Joseph Hubbard. Wit: Narcy (?) (X, his
mark ?) Roby, Wmson Roby, JP. Rec. 23 Jul. 1810.

                        JASPER COUNTY GEORGIA DEED BOOK 3

Pages 1-2.   14 Jul. 1810. Mary Millis and Thomas Ard of
                               Wilkinson Co. to Mark Ray of Baldwin Co. for
$490, 202½ a., lot #38 in the 17th Dist. Baldwin Co., now Randolph, adj.
lots 37, 25, 39, 53. Granted 17 Dec. 1808 to the orphans of Thomas
Millis. s/ Mary Millis, Thomas Ard. Wit: Mary Ard, Reuben Ard, JP.
Rec. 26 Jul. 1810.

Pages 2-4.   31 May 1809. George Ray of Clarke Co. to Samuel
                               Ray (Wray) of same for $300, 202½ a., lot #222
(?) in 16th Dist. adj. lots 223, 199, 221 and Dist. 15. Granted to said
George Ray in the late land lottery, granted 6 Dec. 1808. s/ George Ray.
Wit: Reuben Hill, Nathaniel Williams, Samuel Jackson. Proved by Samuel
Jackson and Reuben Hill before D. Sims, JIC, 2 Oct. 1809 in Clarke Co.
Rec. 26 Jul. 1810.

Pages 5-6.   21 Oct. 1807. Alexander Standridge (Sandridge) of
                               Franklin Co. to Stephen Neal of the Co. afsd.,
for $500, 202½ a., lot #141 in 13th Dist. Baldwin Co. adj. lots 142,
148, 116. s/ Alexander (X) Sandridge. Wit: Richardson Scurry, Jacob
Barrow, John (J) H. (?) Jones. Proved in Baldwin Co. 18 Dec. 1809 by
Richardson O. Scurry before W. Hall, JP. Rec. 30 Jul. 1810.

Pages 7-8.   26 Sep. 1809. Stephen Neal of Franklin Co. to
                               John Wallace of Hancock Co. for $400, lot #141 in
13th Dist. cont. 202½ a. adj. lots 142, 148, 116. s/ Stephen Neal. Wit:
Jeremiah Warren, John Rivers, JP. Rec. 30 Jul. 1810.

Pages 8-10.   16 Dec. 1807. Joseph Dickey of Screven Co. to
                               Benjamin Lucas of (Screven?) Co. for $120, 202½
a., lot #150 in 18th Dist., adj. lot 151, 136. Surveyed by John D. -----,
Dist. Surveyor, 10 Feb. 1807. s/ Joseph Dickey. Wit: Hardy Scarborough,
David Andress. Proved in Jefferson Co. by David <u>Andrew</u> 13 Aug. 1808,
before H. Alexander, JP. Rec. 1 Aug. 1810.

Pages 10-11.   11 Jul. 1809. William Hutchinson to Fields Wilson
                               for $450, lot #201 (?) (101?) in 16th Dist.
Baldwin Co. s/ Wm. Hutchinson. Wit: Thomas W. Harris, James Hammett.

Pages 11-12.   Headed Randolph Co. 11 Jul. 1809. David McCoy
                               and William Hutchinson to Fields Wilson, bond for
$1000 to guarantee title to lot 101 (?) in 16th Dist. Baldwin Co., now
Randolph Co. s/ D. McCoy, Wm. Hutchinson. Wit: Thomas W. Harris, Jno.
Tindill (?). <u>Deed</u> proved by Thomas W. Harris 28 Jul. 1810 before Chs.
Cargile, JP. Rec. 2 Aug. 1810.

Pages 13-14.   Headed Wilkes Co. 7 Apr. 1808. Owen Holiday of
                               Co. afsd. to John John Pugh of same for $300,

202½ a., lot #175 in 18th Dist. Baldwin. s/ Owen Holiday. Wit: John Lewis, Wm. Towns, Jas. Patterson, JP. Rec. 3 Aug. 1810.

Page 15.   26 Oct. 1809. John Batson of Greenville Co., SC
                           to William Hearn of Randolph Co. for $100, lot
#209 in 17th Dist. Baldwin Co. now Randolph, granted to Philip Steed.
Interlined before assigned in three places the name of William Hearn in
place of Joseph Westmoreland (?). s/ John Batson. Wit: Joseph Westmoreland, Joshua Miller, Jno. Cargile, JIC. Rec. 13 Aug. 1810.

Pages 16-17.   16 Aug. 1809. John Steward of Oglethorpe Co. to
                           Charles Walden of Randolph Co. for $800, lot #60
(?) in 18th Dist., cont. 146 a., 2 rods and 36 poles, on the waters of
Bear Cr. adj. lot 81 on the south, and west by the Indian Boundary line.
s/ John Stewart. Wit: Charles Williams, Benjamin Walker. Proved by
Charles Williams 15 Jun. 1810 before Samuel Townsend, JP, in Randolph
Co. Rec. 6 Aug. 1810.

Pages 17-19.   26 Aug. 1809. Joseph Betty of Morgan Co. to
                           Thomas Barren of the Co. afsd. for $350, 202½ a.,
lot #154 in 15th Dist., granted 31 Oct. 1807. s/ Joseph Betty. Wit:
John Davidson, John Park. Proved by John Park in Morgan Co. 25 Jul.
1810 before Samuel Black, JP. Rec. 7 Aug. 1810.

Pages 19-20.   15 Oct. 1808. Theophilus Hill of Wilkes Co. to
                           Hardy Hopson of Washington Co. for $500, 202½ a.
lot #24 in 13th Dist., adj. lots 9, 23, 40, 25 (?), on the waters of
Falling Cr., drawn by the said Theophilus Hill, son of Henry Hill, 24
Dec. 1806. s/ Theophilus Hill. Wit: John Hill, Stephen Johnson, George
Johnson. Rec. 7 Aug. 1810.

Pages 21-22.   29 Jan. 1810. Benjamin Thompson of Hancock Co.
                           to Greene Bailey of Greene Co. for $400, 202½ a.,
lot #105 in 15th Dist., orig. granted to the orphans of Jacob Smith 2
Oct. 1809. s/ Benj. Thompson. Wit: Wm. Gilliland, Wm. (X) Longe (?)
(Pouge ??), William Barnes, JP. Rec. 7 Aug. 1810.

Pages 22-24.   19 Jul. 1810. William Davenport of Hancock Co.
                           to James Stanley of Randolph Co. for $500, lot
#105 in 18th Dist., 202½ a. drawn by said William Davenport in the late
land lottery. s/ Wm. Davenport. Wit: Benjamin Oneil, Solomon Stricklin,
JIC. Rec. Aug. 1810.

Pages 24-25.   2 Nov. 1809. William Burnam of Randolph Co. to
                           Jonathan Phillips of same for $700, lot #154 in
16th Dist. drawn in the name of Petinne (Patience?) Saul of Liberty Co.
s/ William Barnam. Wit: Selby (?) Hearne, Elbert Phillips. Proved in
Randolph Co. by Elbert Phillips 21 Jul. 1810 before Jno. Martin, JIC.
Rec. 8 Aug. 1810.

Pages 26-27.   11 Jan. 1809. Willis Wall of Elbert Co. to
                           William Cardin of Oglethorpe Co. for $700, lot
#7 in the 14th Dist., on the waters of Cedar and Wolf Creeks, adj. the
district line. Drawn by said Willis Wall in the late land lottery, and
granted 8 Jan. 1807. s/ Willis (X) Wall. Wit: Wm. Jones, James Pye
Junr. Rec. 8 Aug. 1810.

Page 28.   (No date) 1810. Henry Haynes of Randolph Co. to
                           William Cleaveland of same for $1,000, lot #30,
bounded by the Dist. 13 and #1 in the 16th Dist., #31 and 29 in said
District. s/ Henry Haynes, Rebecca Haynes. Wit: Phelps (?) Haynes,
Epps (X) Tatom, Eli Glover, Chs. Cargile, JP. Rec. 8 Aug. 1810.

Pages 29-30.   16 Mar. 1810. John Prince of Randolph Co. to
                           John McMichael of same for $600, one half of lot
#49 in the 14th Dist., 101¼ a. s/ John (X) Prince, Nancy (X) Prince.
Wit: John Hamil (?), Johnson Strong, JP. Nancy Prince, wife of John,
relinquished her dower 16 Mar. 1810 before Johnson Strong, JP. Rec. 12
Aug. 1810.

Pages 31-32. Headed Bulloch County. 19 Mar. 1810. Arthur
Williams of Randolph Co. to Mary Patterson of the
county first written for $300, lot #72 in the 16th Dist., adj. lots 71
and 73 granted to Peggy Patterson. s/ Arthur Williams, Peggy Williams.
Wit: Drury Jones, Saml. Lockhart. Proved in Bulloch Co. 25 Mar. 1810
before John Burnet by Samuel Lockart who saw Arthur Williams and his
wife Peggy sign. Rec. 30 Aug. 1810.

Pages 32-34. 29 Feb. 1810. Jesse Holbrook of Franklin Co. to
Benjamin Smith of Randolph Co. for $300, 202½ a.,
lot #174 in the 14th Dist., broadside to lot #147. s/ Jesse Holbrook.
Wit: Allen Bass (?), David (X) Smith, Thomas Griffin. Proved by David
Smith 28 Jul. 1810 before John Bender (?), JP. Rec. 4 Sep. 1810.

Pages 34-35. 2 Sep. 1808. John Hendrick of Wilkes Co. to
James Jennings of said county, for $225, 202½ a.,
lot #66 in 18th Dist., adj. lots 65, 67, 75, 53. s/ John Hendrick.
Wit: Simeon Ellington, Daniel Owen, Archd. Simpson, JP. Rec. 4 Sep. 1810.

Pages 36-38. Headed Jefferson County 3 Jul. 1808. Mary Wilcher
of the state afds. to Elizabeth Barnes of Baldwin
Co. for $100, 202½ a., lot #219 in the 16th Dist., adj. Dist. 15 and
lots 202, 220, 218; surveyed 31 May 1807, granted 31 Oct. 1807, drawn
in the name of Mary Wilcher, widow. s/ Mary (X) Wilcher. Wit: John
McCoy, William (X) Brassell. Proved by William Brassell 18 May 1809
before Gilbert Bardin. Rec. 15 Sep. 1810.

Pages 38-39. 26 May 1810. Stith Daniel to Scynthia Steedman
for "25 dollars cents," 15 head of hogs together
with the increase. s/ Stith Daniel. Wit: James Woodruff. Rec. 19 Sep.
1810.

Page 39. 26 May 1810. Absalom Kenedy to Eady Steedman,
for 12½ cents, 2 feather beds and furniture and
6 chairs. s/ Absalom Kenedy. Wit: James Woodruff. Rec. 19 Sep. 1810.

Pages 40-41. Headed Hancock Co. 28 Dec. 1809. James Miller
Senr. of Hancock Co. to Henry W. Latimer of same
for $600, 202½ a., lot #98 in 19th Dist. adj. lots 99, 91. 97, 121. s/
James (w) Miller. Wit: J. C. Birdsong, Chas. Medlock (?), John Latimer,
JP. Rec. 19 Sep. 1810.

Pages 42-43. Headed Clarke Co. 3 Mar. 1810. William Ross of
Clarke Co. to Bersheeba Kelly of same for $500,
202½ a., lot #119 in 17th Dist. adj. lot 120. s/ William Ross. Wit:
Nancy (X) Bridges, Jacob Kelly Junior. Proved by Jacob Kelly 23 Mar.
1810 in Clarke Co. before George Fenn, JP. Rec. 19 Sep. 1810.

Pages 44-45. 16 Oct. 1807. I, James M. Robertson of Savannah,
Chatham Co., carpenter, appoint Jeremiah Pitman,
butcher, of same place, my lawful attorney to deliver and make title to
a lot of land which I have lately drawn in the last land lottery held at
Louisville in this state; lot #13 in the 14th Dist. s/ Jas. M. Robert-
son. Wit: H. (?) Edward Lloyd, William Davies, Not. Pub. Ack. by
Robertson before William Davies, Not. Pub., 16 Oct. 1807 in Chatham Co.
(Interesting reproduction of Davies' Seal included.) Rec. 25 Sep. 1810.

Pages 46-49. Headed Chatham Co. 10 Nov. 1807. Jeremiah Pitman
of Chatham Co. for James M. Robertson, carpenter,
to William Allen Pitman of same place for $500, lot #13 in 14th Dist.
Baldwin Co. on waters of Wolf Cr., 202½ a. drawn by James M. Robertson,
carpenter, of Pitibones Dist. Chatham Co. in the late land lottery,
surveyed 8 Jan. 1807. s/ Jeremiah Pitman for James M. Robertson. Wit:
Hen. W. Williams, John Poole, JP. Rec. 25 Sep. 1810.

Pages 50-51. 10 Sep. 1810. Thomas Bonner of Morgan Co. to
Arthur Smith of Randolph Co. for $800, 202½ a.,
lot 46 in 14th Dist. granted to William Duke 20 Mar. 1808. s/ Thomas
Bonner. Wit: Martin Gentry, William Wright, Phillip Zimmerman. Proved
by William Wright 22 Sep. 1810 before Johnson Strong, JP in Randolph Co.

Rec. 27 Sep. 1810.

Page 52.   21 Feb. 1809. John Strong of Clarke Co. to
                        Richmond Carroll of Randolph Co., 202½ a., lot
#202 in 10th Dist., adj. lots 201, 183, 203, 215. Drawn in the name of
the said John Strong, Senior. s/ John (X) Strong, Senr. Wit: Robert
Strong, William Strong, JIC. Rec. 27 Sep. 1810.

Pages 53-55.   25 Nov. 1807. Jarrot Campbell and Sally Campbell
                        of Jackson Co. to Jacob B. Warbington of same,
for one dollar, lot #11 in the 14th Dist., on waters of Wolf Cr., granted
to the said Jarrot Campbell 13 Oct. last; 202½ a. adj. lots 12, 10, 22,
13. s/ Jarrot Campbell, Sally ( ) Campbell. "The words'and Sally
Campbell in the third line being first interlined' . . ." Wit: Geo. N.
Lyles, Mark Snow, John McVay. Proved by George N. Lyles 5 Jan. 1809 and
amended (?) 8 May 1809 before David Witt, JIC. Rec. 27 Sep. 1810.

Pages 56-57.   5 Sep. 1808. Isaac Humphries of Clarke Co. to
                        William Colbert of Greene for $440, 202½ a.,
lots #217 in 13 Dist. s/ Isaac Humphries. Wit: Levi Daniel, Isaac
Williams, Pleasant (Tatom?). Proved by Isaac Williams 9 Jun. 1810 before
Jarrel Beasley, JP. Rec. 28 Sep. 1810.

Pages 58-59.   30 Dec. 1808. William Harper of Lincoln Co. to
                        Charles Avington of Putnam Co. for 120, 202½ a.,
lot #267 in 19th Dist., drawn by Harper in the late land lottery. s/
William Harper. Wit: George (X) Lewis, John Wright. Proved by George
Lewis in Morgan Co. before Robt. Gaston, JP. Rec. 29 Sep. 1810.

Pages 60-61 are blank.

Pages 62-63.   2 Aug. 1810. Thomas Snow of Putnam Co. to John
                        McMichael of Randolph Co. for $600, lot #27 in
16th Dist., 202½ a. bounded by lots 4, 28, 34, 26. Drawn by said Thomas
Snow and granted 26 Dec. 1809. s/ Thos. Snow. Wit: Elijah Strong,
James Johnston, Johnson Strong, JP. Rec. 29 Sep. 1810.

Pages 63-65.   13 Nov. 1809. William Stokes Junr. & Jane Stokes
                        his wife of Lincoln Co. to Aquiller Philips of
Elbert Co. for $300, 202½ a., lot #96 in 12th Dist. on Little Falling
Cr., adj. lots 95, 97, 65, district line #17. s/ William Stokes Junr.,
Jane Stokes. Wit: Wm. Wade Stokes, George Storman (?) JP. Rec. 29 Sep.
1810.

Pages 65-66.   7 Nov. 1809. Patrick Butler of Elbert Co. to
                        Claiburn Martin of Oglethorpe Co. for $100, 202½
a., lot #260 in the 19th Dist. s/ Patrick Butler. Wit: William Hightower, James Huft (?). Rec. 30 Sep. 1810.

Pages 66-67.   21 Jul. 1810. Charles Crawford, John Cargile,
                        John Martin, Isaac McLendon and Solomon Strick-
land, Commissioners of the public land of Randolph Co. and the public
buildings in the village of Monticello to Joseph Crockett, merchant of
said Village, for $92, two lots of land in Monticello, #35 & 36. Signed
by all except Charles Crawford. Wit: Adam Glazier, Chs. Cargile, JP.
Rec. 30 Sep. 1810.

Pages 68-69.   11 Jan. 1810. John Johnson Senr. of Hancock Co.
                        to David Henderson of Putnam Co. for $550, 202½
a., lot #85 in 15th Dist. Baldwin Co. now Randolph Co., adj. lots 84,
86, 66, 96. s/ John (X) Johnston. Wit: W. Furlow, W. Galloway, Jno.
Houghton. Proved by William Furlow 6 Mar. 1810 before John Armor, JP.
Rec. 30 Aug. 1810.

Page 70.   John Mitchell of Hancock Co. to Henry Mitchell of
                        the county afsd. for $400, 101¼ a., lot #29 in
15th Dist. adj. lots 28, 32 & 2. s/ John Mitchell. Wit: Samuel Davies,
Wm. Chandler, JP. Rec. 30 Sep. 1810.

Pages 71-73.   14 Aug. 1810. Jonathan Wood and Mary Jamima his

wife of Columbia Co. to Joseph Key of Randolph
Co. for $800, 202½ a., lot #143 in 15th Dist. adj. lots 142, 158, 144,
128. "This deed is given in place of a deed for the same lot of land
dated 21 Dec. 1808 Burnt in the house of Tandy W. Key agreeable to a
copy of his oath made before James Heard JP." s/ Jonathan Wood. Wit:
Geo. Downs, Benjamin H. Berry; Jno. Foster JIC. 14 Aug. 1810, witnessed
by Joseph Key, Mary Jemima Wood certified that on 21 Oct. 1808, she
signed a relinquishment of her dower to the within lot of land that was
unfortunatley burnt. Dower proved by Joseph Key 14 Aug. 1810 before Jno.
Foster JIC in Columbia Co. Rec. 30 Sep. 1810.

Pages 73-74.   Headed Oglethorpe Co. 15 Jun. 1810. William
                        Lumpkin of Co. afsd., attorney for John Gracey to
Andrew Reid of Randolph Co. for $225, 202½ a., lot #1 in 17th Dist.
Power of Atty. from John Gracey was dated 17 Oct. 1808. s/ Wm. Lumpkin.
Wit: James Wiley, Nancy Carden (?), (A. C. McInver?) JP. Rec. 30 Sep.
1810.

Pages 75-77.   25 May 1810. Martin Martin of Liberty Co. to
                        William Harvey of Putnam Co. for $400, 202½ a.,
lot #76 in 14th Dist. s/ Martin Martin. Wit: Samuel Harwill (?), Alex.
Martin, Evans Harvey. Proved by Evans Harvey 28 Jul. 1810 in Putnam Co.
before W. D. Land (?) JP. Rec. 1 Oct. 1810.

Pages 77-80.   17 Oct. 1809. Mary Morgan, admrx., and Robert
                        Morgan and John Carmichael administrators of
Thomas Morgan dec'd. to Phillip Thurmond. Whereas on 23 Nov. 1807,
Thomas Morgan executed his Bond to the said Philip Thurmond to excute
title to lot #166 in 13th Dist. Baldwin Co. but departed this life with-
out making title. . . for $800, title is made. s/ John (X) Carmichael,
Robert (X) Morgan, Mary (X) Morgan. s/ W. Harris, David Will JIC,
William Cobb JP, Robert Couder (?) JP, Edward Adams. Rec. 1 Oct. 1810.

Pages 81-82.   1 Oct. 1810. Abraham Daniel of Burke Co. to
                        Burwell Greene of Randolph Co. for $800, 202½ a.,
lot #134 in 13th Dist. s/ Abram Daniel. Wit: John Knight, Royal Clay,
John Kennaday. Rec. 3 Oct. 1810.

Pages 82-83.   17 Nov. 1807. Sterling Evans of Baldwin Co. to
                        Hugh McConner of the Co. afsd. for $600, lot #206
in 13th Dist. s/ Sterling Evans. Wit: Richard Stokes, James (?) Roe (?),
A. M. Devereaux, JIC. Rec. 4 Oct. 1810.

Pages 84-86.   16 Dec. 1807. Daniel Grantham of Baldwin Co. to
                        Alexander Herring of Hancock Co. for $1,000,
202½ a. on the waters of Murder Cr. in 15th Dist. Baldwin Co.·, lot #24.
s/ Daniel Grantham. Wit: Elisha Gore, Thomas Bloodworth. Proved by
Thomas Bloodworth 14 Jan. 1808 before A. M. (?) Devereux, JIC in Baldwin
Co. Rec. 4 Oct. 1810.

Pages 86-87.   28 Aug. 1810. Willoughby Hammock of Randolph Co.
                        to Moses Trimble of same for $1,000, fractional
lot #181 in 19th Dist. cont. 105 a. s/ Willoughby Hammock. Wit: John
M. Trimble, Micajah H. Fretwell, Wmson Roby, JP. Rec. 8 Oct. 1810.

Pages 87-89.   7 Feb. 1809. William Ronaldson of Jefferson Co.
                        to Benjamin Brown of Clark Co. for $400, 202½ a.,
lot #97 in 19th Dist. Baldwin adj. lots 98, 90, 96, 122. Granted to
Mathew Davis 18 Feb. 1808 and transferred by deed to the said Ronaldson
15 Mar. 1808. s/ Willim. Ronaldson. Wit: Robinson (no first name),
Wm. Wright, JP. Rec. 10 Oct. 1810.

Pages 89-90.   2 Aug. 1810. John McMichal of Randolph Co. to
                        Thomas Snow of Putnam Co. for $500, half of lot
#49 in 14th Dist. adj. the line of the 16th Dist., 101¼ a. s/ John Mc-
Michael. Wit: Elijah Strong, James Johnson, Johnson Strong, JP. Rec.
10 Oct. 1810.

Page 91.   15 Dec. 1807. Gracy Matthews, widow of Columbia
                       Co. to Samuel Arnett of the Co. afsd. for $250,

202½ a., lot #71 in 15th Dist.   s/ Gracy Matthews.   Wit: John Hardin,
Thomas White, JP.   Rec. 10 Oct. 1810.

Page 91.   20 Jul. 1810.   John Gibson of Warren Co. to
                              Thomas Gibson of Baldwin Co. for $500, lot #97
in 17th Dist.   s/ John Gibson.   Wit: George W. Rogers, Henry Cox JP.
Rec. 10 Oct. 1810.

Pages 92-93.   20 Sep. 1810.   Benjamin Walless (Wallace) of
                              Hancock Co. to Nehemiah Schogen of Putnam Co. for
$500, lot 151 in 17th Dist.   s/ Benjamin (X) Walless.   Wit: Nicholas
Lankford, Thomas Traylor.   Proved by Nicholas (X) Lankford 12 Oct. 1810
before Isaac McClendon JIC in Randolph Co.   Rec. 13 Oct. 1810.

Pages 93-94.   4 Dec. 1809.   Joshua Reeves of Randolph Co. to
                              John Evans of same for $400, 103 a., part of lot
#224 in 16th Dist. on Murder Cr. joining lot 225.   Granted to Jacob
Moore 1 Mar. 1809.   s/ Joshua (X) Reeves.   Wit: James Buchanan, Joseph
Buchanan.   Ack. by Reeves 21 Aug. 1810 before Joseph Heard, JP.   Rec.
13 Oct. 1810.

WILLS OF MORGAN COUNTY, GEORGIA

Morgan County was created from Baldwin County by the Legislature on December 10, 1807. The eastern portion of Morgan, districts four and five, was distributed by the 1805 Land Lottery, and the western portion was distributed by the 1807 Land Lottery. This means that the earliest Morgan records would be part of the Baldwin records. For example, the 1807 Baldwin Tax Return covers the area that became eastern Morgan and eastern Putnam.

The wills abstracted below begin with Record of Wills and Marriages A; reference to book and page is at end of abstract. Two wills in this book are omitted from the book's index and from the list in Volume 1 of Historical Collections of the Georgia Chapters of the American Revolution. They are the will of George Lee Atkins and the will of John Jones (proved 1809).

ALLEN, JAMES. Last Will and Testament, dated 2 April 1812, proved 3 Jan. 1814. Lends wife, Lucy Allen, all estate during widowhood; should she marry, a child's part. If negroes in the hands of Nathaniel Allen be recovered, they are to be in the same situation with testator's other property now in testator's possession. Wife, Lucy Allen, Joel Gaar, and David Boring to be executors. Wit: James Hughey, James Head. (A/22)

ATKINS, GEORGE LEE of Morgan County, Last Will and Testament, dated 22 of Oct. 1814, proved 7 Nov. 1814. Gives sister, Lucy Miles, widow, sorrel horse, saddle and briddle. Gives brother, Arnold Atkins, $5. Gives brother, Jeremiah Atkins, $5. Gives sister, Lovecy Atkins, one habit dress of lustring. Gives niece, Unicy Miles, one habit of lustring. Gives balance of estate to brothers and sisters, Lucy Miles, Ransam Atkins, Unicy Brown, Willis Atkins, and Levecy Atkins. Appoints brother, Willis Atkins, executor. Wit: John McCoy, Willis Richards. (A/32,33)

BAILEY, WILLIAM of Morgan County. Last Will and Testament, dated 15 Feb. 1808, partially proved 2 Jan. 1809, entered of record 6 Feb. 1809. Gives 25 cents to daughters, Bethaney Arnold, Ruth Arnold, Alse Lewis, to son, Jeremiah Bailey, to daughter, Elizabeth Bingham, to son, John Bailey, to daughter, Mary Bingham and Temprance Blalock. Gives land "whare on I now live" to sons, William and Fuller. Gives wife, Mary Bailey, negro girl, Cile, and all the rest of testators' property for the support of her family during her natural life or widowhood, and at her death or marriage, property to be equally divided between daughters, Milley Bailey, Gilley Bailey, Salley Bailey, and sons, William Bailey and Fuller Bailey. Wife, Mary Bailey, sons, Jeremiah Bailey, John Bailey and son-in-law, James Lewis, to be executors. Wit: Edwin Lamberth, Isaac Hand. (A/4,5)

BANCKSTON, DANIEL of Morgan County. Last Will and Testament, dated 10 April 1811, proved 7 May 1811. Gives to wife, Rachel Banckston, all lands and plantations and all the rent of the property testator possesses during her lifetime or widowhood. At death of wife, all property to be sold, and daughter, Edeth Patton, to have $50 of proceeds of sale, and the balance to be equally divided among the rest of testator's children. Daughter, Pattey, to have her part in money. Sons, Thomas Banckston and Abner Banckston, and James Malcam to be executors. Wit: James Keelan, Alex, Awtry, and Rob't Bready (Brady). (A/9,10)

BRYANT, PATRICK of Greene County. Last Will and Testament, dated 19 Jan. 1806, proved in Morgan County 7 March 1808. Gives to wife, Elizabeth Bryant, a negro woman, a mare, three cows, two calves, and all the money and notes due testator. Gives eldest son, James Bryant, a mare. Gives to daughter, Rebekah, a filly, cow and calf which she already has. Gives youngest daughter, Nancy, a negro at death of her mother. Gives granddaughter, Mary Simmons, $1.50. Gives daughter, Elizabeth Bryant, $1.50. Gives residue of estate to wife. Wife and John A. Dair to be executors. Wit: John Moore, Susanna Hughey and

366

Jean Adair. (A/1,2)

BUCHANAN, JOSEPH of Morgan County. Last Will and Testament, dated 8
                July 1808, proved 3 Sept. 1810. Gives to wife, Mary
Buchanan, lot #150 in the 4th district of Morgan except for 50 acres
improved by Larkin Cleveland, four negroes, personal estate not other-
wide disposed of, and debts due on accounts not otherwise mentioned.
Gives daughter, Ann Hagerty, half of lot #14 in the 5th district of
Morgan and two negroes. Gives daughter, Sary Cleveland, half of lot
#141 in the 4th district of Morgan whereon Larkin Cleveland's house now
stands, with a field on said lot, cleared by testator, reserved to Mary
Buchanan for four years, and two negroes. Gives daughter, Elizabeth
McAfee, the other half of lot #14 in the 5th district of Morgan and two
negroes. Gives daughter, Jane Buchanan, the other half of lot #150 in
the 4th district including the spring the family now uses, two negroes,
$116 in cash out of money due testator, one good feather bed and furni-
ture, three cows and calves, and $30 more for clothing and other necess-
aries formerly bestowed on the others. If any daughters die without
issue surviving them, the effects to be equally divided between the
surviving sisters. Goods and chattels at wife's death to be equally
divided among heirs. Gives to granddaughter, Mary Clevelend Hagerty,
one small feather bed. Gives to granddaughter, Caroline Cleveland, one
walnut cupboard. Gives to son-in-law, Larkin Cleveland, the other part
of lot #150 in the 4th district, the remaining part of the lot to be 50
acres and to include his improvement. Mary Buchanan, Abel Hagerty, and
Larkin Cleveland to be executors. Wit: Jonathan Anderson, Abraham Mc-
Afee, John Buchannon. (A/5,6)

CARLETON, HENRY of Morgan County. Last Will and Testament, dated 7 Oct.
                1814, proved 7 Nov. 1814. Gives daughter, Nancy Clark
Mitchell, widow of William Mitchell dec'd., all estate except hereafter
excepted. Gives to nephew, Henry Carleton Coxe, $500. Gives nephew,
Henry Carleton, $500. Gives nephew, Thomas Carleton, $200. Gives little
grandchildren, -ary Coxe Mitchell and William Henry Mitchell, 202½
acres, lot #62 in the 5th district of Morgan, granted to Watters Dunn
Senr. of Columbia County. Gives grandson, William Henry Mitchell, shot-
gun and sleeve buttons. Gives negroes to daughter, Nancy C. Mitchell
and her heirs. Daughter, Nancy Clark Mitchell, and James Gillespie to
be executors. Wit: Wm. Johnston, Edw'd Williams, F. S. Cook, William
Askew, and Isham S. Fannen. (A/30,31)

DAVIS, JOHN of Morgan County. Last Will and Testament, dated 27 Sept.
                1813, proved 17 Jan. 1814. Gives to son, Jonathan Davis,
150 acres on the western side of lot testator now lives on, stock, and
furniture. Son, Jonathan, is to take care of his mother out of his
property. Gives son, David Davis, the balance of lot testator now lives
on, stock, and furniture, with all the property that he has received.
Gives to daughter, Nancy Warren, stock and the property she has received.
Gives to son, George Davis, stock the property he has received. Gives
to daughter, Elizabeth, stock and furniture. Gives to daughter, Patsey,
furniture and stock. Gives to son, James Davis, stock and furniture
with all the property he has received. Gives to son, Drewry Davis, stock
with all the property he has received. Gives to my two (relationship
ommitted) William and Martin Davis all the property they have received.
Wife, Nancy Davis, to be executor. Wit: Jesse McIntosh, Daniel Jackson,
and Hudson Allen. (A/23,24,25)

DAVIS, THOMAS. Last Will and Testament, dated 7 Aug. 1811, codicil
                dated 7 April 1812, proved 6 July 1812. Gives to wife
negro girl, bay horse, saddle and bridle, bedstead, bed and clothing,
two trunks, half dozen chairs which were formerly her own, stock, one
thousand weight of pork, two rooms of the house, one above the other,
in the west end, so long as she may see cause to live in them, and ten
acres of the open land or one fifth part of the rent if she sees cause
to remove during her widowhood. Gives to son, Warren W. Davis, negro
boy, Harry, one negro fellow named Ned to be under her dircetion during
her widowhood, or if she marries to be hired out by the executors for
his benefit and schooling. Gives to son, Jeremiah Davis, a negro, $250
to be raised out of testator's estate, and a bed. Gives to daughter, H.
(blank) Davis, negroes and $100 to be raised out of estate, and a bed.

Gives to son, Thomas Jefferson Davis, negroes and a bed. Desires perishable property, stock, household and kitchen furniture, waggon, plantation tools, and the tract lying upon the Apelache granted to Zechariah Butlre to be sold by the executors and profits therefrom to be equally divided among Jeremiah, Nancy, Thomas and Warren as they become of age. Testator's lands, lot #292, #293, another adjoining Pate, to be sold when Thomas becomes of age, and money to be equally divided among the four children, Jeremiah, Nancy, Thomas, and Warren. Thomas and Warren to have four years schooling. William Brown, Arthur Davis, and William McKuen to be executors. Wit: William Spratlen, Sylvanus Walker, John Burney. Codicil gives $600 to be raised out of sale of tract on the Appalache River to child which Testator's wife is now pregnant with. This child to have first child born to negro, Caty. Child to have schooling. Wit: Wm. Brown, Arthur Davis. (A/14,15,16,17)

FIELDER, JAMES of Morgan County. Last Will and Testament, dated 25 Dec. 1812, proved 1 March 1813. Gives wife, Sally Fielder, all estate use and benefit of herself and testator's children. At wife's death or end of widowhood, all property to be sold and an equal division made among all children. With consent of wife, executors to make division when youngest daughter, Tempy Fielder, comes of age. If division takes place before death of wife or during her widowhood, wife to have sufficient maintainance out of testator's estate. Gives son, Isham Fielder, when of age, horse, etc. Gives children, Terrell Fielder, Betsey Fielder, Sally Fielder, Moriah Fielder and Tempy Fielder, as they come of age, horse, etc. At death of wife or with consent of wife to a division, testator's estate not heretofore mentioned to be equally divided among testator's then surviving children; lawful heirs of deceased children to have share of parent. Children of testator are William L. Fielder, Thomas Fielder, Polly Few, John Fielder, Obadiah M. B. Fielder, Josiah Fielder, Isham Fielder, Terrell Fielder, Betsey Fielder, Sally Fielder, Junior, Moriah Fielder, and Tempy Fielder; William L. Fielder, and Obadiah M. B. Fielder to be executors. Wit: Jos. Heard, Harrison Jones, William Silman. (A/18,19)

HAMILTON, ROBERT, planter, of Morgan County. Last Will and Testament, no date, proved 3 Dec. 1810. Sons, James and John, have received what testator intended for them out of testator's estate. Gives daughter, Frances, one cow and calf with what she has already received. Gives son, William, one horse, saddle and cow and calf. Gives son, Peter, one bay horse colt, saddle, and cow and calf at his coming of age or marriage. Gives son, Robert, one sorrel horse colt, saddle, and cow and calf at his coming of age or marriage. Gives to son, Moses, one horse, saddle, and cow and calf at his coming of age or marriage. Gives daughter, Betsey, feather bed and furniture and cow and calf. Gives daughters, Polley and Anne, feather bed and cow and calf each. "It is my will and desire that one yellow girl named Lucy and as much of my property be sold as will discharge my debts and give my two youngest daughters, Polley and Anne, one years schooling at last." Gives wife, Amy, 50 acres of land in the corner where testator lives, with the premises thereof, stock, furniture, tools, and negro woman for her use and support, and children's support, during wife's life. Balance of land to be for benefit of sons, William, Peter, Robert, and Moses to live on or till death of wife. At wife's death, all land to be sold for the equal benefit of testator's children, William, Peter, Robert, Moses, Betsy, Polley, and Anne. Wife and son, William to be executors. Wit: Robert Shaw, Charles Macelroy (McElroy). (A/7,8)

HANSON, EDMUND of Morgan County. Last Will and Testament, dated 4 Aug. 1814, proved 2 Jan. 1815. Gives to wife, Nancy Hanson, all real estate, plantation utensils, household and kitchen furniture, nine negroes, and stock. Gives father, Thomas Hanson, one negro man, one sorrel horse, and one no horned cow. William Jones and William Hanson, Jr. to be executors. Wit: John B. Whatley, William Hanson. Receipt of Thomas Hanson of Jackson County, dated 3 Jan. 1815, for one negro man, one sorrel horse, and one no horned cow. (A/34,35).

JONES, JOHN of Morgan County. Last Will and Testament, dated 18 ----- 1808, proved 2 Jan. 1809. Gives Capt. Thomas Davis ten barrels of corn, etc. Gives Lasors (?) Pearc corn and fodder. Gives

Isaac Briant corn and fodder. Gives $100 in small notes in the hands of Lasors Pearc to Delie (?) Briant. Gives Lasours Pearce one $8 note and $3.75 in the hands of Ezekiel Rankns. Gives Delia Bryant unbrella and trunk. Gives Larso (?) Pearc saddle and clothes. Executors: Thomas Davis and Lazarous Pearc. Wit: Jeremiah Davis, James Cowlom. (A/3)

JONES, JOHN of Morgan County. Last Will and Testament, dated 21 Jan. 1812, proved 4 May 1812. Gives to daughter, Lucy Van, one feather bed and furniture. Gives son, Hasten Jones, eighty acres of land, part of lot #320...running with Fitzpatrick's line, and one bed and furniture. Gives youngest son, John Jones, remainder of my estate, the whole to continue in the possession of wife, Elizabeth, during her lifetime or widowhood. Give each of testator's other children 5 shillings sterling. William Brown and Jesse Gunn to be executors. Wit: Jesse Kelly, Dennis Maddin, Jesse Gunn. (A/12,13)

McMURRAY, WILLIAM of Morgan County. Last Will and Testament, dated 11 Oct. 1815, proved 6 Nov. 1815. Gives wife, Eleanor McMurray, all stock, household and kitchen furniture, plantation whereon testator now lives, and four negroes.* After death of wife, executors to use utmost endeavors to get a law passed by the Legislature to set free and emancipate testator's four negroes above named, together with any child or children they may have after this date. Gives daughter, Elizabeth Evans, two negroes. Gives son, John McMurray four negroes. Gives daughter, Mary Anderson Burney, One dollar. Lends son, William McMurray, three negroes and at his decease, gives them to his heirs. Gives grandson, Franklin Augustus McMurray, a negro. Gives grandson, John McDonald McMurray, a negro. Gives to granddaughter, Augusta Ann McMurray, a negro. Gives to granddaughter, Clarisa Evans, a negro. At death of wife, land where testator lives to be divided equally between negroes, Essex and Jerry, etc. John McMurray and William McMurray, Jr. to be executors. Wit: James Daniell, Reubin Winfrey, William Daniell, John Bassett. (A/38,39,40) *Essex and his wife, Jamima, Jerry and his wife, Peggy.

MITCHELL, WILLIAM of Morgan County. Last Will and Testament, dated 27 J----, 1812, proved 5 April 1813. Executors to collect all money due testator, and pay testator's debts from this money, and invest remainder on money for testator's family. Gives wife, Ann Clark Mitchell, one third part of testator's whole estate for her natural life; then to return to testator's two children, divided equally. Gives daughter, Mary Coxe Mitchell, one third of estate. Gives son, William Henry Mitchell, silver watch, a negro blacksmith, Starling, and one third of estate. Approints friends, Henry Carleton, Thomas Greenwood, and Edward Coxe to be executors. Wit: Graves Harris, Simon Reaves, David Pattillo. (A/20/21)

PATTILLO, DAVID. Last Will and Testament, dated -- Feb. 1815, proved 6 March 1815. Gives to wife, Agathy Patillo, three negroes as her own right and property and to have disposition thereof; also all the claim, right and title of that part of the estate of Jacob Odom deceased to which she was by law entitled previous to intermarriage with testator. Balance of estate, both real and personal, to be equally divided among John Patillo, James Patillo, Elizabeth Hanson (formerly Elizabeth Patillo), William Patillo, Patsey Patillo, Henry Patillo, Tabitha Patillo, Rebecca Patillo, Luren ----(??) Patillo, Sally Patillo, and David Patillo. Appoints ons, John Patillo and James Patillo, and wife, Agathy Patillo as executors. Wit: Isaac Lyda, Wm. Johnston, Samuel Patillo, Robert F. Session. (A/36,37)

SNELLINGS, PETER of Morgan County. Last Will and Testament, dated 25 March 1813, proved 5 July 1813. Gives mother, Salley Snellings, widow of Alexander Snellings, late of Chesterfield Co., Va., $50, a parcel of plank which testator has on the plantation whereon she resides, and the life use of a feather bed, now in Virginia, left testator by his father. At death of mother, bed and furniture to go to nephew Benjamin Laprade. Mother to remain with peaceable possession and enjoyment of the land and premises whereon she now lives as long as she lives. Gives brother, John Snellings, all property in Georgia. Gives brother, George Snellings, all testator's books which are in Virginia. Gives sister, Salley Laprade, negro at death of mother and one fourteenth part of the proceeds of the land and premises whereon testator's mother lives. After deducting the one fourteenth part, the legacy of Sally Laprade, the balance of the proceeds to be equally divided amongst the rest of testator's brothers and sisters except my brother, Alexander Snellings, John Snellings, George Snellings, William Snellings, Nanny Brooks, Molley Elam and Elizabeth Snellings. Gives money, bonds, notes, and accounts due from estate of testator's brothers and sisters except brother, John Snellings, ----- George Snellings, Alexander Snellings, William Snellings, Nanny Brooks, Molly Elam, Sally Laprade, and Elizabeth Snellings. Appoints brothers, John and William Snellings to be executors. Wit: Wilson Whatley, Nathan Swanson, John Swanson, and Salley Whatley. (A/25,26,27,28)

STROUD, JOHN of Morgan County. Last Will and Testament, not dated, proved 6 April 1812. Gives wife, Sarah, during her natural life, negroes, stock, tools, and furniture. Gives eldest son, Ethen Stroud, $10. Gives second child, Pasifi T. Fielder, negro woman in his possession, negro girl and $200 or another negro child. Gives son, Malory Stroud, two negroes and $300 when of age, also horse, bridle and saddle, and household furniture. Balance of estate to be divided among four children, Ethen, Pasfi T., Malory, and Beden. Appoints Ethan Stroud and John Fielder executors. Wit: Levi Benson, John Rice, Thomas Elliot, James Hanes. (A/10,11)

WHATLEY, ELIZABETH of Morgan County. Last Will and Testament, dated 15 June 1810, proved 4 July 1814. Gives son, Ornan Whatley, negro man, all the right that testator had in testator's lifetime to four negroes, household and kitchen furniture, plantation tools, and stock. Appoints son, Robert Whatley, executor. Wit: Jno. Garrett, Tempy Garrett. (A/28,29)

WOOTON, JEREMIAH of Morgan County. Last Will and Testament, 4 Feb. 1810, proved 7 Jan. 1811. Gives wife, Elizabeth Wooton, during her natural life, all estate. After death of wife, estate to go to five children, John Wooton, Prssilla Casey, Amey Cole, Elizabeth Whattley, and Ann Pears. Appoints John Cole and wife, Elizabeth Wooton, executors. Wit: David Ray, Fielding Arnold, Edmund Brantly, JP. (A/8,9)

MORGAN COUNTY, GEORGIA WILL RECORD B, 1818-1830

Will Record B, 1815-1830 contains 168 wills. These wills are abstracted below in alphabetical order with the reference to book and page at the end of each abstract. The index to Will Record B, located in the front of the book, lists all 168 wills. Two wills were omitted from the list in Volume 1 (pp. 79-80) of Historical Collections of the Chapters National Society Daughters of the American Revolution. Those omitted are the wills of William Ball and John Burney. In addition, Historical Collections listed the will of Lemuel Ware which must be misreading of the name of Samuel Watt. Mr. Ted O. Brooke, in his useful book, Georgia Wills 1733-1860, omitted two wills also. These are the wills of William Barton and David Sidwell.

The handwriting in Will Record B is often difficult to read with the added complications of some very faint pages and some pages with faded areas. In general, my reading of the name is based on the signature of the will, how the name was written in the attestation to the will, and how the name was written in the first part of the will. As to be expected, the interpretation of the names in the two references above and the interpretation in these abstracts differ in a number of instances. The interpretation affects the alphabetical order in some cases.

Will Record B can be consulted in the Morgan County Courthouse or viewed on microfilm at the Georgia Department of Archives and History.

AKIN, BARTLEY of Morgan County. Last Will and Testament, dated 3 Dec. 1829, sworn to 4 Jan. 1830. Leaves all estate, real and personal, in the care and charge of beloved wife, ----- Akin, until such time as the child may be born with which she is now pregnant. On the birth of that child, testator leaves to said child the one half of all testator's estate; the other half to wife. If the child dies before age twenty one, the part of estate willed to child to revert to wife. Wife to be executrix and friend Sterling Finny, to be executor. Wife and Sterling Finny to be guardian to said child. Signed: Bartley Akin. Wit: John R. Baldwin, George N. Ware, Wm. Stock. (B/278,279,280)

ALLEN, ELIZABETH J. of Morgan County. Last Will and Testament, dated 22 Aug. 1826, sworn to 7 May 1827. Gives to beloved daughter, Sophia Jenkins of Alabama, one negro lad, Anthony, one third of testator's wearing apparel and bedding after taking out two bed steads & furniture. Gives to beloved granddaughters, Sally, Lucy, Nancey, Patsey, Hetty, and Mary Lewis, daughters of testator's beloved daughter, Patsey Lewis, and to testator's beloved grandsons, Thomas, Jeremiah and John Lewis, and to testator's beloved daughter, Patsey, aforesaid one fifth part of testator's estate as legacies to be paid to them at the discretion of testator's executor, James Head. Gives to granddaughters, before mentioned, one third part of her wearing apparel and bedding, taking out two beds and furniture which is to be sold by her executor. Gives to grandson, James Fortson, one fifth part of estate not herein named as legacies to be paid over to him by executor when collected. Gives to grandchildren, Thomas J. Allen and Eliza C. Allen, one fifth part of estate not otherwise named to be paid to them by executor when it may come into his hands. Gives to daughter, Elizabeth White, one fifth of estate to be paid to her by executor when collected and one third part of wearing apparel and bedding. Gives to beloved son, James Head, one fifth of estate and $50 which testator now has his note for. Appoints beloved son, James Head, executor. Executor to hand over to son-in-law, John Lewis, note of hand testator holds on him for $50 as his legacy. If negro boy, Anthony, should die before coming into the possession of daughter, Sophia, Sophia to have one sixth part of testator's whole estate. Signed: Elizabeth J. Allen. Wit: Hezekiah F. Goss, Robert Cessna, Nathaniel Allen. (B/211,212,213)

ALLEN, WILLIAM of Morgan County. Last Will and Testament, dated 23 Feb. 1815, sworn to 4 Nov. 1816. Gives to beloved wife, Mary Allen, all personal estate consisting of stock, household & kitchen furniture, and plantation utensils, to be at her disposal at her death. Lends and gives beloved wife during her natural life all lands whereon testator now lives. At wife's decease, land to be equally divided among testator's twelve children, Polley Pollard, James Allen, Darcas Allen, John Allen, William Allen, George Allen, Thomas Allen, Susannah Malcom, Rebecca Allen, Elizabeth Allen, Elijah Allen, and Sarah Allen. Has given daughter, Polley Pollard, one feather bed and furniture, which she has received. Has given son, James Allen, two horses, one saddle and bridle which he has received. Has given daughter, Dorcas Allen, one feather bed & furniture which she has received. Has given son, John Allen, one horse, saddle & bridle which he has received. Has given to son, Wm. Allen, one horse which he has received. Has given son, George Allen, one horse, saddle & bridle which he has received. Has given son, Thomas Allen, one horse, saddle & bridle and two cows & calves which he has received. Has given daughter, Susannah Malcom, one feather bed & furniture and cow & calf which she has received. Daughter, Rebecca Allen, to be given one bed & furniture and cow & calf when called for. Appoints wife, Mary, sons, George & John, as executors. Signed: William (X) Allen. Wit: John Bailey, Alexander Awtry, James Bell. (B/24,25)

ANDERSON, WILLIAM of Morgan County. Last Will and Testament, dated 27 Sept. 1824, sworn to 1 Nov. 1824. Gives to beloved wife, Susan E. Anderson, for and during her natural life the following property: one negro woman named -----, testator's house and lot in the Town of Madison where testator now lives, all testator's household and kitchen furniture, all testator's stock of every kind, and at her death to go to testator's son, William W. M. Anderson. Gives to beloved son, William W. M. Anderson, one negro woman named Sereena (?), one negro boy named Eph---- (?). Wife to have use of son's property until he becomes of lawful age for which she is to maintain and educate him. Appoints Elijah E. Jones, executor, and it is testator's wish that he should

manage testator's estate in the way he may think best calculated to pro-
mote the interest of testator's wife and son and particularly that he
direct the manor of testator's son's education. Signed: Wm. Anderson.
Wit: Seaborn J. Johnson, William C. Buffington, Joshua Eckles. (B/162,
163)

BAILEY, JOHN of Morgan County. Last Will and Testament, dated 16 March
          1820, sworn to 3 Sept. 1821. Testator's wish and desire
is that all testator's lands or present place of abode lying in Morgan
County, all testator's negroes together with their increase, all testator's stock of every description, household and kitchen furniture,
plantation tools and apparatus should be in the hands of wife, Mary
Bailey, during her natural life or widowhood to dispose of as she may
deem most advisable and at a period when she may think proper so as to
do equal justice to all my children, Emily Bailey, William Bailey, Sarah
Bailey, John Bailey, Elizabeth Bailey, Caroline Bailey, Martha Bailey,
leaving my wife, Mary Bailey, a complete and sufficient support for herself. Nominates wife, Mary Bailey, executrix and William G. Smith and
Guy Smith, Jr. executors. Signed: John Bailey. Wit: John Hardman, Peter
Hughes. Georgia, Morgan County, Court of Ordinary Sept. Term 1821.
Appeared in open court John Hardman a subscribing witness...and on his
oath sayeth...and believes that with the exception of the erasure of the
name Nancy Bailey the same (i.e., the will) has undergone no alteration.
(B/97,97?)

BAILEY, JOSEPH of Jasper County. Last Will and Testament, dated 5 Nov.
          1815, sworn to in Morgan County 5 May 1817. Lends to
loving wife, Elizabeth, all the property both real and personal during
her natural life or widowhood to keep and raise the small children upon
but not to deprive her of disposing of any part thereof to any of testator's children after coming to a lawful age at the real valuation and to
be considered as part or the whole of what will be coming to them when a
division is to take place. After decease or widowhood of wife, Elizabeth, testator leaves his property then remaining, the whole of it to be
sold, and the net proceeds to be equally divided among all testator's
children then living and the lawful heirs of any that should be dead,
paying due respect to what has been paid (if any) as above mentioned.
Appoints trusty friends, Larkin Clark, Joseph Heard and Ephraim Heard,
executors. Signed: Joseph Bailey. Wit: Joseph Bailey, Caleb Bailey,
George (X) Jackson. (B/38)

BALL, ISAIAH of Morgan County. Last Will and Testament, dated 19 July
          1828, sworn to 3 Nov. 1828. Wills that just debts be paid.
Balance of testator's property to be kept together for the purpose of
raising and schooling testator's children and in the support of wife,
Hannah Ball, during her widowhood and as my children shall become of age
or marry for my executor to give off to each one of them such property
or portion of property as in their judgement the estate can spare so as
to leave a competency for the support of the younger children. When the
youngest child is twenty one, an equal division to take place with all
testator's children and wife, Hannah Ball, to share equally with children. In case wife should marry again before children come of age, she
is to receive a child's part of all my estate after paying just debts.
Appoints Joel Ball, Hudson T. Ware, and Hannah Ball as executors.
Signed: Isaiah Ball. Wit: Thomas Lacey, Richard L. Maguire, George N.
Ware. (B/248,249)

BALL, JOEL of Morgan County. Last Will and Testament, dated 4 April
          1830, sworn to 17 May 1830. Gives to beloved wife, Zelphy
Ball, during her natural life the following property: The lot of land
the houses now sit on, one negro man, Pompey, one negro girl, Marthy,
two beds, bedsteads & furniture, one side board and desk, half dozen
chairs, two horses named Dick and Charley, three cows & calves, one
fifth part of the stock of hogs, one fourth part of the present crop,
the cotton gin, waggon and gear, and two walnut tables. At death of
wife, above property to be equally divided among all testator's children.
The balance of property that is not above disposed of to be equally
divided among all testator's children at the expiration of this year.
Leaves wife, Zelphy Ball, Thomas Lacey, and son, Jepthy Ball, when he
becomes of age, as executors. Signed: Joel Ball. Wit: Hudson T. Ware,

George N. Ware, Wm. P. Melson. (B/291)

BALL, WILLIAM of Morgan County. Last Will and Testament, dated 19 Oct. 1816, sworn to 6 Jan. 1817. Gives all estate, real and personal, to wife, Rebecca Ball, for and during her natural life and after her death the whole of the said estate to be sold and equally divided between testator's children that is Isaiah Ball, Joel Ball, Sarah Deck (?), Elizabeth Lacy, and Jesse Ball & Jonathan Ball son of Esther Ball. Gives one shilling sterling to all the rest of testator's heirs. Appoints Isaiah Ball and Joel Ball as executors. Signed: William (X) Ball. Wit: Hiram Rousseau, Joseph Reed, Samuel McClendon. (B/32)

BANDY, LEWIS of Morgan County. Last Will and Testament, dated 1 Feb. 1827, sworn to 15 March 1827. Gives to beloved wife, Mary Bandy, the tract of land whereon testator now lives containing 152½ acres, three negroes, Stephen, Inny (Jenny?), and her child, one feather bed and furniture, which said property is to be under the full control, use, and enjoyment of wife during her life or widowhood. At the death of wife, the above described land and premises testator gives to son, Absalom B. Baney. Above described woman, Inny (Jenny?), and her child testator gives to daughter, Mary Bandy. The above described negro man, Stephen, testator wishes to be divided among the whole of testator's children except Caty Harris. Gives to son, Absalom B. Bandy, negro boy, Mat. Gives to daughter, Mary, one bed and furniture. Gives to son, Joseph Bandy, one feather bed and furniture. Leaves all estate except property pointed out in the foregoing items subject to be applied to the payment of testator's just debts. After a final settlement of debts, testator desires that whatsoever remains should be equally divided share and share alike among the whole of testator's children except testator's daughter, Catey Harris, to whom testator gives $50 to be paid to her by executors in full of all demands which she might have against estate as one of testator's heirs. Appoints beloved sons, James Bandy, William Bandy, and Absalom Barnes (?) Bandy, as executors. Signed: Lewis Bandy. Wit: Wilson Lumpkin, Hudson Wade, Buddy Bohannon. (B/207,208,209)

BANDY, WILLIAM of Morgan County. Last Will and Testament, dated 29 July 1829, sworn to 7 Sept. 1829. Desires estate to be managed and distributed with as little expense as practicable. Wills that executor and executrix proceed immediately to sell all property real and personal, collect all debts due in particularly a claim against the Tarvers which is now sued for, and then the whole to be equally divided into three equal parts provided the child of which testator's wife, Hannah Bandy, is now pregnant should live. If not, to be equally divided between testator's wife and child, Sarah Ann Bandy. Wills wife to keep in her hands all of the property until it is sold and each child's legacy in her own hands until testor's child or children marries or arrives at the age of twenty one. It is testator's will that wife keep children with her and give them such education as she may deem necessary paying for such education out of each ones respective legacy. Appoints friend, Charter Campbell, as executor and wife, Hannah Bandy, as executrix. Signed: William Bandy. Wit: John Walker, Seth W. Parham, Mark Hemphill. (B/265,266)

BARFIELD, WILLIAM. Last Will and Testament, dated 14 August 1824, sworn to 16 Sept. 1824. Lends loving wife, Winney Barefield, all estate both real and personal during her life except one bed and furniture and two cows and calves which testator gives to daughter, Milley, and to testator's son, John Barefield, one bed and furniture and two cows and calves, and to testator's daughter, Sally, one bed and furniture and two cows and calves, and also to testator's son, Samuel Barefield, one bed and furniture and one cow and calf. Further gives to daughter, Milley, one negro named Biner and to daughter, Sally, one negro named Abram (Hbram?), which two negroes to remain in possession of wife, Winney Barefield, during her life. If Milley and Sally should die without lawfully begotten heirs of their bodies, then said negroes to belong to testator's two sons, John and Samuel Barefield. At wife's death, all the remainder of the property in wife's possession to be equally divided between testator's two sons, John and Samuel after paying $400 out of the estate to testator's son, James Barefield, and $400 to testator's daughter, Betsey Staley (?), and $200 to testator's son, William Barefield

and $450 to testator's daughter, Nancy King, to be the sole property of
said Nancy King and the lawful begotten heirs of her body and testator's
son, Samuel Barefield, to dispose of it to the best advantage for their
use, and $400 to daughter, Winney Sessions. Appoints sons, Samuel and
John Barefield as executors. Signed: William Barefield. Wit: Lewis
Bandy, Wm. Perkins, John Woods. (B/157,158,159)

BARNES, JOHN of Morgan County. Last Will and Testament, dated 24 Sept.
             1822, sworn to 4 Nov. 1822. Gives to dearly beloved father,
Jesse Barnes, residing in the State of North Carolina all estate both
real and personal, to wit, 303 3/4 acres of land in Morgan County adjoining Dukes Carlisle and others whereon testator now lives and five negroes
Dick, Kellis, Jinny, Sofas, and Enoch together with all the rest, residue & remainder of testator's estate of every description. Appoints
father, Jesse Barnes, as executor. Signed: John Barnes. Wit: Thomas B.
Applewhite, William Blackburn, William W. Carlisle JIC. (B/116,117,118)

BARNES, NATHAN of Morgan County. Last Will and Testament, dated 3 Dec.
             1822, sworn to 6 Jan. 1823. Testator wishes children,
Sally Barnes, Luethy Barnes, Alford Barnes, Polly H. Barnes, Matilda
Barnes, and Martha An Barnes to remain undisturbed on testator's lands
on the Oconee River in Morgan Co. whereon testator now lives until
Alford Barnes becomes of age. At which time, testator wishes those
lands to be Alford's own property. At the discretion of executors, all
the aforesaid mentioned children to receive one bed and furniture worth
at least thirty dollars. Testator's horses, cattle & hogs, household &
kitchen furniture to remain on the premesis for the benefit of the aforesaid children. Testator wishes that the lands testator has drawn should
be sold for the payment of testator's debts and the benefit of said
heirs. Gives daughter, Nancy Dingler, one dollar and the bed and furniture she hath received. Gives daughter, Betsy Greene, one dollar and
the bed and furniture she hath received. Gives daughter, Sara (?) Malone, one dollar and the bed and furniture she hath received. Appoints
Absalom Barnes and Joseph Barnes as executors and Sally Barnes as executrix. Signed: Nathan (X) Barnes. Wit: Nancy (X) Malone, John Reed,
Richard S. Park. (B/132,133)

BARNETT, ZADOCK of Morgan County. Last Will and Testament, dated 2 June
             1823, sworn to 7 July 1823. Testator wills beloved wife,
Elizabeth Barnett, all the property she brought to testator at their
intermarriage namely one horse, one feather bed & furniture, one chest,
and the kitchen furniture she brought with her. Lends beloved wife
fifty dollars during her natural life and at her decease to be equally
divided amongst testator's children herein after named. Gives daughter,
Nancy Henderson, thirty dollars to be raised out of estate to make her
equal with what testator's other children have had. Be it further known
that testator has paid fifty seven dollars for son, George Barnett,
which is to be first taken out of the legacy testator leaves to his heirs
before they come in for a division with testator's other children. Also
testator has paid son, James Barnett, twenty four dollars and fifty cents
that his heirs have that much less than my other children. Wills that
negro woman, Bid, be not sold but have her choice of going to any of
testator's children she chooses to live with and for them not to sell
her but to treat her humanely whilst she lives for her service she has
rendered to testator. Remainder of estate not already named to be
equally divided among testator's eight children or heirs as below stated
namely Polly Briant's heirs, George Barnett's heirs, daughter, Carcus
Farrow's heirs, Susannah Sorrel, son, James Barnett's heirs, John Barnett, Nancy Henderson, and Dolley Shaw's heirs. Appoints son, John
Barnett, Greenvill Henderson and William Briant, son & son-in-laws as
executors. Signed: Zaddk Barntt. Wit: Graves Harriss, Sam'l Bellah,
Senr., Sam'l Shields. (B/141,142)

BARTON, PRESLEY of Morgan County. Last Will and Testament, dated 23
             Aug. 1821, sworn to 11 March 1822. Gives to dearly
beloved daughter, Polly, now the wife of Wiley White one hundred dollars
to be raised out of estate in addition to what testator has already
given her. Gives to Jansey, well beloved daughter, now the wife of
Elbert White one hundred dollars to be raised out of estate in addition
to what testator has already given her. Also testator's land which

374

testator now lives on to be sold and Elizabeth Barton, testator's dearly
beloved wife, to have one third of the money that it sells for or otherwise have it rightly divided and take one third of the land, also my
plantation tools of all description and all other tools together with
testator's negroes, Ned, Vut, Delee, Ike, Rachel, Doss, Bob, Nance,
Aaron & Sarah, also five horses, stock of cows & hogs, household and
kitchen furniture, two waggons & gear, one cotton gin, one set blacksmith
tools, one gold watch, two rifles guns, one shot gun and crop of corn
and fodder. For the purpose of paying testator's just debts, present
crop of cotton to be cleaned and sent to Augusta and sold. Also one
note of hand on Thomas Garritt for twenty five dollars, notes on William
H. Ray & one note on Samuel Hemphill & one note on Joseph Tarpley to be
collected and used to pay debts & if any left to be equally divided
between testator's wife & children that is now with her. Names wife,
Elizabeth, and children, Rhoda, Anna, William, Joel, Elias & Beth Hana
Barton. Makes William Barton and Joel Garr executors. Signed: Presly
Barton. Wit: Payton R. Jenkins, John M. Butler. (B/103,105,105)

BARTON, WILLIAM of Morgan County. Last Will and Testament, dated 9
            Sept. 1825, sworn to 13 Sept. 1827. Gives to beloved
wife, Lucy, two negro men, Yett (?) and Stephen, and $600 in cash to be
raised out of estate. Gives daughter, Lucy, a negro woman named Judy
now in her possession. Gives son, Presley, a negro boy named Godfrey,
gives daughter, Rutha Freeman, a negro woman, Imary, now in her possession. Gives son, Samuel, a negro boy, Peter, horse worth $100, saddle &
bridle, one bed & furniture, and one cow & calf. Gives daughter, Nancy
Rutledge, a negro woman, Lotty, now in her possession. Gives daughter,
Elizabeth, a negro woman, Ouida, one horse worth $100, good saddle &
bridle, one bed & furniture, and one cow & calf. Gives daughter, Eliza,
one negro boy, Tom, one horse worth $100, good saddle & bridle, one bed
& furniture, and one cow & calf. Gives daughter Morning, a negro girl,
Mariah, one horse worth $100, good saddle & bridle, one bed & furniture,
and one cow & calf. Gives daughter, Hannah (?), a negro boy, Isaac, one
horse worth $100, good saddle & bridle, one bed and furniture, and one
cow & calf. All the balance of testator's estate to be sold and the net
proceeds to be equally divided between the whole of testator's children,
share and share alike. Appoints Uriah E. Ammons and James Oats executors. Signed: William Barton. Wit: Margaret (X) Head, Samuel Barton,
Thaddeus Beall. (B/219,220,221,222)

BATTLE, LAZARUS of Morgan County. Last Will and Testament, dated 25
            July 182-, sworn to 1 Nov. 1824. Testator recommends
his wife and children to the protection and direction of God. Gives to
loving wife, Margaret Battle, the house & lot in Madison where testator
now lives, her life estate in the plantation near Madison which testator
now cultivates with the waggon and all the stock & tools thereunto belonging, the carriage and grey horses, the household & kitchen furniture, and negro slaves, Sam, John, Tom, Homer, Sally, Milley, Sena &
her three children, and Littleton. Wife Margaret, to give to testator's
two youngest children, Oliver (?) Lazarus and Margaret-Ann, a home for
ten years from my death without charging them or either of them for any
thing more than their clothing & tuition. The little girl, Loucinda,
testator wills and bequeaths to testator's daughter, Margaret-Ann.
Leaves balance of property to two youngest since having heretofore provided for testator's daughter, Martha Gilbert, and advanced her $600
over & above her equal part of testator's estate. Appoints wife, Margaret Battle, William Porter, and Adam G. Saffold executors. Signed:
Laz's Battle. Wit: Elijah E. Jones, Seaborn J. Johnson, Oliver P. Fears.
(B/160,161,162)

BEASLEY, ROBERTSON of Morgan County. Last Will and Testament, dated 12
            April 1826, sworn to 19 July 1826. Gives to dear &
affectionate wife, Mary Beasley, all real and personal estate except
one negro boy, Randal, whom testator gives to testator's little nephew
Robertson B. Brown. Randal to be kept with his mother until he gets of
sufficient size to be serviceable. Gives rifle & shot bag to brother,
Robert Beasley. Gives silver watch to brother, Seymore S. Beasley.
Wills the next child that Sarah may have shall be raised until it gets
of sufficient size to be serviceable whom testator gives to testator's
little nephew, Zeno C. Beasley. Wills that Craven P. Pool shall have

1/6 of that is made upon the plantation during the year 1826. Signed: Robertson Beasley. Wit: J. J. Boswell, Craven P. Pool, Henry Brown. (B/190,191)

BEASLEY, WILLIAM S. of Morgan County. Last Will and Testament, dated 22 April 1826, sworn to 18 May 1826. Estate to be kept in one common stock until testator's dear & affectionate wife, Elizabeth Beasley, or one of testator's dear children should marry or become of age then to be equally divided between them. It is testator's will that as soon as a division should take place the property should be kept in one common stock until the youngest child should marry or become of age. Children to be educated in as good order as the estate will justify. Bay horse, Jolly, to be given to dear mother. Gives clock to wife. Gives dear little daughter, Martha Ann Beasley, small trunk. Gives dear little son, Zeno C. Beasley, shot gun & horn. Gives unto dear little child, William S. Beasley, silver watch. Wife and friends, Nathan Hackny and Henry Brown, executors. Signed: William S. Beasley. Wit: John J. Boswell, Seymore S. Beasly, John P. Smith. (B/176,177)

BELLAH, SAMUEL SENR. of Morgan County. Last Will and Testament, dated 18 Sept. 1826, sworn to 5 May 1828. All estate both real and personal testator leaves in the possession and management of beloved wife, Jane. At death of beloved wife all estate then remaining (except testator's negro, Simon, and some other articles specified) shall be sold and the money from the sale disposed of as follows, to wit, to daughter, Elizabeth Phillips, and sons, Reubin and Samuel Bellah, testator gives one hundred two dollars each to be added to seventy eight dollars which each of them received from testator's son, Moses', estate which testator considered as his own. To son, John Bellah, five dollars to be added to fifty acres of land and other property which testator formerly gave him. To son, James Bellah, five dollars to be added to one hundred one and a fourth acres of land and other property which testator formerly gave him. To daughter, Tempey, wife of William Haynes fifty dollars to be added to fifty acres of land which testator formerly gave them. Also gives daughter, Tempey, sixty dollars in place of a horse. Gives to daughter, Peggy, wife of Ephraim Shaw, testator's corner cupboard & large wash pot & the cupboard furniture & kitchen furniture to be equally divided between Peggy and Tempey. Gives to daughter, Rachel, wife of Thomas Davis, two hundred dollars. Gives to son, Morgan Bellah, a negro boy, Simon, but if he would prefer it three hundred dollars in place of said negro boy. Gives daughter, Pegga, wife of Ephraim Shaw, two hundred dollars but if negro child, Lydia, should live to the age of four years, testator gives Lydia to Pegga in place of two hundred dollars above given at her option which to take. Gives to granddaughter, Pegga Jane, daughter of William Haynes, testator's wife's trunk. It is testator's desire that if any of testator's negroes should be sold that some of the family connection would purchase them and treat them with humanity. Appoints sons, John and James Bellah, executors. Signed: Sam'l Bellah Senr. Wit: Nathan Formby, Leonard Carden, Aaron Formby. (B/238,239,240,241)

BETTY, JOSEPH of Morgan County. Last Will and Testament, dated 25 July 1815, sworn to 6 Jan. 1817. Gives dearly beloved wife, Rebecah Betty, during her natural life time one third part of the land where testator now lives, a negro woman, Alse, (otherwise Alsey), bed & furniture, the property not to be run over from the premesis and at her death to be disposed of as may be herein after mentioned. Gives only son, Henry J. Betty, two thirds of the land where testator now lives which will be the remains of the land when his stepmother takes her part off and at her death the said Henry J. Betty is to have the whole of the land, also three negro boys, Abraham, Benjamin & Jessey, the horse that he now has in possession, a bed & furniture. Gives daughter, Nancy J. Key, a negro man, Titus, which at the age of sixty is to be sat free which will be in 1829, also at the death of her stepmother she is to have Alsey. Gives to daughter, Polly D. Betty, four negroes, Jerry, Elisha, Jinny & Creasy and testator's young horse, Larry, also a bed & furniture & Nancy J. Key shall pay Polly one hundred dollars out of her part of the estate. Gives granddaughter, Peggy D. Key, a negro, Eliza - my horse, stock of cows, hogs & sheep, farming utensils and all other perishable property to be sold and after paying all testator's just debts the balance to be

376

equally divided among testator's just debts the balance to be equally
divided among testator's legatees. Appoints John Ogletree, Tandy W. Key
& Henry J. Betty executors. Signed: Joseph Betty. Wit: John Gill,
Moses Speer, William Finly. (B/28,29)

BILLINGSLEA, CYRUS of Morgan County. Last Will and Testament, dated
(blank) July 1825, sworn to 3 July 1826. Gives wife,
Elizabeth Billingslea, two hundred two & a half acres of land, lot #226,
whereon testator now lives, also one half lot of land lying broad side
and adjoining the above lot #226 on the South East side, also twelve
negroes namely Frank, Betty, Joseph, Patsey, S-m, Sopha, Sulah, Tilly(?),
Lucy, Charles, Joshua, and Hannah, one road wagon and gear, four choice
mules, one large bay mare, all the plantation utensils and the following
furniture belonging to the house...together with all the crockery and
glass ware, two setts of silver table and tea spoons, the desk & bookcase,
one sett of mahogany folding tables, one mahogany side board, one tea
table, one walnut table, all the knives and forks, shovels & tongs and
irons, candlesticks...one eighty gallon still, one forty saw gin and running gear...one cart and choice yoke of oxen...to be left her during her
natural life or widowhood. In case of her intermarriage, she to be entitled to take her dower or a child's part out of the legacy as above
left her. Gives daughter, Sarah Barrow, tract of land containing two
hundred two and a half acres, lot #250, together with the addition of
thirty six acres, part of lot #249, negroes, Henry, Lindsey, Jesse,
Kitty, two horses, the stock of cattle, hogs, sheep, one yoke of oxen
and cart with all the plantation utensils which she has now in possession
and all the household & kitchen furniture. Provided testator's wife,
Elizabeth Billingslea, should abide by testator's will; in that case the
said Sarah Barrow at the death of her mother, Elizabeth Billingslea,
shall have one fifth of the property left by her mother. If Sarah Barrow dies without issue, legacy to revert to testator's estate. Appoints
William Ware and John W. Porter trustees for Sarah Barrow. Gives daughter, Nancy Scott Ware, three negroes, Sam, Esther & Dicey rated at
eleven hundred dollars, one bedstead & furniture amounting to fifty
dollars, one sett silver table & tea spoons amounting to twenty six
dollars, sixteen hundred pounds of pickled port rated at eighty dollars,
one yoke of oxen and cart rated at sixty five dollars and fifty cents,
half dozen fancy chairs cost seventeen dollars...the above property I
have already advanced to the said Nancy Scott Ware. All the property not
mentioned to be equally divided between Nancy S. Ware and Eliza Elizabeth
Park. At death of wife, property in her possession to be equally divided
between Nancy S. Ware & Eliza E. Park after Sarah Barrow has taken 1/5
part. Gives daughter, Eliza Elizabeth Park two negroes, Salina & Harriet
...property already advanced to her. Gives to daughter, Eliza E. Park,
two other negroes, Mason & Mary, at testator's death. Gives son, Frances
James Billingslea, at testator's death or at son's arrival to man's
estate one part of a lot of land containing one hundred sixty six acres,
lot #249, also the fourth part of lot #248, two negroes, Lewis & Bridget,
one patent lever silver watch, one black mare, saddle and bridle, one
rifle, one shot gun, one bedstead and furniture, one sett of blacksmith
tools. At wife's death, son, Francis James Billingslea, to possess land
testator now lives on, lot #226, also one half lot #227. Property not
to be bartered, leased, sold, or conveyed until he has attained the age
of twenty four years. If son dies without a lawful heir, legacy to be
equally divided between Sarah Barrow, Nancy Scott Ware & Eliza Elizabeth
Park. The dividend going to Sarah Barrow shall belong to her during her
natural life and then to her child or children, but if Sarah Barrow has
no lawful issue, legacy to revert back to testator's estate. Appoints
trusty friends, Thomas J. Park, William Ware & Francis James Billingslea
when he comes of age to be executors. Signed: Cyrus Billingslea. Wit:
Wm. Davenport, William Jones, Marcus Hemphill. (B/185,186,187,188,189)

BOON, REBECCA Y. of Morgan County. Last Will and Testament, dated 25
August 1829, sworn to 18 Sept. 1829. Gives mother,
Gilley Boon, for and during her natural life one negro girl, Francis,
one feather bed & furniture and at mother's death. Francis and increase
if any together with the feather bed to be equally divided among testator's brother and sisters namely Patsey Robson, Sally Crawford Buffington, John Rayford Boon, and Catharine Gilley Boon. Gives brother, John
Rayford Boon. Patsey Robson, Sally Crawford Buffington, and Catharine

377

Gilley Boon the balance of testator's estate consisting of an undivided
share of the estate of testator's deceased father. Appoints John Robson
to carry into effect this last will & testament. Signed: Rebecca Y. (X)
Boon. Wit: Hugh J. Ogilby, Lewis Graves, Charter Campbell. (B/273-274)

BOON, SION of Morgan County. Last Will and Testament, dated 7 May 1829,
           sworn to 6 July 1829. Gives wife, Gilley Boon, that part of
plantation in Morgan County known as Irwins (?) place, three negroes,
Sam, Nan, and Luce, one horse, feather bed & furniture and at her death
to be equally divided between her children, Patsey Robson, Sally Crawford Buffington, Gilley Catharine, Rebeccah Yancy & John R. Boon. Gives
son, Joshua Boon, five dollars. Gives children of deceased daughter,
Mary Williams, who was wife of Joseph John Williams, five hundred dollars
in full of their distributive share of testator's estate. Gives Willis
A. Hawkins & Betsey, his wife, six hundred dollars in full of his distributive share of my estate in addition to what I have already given
them. Gives son, Thomas Boon, six hundred dollars in full of his share
of testator's estate; any notes found in testator's possession to be
deducted out of the legacy. Gives daughter, Nancy Brewer, five hundred
dollars in full of her share of testator's estate in addition to what
has already been given her. Gives trusty friends, John Robson & John W.
Porter, as trustees for daughter, Sally Boon, and her children begotten
of Joshua Boon, eight hundred dollars to be raised as hereinafter pointed out to support and maintain said daughter and children. Gives daughter, Gilley Catharine Boon, one negro girl, Caroline, one feather bed &
furniture. Gives daughter, Rebeccah Yancy Boon, one negro girl, Frances,
one feather bed & furniture. Gives son, John R. Boon, one negro boy,
Alfred, one gray horse, saddle & bridle, one feather bed & furniture.
Balance of estate to be equally divided between my children, Patsey
Robson, Sarah Crawford Buffington, Gilley Catharine Boon, Rebecca Yancy
Boon & John Rayford Boon, share and share alike. Friends, John Robson &
John W. Porter, to be executors. Signed: Sion Boon. Wit: Hudson Wade,
Charter Campbell, Lucius L. Wittick (Wittich?). (B/262,263,264)

BRASWELL, BENJAMIN of Morgan County. Last Will and Testament, dated 20
           March ----- (faded), sworn to 1 Sept. 1817 recorded
28 Feb. 1818. Having no children of his own, testator wishes to dispose
of his property so that it may be of benefit to the unfortunate Poor,
etc. Testator wills that any executors hereinafter named shall dispose
of lands, household and furniture with all testator's stock of horses,
cattle and hogs. Secondly, testator wills that the executors dispose of
the following named negroes in the manner hereinafter prescribed. (Negroes named) Each negro is to be sold to such person as they may choose
for a master provided such person will pay at least half the value of
said negroe. After the sale of all testator's property, together with
all the money now in hand and also that is due me, testator's express
will is that the executors take the whole amount of money and lodge it
in the funds of the State Bank. The interest to be use for the sole
purpose of Education of Orphan Children in Morgan County. At death or
refusal to act of testator's Executors, the Court of Ordinary to take
money into their hands to carry out intent of will. Appoints -----(faded
space) John Malcom, Davis Grisham & William ----- (faded) executors.
Signed: Benjamin Braswell. Wit: Epps Duke, David Malcom. (B/135,136,137)

BREWER, NATHAN of Morgan County. Last Will and Testament, dated 26 June
           1818, sworn to 6 July 1818. A tract of land for testator's
wife and children to live on until youngest child becomes sixteen is to
be purchased with what money testator has and with money from sale of
stock or crop or other articles as can best be spared. Tract of land to
belong to wife, Martha Brewer, during her natural life and at her death
to be equally divided amongst testator's surviving children. Desires
children should have a reasonable portion of schooling of their situation will admit of. When youngest child becomes sixteen, remaining part
of testator's property to be equally divided amongst wife & living
children. Appoints wife Martha Brewer, and Douglas Watson executors.
Signed: Nathan Brewer. Wit: John Cook, Joel Dixon, Robert Watson.
(B/56)

GROOM	BRIDE	DATE
Abbot, Hezekiah	Polly McDade	Feb. 25, 1811
Abbot, Zachariah	Margaret Bearding	Dec. 28, 1816
Abbott, John	Ellender Parish	Dec. 20, 1844
Abel, Zachariah	Mary Eliza Timmerman	Feb. 22, 1847
Abrahams, Barnard	Eliz. Gould	Jul. 29, 1826
Adam, Horton B.	Anna E. Hall	Apr. 23, 1846
Adams, Asa	Eliz. Sable	Apr. 10, 1828
Adams, James	Harriet L. Averett	Sept. 14, 1842
Adams, John M.	Sarah L. McMurphy	Oct. 8, 1829
Adams, John Strong	Sarah Eve	Mar. 2, 1803
Adams, Wm.	Emily S. Sandwich	Oct. 10, 1835
Adams, Wm. B.	Cynthia H. Cooper	Dec. 26, 1833
Agelear, John	Salley Lowley or Lawley	Oct. 23, 1821
Aiken, Wm.	Polly Evans	Mar. 9, 1802
Albriton, Amos	Catherine Collins	Jan. 9, 1809
Albritton, James	Sally Pound	Dec. 26, 1813
Aldridge, John B.	Arabelah Mary Jane Anderson	Mar. 2, 1843
Allard, Peter Lewis	Maria A. Magnan	Jul. 2, 1810
Allen, Alexander	Mary Jones	May 14, 1810
Allen, Alexander M.	Mary Palmer	Dec. 22, 1840
Allen, Benjamin	Nancy C. Patterson	Feb. 10, 1809
Allen, Carey W.	Mary An. Y. McMurphy	Feb. 3, 1838
Allen, Elisha A.	Janet J. Evans	Jan. 14, 1840
Allen, Francis M.	Anna Evans	May 29, 1848
Allen, James W.	Eveline A. Rhodes	Nov. 14, 1846
Allen, John	Nelly Nevils	Dec. 23, 1807
Allen, John	Caroline Prater	Jul. 31, 1826
Allen, John R.	Mary Lucy Allen	June 7, 1823
Allen, John W.	Eliz. Lambert	Oct. 1, 1849
Allen, Robert	Eliz. Anderson	June 15, 1798
Allen, Robert A.	Pricilla M. Ward	Jan. 10, 1828
Allen, Samuel	Susanna Ruff	Dec. 27, 1804
Allen, Samuel A.	Mary A. Oliphant	Oct. 19, 1848
Allen, William	Eliz. Calhoun	May 27, 1309
Allen, William	Elisa Ann Primrose	Oct. 11, 1842
Allen, William R.	Martha Netherland	Nov. 28, 1837
Allen, Young	Jane Anderson	Feb. 24, 1804
Alleoud, Marc	C. C. P. Martinet	Feb. 7, 1820
Alston, J. M.	M. A. Fitzsimons	Feb. 23, 1848
Alsup, Edwin	Ann Owens	May 20, 1831
Amburn, Samuel	Mary Abbot	Mar. 11, 1819
Anderson, Edward S.	Sarah Ann Johnson	Sept. 29, 1843
Anderson, Eleazer	Fanny Rowland	June 8, 1808
Anderson, Elijah P.	Martha Bryant	Mar. 20, 1837
Anderson, John M.	Mary Holsombake	May 4, 1813
Anderson, Lawrence	Mary Welsh	Sept. 14, 1847
Anderson, Richard	Adeline Roden	Mar. 13, 1845
Anderson, Robert	Eliza Sullivan	Feb. 12, 1825
Anderson, Thomas	Sarah Anderson	Mar. 26, 1819
Anderson, Wm.	Emily Evlina Rogers	Nov. 23, 1848
Andrew, Benj.	Elizabeth Lee	Feb. 25, 1788
Andrews, Allen	Eliza F. Clark	Sept. 25, 1836
Andrews, David	Barsheba Cellers	Apr. 15, 1830
Ansley, Abel	Lydia Morris	Jan. 30, 1790
Ansley, Jesse	Catherine Urquhart	Dec. 14, 1818
Ansley, Jesse	Anna E. Smith	Oct. 27, 1848
Anthony, Isaac	Tabitha Clanton	Feb. 26, 1813
Anthony, Lavoisier L.	Eliza. A. Brown	Oct. 4, 1838
Appleton, Samuel	Anne L. Duren	Sept. 1, 1823
Archer, Wm. A.	Eliz. Wilkerson	June 11, 1849
Arington, John H.	Elisa Ann Hurst	Dec. 16, 1841
Armour, John B.	Rebecca Hammond	Dec. 9, 1826
Arnett, Bradford T.	Marye E. Rice	Apr. 3, 1849
Arrington, Abner	Ascamitity Whigham	Apr. 19, 1848

GROOM	BRIDE	DATE
Arrington, Henry W.	Martha Young	June 18, 1847
Arrington, James	Jane B. Averit	Jan. 8, 1837
Arrington, John	Nancy Dyass	Aug. 8, 1816
Arrington, Willis	Caroline Adkison	Sept. 29, 1830
Arrington, Henry	Mary Bugg	Apr. 12, 1792
Arterberry, James	Eliza Cogill	Jan. 8, 1840
Ashford, Dennis	Eliza J. Fisher	Oct. 28, 1839
Athey, Elijah	Frances Bell	Jan. 13, 1802
Athey, Zepheniah	Mahaney Coursey	Feb. 14, 1803
Atkinson, Dixon	Ursula Shepherd	Aug. 17, 1802
Atkinson, Robert	Sarah Ann Fudge	Nov. 26, 1832
Attaway, Harkey B.	Mary A. Philpot	Dec. 15, 1846
Atwell, James	Elizabeth Tally	Jan. 4, 1811
Atwell, James	Mary Martin	Dec. 12, 1836
Atwell, Jeremiah	Martha Wall	Sept. 20, 1836
Atwell, John	Lucretia Walls	Apr. 1, 1803
Atwell, John	Amelia Howell	Oct. 19, 1831
Atwell, Redden	Sarah Lambeth	Feb. 5, 1823
Aughtry, David	Catherine Durkee	Mar. 10, 1831
Augustine, John T.	Mariah C. Nickolson	Nov. 23, 1825
Austin, John	Fanny Crittenden	Aug. 12, 1788
Austin, Robert	Anne E. Rinchley	Dec. 20, 1841
Averell, Thomas	Harriet ?. Cart	Sept. 28, 1824
Averett, Thomas	Susan Stanley	Oct. 8, 1807
Averit, Christopher C.	Mary ? ? Allen	Nov. 5, 1833
Averitt, Joseph B.	Amanda McNair	Jan. 2, 1839
Avington, Wm.	Mary Adkison	Feb. 23, 1787
Avret, Alexander	Sarah Luckey	Nov. 22, 1839
Avret, Charles C. P.	Celia Weeks	Nov. 25, 1837
Avret, Christopher C.	Lavinia Murphey	Nov. 26, 1836
Avret, Wm.	Eliz. Tinly	Dec. 5, 1837
Avret, Wm. A.	Eliz. Tinsley	Dec. 5, 1837
Aymav, Sebastien	Adela Menard	May 14, 1818
Ayres, Wm.	Margeret Jones	May 12, 1787
Ayres, Wm. M.	Emmy Branan	Apr. 23, 1849
Bacon, John N.	Mary Ann Roberts	May 13, 1830
Bacon, Lyddal	Mary Beach	Jul. 20, 1832
Bacon, Wm.	Eliza Casten	Dec. 23, 1829
Bacon, Wm.	Lucy Ware	Mar. 5, 1803
Baggs, Elijah	Sophia McCord	June 15, 1787
Bailey, Isaiah	Kesiah A. Andrews	Oct. 6, 1849
Bagley, Wm. P.	Mary G. Pickett	June 13, 1821
Bailey, H.	Margret Wilson	Aug. 20, 1818
Baird, Benj.	Hannah Margaret Camfield	Mar. 13, 1832
Baird, Nelson	Amelia Riddle	Oct. 8, 1829
Baker, Charles	Matilda Carter	Jul. 19, 1848
Baker, Henry	Eliz. T. Hainey	Oct. 19, 1838
Baldwin, Augustus	Rebecca Thompson Cocke	Jan. 11, 1799
Ball, Wm.	Charlotte Lee	Jan. 1, 1796
Bamberg, Wm. G.	Philipine Barthlomew	Feb. 7, 1843
Bardwell, Erastus	Eliz. Stephens	Nov. 12, 1831
Barfoot, Wm.	Eliz. Dees	Oct. 13, 1813
Barham, Charles	Eliz. Whittington	Mar. 17, 1808
Barham, Jesse	Jane Bell	June 13, 1812
Barham, Timothy	Rebecca Savedge	Oct. 13, 1804
Barker, Jno.	Synthia Cooper	Jan. 12, 1839
Barker, Reese	Nancy Bradbury	Sept. 23?, 1802
Barnard, Tomothy	Martha Galphin	Oct. 7, 1800
Barnes, John A.	Eliza Caroline Speights	May 13, 1818
Barnes, John B.	Mary Ann Hammond	Jul. 1, 1806
Barnett, Joel	Elizabeth Crawford	Feb. 5, 1787
Barnitt, Wm.	Anna Crawford	Dec. 3, 1889
Barret, Edward M.	Mary Ann Sharp	Feb. 13, 1834
Barrett, Thomas	Mary Savannah Glascock	Sept. 16, 1830
Barrow, Reuben	Patience Ann Tice	May 13, 1790
Barry, Edward	Caroline Augusta Wray	Jan. 7, 1846
Barry, John	Maria McTyire	Dec. 10, 1810

GROOM	BRIDE	DATE
Bartholomew, Nicholas	Philissim Tignett	May 18, 1839
Bartlett, James	Eliz. Ann Crawford	Nov. 27, 1845
Bartley, Patrick	Marguerite Murphy	Jul. 25, 1841
Bartly, James	Jane Crawford	Sept. 4, 1848
Barton, Benj. T.	Mary A. Sims	June 4, 1829
Barton, David	Hannah Chance	Sept. 25, 1802
Barton, George	Melinda Cullers	1845
Barton, James T.	Jane B. Thomas	Feb. 18, 1829
Bass, Henry	Amelia M. Love	Jan. 4, 1820
Bass, John H.	Martha Cleghorn	June 14, 1837
Basset, Wm.	Jane C. Boyd	Dec. 16, 1849
Bateman, A.	Sarah M. Taylor	Sept. 9, 1846
Battey, Cephas	Mary Agnew Magruder	Oct. 8, 1825
Battey, Geo. M.	Emily A. Verdery	Jan. 19, 1847
Baudry, W. Auguste	Sophie Adelle Tardy	Aug. 13, 1818
Beach, Charles	Mary Redding	Mar. 14, 1807
Beal, James	Ruth Harris	July 15, 1790
Beal, James	Eliz. Ware	Nov. 1, 1809
Beal, John W.	Martha Foster	Apr. 11, 1815
Beal, Littleberry	Mary Ann Silbert	Nov. 8, 1831
Beal, Robert	Martha Cleghorn	Nov. 9, 1831
Beal, Thomas C.	Lavina Rhodes	Feb. 12, 1836
Beal, Wm.	Tabitha Beal	Nov. 29, 1813
Beale, Gaseway	Sarah Ann Day	Dec. 18, 1844
Beale, Reason	Mary Roberts	Feb. 11, 1819
Beall, Francis	Sarah Gregory	Mar. 3, 1801
Bealle, Hezekiah	Dephne Hornsby	Jul. 4, 1816
Bealle, Jno. W.	Pamella Ann Haynie	Dec. 15, 1829
Bean, Joseph S.	Harriet C. Smithe	Mar. 20, 1848
Beard, Thomas I.	Susan Ligon	May 29, 1829
Beasly, Jno.	Frances Briant	Feb. 16, 1820
Beaulard, John Adrain	Eliz. Sayrs	Jan. 1?, 1810
Beazley, Lemuel	Caroline Rosure	Nov. 23, 1819
Beccom, Doyle	Mary Jane Gaines	June 5, 1844
Beck, Jacob L.	Martha Jernagan	June 1, 1846
Beckham, Sherwood	Mary Stevens	Apr. 9, 1794
Beckham, Solomon	Susanna Weathers	Sept. 18, 1737
Bedingfield, Jno.	Harriet Eveline Hargrove	May 27, 1807
Beers, Jonathan S.	Cornilia R. T. Walker	Mar. 1, 1818
Beesley, Bryant	Eleanor Gay	Dec. ?, 1844
Beesley, Jno.	Francis Bryant	Feb. ?, 1820
Beesley, Jno.	Apsibath Purvis	Oct. 5, 1842
Belcher, Ferrel	Sarah Vaughn	Dec. ?, 1794
Bell, Dempsey	Ansley L. Key	Oct. 3, 1829
Bell, Henry D.	Martha Black	Dec. 1?, 1837
Bell, Josiah	Lucretia Bell	Apr. 1?, 1807
Bell, Leaston	Mary Ann Tinley	Mar. 18, 1842
Bell, Thompson	Mary Williamson	Aug. 21, 1832
Bell, Thompson	Eliz. M. A. Tant	Jul. 13, 1834
Bell, W. James	Katey Pearson	Dec. 23, 1814
Bell, Wm.	Lavina Farrer	Jan. 4, 1814
Bell, Wm. A.	Avargia C. Jones	Feb. 2, 1825
Bell, Wm. Harrison	Jane Bell	Oct. 18, 1802
Bell, Zachariah	Eliz. Hall	Mar. 31, 1803
Belt., L. C.	Eliz. T. Jones	May 23, 1846
Benett, John	Sarah Abbott	Jul. 13, 1814
Benjamin, Francis	Julia A. Abraham	Dec. 26, 1848
Bennet, Jacob	Mary Moore	Mar. 7, 1809
Bennet, John	Audrey Walsh	Nov. 13, 1836
Bennett, Jno.	Nancy Hatcher	June 25, 1825
Bennett, Thomas	Eliz. Willcox	Mar. 5, 1823
Benns, Charles	Mary Bosanquet Baley	Aug. 25, 1848
Benton, Amos	Ann B. Owens	Feb. 4, 1831
Benton, Mordicai	Prisilla Pratt	Dec. 8, 1785
Berrey, Dabney	Ann M. Holcombe	Dec. 12, 1818
Berrie, Wm. Jas.	Louisa M. Sandersine	June 15, 1846
Berryhill, Samuel	Ann Hall	Mar. 16, 1795
Bertrand, Jno A.	Mary Watkins	Jan. 4, 1840

GROOM	BRIDE	DATE
Bertrand, Peter	Eliz. Hamet (?)	Nov. 26, 1836
Bethune, Malcolm	Nancy Buck	Aug. 18, 1825
Betts, Philo	Permilia Eliz. Vaughn	Mar. 14, 1849
Betts, Wm. H.	Eliz. Hutchinson	Jan. 18, 1838
Beul, Charles T.	Catherine E. Clanton	Oct. 27, 1831
Bevins, Thomas H.	Angeline Bristenbau	Oct. 10, 1838
Bigelow, Alonzo B.	Martha Ann Danforth	Apr. 23, 1823
Biggs, James	Anna Goodwin	May 28, 1807
Bignon, Barna	Celestine Setze	Jan. 21, 1845
Bignon, Joseph	M. C. Largarde	Apr. 24, 1811
Bignon, Joseph Dominique	Marie C. A. Dugas	Apr. 24, 1810
Bird, Archibald	Eliz. Hall	July 24, 1845
Bird, Eborn	Sally Armstrong	Sept. 14, 1806
Bird, Ezekial	Celia Greenway	Jan. 21, 1832
Bird, James J.	Sarah Ann Parnel	Nov. 12, 1837
Bird, Wm.	Harriet Barton	Oct. 15, 1831
Blache, Anthony	Fanny McTyeire	Feb. 11, 1801
Black, Charles	Janet I. Reid	Dec. 15, 1828
Black, Edward	Mary Singleterry	Apr. 5, 1830
Blackston, Argial	Sarah Burges	Jan. 7, 1819
Blackston, Argyle	Matilda M. Blackston	Apr. 26, 1849
Blackston, James	Rebecca Newman	Sept. 8, 1818
Blackston, John	Catherine Harvey	Apr. 11, 1799
Blackston, Josiah W. B.	Amanda Overton	Dec. 8, 1831
Blackstone, Elbert	Charlotte Rawls	Mar. 24, 1847
Blackstone, Gilbert	Martha Cerilda Washington	Dec. 31, 1848
Blackstone, James	Gerusha Singlet	Oct. 26, 1844
Blackstone, John	Martha M. Rowland	Mar. 8, 1848
Blackstone, Jno.	Martha S. Washington	Dec. 22, 1847
Blackstone, Thos.	Atatha Inglett	Mar. 7, 1840
Blackstop, John	Ateral(?) Ann Blackstop	Nov. 23, 1841
Blain, James T.	Mary E. Russell	May 13, 1837
Blair, Alec	Eliza McKinne	July 2, 1799
	(marriage bond)	
Blalock, Augustus	Sarah Jane Hassell	Oct. 12, 1848
Bland, Charles T.	Harriet A. Sandiford	Feb. 12, 1842
Blease, Thomas W.	Bethany Coleman	July 13, 1818
Blocksom, Geo.	Martha Owens	Nov. 27, 1837
Blodget, Foster	Louisa M. Foster	May 2, 1846
Blome, Alcide L.	Sarah A. Anderson	Jan. 1, 1838
Blount, Stephen	Emily B. Denham	Aug. 17, 1826
Bloxsom, Daniel	Jane Eliz. Crookshanks	Feb. 6, 1817
Bloxsom, Patrick	Ann Buxton	Dec. 23, 1840
Blunt, John	Eliz. Lynch	June 19, 1846
Boartwright, Thomas	Artimitia Wynn	June 21, 1849
Bogan, John	Mary Hutchins	Dec. 2, 1830
Bogan, Shadrack	Ann Few (?) (Fee)	Mar. 2, 1816
Boggs, Archibald	Mary Ann Robertson	Sept. 13, 1827
Bohler, Geo. M.	Josephine Frances McKinney	Nov. 15, 1849
Bohler, John A.	Sarah M. Primrose	Oct. 26, 1843
Boid, N. T.	Nancy Thompson	Feb. 27, 1842
Boisclair, Lewis Forman	Marie Rose Cambry	Sept. 12, 1804
Boisclair, Peter T.	Maria Wray	Jul. 12, 1823
Boisclair, Valentine	Lydia Camfield	Sept. 2, 1839
Bolan, Richard	Margaret Quin	Apr. 11, 1822
Boles, John	Lydia Smith	Oct. 7, 1838
Bond, James	Eliz. Shaw	Mar. 4, 1808
Bond, P. P.	Sarah Savage	Aug. 11, 1843
Bones, John	Maria T. Eve	Apr. 8, 1818
Bones, Samuel	Maria McGraw	Feb. 7, 1835
Bones, Thomas A.	Eliza Phinizy	Jan. 15, 1818
Bones, Wm.	Isabella Spencer	Jan. 4, 1825
Booth, Daniel	Ann Boyd	Apr. 20, 1844
Borage, James	Mary Palmer	Aug. 7, 1816
Born, Jno.	Camilia Green	Dec. 29, 1847
Boron, Edmund H.	Martha Ann Burrough	Oct. 16, 1832
Bostick, Hillery	Elizabeth Jarvis	Apr. 28, 1790
Bostick, Jacob	Rebecca Beal	Feb. 13, 1804

GROOM	BRIDE	DATE
Bostick, John	Elizabeth Hayles	Mar. 5, 1800
Bostick, Jno.	Eloisa Beal	Jan. 24, 1824
Bostick, Littleberry	Polly Philips	Oct. 30, 1792
Bostick, Littleberry	Lucy Evans	June 17, 1801
Bostwick, Leonard	Eliza B. Meigs	Apr. 18, 1837
Bostwick, Rheese	Margaret Jones	Apr. 23, 1803
Bostwick, Wm.	Eliz. A. Howard	Jan. 28, 1829
Bottom, Davis	Sarah Kimble	Mar. 5, 1819
Boulinau, Geo. E.	Mary Ann Riley	1847
Boulineau, Joseph	Savannah Volatin	Dec. 18, 1838
Bourke, Michael	Anne Fishbourne	Mar. 12, 1792
Boutet, David	Melvina Bagleif	no date
Boutet, Peter	Susannah Aldridge	July 2, 1796
Boutet, Peter Davis	Sarah E. Starr	Apr. 3, 1838
Bouyer, Balthazar	Mary Youngblood	Apr. 13, 1822
Bowdre, Hays	Mrs. Harriot Young	Dec. 10, 1827
Bowdre, Preston E.	Mary Z. A. Labuzan	Dec. 30, 1829
Bowen, Taber	Caroline Dennise	May 16, 1801
Bowens, Charles	Elisa Grimsly	Jan. 12, 1848
Bowers, Samuel E.	Mary E. A. Hitt	Nov. 1, 1848
Bouyer, Robt. I.	Mary Ann Dye	Mar. 9, 1836
Boyd, John	Eliza Cane	June 2, 1807
Boyd, Thomas	Betsy Crutchfield	Aug. 1, 1805
Boyd, Wm.	Sarah Collins	Dec. 28, 1812
Boyett, Eli	Mrs. Elen A. Kunze	Sept. 23, 1839
Boyken, James W.	Eliz. Rutherford	Mar. 7, 1839
Boykin, Jas. W.	Eliz. Rutherford	Mar. 7, 1839
Boyle, John	Louisa Holliday	Feb. 2, 1846
Brace, Henry	Sarah Ann Fox	Dec. 15, 1825
Bradberry, Morris	Julian McGehee	June 18, 1811
Bradberry, Morris	Mary Ann McCullen	Jan. 15, 1829
Bradbury, John	Eliz. Dunerent	Dec. --, 1801
Bradbury, Joseph	Eliz. Wood	Jan. 5, 1828
Braden, Reis M.	Eliz. Morris	May 25, 1836
Bradford, M. Fielding	Mary McMillan	June 24, 1819
Bradford, Randolph	Eliz. Rebecca Neal	Oct. 12, 1825
Bradford, Thos. E.	Sarah Wiessinger	Jan. 30, 1813
Bradley, James	Eliz. Miller	May 20, 1801
Bradley, Patrick	Mary Ann Mills	Feb. 8, 1827
Bradshaw, Francis A.	Martha W. Palmer	Mar. 20, 1843
Bradshaw, John	Barbara Pharoah	Jan. 7, 1822
Brazden, Louis	Lucy Weaver	May 1, 1829
Brake, Frederick A.	Mary Virginia Lutheringal (?)	Feb. 17, 1843
Brandon, James	Patsy Tindley	Jan. 12, 1808
Brandon, Jno.	Lydia Knight	Sept. 27, 1810
Brandon, John W.	Sarah Weeks	Aug. 12, 1834
Brantley, Benj.	Susan Fields Blodget	June 19, 1834
Brantley, John	Willie Heath	Sept. 24, 1818
Breitenbaugh, Jno.	Angelim Hill	Oct. 29, 1829
Brenan, Eugine	Martha Moorfield	Jan. 9, 1819
Brewer, Elijah	Rebecca Goss	Jan. 25, 1816
Brickell (?), Thos. H.	Susan B. Hurst	Dec. 18, 1831
Brickmaster, Edw. I.	Amanda Richardson	Feb. 6, 1840
Bridges, Jno.	Laura Danforth	Mar. 3, 1840
Briggs, Wm. H.	Eliz. S. Bruton	Feb. 16, 1824
Bright, Line G.	Emily Fountain	Jan. 21, 1849
Brisco, John	Mary Gray	Mar. 9, 1795
Britton, Samuel	Eliz. M. A. Dame	Nov. 21, 1848
Britton, Samuel T.	Frances B. R. Collins	Sept. 18, 1838
Broadnax, Wm. E.	Adeline Bebee	Dec. 22, 1830
Broadwater, Anderson	Eliza Dyals	July 25, 1841
Broadwater, James A.	Susan Bleckington	Oct. 31, 1844
Brochon, Dominick	Ellen E. Lang	Jan. 3, 1831
Brooke, Jno. F.	Louisa McMillan	Jan. 22, 1840
Brooks, Jordan P.	Ann F. McAlrey	Apr. 19, 1827
Brooks, Thomas	Ann Dick	Jul. 4, 1786
Brown, Absalom N.	Caroline A. Vaughn	Apr. 22, 1842

GROOM	BRIDE	DATE
Brown, Hares (?) G.	Sarah Ann Grant	Mar. 15, 1827
Brown, Henry	Sarah Bennet	Dec. 31, 1839
Brown, James W.	Lucinda Stanton	June 22, 1833
Brown, John	Eliz. Rogar	May 19, 1803
Brown, Joseph	Mary Veach	Jan. 20, 1840
Brown, Joshua	Harriet Sheffield	Oct. 4, 1825
Brown, Patrick	Catherine Smith	Nov. 3, 1830
Brown, Richard	Eliz. O'Keife	Dec. 23, 1830
Brown, Samuel	Eliza Evans	Jan. 12, 1834
Brown, Samuel	Maria Murphey	Jul. 23, 1821
Brown, Sebastian	Nancy Greene	June 11, 1842
Brown, Sidney Smith	Mary Ann Goodman	June 1, 1835
Brown, Theodore	Charlotte Fleming	Oct. 20, 1831
Broxton, Daniel	Rebecca Clark	Jul. 11, 1799
Bruce, Alfred	Catherine Cook	May 4, 1843
Brun, Leon	Cecilia Lafitte	Dec. 8, 1830
Brunce, Daniel M.	Ann Laurence McTyre	1843
Bruner, John D.	Sarah Macdade	May 6, 1808
Brunson, Hezekiah	Obedience McDaniel	Apr. 26, 1810
Brunson, Matthew	Mary Haynes	June 4, 1812
Bryant, James	Martha Parmer	Mar. 20, 1827
Bryant, John	Eliza Ann Rowland	Dec. 21, 1830
Bryant, Wm.	Mary Holly	June 5, 1796
Bryne, Edmund	Milley Walker	Jan. 22, 1799
Bryson, Wm.	Eliza R. Murren	May 13, 1829
Buchanan, Edmund	Amey West	Aug. 29, 1812
Buchanan, James	Jane Chambers	Jul. 9, 1797
Buck, John F.	Nancy Gay	Apr. 22, 1842
Buck, Thomas	Nancy Ann Corleif	Dec. 11, 1843
Buckelew, Joseph	Mrs. Eliza Wilson	Dec. 1?, 1840
Buffington, Jas.	Frances Ganet	Feb. 26, 1829
Buford, Simeon	Caroline E. Leon	Apr. 23, 1835
Bugg, Anselm	Maria M. Coombs	Dec. 18, 1811
Bugg, Edmund	Lyda Andrews	Sept. 17, 1788
Bugg, Geo. F. T.	Eliz. Wildes	May 18, 1833
Bugg, Jacob C.	Eliza Sanders	Jan. 25, 1827
Bugg, Peter	Roanne G. Ellis	Oct. 16, 1815
Bugg, Robt. W.	Caroline C. S. Rhodes	Jul. 7, 1836
Bugg, Samuel	Charlotte Tohler	Dec. 5, 1786
Bugg, Terwood	Mary Ann Jones	May 13, 1788
Bugg, Wm.	Mary Bugg	May 24, 1821
Bugg, Wm. A.	Mary M. Wright	May 3, 1810
Bulfinch, Benj.	Eliz. Beauland	Aug. 24, 1819
Bulger, Daniel	Anna Fears	Nov. 30, 1805
Bulger, Jno.	Eliz. Clarke	Apr. 16, 1810
Bull, Andrew G.	Eluna M. Micon	May 18, 1830
Bullock, Dan	Jane Maxwell	Nov. 11, 1789
Bullock, Zachariah	Frances Edington	Dec. 26, 1812
Bunch, Jeremiah	Clara Fisher Abrahams	Sept. 1, 1847
Bunch, John M.	Mary A. Fraxer	Dec. 6, 1848
Burch, Blanton	Rebecca Barton	June 13, 1825
Burch, Charles	Sarah Howell	Dec. 4, 1798
Burch, Charles	Jane Wiggins	Jan. 7, 1828
Burch, Edmund	Eliza Brandon	Nov. 2, 1810
Burch, Jesse	Martha Daniel	Oct. 19, 1813
Burch, Joseph	Ann Brown	Dec. 13, 1830
Burch, Richard	Priscilla James	Dec. 11, 1799
Burch, Wm. K.	Mary Anderson	Oct. 11, 1845
Burch, Wm. Kelton	Mahala Christian	Mar. 18, 1831
Burch, Wm. R.	Eliz. Loyd	Sept. 3, 1838
Burdell, Ferdinand	Matilda Melville Moss	May 24, 1832
Burdell, Thomas	Sarah Phinizy	Mar. 18, 1807
Burk, Francis	Mary Burk	Feb. 18, 1826
Burke, Michael	Sarah Armstrong	Mar. 26, 1806
Burke, Dr. Michael	Elizabeth Elbert	May 4, 1799
Burke, Thomas	Cornelia Thomas	Sept. 22, 1812
Burkes, Record	Mary Wilkes	Aug. 27, 1813
Burks, Edward	Martha Grinaway	Jan. 30, 1834

384

GROOM	BRIDE	DATE
Burnett, James B.	Matilda Bloxsom	Aug. 29, 1833
Burnett, John	Peggy Turner	Jan. 20, 1799
Burns, Jno.	Keziah Stallings	June 21, 1820
Burr, Wm. H.	Harriet Hill	Jan. 4, 1849
Burroughs, Raymond	Eliza Foster	Mar. 5, 1817
Burroughs, John H.	Susan Heckle	Mar. 23, 1836
Burton, Ira	Eliz. Hammond	Aug. 10, 1825
Burton, Joseph	Hicksey Thorn	Aug. 14, 1832
Burton, Robert	Parthena Green	Nov. 4, 1794
Burts, David	Amelia Fox	May 28, 1831
Bush, Geo. W.	Cemuline Heydenfeldt	May 3, 1838
Bush, Littleberry	Ann Panton	June 21, 1823
Bush, Richard F.	Frances Broadhurst	Mar. 26, 1838
Bussy, Charles	Mary Bugg	Feb. 1, 1830
Butler, Joseph	Williford J. Rabb	Jul. 30, 1823
Butler, Thomas	Margaret Cooper	Apr. 3, 1784
Butler, Wm.	Priscilla Cobb	Jan. 4, 1796
Butterfield, T. E.	Caroline Parker	Mar. 8, 1832
Byne, Edmund	Easter Brack	Aug. 27, 1806
Byne, O. H. P.	Caroline Tarver	Mar. 24, 1838
Byrd, Bunch	Synthia Pitman	Mar. 15, 1827
Byrd, Henry	Ann C. Wingate	Jul. 22, 1820
Byrd, Henry A.	Mary Ann I. Cogle	1847
Byrd, Seaborn	Lucenda Gay	Nov. 4, 1845
Byrd, Wm.	Mary Ann Dillon	Dec. 7, 1849
Cadle, Archibald	Rivanah Greene	May 27, 1845
Cadle, Geo. S.	Eliz. Neugent	Sept. 31, 1849
Cadle, Silas M.	Sarah Foney	Jul. 3, 1847
Caffin, Nicholas Hilaire	Margaret Goodall	Aug. 19, 1820
Cain, Abel	Polly Griffin	Apr. 30, 1802
Cain, Abel	Charlotte Clarke	Jul. 16, 1821
Cain, John	Sarah Harrison	May 27, 1808
Cain, Richard A.	Elizabeth Daniel	Oct. 22, 1826
Caldwell, Isaac W.	Mary Frost	Jul. 31, 1807
Caldwell (Culwell), James	Eliz. Culbreath	Jan. 10, 1787
Caldwell, John	Margaret Culbreath	Jan. 22, 1788
Caldwell, John C.	Eliz. M. Stockton	Apr. 10, 1834
Caldwell, Paul	Sarah Germany	Jul. 9, 1789
Cale, Homer K.	Jane M. Sikes	Dec. 18, 1845
Calhoon, Wm.	Rachel Triplett	Feb. 8, 1792
Calhoun, David W.	Adeline Dickenson	Nov. 21, 1826
Callis, Otho W.	Leonora E. Dinkins	May 13, 1818
Calvert, Mason	Sarah Rogar	Apr. 4, 1806
Calvin, David	Caroline Glover	Oct. 6, 1844
Calvin, James B.	Sarah Calvin	Oct. 4, 1838
Calvin, James B.	Eliz. Ellis	Dec. 31, 1839
Calvin, James P.	Mary Ann Aldridge	Jul. 22, 1833
Cambaa, Reuel	Mary Inglet	June 12, 1824
Camel, Thomas	Sarah Cain	Apr. 3, 1818
Camfield, Abiel	Rebecca Longstreet	May 18, 1809
Camfield, Joseph	Emily A. Flournoy	Jan. 2, 1832
Campbell, Dr. H. T.	Sarah B. Sibley	June 17, 1844
Campbell, James	Mary R. Eve	Apr. 8, 1818
Campbell, Jno. Arch'd.	Margaret H. A. Raiford	Aug. 24, 1847
Campbell, Levi	Eliz. Johnson	Dec. 8, 1817
Campbell, Dr. Robt. A.	Caroline Frances Sibley	June 14, 1848
Capes, John	Mrs. Tempus Johnson	Nov. 30, 1825
Carey, Dr. H. H.	Mary Jane Prouty	Jan. 15, 1849
Caribo, Henry	Eliz. Mason	May 9, 1817
Caribo, Henry	Nelly Stidman	Mar. 25, 1818
Carlin, John	Rachel Jones	Jul. 6, 1797
Carman, Frederick	Eliz. Rony	Aug. 9, 1810
Carmichael, Anderson	Eliz. E. Longstreet	Nov. 21, 1844
Carmichael, James	Mary Eve	Dec. 3, 1807
Carmichael, Jno.	Rachel Davis	May 1, 1804
Carmichael, John C.	Henriette Bishop	Oct. 29, 1841
Carmichael, Robt. D.	Louisa W. Smith	Apr. 8, 1845

385

GROOM	BRIDE	DATE
Carnes, Patrick H.	Anna Matilda Carter	Mar. 5, 1825
Carnes, Thomas P.	Elizabeth Bostick	Nov. 19, 1795
Carney, Arthur	Polly Ryalls	May 8, 1823
Carns, Bartholemew	Ellen Heerry	Feb. 1, 1828
Carolina, David	Diana Thomas	Dec. 28, 1811
Carr, Edward	Malvina Gibbs	June 4, 1839
Carr, Thomas	Francis Bacon	Nov. 11, 1787
Carrie, Peter	Clara Blome	June 18, 1835
Carson, Robert	Louisa W. Coun	Dec. 31, 1823
Carson, Wm.	Mrs. Sarah McLeod	Aug. 3, 1793
Carswell, Edward	Mahala Knight	Sept. 7, 1825
Carswell, Edward R.	Mary G. Walker	June 13, 1835
Carswell, Enoch H.	Nancy Janette McNair	Mar. 6, 1845
Carswell, Eqinardus R.	Sarah Ann Pior	Oct. 26, 1847
Carswell, Jas. A.	Lavina Rhodes	Jan. 18, 1812
Carswell, John F.	Mary J. Kilpatrick	Dec. 21, 1843
Carswell, John W.	Sarah Ann Divine	Jan. 21, 1835
Carswell, Matthew	Mrs. Harriet S. Gordon	Mar. 26, 1831
Carswell, Matthew J.	Harriett E. Kilpatrick	Apr. 27, 1845
Carter, Geo.	Olipbe Conaway	Mar. 15, 1843
Carter, James M.	Sarah R. Barrett	Nov. 25, 1821
Carter, John	Martha M. Flournoy	Jan. 30, 1822
Carter, Robert	E. Nelson	Dec. 30, 1839
Cartlidge, John	Nancy Allen	Nov. 7, 1826
Cary, Ebenezer	Martha B. Stockton	Feb. 21, 1843
Casey, Abraham	Hannah Hattey	Sept. 28, 1802
Cashin, Oswell	Mary Josephine Thomas	Nov. 22, 1843
Castellaw, Wm. H.	Rhody Brewer	Jan. 13, 1810
Casterson, Thomas	Ann Lamkin	Apr. 18, 1798
Cather, David	Eliz. Shannon	Apr. 30, 1828
Cavan, Trevor	Amanda Harkins	Apr. 5, 1832
Caven, David	Eliza Jane Scott	Apr. 15, 1829
Caven, Trava	Amanda Harkins	Apr. 4, 1832
Cavenah, Littleberry	Harriet Bryan	Jan. 22, 1825
Cavender, Philip M.	Martha Kite	May 10, 1837
Cawley, John	Eliz. M. Patterson	June 27, 1832
Chambliss, Thomas	Sarah Aldridge	May 26, 1788
Chance, Isaac	Henrietta Grubbs	Aug. 6, 1791
Chaning, John	Mary Taylor	Jan. 21, 1797
Chapman, Cutter	Sarah J. Smith	Nov. 26, 1838
Chappell, I. S.	S. M. Greene	May 11, 1811
Charity, James	Nancy Smith	Apr. 4, 1795
Charles, Nathaniel	Catherine Kinsley	Sept. 26, 1832
Chavous, Wm.	Amanda Green	July 7, 1847
Cheatam, Anthony	Mary W. Collins	Nov. 12, 1812
Cheatam, Littleberry	Amelia Brown	Feb. 7, 1835
Chew, Benjamin F.	Lucy V. Bufort	May 4, 1828
Christian, Abda	Ann Morse	May 30, 1810
Churchwell, Thomas	Phillis Beckcom	July 18, 1805
Claigg, Allen	Jane Mohaire	Sept. 6, 1828
Clark, Charles E.	Ann Averett	Dec. 4, 1835
Clark, David	Ann Yarborough	Nov. 22, 1832
Clark, Gabriel	Sarah Fears	May 3, 1806
Clark, Gilbert	Milley Avery	Jan. 26, 1788
Clark, James	Mary Loyge	Apr. 11, 1829
Clark, John M.	Sarah A. E. Burler	Apr. 28, 1841
Clark, Richard J. W.	Mary A. E. Stewart	June 20, 1845
Clark, Samuel B.	Martha R. Walker	Nov. 14, 1837
Clark, Wm.	Anne Wood	July 14, 1798
Clark, John M.	Mary Ann Maharrey	Jan. 17, 1830
Clarke, Charles	Sarah Murphey	Sept. 18, 1826
Clarke, Gabriel	Jane Brown	Mar. 6, 1816
Clarke, Gabriel	Jane Boulware	Nov. 20, 1817
Clarke, Gabriel S.	Eliza Gibson	Oct. 24, 1835
Clarke, Geo. W.	Sarah Ann Clarke	Jan. 20, 1830
Clarke, Henry	Jane Bradely	Dec. 22, 1842
Clarke, Henry E.	Caroline Collier	Dec. 16, 1846
Clarke, Henry L.	Ellen M. Thompson	Sept. 19, 1833

GROOM	BRIDE	DATE
Clarke, John M.	Mary Ann Maharrey	Dec. 31, 1829
Clarke, Joseph L.	Caroline E. Mealing	Mar. 29, 1838
Clarke, Michael M.	Tabitha Bloxsom	Aug. 29, 1816
Clarke, Michael	Catherine Johnson	June 26, 1832
Clarke, Nathaniel	Ann M. Redding	May 21, 1819
Clarke, Robert	Eliz. Walton	Jan. 22, 1835
Clarke, Samuel	Adeline E. Moore	Jan. 1, 1824
Clarke, Ulric B.	Catherine A. Watkins	Jan. 12, 1825
Clarke, Wm. C. W.	Tabitha Bolware	Aug. 5, 1816
Clarke, Wm. W.	Sarah Baily	Feb. 20, 1800
Claxton, Wm.	Ellen Moore	June 16, 1842
Clayton, Augustine S.	Julia Carnes	Dec. 19, 1807
Clayton, Edward P.	Mary Eliz. Bradford	Mar. 4, 1839
Clayton, Geo. Roots	Eliza Mildred Hargrove	Jan. 16, 1804
Clayton, John S.	Cecilia L. V. Bignon	June --, 1846
Clayton, Philip	Eliza Carnes	Nov. --, 1801
Clayton, Wm.	Eliza D. Harris	Jan. 23, 1823
Clements, Daniel	Eliz. Ware	Aug. 24, 1819
Clemmons, John	Anne Wilson	Nov. -, 1798
Cleveland, Neil	Jane Carnell	Aug. 24, 1790
Claitt, Isham	Lucy Runnels	July 10, 1817
Claitt, James	Eliza Kinder	Aug. 17, 1833
Claitt, Jehu	Eliz. Savage	Nov. 11, 1818
Claitt, Jesse	France Mosley	Nov. 25, 1812
Cliett, Jeremiah	Mary Ann Skinner	Jan. 30, 1840
Cliett, Jesse	Rhoda Harvey	Mar. 6, 1790
Cliett, John	Eleanor Crawford	Dec. 13, 1810
Cliet, Jonathan	Milley Mosely	Jan. --, 1817
Cliett, Minor J.	Sarah A. Smith	Dec. 20, 1838
Cliett, Richard	Henrietta Buck	Apr. 24, 1840
Cliett, Thos. C.	Mrs. Mary Ann Bacon	Aug. 19, 1836
Cliott, Isaac	Sarah Smars	Dec. 23, 1824
Coats, Jesse	Sarah Lee	July 26, 1798
Cobb, Abraham	Sarah Thompson	Oct. 6, 1837
Cobb, Thomas	Catherine Stith	June 7, 1790
Cobb, Wm. A.	Jane Mac Murphy	Nov. 23, 1819
Cocke, Nathaniel W.	Mary Ann M. Howard	Mar. 20, 1834
Cogil, George Hanson	Nancy Hill	Sept. 6, 1822
Coldwell, Augustus C.	Mary Paine	Aug. 12, 1834
Coleman, Jas. L.	Lucy G. W. Bacon	May 11, 1829
Coleman, James L.	Emeline B. Twiggs	Oct. 17, 1832
Colen, Peter	Martha Malaer	Nov. 24, 1840
Collins, David	Patsey Lyons	Oct. 3, 1810
Collins, George	Mary Sloan	July 17, 1818
Collins, George W.	Catherine Kidd	Dec. 10, 1823
Collins, James	Ann Headspeth	Aug. 2, 1780 (?)
Collins, James	Polly Shepherd	Nov. 21, 1804
Collins, James M.	Rebecca Ponder	June 15, 1849
Collins, Jesse	Eliz. A. Collins	Dec. 5, 1823
Collins, John	Martha Britt	June 12, 1796
Collins, John	Mary Smith	Nov. 1, 1802
Collins, Joseph	Sarah Williams	Apr. 4, 1804
Collins, Joseph	Eliza O. Hartford	Sept. 1, 1830
Collins, Joseph	Ann Rodgers	June 10, 1835
Collins, Lewis	-----(?) Allen	Jan. 2, 1799
Collins, Littleton	Nancy Wood	July 8, 1815
Collins, Major	Mary Triplett	Mar. 4, 1800
Collins, Michael	Minomia Shepherd	Nov. 23, 1805
Collins, Moses	Eliz. Houpt	Jan. 18, 1810
Collins, Moses	----- -----(?)	May 26, 1802
Collins, Robert	Sarah Rooks	May 2, 1812
Collins, Stephen	Sarah Shackleford	Mar. 29, 1787
Collins, Washington	Lavina Goodwin	May 19, 1826
Collins, Wm. S.	Libba Pool	Jan. 21, 1836
Colvin, Henry	Adeline B. Parnell	Aug. 13, 1846
Cone, Edmund L.	Mary Ann Eliz. Osborn	May 6, 1833
Cone, James	Patsey Youngblood	Jan. 6, 1807
Cone, Jno., Jr.	Mary Kirkland	May 20, 1805

GROOM	BRIDE	DATE
Cone, John S.	Rebecca Smith	Apr. 1, 1845
Cone, Wm.	Darcas Bugg	Aug. 21, 1806
Conn, George	Nancy Tyler	Apr. 27, 1799
Conner, Tarrane	Mary E. Picquet	Oct. 15, 1844
Cook, Andrew S.	Eliza Farnet	Nov. 22, 1841
Cook, Isaac	Frances Stan	Aug. 31, 1846
Cook, James R.	Ann Bugg	Sept. 25, 1820
Cook, John	Eliz. Bins	Jan. 8, 1797
Cook, John D.	Mrs. Maria L. Holcombe	July 4, 1838
Cook, Wm.	Ann Hammonds	Dec. 22, 1824
Cooper, James	Susanna Winslow	May 6, 1797
Cooper, James M. V.	Mary Ann Luke	Jan. 18, 1838
Cooper, John	Sarah Hatcher	Nov. 26, 1823
Cooper, John	Maria Moye	Feb. 9, 1829
Cooper, John C.	Elisa Bush	Feb. 2, 1848
Cooper, Wm. H.	Helen S. Henderson	Aug. 7, 1848
Copeland, Massey M.	Mary Ann Jones	May 16, 1830
Copeland, Massey M.	Mrs. Awry Rhodes	Dec. 9, 1831
Corder, H.	Ann T. Johnson	Jan. 5, 1832
Corley, Amos	Winney James	Sept. 16, 1820
Corley, John	Eliz. Fitzgerald	Jan. 5, 1849
Corly, Greenberry	Martha Ann Roshia	Jan. 5, 1848
Cormick, Jno.	Mrs. Catherine Beach	Mar. 18, 1823
Cosby, John	Sarah Glover	Dec. 22, 1793
Cosby, Overton	Elvera Kimbil	Jan. 15, 1829
Coskery, John	Isabella Rones(?)	May 21, 1833
Costar, A. M.	Mary G. Negic(?)	Jan. 7, 1819
Costello, James	Eliz. Flanagan	July 15, 1840
Cotten, John R.	Eliz. Liverman	Mar. 6, 1816
Cotter, Patrick	Eliz. Van	July 17, 1847
Couch, Edward W.	Susan Margaret Ware	Nov. 19, 1831
Couls, Wm.	Ann Merewether	Dec. 8, 1790
Coulter, Henry N.	Hariet E. Starnes	Nov. 7, 1815
Course, Isaac I.	Mrs. Wilhelmina Macky	Mar. 22, 1831
Cousins, Charles	Frances Crittenden	Nov. 20, 1802
Cousins, James	Eliz. Dowry	Nov. 24, 1801
Coutteau, Charles	Mary Bell	Apr. 20, 1809
Cowles, Norman	Mary S. Stockton	Aug. 2, 1839
Cox, Benj.	Ann Crawford	Feb. 5, 1830
Cox, Madison	Anna S. Frazier	Mar. 20, 1838
Cox, Taliaferra	Honor Cox	Nov. 8, 1801
Cox, William R.	Eliz. Carman	Sept. 18, 1826
Crafton, Bennet	Maria Beal	Mar. 15, 1816
Crafton, Thomas	Francis Cooke	Dec. 14, 1840
Craige, Allen	Mary Luther	June 7, 1827
Craig, John	Annabella McKenzie	Sept. 28, 1843
Crane, Moses	Eliz. Roberts	May 24, 1818
Crane, Moses	Eliz. Talley	July 28, 1820
Crawford, David	Mary Wood	Sept. 10, 1793
Crawford, David	Linny Wicker	Nov. 12, 1811
Crawford, George W.	Mary Ann Macintosh	May 4, 1826
Crawford, Joel	Nancy Barnett	Jan. 26, 1790
Crawford, John B.	Eliz. Butler	Dec. 23, 1837
Crawford, Matthew	Sarah Adams	Mar. 9, 1837
Crawford, Nathan	Eliza Roberts	May 17, 1823
Crawford, Robert	Eliz. Maxwell	Dec. 6, 1786
Crawford, Wm.	Mary Ann Downs	June 15, 1812
Crawford, Wm. H.	Susanna Jourdaine	Apr. 28, 1804
Crawford, Wm. H.	Mary Powell	Jan. 5, 1824
Crawley, Martin	Eliza Hannon	May 30, 1829
Crittendon, Wm.	Ann Cousin	May 13, 1789
Crocker, Joseph R.	Eliza Crane	Dec. 13, 1837
Crocker, I. R.	Laura Ann Meredith	Dec. 16, 1841
Crookshank, Patrick	Charity Primrose	Dec. 5, 1793
Crosley, Henry	-----(?) Martin	May 6, 1797
Cross, C. Burdett	Cornelia S. Bird	Oct. 18, 1843
Crothers, Wm.	Mary Wright	Oct. 19, 1829
Crozier, Wm.	Jane Namack	Sept. 16, 1838

GROOM	BRIDE	DATE
Crump, Geo. H.	Sarah L. Taliaferro	Apr. 18, 1849
Crump, Philip	Eliz. Ann Smith	Oct. 3, 1822
Crumpton, Levi I.	Eliz. A. Clark	Mar. 14, 1836
Cruse, Anglehart	Eliz. Trap	Mar. 9, 1796
Cruse, Englehart	Katherine Shaw	Jan. 16, 1802
Culbreath, John	Mary Johns	Dec. 24, 1787
Cullers, John	Matilda Gay	Jan. 23, 1838
Cullins, Augustus A.	Harriet H. Bussey	Apr. 2, 1839
Culver, Erasmus V.	Sarah E. Cooper	Jan. 14, 1845
Cumming, John	Susanna Moore	Apr. 17, 1802
Cumming, John B.	Eliz. Walker	Jan. 18, 1819
Cumming, Wm. H.	Eliz. R. McDowell	Nov. 30, 1847
Cummings, Luther	Caroline Willcox	July 31, 1820
Cunningham, Alexander	Louisa R. T. Baldwin	Nov. 9, 1819
Cunningham, Chas.	Ann Pritchard Eve	Nov. 25, 1800
Cunningham, Chas.	Anna E. White	Apr. 3, 1843
Cunningham, Jno.	Eliza Sturges	May 4, 1819
Cunningham, O. H. P.	Mary S. Roman	--- --, 1843
Cupper, Samuel G.	Mary Hopkins	June 30, 1807
Cuss, Louis	Louisa H. D'Antignac	Jan. 10, 1835
Daggett, Reuben	Betsey Lamkin	Dec. 24, 1812
Dagnal, Elbert Wood B.	Martha Brown	June 18, 1831
Dailey, Henry F.	Catherine Ann Quinn	Jan. 16, 1844
Dailey, Joseph	Mary Hunter	Jan. 5, 1804
Dally, Wm.	Nancy Wright	Dec. 3, 1835
Dalton, Barnabas	Polly Cane	June 18, 1808
Dalton, Henry	Winneford Lamkin	Jan. 8, 1801
Dame, Charles	Sarah Ann Siverman	Sept. 5, 1812
Dameron, Charles	Mary Maise	May 19, 1789
Danely, Daniel	Eliz. Preston	Apr. 10, 1788
Danforth, Abraham	Ann Anderson	Nov. 16, 1824
Danforth, Jacob	Polly Johnston	Dec. 10, 1802
Danforth, Jacob	Mary Ann Avery	Jan. 11, 1849
Danforth, J. R.	Rachael Vanzant	Mar. 18, 1815
Danforth, Joshua	Rachael Doughty	Oct. 9, 1816
Daniel, Bryan	Harriet Rowland	Dec. 14, 1822
Daniel, James L.	Mary Murphy	Oct. 15, 1834
Daniel, Jeptha	Sarah Rowland	Nov. 12, 1808
Daniel, Jesse	Rebecca Tinley	Oct. 19, 1813
Daniel, John	Elizabeth Bone	Jan. 13, 1821
Daniel, John	Eliz. L. Brown	Jan. 30, 1847
Daniel, Robt. W.	Martha Murphy	Mar. 2, 1836
Daniel, Robt. W.	Julia Florence	May 25, 1841
Danielly, Andrew	Jane Harris	Feb. 24, 1790
Danna, Otto	Charlotte Shilling	June 18, 1849
Dannely, John	Ellen Lucky	June 13, 1809
D'Antignac, Lewis C.	Eliz. W. Walker	Dec. 1, 1832
Darby, Jeremiah	Fanny Cook	Mar. 10, 1801
Darby, Wm.	Elisa Lee	Mar. 28, 1848
Darling, Benj.	Mary Lamkin	Jan. 2, 1809
Darling, John	Mary Pace	Dec. 30, 1803
Darling, Joseph	Polly Dunivent	Dec. 31, 1808
Darnell, Needham	Eliz. Carswell	Dec. 31, 1817
Darsey, Joel	Catherine Wright	Dec. 5, 1822
Dart, Benj.	Elizabeth Danforth	Oct. 14, 1848
Dart, Theodore	Ann W. Berry	Mar. 11, 1833
Dasher, Thomas J.	Sophia L. Clarke	May 28, 1828
D'Autel G. Julius	Francis A. Duffy	Aug. 12, 1839
Davenport, John M.	Martha Fuxey	May 12, 1815
Davidson, Paul	Drusella A. Jackson	July 13, 1843
Davies, James W.	Eliz. B. Nesbitt	Feb. 12, 1834
Davis, Aaron	Peggy Cain	Oct. 15, 1814
Davis, Geo.	Martha Pollard	July --, 1836
Davis, George	Margaret Kine	Sept. 10, 1835
Davis, Henry	Mary Reaux	July 22, 1830
Davis, Hightower	Sarah Smith	Oct. 17, 1810
Davis, Jacob R.	Mary Holland	Jan. 21, 1840

GROOM	BRIDE	DATE
Davis, James	Nancy Martin	Feb. 7, 1828
Davis, James	Sarah Hooker	Sept. 20, 1834
Davis, John	Elender King	Dec. 21, 1829
Davis, John	Sarah Simmons	Mar. 7, 1833
Davis, John	Martha Stinson	Jan. 16, 1834
Davis, John	Martha Jane Blackburn	June 11, 1845
Davis, John	Eliz. Waxter	June 29, 1845
Davis, Lorenzo D.	Georgianna Burroughs	Dec. 9, 1845
Davis, Richard Child	Eliza Nettles	Aug. 21, 1794
Davis, Samuel P.	Rebecca B. Whitehead	June 20, 1843
Davis, Samuel S.	Mary C. Cumming	Jan. 5, 1825
Davis, Stephen Edward	Augustae G. Sibley	Nov. 6, 1849
Davis, Thomas	Ruth Philips	Dec. 11, 1789
Davis, Wm. M.	Georgianna E. Cart	Oct. 10, 1838
Dawson, Dread	Elizabeth Patterson	May 30, 1800
Dawsy, Joseph	Ann Chance	Sept. 12, 1816
Day, J. C.	Mary A. Lowery	Sept. (?), 1849
Day, John	Fearibey Bullock	May 31, 1788
Day, John	Jane Frances Barton	Jan. 7, 1846
Day, Richard B.	Eliz. W. Rhodes	Oct. 20, 1823
Day, Wm.	Eliz. Cather	Sept. 11, 1830
Dearing, Wm. E.	Caroline E. Stovall	June 26, 1837
Dearmond, Wm.	Ann Pearce	Dec. 20, 1791
Dearmond, Wm.	Polly Nowland	July 4, 1799
Dearmond, Wm. E.	Eugenia E. Byrd	Dec. 26, 1844
Dearmond, Wm. P.	Eliz. Furey	June 15, 1820
Deas, Alexander	Nancy Culley	Aug. 30, 1837
Deas, Francis	Sally Castalac	Apr. 29, 1814
Deas, Wm.	Elisa Ann Deas	Aug. 2, 1844
Deaves, Edward F.	Eliz. Cooke	July 13, 1837
DeBow, Wm.	Julia Maldin	May 24, 1820
DeCiles, Jose	Eliz. Belcher	May 11, 1816
De Coin, Wm. A.	Leanora E. Brackner	Jan. 7, 1836
De Cottes, Augustus	Susannah C. MacMurphy	Dec. 23, 1839
Deheur, Sebastian	Helener Waber	June 16, 1835
Delaforte, Antony James Joseph D.	Michile Suzanne Victoire Magnan	Dec. 31, 1808
Delaigle, Charles L.	Mary E. M. Watkins	Jan. 21, 1829
Delamar, Thos.	Hannah Longis	Aug. 11, 1819
Delannory, Fortune Theodore	Maria Magdaline C. Reingard	Jan. 17, 1814
Deliac, Antoine Pascall	Sarah Singer	Nov. 26, 1828
Demarest, Benj.	Nancy Lyles	Mar. 13, 1824
Dennard, Wm. L.	Reletha Whitcombe	Nov. 13, 1834
Dent, John	Sarah Macintosh	May 17, 1820
Denton, John	Eliz. Kettles	Aug. 23, 1833
Devilen, Thomas E.	Ardelizar Hightower	Sept. 15, 1823
Dewars, Alex	Margaret Colter	Jan. 12, 1839
Dicken, James T.	Mary Hicks	Jan. 19, 1792
Dickinson, Cosby	Hannah Cockrahain	Jan. 14, 1800
Dickinson, G. W.	? Mustin (marriage bond)	1848
Diehl, Frederick	Mary Gilbert	Feb. 18, 1841
Dill, Andrew J.	Eliza Savage	Aug. 1, 1808
Dill, Daniel	Mary Ann Dill	Feb. 13, 1832
Dill, Jacob	Ann Buxton	Aug. 5, 1809
Dill, Philip	Ann Coleman	May 19, 1818
Dillan, Robert	Sarah Burdell	Apr. 13, 1818
Dillard, Geo.	Zuriah Grubbs	Jan. 15, 1789
Dillard, John	Maria Tarver	May 24, 1830
Dillard, John G.	Nancy Harris	Mar. 6, 1830
Dillon, Wm. C.	Ann Wright	July 7, 1832
Dimon, Robert	Adeline Sterlen	July 26, 1821
Dismukes, Reuben	Elsey Bailey	Mar. 3, 1827
Dixon, Henry	Frances Ann Ashley	Apr. 26, 1820
Dixon, Wm. L.	Mary Tice	Nov. 19, 1846
Dockle, Jacob Christopher	Mrs. Sally Stroder	Aug. 5, 1810
Donaldson, Daniel T.	Emily Powers	Apr. 19, 1834
Donaldson, Peter	Nancy Mann	Feb. 11, 1800

GROOM	BRIDE	DATE
Doonan, Torrence	Ellen Barry	May 16, 1840
Dortic, Germain T.	Ann Frances E. Lafitte	Sept. 6, 1826
Dortic, Sebastian C.	Ann Adelle Parisot	Nov. 10, 1818
Dosset, Wm.	Mary Bell	Dec. 16, 1823
Doubel, Alexandre	Caroline Picquet	Nov. 6, 1848
Dougharty, James A.	Mrs. Pamelia Underhill	Dec. 9, 1821
Dougherty, Michael	Adeline Rudler	Nov. 26, 1846
Doughty, John M.	Louisa Denby	Oct. 16, 1825
Douglas, Samul C.	Phoebe Talbott Cresswell	Apr. 11, 1812
Dow, Jno. M.	Mary McKeen	Nov. 22, 1838
Dowaney, Samuel	Polly Dalton	Mar. 15, 1823
Dowe, John R.	Catherine E. Carmichael	Oct. 4, 1843
Downs, Ambrose	Eliz. McCoy	Oct. 15, 1806
Downs, Isaac	Elizabeth Bennett	Dec. 23, 1827
Downs, Isaac	Mary Ann Critinton	Jan. 9, 1809
Downs, Richard	Jane Crawford	Feb. 8, 1837
Drane, Benj.	Rachel Harris	Feb. 2, 1788
Dreghorn, Jno.	Eliz. Ligon	Nov. 16, 1832
DuBose, Isaac	Emily I. Powers	July 9, 1834
Dudley, John	Eliz. Foster	Aug. 27, 1839
Duffy, Thomas	Catherine Dunbar	Jan. 26, 1829
Dugas, L. P.	Eliz. McKay	June 2, 1819
Dugas, Lewis Alec	Mary C. Barnes	Feb. 6, 1833
Dugas, Louis Alex	Louisa V. Harris	Mar. 16, 1840
Dukes, Robert	Martha Lanthorp	Apr. 24, 1819
Dumingoes, Emanuel	Nancy Netherland	Oct. 6, 1824
Dunbar, Thos. I.	Jane A. Newhouse	Sept. 27, 1845
Duncan, Langdon C.	Mary A. Guedron	Oct. 1, 1840
Duncan, Wm.	Eliz. M. Kain	Feb. 19, 1834
Dunham, Samuel	Rebechah McTyre	Mar. 8, 1796
Dunham, Wm.	Margaret Clementz	Dec. 27, 1828
Dunn, Charles C.	Rebecca Moore	Aug. 12, 1812
Dunwoody, Samuel	Lavinia Snead	Dec. 26, 1825
Duren, George	Charlotte Snead	Nov. 20, 1823
Durham, Wm.	Martha Tully	Feb. 10, 1824
Duval, Beal M.	Ann Underwood	July 24, 1842
Duvall, George W.	Rebecca A. Hack	Jun. 1, 1840
Dwelle, Charles	Eliz. A. I. Honsby	Apr. 30, 1840
Dyas, Henry	Nancy Savage	July 25, 1827
Dyas, Moses	Betsey Lantrip	June 22, 1813
Dye, Benjamin	Nancy Ross	Dec. 19, 1810
Dye, Ethelred	Georgiana Moody	Feb. 27, 1838
Dye, James W.	Virginia C. Richard	Apr. 18, 1848
Dye, Martin M.	Susan Knight	Oct. 27, 1836
Dyer, Moses	Kitty Watson	July 7, 1815
Eads, John	Jane Fee	Nov. 30, 1797
Early, Eleazar	Jane Meriwether Patterson	Oct. 19, 1803
Easter, Wheeler (William)	Milly McDaniel	Jan. 18, 1808
Easterling, Benj.	Barbary Prior	Nov. 9, 1848
Edding, Robert	Eliz. Livingston	Dec. 5, 1839
Edgar, John	Anna E. Carmichael	Jul. 24, 1828
Edings, Benj. L.	Susan Antony	Apr. 3, 1838
Edmonds, Samuel	Louisa J. Hall	Jul. 5, 1843
Edney, John M.	Eliza Fall	Feb. 5, 1817
Edwards, Andrew N. M.	Sarah Clanton	Dec. 22, 1809
Edwards, Andrew N. M.	Charlotte Shadrick	Dec. 12, 1812
Edwards, Andrew N. M.	Ann Norman	Mar. 17, 1818
Edwards, Augustine	Sarah Leigh	Apr. 23, 1799
Edwards, Benj.	Pamelia Adeline Sumner	Apr. 12, 1840
Edwards, Garner	Esther A. Thompson	May 3, 1838
Edwards, Levi	-----(?) Calvin	Oct. 24, 1835
Egan, William H.	Anne Quin	Nov. 7, 1821
Egbert, Peter M.	Nancy Evans	June 1, 1830
Elam, Daniel	Virlinder Johnston	June 23, ----
Elam, George B.	Mary Bugg	Dec. 4, 1816
Elkins, Reuben	Eliz. Davis	Jan. 23, 1797
Elkins, Sion	Mrs. Pening W. Smith	July 4, 1841

GROOM	BRIDE	DATE
Elkins, Sion	Rachel Davis	Dec. 23, 1842
Elligood, Thomas	Louisa Vanzant	Feb. 18, 1819
Ellington, Rice	Nancy Garrett	Apr. 24, 1800
Elliot, Elijah	Nancy Allen	Oct. 6, 1826
Elliot, John	Mrs. Sarah Melhorn	Jan. 18, 1849
Elliott, Abram B.	Lucinda Young	Dec. 31, 1838
Ellis, Jonathan	Abigail Roff	Mar. 9, 1831
Ellott, Randolph	Elizabeth Withers	Mar. 29, 1826
Elmore, Thomas	Lavenia English	Mar. 8, 1838
Elmore, Thomas	Martha Bryant	Oct. 27, 1840
Enecks, Wm.	Mary Oswald	May 14, 1840
Engles, Martin	Mahaly Whiteaker	Sept. 5, 1828
English, James	Louisa Alley	May 18, 1831
Englit, James M.	Mary Ann Eliz. Lovel	Nov. 4, 1844
Entakin, Isaac	Elizabeth Cobb	Dec. 15, 1801
Eubanks, John	Mary Garnett	Jan. 1, 1787
Evalet, Conrad	Catherine Gann	Oct. 17, 1845
Evans, George W.	Eliz. Course	May 25, 1803
Evans, Henry	Darcus Hudson	Nov. 24, 1808
Evans, John	Martha M. Kennedy	May 14, 1828
Evans, John W.	Lucy A. Evans	Oct. 31, 1810
Evans, John W. C.	Judy Washington	Sept. 15, 1825
Evans, Llewellin	Mary Harris	June 25, 1804
Evans, Richard	Ann McCullough	Nov. 6, 1820
Evans, Robert H.	Eliz. Ann Murphy	Nov. 6, 1828
Eve, Dr. Edward A.	Sarah J. Raiford	Feb. 16, 1837
Eve, John	Sarah Carmichael	Jan. 14, 1823
Eve, Dr. Joseph A.	Sarah G. Combs	Apr. 1, 1833
Eve, Joseph C.	Jane M. Ringland	Jan. 26, 1825
Eve, Dr. Paul F.	Sarah Louisa Twiggs	Dec. 16, 1832
Eve, Wm. I.	P. E. Casey	Oct. 21, 1840
Everet, Jesse	Nancy Hudson	Sept. 1, 1808
Everitt, John	Ann Everitt	Mar. 13, 1826
Evingham, Lewis	Martha Green	Jan. 28, 1837
Evingham, Thomas	Mary Shadwick	Feb. 26, 1795
Faillet(?), Wm. B.	Mary Anne Murray	Jan. 19, 1843
Falligant, Louis N.	Eliza Robey Raiford	Jan. 7, 1836
Fargo, Hiram W.	Hannah T. Wray	Apr. 26, 1848
Farmer, Berian B.	Ann Williams	Oct. 14, 1846
Farrar, Absalom	Mildred Clark	Dec. 5, 1790
Farrell, O.	Miss Ramsay	Apr. 15, 1844
Farrington, Wm.	Mary Orr	Aug. 11, 1819
Fausett, Abraham	Sarah Paterson	Dec. 22, 1807
Fennel, Etheldred	Mary Kennedy	Aug. 13, 1803
Fenner, James	Lemendar Wilkins	Sept. 22, 1794
Ferguson, John	Eliz. Cavenis	Oct. 8, 1835
Ferguson, Augustus	Eliz. A. Carswell	May 23, 1848
Ferguson, Wm. J.	Elizabeth Haines	Sept. 28, 1842
Fernanda, Wm. P.	Harriet Bowers	Aug. 14, 1813
Ferrel, Charles A.	Caroline Bird	Nov. 2, 1845
Fetters, John	Abatha M. Eubanks	Apr. 12, 1827
Fickling, Mortimer	Susan E. Hood	May 18, 1848
Fields, Eli	Elizabeth Crawford	July 4, 1801
Fields, S. P.	Ann Pitman	Nov. 19, 1844
Finn, John	Mrs. Ann S. Thomas	Feb. 5, 1828
Finney, James	Bridget Hughes	May 26, 1823
Fischer, Frederick	Frances Mast	Oct. 30, 1849
Fisher, John	Mary A. Williams	May 22, 1835
Fitts, Edgar M.	Mary S. Pond (Mustin)	July 14, 1846
Fitzgerald, Edmund	Eliz. Sloman	Mar. 14, 1833
Fitzgibbons, James	Dicey Joiner	Nov. 14, 1794
Fitzjarrell, John	Mrs. Mary Red	Aug. 10, 1837
Fitzsimons, Paul	Eleanor N. White	Apr. 19, 1827
Flanagan, Gamwell	Winney Snead	Aug. 31, 1824
Fleming, James P.	Mrs. Rebecca Luke	Dec. 23, 1847
Flemming, Porter	Martha Flemming	June 7, 1835
Fletcher, Christopher	Eliz. Townsend	Dec. 28, 1819

392

GROOM	BRIDE	DATE
Fleury, Joseph	Eliza A. Pardue	Jan. 15, 1837
Flint, John	Margaret Butler	June 13, 1807
Flournoy, Thomas	Sophia Davies	July 14, 1801
Floyd, James B.	Mary Bryson	Apr. 15, 1795
Flutcher, John W.	Selina Newman	Apr. 14, 1846
Folds, Amos	Margan Wilkins	June 28, 1798
Foles, Coonrad	Sarah Lamar	Apr. 30, 1787
Foll, George	Lucey Shoemake	May 28, 1794
Ford, N. A.	Martha Pardue	Oct. 7, 1845
Ford, Wm.	Cassiah Jones	Mar. 14, 1786
Forsyth, John, Jr.	Margaret G. Hull	Apr. 22, 1834
Foster, Arthur	Jerusha Garnett	Sept. 1, 1806
Foster, Arthur	Mary Davis	July 14, 1810
Foster, Collier	Lucinda Bowdre	Jan. 4, 1815
Foster, Hardy	Eliza W. Hill	Aug. 9, 1813
Foster, John	Eliz. Savage	Sept. 3, 1785
Foster, Jno.	Jane E. M. Zinn	Feb. 2, 1832
Foster, Joshua	Lucy Savidge	Dec. 5, 1803
Foster, Samuel	Mary Wimberly	Nov. 4, 1824
Foster, Sterling	Eliz. Griffin	Dec. 8, 1828
Foster, Thomas	Lucinda Morgan	Dec. 23, 1830
Foster, Thomas F.	Elizabeth McKinely Gardner	Jan. 9, 1839
Foster, Wm.	Ann Cox	Sept. 18, 1797
Foster, Wm.	Mrs. Ann Bowles	Feb. 3, 1810
Fountain, Gilbert	Rebecca Gladdis	Feb. 27, 1836
Fountain, Kindred	Polly Crawford	Mar. 20, 1845
Fowler, John	Susannah Braden	Nov. 8, 1823
Fowler, John	Nancy Pricket	June 11, 1825
Fowler, Joshua	Ann Marie Suffield	Oct. 2, 1820
Fowler, Wm.	Sally Mauldin	Apr. 27, 1822
Fox, Nicholas	Mrs. Sarah B. Watkins	Dec. 18, 1798
Fox, Wm.	Elizabeth Brown	June 21, 1838
Foyil, John	Catharine Moye	Mar. 3, 1827
Francis, James	Lucy Downs	Mar. 19, 1819
Fraser, Laurence Roger	Agnes Townsend	Nov. 11, 1844
Fraser, Reubin	Levina Heath	Mar. 18, 1823
Frazer, Wm.	Susannah Jones	July 30, 1817
Frederick, Jacob	Rebecca F. Powers	Apr. 30, 1814
Frederick, Jacob	Clarissa Ware	Sept. 22, 1819
Freeland, James M. C.	Caroline Augusta Butler	Aug. 18, 1841
Freeman, John H.	Mary Shermon	May 25, 1822
Freeman, Thomas W.	Caroline E. F. Skinner	Oct. 5, 1842
Fretwell, Charles	Esther Anderson	May 29, 1804
Fretwell, Littleton B.	Lavina Netherland	Jan. 3, 1828
Fridel, John	Lucinda Pond	May 29, 1845
Frith, Joseph	Prudence Rickerson	Aug. 29, 1795
Fryer, John	Mary Godley	Dec. 16, 1819
Fudge, Benjamin	Lydia Collins	Sept. 12, 1806
Fulcher, Armisted	Nancy Daniel	July 23, 1806
Fulcher, James L.	E. F. Daniel	Mar. 27, 1846
Fulcher, John	Mary Coulson	Jan. 30, 1809
Fulcher, Wm.	Nancy Templeton	Sept. 19, 1834
Fullerton, Hugh	Rebecca Love	Jan. 20, 1799
Fullerton, Hugh	Mary Cox	Dec. 29, 1810
Furman, Dr. John Howard	Catherine Eliza Carter	June 23, 1845
Furney, Wm.	Sarah McTyre	Oct. 28, 1815
Fussell, Thomas	Susannah Willis	July 30, 1799
Gaillet, Wm. B.	Mary Ann Mancy	---- --, 1843
Gaines, George G.	Peggy Duhart	July 12, 1800
Gairdner, James P.	Mary M. Gardner	Mar. 1, 1827
Gallagher, John	Ann Scott	July 12, 1827
Gallagher, John W.	Bridget Leslie	May 8, 1846
Gamble, John	Mary Rouse	Mar. 17, 1840
Ganahl, Joseph	Charlotte Elvia Conn	June 17, 1820
Ganas, John	Sarah Atkinson	Dec. 10, 1829
Ganes, Chas.	Mary McNair	Oct. 21, 1849
Ganis, James	Harriet Lions	Feb. 22, 1844

GROOM	BRIDE	DATE
Gant, Richard	Sarah Allen	May 22, 1794
Ganter, Joseph	Mary Ann Lutheringer	Feb. 3, 1842
Gantley, John	Mary McMunn	Oct. 31, 1789
Gantt, Thomas John	Ann Eliza Fell	Dec. 30, 1813
Gardelle, A.	Emma Bignon	Apr. 26, 1831
Gardiner, George W.	Francis P. Fowler	May 8, 1830
Gardiner, Thomas	Sabrinah Lee	June 3, 1825
Gardner, Alexander	Elizabeth Pratt	June 4, 1785
Gardner, James	Sarah Hodgkin	Sept. 5, 1793
Gardner, James	Elizabeth Blair	May 6, 1809
Gardner, John	Elizabeth Thuston	Jan. 5, 1820
Gardner, Thomas	Anna McKinne	Dec. 30, 1804
Garner, John	Sarah A. M. Urquhart	Apr. 10, 1825
Garnett, John	Elizabeth Crawford	Dec. 14, 17-6
Garnett, Zachariah	Susannah Evans	Feb. 21, 1803
Garnett, Zachariah	Susanna Foster	Sept. 2, 1805
Garrard, Wm. W.	Francis J. Urguart	Oct. 10, 1843
Garret, Asa	Charity Holcomb	Feb. 4, 1809
Garret, Edmund	Marriah Whitaker	Jan. 19, 1847
Garrett, John	Catherine Roberts	Sept. 28, 1835
Garrett, Joseph	Elizabeth Pounds	Aug. 8, 1814
Gartrell, John	Elizabeth Jones	May 11, 1787
Garvin, Ignatius	Sarah Ann Anthony	Jan. 25, 1826
Gasque, Nathan	Jane Savage	Dec. 21, 1799
Gass, Fredric	Sophia Miller	July 20, 1812
Gathright, Miles	Mary Collins	Aug. 29, 1795
Gay, Theodore Thos.	Sarah Lambeth	July 29, 1830
Gay, Wm.	Malvina Whitehead	Nov. 28, 1839
Germain, Thos.	Armanella Vaughn	Aug. 29, 1839
Germany, William J.	Olivia E. Watson	Feb. 2, 1827
Germond, William	Susan Cheves	May 5, 1825
Gibbs, John, Jr.	Nancy Spring	Mar. 18, 1838
Gibbs, William	Charlotte Cooke	Jan. 14, 1835
Gibbs, Wm.	Eliz. Vogler	Apr. 30, 1837
Gibson, Alexander	Winney Bullock	Feb. 5, 1794
Gilbert, Mauris	Winfrey Bozman	June 19, 1793
Gilman, Charles	Elsey Robinson	Nov. 29, 1840
Ginn, Thomas	Maria Whittington	Feb. 15, 1819
Girdner, Geo. Washington Franklin	Eliz. Clements	Sept. 30, 1830
Glascock, Edmund B.	Sarah W. Lacy	Mar. 20, 1817
Glascock, Edmund B.	Amelia L. F. Labuzon(?)	Sept. 26, 1829
Glascock, Thomas	Harriot Hayes	May 22, 1813
Glass, John	Susan P. Snead	June 22, 1821
Glendenning, William	Barsheba Hudson	Feb. 8, 1823
Glover, David	Frances Bussy	Nov. 7, 1833
Glover, Robert D.	Martha A. Coombs	Feb. 5, 1835
Glover, William	Susan Megill	Apr. 5, 1815
Godbehere, James	Mary Mann	Mar. 18, 1824
Goetchins, R. V.	Augusta Benl	Oct. 13, 1831
Goff, Ellis H.	Jane C. Page	Apr. 8, 1845
Goff, Samuel	Margaret Downie	June 3, 1813
Golden, Isaiah	Lemilia Daniel	Apr. 27, 1842
Golightly, Hugh	Mary Harris	Dec. 22, 1787
Goodall, William	Margaret Magill	June 19, 1811
Goodman, William	Julia Burton	July 30, 1826
Goodman, Wm. H.	Rachael Payne	Apr. 4, 1837
Goodrich, Luther	Eliza A. Clarke	Apr. 24, 1828
Goodrich, Wm. H.	Susan Caroline Clarke	Nov. 1, 1834
Goodson, Jacob	Nancy Fillips	Mar. 11, 1808
Goodwin, Charles	Sarah Prescott	Nov. 27, 1817
Goodwin, Henry	Sarah Loggan	Feb. 8, 1849
Goodwin, James	Epsy Brown	Jan. 8, 1839
Goodwin, Jesse	Mary Colwell	Nov. 8, 1820
Goodwin, John W.	Eliz. M. Smith	Nov. 28, 1849
Goodwin, Wyche	Anne Powers	Jan. 14, 1798
Goodwyn, James	Jensey Green	May 9, 1802
Googer, Wm. H.	Mary L. Pardue	Dec. 23, 1845

GROOM	BRIDE	DATE
Gordon, Alexander	Rebecca Gordon	Feb. 2, 1820
Gordon, Geo. Ramsey	Melinda M. Guthry	May 30, 1849
Gordon, Patrick	Rebecca Jones	Nov. 4, 1809
Gordon, Wm. H.	Caroline W. Danforth	Mar. 8, 1838
Gorton, Henry	Mary H. Johnson	July 19, 1826
Gorton, Henry	Sarah L. Dunlap	Feb. 4, 1847
Gossage, Henry	Frances Finley	Jan. 19, 1840
Gould, Artemas	Margaret W. Gardner	July 4, 1844
Gould, S.	Sarah Smiley	Mar. 21, 1839
Gould, William T.	Anna McKenne	Oct. 6, 1824
Grace, Samuel	Nancy W. Ladler	Jan. 26, 1825
Grace, Thomas	Elizabeth Allen	Nov. 30, 1818
Grady, John	Adeline Martin	Feb. 17, 1829
Grady, Michael	----- -----	Feb. 4, 1840
Granel, Daniel	Jane A. Lansdale	Sept. 7, 1829
Granger, Benj.	Sarah Allen	Sept. 23, 1830
Grant, Joseph	Ann Lillebridge	Oct. 7, 1801
Grant, Kenneth	May Eblank	Oct. 11, 1828
Grant, Lemuel P.	Laura L. Williams	--- --, 1843
Graves, Edmund H.	Emily C. Hatcher	Jan. 6, 1841
Graves, George	Mary Scott	June 26, 1800
Gray, Wm. W.	Susan N-aly	Apr. 2, 1835
Green, Bartlet C.	Susan Davis	Dec. 21, 1819
Green, Furnifold	Susan Turner	Jan. 3, 1822
Green, Geo. Peter	Elenora Donovan	Aug. 16, 1849
Green, James T.	Sarah Ann Dees	Sept. 20, 1838
Green, John C.	Eliza C. Green	Mar. 8, 1821
Green, John C.	Elenor I. Read	Oct. 18, 1838
Green, W. B., Jr.	Cornelia A. Higgs	Feb. 2, 1842
Green, Wm. G.	Sarah E. Bush	Nov. 20, 1849
Greene, Augusten	Nancy Fisher	Dec. 5, 1844
Greene, John	Eliz. Jenkins	Dec. 19, 1841
Greene, Nathaniel	Maria Barry	Dec. 15, 1844
Greenway, Samuel	Elizabeth Mary McCollough	Dec. 18, 1809
Greenwood, Benjamin L.	E. M. M. Scurry	June 24, 1828
Greenwood, Benj. L.	Letitia A. G. Youngblood	May 26, 1841
Greenwood, Henry	Sarah Dawson	Feb. 17, 1802
Greenwood, Henry	Sally Twiggs	Sept. 9, 1803
Greenwood, Henry D.	Hariet E. Anderson	Dec. 6, 1843
Greer, Thomas	Lettishe Grinnage	Dec. 10, 1788
Gregory, Francis	Mary Hodge	Apr. 9, 1814
Gregory, John	Ann H. Fortinberry	Apr. 9(?), 1828
Greiner, J. P.	Mary Ann Barney	June 3, 1828
Greiner, John L.	Mrs. Julia M. Hamilton	Oct. 11, 1843
Gresham, Edmund B.	Sarah M. Anderson	May 15, 1838
Griffin, Henry	Abigail Hall	Dec. 6, 1825
Griffin, James	Lucy Ann Craig	Aug. 25, 18-3
Griffin, John C.	Mary Bosworth	Feb. 4, 1819
Griffin, Wiley B.	Amanday M. Butler	Sept. 30, 1841
Grothe, Richard W.	Camille Guimarin	May 24, 1837
Groves, Sylvanus B.	Claudia Ann Hornby	Nov. 1, 1821
Grubbs, Joab	Elizabeth Atkison	July 1, 1786
Grubbs, Thomas	Mary Syms	Feb. 22, 1802
Grumbles, George W.	Sarah Sumner	Mar. 17, 1828
Grumbles, William	Anne Oliver	July 29, 1828
Guenebault, Joseph Henry	Leocadie Adelaide Sera	July 28, 1834
Guest, Joseph J.	Sarah D. Burke	Dec. 21, 1833
Gullett, John M., Dr.	Mary Camilla Loving	Mar. 4, 1847
Gumbleton, Robert	Mary Ann Tyrie	Jan. 27, 1821
Gunn, David	Peggy Hickey	Apr. 22, 1828
Gurin, John B.	Virginia M. Cattonett	Oct. 6, 1835
Guthrie, Alfred	Verlendia M. Godley	Apr. 3, 1838
Hack, D. B.	Eliz. Attaway	Oct. 6, 1844
Hack, D. B.	Amelia Winter	Apr. 15, 1846
Hagans, Isom	Nancy Anderson	Nov. 23, 1801
Hagen (?), Hiram	Mary Collins	Nov. 14, 1829
Haggins, Edw. Henry	Sally Youngblood	Jan. 8, 1807

GROOM	BRIDE	DATE
Hahn, John	Cristina Angel	Jan. 27, 1846
Haines, Wm., Jr.	Mary Anne Schley	Apr. 20, 1843
Hale, Eliphalet	Nancy Stewart	Jan. 7, 1819
Haley, John	Mrs. Mary Smith	Aug. 10, 1822
Hall, Benjamin	Harriot Bebe	May 2, 1811
Hall, Charles	Margaret C. C. Reid	Oct. 20, 1820
Hall, Charles H.	Annie M. Cumming	Mar. 2, 1848
Hall, Daniel	Sarah Daniel	Aug. 27, 1824
Hall, David	Eliz. Wigins	Mar. 13, 1842
Hall, James	Nancy Walker	Apr. 2, 1828
Hall, James B.	Jane Kennedy	Feb. 20, 1809
Hall, James M.	Amelia Ogg	June 24, 1809
Hall, Jeremiah	Lucy Hapt King	Nov. 13, 1819
Hall, Lorenzo T.	Eliz. Davis	Nov. 22, 1820
Hall, Raymond	Jeanett Fulcher	May 29, 1838
Hall, Wm.	Mary Brown	Feb. 23, 1841
Halsey, David F.	Mary M. Flournoy	May 19, 1830
Hamilton, Alexander	Mary Ann Kelly	Nov. 28, 1847
Hamilton, Crosir	Martha Anne Peay	June 1, 1848
Hammond, Charles	Mahaly Cone	Nov. 27, 1825
Hammond, James	Christian Allen	May 2, 1793
Hammond, Wm. B.	Sarah Sanderlin	Mar. 17, 1825
Handcock, Joseph	Levina Vall	Dec. 16, 1820
Hanson, Thomas	Eliz. Evans	Feb. 20, 1788
Hard, Wm. J.	Sarah Y. Wanton	Feb. 2, 1836
Hardin, Edward J.	Jane L. Barrett	Mar. 23, 1820
Harkins, James	Francis Mitchel	Jan. 9, 1797
Harkins, Roger	Eliz. Bugg	Oct. 24, 1797
Harmon, Charles	Adeline E. Dinkins	Nov. 22, 1820
Harmon, Isaac	Betsy Collins (colored)	Feb. 14, 1818
Harmon, Matthew	Mary Ruse	Dec. 28, 1819
Harmon, Matthew	Nancy Moore (colored)	July 2, 1825
Harmon, Tippoo S.	Eliz Hammond	Apr. 22, 1820
Harn, John B.	Margaret E. J. Walker	May 15, 1828
Harper, Solomon	Sally Cannon	May 12, 1807
Harper, Wm.	Mary Ann Cashin	May 1, 1823
Harrell, Thomas	Eliz. Lewis	June 29, 1841
Harrigil, Joseph	Rebecca Dudley	Sept. 4, 1799
Harris, Alex T.	Eliz. Burkes	Sept. 5, 1816
Harris, Bennet	Rebecca Ann Baldy	Sept. 9, 1839
Harris, Eligah	Rosa Anderson	May 27, 1840
Harris, Jeremiah	Eleanor Beal	Jan. 28, 1812
Harris, Laird M.	Eliz. Dallas	Jan. 29, 1800
Harris, Michael	Ann M. Turman	Mar. 2, 1804
Harper, Robert A.	Laura F. Ladewere (colored)	Dec. 23, 1847
Harris, Washington G.	Sarah E. Smith	Oct. 23, 1845
Harrison, Samuel	Patsey Hill	Jan. 18, 1810
Harrison, Samuel	Mary Hornby	Dec. 23, 1824
Harrison, Samuel	Eliza Tinley	Sept. 19, 1843
Harrison, Wm.	Fanny Futerill	Feb. 10, 1803
Hart, James B.	Maria V. Collier	Feb. 6, 1838
Hart, Wm.	Eliz. Low	Aug. 16, 1804
Hart, Wm. R.	Sarah H. Carter	Sept. 28, 1834
Hartford, Joshua B.	Eliza Olivia Powers	June 3, 1823
Hartridge, John Earl	Leah Ann Sandwich	Dec. 26, 1807
Harvey, German	Gracy Washington	Feb. 26, 1808
Harvey, John	Rachel Harris	Dec. 21, 1804
Harwood, John	Eliz. Dawson	Oct. 27, 1795
Hassel, Addison	Martha Ann Palmer	Apr. 8, 1845
Hatch, Milo	Emily C. Dye	Mar. 29, 1836
Hatcher, Archibald	Mary Arinton	May 4, 1795
Hatcher, Henry	Anne Wicker	June 14, 1796
Hatcher, John	Sarah Buxton	Feb. 14, 1801
Hatcher, John G.	Ann Eliza Fulcher	Oct. 17, 1843
Hatcher, Jones	Mary Conner	May 30, 1849
Hatfield, Caleb S.	Maria Shaffer	Sept. 14, 1825
Haupt, Philip	Eliz. Smith	Apr. 11, 1804
Hauser (Hansen?), George	Johanah Murphy	Jan. 5, 1847

GROOM	BRIDE	DATE
Hawes, Samuel	Mary Ann Richardson	Feb. 20, 1819
Hawkins, Abimalek	Sarah Raglin	Mar. 8, 1795
Hawkins, Geo. S.	Jane L. Early	May 5, 1832
Hawkins, R. R.	Caroline Philips	Apr. 22, 1839
Haworth, Absalom	Sarah Lang	Mar. 14, 18-6
Hayden, Lawrence	Catharine Heery	Dec. 29, 1828
Haygood, Edwin A.	Eliza G. Barrett	Nov. 25, 1835
Haynes, Francis	Maria Theresa Sanit	June 6, 1812
Haynie, Emelent P.	Louisa A. C. Livingston	---- --, 1849
Haynie, James D.	Mrs. Matilda Hatcher	Dec. 26, 1824
Haynie, James D.	Adeline Brandon	Jan. 24, 1840
Hays, Thomas	Mary Marlbrough	July 15, 1830
Haywood, Wm.	Sarah Andrews	Jan. 28, 1836
Hood, Alfred J.	Sarah Odam	Feb. 23, 1832
Heard, Edmund	Eliz. Thompson	Mar. 6, 1837
Heard, John W.	Martha K. Howard	Feb. 10, 1829
Heard, Isaac T.	Amy M. Collier	May 20, 1834
Heard, Thomas N.	Eliz. Ann Barton	Dec. 23, 1829
Heard, Thomas N.	Emily B. Crews	June 19, 1833
Heath, Royster	Eliz. Parham	Feb. 9, 1789
Heckle, Henry B.	Anne Bohler	Jan. 27, 1842
Heckle, John	Susan McGarr	Sept. 2, 1826
Heckle, Thomas	Frances Jaillett	Dec. 1, 1840
Hemphill, Alexander	Empsy Ann Green	Dec. 5, 1844
Henderson, Joseph	Catharine Edington	Apr. 13, 1805
Henderson, Robert	Eliza W. Pate	June 30, 1819
Hendrick, Lemuel B.	Eliza Dean	Mar. 26, 1840
Henley, John	Phebe Sladen	Mar. 17, 1787
Hendrick, Benj. F.	Jennings, Jane B.	Jan. 8, 1824
Henry, Barney	Mary Callan	Aug. 13, 1846
Henry, Dexter	Nancy Hopkins	Oct. 28, 1828
Henry, John	Mrs. Nancy Gould	Nov. 24, 1821
Henry, John W.	Mrs. Mary Mantz	June 26, 1849
Henry, Walter	Catherine Chiflan (?)	Dec. 2, 1840
Herbert, William	Mary Clancy	Nov. 11, 1843
Herrin, James H.	Julia Bloxsom	Mar. 8, 1849
Herrin, Joseph	Mary Ann Cliat	Jan. 1, 1846
Hester, Wm.	Susannah Weaver	Dec. 21, 1813
Hewlett, Augustine	Margaret Fulcher	Dec. 12, 1808
Hewlett, Augustine	Sevicia Brown	Nov. 17, 1810
Hibler, Isaac A.	Judy S. Keith	Dec. 24, 1833
Hicks, Daniel	Saliva McNeil	Sept. 26, 1842
Hicks, Elijah, Jr.	Sally Corley	Dec. 11, 1845
Higginbotham, James	Julia Tucker	Dec. 16, 1824
Hightower, Wm. B.	Lucinda Hill	May 28, 1839
Hilborn, Levy	Elizabeth Williams	Feb. 1, 1825
Hill, Augustin S.	Matilda A. Jones	Apr. 25, 1838
Hill, Benj. K.	Mrs. Susannah C. Sting	July 3, 1828
Hill, George	Anne B. Sims	Oct. 24, 1826
Hill, Henry B.	Mrs. Ann Walsh	Oct. 23, 1831
Hill, James	Cynthia Burkes	Nov. 8, 1821
Hill, John	Eliz. Champen	Feb. 5, 1797
Hill, John	Mary Davis	July 14, 1808
Hill, John	Eliz. Lantrip	Feb. 5, 1810
Hill, John	Eliz. Carter	Dec. 15, 1810
Hill, John	Mrs. Juneta Pond	Aug. 29, 1844
Hill, John	Rebecca Russell	Nov. 15, 1846
Hill, Wm.	Mary E. Carrie	Mar. 8, 1848
Hills, Nathan	Susannah Reily	June 10, 1792
Hitt, Charles	Susan A. Goodman	Feb. 23, 1832
Hitt, Daniel F.	Elizabeth H. Roberts	Dec. 22, 1831
Hobbs, Wm.	Martha Holley	Apr. 16, 1795
Hobby, Wm. I.	Polly Williamson	Feb. 1, 1803
Hobby, Wm. J.	Lear A. Hartridge	Sept. 29, 1825
Hobby, Wm. J., Jr.	Eliz. A. Mathews	Oct. 14, 18-6
Hodge, David	Rachel Dermot	June 18, 1845
Hodge, John	Mary Washington Carter	July 22, 1808
Hodgen, Wm.	Agness Childrey	Dec. 11, 1787

GROOM	BRIDE	DATE
Hodges, Henry W.	Mary Beal	Apr. 25, 1814
Hodges, James	Nancy Stuart	Mar. 21, 1832
Holcombe, James	Mrs. Ann Gardner	Sept. 29, 1835
Holcombe, Wm. M.	Maria Louisa Bugg	Apr. 23, 1831
Holder, Richard C.	Harriott J. Holder	Dec. 7, 1818
Holderfield, Joseph H.	Martha Ann Tumblefield	Mar. 9, 1840
Holdford, Matthew H.	Mrs. Mary B. Fisher	June 30, 1832
Holland, Alexander S.	Eliz. B. McGruder	Apr. 26, 1838
Holland, Green B.	Mary Cart	July 13, 1826
Holley, Eli	Eliz. Atkinson	Apr. 9, 1827
Holley, James	Mary Bryant	Mar. 21, 1796
Hollinshead, Jno.	Eliz. Dunham	May 22, 1790
Hollinshead, Jno.	Eliza Caroline Cart	Apr. 22, 1824
Hollsonbake, Matthew	Martha Weakley	Feb. 25, 1815
Holly, John	Martha Vaughn	Apr. 10, 1839
Holman, Francis	Mortava Clara	May 29, 1845
Holman, Thornton	Martha Legan	July 20, 1817
Holme, Horatio N.	Margaret McMurray Fleming	Apr. 13, 1824
Holmes, Hodgen	Eliz. Watson	May 21, 1798
Holms, D. G.	Barbara Galphin	May 15, 1805
Holsey, Charles A.	Eliz. Bridget Mageron	May 10, 1849
Holsomback, Thos. L.	Catherine Moore	Dec. 24, 1848
Holsombake, Henry L.	Catherine Moore	Jan. 19, 1849
Holsombake, Matthew	Anna Dismukes	Apr. 16, 1810
Holt, Elbert A.	Rebecca Hart	Oct. 5, 1825
Holt, Thomas Tournay	Eliz. E. E. Burke	June 30, 1825
Holt, Wm.	Martha Clanton	Aug. 30, 1815
Holt, Wm. W.	Mary A. Ware	May 31, 1820
Holtz, Wm.	Nancy Netherland	Mar. 31, 1824
Hood, Benjamin	Ann Barlow	Jan. 5, 1822
Hopkins, Greenbury	Mary Eliz. Jones	Mar. 17, 1841
Hopkins, Seamon P.	Malabeth Byrd	Oct. 20, 1835
Hopkins, Thomas	Rebecca Lambeth	Nov. 2, 1837
Hora, Henry	Sophia T. Flournoy	Mar. 7, 1839
Horn, John	Eliz. Reed	Feb. 13, 1790
Hornaday, Nathan	Ruth Moore	Aug. 11, 1789
Horton, Josiah	Eliz. H. May	Feb. 4, 1841
Houghton, Michael F.	Eliz. Harris	Nov. 2, 1798
Howard, Altemont E. M.	Martha King	Apr. 15, 1847
Howard, Aquila	Eliz. Short	May 9, 1790
Howard, Benjamin	Eliz. Gordon	May 2, 1816
Howard, John	Louisa Stoner	Apr. 3, 1806
Howard, John F.	Rhoda Osborne	Aug. 19, 1831
Howard, Thomas	Agnes Benett	May 30, 1785
Howard, Thomas	Henrietta David	Jan. 14, 1813
Howard, Thomas H.	Martha B. Liverman	May 1, 1841
Howe, Joseph	Eliza Howe	Aug. 25, 1817
Howel, Daniel	Cathrine Wall	Mar. 23, 1798
Howell, Henry	Martha Foster	Nov. 27, 1828
Howell, Malachi	Elizabeth Harris	Sept. 24, 1799
Hubbard, Osborn	Mary Ann Gould	Mar. 5, 1827
Hudsen, David	Juliet M. Hall	Dec. 25, 1834
Hudson, Elbert	Eliz. Hammet	Dec. 13, 1848
Hudson, Hampton A.	Indiana Williams	Dec. 18, 1836
Hudson, Isaac	Mary Shepherd	Dec. 21, 1785
Huestis, Moses B.	Elizabeth Boyd	Mar. 31, 1824
Huff, John	Eliz. Roberts	Jan. 11, 1819
Huggins, Abraham	Eliza Lee	Sept. 28, 1830
Hughes, David	Eliza E. Hicks	Aug. 15, 1844
Hughes, Micajah	Mary Jane Camfield	July 11, 1832
Hughes, Wm. W.	Julia Wanton	Mar. 12, 1823
Hull, George J.	Sarah Williams	Nov. 12, 1795
Hull, James F.	Magdalane Agatha O'Keeffe	Dec. 23, 1802
Hull, Thomas	Levicy Murphey	July 3, 1817
Hungerford, Jno. T.	Susan G. McWharter	Jan. 19, 1840
Hunster, Lewis	Milly Moore	Dec. 26, 1794
Hunt, Edward	----- -----	Dec. 27, 1839
Huntington, Alfred	Caroline Sims	May 19, 1818

GROUP	BRIDE	DATE
Huntington, C. C.	Mary Jane Evans	Sept. 2, 1847
Hurst, Jeremiah	Mary Kelly	Jan. 14, 1847
Hurt, Richard	Eliz. Hall	Jan. 6, 1839
Hust, Harmon	Mary Roney	Mar. 22, 1819
Hutchens, Rigdon	Eliz. Vilanda Aldridge	May 22, 1847
Hutcheson, Adam	Susan D. Nye	Feb. 10, 1825
Hutchinson, John S.	Mary Jane Sophie Burroughs	Feb. 14, 1842
Hutchinson, Joseph J.	Mary A. Jackson	Jan. 1, 1835
Hutchinson, S. P.	J. D. Skinner	Oct. 10, 1848
Hutchinson, Wm.	Anne Burnes	Dec. 7, 1822
Immel, Phillip	Emily Gardner	Oct. 8, 1845
Inabet, John	Arabella Darby	Apr. 23, 1835
Inglet, Abraham	Sarah Fergerson	Oct. 3, 1825
Inglet, Andrew	Mahala Philips	Jan. 12, 1827
Inglet, Andrew Jackson	Martha Matilda Balckston	Nov. 23, 1841
Inglet, Hugh	Milley Dismukes	Dec. 14, 1822
Inglet, Matthew W.	Annis Bagget	Dec. 1, 1828
Inglet, Wm.	Nancy Blackstone	Sept. 8, 1818
Irby, Henry W. M.	Charity Baker	Sept. 13, 1835
Iverson, Alfred	Julia Forsyth	Apr. 7, 1831
Iverson, Robert	Margaret Harris	Mar. 25, 1808
Jackson, George Twiggs	Catherine Wyman Mixer	Dec. 15, 1846
Jackson, James U.	Malvina C. Williamson	Jan. 18, 1838
Jackson, John K.	Louisa Virginia Hardwick	Mar. 8, 1849
Jackson, Jno. W. W.	Eliz. Lee	Feb. 27, 1829
Jackson, Julius	Sally A. Sloan	May 6, 1828
Jackson, Richard	Peggy Hatcher	Feb. 19, 1803
Jacobs, James Madison	Mrs. Emma Barker	Jan. 30, 1840
Jacobs, Methias	Caroline Bowley	Feb. 2, 1846
James, Green B.	Marrandy Dees	Dec. 20, 1845
James, James B.	Mahaly Smith	Oct. 4, 1824
James, John	Nancy King	Mar. 7, 1836
James, John R.	Ann Dees	June 29, 1845
James, Jordan	Nancy Osalt	Jan. 3, 1820
James, Joseph	Eliza Bullard	Apr. 11, 1820
James, Joseph	Lavina Mason	Dec. 9, 1820
James, Josiah	Mary Ann Buck	Dec. 1, 1839
James, Wm.	Mary McGinn	Jan. 27, 1798
James, Wm.	Dicey Rhodes	Oct. 14, 1836
James, Wm. Henry	Nancy Wray	Aug. 16, 1846
James, Wm. W.	Avey Haney	Aug. 14, 1826
Jaroney, Morris	Martha Duke	Feb. 16, 1824
Jarratt, Archelaus	Martha Key	Nov. 14, 1796
Jarvis, Floyd	Sarah Hawkins	Aug. 24, 1799
Jarvis, Floyd	Nancy Sneed	July 11, 1807
Jarvis, Richard	Harriet Roff	Feb. 28, 1836
Jenkins, Arthur	Sarah Morris	Nov. 26, 1785
Jenkins, James	Lucy A. Bryant	May 31, 1845
Jenkins, John	Frances L. Barrett	Nov. 9, 1835
Jenkins, John	Susannah Parish	Aug. 5, 1849
Jenkins, Joshua	Mrs. Mary Watkins	Nov. 19, 1819
Jenkins, Richard	Jane Smith	Mar. 30, 1800
Jernigan, Hardy Rice	Rebecca Lee	Dec. 28, 1791
Jessup, Geo. R.	Minerva Johnston	Apr. 18, 1833
Jewel, Kinchen	Elizabeth Harrison	Apr. 9, 1806
Jewett, Joseph	Margaret J. Stokes	Dec. 16, 1834
Johnson, Benjamin	Caroline Marshall	May 18, 1837
Johnson, Cesar	Prissilla Kelly	Jan. 25, 1807
Johnson, Elijah	Sally Collins	Nov. 26, 1808
Johnson, Elisha R.	Eliz. W. Knight	Sept. 18, 1832
Johnson, Emanuel	Mary Kinklin	Aug. 4, 1824
Johnson, Hardee	Effy Samond	Mar. 14, 1847
Johnson, Henry	Mary B. Rhodes	Oct. 16, 1832
Johnson, James	Mary Nally	Dec. 30, 1824
Johnson, James B.	Sophia Watkins	Oct. 6, 1835
Johnson, Jeremiah	Eliz. Dick	Dec. 25, 1837

GROOM	BRIDE	DATE
Johnson, Jeremiah	Eliz. Tant	Dec. 17, 1844
Johnson, Jesse	Locreshia Watson	Mar. 27, 1823
Johnson, Jesse, Jr.	Louisa Tinley	Jan. 21, 1849
Johnson, John	Nancy Reynolds	Apr. 30, 1826
Johnson, Moses A.	Harriet R. Greene	Feb. 27, 1844
Johnson, Richard H.	Catharine Maclean	Jan. 4, 1823
Johnson, Robert	Jane Lacy	July 9, 1808
Johnson, Thomas	Susanna Dunn	Aug. 8, 1786
Johnson, Walter E.	Sarah W. Walker	Oct. 14, 1840
Johnson, Wm.	Judith Cliatt	July 17, 1821
Johnson, Wm.	Mary Mealy	July 25, 1836
Johnson, Wm. L.	Ann E. Kunze	Oct. 10, 1847
Johnston, Adam	Ann Eliza A. Walker	Apr. 13, 1837
Johnston, Daniel	Cirlenda Ellis	Sept. 2, 1787
Johnston, Hugh	Catherine McPherson	July 22, 1829
Johnston, Dr. Wm.	Mrs. Elizabeth Howard	Dec. 28, 1825
Jones, Abraham	Eliz. Watson Beal	July 27, 1802
Jones, Alexander	Sarah Mattox	Nov. 4, 1841
Jones, Charles	Eliz. Brownson	Jan. 18, 1804
Jones, Chas.	Mrs. Mary Darling	Nov. 26, 1818
Jones, Charles F.	Mrs. Mary Bennet	Jan. 19, 1826
Jones, Charles F.	Nancy Morrison	May 8, 1834
Jones, Chauncey	Mary H. Pearson	Nov. 8, 1821
Jones, David	Emily Williams	Dec. 18, 1831
Jones, Hardy	Sarah Ann Harvey	Dec. 21, 1826
Jones, Henry	Frances Jones	Dec. 21, 1797
Jones, Henry	Amelia Jones	June 18, 1817
Jones, Henry T.	Frances M. Allen	Mar. 20, 1839
Jones, Hezekiah	Obedience Mitchell	Aug. 4, 1792
Jones, James	Mary Darling	July 3, 1792
Jones, Joel	Bathsheba Towtrip	June 23, 1790
Jones, Joel	Nancy Middleton	July 3, 1792
Jones, John	Eliz. Thomas	June 22, 1811
Jones, John Washington	Rebecca Smith	Mar. 2, 1843
Jones, Joseph	Elizabeth Cliatt	Apr. 1, 1819
Jones, Joseph B.	Sarah A. Lewis	Mar. 31, 1842
Jones, Joshua	Sally Morris	Aug. 5, 1795
Jones, Joshua	Elizabeth Loyd	July 23, 1840
Jones, Josiah	Mrs. Eliz. Barham	Mar. 20, 1832
Jones, Rev. Lot	Priscilla McMillan	June 1, 1825
Jones, Lucius	Sarah Daniels	Feb. 25, 1843
Jones, Richard	Mary Shorte	Jan. 26, 1787
Jones, Samuel W.	Christiana Tobler	Nov. 1, 1798
Jones, Seaborn	Eliz. Harris	Oct. 6, 1807
Jones, Stephen	Martha Watson	Sept. 27, 1838
Jones, Thomas	Elizabeth Boyd	Mar. 24, 1792
Jones, Thomas	Catharine Mead	Jan. 20, 1803
Jones, Thomas	Priscilla Jones	Dec. 30, 1818
Jones, Wm.	Corrally Boisclair	July 28, 1810
Kilburn, Joseph K.	Sarah Pucket	Feb. 28, 1844
Kimball, Bartholomew	Mary Kennedy	May 7, 1817
Kimbell, John	Sarah Bush	June 30, 1819
Kimbell, John H.	Elvira Smith	June 10, 1818
Kinder, David	Polly Simpson	Mar. 3, 1802
Kindrick, Wm. O.	Mary McLeam	July 2, 1828
King, Allen	Vine James	Nov. 29, 1846
King, Augustus	Clara H. White	Aug. 13, 1845
King, James L.	Sarah Ann Stubbs	Apr. 30, 1843
King, Jesse	Jane Davis	May 17, 1832
King, John	Celia Reed	Apr. 12, 1797
King, John T.	America M. Pardue	Nov. 2, 1845
King, Reuben	Elisa Ann Dees	Jan. 24, 1847
King, Richard	Dolly Lessoms	Sept. 9, 1808
Kirkpatrick, Daniel	Ann M. St. Marey(?)	Feb. 24, 1823
Kirkpatrick, Daniel, Jr.	Mary A. Robertson	Nov. 16, 1848
Kirkpatrick, James	Lucy S. Wamble	Jan. 29, 1821
Kirkpatrick, John	Mary St. Marys	Jan. 29, 1829

GROOM	BRIDE	DATE
Kitchen, Wm. K.	Sarah Ann Hill	Apr. 30, 1837
Kite, John	Mary Dicks	Oct. 19, 1796
Klein, John	Margaret Jones	Apr. 30, 1836
Knapen, Thomas	Emily Hughes	Aug. 24, 1813
Knaves, John	Sarah Brigs	Apr. 13, 1815
Knaves, John	Eliz. Stokes	Sept. 16, 1816
Knight, Enoch	Susan Bugg	Sept. 3, 1823
Knight, James	Eliz. Vallotton	Nov. 29, 1810
Knight, John	Sarah Tarver	Mar. 9, 1803
Knight, Latty	Polly Burch	Apr. 13, 1802
Knowlten, Augustus	Ann Sims	Nov. 26, 1835
Knox, Peter	Eliza B. Magruder	Oct. 5, 1823
Kraatz, John	Eliz. Tally	Nov. 20, 1799
Kunze, John L.	Ellen A. Lane	Nov. 1, 1833
Kurkendall, Robt.	Rebecca Ennis	Nov. 2, 1837
Labuzan, Bartholomew	Amelia Formon Boisclair	Oct. 7, 1813
Labuzan, Lewis	Mary E. W. Boisclair	Jan. 17, 1828
Lacey, Wm.	Mary Moore	July 20, 1789
Lafitte, Edward	Cecilia Brux	Feb. 4, 1839
Lallerstedt, L. D.	Amanda Clarke	Nov. 7, 1844
Lallerstedt, Larson	Mary Dalton	Nov. 30, 1809
Lallerstedt, Larson	Rebecca Wallace	Apr. 18, 1820
Lamar, Basil	Rebecka Kelly	Jan. 21, 1795
Lamar, G. B.	Jane M. Cresswell	Oct. 17, 1821
Lamar, George W.	Sarah Ann Talbot	May 21, 1823
Lamar, Geo. W.	Sarah W. Green	July 8, 1835
Lamar, James, Jr.	Alasanak Howard	Jan. 24, 1790
Lamar, John T.	Louisa V. Wray	Nov. 21, 1826
Lamb, Bernard	Mary Jane Malone	Sept. 22, 1847
Lamback, Charles F.	Eliz. Sharp	Feb. 3, 1835
Lambeth, John	Sally Sikes	Mar. 31, 1808
Lambeth, John	Mary Bond	Apr. 10, 1812
Lambeth, John	Sarah Hammond	Sept. 7, 1820
Lambeth, Thomas	Lucy Mills	Feb. 5, 1823
Lames, David	Francis Lames	Feb. 3, 1844
Lamkin, Sampson	Martha Carter	Jan. 25, 1811
Landen, Samuel	Misera Weeks	Jan. 10, 1838
Lang, Robert	Helena Prignet	Feb. 10, 1817
Lang, Thomas	Maria E. Savage	Aug. 14, 1823
Lang, Wm. B.	Mary Eliza Brown	Dec. 31, 1845
Langford, Carter	Mary Vigal	Feb. 3, 1821
Langley, James E.	Nancy Brown	Dec. 29, 1835
Lantern, Thomas	Liley White	Apr. 21, 1818
Lanthorn, John	Delilah Morgan	Oct. 2, 1820
Lanthrin, John	Eliz. Prescott	Apr. 9, 1803
Lark, Samuel	Sarah Bugg	Mar. 5, 1818
Lark, Wm. G.	D. Mont	Mar. 24, 1841
Larkin, Patrick	Judy Robertson	Apr. 15, 1844
La Roche, Isaac	Eliza Oliver	June 15, 1809
Latast, Victor	Eliz. A. Hatcher	Feb. 3, 1839
Laventure, Jno. P.	Eugenia Carre	Apr. 22, 1839
Law, Josiah S.	Ellen S. Barrett	Jan. 13, 1831
Lawrence, Garrett	Eliza Humphries	Aug. 29, 1828
Lawrence, Wm. W.	Margaret Ann Moss	Feb. 20, 1846
Lawrence, Wm. Washington	Selty Hargrove	Jan. 6, 1827
Lawrence, Wm. Washington	Catherine Smith	May 21, 1842
Lawson, Albert	Sarah Wyette	Dec. 9, 1828
Lawson, Washington	Sarah Jane Clark	Sept. 4, 1828
Lawson, Wm.	Rachael Felps	Nov. 9, 1786
Lee, Christopher	Cosana Mullen	July 2, 1842
Lee, Ira	Keziah McCready	Apr. 27, 1837
Lee, John	Isabella Fletcher	Aug. 16, 1816
Lee, Jno. J. P.	Mary E. Darby	Nov. 9, 1841
Lee, Lewis	Jenny Triplet	Feb. 22, 1802
Leeds, Nathan	Mary Silbert	Nov. 25, 1820
Leigh, Westly	Ann McCurdy	July 2, 1829
Leith, Charles	Mary Gardner	Jan. 9, 1813

401

GROOM	BRIDE	DATE
Leitner, Henry D.	Mary N. Kirkpatrick	Apr. 28, 1838
Lemeunier, Maturin	Eliz. Mason	May 14, 1818
Lemle, Daniel	Eliz. Webster	Jan. 8, 1801
Lenoir, Fisher	Christianna Jones	Sept. 14, 1802
Leon, Henry L.	Laura Jane Taylor	Jan. 6, 1847
Leon, Lewis	Sarah Meckie	June 15, 1818
Leonard, Samuel	Susannah Birns	Sept. 8, 1821
Leslie, James	Harriott Askew	Mar. 12, 1816
Letherin, John James	Polly Tindley	Apr. 23, 1793
Leverman, Samuel	Boulward Sydney	Jan. 11, 1816
Levy, Isaac	Angelica Hydenfell	Apr. 6, 1841
Levy, Lewis	Jane Florence	Aug. 1, 1827
Lewis, Andrew Jackson	Sarah Rosier	June 13, 1847
Lewis, Oliver J.	Harriet S. Rebo	Dec. 20, 1835
Ligon, Alexander	Caroline Skinner	Feb. 29, 1824
Lin, Rees H.	Amanda M. Sargent	July 29, 1834
Lindsey, Wm.	Martha Dismick	May 10, 1786
Lissenhoff, Frederick H.	Eliza Edrington	Mar. 2, 1814
Little, George	Mary King	Feb. 27, 1845
Little, Isaac A.	Vina Collins	Nov. 2, 1848
Little, Thadeus	Clarissa Bridwell	June 4, 1849
Lively, Mark	Jane Boyd	Feb. 4, 1836
Liverman, John	Eliz. Moore	June 7, 1805
Liverman, Thos. L.	Ann Nichols	Apr. 23, 1835
Livingston, Altamont M.	Frances Wamble	Nov. 1, 1827
Livingston, Geo.	Mrs. Eliz. Wright	Apr. 16, 1822
Livingston, James	Nancy Busby	Aug. 16, 1832
Livingston, James	Emma L. Hartridge	Sept. 30, 1834
Livingston, John	Anngenett Read	July 24, 1845
Livingston, Lewis	Laura T. Stoy	May 17, 1835
Lockhart, John	Sarah Ann Lott	Sept. 10, 1840
Lockhart, Samuel	Mary Moore	Jan. 10, 1798
Lockington, Samuel	Eliz. Fee	Sept. 21, 1799
Locklin, Wm.	Mary Foster	May 30, 1798
Longstreet, Gilbert	Betsy H. Leigh	Nov. 2, 1812
Longstreet, James	Mary Ann Dent	Dec. 30, 1812
Longstreet, Wm.	Mary Ann D. White	Nov. 13, 1823
Lott, George	Jane Eliz. Willingham	July 5, 1830
Lott, John S.	Sarah A. Liverman	June 23, 1825
Loughran, John	Mary Robinson	June 15, 1843
Lowe, Henry H.	Maria J. Tarver	Aug. 25, 1821
Lowell, Wm.	Amanda Melton	Mar. 6, 1838
Loyd, Jesse	Eliz. Watkins	Aug. 20, 1837
Loyless, Elliot B.	Nancy B. Rhodes	Oct. 19, 1829
Luck, James	Mary Reed	Sept. 27, 1848
Luckey, James	Sarah Conner	Nov. 13, 1802
Lucky, Abraham	Maria People	Dec. 6, 1844
Lucky, Isaac	Eliz. Thompson	Feb. 9, 1844
Lucky, John	Mary Prather	Apr. 9, 1823
Lucky, Jno. M.	Mary Averett	Nov. 4, 1836
Lucky, Samuel	Floran Mercer	Nov. 20, 1839
Lucky, Wm.	Martha Collins	July 23, 1822
Lufburrow, Orland H.	Laura L. Wray	Nov. 29, 1849
Luke, Wm. B.	Rebecca Neson	Nov. 2, 1843
Lumpkin, Phillip	Nancy Bugg	Dec. 11, 1813
Lutgert, John C.	Mary Deane	Feb. 15, 1800
Luther, Jeremiah	Mary Ward	Sept. 23, 1819
Luthringer, Valentine	Agnes Simon	Apr. 7, 1842
Lynch, Christopher	Mary Carmon	Sept. 9, 1826
Lynch, James	Johanah Maher	Feb. 22, 1848
Lynch, Michael	Ellen Flannegan	Sept. 1, 1847
Lynch, Peter	Briget Megan	July 1, 1843
Lynes, James	Polly Clanton	July 23, 1823
Lyon, James	Rachael Collins	Sept. 29, 1814
Lyon, James	Mary Newman	July 10, 1823
Lyon, John	Elizabeth Coleman	Aug. 2, 1811
Lyon, Jonathan	Mary Moye	May 7, 1813
Lyons, Benj. F.	Mary Jane Taylor	Aug. 17, 1848

GROOM	BRIDE	DATE
Macafee, James	Sarah Prater	Jan. 2, 1794
McAlister, Archibald	Adeline E. Reines	Apr. 30, 1849
McAllister, James	Sarah Allen	Jan. 5, 1830
McAllister, Moses Sidney	Mary C. Reynolds	Oct. 30, 1843
McAllister, Robt.	Sarah Ann Sidney Clark	Dec. 27, 1838
McCafferty, James	Mary E. Parmelee	Feb. 3, 1841
McCafrey, Lawrence	Mary Muse	May 16, 1837
McCahey, Patrick	Mary B. Reilly	Sept. 27, 1849
McCain, William	Eliz. Watkins	May 19, 1827
McCann, Jordan	Levina Ganas	Nov. 3, 1842
McCarthy, John	Pamelia Philips	Sept. 8, 1818
McCarty, George	Emily S. Duval	July 2, 1846
McCarty, Madison	Henrietta Flawrence	Dec. 28, 1837
McCarty, Sampson	Eliz. Byrd	Dec. 7, 1837
McCaskel, John	Eliza Nelson	July 14, 1810
McCathren, Daniel	Lucinda Ingram	Oct. 24, 1833
McColl, J. M.	Lucia Greenwood	May 18, 1841
McCollough, Jacob	Sukey Lambeth	Jan. 18, 1810
McCollough, Michael	Nancy Nagle	June 1, 1839
McCollough, Samuel	Margaret Allen	June 26, 1816
McComb, Andrew	Zilpha Glenn	Nov. 28, 1813
McCord, Zacheriah	Mary E. Collier	Nov. 18, 1847
McCormick, Daniel	Catherine A. Leitner	Dec. 8, 1831
McCoy, Charles M.	Frances A. Tutt	Aug. 13, 1835
McCoy, Lewis	Jane Brandon	Dec. 24, 1803
McCoy, Wm.	Ann Jane Collins	Nov. 25, 1827
McCue, Patrick	Minerva Ann Bridewell	Dec. 26, 1848
McCullack, Charles	Mary Wilkes	Dec. 4, 1806
McCullough, Henry	Mrs. Sarah Tally	Jan. 17, 1805
McCurdy, John	Susannah Hills	Nov. 30, 1790
McDade, Amanda	Evelina Pool	June 20, 1846
McDade, John	Milly Fortuneberry	Feb. 20, 1801
McDade, John	Eliza McTyre	Dec. 27, 1831
McDade, L. B.	Litha Ann Ingram	Feb. 14, 1834
MacDade, L. B.	Huldy Skinner	Aug. 20, 1849
McDade, Thomas	Martha Wasdon	Dec. 5, 1807
McDade, Wm.	Nancy Fortuneberry	Dec. 24, 1812
McDermatt, Stephen	Eliz. Edney	Dec. 20, 1826
McDonnell, Wm.	Cherry Rooney	Feb. 26, 1826
McDonough, James	Ellen Mitchell	June 1, 1829
McDowall, Thomas	Ann Reid	Dec. 30, 1818
McEachin, Archibald	Esther Stallings	Aug. 1, 1810
McElmurray, Geo.	Mary Ann D. Colson	Dec. 21, 1835
McFeely, Neal	Delia Ann Shaton	June 1, 1845
McGar, Edward	Martha Anderson	Nov. 6, 1804
McGar, John	Martha McGruder	Nov. 2, 1825
McGar, Owen	Mrs. Lear Grifforn	June 23, 1825
McGar, Wm.	Eliza Leath	Oct. 12, 1804
McGee, Jonathan	Rebekah James	Nov. 19, 1793
McGee, Lewis	Susan Culbreth	Jan. 12, 1848
McGlenan, John	Eliza Jordan	Mar. 14, 1822
McGohick(?), H. M.	Henrietta Myers	Feb. 12, 1848
McGowan, Zachariah	Louisa Hargroves	Feb. 5, 1823
McGowen, Jos. K.	Ann Downs	Dec. 3, 1848
McGran, Thomas	Mrs. Eliza Bones	Apr. 8, 1824
McGraw, John	Nancy Kennedy	Aug. 1, 1829
McGraw, Philip	Pamelia E. Greenville	Oct. 9, 1834
McKeen, Van L.	Jane E. Dill	Mar. 30, 1826
McKeen, Robt. W.	Mary Danforth	Oct. 12, 1830
McKeene, Wm. P.	Louisa M. Crawford	Mar. 23, 1826
McKenny, John	Eliza Collins	Jan. 9, 1824
Mackie, Wm.	Sarah Herbert	May 14, 1817
McKinley, Ebenezer D.	Mary A. Torrance	May 30, 1833
McKinne, Barna	Ann Galphin	Sept. 4, 1810
McKinne, Felix	Eliz. S. Law	Apr. 11, 1833
McKinne, John	Eliz. Malone	Dec. 11, 1798
McKinne, John E., Jr.	Maria E. Whitehead	Nov. 7, 1844
McKinne, Joseph P.	Ann Gardner	Apr. 13, 1813

GROOM	BRIDE	DATE
McKinney, David	Constance Sophia Bigar	Mar. 24, 1813
Macklemore, Matthew	Anne Bailey	Mar. 23, 1790
Macky, John	Willhillmina Hunter	Mar. 30, 1824
McLaughlin, Alexander R.	Eliz. W. Bugg	Dec. 28, 1830
McLaughlin, Gerrard	Laura C. Wray	June 3, 1829
McLaughlin, Wm.	Ellen Farrington	Dec. 3, 1833
McLaws, Abram	Sarah T. Porter	Nov. 2, 1848
Maclean, Andrew	Mrs. Jane Stevens	Jan. 12, 1826
McLeod, Hugh	Rebecca L. Lamar (?)	Oct. 24, 1844
McLeod, Robt.	Martha Hudnal	Aug. 14, 1790
McLester, Dr. Francis D.	Emily Rockwell	Feb. 2, 1846
McMahon, Francis	Sarah Ann Hix	Dec. 20, 1833
McMahon, Peter	Eliza Dunn	Feb. 13, 1836
McManes, Jno	Milly Riley	Dec. 15, 1804
McManus, Robert	Polly Cane	June 15, 1810
McMillan, Alexander	Martha Mead	Apr. 21, 1795
McMinn, Richard	Mary Bateman	May 14, 1845
MacMurphy, Daniel	Mary Lamb	May 1, 1816
MacMurphy, Geo. Y.	Keziah P. Martin	Nov. 28, 1805
McNair, Daniel	Ann Martin	Dec. 3, 1805
McNair, James	Eliz. Palmer	Dec. 21, 1825
McNair, John	Mary Lucky	Aug. 13, 1804
McNair, Lewis L.	Mars. Eleanor Pughley(?)	Feb. 4, 1833
McNair, Louis L.	Mrs. Margaret A. Jackson	Sep. 20, 1827
McNatt, Adam	Emeline T. Hurt	June 3, 1839
McNeil, John	Nancy McTyeire	June 12, 1799
McNeill, Daniel	Margret Marshel	Apr. 28, 1788
McNorton, James	Sarah McEvoy	July 5, 1849
McQuinn, Robert M.	Sarah Ann Morris	Nov. 27, 1845
McSweeney, Edmund	Henrietta Lucket	Dec. 22, 1823
McSwine, John	Eliz. Youngblood	Oct. 1, 1794
McTier, Francis	Eliz. H. Cluskey	Sept. 27, 1836
McTyere, Frizzell	Mary Murphy	Mar. 12, 1801
McTyre, Holland	Sarah Sinkfield	Oct. 27, 1795
McTyre, Robert	Eliz. Savage	Feb. 4, 1819
McWhorter, Hugh	Mary Harper	Sept. 3, 1841
Magee, David	Sarah Rooks	July 28, 1809
Magee, Hugh	Mary Dearmond	Oct. 25, 1800
Maginty, Hugh	Mildred Jones	Sept. 9, 1828
Magruder, N. T.	Eliz. B. Bussey	Feb. 21, 1833
Magruder, Samuel	Martha Ellis	Feb. 14, 1788
Maguire, Jas. P.	Sarah McFarland	Jan. 7, 1822
Maharry, Joseph P.	Mary Ann Barom	Sept. 29, 1820
Maher, John	Eliz. Claxton	July 27, 1816
Maher, Richard	Catherine Curran	Oct. 15, 1845
Mahony, Daniel	Mary Elvina Sinderine(?)	Dec. 1, 1838
Maise, David	Aylse McCormack	Jan. 15, 1787
Mallory, A. B.	Harriet R. Walker	Oct. 5, 1837
Malone, John	Ann Glascock	Mar. 7, 1811
Malone, Wm. P.	Keziah O. McMurphy	Oct. 19, 1829
Mann, John H.	Henrietta Stallings	July 13, 1811
Mann, Wm. J.	Eliz. Reiley	Nov. 27, 1841
Margerum, Simon	Bridget Godbee	July 16, 1843
Markes, Christopher	Catharine Shaken	Oct. 15, 1822
Marshall, John	Eliz. McGill	June 8, 1805
Marshall, John	Susan Kelly	June 13, 1838
Marshall, Joseph E.	Louisa Virginia Lamar	Oct. 2, 1842
Martin, Alexander	Nancy Clark	June 30, 1802
Martin, Alexander	Ann Savage	Jan. 2, 1810
Martin, Angus	Eliz. Lowe	Dec. 23, 1797
Martin, Angus	Mrs. Isabel Ringland	May 1, 1805
Martin, Angus	Mrs. Mary Sterrett	Nov. 4, 1818
Martin, Angus W.	Frances L. Thomas	Mar. 23, 1843
Martin, Charles	Eady Harriod	Dec. 28, 1785
Martin, Chas. B.	Amanda M. Millen	Sept. 28, 1837
Martin, Clem	Harriett Carrey(?)	Apr. 6, 1832
Martin, Hamilton	Betsey Brown	Jan. 26, 1832
Martin, James H.	Caroline Nichols	Jan. 4, 1841

GROOM	BRIDE	DATE
Martin, Joseph	Caty Preper	July 14, 1808
Martin, Richard	Eleanor Clarke	July 10, 1799
Marvin, Aaron	Mary M. Bussey	Oct. 21, 1833
Marye, R. V.	Sarah T. Blackwell	Dec. 5, 1816
Massingale, Alfred L.	Mrs. Esther M. Banks	Apr. 14, 1839
Mathews, Albert C.	Sophia F. Wooten	May 13, 1845
Mathews, Charles J.	Susan Frances Greenway	Feb. 22, 1849
Mathews, Geo. G.	Caroline I. Ringgold	Nov. 28, 1839
Mathews, Robert	Mary Murph	Mar. 18, 1849
Matthaei, Jno. Henry	Margaret Gordon	Oct. 6, 1808
Matthews, Graves	Matilda Gipson	July 23, 1819
Matthews, Wm.	Cathrine Collins	Nov. 23, 1812
Matthewson, Daniel	Delilah Cobb	Sept. 7, 1808
Mattox, Chesley	Mary Smith	Feb. 28, 1836
Maury, John O.	Hester Grimsley	Sept. 21, 1848
Maxwell, Edward	Jane Sinquefield	Mar. 12, 1787
Maxwell, James H.	Sarah Frances Dugas	June 24, 1845
May, Alfred	Susan Campbell	Dec. 26, 1840
May, Robt. H.	Josephine A. Calhoon	Feb. 27, 1845
Mays, Sampson	Mrs. Evelina Burgess	Feb. 9, 1843
Mayson, Charles C.	Margaret Eugenia Dubose	Oct. 29, 1823
Mazle, John	Mary Ann Burch	Jan. 28, 1817
Mazo, William	Sarah Prater	May 24, 1817
Mealing, Henry	Teresa Hunster	Mar. 27, 1814
Mealing, Wm.	Eliz. Mobley	June 22, 1822
Meals(?), Joshua	Mildred Jane Bostick	July 10, 1809
Measels, John	Margaret Hill	Jan. 8, 1818
Medlock, George	Mary Perre	Sept. 8, 1789
Megahe, Andre J.	Mary Russell	Nov. 12, 1841
Meigs, Jonathan	Tabitha Anthony	May 27, 1847
Melton, Silas L.	Winney Boyt	Feb. 8, 1846
Meredith, Jas. W.	Ann Knight	Nov. 4, 1840
Meredith, James W., Jr.	Sarah Ann Rigdell	Jan. 1, 1842
Meredith, John	Rebecca Hinton	Jan. 11, 1800
Meredith, Richard C.	Laura Ann Roath	Oct. 14, 1835
Meredith, Wm.	Eleanor Burges	May 15, 1819
Meriwether, James	Susannah Hatcher	May 14, 1790
Meriwether, Nicholas	Emily Glover	Nov. 4, 1845
Merritt, Henry	Malvina Maharry	Feb. 15, 1832
Metcalf, Geo. H.	Lorana D. Cheever	June 30, 1835
Meye, Wm. B.	----- -----	July 20, 1840
Meyer, David	Mary Brewer	Dec. 31, 1821
Meyer, John W.	Mary E. L. Lewis	Aug. 22, 1845
Meyers, James	Sarah Oliver	Sept. 1, 1822
Michael, Wm. H.	Eliza G. Ogletree	Nov. 23, 1833
Micon, Wm. C.	Anna D. Thompson	Feb. 16, 1831
Middleton, John	Eliz. Scott	Feb. 23, 1804
Miles, Byrd Anderson	Lucy Patterson	Aug. 24, 1808
Miller, Andrew J.	Martha B. Olive	Oct. 9, 1828
Miller, Baldwin B.	Rosina S. Morrison	Oct. 25, 1827
Miller, Francis	Hannah Messer	Sept. 2, 1820
Miller, James	Mary Ann Spiers	Nov. 1, 1825
Miller, James	Mary Eliz. Warren	Nov. 29, 1843
Miller, Jonathan M.	Margaret Smith	May 14, 1842
Miller, Nathaniel	Mary Slade(?)	May 14, 1795
Miller, Thomas W.	Julia C. Hardwick	Feb. 16, 1837
Milligan, Dr. Joseph	Eliz. Jones Camfield	Sept. 6, 1842
Milligan, Dr. Joseph A. S.	Octavia P. Camfield	Jan. 2, 1849
Milling, Samuel	Anaise Baudry	Apr. 14, 1842
Mills, Henry	Margaret Horne	July 21, 1831
Milton, Robert J.	Sarah Belcher	Dec. 7, 1832
Mimes, Charles E.	Eliza E. Martin	Dec. 8, 1828
Mims, James L.	Mrs. Amanda M. Cooper	Jan. 27, 1849
Minor, Christopher	Jane C. Robert	June 15, 1837
Mitchell, Benjamin	Morren Harris	July 30, 1789
Mitchell, Bird B.	Mary Ann Bagley	Oct. 21, 1828
Mitchell, Henry	Eliz. Bradberry	Oct. 25, 1826
Mitchell, John	Catherine C. A. Charles	Dec. 7, 1838

GROOM	BRIDE	DATE
Mitchell, Wm. S.	Emily L. Anthony	June 20, 1833
Moderwell, Wm.	Martha M. M. Jones	Jan. 23, 1821
Money, John	Mary Mendinghall	Oct. 8, 1789
Mongin, John D.	Laura E. Malone	July 7, 1836
Monk, Eli	Sarah Willis	Aug. 10, 1821
Monk, Willis	Frances Holly	Sept. 21, 1799
Monroe, Daniel	Sarah McNeill	Dec. 11, 1786
Montgomery, Hugh	Ann Williams	May 30, 1796
Montgomery, Col. Wm. W.	Janet S. Blair	Apr. 29, 1824
Moody, Anderson	Eliz. Williams	Aug. 27, 1828
Moody, James M.	Eliza Marshall Taylor	Aug. 11, 1839
Moody, James Madison	Catherine C. Roberts	Sept. 11, 1837
Moon, James	Ann Amelia Ogg	July 23, 1831
Moore, Augustus	Keziah Louisa Miller	Mar. 18, 1805
Moore, Augustus	Lucretia Hulburd	May 4, 1819
Moore, Jeffery	Isabella Lamar	Feb. 7, 1828
Moore, John	Catharine Thompson	Nov. 16, 1791
Moore, John	Eliz. Young	Jan. 14, 1801
Moore, John	Nancy Olear	Nov. 4, 1815
Moore, Naphthali Byram	Eliza Washington Woolfolk	Sept. 6, 1827
Moore, Thomas	Martha Jones	Mar. 29, 1804
Moore, William	Polly Hooker	Nov. 17, 1829
Moore, Wm.	Martha Ann Johnson	June 28, 1840
Moran, Basel	Winney Blackstone	Nov. 4, 1797
Morand, John	Mary A. C. Tardy	Aug. 15, 1821
Morgan, Andrew	Jane Burnett	Dec. 22, 1792
Morgan, Eldridge	Sally Morris	July 1, 1819
Morgan, Ellis	Margaret Morris	Feb. 14, 1827
Morgan, Frederick A.	Virginia M. Lewis	Jan. 18, 1837
Morgan, Frederick A.	Thank S. Coldwell	July 21, 1841
Morgan, George W.	Matilda A. Micon	Nov. 18, 1835
Morgan, James	Mary Dathney	Apr. 6, 1816
Morgan, James	Mrs. Elizabeth Windsor	Oct. 7, 1819
Morgan, Millenton	Mary Davis	Dec. 12, 1826
Morgan, Millenton	Eliz. Brown	Dec. 13, 1828
Morgan, Millenton	Mary Ann McGinnis	Feb. 21, 1829
Morgan, Moses	Alsie McCain	Dec. 28, 1810
Morgan, William	Frances Ann Seaye (?)	May 28, 1845
Morras, Nicholas	Sarah Harrigan	Sept. 1, 1792
Morris, Augustus F.	Eliz. Hughes	Aug. 13, 1846
Morris, Bartholomew	Olive Horn	Jan. 4, 1847
Morris, Edward	Martha Smith	Aug. 23, 1825
Morris, Jeremiah	Francis E. Bush	Oct. 8, 1840
Morris, John	Nancy Lesley	Apr. 1, 1806
Morris, Joseph	Anne Culbreath	Dec. 3, 1807
Morris, Needham	Eliz. Bradon	June 17, 1841
Morris, Robert	Sarah Haney	Jan. 7, 1833
Morris, Thomas	Nancy Bagget	Dec. 11, 1804
Morrison, John	Mary T. Parker	May 10, 1827
Mote, Jeremiah	Mary Butler	Sept. 4, 1790
Mote, John	Rachel Mote	May 21, 1790
Mountain, Robert	Mrs. Mary Hill	Apr. 24, 1828
Mounthesque, Daniel M.	Mrs. Eliz. Broadwater	Jan. 25, 1822
Moye, Thomas	Janet Fowler	Nov. 4, 1818
Mullen, Philip	Mary Megan	Nov. 9, 1847
Mullin, James	Amanda Lassiter	Dec. 26, 1844
Muncrief, Lewis	Nancy Kennon	June 9, 1831
Munro, R. W. B.	Sarah S. Ames	June 17, 1840
Murdock, Feilding W.	Letty Newman	Nov. 8, 1824
Murphey, Alexander	Muriah Tarver	Jan. 26, 1826
Murphey, Edmund	Eliz. Ann Gibbs	May 16, 1835
Murphey, James	Mary Rhodes	Jan. 30, 1786
Murphey, Leroy H.	Lucinda L. Brown	Oct. 7, 1830
Murphey, Milledge	Emmeline Miles	Dec. 17, 1830
Murphy, Absalem F.	Margaret Smith	Feb. 7, 1830
Murphy, Alexander	Eliz. Allen	Jan. 22, 1823
Murphy, Alexander	Eliza Kindlaw	Nov. 15, 1827
Murphy, James	Mary Fears	Nov. 19, 1804

GROOM	BRIDE	DATE
Murphy, John	Nancy Reynolds	Apr. 5, 1836
Murphy, Nicholas	Ann Collins	Jan. 30, 1805
Murphy, Timothy	Eliz. Atkison	Jan. 13, 1844
Murphy, Wm.	Adeline Sikes	Aug. 29, 1833
Murr (?), Thomas	Henrietta James	Sept. 21, 1843
Murrah, Charles	Mrs. Eliza Ross	Dec. 27, 1829
Murrah, Geo.	Eliz. McCaskell	Feb. 10, 1819
Murray, George	Eliz. McCaskill	Aug. 4, 1825
Murray, James	Catharine A. Pembleton	Feb. 13, 1822
Murray, John	Mary Holt	Aug. 30, 1819
Murray, Michael	Augusttae Primrose	June 12, 1843
Murray, Thomas	Eliz. Thompson	Mar. 17, 1842
Mustin, D. K.	C. P. Beal	Dec. 3, 1844
Musgrove, Edw. H.	Emma J. Thompson	June 11, 1845
Musgrove, Harrison	Amanda Ann McGar	Sept. 8, 1823
Musgrove, Robt. H.	Jane W. Bustin	May 8, 1816
Mustin, David R.	Rebecca Barger	July 31, 1845
Myers, Rev. Edw. H.	Mary A. F. Mackie	Feb. 13, 1845
Myers, Henry	Mrs. S. W. Rush	Oct. 12, 1845
Napier, Thomas	Mrs. Hester Ann Rockwell	Jan. 6, 1831
Nason, Elias	Mira A. Bigelow	Nov. 28, 1836
Nehr, Ambrose	Frances Buhiler	Apr. 30, 1837
Nehrig, Jno. Andrew	Nancy Pittman	Mar. 7, 1838
Neilson, John	Maria Dent	Oct. 10, 1809
Nelhums, Ezekial	Lucy McGowan	Apr. 6, 1842
Nellam, Daniel	Nancy Easter	Apr. 21, 1823
Neloms, Daniel	Mary Sego	Mar. 22, 1827
Nelson, John	Louisa C. Cooper	Feb. 6, 1840
Nelson, Matthew	Mrs. Charlotte Cooper	Sept. 1, 1830
Nelson, Thomas M.	Anna Matilda Carnes	Dec. 20, 1828
Nelson, Wm. H.	Melinda Danforth	Dec. 12, 1842
Nesbitt, Allen	Agnes Ann Taylor	July 30, 1807
Nesbitt, Hugh	Eleanor Lucinda O'Keefe	Feb. 7, 1810
Nesbitt, Hugh	Polly Barden	Feb. 10, 1800
Nesbitt, Thomas	Virginia L. Whitehead	May 23, 1844
Netherlin, James	Betsey Ann Cullers	Oct. 11, 1817
Netherlin, Wm.	Mary Collins	Nov. 10, 1819
Nettles, Israel	Eliz. Clarkson	Dec. 13, 1796
Nettles, Wm.	Nancy Bryson	Aug. 22, 1799
Neugent, Robt. W.	Sarah Neal	Sept. 26, 1835
Newhouse, Adam L.	Mary Jane Hatfield	Feb. 8, 1846
Newman, Geo. W.	Hulda Rachels	Feb. 10, 1846
Newman, James	Srah Blackstone	July 23, 1839
Newman, Martin	Flora Willis	Jan. 28, 1823
Newman, Sylvester P.	Angeline Hutchins	Dec. 7, 1846
Newman, Thomas B.	Nancy Green Rowlan	Apr. 19, 1849
Newman, Thomas J.	Eveline Blackstone	Feb. 21, 1839
Newman, Wm.	Sarah Anderson	Sept. 8, 1833
Newton, Alex I.	Elmina H. F. V. Dye	Dec. 3, 1834
Newton, Amos	Harriet Bonds	Sept. 1, 1806
Neyland, Wm. H.	Eliz. Calvin	July 9, 1840
Neyland, Wm. H.	Mary F. Barton	Apr. 27, 1837
Nickelson, James B.	Anna Maria Willey	Mar. 5, 1833
Nix, John L.	Nancy Busby	Jan. 23, 1840
Nix, John L.	Maria King	Feb. 3, 1831
Niven, James N.	Clarentine Cowling	Aug. 30, 1830
Noles, Gilbert	Johanah Haley	Jan. 5, 1847
Norman, James S.	Leah S. Marks	June 11, 1828
Norman, Joseph	Ann Brown	Feb. 27, 1814
Noris (?), John H.	Mary Ann Zinn	Apr. 14, 1840
Norrell, John B.	Eliza Hudson	May 28, 1827
Norwood, Wm.	Kisiah Langham	May 9, 1806
Nowland, Benj.	Nancy Barton	May 17, 1802
Nunn, James M.	Eleanor Watson	Dec. 27, 1838
Nute, Jeremiah	Hannah Darling	Dec. 14, 1843
Oates, Geo. A.	Sarah A. Wray	Oct. 23, 1849

GROOM	BRIDE	DATE
Oates, James	Sarah Clayton	June 28, 1806
O'Bryan, J.	Mary Ann Swiney	Aug. 8, 1843
Oden, Wm. N.	Jane McDonald	June 11, 1846
Odgen, Moses	Ann Eliza Jones	Aug. 30, 1837
Odom, James	Eliz. Odom	May 5, 1804
Odom, Moses	Nancy Robertson	Nov. 29, 1802
Odom, Richard	Jane Hancock	Feb. 12, 1846
O'Farrell, -----	----- Ramsay	Apr. 13, 1844
Offutt, Ezekiel	Jamima Wilkins	Mar. 26, 1788
Ogg, John	Mildred Garrett	July 24, 1793
Ogg, Thomas	Eliza Suggs	May 15, 1831
Ogg, Thomas	Martha Fulcher	Dec. 10, 1835
Ogletree, Gresham G.	Jane Reynolds	Aug. 22, 1838
O'Keefe, Michael	Mary Ann Galagher	Feb. 28, 1843
O'Keefe, Philip	Eliz. Dove	Sept. 7, 1815
O'Kelly, James	Mary A. Williams	Mar. 4, 1839
Olive, Abel	Matilda Blackston	Mar. 13, 1826
Oliver, Henry G.	Eliz. McDonough	July 24, 1831
Oliver, James	Eliz. Holmes	June 20, 1807
Oliver, James L.	Ann Dickinson	Feb. 25, 1813
Oliver, Stephen H.	Mrs. Mary R. E. Davis	May 8, 1832
Olmstead, Harvy	Mary Ann Pick	June 12, 1827
O'Neal, Wm.	Caroline Eliz. Edes	June 25, 1846
O'Neil, Henry P.	Adeline Quimain(?)	July 17, 1836
O'Neill, Hugh	Flora E. Campbell	Nov. 28, 1844
O'Neill, John	Mrs. Sarah Whiteley	Nov. 8, 1846
Onele, G. W.	Mary Ann -risco	Mar. 31, 1842
O'Reily, John	Eliz. Dove	Feb. 4, 1800
Orr, James	Eliz. Cooper	Dec. 30, 1824
Osborne, Judge Henry	Catharine Howell	Aug. 20, 1791
O'Shea, Jeremiah H.	Mary J. Reddy	Nov. 4, 1843
Oswalt, Hiram	Margaret Branham	Mar. 24, 1830
Oswalt, Samuel	Rosannah Tant	Oct. 2, 1834
Overstreet, Samuel	Margaret Kendely	Oct. 18, 1838
Owen, John	Ann S. Murphy	June 26, 1833
Owen, John G.	Susan R. Frayer	Jan. 23, 1843
Owens, A. B.	Eliz. McCaging	Mar. 24, 1839
Owens, Elisha	Eliz. Smith	Oct. 16, 1813
Owens, Wm. I.	Sarah A. Tarrence	Nov. 5, 1835
Pace, Dreadzil	Eley Tankersley	Apr. 1, 1813
Pace, James	Mrs. Sarah Prescott	Sept. 6, 1827
Page, Ebenezer	Eliza Ann Cook	Oct. 2, 1849
Page, Solomon	Jane Chavons	Dec. 4, 1839
Page, William	Mary Evans	Oct. 2, 1835
Palmblade, John G.	Milly Bradshaw	July 23, 1818
Palmer, Benj.	Isabella Hendrick	Feb. 15, 1817
Palmer, Benj.	Gracey Washington	Oct. 8, 1848
Palmer, David	Martha C. Collins	Aug. 24, 1826
Palmer, Edmund	Jane Allen	Feb. 18, 1819
Palmer, Edmund	Laura M. Antony	July 26, 1837
Palmer, George	Catharine Cawley	Mar. 31, 1842
Palmer, George R.	Levenia A. Rhodes	Apr. 3, 1845
Palmer, Henry A.	Mrs. Jane More	July 13, 1841
Palmer, James	Mary Collins	July 28, 1825
Palmer, John B.	Emily Barlow	Nov. 2, 1835
Palmer, Wm.	Eliz. Fitzgerald	Nov. 9, 1805
Palmer, Willis	Catherine Louisa Collins	May 29, 1832
Pannel, Elijah J. B.	Caroline M. Kepley	Sept. 21, 1837
Panton, James	Ann Savage	Oct. 26, 1811
Pardue, William Anthony	Mrs. Eliz. Lloyd	May 23, 1848
Parish, Greenbery	Eliz. Goodwin	Mar. 12, 1843
Parish, Henry	Martha Browne	Dec. 3, 1848
Parish, Wyatt	Martha Ades	Apr. 14, 1839
Parish, Wyatt	Sarah Berry	Oct. 11, 1845
Park, John T. S.	Tabitha A. Skinner	June 28, 1842
Parker, Ebenezer	Sarah Smarr	Oct. 26, 1839
Parker, Gustavus	Mary Ann Pool	Dec. 19, 1816

GROOM	BRIDE	DATE
Parker, James C.	Mary Ann Fountain	Dec. 6, 1845
Parker, Richard	Sarah Hatley	Sept. 21, 1805
Parks, Aaron	Ann Baldwin	Aug. 7, 1787
Parmela, Henry E.	Mary Broadhurst	Mar. 6, 1838
Parmly, Jahial	Eliza Ann Pleasants	May 3, 1826
Parnell, Henry	Rebecca Lallerstedt	Dec. 27, 1827
Parnell, James	Margarette Wallace	Jan. 28, 1828
Parnell, James	----- -----	Sept. 26, 1836
Parnell, James	Eliza Ann Burch	Nov. 17, 1838
Parnell, James	Mahaley Morris	Feb. 2, 1840
Parr, John	Catharine Boyt	May 20, 1841
Parr, John	Martha Jenkins	Feb. 1, 1846
Parrish, G. F.	Mary A. White	Dec. 6, 1827
Parsons, Henry	Eliza M. Wilson	June 3, 1828
Pate, Thomas D.	Sarah A. D. Holmes	Feb. 2, 1825
Patrick, John	Jane Cleveland	Apr. 12, 1806
Patterson, David	Sarah White	Dec. 28, 1823
Patterson, John	Harriet McNair	Oct. 11, 1816
Paul, Samuel	Hannah Leith	June 16, 1817
Payne, Benj.	Mary Bell	July 5, 1802
Payne, Charles F.	Maria Clark	May 20, 1839
Payne, Wm.	Bridget M. Gehegen	June 29, 1825
Pearce, George W.	Mary A. Fudge	May 22, 1839
Pearre, James	Carandary Graves	Jan. 6, 1790
Pearre, Nathaniel	Anna ----lman	Dec. 22, 1789
Pearson, Geo.	Mrs. Lucy Moore Foll	Sept. 11, 1803
Pearson, Geo.	Catharine Hall	Dec. 14, 1805
Peay, Henry T.	Martha C. Jones	Oct. 29, 1845
Peck, Samuel N.	Mrs. S. A. D. Pate	Dec. 24, 1828
Peiffer, Solomon	Mrs. Johanna Murphey	Apr. 10, 1849
Pemberton, Alton H.	Mrs. Mary H. Jones	Apr. 8, 1824
Pemberton, Wm. F.	Mary H. S. Wightman	Oct. 1, 1840
Penn, George S.	Louisanna Mims	Nov. 20, 1828
Penn, Thomas H.	Mary Ann Pearce	Aug. 26, 1813
Perdieu, Morris	Ann Rosier	Jan. 17, 1794
Perdue, George W.	Ann Perdue	Aug. 3, 1842
Perdue, Peter	Sarah A. Nettles	Dec. 25, 1842
Perdue, Wm.	Ann Palmer	Dec. 21, 1826
Perdue, Wm. J.	Augusta Eliza Foster	May 5, 1846
Perrie, John	Eliz. Simmons	Dec. 5, 1793
Perryman, Elisha	Ruth Cobb	Nov. 28, 1787
Perrymore, Elisha	Martha Watson	Jan. 23, 1826
Perval, Joseph C.	Elizabeth Cowley	Mar. 16, 1826
Peters, John	Eliz. Felders	Jan. 13, 1840
Phelan, John	Catherine Duffie	Feb. 14, 1831
Philips, Asa	Nancy Herrington	Dec. 25, 1834
Phillips, Charles	Mrs. Mary Read	Nov. 19, 1831
Phillips, James	Mary Hill	Jan. 8, 1833
Philpot, David A.	Mary Atwell	June 22, 1845
Philpot, Henry R.	Isabella B. Green	Sept. 6, 1835
Philpot, John N.	Louisa Brennon	Jan. 22, 1825
Philpot, Thomas N.	Catharine Frederick	Feb. 2, 1847
Phinizy, Ferdinand	Harriet H. Bowdre	Feb. 22, 1849
Phinizy, John	Martha Creswell	July 20, 1814
Phinizy, Robert M.	Louisa H. Musgrove	June 13, 1843
Pickering, Alexander B.	Eliz. Miller	Jan. 12, 1840
Picket, Breght	Eliza Cole	Feb. 20, 1828
Picquet, Antonie	Caroline E. Catinell	Feb. 7, 1834
Picquet, Benj.	Matilda Askew	May 9, 1827
Pierce, Benj.	Barbara Kennedy	Oct. 29, 1808
Pierce, Dr. Hamilton R.	Mary G. B. Musgrove	May 8, 1849
Pierce, Thomas F.	Ann D. Malone	Jan. 25, 1849
Pierce, Wm.	Drusella Cousins	Feb. 2, 1819
Pillot, Andrew P.	Matilda M. L. Cowling	June 14, 1831
Pittman, James	Ann Dagnall	Dec. 13, 1835
Platt, Jacob B.	Frances G. Robert	Oct. 2, 1849
Plumb, Daniel B.	Ann S. Hankinson	June 23, 1847
Plunket, Thomas	Francis Cobb	Feb. 26, 1795

409

GROOM	BRIDE	DATE
Poe, Robert	Eliza P. White	Nov. 10, 1822
Poe, Wm.	Frances Winslow	Mar. 5, 1795
Pow, Wm.	Melvina L. M. Walker	Jan. 14, 1823
Polhill, Frederick A.	Mary Williams	Jan. 18, 1843
Pollan, Robert	Eliza Willcox	Jan. 10, 1814
Pomeroy, John W.	Nancy E. Demarest	Jan. 2, 1838
Pond, Wm.	Mary G. Masten	--- --, 1842
Pool, Jacob	Martha Davis	June 5, 1848
Poole, James A.	Marsh Adeline McCarty	Feb. 23, 1845
Porter, Silvester	Ann Maria Goodwin	Oct. 13, 1808
Powell, Frances H.	Ellen Connel	Feb. 23, 1842
Powell, Dr. John	Mrs. Ann Wilkinson	June 4, 1792
Powers, John W. W.	Margaret Stephens	Feb. 16, 1811
Powers, Nicholas Graham	Anne Conn	Mar. 9, 1814
Prather, Edward	Sarah Clayton	Oct. 16, 1806
Prendergast, James	Sarah Rogers	Apr. 17, 1824
Prescott, Milledge	Margaret Robbins	Mar. 13, 1820
Prescott, Patrick	Sarah Bush	Nov. 12, 1818
Preskitt, Seaborn A.	Mrs. Eliz. Johnson	Jan. 27, 1847
Preval, Joseph C.	Martha Harper	May 20, 1830
Price, Wm. E.	Mrs. Emma Wood	June 19, 1849
Prickett, David	Eliz. Trantham	Dec. 28, 1802
Prickett, Elijah	Nancy Averitt	Feb. 13, 1822
Prickett, Elisha	Nancy Hall	Aug. 22, 1830
Prickett, Gideon	Sarah Landers	Dec. 8, 1818
Primrose, James W.	T. A. Ridgdell	Mar. 4, 1849
Primrose, Patrick Henry	Mary Eliz. White	Nov. 26, 1848
Prince, Silvanus	Viney James	July 3, 1813
Pritchard, John W.	Ann West	Apr. 1, 1819
Pritchard, Wm. H.	Mrs. Jane A. Deinon	Aug. 13, 1833
Proctor, Henry	Susannah Lane	Dec. 24, 1838
Proctor, Patrick	Mary Stead	Apr. 28, 1841
Proctor, Thomas	Toyia Bowls	Mar. 3, 1840
Prudhomme, Louis	Mary Jane Lagard	Oct. 15, 1804
Puckett, Chat	Eliz. Aldridge	Jan. 7, 1797
Pumphrey, Jesse	Peggy Robinson	Jan. 10, 1803
Purdee, Thomas	Ellen Fields	Feb. 17, 1832
Pye, Thomas	Isabella Clark	May 3, 1817
Pyne, Benj.	Ellen Carn	June 6, 1838
Pyron, Lewis	Martha R. T. Greenwood	June 15, 1836
Quinn, Isham	Catharine Harvey	Apr. 1, 1799
Quinn, Patrick	Mrs. Mary Ann Cone	Nov. 25, 1847
Quizenberry, Thomas	Rebecca Powers	July 27, 1807
Rabb, Wm.	Hannah James	Jan. 10, 1804
Rachels, Berryam	Mary Allen	Apr. 15, 1849
Rachals, Ezekiel	Bethany Shaw	Mar. 31, 1831
Raiford, Hamilton	May E. W. Wells	Nov. 1, 1832
Rainey, John W.	Nancy Murphy	Dec. 25, 1834
Rall, Charles	Mary Camp	Oct. 21, 1834
Ralston, Alex R.	Mary H. Fox	May 17, 1815
Ralston, David	Ann V. Adams	Aug. 16, 1815
Ramsey, Archibald	Sarah Coghlan	Aug. 27, 1825
Ramsey, George	Mrs. Guthry	May 28, 1849
Ramsey, Joseph B.	Eliz. Zinn	Feb. 19, 1840
Ramsey, Wm. A.	Virginia Ann Dill Snead	Mar. 23, 1849
Ramy, John D.	Susannah Luther	Oct. 22, 1840
Randal, Seaborn	Sarah Whitehead	Jan. 12, 1837
Randolf, John	Emelina Cox	Sept. 13, 1846
Randall, George	Mary Matilda Lee	Dec. 17, 1848
Randall, John S.	Mary Broom	Feb. 10, 1836
Randall, Wm. W.	Mrs. Eliza W. Brower	Jan. 3, 1831
Randolph, Robert	Eliz. Napier	Jan. 10, 1789
Rawls, Hosea	Eliz. Rhodes	May 25, 1841
Raworth, Henry G.	Agnes Wagner	Oct. 2, 1834
Ray, Hector	Lucy Bailey	May 14, 1838
Ray, Hector	Nancy Bailey	Apr. 25, 1833

GROOM	BRIDE	DATE
Reab, Geo. B.	Anna E. E. R. Walker	Nov. 23, 1839
Read, James	----- -----	Feb. 3, 1840
Read, Richard	Eleanor Jane Cart	May 28, 1818
Read, Wm. Burtis	Martha Ann Cart	Oct. 14, 1819
Rearden, John A.	Henrietta G. Ogletree	Jan. 10, 1839
Red, Green B.	Maria S. Byne	Nov. 25, 1830
Redd, Berry	Polly Mason	Nov. 23, 1820
Redding, James	Mary Powers	June 5, 1802
Redman, Wm.	Leuraney Cliatt	Mar. 2, 1824
Redd, Green B.	Adeline Blackstone	Dec. 24, 1839
Reed, John C.	Isabella Lawson	Jan. 3, 1838
Reed, Luke	Barbara W. Murphy	May 3, 1820
Reel, Sterling	Mary Styres	June 1, 1844
Rees, Albert	Sarah Ann Lamar	Oct. 28, 1841
Refo, Charles L.	Sarah A. Starr	Nov. 19, 1845
Reichman, John	Catherine Marks	Oct. 20, 1836
Reid, John B.	Abigal Willcox	June 4, 1817
Reid, Joseph S.	Emilene T. Taylor	Nov. 30, 1846
Reid, Oliver	Mary Oliver	Dec. 4, 1817
Reid, Robert	Martha Russell	Apr. 25, 1831
Reid, Robert	Susanna Bebe	Aug. 5, 1801
Reid, Robt. Raymond	Ann Margaret McLaws	Apr. 3, 1810
Reid, Wm. M.	Georgia A. Cooper	Dec. 30, 1841
Reid, Wm. W.	Felicity M. Guemerin	Sept. 21, 1835
Reilly, James	Mary Ann Conely	Nov. 24, 1846
Reith, Alfred (colored)	Emma Moore (colored)	Apr. 20, 1843
Rethlan, Joseph	Margaret Frala(i?)y	Mar. 13, 1837
Revell, Hardy	Margaret George	Sept. 12, 1825
Revere, Henry L.	Mary Weatherby	Mar. 30, 1799
Reynolds, Anderson J.	Amanda Wright	Feb. 20, 1817
Rheney, Charles	Mary Murphy	Mar. 17, 1809
Rhind, James	Mary M. Gardner	Aug. 1, 1836
Rhodes, Aaron	Nancy Anne Murphey	Dec. 24, 1794
Rhodes, Aaron	Eliz. Beale	Oct. 30, 1832
Rhodes, Absalom	Mary Clayton	Sept. 30, 1808
Rhodes, Absalom, Jr.	Sarah Brown	Jan. 16, 1810
Rhodes, John A.	Cynthia Brown	Apr. 16, 1848
Rhodes, John R.	Arimitta Haney	Dec. 18, 1832
Rhodes, T. V. W.	Mary Fox	Oct. 17, 1844
Rhodes, Thomas R.	Mary Watson	Jan. 26, 1842
Rhodes, W. F.	Georgiana Coker	May 10, 1841
Rhodes, Wm.	Telitha Johnson	Apr. 7, 1807
Rhodes, Wm. J.	Mariah E. Crawford	Sept. 29, 1847
Rhodes, Wm. J.	Martha Allen	Dec. 14, 1819
Rice, Jessee	Susannah Jones	Jan. 23, 1792
Rice, Thomas D.	Sarah A. Burroughs	May 2, 1825
Rice, Wm. J.	Mary E. E. Meigs	Jan. 1, 1831
Rich, Dr. David A.	Amelia O. Holliday	Mar. 7, 1843
Richards, Thomas	Amanda Maria Stoy	Oct. 19, 1824
Richards, Wolcott	Indiana C. Twiggs	May 22, 1827
Richardson, John	Nancy Winters	Nov. 12, 1812
Richer, James	Melvina Gaines	Oct. 19, 1847
Richmond, Henry A.	Eliza A. Dakings	June 20, 1841
Rickitson, Gardias	Eliz. Brown	Oct. 9, 1813
Rickitson, Gordias	Jamima Jones	June 30, 1821
Ridley, John	Lydia Lynes	Dec. 17, 1792
Rigail, Lawrence A.	Anna T. Walker	July 11, 1821
Riley, Ferrel	Ann McNeille	Sept. 20, 1786
Riley, John	Milley Fumey	Apr. 6, 1796
Riley, John	Caroline G. Sneed	Feb. 3, 1825
Riley, John H.	Jane Parr	Jan. 31, 1842
Riley, Moses	Martha M. Pool	Jan. 19, 1818
Ringgold, James G.	Caroline Jane Buckle	May 29, 1827
Ritchie, Wm. H.	Mathilda B. Lomaz	July 23, 1841
Rives, James T.	Amelia E. Williamson	Aug. 17, 1835
Robert, Augustus	Jane Cecilia Lang	Jan. 25, 1843
Robert, Dr. Wm. H.	Barbara M. Skinner	Jan. 30, 1840
Roberts, Augustus R.	Louisa M. Williams	Nov. 28, 1844

411

GROOM	BRIDE	DATE
Roberts, Irwin	Arramenta Lyon	Apr. 8, 1819
Roberts, James L.	Adeline H. Darby	Dec. 12, 1833
Roberts, John	Sarah Dannel	Mar. 20, 1808
Roberts, John	Milly Penny	May 9, 1804
Roberts, John	Mrs. Sally Sargent	Jan. 18, 1810
Roberts, Joseph W.	Sophia L. Gibson	Dec. 21, 1837
Roberts, Stephen	Mary Lyon	July 1, 1819
Roberts, Thomas	Mrs. Mary Ruth Williamson	Dec. 21, 1830
Roberts, Wm.	Mary Ledget	Apr. 17, 1808
Robertson, Abner P.	Mary Bugg	Nov. 13, 1826
Robertson, Henry	Elsey King	Jan. 14, 1819
Robertson, John	Anne Collins	Dec. 20, 1796
Robertson, D. M.	L. A. Kennedy	Apr. 15, 1846
Robertson, Josiah	Eliz. Byrd	Mar. 29, 1829
Robertson, Meshach	Elcey McGill	Sept. 26, 1822
Robertson, Minerah	Caroline Salmons	May 23, 1828
Robertson, Wm.	Henny Berryhill	Nov. 6, 1801
Robertson, Wm. A.	Mary Louisa Watton	Dec. 8, 1842
Robinson, Geo.	Anna Matilda Carter	Nov. 24, 1842
Robinson, Henry	Eliz. Ogden	Jan. 22, 1818
Robinson, James	Eliza Jones	Jan. 31, 1838
Robinson, James B.	Eliz. Bugg	May 31, 1808
Robinson, John	Juriah Landers	Mar. 26, 1788
Robinson, Jonathan	Eliz. Brown	Mar. 30, 1811
Roderick, Joseph	Mary Haley	Jan. 29, 1824
Robinson, Richard	Margaret Newnan	Aug. 17, 1805
Robinson, Wm.	Anna T. Rigail	Oct. 13, 1832
Roff, Aaron	Rebecca L. Camfield	May 17, 1849
(see also Joseph Beau)		
Roff, Aaron	Mary A. Glascock	Aug. 24, 1837
Roff, Freeman T.	Mary E. Soisclair (Labuzan)	Nov. 15, 1838
Roger, Thomas	Isabella Kent	May 21, 1848
Rogers, Elijah	Louisa Ann McCullar	Feb. 24, 1826
Rogers, Moses	Sophia Dantignac	Dec. 12, 1816
Roman, Daniel S.	Mary Ann Liverman	Feb. 17, 1825
Rooney, Hugh	Lucy M. Yarnold	Feb. 15, 1826
Rooney, Patrick	Mrs. Bridget Cline	Oct. 9, 1849
Rose, Authur G.	Eliz. Gardner	Apr. 25, 1837
Ross, Charles L.	Emily H. Moore	Dec. 2, 1838
Rossignol, Paul	Elizabeth Adrienne Dugas	Dec. 24, 1818
Roten, Abram	Nancy Richardson	Jan. 4, 1799
Roundtree, A. W.	Julia Grubbs	Apr. 11, 1849
Roundtree, Geo. R.	Pamella W. Woolfolk	Nov. 15, 1827
Rowe, Bernard	Eliz. Clarke	Nov. 17, 1847
Rowe, Thomas	Mary Smare	Oct. 25, 1823
Rowell, Ezekiel	Mrs. Ann Middleton	Sept. 27, 1827
Rowell, Richard	Martha Knight	May 31, 1827
Rowland, Benj.	Martha Collins	May 26, 1818
Rowland, James	Isabel Palmer	July 28, 1817
Rowland, James T.	Rebecca Bryant	Jan. 24, 1835
Rowland, Merit	Patsey Fitsgerrald	Dec. 16, 1809
Rowland, Williamson	Barshaba Guthery	Aug. 7, 1797
Royal, Wm. S.	Caroline M. Frazer	Sept. 14, 1847
Rozar, Claiborne	Pamelia Atha	May 4, 1814
Rozar, David	Eliz. Calib	Jan. 7, 1801
Ruddell, Geo.	Eliz. H. Greenwood	Oct. 6, 1836
Ruffin, Major Robert R.	Harriett P. Fox	Dec. 23, 1817
Ruise, James	Mary Horton	Oct. 11, 1849
Rush, George W.	Cemuline Heydenfeldt	May 3, 1838
Russell, Benj. B.	Ann E. Broadhurst	Oct. 5, 1845
Russell, Dwight P.	Sarah A. Clarke	Sept. 1, 1836
Russell, Henry F.	Martha A. Danforth	May 31, 1838
Russell, John	Sarah Howard	Jan. 5, 1842
Russell, Simeon	Keziah H. Durkee	Nov. 1, 1818
Ryan, Jeremiah	Unetta Parker	Mar. 23, 1833
Ryan, Wm.	Ellen Fields	Mar. 13, 1832
Sabal, Joseph L. A.	Cephise Ann Cannet	Apr. 16, 1828

GROOM	BRIDE	DATE
Salisbury, David G.	Mrs. Ann Fulcher	Jan. 2, 1831
Salmon, Jefferson D.	Patience W. Barton	July 29, 1821
Salmon, Jefferson D.	Nancy A. Kennedy	Feb. 22, 1838
Salmons, Jefferson D.,Jr.	Adeline Morse	Aug. 9, 1849
Sanders, Thomas	Ann Tunns	Nov. 16, 1789
Sandiford, Wm. A.	Julia A. Courtney	Jan. 1, 1841
Sandwich, Matthew H.	Matilda Wright	Oct. 12, 1834
Sandwich, Thomas	Margaretta Osborne	Dec. 16, 1801
Sante, Augustus	Charlotte Stringfellow	Dec. 26, 1821
Sargant, Thos. H.	Amanda M. Barham	May 5, 1831
Sarling, Isaac	Mary Moses	Oct. 29, 1845
Sassard, John	Henrietta Davis	July 2, 1823
Saturday, Edmund	Ann Midenduff	Sept. 3, 1849
Savage, Asa	Eliz. Amelia Whittle	Feb. 17, 1839
Savage, Caesar A.	Frances M. T. Flournoy	Dec. 14, 1839
Savage, Daniel	Mrs. Susan B. Ware	Dec. 22, 1830
Savage, John	Matilda Caldwell	Apr. 6, 1834
Savage, John	Eliz. Kelly	May 31, 1838
Savage, Nathan W.	Lucinda Adams	Nov. 22, 1832
Savage, Wm. B.	Isabella C. Nicholl	Mar. 9, 1842
Scannell, Daniel	Ellen Haly	Mar. 13, 1838
Scarborough, Benj.	Rebecca Hunter	May 13, 1849
Schley, Geo. H.	Eliz. L. W. Douglass	Apr. 4, 1837
Schley, Wm.	Sophia E. Kerr	Feb. 25, 1846
Schreiner, Chas. W.	Mary T. Johnson	Dec. 2, 1839
Scofield, E. E.	Helen R. Meredith	Oct. 1, 1835
Scott, Elijah	Sarah McAllister	Apr. 19, 1837
Scott, Gamwell T.	Emily F. Guidrat	Oct. 5, 1835
Scott, John	Christian Van Hoose	Jan. 15, 1788
Scott, John	Nancy Ryals	Aug. 22, 1811
Scott, John	Martha Lambert	Jan. 16, 1815
Scott, Thomas	Mary Walton	Mar. 1, 1803
Scott, Wm.	Agnes Kello Walker	June 26, 1805
Scott, Wm. G.	Eliza A. Lewis	May 30, 1835
Scovell, Hezekiah W.	Caroline Matilda Hunter	Jan. 12, 1824
Scruise, James	Nancy Palmer	Oct. 31, 1801
Sea, Jesse	Miriam Baggett	July 4, 1801
Seals, Wm.	Eliz. Pool	Jan. 10, 1843
Seastrunk, Jacob	Priscilla Tutt	Jan. 10, 1840
Seats, Benj.	Eliz. Poll	Sept. 30, 1799
Seay, Willis	Sarah Jane Foster	Aug. 26, 1847
Seeley, Gideon	Sally Glover	Apr. 1, 1802
Seeley, Gideon	Martha Farmer	Jan. 11, 1804
Sego, Abraham	Eliz. Wall	Oct. 14, 1832
Sego, Abraham	Martha Atwell	July 20, 1837
Sego, Alfred	Eliza Sego	July 26, 1837
Sego, Joshua	Nancy Tinley	Aug. 6, 1807
Sego, Levi	Sarah Ann Lovell	Feb. 23, 1833
Sego, Middleton	Mary Neatherlin	Dec. 25, 1822
Sego, Overton	Eliz. Kent	May 2, 1839
Sego, Wm.	Eliz. Netherlin	May 25, 1816
Sellers, Wm.	Sarah A. Grinold	Feb. 7, 1837
Semmes, Andrew G.	Frances Herbert	Sept. 22, 1807
Senges, Jean (John)	Sarah Megar	Feb. 20, 1817
Service, L. C.	C. H. S. Davis	Nov. 27, 1847
Shancleford, Benj.	Sarah Shackleford	Dec. 10, 1797
Shackleford, Geo. W.	Ann Eliz. Meyer	Dec. 22, 1845
Shancleford, Jno. W.	Mildred Evans	Dec. 29, 1801
Shaffer, Daniel S.	Margaret Sears	Aug. 6, 1814
Shannon, Peter J.	Olivia L. N. Morgan	Oct. 10, 1849
Sharp, John	Eliz. Wilcher	Feb. 24, 1842
Shaw, Aaron	Susan Clarke	July 12, 1838
Shaw, Alexander	Margaret Donham	Apr. 10, 1842
Shaw, Caleb T.	Martha Hill	Jan. 1, 1833
Shaw, Frederick R.	Ann M. Wolf	Nov. 10, 1839
Shaw, John	Bethena Naves	Nov. 7, 1826
Shaw, John W.	Mary Rees (?)	Dec. 28, 1845
Shaw, Wm.	Lilla Burks	Jun. 10, 1799

413

GROOM	BRIDE	DATE
Shaw, Wm. C.	Sarah Boyd	Jun. 26, 1836
Shearer, Gilbert	Martha A. Cowles	Feb. 8, 1815
Shelton, Wm. B.	Mrs. Mary Ann Clarke	Oct. 24, 1831
Shepherd, Thompson	Eliz. T. Walker	Oct. 8, 1813
Shepperd, Wm.	Elvy Anderson	Feb. 22, 1802
Sheran, Peter	Rosana Mitchell	--- --, 1849
Sherman, Wm.	Mary F. Buel	June 7, 1842
Sherod, Felix A. M.	Margaret McGraw	Nov. 8, 1832
Shick, Wm.	Larua Backman	Apr. 21, 1835
Shivers, Thomas	Eliz. Smithart	Mar. 16, 1826
Shop, Lawrence T.	Eliz. Watson	Jan. 4, 1838
Shumate, Triplett	Rebecca Bearum	Dec. 5, 1818
Sibley, Wm. (colored)	Nancy Moore (colored)	Apr. 20, 1843
Sikes, James	Sarah Wimpy	Dec. 9, 1793
Sikes, James	Sarah Murphy	Feb. 28, 1801
Sikes, James	Mary Elliot	May 27, 1818
Sikes, Solomon	Jane Daniel	Dec. 9, 1817
Sikes, W. H.	Eliz. S. May	June 6, 1844
Sikes, William	Eliz. Irglet	May 20, 1811
Silcox, John	Charlotte Nelson	Dec. 24, 1840
Silivan, John	Eliz. Boyd	Oct. 23, 1806
Sillivan, H. W.	Penelope Jones	July 9, 1816
Simmone, Jacob	Mary Ann Hall	Feb. 17, 1839
Simmons, Greensville	Eliz. T. Combs	Apr. 27, 1831
Simmons, Henry T.	Eliza Jones	May 19, 1831
Simmons, James S.	Emeline L. L. Robert	Sept. 12, 1844
Simmons, James W. L.	Sophia S. S. Stoner	Dec. 24, 1818
Simmons, Joseph A.	Catherine H. Duhadway	July 20, 1842
Simmons, Thos. M.	Anna Matilda Byrd	May 20, 1835
Simpson, James M.	Mary A. Mealing	Dec. 22, 1840
Sims, Benjamin D.	Jane Mary Jones	Apr. 24, 1823
Sims (Symms), Mann	Marget McGruder	Sept. 11, 1786
Sims, Wm.	Ann Creswell	Apr. 12, 1820
Skinner, Henry	----- -----	Jan. 8, 1798
Skinner, Howard	Gracey Smith	July 24, 1811
Skinner, John	Mary Jones	Dec. 19, 1810
Skinner, John, Jr.	Barberry Jones	Jan. 30, 1834
Skinner, Lucius C.	Mary Francis Morrison	Nov. 8, 1849
Skinner, Seaborn	Martha Ann Hall	Sept. 16, 1830
Skinner, Thomas	Frances Darby	Sept. 29, 1823
Skinner, Wm.	Eliz. Jones	Feb. 4, 1817
Skinner, William	Jane E. Jones	May 26, 1846
Skinner, Wm. S.	Harriet B. Butterfield	Dec. 19, 1845
Slack, Uriah	Sarah A. Glover	Nov. 27, 1839
Slaughter, Augustine	Anna Frances E. Slayter	Sept. 15, 1813
Slaughter, Lawrence	Jane O. Stewart	Dec. 14, 1820
Slaughter, Thos. K.	Thurza Magruder	Feb. 6, 1832
Sloan, John A.	Mary M. Wolf	July 10, 1837
Smar, John	Ann Caroline Ingram	Feb. 17, 1824
Smar, Perril (?)	Sarah Martin	Apr. 11, 1825
Smead, Hamilton P.	Ann G. Savage	Apr. 7, 1836
Smead (?), Patrick H.	Mary Agnes Malone	Mar. 11, 1830
Smedes, Abraham K.	Eliza Isaacs	May 18, 1809
Smith, Alexander P.	Sarah L. Brooknar	Nov. 10, 1831
Smith, Archibald J.	Ruby M. Johnson	Aug. 31, 1830
Smith, Asaph	Catherine Smith	Jan. 8, 1837
Smith, Benj. T. L.	Janette J. Palmer	Apr. 1, 1847
Smith, Charles	Lydia Wroton	Aug. 7, 1816
Smith, Clement	Martha June Brown	Jan. 4, 1847
Smith, David	Margaret Bowers	Feb. 5, 1824
Smith, Ebennezzar	Marget Chambers	Nov. 14, 1788
Smith, Ezekiel	Rebecca Smars	Dec. 19, 1825
Smith, Ezekiel	Sarah Lassitor	Mar. 2, 1826
Smith, Frederick	Eliz. Berryhill	Oct. 30, 1797
Smith, Henry	Caroline Fulcher	Apr. 27, 1826
Smith, Henry	Eliz. Borem	Dec. 24, 1834
Smith, Henry I.	Caroline M. Martin	Dec. 18, 1830
Smith, Isaac W.	Ruth Roberts	Jan. 4, 1849

GROOM	BRIDE	DATE
Smith, Jackson	Martha Ann Jones	Jan. 9, 1845
Smith, Jacob	Cristian Carter	Jan. 6, 1789
Smith, James	Martha Smith	June 23, 1787
Smith, James	Ellinor Barnett	Jan. 27, 1790
Smith, James	Judy Johnson	Jan. 31, 1826
Smith, Jeremiah	Mary Ann F. Watson	Aug. 27, 1829
Smith, Jesse	Catherine Gordon	Aug. 18, 1808
Smith, John	Caroline Doolittle	Dec. 5, 1848
Smith, John R.	Jane Teal	Mar. 5, 1832
Smith, John R.	Eliza W. C. Blain	July 31, 1837
Smith, Leonard	Mary McMannis	Dec. 14, 1796
Smith, Nathaniel	Rebecca Gibbs	Feb. 2, 1828
Smith, Noah	Eliz. Palmer	Dec. 24, 1798
Smith, Peter Sken	Anne E. Cumming	Dec. 20, 1836
Smith, Philip	Priscilla Buck	Dec. 14, 1836
Smith, Radford	Rebekah Hill	Jan. 1, 1795
Smith, Robt. King	Mary Antonia	June 17, 1807
Smith, Samuel	Nancy Rial	July 31, 1815
Smith, Samuel	Susan Hearton	Oct. 11, 1827
Smith, Samuel Jenks	Sarah M. Wheeler	Oct. 12, 1835
Smith, Thomas	Lydia Reddick	Mar. 4, 1838
Smith, Wm.	Eliz. Ramsay	Sept. 8, 1786
Smith, Wm.	(Free) Suckey Meals	Mar. 4, 1795
Smith, Wm.	Louisa Watkins	Apr. 24, 1817
Smith, William	Emma O. Eve	Apr. 5, 1831
Smith, William B.	Harriet A. Butler (Burton)	Aug. 10, 1848
Smith, Wm. F.	Frances Goldworth	Apr. 23, 1848
Smith, Zakeriah	Mary Ann Frances Nevin	Sept. 17, 1849
Snarl, John	Polly Kelly	Dec. 21, 1813
Snead, John C.	Julia Ann Dill	Jan. 17, 1827
Sneed, Nathaniel	Winey Dalton	Jan. 19, 1809
Spear, Charles	Jane Gibson	Feb. 12, 1814
Spears, Joseph Y.	Ellenda Gay	Mar. 31, 1839
Speed, George W.	Mary Eliz. Airey	May 27, 1828
Speed, Wm.	Susanna Collins	June 13, 1799
Spelman, R. P.	Lavenia Fraser	Nov. 9, 1827
Spelman, R. P., Jr.	Frances Foster	Dec. 17, 1844
Spelman, Richard P.	Sarah Randall	June 9, 1821
Spencer, Amasa	Eliza Crayton	Apr. 6, 1824
Spires, Hezekiah	Eliz. Barnett	Aug. 23, 1788
Springs, Joseph L.	Mary Ann Cooke	June --, 1845
Spruce, William	Sarah P. Dixon	Mar. 30, 1797
Stallings, Ezekill	Ann Clark	Aug. 31, 1790
Stansell, Thomas	Sarah Amanda Lewis	Jan. 14, 1845
Stanton, Henry	Martha Ann Stallings	Oct. 29, 1811
Stanton, Henry	Lucinda Foster	June 26, 1817
Stanton, Joseph B.	Lucy T. Howel	Mar. 1, 1810
Stanton, Malachi	Sarah McManes	Mar. 19, 1800
Stark, Wyatt W.	Mrs. Sarah Ann Davis	Oct. 5, 1840
Starling, Bias	Poly Meeks	Dec. 17, 1834
Starnes, Daniel	Harriet E. Russell	Sept. 17, 1808
Starnes, Ebenezar	Winefred Harvy	Oct. 24, 1812
Starnes, Ebenezer	Mary Anne W. Nesbitt	Nov. 26, 1844
Starnes, John	Jane Ware	Feb. 13, 1822
Starr, John	Eliza McDade	Oct. 4, 1815
Stations, Harbert	Harriet P. Keener	Oct. 17, 1824
Staton, Wm.	Nancy Richardson	May 31, 1800
Steaveley, Robert	Eliz. Bowdre	Apr. 14, 1790
Steele, Andrew	Mary Johnson	Nov. 13, 1837
Stephens, Andrew	Matilda C. Ogden	Sept. 26, 1843
Stephens, Wm.	Mrs. Jane Graham	Oct. 17, 1832
Sterling, Walter T.	Bridget McTier	Apr. 30, 1842
Stevens, Micajah	Sarah Bogan	Aug. 22, 1808
Stevens, Micajah	Mrs. Jane Gasque	May 5, 1822
Stewart, James	Mary Treadwell	July 22, 1815
Stewart, George	Angellina G. Ogletree	Dec. 31, 1837
Stewart, Theophilus S.	Susan McDowall	June 5, 1849
Stillman, James	Rebecca Tulane	Apr. 25, 1823

GROOM	BRIDE	DATE
Stilwell, Chas. H.	Mary Marshall	July 9, 1832
Stinson, Wm.	Kitty White	Oct. 2, 1793
Stockton, G. H.	Caroline E. Langston	Oct. 15, 1846
Stone, Isaac	Lucy Jones	Oct. 18, 1832
Stone, Lemuel W.	Elisabeth Blackston	May 21, 1824
Stovall, Charles	Lucy Ashton	Dec. 23, 1809
Stovall, Marcellus A.	Sarah G. McKinne	July 28, 1842
Stovall, Pleasant	Mrs. Frances C. V. Hill	Feb. 11, 1845
Stoy, Thadias S.	Anna M. Winter	May 29, 1835
Strange, John H.	Martha Bass	Oct. 1, 1830
Street, George	Eliz. Farington	June 12, 1845
Streets, Daniel	Matilda Gay	Oct. 17, 1838
Stringfellow, Samuel L.	Mary Ann Thornberry	Jan. 13, 1821
Stringfellow, Wm.	Nancy B. I. Fisher	Feb. 18, 1830
Stringfield, Elisha	Susannah Hammack	Aug. 18, 1817
Strobel, Godfrey	Marguerite Perry	May 3, 1849
Stuart, Andrew	Eliz. G. Robert	Nov. 6, 1833
Stuart, Thomas	Jane Sloan	Oct. 29, 1822
Stuckey, Edmund	Ruth Lamberth	July 4, 1826
Stuckey, Wm. B.	Susan A. H. Martin	Jan. 21, 1834
Stuckey, Wm. B.	Thirzal Elkins	Jan. 7, 1843
Sturges, Andrew B.	Mrs. Louisa Trouchlett	Sept. 16, 1827
Sturges, Columbus F.	Almina Plumb	Jan. 2, 1837
Sturges, John	Mary Parks	Nov. 22, 1806
Sturges, Oliver	Eliz. Nail	Jun. 5, 1802
Sturges, William U.	Georgia Ann Ward	Aug. 10, 1847
Sturgis, Wm. G.	Ann Pool	Nov. 28, 1808
Sullivan, Daniel	Lucretia Cobb	Aug. 8, 1807
Sullivan, Patrick	Mary Buckly	Jan. 21, 1845
Sullivan, Reason H.	Anna R. Stockton	Mar. 26, 1846
Summers, Geo. W.	Mary A. Creswell	Sept. 21, 1837
Sumner, Holland	Vicy Cobb	Jan. 8, 1813
Sumurl(?), William	Mary Brunt	June 27, 1830
Sutcliffe, Sylvester	Eliza Bogan	Dec. 9, 1818
Sutherland, John	Eliz. Purkins	Sept. 12, 1789
Sweeney, Thomas	Margaret A. Duffy	Jan. 31, 1848
Swinden, Matthew Henry	Ann M. Rice	June 15, 1840
Sykes, Wm.	Margaret Howell	July 9, 1797
Taber, John	Eliz. Parker	May 17, 1785
Talcott, Geo. H.	Catherine J. Starke	Nov. 9, 1843
Taliaferro, Christopher	Sarah K. Newby	Apr. 2, 1829
Talley, Jno.	Rebecca McCullough	Jan. 11, 1802
Tant, Isaac L.	Phoebe A. Luct (?)	July 9, 1836
Tant, Isaac S.	Eliza Davis	July 10, 1834
Tant, Wm. R.	Cornelia C. West	Mar. 23, 1837
Tarver, Etheldred J.	Jane McNair	Feb. 5, 1835
Tarver, John R.	Eliz. Shaw	Jan. 9, 1824
Tarver, Robert	Mason Tarver	Oct. 7, 1805
Tarver, Robt.	Ava Smith	June 7, 1822
Tarver, Samuel	Charlotte Tarver	Mar. 11, 1805
Tarver, Samuel	Frances A. Vollotton	Dec. 21, 1818
Tate, Horatio G.	Anna Maria Hook	Dec. 19, 1843
Taylor, Abraham	Mary Mitchell	Sept. 4, 1792
Taylor, Alsey	Charlotte Shepheurd	June 3, 1826
Taylor, David	Sarah Pinchbeck Mead	Sept. 3, 1803
Taylor, Francis C.	Hannah Church	Feb. 25, 1819
Taylor, Francis L.	Peggy Mabry	Apr. 28, 1808
Taylor, Geo.	Mahala Davis	Sept. 22, 1841
Taylor, James	Jensy Green	Dec. 21, 1801
Taylor, James	Susannah Brown	Aug. 22, 1808
Taylor, James	Rhody Hall	Mar. 14, 1809
Taylor, James I.	Jane H. Burke	Dec. 13, 1842
Taylor, Jefferson W.	Mary Ann Langley	Jan. 31, 18-9
Taylor, John	Mary Cocke	Mar. 6, 1821
Taylor, John T.	Ann E. Marshall	Oct. 19, 1826
Taylor, Joseph	Anna Frances Kneeland	Mar. 28, 1837
Taylor, Joseph F.	Caroline Watkins	May 25, 1829

416

GROOM	BRIDE	DATE
Taylor, Walter, Jr.	Nancy Kennedy	Aug. 4, 1800
Taylor, Wm.	Catharine Briggs	Apr. 5, 1827
Taylor, Wm.	Roan Reynolds	Oct. 28, 1828
Templeton, Alexander	Eliz. Walker	Mar. 12, 1806
Templeton, James A.	Harriet E. Williams	Dec. 16, 1834
Templeton, Jas. A.	Mary Ellen Daniel	Oct. 21, 1847
Tennic, Peter	Mrs. Sarah Collins	Mar. 17, 1846
Tennison, James	Mary Atwell	Jan. 28, 18-4
Tennison, Jas. Alex	I-thieia Collins	Oct. 26, 1846
Terry, Benjamin	Sabrina Adams	Jan. 27, 1836
Terry, James	Mary A. L. Hutchinson	June 12, 1827
Thayer, Henry B.	Lucy M. Stokes	Dec. 19, 1849
Thomas, C. C.	Eliz. A. Boulinau	May -, 1846
Thomas, Camm	Eliz. Johnston	Oct. 3, 1790
Thomas, Edward	Sarah Jane Hutchinson	May 29, 1822
Thomas, Floyd	Mary Wilson	June 23, 1836
Thomas, George	Rose Ann Henry	Jan. 8, 1840
Thomas, Henry P.	Ellen E. D. Burroughs	Dec. 5, 1837
Thomas, Joseph B.	Caroline S. Few	Oct. 16, 1834
Thomas, Richard J.	Ann L. Appleton (Mrs.)	Mar. 14, 1827
Thomas, Western B.	Emeline F. Howard	Mar. 4, 1828
Thomas, Wm.	Harriot Shaw	Jan. 12, 1810
Thomas, Wm. M.	Jane Caroline Minor	Aug. 24, 1843
Thompson, Alexander	Lida Newman	Apr. 1, 1789
Thompson, Bartlett	Obedience Hatcher	Dec. 14, 1802
Thompson, Wm. T.	Caroline L. Carrie	July 13, 1837
Thornton, Henry	Mrs. Ann Bigniel	Aug. 25, 1815
Tilley, James R.	Mary Rowland	Jan. 27, 1820
Tilley, John	Eliz. Lambeth	July 9, 1822
Timmerman, John	Eliza Lee	Sept. 28, 1830
Tindall, Pleasant	Polly Hobbs	Nov. 2, 1793
Tindale, James	Alcina Kern	June 26, 1838
Tindley, David	Martha Weathers	Feb. 21, 1816
Tindley, John	Eliz. Weathers	Mar. 21, 1816
Tinlay, John	Mary McCollough	Dec. 7, 1819
Tinley, David	Susan Ward	Feb. 3, 1842
Tinley, James	Rebecca Sego	Feb. 2, 1826
Tinley, Philip	Mary Hill	Jan. 18, 1819
Tinley, Philip	Mary Shaw	Jan. 29, 1837
Tinley, Thomas	Luthia Anne Green	Mar. 9, 1842
Tinley, Vincent	Sarah Birch	Aug. 13, 1818
Tinley, Vincent	Emely Arrington	Jan. 18, 1849
Tinley, Wm.	Nancy Usher	Feb. 20, 1812
Tinley, Wm.	Marsilla Burdick	July 14, 1842
Tinney, Benj.	Ann Beal	Feb. 3, 1789
Tinsley, Elias C.	Alletha Frances May	Sept. 7, 1837
Tinsley, James Z.	Hester Ann Hogg (?)	May 13, 1813
Tinsley, John L.	Lurrency (?) Reynolds	Oct. 15, 1847
Titus, Josiah	Eliz. Neighbours	June 19, 1824
Tobin, Daniel	Agnes Lartique	Apr. 17, 1817
Tobin, Thomas	Athenae Canuch	Dec. 26, 1833
Todd, David	Asarebecca McCullough	July 18, 1799
Todd, Joshua	Mary Burch	May 23, 1797
Tomlin, John	Martha Williams	Sept. 4, 1834
Towns, Richard	Francis Vaughn	Dec. 15, 1840
Tracy, Edward D.	Rebecca C. Campbell	Aug. 4, 1835
Tradewell, A.	Eugania Harris	Aug. 31, 1816
Trembley, Wm. W.	Mrs. Catherine E. Fabin	Oct. 20, 1838
Triplet, Daniel	Mary Hutchinson	Feb. 19, 1810
Tripp, John M.	Sarah Ann Crabb	Nov. 21, 1844
Trippe, John H.	Eveline S. Bowdre	Dec. 2, 1845
Trotti, Francis	Hannah McRyeire	Sept. 19, 1799
Trotti, Laurance	Nancy McTyer of McAyer	Apr. 19, 1797
Trowbridge, John	S. M. Vallotton	Mar. 20, 1843
Trowbridge, Nelson	Evelina F. Oline	Nov. 10, 1836
Trowbridge, Samuel	Julia A. Wilson	Dec. 24, 1834
Truchelet, Jos. A.	Mary H. Steifle	Feb. 5, 1840
Tubman, Richard	Emmily Thomas	June 25, 1818

GROOM	BRIDE	DATE
Tucker, Joseph	Margaret Young	June 22, 1833
Tuder, Jno.	Ann Adkinson	July 23, 1788
Tufts, Francis	Charity Garrett	Dec. 20, 1819
Tulloss, Rodham	Orpha Haywood Carnes	Dec. 26, 1802
Tulloss, Rodham	Mary Starnes	May 22, 1808
Turknet, Henry	Mary Allen	July 2, 1795
Turley, Allen	Eliz. Darby	July 29, 1835
Turman, Joel C.	Martha McCune	Sept. 7, 1816
Turner, Charles W.	Teresa Ryan	Apr. 8, 1822
Turner, Charles	Susannah Martin	Feb. 2, 1843
Turner, John M.	Martha G. Coombs	Sept. 9, 1834
Turner, Shadrach	Mary Taylor	July 14, 1836
Turner, Wm.	Eliz. Roland	Apr. 20, 1804
Turner, Wm. P.	Eliza Brown	Jan. 2, 1839
Turpin, Geo. T.	Heloise T. Bonyer	Apr. 23, 1828
Turpin, J. F.	Catherine M. Barnes	Dec. 2, 1841
Tutt, Wm. H.	Miss Bell	Nov. 21, 1846
Tuttle, Isaac S.	Harriet Newton	Oct. 22, 1814
Tuttle, John M.	Matilda A. Hopkins	Mar. 7, 1842
Twiggs, David E.	Eliz. Ware Hunter	Mar. 28, 1830
Twiggs, George	Sarah Low	May 7, 1811
Urquhart, Wm.	Ann Bowen	Apr. 15, 1805
Usher, Henry	Mary Ann Grace	June 4, 1818
Usher, Henry	Catherine Knowland	Oct. 3, 1831
Vallotton, Hugh	Jane Neighbours	May 14, 1822
Vance, Wm.	Harriet F. Keith	Mar. 16, 1837
Van Riper, Harman	Sarah Prater	Oct. 30, 1802
Vanzant, Abel	Louisa B. Goodwin	Mar. 18, 1815
Vardell, John	----- Danby	June 15, 1838
Basser, Jonathan	Eliz. Buford	May 9, 1807
Vaughn, James	Nancy Churchill	May 16, 1809
Vaughn, Wiley	Nancy Goodson	Sept. 25, 1834
Veitch, Walter	Mary Ann L. Ware	Jan. 6, 1829
Verdell, Jeremiah	Patsey Holmes	May 16, 1814
Verdery, Augustus N.	Susan H. Burton	Sept. 1, 1824
Verdery, Banj. F.	Mary Ann Jackson	Nov. 23, 1826
Verdery, Eugene	Georgianna V. Paul	July 12, 1838
Verdery, Wm. M.	Cornelia F. Skinner	Dec. 15, 1847
Vigal, George	Sarah Trentham	Apr. 25, 1818
Vinson, David	Eliz. Newman	Mar. 22, 1827
Vinson, Tully	Ann Anderson	May 20, 1841
Wafford, Isaiah	Lucy Weakley	May 23, 1818
Wagers, William	Katey Ross	Apr. 19, 1815
Wagner, Michael	Frances M. Brenan	Feb. 8, 1827
Wainwright, Joseph	Lavina Willy	Mar. 5, 1825
Wakeham, John	Ann Johnston	Oct. 8, 1846
Walker, Ambrose	Mary Williams	Dec. 5, 1809
Walker, David	Eliz. Harvey	June 30, 1788
Walker, Darling J.	Kella Wilkinson	Nov. 8, 1832
Walker, Elijah	Eliz. Collins	Jan. 1, 1799
Walker, Freeman	Mary G. Creswell	Apr. 29, 1803
Walker, Freeman W.	Jane E. Wilcox	Apr. 27, 1843
Walker, Geo. A. B.	Arabella L. Pearson	Apr. 4, 1832
Walker, Geo. B.	Amelia McTyeire	Aug. 12, 1819
Walker, Geo. M.	Mary T. Walker	Mar. 3, 1810
Walker, Geo. A. B.	Arobella Pearsen	Apr. 4, 1832
Walker, James	Eliz. Meals	Oct. 17, 1797
Walker, James B.	Louisa M. Woolfolk	Sept. 21, 1830
Walker, John I.	Eliza. Powers	Apr. 11, 1811
Walker, Joseph P.	Hannah West	Dec. 14, 1833
Walker, Joshua S.	Margula Lee	Mar. 19, 1835
Walker, Mathew T.	Maria L. Bohler	Oct. 14, 1847
Walker, Needham	Nancy Berryhill	Sept. 12, 1794
Walker, Robert	Ann Cooper	Jan. 2, 1799
Walker, Robt. T.	Ann F. Polk	June 5, 1828

GROOM	BRIDE	DATE
Walker, Samuel	Mary Ann Hood	Apr. 5, 1846
Walker, Semard (?)	Eliz. Odum	Feb. 20, 1835
Walker, Solomon	Mary Davis	Dec. 8, 1827
Walker, Valentine	Mary Arinton	May 5, 1807
Walker, Gen. Valentine	Mrs. Zemula Whitehead	June 18, 1819
Walker, Wm. W.	Mary B. Rhodes	Oct. 29, 1848
Walker, Zachariah	Susannah Kittle	Mar. 17, 1812
Wall, S. B.	Sarah Darling	May 1, 1828
Wall, Thomas	Eliz. Bird	Dec. 18, 1795
Wall, Wm. W.	Rosina E. Carrie	Jan. 13, 1847
Wallace, William	Jinsey Morgan	Aug. 5, 1830
Warpole, John H.	Mary Ann Lynes	Dec. 12, 1827
Walratt (?), Charles	Jane Brown	Jan. 9, 1840
Walsh, John G.	Odry Tant	June 3, 1824
Walters, Charles	Mary Mills	Feb. 18, 1810
Walthall, Richard	Adeliade Convert	July 28, 1825
Walton, Geo.	Sarah M. Walker	Jan. 10, 1809
Walton, Robert	Evelina S. Watkins	Dec. 23, 1813
Walton, Thos. I.	Mrs. Kesia Wright	Aug. 3, 1845
Walton, Thomas J.	----- -----	Feb. 6, 1833
Walton, Wm. A.	Eliz. A. Moore	Jan. 25, 1849
Ward, Bartholomew	Emily Carson	June 24, 1839
Ward, David	Sarah Stuner	Dec. 9, 1828
Ward, Elija	Naresetta Ward	May 17, 1849
Ward, James	Fereby Goodson	May 29, 1834
Ward, John	Sarah O. Ely	July 23, 1823
Ward, John	Rachel C. Cheves	Sept. 27, 1824
Ward, John	Charity Smith	July 25, 1828
Ward, John Thomas	Eliz. Ann Morris	Dec. 23, 1847
Ward, Simon	Polly King	Aug. 2, 1830
Wardlaw, David L.	Sarah Rosalie Allen	Jan. 13, 1825
Ware, Nicholas	Mary F. Randolph	Dec. 2, 1799
Ware, Robert D.	Clarissa Coleman	Oct. 27, 1825
Ware, Thomas C.	Ophelia Pace	June 4, 1835
Ware, Thompson	Eliza D. Howell	Feb. 2, 1807
Ware, Wm. C.	Ann McMurphy	July 16, 1817
Warner, Geo. W.	Margaret M. Hopkins	Mar. 6, 1821
Warrel, James G. H.	Nancy Davis	Nov. 12, 1834
Warren, Benjamin H.	Mary Ann Coleman	Dec. 22, 1818
Washburn, Abner S.	Margaret C. Micon	July 25, 1833
Waterman, Asaph	Mildred J. Meals	Nov. 8, 1828
Watkins, Anderson	Catharine Eve	Jan. 26, 1804
Watkins, James	Jane E. Urquhart	May 8, 1823
Watkins, James	Amanda Wilcox	Mar. 12, 1838
Watkins, Jason	Hannah Wages	Feb. 1, 1816
Watkins, Jason	Mary Ann Davis	Aug. 15, 1833
Watkins, Jason	Louisa Perdue	Aug. 21, 1838
Watkins, Jesse	Eliz. Hill (?)	Nov. 11, 1805
Watkins, Jesse	Eliz. Wilcox	Mar. 2, 1843
Watkins, Robert A.	Harriet T. Hale	Mar. 5, 1834
Watkins, Thos.	Eliz. H. Arington	Feb. 22, 1809
Watkins, Thomas H.	Nancy L. Cliatt	Oct. 8, 1835
Watkins, Wilson	Mary Hill	Nov. 4, 1802
Watkins, Wilson	Elinder Wages	Apr. 23, 1848
Watson, Geo.	Sarah Boyde	Mar. 10, 1824
Watson, James	Isabella White	Nov. 11, 1813
Watson, Jno.	Sally Wilkes	Oct. 21, 1807
Watson, Kimbrough	Mary Ann Tinsley	Nov. 30, 1837
Watson, Peter	Lucretia Griffin	Apr. 13, 1810
Way, John	Eliza Ann Collins	Jan. 10, 1807
Wayne, Richard, Jr.	Juliana Smyth	Jan. 29, 1800
Wayne, Wm.	Ann Gordon	Feb. 28, 1815
Weathers, Wm.	Ruth Sykes	Apr. 20, 1798
Weaver, Aaron	Mary Beaton	Sept. 21, 1807
Weaver, John H.	Amanda Gould	Mar. 24, 1831
Weaver, John M.	Elizabeth Brewer	Aug. 15, 1846
Weaver, Jonathan	Nancy Weaver	June 18, 1810
Weaver, Jonathan Lewellen	Rebeckah -----	July 15, 1793

419

GROOM	BRIDE	DATE
Weaver, Wm.	Rachel Whiteacre	Sept. 10, 1807
Webb, Robert	Mary Garrett	Jan. 11, 1838
Webb, Thomas	Patsey Penny	May 27, 1813
Weeden, Wm.	Mrs. Jane Eliza Watkins	Feb. 2, 1830
Weeks, Aaron	Mary West	July 23, 1840
Weeks, Caleb C.	Amelia Atwell	Apr. 27, 1843
Weeks, James	Eliz. Morgan	Mar. 8, 1817
Weeks, Joseph W.	Eliz. Bell	July 13, 1834
Weeks, Nathaniel	Joanna Burch	Dec. 30, 1846
Weeks, Wm.	Rhoda Carter	May 17, 1817
Weeks, Wm.	Polly Adkinson	Nov. 8, 1834
Weigell, George	Tokanne Weber	Feb. 9, 1836
Weigell, John	Margaret Thomas	June 1, 1844
Weigle, George	Catherine Larks	Feb. 17, 1835
Weker, Wm.	Eliz. Worthy	Nov. 1, 1804
Wellauer, John	Mary Purvis	July 8, 1841
Welch, Archibald	Rachel Angel	Sept. 16, 1799
Welch, George	Miley Newman	June 11, 1834
Welch, James	Lydia Buck	Oct. 31, 1825
Welch, Jesse	Sarah Walker	--- --, 1792
West, Charles W.	Eliza A. Whitehead	Oct. 22, 1840
West, David	Dicey Mann	Apr. 29, 1801
West, James	Ann Stroud	Nov. 2, 1785
Wheaton, Wm. H.	Anna Thomas Church	Dec. 18, 1817
Wheeler, Charles A.	Rebecca C. Mackenzie	May 26, 1844
Wheeler, Wm. J.	Amonela Vaughan	Oct. 6, 1844
Whidby (?), Daniel	Mary Bailey	Jan. 18, 1832
Whitaker, Wm.	Winney Williams	Mar. 5, 1838
Whitcombe, Wm.	Relete W. Culler	Jan. 19, 1825
White, Benedick	Sarah Hagins	Dec. 15, 1807
White, Benedict	Mary Roberts	Jan. 4, 1835
White, Benedict	Mrs. Mary Crawford	Jan. 25, 1844
White, Washington	Sarah Fitzjarrell	Dec. 6, 1824
White, Wm.	Mary Ann O'Keeffe	May 18, 1801
White, Wm.	Mary Morell	June 5, 1816
White, Wm. Parker	Sarah E. B. Dowse	Nov. 16, 1843
Whiteaker, John	Nancy Wood	July 27, 1825
Whiteaker, Mark	Mary Brooks	Feb. 28, 1808
Whitehead, Amos	Lemula (?) Cresswell	July 20, 1812
Whitehead, Amos G.	Eliz. McKinne	Jan. 13, 1835
Whitehead, Henry W.	Nancy Ann Cogil	Feb. 12, 1846
Whitehead, John	Mary Wilcox	July 13, 1816
Whitehead, Jno. Berrien	Catharine Matilda Harper	Oct. 3, 1842
Whitehead, Robert W.	Peggy Perdue	July 12, 1839
Whiting, Willard	Julia E. Bradley	Oct. 18, 1836
Whitlock, J. W.	Elisa B. Evans	Feb. 15, 1834
Whitlock, James	Mrs. Amy Buckhanon	Feb. 8, 1821
Whitlock, William S.	Jane E. West	Oct. 3, 1844
Whittington, Ephraim	Martha Magruder	Jan. 4, 1823
Whittle, James	Eliza A. Anderson	Apr. 7, 1835
Wigans, Wm.	Mrs. Eliz. Tindley	Oct. 1, 1823
Wiggins, Stephen	Unity Watkins	Dec. 1, 1806
Wiggins, John, Senior	Betsey Elliott	Sept. 5, 1832
Wiggins, John	Lurana Seago	Dec. 23, 1834
Wiggins, Robert	Caroline E. Wolf	Nov. 23, 1839
Wiggins, Wm.	Barbara Tindala	Feb. 8, 1809
Wiggins, Wm.	Sarah McCollough	Dec. 30, 1847
Wightman, John	Amy F. Campfield	Feb. 2, 1842
Wightman, Thomas	Isabella I. Morris	Feb. 17, 1837
Wilcox, Isaac	Jean Clark	June 1, 1795
Wilcox, Jonathan Samuel	Sarah Jane Ansley	June 9, 1846
Wilcox, Martin	Mary Dunham	June 26, 1816
Wilcox, John	Elisa Dunlan	Mar. 12, 1817
Wilde, John W.	Ann Eliz. McMillan	May 1, 1822
Wilde, John W.	Emily McMillan	May 21, 1824
Wilde, R. H.	C. J. Buckle	Feb. 6, 1819
Wilds, Thomas	Ann Bugg	Dec. 3, 1835
Wiles, Chas.	Creasey Combs	Nov. 7, 1794

GROOM	BRIDE	DATE
Wilkerson, Micajah	Mary Kennedy	Aug. 8, 1791
Wilkinson, James R.	Martha Ann Berry	Nov. 21, 1825
Wilkinson, Jno. B.	Eliz. Rae	Nov. 1, 1798
Wilki---, -----	----- Hill	Feb. 28, 1828
Willcox, John	Eliza Dunham	Mar. 13, 1817
Willcox, John	Martha McDade	Nov. 10, 1818
Willcox, Toliver	Eliza Danforth	Mar. 1, 1821
Willebee, Wm.	Jerusha Jones	Jan. 20, 1790
Williams, Chas. D.	Sarah Ann Flournoy	Apr. 15, 1824
Williams, Edward W.	Catherine B. Dailey	Jan. 23, 1835
Williams, Geo. W.	Louisa A. Wightman	May 8, 1843
Williams, Henry	Zilpah Morris	May 9, 1790
Williams, Henry I. G.	Helen M. Castens	Nov. 5, 1829
Williams, Hezekiah	Mary Ann Green	Sept. 5, 1833
Williams, Holston	Peggy Abbot	Mar. 6, 1823
Williams, Isaac	Nancy Bryant	Feb. 20, 1825
Williams, James	Ardiminda Parnel	Feb. 24, 1823
Williams, James	Patsey Sweeta	May 25, 1824
Williams, Jno.	Hester Carson	Feb. 27, 1790
Williams, John	Nancy Knight	Feb. 20, 1805
Williams, Josiah	Mary Mauldin	July 29, 1819
Williams, Lewis	Martha Davis	Mar. 3, 1838
Williams, M. H.	Rachael Florance	Oct. 20, 1842
Williams, Nathaniel	Susanna Haten	Nov. 30, 1785
Williams, Robt.	Rebecca Green	Apr. 18, 1804
Williams, Samuel	Hannah Collins	May 26, 1802
Williams, Samuel	Ann Prather	Jan. 15, 1824
Williams, Simeon	Polly Briant	May 10, 1824
Williams, Thomas	Catherine Clegg	Sept. 6, 1837
Williams, Washington A.	Carolina V. Harris	Oct. 23, 1847
Williams, Zachariah	Martha Walton	Oct. 2, 1800
Williams, Zachariah	Sarah Anderson	June 23, 1807
Williamson, Elias	Martha Holly	Apr. 29, 1815
Williamson, Robt.	Nancy Davis	Oct. 5, 1826
Williamson, Stephen	Mourning David	Jan. 17, 1828
Willson, James	Sarah Critington	Oct. 29, 1812
Wilson, Alexander	Abbigal Finley	July 26, 1796
Wilson, Francis	Sarah Ann Kelly	Oct. 15, 1825
Wilson, Geo. T.	Ellen J. Duer	May 17, 1838
Wilson, James B.	Maria L. Shannon	Sept. 1, 1842
Wilson, James W.	Maria L. Shannon	Aug. 29, 1842
Wilson, Joel	Sarah Preskitt	July 11, 1816
Wilson, John	Margaret Baker	Nov. 4, 1791
Wilson, John	Emery Wright	Oct. 28, 1849
Wilson, John J.	Margaret Gardner	Nov. 20, 1834
Wilson, Joseph H. C.	Nancy Lane	Sept. 7, 1837
Wilson, Wm.	Eliza Greene	Oct. 3, 1837
Wilson, Wm.	Martha Jane Frazer	Apr. 29, 1845
Wimberley, John	Patsey Bush	Dec. 2, 1813
Wimberly, Lewis	Mary Ann Hall	Dec. 17, 1849
Wimberly, Thomas	Eliz. Catlin	Dec. 24, 1829
Windsor, Anderson	Clarrisa Brown	Feb. 12, 1825
Wingard, E. D.	Eliz. B. Worsdick	Dec. 3, 1848
Winter, Berry G.	Eliz. Fulcher	Oct. 28, 1841
Winter, Frederick	Martha Sego	Dec. 8, 1840
Winter, G. W.	Ann McKinne	Nov. 6, 1845
Winter, James	Mahaley M. Howell	July 6, 1831
Winter, John	Ann Bulger	Feb. 7, 1829
Winters, Jeremiah	Mary Daniels	June 10, 1813
Winters, Jeremiah	Eliz. Kelly	Dec. 17, 1818
Winters, James	Jane Gilkie	Dec. 2, 1813
Winters, James	Martha Netherlin	June 8, 1845
Wisenger, Geo.	Winny Anderson	June 30, 1792
Wolfe, David	Anna Copeland	Mar. 23, 1844
Wood, David	Eliz. Underwood	Oct. 22, 1785
Wood, George	Rosy Henderson	Feb. 11, 1849
Wood, Jeremiah	Sarah Bacon	Feb. 22, 1797
Wood, Jonathan	Mary Gemima Barnes	July 18, 1795

GROOM	BRIDE	DATE
Wood, Jonathan	Eliz. Pervis (?)	Nov. 12, 1796 (?)
Wood, Jonathan	Eliza Julia Walker	Mar. 29, 1814
Wood, Jonathan	Blanche L. Walton	Feb. 21, 1818
Wood, Jonathan, Jr.	Polly Naomy Ramsey	May 19, 1816
Wood, Nathaniel	Lavina Anderson	Nov. 6, 1827
Wood, Wiley	Rachael Inglet	Dec. 23, 1825
Wood, Wm.	Rebecca Cooper	Aug. 11, 1812
Wood, Wm.	Casy Ann Blackburn	Feb. 20, 1845
Wood, Wm.	Frances Downs	Oct. 16, 1845
Woodruff, Michael	Abby T. Wells	Jan. 1, 1834
Woodstock, Wm. George	Maria Gordan	Oct. 10, 1841
Woolhopter, P. D.	Eliz. M. Selleck	Jan. 11, 1847
Wooten, Thomas	Hester Stuckey	Dec. 23, 1824
Worrell, Exum	Eliz. Hill	Oct. 5, 1812
Wray, James L.	Caroline A. Andrews	May 15, 1838
Wright, Augustus R.	Eliz. R. Richardson	Mar. 15, 1834
Wright, Benj.	Catherine Collins	Sept. 15, 1808
Wright, David R.	Margaret Bones	Dec. 15, 1847
Wright, Habbakkuh	Susannah Bacon	June 18, 1787
Wright, Isaiah	Rebekah Briscoe	Nov. 24, 1787
Wright, John (negro)	Polly Evans (negro)	Jan. 26, 1819
Wright, John	Emily Allen	Feb. 13, 1848
Wright, Peter	Sally Barden	Apr. 2, 1800
Wright, Samuel W.	Eliz. I. Christian	May 13, 1841
Wright, Wm. H. B.	Keziah Dillon	Jan. 13, 1831
Wyche, Littleton	Susanna Mitchell	May 2, 1798
Wyche, Robert	Mary Harris	July 14, 1795
Wynn, Thomas	Betsey Farrer	July 23, 1805
Yarborough, Levi Hamilton	Eliz. Byrd	Dec. 23, 1849
Yarborough, Littleton	Eliz. Beal	Apr. 29, 1788
Yarnold, Benj.	Lucy Moore Pearson	June 26, 1819
Young, Benj.	Eliz. C. Dye	Jan. 1, 1832
Young, George	Priscilla Wright	Nov. 4, 1841
Young, George	Pheny Goodwin	Feb. 12, 1843
Young, Geo. W.	Lucinda Collier	Sept. 14, 1829
Young, Henry	Mary Williams	May 2, 1843
Young, Lemuel	Mary Evans	Apr. 21, 1795
Young, Mitchell	Serrea Holly	Oct. 20, 1834
Young, Wm. Reilly	Sarah Rewis (?)	Nov. 8, 1841
Young, Wm.	Katherine Fox	July 2, 1801
Young, William	Martha Purvis	Dec. 20, 1844
Young, Wm. T.	Ellen G. Stewart	Apr. 1, 1819
Youngblood, Abraham	Amey McNeill	Mar. 1, 1787
Youngblood, Bazil	Ann Fleming	Dec. 26, 1833
Youngblood, Benj.	Susannah Collins	Dec. 20, 1794
Youngblood, Benj.	Polly Dillard	Jan. 20, 1810
Youngblood, George	Nancy Simpkins	Oct. 24, 1788
Youngblood, Isaac	Eliz. Youngblood	July 2, 1788
Youngblood, Joshua	Catherine McNeill	May 30, 1789
Zachry, A. G. S. L.	Mrs. Nancy H. Griffin	Sept. 29, 1828
Zammotey, Joseph	Polly Dismukes	Apr. 8, 1813
Zinn, John W. H.	Resella C. Leon	May 1, 1839
Zinn, Valentine	Nancy Carter	July 26, 1817

?,ANDREW,327;ARCHIBALD
. 320;BRITON,329
. CLEMENT A,277
. ELIZABETH,321;EPHRIAM
. 247,262;FALBY,282
. FRANCIS S,267,269;GEO
. 269;J W,278;JAMES M
. 278,287;JAMES N,287
. JESSE,346;JOHN I,283
. JOHN W M,286;JONATHAN
. 328;JOSEPH R,247
. JOSHUA,346;KNUDSON W
. 325;MARY J M,204
. NATHAN,247;R A,279
. REBECKAH,419;ROBERT
. 325;SAMUEL,24
. STARLING,326;THOMAS
. 276,345;THOS,278
. VINCENT R,247;WILLIAM
. 321,378;WM,319;WM K
. 273;ZORL,327;ZYMONIA
. 281
?----LLING,POLLY,256
?----RD,CAROLINE,264
?---EY,JOHN,282
?-----LY,LEWIS,320
?---STON,MOSES,320
?--LMAN,ANNA,409
?--REEN---,
  MARGARET J,251
?-EARS,DAVID,7
?-RISCO,MARY ANN,408
AARON,EDWARD,235
. FRANCES,274;GEO,235
. JAMES C,333;JOHN L
. 333;JOHN M,333
. MICHAEL,333;MITCHEL
. 331;THOS B,235
AARONS,MARY,197
ABBOT,HEZEKIAH,379;JOHN
. O,11;MARY,379;PEGGY
. 421;ZACHARIAH,379
ABBOTT,EZEKIEL,333
. JAMES O,27;JOHN,379
. SARAH,381
ABEL,WM A,235;ZACHARIAH
  379
ABENTER,POLLY,47
ABERCROMBIE,235,329
. ABNER,304;CHARLES,289
. 294;CHAS,288;CHS,233
. EDMD,310;L,303,311
. LEA,302;LEON,231
. ROBERT,293;S,290
. WILIE,288;WILLIE,288
ABERNATHIE,J,217
ABRAHAM,JULIA A,381
ABRAHAMS,BARNARD,379
  CLARA FISHER,384
ACOCK,ELIZABETH,208
ACRE,MATLIDA,248
ACREE,JAMES M,235;MARIA
  255
ADAIR,BABSY,235
. ELIZABETH,241;JEAN
. 367;ROBERT,235;VIRGIL
.. J,235;WM,86,96
ADAM,ARCHD,183;ARCHD H
. 183;ELIFARE L,42
. HORTON B,379;JAMES,63
ADAMS,AMANDA,193;ANN V
. 410;ANNA,196;ASA,379
. BETSEY,228;BRITAIN,77
. C B,88;D,328;DAVID,75
. 78,222,228,290,294
. 303,307,311,317,329
. 344;DAVID L,333
. DILSEY,39;EDWARD,364

. ELCY,2;ELEAZER,74
. ELIZABETH L,333
. GEORGE W,333;GINNEY
. 274;JAMES,217,222,228
. 291-292,305,311,331
. 333,379;JAMES C,291
. JAS,220,290-291,304
. 311;JEFFERSON,142;JNO
. 292,303-304,311
. JNOTHAN,291;JOHN,99
. 235,311;JOHN M,379
. JOHN STRONG,379;JON
. 290,304,306,317
. JONATH,228;JONATHAN
. 85,290,311,317,333
. LUCINDA,413;MARY,222
. 290,318;MARYAN,210
. MERIDITH,333;MILES,7
. NOAH,7,11,27;PARMELIA
. 242;S K,105;S M,70
. SABRINA,417;SARAH,388
. SETH K,127,147;THOMAS
. 232;WILLIAM,311,317
. WM,235,290-291,379;WM
. B,379;WM E,235,321
ADAMSON,DOROTHY,303,305
ADCOCK,A W,142;JOSEPH
  291,293
ADDCOCK,A H,126
ADDINGTON,NANCY,357
ADDISON,CHARLES,149
  THOMAS,36
ADERHOLD,JOHN H P,235
ADES,MARTHA,408
ADKINS,
. ADALINE TUGGLE,235
. BOOKER,235;JAMES C,66
. JOSEPH,235;MARY
. ELIZABETH,267
ADKINSON,A W,214;ANN
. 418;ARNOLD,344
. JURASHA,256;LORENA
. 270;POLLY,42,420;THOS
. 10
ADKISON,CAROLINE,380
  MARY,380
AERATT,ARCH,307
AGELEAR,JOHN,379
AIKEN,CHARLES P,333
. DANIEL,333;JAMES,333
. JOHN C,333;SAMUEL S
. 333;THOMAS,333;WM,379
AIKENS,SARAH,282;WM,235
AIKIN,W,97
AKEN,JAMES,331
AKERS,ELIZABETH,275
  JOHN,235;SAMUEL,235
AKIN,371;ANN,206
. BARTLEY,370-371
. EDMOND,235;FRANK,312
. WILLIAM,90;WILLIAM
. 132;WM,85
AKIND,BECKY,253
AKINS,ELIJAH,235;HENRY
. 235;JAMES,235;JOHN,91
. JOSEPH,235;NANCY,274
. 283;SAMUEL S,331
. TEMPERANCE,260;THOMAS
. 331;W,100;WILLIAM,82
. 91;WM A,235
ALBRITAIN,JESSE,177
ALBRITON,AMOS,379
ALBRITTON,AMOS,192
. ANSEL M,235;AUSIL,192
. JAMES,379;JESSE,192
. MARTHA,192;MATHEW,10
. 11,27;MATILDA,192

. MATTHEW,48;MELTON,192
. NANCY LEE,192;ROBERT
. L,48;TOMIL,192
ALDAY,JOHN,9;JOSEPH,36
ALDMON,PATSEY,266
ALDMOND,LUDA,211
ALDRIDGE,ARON,178;ELIZ
. 410;ELIZ VILANDA,399
. JOHN B,379;MARY ANN
. 385;SAMUEL R,235
. SARAH,386;SUSANNAH
. 383
ALDSY,JONAH,6
ALEXANDER,124-125,229
. ADAM,333;ALDEN,333
. ALFRED T,201;ASA,321
. 328;BITHIAH,215;C W
. 77;CAROLINE,43
. CHARLES,74;ELIZA,333
. EZ,350;GEORGE,333
. JAMES,69,72;JANE,331
. JOSEPH,235;JOSEPHINE
. 282;MARGARET A,259
. MARTHA,256;P,360
. PATIENCE C,265
. RIMARDO,235;ROBERT J
. 333;SAML,215;SAMUEL
. 217,329;W,244
ALFORD,219;BALDE,343
. BERTUS,235;BETSEY,238
. BRITON,235;BRITTON,64
. CHINCHEZ,235;COLLIER
. 324,329;CULLEN,342
. ELIZABETH,237;H,11
. HAYWOOD,27;JAMES,224
. 229,306-307,325;JAS
. 329;JNO,302;JOHN,321
. 328;JULIUS,215,235
. 248;LODOWICH,235;MARY
. 251,269;OWEN,315
. POLLY,274;REBECCA,265
. RECKAH,247;SIPPY,62
. TALULA E,236;WILLIAM
. 307;WIN,241;WM,235
. 287;ZADOCK,235
ALFRED,HAYWOOD,11
ALFRIEND,ADELINE,244
. BENJAMIN,235;BENJAMIN
. C,235;E W,312;EDWARD
. W,235;ELIZA J,285;H L
. 312;PATIENCE T,235
. SARAH,266;WM L,235
ALISON,215
ALLAN,JANE,233;MARGARET
. 233-234;WILLIAM,233
. 234
ALLARD,PETER LEWIS,379
ALLBRITTEN,M,52;MATHEW
. 52;ROBERT,52
ALLBRITTON,ISAAC,2
ALLDAY,CHARLES,36;JOHN
. P,27,49;JOSIAH,27,49
. NANCY,27,49;PETER,8
. 27,49
ALLDY,A,207
ALLEGOOD,SAMUEL,8
ALLEN,387;A·M,27
. ALEXANDER,379
. ALEXANDER M,8,11,379
. ALICE,150;AMANDA,242
. ANDREW T J,47;ANN,284
. ANN T,164;ANNE,150
. ARABELLA,262;BENJ,235
. BENJAMIN,379;BEVERLY
. 72;CAREY W,379
. CHARLES,27,58,305
. CHARLOTTE,150
. CHRISTIAN,396;DARCAS

ALLEN(cont)
. 371;DAVID,2,333,347
. DICKSON,235;E M,235
. EASON,11;ELIJAH,371
. ELISHA A,379;ELISHA E
. 36;ELIZ,406;ELIZA C
. 371;ELIZABETH,150,164
. 257,371,395;ELIZABETH
. J,371;EMILY,422
. FRANCES,150;FRANCES M
. 400;FRANCIS M,379
. FRANCIS T,191;FREEMAN
. 324;GEORGE,371;HANDY
. 36;HARRIET,150;HARRIS
. 331,333;HUDSON,367
. HUGH,27,50;J H,235
. J L,158;J T,191;JACK
. 150;JAMES,11,27,49,52
. 150,164,235,366,371
. JAMES P,48,50;JAMES S
. 49;JAMES W,379;JANE
. 324,408;JASPER N,312
. JEREMIAH,47;JESSE,305
. JOHN,6,27,150,235,333
. 371,379;JOHN G,36
. JOHN P,52;JOHN R,379
. JOHN T,150,152;JOHN W
. 312,379;JOSEPH,150
. 152;JOSIAH,235;LUCY
. 366;M B,38;MACON,333
. MARGARET,403;MARGARET
. H,37;MARTHA,52,411
. MARTHA A,240;MARY,52
. 371,380,410,418;MARY
. ELIZABETH,255;MARY
. LUCY,379;MATTHEW,114
. NANCY,237,386,392
. NATHANIEL,366,371
. OLIVER,36;PETER,36
. PHOEBE,333;PLEASANT
. JOSIAH,235;POLLY,248
. REBECCA,371;REUBEN
. 150;ROBERT,10,27,52
. 379;ROBERT A,50,333
. 379;SALLY,150;SAMUEL
. 331,333,379;SAMUEL A
. 379;SARAH,27,36,40,45
. 191,234,371,394-395
. 403;SARAH ANN,57
. SARAH E,278;SARAH
. ROSALIE,419;SMITH,150
. SOPHIA,371;STEPHEN
. 235;SUSAN,331;SUSANNA
. 150;T S,152;THOMAS,27
. 50,371;THOMAS J,312
. 371;W A,235;W W,333
. WILEY,235;WILLIAM,52
. 234,331,333,351,355
. 371,379;WILLIAM P,52
. WILLIAM R,379;WM,290
. WM P,48;YOUNG,379
. YOUNG J,36
ALLEOUD,MARC,379
ALLEY,LOUISA,392
ALLFORD,JAMES,291
    JULIUS,294
ALLIN,JOSIAH,226
ALLISON,223;ALEX H,190
. ALEXANDER,183
. ALEXANDER H,182;LUCY
. 183;REUBEN,236;W P
. 236;WILLIAM,91-92,94
. 95,101-102,108,126
. 224;WM,223,236
ALLMAN,JOHN,27;WILLIAM
    27
ALLMAND,ELZEA,201
ALLMOND,JOHN,6,52

MATHEW,52
ALLRED,WM,236
ALLUMS,MARY,39
ALMOND,E G,201
ALSTON,ANGELINA,80;J M
. 379;JAMES,329;WILLIS
. 236
ALSUP,EDWIN,379
ALVIN,ASHLEY,236
AMBROSE,WARREN,333
AMBURN,SAMUEL,379
AMES,SARAH S,406
AMMONS,RICHARD,236
. STERLING,307;URIAH E
. 375
AMONS,WILLIAM,312
AMOS,CASPER M,80;J K
. 100;MAULDON,159
AMOSS,GEORGE M,236
AMROR,REUBEN,260
ANDERS,SARAH,201;WM,329
ANDERSON,235;ANN,112
. 389,418;ARABELAH MARY
. JANE,379;ARELZA,213
. AUG H,49;AUGUSTUS,27
. BARBARA,200;BENJA,291
. BENJAMIN,316;CALVIN
. 201;CAROLUS,10-11,27
. D M,89;DAVID,84,114
. 149;EDWARD S,379
. ELEAZER,379;ELIJAH P
. 379;ELISHA,2,4,10,27
. ELIZ,379;ELIZA,195
. 203;ELIZA A,420
. ELIZABETH,107,114,121
. 205,266,279;ELVY,414
. ESTHER,393;GEORGE T
. 69;HARIET E,395;HENRY
. 76;ISHAM,96,107,109
. 112,114,119,134;J,112
. 113;J S,100,140,148
. JAMED,87;JAMES,6,10
. 27,49,76-77,84,87,92
. 109,114;JANE,48,379
. JAS,245;JOEL,194;JOHN
. 84,87,90,92,107,109
. 114,122,142,156-157
. 194,275,342;JOHN D G
. 194;JOHN L,131,194
. 201;JOHN M,379;JOHN S
. 142;JONATHAN,367
. JOSEPH,212;JOSEPH C
. 194;JOSEPHINE,240
. JULIA E,40;LAVINA,422
. LAWRENCE,379;LOU,206
. LUCY C,251;MARTHA,107
. 114,120,129,134,403
. MARY,84,92,107,109
. 114,119-121,129,134
. 137,148,195,200,278
. 384;MARY ANDY,206
. MATTHEW,87;MAY,274
. NANCY,395;NANCY A,281
. NANNIE,208;NATHAN,114
. NATHANIEL,83-84,146
. P H,92;PHEBE,272
. POLLY,96;POLLY ANN
. 103;R W,100;RACHEL
. 270,316;RICHARD,379
. ROBERT,379;ROSA,396
. ROXEY ANN,42;RUTH,38
. S M,333;SALLY,239
. SAMUEL,333;SARAH,4
. 279,379,407,421;SARAH
. A,382;SARAH M,395
. SEASY,207;STAFFORD
. 316;SUSAN,256;SUSAN E
. 371;SUSANNAH,261

. SWAIN M,201;THOMAS
. 379;URIAH,201;W R,113
. WILLIAM,27,218,371
. WILLIAM R,68,97,100
. WILLIAM W M,371;WINNY
. 421;WM,372,379
ANDLETON,JNO,10
ANDRES,LYDA,384
ANDRESA,113;W G,116
ANDRESS,DAVID,360
ANDREW,119,148;BENJ,379
. DAVID,360;J O,261;JAS
. ASGOOD,243;NANCY,280
ANDREWS,87,100,112-113
. 118,120-123,129,138
. 143,148,309;ABBEY,283
. ALLEN,379;CAROLINE A
. 422;COLUMBUS,201
. DAVID,62,82,88,91,148
. 379;DAVIS R,333;DRURY
. 309;ELIZABETH,235,267
. FARRER,129;GARNETT W
. 201;GEORGE,201
. GEORGIA ANN,268
. GREENE,333;H H,129
. HARVEY,6,49,52;HARVY
. 27;J,100,140;JAMES A
. 268;JAMISON,306;JOHN
. 27,49,62,82,88,90,93
. 105,108,111,113,116
. 121-123,129,131,136
. 137,146;JOHN L,144
. JOSEPH,27;KESIAH A
. 380;LEWIS,108
. MARGARET,111;MARTHA
. 108,111,123,129,136
. 146,148;MARY,111;MARY
. JANE,268;MILLY,200
. ROBERT,63,93,95,105
. 108,111,116,121,123
. 129,136,146,333
. SAMUEL,49,85;SAMUEL W
. 130;SARAH,108,111,123
. 129,136,146,285,397
. SARAH F,241;THOMAS,36
. W G,111,136;W S,108
. 111,147;WALTER,82,100
. 147;WALTER S,105,111
. 121,123,129,136,147
. WIDOW,79;WILIAM,108
. WILLIAM,111,123,129
. 136,201;WILLIAM H,71
. 88;WILLIE,52;WLATER S
. 90;WM,111;WM H,86
ANGEL,RACHEL,420
ANGLE,CRISTINA,396
ANNIS,EMERSON B,333
    MARTHA G,333
ANSLEY,ABEL,379;JESSE
. 379;PERMELIA,276
. SARAH,238;SARAH JANE
. 420;WILLIAM,151
ANTHONY,BOLING,357
. EMILY L,406;ISAAC,379
. JAMES,333;L,52
. LAVOISIER L,379
. MARGARET C,57;SARAH
. ANN,394;TABITHA,405
ANTONET,CELESTIA,146
ANTONIA,MARY,415
ANTONY,LAURA M,408
    MILTON,333;SUSAN,391
APPERSON,JAMES,104
APPLETON,ANN L,417
    SAMUEL,379
APPLEWHITE,JOHN,47,52
. PETER,47;STEPHEN,47
. THOMAS B,374

APPLING,A,161,188
. DANIEL,165;ELENOR,165
. J,155;JOHN,157,165
. OTHO H,333;REBEKAH
. 165
ARCHER,ALEXNDER,27
. JAMES,10;JANE,52;JOHN
. 52;THOMAS,9,57;WM A
. 379
ARD,MARY,360;REUBEN,360
  THOMAS,360
ARHTUR,JAMES,96
ARI---,MARGARET,262
ARINGTON,ELIZ H,419
  JOHN H,379
ARINTON,MARY,396,419
ARLIN,SARAH ANN,197
ARLINGTON,WILLIAM,52
ARM,JOHN,257
ARMER,REUBEN B,245
ARMOLY,MARGARET,52
ARMOR,BETSEY ANN,255
. EFFIE J,278;JAMES,333
. JIMMY,276;JNO,227,230
. JOHN,219,222,226-227
. 228-229,275,285,354
. 363;JOS,229;LINNIE
. 275;MARY,273;MARY ANN
. W,270;REUBEN,245,263
. REUBEN B,271;SUSAN M
. E,278;WM,270
ARMOUR,JNO,231;JOHN B
  379;PERRY,236
ARMSTRONG,ELIZABETH,255
. EMILY,248;HATTIE,246
. JAMES,135,356;JNO,240
. 352;JOHN,36,97,135
. 235,257,280,284,303
. 309,351,358;JOSEPH
. 356;M,319;NANCY,135
. REBECCA,247;SALLY,382
. SARAH,135,384;WILLIAM
. 135,331,333
ARNALL,STEPHEN,323
  WILLIAM,323
ARNETT,BRADFORD T,379
  SAMUEL,364
ARNOLD,
. ALMIRA SOPHRONIA,238
. ANNA N,235;BETHANEY
. 366;CYNTHIA,251
. ELIZABETH,241;EMMA P
. 245;FIELDING,370
. FRANCES L,239;JAMES
. 90;M W,238,249;MARTHA
. H,248;N M,250;OLIVE M
. 248;P M W,281;REUBEN
. 270-271;REUBEN B,263
. RUTH,366;WESLEY,256
. 287;WESLEY P,235
. WILLIAM W,333;WIOT,27
. WIOTT,7;WM,245,269
. 323
ARON,CYNTHA,209
ARONS,WILLIAM,213
ARP,DANIEL,130
ARRINGTON,ABNER,379
. ELIZABETH,333;EMELY
. 417;HENRY,380;HENRY W
. 380;JAMES,380;JAS,310
. JNO,13;JOHN,15,380
. SHERROD,11;WILLIAM,15
. WILLIS,380;WM,13
ARTER,JAMES,308
ARTERBERRY,JAMES,380
ARTHUR,JAMES,325
ASBERY,NANCEY,269
ASBURY,BETSEY,232;ELIZ

. 230;ELIZABETH,230,232
. ELIZABETH I,283
. MATILDA,284;NANCY,268
. RICHARD,127,230,232
. RICHARD C,127
ASHBERRY,JONATHAN,27
ASHBERY,JONATHAN,8
ASHE,MARY A,241
ASHFIELD,FREDERICK,291
ASHFORD,DENNIS,380
ASHLEY,FRANCES ANN,390
ASHLOCK,JESSE,288
ASHTON,LUCY,416
ASHURST,JOSIAH T,333
ASKEW,CASY,300;HARRIOTT
. 402;MATILIDA,409
. RHODA C,239;ROBINSON
. 13;WILLIAM,333,367
ASKEY,CASEY,308;JOSHUA
. 297,308;JOSIA,327
. URIAH,297
ASTEN,WM L,287
ASTIN,POLLY,270;REBECCA
  270;ROBERT,226
ASTON,WM,275
ATAWAY,PARALEE,58
  WILLIAM W,58
ATCHESON,JAMES A,333
ATHA,PAMELIA,412
ATHEY,ELIJAH,380
  ZEPHENIAH,380
ATKERSON,ABNER,330;R R
  50
ATKINS,ARNOLD,366;ASA
. 349;GEORGE LEE,366
. JEREMIAH,366;JOA,353
. JOSEPH C,65;LEVECY
. 366;LOVECY,366;NANCY
. 285;RANSAM,366;WILLIS
. 366
ATKINSON,A,98;ABNER,311
. AGRIPPA,218,220;ANER
. 216;ARTHUR C,58,139
. 140;C,101,105
. CORNELIUS,62,89,98
. 113,137;DIXON,380
. ELIZ,398;ELIZABETH
. 140,237,269,283,285
. EMILY,285;J C,52
. JAMES C,236;JINCEY
. 268;JOHN,36,49,52,236
. LAZARUS,236;LEMUEL,86
. NANCY,204,268,273
. NATHAN,236;NATHAN L
. 236;PATIENCE,278
. ROBERT,9,380;ROBERT R
. 27;SAMUEL,218;SARAH
. 27,49,393;T P,108
. THOMAS,93,236
. THOMAS L B,236;THOMAS
. P,58,83-84,88,91,96
. 106,117,130,132,140
. THOMS P,114;THOS P,85
. 92,99,110,113,116-117
. 119,123-124,126,136
. 139-140,144;W D,281
. W G,108,114,118,124
. 126,140;WASHINGTON
. 105,141;WASHINGTON G
. 58,82-83,103,116,118
. 139-140;WILLIAM,201
. WILLIAM F,36
ATKISON,ALEXANDER W,194
. ELIZ,407;ELIZABETH
. 395;JOHN,322
ATKNSON,THOS P,118
ATTAWAY,AMOS,36;CANDACY
. 47,52;CATHERINE M,41

. DAVID,27,52;ELIJAH,27
. 48,52;ELIZ,395
. EZEKIEL,36;FLORENCE
. 38;HARKEY B,380
. HARLEY,52;HARLY,27
. JAMES W,312;JESSE,27
. 52;JOHN J,36;JOSEPH
. 27;LAVINA,46;WILLIAM
. 36
ATTEBERRY,DARLING C,36
ATTOWAY,DAVID,6;HARLEY
  6;JOSPEH,6;WILLIAM,9
ATWELL,AMELIA,420
. ELIZABETH,37;JAMES
. 380;JEREMIAH,380;JOHN
. 380;MARTHA,413;MARY
. 409,417;REDDEN,380
AUBREY,LEWIS,236;MARTHA
. 247;REBEKAH,267;SALLY
. 267
AUEIAU,NICHOLAS,2
AUGHTRY,DAVID,380
AUGUSTINE,JOHN T,380
AURET,NATHANIEL,36
AUSTELL,A,149
AUSTIN,HARRIS,27;NANCY
. 206;ROBERT,380;WM,242
. 271,276;WM L,258
AUTHONY,ISAAC,181
AUTREY,ELIZABETH,238
  JACOB,236;O P,236
AVANT,HENRY,331,333
AVARY,ARCHER,159,161
. 172;ASA,161,185
. HERBERT,164;JOHN,187
AVERA,JOHN,154
AVERAT,ALBRIGHT,307
. BENJAMIN,307;DAVID
. 307;JOHN,307;WM,307
AVERELL,THOMAS,380
AVERETT,ANN,386;HARRIET
. L,379;JAMES,333;MARY
. 402;THOMAS,380
AVERIT,CHRISTOPHER C
  380;JANE B,380
AVERITT,ELIZABETH,342
. JOSEPH B,380;NANCY
. 410
AVERY,ARCHER,163,165
. 186-187;ASA,186;ASA G
. 333;HARBERT,186
. HERBET,333;JOHN,179
. 186;JOSEPH,236;MARY
. ANN,389;MILLEY,386
. MILLY,186;ROSE ANN
. 333;SAMUEL,331,333
. SARAH A,275;SARAH H
. 163;WILLIAM,333
AVINGTON,CHARLES,363;WM
  380
AVRET,ALEXANDER,380
. CHARLES C P,380
. CHRISTOPHER C,380;WM
. 380;WM A,380
AWSBY,SARAH,244
AWTREY,ALEXANDER,223
  JOHN,236;REYNOLDS,236
AWTRY,ALEXANDER,366,371
AXON,J S R,286
AXSON,J S K,283;SAMUEL
  E,236
AYCOCK,ELIZABETH,208;J
  116;NANCY,200
AYMAV,SEBASTIEN,380
AYRES,JOHN,154;WILLIAM
  215;WM,380;WM M,380
B---NS,MARTHA,263
B--L--,LUCY,274

BABB,WM,236
BABCOCK,11;JAMES,8;JAS
  5;JOS B,312
BACHELOR,ARCHIBALD,236
  CON,236;RICHARD,236
BACKMAN,LARUA,414
BACON,FRANCIS,386;JOHN
. N,380;LUCY G·W,387
. LYDDAL,380;MARY ANN
. 387;SARAH,421;SIDWELL
. 161;SUSANNAH,422;WM
. 380
BACONE,MARY E,281
BADGET,321
BADULY,JOHN,27;JOHN G
  52;MARY,52;WILLIAM,4
BAER,JOSIE,36
BAGBY,CHAS L,236;DICEY
. 286;GEO E R,236
. THOMAS,129
BAGET,W W,67
BAGGERLY,DAVID,88
BAGGET,329;ANNIS,399
  NANCY,406
BAGGETT,MIRIAM,413
  RHODA,256
BAGGS,ELIJAH,380;JOHN
  13,15;WM,13,15-16
BAGLEIF,MELVINA,383
BAGLEY,ELIZABETH A,236
. GELLY D,286;MARY ANN
. 405;PERETHENE,286;WM
. P,380
BAGLY,THOMAS,130
BAGWELL,LITTLEBURY,82
  LOUISA,90
BAILEY & HUNTER131
BAILEY,11-12,113,118
. 121-122,129,138;ANNE
. 404;C,113;CALEB,372
. CAROLINE,372;CHARLES
. 60,62,70-71,74,78-79
. 80-81,86,95,102,108
. 113,119,124,131-132
. 137-138,142;D J,87,89
. 100-101,104,113,116
. 129,131,136,140,145
. 149;D L,112,120,142
. DAVID,36,52,110;DAVID
. J,68,74,89,103,119
. 121,130,138;DAVID L
. 96;DAVIS,50;ELIAS,27
. ELIZABETH,372;ELSEY
. 390;EMILY,43,372
. FREDERICK A,64;FULLER
. 366;GILLEY,366;GREENE
. 361;H,380;HENRY,60,67
. HENRY J,60,62,64,70-71
. 74-75,78;JAMES,27,89
. 93-94,97-98,146;JANE
. 74;JANES,27;JAS,100
. JEREMIAH,366;JNO,301
. JOEL,63,67-68,71,78
. JOHN,82,327,366,371
. 372;JOSEPH,372;KITTY
. 262;LOUISA,249;LUCY
. 410;LYDIA,37;MARTHA
. 372;MARY,372,420;MARY
. ANN,67;MILLEY,366
. NANCY,372,410
. NATHANIEL,236;RICHARD
. 64,78,80,353;ROBERT
. 67;S,100,118,133,140
. S P,68;S T,112;SALLEY
. 366;SAMUEL ARMSTRONG
. 236;SARAH,372;STEPHEN
. 64,67,85,91,94,100-101
. 103-104,107-108,110

. 111,113-115,117,119
. 121-122,132,137,139
. 146,148-149;STEPHEN P
. 67;THOMAS,86;THOMAS B
. 67,79;THOROGOOD,75
. THOS,126;WILLIAM,60
. 366,372;WILLIAM H,331
. 333;WILLIAMSON,331
. 333
BAILY,SARAH,387;STEPHEN
  148
BAINE,SALLY,277
BAIRD,BENJ,380;EMALINE
  D,253;NELSON,380
BAKER,ARCHD,10
. ARCHIBALD,27;ASA,21
. 23-24;BASEL,201
. CHARITY,399;CHARLES
. 380;CHRISTOPHER,236
. DANIEL,72;EDNA A,128
. 135,140;ELISHA,8
. ELIZABETH,279;FANNY V
. 258;HENRY,380;HENRY H
. 68;JERRY,232;JESSE
. 302;JETHRO,108;JOEL
. 128,135,140;JOHN,10
. JONATHAN,236;JORDAN
. 356;JORDON,9;JOSEPH
. 303,360;JOSHUA,343
. JOURDON,354;M F,271
. MARGARET,421;MARGIT
. 360;MARY,251;MARY C
. 72;NANCY,262;REBEKAH
. 281;SALLY,275;SARAH
. 294;SILAS,236;STEPHEN
. H,128,135;STEVEN,140
. SUSANNAH,294;WILLIAM
. 92;WILLIAM T,72;WM
. 236
BAKS,EATON,334
BAKSTON,REUBEN,96
BALDWIN,226,234;A C,52
. ANN,409;AUGUSTUS,380
. BENJ,236;BETSY,222
. CATHERINE,255;CHARLES
. 270;CHAS,236;DAVID
. 236;ELIZABETH,222
. FRANCES,236;JAMES,236
. 278;JAS,245,247;JOHN
. 36,333;JOHN R,371
. JOSEPH H,236;LOUISA R
. T,389;LUCY,256;MARCUS
. A,333;MARGARET,255
. MORDECAI,230;NANCY
. 285;OWEN,168;OWNE,185
. PERMELIA,285;REBECCA
. 260;RICHARD,184;ROBT
. 236;SAMUEL,236;THO
. 220-221,224,228
. THOMAS,225;THOS,223
. THOS B,236;WILLIAM
. 222,234;WM,225,229
BALDY,REBECCA ANN,396
BALES,ROBELIA H,251
BALEY,ISAIAH,380;JAMES
. 102;JOEL,67;MARY
. BOSANQUET,381;S P,67
BALFLOWER,ROBERT,342
BALINGER,WILLIAM,354
BALIS,163
BALL,ALEY,284;ELIZA,235
. ESTHER,373;G H,52
. HANNAH,372;ISAAC,341
. ISAIAH,372-373;JEPTHY
. 372;JESSE,131,373
. JOEL,372-373;JOHN,142
. JONATHAN,373;REBECCA
. 373;SARAH,260

. WILLIAIM,373;WILLIAM
. 370;WM,380;ZELPHY,372
BALLANGER,DAVID,354
BALLARD,EDWARD,2,9,27
. EDWD,9;ELIJAH,127
. ELLA F,43;GEO,236
. HARRIETT C,244;JAMES
. 324;JOHN,236;MARY,48
. MILLEY,47;REDDICK,8
. 27,52;SARAH,262;W E
. 331,333;WM,232,236
. 290
BALLENGER,WILLIAM,354
BAMBERG,WM G,380
BANBRAY,WILLIAM,97
BANCKSTON,ABNER,341,366
. DANIEL,366;EDETH,366
. JACOB,216;JOEL,216
. PATTEY,366;RACHEL,366
. THOMAS,366
BANDERFORD,RICHARD,289
BANDY,HANNAH,373;JAMES
. 373;JOSEPH,373;LEWIS
. 302,373-374;MARY,373
. SARAH ANN,373;WILLIAM
. 373
BANEY,ABSALOM B,373
BANION,JOHN O,51
BANK,AUGUSTA,177
BANKS,ANN C,284
. BENJAMIN W,331,333
. CHARLES,333
. CHRISTOPHER C,333
. DUNSTAN,334;ELIZABETH
. 203;ESTHER M,405
. JAMES,334;JAMES E,90
. JOHN C,331,334;JOHN T
. 334;JOSIAH C,331,334
. MARY,331;NANCY,331
BANKSTON,108,119-121
. 126,217;A,93,111;AB
. 100;ABNER,73,80,82
. 146;ABRIM,349;ALFRED
. 90;BOLYN K,92;C,105
. COLEMAN,97;DANIEL,216
. ELAM J,90;ELIZABETH
. 149;HENRY,84,87;HENRY
. M,91;HENRY S,97;ISAAC
. 97,216;J,100;J S,113
. JAMES E,146,149;JAMES
. L,64;JAMES R,149
. JAMES S,82;JANE,97
. JOHN,82,125;JOHNNATHAN
. 87;MARTHA,97,113
. REUBEN,69;THOMAS,73
. W R,101,116,130
. WILLIAM R,90,97,107
. WM R,145,149
BANNING,J L,143
BANYAN,JOHN,9
BAR,CLARKE,36
BARBEE,JOSEPH,334
BARBEL,THOMAS,104
BARBER,A,105;AUGUSTUS
. 36;ELIZA,210;G,97;G W
. 87,100,122,141;GEORGE
. 132;GEORGE W,95,131
. HOLDEN,11;HOLDING,48
. JOHN,201;JOSIAH,133
. 143;JOSIAH W,94-95,98
. 102,116,119,129;M,121
. MATTHEW,91,100
. MISSOURI,44;RICHARD
. 349;RICHARD J,236
. SAMUEL,65;WILLIAM,345
. 349
BARCLAY,LEROY P,334
  WILLIAM,334

BARD,WILIBY,198
BARDELL,ROBT W,287
BARDEN,GBT,353;POLLY
  407;SALLY,422
BARDIN,GBT,350
BARDLEY,WILLIAM,64
BARDWELL,ERASTUS,380
BAREFIELD,ARTHUR,236
. COLLIN,9;CULLEN,50
. JAMES J,36;JESSE,49
. JOHN,6,36,373-374
. LUCRETIA,41;MILLEY
. 373;SALLY,373;SAMUEL
. 373-374;VINCENT,9
. VINSON,50;WILLIAM,311
. 373-374;WINNEY,373;WM
. 9
BARER,L L,113
BARERON,JACK,36
BARFIELD,A,147;COLLIN
. 27;JOHN,49;SAMPSON
. 236;SOLOMON,147,311
. VINCENT,27;WILLIAM,27
. 373
BARFOOT,WM,380
BARGER,REBECCA,407
BARGERON,ABIGAIL,49
. BENJ,8;BENJAMIN,36
. BENJAMIN F,36;ELIJAH
. 51-52;ELISHA,49;ELITA
. 52;GEORGE W,36;JANE M
. 39;LOUISA,37,40;NANCY
. ANN,45;WILLIAM,36
BARHAM,AMANDA M,413
. CHARLES,151;ELIZ,400
. ELIZABETH WHITTINGTON
. 190;REBECCA,183
. TIMOTHY,183;TIMOTHY T
. 188,190
BARKER,EMMA,399;HELEN
. 27;JAMES,236;JNO,380
. JOHN,179;NANCY,274
. PATSEY,254;PHANEY,256
. REESE,380;SARAH,263
. THO R,73;THOMAS A,69
. THOMAS R,69
BARKLEY,ANDREW,67
. ELIZABETH A,129
. ELIZABETH ANN,107
. JAMES,98;JANE,67,98
. 107,112,129,147;JOHN
. 67,98,107,112,129
. JOHN H,129;WILLIAM,59
. 67-68,74,80,334
BARKSDALE,ALFRED,312
. COLLIER,328;GREEN B
. 236;JAS,318;JEFRY,305
. JOSEPH,318;SARAH ANN
. 274;WM C,327
BARKWELL,JOHN W,97
. JULIUS,236;R W,97
BARLEY,BATES,27;CELIA
. 51;JOHN B,52
BARLOW,ANN,398;EMILY
. 408;G,105;GEORGE,100
. R,100,113;RICHARD,100
. 113,138,146;RICHRD,97
. 137
BARNADORE,MATTHEW,93
BARNAM,WILLIAM,361
BARNARD,TOMOTHY,380
BARNES,A,328;ABEL,320
. ABSALOM,374;ABSOLOM
. 321;ALFORD,374;ANDREW
. 222;ASA,236;BAT,9
. BENJ,72;CAROLINE,276
. CATHERINE M,418;DAVID
. 48;DEMPSEY,9,48

. DEMPSY,27;DOLLY,46
. ELIZABETH,320,362
. EMALINE,248;EPHRAIM
. 320-321;HANNAH,44
. HENRY,86-87,89,95,106
. 126,134;JAMES,301,314
. JAMES H,194;JESSE,320
. 374;JILPAH,320;JOHN
. 102,106,312,315,374
. JOHN A,380;JOHN B,380
. JOHN W M,253;JOSEPH
. 374;JOSHUA,236;JULIA
. 198;LEWIS,295,300,302
. LUETHY,374;MARTHA AN
. 374;MARY C,391;MARY
. GEMIMA,421;MATILDA
. 374;NANCY,331,334
. NATHAN,374;POLLY H
. 374;ROBERT,232;SALLY
. 374;SAMUEL,236
. WILLIAM,48,52,341,361
. WILLIAM E,346;WM,236
BARNET,BETSEY ANN,280
BARNETT,ANN,237,255
. ELIJAH F,334;ELIZ,415
. ELIZA,334;ELIZABETH
. 374;ELLINOR,415
. GEORGE,374;GREEN,82
. JAMES,374;JAMES L,95
. JOEL,175,380;JOHN,236
. JOHN L,102,116;LUCY
. 260;MARGARET,262
. NANCY,256,388;NATHAN
. 64;NATHAN B,95
. NATHANIEL,331,334
. SAMUEL,223;SUSAN,248
. SUSANNAH,246;THO,234
. W B,253,268;WILLIAM
. 189;WM,236;ZADOCK,374
BARNETTE,MARY,248
BARNEY,JONATHAN,63;MARY
. ANN,395
BARNHARDT,JANE,271
. MARY A E,242;NANNIE
. 242;REBEKAH,270
BARNHART,322;BRUCE,236
. ELIZABETH,236,266
. LEROY,236;MARTHA ANN
. 238;MARTHA J,235;MARY
. ANN,251;PHILLIP,303
. SEABORN R,236
. VIRGINIA,265
BARNHEART,PHILIP,330
. RACHEL,303
BARNITT,WM,380
BARNS,HENRY,95;JOHANN
. 213
BARNTT,ZADDK,374
BARNWELL,ALEXANDER,236
. BENJ,236;ELIZABETH A
. 334;H,105,113;HENRY
. 97,237;JESSE,237
BAROM,MARY ANN,404
BARON,SAMUEL,27;WILLIAM
. 27
BARR,HARRIETT N,334
. JAMES,117;NATHAN D,27
. OLIVER,237;WILLIAM J
. 334
BARREN,HENRY,90,117
. JOHN,294;NANCY,86
. THOMAS,89,361
BARRET,EDWARD M,380
BARRETT,ELIZA G,397
. ELLEN S,401;FRANCES L
. 399;JANE L,396;JOHN
. 237;SARAH R,386
. THOMAS,380

BARRON,234;ANDREW J,334
. HENRY,107,139,147
. JOHN,52,60,78,186,226
. 319;JOSEPH,2;LOUISA E
. 43;SAML,288,294
. SAMUEL,311;SMITH,68
. 78;SUSAN,60;THOMAS
. 155;THOS,237;WILIAM
. 49;WILLIAM,52,57,60
. 78,299,310;WM,2
BARRONHART,PHILLIP,303
BARRONHEART,PHILLIP,311
BARROW,AARON,10,51-52
. BENJAMIN L,36;CHARLES
. W,36;CYRUS B,237
. HOMER W,36;ISAIAH,51
. ISIAH,52;JACOB,309
. 360;JAMES,290
. JANE SARAH ANN,45;JAS
. 309;JOHN,48,293
. MARTHA,27;NANCY,290
. 293;REBECCA,41;REUBEN
. 380;SAMUEL,52;SARAH
. 52;SARAH BILLINGSLEA
. 377;SARAH J,45
. WILLIAM,52
BARRY,EDWARD,380;ELLEN
. 391;JOHN,380;M M,237
. MARIA,395;THOMAS H,36
BARSH,ANNE C,221
. EUGENIA I,221;GEORGE
. 221
BARTEE,ROBERT,160
BARTHLOMEW,PHILIPINE
. 380
BARTHOLOMEW,JOHN,3
. NICHOLAS,381
BARTHOLOMEY,JOHN,2
BARTLET,EUGENE S,334
. GEORGE T,334;WILLIAM
. 82
BARTLETT,104,109,138
. ABNER,237,334;C,92
. EUGENE S,331;GEORGE T
. 331;J,142;JAMES,381;L
. 102;M,93,101,103,105
. 108,119,140;MARION,84
. MARY,331,334;MYRON,87
. 96,102;NATHAN B,102
. O M,94;SAMUEL EUGENE
. 334
BARTLEY,FANNY,42;HENRY
. C,36;PATRICK,381
BARTLY,JAMES,381
BARTON,86-87;ANNA,375
. BENJ T,381;BETH HANA
. 375;DAVID,51,381
. ELIAS,375;ELIZ ANN
. 397;ELIZABETH,375
. EUGENIA C,39;GEORGE
. 381;HANNAH,375
. HARRIET,382;HULDY,43
. JAMES T,381;JANE
. FRANCES,390;JANSEY
. 374;JOEL,375;JOHN H M
. 236;LARKIN,349;LOUISA
. 41;LUCY,375;MARY F
. 407;MORNING,375;NANCY
. 375,407;PATIENCE W
. 413;POLLY,374;PRESLEY
. 374;PRESLY,375
. REBECCA,384;RHODA,375
. RUTHA,375;SAMUEL,375
. STEPHEN,50,52
. THOMPSON,237;WILLIAM
. 36,370,375;WILLOUGHBY
. 36
BARWICK,BERRY,201

BARWICK(cont)
. CAROLINE,197
. ELIZABETH,212;ELIZEAR
. ANN,201;GEORGE J,201
. JAMES,201;JANE,208
. LOTT,213;LUCIAN,201
. LUCY ANN,199;MARGARET
. 210;MARY,205;NANCY A
. 195;NATHAN,213-214
. OZENA,202;PHRABEY,198
. SERENE,206;SUSANAH
. 195;WILLIAM W,194
. WINNIFORD,206
BASEMORE,JOHN,194;SARAH
201
BASOR,SARAH,296
BASS,A S,313;ALLEN,362
. BRYAN,27;ELI,9;ENOCH
. 52;EPHRAIM,7,27;ESAU
. 10;GEORGE,10,315
. HENRY,381;JAMES A,237
. JARED E,10;JESSE,7,11
. 27,48;JOHN,7,48,60
. JOHN H,381;JONATHAN,7
. LIZZIE,246;MARTHA,416
. MARY,278;MATTHEW,3
. MATTHEWS,2;MICTHEL
. 334;SIMON D,315;WESTS
. 194;WILLIAM,52
. WILLIAM A,334;WM C
. 246
BASSER,JONATHAN,418
BASSET,WM,381
BASSETT,JOHN,369
BASTON,C B,36;LUTHER,36
MARTIN V,36
BAT---,SUSAN M A,270
BATCHELOR,AMEY,278
. CORNELIUS,215,219
. JESSE,237
BATEMAN,A,381;J B,89
104;MARY,404
BATES,JOHN,27,52,237
. 306;JOHN F,36;JOSEPH
. W,36;NANCY,272
. NATHANIEL,237;RHODA
. 253;ROBERT,237;SUSAN
. 237;WILLIAM,151
. WILLIAM C,52;WM,237
BATSON,JOHN,361
BATTER,WILLIAM,52
BATTEY,CEPHAS,381;GEO M
381;W,11
BATTLE,219;ISAAC,327
. JOHN,237;LAZARUS,304
. 309,375;LAZR,303
. MARGARET,375
. MARGARET-ANN,375
. MARTHA,375;MATTIE,269
. OLIVER LAZARUS,375
. SUSANNA,273;THOMAS,3
. THOS,2,341;WILLIAM
. 216,218,305;WM,305
BAUCHCUM,AARON,237
. PINCKNEY,237;VERNECEY
. 261
BAUDRY,ANAISE,405
W AUGUSTE,381
BAUGH,ABRAHAM,275;ABRAM
. 237;ABSALOM,282
. ABSOLEM,237;CHARLOTTE
. 263;ELLEN,247;JAS E
. 237;JOS C,312;LUCY
. 286;PRISCILLA,254;R
. 248;RICHARD,284
. RICHARD HENRY,237
. SARAH JANE,253
BAUGHAN,JAMES,147

BAUGHCUM,W W,237
BAUGHTRIGHT,MARYANN,195
BAUGHTRITE,DANIEL,194
REUBEN,194
BAXLEY,AARON,237;CALEB
9,27;WILLIAM,36
BAXTER,ANDREW,290,305
. 323,326,328;ANDW,301
. 302,304;BURCHET,240
. CHARLES,7,26-27,47
. JEREMIAH,325;MARY,47
. R,57;THOMAS,52;THOS W
. 299;WM,237
BAYLEY,JAMES,15
BAYLIS,ISHAM,163
BAYN,JOHN,157
BAYNE,EDWARD,1;JOHN,157
BAYNES,ALFRED J,334
. ELBERT W,331,334;GENE
. 334;JOHN H,331,334
. SARAH ELIZABETH,334
BAYNON,WATKINS,237
BAYS,JOSEPH,237;MARY
279
BAYSDEN,MARY,334
BAZER,CALEB,304,309;ED
319;WM,309,319
BEACH,CATHERINE,388
. CHARLES,381;JAMES,297
. 334;MARY,380
BEACHAM,DANIEL,90;LEWIS
194,213;MINNIE,205
BEAK,60
BEAL,328;ANN,417;C P
. 407;E J,201;ELEANOR
. 396;ELIZ,422;ELIZ
. WATSON,400;ELIZABETH
. 334;ELOISA,383;HENRY
. 1;JAMES,113,381;JOHN
. W,381;LITTLEBERRY,381
. MARIA,388;MARY,398
. NATHAN,28;REBECCA,382
. ROBERT,381;TABITHA
. 381;THOMAS C,381;WM
. 381;YALLULAH,37;Z,223
BEALE,AUGUSTUS,185
. BETSEY ANN,192
. CHARLES SIMMONS,185
. EDITH,189;ELEANOR,166
. ELIZ,411;FRANCIS,381
. GASEWAY,381;JOHN W,36
. MARYANN,185;NANCY,176
. REASON,381;THAD,164
. 165;WILLIAM,185
. WILLIAM L,185;WILLIAM
. P,187;WM P,187
BEALL,ALPHEUS,104
. AUGUSTUS,174;CHARLES
. T,161,174;ELIAS,124
. FRANCIS S,174;FRANCIS
. SHEPPERD,174;JAMES D
. 334;JANE,174;JOHN S
. 174;LYDDIA,189;MARTHA
. TENNASON,174
. NATHANIEL,51;R A,314
. REASON D,174;THADDEUS
. 375;THOMAS,174-175
. WILLIAM,52;WILLIAM L
. 174
BEALLE,CHARLES T,172
. 179-180;HEZEKIAH,172
. 381;JNO W,381;JOHN
. 172;JOHN T,176;MARY
. 172;NANCY,172;WILLIAM
. 172;WILLIAM PENN,172
. WM P,191
BEALT,WILLIAM,7
BEAM,STEPHEN D,76

BEAMAN,THOMAS,315
BEAN,JOSEPH S,381
BEARD,EDMOND,319-320
. JOHN,180;LOUISA,281
. MATTHEW,180;STEPHEN
. 180;THOMAS I,381
BEARDEN,AMY,272;J,116
. JOHN,342;RICHARD,237
. THOS,85
BEARDIN,HANNAH,274
THOMAS,64
BEARDING,ARTHUR,237
MARGARET,379
BEARDS,WASHINGTON,237
BEARFIELD,JAMES I,36
. JESSE,52;JOHN,52;MARY
. FRANCES,45;VINSON,52
BEARROW,MARTHA,40
BEARUM,REBECCA,414
BEASLEY,ADELLA,211;ASA
. 194;BURRELL,199
. DELILA,210;ELBERT,194
. ELIAS,201;ELIJAH,201
. ELIZABETH,376;HIRAM
. 237;JARREL,355,363
. JOHN,79,194,201;LAURA
. 280;MARGARET,263
. MARIANN,201;MARTHA A
. 238;MARTHA ANN,376
. MARY,237,375;MARY ANN
. 203;MILLEY,197
. REBECCA,199;ROBERT
. 216,375;ROBERT C,76-77
. 334;ROBERTSON,375
. SEYMORE S,375;STEPHEN
. W,334;WILLIAM,194,355
. WILLIAM A,201;WILLIAM
. S,376;WM,237;ZENO C
. 375-376
BEASLY,CATHARINE,205
JNO,381;SEYMORE S,376
BEATHLEM,T C,114
BEATIE,JOHN,237
BEATON,MARY,419
BEATTIE,JOHN,269,278
BEATY,JAMES,28,349;JAS
3,10;JOHN,11;THOS,3
BEATYS,JAMES,10
BEAU,JOSEPH,412
BEAUCAMP,DANIEL,93
BEAUCHAMP,102;DANIEL
. 231;LITTLETON,323
. WILLIAM,220,323
BEAUFORT,RICHARD,201
BEAULAND,ELIZ,384
BEAULARD,JOHN ADRAIN
381
BEAVERS,B,149;DANIEL
. 237;ELIZA L,131,150
. HARRIET,149;HARRIET A
. 131,150;HARRIET B,149
. JANE,232;MILES,228
. NATHAN,237;POLLY,287
. R C,147;ROBERT,232
. SARAH E,131,150;SILAS
. M,131,149-150
BEAZLEY,LEMUEL,381;MARY
V,248
BEBE,HARRIOT,396
SUSANNA,411
BEBEE,ADELINE,383
BECCOM,DOYLE,381
BECK,I J,278,281;JACOB
. L,381;JOHN B,28;T J
. 237
BECKAM,CAMEL,36
BECKCOM,PHILLIS,386
BECKEM,CAMBELL,312

BECKEM(cont)
  WILLIAM,312
BECKERS,ELIZABETH,258
BECKET,WM G,142
BECKHAM,SHERWOOD,381
. SOLOMON,381;SUSAN,255
. YOUNG,353
BECKLEY,SALLY,246
BECKOM,JOHN,237;MARY
  251
BECKWITH,GRACE,80;W B
  334;WILLIAM S,334
BECTON,ANDREW·F,36
BECTUR,ANN,52;LEWIS,52
BEDELL,A,218;CLAIRSSA
. 260;ELIZABETH,277
. JOHN,237;MICAJAH,237
. SUSAN,260
BEDFORD,LUCY,249
BEDGOOD,AXEY,196;JANE
. 200;JOHN,194;MARY,52
. MATTHEW,28,52
BEDINGFIELD,DAVID,8,350
. HARDY,9;JNO,381
. MARTHA,28;NEEDHAM,10
BEDSON,GEORGE W,36
BEEKHAM,WILLIAM,155;WM
  155
BEEKIN,SAMUEL,289
  SOLOMON,289
BEEKS,94;WILLIAM A,113
BEEMAN,C P,257;C T,253
. 278;HENRY,237;NATHAN
. 237;SAMUEL H,237
BEEN,BURRELL,85
BEENEY,W V,60
BEERS,JONATHAN S,381
  WILLIAM P,52
BEESLEY,BRYANT,381;JNO
  381
BEGHAM,JAMES,22,24
BEGNON,CASSMERE J,237
BEGOOD,MARY,199
BEHTUNE,L,279
BELAND,BENJAMIN,343
  JAMES,237,343
BELANDER,52
BELANGER,WILLIAM,48
BELCHER,ABNER,11,28
. ABRAHAM,9;ABRAM,9,52
. BENJAMIN B,201;DANIEL
. 11;ELIZ,390;ELLEN,42
. FERREL,381;GREEN B
. 334;HARRIET,42
. HARRIET M,45;ISHAM S
. 334;J ABNER,11;JAMES
. 36;MARTHA,11;MARY,28
. MOURNIN,28;MOURNING
. 49,52;O,348;OBADIAH
. 219,354;OBADIAH R,334
. OBEDIAH,218;PHILLIP
. 11;SARAH,405;WILEY,7
. 11,28;WILLIAM D,334
BELE,RUFUS,57
BELL,1,112,125,418;A H
. 237;ALBERT,37;ALVINA
. 37;AMOS,36;ANNA,46
. ARCHD,9,28;ARCHIBALD
. 49;ARTHER,9;ARTHUR,28
. 52;BENJAMIN,28;DAVID
. 194;DELAEY,49;DEMPSEY
. 49,52,381;DEMPSY,6
. DOROTHY,273;ELIAS,49
. 243;ELISHA,28;ELIZ
. 420;EMMA,37;FRANCES
. 380;FREDERICK,49,52
. GEORGIA,47;GREEN,9,28
. 52,202;HENDY J,36

. HENRY,6,28,52;HENRY D
. 381;HETTY,40;HIRAM,49
. 52;HUGH,183;J P,201
, JACOB,37;JAMES,28,52
. 237,371;JAMES K,36
. JAMES W,36;JANE,380
. 381;JARARD,237;JARED
. 344,348;JEREMIAH,52
. JESSE,298,309;JOHN,6
. 28,37,183,237,334
. JOHN W,36;JORDAN,28
. 49;JOSEPH,9;JOSEPH R
. 36;JOSEPH W H,36
. JOSIAH,381;KENDALL
. 237;LAVINA,275;LEMUEL
. 36;LUCRETIA,381
. MALCOMB,36;MARRY,183
. MARTHA,28;MARTHA C
. 271;MARY,207,236,257
. 388,391,409;MATHEW,9
. 201;MOSES,37;NANCY,40
. NATHAN,9;NATHANIEL
. 237;PAMELIA,239
. PIERCE,237;RACHEL,36
. REBECCA,36;RHODA,39
. RICHARD,28;SEARBORN
. 36;SIMEON,49,52
. THOMAS,8,28;THOMPSON
. 381;V A,269,271
. W JAMES,381;WILLIAM,6
. 28;WM,237,381;WM A
. 381;WM HARRISON,381
. ZACHARIAH,381
BELLAH,HIRAM,84;JAMES
. 376;JANE,376;JAS W
. 237;JOHN,60,67,376
. MORGAN,376;MOSES,376
. PEGGA JANE,376;PEGGY
. 376;RACHEL,376;REUBEN
. L,149;REUBIN,376;SAML
. 374;SAMUEL,60,63,69-70
. 71,84,86,94,96,104
. 124-125,130,136-137
. 143,149,376;TEMPEY
. 376
BELLAMY,C,124;N,107
BELLE,WILLIAM,202
BELLINGSBY,SALLY,249
BELSHER,A,57
BELT,C T,202;L C,381
BEMAN,WILLIAM,89
BENCE,WILLIAM,84,86-87
  90,92,96;WM,103
BENDER,JOHN,351,353,359
  362;JOHN S,334
BENDICT,52
BENEDICT,JOHN C,237
BENET,LEWIS,94
BENETT,AGNES,398;JOHN
  381
BENFO,LEONARD,226
BENHAM,LYMAN,237;SARAH
  E,272
BENION,THOMAS M,52
BENJAMIN,FRANCIS,381
BENL,AUGUSTA,394
BENNEFIELD,SUSAN,42
BENNET,BENJAMIN,213,349
. ELIZABETH,213;JACOB
. 381;JAMES,19;JOHN,381
. L,91;LEWIS,85,93;MARY
. 400;SARAH,384
BENNETH,MARTHA,245
BENNETT,AARON,202;ALEX.
. 37;AMANDA,211,240;ANN
. 233;BENJAMIN,349
. BENJAMIN L,202
. CHARLES,202;CHAS,237

. ELIABETH,209;ELIAS
. 237;ELIZ R,242
. ELIZABETH,262,274,391
. EMMA,273;GEORGE ANN
. 198;H G,98;ISAAC,202
. JACOB,233;JAMES,237
. JANE,239;JAS,237;JNO
. 381;JOHN,194,213,233
. JOHN FRANKLIN,193
. LAURA,39;LEWIS,88,90
. 98,100,102,126,131
. 141;LOVEL J,202
. MARTHA ANN,204;MARY
. 238;NANCY,243;NANCY
. AURENA,249;REUBEN,237
. RILEY W,237;SUSAN,275
. THOMAS,194,381
. VIRGINIA,249;WILLIAM
. 48,233;WM,237
BENNING,JANE,171;JOHN
. 164;JOSEPH,164,171
. MARTHA D,164;NANCY
. 164;PLEASANT,164
. ROWANNA,164;SALLY C
. 164;SUSANNAH,164
. THOMAS,164
BENNITS,BENJAMIN,349
BENNS,CHARLES,381
BENNTT,JOHN,169
BENSON,325;ABBA,334
. ISAAC,298,320;JAMES
. 334;JAMES M,334
. JEREMIAH,334;JOHN,334
. JOSEPH,309;LEVI,298
. 370;LUCIAN,334;OTIS M
. 334;SARAH J,334
. THOMAS J,37;WILLIAM
. 37,101
BENSTON,AARON,310;LEVI
  347
BENT,JOHN,237
BENTLEY,EDMUND J,97
  JAMES,59,115,126
BENTLY,JAMES,59,62
BENTON,ABBA,331;ADAM
. 194;AMOS,381;JAMES L
. 80;JESSE,72;JOHN,305
. MORDICAI,381;ROBERT F
. 62,81-82
BERGE,ALBERT H,92
BERGER,CAREY W,237
BERGERON,ABIGAIL,28
. ELIJAH,28;ELIZABETH
. 28
BERNER,WILLIAM R,334
BERNETT,ELARRINDA,206
BERREY,DABNEY,381
BERRIAN,ALECK,37;SARAH
  204
BERRICE,317
BERRIE,WM JAS,381
BERRIEN,J M,10;SARAH,39
  THOMAS M,52
BERRY,A T,334;ANDERSON
. 334;ANN W,389
. BENJAMIN,189;BENJAMIN
. H,364;CHAS S,238
. DAVID,113,132,136,138
. 149;G J,312;J,98
. JAMES,138;JOHN,98,114
. JOHN J D,135,149;JOHN
. V,113,130,135,137
. JULIA,135;MARTHA,135
. MARTHA ANN,421;MARY
. 135;SARAH,408
BERRYHILL,ELIZ,414
. HENNY,412;NANCY,418
. SAMUEL,381;THOMAS,23

BLAND,CHARLES T,382;EDY
  196;THOMAS,132
BLANKENSHIP,HEZEKIAH
. 294;JENNY,279;JOHN
. 238;NANCY C,248
. SAMUEL,325
BLANKES,DEMSEY,238
BLANKINSHIP,REUBIN,294
  309
BLANKS,MARTHA,250
. MATILDA,255;POLLY,284
. WM,238
BLANN,THOMAS S,84;THOS
  G,85
BLANTON,EDM,224;JAMES L
  73,77;W M,238
BLASENGAME,BENJAMIN,217
  PHILLIP,217
BLASIGAME,239
BLASINGAME,2;JAMES,261
BLASINGHAM,HARVEY,1
BLASSINGAME,JAS T,238
  SALLY,239
BLEASE,THOMAS W,382
BLECKINGTON,SUSAN,383
BLEDSOE,100;A,244;AARON
. 238;BENJAMIN,160
. ELIZABETH,274;ELVINA
. 256;F G,131;GILES,160
. JAMES,128,138;JAMES M
. 105,137-139;JANE,124
. 125;JOHN,129,238
. JOSEPH,97,112,238;M
. 129,140;M E,281
. MARGARET,287;MARTIN
. 112;MARY,135,281
. MARY ANN M,135;MELTON
. 74;MILLER,261;MORGON
. 144;MORTON,75,91,93
. 97,100,104-105,108
. 113,128-129,135,138
. 139-140;PEACHY,86
. RICHMOND,160;T G,92
. 108,137,143-144;T J
. 106;TRAVY G,104,119
. 148;WILLIAM A,90;WM
. 238
BLESSET,JOHN,115;R,105
BLESSIT,ELISHA,107
. GEORGE,95;J,116;NANCY
. 84;RASON,88;REASON,84
. 90,107-108;WILLIAM S
. 107
BLISON,HENRIETTA,205
BLISSET,STEPHEN,78-80
BLISSIT,GEORGE,94;JNO
. 96;JOHN,90;NANCY,111
. R,146;REASON,92,149
. WILLIAM,91,94;WILLIAM
. S,147;WM S,147,149
BLITCH,JOS L,238
BLIZZARD,HENRY,334
BLOCK,202
BLOCKER,BARKLEY M,37
  MICHAEL,321
BLOCKSOM,GEO,382
BLODGET,FOSTER,382
  SUSAN FIELDS,383
BLOME,ALCIDE L,382
  CLARA,386
BLOODSWORTH,118
BLOODWORTH,93,98,104
. 112,127,144;D M,85
. THOMAS,364
BLOUNT,EDWARD,52;EDWIN
. F,37;HENRY,37;HENRY L
. 52;HESTER,53;JAMES,9
. 28;L,52;LEROY,57;LUCY

. 42;MARTHA VIRGINIA,44
. O P,202;ROBERT B,37
. S W,11,28;STEPHEN,382
. STEPHEN W,26,37
. STPEHEN M,48;SUSAN
. 334;VIOLET,41;WILLIAM
. 53
BLOUNTS,S W,27
BLOXSOM,DANIEL,382
. JULIA,397;MATILDA,385
. PATRICK,382;TABITHA
. 387
BLUNT,DANIEL,195;EDMOND
. 158;JOHN,382;JOSEPH G
. 177
BLURTON,SALLY,237
BLYTHE,DELILA,277
. ELIZABETH L,277
. FANNIE L,245;JAMES
. 238;JOS,238;LEROY,238
. N H,285;SARAH,243;W H
. 240,243,251,261-262
. 263,265,268,271,273
. 275,278,282-283;W R
. 275;WM H,238,244
BOALES,MARY.280;SEABORN
  W,71
BOAN,ISAAC,37
BOARTWRIGHT,THOMAS,382
BOATRIGHT,ANNIE,209
. FANNIE,204;JOHN,202
. LUCY,204;MARTHA,200
. REUBEN,21,195,214
. REUBIN,22;WILLIAM,195
BOATSMAN,AVARILLA,273
BOATWRIGHT,ANDREW J,37
  JAMES H,37;JNO,9
BOBLER,QUINSTEN,173
BOCHRIST,CHARLES F,11-12
BODE,PHILLIP L,146
BOGAN,ELIZA,416;JOHN
. 331,334,382;SARAH,415
. SHADRACK,382
BOGGER,ELIZABETH,249
BOGGS,ARCHIBALD,382
  SAMUEL,238
BOHAN,JOSEPH,51
BOHANNON,BUDDY,373
BOHLER,ANNE,397;GEO M
. 382;JOHN A,382;MARIA
. L,418
BOID,N T,382
BOILES,WILLIAM,126
BOINGS,ELIZABETH,299
  MARY,299
BOISCLAIR,
. AMELIA FORMON,401
. CORRALLY,400;LEWIS
. FORMAN,382;MARY E W
. 401;PETER T,382
. VALENTINE,382
BOLAN,RICHARD,382
BOLES,DAVID,23,25
. FANNIE,201;HANNAH,209
. JACKSON,238;JESSE,136
. JOHN,382;POLLY,249
. TURNER,238
BOLING,JOHN,238
BOLLER,ELLEN,210
BOLLES,ELIZABETH,267
BOLLING,FRANCES,200
  SMITH,64
BOLLS,STEPHEN W,80
BOLT,BENJMAIN,310
  JOSEPH,304
BOLTON,JAMES,28,354
BOLWARE,TABITHA,387
BOMAN,134

BOMER,A,135
BOND,GIDEON,299,309
. HENRY,309;J M D,67
. JAMES,100,382;JOHN
. 299,309;MARY,401;P P
. 382;WILLIAM S,334
. WILLIAM W,73
BONDS,HARRIET,407;WM,2
BONE,ELIZABETH,389
BONER,CARY,235;CATY,235
  CHARLES,235
BONES,ELIZA,403;JAMES
. 80;JOHN,91,382;JOHN H
. 238;MARGARET,422;SAM
. 91;SAMUEL,382;THOMAS
. A,382;WM,382
BONING,SARAH,236
BONNELL,28;ANTHONY,28
. ARCHIBALD,50-51
. CHARLES E,37;CHAS,6
. JAMES H,37;JOHN C,37
. REBECCA,46;WM,6
BONNER,ABR,344;ALLEN
. 344;HUDB,352;JAMES
. 289,305;JEREMIAH,218
. 219;JOS,291;THO,224
. THOMAS,230,362
. WHITMELL,341;WHITMILL
. 224;WILLIAM,312;WM
. 317;WYAT,341
BONOW,GRESSY,254
BONYER,HELOISE T,418
BOOKER,JOHN,222;LOUISA
  239;WILLIAM,187
BOOKES,SAMUEL,238
BOOKS,WILLIAM,160
BOOLES,119;ALLEN,238
. ALVINA,247;BEVAN,238
. DELILA,237;ELIZABETH
. 277;EMILY F,284
. JACKSON,238;JANE F
. 285;JEREMIAH,238;JOHN
. 238;JUDITH,253;MARY E
. 238;NANCY,267;S W,113
. 124,142;WILLOUGHBY
. 238;WM T,238
BOOLS,JOHN,238
BOON,ALFRED C,238;BENJ
. 238;CATHARINE GILLEY
. 377;ELIZA JANE,265
. EXUM,334;FRANCIS,238
. GILLEY,377-378;GILLEY
. CATHARINE,378;JACOB
. 334;JESSE,238;JOHN R
. 378;JOHN RAYFORD,377
. 378;JOSHUA,65,67,378
. MARTHA A,243;MARY,285
. PATSEY,243,266;POLLY
. 285;REBECCA Y,377-378
. REBECCAH YANCY,378
. SALLY,378;SION,238
. 378;THOMAS,378
. WILLIAM,8
BOONE,ALLEN R,238;DAVID
. L,238;HARRIET A,242
. JOHN D,238;MARY,235
. NANCY,247;REBECCA,266
. WARREN,238
BOONER,WHITMILL,334
BOOTH,BEVERLY,238
. DANIEL,382;DREAD,2
. JOHN,289;PAMELY ANN
. 238;ROBERT,115,236
. 258,271,278;ROBT,238
. 273;ZACHRY,289
BOOTY,NICHOLAS,306,321
BOOTZ,WM R,26
BOUNT,JOHN,334

BORACH,LUCY,262
BORAGE,JAMES,382
BORAM,GEORGE,334;JOHN
  334
BORAN,JESSE,305;JOHN
  304;NANCY,305
BORDERS,SEVENER ANN,279
BOREDICT,198
BORELAND,ABR,305;ABS
. 321;ANDREW,289,291
. 293,309
BOREM,ELIZ,414
BORING,DAVID,366
  SUSANNAH,264
BORLAND,ANDREW,231
BORN,JNO,382
BORON,EDMUND H,382
BORQUST,ROBT,238
BORTH,ROBERT,256
BORUM,GEORGE,331
BOSTICK,BERY,223
. COLUMBUS WASHINGTON,4
. ELIZABETH,386;H G,4
. HELLORY,11;HILLERY
. 382;HILLORY,7;HOLMES
. G,7;J,28;JACOB,8,28
. 382;JANE,45;JNO,383
. JOHN,223,383;LEONARD
. 383;LITTLEBERRY,222
. 223,383;MILDRED JANE
. 405;NATHAN,298;OLIVE
. 45;RHEESE,383;RHESY
. 10;THOMAS,28;WM,383
BOSTON,JOHN,312
BOSTWICK,A B,129
. CAROLINE L,40;JOHN
. 222;JOSEPH,37;LITTLE
. BURY,235;LITTLEBERRY
. 222,224;LUCY,263;LUCY
. WILLIAMSON,235;NATHAN
. 235,238;PETER,37
. RHESA,48;THOMAS,49
. WESTLEY,37
BOSWELL,CAROLINE F,247
. FANNIE J,243;HENRY
. 334;J J,376;JAMES,330
. JOHN J,376;REUBEN B
. 238;SARAH C,247;WM
. 238
BOSWORTH,MARY,395;SARAH
  192
BOTHWELL,JAMES J,28
  JOHN,13,15;JOHN W,13
BOTRIGHT,REUBEN,24
BOTTOM,DAVIS,383
BOTTY,NICHOLAS,311
  NICHOLS,323
BOUDEN,HARRIETT,253
BOUGHAM,JAMES,100,114
  JAS,100
BOUGHAN,J,149;JAMES,107
  136,147
BOULINAU,ELIZ A,417;GEO
  E,383
BOULWARE,JANE,386
BOURKE,MICHAEL,383
BOURKS,28;EDWARD,28
BOURLAND,ANDREW,292
BOUT,202
BOUTET,DAVID,383;PETER
  383;PETER DAVIS,383
BOUYER,BALTHAZAR,383
  ROBERT I,383
BOUYT,W H,202
BOW---,FRANCIS,280
BOWAN,SALLY,258
BOWDEN,ALMIRA A,285
. AMANDA M,334;ELIZA

. MAY,277;ELIZABETH,250
. 264;ELLIOTT C,239
. FLORNOY,269;FRANCES
. 287;FRANCES L,248;GEO
. THOMAS,239;GEORGIA A
. P,236;JAMES,355
. NANCEY,331;NANCY,334
. REBECCA,262;REBECCA H
. 272;RICHAD,239;ROBT
. 239;WM,239
BOWDER,MARIAH,160
  SAMUEL,160
BOWDERS,166
BOWDIRE,EDMOND,174
  SAMUEL,174
BOWDRE,E,151;ELIZ,415
. EVELINE S,417;HARRIET
. H,409;HAYS,383
. LUCINDA,393;PRESTON E
. 383;SARAH,253
BOWDRIE,E,167
BOWE,SHADRACK,305
BOWELS,SARAH,247
BOWEN,ANN,418;BURELL
. 345;EPHRAIM,299;T J
. 239-240,246,266,273
. TABER,383;WILLIAM,48
BOWENS,CHARLES,383
BOWER,BEN,18;BENAMUD,13
  BENAMUND,14
BOWERS,BENJ,17;HARRIET
. 392;MARGARET,414
. SAMUEL E,383
BOWIE,REASON,224
BOWIES,JOHN,161
BOWIN,EXA,197
BOWINGS,EPHRAIM,299
BOWLES,114;ANN,393
. HENRY,239;JACKSON,127
. JESSE,239;JOHN,239
. 274;LITTLEBERRY,239
. LUCINDA,239,258
. MARGARET JANE,264
. MARY B,119;MARY J,276
. MARY JANE,249;NANCY
. 249;SARAH E H,250
. THOS,239;WM,239;WM H
. 239;WM V,239
BOWLEY,CAROLINE,399
BOWLING,14;ROBERT,13-14
  16-19,25
BOWLS,TOYIA,410
BOWMAN,FRANCIS,235,238
. 240-241,243,246,251
. 253,256-258,260,263
. 264,266-268,273-274
. 276,278,282-283,286
. JANE,280;LEONARD,319
. 328
BOYCE,239;ELISHA,330
  GEO,239
BOYD,ABRAHAM,37;ANN,382
. BANIA,24;BANIAH,23
. BENNIAH,21;DAVID,2
. ELIZ,414;ELIZABETH
. 398,400;HENRY,202;J F
. 136;JAMES,21,161;JANE
. 402;JANE C,381;JOANNA
. 40;JOHN,193,383;LINDY
. 40;MARY,43,45;MARY E
. 266;RICHARD,89-90,331
. SAMUEL,334;SARAH,414
. SARAH M,40;STEPHEN,21
. 23-24,202;THOMAS,26
. WM,383
BOYDE,SARAH,419
BOYED,JOHN R,37
BOYER,JOHN,319

BOYETT,ELI,383
BOYKEN,JAMES W,383
BOYKIN,FRANCIS,334;JAS
. W,383;JESSE W,334
. JOHN,9;LEROY H,239
. WILLIAM P,334
BOYLE,326;JOHN,383;P
  303,308;PR,287
BOYNTON,JAS,89;STEWART
  334;WILLIARD,68
BOYT,ABRAHAM,28,51
. CATHARINE,409;ELBERT
. 48;ELIJAH,195;JAMES
. 10,23,28,50;JAMES E
. 202;JOHN,10,28
. PERMELIA,201;SARAH E
. 204;STEPHEN,10,28,48
. WINNEY,405
BOZEMAN,ANNE,255;JAMES
  239;SAMUEL,334
BOZMAN,MEDE,228;MEDY
. 228;WILEY,227;WINFREY
. 394
BRACE,HENRY,383
BRACEWELL,B W,140
BRACK,BENJAMIN,28
. EASTER,385;HARDEN,10
. MARY,28;RICHARD,28
. RICHD,8;WILLIAM,6,28
. WM H,239
BRACKET,JOHN,15
BRACKETT,JNO,13
BRACKNER,LEANORA E,390
BRADBERRY,ELIZ,405
. ELIZABETH,158;JOHN
. 161;MORRIS,383
BRADBURY,EDMUND,294
. JOSEPH,383;JOSH,383
. NANCY,380
BRADDY,212;JOHN,239;JOS
. E,239;MARY C,272
. ZILPHA,199
BRADELY,JANE,386
BRADEN,REIS M,383
  SUSANNAH,393
BRADFORD,BARBARA,310
. BARBARY,299;EDMUND
. 334;HOSEA,299
. M FIELDING,383;MARY
. ELIZ,387;RANDOLPH,383
. SABRY,299;THOMAS,306
. THOS E,383
BRADLEY,CHARLES,330
. CHAS,239;EMILY,269
. HARRELSON,239;JAMES
. 383;JOHN,239;JULIA E
. 420;MILLER,11;PATRICK
. 383;RICH,228;WILLARD
. 71,75,77,80;WILLIAM
. 71,75,77;WM,80
BRADON,ELIZ,406
BRADSHAW,ASA,239;ELIJAH
. 239;ELIZABETH,270
. ERASTUS,239;FANNY,267
. FRANCIS A,383;GEDIDA
. 244;GEORGE,239;JOHN,8
. 50,383;MILLY,408
. SALLY,249;SM,239
BRADSHOW,JOHN,28
BRADY,EMA ELIZA,208
. JAMES,71,82,90,99,131
. 136-137,143,149;JAS
. 111;JOSHUA,195
. LUCINDA,211;MOSES H
. 90;OLIVER B,202
. PHEREBA,205;SAML,294
. SAMUEL,306;THOMAS,294
. 334

BRADY?,366
BRAGDEN,JOHN,49
BRAGG,CHARLOTTE,279;J H
. 235;MATHEW,239;THOS
. 239;WILLIAM,21,23
BRAHAM,CHARLES,380
  JESSE,380;TIMOTHY,380
BRAKE,FREDERICK A,383
  LATHA,268
BRANAN,EMMY,380
BRANBY,CHARLOTT C,197
BRANCH,A,60;ALBERT H,37
. BAELUM,202;BECKY,38;C
. 203;FRANCES E,273
. JOHN,239;LETITIA M
. 246;ROBT M,239;SARAH
. 246,269;SCOTT,287
. WILLIAM A,37;WM H H
. 239
BRANDON,ADELINE,397
. ELIZA,384;JAMES,334
. 383;JANE,403;JNO,383
. JOHN,331,334;JOHN W
. 383
BRANDS,198
BRANDY,LEWIS,321
BRANHAM,MARGARET,408
BRANNAN,HARRIS,348
BRANTLEY,AMOS,309;BENJ
. 383;CELIA E,205;GREEN
. D,334;J J,260,268,276
. JAMES,2;JAMES M,202
. JESSE,328;JOHN,328
. 383;JOSEPH,214
. W HENRY,312;WM,312;WM
. D,312
BRANTLY,EDMUND,370
. JAMES,315;JOS,2;LEWIS
. 315;MALICA,308;MARY
. 28
BRANUM,HARRIS,334
BRASEL,TOBIAS,104
BRASSEL,BETSEY,235
  JACOB,344;JAMES,239
BRASSELL,WILLIAM,362
BRASWELL,BENJAMIN,378
. ISOM,239;NANCY,269
. RICHARD,344;SAMUEL
. 345
BRAWDIS,THOMAS,311
BRAZDEN,LOUIS,383
BRAZELL,SAML,302
BRAZEWELL,JAMES,302
BRAZIL,SAMUEL,334
  WILLIAM,334
BRAZWELL,AARON,334
BRAZZ,BIRD,325
BRAZZELL,TABITHA C,237
BREADY,ROBT,366
BREATTAN,JOSHUA,297
BREEDLOVE,ANN,334
  THOMAS,297,319
BREITENBAUGH,JNO,383
BRENAN,EUGINE,383
  FRANCES M,418
BRENNON,LOUISA,409
BREUSON,MARIAH JANE,40
BREWER;217;ABAGAIL,283
. ALFRED,110;BETHIS,317
. BETSEY,267,317
. CATHERINE,118;DAVID
. BREWER,239;ELIJAH,383
. ELISHA W,334
. ELIZABETH,419;GEO,239
. HENRY,239;HOWELL,304
. JNO,290-291;JOHN,224
. 291-293,306,317-318
. MARIA,317;MARTHA,378

. MARY,405;NANCY,317
. 378;NATHAN,378;OSBORN
. 288,294;POLLEY,317
. POLLY,254;R C,147
. RHODY,386;SIMON,304
. SUSANNAH,265;WILEY
. 239;WM,239
BREWSTER,115
BREZEAL,C W,102
BRIANT,DELIE,369;EADY
. 194;ELIZABETH,199
. FRANCES,381;ISAAC,369
. JACOB,11;JOHN,239
. NEEDHAM W,202;POLLY
. 374,421;WILLIAM,374
BRIBERRY,W H,248
BRICE,ALFRED,239;MILES
  2
BRICKELL,THOS H,383
BRICKEST,MARIA E,47
BRICKMASTER,EDW I,383
BRIDEWELL,
  MINERVA ANN,403
BRIDGE,HARDY,239
BRIDGES,BENNETT,334
. BENNETT R,331;BERRY Y
. 353;BURRELL,60;ELIZA
. C,269;ELIZABETH F,268
. EZEKIEL,239;H,280
. HARDY,239,266;JAMES
. 239,304;JNO,383;JOHN
. 303-304,306,310
. JOHN J C,239;JOSEPH
. 304;MARTHA,243;MARY A
. 240;NANCY,362;REBECCA
. 240;ROBERT C,239
. SUSAN,239;SUSAN A,266
. SUSANNAH,275;WISEMAN
. 334;WM,239
BRIDWELL,CLARISSA,402
BRIER,GREEN,160
BRIERS,JOHN,334
BRIGGS,CATHARINE,417
  SAMUEL,2;WM H,383
BRIGHAM,CALVIN,37;JOHN
  28,51;MELISIA,41
BRIGHT,ABSALOM,11,28,48
  G,259,271;LINE G,383
BRIGS,SARAH,401
BRIMBERRY,MARTHA,281
  MATTHAIS,239
BRINCKLEY,SARAH ANNE
  249
BRINLEY,MARTHA A,244
BRINSOM,MATHEW,9
BRINSON,ADAM,6-7,11
. ALEXANDER,195
. BENJAMIN,49;BENJAMIN
. E,214;CYPRIAN,49,57
. CYPRON,28;DAVID M,202
. ELEZEA,195;ELIZA,195
. ELVIRA,42;HARRIET E
. 39;HESTER,46;ISAAC
. 195;ISAAC M,37;JANE
. 197;JASPER L,37;JESSE
. A,195;JOHN,28,49,76
. KATE,207;MARGARET E
. 209;MARTHA,206;MARY
. 28,49;MARY A E,37
. MARY E,195;MATHEW S
. 202;MATTHEW,202
. MIDDLETON F,37;MOSES
. 2;NANCY,43;NANCY J,43
. NOAH M,195;PENELOPY
. 196;RIELA,210;SARAH L
. 39;SARAH M,203
. SHEPHERD,28,49;SIMION
. C,37;STEPHEN,8,28,49

. STERLING,9;STIRING,49
. SUSAN,44;SUSAN L,200
. SUSANNAH,43;THOMAS,28
. VIRGINIA,46;WILLIAM
. 47;WILLIM T,37
BRISCO,JOHN,383
BRISCO?,MARY ANN,408
BRISCOE,CATHARINE,162
. JOHN,162,173,239
. LUCIUS M,239;REBEKAH
. 422
BRISTENBAU,ANGELINE,382
BRISTOE,CHESLEY,268
BRISTOW,CHESLEY,248,279
BRITAIN,HENRY,239;WM
  239,247
BRITT,MARTHA,387;WILLIS
  334
BRITTON,G,100;GEORGE,75
. JAMES,82,95,100,105
. 122,142;JOHN,75,90
. SAMUEL,383;SAMUEL T
. 383
BROACH,ALEXANDER,239
. ANNA A,285;AVERYELA
. 238;J E,239;JAMES,239
. MATILDA,262;WM,239;WM
. H,239
BROADAWAY,EDITH,237
BROADDERS,THOMAS,75
BROADDUS,THOS,341,353
BROADHURST,ANN E,412
  FRANCES,385;MARY,409
BROADNAX,EDWD B,329
. JANE,4;JOHN,330
. ROBERT E,52;ROBT,4;WM
. E,383
BROADWATER,ANDERSON,383
  ELIZ,406;JAMES A,383
BROADWAY,SULTANA,235
BROCHON,DOMINICK,383
BROCK,JAMES,119;JAMES L
. 105;MARY,239;V,119
. 137;VALENTINE,105,128
BROCKMAN,GEO M T,112
. GEORGE M T,91,97,129
. 138,144;ISAAC,280
. JAMES,257,286;JAS,236
. 238;MARY,274;MOSES
. 240;PERMELIA H,268
BROCKSTON,JOHN,7;SILAS
  10
BRODDIS,ED A,120
BRODDUS,EDWARD A,334
. EDWARD S,334;THOMAS
. 331,334;THOS,240
BRODDY,MILLER,11
BRODNAX,JOHN,291;R E,28
BROGDEN,PETERSON G,88
BROGDON,P G,88,100,113
. P G B,111;PETERSON G
. 82,97
BROME,JOHN,319
BRONSON,MARTHA D,203
BROOK,ELIZABETH F,267
. JAS,240;JOHN S,240
. JOHN T,240;LORENA H
. 264;SUSAN,267
BROOKE,J F,312;JNO F
. 383;JORDAN P,383;TED
. O,370;THOMAS,383
BROOKER,ELIZABETH,254
  MARY,263
BROOKINGS,SAMUEL,49
BROOKINS,ELIZABETH J,38
. MARTHA C,36;SAMUEL,9
. 28;STEPHEN,6
BROOKNAR,SARAH L,414

BROOKS,11;AMANDA,40
. ARCHIBALD D,240
. AUGUSTUS G,240
. CELESTIA,277
. COVINGTON,240
. ELIZABETH C,271
. HARRIETT,284;HIRAM,74
. ISHAM,303,309;IVERSON
. A,334;JAMES,74,334
. JESSE,240;JIMMY,259
. LEE,312;MARY,420
. MARY A E,259;MINNIE
. 266;NANCY,238;NANNY
. 370;NAOMI,266;R,100
. ROGER,215;RUSSELL,122
. 130,139,334;SARAH,248
. SUSAN P,242;SUSANNA
. 253;THOMAS,240
. WILLIAM,309,334
. WILSON L,240
BROOM,MARTHA ANN,258
. MARY,410;NANCY L,256
. WILLIAM,51
BROOME,ALPHEUS,240
. CICERO,315;JOHN,4;L C
. 277;LUCIUS,240;LUCIUS
. C,250;LUCUIS C,262
. 286
BROOX,HENRY,240;SARAH
. 240
BROUGHTON,ANN,282
. BELITHA,334;CHARLES
. 334;EDWARD,240
. ELIZABETH,263;ESSEY
. 240;GANETT L,240;JOHN
. R,240;JOHN T,240
. SARAH,239
BROWER,ELIZA W,410
BROWIN,HEZEKIAH,60
BROWN,268,309,323,325
. A M,205;AARON,310
. ABRAHAM,354;ABSALOM N
. 383;ADELINE,47;ALEK
. 37;ALEXR,228;ALFRED
. 37;ALLEN T,37;AMANDA
. 41,211;AMELIA,37,386
. ANDERSON,68,122
. ANDREW,202;ANDREW W
. 88;ANN,384,407;AVY
. 196;BARTLETT,334;BENJ
. 240;BENJ F,240
. BENJAMIN,28,48,73,364
. BETSEY,404;BURELL,345
. BURREL,11,28,48
. BURWELL,240;CHARLES
. 11,28,49;CHAS,240
. CLARRISA,421;CYNTHIA
. 411;DANIEL,223,240
. DAVID,37,345;E G,60
. EARNIST G,44;EDWARD
. 311,334;ELIJAH,2-3
. ELIZ,406,411-412;ELIZ
. L,389;ELIZA,418;ELIZA
. A,379;ELIZABETH,48,51
. 251,282,393;ELIZABETH
. ANN,207;EPPS,347;EPSY
. 394;ERVIN,161;EZEKIEL
. 240;FANNY,39,240
. FIELDING,52;FRANCES
. 243;G E,202;GASTON
. 312;GEO O,162;GEORGE
. 68;GEORGE A,334
. GEORGE ARCHER,171
. GREEN,202;HARES G,384
. HARRINGTON,37
. HENRIETTA,243;HENRY
. 37,161,213,295,376
. 384;HENRY L,202

. HERBERT,304;HEZEKIAH
. 60;HUBERT,294,328;J E
. 202;J R,140;JAMES,8
. 28,48,86,195,213,334
. JAMES B,50,202;JAMES
. R,103,113;JAMES S,67
. JAMES W,384;JANE,45
. 206,386,419;JAS L,240
. JEREMIAH,334;JERRY,37
. JESSE,195,213;JESSE F
. 240;JNO,296,307;JOHN
. 7,37,64,73,161,202
. 223,240,289,295-296
. 300,309,319,326,342
. 343,384;JOHN T,195
. 202;JOHN W,334;JOSEPH
. 161,384;JOSHUA,384
. JOSIAH,334;JULIA K
. 274;L E,202;LOTTIE
. 244;LUCINDA,203
. LUCINDA L,406;MARIA
. 45;MARIANN,195;MARTHA
. 389;MARTHA A,210
. MARTHA JUNE,414;MARY
. 254,396;MARY A,57
. MARY ANN,272;MARY
. ELIZ,401;MARY P,261
. MARY T,57;MATTHEW L
. 202;MELVINY,205;MILLY
. 310;MOSES,310;NANCEY
. 161;NANCY,206,264,401
. PATRICK,37,384;PATSEY
. 161;PHEREBA,250
. PHRONY,202;PHYLLIS,36
. POLLEY,223;POLLY,157
. RACHEL,210;RHODA,274
. RICHARD,28,384
. RICHARD G,309;ROBERT
. 60,62,71,79-80,96,110
. 202,334;ROBERTSON B
. 375;RUSSELL J,334
. SABRINA,272;SALLY C
. 279;SAM,195;SAMUEL
. 384;SAMUEL J,50;SARAH
. 310,411;SEBASTIAN,384
. SEVICIA,397;SHILDRAK
. 288;SHILDRAKE,288
. SIDNEY SMITH,384
. SUCKY,334;SUSAN,202
. SUSANNAH,416;TEAAC,37
. TEINA,211;THEODORE
. 384;THOMAS,37;THOS
. 240;THURSBY,310
. TURNER F,312;UNICY
. 366;WADE,50;WALLAR
. 325;WALLER,329
. WASHINGTON H,85
. WILLIAM,7,28,368-369
. WILLIAM A,37;WILLIAM
. E,202;WILLIAM H,37
. WILLIAM J,202;WM,240
. 294
BROWNE,MARTHA,408
BROWNING,DANIEL,240;E B
. 11;JNO,241;JOHN,245
. 251,259,262,273-274
. 279,285,287;NATHAN
. 240;WM,231-232,238
. 240,249,256,259,261
. 284,287
BROWNLEE,JAMES,111,113
. 114,147;JOHN,117
BROWNSON,ELIZ,400
BROXTON,DANIEL,384;JOHN
. 28,52;MARY,210;SARAH
. 52;SILAS,28;THOMAS,28
. 50
BRUCE,ABNER W,240

. ALFRED,384;ANDERSON
. 240;BENJ F,240
. CATHERINE,242-243
. CHRISALINE,255
. CLARISSA,277;EDWARD D
. 240;ELLA DORA,285
. EMILY,265;EPHRAIM,236
. 239-245,251;EPHRAIM M
. 240;EPHRIAM,249,254
. 260,263,265-266,268
. 270,272-275,277-278
. 283,285;HENRIETTA,275
. HENRY C,240;JAMES,240
. JAS,240;JOEL,240;JOHN
. 240;JONATHAN,240
. MARTHA,244,260;NANCY
. 28;NANCY ANNE,276
. PRISCILLA,267;S M,275
. SALLIE F,277
. SARAH ANN M,285
. SEABORN,240;TOWNLEY,2
. TURNELL,240;WILSON
. 240
BRUCH,FRANKEY,275
BRUEC,
. JULIA PRISCILLA,239
BRUN,LEON,384
BRUNCE,DANIEL M,384
BRUNER,JOHN D,384
BRUNSON,HEZEKIAH,384
. MATTHEW,384
BRUNT,ELIZABETH,286;JAS
. 240;JOHN,240;MARIA
. 287;MARTHA,249;MARY
. 416;MARY F,275
. WILLIBY,240
BRUSTER,HUGH,2;LEVINAH
. 289;LOUISA,293
BRUTTRILL,ASA,141
BRUX,CECILIA,401
BRYAN,264;ANN,327
. ASBURY,240;CENA,270
. ELIZABETH,264;FANNIE
. A,244;FRANCES,271
. HARRIET,386;JACOB,11
. 28;JAMES H,28;JAS,240
. JESSE,240;JOSEPH,297
. 307,327;LEWIS,28
. LITTLETON J,240
. LUCIENDA,263;MALINDA
. 263;MARTHA,240,266
. MARTHA A F,263;MARY A
. 241;MARY F,280;MOSES
. 28;NANCY ANN,272
. NATHAN,240;NEDHAM,11
. NEEDHAM,28,213
. READING D,28;RICHARD
. 240;ROBERT,219,298
. 307,309;SALLY,298
. SARAH,280;SARAH C,277
. SARAH F R,275
. SILVANUS S,59;THOS M
. 240;W M,240;WADE,8
. WILLIAM,8,28;WM,47
. 235,238-240,243-244
. 245-248,251,254,256
. 260-261,263,265,267
. 271-272,275,277-278
. 279,281,283,285,287
BRYANT,175;A,63;ABSALOM
. 346;ANNA,48;ARTEMUS
. 334;B,63;BERRIEN,37;C
. 63;CHAS J,240;DAVID
. 15;DD,14;DELIA,369
. ELIZABETH,366;FRANCIS
. 257,381;GUS,202;HENRY
. 2;J J,11;JACOB,9
. JAMES,37,366,384

BRYANT(cont)
. JARED,82;JOHN,334,384
. JOHN O,241;LEWIS,202
. LUCY A,399;MARTHA,379
. 392;MARY,346,398;MARY
. ANN,43;MOSES,11;NANCY
. 366,421;NEEDHAM,48
. PATRICK,366;READING D
. 9;REBECCA,412;REBEKAH
. 366;REDDING,15
. REDDING D,13;ROBERT
. 298;RUSSELL,241;S J
. 11;SARAH,50,298;SARAH
. ANN,283;SELINA,51
. TABITHA,195;TELITHA
. 195;TEMPERANCE,346
. WHIT,241;WILLIAM,9
. 158;WM,264,271,384
BRYNE,EDMUND,384
BRYON,WM,274
BRYSON,A,309;MARY,393
. NANCY,407;WILLIAM J
. 82
BUCH,LUCY,206
BUCHANAN,BENJAMIN,334
. JAMES,350,365,384
. JANE,350,367;JOSEPH
. 365,367;MARY,367;R
. 312;SALLY,243
BUCHANNAN,232;ALEXANDER
N,334;JAMES,345
BUCHANNON,JAMES,109,334
. JOHN,334,367;MARY,279
. SARAH,319
BUCK,HENRIETTA,387;JOHN
. F,384;LYDIA,420;MARY
. ANN,399;NANCY,382
. PRISCILLA,415;THOMAS
. 384
BUCKANNAN,JAMES,340
BUCKELEW,JOSEPH,384
BUCKER,JOEL,297;MORRIS
297;WILLIAM,297
BUCKET,SAMUEL,147
BUCKHALTER,JOHN,8
BUCKHAM,WILLIAM,165
BUCKHANNON,ANNA,254
ROBERT,319
BUCKHANON,AMY,420
BUCKHART,J,143;JACOB,99
BUCKING,PETER,241
BUCKLE,C J,420;CAROLINE
JANE,411
BUCKLEY,BARTLET,28;BENJ
. 8;BENJAMIN,28;ELIJAH
. 342
BUCKLY,MARY,416
BUCKNER,DAVID,241;ELI
. 135;JOEL,295-296;JOHN
. 309,319-320;LESTER
. 296;PARHAM,310
. RICHMOND,297;TABITHA
. 295;WILLIAM,295-296
BUCKOLD,JAMES,95
BUEL,MARY F,414
BUFFINGTON,JAS,384
. SALLY CRAWFORD,377
. SAML,309;SARAH
. CRAWFORD,378;WILLIAM
. C,372
BUFORD,ELIZ,418;SIMEON
384;THOS B,105
BUFORT,LUCY V,386
BUGBY,MARY,237
BUGG,ANN,388,420;ANSELM
. 384;DARCAS,388;EDMUND
. 384;ELIZ,396,412;ELIZ
. W,404;GEO F T,384

. HAMPTON,241;HOBSON
. 174;JACOB C,384;MARIA
. LOUISA,398;MARY,242
. 380,384-385,391,412
. N H,174;NANCY,402
. PETER,384;ROBT W,384
. SAMUEL,4,7,384;SARAH
. 401;SUSAN,401;TERWOOD
. 384;WM,384;WM A,384
. WM B,241
BUHILER,FRANCES,407
BUIE,JOHN,213;MARY,213
MATHEW,213
BUIS,JOHN,334
BUJKLEY,ALBERT G,70
BUKHAM,CATHARENE,172
WILLIAM,172;WM,173
BULFINCH,BENJ,384
BULGER,ANN,421;DANIEL
384;JNO,384
BULKLEY,R E C,105
BULL,ANDREW G,384;JESSE
. 155,159;JONATHON,105
. MARTHA,155;SAVANNAH V
. 38
BULLARD,329;AMOS,11,28
. 48;ASHLEY,202;ELIZA
. 399;ELIZABETH,41
. HENRY,11,28;JAMES,48
. 324,334;JANE,199,210
. JOHN,77,80;LEWIS,248
. RANDOLPH,327;SION R
. 85;TENAH,47;WILEY,334
. WILLIAM,334
BULLOCK,ARCH,157
. ARCHIBALD,156;BATSON
. 353;DAN,384;FEARIBEY
. 390;GEORGE,185;JOSEPH
. 308;MARGARET,301
. SHADRICK,96;W H,140
. WINNEY,394;ZACHARIAH
. 384
BULLWOOD,PEARLY,259
BULTER,BRYAN,319;EDMOND
. 318;EDMUND,294,320
. JESSE,300;JOHN,342
. JOHN M,375
BUMLEY,R,125;RICHARD
124
BUNCH,JEREMIAH,384;JOHN
. M,384;MARTHA,283
. PENELOPE,240
BUNKLEY,ELIZABETH,255
. H F,270;HOWELL,241
. JAMES,59,68;JOHN,70
. SALLIE K,279;WILLIAM
. 323
BUNN,ALDREDGE,241
. MARTHA,286;MATHEW,195
. MOSES,28,48,57
BUNT,STEPHEN,2
BUNTYN,JAMES E,114
BUNY,WILLIAM V,59
BURCH,BLANTON,384
. CHARLES,384;EDMUND
. 384;EDWARD,6;ELIZA
. ANN,409;JERARD,300
. JESSE,37,384;JESSEE
. 28;JOANNA,420;JOE L,4
. JOHN,298,300;JOSEPH
. 384;L B,49;LB,28
. LITTLEBERRY,9;MARY
. 417;MARY ANN,405
. POLLY,401;RICHARD,384
. WM K,384;WM KELTON
. 384;WM R,384
BURCK,327
BURDELL,FERDINAND,384

. ROBT,276,286;SARAH
. 390;THOMAS,384
BURDICK,MARSILLA,417
BURDILE,ROBT,241
BURFIT,WILLIAM,220
BURFORD,ANN B,272
. BURGET ANN,255
. CHARLES,95;CHARLES T
. 148;DANIEL,218,220
. 229;ELIZABETH,128
. JOHN,128,241;JOHN B
. 69,126,142;JOHN E,241
. JUDAN,215;JUDITH,215
. LEONARD,223,228,241
. LUCY,243;MITCHEL,220
. MITCHELL,224;NANCY
. 220;S P,83,133;S T
. 139;SAMUEL,86;SAMUEL
. B,132;SAMUEL P,60,83
. 90,118,128,138,142
. 147;SAMUEL P B,126
. SOLMON,220;SOLOMON
. 221;SUSANNA,249
. THOMAS,92,118,131
. THOMAS B,103,108,125
. 126,138,142,147-148
. 149;THOS B,69,114,119
. 124,128,141;WILLIAM
. 69,90,120,126,128,131
. 142,215,219;WM,221
. 234
BURGAY,WILLIAM,309
BURGE,309;JOHN,69,85,87
94;WILEY,347;WM,241
BURGEN,DANIEL,188
BURGENS,WM,241
BURGER,MARY,286;NOAH
241
BURGES,ELEANOR,405;JOS
330;SARAH,382
BURGESS,A C,241;E A,237
. 241,248,265,276;E H
. 272;EDWARD A,241
. EVELINA,405;JAS,241
. JONATHAN,241;JOSIAH
. 352;NANCY,39;R L,238 •
. 265;ROBERT L,241
. SARAH ANN,256;THOS L
. 241;VIRGINIA E,265;WM
. 241
BURK,CHARLES,217,226
. 289;COLUMBUS,241
. ELMIRA,250;FRANCIS
. 384;HUGH L,195;JAS
. 241;JOHN,115,348;L A
. 287;LITTLETON L,98
. LOUISA,244;LUCY,238
. MARY,384;MILDRED J P
. 285;NANCY J,267
. SEABORN,241;SUSANNAH
. 274;WILLIAM,348
BURKE,AVERY ANN,41;CHAS
. 241;CHRLES,217;ELIZ E
. E,398;ELIZABETH,257
. JANE H,416;JAS,241
. LITTLETON L,145
. MATHEW,9;MATTHEW,28
. 49;MICHAEL,384;MICHL
. 14,16;MICL,13;SARAH
. 257,273;SARAH D,395
. SUSAN EVILINE,38
. THOMAS S,9,28,49,384
. THOMAS S,52;VALERIOUS
. J,241;WILLIAM,8
BURKES,ALVINA ANNE,273
. CYNTHIA,397;ELIZ,396
. NIMROD,51;RECORD,384
BURKS,EDWARD,384;LILLA

==

CALDWELL(cont)
. L D,240-241,243,250
. 258,260,266,268-269
. 270,277-278;LITTLETON
. 241;LITTLETON D,241
. 246;LOUSA,258;M A,270
. MAHALLA,238;MARGARET
. E,42;MARITA ANNE,267
. MARY,28,256;MARY ANN
. 241;MATILDA,413
. MATILDA MARIE,260
. MILES,241;NANCY,240
. PAUL,385;ROSAMOND A
. 254;SARAH JANE,267
. WILLIAM,232;WILLIAM D
. 334;WILLIAM R,52;WM,6
. 232,234,241;WM H,241
CALE,AMANDA,210;HOMER K
  385
CALHOON,JOSEPHINE A,405
  WM,385
CALHOUN,DAVID W,385
. ELIZ,379;LEVI,28
. LONDA,241;WILLIAM,161
CALIB,ELIZ,412
CALLAHAN,AMY W,258
. ANDREW,241;EDWARD,242
. HENRY,242;JAS,242
. JOHN,242;MARY A,263
. MIRIAM J,287;SALLIE
. 263;T,274;THOS,240;WM
. 242
CALLAN,MARY,397
CALLAWAY,E H,11;ENOCH
. 248;JAMES C,334;JAMES
. H,141;JOHN,334;JOHN S
. 247,274;JOSHUA,334
. 347;LEMUEL L,242
. LEWIS,242;R S,242
. SARAH A,247;SARAH ANN
. 242;WILLIS B,242;WM
. 242;WM R,242
CALLIDAY,A F,53
CALLIS,J A,137;OTHO W
  385
CALLOWAY,ENOCH,266;J S
  241;MARY ANN,268
CALLWELL,CHARLES,313
  JOHN,313
CALLY,FRANCIS,264
CALLYER,ABRAM,37
CALVERT,MASON,385;SUSAN
  E,334
CALVIN,391;DAVID,385
. ELIZ,407;J C,266
. JAMES B,385;JAMES P
. 385;SARAH,385
CALWAY,NIGHT,242
CAMACK,11-12
CAMBAA,REUEL,385
CAMBRY,MARIE ROSE,382
CAMEL,ELI,202;J W,93
  THOMAS,385
CAMERON,DUNCAN,233
. HENRY C,242;MOLLY,233
. SALLY,278
CAMFIELD,ABIEL,385;ELIZ
. JONES,405;HANNAH
. MARGARET,380;JOSEPH
. 385;LYDIA,382;MARY
. JANE,398;OCTAVIA P
. 405;REBECCA L,412
CAMINAINGS,ELSEY,38
CAMMORRON,DUNCAN,221
CAMMRAN,DUNKIN,221
CAMMRON,DUNKIN,223
CAMP,A A,149;BENJAMIN
. 149;CECIL,300;EVELINE

. 83;JAMES,83,87,97,103
. 107,114,123,136,145
. JOHN,86,103;JOSEPH T
. 60;JOSEPHUS,202
. LAWRENCE,10;MARY,86-87
. 96-97,237,410;MOLLIE
. E,208;NATHAN,83,87,97
. 107;NATHAN F,90,103
. 114,136,145;POLLY,83
. 87,90,94,97;SEABORN
. 86;STERLING,83,86-87
. 90,94,96-97,103,107
. 114,123,136,145;THOS
. 147;WESLEY,65
CAMPBELL,ANNA,356;C,123
. 140;CATLETT,81
. CHARLES,334;CHARLES G
. 334;CHARTER,373,378
. COOLEY,334;DAVID,108
. DORCAS,334;FLORA E
. 408;H T,385;IRBY,195
. JAMES,88,242,385
. JAMES H,82,90,93,104
. 131,146;JAMES L,334
. JARIOT,348;JARRERT
. 334;JARROT,347-348
. 363;JNO ARCHD,385
. JOHN,11,348;JOSEPH,85
. 90-91,348;LEVI,385
. MALISSA,279;MARY,259
. OBEDIAH,242;PATSEY
. 237;PERMELIA D,146
. PETER,149;REBECCA C
. 417;RICHARD,331,334
. RICHARD S,334;ROBT A
. 385;SALLY,363;SAMUEL
. 242;SUSAN,405;T J,111
. THOMAS,356;WILLIAM C
. 334
CAMPFIELD,AMY F,420
CANADA,JOHN,2
CANADAY,NARCISSA,196
CANADY,LINDY,206;SETH
  289
CANDLER,HENRY,168;JOHN
. 170;MARY,170;WILLAM
. 169
CANE,ELIZA,383;POLLY
  389,404
CANEL,HECTOR,37
CANLEY,GEORGE W,37
CANNADAY,196;MARTHA,199
  MARY,196
CANNADEY,WILLIAM,203
CANNADY,JOHN,202;JOHN W
. 202;REBECCA,207
. SOLOMON,195;WILLIAM
. 203,214
CANNAY,LENNA,196;SUSAN
  196
CANNEDAY,SOLOMON,195
CANNEDY,SARAH T,204
CANNET,CEPHISE ANN,412
CANNON,BURWELL,82,84,94
. JAMES,79,81,115
. JOSHUA,235,254,257
. 259,273-274,283
. ROBERT D,91;SALLY,396
. WILLOUGHBY,2
CANT,MARY A,257
CANUCH,ATHENAE,417
CAPEHEART,JOHN,90
CAPES,B,96;JOHN,385
CARDEL,JOHN C,334
CARDELL,PETER,334
CARDEN,JAMES,334
  LEONARD,376;NANCY,364
CARDIN,WILLIAM,334,361

CARDWICK,JESSE F,53
CARELTON,HENRY,369
CAREY,ELLA,271;H H,385
CARGILE,A,143,149
. AUGUSTUS,130,142,147
. CHARLES,334,353,360
. CHS,361;JAMES,353
. JOHN,334,352-353,363
. JOHN R,75-77;MARY,101
. 131,134;R S,59;THOMAS
. 334
CARGILL,CHARLES,343,348
. 357;CHAS,347;CHRLES
. 344;JNO,344,346;JOHN
. 343,345,351,359;JONA
. 358
CARHART,118
CARIBO,HENRY,385
CARLE,THOMAS,251
CARLETON,COXE,367;ELIZA
. 235;HEN,230,232;HENRY
. 221,229,233,357,367
. THO,223,225-229,232
. 234-235;THOMAS,221
. 367;THOS,231;WILLIAM
. HENRY,367
CARLEY,325
CARLILE,GEORGE,82
CARLIN,JOHN,385
CARLISLE,DUKES,374;MARY
  334;WILLIAM W,374
CARLTON,ELVIA,277;EMILY
. A,270;EMMA A,259
. HENRY,311;L D,265,276
. 277;L O,278;LAURA R
. 247;LORENGO D,245-246
. LORENZO D,275;MAGGIE
. W,269;MARY E,261
. NANCY,286;THO,227
CARMAN,ELIZ,388
  FREDERICK,385
CARMEL,MOUNT,168
CARMET,FREDRICK A,37
CARMICAL,JOSEPH,80
CARMICHAEL,ANDERSON,385
. ANNA E,391;CATHERINE
. E,391;ELIZABETH,248
. H W,111;HUGH W,80,90
. J,120-121;J B,111,116
. 123;JAMES,69,80,95
. 385;JNO,225,385;JOHN
. 88,334,364;JOHN B,90
. 111,122,129,136;JOHN
. C,385;JOSEPH,69,90,93
. 111;JOSEPH E,80
. JOSEPH H,193;MARY,111
. POLLY,266;ROBT D,385
. SARAH,182,392;WM,90
CARMICHALL,215;JOSEPH
  222
CARMON,MARY,402
CARN,ELLEN,410
CARNE,WM,19
CARNEL,WRIGHT,37
CARNELL,JANE,387
CARNES,ANNA MATILDA,407
. ELIZA,387;JULIA,387
. ORPHA HAYWOOD,418
. PATRICK H,386;THOMAS
. P,386
CARNEY,ARTHUR,386
CARNS,BARTHOLEMEW,386
CAROLINA,DAVID,386
CAROTHERS,WM,10
CARPENTER,BAILEY,28,49
. 53;BAILY,2;BARBARA
. 356;CELLINISE M,39
. ENSIGN JESSE,9

CARPENTER(cont)
. GEORGE W A,36;JOHN,28
. 52;LEROY,202;LEWIS,37
. LOU,40;SUSAN,45
CARR,215;D S,149;DAVID
. S,86,90;EDWARD,386
. ELIZABETH,271
. ELIZABETH ANN,280
. FANNY,176;LOUISA JANE
. 209;MARTHA,236
. PATRICK,3;REBECCA,243
. ROBERT,302;THOMAS,176
. 386;W S,149;WILLIAM
. 313
CARRE,EUGENIA,401
CARREL,ANGELINA,276
. PATSEY,273
CARRELL,HARRIETT,253
. ROSETTA,37;THOMAS,310
. THOS,319,327
CARREY,HARRIETT,404
CARRIE,CAROLINE L,417
. MARY E,397;PETER,386
. ROSINA E,419
CARRIEL,GRIEF,341;JOHN
. D,341
CARRIERS,CHAIN,231
CARRIL,GRIEF,341
CARROL,POLLY,239
CARROLE,LUCY,38
CARROLL,28;A A V,240
. HECTOR,38;JAMES,63
. JAS,147;JOHN,346
. RICHMOND,363;ROBERT
. 363;WILLIAM,363
CARROUTH,WM,90
CARRUTHERS,JOSEPH,140
CARSON,ADAM,228,342
. ANDREW,48,53;ANNA,258
. EDWARD,38;EFFIE L,279
. ELIZ,247;EMILY,419
. HESTER,421;JOSEPH,222
. MARY GREEN,47;ROBERT
. 386;SARAH A,46;SARAH
. M,265;WM,294,386
CARSWELL,ALEXANDER,4,10
. 28,53;CUDJAI GOLDING
. 38;EDWARD,386;EDWARD
. R,386;ELIZ,389;ELIZ A
. 392;ELIZABETH,28
. ENOCH H,386;EQINARDUS
. R,386;JAS A,386;JOHN
. 53;JOHN D,38;JOHN F
. 386;JOHN W,386
. MATTHEW,28,50,53,386
. MATTHEW J,386;REBECCA
. 41;SARAH,4
CART,ELEANOR JANE,411
. ELIZA CAROLINE,398
. GEORGIANNA E,390
. HARRIET,380;MARTHA
. ANN,411;MARY,398
CARTAIN,JAS,2
CARTER,ALEXANDER,28
. ANNA MATILDA,386,412
. B S,100,105,113
. BEDFORD S,97;BEN,202
. BRADFORD,136;CADER
. 321;CATHERINE ELIZA
. 393;CHARLOTTE E,44
. CRISTIAN,415;CYNTHIA
. 237;EBENEZAR,114,122
. EDWARD,53;EDWARD A,38
. ELIZ,244,397;ELIZA,38
. GEO,386;ISAAC,297
. ISAIAH,4;ISIAH W,38
. JACOB,19;JAMES,74-75
. 82,84,86,90,93,99,109

. 118,120,126-127,131
. 133-134,143;JAMES M
. 386;JOHN,38,65,90,102
. 386;JOHN A,349;JOHN
. ALEXANDER,351
. JOHNATHAN,122
. JONATHAN,102,114
. JOSIAH,218;KINCHEN
. 303;KISSIAH,334
. LANDON,334;LEWIS,38
. LITTLETON,307;LOUISA
. 45;MAILDA,53;MARCUS E
. 108,111,123;MARGARET
. 245;MARTHA,126,401
. MARY,4;MARY ANN,37
. MARY WASHINGTON,397
. MATILDA,380;NANCY,274
. 422;NELSON,85,91
. RHODA,420;RICHARD,334
. 346,348-349,351-352
. 358;ROBERT,386;SARAH
. 53;SARAH H,396;SUSAN
. 42;TEMPERANCE,331
. THOMAS,321;WM B,147
CARTLEDGE,JAMES,188
. JOHN,185;JOSEPH,188
CARTLIDGE,JOHN,386
CARTWRIGHT,ANN B,276
. BETSEY,251;JNO,224
. JOHN,317;JOS,224;JUNE
. 266;MARGARET,254
. MARTHA,239;MARY H,269
. MATILDA,281;NANCY,238
. 269;NANCY H,239;PETER
. 224;SARAH,263;SUSAN
. 263
CARUTHERS,J,140;JAMES
. 47;NANCY,28,47;SAMUEL
. 47,53;WILLIAM,28
CARVER,JOS,2;JOSEPH,2
. THOS,2
CARVY,JAS,14
CARY,EBENEZER,386
. RICHARD,320
CASE,E,59;ERMINE,67,71
. HARMON H,38;WILLEY J
. 334;WILLIS,125
CASEY,ABRAHAM,386
. ELIJAH,213;P E,392
. PRISCILLA,370;RICHARD
. G,214;RIGHT,213
. THOMAS,202,213
CASH,F A,73;JOHN,351
. 357;JOHN H,108
CASHIN,JOHN,353,359
. MARY ANN,396;OSWELL
. 386
CASNAHAN,LUCY,40
CASON,JOHN,2,10
CASSELS,SAM J,254
CASTALAC,SALLY,390
CASTELEN,THO,229
CASTELLAW,WM H,386
CASTEN,ELIZA,380
CASTENS,HELEN M,421
CASTERSON,THOMAS,386
CASTLEBERRY,EDWARD,299
. JAMES,308;JEREMIAH
. 308;JOHN,69,287,293
. 308;MARY ANN,308-309
. RICHARD,300;THOMAS
. 334
CASTLEBURY,JEREMIAH,293
. JOHN,287
CASTLELOW,JOHN B,334
CASWELL,ALEXANDER,4
CATCHETT,FLORA M,36
CATCHING,SAYMER,218

. SEYMORE,218
CATCHINGS,ELBERT C,334
. ELIZABETH,267;LAVINIA
. 283;MARY E,281;NANCY
. 251
CATCHINS,BENJ,228
CATER,EDWARD,188
CATES,ALICE G,41
. ARMAMINTA,36;JAMES,28
. 48,53;JOHN,28,38
. JOSEPH,48;JOSEPH L,53
. MARTHA,43;THOMAS,53
. 297,321;THOMAS W,38
CATHAN,W,117
CATHELL,JAMES,294;JEAN
. 294
CATHER,DAVID,386;ELIZ
. 390
CATHERN,WILLIAM,124
CATINELL,CAROLINE E,409
CATLEGE,JOSEPH,152
CATLET,POLLY,28
CATLETT,JOHN,10
CATLIN,ELIZ,421
CATO,28;AMANDA,285;BUTT
. L,237,242,274;BUTTS L
. 283;GREEN,291,321,326
. GREENE,328;JINNY,28
. PHILIP,328;STERLING
. 291,328;WILLIAM,15-16
. WM,14,17,242;WYCHE
. 242,326,328
CATOE,STERLING,291,321
. WYCHE,321
CATREHEAD,JOHN,242
CATTONETT,VIRGINIA M
. 395
CAUDLE,GREEN,115;JNO
. 307
CAUDLER,J A,190;M A,190
CAUGHLIN,JAMES,53;MARY
. 38
CAULIE,JOHN,15;REASON
. 15,17
CAULIR,JOHN,14
CAUSEY,ALLEN,22,25
. ELIZABETH,201;PHILIP
. 28;PHILIPS,242
CAUSTIN,HESTER,28
CAUTHON,J W,242
CAVAN,TREVOR,386
CAVARITT,BRIGHT,2
CAVEN,DAVID,386;TRAVA
. 386
CAVENA,2
CAVENAH,CHARLES,49;JANE
. ANN,207;LITTLEBERRY
. 386
CAVENDER,PHILLIP M,386
CAVENIS,ELIZ,392
CAVENNET,SARAH,53
CAWHORN,J,100
CAWHORR,J,113
CAWLEY,218;CATHARINE
. 408;CHANY,82;JAMES,50
. JOHN,386;JUNE,46
CAWLY,CHANY,95
CAWTHON,DABNEY,290
. JAMES,90,103;JOHN W
. 242
CAWTHORN,JESSE H,95
CEALEY,A NEGRO,292
CELLERS,BARSHEBA,379
CENTALL,JOSEPH,91
CESSEND,SARAH ELIZ,245
CESSIOM,34
CESSNA,CHALRES,221
. CHARLES,218,223;CHS

CESSNA(cont)
. 228;ELIZABETH,267;JNO
. 231;JOHN,221,223
. ROBERT,371;SAMUEL,223
CESSNES,G K,92
CESSUMS,PATRICK,28
CETCHREWS,W F,53
CHAFFIN,BEVERLY,334
JOHN T,334
CHAFIN,JOHN J,147
NATHAN,355;THOS,242
CHAIFFIN,J J,118
CHAIN,ANGELINE,248
CHAIRES,BEN,348
BENJAMIN,349
CHAIRS,BENJAMIN,349
CHAISON,JAMES,11
CHAMBER,232,234
CHAMBERLAIN,
ELLIOTT R,242
CHAMBERS,EMILY,263
. HENRY,195,227;JAMES,2
. JANE,384;JOHN,13-14
. JOHN FINCH,242;JOSEPH
. 291;LENA,249;MARGET
. 414;MARTHA ANN,254
. ROBERT,341,346;ROBT
. 290;SARAH V,268
. THOMAS,38
CHAMBLERS,A,38
CHAMBLISS,THOMAS,386
CHAMPEN,ELIZ,397
CHAMPION,89,101
. ALEXANDER,288
. AMORETTE C,263;ELI
. 288;ELIAS,288
. ELIZABETH,288
. HARRIETT L,258;HART
. 287-288;HENRY,242,288
. JAS,242;JESSE,242,288
. JESSE W,242;JNO,327
. JOHN,287-288;LUCY,288
. MARTHA J,258;MARY A E
. 261;MARY V,242;MOSES
. 334;PATSEY,288;PEGGY
. 288;WM,243
CHANCE,ALFRED W,38;ANN
. 390;AUGUSTUS,38
. BENJAMIN,38;BETHA,53
. CALVIN,203;CARY,201
. COLONEL,203;EDWARD,53
. FLORENCE M,44;FRANCE
. M,42;GRANVILLE,38
. HANNAH,381;HENRY,2,8
. 28,49,53;ISAAC,386
. IVENA,45;JACOB,53
. JAMES,53;JESSE,8,28
. JOHN,48,53;JOHN B,53
. JOSEPH,9,28;LIZZIE,36
. MARY,53;PHILEMON,2
. RACHEL,206,212
. REBECCA,42;REUBEN,28
. REUBIN,6;SILVA,204
. STEPHEN,28;SUSAN,40
. WILLIAM,28,38;WILLIAM
. C,203;WILLOUGHBY,38
CHANDLER,ALLY,47;DANIEL
. B,242;DEANA,45;GEORGE
. 28,51;M G A,279
. MILLER,259;ROBERT,38
. SALLIE,43;SUSANNAH,53
. WALTON,242;WM,310,363
CHANING,JOHN,386
CHANNEL,ISHAM,242
. REBEKAH,278;SOPHRONIA
. ANN,277
CHANNELL,LITLETON,242
. LOUEZA,243;MANISSA P

. 261;MICHAEL,242;NANCY
. 237;RENA,245;SAPHRONE
. 264;SUSAN,277;THOS
. 242;WM,242
CHAPEL,A H,91
CHAPELL,JOHN,311
CHAPLIN,JOS,2
CHAPMAN,ABNER,89,334
. ASA W,334;ASA W F,331
. B W,113;BERRY,309
. BRITTON,82;CUTTER,386
. EDMOND,334;ELIZABETH
. D,264;ISAAC,309
. ISAIAH,309;ISRAEL,28
. JOHN,334;JOHN M,242
. MATTIE L,240;MILES
. 242;R C,64;RANDLE,242
. RANDOL,242;THOS,242
. W H,246;W M,260,270
. WM,261;WM G,237;WM H
. 237,242;WM M,242,280
CHAPPEL,J B,275
CHAPPELL,A H,92,120
. BENJA,311;BENJAMIN
. 311;ELIZABETH,259;G A
. 265,273;I S,386;JOHN
. 217,228,242,311;JOHN
. B,254;JOSEPH,217,311
. MARY,259;ROBT,242
CHAPPLE,SARAH,249
CHARITY,JAMES,386
CHARLES,
. CATHERINE C A,405
. NATHANIEL,386
CHARLES-CLARK,ENSIGN,8
CHATHAM,323;JOSIAH,84
MARY,255
CHATMAN,MILES,242
CHATTELS,113
CHAVES,DRURY,304,311
CHAVONS,JANE,408
CHAVOUS,WM,386
CHEATAIN,ELIZABETH,207
CHEATAM,ANTHONY,386
CHEATHAM,O P,60,62,64
. 71,77,79,88;OBEDIAH P
. 63;TABITHA,257
CHEATMAN,LOVERA B,242
CHEEK,ASBELL,242;BURD
. 87;BURGES,90;EDNA,278
. ELIZABETH,250;JAMES
. 315;JOHN,315;JOHN W
. 334;LAFAYETTE,334;PAT
. F,314;WILLIAM,331,334
CHEEKY,MARY,312
CHEENY,THOS B,149
CHEEVER,LORANA D,405
CHENEY,ALMARINE C,266
. ANN,239;JOHN F,242
. MARTHA,248;MARY E,266
. RHODA,284;RHONDA ANN
. 242;SARAH,239;W A,285
. WILLIAM R,334;WM O
. 242
CHERRY,JESSE,334;NATHAN
2
CHESSER,MARY,272
CHESTER,FRANCIS,242
JOHN A,38;W G,38
CHEVES,ADONIRAM,242
. GREEF,242;JOSEPH,242
. RACHEL C,419;SUSAN
. 394
CHEW,B F,68;BENJAMIN F.
. 386;ELIZABETH J,268
. JOHN,242,256,268;JOHN
. C,38;MARGARET ANN,285
. MARY S,251;THOS,242

CHEWNING,MARY,237
SAMUEL,325;WM I,242
CHEWNINGS,PAMELIA,276
CHHINGS,RHODY,262
CHIFLAN,CATHERINE,397
CHILDERS,87,101;F J,140
. FLEMING,144;FLEMUEL
. 90
CHILDREY,AGNESS,397
CHILDS,HENRY,334;JACK
334;JAMES,95,143,148
CHILES,JAMES,147
CHIRSTOPHER,TOMAS,115
CHISHOLM,M A,70;THOMAS
3
CHISOLM,16;JOHN,347
. MARY,4;THOMAS,4-5
. THOS,2
CHOICE,TULLEY,291;TULLY
294,306;WM,245
CHONN,CHAS C,242
CHRISTIAN,ABDA,178,386
. ELIZ I,422;GEO,350
. JOHN,313;MAHALA,384
. THEOPHILUS,203;W,344
CHRISTOPER,JAS,294
CHRISTOPHER,D,297;DAVID
. 115,297,306;HENRY,242
. JAMES,297;JAS,306
. MARY,238,279;SEABORN
. 242;WM,242-243
CHRISWELL,JOHN,243;WM
243
CHUNING,DAVID,298
SAMUEL,298
CHURCH,HANNAH,416
CHURCHILL,AUGUSTA V,40
. CALVIN B,53;GEORGE,38
. HANNAH L,207;NANCY
. 418
CHURCHWELL,THOMAS,386
CHURSH,ANNA THOMAS,420
CIMBROUS,217
CISSNA,JNO,221
CLAGG,DAVID,28
CLAIGG,ALLEN,386
CLAITT,ISHAM,387;JAMES
. 387;JEHU,387;JEREMIAH
. 387;JESSE,387;JOHN
. 387
CLAMES,J,254
CLANCY,MARY,397
CLANTON,CATHERINE E,382
. MARTHA,398;POLLY,402
. SARAH,391;TABITHA,379
CLARA,MORTAVA,398
CLARK,94,289;ALLEN,331
. ANN,415;ARTHUR,243
. BENJ,243;BETSEY,53;C
. 291-292;CELESLIA V,43
. CHARLES,50;CHARLES E
. 386;CHRISTOPHER,29,49
. CONELIUS,311
. CORNELIUS,289,291,303
. DAVID,386;DORCAS,213
. EDWARD,38;ELIZ A,389
. ELIZA F,379;ELIZABETH
. 58;EMILY,334;ESTHER M
. 37;FANNY M,246
. FRANCIS A,243,334
. GABRIEL,386;GEO O,242
. GEORGE,331;GEORGE W
. 38,334;GILBERT,331
. 334,386;H,148;HENRY
. 149;ISABELLA,410;J S
. 243;JAMES,306;JAMES A
. 203;JAS,243;JEAN,420
. JESSE,297,302,306

===
index to Some Georgia County Records, volume 4   PAGE 439

CLARK(cont)
. JOHN,38,67,170-171
. 331,334;JOHN M,386
. JOSEPH,334;JOSHUA,334
. JOSHUA R,334;LARKIN
. 372;LEAMA,331;LILLY
. ANN,206;LINDSEY,334
. LOUISA,36;LUCINDA,261
. LUCIUS,203;MARGATE
. 303;MARIA,262,409
. MARTHA,331;MARY,42
. MARY ANN,240;MILDRED
. 392;NANCY,36,254,273
. 404;OLIVE,52;PATSY
. 346;PHILLIP,38
. REBECCA,384;REBEKAH
. 292,306;RICHARD J W
. 386;RICHD,329;ROBERT
. 291-292,303-306,311
. RUTHA,37;SALLIE,201
. SAMUEL,11,60,146
. SAMUEL B,386;SARAH,36
. SARAH ANN SIDNEY,403
. SARAH JANE,401
. TABITHA,291;THOMAS
. 297,306,334;WARREN,10
. 51;WILLIAM,48,51,106
. 195,297,303-304,310
. WILLIAMSON,346;WM,304
. 306,386;WM H,149;WM J
. 243;Z,108
CLARKE,AMANDA,401
. CHARLES,29,53,386
. CHARLOTTE,385;D,25
. DAVID,20-22,24;DIANA
. 153;E,53;ELEANOR,405
. ELIZ,384,412;ELIZA A
. 394;FANNY,29;GABRIEL
. 386;GABRIEL S,386;GEO
. C,244,250-251,259-260
. 286;GEO W,386;HENRY
. 386;HENRY E,386;HENRY
. L,386;JAMES,20,22,24
. 53;JOHN,7,9,29,359
. JOHN M,387;JOSEPH,53
. JOSEPH L,387;LUCY,284
. LYDIA D,41;MARY,278
. MARY ANN,414;MICHAEL
. M,387;NATHANIEL,387
. ROBERT,387;SAMUEL,387
. SARAH,53,57,276;SARAH
. A,412;SARAH ANN,386
. SOPHIA L,389;SUSAN
. 413;SUSAN CAROLINE
. 394;ULRIC B,387
. WARREN,53;WILLIAM E
. 38;WM,243;WM C W,387
. WM W,387
CLARKSON,ELIZ,407
. JOSEPH,223
CLARY,JAMES,10
CLATON,DANIEL W,53
CLAUDEN,CHALY,38
CLAXTON,AUGUSTINE S,387
. EDWARD P,387;ELIZ,404
. GEO ROOTS,387;JOHN S
. 387;PHILIP,387
. WILLIAIM,38;WM,387
CLAY,DELPHY,276
. HEZEKIAH,334;JAMES C
. 334;JESSE,334,345,355
. MARTHA S,334;NATHAN
. 215;P G,79,81
. PLEASANT G,59;ROYAL
. 364;S,76;SALLY,237
. SAMUEL,59,62,79,81
. 243,355
CLAYTON,AUSTIN,90;BILLY

. 171;CHARLES,171;ELIZA
. 171;HANNAH,171;I I,53
. JAMES,65-66,75;KEFSA
. 171;L R,203;LENORA
. 281;MARY,411;MARY ANN
. 171;NAN,171;NANCY,171
. PHILL,171;PHILLIPS
. 243;SAMUEL,171;SARAH
. 408,410
CLE,MARTHA MELVINA,45
CLEARSHAW,J H,113
CLEATON,AUSTIN,126
CLEAVELAND,WILLIAM,361
CLECKLEY,JACOB,334
CLEGG,CATHERINE,421
CLEGHORN,176;GEORGE,180
. MARTHA,381;MARTHA I
. 189
CLELLAND,MAX,331,333
CLEMANCE,ELLIS,243
CLEMANS,DELILA,200
CLEMENTS,215,219,329
. AARON,243;ALLEN,334
. ANDERSON,243;BETSY
. NORTH,316;CHLOE,316;D
. 303;DANIEL,387;DAVID
. 292,302,316,318,321
. ELIZ,394;ELIZA,316
. ELIZABETH,223,231,255
. FRANKLIN,243;GREZIL
. 245;HANNAH,243;JACOB
. 29;JESSE,195,243,294
. 306;JOHN,316,318-319
. LOUISA H,266;LUCY,266
. MARY,239;MARY A,29
. MORTIMER,195;PEYTON
. 243,334;PHILLIP,240
. 243,294;PHILLIPS,243
. SARAH,253;STEPHEN,316
. 318-319;TONEY,316
. TYRE,215,221,223;WM B
. 243
CLEMENTZ,MARGARET,391
CLEMMENTS,GABRIEL,10
CLEMMOND,WILEY,85
CLEMMONS,JOHN,387
CLEPBON,DANIEL,243
CLEVELAND,ALLEN,69,71
. BENJ,345;BENJAMIN,345
. JACOB,86;JANE,409
. JOHN D,275;LARKIN,243
. 367;NEIL,387;O C,96
. RICE,71;SARY,367
. WILLIAM C,91
CLIAT,MARY ANN,397
CLIATT,ELIZABETH,400
. JAMES,65;JUDITH,400
. LEURANEY,411;NANCY L
. 419
CLIET,JONATHAN,387
CLIETT,JONATHAN,172,183
. MINOR J,387;RICHARD
. 387;THOS C,387
. WILLIAM,127
CLIFTON,ABIGAIL,211
. ALANSON,243;ANN MAY
. 196;ANNA,237;CHAS,243
. EDWIN,290;EZEKIEL,212
. GEORGE W,213;JANE H
. 261;JOHN,213;JOHN R
. 243;L,290;LEMUEL,290
. MARY A,273;MARY ANN
. 262;PATIENCE F,240
. R L,243;WILLIAM,7;WM
. 243
CLINE,BRIDGET,412
CLINTON,ANGELINA,53;D W
. 38

CLIOTT,ISAAC,387
CLOER,ASA,168
CLOPTON,124
CLOWER,GEORGE,311;J,232
. JONATHAN,305,310-311
. 318,321;WM,306
CLOWERS,WILLIAM,291
CLRK,ROBERT,304
CLUSKEY,ELIZ H,404
CLUTSION,HENSIAN,38
CLYMA,PETER,2
CLYMAN,E,216
COADY,LEWIS,6
COATES,SUSANNAH,2
COATS,JAMES,334;JAS,243
. JESSE,387
COAVY,DAVID,9
COB,ANNY,250
COBB,89;ABRAHAM,387
. ADELINE,172;BRITIAN
. 195;BRITON,29
. CATHERINE E,172
. CURTIS,10,48,213
. DELILAH,405;EDMUND,85
. ELIZABETH,201,392
. FRANCIS,409;JACOB,48
. 293;JAMES,14-15;JOHN
. 172,186,243;JOHN S,58
. LEWIS,172;LUCRETIA
. 416;MABLE,195;PHILIP
. M,8;POLLY W,172
. PRISCILLA,385;RASH,19
. RUTH,409;THOMAS,156
. 166,171,387;THOMAS W
. 170,172-173;THOS,156
. 158,165,167;VICY,416
. WILLIAM,172,364
. WILLIAM BUKHAM,172;WM
. A,387
COCHRAM,CENA,239
COCHRAN,221;CHEADLE,334
. HANNAH,246;JAS,243
. JOHN,130,243,334
. JUBIL,334;MARTHA,275
. MARY F,244;REBECCAH
. 271;ROBERT,69;SALLY
. 269;SAMUEL,243;THOMAS
. G,90;WM,215,217-218
. 219-220,228
COCHRANE,JAMES J,38
COCHRUM,THOS,244
COCK,JOHN,11,29
COCKE,MARY,416
. NATHANIEL W,387
. REBECCA THOMPSON,380
COCKRAHAIN,HANNAH,390
COCKRAM,MARTHA A,272
COCKRAN,WM,216,222-223
. 224
COCRAFT,ANNA,246;JAS
. 243
COCROFT,CELINA,246
COELMAN,JEREMIAH,195
COF,LEWIS C,243
COFER,ALICE,283
COFFEE,JNO,329;JOHN,325
. JOSHUA,325;PATSY,325
. PETER,325-326,329
. POLLY,325;SALLEY,325
. SINTHY,325
COFFIELD,EMELINE R,241
. IRENA C,263;MARY JANE
. 241;SARAH FRANCES;239
COGBOURNE,GEORGE,7
COGEN,JACOB H,243
COGHLAN,SARAH,410
COGIL,GEORGE HANSON,387
. NANCY ANN,420

COGILL,ELIZA,380
COGLAND,EDWARD,38
COGLE,MARY ANN I,385
COHN,29
COHOON,JOHN,309
COHORN,JOHN,97
COIL,GIDEON M,29
COILE,ELIZABETH,51
COK,LOURINA,263
COKER,87;ELISHA,82,84
. 90;GEORGIANA,411
. ISAAC,96;JACOB,96
. THOMAS,71,91;WM,149
COLBERT,FRED K,243;J B
. 113;WILLIAM,363
COLCLOUGH,CORDELIA E
. 238;ELIZABETH,270
. PATSEY,268;SARAH
. ISADORE,287;W.A,241
. 286;WM A,265
COLCOUGH,ELIZA C,259
. JOHN M,243;WM A,243
COLDING,BENJ,288
COLDOUGH,RACHEL,235
COLDWELL,AUGUSTUS C,387
. THANK S,406
COLE,29,210;AMEY,370
. ANN ELIZA,42;BETSEY
. ANN,250;BUD G,38
. ELIZA,409;ELIZABETH L
. 334;ELIZABETH P,210
. JOHN,47,370;JOHN L
. 131;RENE,334;THOS,243
. WILLIAM,334
COLEMAN,29;A H,203
. ALFRED,195;AMELIA,275
. ANDREW,203;ANN,390
. ANNE,253;B F,203
. BETHANY,382;C,203
. CHARLES,7,29,48,203
. 214;CHARLES M,203
. CLARISSA,419;CORD,203
. DANIEL,243;DAVID,213
. DELENGIST,207;E L,204
. ELIAS,195;ELISHA,7,29
. 48,195,213-214;ELISHA
. S,195;ELIZ,243;ELIZA
. 270;ELIZA T,197
. ELIZABETH,207,250,402
. ELLENDER,309;ELZEAR
. 199;F J,203;FRANCIS
. 291,325;GEORGE,203
. HATTIE,207;HETTY,205
. ISAAC,11,14,203;JAMES
. 203;JAMES E,203;JAMES
. L,387;JANE,203,211
. JAS L,387;JEREMIAH
. 203,214;JEREMIAH H
. 203;JESSE,11,29,48
. JOHN,14-15,170,214
. JOHN L,197;JS,228
. JULIA ANN,205;L,210
. L B,203;L V,196;LAURA
. A,210;LINDSEY,213
. LOUISA,256;LUCINDY
. 208;LUCRECIA,196
. LUVENA E,202;MALCUM C
. 203;MARY,90,104;MARY
. ANN,419;MILLY,11,53
. MILTON,203;NANCY,53
. 282;PHRONA,207;POLLY
. 204,275;R,140;RACHAEL
. 213;RACHEL,195,210
. RACHEL R,197;REUBEN,5
. ROBERT,99-100;ROBERT
. P,90,116;ROBT,84
. SALLY,273;SAML,216
. SAMUEL,243;SARAH,199

. STEPHEN,192
. TEMPERANCE,268;THOS
. 243;TILDA,202;WADE,15
. WELCOM,195;WELCOMB L
. 203;WELCOME,195
. WILLIAM,195,212
. WILLIAM A,203
COLEMAND,DAVID ANN,110
. DAVID LEWIS,110
. DOROTHY,110;FRANCIS
. HARRIS,110
COLEN,PETER,387
COLEY,265;JOHN,243
. SARAH F,251;WM,243
COLHOUN,LEVI,11
COLIDAY,JOHN,14
COLIE,READON,13
COLLEMAN,KITTEY,257
COLLEN,ROSS,90
COLLENS,ANNA ELIZA,208
. JULIA ANN,207;MARY C
. 208;MELVINA,203;SUSAN
. LAFAYETT,211
COLLERSON,WILLIAM,11
COLLEY,AMANDA,271;F S
. 240;FRANCIS,240
. FRANCIS S,240,280
. NANCY,273;RIETLEY,237
COLLIDAY,JOHN,9
COLLIER,AMY M,397;ARON
. 178;BENJAMIN,62
. BETSEY,269;CAROLINE
. 386;CLINCH,38;EDWARD
. 178;EDWIN,243;ELIZ
. 244;HENDERSON,327
. JACKSON,97;JANE,263
. JAS,243;JOHN,178,334
. 353,357;LUCINDA,422
. MARIA V,396;MARY E
. 403;REBAKAH,263;SARAH
. 178;THOMAS,62;THOS
. 243;WIETTE,318
. WILLIAM,178,334;WMNSN
. 243
COLLINS,232;ANDREW,48
. ANN,407;ANN JANE,403
. ANNE,412;BETSY,396
. CATHERINE,379,422
. CATHERINE LOUISA,408
. CATHRINE,405;CHARLES
. 72;DAVID,387;DICEY,37
. ELIZ,418;ELIZA,293
. 403;ELIZA A,387;ELIZA
. ANN,419;ELIZABETH,208
. EMELINE,202;FRANCES B
. R,383;GEORGE,293,330
. 387;GEORGE W,387
. HANNAH,421;ITHIEIA
. 417;JACOB,53,289,304
. JAMES,159,387;JAMES M
. 387;JAS,243;JESSE,387
. JOHN,29,52-53,224,387
. JONES,243;JOSEPH,387
. LEVIN,10,29;LEWIS,8
. 387;LITTLETON,387
. LOUISA M,46;LYDIA,393
. MAJOR,387;MARTHA,159
. 402,412;MARTHA C,408
. MARY,394-395,407-408
. MARY W,386;MICHAEL
. 307,387;MOSES,387;N H
. 181;NATHANIEL,243
. PERRY,203;Q H,206
. RACHAEL,402;RICHARD
. 243;ROBERT,387;S,111
. 149;SALLY,4,399
. SAMUEL,60,84,87,147
. 149;SARAH,49,383,417

. SEABORN,10;SEBERN,213
. STEPHEN,387;SUSANNA
. 415;SUSANNAH,422
. THOMAS,329;THOS,148
. TRUITT,329;VINA,402
. WASINGTON,387;WILLIAM
. 159,346;WM S,387;ZOAH
. 204
COLLOCAN,CHRISTIAN,280
COLLUM,DAVID,310
COLON,JAS,243
COLQUIT,JOHN TERRY,334
COLQUITT,MARTHA,250
. MARTHA I,282;MARY,244
. SARAH,251
COLSON,AMANDA F,46
. CHANEY,39;MARY ANN D
. 403;SARAH,42;WILLIAM
. 51,53
COLTER,GEORGE,53
. MARGARET,390
COLVARD,WM,160
COLVES,JOHN,169
COLVIN,HENRY,387;THOS
. 86
COLWELL,EDWARD,243;MARY
. 394
COMBER,JOHN,2
COMBS,CREASEY,420;ELIZ
. T,414;F A,60;SARAH G
. 392
COMER,A,233,294
. ANDERSON,217,288;H M
. 321;HUGH,291;J,290-291
. 293;JAMES,296;JAS,294
. 308;JESSE,330;JOHN
. 303;LYDIA,335;MARY B
. 331,335;SALLIE E,281
. THOMAS J,331,335
COMPTON,85,93,103-104
. 108,112-114,119,128
. 134,138;FRANKLIN,82
. JAMES L,113,118,121
. 140;JEMIAH J,262;JOHN
. W,335;JORDA,335
. JORDAN,82,85,331;P M
. 90,100,105,108,113
. 116,118-123,130-131
. 140,142,145;PLEASANT
. 331,335;PLEASANT M
. 107;POLLY ANN,335
CONANT,WILLIAM L,122
CONAWAY,OLIPBE,386
CONDEN,DAVID,347
CONDON,WM D,243
CONDUS,ROYALS,46
CONE,14;CATHERINE,277
. EDMUND L,387
. ELIZABETH,262;EZEKIEL
. 243;FRANCIS,243
. FRANCIS JULIA ANN,237
. JAMES,387;JANE
. VICTORIA,246;JAS T
. 243;JNO,387;JOHN S
. 388;MAHALY,396;MARY
. ANN,269,410;NANCY,241
. P,19;PETER,18,63;RICH
. 243;ROBT,243;W,237
. 272;W H,261;W H C,243
. 254,256,276,284
. WINNEY,259,273;WM,238
. 239,241-242,245,247
. 248-249,253,257-258
. 262,266,271,273,277
. 281-282,388
CONELY,MARY ANN,411
CONGER,A A,137,147,149
. AMOS,86,118;AMOS A

CONGER(cont)
. 128,143;E,137;E M,128
. ELI,62,69,71,83,117
. 118,124,126,128,136
. 142-144;ELI M,147
CONINE,RICHARD,243;WM
  243
CONLEY,HARRIET,43;S W
  244
CONN,ANNE,410;CHARLOTTE
  ELVIA,393;GEORGE,388
CONNAL,JOHN,60
CONNEL,CYNTHIA,251
. ELLEN,410;JOHN,60
. SUSAN JANE,237;T,101
. T H;136;THOMAS,225
. THOMAS H,123;THOMAS W
. 129;THOS H,105
CONNELL,ASENETH,263
. CARY ANN,272;CELIA
. 236;D,313;DANEY,272
. DAVID,244;HARTWELL
. 244;JEMIMA,264;JESSE
. 295,306,318;JOHN,244
. MARGARET,111;MARY,242
. 256;NANCY,282;SYDNEY
. 268;T,149;THOMAS H
. 111;WM,111
CONNELLY,PATRICK P,11
  POLLY,348
CONNER,ABEL,244;BURILL
. 244;ISAAC,21,23,25
. JAMES G,18;JOHN,29
. JOHN W,335;MARY,29
. 287,396;MARY ANN,36
. REBEKAH,299;SALLEY
. 322;SARAH,402;TARRANE
. 388;THOMAS,304
. WILLIAM,19
CONNOR,JOHN,5;MARY,29
CONVERT,ADELIADE,419
CONY,NANCY,280
CONYERS,ELIZABETH R,254
. ELIZABETH S,207;SARAH
. 260
COODY,C M,62-63,69-70
. 72,92,100,105,107,113
. 122,145;CLAYTON M,82
. LEWIS,29
COOK,89,97,124;ABRAHAM
. 8;ABRAM,29;ALHEE,45
. ALLEN,91,291,294
. ANDREW L,53;ANDREW S
. 388;ANNA JONES,39
. ANNY,282;ANTHONY,320
. B,330;BENJ,10,319
. BENJAMIN,310-311
. BENJAMIN W,335
. BURRELL,293;CATHERINE
. 384;DELILA,263;DINAH
. 47;DRURY,216,293,307
. 308,310-311;DUDLEY,85
. ELIZ,218;ELIZA,235
. ELIZA ANN,408
. ELIZABETH,217,270
. EMMA,37;EMORY,244;F
. 97;F S,367;FANNY,389
. FERGUSON,9;FRANCES,44
. GEORGE R,38;GRACY,288
. HARRIETT,243;HENRY,18
. HENRY A,78;ISAAC,238
. 244,388;ISRAEL,10
. JAMES,7,10,29,115
. JAMES R,388;JANE W
. 243;JAS,244;JASPER T
. 244;JOHN,11,48,215
. 218,244,288,293,296
. 304,306,317-318,320

. 321,330,378,388;JOHN
. D,388;JOHN R,13,18
. 244;JOHN W,335;JOSEPH
. 226,244;JOSHUA,244
. LUCRETIA,237;MALINDA
. 271;MARY,273;MCKEEN
. 146;NATHAN,303;P,309
. PATIENCE,304;PERKINS
. 107;PHILIP,302
. PHILLIP,288,303-304
. ROBERT,217-218;SHEROD
. A,53;THOMAS,65-66
. THOS,102,244,342
. WILLIAM,10,343,346
. 348;WM,244,388
COOKE,ABRAAM,51;ARTHUR
. S,51;CHARLOTTE,394
. ELIZ,390;FRANCIS,388
. JAMES,51;JOHN,329
. JOHN D,50;MARY ANN
. 415
COOKSEY,HANNAH,118;MAY
. 197;THOMAS B,203
COOLY,105
COOMBS,MARIA M,384
. MARTHA A,394;MARTHA G
. 418
COONAMAN,ELIZABETH,40
COONER,ELLEN,208;JASPER
  203
COOP,SAMUEL J,57
COOPER,306;AMANDA M,405
. AMOS,244;ANN,418
. ANTHONY,173;BETSEY
. 232,235,268;BEVERLY
. 89;CHARLOTTE,407
. CYNTHIA H,379;DAVID
. 190,194;ELI,78;ELIJAH
. 222,226;ELIZ,408
. GEORGIA A,411;JAMES
. 226,232,234,311,388
. JAMES M V,388;JANE,47
. JAS,290,296,359;JOHN
. 173,297,325,388;JOHN
. C,388;JOS,290;JOSEPH
. 29,173,297;LOUISA C
. 407;MARGARET,385
. MARTHA,182;MICAJAH
. 290;PATSEY,295
. PENELOPE,269;REBECCA
. 422;REBECKAH,173
. SANOLINE,37;SARAH E
. 389;SYNTHIA,380;T,318
. THOMAS,290,295;THOMAS
. B,262,285;THOS,288
. 325;THOS B,244
. WILLIAM,53;WM,244;WM
. H,388
COOS,57
COOSA,HUGH,29
COPELAN,A H,239,244
. ANNIE V,244;DANIEL E
. 244;ELIAS D,244;ELIZA
. 264;ELIZA B,286
. ELIZABETH,284
. ELIZABETH F,239;JILES
. 244;JOHN,239,244-245
. JOHN B,244;JOHN D,244
. MAJOR,244;MARY E,261
. MARY N,286;NANCY,239
. 251;OBIDIAH G,244
. ROWAN,244;SUSAN,239
. 264;SUSAN A,285;THOS
. M,244;UNITY,246;WILEY
. R,244;WINNIE F,263
COPELAND,ALEXR,244;ANNA
. 421;ARCHIBALD H,244
. COALSON,244;DORA,261

. ELISHA,291;ELIZA,283
. JANE,265;JASPER,244
. JOHN,242,244;JOHN D
. 275;MARANDA,248;MARY
. 239,256;MASSEY M,388
. N,244;PETER,244;POLLY
. 278;RACHEL,266;SALLIE
. E,235;SUSANNAH,277;WM
. 244;WM D,244
COPELIN,RICHARD,233
COPLAN,SALLY,256
COPLAND,RICHARD,220
COPPER,JAS,294
COPPOCK,NANCY,212
. SALLIE NANCY,209
. SAMPSON,203;TOBY,203
COPPS,JOHN,74
CORBAN,TEMPY,204
CORBIN,JANE,204;LUCINDA
. 197;NELSON,202-203
. WELLINGTON,203
CORDER,H,388
CORE,RICHARD,244
CORKE,AMELIA,44
CORKER,DREWRY,49,53
. JOHN,2;STEPHEN,11,29
. 48,53
CORKINS,STEPHEN,11
CORLEIF,NANCY ANN,384
CORLEW,CASANDRIA,258
CORLEY,AMOS,388;CHANY
. 88;EDMOND,300,306
. EDMUND,300;JOHN,388
. SALLY,397
CORLY,GREENBERRY,388
. SARA,36
CORMICK,JNO,388
CORNELIUS,4
CORNET,ELI,10,29;JOSIAH
. 9
CORNWELL,ELIJAH,335
. GEORGE W,331,335
. GIBSON H,335;OBADIAH
. 335;WILLIAM D,335
CORRY,DANIEL,244;G T
. 244;JAS THOS,244;JOHN
. 244;JOHN A,244;MARY
. 258;MISSOURI A,254
. NANCY,253;W A,241,245
. 258;WM A,240-241,244
. 260
CORSSLEY,NANCY,239
CORZART,215
COSBY,GARLAND,158;HICK
. 158;HICKERSON,158
. JOHN,388;LOUISA,237
. OVERTON,388
COSKERY,JOHN,388
COSNAHAM,THOMAS,51
COSNAHAN,CHARLES A,38
  NANCY,42
COSNOHAN,S Z,44
COSTAR,A M,388
COSTELLO,JAMES,388;JOS
  312
COTHERN,JESSE H,118
. WILLIAM,118
COTHERON,ROBERT,19
COTHRINE,ACINTHA,239
COTTEN,GEORGE,218-219
. JOHN R,388
COTTER,PATRICK,388;W J
. 257,275
COTTON,219;HENRY,244
. PLEASANT,29
COUCH,EDWARD W,388
. MOSES,335;N H,331,335
. NANCY,335

COUDER,ROBERT,364
COUDREY,W D,268
COUDY,A B,49
COUGHRAN,JOHN,100,122
    124
COULS,WM,388
COULSON,JOHN,29;MARY
    393;WILLIAM,7,29
COULTEAU,MARY,51
COULTER,HENRY N,388
. JOHN,289-290,323;THOS
. D,96;WILLIAM,329
COUN,LOUISA W,386
COURSE,ELIZ,392;ISAAC I
    388
COURSEY,ALLEN,20;HOWELL
. 203;MAHANEY,380
. WILLIAM P,203
COURTNAY,JAMES,351
COURTNEY,JULIA A,413
COUSIN,ANN,388
COUSINS,CHARLES,388
. DRUSELLA,409;JAMES
. 388;THOMAS,335
COUTTEAU,CHARLES,29,388
COVE,LEVI,315
COVENDER,MARY JANE,40
COVENNAH,CHARLES,29;LB
    29
COVENTON,WILLIAM,323
COWARD,ANDREW I,53;JOHN
. 19;JOHN W,11
. ZACHARIAH,11
COWART,A L,195;ANNA,209
. AUGUSTUS M,213;CURTIS
. 203;DAVID C,203
. ELEAZER L,212
. ELIZABETH,199;ELIZZIE
. 202;GEORGE,203
. HEZEKIAH P,203;ISAIAH
. 203;JAMES J,203,213
. JOHN H,213;JOSEPH W
. 203;LUCY,207;LYDIA
. 198;M,209;MARTHA,195
. 213;MARTHA A,209;MARY
. 198;MARY JANE,202
. NANCY,202;NATHAN E
. 195;NATHANIEL,213
. SEBERN,213;STEPHEN
. 213;WILLIAM D,203
. ZACH,7;ZACHARIAH,29
. ZACK,203
COWEN,ANN HENDLY,180
COWLES,MARTHA A,414
. NORMAN,388;SAMUEL,244
. 271
COWLEY,ELIZABETH,409
COWLING,CLARENTINE,407
    MATILDA M L,409
COWLOM,JAMES,369
COWMA,FRANCIS,256
COX,AARON,29;ANN,393
. ANN F,63;ASA,63;BENJ
. 388;CALEB,1;DANIEL,38
. DREWERY C,146;DUNKIN
. P,38;ELIZABETH,36,281
. ELMIRA,39;EMELINA,410
. EPHRAIM,58;ESTHER,47
. HELLEN J,38;HENRY,365
. HONOR,174,388;JAMES
. 49;JAS M,244;JESSE,11
. 29,48,335;JNO,232,241
. JOHN,10,53,229,234
. 283;JOHN M,271;JOHN T
. 244,269;JOHN W,262
. JON,256;JOSEPH,288
. 304;JULIA L,41
. MADISON,388;MARTHA

. 352;MARY,53,393;MILLY
. 29;MOSES,29,58;PEGGY
. 29;SARAH,331
. SEABORN J M,38;SEBORN
. 53;TALIAFERRA,388
. THOMAS,352;THOMAS R
. 38;WILEY J,331,335
. WILLIAM,29,38;WILLIAM
. R,388;WM,7,291;ZACK
. 226
COXAN,THOMAS W,297
COXE,EDWARD,369;HENRY
    CARLETON,367
COY,D M,343
COYNE,PHENIAS,20,22,24
    25
CRABB,BENJ,244;SAMUEL
    167;SARAH ANN,417
CRADDOCK,MARY A,245
CRAFT,140;HUGH,244
    JESSE,29
CRAFTON,BENNET,388
    THOMAS,388
CRAIG,ALEXANDER,128
    JOHN,388;LUCY ANN,395
CRAIGE,ALLEN,388
CRAIGHEAD,GEORGE,227
CRAIN,JAMES,321;JOHN,9
. JOSIAH,86,125-126,143
. LEVY,7;LEWIS,219
. REESY,38;SPENCER,335
CRALL,JAMES,335
CRANE,ELIZA,388
. HENRIETTA W,247;JAMES
. 319;JOHN,29;LEVI,29
. MOSES,29,388;RESEY,38
. STEPHEN D,65;W H,89
. WM,244
CRANFORD,LEONARD,310
    SAMUEL,216-217
CRAPS,SAMUEL,19
CRAVY,HENRY,9;HUGH,9
    JAMES,7
CRAWFORD,187;A,151-152
. 153-156,158-159,161
. 162-163,167,175,182
. 187;ABIGAL,198
. ALEXANDER,187
. ANDERSON,150,157,167
. 174,178-179,186
. ANDREW,331,335;ANN
. 388;ANNA,380;AUGUSTUS
. 176;BEN,257;BENNETT
. 244,259;C A,250
. CHARLES,175,343-344
. 346-347,349-352,354
. 359,363;DAVID,388
. DAVID MAXWELL,176
. DAVID W,174;ELEANOR
. 387;ELIZ ANN,381
. ELIZABETH,257,380,392
. 394;ELIZABETH ANN,270
. EMMA,253;GEOR,244
. GEORGE W,388;H,241
. 243,245;HARRIET,249
. HENRY,38;HINTON,236
. 237,239,241,243-244
. 247,250,254,256,260
. 264-265,267,269-270
. 271,275,279-282
. JACKANN,266;JANE,175
. 381,391;JAS,244;JOEL
. 133,175,320,388;JOEL
. J,141;JOEL T,117
. JOEL T L,148;JOHN B
. 388;JOSIAH,244;JUNIOR
. 152;LOUISA M,403

. LOUSA F,266;M M,272
. MARIAH E,411;MARTHA
. 271;MARY,420;MARY ANN
. 172,175;MARY B,277
. MARY F,235;MATTHEW
. 388;N M,239,242,246
. 257,276,279,285-286
. NANCY,244;NATHAN,160
. 165,175,188,242,388
. NOWELL,244;PETER,154
. 161,165,170,172,174
. 178-183,187,189,191
. POLLY,160,393;R L,149
. ROBERT,187,388;SALLY
. 160,378;SAMUEL,335
. 353;SARAH,267;SARAH
. ANN,279;SARAH H,267
. SARAH J,266;THO,232
. THOMAS,247,258,261
. 270,275,285;THOS,235
. 237,245-247,259;TITUS
. 244;W L,134;WILLIAM L
. 134;WM,244,353,388;WM
. H,244,388
CRAWL,MARGARET,245
CRAWLEY,JAMES,341,343
. 346;MARTIN,388
. SANDERS,351
CRAWMAN,MARY,331,335
CRAYTON,148;ELIZA,415
CREAGH,THOMAS B,335
CREBS,223
CREDDELLE,MARY ANN,268
CREDDILE,FRANCINA,240
    SARAH E,261
CREDELLE,R A,248,273
CREDILLE,ARENA,245
. BETSEY ANN,244;CULLEN
. S,245;DOLY,238;ELIZ
. 246;FREDONIA,278;GRAY
. 245;HENRY,245;JESSE
. 245;LAURANA,281;MARY
. A,256;MARY ANN,239
. MINNY,256;NANCY,281
. NANCY L,277;REUBEN A
. 245;RHODA,242;SARAH
. H,261;SARAH R,244
. THOS,215,346;WM,245
. WM G,245;WM H,245;WM
. S,245
CREMER,LUCY A,240
CRENSHAW,JARRELL,335
. MARY E,254;WM H,245
. WM L,245
CRESSWELL,JANE M,401
. LEMULA,420;PHOEBE
. TALBOTT,391
CRESWELL,ANN,414;DAVID
. 4;MARTHA,409;MARY A
. 416;MARY G,418;ZEMALA
. 4
CREVERE,JUSTINE,80
CREW,ELBERT,29;ELISHA
. 89;HENRY,29;ROBERT,95
. ROBERT H,89
CREWS,EMILY B,397;JAMES
. 100;JOHN,53;MARTHA
. 242;STANLEY,69
CREWSE,VALENTINE,69
CRIBBS,GILBERT,222;W
    219
CRIBS,GILBERT,224-225
. 226-228,231;MARGARET
. 225-226;THOMAS,231
. WILLIAM,228
CRIDDILE,THOMAS,215
CRISWELL,PERMELIA D,253
CRITINGTON,SARAH,421

==

CRITINTON,MARY ANN,391
CRITTENDEN,FANNY,380
. FRANCES,388;ISAAC,245
CRITTENDON,WM,388
CROAN,29
CROCKER,I R,388;JOSEPH
. R,388
CROCKET,289;FLOYD,29
. JOSEPH,344
CROCKETT,AUGUSTUS C,245
. FLOYD,51;JOSEPH,363
. MARIAH,40
CROMER,JERRY,195
CROOKSHANK,PATRICK,388
CROOKSHANKS,
. JANE ELIZ,382
CROSBY,ANDREW,20
CROSKY,C M,245;COLUMBUS
. M,245;EDWARD,245
CROSLEY,HENRY,388
. MARTHA ANN,283;W H
. 313
CROSS,ALLEN,203;AUREND
. 203;C BURDETT,388
. ELISHA,335;EURON,53
. FETHERSHAUX,245
. FRANCEWS,53;GEORGE
. 335,348;ISAAC,9,29,48
. 53,203;JAMES,48,203
. JOHN,331,335;JOHN M
. 335;JOSEPH,48,53
. LITTLETON,53;MANDA
. 201;MANDY,207;MARY,42
. NATHAN,203;SARDIS E
. 48;STEPHEN,29;THOMAS
. 48,53;WILLIAM,29,47
. WINNIE,205
CROSSBY,ANDREW,22,25
CROSSLEY,ANN,285;EDWAD
. 245;EDWIN,245;EMILY
. 254;JOSIAH,245;LEMUEL
. 245;LEMUEL T,261,275
. WILEY A,245
CROTHERS,WM,388
CROUCH,JOS,245
CROW,ISAAC,289;STEPHEN
. 245
CROWLEY,THOS,245
CROWSER,RICHARD,245
CROZIER,JOHN,49;NANCY
. 29;THOMAS,9,29,49
. WILLIAM,8;WM,388
CRUCE,JOHN,29
CRUMBY,WM M,273
CRUMMER,E S,238
CRUMMOND,MANDY,43
CRUMP,ELIZA J,199;GEO H
. 389;JOHN C,213
. MISSOURI A,207;PHILIP
. 389
CRUMPTON,LEVI I,389
CRUSE,ANGLEHART,389
. CATHERINE,240
. ENGLEHART,389;JOHN,48
CRUTCHFIELD,BETSY,383
. GEO,245;JOHN,245;JOHN
. W,245;LOUISA,266;LUCY
. 251;MARY E,281;ROBT
. 245
CRUTE,HANNAH,155
. REBEKEH,155
CUCHANAN,ELIZABETH,261
CUE,JAMES,38
CUISE,JEREMIAH,10
CULBERSON,JAMES,254,256

260;JAS,245
CULBERT,NANCY,256
CULBERTSON,DAVID,245
. JEREMIAH F,245;SAMUEL
. 335;WM B,245
CULBREATH,ANN,153;ANNE
. 406;ELIZ,385
. ELIZABETH,166;JAMES
. 166;JAMES MCNEAL,179
. JOHN,162-163,179-180
. 389;LUCY,179;MARY,179
. MARY ANN,248;NANCY
. 179;PATRICK,179
. SUSANNAH,166;THOMAS
. 179;WEST,179
CULBRETH,SUSAN,403
CULLEN,A A,312
CULLENS,THOMAS W,38
CULLER,JOHN,389;RELETE
. W,420
CULLERS,BETSEY ANN,407
. MELINDA,381
CULLEY,NANCY,390
CULLINS,AUGUSTUS A,389
CULLOCHE,CATHERINE W
. 282
CULP,MARGARET,267;PETER
. 245
CULVER,ALFRED,245;B C
. 314;ERASMUS A,389
. EVERARD H,315;G P,314
. GEO P,245;H C,312;J L
. 313;JOHN P,245;JOSHUA
. T,245;L E,268
. NATHANIEL,302
CULVERHOUSE,JEREMIAH
. 309
CULWELL,385
CUMBIE,PETER,245
CUMBREE,MARY,250
CUMMING,ANNE E,415
. ANNIE M,396;JOHN,389
. JOHN B,389;MARY C,390
. WM H,389
CUMMINGS,ELIZABETH,46
. LAURA,47;LUTHER,389
CUMMINS,ELI,169;F,243
. FRANCES,246;FRANCIS
. 235,242-245,250,254
. 258-261,266,270,275
. 276-277,285;POLLY,249
. RHODA,287
CUNA,POLLY,275
CUNARD,JOHN,331,335
. JUMINA,331,335
CUNNELEY,DANIEL,38
CUNNINGHAM,ALEXANDER
. 389;CHAS,389
. CORNELIUS,245;ELIZA
. 247,253;HARRIET F,270
. JNO,389;JOHN,14
. MARTHA,265;MARY,263
. MARY FRANCIS,256;O H
. P,389;PHARABE,260
. REBECCA,286;REBECCAH
. 284;ROBERT M,316,324
. ROBT M,251;SAML,230
. THOS,245;WM,85,245;WM
. H,245
CUNNINS,FRANCES,253
CUPPER,SAMUEL G,389
CURENTON,BOLIN,307
CURETON,BOLIN,299
. HANNAH,299;JEAN,299
. JOHN,299;MARTHA,299
. REZON,299;RICHARD,299
. ROBERT,299;WILLIAM
. 220,299,307;WINNEFRED

. 299;WM,245,291
CURL,ELIJAH,195,203
. ELIZABETH,205;KINCHEN
. 203;LUCY,205;MATHEW
. 214;MATTHEW,203;PETER
. 203;REUBEN,195;SUSAN
. 208;WILSON,16
CURRAN,A E,314
. CATHERINE,404
CURRUTHERS,JAMES,53
. WILLIAM,53
CURRY,AGGY,115-116,125
. CARY,323;DANIEL,115
. 116-117,125;DUDLEY
. 290;HARRIET ANN,117
. 131,137,144;HARRIETT
. ANN,125;JAMES,86,90
. 245;JOHN,335;KITTY
. 271;NANCY,267,273
. ROBERT,63;SARAH,264
. 278;THOMAS,170
. THOMPSON,331,335
. WILEY,86,108,125
. WILLIAM,117,136,139
. 141;WM H,245;WYLIE,92
CURT,SAMUEL,279
CURTIS,AGNES,266;ANNE
. 244;JOHNSON,245;MARY
. 37;PATSEY,253;ROBT
. 245;WM,88,245
CURTWRIGHT,JOHN,245
. LEVINIA,279;MARY,279
. SAMUEL,245
CUSHMAN,R,87
CUSS,LOUIS,389
CUTHBERT,ALFRED,335;J A
. 101;JOHN A,84
CUTWRIGHT,
. SARAH VIRGINIA,275
CUYLES,EMMA,40
CYRUS,WILLIAM,90;WM,86
D'ANTIGNAC,LEWIS C,389
. LOUISA H,389
D'AUTEL,G JULIUS,389
D----,LOUNZA,282;THOMAS
. H,282
D-----?,JAMES M,251
DABNEY,ANDERSON,335
. HANNAH,335
DAELY,CHRISTUN,206
DAGG,ELIZABETH T,256
. J L,246;M J,264
DAGGETT,REUBEN,389
DAGNAL,ELBERT WOOD B
. 389
DAGNALL,ANN,409
DAILEY,CATHERINE B,421
. GEORGIANN,197;HENRY F
. 389;JOSEPH,389;MARY
. 47
DAILY,MARY,53
DAIR,JOHN A,366
DAKES,AZARIAH,7
DAKINGS,ELIZA A,411
DALE,ARCHIBALD,245
. MARTHA,352;ROBERT,282
. SAML,352
DALEY,JOSEPH,183;THOMAS
. 195
DALLAS,ELIZ,396
DALLIS,GEORGE,203
DALLISON,CATHARINE T
. 204
DALLY,WM,389
DALTON,BARNABAS,389
. HENRY,389;MARY,401
. POLLY,391;WINEY,415
DAME,CHARLES,389;ELIA M

DAME(cont)
A,383
DAMERON,CHARLES,389
DAMRON,JOHN,307
DANALY,JAMES,224
DANBY,418
DANCE,GEDEON,53
DANELY,DANIEL,389
DANES,MATEL,212
DANFORD,JESSE,7
DANFORTH,ABRAHAM,389
. CAROLINE W,395;ELIZA
. 421;ELIZABETH,389;J R
. 389;JACOB,389;JOSHUA
. 389;LAURA,383;MARTHA
. A,412;MARTHA ANN,382
. MARY,403;MELINDA,407
DANIEL,32;ABRAHAM,364
. ALEXANDER,335;ALLEN
. 348,354;AMOS,321;AMY
. 259;ANNA,276;ANNIS M
. 29;BETSEY,325;BETSEY
. C,263;BRYAN,389;C N
. 127;CATHERINE,246
. CHARLOTTE,249;CHAS S
. 245;CHAS W,245
. CHESLEY,53;DANA B,245
. DAVID,7,9,26;DENTON
. 245;DICY,206;E F,393
. E M C,65;EGGBERT P,85
. 91,101;ELIAS,8;ELIZA
. J,235;ELIZABETH,251
. 385;EMILEY C,36
. ENSIGN JNO,7;FRANCIS
. 40;GEORGE,349;GEORGIA
. ANNA,285;HAMBLETON G
. 203;HARRIETT A,259
. HENRIETTA E,274;HENRY
. F,245;IRA A M,245
. ISAAC,331,335;J,149
. JAMES,128,245,290,309
. JAMES W,232;JANE,414
. JEAN,263;JEPTHA,389
. JESSE,389;JMES L,389
. JOHN,245,389;JOHN M
. 131;JOHN R,11;JOHN W
. 335;JOSEPH,8,29;JUNE
. 259;LEMILIA,394;LEVI
. 309,335,363;MAJOR,53
. MALISSA ANN,270
. MARGARET,237,276
. MARTHA,29,200,384
. MARY,11,29,281,283
. MARY ELLEN,417;MARY H
. 262;MARY J,196
. MATTHEW,53;MOSES,335
. 353,357;NANCY,236,290
. 393;NATHAN,297,307
. OLIVER P,246;OLIVER T
. 246;ROBERT,53;ROBERT
. C,29;ROBERT W,389
. SAMUEL B,246;SARAH
. 237,396;SIMEON,58
. SOLOMON,6;STEPHEN,297
. STITH,362;THOMAS,224
. 335;THOMAS M,312;THOS
. B,85;WM,246;WM T,246
. ZACHARIAH,38
. ZACHARRIAH,53
DANIEL?,NANCY,251
DANIELL,225;BETSEY,221
. 229,277;CATHERINE,302
. CHARLES,223,229,231
. CHAS,329;CHRISTOPHER
. 50;DAVID,51;EDMD,223
. 232;EUSTACE,221-222
. HAMBLETON G,203;JAMES
. 289-290,293,302,369

. JAS,215;LEVI,289-290
. 293,302-303;MARTHA
. 302-303;MARY,222;MARY
. K,224;MARY KEMP,231
. MATTHEW,52;MOSES,47
. NANCY,289,293,302-303
. 309;POLLY,249;ROBERT
. C,50;SARAH,221,229
. SARAH R,282;STEPHEN
. 300,308;THOMAS,216
. 221,223-224,229
. WILIAM,220,225
. WILLIAM,218,221,224
. 229,369;WM,215-216
. 218-219,222,226,231
. ZACHARIAH,52
DANIELLY,ANDREW,389
DANIELS,FREEMAN,203
. MARY,421;MARY ANNE-
. 279;MARY J,204;NANCY
. 285;NANCY J,203;SARAH
. 400
DANLEY,WM L,246
DANNA,OTTO,389
DANNEL,SARAH,412
DANNELLY,ARTHUR,306,311
. ELIZABETH,307;FRANCIS
. 294,306;JANE,307
DANNELY,JOHN,389
DANNIELL,232
DANNIELY,NANCY,335
DANS,
. MARTHA ANN ELIZA,259
. SARAH,258
DANSBY,CATEREEN,220
JACOB,220
DANSEL,DAVID,274
DANTIGNAC,SOPHIA,412
DARBY,ADELINE H,412
. ARABELLA,399;ELIZ,418
. ELIZABETH P,198
. FRANCES,414;JEREMIAH
. 389;MARY E,401;S,206
. WM,389
DARDEN,B H,82,86,100
. 116;BEDFORD H,82,89
. 93,95,128;BERRIEN W
. 203;BURFORD H,130;G H
. 110;JAMES M,88,335
. JOHN,335;JOHN B,335
. MARY JANE,205;WILLIAM
. 11
DARDIN,GEORGE,228
DARLEY,THOMAS,257
DARLING,BENJ,389;HANNAH
. 407;JOHN,389;JOSEPH
. 389;MARY,400;SARAH
. 419
DARLINGTON,MARTHA,53,58
247;SARAH,39
DARLY,CHRISTIANNER,206
DARNALL,D,147;HENRY,295
RICHARD H,147
DARNEL,SALLY B,276
DARNELL,CATO,319;D,149
. HENRY,319;NEEDHAM,389
. RICHRD H,149
. ZACHARIAH,246
DARNY,JOSEP,20
DARROCOTT,WM,246
DARSEY,JOEL,389;JOSEPH
22,24
DARSY,JOHN,29
DART,BENJ,389;THEODORE
389
DASHER,MARGARET E,211
. MCLARY FRANCIS,208
. THOMAS J,389

DATHNEY,MARY,406
DAUGGIN,JOHN,38
DAUGHERTY,A H,83,88,92
. 114,118,122,128
. ALEXANDER H,130
DAUGHTERTY,A H,126
ALEXANDER H,90
DAUGHTERY,BERRIEN,212
SARAH J,46
DAUGHTEY,SIMEON C,39
DAUGHTRY,JAMES,204
RACHAEL,209
DAUGLASS,THOMAS,93
DAVANT,AMELIA M,44;JAS
. 246;P E,246;SAMUEL
. 246;WM F,246
DAVENEY,JOHN THOS,246
WM,246
DAVENPORT,AMANDA,283
. BURKETT,246;ELIABETH
. E,264;H,260;HENRY,246
. JOHN,11,350;JOHN M,67
. 389;REBECCA CAROLINE
. 67;STEPHEN,47;URIAH
. 53;W,377;WILLIAM,297
. 361
DAVID,ALOIS P,145
. ARTHUR,53;CORNELIS
. 247;DICI,38;EVAS,53
. FRANCES ELLA,254;H,53
. HENRIETTA,398;ISHMAEL
. 330;JOHN F,59
. JONATHAN,330;JOSEPH
. 21,23;LEWIS C,145
. MOSES,53;MOURNING,421
. OWEN,291;RABLIN,6
. ROBBIN,53;SAMUEL,53
. SARAH ANN,53;THOMAS
. 53;TOLIVER,101
. WILLIAM,8,97
DAVIDSON,AQUILA,311;J M
. 240;JAMES,250,271,311
. JAMES M,263;JAS,240
. 242-243;JNO,226;JOHN
. 225,311,335,361
. LEMUEL,310-311
. MARGARET,239;PAUL,389
. ROBERT,335
DAVIE,RANDOLPH,189
SARAH HAMPTON,189
DAVIES,J,1;JAMES J,51
. JAMES W,389;JOHN O
. 246;SAMUEL,363;SOPHIA
. 393;THOMAS W,52
. WILLIAM,362;WILLIAM W
. 29;WM,246
DAVIS,216;A W,147;AARON
. 389;AARON L B,246
. ABNER,246;ANNA,41
. ARTHUR,50,368;ASA A
. 38;AUGUSTUS B,246
. BENJ,7;BENJAMIN,10
. 216;BLAUFORD,182;C
. 101;C A,246;C H S,413
. CELIA,29;CHARLOTTE
. 201;CORNELIA C,273;D
. 149,233;DAVID,124-125
. 204,214,232,234,246
. 367;DEMPSY,9;DREWRY
. 367;ELENER,182;ELENOR
. 182;ELIZ,391,396
. ELIZA,416;ELIZABETH
. 196,262,367;ELNATHAN
. 11,29;FRANCES A,279
. GASSICVAY,182;GEO,389
. GEO C,246;GEO W,82
. GEORGE,367;GEORGE C
. 195,204;H,367

DAVIS(cont)
. HARRIETTE,46
. HENRIETTA,413;HENRY
. 38,389;HIGHTOWER,389
. ISHMAIL,292;J H,131
. JACOB R,389;JAMES,195
. 232,234,292,330,367
. 390;JAMES A,-195,204
. JAMES G,90;JAMES N,91
. JANE,46,234,283,400
. JAS,330;JEREMIAH,367
. 368-369;JESSE H,11
. JOHN,4,6-7,232,246
. 367,390;JOHN E,38
. JOHN F,49;JOHN G,194
. JOHN J,204;JOHN R,195
. JONATHAN,260,281,284
. 293,311,319,367;JOS,2
. JOSEPH,78;JOSEPHINE M
. 276;JOSIAH,204;JULIA
. 284;LATHA A,199;LEROY
. 246;LEWIS,169,214
. LINEY E,204;LORENZO D
. 390;LOUIS J,204
. LURANA,239;MAHALA,416
. MARK PRICE,191;MARTHA
. 198,421;MARTIN,246
. 367;MARY,43,82,182
. 393,397,406,419;MARY
. ANN,197,419;MARY
. PRICE,182;MARY R E
. 408;MATHEW,364
. MATTHIAS M,204;MOSES
. 7,14-15;NANCY,272,367
. 368,419,421;NEWTON,90
. PATSEY,41,367;POLLY
. 239;RACHEL,385,392
. RACHEL BELLAH,376
. REUBEN,246;REYNOLDS
. 246;RICHARD CHILD,390
. ROBBIN,29;ROBERT,67
. ROBERT S,6;ROBLIN,50
. SALLY,239;SAMUEL,8,29
. 350;SAMUEL P,390
. SAMUEL S,390;SARAH,29
. SARAH ANN,415;SARAH
. JANE,270;SIMEON,29
. STEPHEN A,86;STEPHEN
. EDWARD,390;SUSAN,395
. THO,357;THOMAS,50,213
. 335,367-369,376,390
. THOMAS JEFFERSON,368
. THOMAS LAMAR,182
. THOMAS LEMAR,182
. THOMAS W,29;THOS,86
. 246;THOS W,246;TOBER
. 38;VACHEL,182;WARREN
. 368;WARREN W,367
. WILLIAM,29,204,213
. 341,367;WILLIAM G,195
. WILLIAM J,195;WILSON
. O,38;WM,246;WM M,246,390
. WM S,246;WYLIE,155
DAVISON,170;C C,243,271
. DANIEL,292;HENRY,53
. J M,262,271;JAMES,249
. 254,266-267,274,285
. JAMES M,286;JAS,246
. JAS M,246;JOHN,322
. REUBEN,246;ROBT E,246
DAWDLE,JOSEPH,308
DAWKINS,GEORGE,82,293
. 335;PARTHENY,335
DAWSEY,DANIEL,246
DAWSON,222;BETSEY,268
. BRITON,29;DREAD,390
. E G,312;ELIZ,396

. EMMA H J,256;EPHRONIA
. M,267;GEO,246;GEO M
. 246;GEORGE,223
. HENRIETTA W,256;HENRY
. C,349;J C,312;JAMES B
. 38;JAS,246;JOHN,85,90
. 91,113,126,142,224
. 236;JOHN E,319;JOHN T
. 246;JOSEPH,82,86,94
. JOSPEH,85;KISSIAH,115
. LORENOR,281;MARY,48
. POLLY,266;RUTH,253
. SALLIE A,45;SALLY,249
. SARAH,395;W H,127
. WILLIAM C,127;WM
. CROSBY,246
DAWSY,JOSEPH,390
DAY,J C,390;JANTH,329
. JEREMIAH,153;JOHN,246
. 390;JONATHAN,319,321
. JONTHAN,360;JOSEPH
. 175;REBECAH,274
. RICHARD B,390;ROBERT
. C,357;SARAH ANN,381
. SIMON,310;WILEY,246
. WM,390
DE COIN,WM A,390
DE COTES,AUGUSTUS,390
DEADWILDER,EVA,335
DEAKLE,G W,204;JOHN,195
. NANCY,194;SUSAN,206
DEAL,ARGENT,53
. ELIZABETH,205;EZEKIEL
. 29;FANEY,14;FERNEY,15
. FURNEY,214;JAMES,53
. 204;JANE,201;JOHN,214
. NANCY,202;WILLIAM,213
. 335
DEALL,EZEKIEL,47
DEALY,JOHN,195
DEAMOND,LOUISA,203
DEAN,ELIZA,397;JAMES,2
. MARTHA,280;WILLIAM,88
DEANE,BURKIT,229;MARY
. 402;NATHANIEL,335
. THOMAS,335
DEANES,WILLIS,343
DEANS,WILLIS,343
DEARING,SIMEON,88;WM E
. 390
DEARMOND,MARY,404
. WILLIAM P,185;WM,390
. WM E,390;WM P,390
DEAS,ALEXANDER,390
. ELISA ANN,390;FRANCIS
. 390;JOEL,96;JOS A,312
. JOSEPH F,313;WM,390
. WM A,313
DEASON,87;BENJ,102
. BENJAMIN,94,102;J R
. 144;WILLIAM,38
. ZACHARIAH,65
. ZECHARIAH,62,65
DEATH,D,149
DEAVES,EDWARD F,390
DEAVOURS,JOHN,131
DEAWDAY,JAMES,23
DEAY,THOMAS,222
DEBOW,WM,390
DECILES,JOSE,390
DECK,SARAH,373
DECKLE,BERYAN,204;JULIA
. 207;MARTHA,207;MARY
. 195
DEEKLE,ANNA,211
DEES,ANN,399;ELISA ANN
. 400;ELIZ,380;MARRANDY
. 399;SARAH ANN,395

DEFOUR,JOS,246;WM,246
DEFRAFFENREID,265
DEHEUR,SEBASTIAN,390
DEINON,JANE A,410
DEJARNETT,REUBEN,246
DEJERNATT,R,220;REUBEN
. 219
DEJERNATTE,R,223-224
DEJERNETT,REUBEN,233
DEKLE,CAROLINE,210;CATY
. 212;GEORGE,212;MONDA
. 204;NANCY,195,204
. PETER,204;SARAH,210
DELAFORTE,
. ANTONY JAMES -
. JOSEPH D,390
DELAIGLE,CHARLES L,390
DELAMAR,THOS,390
DELANEY,DRURY,246
DELANNORY,
. FORTUNE THEODORE,390
DELIAC,
. ANTOINE PASCALL,390
DELLO,SAMUEL B,337
DELLON,ROBERT,11
DELOACH,FRANCES,264
. REBECCA,278;SARAH S
. 53;SOPHIA B,204
. WILLIAM,21,23,25
DELOUCH,ELIZABETH,264
DEMAREST,BENJ,390;NANCY
. E,410
DEMBY,JAMES H,82
DENBY,LOUISA,391
DENDEN,SIMEON,195
DENHAM,172;CHARLES,154
. CHARLEY,154;CHAS,155
. EMILY B,382;JAMES,154
. 155
DENMARK,CLABORN,356
DENNARD,JARRED,246;WM L
. 390
DENNING,GEO,246
DENNIS,229;ABRAHAM,2
. E C,135,144;E W,137
. ELIZABETH C,135-136
. 137-139,143,148-149
. ISAAC,135,137,168,320
. J,100,137;JACOB,220
. JESSE,335;JOHN,100
. 135,137;JOSEPH,288
. JOSIAH,149,213,293
. 295,310;MARGARET M
. 239;MATTHEW,292
. MATTHIAS,293
DENNISE,CAROLINE,383
DENSLIE,HENRY,295
DENSON,JAMES,267;JESSE
. 11;JOSEPH,288,293,304
DENT,ANN M,175;DENNIS
. 175;GEORGE,175;GEORGE
. COLUMBUS,175,181
. JAMES T,175,181;JOHN
. 175,181,390;MARIA,407
. MARSHALL,176;MARY ANN
. 402;PARTHENIA,37
. PETER,297;SAML,295
. SAMUEL,297;THOMAS,288
. 293;THOMAS M,175;WILL
. 295,298,301
DENTINACK,ELIZABETH,159
DENTON,EDWARD,307;JOHN
. 390;SARAH,243
DERING,SIMEON,79
DERISCO,J E,204
DERISO,CATHARINE,204
. SARAH,208
DERMOT,RACHEL,397

DERRY,W C,105;WM C,97
DESALEAYE,MARK,48
DEVANEY,LUCY A V,270
. POLLY,271
DEVANT,ISABELL L,37;JAS
. 246
DEVENPORT,STEPHEN,11,29
DEVÉRAUX,321;WM,347
DEVEREAUSE,
. ELIZABETH FEW,170
. WILLIAM,170
DEVEREAUX,A M,364;L A
. 257;SAMUEL,168
DEVEREUX,AM,349;J W,309
. 349;JNO WM,231;JOHN B
. 302;JOHN WM,316;S,319
DEVILEN,THOMAS E,390
DEVINE,JOHN,5
DEVINEY,JAS M,246
DEWARS,ALEX,390
DEWBERY,JOHN,291
DEWOLF,WILLIAM,7
DEYAMPERT,JNO,291
DIAMOND,REUBIN,10
DICK,ANN,383;ELIZ,399
. WM,246
DICKEN,118;H T,100,102
. H Y,82;HAMPTON T,90
. J R,101,105;JAMES T
. 390;JOHN R,85,91-92
. 96,107,121;M M,104
. MONROE,90,93
DICKENS,H T,113;JAMES
. 108;JOHN R,97;M M,100
. R L,314;R LEE,313
. ROBERT,358
DICKENSON,ADELINE,385
DICKER,M M,100
DICKERMAN,MARIA F,276
DICKERSON,ALIC,38
. AUGUSTUS,38;ELIZABETH
. 205;EMANUEL,38
. FRANCIS,246;FRED,38
. JESSE,38;JOHN T,246
. PATTY,320;R I,284
. ROGER,246;STEPHEN,204
. W R,204;WILBORNE,299
. WILLIAM B,91;WM,246
. 247;WM B,85
DICKERY,J M,271
DICKEY,J M,251,259,272
. 273,275;JOHN,53
. JOSEPH,360;JOSEPH W
. 53,204;L M,242;M M,39
. MARY,53;OLIVE,43
. ROPEY ANN,36;SARAH
. ANN,43
DICKIN,T,97
DICKINS,LUCY J,249
. TILLMAN,246
DICKINSON,ANN,408
. CATHERINE D,280;COSBY
. 390;G W,390;HENRY,325
. HENRY A,335;JACOB,325
. JUDAH,325;R L,237
. ROGER,245;WENBURN,321
. WILBOURN,328
DICKS,GEO,247;JOHN H
. 195;MARY,401
DICKSON,BENJAMIN,324-325
. CHANEY,37;CURRY,324
. 325;CYRUS,325;DAVID
. 290,325;JAMES,291
. JOHH,325;JOHN,325,328
. JOSEPH C,314;MARTHA
. 325;MARTHA L,253
. MICHAEL,324-325;NANCY
. 265;Q L,314;ROSA,46

. THOMAS,307,324-325
. WILLIAM,324-325;WM
. 313
DICKY,JOHN,52;JOSEPH,49
DICY,PHILLIPS,212
DIEHL,FREDERICK,390
DIEMOND,MARY,46
DIFFEY,SAMUEL F,125
DIGBY,BENJAMIN,335
. BERRY T,331,335;JOHN
. 335;JOHN B,335
DIKES,DANIEL,289,293
. STEPHEN,293
DILDER,ELIZABETH,241
DILKS,FRANCES,39
DILL,ANDREW J,390
. DANIEL,390;JACOB,390
. JANE E,403;JULIA ANN
. 415;MARY ANN,390
. PHILIP,390
DILLAN,ROBERT,390
DILLARD,ELIZABETH,29
. GEO,247,264,283,390
. ISAAC,10,29;JOHN,7,50
. 53,390;JOHN A,335
. JOHN G,51,390;JOSEPH
. 53;JULIA ANN,265
. LOUISE A,37;LUCY,264
. MARY J,45;PHILIP,8,29
. POLLY,422;THOMAS,335
. TOLIVER,53;TOLLIVER,8
. 39;WILLIAM,29;WM C
. 390
DILLEN,H,130
DILLION,MARY ANN,385
DILLON,GEORGE W,39;H
. 100,105,113,122,140
. HENRY,100;JOHN,247
. 335;KEZIAH,422
. TOLLIVER,29
DIMON,ROBERT,390
DINGLER,JOHN,82,251,256
. NANCY,285,374;WILLIAM
. 335
DINKINS,ADELINE E,396
. LEONORA E,385
DISMICK,MARTHA,402
DISMUKES,ANNA,398;FINNY
. 288;JAMES,358;JOHN
. 234;MARTHA D,335
. MILLEY,399;POLLY,422
. REUBEN,390
DIVINE,
. MARGARET ELIZA,285
. MARY ANN,251;SARAH
. ANN,386
DIVIS,BENJ,5
DIX,JOHN W K,247
DIXON,ALIS,257;ANITA A
. M,273;CARTER,39;DAVID
. 247,302,305;DELAWARE
. 58;DENNIS B,39;HENRY
. 322,390;HUGH,247
. JAMES,39;JANE ADALADE
. 43;JOEL,247,378;JOHN
. 10;JOSEPHINE R,37
. MANDA,44;MARY,272;N
. 321;NICHOLAS,328
. ROBERT,6,29,47,53
. ROBERT J,51;SARAH P
. 415;THOMAS,53;THOMAS
. J,52;THOS,307;WEAMES
. R,39;WILLIAM,53;WM L
. 390
DOBBS,LAURA,237
DOBLE,JOSHUA,247
DOCKLE,
. JACOB CHRISTOPHER,390

DODD,CATHERINE,217;JANE
. 58;R T,98;ROBERT T
. 113;ROBT T,82;WILLIAM
. L,53
DODDRIDGE,NOAH,304,318
. NOEL,293
DODEN,J,317
DODRIDGE,NOAH,293,330
. NOE,291
DODSON,91;ELIJAH,335
. JOHN D,83
DOGGETT,ASA,159,171
. GARNER,159,335;JOHN
. 331,335;RICHARD,82
DOKES,CAMPBELL S,23,25
DOLVIN,HARRIETT C,235
. J I,236;JAS,247;JAS H
. 247;JOHN,275;JOHN F
. 286;JOHN I,286;JOHN T
. 239,244,271
. MARTHA ANN REBECCA
. 257;NANCY,260;PATSEY
. 271;WM B,247
DONAGHEY,293
DONALDSON,
. CATHARINE T,196
. DANIEL T,390;PETER
. 342,351,390;WILLIAM
. 21,23
DONHAM,MARGARET,413
DONNELLY,JAMES,258
DONOVAN,ELENORA,395
DOOLEY,L J,247
DOOLITTLE,CAROLINE,415
DOOLY,MARTHA W,268
DOONAN,TORRENCE,391
DORITY,MARY,269
DORMAN,ALLEN,300
DOROUGH,BETSEY,269
. PETTY,243
DORSE,JOHN,309
DORSET,J F,39
DORSETT,PALEMON W,335
DORSEY,CORNELIA C,254
DORTIC,GERMAIN T,391
. SEBASTIAN C,391
DORTON,JOHN,147
DOSS,HIRAM,77;J W,147
DOSSETT,WM,391
DOSSEY,JOHN,247
DOSTA,JONATHAN,247;WM T
. 247
DOSTER,JAMES C,331,335
. JAMES W,335;WM T,263
DOUBEL,ALEXANDRE,391
DOUGHARTY,JAMES A,391
. PATR,172
DOUGHERTY,MICHAEL,391
. PATRICK,171,173;SUSAN
. A,212
DOUGHTER,WM,247
DOUGHTERTY,WILLIAM,335
DOUGHTY,306;EBENEEZER
. 325;JOHN M,391
. RACHAEL,389
DOUGLAS,MARSHAL,81
. SAMUL C,391;SARAH ANN
. 40;W B,29
DOUGLASS,DAVID,204
. ELBERT,10;ELIZ L W
. 413;EUGENIOUS L,112
. EUGENIUS,123,149
. EUGENIUS L,103,134
. EUGENIUS LAFAYETTE,88
. 100,103,108,112,130
. 140;FRANCES,89,145
. FRANCIS,83,88,91,93

DOUGLASS(cont)
. 104,114,130,134;JACOB
. 39;JAMES,2;JANE,145
. JOHN B,84,96;LADUSKA
. 200;LUCIA,200
. MARCELIUS,103
. MARCELLA,123
. MARCELLUS,88,112,149
. MARTHA ANN,198
. MERCELUS,134;NANCY
. 200;NARCISSA,112,121
. 134,145,149;NARCISSA
. WEAKLEY,88;R F,145
. ROBERT,90,93,104,118
. 145;ROBT,86;SARAH J
. 90,145;SARAH JANE,93
. T,112;THOMAS,89,93,97
. 103-104,107,111,113
. 114,121,123,130,134
. 145,149;THOS,88
. TILMON,53;VINA,210
. W S,103-104,121,123
. WILLIAM,4,9,90,123
. WILLIAM B,53;WILLIAM
. G,89,93;WILLIAM R,195
. WILLIAM S,88,113,130
. 134,145,149;WINA,195
. WM,111;WM B,47;WM S
. 112
DOVE,BETSEY,267;ELIZ
. 408;RICHARD,10,29
. WILLIAM,39
DOW,JNO M,391
DOWANEY,SAMUEL,391
DOWDE,NANCY,53;SAMUEL
. 53
DOWDLE,BARTHL. T,297
. JOHN,319
DOWE,JOHN R,391
DOWELL,JAS,247
DOWLIN,THOMAS P,29
DOWMAN,SARAH L,316
DOWNEY,ELIZ,246
DOWNIE,MARGARET,394
DOWNING,ANTIONETTE W
. 244;JUNR,166;THOS,247
. WILLIAM,166
DOWNMAN,WILLIAM,318
. WILLIAM P,318;WM,319
. 329
DOWNS,AMBROSE,391;ANN
. 403;FRANCES,422;GEO
. 364;ISAAC,295,391
. JOHN,289,331;JOSEPH
. 158;LUCY,393;MARY ANN
. 388;RICHARD,153,391
. S P,335;SKELLY,335;WM
. A,247
DOWRY,ELIZ,388
DOWSE,CHARLES,39;SAMUEL
. 29;SARAH E B,420
DOWSING,WM,233
DOYAL,F,164
DOYLE,D,309;FRANCES,41
. WILLIAM,29
DOZIER,ABNER C,331,335
. ADALINE B,331;GEORGE
. R,335;THOMAS,68;WOODY
. 59,335
DRAIGHAN,BIAL,2
DRAKE,
. BATHSHEBA WINFREY,196
. ELIAS,9,11,29;EPAPHROD
. ITUS,297-298;HARRIETT
. 245;JAS V,247;JAS W
. 247;JOHN,247;MILLY,53
. N J,204;PATRICK HENRY
. 247;QUEEN ELIZABETH

. 43;SARAH,48;SUSAN,266
. SUVANNAH A,44;THOMAS
. 53;THOS R,247;TOURNER
. 204;VIRGINIA,207
. WILLIAM,53;WILLIAM L
. 204
DRANE,ALSE,166;ALTETHA
. MAGRUDER,166;ALTHETHA
. 166;BENJ,391
. CASSANDER,166;ELSIE?
. (ALCE),166;WILLIAM
. 153
DRANES,ALLETHE,160;ANNA
. 160;BETSEY,160
. CASSANDER,160;EFEY
. 160;POLLY,160;WALTER
. 160;WILLIAM,160
DRAPER,JAMES,86,90,94
. 102;JOSIAH,83
DRAWDY,JAMES,21
DRAYTON,NED,39;PETER,39
DREADWILDER,
. CHRISTOPHER,346
DREGHORN,JNO,391
DRENNAN,J W,266,283
. JOSEPH W,249,265
DRENNON,JOSEPH W,271
. MARY,269;RHODA C,275
DREW,ACY,11;ASA,29;J D
. 204;JANE R,196;JOHN
. 21;JOSIAH,29,39,213
. LEVIE,214;MARY,48,200
. SABRA,200;SARAH,198
. SUSAN,200;THOMAS,204
. 213;WILLIAM,29
. WILLOUGBY,9;WILSON,29
. 213
DREWRY,MILLS,343
DRIDON,JESSE,2
DRIGGERS,SIMEON,19
DRISKELL,JAMES B,335
. JOHN,335;JULIA G,331
. 335
DRISKEW,145
DRISKILL,145-146;JAMES
. 94
DRUMMOND,JOHN,319
DU----,SUSAN,251
DUBERRY,LEWANSE,237
DUBOSE,ANN,185;CLEMENT
. 185;DAVID,185
. ELIZABETH,185;FRA---Y
. 185;HANNAH,185;ISAAC
. 185,391;MARGARET
. EUGENIA,405;MARTHA
. 185;SARAH,185
DUCE,JOHN,22
DUCKWORTH,JAMES,356
. RANDOL,356
DUDLASS,ROBT,2
DUDLEY,G A,97,123;G W
. 314;GEO A,113;GEORGE
. A,100;JACKLY,123
. JAMES,64,195,214;JNO
. 328;JOHN,327,391
. KINCHEN,53;KINCHEN C
. 53;REBECCA,396
DUDLY,FANNY,205;KINCHEN
. C,29
DUER,ELLEN J,421
DUERRGUAL,228
DUFFEE,JOHN,90;WILLIAM
. 90
DUFFEY,94,121,129;D L
. 92,98,102,105,111,114
. DANL,155;JOHN,119,128
. 139,147;L,101;S F,111
. SAMUEL,141;SAMUEL F

. 87
DUFFIE,CATHERINE,409
DUFFY,D L,107;FRANCIS A
. 389;JOHN,74;MARGARET
. A,416;SAMUEL,90
. THOMAS,391;WILLIAM,85
DUGAS,
. ELIZABETH ADRIENNE
. 412;L P,29,391;LEWIS
. ALEC,391;LOUIS ALEX
. 391;MARIE C A,382
. SARAH FRANCES,405
DUGERS,SARAH,196
DUGGAN,JAY W,313
DUGGEN,IVY W,314
DUHADWAY,CATHERINE H
. 414
DUHART,PEGGY,4,393
DUKE,A G,117,124,128
. 137,142-143;ANN,117
. ARISTOTLE,92,117,124
. 128,137;ARISTOTLE G
. 65,83-84,118,124
. AZARIAH,29,47;BUCKNER
. 308;CHARLES P,117-118
. CHRISTIANA,47
. COATSWORTH,117,124
. 128,137,143;DANIEL,29
. DREWRY,29;E,65;ELISHA
. 47;ELIZABETH,117,124
. 128,137,143;ELLA M
. 246;EPPS,378;GREEN
. 247;H,101,149;HARDMAN
. 113;HARDY,343;HENRY
. 82,86,89,93,107,112
. 113,130,149;HENRY M
. 89;HENRY P,89;ISHAM
. 247,335;JAMES,29,47
. 90;JAMES H,53;JOHN,53
. 294,319;JOSEPH,352
. MARIA,46;MARTHA,399
. MARTHA ANN,124,128
. 137,142;MARY,29,47
. 128,137,143;MOSES,352
. NANCY,47,53;POLLY,117
. 124;R G,93;REUBEN,53
. ROBERT,100,149;ROBERT
. G,84,88,90,93,104
. ROBT,247;ROSALINE,46
. SAMUEL,89;SARAH,117
. 118,128,137,142-143
. STEPHEN,352;THOMAS
. 220,356;TURNER,29
. WEEKLY,90;WILLIAM,53
. 90,117,124,128,143
. 362;WILLIS,26;WM N,97
DUKES,DANIEL,7;DOLES,10
. DRUREY,7;ELBERT,39
. GREEN,9;JOHN,10
. MATTIE A,44;ROBERT
. 391;TURNER,9;WILLIS
. 27
DUMINGOES,EMANUEL,391
DUNAWAY,JOHN,247
DUNBAR,CATHERINE,391
. JOHN,11;THOS I,391
DUNCAN,BETSEY,259
. DANIEL,247;FLORIDA C
. 285;FRANCES,286;J A
. 258,261-262,285;JAMES
. 85;JAS,247;JESSE,95
. JOHN P,279;LANGDON C
. 391;RACHEL A,249
. THOMAS,335;WM,391
DUNERENT,ELIZ,383
DUNFORD,ADISON,53;ANNA
. 202;DANIEL,29;JAMES A

DUNFORD(cont)
. 204;MARY ANN,203
. SUSANNAH,29,49
DUNHAM,ELIZ,398;ELIZA
. 421;MARY,420;SAMUEL
. 391;WM,391
DUNIGEN,SARAH,202
DUNIVAN,HARBAND,158
. HARBERD,158;MAN,158
. MARY,158;POLLY,158
. WILLIAM,158
DUNIVENT,POLLY,389
DUNKIN,JESSE W,90
. WILLIAM,8
DUNLAN,ELISA,420
DUNLAP,JOHN,82,89;SARAH
. L,395
DUNN,A F,314;ALBERT G
. 335;ALEXANDER,302
. ALEXR,291;ALFRED
. JEFFERSON,162;CHARLES
. C,391;DOCK,313;ELBERT
. BALDWIN,162;ELIJAH
. 250;ELIZA,404
. ELIZABETH,162,239
. ENSIGN MATHEW,6;G P
. 314;GATEWOOD,335
. GEORGE WASHINGTON,162
. HENRY,300-301,308
. HIRAM,247;ISHMAEL,247
. JAMES,188,267;JANE,29
. JOHN,2,29,231;JOHN V
. 60;JOS M,313;JOSEE,79
. LEWIS,6;MALINDA,254
. MARY,29,244;MARY E
. 235;NANCY,300;SARAH
. FRANCES,235;SUSANNA
. 301,400;THOS J,313
. WATERS,162;WATTERS
. 367;WILLIAM,301
. WILLIAM G,331,335
. WINNY,162;WM,247
DUNSIETH,J C,60,102,126
. 142;JAMES C,63,79,90
. 94;JOS C,74
DUNSON,MARY JANE,256
DUNWOODY,SAMUEL,391
DUPREE,ABRAM,247
. COLUMBUS,247;DAVID D
. 313;GEO W,247;HENRY H
. 247;J D,247;JAS,247
. JAS M,247;JOHN C,247
. JONATHAN D,247;JOS V
. 247;SAMUEL D,247
. SAMUEL J,247;SILAS
. 247;WM,247;WM J,247
DURAT,ALDOLPHUS F,247
DURDAN,ELIZABETH,196
. LOUISA M,200;MARY ANN
. 195,200;STEPHEN,305
. 306
DURDEN,ALBERT,204
. ALBERT N,195;ALJAREON
. 204;AUGUST G,204
. CHRISTIAN,205;DENIS S
. 204;DENNIS,212;DENNIS
. J,204;ELEAZER,214
. ELIZA,205;F J,204
. GEORGE D,204;HENRY,11
. 214;JACK,204;JOHN,173
. 195,214;JOHN G,204
. LOTT,204;MAHALA H,210
. MARGARET,204;MARTHA
. 199;MARTHA C,205;MARY
. 205;MELBERRY ANN,197
. NANCY M,211;NATHAN N
. 195;REBECKAH,214
. ROBERT,204;ROWAN,204

. ROWAN N,195;SALLY P
. 210;SIMEON,212
. STEPHEN,311;STEPHEN J
. 335;TENER,210;WILLIAM
. 212,214;WILLIAM R,204
DURDIN,JACOB,11;STEPHEN
. 345
DURDON,ELIMASON,195
. ELIZABETH,195;WILLIAM
. 195
DUREN,ANNE L,379;GEORGE
. 391
DURHAM,ABNER,353;ALSEY
. 82,99,111;ANNIE,253
. ELECTRA A,274;ELIZ
. 247;ELLEN A,286;EMILY
. 270;JOAB,308,320;JOHN
. 309;MARTHA E,282
. MARTHA J,249;MARY,248
. MATHEW,304;MATTHEW
. 288,303,319,329;NANCY
. 239;SARAH E,267
. SELINA S,250;WM,391
DURKE,CAROLINE,286
DURKEE,CATHERINE,380
. KEZIAH H,412
DUVAL,BEAL M,391;EMILY
. S,403;EZEKIEL,247
DUVALL,GEORGE W,391
DUVELLE,GEORGE W,39
DWELLE,CHARLES,391
DYALS,ELIZA,383
DYAS,HENRY,391;MOSES
. 391
DYASS,NANCY,380
DYE,ANNA E,204;AVERY,29
. 50,53;BENJ,7;BENJAMIN
. 29,391;BENJAMIN G,39
. D C,53;ELIZ C,422
. ELMINA H F V,407
. EMILY C,396;ETHELRED
. 391;HOPKIN,29;JAMES M
. 8;JAMES W,391;JNO M
. 10;MARTIN M,8,29,50
. 391;MARY ANN,383
. OPHELA,202;WILLIAM,39
DYER,ANTHONY,80,331,335
. ELIJAH,357;J R,149
. JOHN,247,358-359;JOHN
. P,335;JOHN R,144
. MOSES,391
DYES,ANTHONY,79
DYKES,HUBBARD,291
DYOORT,JOHN,168
DYSON,WILLIAM,354
DYUS,JOHN,51;MOSES,51
E-----,DAVID R,272
EADES,W,247
EADS,JOHN,391
EALY,JAMES,9
EARLEY,BETSEY,216
. RHONDA,170
EARLY,14;ANN,277;ANN
. ELIZA,245;ELEAZAR,391
. GEOFFRY,169;JANE L
. 397;JEREMIAH,247;LUCY
. 265;PETER,244,273
. POLLY,283;RICHARD,170
. SEABORN,247
EARP,D,113;DANIEL,146
EASLEY,CLEMENT,247
. WARSHAM,328
EASLIN,JAMES M,247
EASON,E,53;HANNA,206
. SETH,49;STERLING,11
. THOMAS T,247
EAST,NANCY,257
EASTER,NANCY,407

. WHEELER,391;WILLIAM
. 391
EASTERLING,BENJ,391
EATERKIN,WM,2
EATES,JOSEPH I,53
EAVENS,ZACCHUS,213
EAVNS,STEPHEN,216
. WILLIAM,301
EBLANK,MAY,395
ECHOLS,ELIZABETH,335
. FREDERICK,300
. JOSEPHINE,261;JOSHUA
. 60;MILNER,355;PETER
. 312;ROBERT,247;SAMUEL
. D,60;SILAS M,247;WM
. 85
ECKLES,JOSHUA,372
ECKLEY,L,105;LEVI,113
ECTON,HUGH W,70
ECTOR,WILLIE B,59,73
EDDING,ROBERT,391
EDEN,MARY JANE,246
. THOMAS,72
EDENFIELD,ADALINE,202
. ANDREW J,204;BETTY
. 202;CALCIA N,204
. DAVID,214;DAVID J,196
. 204;ELI,196;ELIS,212
. ELIZABETH,194-195,198
. EPHRAIM,204;EPHRAIM H
. 196;EPHRAM,204;GEORGE
. W,204;JAMES,196,212
. JAMES A,196;JAMES W
. 204;JESSE,212;JOHN
. 196;L H,204;LUCRETIA
. 202;M A E,208;MANORD
. 204;MARTHA,201,209
. MARTHA A,207;MARTHY L
. 211;MARY,208,212;MARY
. ANN,212;MARY C,208
. PHILENA,195;RICHMOND
. 196;SINTHA,201;THOMAS
. 204;WILLIAM,212
. WILLIAM D,196;WILLIAM
. H,196
EDES,CAROLINE ELIZ,408
EDGAR,JOHN,391
EDGE,AMANDA,247
EDGEWORTH,A E,148
EDINGS,BENJ L,391
EDINGTON,CATHARINE,397
. FRANCES,384
EDISON,ANNA,139
. ELIZABETH,139;FRANCES
. 139;FRANCES MARIES
. 139;HARRIET,139;JAMES
. 139;JOHN,86,138-139
. 141;MARY,138-139
. NANCY,139;SARAH A,139
. WILLIAM T,139
EDMONDS,AMOS,143
. CATHERINE S,249
. ELIZABETH,250;RACHEL
. 331,335;REUBEN B,247
. SAMUEL,391;WM,247
EDMONDSON,ADALINE,266
. AUGUSTUS,247;B C,355
. 359;BENJ,342;BENJAMIN
. 343-344,346,348
. BENJAMIN C,335
. CRAWFORD,335;ELIZA W
. 269;HARRIET E,236
. JOHN,248,293,304
. JOSEPH,248;JULIA M
. 261;JULIAN,263;MARTHA
. G,287;SAMUEL,335
EDMONSON,B C,357
EDMUND,AMOS,89

EDMUNDS,WILLIAM,29
EDMUNDSON,B,115;BRYANT
. 115;ELIZABETH,280
. ISAAC,300;JAMES,248
. WILEY,130;WILEY L,115
EDNEY,ELIZ,403;JOHN M
391
EDRINGTON,ELIZA,402
EDWARD,BENJAMIN,3,5
EDWARDS,AMBROSE,230,248
. ANDREW N M,391
. AUGUSTINE,391;BENJ
. 391;CHARITY,242
. ETHELBRED,248;FANNIE
. C,247;GARNER,391
. GRESHAM,248;HERBERT
. 335;JACOB,248;JAMES,6
. 335;JAMES H,60,70
. JOEL,91;JOEL J,335
. JOHN,78,248,335
. LEDFERD,78;LEDFORD,59
. LEROY,248;LEVI,391
. NANCY,263;PITMAN,248
. PRYOR,78;REUBEN,219
. 231,331,335;ROBERT S
. 335;STEPHEN,220
. THOMAS,248;WILLIAM
. 230,354;WILLIAM J,335
EGAN,WILLIAM H,391
EGBERT,PETER M,391
EGERTON,JOHN WILLIAM,39
EGNEW,WILLIAM,335
EIDESON,JOHN,83
EIDSON,ELIZABETH,260
. ELLIS,248;JOHN,84,104
. JOHN R,248;SARAH,261
. THOMAS,248;WILLIS,90
. 248
ELAM,DANIEL,391;GEORGE
B,391;MOLLEY,370
ELBERT,ELIZABETH,384
ELDER,B R,282,285;D,116
. D W,282;DAIVD,130
. EDWARD A,335;HENRY
. 335;JOHN,248;SUSAN
. 335;TURNER,335;VIOLET
. 254;W A,149;WM A,130
. 141;WM H,248
ELERSON,JAMES,321
ELEY,ELIZABETH B,280
. SAMUEL,248;WILBORN
. 248
ELIOTT,SILAS,68
ELIS,PHADA,194
ELKINS,REUBEN,391;SION
391-392;THIRZAL,416
ELLEFAIR,BURTON,36
ELLIBY,DICK,29
ELIZABETH,29
ELLIGOOD,RICE,392
THOMAS,392
ELLILEY,DICK,50
ELLINGTON,ENOCH,248
. HEKEKIAH,248;MARY ANN
. F,198;RICHARD,248
. SIMEON,362
ELLIOT,ELIJAH,392
. ELIZABETH,44;JOHN,6
. 53,392;MARY,414;MARY
. JANE,42;SILAS,76
. THOMAS,351,370;THOS
. 351
ELLIOTT,87;ABRAM B,392
. BENJ,248;BETSEY,420
. DAVID,248;DREWRY,29
. 49;ELISHA,282;GEORGE
. 248;JOHN,29,49;LAURA
. 246;MARY,44,50;S,86

. SAVANNAH,39;SILAS,29
. 58,69-72,86;THOMAS,3
. WM,2
ELLIS,ABIGAIL,330
. ALFRED,172;AMY,278
. ANN TREEL,161;CHARLES
. G,172;CIRLENDA,400
. D H,95,116,124-125
. 143;DANIEL B,86
. DANIEL H,106;DANIEL R
. 90;ELISHA,293-294,308
. 330;ELIZ,385
. ELIZABETH,248,269
. ELLISON,229;EMELINE F
. 240;EPHRAIM,360;G E
. BUKHAM,172-173;HENRY
. 331,335;ISAAC,288,297
. 330;J A,74;J H,113
. JAMES,330,335;JAMES H
. 248;JESSE,297,330
. JOHN,228;JOHN B,335
. JOHN H,148;JOHN W,248
. JONATHAN,392;JOSHUA
. 330;LEVEN,218-219
. LEVI,330;MARTHA,275
. 404;MATHEW,248;NANCY
. 249;PHOEBE,74;RADFORD
. 331,335,345;ROANNE G
. 384;SARAH,263;SIMPSON
. 172;SOLOMON,9;STEPHEN
. 330;THO,228;W,113
. WALTER,351
ELLISON,228;BENJAMIN,50
. 53;EMMA,43;JACOB,7
. JOSEPH,10;LABAN,39
. ROBERT,52-53;ROSA,37
. SARAH,53;SARAH M,42
. T J,39;THOMAS,53
ELLISS,JOHN,228;THOMAS
228
ELLISTON,GEORGE,29
JOSEPH,29;ROBERT,29
ELLOTSON,JACOB,29
ELLOTT,RANDOLPH,392
ELMORE,THOMAS,392
ELSEY,M,53
ELTON,NANCY,247
ELY,BENNET A,283;ELIZA
. 280;FANNY,282;JAMES J
. 248;JOHN,248;MARY,268
. MARY M,259;MATTIE,267
. PRISCILLA,284;SAMUEL
. 238,247,267,284;SARAH
. O,419;VA A,246
EMANUEL,AMOS,19;DAVID,1
5;JOHN,1;LEWIS,7
EMBERSON,WILLIAM,310
EMBREE,JNO,182;JOHN,184
EMERSON,JAMES,234
EMERY,JOHN,182
ENABERY,SAMUEL,291
ENECKS,WM,392
ENGLES,MARTIN,392
ENGLINS,216
ENGLISH,AUGUSTUS,335
. CHARLES F,76;HENRY
. 232,248,272,278;INEZ
. 285;J H,248;JAMES,392
. JAMES N,248;JOHN,248
. JOHN H,248;LAVENIA
. 392;LOUISA JANE,283
. LUCY,254;MARY,280
. MARY F,242;NANCY,237
. SALLY,272;SARAH H,242
. STEPHEN,248;WM,247-248
. 260,272
ENGLIT,JAMES M,392
ENNIS,PEGGY,29;REBECCA

401;WILLIAM B,10
ENTAKIN,ISAAC,392
EPES,JNO,225
EPPS,ALEXANDER,248
. CHESLEY,248;JOSEPH
. 335;SUSAN J,283;WM
. 248;WM C,248
ERRICK,CHARLES C,248
ERVING,DAVID,348
ERWIN,RICHARD,29;ROBERT
29
ESON,SETH,7
ESPEY,THOMAS,219
ESPRY,ROBERT,248
ESTER,J B,312
ESTIS,ZACHARY,344
ZACHERY,342
ETHRAGE,C,86
ETHRIDGE,CASWELL,68
. HENRY C,248;J F,39
. LEWIS,130
ETTER,ANNA E,36;GODFREY
DEGILSE,39
EUBANK,CHAS H,314
. EASTER,167;GEORGE,73
. JAMES,167;L B,73
. LITTLEBERRY,73;MAJOR
. 167;MILLY,167;REUBEN
. 167;RHODA,167;RICHARD
. 167;THOMAS,167
EUBANKS,ABATHA M,392
. DANIEL,2;ELIZABETH
. 185;GEORGE,64;GOERGE
. 85;JOHN,159,162,392
. L B,88;MAGERS,335
. REBECAH,162;RICHARD
. 151,159,162,187
. WILLIAM,162
EVALET,CONRAD,392
EVANS,1,323;A R,86,101
. 111;ABNER,216,311,321
. AGNES R,86;ANNA,379
. ARDEN,248;ARDIN B C
. 248;AUGUSTINE,247
. BENJ,248,319;BENJAMIN
. 220;BEVERLY,100,109
. 119,131;CAROLINE,46
. CLARISA MCMURRAY,369
. D,144;DANIEL,1,4,29
. DANIEL G,51;DAVID,69
. 82,91,111,114,116,120
. 121,321;ELENDER T,255
. ELIJAH,248;ELISA B
. 420;ELIZ,396;ELIZA
. 384;ELIZABETH,369
. EMILY,280;FRANCES,277
. GEORGE W,29,47,53,392
. HENRY,392;HENRY W,335
. ISAAC,218,310-311
. ISSAC,220;J,352,355
. 359;J J,98;J W,86
. JABIN,359;JACBIN,359
. JACOB,50,53;JAMES,95
. 329;JANET J,379
. JENNETT,275;JEREMIAH
. 59,65;JESSE,335,352
. 356;JOHN,2,344,359
. 365,392;JOHN W,392
. JOHN W C,392;JOSHUA J
. 60,62,82;JOSIAH J,335
. LELWELLIN,392;LUCY
. 383;LUCY A,392;MARTHA
. 4;MARY,99,408,422
. MARY JANE,399;MICAH
. 161;MILDRED,413;MILLY
. 274;MIRAH,164;NANCY
. 258,391;NICHOLAS H
. 248;POLLY,379,422

EVANS(cont)
. RICHARD,29,50,392
. RICHARD H,51;RICHD,10
. ROBERT H,51,392;SALLY
. 243;STEPHEN,291,302
. 307,311,359;STERLING
. 364;SUSANNAH,394
. TABITHA,258;THOS,357
. TILLITHA J,250;W H
. 279;WILLIAM,53
. WILLIAM G,51;WINSTON
. 248;WM,14,231,294;WM
. E,47
EVE,ANN PRITCHARD,389
. CATHARINE,419;EDWARD
. A,392;EMMA O,415;JOHN
. 392;JOSEPH A,392
. JOSEPH C,392;MARIA T
. 382;MARY,385;MARY R
. 385;PAUL F,392;SARAH
. 379;WM I,392
EVENS,D T,149;DAVID,146
EVERET,JESSE,392
EVERETT,PRUNELEA,202
  SARAH ANN,242
EVERITT,ANN,392;BENJ
  353;JAMES,53;JOHN,392
EVERSTEET,WILLIAM,53
EVINGHAM,LEWIS,392
  THOMAS,392
EVINS,SAMUEL,296
  WILLISM,15
EWING,SAMUEL,296-297
  319;WILLIAM,291
EZELL,BRAXTON R,335
. HENRY CLAY,248;JAMES
. M,248;JOHN,335;ROBERT
. 335
F---,ELIAS G,249
FABB,DAVIS,53
FABIN,CATHERINE E,417
FAIL,ARTHUR,306,329-330
. CHLOE,328-329;FRANCIS
. 308,330;GRACY,329
. JAMES,288,308,319,328
. 330;THOMAS,308,330
. THOS,2,329
FAILLET,WM B,392
FAIN,WILLIAM,215;WM,215
FAIR,GILMORE,39
FAIRCHILD,ABRAHAM,309
FAIRCLOTH,ALEX,204
. ANDREW,204;CHARLES
. 204;CHESLY,204
. ELIZURE,195;ELLY,204
. ENOCH J,196;G N,204
. GEORGE,196;J L B,214
. JAMES,204;JOHN,214
. JOHN R,204;LAVINAH
. 199;MARTHA,199;REDDIN
. 29;WASHINGTON,196
FALKNER,J W,111
FALL,ELIZA,391;JOHN N
  90
FALLIGANT,LOUIS N,392
FAMBOROUGH,T M,269
FAMBRER,233
FAMBRO,A G,97;ELIZABETH
. 238;JULIA NN,286;W P
. 97
FAMBROUGH,ABILGAIL,255
. ANDERSON,233;AUGUSTA
. F,241;CAREY,283
. ELEANOR,262;EMMA E
. 241;JAMES,249;JANE
. 284;JESSE,249;MARY
. 258;MATTIE D,272;O M
. 282;SATIRA J,241;T M

. 249,274;THOMAS M,249
. WM,249;ZACHARIAH,249
FAMBRUGH,ARRY,284
FANER,BETSEY,308;JAMES
. 308;JEREMIAH,308;JOHN
. 308;JOSIAH,308;KESIAH
. 308;MARY,308;NANCY
. 308
FANN,ISAAC,310;MILLEY
  50;WILLOBY,310
FANNE,ISHAM S,367
FANNIN,ISHAM,249;J H
. 359;JAS B,329;JEPTHAH
. 249;T W,359;WM,249
FANNING,JOHN,321
FAR,JEREMIAH,141
FARABEE,P W,262
FARE,WILLIAM H,90
FARECLOTH,JOHN,97
FARGASON,JOHN,144
FARGO,HIRAM W,392
FARINGTON,ELIZ,416
FARLEY,JAMES,344;JOHN
. 335;PRUDENCE,260
. STEPHEN,359;THOMAS
. 295;WILLIAM,26
FARLMER,ELEY,198
FARMELL,MARTHA,36
FARMER,ABEL,9;BERIAN B
. 392;DAVID,8;E F,204
. ELIZABETH,323;ENOCH
. 213;ISAAC,8-9,29,53
. JAMES,29;JOHN,50
. MARTHA,413;MARY,239
. NANCY,29;RACHEL,203
. VERITY,7,29,53;WM,249
FARNEL,BENJAMIN,26
FARNELL,BENJ,9;JOHN,9
  THERESA,49
FARR,JEREMIAH,83;LILATH
  352
FARRAR,ABSALOM,392
. MILLY AVERY,186
. WILLIAM G,335;WM J
. 249
FARREL,BENDER,29
FARRELL,ELIZABETH,283;O
  392;WM,302
FARRER,BETSEY,422;HENRY
  123;LAVINA,381
FARRILL,LUCY,211
FARRINGTON,ELLEN,404;WM
  392
FARRIS,JAMES,249;NANCY
  239
FARROW,CARCUS,374
. CHANEY,96;DANIEL,53
. FANNEY,48;FRANCES,48
. JESSE,29;JESSE P,196
. MARY,53;NATHANIEL,249
. SHELDON,49,53
FART,JULIA,240
FARWATER,JAMES L,249
FASSETT,EARLY P,249
FATLIN,PENELOPE F,281
FAUCH,JONAS,249
FAUKNER,W,149
FAULKNER,
. JAMES HILTON,335
. JAMES W,86,101;JOHN
. 331,335;MASTON,331
. 335;Z,141;ZACHARIAH
. 249,335
FAUNLAIN,THOMAS,168
FAUNTHEROY,GEO,250
FAUSETT,ABRAHAM,392
FAUVER,BENJAMIN,215
FAVOR,H,354

FAVORS,JOSEPH C,335
FAY,DOROTHY,238;FRANK
  250
FEARS,AILSEY,331;ALSEA
. 335;ANNA,384;BENJAMIN
. FRANKLIN,335;EZEKIAL
. 335;EZEKIEL,250,357;F
. 319;JAMES P,250;JESSE
. W,250;JOICE,260;MARY
. 406;OLIVER P,375
. SARAH,386;WILLIAM Q
. 335;WYLY,335
FEATHERSTON,RICHARD,335
FEE,382;ELIZ,402;JANE
  391
FEELOY,JAMES,57
FELDER,THOMAS B,39
FELDERS,ELIZ,409
FELL,ANN ELIZA,394
FELLERS,JOHN A,90
FELLOWS,A,96;J A,98,100
  101;JOHN A,106
FELPS,JOHN,319;RACHAEL
  401;SAMUEL,304
FENDALL,SARAH M,181
FENDLEY,MALACHIA F,204
FENDLY,ELIZA,209;MARY
  208;MIRUM,212
FENISON,JOSEPH,53
FENLY,WM,309
FENN,GEORGE,362;MARY
  269
FENNEL,CULLEN,196
. ELIZABETH,199
. ETHELDRED,392;MARY
. 198;MILLY ANN,202
. NATHAN,196,204
FENNELL,CLARKY,196,205
  MILLY ANN,195
FENNER,JAMES,392
FERGERSON,SARAH,399
FERGUSON,A W,82,89
. AUGUSTUS,392;DANIEL
. 108;JOHN,392;NEILL,89
. ROSABELL,209;SAMUEL
. 305,328;T J,111,127
. THOMAS J,82,122;THOS
. L,105;WILLIAM,108;WM
. J,392
FERNANDA,WM P,392
FERREL,85;CHARLES,15
. CHARLES A,392;CHARS
. 13;HUBARD,294;T,101
. T P,85,92,96,99
. THOMAS,101;W G,85;W S
. 92,99;WILEY S,96
FERRELL,BENNET,349
. HUBARD,308;JOHN,72
. JOHN D,345;MICAJAH
. 133;SARAH D,286;T P
. 92;T S,96;W S,96
. WYLIE,92,139
FERRIL,ARCHELAUS,250
FERRILL,BIRD,319
  HUBBARD,325;J D,313
FERS,EZEKIEL,250
FETTEN,ELIZA,250
FETTERS,JOHN,392
FETTS,ANNA E,37
FEUTRAL,JOHN J,39
FEW,186;ALFRED,168-169
. 170-171;AMELIA,190
. ANN,382;BENJAMIN,51
. 170,222-224;CAMILLUS
. 168-170;CAMMILLES,171
. CAROLINE S,417
. CRASSUS,169-171;ELIZA
. 190;ELIZA W,287

FEW(cont)
. ELIZABETH,170;EMILUS
. 190;EMILY,51;FRANCES
. 190;HANNAH,190
. IGNATIUS,168-171,190
. IGNATUS,168;J,162
. JOSEPH,250;LADUSKA
. 168-169,171;LAVINIA
. 168-169,171;LEONIDAS
. 168-171;LODOISKA,169
. LODUSKA,171;MARY,170
. PAULLUS,190;POLLY,368
. THOMAS,169;WILLIAM
. 168-171,190
FICKLAND,SAMUEL,52
FICKLIN,SAMUEL,53
FICKLING,MORTIMER,392
  MORTIMORE C,39
FIELDER,AGNES,240
. BETSEY,368;ISHAM,368
. J H,144;J M,107,122
. JAMES,368;JAMES M,114
. 118,121,130;JOHN,368
. 370;JOSEPH,123,137
. JOSEPH H,150;JOSIAH
. 368;MORIAH,368
. OBADIAH M B,368
. PASIFI T,370;SALLY
. 368;SAM B,257;TEMPY
. 368;TERRELL,368
FIELDS,CHARLES,204;ELI
. 392;ELLEN,410,412
. FANNY,250;J W,204
. JAMES,7;JAS,2;JOSEPH
. W,250;LEWIS,250;MARY
. 29;MILES,11,21-22,24
. 25,29;S P,392;SETH,9
. THOMAS,250
FIGGS,MARY,244-245
FILDER,JAMES,107
FILES,SAML,309
FILLINGGAME,NANCY,281
FILLINGHAM,COUNSEL,250
. HENRY C,250;JARVIS W
. 250
FILLINGIM,MATTIE J,261
FILLINGIN,MARY L,282
FILLIPS,NANCY,394
FINCH,ELIZABETH,236
. GEORGE,250;JAMES,323
. JOHN E,250;ROBERT,294
. 304;WM,250
FINCHER,ARCHIBALD,60
. LEONARD C,335;WM M
. 142
FINDLEY,BETSEY,241
. DIONIA,248;ELIZABETH
. 239;J,246;J F,236,245
. J I,285;J T,270,285
. JAMES,147,264;JAMES F
. 260;JAMES P,260;JAMES
. T,266;JAS F,238;JAS T
. 237;JOHN,29;LEANDER
. 204;MARGARET,249,254
. R,113
FINDLY,MARY,208
FINITY,JAMES P,205
FINLEY,ABBIGAL,421
. DELLA,276;ELIZABETH
. 274,282;FRANCES,395
. GRACE,275;J T,275
. JACOB,225;JANE,244
. 250,265;JOHN,9,48,250
. LEROY I,250;LUCENDIA
. 250;MARGARET,280;MARY
. S,271;NELLE,260
. NORWOOD H,250;POLLY
. 276;REBECCA,257

. ROBERT,250,342;THOMAS
. 250;THOMAS L,250;WM
. 250
FINLY,JACOB,345;WILLIAM
  377
FINN,JOHN,392
FINNELL,CHARLES,177
. COLLINS,177;HITURAH
. 177;LEROY,177;NANCEY
. 177;SKILTON,177
. UGEANE,177
FINNEY,JAMES,392;MOHN,2
  MURREL,8;SARAH,50
FINNY,ANN,172;BENJAMIN
. 172;PATSEY,172;SARAH
. 30;STERLING,371
FIRTH,ZACHERY,57
FISBOURNE,ANNE,383
FISCHER,FREDERICK,392
FISH,CALVIN,86,331,335
. EMILY B,331;NATHAN,86
. 335,354;R,121;RUSSEL
. 86-87,90,96-97
. RUSSELL,84,87
FISHER,A A,73;AMANDA
. 256;GEORGIA ANN,285
. JOHN,392;JOSEPH,250
. MARY B,398;NANCY,395
. NANCY B I,416;NANCY F
. 264;WM,18
FISHTER,ELIZA J,380
FISSELL,WM,1
FITCH,I D,53
FITSGERRALD,PATSEY,412
FITSH,H,148
FITTS,EDGAR M,392
FITZGARRALD,ANN,154
. JOHN,154;SARAH,154
. SILAS,154
FITZGERALD,BIRD,250
. DAVID,30;EDMUND,392
. ELIZ,388,408;JOHN,30
. JOSEPH,250;RENE,250
FITZGIBBONS,JAMES,392
FITZJARELD,DAVID,7
FITZJARRELL,216;JOHN
. 392;SARAH,420
FITZPATRICK,218,369
. BENJ,232;BENJAMIN,348
. BOUTH,221,335,342
. BOUTH W,357;ELIZ,243
. ELIZABETH,262,283
. FRANCES,280;H H,253
. JO,263;JOHN,47;JOS
. 227;JOSEPH,227;LUCY
. 266;MARY,271;MARY ANN
. 256;NANCY,279;P,344
. PHILLIP,355;PHILLIPS
. 353,355-358;REANE,220
. RENE,227;SALLY,238
. WILLIAM,227-228,232
. 335;WM,227
FITZSIMMONS,EMMA,335
  HENRY,250
FITZSIMONS,M A,379;PAUL
  392
FLAKE,JOHN P,62
FLANAGAN,EDWARD,250
. ELIZ,388;GAMWELL,392
. MARY J,57;WM,250
FLANDER,JORDEN,214
FLANDERS,89,97,124
. ALEXANDER C,196,205
. BARNABAS,196
. CATHARINE,198
. ELIZABETH W,194
. FRANCIS D,206;FRANCIS
. T,196;FRANCIS Y,196

. FREDERICK W,196
. JAMIMA,201;JOHN,196
. JOHN R,205,214;JORDAN
. 196;JOSEPH P,205
. JOSEPH S,196;MARIANNA
. 199;MARTHA,196;NANCY
. G,210;PAUL F,205
. RACHEL MARYANN,200
. RICHARD B,196,205
. SALLIE,211;SALLIE E
. 203;SARAH,205;WILLIAM
. A,196;WILLIAM J,196
. 205;WILLIAM T,205
FLANIKIN,226
FLANNEGAN,ELLEN,402
FLAUNDERS,SARAH,204
FLAWRENCE,HENRIETTA,403
FLEETWOOD,
. HARRIETT A M,266
. LITTLEBERRY,250;MARY
. LENORA,282;WILLIAM
. 250
FLEMING,ANN,422
. CHARLOTTE,384;JAMES P
. 392;JNO B,185;L B,15
. LAIRD B,14,16
. MARGARET MCMURRAY,398
. PETER L,39;REBECCA
. 261;ROBERT,11
FLEMISTER,ELLENDER G
  335;JAMES C,335
FLEMMING,MARTHA,392
  PORTER,392
FLENNIKEN,SAML,222
FLETCHER,324
. CHRISTOPHER,392
. ISABELLA,401;R B,358
. RICHARD B,346
FLEWELLEN,C,63
FLINN,MICHAEL,194
FLINT,AQUELLA,165
. AQUILLA,157;ELIZABETH
. 165;JAMES,157;JANE
. 165;JOHN,157,393
. REBECCA,157;SARAH,157
. 165;THOMAS,157;THOMAS
. H,165;WILLIAM,157
. WILLIAM T,250
FLORANCE,RACHAEL,421
  W A,104
FLORENCE,A S,335;BETTIE
. A,257;FRANK S,250
. JANE,402;JULIA,389
. L D,284;W A,98,100
. 111-113,122,127,129
. 131-132,134,139,143
. 148,239,242,267,284
. WILLIAM A,90-91,93,95
. 103,105,118,129;WM A
. 250
FLOREY,JOHN,60
FLOURNEY,GIBSON,250
  ROBT,287
FLOURNOY,119;EMILY A
. 385;FRANCES M T,413
. JOSIAH,335;MARTHA M
. 386;MARY M,396;PETER
. 304;PETER F,319
. ROBERT,218,360;SAMUEL
. A,335;SARAH ANN,421
. SOPHIA T,398;THOMS
. 393;WILLIAM F,335;WM
. 291
FLOW,COLEMAN,250
FLOWERS,EDWARD,297
FLOYD,ABRAM,6;ANDREW,53
. BARBARA,44;FRANCIS,8
. GEORGE F,248;JAMES,12

FLOYD(cont)
. 30;JAMES B,393;JOHN
. 10,30,82,100,248
. JOSEPH,12,14-15
. MARGARET,12;MATHEW,10
. MATTHEW,30;PALEMON,10
. STEPHEN,6;THOMAS,9,30
. THOMPSON,144;W,98;WZT
. 10
FLOYNOY,PETER F,328-329
  WILLIAM,328
FLUERY,JOSEPH,393
FLUKER,230;A A,270;B,60
. BETSEY,270;ISAAC,217
. JESSE M,248;JOHN C
. 248;OSCAR S,248
. WILLIAM,217
FLURY,JOSEPH,314
FLUTCHER,JOHN W,393
FLYNN,JOHN,53
FOALDS,FERNEY,39
FOBBIS,W,354
FOKES,SHADI,20;SHADRACK
  25;SHADRICK,24
FOLDS,AMOS,393;CHARLES
. J,335;GEORGE,53
. GRANDASON,335;JACOB
. 335;JOHN,65,335;JOHN
. RICHARD,53;RICHARD,30
. 50;THOMAS,65,82,96
. 124;THOS,111
FOLES,COONRAD,393
FOLIS,TURNER P,248
FOLKES,SARAH,196;SHADI
  22
FOLKS,JOHN,50
FOLL,GEORGE,393;LUCY
  MOORE,409
FOLLY,WM,248
FONEY,SARAH,385
FOOL,AGNES S,241
FOOTE,W R,247,254
FORBES,EDWARD,151;ENOCH
  354;WESLEY,354
FORCE,ALBERT W,248
. BENJAMIN W,248;JOHN P
. 60
FORD,JOHN,20,22;JOHN S
. 248;N A,393;SAML,14
. SAMUEL,15;WASHINGTON
. 335;WILLIAM W,82;WM
. 248-249,393
FORDE,PERLY,96
FOREHAND,BERRIEN A,39
. DREWRY,30,49;DRURY,10
. JEREMIAH,97;LAVINA,45
. MARTHA ANN,44;W H,39
FOREMAN,DAVID,349
. EDMUND,348;ISAAC,341
. JACOB,335;REUBEN,291
. 307
FORISTER,GEO,128
FORKNER,198
FORMBY,AARON,376;NATHAN
  376
FORREST,JAMES N,249
FORRESTER,118,124;ADDIE
. 244;ANNE,242
. ELIZABETH,267-268
. GEORGE,115;GRESHAM
. 249;JANE,283;JESSE M
. 249;JOEL,249;MARY,237
. 245,256,276;NANCY,283
. REDMAN,249;SARAH,237
. WILLIAM,249;WM,249
FORRISTER,126
FORSYTH,A B,130,140
  JOHN,393;JULIA,399

FORT,124;FERUCH S,249
FORTH,JOEL L,26,30,48
. JOHN T,30,48;THOMAS
. 30
FORTINBERRY,ANN H,395
FORTNER,MICHEL J,196
  MITCHEL,214;THOMAS,39
FORTSON,JAMES,371
FORTUNEBERRY,MILLY,403
  NANCY,403
FOS,LOUISA A,251
FOSKIN,ALLEN M,196
FOSTE,W R,267
FOSTER,87,180;A G,312
. A S,147;ANDERSON,249
. ANN MARTIN,272;ANNE M
. 269;ARTHUR,190,231
. 239,249,251,274,393
. ARTHUR R,249;AUGUSTA
. ELIZA,409;BASDEL,306
. BROOKS,87;CHRISTIAN
. 126;COLLIER,171,182
. 393;ELIZ,391;ELIZ
. FORTE,246;ELIZA,385
. ELIZABETH,171,183,241
. EMILY,250;ENOCH,353
. EVALINE H,273;FRANCES
. 42,415;G W,217,220
. 224;GEO W,225;GEORGE
. W,221,229-230;GEORGE
. WELLS,298;HARDY,171
. 393;J,164;J M,100
. JAMES,166,188,190,311
. JAMES F,249;JAS,151
. JNO,159,182,364,393
. JOANAH,88;JOEL,147
. JOHN,150-155,157-158
. 160-165,168,171-172
. 173,175-181,183-184
. 185-188,191,249,291
. 306-307,311,393;JOHN
. M,97;JOHN W,57;JOSEPH
. 249;JOSHUA,393;JULIA
. 285;LOUISA M,382
. LUCINDA,415;LUCY S
. 255;M G,250;MARTHA
. 259,381,398;MARY,112
. 240,345,402;NANCEY
. 270;PENELOPE,87;PETER
. 192;PHEBE,242
. PHILEMON,311;REBEKEH
. CRUTE,155;RICHARD,30
. 196;ROBERT,172,249
. ROBERT M,249;ROBERT S
. 182;SAL,329;SALEY,306
. SALLEY,306;SAMUEL,51
. 53,249,393;SARAH,286
. SARAH JANE,413
. SEABORN,249;STERLING
. 50,393;SUSANNA,394;T
. 101;T J,147;THOMAS,82
. 95,249,393;THOMAS F
. 393;THOS,111;W T,263
. 279;WILLIAM,112,357
. WILLIAM J,87,96,129
. WM,249,393
FOUNTAIN,BRINSON,48,53
. DEMPSY,30;GILBERT,393
. KINDRED,393;MARTHA
. 209;MARY,201;MARY ANN
. 409;MARY JANE,242
FOURDE,PURLEY,101
FOWLER,DAVID,224
. FRANCIS P,394;JANET
. 406;JOHN,393;JOSHUA
. 393;WM,393
FOX,AMELIA,385;GILLIAM
. 319;HARRIETT P,412

. KATHERINE,422;MARY
. 411;MARY H,410
. NICHOLAS,393;SARAH
. ANN,383;WM,393
FOYD,JOHN,53
FOYIL,JOHN,393
FRAIL,MARY,169-170
FRAILS,MARY,170
FRALA,MARGARET,411
FRANCIS,JAMES,393;JAMES
. C,39;SARAH,187;THOMAS
. 10,52-53
FRANET,ELIZA,388
FRANKLIN,ABRAHAM,155
. AUGUSTUS F,39;ELIZY
. 45;ESOM,330;JOHN C
. 335;JOHN CARTER,331
. MARY ANNE,260;MAUDA
. 206;Z,160
FRASER,
. LAURENCE ROGER,393
. LAVENIA,415;REUBIN
. 393
FRASIER,WM F,313
FRAXER,MARY A,384
FRAYER,SUSAN R,408
FRAZER,CAROLINE M.412
. MARTHA JANE,421;WM
. 393
FRAZIER,ANDREW,335;ANNA
  S,388;WILLIAM,96,112
FRAZOR,ROBERT,173
FRAZURE,ROBERT,173
FREADWELL,JOSHUA,8
FREDERICK,CATHARINE,409
. JACOB,393;STEPHEN,191
. THOS,2
FREDUWAY,J,106
FREELAND,JAMES M C,393
. JOHN H,393;THOMAS W
. 393
FREEMAN,89,107;BAILEY
. 335,352;BEASLEY,249
. BENJAMIN B,335
. CATHERINE S,267
. CYNTHIA A,331;DANIEL
. 335;DELILAH JANE,249
. FLOYD,331;FRANCES E
. 241;GABRIEL,352
. GEORGE,335;GEORGE A
. 249;HAMLIM,68;HAMLIN
. 58,70,73,78;HARRIET
. 71;HARTWELL,335
. HOLMAN,349;HOPSON,335
. ISAAC H,335;ISHAM,71
. 82,86,102;JAMES,331
. 335;JANE,249;JARIAH
. 265;JNO,292;JOHN,2
. 291,302,310,319,347
. JOHN G,249;JOSIAH,331
. 335;MARGARET,237
. MARTHA,248;MARTHA J
. 274;MARY,255;MARY C
. 331;POLLY,247;RERRICK
. 39;RUTHA BARTON,375
. SALLY,236;TIMOTHY,359
. VALENTINE,249
. ZACHARIA,249
FREENEY,ELIJAH,317
. ELIZABETH,321;NANCY
. 317,319,321;THOMAS
. 317
FREENY,GILLAH,321
FRENCE,ROBERT,14
FRENCH,CHARLES,15;CHARS
. 14;LEWIS,249;REASE,14
. 15;ROBERT,15,18
FRETWELL,CHARLES,393

FRETWELL(cont)
. LITTLETON B,393
. MICAJAH,249;MICAJAH H
. 364;RICHARD,294
FRIDEL,JOHN,393
FRITH,JOSEPH,393
FROGIER,JOHN V,249
FROST,JAMES,30;MARY,385
FRYER,A G,53;FIELDING
. 30,50,53;JOHN,10,30
. 51,53,393;ROBERT,7,30
. 52;WINNIFRED,30;ZACH
. L,8;ZACHARIAH L,30
. ZACKARIAH,4;ZACKARIAH
. L,1
FUDGE,BENJAMIN,393;MARY
. A,409;SARAH ANN,380
FUGUAY,PRATER,289
FULCHER,ALANA,38;ANN
. 413;ANN C,45;ANN
. ELIZA,396;ANNIE F,39
. ARMISTED,393;CAROLINE
. 414;ELIZ,421;HARRIET
. C,38;JAMES A,53;JAMES
. L,393;JEANETT,396
. JOHN,10,30,51,393
. JOHN W,39;MARGARET
. 397;MARTHA,408;MARY V
. 43;WM,393
FULFORD,CAROLINE,53
. OWEN,196
FULFORT,NANCY,197
FULLER,AGNESS,126
. ALFRED,126,142;CELIA
. 248;DAVID,249;ELIJAH
. 58-59,249;ELIZA,272
. FREDERICK C,249;GREEN
. 126;GREENE,249;ISHAM
. 165;J C,353;JESSE,249
. MILLY,251;PHOEBE,238
. POLLY,245;SAMUEL,165
. SIMON,249;SUSANNA,126
. WM S,249
FULLERTON,HUGH,393
FULLERWOOD,JIM,39
FULLINGHAM,MARTHA,258
FULSOME,BUD,300
FULTON,SAMUEL,89
FULWOOD,JOHN THOMAS,249
FUMEY,MILLEY,411
FUNDERBURK,WILLIAM A
. 335
FUR,ELIZABETH,164
FUREY,ELIZ,390
FURGASON,DANIEL T,90
FURGE,REBECCA,263
FURLOUGH,CHARLES,249
FURLOW,ASHLEY,280;DAVID
. 249;ELIZ P,243;GEO W
. 249;JAMES,249;JAMES T
. 249;MARY E,244;OSBORN
. 249;SALLY,243;SARAH
. 241;SARAH ANN,235;W
. 363;WILLIAM,363
FURMAN,JOHN HOWARD,393
FURNEY,WM,393
FUSSELL,1;DORCAS,322
. THOMAS,5,393;WM,1
FUTCH,JOHN,26;O,53
FUTERELL,JOEL,48
FUTERILL,FANNY,396
FUTRAL,BENJAMIN,249
. MARY,53
FUTREL,LEVI,57
FUXEY,MARTHA,389
G----,J N,276;LEWIS T
. 205
G?,MARK,327

GAAR,JOEL,366
GABARD,THOMAS,30
GABLE,LUTHER,76
GACHET,309
GAFFORD,DANIEL,352;DANL
. 309;THOMAS,250
GAGE,A NEGRO,62
GAGOOD,BENJAMIN,292
GAHAGAN,LAWRENCE,59,64
. 67,75-77;LAWSON,60
GAHAN,LAWRENCE,76
GAILLET,WM B,393
GAILSFIELD,THOMAS,250
GAINES,AMARENTHA E,38
. CHARLES,53;DUNCAN,10
. 26,30,48,53;GEO,4
. GEORGE G,393;HENRY
. 302;JAMES,2;JOHN,53
. JOHN L,53;LEVI,57
. MARY JANE,381;MELVINA
. 411;MIKEL,19;NUNROE
. 39;SARAH,53;SEABORN
. 39;THEOPHILUS,30
GAINEY,97
GAINS,THEOPHILUS,14-15
. WILLIAM,101
GAINUS,COOPERUR,50;JOHN
. 50
GAIRCLOTH,JAMES,214
. WILLIAM,214
GAIRDNER,JAMES P,393
GAITHER,227-228;A B,97
. BRICE,301,318;HENRY
. 310;W W,89;WILEY W,90
. 97
GAITHERS,WILEY W,130
GALAGHER,MARY ANN,408
GALLAGHER,JOHN,393;JOHN
. W,393
GALLMAN,JOHN C,335
GALLOWAY,30;W,363
GALMAN,JOHN,96
GALMON,JOHN,101
GALPHIN,ANN,403;BARBARA
. 398;MARTHA,380
GALTIN,ADALINE,247
GAMAWAY,EDWARD,39
GAMBLE,JOHN,13-14,16
. 393;R L,13;ROGER L,14
. 16-18
GANAHL,JOSEPH,393
GANAS,JOHN,393;LEVINA
. 403
GANES,CHAS,393
GANET,FRANCES,384
GANEY,BENJAMIN,57
GANIS,JAMES,393
GANN,CATHERINE,392;JOHN
. 250;MARION,250;SAMUEL
. 250;WILLIAM,94,100
GANT,RICHARD,394
GANTER,JOSEPH,50,394
GANTLEY,JOHN,394
GANTT,ELI,250;MARY E
. 282;THOMAS JOHN,394
GARBETT,MARY W,72
. WILLIAM,72
GARDELLE,A,394
GARDENER,AARON,17
GARDINER,GEORGE W,394
. JOHN F,225;THOMAS,394
GARDNER,AARON,14-15
. ALEXANDER,394;ANN,398
. 403;ELIZ,412;ELIZA
. BROWN,167;ELIZABETH
. MCKINELY,393;EMILY
. 399;ETHELRED,335
. JACOB,60,90;JAMES,53

. 90,394;JESSE,167;JOHN
. 394;LEWIS,166-167
. MARGARET,421;MARGARET
. W,395;MARY,167,401
. MARY M,393,411;S A
. 250;SAMUEL,86,250
. STERLING,310;THOMAS
. 394;WILLIAIM,53
. WILLIAM,167,181
GARET,MARY,30
GARLAND,JOHN,335
GARLICK,EDWARD,52-53
. JUDAH,52;SAMUEL,9,12
. 30
GARLINGTON,ANN,51;JOHN
. 250;THOMAS C,250
GARLINTON,BENJAMIN,39
GARNER,JOHN,311,394
. JOHN J,250;M F,264
. RICHARD,48,359;SALLY
. 250;SAM,39;THOMAS,250
. WM,250;WM B,250;WM W
. 250
GARNETT,ANTHONY,159
. JERUSHA,393;JOHN,394
. MARY,392;REBECAH,159
. SUSANNAH,183
. ZACHARIAH,183,394
GARR,JOEL,375;M D,85
. WILLIAM,346
GARRARD,WM W,394
GARRET,ASA,394;EDMUND
. 394;J,121;JOHN,250
. JOSIAH,90,97,103
GARRETT,328;BLUNTY,335
. CHARITY,418;ELI,177
. ELIZ,246;FANNIE,241
. GEORGE S,335;HENRY
. 318;J C,136;JAS,294
. JNO,370;JOHN,218,250
. 394;JOHN C,82;JOSEPH
. 394;JOSIAH,87;MARY
. 420;MILDRED,408;NANCY
. 238,392;RICHARD,145
. ROBERT,250;SARAH,177
. SUSANNAH,188,190
. TEMPY,370;THOMAS,313
. THOMAS B,250;WILLIAM
. 328
GARRITT,THOMAS,375
GARROTT,CATHARINE,218
. JOHN,218;MARY,50
GARROW,CHANEY,112
GARTRELL,FRANCIS,359
. JOHN,187,394
GARTRELLE,JOHN O,250;WM
. J,250
GARTRETE,JOHN,165
GARTRETH,JOHN,154-155
GARVIN,ANN,42;IGNATIUS
. 394;IGNATIUS P,51
. JIMMIS,44;JOHN,39,170
GARY,JAMES,310,326
GASDEN,P,92
GASKINS,ISAAC,222
GASQUE,JANE,415;NATHAN
. 394
GASS,FREDRIC,394
GASTIN,ALEXANDER,250
. JANE FEREBA,245;JOHN
. 250;MATTHEW,250
GASTON,AGGY,117
. CATHARINE,335;MARY
. ANN,277;MARY E,282
. MATTHEW,116-117,125
. 131,136-137,139,144
. MOSES,60;NANCY A,335
. P F,335;PEGGY,271

GASTON(cont)
. SARAH JANE,246;THOMAS
. 335,340;W F,243,247
. W T,243,251,261-262
. 263;WILLIAM,251;WM F
. 242,246
GATES,309;SAMUEL,2
GATEWOOD,PHILLIP,251
GATHER,226;ELI E,59
GATHRELL,
  NANCY PRUDESON,177
GATHRIGHT,MILES,394
GATLIN,247;ALLAH,240
. ALPHEUS,251;CAROLINE
. 284;CHURCHWELL,251
. DARKES,251;ELIZABETH
. 257;H,269;JAMES,357
. LEMUEL M,251;MAJOR
. 251;MARIAH,251;PATSY
. 277;RADFORD,251;S,251
. SARAH,266;STEPHEN,280
. 285
GAUGH,GEORGE,7
GAULDING,CNOJO,39
GAVERT,JOHN MATHEWS,250
GAY,ABRAHAM,213;ALLEN
. 308-309;BATT,196
. CALVIN C,205;ELEANOR
. 381;ELLENDA,415
. GEORGE,205;GILBERT
. 343;HENRY,10;JACOB,39
. JOEL,30;JOHN,79,295
. 300,310;L,205;LEWIS
. 213;LUCENDA,385
. MARGARET,209;MARY,30
. MATHEW,205,213
. MATILDA,389,416
. MATTHEW,79;MICHAEL
. 196;NANCY,47,384
. SHERROD H,331,335
. SUSAN L,206;THEODORE
. THOS,394;THOMAS,30
. WILLIAM,311;WINNIE
. 209;WM,394;ZENY,208
GAYLORD,GILES,251
GEE,SAMUEL,59,62
GEER,HELEN MARY,265
  JAMES,256
GEHEGEN,BRIDGET M,409
GEIGER,ELIZABETH,331
. 335;FELIX,359;HARMAN
. H,331;HARMON H,335
. JOHN C,205;RANDAL H
. 335;WASHINGTON,335
GENINGS,ANNIE,44
GENTRY,ANN,259;BURGESS
. 251;ELIZABETH,265
. JOHN D,251;JUDITH,243
. MARTHA A,286;MARTIN
. 362;OPHELIA T,257
. PATSEY,241;SAMUEL,251
. SEBORN,251;WM,251;WM
. H,251
GEORGE,DAVID,30;ELIJAH
. 295,298,306;J V,89
. JACOB,39;JAMES,176
. 335;JORDAN,176
. MARGARET,411;NANCY
. 306;POLLY,266;ROBERT
. 176;SILAS,39;WILLIAM
. 251;WILLIAM B,73
GERALD,R,190
GERDINE,
  GEORGE AUGUSTUS L,251
GERMAIN,THOS,394
GERMAN,JNO,166
GERMANY,BENJAMIN,177
. CLAUISA,181;ELEANOR

. 181;ELLENDER,177
. FANNY WASHINGTON,185
. JAMES,177;JOHN,162
. 177,251;JOSEPH,177
. ROBERT,177;ROBT,358
. SAMUEL,177,181,185
. SARAH,385;THOMAS,181
. WASHINGTON,165,177
. WILLIAM,177,353
. WILLIAM J,394
GERMOND,WILLIAM,394
GEROLD,RANDAL,190
GETTATHEWS,GEORGE,251
GHEEN,J N,258
GHOLSON,323;ANTHONY,323
. EGGLESTON,323;J,317
. JOHN,288,304,323
. SINTHE,323
GHOLSTON,ANTHONY,321
. 323,335;JOHN,323
GHOLSTONE,JOHN,321
GIBBONS,BARACK,186
. CHARLOTTE,4;WILLIAM
. 186
GIBBS,ELIZ ANN,406;JOHN
. 394;MALVINA,386;MILES
. 251;REBECCA,415
. THOMAS,251;TIBITHA
. 254;WILLIAM,394
GIBBSON,SHADRICK W,192
GIBNEY,JNO,320
GIBONEY,354;WM,271
GIBONY,WM,230,355
GIBSON,A C,104;ABRAM
. 151-152;ALEXANDER,394
. DEXTER,151-152;ELIZA
. 386;ELIZABETH,151
. HENRY A,251;ISAIAH
. 251;J C,76;J W,189
. JANE,415;JOHN,365
. JOHN C,335;S W,189
. SARAH,151;SHADRACH
. 151;SHADRICK W,189
. SHADRIEK W,192;SOPHIA
. L,412;SYLVANUS,248
. TARRESA,151;THOMAS
. 365;THOMAS C,251
GIDENS,ALI,53
GIDEON,CHARLES,65
  CHARLES GIDEON,65
GIGER,ABRAHAM,359
GILAMS,CLARENCE,196
GILBERT,ANN,255
. BENJAMIN,297-298,317
. EADY ANN,195;EDMOND
. 317;ELIZABETH,282
. FANNY,317;J,149;J G
. 268;JABEZ,80,119;JOHN
. 317;MARTHA,268;MARTHA
. BATTLE,375;MARTIN,298
. MARY,390;MAURIS,394
. MICHAEL,298,327
. MOTTEN,354;PATSEY,317
. POLLEY,317;RICH,271
. ROBERT,251,265,298
. SAML,294,321;SAMUEL
. 317;W,119;WILLIAM,60
. 105,119
GILBREA,DANIEL,251
GILBREATH,247
GILDERS,BENJ,276
GILDING,CHARLES,251
GILES,259;DAVID S,79
. JAMES D,102,113-114
. RACHEL,294;REDDEN,259
. RUBEN,259;SALLY,106
. T J,98;THOMAS,251,294
. THOMAS G,144;THOMAS J

. 95,102,114,121,141
. 146-148;THOS J,144;W
. 101;WADE H,91,98,100
. 119;WAID H,94;WILLIAM
. 60,80,85,95,121,251
. 311;WILLIS,259;WM,98
GILHAM,EZEKIEL,64
GILKIE,JANE,421
GILL,217;BENJAMIN,340
  JOHN,217,224,377
GILLEN,JOHN,251;SAMUEL
  I,251
GILLEON,JOHN,304
GILLESPIE,JAMES,367
  JOHN,68
GILLIAM,233
GILLILAND,WILLIAM,307
  320;WM,361
GILLION,JOHN,310
GILLIS,ANDREW J,196
. AUGUS A,205;JOHN D
. 214;MARGARET G,212
. MATHEW,205;N C,205
. SANDY,205;THOMAS,205
GILLMAN,NANCEY,269
GILLSON,DENNIS T,39
. EVAN C,39;J W,39
. JAMES T,39
GILMAN,CHARLES,394;WM W
  86-87
GILMER,140;ELIJAH,356
. JOSEPH,251;MARY,251
. NAOMI,286
GILMORE,AGRILLA,102
. ANTHONY,86;AQUILLA,95
. 106;BETSEY,272;ELIJAH
. S,89;H,99;H J,90;H J
. W,91;H W,91;HUM,231
. HUMPHREY,81,99,115
. 226-227,231;JOHN,251
. QUILLA,94;ROBERT,85
. 89,287,297;UMPHREY,88
. WILLIAM,81,90,117,125
. WM,97
GILPHIN,THOMAS,105
GILPIN,IGNATIUS,175
  NANCEY,154
GILSON,DAVID B,59
GILSTRAP,BENJAMIN E,53
. HENRY,30,49;JOHN B
. 335;MINGO,39;R W,53
. WILLIAM,8,30,49
GINDRAT,JOHN,12
GINN,THOMAS,394
GIPSON,MATILDA,405;S C
  53
GIRDNER,
. GEO WASHINGTON -
. FRANKLIN,394
GIRTMAN,JOHN C,140
GIVENS,MARY,201
GLA---,HYRAM,251;SAMUEL
  251
GLA----,ELIZABETH,251
GLADDIS,REBECCA,393
GLASCOCK,ANN,404;E,30
. EDMUND B,394;MARY A
. 412;MARY SAVANNAH,380
. THOMAS,394;THOS,319
GLASS,ASSENATH,198;B
. 251;ELIAS,251;JAMES
. 251;JOHN,394;JONATHAN
. 251;LEVY,14-15;NANCY
. 218,220;PLEASANT M
. 114;SARAH,216;TABITHA
. 286;THOMAS,65,67
. WILLIAM,216,311;WM,2
. Z,251;ZACHARIAH,216

GLASS(cont)
  218,220,311
GLASSCOCK,WILLIAM,181
GLAWSON,ELI,251
GLAZE,ELIZ,246
GLAZIER,ADAM,352,363
. ELIZA ANN,269;HIRAM
. 62
GLEEN,I,241;J W,279
  LIZA ANN,281
GLENDENNING,WILLIAM,394
GLENN,229;CLEMT,291
. ELIZABETH,249;J N,272
. JOHN,63;OPHELIA
. ELIZABET,146;THOMAS
. 304,321,329;THORNTON
. I,335;ZILPHA,403
GLISSON,AMELIA,37
. DENNIS,8,30,51,53
. EVAN,51;HETTY,208
. JOHN,7,99;JOHN B,49
. LYDIA,30;PHEROH,30
. ROBERT,205;TILLY,30
GLOVER,CAROLINE,385
. DAVID,394;ELI,331,335
. 357,359,361;ELI S,335
. EMILY,405;HANNAH,41
. HENRY S,335;JOHN,335
. JOHN E,335;L L,251
. ROBERT D,394;SALL,413
. SARAH,388;SARAH A,414
. WILLIAM,65,80,394
GOAR,JACOB,297
GOARE,J,328
GOCH,NATHAN,251
GODARD,JOSEPH,118,127
  128
GODBE,SAMUEL,8
GODBEE,ALFRED A,30,39
. 51,53;AMELIA,37;ANN
. 40;BRIDGET,404
. CARSWELL G,39;CHARLES
. 39;CHARLOTTE,38,45
. COPER,39;DAVE,39
. DRUSILLA,51;E,53
. ELBERT,30;ELIZA,53
. EZEKIEL S,39;FLORENCE
. A,41;FREEMAN,53;HENRY
. 30,51,53,58;JAMES,8
. 30,50-51,53;JAMES A
. 58;JAMES F,53;JAMES H
. 53,58;JAMES M,39
. JAMES W,39;JASON,39
. JULIA B,40;LOUSIA,42
. MALISSA,45;MARGARET
. 51,53;MARIAH,46
. MARTHA,42-43;MARTIN
. 53;MARY,30,51,53,58
. MARY J,39;MERCHANT,53
. MILLEDGE,53;MOSES,51
. 53;OCTAVIA,40;PALMYRA
. V,58;POLLY ANN,40
. RAYFORD,39;SAMUEL,51
. 53,58;SARAH M,40
. SIMEON,53;STEPHEN,39
. STPEHEN,30;SUSAN,40
. WILLIAM,30;WM,9
GODBEHERE,JAMES,394
GODBY,ELIPPEY P,39
  JAMES,342
GODDARD,J,143;JOSEPH
  148;L,134
GODDEN,STEPHEN,14
GODDING,WILEY,14
GODDWIN,CLARA C,45
GODEN,STEPHEN,17;WILEY
  17
GODFREY,ENOCH,30

  WILLIAM,214
GODFREYS,FRANCIS H,12
GODING,STEPHEN,15;WILEY
  15
GODKIN,CATHERINE,257
. J W,237,239,241,244
. 248,258,264-265,267
. 268,287;JAMES,275
. JAMES W,251,257,259
. 261,266-267,270,272
. 273,276,278-279,281
. 284-286;JAS M,247;JAS
. W,235-236,244,256
. JOHN W,239
GODKINS,JAMES W,266,271
  277
GODLEY,JOHN A,8;MARY
  393;VERLENDIA M,395
GODPHREY,MARTHA,52
GODWIN,EDMOND,321
. ELIZABETH,319;JAS W
. 236;JONATHAN,309
. MICAJAH,297
GOEN,HUGH,90;ROBERT,90
GOETCHINS,R V,394
GOFF,ELLIS H,394
. NATHANIEL,82;SAMUEL
. 394
GOGGINS,MADISON,335
GOHAGAN,76
GOIN,HUGH,63,85,131
GOING,MOSES,216-217,290
GOINS,HUGH,70
GOLDEN,ISAIAH,394
  LANKUTER,39
GOLDIN,ABRAHAM,112
GOLDING,F R,235,248,275
  279
GOLDSBY,LYDIA,280
GOLDSMITH,WILLIAM H,69
GOLDSON,ANTHONY,320
. EGLESTON,320;JACKEY
. 320;JOHN,320
GOLDWARE,DENNIS,22
GOLDWORTH,FRANCES,415
GOLIGHTLY,HUGH,394
GOLPHIN,FRANCE,30
GONDEN,MARK,293
GOOCH,MARY,286;WINNEY
  251
GOOD,DAVID W,251;LAURA
. C,46;STERLING,335
. THEOPHILUS,335
GOODALL,MARGARET,385
  PARKS,8;WILLIAM,394
GOODBEE,ALBERT,51
  ALFRED,7;HENRY,51
GOODE,CLAREY,275;J W
. 171;JAMES H,335;JAMES
. HENDERSON,331;JESSE
. 331,335;JOHN,309;JOHN
. C,331,335;SAMUEL,177
. SAMUEL W,187;WILLIAM
. 335,346
GOODEN,JOHN,17
GOODING,JOHN,14-15
GOODKIN,J W,242
GOODMAN,85,88,90,92,94
. 96,98,102,106,112,114
. 118,120-121,123,129
. 138,141,143,148
. BARNEY,335;DENNIS,20
. HENRY,18-19;J,100,130
. 149;JOHN,65,70,82,85
. 86,88,90-91,93,101
. 104-105,108,110,112
. 113,122,128-129,131
. 132-134,137-139,143

. 146-147,149;MARY ANN
. 384;SUSAN A,397;SUSAN
. L,272;WILLIAM,23,394
. WM H,394
GOODRICH,E R,70,73;ELI
. R,71;LUTHER,394;WM H
. 394
GOODROE,MATILDA,285
GOODS,113
GOODSON,FEREBY,419
. JACOB,394;JCABO,51
. NANCY,418;WILLIAM,355
GOODWIN,ANN MARIA,410
. ANNA,382;CHARLES,30
. 394;CHAS,165;ELIZ,408
. HENRY,394;JAMES,394
. JESSE,70,75,79,394
. JOHN,49,53;JOHN W,394
. LAVINA,387;LOUISA B
. 418;MATHEW,7;MATTHEW
. 51;MATTHEWS,30;PHENY
. 422;WILLIAM,30;WYCHE
. 394
GOODWYN,JAMES,394;MACK
  142,148;STETH H,86
GOOGER,WILLIAM,298;WM H
  394
GOOLSBY,CARDEN,331
. CINCINATTUS L,335
. CINCINNATIUS L,331
. DENNIS,335;JACOB,331
. 335;JAMES B,335;JOHN
. 335;LEVI,335;WADE B
. 335;WILLIAM,331,336
GOOMAN,JAMES,91
GORDAN,MARIA,422
  PATRICK,178
GORDEN,107;DELILAH,258
  ROBERT,39
GORDEYS,JAMES,12
GORDIN,WILLIAM,53
GORDON,ALEXANDER,321
. 395;ANN,419;CATHERINE
. 415;CHARLES P,336
. CHARLOTTE,4;DUNCAN,50
. ELENCY,53;ELIZ,398
. GEO RAMSEY,395
. GERALDINE A,46
. HARRIET S,386;HUGH,9
. IDA O,46;JAMES,20,22
. 24-25,47;JOHN,39,51
. JOHN B,53;LOUISA,336
. LOUISE,331;MARGARET
. 405;MARIE LOUISA,45
. MARY D,336;MARY F,274
. MISSOURI,208;PATRICK
. 395;REBECCA,395
. ROBERT,30;ROBT,3
. SARAH F,39;THOMAS A
. 336;W F,244;WILLIAIM
. 30;WILLIAM,7,48
GORDY,ELI,10,30;ELIJAH
. 49,53;ELIZABETH,30
. GEORGE,9;GEORGIA A
. 207;JAMES,7,30
. LEONARD,293;MOSES,30
. PETER,53
GORE,ELISHA,364;THOMAS
  251
GOREE,AMOS,75
GOREY,A,89
GORIE,AMOS,85
GORLEY,JONATHAN,251
GORNTO,BENJAMIN,196
  NATHAN,196
GORTON,HENRY,395
GOSDEN,E,96;EZEKIEL,84
  WATEMAN,86

GOSLIN,SIMON,289
GOSS,HEZEKIAH F,371
. ISOM,263;JOHN M,205
. MARY,279;MATILDA,268
. REBECCA,383
GOSSAGE,HENRY,395
GOSTER,G W,224
GOTSEN,ABRAHAM,96
GOUGER,STEPHEN,251
GOUGH,GEORGE,48,53
GOULD,AMANDA,419
. ARTEMAS,395;ELIZ,379
. MARY ANN,398;NANCY
. 397;S,395;WILLIAM T
. 395
GOULDING,PETER I,30
    WILLIAM,53
GOULDMAN,FRANCIS,166
GOVEN,JAMES,357
GRABILL,HENRY,297
GRACE,ELIZABETH,30
. JAMES,292;JAS,292,358
. JOHN,336;MARY ANN,418
. SAMUEL,395;SARAH,218
. THOMAS,218,305,395
GRACEY,JOHN,364
GRADEY,WILLIAM,72
GRADY,JOHN,395;MICHAEL
    395
GRAHAM,ANDREW,30;ANSON
. B,53;JAMES,336;JANE
. 415;JOSEPH,251;MARTHA
. L,37;MARY L,46;POLLY
. 263,282;SARAH,30
GRAMMAR,JOHN,295;PETER
    295
GRANBERRY,JAMES M,73
    S M,73
GRANEL,DANIEL,395
GRANGER,BENJ,395
GRANT,323;A E,246;ALLEN
. 251;CATHARINE,205
. CULLAN E,251;DANIEL
. 251;ELIZA T,251
. ELIZABETH,195,323
. ISAAC,30;J T,251
. JAMES,251;JAMES T,251
. JOHN C,251;JOHN G,251
. JOSEPH,251,305,395
. KENNETH,395;LEMUEL P
. 395;MARY,30,53;SAMUEL
. 336;SARAH A,237;SARAH
. ANN,384;SUSANNAH,202
. THOMAS,13,15,205,251
. 336;VENUS,44;WILLIAM
. 73;WILLIAM G,205;WM S
. 251;ZELPHA,202
GRANTHAM,DANIEL,364
    WILLIAM,76,320
GRANVILLE,CHARLES,10
GRASS,CHARLES,325
    SOLOMON,2
GRAV,YOUNG W,251
GRAVER,WM,309
GRAVES,CARANDARY,409
. CLOE,191;DANIEL,12
. E W R R,113;EDMUND H
. 395;GEORGE,191-192
. 395;HUMPHREY,191
. JAMES,163;JOHN,307
. JOSEPH,251;LEWIS,336
. 378;PERRY,191;R R,126
. RUFUS R,97;THOMAS,191
. THOMAS S,145;WILLIAM
. M,82
GRAY,1,170;A,250,259
. 278,280;A T,336
. ALBERT,244,249,256

. 263-264,275,279,281
. 286;ANDREW,87
. ARCHIBALD,251;BARBARY
. 51;BAZIL,30;BETSEY,36
. BUCKNER,10;EDMUND,30
. ELIZABETH,131;EMILY
. 45;EMOND,8;FRANCIS
. 319,329;GEO,310
. GEORGE,309;GIBSON,30
. GO,329;HEZEKIAH,2
. ISHAM,205;J A,131
. JAMES,4-5,131,300
. JANNIE L,39;JOHN,5-7
. 30,167,185,293,304
. 319,329;JOHNSON A,131
. JOSEPHINE,261
. JOSEPHINE L,37;JOSHUA
. 8,10,49,53;KEZIAH,4
. MENCHES,6;MINCHA,30
. MINCHEY,49;MINTHE,53
. MORTON,294,304;NELLIE
. 206;PORTUS,39;RACHEL
. 131;ROBERT R,53;S O
. 47;THOMAS,97,320
. VIRGINIA M,41
. WILLIAIM,53;WILLIAM,9
. 30,97,131;WM W,395
GRAYBILL,325;HARDIMAN
. 124;HEN,219,317-318
. HENRY,290,320,349
. MARY,349
GRAYTON,JOHN,60
GREAR,JOHN,310
GREE,JASON,82
GREEN,ABRAM,30;ABRM,7
. AMANDA,386;AMORETTE
. 255;ANN H G,251;AVY
. 205;BARTLET C,395
. BENJAMIN,1,12,48
. CAMILIA,382;DANIEL,19
. 48,196,213;DANIEL A
. 205;DANL,9;DAVID,10
. DAVID E,30,51;E L,205
. ELISHA,19;ELIVIRA,44
. ELIZA C,395;ELIZABETH
. 255;ELIZABETH E,51
. ELIZABETH PRISSILLA
. 200;EMILY,211;EMPSY
. ANN,397;FELIX,205
. FURNIFOLD,395;GEO
. PETER,395;HENRY,303
. 309;HETY,197;ISAAC N
. 253;ISABELLA B,409
. JAMES T,395;JASON,105
. JENSEY,394;JENSY,416
. JESSE P,40,51,53;JOHN
. 3,5,40;JOHN C,395;JOS
. 305;LAURA,38,203
. LEMUEL,235,238,355
. LEWIS,19;LUCINDA,47
. LUCY A G,248;LUTHIA
. ANNE,417;M,321;MARTHA
. 392;MARTHA P,207;MARY
. 208;MARY ANN,421
. MATILDA,202;MULES,290
. MYLES,295,305,311,320
. 321,323;NANCY,278
. PARTHENA,385;PLEASANT
. 88,336;R T,124
. RALEIGH,242;REBECCA
. 421;RILEY,40;SAM,40
. SAMUEL,213;SARAH W
. 401;SCILLA,41
. SUSANNAH,39;THOMAS
. 205;TOBY,40;VINA,208
. W B,395;W D,30;WARREN
. 11-12,30;WILLIAM,5,53
. 205,336;WINFOREE,211

. WM,1;WM G,395;WM H
. 313
GREENAWAY,MARGARET,199
. 209;SAML,10;WM,7
GREENE,ALEXANDER,328
. ALSTON T,355;ARGUSTUS
. F,253;AUGUSTEN,395
. AUGUSTINE,281-282
. BENJ,5;BENJAMIN F,253
. BETSY,374;BURWELL,336
. 364;ELIZA,421
. ELIZABETH,241;EMILY
. 240;EVELINA A,258
. FARNAFALD,253;HARRIET
. R,400;HARRIETT A,238
. HENRY,299,310;JAMES
. 291;JAMES H,253;JAS
. 329;JOHN,253,395
. JOSEPH,253;LEMUEL,240
. 249,253,259,263,269
. 272,280;LEMUEL H,253
. M,292,303,319;MARY A
. 279;MYLES,291,295,300
. 302,305,316-317,319
. 324,328-329;NANCY,384
. NANCY F,286;NATHANIEL
. 395;RAWLEIGH,296
. REBECCA,280;RIVANAH
. 385;S M,386;SUSAN
. AMORETTE,253;TERZA
. 261;THOS,322;WALTER
. 253;WILLIAM B,51;WM
. 253
GREENVILLE,PAMELIA E
    403
GREENWAY,BERRYAN,196
. CELIA,382;JOHN,50
. LUCRETIA,30;SAMUEL,50
. 395;SUSAN FRANCES,405
. WILLIAM,30,50
GREENWOOD,176;BENJAMIN
. L,395;CAROLINE,261
. ELIZ H,412;HENRY,395
. HENRY D,395;LUCIA,403
. MARTHA R T,410;THOMAS
. 253,369;THOMAS E,253
GREER,217-218;AARON,336
. ABRAHAM,336;ALLATHA
. 238;AQUILA,253
. AQUILLA,253;ARCHIBALD
. 253;CRAWFORD H,336
. D L,253;DAVID,135-136
. 137,148,253;ELIZABETH
. 148,238,253;ELIZABETH
. L,148;ELLA,254;EMILY
. 275;EVALINE C,238
. FRANCES G,247;HATTIE
. 336;HENRY,253;HENRY F
. 253;HENRY H,253;ISAAC
. 253;J,100;JAMES,248
. 253;JANE,148;JASON,90
. 98,108,137,144,147
. JEAN,250;JEFFERSON
. 336;JIMMY,239;JOHN,90
. 104,107-108,113,116
. 120,132,135-137,139
. 141-143,149,218,220
. 253,309;JOHN R,336
. JOHN S,148;JOHN W G
. 238;JOHNSTON,148
. JUDSON,102;LUCY,253
. LYDIA L,286;MARY,148
. MARY ANN,285;NANCY
. 148,258,280,286;NANCY
. L,135;PATSEY,262
. PRISCILLA,259;RICHARD
. 253;ROBERT,253;ROBERT
. S,336;SALLIE M,248

GREER(cont)
. SAMUEL,148;SARAH,220
. 253,257;SARAH ANN,148
. 267;SOPHIA,277
. SUSANNAH,282;THOMAS
. 342,395;THOMAS G,253
. THOMAS H,148;THOMAS L
. 253,336;URIAH,225
. VINSO,216;WILLIAM,147
. 217,219-221,253;WM
. 215-216,222,226,228
. 230-232,236,254,266
. 267,269,272,274,277
GREESON,P C,100
GREEY,M,329
GREGEOREY,SAML,17
GREGNOREY,SAML,15
GREGORY,ARTHUR,349;BENJ
. F,253;CAROLINE M,280
. CATHARINE,202;FRANCIS
. 395;HARDY,30;J K,342
. JAMES,185;JOHN,9,47
. 319,395;JOHN R,309
. LEWIS,332,336;MARTHA
. 30;MARY,349;MATTHEW
. 336;NANCY,53,250;SAML
. 14,17;SAMUEL,18;SARAH
. 381;SARAH H,42
. WILLIAM,140,144;WM
. 149
GREINER,J P,395;JOHN L
. 395
GRENWAY,SAMUEL,214
GRESHAM,92,94,101,221;A
. 225,228-229,247,263
. 264,275,281;ALBERT
. 253;ALBERT W,253
. ARCHERBALD,226;DAVID
. 230;DAVIS,222,226-227
. 230,234;EDMUND B,395
. EDWARD,53;ENSIGN JOB
. 8;FRANCES,274,282
. J JONES,40;JOB,30
. JOHN,4,54;JOHN H,253
. LAURA,274;LITTLE B
. 233-234;MARCALINE A
. 237;MARY E,263,272
. MARY J,40;MILLY,259
. STERLING A,253;T J,88
. THOMAS J,88,90
. WILLIAM,68;YOUNG
. FELIX,253
GREVOR,JOHN,299
GREYER,GEORGE,289
GRICE,JOHN,8
GRIER,A S,128;AARON,357
. AARON W,336;JOHN W
. 243;LETITIA,247;LUCY
. ANN,286;MARY,259;R
. 100;ROBERT,80,128,233
. 357;SARAH,245;THOMAS
. 332;WM,226
GRIEVE,91
GRIFF,R F,251,269
GRIFFEN,JAMES,266;JAMES
. M,280;JANE,271;NANCEY
. 262;R F,265,270,282
. 283-284;ROBERT I,283
. ROBT F,286
GRIFFETH,JOHN T,313
GRIFFEY,JOHN,253
GRIFFI,R F,278
GRIFFIN,AARON,54;ANDREW
. B,60;ANDREW J,253
. AVEY,39;B F,251
. BENJAMIN E,205
. BENJAMIN F,40;DEMPSEY
. 52;DEWEY,40;ELIZ,393

. ELIZABETH,54;GEORGE,8
. 51;HENRY,395;ISAAC,54
. ISHAM,153;JAMES,2,54
. 212,395;JAMES M,269
. JEFFERSON L,40
. JEREMIAH,190;JNO,7
. JOB,7;JOE,40;JOHN,30
. 153;JOHN A,253;JOHN C
. 395;JOSEPH,54;LAMIRA
. L,45;LUCRETIA,419
. MARY,30,50,52,257
. MATTHEW,253;MOSES,51
. 54;NANCY,272;NANCY H
. 422;NOAH,30;PATTY,307
. POLLY,385;R F,236-237
. 240,245,262,273;R G
. 275;RICHARD,64;ROBERT
. 253;ROBERT A,82,90
. ROBERT F,249,251,263
. 270;ROBERT T,258
. ROLAND,153;ROYAL,40
. SARAH,30,45,52,206
. SARAH E,41;STEPHEN,50
. T W,54,205;THOMAS,362
. THOMAS W,52;WALTER
. 253;WILEY B,395
. WILLIAM,10,54
GRIFFIS,AMERICA,203
. CASANDA,207;EMILLIA
. 197;FRANCIS,322;MARY
. 198;WILLIAM S,205
GRIFFITH,JEDEKIAH,253
. MORGAN,340;NATHAN,253
. THOMAS,253;WILLIAM,60
. WM P,253;WM V,253
GRIFFITY,CHRISTIAN,210
GRIFFORN,LEAR,403
GRIGG,JESSE,291,302
GRIGGS,JOHN,291,302
. JOHN T,336;MARY ANN
. 240;WILLIAM,300,308
GRIGSBY,BETSY ANN,235
. WILLIAM,216
GRIMES,AMANDA,265
. CHARITY N,276;DANIEL
. 196;ELIZABETH,204,251
. ELIZABETH C,238;HENRY
. 253;I M,286;I M,286
. JAMES,253;JEREMIAH
. 213;JESSE,253;JOHN
. 313;JOSEPH,253;LUKY
. 268;MALIDDA,210
. MARTHA INORANS,263
. MARTHA JANE,264;MARY
. 243;MARY JANE,281;R M
. 253;ROBERT M,253;RUTH
. 248;SARAH J,42
. STERLING F,253;SYDNEY
. 235;T W,237-238,254
. 287;THOMAS,222,253
. 272,276,279;THOMAS W
. 253,260,264,276,280
. 281,286;THOS W,235-236
. 240,245,259;WILLIAM
. 205;WM P,253
GRIMES?,THOS W,266
GRIMKE,C,89
GRIMMET,A J,95,119,132
. A L,105;ALFRED J,141
. 142;ELIZABETH,119,127
. 132;J H,127;JACKSON
. 128;JAMES H,127,132
. MARY,119,132;ROBERT
. 95,105,119,127,132
. T L,119;THOMAS,128
. THOMAS L,119,132
. WILLIAM,127,132
. WILLIAM M,105

GRIMMETT,A J,117;J H
. 117;JAMES T,336
. ROBERT,108,117,253
. SARAH E,336;THOMAS L
. 117;WILLIAM,336
. WILLIAM E,117
GRIMMIT,J H,133
GRIMMITT,A J,108
. ELIZABETH,108;J H,108
. JAMES H,108;MARY,108
. ROBERT,108;T L,108
. THOMAS L,108;WILLIAM
. 108
GRIMSLEY,HESTER,405
. RICHARD,292
GRIMSLY,ELISA,383
GRINAGE,JOSHUA,172
GRINAWAY,MARTHA,384
GRINER,JOHN,351
GRINEWAY,JAMES,54
. WILLIAM,54
GRINGES,175
GRINKLE,G,106
GRINNAGE,LETTISHE,395
GRINNELL,BENJAMIN,336
. CHARLES,336
GRINOLD,SARAH A,413
GRISBY,BEHEATHALON,277
GRISHAM,A,225-226;DAVID
. 226;DAVIS,378
GRITMAN,JOHN,216
GRIVE,140
GRIZARD,JOSEPH,323
GROOM,THOMAS,196
GROSS,EDWARD,196;JOHN
. 336;SOLOMON,345
GROTHE,RICHARD W,395
GROUGHTON,GENETTE,280
GROVES,SYLVANUS B,395
GRUBBS,ADALAID,38
. DANIEL G,40;ELISHA C
. 336;HENRIETTA,386
. JAMES,12,40,48,54
. JOAB,395;JOHN,48,54
. JULIA,412;LEVENA,202
. MARTHA,262;MARY J,41
. THOMAS,30,395;WILEY B
. 336;WILLIAM,54;ZURIAH
. 390
GRUBS,THOMAS,9
GRUDER,JOHN M,12
GRUMBELS,GEORGE,324
GRUMBLES,GEORGE,51
. GEORGE W,395;JOHN S
. 51,54;WILLIAM,395
GRUNBIE,ELIZABETH,321
GRUSON,S T,100
GUANN,JACOB,358
GUAY,CHARLTON,205;SUSAN
. J,206
GUEDRON,MARY A,391
GUEMERIN,FELICITY M,411
GUEN,SARAH,54;WILLIAM
. 54
GUENEBAULT,
. JOSEPH HENRY,395
GUERY,SAMUEL,319
GUEST,ADAM,177;ANN,38
. BENJ,7;BENJAMIN,30
. E B,30;JOSEPH J,395
. SARAH,51
GUIDRAT,EMILY F,413
GUILDER,GUILFORD,86
GUILL,WM B,253
GUIMARIN,CAMILLE,395
GUINN,FRANKLIN,336
. POLLY,276
GUIRM,JAMES,2

HAMMEL,G A,336
HAMMER,M,302
HAMMET,ELIZ,398
HAMMETT,JAMES,254,360
. WALTER,205;WILLIAM
. 352-353,355
HAMMILL,ABSALOM,351
HAMMOCK,DAVID,2
. WILLOUGHBY,364
HAMMON,CHARLES,87;NANCY
. 87;WILLIAM JAMES,87
HAMMOND,A L,142;ABNER
. 145-146;CARRIE,41
. CHARLES,101,108,118
. 124,126,133,141,148
. 396;DANIEL,22;DANL,21
. ELIJAH,147;ELIZ,385
. 396;ELIZABETH,268
. JAMES,396;MARTIN,288
. MARY ANN,380;NANCY
. 124,244;REBECCA,379
. ROBERT,254;SARAH,401
. SUSANNAH,288;WILLIAM
. J,108,118,126,133,141
. 148;WM,254;WM B,396
HAMMONDS,ANN,388;SARAH
. C,247
HAMMONS,SARAH,286
HAMOND,SUSANNAH,288
HAMPTON,H,165,215;HENRY
. 154;JAMES,26-27,30,49
. 54;JOHN,26-27,73
. REASON,214;SALLY,49
. SIMEON,30,49;SIMON,54
. THOMAS,8,30,67,73
. VIRGINIA,36;WILLIAM E
. 57
HANBERG,SOLOMON,40
HANBERRY,A,54;HESEKIAH
. 205;JOHN,15
HANBURY,E,207
HANCOCK,CHARLOTTE,270
. ELIZABETH,246;GEORGE
. 254;GEORGE P,254
. HENRY L,254;HENRY W
. 254;JAMES,12;JAMES A
. 254;JANE,408;JOSEPH
. 51;NERO,30,50;SAMUEL
. 83,143;SARAH J,277
. THOMAS,63;W,87
. WILLIAM,88,121,336
HAND,86;ABERAHAM,173
. GENTRY,87;H H,18
. H HENRY,20;HENRY,155
. 168,173;ISAAC,366
. JOHN,51,168,173;JOHN
. J,30,54;MARGARET,173
. MARY,173;REBEA,173
. RICHARD,254;ROBERT
. 168,173;RODY,173;SARAH
. 168,173;THOMAS,173
. WILLIAM,155,173
HANDBERRY,JAMES,205
. JOHN,7;SARAH JANE,37
HANDBURG,ISRAEL,30
HANDBURY,JNO,14;JOHN,2
. LUCKY,205;SOLOMON,205
HANDCOCK,JOSEPH,396
HANDEE,HOMER,286
HANDLEY,THOMAS,24
HANDLY,GEORGE,215
HANDS,RICHARD,353
HANES,CHARLES,176;JAMES
. 370;WM,83
HANEY,ARIMITTA,411;AVEY
. 399;SARAH,406
HANKERSON,EASTER,45
. MARTHA,38;WM,58

HANKINSON,ANN S,409
HANLEY,W J,251
HANNAH,JOHN,9,30
HANNIBEL,17
HANNON,BARTON,216;ELIZA
. 388;JOHN,194
HANSEN,396
HANSFORD,JAMES,89
HANSON,EDMUND,368;ELIZA
. 161;ELIZABETH,369
. JAMES B,118;JAS B,110
. NANCY,368;PEGGY,180
. THOMAS,396;WILLIAM
. 368
HARALSON,BRADDY B,254
. EUNICE,240;HUGH,254
. JESSE B,254;KINCHIN L
. 254;VINCENT,254
HARBEY,217
HARBIN,JAMES T,254
HARBIRG,JOHN,304
HARBIRT,ALICE WRIGHT
. 293;GEORGE,293;HARDY
. 293;JOHN,288,290,293
. 302-304,309;THOMAS
. 290,293
HARBIT,JOHN,305
HARD,CORDELIA E,276;W M
. I,251;WM J,396
HARDAGE,WILLIAM,309,329
HARDAMAN,BENJAMIN J,95
. J,86
HARDEMAN,MARITA ANNE
. 282
HARDEN,B A,100;EDWARD J
. 12;HENRY,254;PATSEY
. 179;REBEKAH,250
. THOMAS M,12;WILLIAM
. 90
HARDEYS,PELEE,257
HARDIMAN,JOHN,79
HARDIN,EDWARD J,396
. HENRY,82,88;ISAAC B
. 30;JAMES,254;JOEL,100
. JOHN,365;JOHN S,336
. SILAS M,336;WILLIAM
. 101
HARDMAN,ALPHONSO,332
. ALPHONZO,336;JOHN,372
HARDRICH,ANDREW,9
. PHILIP,9
HARDWICK,ANDREW,30
. CHARITY,332;G,346,348
. 356;GARLAND,293
. GEORGE,190;HANNAH,54
. HENRY,54;JAMES,254
. JULIA C,405;LOUISA
. VIRGINIA,399;PLEASANT
. 234;THOMAS,312;W,305
. W H,313;WILLIAM,289
. 290,322,336;WM,288
HARDY,BENAJAH,336
. CORNELIUS,336;E,98
. ELBERT,95,98;J,118
. JOSIAH,86,91,95,102
. 106;W J,254;WILLIAM
. 91,139;WILLIAM P,336
HARE,114,197
HAREL,EDWARD,205
HARELL,MILLY,345
HARG---,ALEX,254
HARGERTY,ABEL,233
HARGRAVES,GEORGE,302
HARGROOVER,SANFORD,254
HARGROVE,
. ELIZA MILDRED,387
. HARRIET EVELINE,381
. HENRY,50;JACOB,30,50

. JOANNA M,37;MARY A
. 278;NANCY,209;NANCY A
. 36;SELTY,401;SUSAN E
. 37;WILLIAM H,357
HARGROVES,DUDLEY,317
. 321;LOUISA,403
HARISS,ISABEL,354
HARKINS,AMANDA,386
. JAMES,396;ROGER,396
. THOS,357
HARKNESS,HARRIET,135;J
. 100,105;J B,119;JAMES
. 82,90,93,107,111,113
. 119,141;JAMES W,114
. 121,136-137,149;JAS
. 100;JOHN,141;JOHN B
. 130,139;R W,76,80,100
. 105,107,113;ROBERT,71
. 127;ROBERT W,59,62,64
. 70,72,79,81,128-129
. 139;THOMAS,113;THOMAS
. B,138;THOMAS M,90,149
. THOS,144;THOS M,136
. 143,149;W,100;W S B
. 93,100,107,147,149
. WILLIAM,90,113
HARLBERT,ROSWELL,254
HARLEY,ELLEN J,39
HARLOW,JAMES B,254
. REBECCA,54;SOUTHWORTH
. 30
HARMON,CHARLES,396;HETE
. 256;ISAAC,396;JOSEPH
. 69;MATTHEW,396;TIPPOO
. S,396;WILLIAM,114
HARN,JOHN B,396
HAROLD,ELIJAH,54
HARP,A,277;DIXON,288
. ELIZABETH,286;IONE
. 253;MILLY,283;POLLY
. 272;SAMUEL,254
. WILLIAM,254
HARPER,ALLEN,254
. AVARILLA,280;AXAMINS
. 254;B,329;B H,132
. CATHARINE MATILDA,420
. DARCAS,354;EMALIZA L
. 237;EVERET,354
. FRANCES,246;GEORGE A
. 254;H,149;HENRY,40
. JANE L,249;JOHN,216
. JOSEPH,328;JULIA NN
. 248;LENORA,243;LUCY
. ANN,280;MARGARET,242
. MARIA,273;MARTHA,410
. MARY,216,404;MARY D
. 260;POLLY,239,279;R J
. 143;RICHARD,76;ROBERT
. 216,290;ROBERT A,396
. RUTH,236;SALLY,260
. SAML,231,234-235
. SAMUEL,249;SARAH,253
. SOLOMON,396;WILLIAM
. 80-81,84,91-92,94,107
. 363;WM,291,396
HARRAL,JAMES,336
HARREL,CYNTHIA,45;LAURA
. 210
HARRELL,ELIJA,8;ELISHA
. 2,50;ELIZABETH,92
. JOHN D,40;P O,54
. REBEKAH,272;THOMAS,50
. 54,396;WM,103
. ZACHARIAH,345
HARRELSON,ELIZABETH,284
. HUGH A,84
HARREN,JAMES H,254
HARRIEL,HUGH,358

HARRIGAN,SARAH,406
HARRIGIL,JOSEPH,396
HARRILL,SAMUEL,341
HARRINGTON,MARTIN,54
HARRIOD,EADY,404
HARRIS,279,359;ABSALOM
. 291,311,321;ADALINE M
. 282;ALEX T,396;ALICE
. J,245;AUGUSTIN,227;B
. 341;BENJAMIN,30,254
. 321;BENNET,396
. BUCKNER,216;CATY,373
. CHARLES,254;CHARLES F
. 254;D,160;DAVID,160
. 336;DINAH,236;EDWARD
. 160;ELI,304-305,317
. 328;ELIGAH,396;ELIOS
. 254;ELISHA,219;ELIZ
. 398,400;ELIZA D,387
. ELIZA R,321;ELIZABETH
. 284,398;EMALINE,239
. EMALLINE,239;EMILY
. 246;EUGANIA,417
. EZEKIEL,353;FLORENCE
. M,45;FRANCES,246
. FRANKLIN,40;GEORGE H
. 54;GIDEON,30;GRAVES
. 369;HENRY,106,311,321
. HENRY C,254;ISABEL
. 354;ISHAM,336;J P,255
. JAMES,151,254-255
. JANE,270,389;JANE
. AMANDA,284;JANE E,244
. JAS,2;JEREMIAH,396
. JESSE,255;JNO,241
. JOHN,72,82,160-161
. 235,237-238,244,254
. 255,258,262-263,265
. 266,268,272-275,277
. 278,281-284,287,336
. 343;JOHN M,255;JOHN N
. 269;JOHN T,50,255
. JOHN W,97,264;JOSEPH
. 222,225,227;LA
. FAYETTE,40;LAIRD M
. 396;LAURA,210;LIVEY
. 37;LOUISA RA----,255
. LOUISA V,391
. LUCY ELIZABETH S--Y--
. 255;LUKE,205;MARGARET
. 399;MARIAL,268;MARTHA
. 260,281;MARY,44,63
. 160,248,283,336,392
. 394,422;MARY ANN,54
. MARY E,259;MARY JANE
. 286;MATILDA,271
. MATTIE J,265;MICHAEL
. 396;MORREN,405;MYLES
. G,255;N H,263;NANCEY
. 256;NANCY,247,341,390
. NANCY R,279;NARCISA
. 275;NAT,263,275
. NATHANIEL N,255
. NATHANL,10;PATIENCE
. 259;PATSEY,270;POLLEY
. 321;POLLY,160,276,321
. RACHEL,391,396;ROBERT
. 158,255;ROBERT L,255
. RUTH,381;S B,255
. SALLY,325;SAMUEL,317
. 326;SEABORN,255
. SINGLETON,255;T,108
. T W,343-344
. TEMPERANCE,277;THOMAS
. 324,350;THOMAS MCCALL
. 255;THOMAS W,347,353
. 358,360;W,364;WALTON
. 216;WASHINGTON G,396

. WEST,271;WILIE,341
. WILLIAM,91,156,326;WM
. 141,255;WM L,255
. YOUNG R,82,90
HARRISON,145;B,98;BEN
. 100,113;BENJ,82
. BENJAMIN,82,88,90,97
. 114,255;BETTY,184
. DAVIS,229;DICK,184
. DICK FRANKLIN,184
. DINWIDDIE,184
. ELIZABETH,99,143,283
. 399;EPTHPATHA,336
. GADWELL REINES,184
. GIDEON,222,231;HENRY
. 336;HENSON,253;J,105
. JAMES,64,84,94,99,143
. 184,255;JANE W,255
. JNO,227;JOHN,234;JOHN
. P,40;LIZA,260
. MARGARET J,4;MARY,255
. 266;MAT RICHARD
. TYRREL,184;MONT,314
. PERRYMAN NUPLICRD,184
. RICHARD,184;ROBERT
. 255;SAMUEL,396;SARAH
. 385;SEABORN,52
. SULLIVAN,184;TERREL
. COOK,184;THOMAS,99
. THOS,143;TYRREL COOK
. 184;WILLIAM,84,94,99
. WM,143,396
HARRISS,GRAVES,374
. JOSEPH,233;JURIAH,180
. SAMUEL,222
HARROD,309
HARROWAY,JUDITH,244
HARRUP,JAMES,255;MANING
. 291;RIDLEY,255;WARREN
. 255
HART,276;AMOS,197;BERRY
. 205;GEORGIANNA A,257
. HARDY,65;HENRY,205
. ISAAC,255;JAMES B,396
. JESSE,197;JOHN S,255
. JOSEPH,197;MARSHALL
. 212;REBECCA,398;SAML
. 298;SAMUEL,298;SARAH
. JANE,206;THOMAS,7,30
. 255;W P,312;WATKINS,9
. WM,396;WM M,255;WM R
. 396
HARTES,MARY S,273
HARTFORD,ELIZA O,387
. JOSHUA B,396
HARTLEY,JOSEPH,300
. ROBERT,300
HARTON,321
HARTRIDGE,EMMA L,402
. JOHN EARL,396;LEAR A
. 397
HARTSFIELD,91;G,101
. GODFREY M,82
. MIDDLETON,82,88,332
. 336
HARVARD,STEPHEN,7
HARVELL,DANIEL,255
HARVEY,BLAS,2
. BLASINGAME,3;BLASS,12
. CALEB P,12;CATHARINE
. 410;CATHERINE,382
. CHARLES,1;ELIAS,1
. ELIZ,418;ELIZABETH,49
. EVAN,297;EVANS,364
. GALPHIN B,12;GERMAN
. 396;JAMES,3,297,306
. 317,325;JAS,1,218-219
. 297;JOHN,297,396;JOHN

. N,284;MICHAEL,358
. NANCY,268,327;RHODA
. 387;SARAH ANN,400
. WILLIAM,364;ZEPHENIAH
. 336
HARVILL,THOMAS,255
HARVY,BLASSINGAME,30
. G B,30;WINEFRED,415
HARWELL,358;ABSALOM,30
. ANDERSON,291-292
. HOLLY,259;JAMES M,255
. MASON,336;MILLY,345
. WM,255
HARWILL,RANSOM,297
. SAMUEL,364
HARWOOD,JOHN,396
HASE,HAMILTON,101
HASLIP,JONAS,48;LOTT W
. 48;R G,349
HASMER,DAVID,9
HASSEL,ADDISON,396
HASSELL,SARAH JANE,382
HASSELTON,WALTER,317
HASTY,WILLIS,47,54
HATCH,J D,43;MILO,396
HATCHER,ARCHIBALD,396
. BERRY,40;CHARLOTA,46
. EDWARD,8,12,30,40,51
. 54,307;ELIZ A,401
. ELLINGTON,57;EMILY C
. 395;FANNY,46;HENRY
. 396;JOHN,358,396;JOHN
. G,396;JONES,396
. JOSIAH,30;LEONIDAS B
. 40;MATILDA,397;N J,40
. NANCY,381;OBEDIENCE
. 417;PEGGY,399;SARAH
. 51,388;SUSANNAH,405
. THOMAS,8;URIAH,336
. WILLIAM,54,62
HATCHETT,JOHN,255,280
HATELY,H,96;HENRY,59-60
. 63-64,69-70,72-73,77
HATEN,SUSANNA,421
HATFIELD,CALEB S,396
. MARY JANE,407
HATLEY,HENRY,64;SARAH
. 409
HATTEY,HANNAH,386
HATTON,THOMAS,255
HAUBERRY,JANE,211
HAUPT,PHILIP,396
HAUSER,GEORGE,396
HAVENS,ANDREW,79
HAW,AARON,21,23
HAWES,SAMUEL,397;SARAH
. 30
HAWK,HENRY,332;SEABORN
. J,336
HAWKE,JOHN,255;PETER
. 255
HAWKINS,299;ABIMALEK
. 397;BETSEY,378;GEO S
. 397;GILLY,238;HARDY
. 305;J F,314;JOHN W
. 336;MATTHEW,304;R R
. 397;SARAH,399;WILLIS
. A,378
HAWL,WINNEFRED,196
HAWORTH,ABSALOM,397
HAWS,JOSEPH W,40
HAWTHRON,EDWD,234
HAY,EDMOND,336;HARDY,9
. 30;JAEMS,10;STEPHEN
. 336;WASHINGTON,336
. WILLIAM T,336
HAYAT,WASHINGTON,85
HAYDEN,LAWRENCE,397

HAYES,A,260;ADAM,216
. 220;EZEKIAL,255
. HARRIOT,394;JAMES,10
. JON,205;PATRICK,220
. 221,291;RICHARD,30
. ROBERT,255;WM,255
HAYGOOD,AARON,77;EDWIN
A,397
HAYLES,ELIZABETH,383
HAYLEY,JAMES,14
HAYMAN,ELISHA,40
. EVERETT,40;STEPHEN,30
. WILLIAM,30
HAYMON,CLAY,54;JAMES,54
SARAH,54
HAYMOND,ELISHA,50
STEPHEN,50
HAYMONS,WILLIAM,7
HAYNE,EDWARD,40;JAMES B
40
HAYNES,D S,312;DELILAH
. 253;FRANCIS,397;HENRY
. 361;JASPER,255;JIMMY
. 257;JOHN,255;MARY,384
. MARY S,236;MOSES P,90
. NANCY,266;PARMEN,255
. PEGGA JANE BELLAH,376
. PEGGY,256;PHELPS,361
. REBECCA,361;ROBERT
. 255;SALLY,272;SARAH
. ANN,281;TEMPEY BELLAH
. 376;WILLIAM,376;Y,113
HAYNIE,EMELENT P,397
. JAMES D,397;PAMELLA
. ANN,381
HAYS,A,262;ADAM,257,286
. DELILA,205;GARRY,205
. 214;GARY,197;HARRIETT
. 205;HIRAM,345;HOWARD
. 255;JAMES,205;JANE
. 287;MARGARET,241
. MARSHALL,205;MARY H
. 203;PEGGY,266;PHERABA
. 203;RACHEL,196
. REBECCA,336;THOMAS
. 397;WASHINGTON,94;WM
. 255
HAYSLIP,ELIJAH,54;JAMES
. 54;JOHN,30,54;KENDAL
. C,30;LOTT,54;SUSANNAH
. 30
HAYTLY,HENRY,69
HAYWOOD,LUKE,40;WM,397
HAZEL,JOHN,255
HAZLEHURST,CARRIE C,47
HAZLETT,WILSON,255
HEAD,EDMUND,91,101
. ELIZA,280;G M,108
. GEORGE M,86,128;JAMES
. 366,371;MARGARET,375
. MARY,255;POLLY,255
. RICHARD,353;SUSAN L
. 255;W J,98;WILLIAM B
. 83;WILLIAM J,144,146
. WILLIAM P,99;WILLIAM
. R,99,111,119;WM,358
HEADSPETH,ANN,387
HEAGERTY,WILIAM,233
HEAIL,JOHN,86
HEARD,87,113;A,228
. ABRAHAM,223-224,228
. BARNARD,226;BARNEY
. 227;CATHERINE,271
. CHARLES,67;CLEM
. FREENA,255;COLUMBUS
. 247;EDMUND,397
. ELIZABETH,271,280
. EPHRAIM,372;FRANKLIN

. 255;FRANKLIN C,78;GEO
. 240,257,284;GEORGE,67
. 271;HUGH,141;HUGH H
. 117;ISAAC T,397;JAMES
. 364;JAMES T,255;JANE
. 269;JAS,345;JESSE,228
. JOHN,67,223,225-226
. 228,255;JOHN T,255
. JOHN W,397;JON,257
. JOS,341,356,368
. JOSEPH,365,372;JULIA
. 262;JULIA F,269
. MAGGIE,269;MARTH A
. 281;NANCY,286;OLIVIA
. 263;SAMUEL,351;SARAH
. 260;SOPHRONIA A,258
. STEPHEN,218,224
. STEPHEN I,255;SUSANNA
. 236;THOMAS,215,223
. 255;THOMAS N,397;W T
. 255;WILLIAM,224;WM I
. 249;WOODROW,255
HEARN,119;ELIJAH,293
. 309;JOHN,305;WILLIAM
. 361;WM T,255
HEARNE,GEORGE,358;SELBY
345;WM,215,345
HEARST,WILLIAM,64
HEART,MARY,258;SAL,204
HEARTON,SUSAN,415
HEATH,ABRAM,8;CAROLINE
. A,267;CHAPEL,311
. CHAPPELL,311;COLSON
. 303,306;D,116;DAWSON
. 84-85,90,101,105,111
. 131;DRUCILLA,30
. ELIZABETH,197
. ELIZABETH A,45;GEORGE
. W,40;HENRY,30,52,54
. HOMER V,40;ISAAC J,54
. JAMES,30,51,54;JIM,40
. JOHN,54;JORDAN,30,51
. 52,54;JUDSON L,40
. JULUIS V,40;JUSTIN B
. 40;LAURIA,38;LEVINA
. 393;LEWIS,10;LOUISA
. 52;LOUISA C,45;LUCY E
. 247;MARY,200;MATTHEW
. 255;MOSES,51,54
. PETERSON,312;RADASKEY
. 44;RICHARD,30,336
. RIGDON,49,54;ROYSTER
. 397;RYLAN,255;SAMUEL
. 8,30;SAMUEL J,40
. SAMUEL L,40;SUSAN M
. 266;THOMAS,303,341
. WASHINGTON,40;WILLIE
. 383
HEATHERINGTON,MARTHA,2
HECK,THOMAS,255
HECKEL,JOHN,197
HECKLE,HENRY B,397;JOHN
. 397;SUSAN,385;THOMS
. 397
HEDGE,WHITFIELD,255
HEDGES,ENOCH,215
HEERRY,ELLEN,386
HEERY,CATHARINE,397
HEFLIN,JAMES,256;JOSHUA
70
HEGGS,JESSE,22
HEGINBOTHAM,JOSEPH,308
HEISLAR,SAMUEL,30,48
HEIST,E,275
HELLAMER,BENNETT,283
HELMLEY,ROSALINE E,39
HELTON,J T,205
HEMBREE,HOMER,237

HEMPHILL,ALEXANDER,397
. HIRAM,256;MARCUS,377
. MARK,373;NANCY,244;S
. 357;SAMUEL,375;THOMAS
. 154;THOMPSON,256;WM
. 256
HEND----,HOMER,249
HENDEE,HOMER,248
HENDEL,HOMER,256
HENDER,JOHN,256
HENDERICKS,JULIA A F
266
HENDERSON,233;CHARLES
. 332,336:D,327;DAVID
. 363;FRANKIE,336
. GEORGE,30;GEORGE E,52
. GREENVILL,374;HELEN S
. 388;ISAAC W,336;JACOB
. 131;JAMES,4,10,96,332
. 336;JANE L,336;JOEPH
. 397;JOHN,298,300,336
. JOSEPH,256,336;NANCY
. 374;NOBBY,54;ROBERT
. 397;ROSY,421;SABRA,58
. SAMUEL,233,332,336
. 340,345,356;W N,40
. WILLIAM,54,336
. WILLIAM WESLEY,85
HENDLEY,ABRAHAM,213
. JANE,211;JOHN,213
. RIGHT,213;THOMAS,20
. 22
HENDON,HATTIE M,247
. JOHNSTON,351;ROBINSON
. 351
HENDREY,MARY E,276
HENDRICK,85,90,92,96,98
. 102,105-106,114
. ABSOLEM,350;ALEX,2
. ALFRED,110;BENJ F,397
. G,92,104,118,127-128
. 131,136-139;GUSTAVUS
. 62,68,90,116,122-123
. GUSTUVAS,92;ISAAC,85
. ISABELLA,408;JAMES
. 256;JOHN,58,63,65,68
. 70-72,75,77,79-81,84
. 86,92,95,110,113,117
. 119-120,126,133,136
. 139,359,362;LEMUEL B
. 397;M D,90;MARTIN D
. 93;MASTIN,146
. NATHANIEL,291;ROBERT
. 290;ROBT,303;SAMUEL
. 89
HENDRICKS,FRANCES,259
. LOUISA,270;LUCIENDA
. 248;WILEY,205
HENDRIX,JOHN,19-20,126
. MARIDA,205;ROBERY,205
. WILLIAM,197
HENDRY,ANNA L J,278;C M
256;J W,205
HENER,ADAM,8;GRO,6
HENERY,CHAS,2
HENIOR,JOHN,30;MARY,30
HENLEY,JOHN;397;NANCY
281
HENLY,ABIJAH,336;SALLY
277
HENNING,JOHN,12
HENRY,320,325;BARNEY
. 397;BENJAMIN,325;DAV
. 306;DAVID,305;DEXTER
. 397;J T,206;JOHN,320
. 397;JOHN W,397;JOSEPH
. 297;LAURA,206;ROSE
. ANN,417;STEPHEN,306

HENRY(cont)
. THOMAS WYTT,256
. WALTER,397;WILLIAM P
. 59;WM,86
HENSON,LOUDEN,256;SUT
40;THOMAS,296
HERALD,W R,206
HERBAY,JOHN,12
HERBERT,FRANCES,413
. ISAAC,174;SARAH,403
. WILLIAM,397
HERD,FRANCES,239;OMELIA
202
HERINGTO,DICY,204
HERINGTON,BERIAN,206
F E,212;MANNING,197
HERMON,
. BETSEY R N--LTON,256
. WM,256
HERN,ELISHA,215;WM,256
ZABAD,256
HERNDON,JOSEPH,347
REUBEN,291
HERRIN,JAMES W,397
JOSEPH,397
HERRING,ALEXANDER,364
. ARTHUR,307,320,345
. MILLY,345;MOSES,227
. SANDERS,307
HERRINGTON,CRAWFORD,40
. DANIEL,40;ELLA,37
. EPHRAIM,197;EUGENIA
. 36;JOHN,206;JOHN C
. 206;LUCRETIA,207
. MALISSA,211;MARTIN,9
. 30,50;MARTIN E,40
. MOSES,14-15;NANCY,36
. 409;SARAH A,39
. STEPHEN M,40
HERRON,SUSAN,280
HERSTON,JAMES M,78
HESTER,DAVID,30,50;ELI
. 7;ELIZABETH S,238
. FRANCES,251;FRANCIS
. 256;HARRIETT,200;JOHN
. 291,298;MACON,254
. MARTHA L,255;MARY W
. 265;NANCY,285;ROBERT
. 256;SARAH ELIZABETH
. 258;SIMEON,256;TAPLEY
. 26;WILLIAM,26,30,50
. WILLIS,26;WILSON,7;WM
. 7,397
HETTON,205
HEWBY,JESSE,328
HEWLETT,AUGUSTINE,397
HEWLIT,AUGUSTIN,9
HEWSTON,JOHN,256
HEYDENFELDT,CEMULINE
385,412
HIATES,SARAH M,37
HIBBLES,ELDRED M,59
HIBLER,ISAAC A,397
HICKERSON,GARLAND,158
HICKES,WILLIAM P,197
HICKEY,JAMES,51;PEGGY
395;WM,256
HICKMAN,ANDREW,40;HENRY
. A,40;POASCHAL,47
. STEPHEN,31,51,54
. WILLIAM,40
HICKS,170-171;DANIEL
. 397;DOROTHY,250;E,74
. ELIJAH,397;ELIZA ANN
. E,210;ELIZA E,398
. JAMES M,54;JEFFERSON
. 85,91;JOHN,162,300-301
. 336,343;JOHN J,336

. JOSEPH,336;LUCY,264
. MARY,161,169-170,390
. ROBERT,311;SARAH,238
HICKY,JAMES,31
HIEAR,CORNELIUS,256
HIERS,SOLOMON,19-20
HIGDON,ROBERT,197;ROBT
2
HIGENBOTHAM,ROBERT H
343
HIGGINBOTHAM,A,261
. JACOB,336;JAMES,397
. JOSEPH,336;RILEY N
. 256;ROBERT,336
HIGGINBOTHAMS,MARY,249
HIGGINS,ALICE,241;B A
. 113;D,98,100;DAVID,79
. 88,90,102,121,141
. 119,140;JAMES,98,100
. 101;JOHN,82,90,97-98
. 100,107,113;JOSEPH
. 106,126,141;NANCY,146
. NATHAN,40;P A,85-86
. 90,97,100,113-114
. PALMER,86;PALMER A,77
. 86,89,95;PARMOUR A,69
. R A,100;S T,97,100
. 105,112-113,126,131
. 144;STERLING T,93,131
. 150;TILMAN,90;TUCKER
. 90,93;WILLIAM,3,60,69
. 144;WM,85,97
HIGGS,CORNELIA A,395
HIGH,DANIEL,279
HIGHTOWER,AREDLIZAR,390
. D,267-268;DANIEL,251
. 256,258,276,279
. DANIEL LEE,256;ELISHA
. 256;ELIZABETH,271
. JACOB,256;JAMES,197
. JOHN,197;LOUISA M,260
. MARIA D,244;MARIETTA
. R,238;MARY,263;MARY A
. 247;MATTHEW,256;MILLY
. 278;OSCAR T,256
. PATSEY,260;POLLY
. ----LLING,256;PRESSLY
. 256;STEPHEN,244,256
. 267;SUSANNAH,263
. THOMAS,256;TREACY,197
. WILLIAM,233,363;WM
. 225,256;WM B,397
HIGLEY,H H,85
HILBORN,LUCY,397
HILL,421;A,54;ABNER R
. 256,269;ANGELIM,383
. ANNA J,43;AUGUSTIN S
. 397;B D,40,54;BENJ
. 352;BENJ K,397
. BENJAMIN,40,319;E,114
. E Y,87;EDWARD YOUNG
. 79;ELIJAH,8,31,51
. ELIZ,419,422;ELIZA W
. 393;ENIAS,336
. FRANCES C V,416
. FREDERICK,51,54;G,145
. 31;GILLAM,8;GILLEEM
. 57;GILLIUM,51
. GRANBERRY,31;H G,54
. HARRIET,385;HENRY,361
. HENRY B,397;ISAAC,336
. 345;J,87;JACOB,40
. JAMES,256,306,336,397
. JAMES H,74;JOE,312
. JOHN,54,77,336,361
. 397;JOHN G,40,97;JOHN

. W,88,141;JOSEPH,256
. JOSHUA,139;LAWRENCE
. 336;LUCINDA,397
. MARGARET,405;MARTHA
. 413;MARY,182,406,409
. 417,419;MARY A,238
. N H,266,272,284;NANCY
. 387;PATSEY,396
. PLEASANT,40;POLLY,70
. 286;REBEKAH,415
. REUBEN,360;ROBERT,256
. 290-291,293-294,304
. 306-307,311,321,323
. ROBT,228;RT,319;SALLY
. 275;SARAH,54;SARAH
. ANN,401;SARAH RAY,151
. SCINTHA,242
. THEOPHILUS,336,361
. THO,227;THOMAS,297
. WHITMAN,262;WILLIAM
. 309-310,336;WILLIAM J
. 40;WILLIAM P,70;WM
. 227,256,299,346,397
HILLARD,WILLIE,300
WYLIE,293
HILLIARD,HENRY,2,12,31
. JAMES,12;JANE,12,31
. WILIE,322
HILLIS,ALEXANDER,40
. HENRY,40;JACOB,40
. JANE,31;JOHN,31,54
. MARY JANE E,39
. NARCISSA,39;SIMEON,40
. WILLIAM,31,54;WILLIAM
. P,58;WILLIS,8;WM,2
HILLISS,JOHN,51
HILLS,WILLY,39;NATHAN
. 397;ROBERT,310
. SUSANNAH,403
HILLSMAN,JEFFRE E,256
MICAPH,256
HILLYER,JOHN,264;L G
. 250,269;S G,242,251
. 256,258,276,284;S H
. 259;SHALES G,259
. TRUEMAN,5
HILMAN,E,86
HILSON,DIANA,358
HILTON,JED,20;JEREMIAH
. 22;JOSEPH,40;SELINA
. 40
HINES,11-12;ALLEN,206
. ANN,37;CARALINE E,41
. CHURCHWELL,10;ENSIGN
. JOHN,10;HETTY,38
. JAMES,31,332,355
. JAMES E,49;JAMES P,54
. JOHN,31,48;JOHN H,48
. 54;JOSEPH,12,31
. JOSEPHINE A,42
. JULIANNA,36;LOVY,254
. MARY A,245;MARY ANN
. 36;NANCY,284
. NATHANIEL,256;RICHARD
. 8;SABURY R,256
. STEPHEN,9,31;WILLIAM
. 49;WM,76
HINLY,MARY,31
HINSON,JOSEPH,12;LEWIS
2
HINTER,ROBERT W,116
HINTON,BETSEY,239;L H
256;REBECCA,405
HISTER,WILLIS,10
HITCHCOCK,DAVID,313;JAS
. 343;JOS,18;MATTHEW
. 336;SAMUEL CH---ER
. 256;WILLIAM,63,336

HITT,CHARLES,397;DANIEL
F,397;MARY E A,383
HIX,EPHRIAM,256;JOHN
. 300;MARTHA C,238
. NATHANIEL,163;SAMUEL
. 163;SARAH ANN,404
HIXON,E C,256
HNEDERSON,HENRY,86
HOARD,J M,145;JAMES,142
HOBB,SALLY,278;WILLIAM
26
HOBBS,CAROLINE B,262
. CHARLES,91,100;ISHAM
. 256;JAMES,256;JOHN,2
. 178;JOSEPH,256;LEWIS
. 178;MERON L,259
. NATHAN,239-240,250
. 256-257,265,268,274
. 278;POLLY,255,417
. REBECCA,272;ROBERT
. 343;ROBIN,216;SARAH
. 178;WILLIAM,178
. WILLIAM M,9;WM,397
HOBBY,MARMADUKE,10;WM I
397;WM J,397
HOBKIRK,JOHN B,27
HOBS,WILLIAM,90
HOBSON,CHRISTOPHER,336
JOHN,293,336
HODGE,A,327;ALSTON,256
. D R,332;DAVID,397
. DUKE R,336;ELIZABETH
. 31;ELIZABETH M,274
. GEORGE,119;GEORGE E
. 108,117,127,132;JAMES
. 256,336;JOHN,256,397
. MARY,395;NANCY,31
. RUTH,250;WILLIAM,336
. WM,329
HODGEN,WM,397
HODGES,87;ANDREW,95;ANN
. 222,224;ANNE,225;C C
. 146;ELIZABETH,47
. FRANCIS,7;HENRY W,398
. J,106;JAMES,398;JESSE
. 87,90,94;JOSHUA,344
. MARY,248;RUTHEY,256
. WILL,298
HODGKIN,SARAH,394
HODNETT,BENJAMIN,336
HODNETTE,JAMES,257
HODSON,GRACY,44
HOFF,THOMAS,225
HOG,HESTER ANN,417
HOGAN,MARY,155;THOMAS
155;WILLIAM,90
HOGATHA,JOSHUA,232
HOGE,CASANDIA,153;JACOB
. 153;POLLY,153;SOL,192
. SOLOMON,153;STEPHEN
. 153;WILLIAM,153
HOGER,ELTON,54
HOGG,227;HANNAH,255
. HENKY,256;HUGH,256
. ISAAC,256;JAMES,322
. JAMES V,58,60,68,77
. JOHN,256;MARGARET,284
. MARGARET E,268;MARY
. 264;MATHEW,256
. MATTHEW,321;PEGGY,237
. WILLIAM,322;WM,256;WM
. D,256
HOGGAHAM,J S,124
HOGINS,DANIEL,305
HOLAWAY,ISHAM,360
HOLBROOK,JESSE,362
WILLIAM,108
HOLCOMB,CHARITY,394;H L

. 257;JOEL,292,305;JOHN
. 292,297
HOLCOMBE,ANN M,381
. JAMES,398;MARIA L,388
. WM M,398
HOLD,BAILEY,112
HOLDEFIELD,WILLIS,78
HOLDER,HARRIOTT J,398
. MARIETTA,250;MARTHA
. 237;RICHARD C,398
. SARAH JANE,277
HOLDERFIELD,JOSEPH H
398
HOLDFORD,MATTHEW H,398
HOLEFIELD,W P,88
HOLF,11
HOLIDAY,OWEN,360-361
THOMAS,10
HOLIFIELD,
. CHRISTOPHER H,145
. POLLY,336;WILEY,336
. WILLIS,87,102,118,126
. 145
HOLLAMON,WILLIAM,342
HOLLAND,ALEXANDER S,398
. ANNA,51;BETSEY,278
. CATHERINE,40;CIVILITY
. 51;DANIEL,31
. ELIZABETH,54;GEORGE W
. 40;GREEN B,398
. HARRISON,257;HENRY J
. 336;IASIAH,40;ISAAC
. 325;J L,336;JAMES,8
. 51,54;JAMES W,336
. JEREMIAH,31;JONAS H
. 336;JOSEPH,54;JOSIAH
. 206;JULIA ANN,42
. LAWSON S,336;LEVINIA
. 336;LEWIS C,336
. MARGARETT,336;MARION
. 40;MARY,389;MARY A
. 336;REBECCAH,270
. SALLY,269;SYDNEY ANN
. 40;THOMAS,257;TOBIAS
. 257;URSULA,39;W A,54
. WILLIAM T,336
HOLLAWAY,PERRY,206
HOLLEY,ELI,398;JAMES
398;MARTHA,397
HOLLIDAY,325;ABNER,31
. ABNER E,48;AMELIA O
. 411;ASHLEY,48;CEVILLE
. 54;FERNEY,9;FERNY,31
. FURNEY,49;JAS,318
. JOHN,257,312;JOSEPH
. 31;LOUISA,383;MILNER
. 31;THOMAS,7,31,49
. WILLIAM,31;WM,257
HOLLIMAN,JOHN,10;THOAS
342;WILLIAM,342
HOLLINGSHEAD,JOHN,170
HOLLINGSWORTH,JACOB,9
HOLLINSHEAD,JNO,398
HOLLINSWORTH,SARAH A
208
HOLLODAY,DENNIS L,48
HOLLOMAN,THOMAS,342
WILLIAM,342
HOLLOMON,ELIJAH,54
HOLLOWAY,ABNER,12;ADAM
. 206;ALSEY,336;DABNEY
. P,332,336;DAVID,31
. 257;E H,12;ELIZABETH
. 336;ISAM,336;ISHAM
. 227;JAMES M,336;JESSE
. 332,336;MARTIN,88
. MARY,46;NANCY,257
. NORWELL,82;SAML,226

. 227-228;SAMUEL,336
. THOS,229;WILLIAM,91
. 107
HOLLSONBAKE,MATTHEW,398
HOLLY,ELI,10,50
. ELIZABETH,54;FRANCES
. 406;GREENLEE,58
. HOWELL,62;JAMES,31
. JOHN,31,398;MARTHA
. 421;MARY,384;SERREA
. 422
HOLMAN,FRANCIS,398
THORNTON,398
HOLME,HORATIO N,398
HOLMES,DAVID,3;ELIZ,408
. GEO P,257;GEORGE,40
. HODGEN,398;JAMES,358
. JOHN,206;M,206;PATSEY
. 418;RICHARD,302,359
. SARAH A D,409
HOLMS,D G,398;RICHARD
355
HOLNS,JOHN,257
HOLOMON,ANN,319
HOLOWAY,BARNES,348
HOLSENBECK,ALFRED,336
HOLSEY,CHARLES A,398
GEORGE,336
HOLSOMBACK,THOS L,398
HOLSOMBAKE,HENRY L,398
MARY,379;MATTHEW,398
HOLSTED,JOHN,329
HOLT,ALFORD B,75;AMELIA
. 271;ASA,64;DAVID S
. 257;ELBERT A,398;H
. 290;HINES,233,297
. HIRAM,233;J,263,278
. JAMES,261,266,272,282
. 284;JAS,236,245;JNO
. 174;JULIA B,38;MARY
. 407;ROBERT,257,297
. 327;SIMON,327
. SINGLETON,295,321
. THAD,309;THADEUS,302
. THADS,302;THOMAS,257
. THOMAS TOURNAY,398;WM
. 398;WM W,398
HOLTEN,ISAAC,8;JONIAH,6
HOLTON,BENJAMIN,41
. DANIEL,206;F J,206
. G J,206;GEORGE J,40
. ISAAC,31,49,54,197
. 206;ISAAC B,206;JAMES
. 31;JOSIAH,31;MILLY
. 212;PRISCILLA,39
. SARAH A,36;THOMAS,31
. WILLIAM S,206
HOLTZ,WM,398
HOLTZCHAW,JOHN,264
HOLTZCLAW,ANN,248
. ELIJAH,273;J F,272
. J G,253;JNO G,235,239
. JOHN B,253;JOHN G,247
. 248,257,259,262,267
. 272,280;JOHN I,245
. JOHN R,275;JOHN T,262
. JULIA,248;MARTHA E
. 249,251;MARY,280
HOLYFIELD,WILLIS,132
136
HOMER,249
HOMES,JOHN,112;MATTIE
39
HONSBY,ELIZ A I,391
HOOD,ALFRED J,397
. BENJAMIN,398;DEMCY
. 230;G R,312;ICHABOD
. 82,85,88,91,130,141;J

HOOD(cont)
. 82,113,131;JOHN,100
. 232;MARY,238;MARY ANN
. 419;SUSAN E,392;WILEY
. 336
HOOK,ANNA MARIA,416
  JACOB,197
HOOKER,ELISHA,2;POLLY
  406;SARAH,390
HOOKS,ALLEN,197;EPHRAIM
. 206;G L,314;H MAT,314
. HARDY,197,206;J W,206
. JACK,206;JOHN,197
. JOHN W,336;JONATHON
. 214;MARY,206;MARY A E
. 204;MARY ANN ABIELLA
. 210;MARY F,275
. MICHAEL,48,54,206
. MISSOURI A,235;NANCY
. 205;RACHEL,208;THOS
. 353;V,209;WILLIAM,31
HOOSE,CHRISTIAN VAN,413
HOOTEN,ELISHA,336;JAMES
. 336;MARY JANE,336
. SEABORN R,336
HOPKINS,CARNELAI S,43
. ELIZABETH,237
. GREENBURY,398;JENNY
. 246;LAMBETH,220
. MARGARET M,419;MARY
. 389;MATILDA A,418
. MATTHEW,294;NANCY,397
. O B,76;PRISSILER,220
. SEAMON P,398;THOMAS
. 398
HOPSON,HARDY,361
HORA,HENRY,398
HOREL,205
HORN,BENJAMIN,156-157
. EDWARD,257;ELIZA JANE
. 280;ELIZABETH,271
. HENRY,3;JOHN,257,398
. LETISHIA,203;MARY ANN
. 284;NANCY,241;OLIVE
. 406;PRESTON A,257
. SHURARD H,85;WILLIAM
. 41
HORNADAY,NATHAN,398
HORNBY,CLAUDIA ANN,395
  DAPLEUE,181;MARY,396
HORNE,MARGARET,405
HORNES,JOHN,96
HORNSBY,DAPLINE,175
. DEPHNE,381;J,119;N
. 119
HORSEFORD,DANIEL,8
HORTEN,PROPER,293
HORTO,JAMES,288;WILLIAM
  288
HORTON,329;C T,284
. CAROLINE,274;ELISHA
. 332;JAMES,288,296,304
. 321,329;JAMES C,92
. JAMES W,257;JOSIAH
. 398;MARY,412;STEPHEN
. 290,302-304,309
. WILLIAM,217,293,309
. WM,215,328,330
HOSEA,JONATHAN,218,295
HOSEY,AMELIA,43
HOSKEY,STANDLY M,197
HOSTELLO,LUCRETIA,208
HOUGH,NANCY,278;SAMUEL
  223;SARAH,223
HOUGHTON,222,271;ALEX
. 257;ALEXANDER,257
. BETSEY,223;DILLY,273
. ELIZABETH,278;EMILY

. 283;HARRIETT,282
. HENRY W,257;JAMES,257
. JANE E,278;JNO,233
. 363;JOSHUA,218-220
. 228;JOSIAH,257,332
. 336;LUCY A A,241;MARY
. ANN,280;MATILDA,249
. MATTHEW,257;MICHAEL F
. 398;NANCEY,263;NANCY
. 218-220,228,265,273
. REBECCA S,264;SALLY
. 269;SARAH T,244
. SEABORN,257;SM,224
. TABATHA,281;THO,220
. 222;THOMAS,224,227
. THOS,221;WILLIAM,223
. WM,232,257;WM M,257
HOUPT,ELIZ,387
HOUSE,BENJAMIN L,206
. JOHN W,257;LION S,257
. MARY JANE,246;R A,254
. REBECCA A,246;THOMAS
. 89,96,105,121;WILLIAM
. 20;WM,19
HOUSTON,ALICE,39
. AUGUSTUS,41;CHRISR
. 230;E N,41;FRANCES,51
. FRANCES E,40;P A,244
. R A,244,246,256-257
. 261,272,278-279;R W
. 247;RUFUS,41
HOWARD,170,186;ALASANAK
. 401;ALTEMONT E M,398
. AQUILA,398;AQUILLA
. 184,191;AQUILLA E,184
. BENJAMIN,398;CHARITY
. 280;DORSEY,191;ELIZ A
. 383;ELIZA,236
. ELIZABETH,191,400
. EMELINE F,417;FANNY
. 191;J B,332;JACK,206
. JAMES,74,257;JAMES B
. 336;JAS,3;JOHN,54,59
. 170,191,398;JOHN F
. 398;JOHN GORDON,41
. JOSEPH,220-221,299
. MARTHA K,397;MARY ANN
. 191;MARY ANN M,387
. RUTH WHITAKER,191
. SAMUEL,336;SARAH,412
. STEPHEN,332,336
. STERLING,302;THO,233
. THOMAS,191,398;THOMAS
. H,398;WILLIAM,31
. WILLIAM J,68
HOWE,CATHERINE,272
. ELIZA,398;JOSEPH,398
. WM,357
HOWEL,DANIEL,398;LUCY T
  415
HOWELL,264;A,318;ALLEN
. 257;ALONZO,257;AMELIA
. 380;BARBARA,245;BETSY
. 272;BURRELL,75
. BURWELL,78;C W,312
. CATHARINE,408
. CHARLOTTE,272;CLARK
. 257;DANIEL,2,257
. DAVID,257;ELIZ,243
. ELIZA D,419;GEORGIA A
. 267;GREEN,41;HENRY
. 398;HEZEKIAH,300,311
. 321-322;HIRAM,322
. IRENE,248;J J,256,258
. 259,268,287;JAMES,41
. 322;JOAB T,49;JOHN
. 235,245,249,256,321
. JOHN I,261;JOSEPH,300

. 322;LUCY,208;MAHALEY
. M,421;MALACHI,398
. MARGARET,416;MARIAH
. ANN,254;MARY JANE,268
. MATHEW,303;MATTHEW C
. 257;N N,115;NANCY,237
. 242;NATHANIEL,222,257
. 311;PATTY,157;PEGGY
. 322;RACHEL,322
. RACHELL,322;REBKAH
. 236;SARAH,384;SARAH A
. 208;TEXANA,251;THOMAS
. 206;WM,2;WM J,257
. WYLY,257
HOWLAND,C D,105;C L,105
HOWSON,ROBT,224
HOWZE,MARY,244
HOYLE,JANE C,40
HOYT,MARGARET J,236;N
  236;NATHAN,280,282
HUBBARD,308;ANDREW
. JACKSON,257;AUGUSTUS
. 257;C W,262;DAVIS,231
. DEMARIAS CARTER,272
. ELIZ,246;ELIZABETH
. 241;JAMES,257;JOSEPH
. 227,231,360;LARKIN
. 257;M H,267;MARTHA
. 280;MATTHEW,292;NANCY
. 265,281;OSBORN,398
. SAML,231;SAMUEL,336
. THOMAS,257;WM H,257
HUBBURD,JOSEPH,227
HUBERT,B,309,358;M,341
HUCHINGSON,JO,225
HUCKABEE,ISHAM,307
HUCKABOO,JOEL,51
HUCKABY,ISHAM,310;JAMES
  257;JNO,294;SARAH,310
HUCKEBEY,ISHAM,308
  SARAH,308
HUCKEBY,RICHARD,310
HUCKLEY,LETTA,206
HUDDLESTON,JAMES,291
HUDGENS,MARY ANN,268
HUDGINS,ANNIE,294
  THORNTON,294
HUDMAN,GARRETT,329;JOHN
  304
HUDMON,JOHN,294
HUDNAL,MARTHA,404
HUDSEN,DAVID,398
HUDSON,ALLEN,328,330
. BARSHEBA,394;BIRD,7
. DARCUS,392;ELBERT,398
. ELIZA,407;GARRETT,257
. HAMPTON,7;HAMPTON A
. 398;IRBY,328;ISAAC
. 398;JENNIE,209;JOHN,9
. 31,257;JULIA A,259
. MARY,241;NANCY,392
. NANCY W,254;S,54
. SALLIE M,275;SARAH
. 135;SARAH F,258
. THOMAS,257,318;WARD
. 257;WILLIAM,312;WM
. 270,328
HUDSPETH,ANNY,356;ANY
. 356;GEORGE,356
. RICHARD,347
HUESTIS,MOSES B,398
HUFF,CLATYON W,336
. FRANCES,284;GEORGE
. 330;JOHN,257,398
. RALPH,257,336;THMAS
. 336
HUFFIN,HARRIET,212
HUFFMAN,JUDY ANN,198

HUFT,JAMES,363
HUGERFORD,JNO T,398
HUGGINS,ABRAHAM,398
  GEORGE W,41;WM,2
HUGHES,AGNES E,41;ALLA
. G,39;ANNA J,44
. AUGUSTUS B,41;BRIDGET
. 392;CHARLES T,41
. CONWAY,7;DAVID,398
. DELACY,250;ELIZ,406
. EMILY,4,401;F G,259
. HENRY,4;JAMES,73;JANE
. 31;JOHN,257;MATILDA
. 41;MICAJAH,398;NANCY
. 256;PETER,372;ROBERT
. 41;THOS G,5;WARD H,41
. WEST,41;WM,257;WM W
. 398
HUGHEY,JAMES,366
. SUSANNA,366;THOMAS
. 257
HUGHS,GEORGE,357
  WILLIAM H,54
HUGHSTON,LEWIS,54
HUGHTON,THO,223
HUIE,JAS,348;ROBT,348
HUISLIP,KENDAL,9
HUITT,ELIZABETH,220
  WILLIAM,220
HULL,ANSULUM,86;B F,143
. BENJAMIN H,118;DELILA
. 54;EZEKIEL,7,31,47
. GEORGE J,398;HOPE,170
. 348;JAMES F,398;JOHN
. G,213;MARGARET G,393
. THOMAS,398
HULLEY,SAMUEL,303
HULME,B L,240
HUMBER,ROBERT,62,131
HUMPHERVILLE,
  TIMOTHY B,340
HUMPHREY,BEMJAMIN,311
. BENJAMIN,300;CHAS,313
. D F,313;DANL,17
. ELIZABETH,248;MATTHEW
. 311;URIAH,170
HUMPHREYS,JOHN,289
HUMPHRIES,31;ELIZA,401
. ISAAC,363;JAMES,87
. JAMES C,310;JOHN,293
. 304,309-310;JOHN R
. 142;NEIL M,257;SEXTON
. 103;STEPHEN,87,96
. STERLING,103
HUMPHRIS,JOSEPH,86
HUMPHYS,JAMES,322
HUMPRY,ISHAM,292
HUNDLEY,WILLIAM B,62
HUNGERFORD,113,134,136
. 146,148;ANSON,336;C
. 142,145
HUNNICUTT,MATTHEW R,257
HUNSTER,LEWIS,398
  TERESA,405
HUNT,230;AGNES,257
. ALICE,281;ALSAY,284
. ANDERSON,257
. CONSTANCE,165;CURTIS
. 292;DANIEL,291-292
. 299;DIMMY,273;DIMNY
. 271;EDWARD,398;F M
. 182;GEORGE,257;HENRY
. 165,230,291;J,293
. JAMES,72,257,317,336
. JAMES T,257;JANNET
. 165;JESSE,336;JOEL
. 330;JOHN,257,291-292
. JUDKINS,291,303,330

. 352;LETTY,291;LURIAH
. 247;MICHAEL C,292
. REBECCA,265;REBEKAH
. 291;SARAH,249;THOMAS
. 170-171,291-292
. TIMOTHY,258;TURNER
. 291,321;W H,336
. WILLIAM,165,167,170
. 171,330
HUNTER,118,121,129,142
. A,132;ALEXANDER,58,79
. 90,111,113,117,119
. 121,130-131,133,141
. 148;ALEXANDER A,332
. ANN,280;CAROLINE
. MATILDA,413;DOCTOR
. 113;E S,237-239,244
. 256,262,267,272-273
. 283,285;E SPARKS,245
. EDWARD,258;ELISHA C
. 258;ELIZ ARE,418
. ELIZAR,198;HENRY,336
. HENRY M,258;I P,336
. JAMES T,332,336;JOHN
. 2;JULIA F,245;L J,148
. LAURA E,239;LOUISA
. 248;LYDDIA ISABELLA
. 141;LYDIA ISABELLA
. 116,133;LYDIA
. ISSABELLA,117;MAHALA
. 281;MARGARET,113,116
. 117,119,130;MARY,242
. 389;MARY L,274;MILLER
. 250;MIRIUM,273
. PHILLIP,258;R W,103
. REBECCA,413;ROBERT B
. 130;ROBERT H,119
. ROBERT M,58;ROBERT W
. 76,79,98,110,113,116
. 117,133,141,148;ROBET
. W,121;S A,336;SAMUEL
. 258;SAMUEL B,119
. SAMUEL H,148;SAMUEL S
. 108,117,119;SARAH,40
. SARAH ANN,116;SARAH
. JANE,117,133,141
. WILLHILLMINA,404;WM A
. 258;WM C,258
HUNTINGTON,ALFRED,398
  C C,399
HUNTON,NANCY,153
HUNTOR,
  REBECCA ELIZABETH,276
HURD,ABRAHAM,326;H H
. 148;NANCY,325;NANCY
. ANN,42
HURES,STEPHEN,54
HURLBERT,ROSWELL,258
HURST,ELISA ANN,379
. ELIZABETH,54;GEORGE W
. 54;HARMAN,10;HARMON
. 54;HENRY,7;JEREMIAH
. 399;JESSE,31;JOANNA L
. 36;JOHN,31;MAJOR,31
. MARGARET P,44;MOSES
. 41;NEEDHAM,54;SEABORN
. E,41;SUSAN,54;SUSAN B
. 383;W,54;WILLIAM,31
. 85;WILLIS,54
HURT,CHARLES,308
. EMELINE T,404;GEORGE
. 258;HENRY,299;JOEL
. 299;RICHARD,399
. WILLIAM,295,299,336
. WM,299
HUSE,NANCY,41
HUSETON,ELIZABETH,38
HUSK,HENRY,347

HUSON,DAVID,336
HUST,HARMON,31,399
. JAMES,49;JESSE,51
. JOHN,51
HUSTON,FRANCES,31;LEWIS
  54;ZACH,54
HUTCH,A,254
HUTCHENS,AMANDA,46
. CHARLES,313;ELIZABETH
. 31;RIGDON,399;WILLIAM
. 31;WM E,313
HUTCHENSON,A,267;JOHN
  115
HUTCHERSON,
. AMANDA MELVINA,208
. DELILAH,195;ENOCH,197
. GEORGIA E,271;JAMES
. 197,206;JOHN,197;JOHN
. G,197;JOHN J,197
. JULIA A,275;KATHARINE
. 197;KISIER,201;MARY
. ANN,201,282;SARAH,199
. WILLIAM,197
HUTCHESON,A,248,261,265
. 281,283-285,287;ADAM
. 399;ALBERT M,258
. ALBERT S,258;AMBROSE
. 258;C L,275;C R,263
. CHARLES R,258;FURNEY
. 86;HENRY E,206;JAMES
. 258;JOHN,258;LEWIS
. 197;RICHARD,258
. SEABORN L,258
HUTCHING,ROBERT,318
HUTCHINGS,RICHARD S,336
HUTCHINGSON,JAMES,249
  PETER,316
HUTCHINS,ANGELINE,407
. BERRY,7;DANIEL,48
. ELIZABETH,12,47;MARY
. 382;MATTHEW,54;NANCY
. 48
HUTCHINSON,A,244,246
. 262,279-280;A G,280
. AMBROSE,221;ANDREW E
. 197;BENJAMIN,288;ELIZ
. 243,382;HULACY,197
. HULDAY,206;JAMES,51
. JOHN,250;JOHN P,206
. JOHN S,399;JOSEPH J
. 399;MARY A L,417
. NATHAN,221;S P,399
. SARAH ANN,249;SARAH
. JANE,417;WILLIAM,304
. 319,360;WM,399
HUTCHISON,IRA,197;M H
  336;THOMAS L,336
HUTCINSON,MARY,417
  VIRGINIA A,272
HUTSON,CHARLES,289,295
. 296;ELIZABETH,278
. JOHN,309
HUTSON?,WILLIAM,328
HUTTO,ELI,81,90
. HAMILTON,81,90;JOHN
. 81,89;MARY ANN,81
HYDE,ELIZABETH,227
. JAMES,227;ROBERT,227
. THO,228;THOMAS,227
. 351
HYDENFELL,ANGELICA,402
HYDRICK,GEORGE,3
HYMAN,JOHN H,313
IDLEY,JOHN,97
IDSON,JOHN,258
IEPSEV,THOMAS,54
IHLEY,RICHARD,8
IMMEL,PHILLIP,399

===

INABET,JOHN,399
INGLEMAN,JUANNA,154
INGLET,ABRAHAM,399
. ANDREW,399;ANDREW
. JACKSON,399;HUGH,399
. MARY,385;MATTHEW W
. 399;RACHAEL,422;WM
. 399
INGLETT,ATATHA,382
INGRAM,ABRAHAM,258;ANN
. CAROLINE,414;ARIAM
. 285;BETSEY,158;J S,93
. JAMES G,258;JAMES
. MADISON,141;JOHN S
. 109,140,142;JOHN
. SPIERS,141;LITHA ANN
. 403;LUCINDA,403;MARIA
. 4;NANCY,141,147;NANCY
. ELIZABETH,141;PRESLEY
. 348;THOMAS,311;THOMAS
. W,4;W,158;WILLIAM,304
. WILLIAM BURWEL,141
INMAN,ALFORD,10,54
. ALFRED,31,48;ALFRED G
. 41;ALLEN,49,54;DANIEL
. 11-12,31,48;ELIZA,12
. EZEKIAL,9;EZEKIEL,31
. JEREMIAH,54;JOSHUA,2
. MARY E E,57;MIDDY,54
. MOLLIE F,211;VIRGINIA
. L,41
INNMAN,ELA T,202
IRAM,JOHN,41
IRBY,ABRAHAM,258;EDWARD
. 2;ELI,258;ELISHA,258
. ELIZ,240;ELIZA A,273
. ELIZABETH,264,274
. FANNY,270;HENRY W M
. 399;J S,119;JAMES S
. 79,113;JOHN G,81,117
. JOHN S,90,104,107,111
. 136-138,147;LODUSCA
. 266;LUCIENA,277
. MARTHA,249;MARTHA A
. 278;MARY,275;MARY
. JANE,279;SARAH,264
. THOMAS F,258
IRGLET,ELIZ,414
IRVIN,WILLIAM B,105
IRVINE,W,149;WILL,148
. WILLIAM,118,121,146
. 147;WM,141
IRVING,CARNELL,258
IRVINS,WILLIAM,132
IRWIN,CHAS M,239;JAMES
. 258;LYDIA,38;RICHARD
. 7;ROBERT,8,82;WILLIAM
. P,101
ISAACS,ELIZA,414
ISHAM,323
ISHLEY,MARAH,31
ISLANDS,ASA,288
IVERSON,ALFRED,399
. ROBERT,4,399
IVES,HARDIN,306
IVEY,ANTHONY,96;CHARLES
. 291;HENRY,336;JERREY
. 258;JESSE,342;JOHN
. 258;LOT,336;LUCINDA
. 244;NANCY,235;ROBERT
. W,336;WENNEY,336
IVY,
. FRANCIES PARMELIA,259
. JAMES,258;JEREMIAH
. 258;JORDAN,258;JOSIAH
. 258;MOSES,187;NANCY
. 238
J-----,MARIETTA,265

JACK,JOHN,291,302
. SAMUEL,298;SAMUEL S
. 102;THOMAS,291
JACKS,CARRIE,322;JOHN W
. 258
JACKSON,225;A J,88;A J
. S,239,241,248,275
. ABBE,258;ABRAHAM,54
. ABRAHAM M,60;ADALADE
. 260;ADALINE H,246
. ALBERT,272;ALDRIDGE
. 258;ALEXANDER J S,258
. ALFRED,258;ALFRED H
. 258;ALLEN,258;ANDREW
. F,258;ANNE,284;ARTHUR
. M,258;BENJ,291
. BURWELL,229;CASEY,54
. CATHERINE,248;CECILE
. 272;CLAUDIA,286
. DANIEL,258,367;DAVID
. 235,258;DIANAH,279
. DRUCILLA,45;DRURY,303
. 309;DRUSELLA A,389;E
. 54;EDMOND,258;EDMUND
. 258;EDNA,241;ELIZA
. 336;ELIZABETH,52,239
. 248,274,284;ELIZABETH
. H,251;ELIZABETH JANE
. 249;EMILY,265,275
. ERICK,168;FLOYD,258
. GEORGE,41,372;GEORGE
. A,258;GEORGE TWIGGS
. 399;HANNAH,264
. HENRIETTA,255;HENRY
. 60,62,64-65,68,70,75
. 258,296-297,299,307
. 317;HEZEKIAH,41;IRENE
. 257;ISAAC,232,258,336
. 351;ISAAC M,258
. ISRAEL,258;J DICK,313
. JACK,313;JACOB,258
. JAMES,31,258,344
. JAMES A,258;JAMES U
. 399;JAMES W,54,258
. JANE,288;JAS R,313
. JESSE W,259;JETHRO
. 330;JNO,292;JNO W W
. 399;JOB,258;JOHN,258
. 259,298,336;JOHN E
. 259;JOHN H,259;JOHN K
. 399;JOHN S,259
. JONATHAN,224;JOSEPH
. 231;JOSEPHINE A,282
. JUDITH,235;JULIUS,399
. L B,237-238,243-244
. 250,254,259,266,270
. 275,287;LEAH,46
. LEMUEL,41;LITTLEBERRY
. 259;LOUISA,242;LOVEY
. 39;LUTHER R,259;M H
. 149;MALISSA,243
. MARGARET A,404;MARITA
. 260;MARK,259;MARTHA
. 276;MARTHA A,235
. MARTIN,259;MARY,258
. 275;MARY A,282,399
. MARY ANN,250,418;MARY
. E,282;MARY JANE,267
. MELVINA,281;MOODY,259
. MOSES,156;NANCY,269
. NANCY C,235;NED,41
. OBED,31;P H,149
. PASCAL H,90;PETER,259
. PHILIP,310,329
. PLEASANT,332,336
. POLLY,235,240,249;R H
. 259;REBECCA,285
. RICHARD,399;ROBERT B

. 259;ROBERT HAUSEN,259
. ROLING,259;SALLIE,281
. SAMUEL,360;SARAH,257
. SARAH A M,270;SARAH
. ANN,246;SARAH JANE
. 270;SERENA,40;STEPHEN
. 259,305;STEPHEN A,41
. SUSAN ANN,254;TALISHA
. J,286;THOMAS,259,336
. WILKINS,317;WILL,41
. WILLIAIM,49;WILLIAM
. 219;WINGATE,89;WM,259
. WM JASPER,41
JACOB,BENJAMIN,309
. MORDECAI,288;MORDICAI
. 321
JACOBS,BENJAMIN,288
. JAMES MADISON,399
. JOSEPH,307;JOSHUA,307
. METHIAS,399;MORDECAI
. 304
JAILLETT,FRANCES,397
JAINER,RACHEL,39
JAMES,CALVIN,206;GREEN
. B,399;HANNAH,410
. HELEN,287;HENRIETTA
. 407;HENRY,259;JAMES B
. 399;JOHN,259,399;JOHN
. R,399;JORDAN,399
. JOSEPH,399;JOSIAH,399
. L R L,276;MARTHA,274
. MICHAEL,20;PRISCILLA
. 384;RACHEL,254
. REBEKAH,403;SAMUEL,77
. THOMAS,259;THOMAS G
. 259;VINE,400;VINEY
. 410;WILLIAMSON,259
. WINNEY,388;WM,264,399
. WM HENRY,399;WM W,399
JAMISON,ELIZABETH,167
JANES,SUSANAH P,210
JAREL,WILLIS,60
JARONEY,MORRIS,399
JARRATT,ARCHELAUS,399
JARREL,CYNTHIA,265
. ENOCH,136;WILLIAM,89
. WILLIS,136
JARRELL,94,121,129;E
. 130;E P,245,256,258
. 268,282;ENOCH,90
. JACOB,259;JAMES,90
. MARY,97;NANCY,241,274
. POLLY,97;SARAH,259
. SARAH C,271;W,86,95
. 105,129;WILLIAM,97
. 107,111,114,119,123
. 136,145;WILLIS,70-71
. 75,77-81,83,90,97,107
. 111,113-114,136;WM
. 103
JARVIS,ELIZABETH,382
. FLOYD,399;PATRICK,31
. RICHARD,399
JAWERS,JOHN H,41
JEAN,MARY M,261
JEFFERS,DEALPHA M W,45
. ELIZABETH,49;JAMES M
. 41;JOHN,21,23
. JOHNATHAN,41,54
. JONATHAN,47;JOSIAH,54
. MARGARETT,38;MARY F
. 38;THOMAS,48,54
. W WILLIAM,41;WILLIAIM
. 54
JEFFERSON,FRANCIS M,259
. WM M,259
JEFFREY,THOMAS,259
JEFFRIES,B,220;B S,336

JEFFRIES(cont)
. BOOKER,226;COLBERT
. 336;CORDIAL D,336
. GEORGIA ANN,336
. THOMAS,336;WILLIAM R
. 336;WM,259
JELK,JINNEY W,245
JENKINS,89,130;ABISHAI
. 9;ABISHAL,49;ABRAHAM
. 250,260;AQUILLA,2
. ARTHUR,399;BASSHEBA
. 40;CAROLINE,241
. CHARLES J,41;CHARLIE
. J,206;CHAS,2;CYRUS R
. 336;EDMAN E,197
. EDMOND B,345;EDMUND B
. 350;ELIJAH,259;ELIZ
. 395;ELIZ ANN,245
. ELIZA,283;ELIZABETH
. 43,276;FRANCIS,332
. 336;GEORGE,313
. HARMOND,259;HENRETTA
. 46;HENRY,206;IQATUS
. 41;ISAITUS,49;IZATUS
. 54;JAMES,213,399
. JAMES A T,259;JAMES R
. 259;JESSE,259;JOHN,54
. 213,233,259,399;JOHN
. H,336;JOHN T,138
. JOSHUA,399;LEROY,146
. LOUISA,43;MARGARETT
. 46;MARIA,244;MARION L
. 265;MARTHA,45,90,93
. 130,142,409;MARY J
. 279;MASS,259;MYRAM A
. 43;O R,111;OPHELEB E
. 259;P,130;PENELOPE
. 138;PEYTON R,375
. PHILIP,41;PLEASANT
. 259;POLLY,251,265
. RICHARD,399;ROBERT
. 259;S G,274;S S,130
. SAML,9;SAMPSON,31
. SAMUEL,49,346;SARAH J
. 198;SIMEON C,138
. SOPHIA,371;SPANE,41
. STARLING,54;STEPHEN
. 31,49,54;STERLING,9
. 49,90,93;STERLING S
. 130,142,145;THOMAS
. 349;W,97;W C,92,97
. 104,113;WAITES,259
. WILLIA C,122,137-138
. WILLIAM,54,226,332
. 336;WILLIAM F,138
. WILLIAM L,122;WILLIAM
. T,89;WILLIS,116
. WILLIS C,90,93,130
. 138,142,145;WINNEFRED
. 159
JENNINGS,A,189;CALEB
. 134;CATY D,155
. CHARLES,164;GILES,259
. HENRY,259;JAMES,362
. JANE B,397;L R L,241
. 259,261,270,278
JENT,CHARLES,345
JEPPSON,POLLENA,36
JERKINS,JOSEPHINE,44
JERNAGAN,MARTHA,381
NEEDHAM,287-288
JERNIGAN,A A,281;ALBERT
. 259;ANNE,257;EMMA,268
. FRANCES,241,248;HARDY
. E,259;HARDY RICE,399
. HENRY,297;JOHN E,259
. JOHN R,259;LEILA M
. 253;LUCY M,253;LUCY P

. 279;N,235;NEEDHAM,325
. SEABORN J,259
JERRELL,MARY,96
JERRERS,MARTHA D,38
JERVIN,ROBERT,12
JESSUP,GEO R,399
JESTER,A,101;ABNER,87
. 101,104,112,124,129;B
. 101;BENJ,87;BENJAMIN
. 101,112,124,129;HENRY
. 87,95,101,104,108,112
. 124,129;JAMES,87-88
. 95-96,101,104,108,112
. LEVI,101,124-125,129
. M,101;MARY,87,101,104
. 112,124;ROSANA,101
. ROSANN,87;ROSANNA,124
JETER,ANDREW,291,317
. ELIZABETH,89,271
. FRANCIS,321;SAMUEL
. 259;WM P,259
JETT,FRANCIS,259;JUDITH
. 272;SARAH,260
JETTER,LUCY R,264
JETTON,BENNEDICK,348
JEWEL,KINCHEN,399
. WILLIAM,197
JEWELL,J G,140;JAMES
. 259;NANCY,196
JEWETT,JOSEPH,399
. MARTHA,336
JINKINS,GEORGIA,47;JOHN
. 233;LEWIS,227;MARTHA
. 121;MARY,46;MARY ANN
. 43;MELVINA,36;W C,100
JINKS,118,124,126
. BURREL,74;BURRELL,107
. BURWELL,99,103,114
. 128,147;GALES,74,86
. 126,147;GILES,105
. JOHN,118;LAURA,74
. MINTON,147;SPENCER,86
. 90,94,118,131;WM,86
JOAN,ARTHUR,304
JOHN,WILLIAM,320,345
JOHNS,ANDREW J,206
. ELIZA,205;ELIZABETH
. 201;GRACY JANE,203
. GRIFFITH,197;JAMES
. 206;JAMES S,153;JESSE
. 9,31,47,54;JOHN,125
. JOHN M,313;JONATHAN
. 48,304,310;MARY,389
. MARY ANN,201;R,187
. ROBERT,190;SARAH,57
. THOMAS,336;WILLIAM R
. 206
JOHNSON,96,216,248;A S
. 265;ADELIA M,207
. ADELINE,46;ALEX,260
. 278;ALEXANDER,336
. ALFRED,336;ALLEN,260
. ALMEDA T,267;AMOS,260
. ANN T,191,388;ANNIS T
. 336;AQUITTA FELPS,85
. ARNOLD,98,120,146-147
. B,137;BARNARD,260
. BENJAMIN,206,399
. BENJAMIN J,130
. BENJAMIN W,197;BENY
. 206;BETSE,256;BETSEY
. 236;BRADUS,41;BURWELL
. 98,146;C,197;CAROLINE
. 41;CATHARINE,208
. CATHERINE,387;CESAR
. 399;CHARLOTH,12
. CHARLOTTE,31;COLONEL

. 206;DACUS SUSAN,199
. DANIEL W,206;DAVID,85
. ELEANOR,260,287
. ELHANNON,50;ELIAS,19
. 197;ELIJA,7;ELIJAH,4
. 31,399;ELISHA,354
. ELISHA R,399;ELIZ,385
. 410;ELIZA ANN,240
. ELIZABETH,31,41,202
. 259,266,283;ELIZABETH
. AMANDA,273;ELLEN A
. 260;EMANUEL,399;ERICK
. 168;FANNIE M,270
. FELIX,336;FINNY,197
. FRANCIS,206;FREDERICK
. 260;GABRIEL,355;GEO
. 284;GEORGE,8,31,361
. GEORGE W,59,260
. GILBERT,260;H G,89
. HANEY,336;HANNAH,359
. HARRIS,9;HENRY,197
. 213,399;HERSHEL V,312
. HRDEE,399;ISHAM,206;J
. 148;J C,258;JACK,206
. JACOB,31;JAMES,2,27
. 31,41,206,364,399
. JAMES B,399;JAMES M
. 336;JAMES T,260;JAMES
. W,197,260;JANE,253
. JARED,31;JAS,26
. JEREMIAH,346,399-400
. JESSE,260,352,400
. JOHN,41,206,213,260
. 336,363,400;JOHN
. CALVIN,265;JOHN D,197
. JOHN R,260;JOHN S,260
. JOHN W,82;JOSEPH,54
. 311;JOSHUA,10
. JUDITH ANN A,271;JUDY
. 415;KINARD,197
. KINCHEN,260;L B,147
. 238;L D,41;LABAN
. SCOTT,260;LEBON,206
. LEONIDAS B,260;LEWIS
. 9,206;LEWSIDAH,198
. LITTLEBERRY,65,260
. LOUISA EMILY,285
. LOUVENIA A,207;LUCY W
. O,206;LUKE,97;M A B
. 201;MANNY,199
. MARIETTA,202;MARTHA
. 265;MARTHA ANN,406
. MARTHA H,243;MARY,208
. 254,415;MARY ANN,54
. 198,202;MARY H,395
. MARY J,202;MARY S,268
. MARY T,413;MARY Z,237
. MICHAEL,140;MINOR W P
. 349;MINOR W S,359
. MONES,191;MOSES,7,31
. 50,54;MOSES A,400;N
. 98;N M,239;NANCY,82
. 260;NANCY ANN,256
. NANCY E,209;NATHAN
. 213;NEHEMIAH,10;O B
. 260;OBADIAH,128,138
. P C,271,273;P P,146
. PARISH,41;PATIENCE
. 271;PATSEY,211,235
. PATY,247;PETER,260
. 271;PETER C,260,273
. PETER G,260;PHOBE J
. 267;PICKINS,98
. PLEASANT,98;POLLY,85
. R A,242;R W,312
. RACHEL,203;RICHARD H
. 400;ROBERT,260,400
. ROBERT G,260;ROCKEY

JOHNSON(cont)
. 209;ROWAN,213;RUBY M
. 414;S M,203;SAMUEL,98
. 120,206,260;SAPHRONIA
. 202;SARAH,31,54,245
. 264,271;SARAH ANN,379
. SARAH B,259,272;SARAH
. F,255;SEABORN J,372
. 375;SEBRIN,213
. SEMENTHA D,255
. SILVESTER,260;SIMON
. 346;SNELLEN,336
. SOPHIA,206;STEPHEN
. 361;SUSAN,197,206,250
. 256;SUSANNAH,205
. TELITHA,411;TEMPUS
. 385;TERRY,261;THOMAS
. 59,62-63,156,206,248
. 251,253,260-261,264
. 265,269,276,280,282
. 284,297,400;THOMAS M
. 336;THOS,241,247;THOS
. D,86;TILDA,37;UNITY
. 284;W,237,254,286;W G
. 245,261,263,268;W M
. 262,266,273,286;W P
. 349;W R,235;W T,261
. WALTER,336;WALTER E
. 400;WILEY G,269
. WILLIAM,54,82,84-85
. 122,130,132,213,297
. 336,357;WILLIAM R,206
. WINNEFRED,156;WM,242
. 248,260-261,283,294
. 318,400;WM B,261;WM L
. 400
JOHNSTON,156,328-329
. ABEL,320;ADAM,400;ANN
. 418;BELLOM,2;BENJAMIN
. 346;BUSHWOOD,59
. DANIEL,197,400;ELIZ
. 417;ELIZA ANN,268
. EMANUEL B,197;FRANCIS
. 88,109-110;GEO,261
. HUGH,400;ISAIAH,49
. JAMES,12,72,230;JAMES
. M,332;JARED,15,48
. JOHN,13,15,17,79,229
. 321,332,357,363
. LITTLETON,88,93
. MARTHA,332;MARTHA M
. 336;MINERVA,399
. MONROE,110;MOSES,4,31
. NATHAN,336;POLLY,389
. RAMON,2;REBECKAH,328
. RICHARD,88;SAMSON,2
. SIMON,346;TABITHA,261
. THOMAS,328,332,336
. VIRLINDER,391;WILLIAM
. 110,298,327;WILLIAM A
. 336;WILLIAM H,88,93
. 109,336;WM,249,318
. 367,369,400;WM H,88
JOINER,DICEY,392;ELIZ
. 245;HENRY,261;JACOB,6
. MATHEW,54;MILLY,43
. NELLY,207;THOMAS,31
. 49,54;THOS,6
JOLLY,JESSE,94,98,102
. 114,126;WILLIAM,95
JONE,CHENY,37;EMMA,39
JONES,164,227;A E MARY
. 42;ABRAHAM,49,54,400
. ADAM,155,184;ADDISON
. 107;ADELINE,245;AFFIE
. 46;ALEXANDER,400
. ALFRED,41;ALICE A,259
. ALLEN,297-298;AMANDA

. 283;AMBROSE,163
. AMELIA,400;ANABY,44
. ANDREW,260;ANN,38,152
. ANN ELIZA,408;ANNY
. 203;AUGUSTUS,41
. AVARGIA C,381;B F,260
. BARBERRY,414;BATT,1
. 31,41;BECKY,47;BEN
. 206;BENJA,358
. BENJAMIN,297,327
. BETSEY,265;BRITAIN
. 298;CASSIAH,393
. CATHARINE E,163
. CHARLES,9,31,41,50
. 291,400;CHARLES F,400
. CHARLES P,260;CHAS
. 400;CHAUNCEY,400
. CHRISTIANNA,402
. CORNELIA M,276;DADNEY
. 239;DALLIE,38;DAVID,2
. 41,400;DAVID C,332
. 336;DICKERSON,253
. DICKINSON,260;DINAH
. 38;DRURY,362;E,118
. EDIE,47;EDWARD,336
. ELENDER,202;ELIAS,152
. ELIJAH E,145,243,371
. 375;ELIZ,414;ELIZ T
. 381;ELIZ WILSON,246
. ELIZA,204,412,414
. ELIZABETH,5,54,271
. 286,369,394;EMMA,270
. FERREBY,251;FORNEY,41
. FRANCES,41,273,400
. FRANCIS,2,48;GABRIEL
. 163;GEORGE,8,41
. GEORGE W,41;HARDY,400
. HARRIET E,43;HARRISON
. 368;HASTEN,369
. HENRIETTA,46;HENRY,41
. 322,400;HENRY J,9
. HENRY P,9,12,49,54,76
. HENRY S,43,49;HENRY T
. 31,400;HEZEKIAH,157
. 260,400;HIRAM,212
. HUGH,226;ISAAC,260
. ISAM,41;J E,105;J J
. 148,242;J M,54;J W
. 140;JAMES,5,41,152
. 197,236,248,257,260
. 278,285,315-316,400
. JAMES A,260;JAMES E
. 90;JAMES H,297,319
. JAMES J,260;JAMES M
. 57;JAMES W,31,54
. JAMIMA,411;JANE,31,45
. JANE E,414;JANE MARY
. 414;JAS,2-3,239-240
. 245;JEMIMA,31;JERRY
. 41;JERUSHA,421;JOEL
. 400;JOHN,1,7,31,41,54
. 85,89,91,96-97,106-107
. 115-116,124-125,136
. 142,144,151,260,297
. 306,309,360,366,368
. 369,400;JOHN E,85,92
. 94,101,113;JOHN F,206
. JOHN L,113,118;JOHN M
. 50;JOHN P,260;JOHN
. WASHINGTON,400
. JOHNSON,136;JOSEPH
. 188,190,227,260,336
. 400;JOSEPH A,260
. JOSEPH B,400;JOSEPH W
. 355;JOSHUA,400;JOSIAH
. 65,400;L H,54;L N,260
. LETTIE,40;LILLY V,259
. LIZZY,275;LOT,400

. LUCIUS,400;LUCRETIA
. 254;LUCY,152,204,284
. 416;M E,39;MALCOMB D
. 41;MARGARET,54,383
. 401;MARGERET,380
. MARTHA,41,257,406
. MARTHA ANN,415;MARTHA
. C,409;MARTHA E,124
. 144;MARTHA M M,406
. MARY,152,163,336,379
. 414;MARY A,281;MARY
. ANN,247,298,384,388
. MARY B,273;MARY E,276
. MARY ELIZ,398;MARY H
. 409;MARY S,242
. MATILDA A,397;MATTHEW
. 48,291;MILDRED,404
. MILLY,41;MORRIS,41
. N M,239,247,273,278
. 281;NANCY,4,151,217
. 287;NANCY W,266
. NATHAN,217,219,224
. 229-231,260;NICHOLAS
. M,260;NOBLE W,186;P T
. 312;PENELOPE,414
. PHILIP,5;POLLY,276
. PRESTON,41;PRISCILLA
. 269,400;RACHEL,41,385
. RANDOL,152;RAZE,38
. REBECCA,395;REBEKAH
. 268,306;REUBEN,109
. REUBIN,293,305
. RICHARD,87,156,163
. 184,217,400;RICHRD
. 217;ROBERT,8-9,31,152
. 177,260;ROBERT S,260
. ROBERT W,260;ROBT W
. 314;ROSS,41;RUSSELL
. 260;SADDY,245;SALLIE
. 202;SAMUEL,41,59
. SAMUEL W,400;SANDERS
. 260;SARAH,89,152,163
. 239;SARAH A,251;SARAH
. ANN,4;SARAH E,242
. SARAH ELIZABETH,280
. SARAH J,43;SARAH P
. 245;SEABORN,41,77,107
. 174,218,400;SEABORN A
. 206;SEABORN H,31;SERM
. 41;SIMEON,41;SIMON,31
. 107,358;SMITH,31
. STARLING,260;STEPHEN
. 325,400;SUSAN,247
. SUSANNAH,393,411;T
. 329;TAMERLANE,329
. TANDY,13;TANDY C,15
. THOMAS,12,31,41,152
. 163,173,187,206,212
. 214,260,329,348,400
. THOMAS D,260;THOMAS J
. 50;THOMAS REED,41
. THOS,152,159;THOS H
. 10;VINCENT,336;VINSON
. 54;W,100,105;W A,140
. W E,113;W T,260
. WALTER,187;WILEY,91
. 95,98,260;WILLIAM,5,7
. 12,31,54,71,82,91,97
. 118,141,151-152,162
. 167,177-178,182,206
. 212-213,309,332,336
. 368,377;WILLIAM E,117
. 118;WILLIAM L,185,336
. WILLIE,43;WILLIM,6
. WILLIS,329;WM,88,97
. 185,244,259-260,290
. 361,400;WM E,97,100
. ZACHARIAH,260

JONICAN,234
JORDAN,ARTEMI,276
. BENJAMIN,336;BETHINE
. 268;BILL,336;CHAS,2
. DANIEL,26,31;DAVID,16
. DEMSEY,215;EDWARD,261
. ELIZA,403;ELIZABETH
. 322;FLEMING,332,336
. 344;GEORGE,82;HARRIET
. 209;JACK,336;JOHN,17
. 344;JOSHUA,72;OVEROFF
. 320;PENELOPE,294
. RADFORD,322;REUBEN
. 332,336;SOLOMON,327
. SPENCER,336;STERLING
. 336;THOMAS H,336
. WILLIAM P,336;WILLIAM
. W,72;ZACHARIAH,261
JORDEN,SOLOMON,327
JORDIN,MAGGA F,38
JORDON,ASSA,307;DANIEL
. 27;DAVID,14;JAMES,41
. JOHN,18
JOSEY,35;WILLIS,31
JOSSEY,CATHERINE A,277
JOURDAINE,SUSANNA,388
JOURDAN,ELIJAH,261
JOURNICKIN,232
JOYNER,PETER,269
JUNE,JOHN HOUGHTON,261
JUNES,ELIZABETH,202
JUNIGAN,A A,273
JUSTIC,MARY,182
JUSTICE,JOHN,322
. STEPHEN,322
JUSTIES,THOMAS,7
JUSTIN,THOMAS,26
JUSTUS',DEMCY,293
KAIN,ELIZ M,391
KANNON,CHARLES,359;WM W
. 62
KARNEL,SARAH,97
KARR,226
KAY,CALEB W,238
KEA,ARRENA R,200;BELIDA
. 195;BENNETT,197
. DELILA,201;ELIZABETH
. J,208;FRANCES DELILA
. 210;JAMES,206;MARY H
. 200;MARY JANE,207
. NANCY M,204;VIOLET
. 208;WARREN W,206
KEAL,WILLIAM B,197,206
KEARNEY,RICHARD B,261
KEARNS,A,266
KEATON,JAMES K,261
. NANCY,244
KECKER,NANCY,267
KEE,H S,147
KEELAN,JAMES,366
KEELER,WARD,100,105,110
. 114,122-123,128
KEELIN,JULIA ANN,207
KEELING,WILL,293
. WILLIAM,337
KEELY,ELIZABETH,278
KEEN,E,54
KEENE,ANN T,332,337
. BENJAMIN F,337;WILSON
. J,214
KEENER,HARRIET P,415
. JNO,342
KEET,HENRY,197
KEITH,CATHERINE E,258
. FARLTON FLEMING,191
. HARRIET F,418;ISHAM
. 191;JAMES,191;JUDY S
. 397;MARSHALL,178,184

. 191;PETER GRANT,191
KELCY,NOAH,329
KELL,PHINEAS,86;PHINIAS
. 63
KELLAN,101
KELLER,DAVID C,261
KELLEY,ARNOLD,311;D,121
. DANIEL,311;DAVID,329
. JAMES,261;JAMES M,275
. JENNEY,223;JOHN,293
. 327-328;LOYD,300,308
. 310-311,322;PETER,223
. POLLY,284;REUBEN B
. 261
KELLY,ABRAHAM,51;ALLAN
. 341;ALLEN,337,341
. BERSHEBA,357
. BERSHEEBA,362;BI,311
. C,297;CHARLES,261
. DANIEL,337;EATON S
. 337;EDWARD,206;ELIZ
. 413,421;ELIZABETH,254
. 251,266,277-278,281
. 285;JACOB,357,362
. JAMES M,253,261-262
. JANE E,337;JANE
. FRANCES,40;JARRETT B
. 337;JAS M,235,242-243
. 246;JESSE,31,369;JNO
. 13;JOHN,16,31,41,54
. 343;JOHN C,337;JOHN H
. 337;JOHN R,332,337
. JOHN W,41,332,337
. LOYD,293,300,310;MARY
. 337,399;MARY ANN,396
. POLLY,415;PRISSILLA
. 399;R B,237,242,246
. 269,274,277;REBECKA
. 401;REUBEN,249;SARAH
. 54;SARAH ANN,421
. SEABORN C,337;SUSAN
. 404;SUSANNAH,31,207
. WILLIAM,233,319,343
. WILLIAM S,3;WM,2
KELSEY,D,123;DANIEL,142
. DAVID,122,124,134
. JANE,46;ROBERT,41
. WILLIAM D,127
KELTON,BELL,143
KEMP,A C,206;HENRY,197
. JAMES,21-22;JINCY,204
. JOHN,197,207;JOHN A
. 207,214;JOHN S,207
. JOSHUA,197;KINCHEN
. 197;SOPHRONIA,207
. STERLING,78;VIANNA
. 201;WILLIAM A,207
KEMPE,CICTY,199
KENADY,NANCY,200
KENDALL,ISAAC,347;JOHN
. 226;MARY A E,274
. THOMAS,261
KENDEL,HAMER,247
KENDELY,MARGARET,408
KENDRICK,JOHN,82;M N
. 197;ROBERT,261;SAMUEL
. 105;SHADRACK,337
KENDRIX,ANGIE,337
KENEDY,ABSALOM,362
. FRANCIS,9;JOHN,9
. JOSEPH PULOSKY,357
KENNADAY,JOHN,364
KENNADY,JINCY,195
. WILLIAM F,41
KENNEBREW,C D,261,283
. MARCUS B,261
KENNEDA,SAMUEL,213

KENNEDY,229;ADISON L
. 209;BARBARA,409;CASSA
. 212;DAVID,337;DELILA
. 250;ELIZA JANE,196
. 204;FIELDS,229;GIDEON
. 213;GIDEON H,207
. HENRY A,207;ISABELLA
. 267;J B,197;J D,207
. JAMES,261;JANE,209
. 332,396;JHN,261;JOHN
. 261;JOHN E,261;JOHN P
. 207;L A,412;MARTHA M
. 392;MARY,274,392,400
. 421;MIRIAM,247
. MISSORI,209;NANCY,403
. 417;NANCY A,413;NANCY
. SUSAN,264;POLLY,283
. SALLIE,208;SARAH ANN
. 196,204;SETH,288,304
. WILLIAM,3,221
KENNER,342;WILLIAM,342
KENNEY,JAMES,261;SABORN
. 261
KENNON,225;NANCY,406
. WILLIAM W,354
KENNY,ANDERSON,307
. BETSY,307;CATHERINE
. 307;JESSE,261;JOSHIA
. 261;JOSHUA,307,309
. NANNY,307;SEABORN,261
KENOUGH,WM L,261
KENT,ANNA A,195
. AUGUSTUS,207;CELIA,40
. DANIEL,213;ELIZ,413
. ISABELLA,412;MAHALIN
. 208;MARIETTA,211;MARY
. 197;POLLY,238;THOMAS
. 213
KENYAN,JOHN L,41
KENYON,JAMES,12
KEOUGH,WM L,261
KEPLEY,CAROLINE M,408
KERBY,HIRAM,197
KERCY,JOHN B,197
KERKLAND,RICHARD,207
KERN,ALCINA,417
KERR,SOPHIA E,413
KERSEY,AILSEY,52;ELIS
. 210;JOHN D,197
. SOLOMON,197;WESLEY,54
KERSY,31;BUD,31;JOHN,31
KESLER,WARD,98
KETTLES,ELIZ,390
KEY,ANSLEY L,381;B P
. 106,332,337;BURREL
. 214;BURRELL P,62
. BURWELL P,95;C W,274
. COBB M,235;DELILA,200
. J L,106;J S,264;JARY
. G,337;JESSE B,145
. JOSEPH,64-65,71,75-76
. 77,79,87,91,94,102
. 106,149,364;JOSHUA,54
. MARTHA,399;NANCY J
. BETTY,376;PEGGY D,376
. SARAH,65-67;SION,214
. SPENCER,214;TANDY W
. 364,377;THOMAS,65-66
. 67;WARREN,214;WESLEY
. 197;WESTLY,197;WILEY
. 197;WILLIAM,31
KEY?,ARRENA R,200
KEYLAND,33;JANE,31
KEYS,HUGH,2
KIBBEE,THOMAS H,207
KICKER,ELIZA,275;WM G
. 261
KICKLIGHTER,

KICKLIGHTER(cont)
  SPENCER C,261
KID,EDWARD,54
KIDD,AUGUSTUS,51
. CATHERINE,387;HENRY
. 31
KIERCE,WILSON J,214
KIETH,ALLEN,158
  MARSHALL,158
KIGHT,STEPHEN,67
KILBURN,JOSEPH K,400
KILBY,WILLIAM,337
KILCREASE,DANIEL,70,97
  EMILY,97
KILGOAR,WM,261
KILGORE,CHARLES,322
. NANCY,322;SALLY,250
. WILLIAM,337
KILLGORE,CHARLES,124
. 142;CHARLES A,83-84
. 92,117-118,124;JOHN
. 322
KILLINGSWORTH,DANIEL
. 192;FREEMAN,192;JOHN
. 192;LIZA,192;MATTHEW
. 192;SARAH,192
. SUSANNAH,192
KILLPATRICK,J H T,49
. JAMES H,261;ROBERT,50
. SPENCER,50
KILPARTRICK,
  BETSEY ANN,41
KILPATRICK,ELIZA,54;J H
. 235,241,244-246,250
. 251,257-260,264-265
. 267-268,271,273,279
. 280,282;J M,274;JAMES
. 264;JAS H,246,261
. JOHN,7,31;MARGARET,39
. MARY J,386;PATRICK,2
. SPENCER,8,31,54
KILTZ,JOHN,262
KIMBAL,DAVID,90
KIMBALL,BARTHOLOMEW,400
. BENJAMIN,337;CHARLES
. 9;DAVID,62,261;JAMES
. 31;JAS,6;JOHN,400
. JOHN H,400;JOSEPH,6
. 31;JOSHUA,50;MARY,31
. WILLIAM,31,50
KIMBEL,JEREMIAH,10
KIMBELL,BENJ,84,90
. CHARLES,31;CREASY,42
. DANIEL,77;DAVID,67,84
. 86-87,92,96,109,114
. 149;J T,146;JAMES G
. 148;MARTHA,148;ROBERT
. 67
KIMBIL,ELVERA,388
KIMBILL,DAVID,107
KIMBLE,DAVID,337;SARAH
  38,383
KIMBREL,BENJAMIN,87
  ELIZABETH,42;ELLEN,38
KIMBRELL,DALLIS,41;JANE
. 204;SIMEON,41;WILLIAM
. 54,207
KIMBREW,JOHN,347
KIMBRIL,DAVID,60
KIMBRLL,JOHN,84
KIMBRO,ANN S,246;ISAAC
. 261;JOHN,298;SALLY
. 266
KIMBROE,CECIL,328;WM
  328
KIMBROUGH,217;ALEXANDER
. 261;ASBURY,261
. AUGUSTUS L,261;BETSEY

. 248;BRADLEY,261
. ELEANOR,276;ELIZABETH
. 264,277;JESSE,261
. JOHN,63,217,224,226
. 227,261;JOHN P,261
. LOCKET M,261;LOUISA
. 287;MARTHA ANN,265
. MARY,63,224,227,258
. NANCY,277;REBECCA,225
. 227;SARAH,278,285
. SHADRACK,82,224
. STEPHEN T,261;THOMAS
. 217,261;WILLIAM,222
. 225,227;WM,226-227
. 261;WM A,261;WM G,261
KIMBROW,JOHN,356
KIMSEY,J L,207
KINARD,FRANCIS M,337
  JOHN H,337
KINCHEN,JOHN,321;MARY
. 321;MATTHEW,288,290
. 304,309,319;WILLIAM
. 321,330
KINCHIN,MAT,293
KINDER,DAVID,400;ELIZA
  387
KINDLAW,ELIZA,406
KINDRICK,JOHN,304
. NANCEY M,193;R R,71
. SUSANNAH,192;WM O,400
KINDRICKS,MARY,304
KINE,MARGARET,389
KINEBREW,SHADRACK,337
KINEMAN,BETSEY,274
KING,A,100;ADELAID,275
. ALEX,354;ALEXANDER
. 297,353;ALEXR,232,298
. ALFRED,107;ALFRED A
. 147;ALFRED H,120
. ALLEN,400;AMANDA E
. 268;AMY,271;ANN J,258
. AUGUSTUS,400;B G,337
. CATTEL,337;CHARLES M
. 261;CYNTHIA,261
. DANIEL,12;DANL,10
. DOLLY,332,337;DRURY
. 261;EDWIN D,261-262
. ELENDER,390;ELISHA
. 261;ELIZA,200;ELIZA F
. 281;ELIZABETH,253,257
. 264;ELSEY,412;EPHRAIM
. 31;EUGENIUS L,272
. EZEKIEL,261;FRANCES
. 256;FRANCIS,253;HENRY
. 261;HUGH MOORE,261
. ISAAC,304;JACOB,253
. JAMES,141,147,261
. JAMES L,400;JAMES R
. 262;JAMES WILLIAM,262
. JESSE,262,400;JOHN
. 222-224,262,400;JOHN
. MITCHEL,337;JOHN T
. 400;JOSEPH,262,354
. LOUISA,272;LOUISIANA
. 236;LUCINDA,253
. LUCINDA P,242;LUCY
. HAPT,396;MARIA,400
. MARTHA,270,354,398.
. MARTHA A,241;MARY,246
. 402;MARY L,237;MARY W
. 253;MITCHEL,337;NANCY
. 236,241,324,374,399
. NEHEMIAH,77;O P,67-68
. POLLY,4,419;RAWLS,140
. REUBEN,400;RICHARD
. 400;RICHARD D,337
. SAMUEL B,132;SARAH
. 237;SARAH E M,273

. SUSAN,241;TENNESE,240
. THOMAS,305;ULYSSES B
. 262;WILLIAM,325,337
. WILSON,19-20;WM,262
. WM C,262
KINKLIN,MARY,399
KINMAN,JOHN,262
KINMONS,227
KINMORE,JOHN,262
KINNEBREW,C D,241
KINNEWBREW,BARBY ANN
  243
KINNEY,ARIADNE,242
. JAMES,262;NANCY,263
. PATIENCE,243;REBECCA
. 245;SARAH ANN,244,263
. THOMAS,64,71;WINNEY
. 243;WM R,262
KINNIE,REBECCA,245
KINNION,JAMES,262
KINSLEY,CATHERINE,386
KIRBY,DAVID D,337
  GEORGE,10;P H,269
KIRK,ANNEY,342;JOHN,262
. JOSEP,20;JOSEPH,22
. ROLLIN H,41;STEPHEN
. 295,341-342
KIRKENDALL,MARY,270
KIRKLAND,207;A L,213
. ABRAHAM L,197;ALFRED
. 207;B L,54;E L,197
. 207;ELIZABETH J,200
. 211;GEO,191;H C C,207
. HENRY T,207;ISAAC,207
. LAVINA,203;MARY,387
. SARAH ANN,203;THOMAS
. B,207
KIRKLEY,MARTHA,280
KIRKPATRICK,DANIEL,400
. JAMES,400;JOHN,400
. MARY N,402
KIRKSEY,A J,100;E F,85
. E S,82,85-86,89,93
. ELISHA F,101;ELISHA G
. 85;W,88
KIRKWOOD,CYLIS,197
KIRSY,31
KIRTON,JAMES,8
KITCHEN,WM K,401
KITCHENS,ANN,197
. CHARLES,332,337
. GASTON A,207;JAMES
. 197,214;JOHN W,207
. JOSEPH H,207
. KATHARINE,200;MARY C
. 205;SARAH JAN,200
. TEREL,313
KITCHINS,BENJ,343
KITE,GREEN,197;JOHN,401
. MARTHA,386;SHADRACK
. 214;SHADRICK,198
. WILLIAM,198
KITTELL,ELIZA T,286
KITTERALL,SARAH I,287
KITTLE,SUSANNAH,419
KITTWELL,JACOB,234
KIZERK,MARY,275
KLEIN,JOHN,401
KNAPEN,THOMAS,4,401
KNAVES,JOHN,401
KNEELAND,
  ANNA FRANCES,416
KNIGHT,31;ANN,405;C F
. 65,84;CALVARY F,71
. 118;CALVERY F,108,133
. COFFIELD,262;DEMCY,54
. DEMPSY,7;ELI,84,118
. 133;ELISHA,343;ELIZ W

LANIER(cont)
. 207;THOMAS W,42
. WILLIAM,207,337
LANKEFORD,MARY,256
LANKFORD,DANIEL,262
. EMMA,286;JAMES C,262
. MARTHA,256;MARY,271
. MARY F,286;MARY I,286
. ROBERT,262;ROBERT C
. 262;SALLY,239;WILLIS
. J,262;WM,14,16-17
LANNER,MARGARET,194
LANOR,BENJAMIN,42
LANR,JOHN,213
LANSDALE,JANE A,395
LANTERN,THOMAS,401
LANTHORN,JOHN,401
LANTHRIN,JOHN,401
LANTHROP,MARTHA,391
LANTRIP,BETSEY,391;ELIZ
397
LAPRADE,BENJAMIN,369
SALLEY,370
LARD,CLAUDIUS,8
LARGARDE,M C,382
LARK,DENNIS,5;SAMUEL
401;WM G,401
LARKIN,PATRICK,401
THOMAS,172
LARKS,CATHERINE,420
LARTIQUE,AGNES,417
LARY,DANBY,300;DARBY
. 345;HINCHIER,300
. ISAAC,345;JEREMIAH
. 300,322;JESSE,348
. JOHN,300
LASENBY,DEBORAH,192
. ELIAS,192;MARTHA,192
. NANCEY,192
LASETER,CHRISTIAN,256
LASITER,BENJAMIN,353
EMERY,6;JOHN,1
LASLEY,DAVID,262
LASSETER,ELLA ULLA,40
. JOHN,356;MARTHA,279
. MIDDLETON T,42;PAD,42
. WILLIAM E,42
LASSITER,AMANDA,406
. BROWN,262;DAVID,2
. EDWARD,31;ELISHA,262
. ELIZA,39;JESSE,262
. JOHN,262;LEMUEL,31
. MARY,31;NANCY,251
. THOMAS H,42;WILLIAIM
. 31;WILLIAM,8,49,54
LASSITOR,SARAH,414
LASTER,BENJAMIN,303
LASTINGER,ANDREW,351
. DAVID,350-351;DINAH
. 351;GEORGE,350
LASTLY,ANN,153
LATAST,VICTOR,401
LATIMER,HENRY W,362;J B
. 312;JOHN,311,362;MARK
. 313;MRK,312;T H,313
. THOMAS H,312
LATIMORE,ALF,312;ED,313
JOHN,313;THOS H,313
LATTIMORE,JAMES H,313
LAUGHLIN,JOHN,313
LAUNIS,C W,253;CHAS W
239
LAURENCE,ABRAM,305;E C
. 262;ELIZABETH,287
. ENOCH C,262;H H,236
. 266;HARTWELL,262
. HARTWELL H,249;J D
. 207;JAMES,262;JAMES J

. 265;JAS J,312;JOHN
. 262;MARY ANN,282
. ORSON,262;SARAH,285
. THOMAS,262
LAVENTURE,JNO P,401
LAW,BENJAMIN L,198;DICK
. 42;ELIZ S,403;GEORGE
. 54;ISAAC,90;JOSIAH S
. 401;THOMAS,198
LAWLEY,379
LAWRENCE,ABRAHAM,305
. ABRAM,318;GARRETT,401
. H H,237,240,249,278
. HARRIETT L,258;JAMES
. 329,337;JANE,301;JAS
. L,237;JOSEPH W,145
. LEAN,199;LENORA,42
. LEROY,332,337;MARTHA
. A,243;PATSEY,273
. POLLY,274;SEABORN,337
. WILLIAM,332,337
. WILLIS,82;WM W,401;WM
. WASHINGTON,401
LAWS,BENNETT,262;ELIZ
. 243;ISARN,262;JOHN T
. 262;MARTIN,337;SARAH
. 242;SHELTON,262
LAWSON,86,143;A,88;A B
. 48,54;A J,31;ALBERT
. 401;ALEXR J,52;ARTHUR
. 88-90;AUGUSTA L,38
. DAVID,63,67,301,337
. DINAH,41;DUDLEY,301
. ELLA,42;FANNIE J,57
. FANNY,265;FRANCES,309
. 310;GINNEY,262;HUGH,1
. ISABELLA,411;JAMES,54
. JANE,301;JOHN,67,88
. 301;JONATHAN S,63
. MARY,337;MARY E,208
. MOSES,42;MOUNFORD,301
. NATHAN,42;POLLY,277
. ROBERT,89-90,93,100
. ROBT,88;S B,31;SARAH
. 36,301;SARAH A,337
. THOMAS,301;WASHINGTON
. 401;WILL,298;WILLIAM
. 301,308,337;WM,290
. 295,401
LAYERS,WM,262
LAYFIELD,JOHN,315
LAYSON,C C,337
LAZENBY,ELIAS,173,192
. ELLENDER,337;MARY A
. 332;ROBERT,151,194
. WILLIAM,337
LE ROY,F R,228
LEA,TEMPLE,310
LEACH,JOHN B,262;JOHN W
263
LEAGER,J,357
LEAIUVE,MEDIA,12
LEAK,G,91;T,91,112
. TILMAN,88,91;WILLIAM
. M,85
LEAPTROT,JAMES,12;JOHN
12
LEASLIE,CYNTHIA A E,245
LEAT,SOLOMON,59
LEATH,ELIZA,403
LEAVITT,MARY,5;THOMAS,5
LEDBETTER,AGATHY,244
. AGNES,246;ALICE A,44
. CAROLINE,236;CORNELIA
. J,260;ELIZA,243;ELIZA
. JOHNSON,263;HENRY,337
. ISCHABAD,7;JAMES,263

. JAMES C,263
. LITTLEBERRY,263
. MALDEN S,263;MARY,31
. MATTIE,275;NELL,248
. SARAH V,267;SAVANNAH
. W,274;WM T,263
LEDGET,MARY,412
LEE,306,318;ANN,280
. BERNARD,93;BRUANT,342
. C B,88;CHARLES,263
. CHARLES B,90
. CHARLOTTE,380
. CHRISTOPHER,401
. EDWARD,91;ELIJAH,263
. ELISA,389;ELIZ,399
. ELIZA,398,417
. ELIZABETH,259,379
. ELIZABETH S,261;FRANK
. 313;GENERAL W,207
. GEORGE W,207
. GREENBERRY,169,174
. H G,129;H S,126,137
. 147-148;HARRY G,118
. HARVA S,128;HARVY,95
. HENRY,77,90-91,95,102
. 112,133,141;HENRY S
. 138;IRA,401;JAMES,207
. 263;JERUSHIA,198
. JNO J P,401;JOHN,169
. 170,298,401;JOHN C,31
. JOSHUA K,207;LARKIN
. 91;LARKIN D,143,147
. LEVI,21,23,25;LEWIS
. 401;LILLIS,91,133,141
. MALACHI,207;MARGULA
. 418;MARY MATILDA,410
. MATILDA M,264;MOSES
. 145;NATHAN,263;NATHAN
. P,144;OBADIAH,207;R H
. 292,307;RACHEL,210
. REBECCA,399;RICHARD
. 292;SABRINAH,394
. SARAH,387;STEWARD,75
. STEWART,86,91,94-95
. 102,112-113;SUSANNA
. 284;TEMPLE,305,322
. THOMAS M,207;WILL,356
. WILLIAM,88,168-170
. 329,337;WM,263
LEEDS,NATHAN,401
LEEKS,JAMES,160
LEFEVER,ABRAHAM,2
LEFTWICH,J A,274;JOHN
245,263
LEGACY,ROSEY WISE,94
LEGAN,MARTHA,398
LEGATE,JORDAN,12
LEGET,LEWIS,311
LEGETT,JAMES,233;NANCY
249
LEGGATE,BENJAMIN,12
LEGGET,31-32
LEGGETT,C R,337;DANIEL
54;DAVID,48
LEGGIT,BENJAMIN,31
DAVID,31
LEGGITT,JAMES,222
LEGNEX,MARTHA,54
LEGON,JOHN,263;THOMAS
263
LEGUE,THOMAS,268
LEGUR,EMANUEL,54
LEIGH,BENJAMIN,160,166
. BETSY H,402;MARY,166
. SARAH,391
LEIGHT,WESTLY,401
LEITH,CHARLES,401
HANNAH,409

LEITNER,CATHERINE A,403
  HENRY D,402
LELY,JOHN E,263
LEMEUNIER,MATURIN,402
LEMLE,DANIEL,402
LEMLO,DANIEL,12
LEMMON,W A,106
LEMMONS,JOHN,60
LEMON,JAMES,68;JOSEPH
  217
LENNEAR,AMANDA,202
LENNINGTON,SION,12
LENNUP,MARY,195
LENOIR,FISHER,402
  ROBERT C,31
LENZY,WESLEY,207
LEON;CAROLINE E,384
. HENRY L,402;LEWIS,402
. RESELLA C,422
LEONARD,A K,67;COLEMAN
. 263;IRBANE,263;POLLY
. 277;ROANCK,67;RODRICK
. 353;SAMUEL,402;WM,263
LEPTROT,JAMES,12
LEQUIEUX,PETER,4
LEQUOUX,PETER,31
LERABOUR,B A,263
LESETTER,ELISHA,337
LESLEY,NANCY,406
LESLIE,BRIDGET,393
. FRANCES C,255;JAMES
. 402;JULIUS,263
LESSEY,ANN,213
LESSOMS,DOLLY,400
LESTEE,JOHN,12
LESTER,BENJ,263;DANL,6
. ELIZABETH,49;EZEKIAL
. 8;EZEKIEL,12,31,49,54
. HIRAM,91;JOHN,8,31
. 231;JOHN A,42;JOSIAH
. 263;NEEL,31;NIXON,6
LET,ISHAM,311
LETBETTER,FRANCIS M,263
. GEORGE,263;JOEL,263
. L D,263;WASHINGTON
. 263;WM,263
LETHERIN,JOHN JAMES,402
LETSON,ROBERT,337
LETT,ISHAM,291;JOHN H
  291
LEVEREST,J P,251
LEVERETT,A,54;ELIJAH,85
. ELIZABETH,31;FERRIBY
. 54;HARRIET T,249;J P
. 240,254,257,263,270
. 271,283;J R,238;JESSE
. 337;L P,283;MARTHA
. CAROLINE,332;MARTHA J
. 255;MARTIN,54;NANCY E
. 254;ROBERT,354
. WILLIAM C,337
LEVERETTE,J P,258
LEVERITT,FRANCES A,282
. J P,240,243,247,258
. 259-262,270,277,282
. JOHN B,50;L P,287
. MASTON,49;PHEROBE,51
LEVERMAN,SAMUEL,402
LEVERT,JACOB,299
LEVESTON,MICHAEL,2
LEVETT,A L,54;GEORGE,54
. JAMES,54;PAYNE,54
. SAMUEL,54;THOMAS,31
LEVIGN,CLARRA,37
LEVINE,LEONARD,255
  MOSELLE,40
LEVSAY,JEMIMA,71
LEVY,ISAAC,402;LEWIS

  402
LEW,112
LEWAS,MOSES,217
LEWIS,140,366;A P,31
. ABEL,32,54;ABRAM,32
. ADDIE,269;ALEXANDER
. 54;ALFRED,42;AMARIAH
. 207;AMASEAH,207
. ANDREW JACKSON,402
. ANN,46;ANNA,46
. ASENTHA,287;BARNETT B
. 42;BENJAMIN,54
. BENJAMIN S,57;BEVERLY
. ?,162;BILL,42;C E,207
. CAROLINE B,243
. CAROLINE M,254;CEPHAS
. 263;CHARLES,16
. CHARLOTTE L,240;CHLOE
. 267;CURTIS,263;CYHAS
. 263;CYNTHIA,277
. DANIEL,49,207;DAVID,7
. EDNEY,45;ELAM B,54,57
. ELEAZAR,32;ELEAZER,12
. 48;ELEAZOR,11
. ELIABETH,262;ELIZ,396
. ELIZA,39,206;ELIZA A
. 413;ELIZABETH A,195
. EMMA,272;EUGENIA,57
. EVAN,26;FIELDS,263
. FRANCIS,291,309,317
. 319;FREEMAN,302,309
. FRISMAN,263;GABRIEL
. 263;GALE,318-319,328
. GAYLE,288;GEORGE,263
. 297,363;GEORGE ANN
. 205;GILLFORD,54;H,321
. HAMBLIN,302;HAMLIN
. 314,323;HENRY,54,263
. HENRY S,42;HETTY,371
. HEZEKIAH,9,32;IRA,263
. JACOB,1;JAMES,32,49
. 366;JAMES B,337;JANE
. W,254;JEREMIAH,8,371
. JOHN,42,49,54,82,263
. 291,310,317,320,329
. 354,361,371;JOHN C,32
. JONATHAN,32,47;JOSHUA
. K,198;JOSIAH,26,32,54
. JULIA,57;LITTLEBERRY
. 32;LIZZIE,38;LUCINDA
. 199,270;LUCISSS,270
. LUCY,371;LURANEY,237
. MARTHA,275;MARY,213
. 240,274,371;MARY ANN
. 337;MARY E,271;MARY E
. L,405;MATHEW,9;MILES
. W,263;MILHAN A R W M
. 199;MOSELLE,197;N,251
. NANCE ?,162;NANCEY
. 371;NANCY,258,277;NED
. 42;NEMROD,16;NICHOLAS
. 237,276;NIMROD,14,26
. OLIVER J,402;PATSEY
. 371;PLES,313;RACHEL
. 54,258;RANSOM,49,54
. REBECCA W,277;RICHARD
. 225,263;ROSA,46;SALLY
. 371;SARAH,287;SARAH A
. 400;SARAH AMANDA,415
. SARAH C,242;SAVANNAH
. 57;STEPHEN,213
. SUSAN A M,208;SUSAN M
. 354;SUSANNAH,238
. SUVANNAH J,206
. TEMPERANCE,263
. THEOPHILUS,263;THOMAS
. 1,5,42,49,54,371
. THOMAS S,263;THOMAS W

. 263;TILMAN,134
. VIRGINIA M,406;W J
. 111;WALDER,244;WALKER
. 240,256,263,267,269
. 277;WALTER,263
. WILLIAM,6,32,50,54
. 149,213;WM,263;WM W
. 263;ZACHARIAH,198
LEWOOD,ELIZABETH,249
LICOR,309
LIGGET,JORDAN,32
LIGGIN,MARSHALL,32
LIGHT,OBADIAH,341
LIGHTFOOT,ARCHA,42
. ARCHER,54;BENJAMIN,47
. C,54;ELIZABETH,36
. JAMES,42;LUCINDA,46
. MARY E,43;MOSES,42
. PHILIP,3,9,32;SALLIE
. C,274;THOMAS,343-344
. 358
LIGON,ALEXANDER,402
. ELIZ,391;JOSEPH,234
. SUSAN,381
LILES,JOHN,114
LILLAN,AREAN M,283
LILLEBRIDGE,ANN,395
LIN,REES H,402
LINC,PARMELIA,245
LINCH,BELLINA,261
. BENJAMIN,54;ELIHUE
. 263;HENRY,48;JAMES C
. 263;JULIA ANN,285
. ROBERT,42;WM,263
LINDALL,MARY,259
LINDER,MARTHA,209
LINDSAY,ELLA,246;JANE
. 237;JEREMIAH,238
. PARHAM,58,69
LINDSEY,87;ALEX,97;BEN
. 9;BETSEY,238;CLABOURN
. 263;D,101,121;DOLPHIN
. 96,104,124-125,143
. 149;ELIZABETH,267
. EMMA E,253;JEREMIAH
. 262-263;JOHN,263;JOHN♦
. L,337;LUCY,281;MARTHA
. B---NS,263;NANCY,280
. P,97;PARHAM,82-83,85
. 86,90-91,94,97,100-101
. 112-113,132,137-138
. 142,146;PARHAN,82
. POLLY,280;REASON,54
. SAMUEL,337;SUSAN,280
. WM,263,402;WM T,263
LINEAR,ALLEN,212;BURREL
. 213
LINGO,PETER,50
LINNEAR,GUY,198
LINTON,A B,59;ALEXANDER
. 263;ANN,278;SAMUEL D
. 263;WM,263
LIONS,HARRIET,393
LIPHAM,FREDERICK,319
LIPMAN,FREDK,329
LIPREY,197
LIPSEY,WILLIAM,42,48
LIPTROOT,JAMES,48
LIPTROT,BOWLING,2
. ELIJAH,54;J A,54
. JAMES,32,54;JEPTHA,2
. JOHN,12,32;LOVEN,54
. NELLY,32;SARAH,32
LIPTROTT,HOPKIN,47;JAS
. 7;JOHN,9
LISSENBY,WILLIAM,32
LISSENHOFF,
  FREDERICK H,402

LISTER,231;GEO,231
LITTLE,148;ANDERSON,263
. CHARLES E,263
. ELIZABETH,32;GEORGE
. 402;ISAAC A,402;JAMES
. 313;JAMES F,263;JESSE
. 59;JOHN,313,329;JOHN
. W,263;JOSEPH·C,149
. MARTHA,256;MICAJAH
. 329;NANCY,277;POLLY
. 254;ROBERT,59;THADEUS
. 402;THOMAS,3;WALTER G
. 263;WILLIAM,6;WILLIS
. 102;WM,1,263
LITTLEBERRY,MARSH,12
LITTLEJOHN,THOMAS,263
. 337
LITTLETON,ABBIGAIL B
. 270;EMMA F,248
. LUCRETIA C,251;MARY E
. 240
LIVECORD,DAVID,7
LIVELY,ABEL,342
. ALEXANDER,42
. ELIZABETH,32,54;EMILY
. 54;GEORGE ANN,212
. GEORGE P,42;GREEN B
. 42;JAMES D,32;JOANNA
. 36;JOHN,54;JOHN G,42
. LEWIS,54;LUKE,51;MARK
. 10,54,402;MARTHA,43
. MATHEW,7;MATTHEW,32
. 51;REUBIN,7;SAVANNAH
. 44
LIVERMAN,ELIZ,388;JOHN
. 402;MARTHA B,398;MARY
. ANN,412;SARAH A,402
. THOS·L,402
LIVINGSTON,AARON,232
. ALFRED,80;ALTAMONT M
. 402;ARON,223;ELIZ,391
. GEO,402;JMES,402;JOHN
. 402;LEWIS,402
. LOUISA A C,397;PETER
. L,32;ROBERT,80
LIVINGSTONE,AARON,264
LLOYD,EDMUND,337;EDWARD
. 362;ELIZ,408;REBECCA
. F,236
LOCKE,JOSIAH,264
LOCKETE,REUBEN,358
LOCKETT,ABNER,317
. REUBEN,358;SOL,286
LOCKEY,JAMES,300;POLLEY
. 295;POLLY,300
LOCKHART,ADALINE,36
. ANDREW,42;JOHN,352
. 402;MARY,305;RICHARD
. 305;SAML,362;SAMUEL
. 402
LOCKHEART,RICHARD,305
LOCKINGTON,SAMUEL,402
LOCKLIN,WM,402
LOCKWOOD,JAMES,337
LODGE,JOHN,12,32,48
. JOSIAH,2;LEVI,32
. LEWIS,32;RUTH,32
. SIMEON,48
LODGES,RUTH,12
LOE,113
LOFTON,127,129,138,143
. 148;JOHN,60,64-65,70
. 73,75-76,79-81,87,92
. 104,124,128,138;SARAH
. WILLIAM JAMES,87
LOGAN,LILLIAN H,273
. ROBT,273;WYATE,161

LOGGAN,SARAH,394
LOGUE,MARY,198
LOMAZ,MATHILDA B,411
LOMMIS,SIMEON,329
LONDON,J W,54
LONG,ELIZABETH,51,54
. GEORGE,88,332,337
. HENRY,309,318;JACKSON
. 313;LARKIN,313
. LITTLETON,91;N,224
. NICHOLAS,224,229
. RICHARD,325;ROBERT,21
. W R,105;WILLIAM,42;WM
. 100
LONGE,WM,361
LONGIS,HANNAH,390
LONGSTREET,A B,253;AUG
. B,287;ELIZ E,385
. GILBERT,402;JAMES,402
. REBECCA,385;WM,402
LOPER,CHARLES,54;LAPSY
. 55
LORD,MARY,50;SAMUEL,325
. WILLIAM,297
LOTT,ARTHUR,2,347
. GEORGE,402;JOHN S,402
. REUBEN,1;SARAH ANN
. 402;T,212
LOUDANDALE,SAMUEL,12
LOUDERMILK,J J,248,258
. 260,268
LOUGHRAN,JOHN,402
LOURY,J M,245,269;JOHN
. M,286
LOVE,224,293;AMELIA M
. 381;BEDA ANN,42;CALOP
. 207;CATHARINE E,196
. DAVID,217,223,264
. FRANCES,276;HENRY,264
. JAMES,198;JOHN,12,213
. 359;JOSEPHUS,298
. LEMUEL,214;LILA,205
. PARIZADE,267;R A,213
. REBECCA,393;ROBERTUS
. 294;SENETH,197
. SUSANNAH,236;VIRTUOUS
. 281
LOVEJOY,COLMAN B,337
. ELEAZER,337;JEMIMA,63
. JOHN D,337;PLEASANT R
. 337;S,108;SAMUEL,80
. 347;SIMEON,60,85
LOVEL,MARY ANN ELIZ,392
LOVELACE,ALLEN,164,180
. 186;ELEANOR,164,186
. JAMES,165
LOVELL,SARAH ANN,413
. VIRGINIA,40;WILLIAM
. 51
LOVEN,BAILIFF,311
LOVET,CUYLER,18
LOVETT,ELIZA,40;J,314
. LUDIA S,46;NANCY,42
. PAYNE,55;ROBERT,264
. TERESA C,39;THOS C,19
. W J,314
LOVETTE,ALEX,42;GRACE
. 43
LOVING,MARY CAMILLA,395
LOVLACE,JAMES,172
LOVVORN,JAMES,347
LOW,90,93,102-104,108
. 112-113,121;ANDREW,12
. CHRITY,305;DANIEL,176
. 291,303,307,311,329
. DANIEL JOHNSON,307
. DANL,330;ELIZ,396
. ELIZABETH,307;HENRY

. 288,293,303-304;I,105
. ISAAC,72,93,104,136
. JOHN,329;JOHN H,141
. JOSHUA,295;MARY ANN
. 207;RALPH,329;SARAH
. 418;THOMAS,176,302
. WILLIAM,86,176,185
. 307,317,330;WILLIAM
. DANIEL,207
LOWE,BEVERLY,166;CURTIS
. 156;DAVID WALKER,156
. E W,123;EDMOND,2;ELIZ
. 404;ELIZABETH,156
. GEORGE,156;HENRY,2
. 309;HENRY H,402;ISAAC
. 156;JOHN,2;JUDITH,166
. MARTHA SLAYTON,156
. MATILDA,156;OBADIAH
. 166;POLLY,156;RALPH
. 295;REBECCA R,156
. SARAH,156
LOWELL,WM,402
LOWERY,AMANDA,39;ANN
. 337;GEO W,94;KIRBY D
. 337;MARY A,390;OSBORN
. 55;SIMEON,32
LOWLEY,SALLEY,379
LOWNEY,J M,263-264
LOWREY,BENJAMIN,264
. SIMEON,49;SIMON,12
LOWRY,ANN,332;ELIZABETH
. 332,337;J M,272,274
LOYAL,JESSE,79,91,93
LOYALL,JESSE,85,122,129
. 142,146,337
LOYD,329;ALFRED,264
. ELIZ,384;ELIZABETH
. 271,400;JAMES T,264
. JESSE,402;THOMAS,337
. WILLIAM,328
LOYGE,MARY,386
LOYLESS,ELLIOT B,402
. HENRY,68
LUCAS,320,325;BENJAMIN
. 360;EDITH,256
. ELIZABETH,280,323;J C
. 239;JAMES,300,319,323
. JAMES T,264;JANE,277
. JANE E,240;JAS,318
. JNO,296;JOHN,264,302
. 321,323,329,337;JOHN
. C,260,285;MARY ANN
. 282;MILDRED,323
. MILDREN,323;NANCY B
. 280;WALTER,323
. WILLIAM,340
LUCK,ANNIE,245;JAMES
. 402;WM F,264
LUCKET,HENRIETTA,404
LUCKEY,JAMES,402;MARY F
. 269;NELL,255;SARAH
. 380
LUCKIE,JNO,351,353
. WILLIAM D,110;WILLIAM
. G,337
LUCKY,ABRAHAM,402;ELLEN
. 389;ISAAC,402;JNO M
. 402;JOHN,402;MARCUS A
. 42;MARY,404;NANCY A
. 276;SAMUEL,402;WM,402
LUCRETT,J P,250
LUCT,PHOEBE A,416
LUDWIG,L KOHL,264
LUFBURROW,ORLAND H,402
LUGS,JOHN,6
LUKE,DAVID,264;EDWARD
. 47,55;ELIZABETH,180
. JAMES,177,180-181

LUKE(cont)
. JANE,185;MARY,180
. MARY ANN,388;REBECCA
. 392;WM B,402.
LUKERS,JEFF,115
LUMKIN,ANNE,343
. DRUCILLA,357;GEORGE
. 357;JOSEPH,343;JOSEPH
. L,42;JOSEPH S,42
. POLLY,357;WALTER,357
LUMPKIN,ANN,343
. CORDELIA ANN,268;E W
. 48;EDMUND,55,264
. EDMUND W,32;GEO,273
. GEORGE,357;JACK,236
. 242,247,250,253,256
. 267,269,280-281;JAMCK
. 266;JAMES,264;JOHN
. 337;JOS HENRY,312
. JOSEPH,220,343;LEROY
. 264;MAR,337;MARTHA,4
. N M,284;NANCY,267
. NEVILLE,281;NEWELL
. 267;PHILIP,32;PHILLIP
. 402;WILLIAM,60,364
. WILSON,373;WM,264,340
LUMSDEL,JEREMIAH C,85
LUMSDEN,JEREMIAH,337
. JOHN,64;POLLY,280
LUMUS,ELIZABETH,55
LUNCEFORD,C,149;LOVINA
. 239;R L,149
LUNDY,ALEXANDER,264
. ARCHIBALD P,264;ELIZ
. J,244;LEWIS W,264
. MARY J,244;NANCY R
. 251;REBECCA,264;SARAH
. ELIZ,244;WM C D,264
LUNSFORD,LEONARD L,332
. 337;MATTIE,273
LUPE,283
LUPO,JAMES M,264
LUTGERT,PHILLIP,402
LUTHER,JEREMIAH,402
. MARY,388;SUSANNAH,410
LUTHERINGAL,
. MARY VIRGINIA,383
LUTHERINGER,MARY ANN
. 394
LUTHRINGER,VALENTINE
. 402
LYALL,ALEXANDER,309
LYDA,ISAAC,369
LYLE,CHARLES V,264
LYLES,GEO N,363;JAMES
. 119;NANCY,390
LYMAN,E,215-216
LYNCH,ALFRED,42;BERTHA
. 263;CHRISTOPHER,402
. EDLOW,264;ELIZ,382
. GRIF,142;HENRY,10,32
. JAMES,402;JARRETT,332
. 337;MICHAEL,402;PETER
. 402;S,149;SACKVILLE
. 147
LYNCHES,WILLIAM,12
LYNE,ELIZABETH,281
. THOMAS,232,248,275
. 281
LYNES,JAMES,402;LYDIA
. 411;MARY ANN,419
. PHEREBA,281
LYNN,JOHN,230;WILLIAM
. 85
LYON,ARRAMENTA,412
. DENNIS LAURENCE,341
. FANNY,167;HENRY,5
. JAMES,323,402;JOHN

. 167,337,402;JONATHAN
. 402;MARY,342,412
. PETER,32;THOMAS,172
. 308;WILLIAM,342,351
. WILLIAM T,70,81
LYONS,BEERSHEBA,50;BENJ
. F,402;BENJAMIN,55
. BETSEY,308;JESSE,321
. PATSEY,387;W H,114
. WILLIAM T L,122
. WILLIAM Y,115
LYTLE,ROBERT,77
M----,JOHN C,277
MABRY,ADAM,347;ALFRED
. 264;ELIZABETH
. HARRIETT,265;H P,278
. HINCHIA,264;JOEL B
. 146;JOHN,264;MARY,278
. MERIUM,287;MINERVA
. 283;PEGGY,416;THOMAS
. 264
MABYN,DANIEL WEBSTER,42
MACAFEE,JAMES,403
MACDADE,SARAH,384
MACELROY,CHARLES,368
MACINTOSH,MARY ANN,388
. SARAH,390
MACK,FANNY,41
MACKEE,SUSAN M,97;WM M
. 97
MACKELROY,JOHN,108
MACKENZIE,KATIE M,43
. REBECCA C,420
MACKEY,THOMAS,149
MACKIE,MARY A F,407;WM
. 403
MACKLEMORE,MATTHEW,404
MACKY,JOHN,404
. WILHELMINA,388
MACLEAN,ANDREW,404
. CATHARINE,400
MACLIMORE,MILLY,2
MACMURPHY,DANIEL,404
. GEO Y,404;SUSANNAH C
. 390
MACOMB,DAVID B,73
MACON,CATHERINE,32;EMMA
. H,246;EVALINE J,235
. HARRIETT,260;MARGARET
. 32;MARTHA WILLIAMSON
. 332;NANCY,245
. NATHANIEL G,337
MACY,CHARLOTTE,55
MADCALF,ANTHONY,12
MADDEN,DAVID,84-85,91
. JAMES M,42;MAHALEY,85
. TOLIVER,116
MADDIN,DENNIS,369
MADDON,T,98
MADDOX,85,101-102,108
. A M,244;ABRAHAM,85
. ADALINE,271;ANNA,284
. B,236,266,270;BETSEY
. 241;C,241,248,251,267
. 271,287;CALBORN,242
. CASSANDRA,258;CLABORN
. 268;CLABOURN,272
. CLAYBORN,264,269
. DAVID M,64;GEO,295
. IRA H,73;JESSE,64,311
. JOE C,264;JOHN D,264
. JOSEPH,287;JOSEPH D
. 264;JOSHUA,293;MARITA
. E,267;MARTHA C,269
. MARY A,269;MGREEN,64
. MICHAEL,294,304;NANCY
. 251;NANCY W,253
. ROBERT T,264;SAML,291

. SAMUEL,72,82,290,356
. SARAH,280;SPENCER,60
. W D,250;WALTER,159
. WILLIAM,291;WILSON,99
. WM D,264;WM J,264
MADDREY,JAMES,14
MADDUS,WILSON,92
MADDUX,119-121,126,145
. 146,148;BENJA,219
. BENJAMIN,218;BETSEY
. 218-219;DAVID W,90
. J L,76;JAMES,85;JAMES
. L,93;JOHN,332,337
. JOHN C,332;JOSEPH,297
. LEONARD,297;SAMUEL
. 306;WILLIAM,113,218
. 219,297;WILLIAM D,332
. 337;WILSON,91,96
MADE,MARTHA,241
MADISET,CHARLES M,42
MADRAY,EDMOND,10;GEORGE
. 47;JAMES,9;JOSEPH,32
. MILLY,45;RICHD,9
MADRY,BENJAMIN,32;JAMES
. 16;JOHN,17
MAFEE,A,347
MAFFET,309
MAGBEE,HIRAM,104;LABAN
. 104;LABIN,104;LABON
. 108;RACHEL,104;WM,86
MAGBIE,RACHEL,72
MAGEE,DAVID,404;HUGH
. 404;JAMES,10;JOHN,48
. WILSON,60
MAGERON,ELIZ BRIDGET
. 398
MAGILL,MARGARET,394
MAGINTA,ISAAC,88
MAGINTY,HUGH,404
MAGNAN,MARIA A,379
. MICHILE SUZANNE -
. VICTOIRE,390
MAGRUDER,ALTETHA,166
. ELIZA B,401;ELIZABETH
. 166;GEORGE,166,175
. HEZEKIAH,167;JAMES,55
. JNO,7;JOHN,32,48
. MARTHA,420;MARY AGNEW
. 381;N T,404;NANCEY
. 166;NINION B,166
. REBEKAH,166;SAMUEL
. 166,404;THURZA,414;WM
. 179
MAGUE,LABAN,264
MAGUIRE,JAS P,404
. RICHARD L,372
MAHAFFEY,MARGARET S,264
MAHAN,JOHN R,90
MAHARREY,MARY ANN,386
. 387
MAHARRY,JOSEPH P,404
. MALVINA,405
MAHARY,12
MAHER,JOHANAH,402;JOHN
. 404;RICHARD,404
MAHONE,PETER,299,310
. 319;WILLIAM,8
MAHONY,DANIEL,404
MAINER,219;KESIAH,219
MAINOR,HARDY,32;SARAH
. 49;WILLIS,47
MAISE,DAVID,404;MARY
. 389
MAISEY,WM,264
MAISON,ROBERT,221
MAITLAND,THOS,2
MAJORS,ART,18
MALABAR,JOHN,42

MALAER,MARTHA,387
MALAY,JAMES,337
MALCAM,JAMES,366
MALCOM,DAVID,378;JOHN
. 60;JON,378;SUSANNAH
. 371
MALCOMSON,A,108
MALDEN,ELIAS,32
MALDIN,JULIA,390
MALDING,ELIAS,49
MALEAR,L,106
MALIER,L W,86
MALLARD,JOHN,32,51
MALLERY,THOMAS,12
MALLET,JESSE,329,345
MALLORY,A B,404;B D,264
. CAROLINE ----RD,264
. IRVIN,264;JAMES,16
. JOHN,264;JOSEPH,264
. LOUISA ANN,275;LUCY
. ANN,236;NANCEY,249
. ROLLIN D,264;THOMAS
. 16,32,264
MALON,SARAH,238
MALONE,ALLEN M,337;ANN
. D,409;ANNA B,332
. ANNIE B,337;C B,147
. CADER,337;CHARLES B
. 92;DRURY,264;ELIZ,403
. ELIZABETH I,248;EMILY
. 92,148;FLOYD,337
. FRANCIS,337;FRANK,337
. HARRIETT,264;HENRY
. 147;HENRY W,92;JAREL
. 337;JARRETT,337
. JEPTHA,337;JOHN,74
. 224,264,404;JOHN A,92
. 102,114,126,138,148
. JOSEPHINE,238;LAURA E
. 406;MARTHA,92,103,114
. 148;MARY,39,248;MARY
. ADRAAN,92;MARY AGNES
. 414;MARY JANE,401
. MARY LUCY,337;NANCY
. 254,374;SARA,374
. SARAH,92;SHEROD,337
. THOMAS,59;THOMPSON
. 264;W B,337
. WASHINGTON,264
. WILLIAM,337;WM B,264
. WM P,404;Y G,121,136
. 149;YOUNG,264;YOUNG G
. 137
MALOROY,JOHN H,357
MAN,HARRY B,108
MANCY,MARY ANN,393
MANDELL,ANNIE R,43
MANGHAM,JAMES,86,122
. JAMES M,84,95;JAS,90
. JOHN N,140;SOLOMON
. 303-304,309,321;WILEY
. E,88;WILLIAM,288,311
MANGO,CAROLINE M,284
MANGRUM,SOLOMON,288
. WILLIAM,287
MANGUM,JAMES,108;N,108
MANHALL,JOSEPH,181
MANLEY,JOHN,232;LUCY M
. 260;WM,264,266
MANN,ALFRED T,257;DAVID
. 264;DICEY,420;E,106
. E S,106;J J,86;JOHN H
. 404;JOSEPH B,264;MARY
. 394;NANCY,390;R P,121
. SIDERIA D,259
. WASHINGTON,106;WM J
. 404
MANND,CALHOUN,42

MANNING,MICHAEL,264
MANOR,EMORY,198
MANSON,JOHN,3
MANSORY,WILLIAM,174
MANTZ,MARY,397
MAPP,91;AL,264
. ARCHIBALD P.264
. ASENITH W,261;E J,264
. FRANCES A,268;HOWSIN
. 294;HOWSON,224;J,248
. 249,256,259,265,267
. 284;J F,264;JACOB,220
. JAMES,191,264;JAMES H
. 264;JEREMIAH,294,337
. JEREMIAH J M,82;JOHN
. 220,227,274,297
. LITTLETON,220,264,294
. 297;MARIETTA J----
. 265;MARTHA,236
. MARTHA ANN R,272;MARY
. 261;MARY ANN,236
. MOORE,264;R H,241
. R HANSON,264;ROBERT
. 297;ROBERT H,264-265
. SUSAN,287;W,100
. WILLIAM,294,297
. WILLIAM F,82,85,88-89
. 91,93,95-96,98,100
. 105,107,112,115,121
. 122,133,139,142
. WILLIAM T,150;WM,265
. WM B,265;WM E,110;WM
. F,82,88,101;WM J,265
MAPPIN,JAMES,159;JAS
. 191
MARABLE,AUGUSTUS,265
. CHAMPION,265;ERASMUS
. 97;JOHN,85,265;JOHN D
. 97;RASMUR,109
MARBLE,JOHN B,97
MARBURY,WILLIAM,4
MARCHMAN,CATHERINE,243
. CICERO,265;JAMES,265
. 322;JOHN M,265;LEVI
. 265;NANCY,243;NATHAN
. 265;PRISCILLA,260,263
. RISDON,265;TEBATHY
. 242
MARCHMENT,JOHN,340
MARES,JAMES H,42
MARGERUM,SIMON,404
MARIBLE,ERUSMUS G,82
MARK,119;SAMUEL,265
. THOMAS OWENS,225
MARKES,CHRISTOPHER,404
MARKEY,ALEXR,344
MARKS,198;CATHERINE,411
. JAMES,77;JAMES K,337
. JOHN H,348;LEAH S,407
. LEON H,20,22,24
MARKWALTER,MARTIN,265
MARLBROUGH,MARY,397
MARLIN,FRANCIS P,243
MARRABLE,WM,351
MARRITT,BENJ,263
MARS,ALEXANDER,12
MARSH,CAROLINA,270;ELI
. 305;ELIZABETH,198
. ISAAC M,42;JEHU,7
. JOHN,7,32;JOSEPHINE
. 270;L B,47,55;LB,32
. MALLFORD,55;MARTIN,55
. MARY,213;NANCY ANN
. 200;REUBIN,10
MARSHAL,RUTH,77
MARSHALL,164;A,163
. ABRAHAM,77,193;ANN
. 188;ANN E,416

. CAROLINE,399;D,163
. DANIEL,157,160,163
. 187-188,193;ELISA,160
. ELIZA,187;ELIZABETH
. 163;EMELY,160;EMILY
. 187;EUNICE,163;HULDAH
. 188;J,163;JABAL P,188
. JABEZ P,188;JABEZ
. PLAEIDY,193;JAMES,10
. JOHN,21,23,25,160,163
. 404;JOSE,174;JOSEPH
. 160,163,180,187-188
. 190;JOSEPH E,404
. JUBEL ORION,193;LEVI
. 160,187;LEWIS,188
. LOUISA,41;MARIA,41
. MARTHA,188,193;MARY
. 416;MATTHEW,32,77
. MERRIAN,163;MOSES,288
. 304;MUMFORD,191;ONNEL
. PLESDER,188;PETER,187
. S,163;SALUDA,188
. SAMUEL,163;SARAH,160
. 187-188;SARAH ANN,197
. SOLOMON,186;WILLIAM H
. 207;WILLIAM S,32
MARSHEL,MARGARET,404
MARTAIN,JAMES,359
MARTIN,91,112,388;A W
. 107;AARON,405;ADELINE
. 395;ALEX,364
. ALEXANDER,404;ALFA
. 199;ANGUS,404;ANGUS W
. 404;ANN,404;ANN E E
. 58;ANNE,259;ARCHABAL
. 265;ARCHIBALD,170,324
. B H,94;BALLY G,265
. BARTON,96;BENJ F,257
. 273;BETSEY,272
. CALIBURN,363;CAROLINE
. M,414;CATHERINE,249
. CHARLES,404;CHAS B
. 404;CLEM,2,404;DANIEL
. 90;DAVID,32,85,98,102
. DELL,262;ELIJAH,265
. 359;ELIZA E,405
. ELIZABETH,195;F S,88
. 91,133,344;F T,246
. FANIEL,37;FRANCES S
. 258;FRANCIS,7,192,265
. 292;FRANCIS S,82,351
. GEO W,87;GEORGE,8
. HAMILTON,404;HUGH M
. 337;I D,282;ISAAC W
. 207;J R,133;JACOB,122
. 140,164;JAMES,42,49
. 55,152,198,212,258
. 359;JAMES H,404;JANE
. 201;JAS,238;JERRY,42
. JESSE,49,213;JNO,232
. 344,346,357;JOHN,207
. 213,265,343,345,351
. 353,359,363;JOHN
. RUFUS,207;JOSEPH,405
. JOSEPH JOHN,265
. JOSHUA,216-217,232
. JULIA,240;KEZIAH P
. 404;LEVI,59,69;LEWIS
. 64,73;MALINDA,149,257
. MARTHA,192;MARTIN,290
. 294,302,311,316,364
. MARY,216,278,380
. MELANEY,263
. MERENDY HULLY ANN,200
. MISSOURI S,246;NANCY
. 390;NELSON W,207
. NICHOLAS,51;OLIVER,2
. REUBIN,207;RICHARD

MCCANN,BALSORA C,42
  CHARLES,50;JORDAN,403
MCCARDLE,CORNELIUS,169
MCCARRELL,JOHN,8
MCCARROL,28
MCCARROLL,JOHN,32
MCCARTHAN,RIAS,43
MCCARTHUR,JAMES,265
MCCARTHY,DENNIS,85
. JAMES,156;JOHN,156
. 403;KEZIAH,156;MARY
. 156;RHESHA,156;SALOME
. 156
MCCARTY,AMANDA E,265
. DENNIS,98,102;ENNIS
. 82;GEORGE,403;LOU
. ANNA,259;MADISON,403
. MARSH ADELINE,410
. MARY ANN,261;SAMPSON
. 403;WALKER,265;WM,265
MCCARY,S P,112
MCCASKEL,JOHN,403
MCCASKELL,ELIZ,407
MCCASKILL,ELIZ,407;JOHN
326
MCCATHARINE,WALKER,43
MCCATHERINE,DAVID,55
MCCATHREN,DANIEL,403
MCCAUGHLIN,JOHN,43
MCCAY,GEORGE,51;JAMES
63;WILLIAM,207
MCCHUSKEY,G L,245
MCCIBBIN,THOMAS,90
MCCICHAEL,WM,346
MCCLAIN,BENNETT,265
. ELIJAH,265;ELISHA,265
. J,96;JOHN,265;SAMUEL
. H,96
MCCLAMMY,MARK,10
MCCLANARY,G,55
MCCLANE,ISABELLA,236
MCCLANEY,BARBARA,32
  THOMAS,32
MCCLELLAN,EMILY,271
MCCLELLAND,DAVID,337
MCCLELLON,JAMES,265
. JEREMIAH,265;MARVEL
. 265
MCCLENDON,ALLEN,82,85
. 88-89,91-93,95-96,100
. 101,105,112,122,133
. 139,142;BETISH,265
. DAN EL,112;DANIEL,93
. 129,139;DYPE,262
. ETHELRED,337;F,144
. FREEMAN,142;H P,95
. ICH,72;ISAAC,227,229
. 234,283,332,337,344
. 346,352,354-355,357
. 365;ISAACK,344;J F
. 134,144;J W,100
. JEPRTHA,85;JEPTHA,101
. 112,122,142;JEREMIAH
. 92,127,134,142,148
. JEREMIAH M,82
. JEREMIAH P,95,100-101
. 105,110,113,118,144
. JERMEIAH P,143;JESSE
. 32,50,55,121;JOEL,289
. 327,337,346;JONATHAN
. 337;JOSEPH,92,105
. JOSEPH F,95,98,112
. 133,142;MARY,86,92
. MARY S,82,88,90,101
. 122;MOSES J,337;NANCY
. 93,105,112,129,138-139
. O,100;O A P,100;O H
. 98;O H P,98,101,105

. 107,110,112-113,115
. 118,122,127,134,142
. 143-144,147-150
. OLIVER,82,92,116
. REBECCA,134;REBEKAH
. 237;SAMUEL,373;SIMEON
. D,134,142;STEPHEN W
. 332,337;W,127
. WASHINGTON,337;WILEY
. F,337;WILLIAM,90,105
. 112,115,122,142
. WILLIAM C,92,95,98;WM
. 111;WYLIE F,93
MCCLENDOR,O H P,134
MCCLENNAND,VIRGINIA W
45
MCCLESKEY,THOMAS J,78
MCCLESKY,WILLIAM,341
MCCLURE,100,102,113,118
. 119;JAMES,69,94;JAMES
. S,90;JOHN,86,94,99
. 112,126,144,148;MARY
. 143;THOMAS,94,99,126
MCCLUSKEY,THOMAS,265
MCCOLEN,29
MCCOLL,J M,403
MCCOLLOM,ROBERT,100
MCCOLLOUGH,ELIZABETH
. 194;ELIZABETH MARY
. 395;JACOB,20,403;JOHN
. T,43;MARY,417;MICHAEL
. 403;SAMUEL,403;SARAH
. 213,420
MCCOLLUM,J F,116;JOSEPH
. 51;PATSEY,44;R,130
. R H,116
MCCOLOUGH,J E,208
MCCOLUM,JORDAN,55
MCCOMB,ANDREW,403
MCCOMBS,POLLY,275
MCCOMMON,JAMES H,265
MCCON,BALSORA C,42
MCCONNER,HUGH,364
MCCOOK,ALF,313;DAWSON
. 315;ROBERT,307;WM,313
MCCORC,JOHN,128
MCCORD,141,148;J,113
. 118,127;J R,86,93,98
. 106-109,112-115,118
. 120,122,126,128-129
. 131,134,138,140,142
. 143,146-147,149;J W
. 93,98,100,105-106,108
. 109,112-114,118,120
. 122-123,129,131,134
. 136,138,140,142-143
. 149;JAMES,93;JAMES R
. 70,75,116,127-128,134
. JAMES W,110;JOHN,59
. 62-63,65,67-68,71,74
. 78,80,83-84,89,91-92
. 94,96,98-99,101-102
. 104,106-109,112,114
. 118-126,128-131,133
. 134,137-141,143,145
. 148,150;JOHN W,70,75
. 122,127-128,136,143
. 148;SOPHIA,380
. ZACHERIAH,403
MCCORDS,MESSERS,90
MCCORKLE,SAMUEL,73
MCCORMACK,AYLSE,404
  JAMES,306,337
MCCORMICK,DANIEL,403
  SAMUEL,2
MCCOWAN,NANCY,47
MCCOWEN,JOHN W,265;MARY
  ANN,256

MCCOY,ALEXANDER,48
. ARCHIBALD,311
. CAROLINA,253;CHARLES
. M,403;D,352,355;DAVID
. 360;ELIZ,391;EWEL,344
. EWELL,266;GEORGE,8
. GEORGE M,43;HENRY,63
. 70,72,78;JOHN,49,266
. 291,344,359,362,366
. LEVY,344;LEWIS,403
. MARY,55;NEILY,344
. OLIVE,42;SABRA,42
. WILLIAM,43;WM,403
MCCRAM,ELI,55;RHESSA,55
MCCRANEY,MARTHA,55
  RICHARD,55
MCCRARY,JOHN W,235,266
MCCRAY,JASPER,313
MCCREA,WILEY B,266
MCCREADY,KEZIAH,401
MCCROAN,29;JAMES,8
. JAMES I,55;RHESA H C
. 43;ZILPHAY,32
MCCRORY,JOHN W,272
MCCUDE,JAMES A,92
MCCUE,PATRICK,403
MCCUEN,JOHN N,82
MCCULLACK,CHARLES,403
MCCULLAR,LOUISA ANN,412
MCCULLARS,KIRKLING,14
MCCULLEN,MARY ANN,383
MCCULLER,SUSAN,36
MCCULLERS,AVERITT B,342
. JNO,10;JOHN,32
. KIRKLAND,19;MATTHEW
. 48,55;MATTHEW C,32
MCCULLOCK,JNO,302
MCCULLOGH,JACOB,24
MCCULLOIGH,JACOB,22
MCCULLOUGH,275;ANN,392
. ASAREBECCA,417;HENRY
. 403;MARY E,45;REBECCA
. 416;THOS B,87
MCCUMMONS,LEONORA,277
MCCUNE,108,120-121
. CORNELIUS,137
. CORNELIUS M,108,121
. 145;E,98;ELIZABETH,90
. 101,144;J A,143;JAMES
. A,90,102,113,118-119
. 124,139,141,147;JAS A
. 107;JOHN,90;JOHN N
. 101;JOHN T,98;M F,91
. 108;MACAJAH F,101,121
. MARTHA,418;MICAJAH F
. 98,113,137,145
. MICHJAH,90;NANCY,98
. 108,121,137;R,98
. RUFUS,100;SUSAN,62
. THOMAS B,337;WILLIAM
. 83,90,113,137,146
. WILLIAM A,98,101,113
. 121,140,144-145;WM A
. 98,112
MCCURDY,ANN,401;JOHN
403
MCDADE,AMANDA,403;ELIZA
. 415;JOHN,403;L B,403
. MARTHA,421;POLLY,379
. THOMAS,403;WILLIAM
. 344;WM,403
MCDANIEL,29,88,94;A,188
. ANNIE,281;DANIEL,337
. DANL,9;E,98,100,106
. 126;EDMUND,90,113,123
. 127,130,132,137-138
. 139-140,147;ENNIS,12
. JACOB,337;JAMES M,337

MCDANIEL(cont)
. JOHN,32;JOHN C,81
. JOHN H,65,76,82,102
. 103,106,148;JOHN M
. 337;MARY ANN,337
. MICHAEL A,337;MILLY
. 391;OBEDIENCE,384
. RANDAL,32;REBECCA,211
. WILLIAM,337;WILLIAM A
. 337;ZACH,188
MCDANIELS,ZACHERY,179
MCDERMATT,STEPHEN,403
MCDOAL,JANE,265
MCDONALD,A J,198
. ALEXANDER,192,303,350
. ANNA,153;ANNER,303
. CHARLES,288,304,306
. 329;CHARLES J,60
. CHARLES JAMES,303
. CHAS,309;DANIEL,266;E
. 145;ELIZABETH,303
. HUGH,346,357;J,105
. JAMES,234;JANE,408
. MARION,266;MARY,303
. REED,208
MCDONNELL,WM,403
MCDONOUGH,ELIZ,408
. JAMES,403
MCDOWALL,SUSAN,415
. THOMAS,403
MCDOWEL,JAMES,91
MCDOWELL,DANIEL,332
. ELIZ R,389;JAMES,85
. MARY,261;RANDAL,6
MCDUFF,R,96;RICHARD,107
. RUTH,108
MCDUFFEY,JOHN,170
MCDUFFY,R,100
MCEACHIN,ARCHIBALD,403
MCELHENNY,G W,337;JOHN
. 337;VINCENT H,337
. WILLIAM,88
MCELMURRAY,44;GEO,403
. JAMES R,51;JOHN F,43
. NORAH,44;THOMAS J,43
. VIOLET,39
MCELROY,368;A M D,144
. EASTER,237;JOHN,221
. LILLIE B,240;MAGY,221
. ZACHEUS,96
MCENCROE,WILLIAM,337
MCEVOY,SARAH,404
MCEWEN,A,340
MCFARLAN,PETER,329
MCFARLAND,ANN,192;JAMES
. 192;JOHN,192-193
. SARAH,404
MCFARLIN,JAMES,124
. PETER,115-116,118,124
. 140,304,317,321
MCFEELY,NEAL,403
MCGAHEE,BENJAMIN,338
. EDWARD,338
MCGAN,WM HENRY,266
MCGAR,ADELINE,207
. AMANDA,200;EDWARD,213
. 403;GEORGE W,208;JOHN
. 403;OWEN,213,403;WM
. 403
MCGARR,ELIZABETH,200
. SUSAN,397
MCGARTH,JAMES,208
MCGAUGHEY,JAMES,311
. JEAN,290;JOHN,294
. MARTHA,269
MCGAUHEY,WILLIAM,311
MCGEE,CATHARINE,154
. HUGH,154;JOHN,188

. JONATHAN,403;JOSIAH
. 188;JUDATH,188;JULIA
. 154;LEVIN,188;LEWIS
. 403;LORENA,261;MARY
. ANN,188;MELBY,329
. MILBA,188;NANCY,272
. THOMAS,154
MCGEEHEE,R F,85
MCGEHE,JAMES,318
MCGEHEE,EDWARD,347
. JULIAN,383
MCGIBONEY,246;J H,241
. LUCRETIA,264;MARIAH
. 282;MATILDA,260,262;W
. 237,243,278;WM,242
. 245,251,261-262,264
. 268,270,273,276-277
. 282-283;WM R,266
MCGIBONY,REBECCA,258;W
. 258,279
MCGILL,ELCEY,412;ELIZ
. 404;JOHN,12,228
. MARGARET,159
MCGINN,MARY,399
MCGINNIS,MARY ANN,406
MCGINTA,ISAAC,88
MCGINTY,JOS,309;JOSEPH
. 303,319;ROBERT,218
. 289-290,302-303,309
. ROBT,219,309
MCGIVIER,HARRIETT L,244
MCGLAUGHLIN,JAMES,332
MCGLENAN,JOHN,403
MCGOHICK,H M,403
MCGOODWIN,90
MCGOWAN,LUCY,407
. ZACHARIAH,403
MCGOWEN,JOS K,403;NANCY
. 55
MCGR,AMANDA ANN,407
MCGRADY,R,100;ROBERT,82
. 85,88,90;ROBT,88
MCGRAN,THOS,403
MCGRATH,JAMES,198
MCGRAW,JOHN,403
. MARGARET,414;MARIA
. 382;MARTHA L,257
. PHILIP,403
MCGRAY,RICHARD T,266
MCGREGOR,ELIZABETH,211
MCGRUDER,BRYAN,266;ELIZ
. B,398;GREEN,208;J A
. 208;MARGET,414;MARTHA
. 403
MCGUINNES,ELIZABETH,350
MCGUIRE,A,266;JAMES,266
. MATILDA,276;THOMAS
. 266
MCGUIRT,JOHN,294
MCGUYNES,JAMES,350
MCHARGUE,CYNTHIA,241
. JANE H,259;MARTHA,248
. MARY,259;PEGGY ANNE
. 247
MCHARGUS,WM T,266
MCHENRY,EDWARD A L,43
. JAMES H,266;MARIAN B
. 268
MCINTOSH,221;CATHERINE
. 236;JAMES,297;JESSE
. 266,367;MARIA M,42
. NANCY,279;SUSANAH,306
MCINTOSLE,DAVID,266
MCINTYRE,JANE S,285
MCINVAIL,BENJAMIN,289
MCINVALE,ROBERT,118,124
MCINVER,A C,364
MCIVER,ZILPHA,52

MCJUNKINS,D L,106
MCK----,JAMES,248
MCKAY,ELIZ,391;GEORGE
. 32;JAMES,5;SAMUEL,3
MCKEE,JOHN F M,332
. LEWIS W,338;SAMUEL,2
MCKEEN,MARY,391;ROBT W
. 403;VAN L,403
MCKEENE,WM P,403
MCKELBERRY,ALDEN,93
MCKELHANEY,JOHN,85
MCKELROY,ISAAC,352
MCKEMIE,JAMES,338;JOHN
. 338
MCKENNE,ANNA,395
MCKENNON,WILLIAM,352
MCKENNY,JOHN,403
MCKENSEY,ISUM,43
MCKENZIE,AARON,294
. ANNABELLA,388;JAMES
. 43,261;JOHN,1,208
. JOSEPHUS,266
MCKEY,ALEXANDER,343
MCKIBBEN,JAMES S,95
. THOMAS,84
MCKIBBIN,THOS,111
MCKIGNEY,B,348
MCKINLEY,161;C,266
. CLAUDIA F,280
. EBENEZER D,403;F C
. 142;LULA,338
MCKINNA,JANETT,37
MCKINNE,ANN,421;ANNA
. 394;ELIZ,420;ELIZA
. 382;FELIX,403;JESSE
. 300;JOHN,403;JOHN E
. 403;JOSEPH P,403
. SARAH G,416
MCKINNER,WILLIAM,208
MCKINNEY,BARNA,403
. DAVID,404;JOSEPHINE
. FRANCES,382
MCKINNIE,JOHN,55
. PATIENCE,203
MCKINSEY,GEORGE,213
. SARAH,196;WILLIAM E
. 208
MCKINSY,G,204
MCKINZE,GEORGE,168
MCKINZEY,JOHN,233;WM
. 289
MCKISSACK,DUCNAN,338
. JAMES,306;JOHN,338
. JONATHAN,294;JONN,294
. THOMAS,294,332,338
. WILLIAM T,338
MCKLEROY,DAWSON,83,141
. 143;JAMES,83;JOHN,83
MCKNIGHT,ELIZABETH,255
. JOHN,266
MCKOWAN,ELIZABETH G,237
MCKUEN,WILLIAM,368
MCLAIN,GEORGE,59;JAMES
. 115,266;MARY,245
. NANCY,236;SAMUEL,266
MCLANE,JOHN,266;LAVINIA
. 210;MARY,203-204,265
. WM,97
MCLARGE,G,148
MCLARK,DANIEL,115
MCLAUCHLIN,DUNKIN,232
MCLAUGHLIN,
. ALEXANDER R,404
. GERRARD,404;JAMES,338
. OWEN A,266;WM,404
MCLAURIN,MARTHA E,260
MCLAWS,ABRAM,404;ANN
. MARGARET,411

MEDLOCK(cont)
. 405;J M,312;JAMES E
. 315
MEDOWS,DANL,9
MEEDON,JOHN,191
MEEK,FRANCY,197;JAMES S
. 68,96;SUSAN,201
. ZELPHA,197
MEEKAN,ALLEN T,198
MEEKES,JONAH,198
MEEKS,ADALINE,210
. ALBERT H,266
. ELIZABETH,197
. MARGARET,210;MARTHA
. 194;POLY,415;R,96
. SARAH,211;WILLIAM R
. 208;WINNY,196
MEGAHE,ANDRE J,405
MEGAN,BRIGET,402;MARY
. 406
MEGAR,SARAH,413
MEGILL,SUSAN,394
MEHONE,PETER,309
MEIGS,ELIZA B,383
. JONATHAN,405;MARY E E
. 411
MELBORN,LEVI T,266
MELHORN,SARAH,392
MELL,P H,240,242,244
. 246-248,256,263,265
. 266,268-269,274,279
. 282,284,286
MELSON,J W,73,80;WM P
. 373
MELTON,AMANDA,402;ELIZ
. 229;ELIZABETH,229
. ISAAC,350;JAMES K,266
. JONATHAN,289;LOUISA
. 267;LUCY,225;PETER,50
. POLLY,275;REBEKAH,187
. ROBERT,225,229-230
. 266;SILAS L,405
. TIMOTHY,337;WILLIAM
. 220,225-226,228;WM
. 223;WM ALLEN,266
MELVIN,NATHAN,287,293
. THOMAS,287,321
MEMSE,DAVID,12
MENARD,ADELA,380
MENDINGHALL,MARY,406
MERCER,FLORAN,402
. GRIFFIN,213;HERMAN
. 281;HERMON,263;JAMES
. 9;JANE,130;JESSE,130
. 259,263,269,274,282
. 285-286;JOE,208
. MALAKIAH,208;MERMON
. 257;MOLEN,204;RODA
. 175;SILAS,215;SOLOMON
. 208,348;STEPHEN,32
. WILLIAM,337;WILLIAM E
. 115;WILLIBY,32
. WILLOUGHBY,8
MERCHANT,ISAAC,97
MEREDITH,HELEN R,413
. J W,80;JAMES,266
. JAMES W,405;JAS W,405
. JOHN,405;LAURA ANN
. 388;NANCY,275;NELSON
. 98;RICHARD C,405
. WILLIAM H,32;WM,405
MEREWETHER,ANN,388
. FRANCES,171;FRANCIS
. 165;JANE,165;MATILDA
. 165;NICHOLAS,164
. ROBERT,165,171;THOMAS
. 164-165;WILLIAM,164
. 165,171-173

MEREWITHER,JAMES,59
MERIDA,N,100
MERIDITH,ELIZABETH M
. 140;JAMES A,140
. MAHALA,140
. NANCY LOUIZA M,140
. NELSON,140,144
. WILLIAM H,140;WILSON
. 90
MERIL,S P,145
MERIT,ABSCILLA,32
. COTTON,32;EMANUEL,321
. JESSE,32;WILLIAM,222
MERIWETHER,A,22
. ALEXANDER,20;CHARLES
. 337;DAVID,332,337,341
. FRANCES,253;GEORGE M
. 337;JAMES,341,405
. LULA,337;MATILDA A
. 337;NICHOLAS,161,405
. SALLIE A,332,337
. THOMAS,154,161
MERONEY,WM,73
MERRELL,ARTHUR,2;THOS W
. 155
MERRETT,MARY,236
MERRIT,COMFORT,55
. COTTON,6;GEORGE W,55
. JOHN,92
MERRITS,CORNELIA,280
MERRITT,ABSCILLA,52
. ALLEN,266;BENJ,239
. 266;COMFORT,52;ELIZA
. A,240;ELIZABETH,240
. 284;FRANKLIN,266
. HENRY,266,405;JAMES
. 266;JNO E,243;JOHN
. 266;JOHN C,242,244
. 266-267,274,278
. LOVETT,266;MARIA J E
. 272;MRTHA,243;NANCY
. 253;PANSEY,253;POLLY
. 255;STEPHEN,266
. THOMAS,266-267;WM,267
. WM T,258
MERRIWETHER,FRANCIS,267
. JAMES,267;LUCY,274
MERRY,BRADFORD,42
MESSE,THOMAS,289
MESSER,HANNAH,405
. WILLIAM,337,356
MESSEX,GEORGIA,40;JANE
. 37;JESSE,42;VIRGINIA
. 36
METCALF,ANTHONY,32
. EDWARD,267;GEO W,405
. ISAAC,32;WILLIAM,32
METCLAF,WM,10
METHIERS,THOMAS,321
METHRIN,THOMAS,321
METHVIN,NATHAN,293
. THOMAS,293;THOS,287
METTS,REDDING,6
METTZ,REDDING,16
MEYE,WM B,405
MEYER,ANN ELIZ,413
. DAVID,405;JOHN W,405
MEYERS,JAMES,405
MICHAEL,ADELINE,271;JNO
. 306;JOHN,300,325;S M
. 261;S W,256;THOMAS J
. 267;WM H,405;Z,346
MICKELBERRY,A,119;ALDEN
. 84,89,100,104,107
MICKELROY,DAWSON,149
MICKLEBERRY,ALDEN,82
. 121
MICON,ELUNA M,384

. MARGARET C,419
. MATILDA A,406;WM C
. 405
MIDDLEBROOKS,323
. ANDERSON,328;G C,314
. JAMES P,121;JAS T,315
. JOSEPH,306,321;JOSEPH
. A,337;M,305;MICAJAH
. 330;ROBERT,306;ZARA B
. 267
MIDDLETON,ANN,412;HUKE
. 174;JOHN,405;NANCY
. 248,400;R,317;ROBERT
. 222-223,233;WM,267;Z
. 298
MIDENDUFF,ANN,413
MIDLETON,ROBERT,224
MIFFLIN,GEORGE,297
MIKEL,THOMAS,213
MIKUS,195
MILAM,JORDAN,85
MILBER,WILLIAM B,198
MILES,A,321;ABRIM,309
. BYRD ANDERSON,405
. ELIJAH,99;EMMELINE
. 406;JOHN,294,360;L M
. 55;LEVISA,32;LOISESA
. 12;LUCY,366;MARY,158
. RICHARD,166;THOS,309
. UNICY,366;WILLIAM,158
. 159
MILESBERRY,A,87
MILICAN,JOHN A,42
MILLEN,AMANDA M,404;D
. 97;G D,97,113;GEORGE
. 52;GEORGE D,123,337
. HENRY,337;JOHN,337
MILLER,ALFRED,42;ANDREW
. J,405;ANDREW T,89
. ANNA E,278;BALDWIN B
. 405;BRICE,299,309
. CHARLES,75,79,213,304
. 319;CHARLEY,267
. CHRLES,288;COSTELL,42
. D B B,55;DANIEL,337
. 342,351;ELIZ,383,409
. ELIZABETH,38;EMMA,43
. EZEKIEL,169;FRANCES
. 143;FRANCIS,65,95,106
. 119,125,326,405;HENRY
. 42;JAMES,213,300,305
. 310,362,405;JOE,208
. JOEL,208;JOHN,3,12,32
. 76,79,267;JOHN A,215
. 267;JOHN ADAM,215,224
. JONATHAN,326;JONATHAN
. M,405;JOSEPH,14,16
. 168;JOSHUA,361;KEZIAH
. LOUISA,406;LEWIS,326
. LINA,205;MARTHA A,278
. MARY,177,326;NANCY
. 265;NATHANIEL,3,405
. PENNY JANE,197;PRKER
. C,267;RANDALL,42;ROXY
. ANN,206;SALETA A,203
. SARAH,3,213;SEABORN
. 18,20;SOLOMON K,42
. SOPHIA,394;STEPHEN,7
. THOMAS S,267;THOMAS W
. 405;THOMPSON,170;W H
. 106,116,124;WILLIAM
. 42,75,198,213,337
. WILLIAM B,213;WILLIAM
. K,42
MILLIGAN,JAMES,267
. JOSEPH,405
MILLIN,GEORGE,32;JAMES
. H,32

MILLING,SAMUEL,405
MILLIS,MARY,360;THOMAS
  360
MILLS,ABRAHAM,303
. ANTHONY,32,50,55
. ARCHIBALD,50,55;ELIZ
. 243;ELIZABETH,50,55
. ESTHER,290;HENRY,267
. 405;J,12;LAURA,38
. LUCY,401;MARY,419
. MARY ANN,383;NANCY,42
. PHEBE,41;RICHARD,302
. ROBERT,193,305
. STEPHEN,55;SUSAN,44
. THOS,97;WILLIAM,55
. WM H C,47
MILNER,OBADIAH,267;S B
  136
MILSAPS,JACOB,344
MILSON,DANIEL,292
MILSTED,ZEAL,220
MILTON,FABIRE MAXIMUS,5
. HANNAH E,32;JOHN,5
. JULIUS CEASAR,5
. MARY ANNE ARMSTRONG,4
. PETER,8,32,55;ROBERT
. J,405
MIMES,CHARLES E,405
MIMMS,A,108;DAVID,21
  SARAH,214
MIMS,HARRIET,198;JAMES
. L,405;JOHN,198;JUDE
. 153;LOUISANNA,409
. MARSHALL,171;THOMAS S
. 43
MINCHEV,SARAH,49
MINCHEY,HILL,55;SARAH
  55
MINCY,T,205
MINER,HERMON,267
MINIS,JUDITH,5
MINNIS,SARAH,198
MINOR,CHRISTOPHER,405
. JANE CAROLINE,417;JNO
. B,172;JOHN,295;WM,295
MINS,DAVID,22
MINSEY,DENNIS,208
MINTER,F B,337;JEREMIAH
. P,332,337;JOE,337
. JOHN W,337;RICHARD
. 101,337;ROBERT J,337
. THOMAS C,337;WILLIAM
. S,337
MIRES,FALIMA,195
  SEABORN F,208
MIRNNER,WM,267
MISER,JOSEPH,337
MITCALF,ANTHONY,10
MITCHEL,DANIEL,337
. FRANCIS,396;WILLIAM
. 94
MITCHELL,323;ANN CLARK
. 369;BENJAMIN,405;BIRD
. B,405;BORELAND,302
. C A,240,259;C D,239
. CICERO,267;DANIEL,288
. 325;EDWARD,267
. ELIZABETH,264
. ELIZABETH T,248;ELLEN
. 403;HENRY,310,319,363
. 405;IDA J,276;ISAAC
. 267;JAMES,223;JOHN,5
. 14,16,49,267,363,405
. JOSHUA,304;JOSHUA M
. 267;LOCKETTE,293
. LUKEY,239;MARGARET
. 274;MARGARET F,255
. MARTHA J,235;MARY,416

. MARY CLARK,367;MARY
. COXE,369;N,108;NANCEY
. 253;NANCY CLARK,367
. NEWTON,43;OBEDIENCE
. 400;PETER,108;RANSOM
. 303;REUBEN,268;REUBEN
. S,267;RICHARD,332,337
. ROBERT,291,311,328
. ROSANA,414;SARAH A
. 268;SARAH ANN,249
. STEPHEN,108;STERLING
. 267;SUSANNA,422
. THOMAS,312;WILLIAM,5
. 51,84,346-347;355,367
. 369;WILLIAM HENRY,369
. WM,341;WM S,406
MITEN,ROBERT,226
MITIN,ROBERT,226;WM,226
MITSHEL,SAMUEL,88
MIXER,
  CATHERINE WYMAN,399
MIXON,GEORGE,8,32,51,55
. JEP,55;JES,55;JOHN,43
. MICHAEL,7,32,51,55
. MIKEL,198;NANCY,32
MIZE,ANDERSON,267;JAMES
  337;JO,267
MIZEL,GRIFFIN,344
MIZELL,GRIFFIN,344
MOAT,FREEMAN,313;JOE
  313
MOBLEY,ALEXR,10;BENJ,7
. BENJAMIN,51,55;CHRISTO
. PHER,57;CIVILITY,37
. ELDRIDGE H,77;ELEAZA
. 76;ELEAZER,58,62,68
. 75,77;ELIZ,405
. JACKSON,89;JAMES,49
. JAMES A,55;JAMES R,55
. JETHRO,347;MARY,55
. MARY E,210;SARAH,51
. SMITH,86;STEPHEN,89
. 337;SUSANNAH C,45
. WILLIAM,51
MOBLY,BENJAMIN,32
  JETHRO,347;SARAH,32
MOCK,ARTHUR,7,32
MOCKS,93
MODERWELL,WM,406
MODISDA,FANNY,42
MODY,ALMIRA,250
MOGIN,WM,289
MOHAIRE,JANE,386
MONCRIEF,D H,127,131
. DAVID,267;ISAAC,267
. LIZZIE,284;MARSHALL
. 267;MARTHA,269
. SEABORN L,43;THOMAS I
. 267;WM,259,267
MOND,ENSIGN MALACHI,7
MONDY,WILLIS,208
MONELIA,ESTHER,55
MONEY,JOHN,406
MONFORT,JANE,268
MONGIN,JOHN D,406
MONK,ELI,406;TEARSON B
  267;WILLIS,406;WM,309
MONNOX,JMGM,232
MONRO,DONALD,208
MONROE,DANIEL,406;DAVID
. 32,48;JOHN,55;JOSEPH
. 32,48,55;NANCY,55,178
. POLLY A,198;STEPHEN
. 10,48
MONROW,DAVID,12;JOSEPH
  12
MONT,D,401
MONTFORD,ANN,242

MONTFORT,ALEXANDER,267
. JOHN,267;JOHN C,267
. NANCY,273;OSCAR L,267
. REBECCA,268;WM,267
MONTGOMERY,ADALINE,265
. BENJAMIN H,337;DAVID
. 91,337;ELIZ,242;HUGH
. 291,406;JAMES,267
. JAMES H,337;JAMES N
. 332;JAS M,288;JOSEPH
. 288,304;JOSEPH C,208
. JOSIAH,288;LIDDIER
. 322;ROBERT,288-289;WM
. 267,319;WM W,406
MONTREY,JOHN D,75
MOOCSETT,LEWIS Y,43
MOODY,ANDERSON,406;E B
. 247;ELIAS B,267
. EMELINE,267;EMMA,274
. EMMELIN,269;GEORGE
. 267;GEORGE W,267
. GEORGIANA,391;GREEN
. 64,114;GREENE,267
. HENRY,267;JAMES A,267
. JAMES M,406;JAMES
. MADISON,406;JOEL,357
. JOHN,267;JOHN C,267
. LOUISA,271;MARTHA A
. 271;MARY A,269;MARY T
. 263;S E,269;VIRGINIA
. 253;WALDMAN,267
. WALTER F,43
MOON,ARTHUR,2;CATHERINE
. 260;CAUSBY,267
. FRANKLIN H,267;GEORGE
. W,267;JAMES,270,406
. JAS,240;JOHN,343;JOHN
. F,208;LEWIS,72
. MARGARET,272;REBEKAH
. 264;SARAH M,240;WM L
. 267
MOOR,DAVID,267;GEORGE
. 82;ISAAC,267;LUCINDA
. 212;MARY ANN,206
. MILLY,204;THOMAS,83
. YOUNG,267
MOORE,145,234,302;A L
. 208;AARON,348;AAUG,21
. ABNER,8;ABNER R,55
. ADALINE,246;ADELINE E
. 387;ALDRIDGE,20,22,25
. ALFORD,212;AMANDA M
. 37;ANDERSON C,267
. ANDREW,2;ASBURY GREEN
. 267;AUGUSTUS,22,25
. 406;AUGUSTUS C,337
. AUGUSTUS M,198;BALDY
. 6;BENJAMIN,71;BERTAM
. 267;BETSEY,203;BETTIE
. C,208;C,142;CASWELL
. 20,22;CATHERINE,398
. CHARLES,298;CLEMENT
. 84,86,93,101-102,303
. CORRINNE C,260;CRESSA
. 270;CURTIS,267;D B M
. 89,131;DANIEL L,57
. DAVID BRADY,90;DAVID
. C,267;DEMPSEY,198
. DILLY,42;DREWRY S,198
. E,106;EDMD,302;EDW
. 359;EDWARD,293;ELIJAH
. 293;ELIZ,402;ELIZ A
. 419;ELIZA,277;ELIZA J
. 259;ELIZABETH,32,261
. ELLEN,387;EMILY,257
. EMILY H,412;EMMA,411
. EPHRAIM,310-311
. ETHELDRED,20;ETHELRED

MOORE(cont)
. 22,24;F D,208;FRANCES
. 36;FRANCES A,271
. FREELING H,267;G W
. 141;GEORGE,267-268
. GEORGE W,268;GEORGIA
. ANN,267;GILLIS,268
. GILLY,240,256,261-262
. 277;HENRY H,268;HIRAM
. 168,268,337;HIRUM,230
. HORTENSE,246;IRENE P
. 262;ISAAC,226,261,268
. ISAAC D,268;ISAAC J
. 268;J D,268;J W,268
. JACKSON,268;JACOB,350
. 365;JAMES,10,32,168
. 208,249,251,259,262
. 263-265,268-270,272
. 276-277,279,283,286
. 287,318,355;JAMES B
. 208;JAMES M,268;JAMES
. W,313;JANE,256;JANE
. MARY,43;JAS,236,238
. 241,243;JEFFERY,406
. JENNY,263;JEREMIAH
. 268,291,301-302;JESSE
. 214;JESSE I,268;JOHN
. 8,43,55,97,159,168
. 198,208,268,337,366
. 406;JOHN A,208;JOHN B
. 268;JOHN C,268;JOHN H
. 82;JOHN R,32;JONATHAN
. 298,318;JOSEPH J,173
. JOSHIAH,89;JOSIAH,55
. 86,93;LAURA,241
. LEAVEN,289;LELLA W
. 250;LEVIN,310-311
. LEWIS,59,71,80,84,90
. 113,118,120-121,128
. 130,132-133,136-137
. 138-139,142,147-148
. LEWIS M,208;LUCIUS A
. 314;LULA W,255;MANNEN
. 198;MANNING,214
. MARGARET,246;MARTHA
. 236,241;MARTHA
. MATILDA,245;MARTHA S
. 245;MARTIN B,198;MARY
. 273,381,401-402;MARY
. A,247;MARY J,282;MARY
. M,210;MARY S,284
. MATILDA J,243;METSEY
. 274;MILLY,398;MIRIAM
. 195;MORIN,341
. MOURNING,51;NANCY,261
. 310,396,414;NANCY
. LOURANA,208;NAPHTHALI
. BYRAM,406;NEUBIL,310
. OBSORN,268;CSCAR D
. 268;PALATINE,337
. PATSEY,251,264;PEGGY
. 279;PLEASANT,32;POLLY
. 239,265,284;R,288,295
. R M,97;RANSOM,268
. REBECCA,143,147,391
. REBECCA B,287;REUBIN
. 7;RICHARD,168,184-185
. RICHD,6;RISDO,301
. RISDON,295,297-298
. 320;ROBERT,268,355
. ROWLAND,48;RUTH,268
. S J,39;SAM,2;SAMUEL,3
. 268,289;SARAH,32,241
. 273;SARAH JANE,264
. SARAH L,208;SARAH LOU
. SMITH,255;SEABORN S
. 208;SIMEON,198
. SPENCER,268;SUSAN,204

. SUSANNA,389;TABITH
. 310;TAYLOR B,9;THOMAS
. 7,32,43,55,89,93,141
. 198,406;THOS,82,144
. TURNER B,52;TURNER R
. 32;W A,239,256;W E,43
. W W,236,241,256,258
. 268,270,272,286
. WILLIAM,32,198,298
. 310,406;WILLIS,71-72
. WINFIELD,49;WINFRED
. 32;WM,253,268,282;WM
. B,268;WM H,268;WM W
. 260,264
MOORFIELD,MARTHA,383
MOORS,WILLIAM,7
MOOSE,FRANCES R,250
MOOT,ANDREW,208
MORAN,BASEL,406;BASIL
  268
MORAND,JOHN,406
MORE,232;JANE,408;MARK
  318
MORELAND,228;FRANCES
. 332;FRANCIS,337;ISAAC
. 290-291,302;JAMES M
. 268;JOHN,337;MATTIE N
. 278;POLLY,262;ROBERT
. 328;ROBT,292;SALLY
. 236;THOMAS,337
MORELL,MARY,420
MORES,MARTHA,196
MORGAN,ADRAIN S,268
. ANDREW,406;AUGUSTUS F
. 406;BARTHOLOMEW,406
. CHARLES,337
. CHRISTOPHER C,43
. DELILAH,401;DRURY
. CHIPSON,268;EDWARD
. 406;ELDRIDGE,406;ELIZ
. 420;ELLINGTON,309-310
. ELLIS,406;ENOCH C,268
. FRANCIS,343;FREDERICK
. A,406;GEORGE W,406
. HENRIETTA,247;J,327
. JAMES,406;JANE,266
. JEREMIAH,406;JESSE C
. 208;JINSEY,419;JOHN
. 406;JOSEPH,406
. LUCINDA,393;MARY,364
. MARY A,266;MARY E,246
. MIL,207;MILLENTON,406
. MILTON,337;MOSES,406
. NATHAN,304;NEEDHAM
. 406;NICHOLAS,406
. OLIVIA L N,413;ROBERT
. 364,406;STOKELY,359
. STOKLEY,337;SUSAN M
. 204;T R,280;THOMAS
. 364,406;THOMAS H,268
. W H,268;WILLIAM,406
. WILLIAM J,337;WM,268
. 289
MORGON,WM T,356
MORING,ANDREW,208;CLARA
. 208;CLARRA,208
. EMELINE,207;JOEL J
. 208;P B,208;THOMAS
. 208;W T,208
MORIS,NANCY,201
MORLAND,BARTLEY,230
MORLEY,WILLIAM,55
MORRAN,JOSEPH,289
MORREL,SIMEON,268
MORRIS,179;ALBERT,208
. ANDREW,268;BENJAMIN F
. 332,337;C C,147,149
. CARRIE E,286

. CHRISTOPHER C,147
. COLY,43;ELIZ,383;ELIZ
. ANN,419;ELIZABETH,45
. 259;FRANCES,268;G,163
. GEORGE,268;GERALD,187
. GERARD,159;HANNAH R
. 270;HARPER,208;I,236
. ISABELLA I,420;J Y
. 100,116,130;JAMES,59
. 81,85,122,136,295
. JAMES E,32;JAMES S
. 146;JOHN,82,105,126
. 144;JOHN C,90,100
. JOHN G,337;JORDAN,130
. 146;JOSIAH,100;LEMON
. 268;LYDIA,379;MAHALEY
. 409;MARGARET,406;MARY
. 239;MARY ANN,277
. MOSES,7,14,16;NANCY
. 212;POLLY,282,284
. SALLIE F,240;SALLY
. 400,406;SARAH,69,399
. SARAH ANN,404;SARAH M
. 332,337;SARAH R,260
. SIMON,230;STEPHEN,337
. TENA,38;WILLIAM,337
. WILLIAM T,55;WM F,130
. ZILPAH,421
MORRISON,ELIZABETH,5
. ISAAC,268;JOHN,1,5
. 406;JOHN B,32;MARY
. FRANCIS,414;NANCY,400
. ROSINA S,405;WILLIAM
. 21,23;WM J,268
MORRISS,
. MERRIAN MARSHALL,163
. MITCHEL,307-308
. THOMAS,302
MORROW,EWING,284;HUGH E
  268;SARAH,264
MORSE,ADALINE,37
  ADELINE,413;ANN,386
MORTON,WM T,359
MOSELEY,BENJAMIN,268
. HENRY,332;JOHN A,268
. JOSHUA,323;LEWIS,268
. W R H,257;W R M,268
. W S,208
MOSELY,C T,212;E B,231
. E W,198;ELBERT,198
. ELIZABETH,212;ELNAR
. 198;HENRY,337
. MARGARET,200;MARY I
. 286;POLLY,276;W R,337
. W R N,263;WILLIAM S
. 212
MOSES,JOHN,337;MARY,413
  OBEDIER,289;WRIGHT,19
MOSLEY,32;ASHLEY I,208
. CHAMPION,268;CLEMENT
. T,208;FRANCE,387;MARY
. R,211;MILLEY,387
. WILLIAM W,208
MOSS,ARCHIBALD,337
. CARSON F,268;FOUNTAIN
. 8,26;GEORGIA A,242
. HENRY,268,319;JOHN D
. 79;JOSEPH,75;LEWIS
. 322,329,350;MARGARET
. ANN,401;MATILDA
. MELVILLE,384;PETER M
. 268;SUSANNAH C,337;VA
. A,247
MOTE,JEREMIAH,406;JOHN
. 406;RACHEL,406;SILAS
. 168
MOTLEY,ISAAC,311
MOTTE,LEVI S,268

MOUNCE,M,100,113
MOUNGER,LENORA ANN,253
. MARY,268
MOUNSE.S,105
MOUNT,MOSES,82,88-89,97
MOUNTAIN,ROBERT,406
MOUNTCASTLE,DAVID,95
MOUNTHESQUE,DANIEL M
406
MOUNTS,IRVIN,100;MOSES
88,100;URBIN,97
MOURLAND,JOHN,226
MOXLEY,BENJAMIN,32,47
. 55;BENJAMIN A,198
. DANIEL,7,32,48,55
. HENRY M,208;J T,208
. JAMES,7;JANE,201;JNO
. 10;JOHN,47,55;JOSEPH
. 208;MATHER,55;MATTHEW
. 47;NATHANIEL,32
. RACHEL,196;SARAH,198
. WILLIAM,7;WM,47
MOY,EDWIN,24
MOYE,CATHARINE,393
. MARIA,388;MARY,402
. THOMAS,406;THOMAS W
. 337
MOYNE,EDWIN,25
MRCAY,ROSEY,268
MRTIN,JOHN,352
MULFORD,THOMAS,55
. WILLIAM B,32,50
MULKEV,HOMER V,50
MULKEY,HOMER V,55;ISAAC
. 52,55;JAMES,268;JNO,9
. MOCKEY,55;MOSES,50,55
. 342;SARAH,39
. WASHINGTON,55
MULKY,ISAAC,32;MOSES,32
. WILLIAM,32
MULLALLY,WM T,313
MULLEN,COSANA,401
. PHILIP,406;WILLIAM
. 191
MULLER,JAMES,187
MULLIN,JAMES,406;JNO
352
MULLING,ANN E,211;EMMA
205
MULLINS,
. ANNA JOSEPHINE,242
. CHARLES,268;G D,97
. GEORGIANNA J,235;JOHN
. 268;JULIUS S,268
. LOUISA C,269;MALONE
. 299,328-329;MARTHA
. ANN,235;NANCY,255
. NATHANIEL,309;NATHL
. 310;THOMAS K,268
. WILLIAM,97;WM,97
MULLOY,JEREMIAH,58
MUNCRIEF,LEWIS,406
MUNDAY,REUBEN,70
MUNNERLYN,JOHN D,43
MUNPHREE,208
MUNRO,R W B,406
MUNROE,JOSEPH,10
MURDEN,H D,246;HENNING
. D,268;MALACHI,236,248
. MALICHI,266,270,278
. MALICIA,268;REDMOND
. 268;W D,235
MURDOCK,FEILDING W,406
. M J,211;THOMAS P,55
MURDOW,MALICHI,268
MURKISON,JOHN,60
MURPH,MARY,405
MURPHEE,EMILY,42

MURPHEY,ALEXANDER,50
. 406;ANDREW,268;BETSEY
. 282;EDEY,262;EDMUND
. 406;JAMES,294;JMES
. 406;JOHANNA,409;JOHN
. 48,269;LAVINA,380
. LEROY H,406;LEVICY
. 398;MARIA,384;MICHAEL
. 208;MILLEDGE,406
. NANCY ANNE,411;SALLY
. 233;SARAH,386;WILLIAM
. 48
MURPHREE,ALEXANDER,55
. EMILY V,57;JOSIAH,10
. 48;L,203;MARGARET J
. 37;WILLIAM,11-12,48
. 55;WM,9;WRIGHT,9,12
. 48,55
MURPHREY,JOSIAH,55
MURPHY,ABSALEM F,406
. ALEXANDER,406;ANN S
. 408;BARBARA W,411
. BARTHOLOMEW,233;ELIZ
. ANN,392;ELIZABETH,233
. JAMES,32,406;JANE MAC
. 387;JOHANAH,396;JOHN
. 32,64,296,304,407
. JOSIAH,32;LYDIA,209
. MALACHI,47;MARGUERITE
. 381;MARTHA,389;MARY
. 389,404,411;MICHELL
. 208;NANCY,410
. NICHOLAS,407;ROBERT A
. 43;SARAH,296,414;SARY
. 233;SOPHIA A,44
. TIMOTHY,407;WILLIAM
. 32,208;WILLIAM D,43
. WM,407;WRIGHT,32
MURR,THOMAS,407
MURRAH,CHARLES,355,407
. GEO,407;JAMES,269
. MARY,280
MURRAY,ADALINE,43
. AMANDA,36;CALEB,43
. CHARLOTTE,42;DAVID,6
. 32;ENOCH,43;GEORGE
. 269,407;HENRY,49
. JAMES,32,50,407
. JEREMIAH,50;JOHN,6,32
. 407;MARY,32,188;MARY
. A,40;MATTHEW,155
. MICHAEL,407;STEPHEN,6
. 9;THOMAS,407;TIMOTHY
. 6,32,50
MURREL,THOMAS W,186
MURRELL,
. THOMAS WILLIAM,153
MURREN,ELIZA R,384
MURREY,JASPER,208
MURRY,BENJAMIN E,208
. HENRY,55,85;JANE,85
. JOHN,85,132;MARTHA
. 132;MARTHW,85;MARY
. ANNE,392;ROSA ANN,204
. SEPEY,55
MUSE,MARY,403;MAY,195
MUSGROVE,CATHERINE,270
. EDW H,407;ELIZABETH
. 279;HARRISON,407
. LOUISA H,409;MARY G B
. 409;NANCY,254;ROBT H
. 407
MUSSA,POLLEY,49
MUSTIN,390,392;D K,407
. DAVID R,407
MYER,L B,55
MYERS,EDW H,407
. HENRIETTA,403;HENRY

. 407
MYGATT,GEORGE,337
MYLES,WILLIAM H,337
MYRICK,CAROLYN,237;EVAN
. 254;EVANS,235,269
. JOHN,268,271,274,306
. JOSHUA,6;ROBERT,97
. ROBERT T,82
N--LTON,BETSEY R,256
NABB,MARGARET,200-201
. MARTHA,211;WILLIAM B
. 213
NAGLE,NANCY,403
NAIL,ELIZ,416;JAMES,9
NAIPER,WILLIAM,140
NALL,NATHAN,338
NALLS,RICHARD,170
NALLY,DANIEL,95;MARY
399
NALY,SUSAN,395
NAMACK,JANE,388
NANCE,JANE,268;JOHN,60
NANCE?,162
NANCY,ANNE W,238
NAPIER,215;CLOE,215
. ELIZ,410;MYRICK,97
. 107;THOMAS,215,407
. URIAH,89
NAPP,JNO,223
NAPPIER,PATRICK,232
NARES,JOHN,32
NASH,CAROLINE,262
. CLEMENT,224,233;SARAH
. N,280
NASON,ELIAS,407
NASWORTHY,GEORGE,55
. GEORGE WASHINGTON,198
. JOHN,43;MITCHELL O,43
. THOMAS J,43;URIAH,55
. VIRGINIA,39;WILLIAM
. 48,55
NATHAN,HANNAH,45
NAVE,MARY E,255
NAVES,BETHENA,413;JOHN
52
NAVEY,WILSON,4
NAVY,WILSON,32
NAYWORTHY,JOHN,12
NAZERY,HENRY,269
NAZWORTHY,JOHN,32
. OGBURN,32
NCNELLY,JOHN,22
NEAL,ALDER,269;ANN G
. 242;BASSEL,150;ELIZ
. REBECCA,383;ELIZABETH
. 150;GEO W,269;JAMES
. 82,91;JERRY,122;JOHN
. 88;JOHN W,198;MARYANN
. JOAN,200;RICHARD,150
. ROBERT,269;SARAH,407
. STEPHEN,360
NEALY,JAMES M,43
NEATHERLIN,MARY,413
NEAVES,JOHN,309
NEED,ELIZA ANN,210
NEEL,AARON,227
. ELIZABETH,257;JAMES L
. 209;JOHN H,314
. SARIANN,200;WM S,314
NEELY,JOHN F,269
NEEVES,DANIEL,321
NEGIC,MARY G,388
NEGRO,AARON,150,175,327
. 375;ABBY,302;ABEDNEGO
. 329;ABERDEEDN,316
. ABERDEEN,319;ABIGAIL
. 153,327;ABNER,185
. ABRAHAM,160,162,189

NEGRO(cont)
. 230,301,303,376
. ABRAHM,301;ABRAM,130
. 164,174,179,188,290
. 291-292,302,305-306
. 373;ABRAM (YOUNG
. ABRAM),188;ABSOM,289
. ACRE,293;ADAM,164,299
. 317,320;ADSTON,317
. AGG,164;AGGE,304,318
. AGGEY,327;AGGY,60,153
. 160,175,187,193,324
. AGNES,109;AILSEY,164
. 174;ALBERT,155,175
. ALCE,162;ALECK,302
. 316;ALEK,157;ALEX,154
. 169;ALFRED,162,192
. 378;ALICE,172;ALICK
. 168,186;ALLEN,65,154
. 159,171,175,179;ALSA
. 307;ALSE,307;ALSEY
. 109,376;AMELIA,229
. AMEY,155,234,298,309
. 316,318;AMOS,190;AMY
. 184,186,299,306,318
. ANDERSON,169;ANDREW
. 163;ANDREWS,127;ANN
. 302;ANNA,329;ANNE,186
. ANTHONY,74,153,185
. 288,296,304,371;ARCH
. 189;ARMOR,302;ARTHUR
. 164,184,288,296,304
. 317,320;ARVA,181
. AUGUST,170,186;AUSTIN
. 162,189;AVINGTON,169
. BAALAW,189;BANISTER
. 189;BANJAMIN,182
. BARBARY,322;BARTLETT
. 114,301;BATCHELL,324
. BATH,165;BATTY,162
. BAZIL,185;BECK,160
. 287,301-302,318;BECKE
. 168;BECKY,78,293
. BELLA,186;BEN,108,153
. 154,158,164,172,179
. 181,185,189,234,291
. 302,307,317-319,327
. BENARD,153;BENIR,302
. BENJ,320,324;BENJAMIN
. 91,376;BENN,319
. BERANS,166;BERNEY,108
. BESS,170;BETSEY,70
. 171-172,309,322;BETT
. 60;BETTY,156,164,169
. 171,175,181,185,187
. 189,327,377;BEUAH,185
. BIBB,163;BIG SAM,293
. BIGG,185;BILL,160,165
. 174,187,301-302
. BILLER,306;BILLY,293
. BINAH,186;BINER,293
. 373;BIRD,164;BOB,161
. 164,169,172-173,177
. 179,186,189,293,302
. 311,318,329,375
. BOB (BIG BOB),164
. BOBB,172;BRIDGET,172
. 177,377;BUKY (LITTLE
. BUKY),171;CADER,229
. CAESAR,186,326;CAGEY
. 135;CANDACE,160
. CANDIS,160;CAPS,164
. CAPTIN,296;CAREY,164
. CARMELIA,169;CAROLINE
. 108,378;CARY,302
. CASSAE,182;CATE,155
. 157-160,162,177,181
. 185;CATERINE,318;CATO

. 302,307;CATOE,307,318
. CATY,293,368;CEALEY
. 292;CEASER,189;CELIA
. 158;CENA,167;CESAR
. 292;CHANDIS,172
. CHANEY,192,293,317
. 327;CHANY,287;CHARITY
. 189,302,319;CHARLES
. 163-164,168,172,176
. 179,182,305,318,329
. 377;CHARLES MAY,186
. CHARLEY,156;CHARLOTT
. 303;CHARLOTTE,63,71
. 160,162,179,183,186
. 187,189,192,293,298
. 305,328;CHARLY,160
. 177;CHINA,177,183,189
. 190;CHLOA,189;CHLOE
. 183,189,293,319
. CICERO,162;CILE,366
. CINDA,170;CINDY,326
. CINTHA,289;CLABON,322
. CLAEY,161;CLAR,60
. CLARK,135;CLARY,162
. 168,179,185;CLEARTOLL
. 179;CLEB,175;CLEM,108
. CLO,310;CLOE,191,234
. 293,311;CLOEY,290,317
. CLOLE,175;COOK,155
. CORNELIUS,297;CREASY
. 179,376;CUD,169
. CUDJOE,317;CUMBERLAND
. 164;CUSSIA,186
. CYNTHIA,302;CYRUS,158
. 169,189;DAFNEY,109
. DAN,329;DANIEL,60,104
. 153,155,164,169,180
. 181,184,189,292,301
. 307,318,325,329
. DAPHNE,158,170
. DAPHNEY,177,185,293
. DARCAS,193;DAVE,110
. 159-160,193,301,311
. DAVID,163,185,317,321
. 324,327,329;DAVIE,186
. DAVIE (LITTLE DAVIE)
. 186;DAVY,70,302;DAWL
. 151;DEADON,289;DEDAN
. 290;DELCE,190;DELCY
. 156,159;DELEE,375
. DELIA,186;DELILAH,327
. 351;DELPHA,165;DENNIS
. 154;DERRY,155;DIANAH
. 181;DICE,162,318
. DICEY,156,160,318,328
. 377;DICK,78,155,160
. 161-162,166,169,176
. 179,187,189,288,296
. 301-302,307,309,319
. 324,352,374
. DICK (LITTLE DICK)
. 307;DICY,302;DILSEY
. 172,234;DILSY,186
. DINA,179,298;DINAH,75
. 104,158,171,192,298
. 302,327;DINAH (LITTLE
. DINAH),182;DINAH (OLD
. DINAH),182;DINE,346
. DINER,289,316;DOCTOR
. 193-194;DOLL,157,164
. 186,288,301,318
. DOLLEY,234,318;DORCAS
. 299;DOSS,375;DOVER
. 293;DRIVER,293;DUKE
. 289;EADY,166;EARLY,60
. EASTER,157,167,179
. 296;EDD,69;EDE,311
. EDENBOROUGH,182;EDEY

. 327;EDIE,169
. EDINBURGH,187;EDITH
. 288,296,304;EDMOND
. 155;EDMUND,104,162
. EDNEY,327;EDWARD,185
. EDY,229,296;ELENDER
. 163;ELI,135;ELIAS,18
. ELICE,153;ELINON,169
. ELISHA,234,376;ELIZA
. 108,186,375;ELLEN,70
. ELLICK,293,319
. ELLINNEU,293;ELLIS
. 293;ELMINA,169;ELSE
. 162;ELSIE? (ALCE),162
. ELVEY,181;ELVIA,189
. EMANUAL,169;EMELY,160
. ENOCH,374;EPHRAIM,60
. 164;ESSEX,369;ESTER
. 292,296;ESTHER,109
. 179,288-289,302,304
. 359,377;EVE,158;FAIN
. 296;FAN,169;FANN,318
. FANNY,154,158,189,288
. 296,304,317-318,320
. 322-323,327,329
. FARINY,188;FARM,169
. FARY,164;FEBE,317
. FIBBY,155;FIELDING
. 158;FILIS,317;FILL
. 329;FILLIS,322;FITUS
. 191;FLANDER,293;FLORA
. 79,168,170,180,189
. 294,302;FLOYD,94
. FOREST,307;FRANCES
. 377-378;FRANCIS,182
. FRANK,164,179,185,288
. 296,304,307,317,320
. 328,352,377;FRANKEY
. 153;FRANKEY (GIRL),72
. FRANKY,171,184;FRED
. 183;FREDERICK,183
. FRIDAY,302;GADESS,190
. GAGE,62;GARDNER,72
. GARRETT,189;GENNA,168
. GEORGE,60,71,74,150
. 162,164,166,177,179
. 184,186,189,192,293
. 294,297,301-302,317
. 318,330;GERALD,158
. GILBERT,163;GINNEY
. 302,321;GLOSTER,328
. GLOUCESTER,317
. GODFREY,375;GOODMAN
. 127;GRACE,78,164,183
. 231;GUNDY,357;GUY,156
. 329;HAGER,162;HAL,162
. 293;HALL,189,293,318
. HAMILTON,169;HAMPTON
. 164,168,317;HANAH,228
. HANDY,302;HANNAH,64
. 77-78,151,159-160,162
. 164,170,177,187,189
. 235,288,293,296-297
. 301-302,304,317,330
. 352,377;HANNER,317
. 324;HANNIBAL,181
. HANNIBEL,166;HARK,321
. HARREL,324;HARRIET,79
. 377;HARRIETT,110,162
. HARRIOT,302,306
. HARROT,184;HARRY,157
. 160,162,164,169,178
. 181,187,232,288,290
. 301-302,311,316,324
. 325,327,367
. HARRY (LITTLE HARRY)
. 288;HARY,319;HECTOR
. 189,293;HEICENTY,306

NEGRO(cont)
. HEINA,192;HENRY,162
. 171-172,179,185,189
. 291,377;HERCULEAS,182
. HERCULUS,163;HESTER
. 293;HETHY,306;HETTY
. 186,306;HICTOR,293
. HIOTT,168;HOMER,375
. HUFFY,292;IBBEY,292
. IBBY,311;IKE,375
. IMARY,375;INNY,373
. ISAAC,162,164,170,185
. 297,302-303,305-306
. 327,329,375
. ISAAC (LITTLE ISAAC)
. 185;ISAC,317;ISAM,159
. ISBEL,154,165,189
. ISHAM,162,179,189
. ISHAMAEL,187;ISOM,323
. ISRAEL,292;ISSABEL
. 192;IVEY,302;JACK,80
. 153-154,156,170,178
. 192,293,297,301-302
. 303,305,317,320,325
. JACOB,162,164-165,175
. 288,293,296,299,329
. JACOB ANN,164;JAME
. 299;JAMES,166-168,183
. 229,301,324;JAMIMA
. 369;JAMY,155;JANE,164
. 177,230,234,328
. JANREY,188;JARRATT
. 154;JEFF,108;JEFFERY
. 186,189;JEFFRY,78
. JEFRY,307;JEM,159
. JENCEY,172;JENCY,229
. JENNY,78,164-165,186.
. 192,311,322,373;JENY
. 188;JEPETER,299
. JEREMIAH,155;JERRY,78
. 91,163,172,182,187
. 189,298,320-321,323
. 369,376;JERY,79,309
. JESSE,108,172,178-179
. 316,377;JESSEY,376
. JIM,177,181,186-187
. 192,288,306,327
. JIMIMY,78;JIN,184,289
. 296;JINCY,310;JINNEY
. 229,291-292,322;JINNY
. 160,181,185,288,290
. 296,304,311,374,376
. JO,322;JOAN,288,296
. 304;JOBE,231;JOE,155
. 162,167,169,176,184
. 186,288-290,296,302
. 304;JOE (LITTLE JOE)
. 186;JOEL,327;JOHH,302
. JOHN,78,155,160,162
. 182,184,189,307,309
. 317-318,328,375
. JOHNSTON,162;JORDAN
. 71;JORDIN,155;JOSEPH
. 104,160,322,377
. JOSHUA,162,186,377
. JUD,309;JUDA,305,307
. 330;JUDAH,155,229
. JUDE,163,165,167,169
. 179,291,324;JUDITH
. 328;JUDY,67,171,178
. 183,186,290-291,298
. 375;JULIETT,302
. JULIUS,104,318;JULY
. 185,302;JUM,318;JUNE
. 24-25;JUPITER,293
. KATE,153,316;KATY,189
. KELLIS,374;KELLY,175
. KET,189;KEZIAH,172

. 316;KING,230;KITTY
. 177,377;KIZIA,192
. KUFFEY,292;LAFAYETTE
. 110;LARRY,355;LAURA
. 175;LEACH,172;LEAH
. 187,317;LEEANNER,124
. LEMERICK,186;LEN,319
. LEROY,74,135;LETLY
. 189;LETT,301;LETTUCE
. 24-25;LETTY,162,193
. 318;LEVEN,311;LEVER
. 317;LEVI,316;LEVIN
. 293;LEWIS,60,73,160
. 163-164,172,176-177
. 183,186-187,189,316
. 319,327,329,377
. LIDDEY,193;LIDDY,193
. LILL,185;LILLIE,156
. LIMUS,169;LINDER,175
. LINDSEY,377;LINNEY
. 193;LINNY,192;LITTLE
. 160;LITTLETON,375
. LIVISIA,181;LOISHAM
. 60;LOTT,306;LOTTY,375
. LOUCINDA,375;LOUIS
. 179;LOUISA,160;LOVEY
. 189;LUCE,302,378
. LUCEY,289;LUCINDA,169
. LUCY,58,78,104,154
. 162-164,168-169,172
. 181,189,229-232,234
. 291,301-302,304,307
. 323,327,329,377
. LUCY (YOUNG LUCY),189
. LUCY EDD,69;LUKE,168
. 316;LYDA,317;LYDDA
. 151,311,327;LYDIA,70
. 180,189,376;LYLLA,169
. MAGE,164;MAGGY,302
. MALCUM,328;MANERVY
. 108;MANSFIELD,189
. MARCH,151,288,296,302
. MARCUS,186;MARIA,156
. 169;MARIAH,155,176
. 184-185,189-190,375
. MARK,170;MARLIN,164
. MARTHA,182,291,317
. 320,357;MARTHY,372
. MARTIN,288,290;MARY
. 108,150,153,162-163
. 164,169,175-176,179
. 181,185,189,291,317
. 318,320-321,323,327
. 377;MASON,377;MAT,187
. 317,373;MATDIGON,174
. MATILDA,104,170,176
. 189;MAURICE,186;MAYS
. 114;MEAL,185;MELINDA
. 188;MELVINA,171
. MERCAR,164;MERIAH,189
. MILL,301-302;MILLA
. 155;MILLEN,292;MILLEY
. 162,287,292,302,316
. 375;MILLY,104,150,160
. 164,167,169,183,188
. MIMA,192;MINGO,327
. MINOR,189;MIRA,175
. MOLIDA,226;MOLL,292
. 307,320;MOLLEY,302
. MOLLY,164;MONDAY,160
. 182;MONOAH,108;MORIAH
. 234,293;MOSES,156,164
. 168-169,186,188-189
. 302,317,320;MOURNING
. 299;MURRIBER,326;NAN
. 288,296,301-302,304
. 307,378;NANCE,78,160
. 189,290-291,311,375

. NANCEY,154,156,166
. 172,181-182,189;NANCY
. 164,168,177,288-289
. 296;NANEE,160;NANN,60
. NANNY,171,186;NANY
. 307;NASE,325;NAT,170
. NATHAN,184;NATHANIEL
. 154;NATT,160;NEAL,189
. 301;NED,164,169,178
. 186,293,302,307,323
. 367,375;NEDD,156;NEIL
. 301;NELL,153,166,179
. 181,235,289,307;NELLY
. 155-156,164,169,193
. NELSON,179,182,186
. NICK,160,185;NICY,164
. NUTT,306;NUTTY,306
. OBEY,292;OERA,186
. ORRY,185;OSTIN,16.1
. OUIDA,375;PAGE,158
. PALLAS,172;PAMELA,186
. PARROT,189;PARTERICK
. 319;PAT,153,157
. PATIENCE,184,291,317
. PATRICK,164,172
. PATSEY,377;PATT,164
. 215,288,290,297,302
. 317;PATTY,162;PEARSON
. 70;PEG,184,298;PEGG
. 298,302;PEGGY,175,186
. 187,293,369;PETER,153
. 156,158-159,162,164
. 168-169,171-173,175
. 176,183-184,186-187
. 188-189,288,293,296
. 298,301,304-305,325
. 357,375;PETER (BIG
. PETER),163;PETER (OLD
. PETER),162;PHEBE,186
. 305;PHERBY,160;PHIL
. 160,172,181,324
. PHILIP,327;PHILIS,177
. 190;PHILL,158,164,302
. PHILLIS,164,172,179
. 189,230,322;PHILLY
. 157,166;PINK,181
. PLATO,170;POE (OLE
. POE),301;POLADORE,153
. POLL,177,307;POLLEY
. 291,298,309,317,322
. POLLY,162,164,166,170
. 177,185,189;POLYDORE
. 164,189;POMP,310
. POMPEY,168,185,301
. 311,372;POMPY,293
. POOL,325;PRESCILLA
. 186;PRESKY,166;PRICES
. 189;PRISCILLA,328
. QUAMINA,186;QUAMMONY
. 158-159;RACHAEL,187
. RACHEL,108,135,155
. 160,162,164,166-167
. 169-170,172,176,186
. 212,234,293,299,301
. 327,375;RACHEL (OLD
. RACHEL),293;RALPH,162
. 179;RANDAL,375;RANSOM
. 305;REASON,180
. REBECCA,328;REUBEN
. 177,293,328;REUBIN
. 293;RHODA,190,317
. RHOENE (FEMALE),74
. RICHA,155;RICHARD,175
. 298;ROBEN,185;ROBERT
. 70,167,309,317-318
. ROBIE,150;ROBIN,162
. 318;RODERICK,175,186
. ROGER,318;ROSE,74,154

NEGRO(cont)
. 158-159,161,170,179
. 186,292,300,302,323
. SAL,169,186;SAL (OLD
. SAL),162;SALINA,377
. SALL,158,230,304,307
. SALLEY,288,293,296
. 307;SALLY,60,155,165
. 172,176,186,293,375
. SALLY (LITTLE SALLY)
. 189;SALLY (OLD SALLY)
. 189;SALTAGE,186;SAM
. 108,154-155,162,164
. 169,177,181,183-184
. 189,229,288,290,292
. 293-294,296,301-302
. 304,311,323,346,375
. 377-378;SAM "BLACK
. SAM",104;SAM (LITTLE
. SAM),171;SAMBO,154
. 297;SAMPSON,192,291
. 302;SAMUEL,104,163
. 178,317,321;SANCO,293
. SARA,326;SARA (YOUNG
. SARA),179;SARAH,108
. 135,168,173,175,177
. 182,184,188-189,307
. 317-318,320,326-327
. 329,375;SARAH (OLD
. SARAH),301;SARAH ANN
. 108;SARAH SUBRINE,172
. SARRY (OLD SARRY),177
. SARRY (YOUNG SARRY)
. 177;SARY,291,302
. SAURA,168;SAWNEY,164
. SAWYER,78;SEALEY,290
. SEMORE,210;SENA,375
. SEPTEMBER,186;SEREENA
. 371;SIDNEY,162;SILLAH
. 104;SILLAR,178;SILLER
. 226,293,302,330
. SILMAN,323;SILVEY,182
. 234,305,330,349;SILVY
. 301,307;SIMION,181
. SIMON,162,166-169,175
. 292,302,308,376
. SINDYRILLA,306
. SINTHEA,177;SIRE,164
. SISERO,357;SISLEY,164
. SOFAS,374;SOL,172
. SOLOMON,168,172,179
. 185,318,325;SOMERSAT
. 175;SOOK,290-291
. SOOKY,210;SOPHA,176
. 377;SOPHIA,297;SOPHY
. 186;SOPLEY,184
. SPENCER,114,317
. SQUIRE,185,289-290
. 306;STACE,301;STACY
. 324;STAFFORD,234
. STEPHEN,77-78,164,179
. 193,297,307,321,323
. 373,375;STEPHENY,320
. STEPNEY,109;STIFF,305
. SUCH,172;SUCK,289,307
. 320;SUCKEY,184;SUCKY
. 293;SUE,302,318;SUK
. 153;SUKE,307;SUKEE
. 299;SUKEY,317;SUKY
. 162;SULAH,377;SURRY
. 184;SUSAN,162,167,169
. 181;SUSANNAH,154,177
. SUTON,321;SUTTON,301
. 323;SYBBA,297;SYLVIA
. 154,169,184,189;TAGGY
. 189;TANNER,172;TENAR
. 179;TENER,317;TERRY
. 164;THENY,164;THOMAS

. 192,319;THONY,301
. THOS,156;TILLA,169
. 327;TILLER,162,230
. TILLY,377;TIM,170
. TIM (OLD TIM),301
. TITUS,189,376;TOBE
. 328;TOBY,302;TOLBERT
. 155;TOLIFERRO,155;TOM
. 155,162-164,167-168
. 172,186,231,234,300
. 302,322,327-328,375
. TOM (OLD TOM),293
. TONE,181;TONEY,186
. 319,326;TONY,319;TOW
. 189;TRREY,172;TURNER
. 321;ULEADON,172
. URELEY,164;VANDY,189
. VENUS,164,179,302
. VILET,183-184,293,307
. 318;VILETT,327;VINEY
. 317;VINNS,172;VIOLET
. 175,293,329;VOL,288
. 296,304;VOLENTIN,161
. VUT,375;WALLY,183,189
. WARREN,317;WASHINGTON
. 77-78;WATTY,186;WILEY
. 109;WILL,166,174,292
. 302,310-311,317
. WILLEY,163;WILLIAM
. 104,162-163;WILLIE
. 316,319;WILLINGHAM
. 114;WILLIS,77,158
. WILSON,169,189;WINNEY
. 162,170,317;WINNY,153
. 164,188;WYETT,60
. YELLOW AARON,104;YETT
. 375;YORK,60,167,170
. 186,212;YORK (LITTLE
. YORK),186;ZOUER,293
NEHR,AMBROSE,407
NEHRIG,JNO ANDREW,407
NEIGHBOURS,ELIZ,417
. JANE,418
NEIL,ALBERT,213;DAVID
. 340;JOHN,198
NEILL,AARON,226
NEILSON,JOHN,407;SAMUEL
. 175,181
NELAM,ISAAC,85
NELHUMS,EZEKIAL,407
NELL,323
NELLAM,DANIEL,407
NELLEMS,WILLIAM,84
NELMS,MARY,32;MARY ANN
. 276;OLIVER,269;SAMUEL
. 269;THOMAS,269
NELOMS,DANIEL,407
NELSON,328;A,241;ABRAMS
. 269;ALEXANDER,345
. ANNA,51,55;ANNIE,264
. CHARLES,155;CHARLOTTE
. 414;DODD,144;E,386
. ELIZA,403;EUNICE,270
. FRANCES Z Y,279;G W
. 314;GEO W,269;J,149
. 302-303,311;J W,314
. JAMES,168;JANMIA,168
. JEREMIAH,291,306,321
. JOHN,407;JOHN B,269
. JOHN W,269;JOSEPH F
. 269;JULIA V,58;LIDY
. 168;LYDDA,155;M,91
. MARGARET,279;MATTHEW
. 407;MEREDITH,85,90
. 113,131;MERIDITH,83
. PERRY,269;POLLY,264
. RACHEL,237;ROBERT,113
. SARAH,284;TAYLOR,297

. 308;TAYOR,308;THOMAS
. M,407;WM H,407
NESBET,JOHN,105
NESBIT,124;ELIZ B,389
. JAMES,218,269;JAS,290
NESBITS,JAS,290
NESBITT,ALLEN,407;HUGH
. 407;MARY ANNE W,415
. THOMAS,407
NESMITH,CHARLES,32
. HITTY,45
NESON,REBECCA,402
NESSMITH,CHARLES,55
. CHARLES R,51;JAMES,5
. MARY,5;THOS,5
NETHERLAND,B,216;L B,55
. LAVINA,393;MARTHA,379
. NANCY,391,398;WILLIAM
. P,43
NETHERLIN,ELIZ,413
. JAMES,407;MARTHA,421
. WM,407
NETTLES,ELIZA,390
. ISRAEL,407;SARAH A
. 409;WM,407
NEUGENT,ELIZ,385;ROBT W
. 407
NEVILS,MOLLIE,206;NELLY
. 379
NEVIN,
. MARY ANN FRANCES,415
NEWBERN,DRED,20
NEWBERRY,ELIZABETH,276
. JABECK,168;JACOB,168
. LEVY,168;WILLIAM,311
NEWBORN,DRED,19
NEWBY,JOHN,338;NANCY
. 240;SARAH K,416
NEWCOME,LUCY M,257
NEWELL,LUCINDA,276;WM
. 269
NEWHOUSE,ADAM L,407
. JANE A,391
NEWMAN,ALEX I,407;AMOS
. 407;ELIZ,418;GEO W
. 407;JAMES,350-351,407
. JOSIAH,142;LETTY,406
. LIDA,417;MARTIN,407
. MARY,402;MILEY,420
. MOURNING,350;N,125
. N W,115;REBECCA,382
. SELINA,393;SUSAN E
. 204;SYLVESTER P,407
. THOMAS B,407;THOMAS J
. 407;WILDER,305;WM,407
NEWNAN,MARGARET,412
NEWNUS,ARAMITTA,39
NEWSOM,ANN,257;DAVID A
. 269;ELIZABETH,249
. JOSEPH N,269;M R,245
. MARTHA,273;MARY,248
. MATTIE,268;ROBERT,265
. 269,280-281,301;ROBT
. 283;SARAH,273
. TEMPERANCE,281
. WILLIAM,330;WM J,269
NEWSOME,JOEL',232;ROBERT
. 253,285;ROBT,242,245
. 284;RUTH,241
NEWSON,JOHN,293;ROBERT
. 244,249
NEWTON,143,145,148,209
. ANN,45;ARIS,338
. ARISTARCHUS,332
. BENJAMIN F,209
. BENJAMIN L,213;BIRD L
. 213;C F,118,121,123
. 127,133-134,138,142

NEWTON(cont)
. 144,146;ELIJAH,269
. ELIZABETH,207;FANNEY
. 286;HARRIET,418;HENRY
. 241,243-246,254,260
. 263,274,281,283
. ISEBELLA,207;J C,209
. JAMES B,209;JOHN,213
. JULIA,338;JULIA ANN
. 249;LIZZIE A,274
. LUCINE B,338;MARK L
. 338;MARTH(A),205
. MARTHA B,338;MARY F
. 338;O H P,338;OLIVER
. H,338;PHILLIP,198,213
. REBECCA,282;WILLIA
. 231;WILLIS,338;WINNIE
. R,275;WM,269
NEYLAND,31;CHARLOTTE,33
. GILBERT,4-5,7,350
. HENRY,9,33;JOSEPH,10
. MARY H,52;WM H,407
NICHELSON,ARCHIBALD,269
. GEO W,269;GEORGE,269
. GOERGE,269;HARRIET M
. 283;HENRY CLAY,269
. OSCAR E,269;SAMUEL
. 269;WM,269;WM B,269
NICHERE,FREDERICK,12
NICHLOS,320
NICHOLL,ISABELLA C,413
NICHOLS,AMELIA A,48
. AMOS,7,33;ANN,402
. CAROLINE,404;CHARLES
. 33,48;CHAS,10;DAVID,2
. 33;ELIAS,7;EMELIA,33
. JEFF,338;JONATHAN,59
. 320,343;NANCY,277
. POLLY,253;THOMAS,33
. 269;WM,10
NICHOLSON,ANN,236
. GRIMES,176;JNO,319
. MALCOLM,33;MALCOM,12
NICHSON,JOSEPH W,76
NICKELSON,JAMES B,407
. JAS B,236;JULIA E,265
. JULIA M,249;MARGARET
. 276;SIDNEY E A,278
NICKERSTAFF,ROBERT,114
NICKLES,MORRIS,55
NICKLESON,GEORGE,115
. POLLY,274
NICKOLSON,JAMES H,233
. MARIAH C,380
NICKS,BENIAH,10;HENRY
. 269
NIEDA,WILLIAM,63
NIELAY,JOHN,320
NIGHT,31;ELISHA,347
. JESSE,33;MATTHEW,33
. ROBERT,33;WESTLY,33
. WILLIAM,33
NILLOMS,WILEY,7
NIME,GEORGE W,172
NISBET,231;AMANDA,258
. JAMES,226,230;JAS,228
. JOHN,230
NISBIT,JAS,222,224
NIVEN,JAMES N,407
NIX,JOHN L,407
NIXON,BENJ,9;BENJAMIN
. 33;ELDRED,85;JOHN,111
NOALS,D,10
NOBLE,JOHN,198,212
. SARAH ANN,212
NOBLES,JAMES,33
NOBLY,JAMES,166;LEAVEL
. 166;MARY,166

NOEL,MCCORANCH,64
NOLAN,ELIZABETH C,332
NOLAND,198;A,55
NOLEN,89;ABNER,147
. ISAAC,69-70,72-73,82
. 85,88,90;JAMES,87
. JOHN,93;R,100;RICHARD
. 100,105,126;ROBERT,73
. STEPHEN,111;WILLIAM
. 105
NOLES,ELINOR,338
. EPHRAIM,33,48,55
. GILBERT,407;J H,338
. JAMES,108;JOHN W,338
. WILLIAM D,338;ZACH,24
. ZACHARIAH,12;ZACHR,14
NOOBES,NANCY,253
NORIS,ISAAC,198;JOHN H
. 407
NORMAN,A B,21,23;ANN
. 391;G G,260;J M,21
. JAMES M,23;JAMES S
. 407;JOSEPH,407
. WILLIAM,350
NORMOND,164
NORRELL,JOHN B,407
NORRICE,JOHN M,60;YOUNG
. R,60
NORRILL,SAMUEL,2
NORRIS,ELIZABETH W,209
. ISAAC,214;JACOB,269
. JAMES,23,269;JAMES M
. 132;JEANETTE,242;JOHN
. 55,60;JORDAN,198
. LURIA,242;MARTHA,132
. 135,138,200,283
. MARTHA J,243;MARY,195
. MILLY,198;NANCY L,260
. REBECCAH,247;WILLIAM
. 214;WILLIAM C,51
. WILLIAM DAVID,132;Y R
. 113,136;YOUNG R,81
. 132,144
NORSWORTHY,BETSEY,317
. FREDERICK,269,316-317
. GEORGE,289,316-317
. JAMES,89;MARTHA,247
. SALLEY,316-317;WILLY
. 198
NORTH,JOHN,158
NORTHERN,SARAH A M,265
NORTHINGTON,JAMES,269
NORTON,CHARLES C,269
NORWOOD,JAMES M,269,271
. WM,269,407
NORWORTHY,JOHN,12
NOUNDER,JONAS,2
NOWELL,ROBERT,269
NOWLAND,BENJ,407;POLLY
. 390
NRUN,PRUDENCE W,159
NUMIS,JESSE,55;JOSEPH
. 55
NUNAS,PHILLIP H,209
NUNES,CHARLES,50;JANET
. 50;JOSEPH,50;PHILIP H
. 198;ROBERT,50
NUNIS,ALEXANDER,33
NUNN,ADALINE,205;C W
. 269;ELIZABETH,197;F L
. 269;HIRAM,33,49
. HOLLEY J,196;JAMES M
. 407;JAMES R,214;JOHN
. B,269;JOSHUA,198
. LOHOIRY,197;SARAH
. FRANCES,273
NUNNALLY,HORATIO,256
NUNNELLY,HORATIO,279

NUTE,JEREMIAH,407
NUTON,PHILLIP D,209
NUTT,ANDREW,87,90;DAVID
. M,117,130;DINAH,76
. J B,111;S R,129
. SAMUEL,67,90;SAMUEL R
. 67,69,74,78-79,107
. 130;W B,107;WILLIAM B
. 116;WM B,100,103,147
NYE,SUSAN D,399
OATEN,DAVID,12
OATES,CHARLES,48;GEO A
. 407;JAMES,408;JOHN S
. 57
OATS,CHARLES,10,33
. JAMES,166,375
OBANION,BRYANT,12,33
. JOHN,33,43,55
OBANNION,LOUISA,44
OBERRY,JAMES,355
OBLEBY,ELIZABETH,197
OBLESBEY,ELIZA,211
OBRIEN,WILLIAM,209
OBRYAN,J,408
OCERTON,W A,274
OCHELER,JOHN F,43
OCONNER,JOHN,269
ODAM,CISAS,7;E A J,206
. GIDEON,8;JOSHUA,8,33
. LABAN,9;RICHARD,344
. SARAH,397;SILAS,8
ODAN,RICH,2
ODEM,JANE D,44
ODEN,MELVINA,40;WM N
. 408
ODGEN,MOSES,408
ODOM,BENNETT W,209;ELIZ
. 408;ELIZABETH,2,211
. GIDEON,33;JACOB,369
. JAMES,408;JOHN,198
. KATHARINE,210;LABEN
. 33;LABON,55;MOSES,408
. NANCY,210;RICHARD,408
. SAVANNAH,44;SCOTT,209
ODOMS,S E,338
ODUM,CELIA,52;ELIZ,419
. JAMES P,43;LABAN,51
. WINBURN,338;WINEFORD
. 194
OFARRELL,408
OFFUTT,EZEKIEL,226,408
OGDEN,ELIZ,412;MATILDA
. C,415
OGG,AMELIA,396;ANN
. AMELIA,406;JOHN,408
. THOMAS,408
OGILBY,HUGH J,378
OGLE,REBECCAH,287
OGLESBEE,ELMINA G,44
. NANCY,40
OGLESBY,ALLEN,213;ALLEN
. F,209;B J,43;BENJAMIN
. S,209;DANIEL,55,209
. ELIJAH,55;ELIZABETH
. ANN,194;HENRY,43;JACK
. 209;JAMES,213;JAMES H
. W,209;JOHN,43,213
. JOHN W,209;MARY,45
. 195;RACHEL L,204
. RICHARD,43;SARAH,206
. SEABORN,198;SUSAN M
. 211;THOMAS,72,269
. WILLIAM,209
OGLETREE,223;ANGELLINA
. G,415;ELIZA G,405
. GRESHAM G,408
. HENRIETTA,279
. HENRIETTA G,411;JOHN

OGLETREE(cont)
. 377;JULIE,248
. PHILEMON,262;SAMUEL T
. 269;WM D,269
OINS,AARON,292
OKEEFE,D C,269;DANIEL
. 269;ELEANOR LUCINDA
. 407;MICHAEL,408
. PHILIP,408
OKEEFFE,
. MAGDALANE AGATHA,398
. MARY ANN,420
OKEIFE,ELIZ,384
OKELLEY,PATRICK,269
OKELLY,JMES,408
OLCOTT,JOHN,269
OLDS,ALEX,209
OLEAR,NANCY,406
OLEPHANT,MATILDA,281
OLIEF,BENJAMIN,16;BENJN
14;JOHN,14,16
OLIFF,ANN,202;BENJAMINE
209;MATTHEW,209
OLINE,EVELINA F,417
OLIPHANT,AARON P,269
JOSEPH,33;MARY A,379
OLIVE,ABEL,408;JOHN,21
. MARTHA B,405;WILEY
. 153
OLIVER,AGIAH,196
. ALEXANDER,269;ANDREW
. 269;ANN,47;ANNE,395
. BENJAMIN,300;BENJMAIN
. 310;CHARLES C,269
. CHARLES T,43;COLUMBUS
. C,269;ELIZA,401
. ELIZABETH CATHERINE
. 278;EMALINE,282;HENRY
. G,408;JAMES,6,121,408
. JAMES L,408;JOHN,269
. 319,329;JOHN G,269
. JOHN L,245;JOSEPH,23
. LUCINDA,240
. MARGARET A E,278;MARK
. 209;MARTHA S,281;MARY
. 411;MARY ANN,240;MARY
. H,43;MARY JANE,278
. MATHEW,277;MILUS W
. 269;NATHAN,277
. PRISCILLA,6;QUILPHA
. 55;RISDON,10;RT,319
. SARAH,211,405;SARAH
. ANN,240;SOLOMON,288
. 319;STEPHEN H,408
. THOMAS A,269;THOS,2
. WM,269;WM I,270
OLIVIA,MATTHEW,261
OLMS,EDWD,290
OLMSTEAD,HARVY,408
ONAIL,AARON,95,116,122
. 124-126,143;ARON,106
. E W,125,147;EDWARD
. 108,128,141;EDWARD W
. 86,118,126,143
. FRANCES,125;ZACHARIAH
. 83
ONEAL,164,329;ADALINE M
. 241,258;ALEXANDER S
. 270;ALFRED,270
. ANGELINE C,269
. AUGUSTUS,270;AXIOM
. 302,308;DANIEL,55
. DANIEL H,270;EDMUND
. 302;EDWARD,270
. ELIZABETH,254,277
. HAMPTON,270;HARRISON
. 270;JAMES,270,291
. JOHN,229,236,248,254

. 267,270;JOSHUA,270
. M E,260;MARTHA,246
. 265;MARY,277;NATHAN
. 302;REBECAH,166
. SAMUEL,177;SARAH ANN
. 279;SUSAN C,266
. WILLIAMSON,270;WM,408
. WM H,270;WOOTEN,241
. 264,267,270,302
. WOOTON,324;ZECHARIAH
. 72
ONEALE,BAZZEL,186
. EDWARD,185-186;JULY
. 185-186;PEGGY,185
. POLLY,186;REBECCA,185
. 186;SUSANNAH,185
. WOOTEN,281
ONEIL,BENJAMIN,361;EXUM
215;HENRY P,408
ONEILL,HUGH,408;JOHN
408
ONELE,G W,408
OQUINN,WILLIAM,33
OR----,LOUISA J,281
OR---?,JOSIAH,270
OR-SS?,BENJ,270
ORARE,BENJAMIN,328
. DANIEL,328;LIZER,328
. MIRIAM,328;SILEATIA
. 328;WILLIAM,328
OREAR,DANIEL,321;ELLEN
. 244;MARY,266;OSBURN
. 270;ROBERT,270
. WILLIAM,71
OREILY,JOHN,408
ORGAN,MATTHEW,338
ORGOOD,DANL,329
ORM,91
ORME,140
ORR,ALLEN,338;HANNAH
. 287;J B,118,143;JAMES
. 408;MARY,274,392
. MATTHEW,85;WM,270;Y
. 124
OSALT,NANCY,399
OSBORN,DANIEL,90-91;LOU
. 312;MARY ANN ELIZ,387
. MOSES,43;SAMUEL,90,96
. 112;WM T,270
OSBORNE,HENRY,408
. MARGARETTA,413;RHODA
. 398;WILLIAM,338
OSBURN,EDY,45;JAMES,59
OSHEA,JEREMIAH H,408
OSLIN,HANNAH,240;JOS
. 225;MARY,257;SARAH E
. 237
OSLING,JOHN,225
OSTEEN,ROBERT,354
OSTIN,JOHN,270
OSTON,HARRIS,2;JESSE
309
OSWALD,MARY,392
OSWALT,HIRAM,408;SAMUEL
408
OTOM,198
OTWELL,JAMES,76
OUSTREETER,HENRY,198
MATHEW,198
OUTLAW,CHARLES C,198
. ELIZABETH JANE,197
. HARRIET,203;JEREMIAH
. 9;KISIAH,200;MARY,201
. 211;MORGAN,198
. WILLIAM D,209;WILLIAM
. L,198
OVERBAY,BENJAMIN,187
. PETER,187;SAMUEL,187

. SUSANNAH,187;WILLIAM
. 187
OVERBY,B H,270
OVERSTEET,ELIZA,58
WILLIAM,52
OVERSTREE,MARY,203
OVERSTREET,BRASWELL,342
. ELEFAIR,47;HENRY,209
. JAMES,199,214;JOHN
. 209,213;MARTHA A,202
. MARY,206;MATHEW HENRY
. 213;MATTHEW,209;MOSES
. 10,33,52;SALLIE J,203
. SAMUEL,408;STEPHN,14
. 16;WILLIAM,33
OVERTON,AMANDA,382;DORA
. 281;JOSEPH,184;M C
. 270;MARY V,260;SIMEON
. 270;W A,238,246,248
. 254,259,263,265-266
. 268-270,278,282,286
. WM A,235,237,240,246
. 248-249,274,276,279
. 281
OWEN,A B,408;ALEXANDER
. 43;ARON,293;CALEB,33
. CATHERINE,38;DANIEL
. 362;ELISHA,408;EMILY
. 40;GEO,263;GEORGE,63
. GREEN,86;JACOB,310
. 358;JOHN,33,47,50,101
. 270,408;JOHN B,43
. JOHN G,408;MARY H,262
. MARY J,275;NANCY,33
. PHILLMAN,270;ROBERT
. 358;WILLIAM,33,50;WM
. 245,270;WM I,408
OWENS,ANN,379;ANN B,381
. ANNIE E,40;CHARLES
. 270;DANIEL,246,270
. DAVID,8;ELIZA,236
. ELIZABETH,58;GEO,269
. JACOB,338;JAMES,43
. JEFFERSON,270;JESSE,9
. 21,23;JOHN,7,55
. LANCASTER,43;MARTHA •
. 382;MOREFIELD,270
. POLLY,157;STEWART,338
. SUSANNAH C,338
. WILLIAM,10
OWLSEY,THOMAS,310
OWNE,REBECCA,168
OWSLEY,CHARLES,309
. ROBERT,297;THOMAS,299
. 309;WELDON,310
. WILLIAM,233,297,306
. WILSON,319;WM,297,305
. 306
OXFORD,JAMES W,338;R L
338;WASHINGTON,332
OXLEY,SARAH ANN,33
WILLIAM,33
OZBORN,JAMES,338
P----ST,MILES M,273
PA----,J S (REV),272
PACE,ANDREW,43;B,354
. BARNABUS,270;DREADZIL
. 408;JAMES,408;KINDRED
. 8;MARY,389;OPHELIA
. 419;PENNY,251;WILLIAM
. 343;WILLSON,9
PACKARD,FRANCES,46
PAGE,ALLEN,9;EBENEZER
. 408;JAMES,307;JANE C
. 394;LEWIS,289;SOLOMON
. 9,408;TABITHA,200
. THIMOTHY,9;THOMAS T
. 199;WILIAM,408

PAIN,EDWARD C,97;O,69
PAINE,MARY,387;THOMAS
. 338
PALLOCK,GEORGE W,43
PALLSEY,WM,306
PALMBLADE,JOHN G,408
PALMER,ABEL,33;ANN,55
. 409;ANNIE,46;BENJ,408
. BENJAMIN,33,50,55
. CATHERINE,241;DAVID
. 408;EDMUND,51,55,408
. EDWIN N,43;ELBERT,43
. ELIZ,404,415;ELIZA
. 253;EMILY,43;GEORGE
. 33,408;GEORGE A,43
. GEORGE R,408;HENRY A
. 408;ISABEL,412;JAMES
. 408;JANETTE J,414
. JOHN B,408;LAURA,43
. MARTHA ANN,396;MARTHA
. W,383;MARY,4,299,379
. 382;MARY ANN,246
. NANCY,4,413;RICHARD,8
. ROBERT,33;SALLY,33
. SARAH H,42;WILLIAM,50
. WILLIS,408;WM,408
PALMORE,ELIZABETH,273
. FRANCIS,270;JAMES,270
. JAMES C,270;JAMES M
. 270;LANDO,270;POLLY
. 257;WM W,270
PANE,ASA,86;EDWARD,121
. P,75;SAVANNAH,203
PANIL,215
PANNEL,ELIJAH J B,408
PANNELL,226
PANTON,ABNER,270;ANN
. 385;JAMES,408
. REBECCAH,274
PAR---,W A,287
PARA,C,259
PARDUE,AMERICA M,400
. ELIZA A,393;MARTHA
. 393;MARY L,394
. WILLIAM ANTHONY,408
PARDUE?,EMILY A,278
PARHAM,DARLING P,270
. DICKSON,60;ELIZ,397
. ELIZA ANN,247;JAMES
. 320;JOHN,320;LEWIS
. 320;NATHANIEL,320
. NATHL,320;POLLY,320
. 338;REBEKAH,320
. ROBERT,293,328;SETH W
. 373;TANIZEY,320;TANZY
. 320
PARIS,FRANCIS,3,33;JACK
. 33;MOSE,43
PARISH,ANN,206;ELIZ,246
. ELLENDER,379;EZEKIEL
. 212;GEORGE,157
. GREENBERY,408;HARRIS
. 115;HENRY,408;HENRY J
. 213;HEZEKIAH,212
. NANCY,205;SOLOMON,209
. SUSANNAH,399;WYATT
. 408
PARK,BETSEY A,246
. BETSEY ANN,250
. CATHERINE,282
. COLUMBUS M,277;E,222
. E C,268
. ELIZA ELIZABETH -
. BILLINGSLEA,377
. ELIZABETH,261;EZEKIEL
. E,222;EZEKIEL E P,270
. HARRIETT,278;HUGH H
. 270;JAMES,263,265,280

. JAMES B,270;JAMES L
. 270;JANE,236;JAS,238
. JAS A,241;JOHN,244
. 248,250,266,275,279
. 361;JOHN T S,408
. LUCINDA,285;MARGRET A
. 257;MARY E,275
. MATILDA,271;NANCY J
. 279;RICHARD,270
. RICHARD S,270,374
. SARAH,248;SOPHIA,246
. SOPHIA I,286;THOMAS
. 270;THOMAS I,285
. THOMAS J,280,377;W J
. 279;WM,90,253;WM J
. 270,275
PARKER,AARON,270,292
. ANN ELIZA,338;ASA J
. 270;ASENETH,277
. AUSTIN,270;BENJA,309
. BETSEY,242;CAROLINE
. 385;DAVID,270
. EBENEZER,408;EDWIN
. 270;ELIZ,416;ELIZ M
. 243;ELIZA,282
. ELIZABETH,203;EMANUEL
. 270;FAITHEY,236
. FRANCINA,275
. FRANCIS S E,264
. GUSTAVUS,408;HARDEE,8
. HENRY,43;ISAAC L,338
. ISAIAH,310;J F,270
. J R,264-266,271;JACOB
. 12,33,48;JAMES,33
. JAMES B,270;JAMES C
. 409;JEAN,282;JESSE,7
. JOE,313;JOE R,271
. JOHN,300,311,322;JOS
. C,100;JOS R,258
. JOSEPH,357;JOSEPH R
. 251,267,285;LEWIS,12
. 33,239,264,270,306
. 309;LEWIS S,338;M,102
. MARTHA,270;MARTIN,315
. MARY,290;MARY JANE,38
. MARY M,269;MARY T,406
. MILES,10,12,94,112
. MOSES,217,227;NANCY
. 237,242,266;PATSEY
. 279;POLLY,236,239,241
. 257,277;RICHARD,229
. 409;ROBERT F,270
. SALLY,250;SAML,227
. 231,360;SAMUEL,62,227
. 288,303,309;SANDERS
. 62;SARAH,236;SIMON,7
. 33;STARLING,21,23,25
. SUSAN ANN,283
. SUSAN M A BAT---,270
. SUSANNAH,217;TALBOT
. 217;THOMAS,43,161,175
. 180;UNETTA,412;URANIA
. ELIZABETH,332;W B,113
. WILLIAM,288;WILLIAM C
. 338;WILLIAM H,85,209
. WM,97,270;WM H,82,85
. ZILPHA,47
PARKERSON,JOHN C,88
PARKMAN,DANIEL,65
PARKS,AARON,159,409
. AMANDA M,277;DAVID
. 209;ELI,82,97,112,115
. 146;H H,268;ISAAC,85
. JOHN,177,281;JOHN B
. 338,356;MARY,416;W J
. 278-279;WEKEM
. (WELCOME),359;WILLIAM
. 338;WM,258;WM I,242

. 265,277,287;WM J,271
. 275;WM M,270;WM S,243
PARMELA,HENRY E,409
PARMELEE,MARY E,403
PARMENTREE,JASON,271
PARMER,JOSEPH,346
. MARTHA,384;WILLIAM,55
PARMLY,JAHIAL,409
PARNEL,ARDIMINDA,421
. SARAH ANN,382
PARNELL,ADELINE B,387
. ELIZA,276;HENRY,6,409
. J R,314;JAMES,6,55
. 175,409;JOHN,338
PARR,JANE,411;JOHN,409
PARRAM,BILL,341;DENT
. 341;MATHEW,341
PARRAMORE,ROBERT R,43
PARRIS,17;CARRIE,39
. FRANICS,6;HENRY A,50
. MARY,39
PARRISH,G F,409
. HEZAKIAH,209;LOUVENIA
. 202;P,209;POLLY,251
PARROLT,REBECCA A,259
PARROT,HENRY,338;KISIAH
. 199
PARROTT,A B,314;ANNETT
. 257;ASBERRY L,271
. ASBURY L,271;BENJAMIN
. 271,328;CURTIS,271
. ELIZABETH,275-276
. ELIZABETH ANN,236
. EMMA L,285;HENRY,271
. JAMES,271;JULIA E,258
. LOUISA R,285;MARTHA C
. 264;NANCY,256;OBADIAH
. 271;TRANQUILLA C,282
PARSON,
. MARTHA MATILDA,199
PARSONS,HENRY,409;JOHN
. A,55;JOS,2;MARY,195
. SAMUEL,307,322;THOMAS
. A,55
PART,ELIZA CATHERINE
. 235
PARTEE,272;W A,237,239
. 241,249,273,286;W W
. 273;WALTER A,271
PARTRIDGE,JOHN,183
. THOMAS,271
PASCHALL,SAMUEL,338
PASCHEL,SAMUEL D,271
PASHAM,JOHN,92
PASSONS,TURNER,341
PATE,EDWARD,271;ELIZA W
. 397;REDDING,10;S A D
. 409;THOMAS D,409
PATERSON,EMELIA,260
. SARAH,392
PATILLO,DAVID,298;JAMES
. 369;JOHN,369;JOHN V
. 304;LITTLEBERRY,310
. SAMUEL,369
PATILLOS,DAVID,369
. HENRY,369;LUREN,369
. PATSEY,369;REBECCA
. 369;SALLY,369;TABITHA
. 369;WILLIAM,369
PATRICK,ALEXANDER F,348
. BENJ B,271;C,319
. CHARLES L,271
. CONSTANTINE,271
. ELIZABETH,237,257
. EMMA,271;FRANCES,267
. HUGH,190;IRABELLAH
. 286;JANEY,272;JOHN
. 409;JOSHUA,119,121

PINCKNEY,14
PINCKSTON,JAMES,319
PINDER,JAMES,88
PINKARD,FRANCES,287;J
. 113;JANE,253;JOHN,100
PINKERTON,DAVID,329;S I
. 249;S J,281
PINKIN,URIAH,16
PINKSON,JOHN,324
PINKSTON,324;CORNELIA F
. 268;GREENBERRY,320
. GREENBURY,324;HENRY
. 324;HENRY B,313;JAMES
. 324;JAS,303;JOHN,324
. 327;MARY,324
PINTHART,JOHN,272
PIOER,WM,272
PIOR,EDMUND,33,350
. ROBERT,2;SARAH ANN
. 386
PIPER,THOMAS L,338
. ZADICK,272
PIPKIN,URIAH,13
PITMAN,ANN,392;FANNY
. 254;JEREMIAH,362;JOEL
. L,272;MARSHAL,188
. PHILIP,2;SYNTHIA,385
. WILLIAM ALLEN,362
PITTMAN,JAMES,409
. MARSHALL,193;NANCY
. 407;PRISCILLA,193
. TERESA,265;TIMOTHY
. 160,180
PITTS,JOHN D,338;JOSEPH
. A,338;NESTER,338
. PERMELIA,338
PLASK,JAMES,33
PLATT,DAVID,8;GEORGE
. 338;JACOB B,409;JOHN
. 7
PLEASANTS,ELIZA ANN,409
PLUMB,ALMINA,416;DANIEL
. B,409
PLUMER,CAROLINE,43
PLUMMER,SAMUEL,338
PLUNKET,MARY EMALENE
. 210;THOMAS,409
PLUNKETT,SILAS,87
PLYTHRESS,WILLIAM,8
PO---,JAMES M,249
POE,124;ROBERT,410
. WASHINGTON,78;WM,410
POLARD,ROBERT,310
POLHILL,FREDERICK A,410
. JAMES,33,52;JOHN G,12
. 33;NATHAN,33
. NATHANIEL,50;REBECCAH
. 50
POLK,164;ANN F,418
. CHARLES E,338;JOSHUA
. F,338
POLL,ELIZ,413
POLLACK,ELIZABETH,39
POLLAN,ROBERT,410
POLLAR,ELIZABETH,262
POLLARD,BRITTIAN C,272
. FRANCES V,256
. FREDERICK,272;JAMES
. 272;JOHN,298;JOSEPH
. 321;JOSIAH,272;MARTHA
. 389;POLLEY,371
. RICHARD,338;STEPHEN
. 272
POLLETTE,JOHN G,214
POLLOCK,ALICE P,36
POLSY,BENNETT,272
POMBERTON,33
POMEROY,JOHN W,410;SAML

17
POMROY,SAMUEL,13,16
PON,JOHN T,338;TAYLOR
. 338
POND,JUNETA,397;LUCINDA
. 393;MARY S,392;WM,410
PONDER,DAWSON,33
. EPHRAIM,33,50;H,55
. JAMES,351;REBECCA,387
. RICHARD,33,50;SARAH Y
. 57
PONSONBRY,GEORGE,272
POOL,ADAM,358;ANN,416
. ANNE,351;BAXTER,351
. CRAVEN P,375-376;ELIZ
. 413;EVELINA,403;FRED
. B,313;GILMON,272
. HARDY,313;LIBBA,387
. MARTHA M,411;MARY ANN
. 408;PETER,313;THOMAS
. 342,344;TURNER,209
. W B,44
POOLE,ABRAM,338;JAMES A
. 410;JOHN,272,362
. THOMAS,338
POOLER,BURKE,5
POPE,A B,59,76;ANNIE J
. 338;AUGUSTEN B,70
. AUGUSTIN B,68,71,75
. 78;AUGUSTINE B,67-68
. AUGUSTUS B,60
. BARZILLA,7;CHRISTIAN
. 359;COLLIN,305;HENRY
. 346;JESSE,287,305
. JESSE MCKINNE,230
. JOHN,297,305;JOHN C
. 338;JOHN HARDEMAN,272
. JOSIAH,338
. LITTLEBERRY,272
. MILLER W,338;SUSANNAH
. 359;WILIE,353;WILLIAM
. K,338;WILLSON,272
POR---,JAMES,249
PORCH,HENRY,321
PORT,BASIL,44
PORTER,221,234,323;A
. 227;ANTHONY,349
. BRADFORD,178
. CATHARINE,338
. CATHERINE,249;CHARLES
. 177;CHARLES HANSFORD
. 178;DAVID O,272
. ELIZABETH,177,338
. FAYETTE,178;GEORGE
. NICHOLAS,177
. HENRIETTA,244;I,260
. J L M,239;JAMES M,248
. 254,287;JOHN,272;JOHN
. S,33;JOHN W,149,377
. 378;MARY,284;MARY E
. 264;MATILDA M,332,338
. NANCY,247;O,230,232
. 235,246-247,257-258
. 273-275,278,280,342
. PEGGY,249;ROBERT,226
. 272;SARAH E,276;SARAH
. T,404;SILVESTER,410
. STANTON,178;VINEY J
. 271;W A,239,241,272
. W S,238;WILLIAM,67
. 338,375
PORTWOOD,CATHERINE,338
POSEY,BENJAMIN,217,224
. J H,358;POTTER E,78
POSH,11
POST,SAMUEL,332,338
POTTER,ADAM C,338
. AUGUSTIN,298;AUSTON

. 327;B G,107;BOSDELL G
. 87,141;CHARLES,272
. DAVID,300;GEO,273;J S
. 239;PLEASANT,80,90
. 338;RILEY,90,94,102
POTTS,REBECCA,277
. STEPHEN,338;WM,273
POU,JOHN T,332
POULAIN,ELLA F,256
POULLAIN,FELIZ,273
. HARRIETT M,269;SARAH
. G,266;SARAH N,286
. THOMAS N,273
POUND,ED F,313;R,58
. RICHARD,68;SALLY,379
POUNDS,ELIZABETH,394
. JARED,164,186;NEWMAN
. 215
POW,WM,410
POWEL,89;ALLEN,59
. ARTEMEW,8;CALVIN,214
. ELIAS,214;JOHN,85
. SAMPSON,214;SILAS,214
. SUSANNAH,351;ZACHEUS
. 351
POWELL,101,217;A L,332
. ADEN,199;ALLEN B,346
. ALLIE LAURA,338
. ALPHORD,209;ANN,40
. ARTEMAS,52;ARTEMUS,33
. ARTHUR,8;ASHLEY,209
. BARRY,44;BENJAMIN,33
. BOB,52;BRETTEN,199
. BRITIAN D,209;CADER R
. 52,55;CALVIN,199
. CARTER,302;CLARA N,42
. DANIEL,321;DOBEY,194
. E A,39;EDLA C,47
. ELIJAH,7;ELIZABETH,33
. 50,198,201;ENOCH,131
. EVAN H,332,338
. FRANCES H,410;JOHN,1
. 33,44,410;JOHN F,209
. JOHN G,338;JOHNSON
. 104;L F,55;LAFAYETTE
. 44;LAMAR,199;LEWIS,8
. 33;LEWIS T,50;LINEAR
. 214;MALINDA,212;MARK
. M,128;MARTHA,295;MARY
. 48,199,388;MOSES,297
. 338,342;NANCY,195,207
. QUINNY,296;RACHEL,332
. SARAH F,265;STEPHEN
. 199,209,302;T O,313
. WHIT,338;WILLIAM R
. 338
POWERS,ALLINUS,273;ANNE
. 394;ELIZA,418;ELIZA
. OLIVIA,396;EMILY,390
. EMILY I,391;ISAAC,273
. JNO,222-223;JOHN,229
. 273,314;JOHN W W,410
. MARIA,237;MARY,411
. NICHOLAS GRAHAM,410
. PENELOPE,235;REBECCA
. 410;REBECCA F,393
. ROBERT,90;SARAH,90
. 277;TEMPY,243;WILLIAM
. 229;WM,273
POYHRESS,EDWARD,7
POYTHRESS,GEORGE,9,225
. JOHN,55;JOHN C,52
. THOS,2
POYTHRYSS,FRANCIS,215
PRATER,CAROLINE,379
. SARAH,403,405,418
. TABITHA,193
PRATHER,ANN,421;EDWARD

PRATHER(cont)
410;MARY,402
PRATT,ELIZABETH,394
. JAMES,273;PRISILLA
. 381;THOMAS S,273
PREE,E,198
PRENDERGAST,JAMES,410
PREPER,CATY,405
PRESCOT,ANTHONY,8;JOHN
8;SAMUEL,8
PRESCOTT,
. ANDERSON AUGUSTUS,44
. ANTHONY,33;BENIJAH,51
. CHRISTANNA,44;ELIZ
. 401;GEORGIAN,207
. JAMES,48;JANE,210
. JOHN,51,55,193;KITTIA
. 44;MILLEDGE,410;MOSES
. 51,55;NANCY,51
. PATRICK,410;SAMUEL F
. 33;SARAH,33,51,394
. 408;THOMAS,44;WILLIAM
. 33;WILLIS,55
PRESKITT,BRITTON,44
. SAMUEL,52;SARAH,421
. SEABORN A,410
PRESLEY,A,93
PRESTON,CHARLES T,338;E
. 144;E J,90-91,140-141
. ELIJAH,97;ELISHA J,91
. 142,144,146;ELIZ,389
. ESTHER,37;GILLIAM,91
. 144;J A,236,245;JAMES
. 91;JAMES A,273;JOHN F
. 82,93,144;SALLY,91
. THOMAS J,144;WILLIAM
. 345;WILLIAM G,85,89
. WILLIAM H,332,338
PREVAL,JOSEPH C,410
PREVATT,WILLIAM A,72
PRI---,F W,276
PRICE,ADAM A,273;ALFRED
. 199;ANNA,197;BERRY
. 199;CAROLINE,199,209
. CLEMENT,199;EDWARD
. 294,338;ELIZABETH,201
. ENOCH N,273;EPHRUM
. 273;FRANCES,276;G W
. 92;HAMSFORD,273;HENRY
. P,199;HULDY,200;J H
. 199;JAMES,214;JAMES T
. 273;JAS,2;JOHN,8,82
. 338;JOSEPH,294;JULIA
. M,135;LOYD,214;MARTHA
. 199,236;MARTHA E,135
. MARY,264,332;MARY A
. 260;MATILDA,195,204
. NANCY,267,274;POLLY
. 246,256,280;ROBERT,91
. 338;S W,86,108,119
. 123,131,136-138,140
. 149;SALLY,261;SAMUEL
. 86;STEPHEN W,82,90,99
. 132;TEMPERANCE,197
. THEOPHILUS,A,273
. WILEY SMALL,199
. WILLIAM,325;WILLIAM
. HENRY,133;WM,97;WM E
. 273,410;WM H,267
PRICEHAY,DAVID,6
PRICHET,GUILFORD,33
PRICKET,ISRAEL,147
. NANCY,393
PRICKETT,DAVID,410
. ELIJAH,410;ELISHA,410
. GIDEON,410
PRIDE,WILLIAM,310,329
PRIDGEN,JAMES,67;LUKE

353;WILLIAM,353
PRIDGEON,JAMES,82,95
102
PRIDGES,
. LAURENCE (ALONZO) G
. 273
PRIDGON,JAMES,98;JOHN
98
PRIGIN,LUKE,354
PRIGNET,HELENA,401
PRIMROSE,AUGUSTTAE,407
. CHARITY,388;ELISA ANN
. 379;JAMES,273;JAMES W
. 410;PATRICK HENRY,410
. SARAH M,382
PRINCE,BETSEY,243
. DENNIS,44;GEORGE,273
. 325;JOHN,273,361;MARY
. 265;SILVANUS,410
PRINTER,328
PRINTUP,EMMA A,242
PRIOR,ASA,72;BARBARY
. 391;HADEN,291;HARDEN
. M,273;MARY,104;PHILIP
. 72;ROBERT,48,55
. VIRGINIA,37;WILLIAM
. 104
PRITCHARD,C B,199;CELIA
. 210;JOHN W,410;L J
. 209;MARCUS,209;MARTHA
. E,202;WM H,410
PRITCHELL,JAMES,273
PRITCHET,ASHLEY,199
PRITCHETT,ALFRED M,338
. GEORGE,349;GUILFORD
. 50;JAMES,310;PHILLIP
. 302;T J,338;WILLIAM
. 300;WILLIAM H,338
PRITCHIT,WM,307
PROCTER,JONA,7;WILLIAM
346
PROCTOR,ABRAHAM,33,55
. ADESON E,209;ALLEN
. 213;AUGUSTUS D,199
. BARNEY,45;DANIEL J
. 213;EMILY A,203
. GEORGE W,209;HARMON
. 99;HENRY,410;JOHN,213
. JOHNSTON,199;JONAS,33
. JONES,210;LAVINA,41
. MARY,46;MOSES T,50
. PATRICK,410;ROBERT
. 199;SAMUEL,8,33,49
. SARAH,36;THOMAS,55
. 199,410;WILLIAM,213
. WILLIAM A,210;WILLIAM
. P,44
PROUDFIT,ANDREW,12
PROUTY,MARY JANE,385
PRUDDEN,SYDNEY C,273
PRUDHOMME,LOUIS,410
PRUET,JACOB,299;JAMES
299;SAML,294
PRUIT,JACOB,309-310
JAMES,310
PRUITT,MARTIN,311
PRUR,GEORGE,199
PRYER,ELIJAH,55;JACKSON
273;MARLOW,273
PRYOR,A W,112;ALLEN W
. 88;ASA,72;ELIZABETH
. CA----,273;MARTHA M
. 279;PHILLIS,39;SUSAN
. 271;WILLIAM,85,91,101
. 112
PUBH,WILLIAM,10
PUCKELL,JOHN,273
PUCKET,SARAH,400

PUCKETT,CHAT,410;MARTIN
338
PUGH,BERRY,273;JAMES
. 273;JOHN,359-360;NEY
. 119;ROBERT,9,12,33
. WHITSON,12;WM,10
PUGHLEY,ELEANOR,404
PUGNE,PEGGY,249
PUGSLEY,JACOB P,210
MATTIE S,208
PULLEN,164;ARENATH,286
. MARTHA,180;PENELOPE S
. 260;SANFORD,273
. SUSANNAH,273;WM L,275
PUMPHREY,JESSE,410
PUNCH,TOM,300
PURDEE,GEORGE,273;JOHN
273;THOMAS,410
PURDELL,JOHN THOMAS,273
PURDUE,JOHN T,273;LUCY
256;MARY ANN,257
PUREFOY,CHARLES,97
PURIFOY,133;CASWELL,122
. 142;M P,281;NICHOLAS
. 85,112
PURIFY,JOHN,300;WILLIAM
308
PURKINS,33;ALLEN,33
. DANIEL,338;DAVID,33
. ELIZ,416;LEAH,33
. NEWTON,33;TABITHA,33
. WILLIAM,33
PURKS,WM,273
PURSY,NANCY,237
PURVIS,APSIBATH,381
. JEPTHAH,213;MARTHA
. 422;MARY,420
PYE,BARTHENY,338
. GRIFFIN L,338;HARMON
. W,338;JAMES,19,82,332
. 338,361;JORDAN,332
. 338;THADEUS,338
. THEOPHILUS,332,338
. THOMAS,410;THOMAS W
. 338
PYN,BENJ,410
PYOR,EDMOND,10
PYRAN,MARTHA,235
PYRON,CHARLES,273
. ELIZABETH R,259;LEWIS
. 258,410;NANCY,273
. SARAH,254;SUSAN,254
QUENN,C D,136;T,136
QUICK,CAMERON,44
QUILL,ELIZABETH H,267
MARTHA FRANCES,242
QUIMAIN,ADELINE,408
QUIN,ANNE,391;MARGARET
382
QUINCY,MATILDA A,207
QUINN,BRYANT O,55
. CATHERINE ANN,389
. CHARLES,273;ISHAM,410
. JOHN C,273;PATRICK
. 410;SARAH,36
QUIZENBERRY,THOMAS,410
QUORUM,J,357
QWEN,REUBEN,242
RA----,LOUISA,255
RABB,WILLIFORD J,385;WM
410
RABON,MATT,287-288,317
WILLIAM,317
RABUN,MATT,216,288
. MATTHEW,350;WILLIAM
. 218;WM,300,305,322
RABURN,MATHEW,218,273
RACHALS,EZEKIAL,410

RACHELS,BERRYAM,410
. EZEKIEL,8,33,51;HULDA
. 407;JOHN,315;PLEASANT
. W,313;WILLIAM,10,33
. 51
RACKLEY,ELIZA A M,46
. JOEL,50,55;MARY,41
. NATHAN,9
RAD,ANN,253
RADCLIFF,MARK,10;MOSES
338
RADEN,J N,273;JOHN,273
MARY A,260
RADFORD,210;BETSY,344
. ELIZABETH,344;REUBEN
. 344,359
RADIN,GEORGE,273
RADMORE,LYDIA,270
RAE,ELIZ,421;EMMA,276
JOHN,2
RAGAN,ANN A,253;ASA,338
. IBZAN,273;J,265
. JEREMIAH,253,259;JNO
. 293;JOHN,218-219,273
. 288,290,296,302,306
. 309,319;MOSES,273
RAGARD,JOHN,273
RAGIN,JEHU,349
. NATHANIEL,226
. NATHANILE,226
RAGLAND,JOHN A,88;MARY
. R,332;PETTUS,338;T
. 122;THOMAS,114,142
RAGLIN,SARAH,397
RAGSDALL,WM,222
RAIFORD,ALEXANDER G,24
. ALEXR G,20,22;ELIZA
. ROBEY,392;HAMILTON
. 410;MARGARET H,385
. ROBERT,21;SARAH J,392
RAINES,HARDY,341
RAINEY,55;CHARLES,55
. D M,73;ETHELDRED,273
. FRANCES,253;HARRIET
. 283;JOHN H,273;JOHN W
. 55,410;MATTHEW,338
. NATHANIEL H,338
. WILLIAM,338;WM J,273
RAINS,MITCHAEL,210
RAINWATER,ALOY C,313
. CHARLES A,273;FRANCES
. E,257;JOSEPH H,273
. LACY D,273;THED W,313
. VERGAL,313;W T,273
RAINY,FRANCES,39
RAITON,JNO,358
RALL,CHARLES,410
RALLENDEN,T M,17
RALLS,HECTOR,273;JAMES
. H,273;JULIA CORNELIA
. 251;MARY,238
RALLY,ANN E,258
RALSTON,ALEX R,410
DAVID,62,410
RAMEY,A,87;ABSALOM,338
. ALLICE,338;CHARLES,71
. CLARISSA,338;DANIEL M
. 338;ELIZABETH P,338
RAMSAY,408;ELIZ,415
MISS,392
RAMSEY,164,229
. ARCHIBALD,78,410
. ELEANOR,163;ELENOR
. FRAZER,167;GEORGE,95
. 410;H,132;HIRAM,108
. 119,122;ISAAC,162-163
. 167;JOHN,162-163
. JOSEPH B,410;MARTHA

. 162;MARY,162-163
. POLLY N,176;POLLY
. NAOMY,422;R P,149
. RANDAL,162-163;SAMUEL
. 162,176;SUSAN P,285
. WM A,410
RAMY,JOHN D,410
RAND,JOSIAH,254
RANDAL,JOSIAS,257
SEABORN,410
RANDALL,ABRAM,44
. AUGUSTUS HENRY,273
. GEORGE,410;J W,273
. JAMES G,273;JOHN S
. 410;SARAH,415;THOMAS
. 273;THOMAS W,273;WM C
. 273;WM W,410
RANDLE,329;BEVERLY,318
. CLAVENDIA A R,243
. EDMOND,318;HARRIET,41
. JAMES,298,318;JOHN
. 318,328;JOHN GRAVES
. 318;JONA,166;JOSIA
. 251;JOSIAH,243;JOSIAS
. 272;MARY A W,250
. PETER,318;ROSALINA O
. 41;ROSANNA,318;SARAH
. 264;VALERIA T,267
. WASHINGTON,318
. WILLIAM,318;WM,318
RANDLESON,ANDREW,47
RANDOL,SUSANNAH,325
RANDOLF,JOHN,410
RANDOLPH,B,33;BEVERLEY
. 49;BEVERLY,26,33;JOHN
. 343;MARY F,419;ROBERT
. 410
RANDOLSON,MARGET,55
RANDON,SUSAN,45
RANDY,SAMUEL,23
RANEY,112,122;ELLEN,41
JOHN D,97
RANFROE,SAMSON,223;ZACH
223
RANKIN,ADAM W,273;DAVID
. 273;ILLISA,279;JAMES
. R,273;MARGARET,259
. SARAH J,260;SARAH L
. 262
RANKNS,EZEKIEL,369
RANSOM,ELIZ,244;H,244
. HENRY,309;JAMES,88
. NANCY,272;POLLY,274;R
. 82;REBECCA,262;ROBERT
. 274,301;ROBERT S,308
. SARAH,240;THOMAS H
. 274
RANSOME,JENNY,281
RANSON,JAMES,82;JOSEPH
273;SARAH,265
RAPE,J,119;JACOB,142
RAPLEY,SARAH,240
RATCHFORD,M N,210
RATCLIFF,MOSES,332
RATCLIFT,BENJAMIN,5
RATFORD,ANDERSON,210
RATLIFF,JAMES,8;MARK,33
RATTERLL,ALEXANDER,108
RAWLES,ALAN,63;HOSEA,51
SARAH,196
RAWLINGS,ELIZABETH,49
RAWLS,A,327;CHARLOTTE
. 382;HOSEA,410;JAS,2
. JOHN,18,20;JOSEPH,19
. SARAH A,244;SARAH M
. 287;WILLIAM,213
RAWORTH,HENRY G,410
RAY,A,266;ADALINE,95

. ANDERSON,259,280,287
. ANDREW,274;ANN C,253
. BENJAMIN,151,274
. BETSEY,189-190;C L,83
. 95-96,106,124;CAIN
. 291;CATHARINE,151
. COLEMAN L,95-96;DAVID
. 274,370;ELIZABETH,95
. 106,116,124,190,273
. EMANUEL,274;GEORGE
. 150-151,360;HECTOR
. 410;HENRY,154;ISAAC
. 274;J L,106,116;JAMES
. 75,87,96,154-155,165
. 166;JAMES A,314;JESSE
. B,134;JOHN,151,154
. 189-190;JOHN H,274
. JOHN L,95;JOHN T,274
. JOSEPH,154;JOSEPH C
. 190;LEVY,210;LEWIS
. 190;MARGARET,256;MARK
. 360;MARTHA,246;MARY
. 151,250;MATILDA,280
. NANCEY,154;NANCY,226
. 274;NANCY M,190
. NIMROD,274;PHEBE,190
. R Y,106,116,124;ROSA
. 265;SALLY,190;SALLY
. WEST<,154;SAMUEL,360
. SARAH,151;SARAH N,286
. SHADRACH,274;SOLOMON
. 96;U,282;W G,58,106
. 143;W H,106,116,124
. 96,106,116,123,151
. 154;WILLIAM G,95,106
. 124;WILLIAM H,375;WM
. 274;WM A,314;WM G,95
RAYBUN,WILLIAM,311
RAYN,D L,321
RBOINSON,SALLY,243
RE----,ROBERT,254
REA,BENJ,274;FRANCES
. 268;MARY,235;ROBERT
. 237,249,261,266,271
. 274-275,277-279,283
. 284;ROBT,236,238,243
. SARAH,284
REAB,GEO B,411
READ,AJONADAB,298,306
. ALEXANDER,292;AMY,262
. ANNGENETT,402
. BENJAMIN,346;DANIEL R
. 91;EDMOND,358;ELENOR
. I,395;JAMES,274,358
. 411;JAMES D,97;JOHN
. 219,307;M,80;MARY,409
. REBECKAH,358;REUBEN
. 325;RICHARD,411;SHEAR
. 325;WM BURTIS,411
. WM L C,97
READING,W W,359
REAMS,AZARIAH,59
REARDEN,JOHN A,411
REAUX,MARY,389
REAVES,SIMON,369;SPIVY
7;WILLIAM,289
REBO,HARRIET S,402
REBUN,MATTHEW,220
RECDICK,JACOB,2;PETER,2
SHADRICK,2
RECTOR,SAMPSON,55
RED,AJONADAB,217;ALLEN
. B,55;AMELIA,238
. BARBARA,55;GREEN B,55
. 411;HIRAM,51;HOLLAND
. 50,55;JAMES,10;MARY
. 392;NOAH,55;WELCOME

RED(cont)
. 55;WILLIAM,55
. WILLIAMI,51
REDD,ALBERT G,274;BERRY
. 411;FRANCES A,270
. GREEN B,411;JAMES,274
. VIRGINIA,38;WILLIAM
. 33
REDDEN,DAVID,338
REDDICK,ABRAHAM,220,309
. ALEX,323;GEORGE,338
. HANNAH,220;HENRY,338
. JACOB,33;JOHN,33,49
. JOSIAH,229;LYDIA,415
. MARY ANN,55;NICHOLAS
. 49,55;SARAH,49,55
REDDIN,JAMES,274
REDDING,ANN M,387;JAMES
. 411;JINNIE M,202;MARY
. 381;SARAH M L G,206
. THOMAS,274;WM,3
REDDOCK,ABRAHAM,294
. ALEXANDER,289;ALEXR
. 230;DAVID,289;JOHN
. 289,299;MARY,289
. WILLIAM,230,289
REDDY,DAVID,21,23,25
. MARY J,408
REDFERN,ANDREW,313;J D
. 313
REDICK,ABRAHAM,218,220
. HANNAH,218
REDING,W H,350-351
REDMAN,ELIZABETH,84,93
. 99,134,143;MARTHA,84
. 93,99,109,120,127,133
. 134,143;MARY,84,93,99
. 109,118,120,127,131
. 134;MARY C,126;THOMAS
. 99;W T C,120;WILLIAM
. 59,84,93,99,109,118
. 120,126-127,134,143
. WILLIAM T C,126-127
. 134;WM,411;WM T C,143
REDMOND,D,312;JOHN,274
REDWINE,119;J,119;JACOB
. 105;JOHN,108
REECE,148;CHARLES,274
. DRURY,274;EMILY
. VIRGINIA,202;JAMES,50
. 55
REED,A D,133;AJONADAB
. 224,298;ALEX,291
. ALEXR,228,292;ANDREW
. 291;BETSEY,261;CELIA
. 400;D,133;ELIZ,398
. ELIZABETH,37;FELIX C
. 274;FREEMAN,274;GRACY
. 180;H,245;J W,247
. JAMES,159,162,179-180
. 274,358;JANE,179-180
. JOHN,91,188,219,223
. 227,293,309,319,374
. JOHN C,411;JOHN W,254
. JOSEPH,373;LUCY,256
. LUKE,76,411;M,274
. MARY,402;NANCY,269
. ROBERT N,274;SAML,291
. SAMUEL,222;W M,65;WM
. 274;ZACHRIAH,274
REEDE,ALEXANDER,330
REEDS,ROBERT,152
REEL,STERLING,411
REES,328;ALBERT,155,411
. BENJAMIN,155;EPHATHA
. 155;ISHAM,300;JAMES,7
. 155,300;JEREMIAH,155
. JOEL,292,321;JOHN D

. 131;LITTLETON,321
. MARY,413;RICHA,155
. SALLY PORTER,177
. SARAH,155;TALLIFERO
. 155;TOLBERT,155
REESE,112,291;CUTHBERT
. 332,338;DAND,44
. GEORGE W,44;H A,319
. ISHAM,295;JAMES,33
. JOEL,33;JOEL A,338
. JOHN C,60;JOHN T,44
. JOHN T A,44;JOSEPH
. 338;TOBY,44;WESLEY W
. 49;WILLIAM,310,317
. 329;WM,310
REEVE,JOHN,153;SARAH
. 153
REEVES,ABBIE A,40;ANNA
. 55;BENJ,2;ESTER,37
. GEORGE W,85;GRACE B
. 84;GREEN B,86,92,104
. 118,125,128,141,149
. ICHABOD,342;J B,93
. J I,274;JASPER,86
. JESSE B,82;JOHN,58,69
. JOHN B,90,93-94,102
. JONATHAN,74;JOSHUA
. 347,350,365;MALICHI
. 358;MICHAEL,342;NANCY
. A,43,86,92,104,118
. 125,128,141,149
. SPEOUS,55;SPIAS,33
. SPIUS,49;THOMAS,298
. WILLIAM,59,63,69,93
REFO,CHARLES L,411
REGISTER,JOSIAH,21,23
. 25
REHEYNEY,CHARLES,9
REICHMAN,JOHN,411
REID,ALEXANDER,291,302
. 304,318,328;ALEXR,222
. ANDREW,364;ANN,403
. BRICE,274;CLEMENTINE
. J,251;ELIZA,235
. ELIZABETH,204,255;GEO
. 217,220;J W,250;JAMES
. 306;JAMES R,210;JANET
. I,382;JNO W,239;JOHN
. 227,232,305,348,351
. JOHN B,411;JOHN L,140
. JOHN W,246,253;JOSEPH
. S,411;LUCY,328
. MARGARET,281
. MARGARET C C,396;MARY
. 209;NANCY,246;OLIVER
. 411;REUBEN,274;ROBERT
. 411;ROBT RAYMOND,411
. SALLY,286;SAMUEL,332
. 338;VIRGIL,338
. WILLIAM A,332,338;WM
. M,411;WM T,274;WM W
. 411;ZACHARIAH,274
REIGS,STEPHEN,359
REILEY,ELIZ,404
REILLY,JAMES,411;MARY B
. 403
REILY,SUSANNAH,397
REINES,ADELINE E,403
REINGARD,
. MARIA MAGDALINE C,390
REINHART,GEORGE,210
REITH,ALFRED,411
RENNOLDS,FREDRICK,227
RENTFORE,ANNE,226
. GEORGE,226
RENTFROE,ZACHARIAH,225
RENTFROW,G,225;SAMPSON
. 226

REPASS,CHURCHWELL,338
RESETER,TIMOTHY,292
RESPESS,JOHN,300;NANCY
. 300;RICHARD,295,300
. THOMAS,300;WIDOW,300
RETHLAN,JOSEPH,411
REVELL,HARDY,411
REVERE,HENRY L,411
REVILL,WILLIAM T,44
REWIS,SARAH,422
REY,WILLIAM,83
REYNOLD,F F,237
REYNOLDS,303;ALICE E
. 287;AMELIUS W,44
. ANDERSON J,411
. CATHERINE,247;CHARLES
. 44;CYNTHIA S,274;D S
. 315;DOROTHY,229;E W
. 114,122;ELIZA,36,278
. EMMA J,246;F F,253;H
. 321;HARDY,313;HERBERT
. 319;HUBERT,293,319
. JAMES,73,82,88,274
. JAMES H,274;JAMES M
. 55;JANE,73,408;JAS R
. 315;JOHN,33,274;JOHN
. W,44,49;JULIA,240
. LEVY,274;LURRENCY,417
. MARY A,244;MARY C,403
. MORDECAI,274
. MORDICIA J,274;NANCY
. 400,407;NANCY A,240
. REBA,247;REBECCA,284
. RICHARD,298;ROAN,417
. SARAH,43,55;THOMAS P
. 73;WILLIAM,9,33,49,73
. WILLIAM M,44;WM E,274
RHANEY,55;ANTHONY,44
. SARAH,55
RHEA,SUSAN,60
RHEINY,CHARLES,33;JOHN
. 33
RHENEY,CHARLES,411
. ELIZA,41
RHEYNER,WASH,210
RHIMES,WM,274
RHIND,JAMES,411
RHINER,JOHN B,199
. JOSEPH A,210;SARAH
. 194;TEMPY,210
RHOADS,WILLIAM,6
RHODELANDER,33
RHODES,A S,274;AARON
. 411;ABSALOM,247,411
. ANN,285;ARNOR,44;AWRY
. 388;BENJAMIN F,84
. BETSEY,244;CAROLINE C
. S,384;CHARLES,309
. DICEY,399;ELBERT,44
. ELIZ,410;ELIZ W,390
. ELIZA,243,274;EVELINE
. A,379;HARRIET C,94
. HENRY,274,320;IRWIA
. 244;JAMES,94,102,344
. JAMES M,83,94;JANE
. 243;JOHN A,411;JOHN R
. 411;JOHNSON,274
. JOSIAH,84,94;JULIA
. ANN,270;LAVINA,381
. 386;LEVENIA A,408
. LEWIS,33;MARTHA N,207
. MARTIN V,274;MARY,406
. MARY B,399,419;NANCY
. 102;NANCY B,402
. SAMUEL P,338;SAVANNAH
. 43;SIMON,44;SUSAN,273
. T V W,411;THOMAS,274
. 284;THOMAS R,411;THOS

RHODES(cont)
. 246;VIRGINIA L,43;W F
. 411;WILEY,274;WILLIAM
. 84;WM,274,309,411;WM
. C,274;WM J.411;WM M
. 94
RHONEY,MORRIS G,51
RHYMES,JOHN,329;SUSAN E
279
RHYMIE,KNO,329
RHYNER,MARTHA,208
RHYNOR,ELIZABETH,194
RIAL,NANCY,415
RICE,AGNES,239;ANN M
. 416;JESSE,152;JESSEE
. 411;JOHN,370;MARYE E
. 379;SAMUEL CLARK,189
. SUSANNA,152;THOMAS D
. 411;THOS S,135;WM J.
. 411
RICH,ARCHIBALD,60
. DANIEL E,210,214
. DAVID A,411;DELILAH
. 205;DEMARIS,194
. ISABELL,212;JOAB,199
. JOSEPH A,199,210;L V
. 210;MARGARET,196
. MARTHA,200;MARTIN V
. 210;SARAH,205;STEPHEN
. 199;STEVEN,199
. WILLIAM J,199,210
RICHARD,ELLA,240;MARTHA
. 244;ROBT,351;VIRGINIA
. C,391
RICHARDS,ANN,255;AZARIA
. 274;CALVUS,274;CANDIS
. 266;DAVID,411;DELANA
. 276;FALBRA,277;GEORGE
. 311;HENRY,12;JANE,258
. JOHN,2,33;LUCY,274
. MARY ANN,272;MATILDA
. 254;PETERS,355
. PICKEREL,274;ROBT,345
. SUSANNAH,259;TABITHA
. 273;TIRAH,274;WILLIS
. 274,366;WM,232;WM A
. 274;WOLCOTT,411
RICHARDSON,325;AMANDA
. 383;BURREL,2;ELIZ R
. 422;GABL,297;JAMES
. 107,184,274;JOHN,12
. 184,411;MARY,248;MARY
. ANN,184,276,397;NANCY
. 412,415;O,306;OBA,297
. OBADIAH,295,297,307
. 320,322;POLLY,280
. ROBERT,274;ROSANNA
. 184;SAMUEL,199,213;WM
. 2
RICHER,JAMES,411
RICHEY,EDWARD J,338
RICHMOND,HENRY A,411
RICHRDSON,E J,210
GEORGE,338
RICHTER,CHARLES W J,274
RICK,MATILDA,210
RICKER,LOUISA,39
RICKERSON,PRUDENCE,393
RICKETTS,RICHARD S,338
RICKITSON,GARDIAS,411
GORDIAS,411
RICKS,ELIZABETH,196
. JACOBS,210;JOHN,199
. LYMAN D,210;M C,205
. RICHARD,358;RICHARD W
. 210;WARREN W,199
. WILLIAM G,210
RICON,JOB,319

RIDDLE,AMELIA,380
RIDGDELL,T A,410
RIDGE,SAMUEL,101
RIDGEWAY,SAMUEL,71,88
101,110
RIDLEY,ARCHIBALD B,338
JOHN,411
RIGAIL,LAWRENCE A,411
RIGDAN,MARY A,197
RIGDELL,SARAH ANN,405
RIGGS,J,149;JESSE,21
RIGHT,GILLIS,85;RANDAL
90
RIGHTONAN,JOHN,33
RIGHTS,JOHN,274
RILEY,ELIZABETH,266
. FERREL,411;HENRY N
. 275;JACOB,275;JAMES
. 272;JAMES G,275;JAS
. 238;JOHN,240,357,411
. JOHN H,411;JOSEPH,275
. MARY ANN,383;MARY D
. 246;MILLY,404;MOSES
. 411;POLLY,277;TEMPSY
. 246;THOMAS,250,254
. 257,259,264,271,275
. 283;THOMAS P,275;THOS
. 236,245;WM M,275
RIMES,HANNAH,254,284;WM
306
RINCHLEY,ANNE E,380
RINER,AMOS,199;JOHN,214
. LAWSON,210;LYDIA,198
. WILLIAM,210,214
. WILSON,199
RINGGOLD,CAROLINE I,405
JAMES G,411
RINGLAND,ISABEL,404
JANE M,392
RINLY,87
RINOR,MATILDA,194
RISE,RILEY,86;ROSEY,86
RISSEL,WM,275
RITCHIE,MARGARET,245;WM
H,411
RITCHY,DAN,151;DANL,153
RIVER,J H B,85
RIVERS,291;BENJAMIN,332
. 338;EMMA,211;FRED,338
. JAMES,338;JOHN,291
. 299,306,316,328,360
. ROBERT,299,309,316
. 329-330;T H B,93
RIVES,JAMES T,411
ROACH,JOHN,348;WILLIAM
329
ROAD,BENJAMIN,275
ROAN,113-114;BENJ,100
. DELILA,98;GEORGE,224
. 306;J W,100;JAMES,306
. JOHN,97;LEONARD,58,97
. MILLEY,219,306
. TUNSTAL,219,298
. TUNSTALL,306;TUNSTEL
. 298
ROARKS,JOEL,275
ROATH,LAURA ANN,405
ROBARTS,DAVID,275;ELIZA
GREEN,275
ROBBERTS,JAMES,108
ROBBINS,MARGARET,410
ROBERDS,12;JOSHUA,219
ROBERNETT,JOHN,229,231
ROBERSON,CEASAR,44
. CYNTHA,165;FLORENCE C
. 43;FORTSON,44;JOHN,12
. 285;JOHN T,44;LAMB,44
. LUCY,44;MACK,44;MARIA

. AN,37;MARY ANN,267
. MINOR,36;NANCY,42
. SARAH,37;WILLIAM,44
ROBERT,AUGUSTUS,411;ELI
. 213;ELIZ G,416
. EMELINE L L,414
. FRANCES G,409;JANE C
. 405;JOSEPH,281
. LAWRENCE WOOD,338
. MOORE,269;SHADRACK
. 152;TABITHA,213;WM H
. 411
ROBERTS,1,219,324
. ABSALOM,48;ABSOLAM
. 152;ADALEN,210;ANDREW
. 275;ANN,198;ANNA,202
. 248;ANNA A,41
. AUGUSTUS R,411
. BARTHOLOMEW G,338
. CATHERINE,394
. CATHERINE C,406
. CHARLES,55;CHARLOTTE
. 37;CLARICEY,158;D,218
. D F,232;DANIEL,218
. DANILE,338;DAVID,152
. DELIA,33;DELILAH,47
. DELLEY,152;ELI,153
. ELISHA,320;ELIZ,388
. 398;ELIZA,388
. ELIZABETH,153,209,270
. ELIZABETH H,397
. ELVIRA,210;EMELINE
. 203;FAITH,152;FANNY
. 152;FREDERICK,275
. GENNY,152;GEORGE,153
. 180;GEORGE D,44
. GRAYSTOCK,7,33;GREEN
. 9,33;GREER,55;HARWOOD
. 174;IRWIN,412;J,113
. JACOB,44;JAMES,10,33
. 50,119,153,179,359
. JAMES H,62,102,338
. JAMES L,412;JAMES M
. 210;JEFF,55;JESSE,162
. 165;JNO,10;JOHN,8,19
. 47,152-153,210,275
. 412;JOHN A,33,52,55
. JOHN W,58;JOS,284
. JOSEPH,152-153;JOSEPH
. W,412;JOSHUA,218,225
. JOSIAH,50,153;JR,258
. 275;KEZIAH TREEL,161
. LIZZIE,45;LOTTIE,41
. MADISON,55;MARGARET
. 194;MARY,2,33,218,381
. 420;MARY ANN,380;MARY
. M,276;MATISON,57
. MILES,55;NATHAN,212
. PATIONS,152;PATSEY
. 284;PATTY,153;POLLY
. 255;R F G,275;RICHARD
. 153,275;RUTH,414
. SARAH,200,209,225,338
. SHADRACK,152;SIMEON,7
. 33;SOPHIA,269;STEPHEN
. 412;TAMENY,55;TAMMEY
. 51;THOMAS,210,412
. THOR,210;THOS,2;W H
. 113,122;W L,210;WILEY
. 153;WILIE,347;WILL M
. 148;WILLARD,33
. WILLIAM,10,44;WILLIS
. 324;WM,10,275,412;WM
. B,275
ROBERTSON,191;ABNER P
. 412;AMANDA JANE,253
. D M,412;DANIEL,234
. DAVID,44;FRANCES A,44

ROBERTSON(cont)
. FRANCES GREENE,238
. HENRY,412;ISAAC,324
. ISAAC E,338;JAMES M
. 362;JESSE,275;JOHN
. 129,259,275,338,356
. 412;JOSIAH,412;JUDY
. 401;MARTHA,241;MARY A
. 400;MARY ANN,382;MARY
. JANE,43;MATHEW,12
. MESHACH,412;MINERAH
. 412;MOSES,2;NANCY,408
. NATHANIEL,302;NATHL
. 302;PEGGY,265;REBECCA
. 267;REBEKAH,166;T,55
. W,264;WILKES,275;WM
. 258,275,412;WM A,412
. Z,275
ROBESON,MARY,153
ROBEY,ELIZA JANE,338
. JOHN N,62;NATHAN,332
. ROBT,359;TIMOTHY,332
ROBINET,EZEKIEL,226
ROBINETT,EZEKIEL,225
. JOHN,222,225
ROBINITTE,RACHEL,237
ROBINS,ALBERT,275
. ARTHUR,9;JAMES R,275
. JOHN,266,275;NANCY
. 235;RACHEL,258;THOMAS
. S,275;WM,275
ROBINSON,105,364;A L,59
. 60,64-65,70,73,76-77
. 79,81,83-84,89,92-93
. 100-101,103-105,107
. 112-113,116,121-122
. 124,129,131-132,135
. 136-137,139,143;ABEL
. L,58-60,62-63-64,68
. 70,72,75,78,116,120
. 130;ABRAM,22,24;ANN
. 247;ARCHIBALD,2;ASKEW
. 15;BENJ,275;BRAM,20
. CHARLOTTE,39;DAVID,8
. 33;ELIZABETH,276
. ELSEY,394;EMILY,271
. GEO,412;HENRY,33,412
. JAMES,48,275,412
. JAMES B,412;JAMES F
. 338;JAMES T,338;JERRY
. 338;JOHN,60,63,72,284
. 309,338,412;JOHN POPE
. 275;JONATHAN,412
. JOSEPH,275;JOSEPH W
. 275;L,134;LEMUEL,51
. LUKE,60,68,73;MARTHA
. A,285;MARY,260,284
. 402;MILFORD,275;NANCY
. 256;NATHAN,44;P B,236
. 274;PEGGY,410;PHILIP
. 33,55,259,263,269,281
. PHILIP B,244,265
. PHILIP H,248;PHILLIP
. 236-237,275;RANDALL
. 63;RICHARD,412;S L,92
. SALLY,269;SARAH
. MARGARET,239;THOMAS
. 59,68,339;THOMAS W
. 275;WALTER,349
. WILLIAM,1,9;WILLIAM A
. 55;WILLIAM C,332,339
. WM,249,412;WM H,275
ROBISON,JOHN,356
. WINFIELD,314;WM F,314
ROBSON,ELIZA M,287;J A
. P,314;JOHN,378;PATSEY
. 377-378

ROBY,MILLEDGE,339;NARCY
. 360;NATHAN,339;THOMAS
. L,339;TIMOTHY,339
. WALTER L,339
. WILLIAMSON,332,350
. 360,364;WILLIAMSON B
. 339
ROCHRIST,12
ROCKER,CHARLES,314
. HERBERT,312
ROCKWELL,EMILY,404
. HESTER ANN,407
RODEN,ADELINE,379
. VANBUREN,210
RODERICK,JOSEPH,412
RODGER,CALEB,191;SANN
. 387
RODGERS,ALOHEUS M,44
. ANDREW J,275;DOCK,313
. JAMES,50,191;JAMES H
. 339;JOHN,313;JOSEPH
. 313;LAURA E,38;R C D
. 205;RUFUS,313;SALLIE
. 42
ROE,A H,55;ELIZABETH,58
. JAMES,364;JOSEPH,33
. 52;JOSEPH A,55,58
. SHAD,306;SHADRACK,305
ROFF,12;AARON,412
. ABIGAIL,392;FREEMAN T
. 412;HARRIET,399
ROGAR,ELIZ,384;SARAH
. 385
ROGER,BRITAIN,292
. THOMAS,412
ROGERS,289;BENJAMIN F
. 44;BRITAIN,295,299
. BRITON,295;CARRAN,104
. DRED,332;EDWARD,6,33
. ELIJAH,112;ELLIS,72
. 80;EMILY EVLINA,379
. ENOCH,44,339;GEORGE
. 353;GEORGE W,365;H
. 312;HENRY,309;J,33
. JAMES,353;JNO,291
. JOEL B,275;JOHN,33,55
. 275,324-325;JONATHAN
. 349;JOS,349;LEMON,85
. LUKE W,210;MARANDA
. 205;MARY,55;MICAJAH
. 358;MOSES,412;OSBORNE
. 278;PELEG,3;RICH,2
. RICHARD,33;RICHARD W
. 44;RICHD,8;ROBERT,339
. RUFUS J,44;SARAH,286
. 410;THOMAS,55;WILLIAM
. 8,33,50
ROLAND,ELIZ,418;PATSEY
. 266;ROBERT A,55
. THOMAS,75;WILLIAM,214
ROLLAND,JAMES,311
ROLLINS,BRANKA J,41
. ELIZA,55;ELIZABETH,33
. JAMES,303;JOHN,6-7,33
. 47,55;RALEIGH,34
. ROLEY,47;ROLLA,7
. SAMUEL,34,55;WILLIAM
. 10,34,55;WILLIAMJ,72
. WM,47
ROMAN,DANIEL S,412;MARY
. S,389
RONALDSON,ANDREW,9
. WILLIAM,364;WILLIM
. 364
RONES,ISABELLA,388
RONEY,MARY,399
RONY,ELIZ,385
ROOKS,SARAH,387,404

ROONEY,CHERRY,403;HUGH
. 412;PATRICK,412
ROOSE,JOHN A,313
ROPER,GEORGE,291-292
. MOSES,96
ROSE,AUTHUR G,412
. ELIZABETH,194;EPHRAIM
. 295-296,299;FREDERICK
. 294,299;FREDK,296
. HOWELL,296,299;HUDSON
. 12;JAMES,328;JOHN,295
. 299;JOSEPH,89;MARY
. 295;PLEASANT,294-295
. 296;S,104,140
. WASHINGTON,295;WM,275
. WYATT,143
ROSHIA,MARTHA NN,388
ROSIER,ANN,409;DANIEL
. 44;JANE E,57;S J,47
. SARAH,402
ROSS,C,116;CHARLES,97
. CHARLES L,412;EDW,171
. ELIZA,407;FRANCIS,244
. 248,274;JAMES,48,199
. 288,291,330;JOHN,169
. 228;KATEY,418;MOATIA
. 199;NANCY,391;SAMUEL
. 275;WILLIAM,12,16,48
. 291,332,339,362;WM,14
ROSSER,BEATRICE H,244
. DAVID,311,317,321
. MARY,245;MOSES,60,62
. 86,97,104,108,147
ROSSETER,APPLETON,295
. T W,295;TIMOTHY,329
ROSSIGNOL,PAUL,412
ROSSITER,APPLETON,305
. TIMOTHY,291
ROSURE,CAROLINE,381
ROTEN,ABRAM,412
ROUM,CHARLES,275
ROUN,SARAH,279
ROUNDTREE,A W,412;ALLEN
. 199;GEO R,412;GEORGE
. 199;JOHN,199;M M,199
. WILLIAM,199
ROUNSAVILLE,JOSIAH,63
ROUNSEVALL,ROBERT,275
ROUNTREE,320-321;ALLEN
. 212;BENJAMIN,210
. DORIANN L,200
. ELIZABETH J,203;ELLEN
. 209;GEORGE C,210
. JAMES,210;JANE,201
. JENCY,211;JOHN,212
. JOSHUA,214;JOSHUA W
. 210;JULIA A,207;K,210
. L J,200;LOU,212
. LUCINDA,200;M,207;M L
. 211;MARY,201;NANCY
. 200;PHERBY,197;ROBERT
. 210;ROCKSANN,195
. SARAH,199;SARAH A,202
. W P,210;WILLIAM,210
. ZILPHA,207
ROUSE,MARY,393
ROUSSEALL,WILLIAM,170
ROUSSEAU,HIRAM,373
ROUTZAHN,L H,44
ROUZEL,HIRAM,275
ROWE,BERNARD,412;DAVID
. 117;JOHN C,339;THOMAS
. 412
ROWEL,HENRY,214;HENRY G
. 210;JOAB,34;WILLIAM
. 214
ROWELL,ELIZABETH,52,55
. ELIZABETH M,201

SANDERS(cont)
. 102,112,132;T J,134
. THOMAS,413;THOMAS J
. 100,114;THOMAS L,276
. THOS J,113,130
. WILLIAM,329;WM,276
. ZADOCK,276
SANDERSINE,LOUISA M,381
SANDERSON,GEO,276
SANDFORD,NATHAN T,12
SANDIFORD,HARRIET A,382
  WM A,413
SANDRIDGE,360
SANDROUS,KYSIAH,341
SANDWICH,EMILY S,379
. LEAH ANN,396;MATTHEW
. H,413;THOMAS,413
SANDYFORD,N T,34
  WILLIAM,34
SANFORD,218;ANNA M,242
. B,319;BEN,276;DANIEL
. 97,124,134;DANL,232
. EDNA,265;ELIZABETH E
. 273;ELIZABETH P,259
. ELLA V,273;GEORGIA
. 236;HENRY,232,276;J
. 319;JESSE,221;MILDRED
. P,273;MOLLIE,248
. SHELTON P,276;THOMAS
. 279;THOS P,235;WM,276
SANIT,MARIA THERESA,397
SANKEY,ANN,281;JOHN T
. 276,296;M D,276
. RICHARD D,276;RICHARD
. T,276
SANSING,BENJAMIN,86
SANSOM,RICHARD,339
SANTE,AUGUSTUS,413
SANTFORD,G,199;J Y,199
  MARTHA MELVERNA,196
SAP,WILEY,6
SAPP,ADDIN,9;ADDISON,34
. ALEY,9;ALLEN,45
. AMANDA,38;ANNIE,38
. ANTHONY,213;CAMERAL
. ZIMON,44;CAROLINE E
. 46;CHARLES,49;DELL,1-2
. DELSON B,8;DENNIS,50
. 55;DOALIN,2;ELIJA,8
. ELIZABETH,34,36;ELLA
. 37;ELLEN,37;ENOS,44
. EVERETT,55,58;EVERITT
. 50;EVERT,34;HARDY C
. 34,50;HARRIET,46
. HENDERSON,45;HENRY,9
. ISAAC,9;ISAIAH,34,50
. JAMES,6,34,50;JANE,45
. JOHN,2,6,8-9,34,45,50
. 55-56;JOIAH,56;JONEN
. 45;KESIAH,36;LEVI,2
. LUKE,2,34,56;MADISON
. 45;MARY,45;MATILDA,43
. MINOCK,45;PEHNICY,50
. PENDLETON,56;PETER,45
. PHILIP,3,8;PHILLIP,2
. RICHARD H,276;SARAH
. ANN,43;SEABORN,44
. SOLOMON,45;THEOPHILUS
. 50;WILEY,34;WILLIAM,5
. 8,34,50,56;ZILPHA,50
SARBOROUGH,REDDICK,24
SARGANT,THOS H,413
SARGEANT,JOHN C,276
SARGENT,AMANDA M,402
  SALLY,412
SARLING,ISAAC,413
SARTIN,JAMES,2,60,62
SASSARD,JOHN,413

SASSER,JOSEPH,23-25
SASSON,JOSEPH,21
SATON,156
SATTER,EDWARD T,20
SATTERWHITE,DAWSON,332
  339;ELIZABETH,258
SATURDAY,EDMUND,413
SAUCER,JOHN,8
SAUL,PATIENCE,361
  PETINNE,361
SAULTER,WILLIAM,199
SAUNDERS,90,97,102;ALEX
. 144,148;ALEXANDER,49
. B M,236,247;JAC,100
. JACOB,95;JOE,77;JOHN
. 75,89,94,102,113,141
. 144,148;NANCY,144-145
. 148-149;R B,98,100
. 113;ROBERT B,89,93
. 104,114,116;S H,135
. 136-139,141,149;S W
. 132;THOMAS,10;THOMAS
. J,89,100,144;THOS J
. 84,142,146;THOS P,135
. WILLIAM,96
SAVAGE,ANN,404,408;ANN
. G,414;ASA,183,413
. CAESAR A,413;DANIEL
. 413;ELIZ,387,393,404
. ELIZA,390;ELIZA MARIA
. 183;JANE,394;JOHN,413
. LOVELESS,183;MARIA E
. 401;NANCY,391;NATHAN
. W,413;SANIEL,34;SARAH
. 382;WM B,413
SAVIDGE,ELIZABETH,183
. 188,190;JAMES,183,188
. 190;JOHN,188,190
. LOVELESS,183;LUCY,393
. REBECCA,188,190
. ROBERT,183
SAXON,ALBERT B,45
. AUGUSTUS A,45;BENJ,9
. BENJAMIN Y,48;CELIA
. 56;ELIZABETH,286
. IRENE,278;JOHN,6,34
. 45,48;JOSHUA,56;LEWIS
. W,276;LINDA,40
. MARGARET,57;MARY,56
. RANSON Y,45;SAMUEL,8
. 34;SARAH H,36;WILLIAM
. 34,52;WILLIAM H,45
SAYER,CATHERINE,279
. CORNLIA,244;ELIZABETH
. 273
SAYERS,CLESTIA M,240
. DAVID,276;ELIZABETH
. 274,277;EUGENIA H,276
. FRANCES DELANEY,264
. HOLLY,276;HOLLY ANN
. 261;JAMES M,276;JOHN
. S,276;JOSHUA L,276
. MARTHA A,253;SARAH
. 253;TEMPSY,240
. VIRGINIA W,270
SAYRES,WILLIAM H,312
SAYRS,ELIZ,381
SCAFFIELD,WILLIAM,45
SCAFFNER,JOHN F,45
SCALES,BARNEY,45;LAURA
  47;MAUDE,44
SCAMPER,DANIEL,276
SCANNELL,DANIEL,413
SCARBER,REDDICK,21-22
SCARBORO,G W,210
SCARBOROUGH,AD,10
. ELIZABETH,12;HARDY
. 360;JACKSON,16;JOAB

. 10;JOEL,34;JONAN,10
. JONATHAN,12;MAY,197
. MILES,10;REDDICK,49
. SAMUEL,34;SAMUEL E
. 210;SARAH,49;SILAS,34
. 48,199;THOMAS,34;THOS
. 10;TURNER,48;WILLIAM
. 12,34,48,199;WM,2,9
SCARBOUGH,NARCISSA,44
SCARBRO,JACKSON,14
SCARBROUGH,A T,56;JOEL
  7;SILAS,7
SCARLET,JAMES,309
SCHACKLEFORD,LUCINDA,60
SCHLEY,ADALINE,42;GEO H
. 413;HENRY,45;M,24
. MARY ANNE,396;MICHAEL
. 20,22;NED,45;RICH,2
. WM,413
SCHLEYS,JOHN,12;PHILLIP
  T,12
SCHNEIDER,GODLEIB,358
SCHNNEIDER,GOTTLEIB,358
SCHOGEN,NEHEMIAH,365
SCHREINER,CHAS W,413
SCOFIELD,E E,413
SCOGGINS,CAROLINE,278
. ELIZABETH,258,264
. JOHN I,276
SCONERS,BARTLY,214;JOHN
  214
SCONGES,I,56;ISAAC,56
. JANE,56;RICHARD,56;T
  56
SCONIERS,JEHU,48;JOHN
. 48;NOAH,48;RICHARD,48
. RICHARD B,48
SCONYEARES,ISAAC,199
SCONYERS,34;ELIZABETH
. 198;J E,210;JOHN,199
. JULIA ANN,195
. MARTHA A A,207;RICHD
. 10;SADAY,195;SARAH J
. 195;SUSANNAH,197
SCOTT,118,198,309;A,351
. A C,142;A H,246,270
. 282;A N,281;ADAM,182
. ANDREW,26-27,34;ANN
. 393;BENJAMIN,169
. BUTTON,213;CHARLES,9
. 34,52,56;DANIEL Z,210
. ELIJAH,413;ELIZ,405
. ELIZA A,250;ELIZA
. JANE,386;ELIZABETH
. 285;EMILY,44;GAMWELL
. T,413;GEORGE,45
. GEORGE ANN,203;HENRY
. 45,199;J A,314;J W,76
. JAMES,5,18;JESSE,199
. JNO,224,296;JOHN,19
. 56,246,309,413;JOHN I
. 276;JOSEPH,125;JOSEPH
. C,80;MARTHA,37;MARY
. 395;OSCAR D,315
. PULSKIE,276;ROBERT,20
. S S,95,106,116,124
. SAMUEL,174;SAMUEL S
. 95;THOMAS,210,280,297
. 413;THOS B,5,215
. VINEY,45;WILLIAM,191
. 352-353,355;WILLIS,45
. WM,171,413;WM G,413
. WOODLEF,328
SCOVELL,HEZEKIAH W,413
SCRBOROUGH,BENJ,413
SCREWS,ENOCH,99;JAMES
. 99-100,109,119,131
. NANCY,99;ZACHARIAH

SCREWS(cont)
210
SCRIVEN,ROSA,206
SCROGGINS,WARREN C,90
SCRUGGS,ABISHA,26
  ABISHAE,34;WM M,8
SCRUISE,JAMES,413
SCRUTCHENS,JOSIAH,34
SCRUTCHENS/SCRATCHENS,
  JOSIAH,12
SCRUTCHINS,JOSIAH,48
SCUDDER,ANN L,253
SCUDDER,
  SAMUEL C,276
SCURLOCK,JOSHUA,289
SCURRY,E M M,395
  RICHARDSON,360
SCUTCHINS,JOSIAH,10
SEA,JESSE,413
SEABORN,RACHEL,56
SEAGAR,BENJ,7;JOHN,10
SEAGO,LURANA,420
SEALES,JOHN,50;WILLIAM
  311
SEALS,H B,313;HENRY,276
. JOHN,56;JOHN H,276
. LIZZY,36;MARTHA J,263
. MARY J,280;THOMAS,70
. W D,313;WM,413
SEARS,MARGARET,413
SEASLEY,BURRELL,199
SEASTRUNK,JACOB,413
SEATS,BENJ,413
SEAWELL,MICHAEL,323
SEAY,DAVID,190;ELLA,236
. JUDA WINFREY,189
. JULIUS,178;PHEBE,190
. WILLIS,413
SEAYE,FRANCES ANN,406
SEEGAR,BENJAMIN,48
. CHARLES F,48;SAMUEL
. 48
SEELEY,GIDEON,413
SEGAR,BENJAMIN,34
. CHARLES T,34;JOAB,34
. SAMUEL,34
SEGO,ABRAHAM,413;ALFRED
. 413;ELIZA,413;JOSHUA
. 413;LEVI,413;MARTHA
. 421;MARY,407
. MIDDLETON,413;OVERTON
. 413;REBECCA,417;WM
. 413
SELF,ELISHA,295;JAMES E
. 276;TABITHA,295
. WILLIAM,341;WM,276
SELLECK,ELIZ M,422
SELLERS,WM,413
SELMAN,H,341
SELMON,WILLIAM,341
  WILLIAM W,95
SEMMES,ANDREW C,413
SENGES,JEAN,413;JOHN
  413
SENTELL,JOSEPH,59,69,73
SERA,
  LEOCADIE ADELAIDE,395
SERGEANTS,JOHN,329
SERVICE,L C,413
SESSION,ROBERT F,369
SESSIONS,34;JEREMIAH M
  276;WINNEY,374
SESSOMS,AMOS,159;CATY
. 159;DOLLY,159;MARY
. 159;NANCY,159
SETZE,CELESTINE,382
SEUKEY,ELIZABETH,154
SEVEDGE,
. (SEE SAVIDGE),183

. REBECCA,380;ZACHARIAH
. 183
SEVIER,JOHN,34
SEW,ALFRED ROATH,45
SEWELL,JOHN E,119
SEXTON,DINAH,42
SEYMORE,EVABON,276;JOHN
  R,339;MARTHA,339
SEYMOUR,HENRY C,276
SHACKELFORD,JAMES,318
  LLOYD,276
SHACKLEFORD,JAMES,226
. 323;JOHN,60,153;SALLY
. 153;SARAH,387,413
SHACKLEY,SARAH,245
SHADRICK,CHARLOTTE,391
SHADWICK,MARY,392
SHAFFER,DANIEL S,413
. HENRIETTA M,259;HENRY
. 2;LUCY G,246;MARIA
. 396
SHAKELFORD,ANN,301
. BETSY,301;EDMOND,301
. FANNY,301;FRANCIS,301
. JAMES,300-301;JOHN
. 301-302;NANCY,301
. POLLEY,301
SHAKEN,CATHARINE,404
SHANCLEFORD,BENJ,413
  GEO W,413;JNO W,413
SHANDLER,GEORGE,8
SHANKLIN,MARTHA,194
SHANNON,ELIZ,386;JOHN
. 88,93;MARIA L,421
. PETER J,413;WILLIAM
. 78;WM,276
SHARD,CORNELIUS,339
SHARK,C,124
SHARKLEY,SILAS,276
SHARMAN,JAMES,339
SHARP,ABEDA,47;BASDIL
. 34;BENJ,276;CADE,7,34
. CADER,47;CAMBELL,210
. CAMMEL,199;CLEMY,34
. ELIZ,401;ELIZABETH,49
. JAMES,339;JOHN,1,3,6
. 276,413;JUDITH,292
. M M,56;MARTIAL,276
. MARY,43;MARY ANN,380
. MICAJAH,56;MICHAEL,1
. POLLY,34;RICHARD,276
. ROBERT,80,276;SAML
. 234;SARAH E,248;WM
. 292
SHARPE,A D,314;J H,314
. LEWIS T,199;POLLY,250
. WILLIAM,57,339
SHATON,DELIA ANN,403
SHAW,234;AARON,413
. ALEXANDER,413;AMOS
. 115;BETHANY,410;CALEB
. T,413;CHARLES,175
. CREYTIN,276;DOLLEY
. 374;ELIZ,382,416
. EPHRAIM,376;FREDERICK
. R,413;GILBERT,232
. HARRIOT,417;JAMES,175
. 276;JANE,41;JOHN,51
. 276,332,339,413;JOHN
. W,413;KATHERINE,389
. MARY,417;PEGGY BELLAH
. 376;POLLY,255;ROBERT
. 175,356,368;SALLY,258
. SAMUEL,276;WATSON,339
. WILLIAM,232;WM,413;WM
. C,414
SHEARER,GILBERT,414
  WILLIAM J,96

SHEART,GEORGE,210
SHEARWARD,BENEATOR,197
SHEATS,BENOJAH,276
  ROBERT,289
SHED,PRELOW,277;WM,277
SHEDD,JANE,247
SHEERER,JOHN,87
SHEFFEL,ELIZABETH,265
SHEFFELD,BARNABEE,339
SHEFFERD,12
SHEFFIELD,GEORGE,216
  HARRIET,384
SHEFTALL,BEN,72;EMANUEL
  8
SHEILDS,LETIA,239
SHELBEY,MOSES,231
SHELL,LUCINENDA,277
. MARTHA,240;REBECCA
. 283;REUBEN R,277;T I
. 277
SHELMAN,JOHN,2
SHELTON,ELIZABETH,265
. GEO,277;JOHN L,277
. MARGRET,239;REBECCA
. 255;SARAH,265;WM B
. 414
SHEPARD,GATHERS,56
. MARTHA,200;RICHARD
. 128;WILLIAM B,45
SHEPHARD,ANDREW,192
SHEPHERD,ABRAHAM,339
. BAZIL,34;ELEAZER W
. 332,339;GEORGE F,98
. JAMES,8,34,49;JOSEPH
. 9;MARTHA,251;MARY,398
. MINOMIA,387;POLLY,387
. RICHARD,66;SARAH,332
. THOMPSON,414;URSULA
. 380;WILLIAM L,339
. WINBURN R,339;WM,19
SHEPHERDSON,ELIZABETH
  34
SHEPHEURD,CHARLOTTE,416
SHEPPARD,JOHN B,19
  WILLIAM,19
SHEPPERD,RICHARD,65;WM
  414
SHERAD,BENJAMIN,199
SHERAN,PETER,414
SHERIDAN,DENNIS,277;R W
  277
SHERLEY,MARY,266
. RICHARD,26;RICHMOND
. 277;WILLIAM,26
. WILLIAM S,22,24
SHERLING,MARY,266
SHERMAN,JOHN,306;WM,414
SHERMON,MARY,393
SHEROD,ELIS,203;ELIZA
  206;FELIX A M,414
SHERRARD,BENJAMIN,199
  JOSEPH L,199
SHERREL,LAVINIA,238
SHERRILL,ELIZ,247
. LITTLEBERRY,277
. PERRIN,235;POLLY,239
. SALLY,283 .
SHERROD,BENJAMIN,210
. ELIZA,44;G,210;INDIA
. 204;JOHN,213;JOHN W
. 210;NANCY,207;RACHEL
. 211;WILLIAM G,199,213
SHERWOOD,ADIAL,277
. ADIEL,243;BENJ,7
. ODIEL,239
SHEWMAKE,JOSEPH,49
SHEWMAKER,ANNIE E,43
. GEORGE,45;JUNNY,45

SHEWMAKER(cont)
. MARY L,44;SARAH J,37
. SAXON,45
SHEY,SAMUEL,277
SHICK,WM,414
SHIDMORE,HARRIETT A,245
SHIELDS,159;BEDDY,167
. HANNAH,167;HENRY G,8
. JAMES,167;JOHN,167
. MARY,167;ROBERT,167
. SAML,374;SUSAN,167
. WILLIAM,167;WM,277
SHILLING,CHARLOTTE,389
SHINGLE,ELY,38
SHIP,DAVID,288;REBECCA
. 263;RESPY,264;RICHARD
. 297,305
SHIPARD,ANDREW,2;JOHN,2
SHIPLEY,ROBERT,215,217
SHIPP,BENJAMIN,288
. GUSTAVUS V,339;JOHN H
. 277;LEMUEL,277;MARY E
. 285;SALLY,245;STEPHEN
. 277
SHIRLEY,ELIZABETH,257
. JOHN,8;MALINDA,251
. WILLIAM,20;WILLIAM S
. 25;WM,7
SHIRLIN,CYNTHIA W,239
SHIRLING,JAMES N,277
. RABUN W,277;RICHARD
. 277
SHIRLY,JOHN,4
SHIVERS,325;EMANUEL,62
. G W C,62;J H,122
. JAMES,62;JOHN,218
. JONAS,287,305,317,322
. MARGARET,124-125
. THOMAS,414;THOMAS J
. 277;WILSON,62
SHOCKLEY,A,116;BENJ,277
. GEORGE W,339;MILLY
. 258;NELLY,241;THOMAS
. 298
SHOEMAKE,LUCEY,393
SHOEMAKER,JOSEPH,56
SHOP,LAWRENCE T,414
SHORES,WILEY,9
SHORRS,RICH,2
SHORT,ELIZ,398
. ELIZABETH,258;P B,191
SHORTE,MARY,400
SHORTER,A,101;ALFRED,92
. ALFRED A,93;MARY,251
. 269;OLIVER,339;R C,76
SHORTS,THOMAS,159
SHOWERS,ELRIDGE,339
. PASCHAL,332,339
SHROPSHIRE,BETSEY,281
. JAMES E,339;JAMES H
. 277;JAMES W,332,339
. JOSHUA,306;M G,339
. OLIVIA J,332;WESLEY
. 277
SHUBERT,ABRAM,45
. CAROLINE JANE,5;FRED
. 5;FREDERICK,5
SHULTZ,CHRISTIAN,79
SHUMAKE,ENSIGN JOSEPH,9
. JOSEPH,34
SHUMATE,TRIPLETT,414
SHURBY,SARAH ANN,134
SHY,FRANK,339;PEYTON
. 339;SAMUEL,339
. SEABORN J,332,339;WM
. H,277
SIBLEY,AUGUSTAE G,390
. CAROLINE FRANCES,385

. SARAH B,385;WM,414
SIDWELL,AMANDA J,271
. DAVID,370;JOHN,277
. MARY E,287;REBECCA A
. 277;SARAH,266
SIGNAW,THOMAS,277
SIKES,ADELINE,407
. EDWARD,45;FRANCES C
. 38;JAMES,45,414;JANE
. M,385;MARY E,36;SALLY
. 401;SOLOMON,414
. THOMAS,56;W H,414
. WILLIAM,414
SILBERT,MARY,401;MARY
. ANN,381
SILCOX,JOHH,414
SILER,WILLIAM D,339
SILIVAN,JOHN,414
SILLIVAN,34;DENNIS,34
. H W,414
SILLIVENT,MARY,199
SILLS,HENRY C,91
. MACKLING,193;NANCY,34
. 50
SILMAN,WILIAM,323
. WILLIAM,323,368
SILVERMAN,SARAH ANN,389
SILVEY,HINTON C,277
SIMES,PATSEY,258
SIMMONE,JACOB,414
SIMMONS,ANN,270;C H,89
. CHARLES,277,305
. CLEMENTINE P,249;ELIZ
. 409;FRANK M,277
. FRANKLIN,277
. GREENSVILLE,414;HENRY
. S,277;HENRY T,414
. HILLORY,193;HULDA,260
. I W,257;ISAAC,329;J C
. 280;J M,113;J W L,12
. JACK,277;JAMES,324
. JAMES M,119;JAMES S
. 414;JAMES W L,414
. JOHN,70,81,148,224
. 279,328;JOSEPH A,414
. M T,113;MARY,36;MARY
. S,277;NANCY L,240
. PATIMA,270;PHERIBY,34
. ROBERT,328;SANDERS W
. 339;SARAH,390;SIMEON
. 277;STEPHENS,277
. THOMAS,318,321;THOS M
. 414;W,113;WILLIAM,90
. 97,306,358;WM,100
SIMMS,BRITTIAN,164
. CHRISTIAN NATURE,164
. ELIZABETH,5;FREDERICK
. 277;JAMES,159,164
. RICHARD S,339;THOMAS
. 5
SIMON,AGNES,402;BAILEY
. 236
SIMONS,215;ISABEL,273
. JOSIAH,299;THOMAS,359
SIMONSON,ISAAC,21,23
SIMONTON,EZEKIEL,277;G
. 101;GILBRAITH,339
. ISABELLA,273;JOEL,277
. JOHN A,277;MARGARET
. 235;MARY,262;NANCY
. 282;PENELOPE,241
. SARAH M,257;THOMAS
. 277
SIMPKINS,EMMA M,261
. JULIA ANN,259;NANCY
. 422
SIMPSON,ARCHD,362
. ARCHIE,345;BRUNETT

. 177;DAVID,178;E WADE
. 314;EASTER,36;ELIZA,2
. ELIZABETH,2-3;G,309
. GEO,309;GEORGE,309
. 321;JAMES M,414;JJOHN
. 339;JOHN J,339;MATTIE
. 254;POLLY,400;W R,100
. WILLIAM,82,86,88,116
. WILLIAM R,93,116;WM
. 88,97,277;WM R,90,130
SIMS,A F,277;ABNER,161
. 180;AGGY,180;ANN,401
. ANNE B,397;BARTLETT
. 291;BENJA,233
. BENJAMIN,185;BENJAMIN
. D,414;BETSEY,283
. BIROM,318;CAROLINE
. 398;D,359-360;DAVID
. 358;E,350;EMILY W,260
. GEORGE,303,311;GREENE
. 303;JAMES,153,357
. JAMES GLENN,359;JNO
. 232;JOHN,80,233;JOHN
. M,277;LENNY,180;MAN
. 161;MANN,180,414
. MARGARET,166;MARTHA
. 248;MARY,353;MARY A
. 381;MARY BEALLE,172
. MARY PENN,161,180
. PHILIP,328;ROBERT,297
. 318,320;WILLIAM,180
. 359;WM,277,414;WYLIE
. 352
SINCLAIR,WM F M,277
SINDERINE,
. MARY ELVINA,404
SINGER,SARAH,390
SINGLETERRY,MARY,382
SINGLETON,CAROLINE,45
. GRANDISON,45;JOHN,94
. JOSEPH,277
SINKFIELD,SARAH,404
SINQUEFIELD,JANE,405
SIPREY,197
SISSON,LARKIN R,273
SISTRUNK,SAMUEL,339
SKELBY,316
SKELLEY,WILLIAM,318
SKELTON,ROBERT,154
SKIDMORE,ANNE E,236
. CROSLEY,277
SKINNER,A R,56;BARBARA
. M,411;CAROLINE,402
. CAROLINE E F,393
. CHARLES,9,34,49,56
. CORNELIA F,418;ELIZA
. J,45;ELIZABETH,36,151
. HANEY,151;HENRY,56
. 414;HETTY,36;HOWARD
. 151,414;HULDY,151
. ISAAC,151;J D,399;J T
. 210;JACOB,48;JANE,38
. 41,56,151;JESSE,47
. JOHN,9,34,49,151,414
. JOHN R,56;JONAS,34,47
. 56;JOSEPH,222;LOTTEY
. 56;LUCH,45;LUCIUS C
. 414;MARY ANN,387
. OLIVER,320;REBECCA,56
. REBECCAH,49;RICHARD
. 151;ROBERT,6,34,49,56
. SALLY,242;SARAH,34,41
. 43;SARAH M,210
. SEABORN,414;SIMEION G
. 45;SIMEON,45;TABITHA
. A,408;THOMAS,57,414
. THOMAS HIRAM ABELH
. 151;UNAH,45;URIAH,34

SMITH(cont)
. MARIETTA A,264
. MARSHAL,321;MARSHALL
. 323;MARTHA,115,260
. 406,415;MARTHA H,287
. MARTHA J,206;MARTHA W
. 247;MARTIN,122;MARY
. 56,193,259,272,284
. 292,387,396,405;MARY
. ANN,42,193,245,281
. MARY S,257;MATTIE A
. 339;MORRIS,51;MOSES M
. 147;N,56,138;NANCY,56
. 202,205,247,249,254
. 386;NANCY R,279
. NATHAN,45,278,328
. NATHANIEL,56,278,415
. NETTIE V,286;NOAH,34
. 50,415;NORRIS,14,16-17
. O L,267,275;OTIS,253
. 276;PATIENCE,263,278
. PATIENCE A,236;PENING
. W,391;PETER SKEN,415
. PEYTON,224;PHILIP,415
. POLLY,241,245,258,261
. 346;PRESLEY,82
. PRESSLEY,124;R C,116
. 124,282;R W,91,100
. 142;RABUN,312;RADFORD
. 415;REBECCA,157,388
. 400;REBEKAH,157
. REDDICK,278;REUBEN
. 223-224,233,297
. REUBEN C,278;RICHARD
. 48,119,129,143,278
. 311,321;RICHARD B,339
. RICHARD P,107;RICHRD
. 133;ROBERT,58,60,63
. 69,73,81,89,96,141
. 229;ROBERT W,79,88-89
. 102,113;ROBT,87;ROBT
. KING,415;RODY,237
. ROLIN,339;ROSA N,204
. S B,142;SALLEY,292
. SALLY,226;SAMUEL,86
. 89,122,415;SAMUEL
. JENKS,415;SAMUEL R
. 339;SARAH,235,245,274
. 389;SARAH A,261,387
. SARAH ANN,238;SARAH E
. 38,396;SARAH F,258
. SARAH J,386;SARAH
. JANE,267;SELATTIA,283
. SENIA,204;SENIO,204
. SIMON,115,126;SOLOMON
. 63,293,319;SOPHIA,39
. STEPHEN,7;SUSAN,40,52
. SUSAN ANN,276;SUSAN R
. 278;SUSANNA,14
. SUSANNAH,56,278;T A
. 320;THOMAS,56,119,226
. 278,306,339,415
. THOMAS H,278;THOMAS J
. 339;THOMAS R,339
. THOMAS W,339;THOS,357
. TONY,211;W,113;W J,45
. W R,214;W R SIMPSON
. 122;WHIT R,200;WHITE
. R,211;WILLIAM,34,45
. 58,60,63,82,89,169
. 213,227,309,352,357
. WILLIAM B,114-115,117
. 415;WILLIAM G,332,339
. 372;WILLIAM H,115,117
. 126,142,148,339
. WILLIAM S,93,131
. WILLIAM T,56;WINNEY
. 217;WM,88,278,354,415

. WM C,278;WM F,415;WM
. G,85,278;WM T,278
. WYATT R,339:ZACHARIAH
. 200;ZACHARIAH A,339
. ZAKERIAH,415;ZILPHA A
. 37;ZIPPORAH A,339
SMITHART,ELIZ,414
SMITHE,HARRIET C,381
SMITHWICK,ELIZABETH,354
. WILLIAM,354
SMITY,YOUNG,278
. YOUNGEST,278
SMYTH,JOURDAN,355
. JULIANA,419;SIMO,355
SMYTHE,ELIJAH,345
SNADERS,THOMAS J,131
SNARL,JOHN,415
SNEAD,CHARLOTTE,391
. DUDLEY,34;JOHN C,415
. LAVINIA,391;LEASTON
. 34;MARY,4;PHILIP,34
. PRINCE,45;SAMUEL,34
. SUSAN P,394
. VIRGINIA ANN DILL,410
SNEED,198,200;CAROLINE
. G,411;DUDLEY,12
. LEASTON,48;NANCY,399
. NATHANIEL,415;ROBT,2
. SAMUEL M,12;WINNEY
. 392;WM,278
SNELL,LIZZIE C,207
. ROXANN M C,198
SNELLING,ANTOINETTE,264
SNELLINGS,ALEXANDER,369
. 370;ELIZABETH,370
. GEORGE,369-370;JOHN
. 369-370;PETER,369
. SALLEY,369;WILLIAM
. 370
SNIDER,ANDREW J,214
. ELIZABETH,198;ROSCIAN
. 40
SNIPES,ELIZA A J,202
SNODDY,89;S,100;SAMUEL
. 85,89-90,92-93,101
. 104-105,112,119,122
. 124
SNOODY,S,113;SAMUEL,95
. 96,99-100
SNOW,ATHERIA L R,283
. JOHN P,278;MARK,363
. SAMUEL G,278;THO,227
. THOMAS,251,259,278
. 363-364;THOS,236-237
SNOWLINSON,W H,104
SOISCLAIR,MARY E,412
SOMER,JAMES,307
SOMERSETT,MARY H,49
SORENSON,ANDREW G,214
SORREL,SUSANNAH,374
SORRELL,ELIZABETH,257
. GEORGE,278;MATILDA
. 284;NANCY,240;POLLY
. 284;ROBERT,225;SALLY
. 236
SORRELS,CHARLES,354
SORRILL,GREENE,233;JOHN
. 231;ROBERT,233
SORROW,JOSEPH C,278
. NICHOLAS,278
SORSBEE,THOS,7
SOUNCERS,THOMAS,191
SOURSBY,THOMAS,34
SOUTH,JAMES,62
SOUTHALL,HALLMAN,278
. JNO,290;JOHN,291,304
. 306,310;REBECCA,289
. REBEKAH,304

SOUTHERLAND,
. ELIZABETH,265;EMILY
. 282;JOHN,278;MARY ANN
. 246;PRISCILLA,268
SPAIN,LEVI,12,34;LEVY,7
. LEWELLIN,11;LUELLEN
. 34;MATTHEW,34,49
. SIMEON,7
SPANN,AGIE,207;JAMES B
. 34
SPARKS,JAMES,278;THOMAS
. 298;THOMAS H,278;THOS
. 353
SPE,DANIEL,97
SPEAIRS,CALEB W,332
SPEAKE,EBENEZER,60;G T
. 60,77;GEORGE P,78
.: GEORGE T,69,80;JAMES
. T,60;RICHARD,87
SPEAR,CHARLES,415;HARRY
. 339;JOHN,288
SPEARMAN,G T,332
. GABRIEL T,339;JOHN
. 333;JOHN F,339;MARTHA
. 333
SPEARS,AUGUSTUS,339
. COLUMBUS A,333,339
. CREED A,333;CREED E
. 339;EATON,339;ELIZA E
. 40;JAMES T,339;JESSE
. 339;JOHN,7,34,333,339
. JOHN WESLEY,339
. JOSEPH Y,415;JOSHUA B
. 339;JOSIAH C,339
. LAVINA,58;SIDNEY,339
. THOMAS J,339;WILLIAM
. 339-340;WILLIAM H,333
. 339
SPEED,GEORGE W,415;WM
. 415
SPEER,E W,283;JOHN,346
. MOSES,377
SPEERS,C,56;CHARLOTTE
. 51;DRUSILLA,160
. WILLIAMSON,160
SPEIGHT,JAS,10
SPEIGHTS,
. ELIZA CAROLINE,380
. JAMES,333,339
SPEIR,WILLIAM,218;WM
. 220
SPELL,CELIA,2
SPELMAN,R P,415;RICHARD
. P,415
SPENCE,EDITH,199;GREEN
. B,200;GREENVILLE,48
. HARRIS,34;ISAAC,14,16
. JEREMIAH,213;JOHN,9
. 14,16;JOHN A,200
. JOSEPH,48;JULIA A,203
. LEDSTON,12;LEWIS,7
. LITTLETON,12,213;MARY
. 34,48,196;MATTHEW,200
. NANCY,34;PAUL,339
. ROBT,2
SPENCER & MAYS131
SPENCER,87-88,90-94,96
. 98,102-104,108,113-114
. 117-122,124,129,134
. 136,138,140-141,145
. 146,148;ABRAHAM,229
. AMASA,415;ANNIE M,268
. B E,273;BLUFORD,12
. DAVID,86,110;DEBY,208
. ISABELLA,382;JESSE M
. 339;JOHN,278;LEVI,278
. T L,62;THOMAS,288,293
. 299,302,309,319,330

STEWART(cont)
. 270;H B,101;HAMILTON
. 85;ISAAC,228;JAMES
. 119,127,132,219,339
. 415;JANE O,414
. JEPTHAH,347;JOHN,223
. 361;JULIA,41
. KATHERINE ELIZABETH
. 254;MARY,41;MARY A E
. 386;MARY C,241;MILLEY
. 51;NANCY,396;NANNIE E
. 254;R M,126;RICHARD M
. 108,117;ROBERT,119
. 228,357;ROBT,351
. SARAH,108;THEOPHILUS
. S,415;VINCENT,45
. VIRGINIA,260;WILLIAM
. 7;WM,10;WM D,279
STICKER,SOLOMON,279
STIDMAN,NELLY,385
STILL,ARCHIBALD,279;B
. 130;BARTHOLONEW,122
STILLMAN,JAMES,415
. SAMUEL,279
STILLWELL,J M,246-247
. RICHARD,111,125
. SQUIRE,90
STILWELL,CHAS H,416;J M
. 259;SQUIRE,82
STINES,HARRIETT,275
STING,SUSANNAH C,397
STINGERS,N L,12;SAMUEL
. 12
STINSON,MARTHA,390
. MICAJAH,343;WM,416
STITH,CATHERINE,387
. JOHN,151;WILL,218;WM
. 288,290,293
STOBO,NANCY,34
STOCK,THOMAS,284;WM,371
STOCKDALE,JOHN,34;NANCY
. 50
STOCKS,CATRON,223
. DANIEL,251;ISAAC,215
. 219,223;JOHN,279;JOHN
. G,279;THOMAS,249,253
. 256,258-259,262-263
. 265,267,269,272-273
. 274,276,279-281,285
. 286;THOS,236-238,240
. 241-242,244;W,235;W H
. 284
STOCKTON,ANNA R,416
. ELIZ M,385;G H,416
. MARY S,388;MRTHA B
. 386
STODGHILL,127,129,138
. 143,148;WM,95
STOKELEY,ELIZABETH,238
. PETER,3
STOKES,ALLEN,347;DRURY
. 9;ELIZ,401;ELIZABETH
. 238;IGNATIUS,339
. JACOB,103;JAMES M,45
. JANE,196,363;LUCY M
. 417;MARCUS,9;MARGARET
. J,399;MARK,34,49,56
. MARTHA,34;MARTIN,10
. RICHARD,364;SARAH F
. 253;THOMAS,273;THOS
. 235,240;WILLIAM,363
. WILLIAM B,339;WM WADE
. 363
STONE,ELIZ,244;EMMA E
. 36;HARDY,279;HENRY,23
. 25;HENRY HOLCOMBE,200
. HEZEKIAH,232;ISAAC
. 416;JAMES G,45;JOHN

. 310,319;JOHN T,279
. JOHN W,279,339;LEMUEL
. W,416;LUCY A,272
. MAHALA ANN,339;MARY
. 181;MICHAEL D,82;R G
. 314;REUBEN S,63
. ROBERT R,45;THOMAS J
. 146;WILLIAM,4,21,23
. 25,191;WM,291
STONER,LOUISA,398
. SOPHIA S S,414
STONUM,BRYON,296
STORES,JAMES,12
STORMAN,GEORGE,363
STORMANT,HENRY,111
STORY,JOHN T,99
STOUTAMIRE,ELIZABETH
. 275
STOVAL,SARAH,245
STOVALL,91,233;CAROLINE
. E,390;CHARLES,416
. ELBA N,283;EMMA B,265
. GEO,105,238,247,256
. JOHN,279;LITTLEBERRY
. 279;MARCELLUS A,416
. MARTHA,272;MARTHA ANN
. 279;MARY LOUISA,273
. MILDRED A,282
. PLEASANT,279
. POWHATTAN,279;THOMAS
. 290;WM H,279
STOW,145;CORRIE A,244
. E B,124
STOWE,CORDELIA,276
STOWERS,THOMAS,344
STOY,AMANDA MARIA,411
. LAURA T,402;THADIAS S
. 416
STRADLEY,DAVID,3;MIROD
. 3
STRAHAM,SAMUEL,69;WM H
. 69
STRAHAN,NEILL,72-73
. SAMUEL,71,75
STRAIN,EMELINE T,265
. ISAAC,56;ISSAC,57;W L
. 279;W W,279
STRAINGER,JAMES,10
STRANGE,AMANDA M,236
. JAMES W,279;JOHN H
. 416;MARTHA,202
. MITCHELL,200;SAMUEL
. 214;SARAH,204
. SUSANNAH,195
STRAUDER,RICH,3
STRAWN,JAMES,353;MARTHA
. 353
STRAWTHER,JAMES,292
. RICHARD,292
STREET,GEORGE,416;JAMES
. F,279;THOMAS,12
STREETMAN,WM,13,16
STREETS,DANIEL,416
STRICKLAND,C C O,279
. C H,254,258,266,273;H
. 350;JAMES K,279
. JEPHTHAH,293;SOLOMON
. 339,343,345,351-352
. 359,363
STRICKLIN,SOLOMON,353
. 361
STRINGER,ABNER,6,12,34
. JAMES,34;M W,56;SMITH
. 6,34;WILLIAM F M,45
STRINGFELLOW,283;ALISEY
. 250;ANNY,275
. CHARLOTTE,413;GEORGE
. W,339;H,89;HENRY,342

. JAMES,339;SAMUEL L
. 416;WM,416
STRINGFIELD,ELISHA,19
. 416
STROBEL,GODFREY,416
STRODER,SALLY,390
STRONG,ELIJAH,363-364
. JOHN,363;JOHNSON,343
. 347-348,354-355,357
. 361-362,364;SHERWOOD
. 345
STROTHER,FRANCIS,309
. RICHARD,319
STROUD,ALBAN,289;ANN
. 420;BARSHEBA,128
. BATHSHEBA,130;BEDEN
. 370;ELI,289;EMILY,130
. ETHEN,370;JAMES,200
. 214;JOHN,200,279,347
. 370;LEVI,289;MALORY
. 370;MARK,289,292
. MARTHA,289;MARY,289
. ORION,289;PASIFI T
. 370;PHILIP,359;SARAH
. 289,370;SARAH A,210
. THOMAS,200;TILLATHA
. 289;WILLIAM,75,119
. 128,130,289;WM,347
STROZIER,
. ANN CATHERINE,239
. ELIZABETH D,268;JOHN
. 234;MARTHA E,245
. REUBEN I,279;SARAH E
. 242
STRUGES,DANIEL,173
. ELEANOR,173;JOHN,173
. ROBERT,173
STUART,34;ANDREW,95,416
. ANNA,34;ISAAC,34;JAKE
. W,200;JAMES,34;JOHN
. 200;NANCY,398;NATHAN
. 200;THOMAS,416
STUBBLEFIELD,
. GUSTAVUS,279;MARY E
. 242;THEODRICK,357
. WILLIAM S,34
STUBBS,309;FRANCIS,303
. 309;JAMES,3,339;JANE
. E,194;JAS,5;JOHN,156
. SARAH ANN,400
STUBS,WILLIAM,320
STUCKEY,EDMUND,416
. HESTER,422;WM B,416
STUDMAN,SALLY,283
STUNER,SARAH,419
STURDIVANT,328;CHARLES
. 309;CHAS,288,294
. EDWIN,352;ELIZABETH
. 255;GEO W,279;JOHN
. 296,299,329;LUCY,352
. SARAH,265
STURGES,ANDREW B,416
. ANNE,351;COLUMBUS F
. 416;ELIZA,389;J,192
. JOHN,173,416;OLIVER
. 416;SAMUEL,52;WILLIAM
. G,351;WILLIAM U,416
. WM G,34
STURGESS,BENJAMIN H,181
. DANIEL,181;JOHN,181
. MARIAH,181;ROBERT,181
STURGIS,CHARLES M,279;J
. 116;MARTHA C
. THOR---TON,279;SAMUEL
. 34;WM G,342
STURRICE,JOHN S,78
STWEART,REBECCA,56
. WILLIAM,56

STYRES,MARY,411
SUBRINE,SARAH,172
SUFFIELD,ANN MARIE,393
SUGGS,ELIZA,408;JOHN,34
  56
SUGS,MOSES,19
SULIVANT,ASTABB,200
SULLIVAN,34;ARABEL,185
. DANIEL,416;ELIZA,379
. JAMES MADISON,185
. MARGARET,263;MARK,185
. MARY,185;OBADIAH,185
. PATRICK,416;REASON H
. 416;SAMUEL,185
SULVANT,MARY,214
SUMELIN,THOS,3
SUMER,SALLIE,202
SUMERAL,DAVID,19
SUMERLIN,JAMES,86
SUMMERLAND,PEGGY,256
SUMMERLIN,HENRY,64,73
. 75-76,96,130,346
. JAMES J,143;JOHN,60
. JOS,80;JOSEPH,75-76
. 81,84,92,116;LAZARUS
. 72;MICHAEL,64,73
SUMMERLINE,MICHAEL,65
SUMMERS,GEO W,416
SUMNER,ALEXANDER C,200
. 214;ALICE,202;BIRD L
. 200,214;CLARISSA,50
. DANIEL T,200;DAVID
. 200;DORA M,210
. ELIZABETH,51,197
. ELIZABETH J,203
. HOLLAND,416;HOLLIN,56
. JETHRO,200;JOHN,214
. JOHN C,200;MARY,205
. NANCY E,209;PAMELIA
. ADELINE,391;RICHARD
. 214;ROBERT,45,200
. RUTH,200;RUTHA,207
. SARAH,395;SUMNER,10
. 34;WILLIAM,200
SUMURL,WILLIAM,416
SUNTER,STEPHEN,223
SURFT,A B,246
SURNDEN,ANNE,279
SUTCLIFFE,SYLVESTER,416
SUTHERLAND,JOHN,416
SUTON,JORDEN,212
SUTTER,C M,116
SUTTLE,G W,86,104
. GEORGE,86;GEORGE W,82
. 85,90
SUTTLES,G W,100
SUTTON,ABNER,212;ANNA
. 211;ARMINDA J,200;ASA
. 304,306,321;D J,211
. ELIZABETH,204
. ELLENDER,201;JAMES
. 311;JAMES E,200;JANE
. L,206;JOHN,169;JORDAN
. 200;LANEY,209;LAURA
. 202;MARTHA ANN,198
. MARY ANN,195;RUBY ANN
. 195;SARAH,195;TEMPA
. ANN,201;WILLIAM,297
. 304,311;WM,321
SWA---,JOHN W,269
SWAGZENS,MARY,343
SWAIN,DARLING,214
. ELDRED,200;JOHN,279
. JOHN L,69;JULIANN
. ABIGAL,198;MARGARET
. 199;MARY ANN,209
. PERMEALEY,198;RICHARD
. 69;STEPHEN,3;WILLIAM

. 200;WILLIAM C,69
SWAN,ELIZA ANN,243;MARY
. R,241;SALLY,275
SWANN,CYNTHIA,285
. GEORGE,279;JOHN,279
. JOHN W,279;JOSEPH,279
. POLLY,284;SALLIE F
. 277
SWANSON,148;F M,339
. GRAVES,279;JOHN,370
. NANCY,277,370;T R,248
SWEARINGEN,VAN,319
SWEENEY,RACHEL,235,281
. THOMAS,416
SWEET,NANCY T,275
SWEETA,PATSEY,421
SWEPSON,JOHN,220
SWIFT,JOHN D,64;WM A,64
SWINDALL,DANIEL,279
. ELIZA,243;MARY JANE
. 257;NANCY JANE,262
. SARAH,282
SWINDALLE,EMILY,283
SWINDELL,CAROLINE M,278
. MARTHA M,282;THOMAS
. 279
SWINDEN,
. MATTHEW HENRY,416
SWINDLE,THOMAS,279
SWINEY,MARY ANN,408
SWINNEY,CELEST C,262
. DUDLEY,302;HENRY,279
. JNO,291,329;JOHN,302
. JOTHRAM,279;LAVINIA A
. 278;MARCUS,279;MARTHA
. 260;RANSOM,302;ROSEY
. 302;WILSON,302;WM,279
SWINT,EDMOND,305
. ELIZABETH,305
. FREDERICK,305;JAMES
. 305;JOHN,305;JOSEPH
. 305;SAML,305;WILLIAM
. 305
SYDNEY,BOULWARD,402
SYHES,THOS,6
SYKES,ARTHER,10;ARTHUR
. 34;JOHN,7,34;RUTH,419
. SARAH,34;THOMAS,34
. WILLIAM,45;WM,416
SYLL,THOMAS,45
SYMES,ROBERT,45
SYMMS,414;LAW M,41
SYMS,ANNIE,39;ELIZABETH
. A,44;MARY,395
TABB,DAVID,26,34;DAVIS
. 27,50;EDWARD,10,34,51
. 56;EMILY F,36;JOHN,51
. 56;JULIA,36;LUCKY A W
. 45;PATENICE P,42
. ROBERT,45;THOMAS,7,51
. VIGINIA,42;WILLIAM,56
TABER,JOHN,416
TAILER,E D,56
TAIT,276;LUCY,248
TALBOT,EMILY,253;JAMES
. 279;JESSE,294;SARAH
. ANN,401
TALCOTT,GEO H,416
TALFREE,ROBT,271
TALIAFERRO,
. CHRISTOPHER,416;SARAH
. L,389
TALL---,J W,258
TALLEY,E,240,243,261
. 271,286;ELIZ,243,388
. ELIZABETH,282;EUGENIA
. I,221;J W,262;JNO,416
. JOHN W,280;MARY,249

. UGENIA J,286;WILLIAM
. D,221;WM L,279
TALLY,E,239,275,287
. ELIZ,242,401
. ELIZABETH,278,380
. ELIZABETH W,264
. ELKANAH,279;LARKIN
. 151;NANCY,244;NATHAN
. 279;SARAH,403;THOMAS
. 279;WM,250,262
TALMADGE,JOHN,339;JOHN
. H,339;SAML K,242
. SAMUEL K,246;STEPHEN
. C,333,339
TALOR,JAMES W,50
TANKERLEY,179
TANKERSLEY,ELEY,408
. JOHN,297;JOS,358
. ROBERT,329;WM,329;WM
. B,179
TANNER,FLOYD,279;GIDEON
. 70,90;JESSE,279
. JUDITH,279;SARAH,274
. WILLIAM,170;WILLIAM H
. 89,95;WM H,90
TANT,ELIZ,400;ELIZ M A
. 381;ISAAC L,416;ISAAC
. S,416;JOHN,56;ODRY
. 419;ROSANNAH,408;WM R
. 416
TAP---?,327
TAPLEY,ELIZABETH,201
. JAMES M,200,214;JOHN
. C,200;LOU,208;MALINDA
. 212;NEEDY,207;SARAH
. 214;T,200;WILLIAM L
. 200
TAPPAN,A B,279
. ALEXANDER,280
. RANDOLPH,280;SAMUEL W
. 280
TARBY,POLLY,250
TARDY,MARY A C,406
. SOPHIE ADELLE,381
TARPLEY,ARCHIBALD,280
. AUGUSTUS,280;DAVID T
. 132;ELIZA ANN,270
. ELIZABETH,122;JAMES J
. 122,132;JAMES T,122
. JNO,96;JOANNA E,148
. JOANNAH,143;JOANNAH E
. 132,139;JOHN,62-63,70
. 76-78,122,131-132,139
. 143,148,280;JOHN L
. 280;JOSEPH,375;MARTHA
. 240;MARY,122,132
. MARY E F,277;MATTHEW
. 132,139,143,148
TARRENCE,JAMES,7;SARAH
. A,408
TARRENTINE,JAMES,311
TARVER,ALLEN,50
. CAROLINE,385
. CHARLOTTE,416
. ETHELDRED J,416;JOHN
. R,416;MARIA,390;MARK
. 56;MASON,416;ROBERT
. 416;SAMUEL,416;SAMUEL
. B,34;SARAH,401
TARWATER,JAMES S,280
. JAS L,237
TATE,HORATIO G,416
TATMAN,JOHN,7
TATOM,EPPS,361;PLEASANT
. 363;THOMAS,115
TATTUM,JOEL,280
TATUM,HENNERIAR,222
. HOWELL,222;SARAH,249

TATUM(cont)
. SETH,297
TAVER,WILLIAM,56
TAY---?,327
TAYLER,THOMAS,289
TAYLOR,108,120-121,264
. 320-321,326;ABRAHAM
. 280,416;ABRAM,45
. AGNES ANN,407;ALSEY
. 416;ANGELINE T,255
. ARCHIBALD,296
. ARCHIBALD E,280;B P
. 242,269;BRANTLY,280
. CALEB,34;CATHARINE,49
. CATHERINE,34;CELEB,9
. CHAS,3;D,118;DAVID,34
. 416;DORY,83,147;EDMD
. W,359;ELIZA MARSHALL
. 406;ELIZABETH,48,254
. 261;EMILENE T,411
. FRANCIS C,416;FRANCIS
. L,416;FRANCIS N,339
. GEO,416;GEORGE D,57
. 78;HENRY,280;J M D,74
. JAMES,5,280,290,309
. 319,416;JAMES H,249
. JAMES I,416;JAS H,242
. JEFFERSON W,416
. JEREMIAH,56;JOB,85,88
. 310-311;JOHN,9-10,73
. 280,416;JOHN JAMES,97
. JOHN M D,62,70;JOHN T
. 416;JORDAN,3;JOSEPH
. 416;JOSEPH F,416
. LAURA JANE,402
. LEONARD,333,339
. MARGARET,51,245
. MARTHA,261;MARY,49,62
. 386,418;MARY JANE,402
. MARY SUSAN,235;MARY W
. 254;N W,100;NOAH,62
. NOAH W,78,84,90,93
. ROUNDTREE,296;RUDOLPH
. 280;SALLY,260;SAMUEL
. 8;SAMUEL S,280;SARAH
. G,242;SARAH M,381
. SEABORN H,280;SEMION
. 280;SHADK,307
. SHADRACK,293;SIR
. WILLIAM,56;SIR WM,48
. T C,112-113;THOMAS
. 164,280,310;THOMAS C
. 90,101,104,108,112
. 121;THOS C,107;TILMON
. 115;WALTER,417
. WILLIAM,8,34,56
. WILLIAM H,339;WM,417
. WM P,48
TAYOR,JORDAN,9
TAYTOR,NANCEY,166
TEADLY,WILLIS P,82
TEAK,ABRAHAM,249
TEAL,JANE,415
TEATER,ABRAHAM,238
TEATES,ABRAHAM,248
TEDDARS,C M,339
TEDDER,JAMES,34
TEDDERS,SAMUEL,339
TEDWELL,MOIL M,106
TELEGRAPH,MACON,124
TELFAIR,ALEX,35
. ALEXANDER,186;ALEXN
. 34;EDWARD,1,169,186
. JOHN G,186;JOSIAH G
. 186;LEWIS O,56
. MARGARET,186;MARY,186
. SARAH,186;THOMAS,186
TEMPLE,JONES,346-347

TEMPLER,STUART,280
TEMPLETON,ALEXANDER,417
. JAMES A,417;JOHN,169
. JOHN C,45;MATTHEW,50
. NANCY,393
TENANT,ANDREW,88,139
. 142;GEORGE,148
TENISON,JOHN L,45
TENNANT,ANDREW,82,91
TENNELL,ELIZA ANN,198
TENNELLE,FRANCIS,233
TENNERSON,MARTHA M,38
TENNIC,PETER,417
TENNISON,JAMES,417;JAS
. ALEX,417;JOHN,6,56
TERREL,JAMES,84
TERRELL,B,349;DAVID,158
. 280;FRANCES,247
. FRANCES W,272;MARY-
. ANN,277;NANCY V,285
. THOMAS,339
TERRILL,JOEL W,67;PETER
. B,158
TERRY,BENJAMIN,417
. JAMES,417;JOHN,147;WM
. 280
TERZEACH,ESSY,267
TESSIER,LEWIS P,51
. MADISON M,45;RUSH E
. 45
TEURNFOG,C D,281
THARPE,JAMES B,5
THAXTON,BAILEY Y,121
. CHARLES,65;CHARLES G
. 96,98;CHARLES GIDEON
. 65;DANIEL,280;E,93
. G C,111;G W,105;J B
. 111;J T,100;JAMES,280
. JAMES N,280;JERMIAH
. 280;MARY,65;NATHANIEL
. 280;S W,96,101,111
. SAMUEL W,82,85;SIMON
. 280;WARD,130;WILEY,60
. 65;WILLIAM,105,136;WM
. 111,130;Y,94,111
. YELVENTON,96,98-99
. 105,120,146;YELVERTON
. 60,64-65,82-84,88
THAYER,HENRY B,417
THERMAN,NANCEY,263
THERSEY,HANEY,49;MARY
. 48
THETFORD,WILLIAM,324;WM
. 329
THIGPEN,LETHEA,247
. MARTHA,240;RHODA,205
. WILLIAM,214;WILLIAM G
. 200;WINNIE,249
THILOSON,THOS,345
THINCEY,ABSALOM,49
THISPEN,JANE,205
THOMAS & THOMPSON132
THOMAS,309;ABSALOM,50
. ABSOLOM,34;ANN S,392
. ANNA,262;AUGUSTIN,290
. C C,417;CAMM,417
. CHARLES,46;CHRISTIAN
. 262;CORNELIA,384
. DANIEL,3;DIANA,386;E
. 329,341;E C I B,282
. EDWARD,417;ELIZ,400
. ELIZABETH,99,264
. EMMILY,417;ETHELDRED
. 34;FLOYD,417;FRANCES
. L,404;FREDERICK S,76
. G,97;G E,312;G W,119
. 122,129,140;GEO W,122
. GEOERGE W,130;GEORGE

. 103,417;GEORGE W,85
. 96,118,124,128,148
. GEORGIA W,137;HANNAH
. 40;HENRY P,417;JAMES
. 165,312-313;JAMES H
. 280;JANE B,381;JESSE
. 340;JOANNA,262;JOHN,9
. 200,280;JOHN I,280
. JOHN R,45;JONATHAN
. 323;JOSEPH A,46
. JOSEPH B,417;JOSEPH D
. 34,51,56;LUCY,262
. MANEN,200;MARGARET
. 420;MARTIN,8;MARY
. JOSEPHINE,386
. NICHOLAS,307;PETER
. 348;REBECCA,198;RED,9
. 26;RICHARD,34,48,56
. RICHARD J,417;RICHD,9
. ROBERD,219;ROBERT,65
. ROBERT F,45;SARAH
. LAWSON,301;SETH,280
. THEOPHILUS,297,302
. THOMAS,59;THOMAS W
. 312;THOS,86;WESTERN B
. 417;WILLIAM,226,297
. 317,333,339;WILLIAM
. JAMES,165;WM,280,417
. WM A,313;WM M,417
THOMASON,ALEXANDER,339
. HANNAH,339;HENRY,333
. JACKSON C,339;JACOB M
. 339;JAMES,339
. JEREMIAH,339;ROBERT M
. 339;SALLIE,339;THOMAS
. 333,339
THOMEN,MARTHA,39
THOMPSON,89,217-218,222
. 325;A F,82,85,88-89
. 92-93,100,105,112-113
. 115,122,127,134,140
. AARON,9,34,50
. ALEXANDER,417;ALLEN
. 200;ALMIRA E,112
. ALMIRIA E,138
. ANDERSON F,82,103-104
. ANN,3,345;ANNA D,405
. ANNE,247,310;ARTEMUS
. 34;ASA,214;B,320;B H
. 262;BARTLETT,417
. BEATRIX,325;BENJ,319
. 320,361;BENJA,216,308
. BENJAMIN,35,56,306
. 309,320,361;CATHARINE
. 406;CHARITY,35,50
. CHARLES,221,312;D,111
. DANIEL,35,49,56;DANL
. 6;EADY,35;ELIHU,49,56
. ELIZ,397,402,407
. ELIZABETH,207,280
. ELLEN M,386;ELMIREY E
. 128;ELMIRY E,104;EMMA
. 37;EMMA J,407;ESTHER
. A,391;G H,237,246;GEO
. S,62;GEOERGE L,128
. GEORGE,92,280,289
. GEORGE L,72,76,92,104
. 105,118,122,125-126
. 141,149;GEORGE S,65
. GIDEON,306;GOERGE L
. 86;GREENE,273;HANNAH
. 85;HENRY B,280;HIRAM
. 280;ISHAM,300,306;J H
. 100;JACOB,9;JAMES,52
. 62,84,86,154,219,280
. 292;JAMES C,104;JANE
. 35;JAS,3;JEREMIAH,280
. 325;JESSE,306,310

THOMPSON(cont)
. JOHN,10,35,46,89,169
. 219,231,280,292,329
. 344;JOHN H,122,128
. JOHN N,104,200;JOSEPH
. 280;JOSEPH M,280
. JULIA,238;KATHERINE
. 197;LAVINA,85;LOUISA
. 46;LUCINDA,164;LUCY
. 285;LUCY ANN,245
. MARGARET R,202;MARTHA
. 35;MARY,46;MARY ANN
. 198;MARY ELIZABETH
. 282;MARY J,195
. MATTHEW,280;MICHAEL
. 105,119;MILLEY,241
. MOODY,280;MOSES,6,280
. NANCY,292;NANCY E,207
. NANCY HESTER ANN,195
. NATHAN,46;NATHANIEL
. 352;NICHODEMUS,50
. PANTHEA T,238
. PRISCILLA,286;R E J
. 46;REUBEN,214;REUBEN
. J,200;RICHARD M,280
. ROBERT,214,233;S,257
. SAMUEL,219,280;SARAH
. 196,216,382,387
. SARAH A D,249;SEBORN
. 56;SOLOMON,35,56;T,56
. TABITHA,51;THOMAS,280
. THOMAS B,280;THOMAS H
. 280;THOMAS P,164;THOS
. B,280;V T,142;VINCENT
. T,141;WILLIAM,6,8,35
. 50,170,216,227;WILLIS
. 272;WM,152,280;WM A
. 280;WM F,280;WM T,417
. ZACHARIAH,95,108
THOMSON,JAMES,3,342,344
THOR---TON,MARTHA C,279
THORN,ELLEN,37;HENRETTA
. 37;HICKSEY,385
. HIGHTOWER,159;JOSHUA
. 159;MIDDLETON,56
. PRESTLY,159;WILLIAM
. 49
THORNBERRY,MARY ANN,416
THORNBURY,WM,280
THORNTON,A,256
. ALEXANDER,328;E R,244
. ELSEY B,83;GREEN,108
. HENRY,417;HENRY C,280
. JAMES A,269,286;JESSE
. 280;JESSE M,280;JOE F
. 280;JOEL F,263
. LOURENA,257;MYRTUS
. 274;OTIS S,280;REDICK
. 19;REDMON,230;REUBEN
. 279;RICHARD,232,280
. ROBERT,131,321;SAML
. 222;SAMUEL,215-217
. 281;SAMUL,229;SARAH
. 262;SOLOMON,288,304
. 328;V R,238-239,241
. 244,247,249-250,254
. 261-262,273-274,277
. 280-283,285;VINCENT
. 236,238,281;VINCENT R
. 237,244,249,267,270
. 272;WILLIAM,288,308
. 327;WM R,281;ZYMONIA
. 281
THRASHER,233;ALEXANDER
. B,281;EARLY W,281;J F
. 277;JOHN F,281;JOSEPH
. 221;JOSEPH C,222
. RICHARD,222-223;WM H

. 238
THREATT,P,145
THREDWELL,GREEN,82
THRONTON,V R,273
THROWER,JEREMIAH,291
. JERMEIAH,303;MARGARET
. 304;MARGARETT,304
. THOMAS,311
THURMAN,136;ELIZABETH
. 100;J B,122;J M,141
. J R,122;JAMES,60,82
. 100,122;JOHN B,82;M
. 97;NANCY,256;P,113
. PHILLIP,97,339,345
. PHILLIPS,357
THURMON,ANNY,249;NANCY
. 256
THURMOND,FOUNTAIN M,339
. MARY,273;PHILLIP,364
. POPE,266
THUSTON,ELIZABETH,394
THWEAT,JAMES,321
THWEATT,296;G----,328
. JAMES,291;JAS,291,293
. 302,309;JOHN,311,319
TICE,MARY,390;PATIENCE
. ANN,380
TICED,DAVID,309
TIDWELL,SEAGORN M,118
. T B,95
TIGNER,HOPE H,281
. PHILIP,281;PHILLIP
. 217
TIGNETT,PHILISSIM,381
TILLER,MARTIN,281
TILLERY,ELIZABETH,69
. GEORGE,342;JOHN,136
TILLEY,GEORGE,8;ISAAC
. 49;JAMES R,417;JOHN
. 51,56,417;JOSEPH,51
. LEVI,56;WILLIAM,50,56
TILLINGHAST,STUTELY,35
TILLMAN,GEO,3;JOHN,339
. PHOEBE,339;ROBT,3
TILLMON,WILLIAM,229
TILLY,BETSY,35;GEORGE
. 35;ISAAC,9,35;JAMES,8
. 10;JOSEPH,35;WILLIAM
. 8,35
TILMAN,JESSE,9;LEWIS,10
TIMMERMAN,JOHN,417;MARY
. ELIZA,379
TIMMONS,CHALRES,115
TIMS,ELIZABETH H,194
TINDAL,BOOKER,176;JAMES
. 6;PLEASANT,178;POLLY
. 178;SALLEY,178;THOMAS
. LEWIS,178;W,281
. WILLIAM,178
TINDALA,BARBARA,420
TINDALE,JAMES,49,57,417
. LOURANIA,57;WILEY,49
. WILLIAM,57
TINDALL,BIRD B,303
. JAMES JR,35;PLEASANT
. 417;SARAH M,175
TINDELL,ANNA T,193
. BETSEY,193;HENRY W
. 193;JOHN B,193
. JONATHAN,176,193
. PLEASANT,176,193
. ROBERT H,193;SALLY C
. 193;WILLIAM,176
TINDIL,JOHN,344
TINDILL,JNO,360
. JONATHAN,339;W,175
TINDLEY,DAVID,417;ELIZ
. 420;JOHN,417;POLLY

. 402;PTSY,383
TINGLE,DANIEL,71-72,115
. DAVID,60;PURIFOY,88
TINLAY,JOHN,417
TINLEY,DAVID,417;ELIZA
. 396;JAMES,417;LOUISA
. 400;MARY ANN,381
. NANCY,413;PHILIP,417
. REBECCA,389;THOMAS
. 417;VINCENT,417;WM
. 417
TINLY,ELIZ,380
TINNEY,BENJ,417
TINNINSON,JOHN,35
TINSLEY,ABRAM,176;ANN
. 176;ELIAS C,417;ELIZ
. 380;JAMES,176;JAMES Z
. 417;JOHN,176;JOHN L
. 417;LUCEY,176;MARY
. ANN,419;MASON A,192
. NANCEY,176;PHILIP,176
. 192;PHILLIP,163;POLLY
. 176;SALLY,176;SAMUEL
. 329;WILLIAM,176
TINSON,WILLIAM,56
TIPPET,MARY,241
TIPPETT,FREDERICK,281
. JOHN,281;LUCY,279
. NANCY,261;SARAH,257
. WM,281
TIPPIN,NOAH,281
TIPTON,AMY,35;JACOB,9
. JONATHAN,26-27,35
. JOSEPH,49;REUBEN,26-27
. 35
TISDEL,JAMES,56;SAMPSON
. 56;WILLIAM H,56
TISON,DANIEL,200;JOB
. 296,327;JOHN,200
. JULIANN,196;KATHARINE
. 214;LYDIA,201,212
. MARY,194,200;NOAH,200
. SELAH,201
TITUS,JOSIAH,417
TOBIN,DANIEL,417;THOMAS
. 417
TOBLER,CHRISTIANA,400
. POLLY,4
TODD,ANNA,237;APHIAH F
. B,250;APPHIA,5;DAVID
. 417;HENRY,1,5;JAMES,8
. JOHN,161;JOHN H,281
. JOSHUA,417;THOMAS B
. 322;VIRGINIA C,261
TOEDWELL,F S,35
TOHLER,CHARLOTTE,384
TOLAND,MICHAEL M,333
. 339;SALLY,339;SAMUEL
. 339
TOLBERT,TOLITHA E,245
TOLEFER,306
TOLER,DANIEL,35
TOLLESON,JESSE,91,122
. 133
TOLLY,BETSY,262;SARAH
. 284
TOLVER,NANCY,242
TOMAS,59
TOMBS,WM,228
TOMLILN,L L F,50
TOMLIN,ATOM,3;HARRIS,7
. 35;JACOB,355;JAS,305
. JOHN,7,35,46,51,56
. 417;MARY,50,56;Y L,56
. ZACHARIAH,8
TOMLINSON,J B,117;JAMES
. 95;JAMES B,97,100,107
. JOHN D,339;L,97;S H

TOMLINSON(cont)
. 81;W,142;WILLIAM,100
. 126
TOMLON,DIANAH,40
TOMPKINS,BURWELL,358
. GILES,348;JAMES M,57
. LUCY ANN,333,339
TOOK,LOU,272
TOOL,HATTIE A,247
  KATHARINE,208
TOOLE,JAS,185
TOOLS,KATHARINE,198
TOOTLE,ROBERT,35
TOPSECK,JESSE,200
TORANCE,ALLEN,213
TORBERT,BENJ F,281;JOHN
  I,281;SAMUEL A,281
TORBET,FRANCIS,95;HUGH
  S,94-95
TORELL,JAMES,86
TORIER,WILLIAM J,68
TORLOW,HARRIETT,258
TORRANCE,JAMES,49;MARY
  A,403
TORRENCE,E,262,264
. EBENEZER,256,281
. JAMES,35;JOHN,281
. MARTHA,56
TORRY,A,321
TOSEY,35
TOUCHSTONE,CALEB,347
  SOLOMON,99;WM,281
TOWERS,MARIA,285
TOWNS,BENJ,281;DRURY
. 281;JOHN G,333,339
. JOHN T C,339;JOHN W
. 281;RICHARD,417;WM
. 361
TOWNSEN,APPY,198;JANE
. 201;MARY,356;WILLIAM
. 356
TOWNSEND,224;AGNES,393
. DENNIS L,135;DUNCAN C
. 281;ELI,292;ELIZ,392
. HANNAH,279;HENRY,299
. ISAAC N,200;SAMUEL
. 361;SILAS,200;THOMAS
. 139;THOMAS J,135
TOWNSING,ANDERSON C,280
TOWNSON,WM,281
TOWTRIP,BATHSHEBA,400
TRACY,EDWARD D,417
TRADEWELL,A,417
TRAMMEL,N R,134
TRANTHAM,ELIZ,410
TRAP,ELIZ,389
TRAPLEY,JAMES J,114
  JOHN,71,114
TRAPNAL,ALGEARNE,200
  CLITHA ORNEA,198
TRAPNALL,SELINA V,201
TRAPNELL,ELIJAH,47,56
. 213;MARY ANN,212
. PERRY,211
TRAVELS,PARKS,328
TRAVER,JARIA J,402
. LAURA,45;MARK,50
. MURIAH,406;ROBERT,50
. SAMUEL,8;WILLIAM,50
TRAVIS,DAVID D,48
  MARTHA,279
TRAWICK,FRANCIS,326
  GEORGE,326
TRAYLOR,ARCHBD,294
. CHAMPION T,333,339
. JOHN,115;THOMAS,333
. 365;WILLIAM H,339
TREADWAY,ELIJAH,281

INDIANA,278
TREADWELL,J L,51;JOHN,9
  MARY,415
TREDWELL,G,116
TREE,LOVETT RASON,46
TREEL,ANN,161;ELIZABETH
. 161-162;JOHN,161-162
. KEZIAH,161;LEWIS,161
TREMBLE,ROBERT,7
  WILLIAM,7
TREMBLEY,WM A,417
TRENTHAM,SARAH,418
TREWETT,ELIJAH,330
TREWITT,DAVID,211
. EDWARD J,211;LAURENCE
. 211
TRIBBLE,
. ELIZA CATHERINE,262
. JOHN,281
TRIBLE,E,87;EZEKIEL,87
TRICE,E,312
TRIGGS,JOHN I,56
TRIMBLE,JANE,243;JOHN
. 21-22,35;JOHN M,364
. MOSES,364
TRIP,JAMES M,281
TRIPLET,219;DANIEL,417
  JENNY,401
TRIPLETT,MARY,387
  RACHEL,385
TRIPP,HENRY,321,341
  JOHN,341;JOHN M,417
TRIPPE,EMILY J L,271
. HENRY,288,304,321,341
. JOHN,317;WILLIAM,339
. WM,291
TROITTI,FRANCIS,417
  LAURANCE,417
TROTER,ROBERT W,119
TROTTER,JOHN W,111
TROUCHLETT,LOUISA,416
TROWBRIDGE,JOHN,417
  NELSON,417;SAMUEL,417
TROWEL,JAMES,35
TRUCHELET,JOS A,417
TRUETT,EDWARD J,200
  EMILY,40;SUSAN,199
TRUIT,JOHN,281;RILEY
  339,346
TRUITT,JOHN,339
TRULL,CAROLINE,203
TRUSSELL,CHARLES H,339
TUBBLE,ELIZA,255
TUBMAN,RICHARD,417
TUCKER,128,134,138
. ALLEN,339;B F,64,72
. 113,119,121;BENJ F,71
. BENJAMIN,59;BENJAMIN
. F,59,68;ELIZABETH,249
. FRANCES,253;H H,237
. 238,248,261,263,268
. JEREMIAH,281;JOHN,281
. JOSEPH,418;JULIA,397
. LEW,294,306;LUCREICY
. 197;MARY,245;NANCY
. 282,287;ROBERT,291
. S J,46;SARAH,339
. THOMAS,59;WILLIAM J
. 211;WILLIAM S,56
TUDER,JNO,418
TUFTS,FRANCIS,418
TUGGLE,232;ADALINE,235
. ANN A,274;ANN
. ELIZABETH,256;ANNE E
. 282;AUGUSTUS SEE,281
. AUGUSTUS W,281
. CATHERINE,246;E B,281
. ELIZABETH,333,339

. EUNICE,232;G H,281
. GEO,272,279,281,284
. 343;GEORGE W,124-125
. HOLLARD,281;JULIA A
. 244;JUNIE A,339
. LEONARD,281
. LITTLEBERRY,281
. LODOWICK,232;MARY,244
. 259;MARY ANNE,255
. MARY J,237;ROBERT,339
. ROBT,232;SALLY,232
. THOMAS,232;WILLIAM J
. L,333,339;WILLIAM R
. 339;WILLIE,339;WM,239
. 244,249
TUGGLES,MARY,260
TULANE,REBECCA,415
TULLIS,FULLER,346;JOHN
  346-347;TEMPLE,346-347
TULLOSS,RODHAM,418
TULLY,MARTHA,391
TUMBLEFIELD,
  MARTHA ANN,398
TUNIS,ROBERT,294
TUNISON,SARAH G,246
TUNNEL,JESSE W,281
TUNNELL,DORA,286;JULIA
. C,259;LAURA,251;MARY
. A,258;NANCY M,280
. SIDNEY W,283
TUNNISON,MARY R,256;WM
  C,281
TUNNS,ANN,413
TURK,JOHN,288,319,333
. 339;JONATHAN,339;THEO
. 317;THEODO,321
. THEODOSIUS,288,296
. WILLIAM C,339
TURKNET,HENRY,418
TURLEY,ALLEN,418
TURMAN,ANN M,396;GEORGE
  352;JOEL C,418
TURNE,320
TURNELL,FRANCES D,240
. MARTHA J,245;SARAH E
. E,247
TURNER,12,302;?,347;A
. 281;A L,211;ABEDNIGO
. 76;ABSALOM,49;ABSOLAM
. 8;ABSOLEM,211;ABSOLOM
. 35;ARMENDA J,203
. BOSWELL,281;BUTLER
. 287-288;CHARLES,6
. CHARLES W,418;DAVID
. 281;EDWARD,293;EDWD
. 287;ELI,281;ELIZA,251
. ELIZABETH I,268;FANNY
. 271;FRANCES,36;G B H
. 100;GABREL,211;HENRY
. 6,10,35,48,326-327
. HENRY C,281;JAMES,233
. 281,293;JAMES W,281
. JANE,209;JANE K,264
. JARRELL L,281;JAS,288
. JOHN,35,47-48,56,258
. 263,268,281,287,320
. 345,347;JOHN G,339
. JOHN L,200;JOHN M,418
. JOSEPH,318,321;JOSHUA
. 292;LARKIN,310;LOUISA
. 283;LOUISA J OR----
. 281;LUCINDA,209
. LUCINDY,46;MARTHA,202
. MARTHA H,270;MARY,207
. MARY E,239;MESHACH,76
. MOSES,46;MOURNING,57
. PEGGY,385;PHILIP,319
. REBECCA,235;REUBEN,35

TURNER(cont)
. 48;REUBEN T,281;S S
. 281;S W,333;SALLIE L
. 40;SAM,46;SARA ANNE
. 247;SHADRACH,418
. SUSAN,395;THOMAS,281
. 349;THOMAS M,312,339
. TOLIVER A,339;WILLIAM
. 213,305;WILLIAM E,46
. WILLIAM H,211;WM,418
. WM P,418
TURNEY,P F,339
TURNING,LUCIUS,35
TURPIN,GEO T,418;J F
418
TUTLE,ROBERT,51
TUTT,FRANCES A,403
. GEORGE C,281;LUCY,174
. MARY,210;PRISCILLA
. 413;WM H,418
TUTTLE,ISAAC S,418;JOHN
M,418
TWER,N,56
TWIGGS,ABRAM,46;DAVID E
. 418;EMELINE B,387;G W
. L,78;GEORGE,418
. INDIANA C,411;SALLY
. 395;SARAH LOUISA,392
TWILLEY,WILLIAM,322
TWILLY,ELIJAH,90,100
TWITTY,JOHN,219
TYE,SAMUEL,211
TYLAR,J,87
TYLER,219;ALEXANDER,281
. ARCHY,257;BARSHEBA
. 262;BETTY,158;FRANCIS
. M,339;JOB,102,339
. JOHN,158,339;MARCUS H
. 339;MARY,243;NANCY
. 388;PEGGY,164;ROBERT
. 281;SAMUEL B,339
. THOMAS,164;WILLIS,281
TYLOR,JOB,121
TYNER,R JOHN,339
TYRE,JAMES,21;JOHN,23
LEWIS,21,23
TYREY,WILLIAM,176
TYRIE,MARY ANN,395
TYSON,ELIZABETH V,210
. HENRY F,339;JANE,108
. MARTHA,200;MARY A,48
UMPHREY,ERASTUS,281
UMPHREYS,DANL,14
WILLIAM,8
UMPHRIES,DANL,16
WILLIAM,35
UNDERHILL,PAMELIA,391
UNDERWOOD,ANN,391;BENJ
. F,281;DANIEL,281;ELIZ
. 421;GEORGE C,281
.. JESSE H,281;LEWIS,309
. LOUISA,260;MARGARET A
. 269;MARY,258;MATILDA
. 282;MILES P,281;SARAH
. 3;SARAH C,269;SARAH M
. 262;THOMAS,63;WILLIAM
. 175
UPTON,BENJAMIN,186
. GEORGE,170;WILLIAM
. 186
URGUART,FRANCIS J,394
URQUHART,ALEX,56
. ALEXANDER,59,339
. CATHERINE,379;JANE E
. 419;MARY E,250;MARY V
. 339;NEILL,353;SARAH A
. M,394;WILLIAM,35;WM
. 418

URSERY,ELIZABETH,49
JOHN,309
USHER,HENRY,418;NANCY
417
USSERY,PETER,105,119
UTLEY,ARAMINTA C,41
. ELISHA H,35;HENRY,35
. 50;HENRY L,46;WILLIAM
. 56
VALENTINE,THOMAS,106
VALL,LEVINA,396
VALLOTON,WINNIE,39
VALLOTTON,ELIZ,401;HUGH
418;S M,417
VAN COARSEY,MARY,201
VAN RIPER,HARMAN,418
VAN TRIEAU,
CONSTANTINE,282
VAN VALKINBURG,
ALONZA WANDISON,282
VAN,ELIZ,388;LUCY,369
VANBIBBER,HENRY,65-66
85
VANCE,WM,418
VANCEY,JAMES,87
VANDEFORD,RICHARD,230
VANDIVERE,A IN N,286
VANHOOKIS,E,12;J W,12
VANN,JOSIAH,35;WILLIAM
86
VANZANT,ABEL,418;LOUISA
392;RACHAEL,389
VARDELL,JOHN,418
VARDEMAN,WILLIAM,339
VARINGTON,BENJAMIN,325
VARNER,JOSEPH W,282
WILLIAM,339
VARNES,ELECTA A,38
VASON,JOHN,282;WILLIAM
224;WM,224
VASSER,
HITURAH FINNELL,177
VASY,VERLENDA,177
VAUGHAN,AMONELA,420
. DANIEL,156;HUNDLEY
. 344;ISAAC,182;JOHN,48
. W W,131;WILLIAM,82
. 304
VAUGHN,ARMANELLA,394
. BENJAMIN T,339
. CAROLINE A,383
. FRANCIS,417;ISAAC,282
. JAMES,35,418;JAMES M
. 339;JOSHUA,160;MARTHA
. 398;MCDANIEL,46
. MCDONALD,46;PARTHENIA
. 272;SARAH,381;STEPHEN
. H,333,339;THOMAS J
. 339;WILEY,418;WILLIAM
. 35,339;WILLIE,44
. WYATT,282
VAUGHTN,
PERMILIA ELIZ,382
VAUGN,JEREMIAH,46;MARY
330
VEACH,MARY,384
VEAGEY,A,249
VEAL,JAMES H,282;NATHAN
326
VEASEY,EZEKIEL,298
JESSE,319;WM,291
VEAZEY,A,278,284;ALBERT
. A,282;ALLANSON E,282
. CORNELIA J,273
. EMELINE,282;FRANCINE
. 281;JNO,327;JOHN L
. 250,269,282,284;JULIA
. 251;MARGARY,268;MARY

. 245,281;NANCY A,250
. PERMELIA,282;REBEKAH
. 272;RUTH,282;SARAH A
. 260;SARAH ANN,235;W C
. 240;WM C,261;WM I,282
VEAZY,ELI A,282
. ELIZABETH,281;EZEKIEL
. 282;JAMES,282;JOHN
. 282;TIMOTHY,282;WM C
. 282;WM D,282
VEITCH,WALTER,418
VELVIN,ELIZA,267;NANCY
267;THOMAS,282
VENABLE,ROBERT A,282
VERDELL,JEREMIAH,418
VERDERY,AUGUSTUS. N,418
. B F,51;BANJ E,418
. EMILY A,381;EUGENE
. 418;M P,49;WM M,418
VEST,GEORGE,294;JOHN
319;MARY,294
VEZGEY,A,249
VICKARS,WILLIAM,90
VICKERS,ABRAHAM,3;ANNA
. 91,102,114;ARTHUR,12
. ELIJAH,339;ELIZABETH
. 130;FREDERICK,12,35
. HOWARD,130;HOWRD,144
. JACOB,144;JEFFERSON
. 115;JOSHUA,3;NATHAN
. 10,13,35;PENELOPE,35
. PRUDY,144;WILLIAM,85
. 91,100,102,109,114
. 121,123,130,137,144
VICKERY,WILLIAM,21,25
VICKORY,HESEKIAH,46
VICTORY,ELIZABETH,238
ELLEN N,255
VIDETTA,PAYTON L,46
VIDITTO,HENRY A,46
VIGAL,GEORGE,418;MARY
401
VINCE,ANN BARBARA,4
VINCENT,CHARLES A,282
. HENRY,106,119;MARY
. 106,113,119;NATHANIEL
. 106,119;POWEL P,119
. RICHARD,35;SANFORD
. 282;THOMAS,119;WILL
. 106;WILLIAM,106;WM
. 282
VINE,MARTHA J,273
VINING,BEN,4
VINSON,DAVID,418;HENRY
96;TULLY,418
VIRGES,MARY,46
VISON,JOHN,330
VOGLER,ELIZ,394
VOLATIN,SAVANNAH,383
VOLLETIN,HUGH,7
VOLLINTINE,FRANCIS,56
VOLLOTTON,FRANCES A,416
. FRANCIS,50;FRANCIS S
. 35;RACHEL,35
VOUGHT,J L,282
VOULLARD,E A,312
VURGER,EMALINE,241
W A P?273
W----,JOHN,283;SALLY
254
W-----,ALFRED L,250
EZEKELL S,250
WAAGE,M G,17-18,25-26
WABER,HELENER,390
WADDAILL,JOSEPH,341
WADDELL,JANE,249
MARSHALL,282
WADDINGTON,ROBERT,218

WADDLE,ISAAC W,282
WADE,ANNE,285;BARSHEBA
. 286;BENJAMIN,333,339
. ELIZABETH L,339;H;339
. HEZEKIAH,3,10;HUDSON
. 373,378;JAMES,282,339
. JINCEY,239;JOHN,282
. JOSHUA,282;MAHALA
. FRANCES,285;MARY A E
. 339;REBECCA,286
. WILLIAM,56;Z,309
WADKINS,A A,141
   BENJAMIN,56
WADSWORTH,JAS,307
WAGERS,WILLIAM,418
WAGES,ELINDER,419
   HANNAH,419;WILLIAM,7
WAGGE,M G,20
WAGGMER,ANNA,250
WAGGONER,SARAH,273
   THOMAS,282;WM,282
WAGNER,AGNES,410
. ELIZABETH,257;JOHN A
. 97;MICHAEL,418
. SAMPSON,339
WAGNON,DANIEL,282,324
. EUGENIUS N,282;GEO H
. 282;J P,224;JOHN P
. 222,275,282;JOHN
. PETER,1,223-225
. JOSHUA H,282;JULIA A
. 265;PHERABY,268
. PITTMAN M,282;REBECCA
. 225;REBECCA A,268;THO
. 224;THOMAS,222-224
. 282;THOMAS P,222;THOS
. 341;WM S,282
WAGONER,GEORGE,217
   HIRAM,340
WAINWRIGHT,GEORGE,169
   JOSEPH,418
WAITERS,17
WAITS,ALEXANDER,340;AMY
. 340;BENJAMIN,333,340
. JOHN,340;LEROY,333
WAKEFIELD,CHARLES,86,95
   133,141;SAMUEL,147
WAKEHAM,JOHN,418
WAKINS,GEO,285
WALA,SEVERN,213
WALCH,ANN,269;NICHOLAS
   S,46
WALDEN,CHARLES,361
. LEWIS,234;RICHARD,234
. SAML,13;SMITH,282
. TOWNER,282;WILLIAM
. 234
WALDING,SAML,16
WALDREP,LEECEL,340
WALDRON,JOHN,19
WALDROP,DELPHIA A,340
. JOHNSON,340;SOLOMON
. 340
WALDRUP,SIMEON N G,88
WALEA,ELIZABETH,207
. THOMAS,211;WILLIAM W
. 211
WALEY,MARGARET,195
   WILLIAM,35
WALKER,89,232;A,35
. ABRAM,46;ADALINE,282
. ADAM,181;AGNES KELLO
. 413;AMBROSE,418;AMOS
. 50;ANDREW,282
. ANN ELIZA A,400
. ANNA E E R,411;ANNA T
. 411;BARTHL,297
. BATHIAH,35;BENJAMIN

. 361;CAPERS,46
. CORNILIA R T,381
. DARLING J,418;DAVID
. 311,321,323,418
. DIANAH D,275;E,86,107
. 114,117,122;EDWIN I
. 282;ELIJAH,35,418
. ELIZ,389,417;ELIZ T
. 414;ELIZ W,389;ELIZA
. JULIA,422;ELIZABETH,4
. 56,283,323;EZEKIEL,59
. 60,83-84,90,117;F,35
. FALBY,282;FRANCES ANN
. 244;FRANCES I,56
. FRANCIS A E,282
. FREEMAN,170,418
. FREEMAN W,418;GEO A B
. 418;GEO B,418;GEO M
. 418;GEORGE,319;H,352
. 354,359;HACK,227
. HACKEY,333,340
. HARRIET R,404
. HARRIETT,36;HARRY,355
. HENERY,355;HENRY,282
. 323,333,340,343-344
. 349,355,357;ISAAC,4-5
. JAMES,182,320,340,418
. JAMES B,418;JAMES G
. 89;JAMES T,282;JAMES
. W,200;JANE,258;JANE E
. 281;JEREMIAH,288,304
. JEREMIAH S,67;JERMIAH
. S,74;JOHN,8,46,88,93
. 282,323,373;JOHN A,56
. JOHN E,282;JOHN H,323
. JOHN I,418;JOSEPH P
. 418;JOSHUA S,418
. JULIA WINFREY,181
. LOU--- MARION,256
. MAGERS,340;MARGARET E
. J,396;MARION,256
. MARTHA R,386;MARY A E
. 244;MARY G,386;MARY M
. 236;MARY T,418;MATHEW
. T,418;MELVINA L M,410
. MENA M,282;MILLEY,384
. MOSES,8,35,56,340
. NANCY,240,396;NANCY T
. 270;NEEDHAM,418;R,72
. REBECCA I,245;REUBEN
. 4;ROBERT,282,418
. ROBERT T,50;ROBERT W
. 181;ROBT T,418;SAMUEL
. 92,128,137,419;SAMUEL
. R,282;SANDERS,222
. SARAH,420;SARAH A V
. 255;SARAH M,419;SARAH
. W,400;SEMARD,419
. SMITH,84;SOLOMON,419
. STEPHEN,46;SUSANNAH
. 260;SYLVANUS,368
. TABITHA,272;THOMAS J
. 109;THOMAS P,48;V,35
. VALENTINE,419;WANEN
. 46;WILLIAM,46,311,321
. 323;WILLIAM W,340;WEN
. 282,290,321,329;WM H
. 282;WM I,282;WM R,282
. WM W,419;Z I,282
. ZACHARIAH,419
WALL,220;BARGES,8
. CATHRINE,398;COONROD
. 151;DAVID H,84;ELIZ
. 413;ELIZABETH,257
. FRANK,282;ISAAC D,50
. J N,211;MARTHA,247
. 380;POLLY,238;RICHARD
. W,282;ROBERT,56;S B

. 419;THOMAS,35,419
. WILLIS,361;WM W,419
WALLACE,365;AARON B,282
. ADAM,49,56;AUGUSTUS
. 283;AUSTIN,358;B G
. 283;BALAAM,310
. BARTLEY,283;DICY,210
. DRUCILA,206;ELIZABETH
. 282;ELLEN J,42
. FRANCES,37;J J,246
. JAMES S,200;JESSE,47
. JNO,311;JOHN,6,35,49
. 56,215,304,330,360
. JOSEPH,343;JOSEPHINE
. 41;JOSIAH,35;LOW,13
. MARGARETTE,409;MARY
. 195;MARY ANN,43
. NEWTON S,46;PHERIBY
. 35;REBECCA,401;S B,56
. SEMION,46;SIMEON,56
. STIRING B,49;STIRLING
. 35;STIVING,8;STYING C
. 46;SUSAN,43;VERLINDA
. 115;W SIMEON,46
. WILIAM,49;WILLIAM,8
. 35,56,304,330,419
. WILLIAM B,46;WOOLFORD
. 283
WALLER,BEN,313;BENJ B
. 283;BENJAMIN,287,293
. 307;CHARLES,309-310
. CHARLES R,71-72,82,91
. DAVID S,130;ELISHA
. 288,304,319,321;GEO L
. 314;J,317;JAMES,62
. 283,307,322;JAMES B
. 90;JESSE,8;JOHN,62
. 287,290,293,309;JOHN
. K,91;JONATHAN,341
. JOSEPH,309-310;NAT
. 140;NATHANIEL,90,288
. 293;NATHANIEL G,90
. NATHL,341;NATT,319
. RACHEL,310;S,288
. SMITH,341;STEPHEN,288
. 304,307,310,321
. THOMAS,283;WILLIAM
. 289,310;WM,283
WALLESS,BENJAMIN,365
WALLIS,BENJAMIN,304
   NANCY,255
WALLS,ARCHIBALD,250
. HANNAH,273;HUMPHREY
. 183;JANE,46;JOHN,318
. JUBAL,283;LUCRETIA
. 380;REBAKAH,264
. THOMAS,10
WALLTHALL,TURMAN,131
WALRATT,CHARLES,419
WALSH,ANN,397;AUBREY
   381;JOHN G,419
WALSINGHAM,JNO G,358
WALTERS,CHARLES,419
   JOSEPH,200
WALTHALL,EDWARD,340
. RICHARD,419;T,123
. THURMAN,136,140,144
. TURMAN,132
WALTOM,RICHARD,9;THOS
   10
WALTON,AMEY,42;BLANCHE
. L,422;BLUFORD M,340
. DANIEL,35,48;DANL,14
. 16;DAVID,56;ELIZ,387
. ELIZA,215;EMORY S,46
. EVERET,7;EVERT,35
. FRANCES GEORGE,189
. GEO,419;GEORGE,1,174

WALTON(cont)
. GEORGIA S,42;HENRY B
. 340;HIRAM,340;HUGH,56
. J C,290;JAMES,163,179
. JAMES S,174;JESSE,35
. 189;JESSE SIMS,189
. JOHN,51,163,173;JOHN
. W,191;LIZZIE,41
. MARTHA,421;MARTHA A
. 236;MARY,413;PETER W
. 101;ROBERT,7,46,51
. 166,187,215,419
. ROBERT J,340;SARAH
. 189;THOMAS J,419;THOS
. I,419;WILLIAM,7,183
. 189;WILLIAM F,46
. WILLIAM FAIRFAX,189
. WM A,419
WAMBLE,FRANCES,402
    HENRY,13;LUCY S,400
WAMMACK,JAMES,340
. SHEARWARD,329
. WILLIAMSON L B,340
WANNAH,SARAH,69
WANTON,JULIA,398;SARAH
    Y,396
WARBINGTON,
. ELLEMANDER,348
. ELLENDER,348;JACOB B
. 348,363
WARD,ANNE,294;AUSTIN
. 283;B F,88,100,113
. BARTHOLOMEW,419;BENJ
. F,88;BETHENEY,238
. CHANEY,45;CHARLES,8
. 51,56;CHARLOTTE,42
. DAVID,8,35,56,419;E
. 254;EDWARD H,283
. EDWIN L A,46;ELAM,294
. ELIJA,419;ELIZA,202
. ENEAS,283;ENOS WESLEY
. 283;EUNICE,279;F,74
. FRANCIS,9,35,52,67
. GEORGE,283;GEORGIA
. ANN,416;HARRIET,46
. HARRIETT,262;HENRY C
. 46,283;HUDSON,283
. JAMES,26-27,35,51-52
. 217,283,419;JAMES D S
. 340;JAMES S,283;JANE
. 35;JOHN,9,35,49,283
. 419;JOHN E,340;JOHN
. THOMAS,419;JOSEPH,46
. JOSEPH S,283;LUCY,268
. LURANIA R,245;M B,35
. MARTHA,46;MARY,51,58
. 402;MARY A,240
. MARY ANN TARPLEY,240
. NANCY,51,266
. NARESETTA,419;POLLY
. 243;PRICILLA M,379
. RACHAEL,262;REBECCA E
. 36;RICHARD,283;ROBERT
. 51,283;SIMON,419
. STEPHEN,283;SUSAN,417
. THOMAS,6,35,52,283
. VIRGINIA,237;WILEY
. 283;WM,283
WARDE,ISENA,245
WARDLAW,DAVID L,419
WARE,CLARISSA,393;ELIZ
. 381,387;GEORGE N,371
. 372-373;HENRY,215,333
. 340;HUDSON T,372
. JAMES,56,226;JANE,415
. JOSEPH H,340;LEMUEL
. 370;LUCY,380;MARTHA
. 279;MARY A,398

. MARY ANN L,418;MARY E
. 242;NANCY,56
. NANCY SCOTT -
. BILLNGSLEA,377
. NICHOLAS,180,419
. ROBERT D,419;SMITH
. 223;SUSAN B,413;SUSAN
. MARGARET,388;SUSANNAH
. 257;THOMAS C,419
. THOMPSON,419;W,157
. WILLIAM,377;WM,302;WM
. C,419
WARLICK,JEFFERSON,74
. 140,147;NANCY,74
. SOLOMON,74
WARMOCK,SARAH,47;SUSAN
    202
WARNER,GEO W,419;MARY
. ANN,266;ROBERT,283-
. SAMUEL,46;WM,283
WARNOCK,DAVID,26
. ELIZABETH,57
. ELIZABETH F,44;ELLA
. 56;H J,209;HENRIETTA
. JANE,209;J F,211
. JESSE K,201;JOHN,56
. 211;MARTHA,44;MARY
. 203;SARAH,56;SIMEON
. 46,211
WARNUCK,SUSANNAH,204
WARPOLE,JOHN H,419
WARREL,JAMES G H,419
WARREN,296;ALLEN,161
. ARCHD,6;BENJAMIN H
. 419;BRAY,340;CARLOS
. 35;DAVIS,211;E W,250
. EDMOND,340;EDWARD,340
. ELEAYAR,211;FRANCIS M
. 211;GEO W,283;HENRY G
. 211;JAMES,201,211
. JAMES J,211;JAMES R
. 283;JANE,197;JASPER
. 211;JEREMIAH,360
. JESSE,296,329;MALICHA
. 7;MARTHA,200-201;MARY
. 4;MARY ELIZ,405;MOSES
. 201,211-212;NANCY,202
. 208,367;PETER,116
. SIPPER,212;SLADY,283
. WALLES,98;WILLIAM,211
WARREN/WARNER,J R,13
WARS,BETSEY CAROLINE
    238
WARTHEN,DAVID,313
. ELIZABETH,299;G W,313
. GEORGE W,312
. W RICHARD,312;W T,314
WARTZFELDER,E,312
WASDEN,JOSEPH,312
WASDON,MARTHA,403
WASHAM,JOHN,283
WASHBURN,ABNER S,419
WASHINGTON,ANDREW,46
. EPHRAIM,295;ETHELDRED
. 295;GEORGE,46;GRACEY
. 408;GRACY,396;JOHN
. 295;JUDY,392;MARTHA
. CERILDA,382;MARY,295
. PHILLIS,42;SARAH,295
. SHIPPEORD,46;SOPHIA
. 50;WILLIAM,295-296
. 299
WATER,GEORGE,23
WATERMAN,ASAPH,419
WATERS,ARTHUR,283
. CHARLES,56;CHARLES W
. 50;GABRIEL,201;GEORGE
. 21;ISAAC,283;JAMES W

. 283;JOSEPH,201;MARY
. MATILDA,198;MATTHEW
. 283;ROBERT P,340
. SARAH,204;WM,19
WATHALL,S M,236
WATKINS,ALBERT A,95
. ALEXANDER,340
. ANDERSON,419;C A,52
. CAROLINE,416
. CATHERINE A,387;CHLOE
. 41;DELPHA,285;ELISHA
. 211;ELIZ,402-403
. EVELINA S,419;GEO,244
. 256;GEORGE,279,283
. J W,75,86,113,116,124
. JAMES,419;JAMES W,70
. 80;JANE,249;JANE
. ELIZA,420;JAS W,119
. JASON,419;JESSE,419
. JOHN,283,316;JOSIAH
. 283;LOUISA,415;MARY
. 381,399;MARY ANNE,284
. MARY E,42;MARY E M
. 390;RHODA,35,50
. ROBERT A,419;SARAH B
. 393;SOPHIA,399
. STEPHEN,46;THOMAS H
. 419;THOS,419;UNITY
. 420;WILSON,419;WM,283
WATSON,ALZIRA E,247
. ANDREW JACKSON,283
. ANN,283;ANNA,237
. BECKEY,286;BRIANT,283
. CATHERINE,236;DOUGLAS
. 231,378;DOUGLAS C,283
. ELEANOR,407;ELIAS,283
. ELIZ,398,414
. ELIZABETH,264;GEO,419
. GEORGE,211;JACOB,352
. JAMES,340,419;JAMES H
. 75;JESSE,283;JESSE H
. 239,249;JNO,419;JOHN
. 283;JOHN A,283
. KIMBROUGH,419;KITTY
. 391;LOCRESHIA,400
. LUCRETIA,238;MARCUS L
. 283;MARGARET,265
. MARTHA,400,409;MARY
. 411;MARY A,257;MARY
. ANN,254;MARY ANN F
. 415;MARY K,242;MRTHA
. 243;NANCY,247
. NICHOLAS A,283;OLIVIA
. E,394;PETER,158-159
. 191,419;REBECCA,236
. ROBERT,65,378;SARAH
. 281;SOLOMON,211,283
. SUSAN E,211;W,358
. WILLIAM,93,211;WILLIS
. 1;WM,258,271,283;WM B
. 283
WATT,SAMUEL,370
WATTERS,D,293;JANE,340
. JOHN C,333,340;MARY C
. 340;ROBERT P,333
. WILLIAM,20
WATTON,MARY LOUISA,412
    PETER W,91
WATTS,A,277;ANN ELIZ
. 245;ARCHIBALD,237,243
. 272;CATHERINE,236
. ELIZABETH,198,209,240
. HAMPTON,283;HARDY K
. 283;HARRISON,283
. HARRISON H,283;HOLTON
. 283;JACOBY,283;JOHN R
. 283;JOSEPH,201,283
. JUBAL,127-128,134,142

WATTS(cont)
. LILLTE B,283;MARTHA
. 267,283;MARY,209,271
. MARY M,276;MARY S,283
. NANCY,249;NANNIE S
. 274;NAUCIE,312;POLLY
. 250;PRESLEY,283
. RICHARD,283;RICHARD N
. 283;RILEY,214;SARAH
. 127-128,134,142,267
. SARAH ANN,206;SARAH J
. 246;THOMAS,347
. WILLIAM,222;WM,283;WM
. H,284
WAXTER,ELIZ,390
WAY,JIM,46;JOHN,419
WAYNE,RICHARD,419;WM
419
WEAKLEY,LUCY,418;MARTHA
398
WEALCH,JOSEPH,3
WEATHERBY,309;GEORGE
. 297;L,324;MARY,411
. SEPTIMUS,307
WEATHERLY,JOHN S,284
SEPTIMUS,302;WM,284
WEATHERS,BETSEY,241
. EDWARD,156-157;ELIZ
. 417;JESSE,284;JOHN
. 284;MARTHA,417;NANCY
. 56;SUSANNA,381
. WILLIAM,10;WM,419
WEATHERSBEE,OWEN,340
WEATHERSLY,WILLIAM,58
WEAVER,AARON,7,419
. AUGUSTA,279;BETSEY
. 264;CLAUD M,265
. EDWARD,59,63-64,69,79
. 82;ELLA,46;FRANCIS
. 284;GEORGE W,96;HENRY
. C,46,271;JAMES M,284
. JARRETT,69,90;JOHN
. 284;JOHN H,82,90,419
. JOHN M,419;JONATHAN
. 419;JONATHAN LEWELLEN
. 419;LUCY,383;NANCY
. 419;SUSANNAH,397;WM
. 420;WM M,284
WEAY,JAMES M,211
WEBB,202;ALFORD G,201
. ANNIE J,340;C,100;C G
. 113;CHARLES,358;ELIAS
. G,201;ELIZA,340
. ELIZABETH,250;JAMES
. 340;JAMES A,201;JOHN
. 82,236,284;JOHN G,284
. KINCHEN J,201;LEVI
. 201;LEVI E,211;LUCY
. 241;MARTHA,250;MARY
. 259;NANCY,205;P A,340
. ROBERT,284,420;SALLY
. 100;SARAH,352;THOMAS
. 420;THOMAS P,340
. WILLIAM A,201,211
. WILLIE,20,22,25
WEBER,TOKANNE,420
WEBSTER,ELIZ,402;SAMUEL
17
WEED,E B,148
WEEDEN,WM,420
WEEDON,JOHN,191
WEEKES,THOMAS,7
WEEKLY,THOMAS,169
WEEKS,AARON,420;AM,327
. BENJAMIN L,56;CALEB C
. 420;CELIA,380
. ELIZABETH,237,327
. JAMES,420;JOHN,290

. 297;JOSEPH W,420
. MISERA,401;NANCY,327
. NATHANIEL,420;SAMUEL
. 284;SARAH,383;THOMAS
. 35,48,297;WILLIAM,309
. WM,289,420
WEESE,ELIZA,208
WEEVER,J H,111
WEIGELL,GEORGE,420;JOHN
420
WEIGHTS,JOHN,340
WEIGLE,GEORGE,420
WEKER,WM,420
WELBORN,CHAPLEY ROSS
. 349;CHRIS,230;CURTIS
. 219;ELIAS,150;ELIJAH
. 219;HOLMAND,219
. JOHNSON,349;JONATHAN
. 284;MARTHA,186;MARY
. 219;THOMAS,217,219;WM
. 284
WELBOURN,JEREMIAH,284
WELBURN,JAMES,284
WELCH,ARCHIBALD,420;BEN
. 215;F S,140;GEORGE
. 420;HANDY,46;HENRY
. 211;ISAAC,13-14;JAMES
. 35,173,420;JAMES A
. 140;JESSE,420
WELDING,ISAAC,353
WELDON,ANDREW,340,358
ISAAC,340;MARY,340
WELLAUER,JOHN,420
WELLBORN,
. ELIZABETH WINFREY,189
. SARAH,349;SHELTON,359
. WILLIAM T,340
WELLMAKER,SUSAN,273
WELLS,56;ABBY T,422
. ABSOLEM,3;CASSANDRA
. 251;DANIEL,329;E W,88
. ELLIN,211;GEORGE,284
. GEORGE D,211;JOHN,3
. 284;JOHN T,119;JULIUS
. 3;MARY,253;MAY E W
. 410;NANCY,257;SARAH
. 320-321
WELSH,ISAAC,8;JOHN,7
MARY,379;WARREN,10
WELTON,PETER W,112
WENDORWEDDLE,309
WESCOTT,JAMES D,73
WESH,WM,3
WEST,AMEY,384;ANDREW
. 333;ANN,410;ARTHUR,35
. CHARLES W,420
. CORDELIA,247;CORNELIA
. C,416;DAVID,420
. EDWARD,284;ELIJAH,284
. ELIZABETH,232,256
. ELLIS,221,231-232
. EMILY,260;EMMA J,285
. EPHRAIM,328;FRANCIS
. 221,237,243,247,259
. 274;G W,276;GEO,284
. GEORGE,284;GIBSON,35
. 50,56;HAMBLIN,291
. HANNAH,418;HENRY,154
. J A J,340;J I,284;J N
. 97;JAMES,420;JANE E
. 420;LUCY,46;MALINDA
. 259;MARTHA K,56;MARY
. 420;PHILLIS,45;REUBEN
. 284;SARAH,263;SARAH E
. 243;THOMAS J,284
. WARREN,284,298,327
. WILLIAM,7,35,47,220
. 221,321,323;WILLIAM R

. 56;WM,284;WM E,284;WM
. M,284
WESTBROOKS,ALLIN,284
. SARAH,242;THOMAS,284
. W A,97;WM,284
WESTER,ANNE,284;EDWARD
. 284;HENRY,14,16-17
. JOHN,284;PRUDY,280
. RACHEL,239
WESTFIELD,221
WESTMORELAND,
. ELIZABETH,329;ISHAM
. 329;JOS,294;JOSEPH
. 291,361;REUBEN,291
. 296;REUBIN,294
WETHERBY,CAROLINE,35
WETHERSBEE,
. CHARLOTT M,340
WFFORD,ISAIAH,418
WHALEY,BETSEY,284
. BURWELL,284;CHARLES
. 356;EDWARD,284;JAMES
. 284,324;JOHN,232
. THOMAS,284;THOS,245
WHATLEY,217-218;ALLEN
. 287,293;ANN,215,219
. ANNA,215;CATHERON,296
. CHARITY,258;CURBY,215
. 219;DANIEL,311;E L
. 267,284;ELISHA,311
. ELIZABETH,282,370
. FANNY,278;FLOYD,284
. GENNIT,296;GREENE,296
. HIRAM,311;JAMES,324
. JNO H,357;JOHH H,349
. JOHN,284;JOHN B,368
. JOHN H,348-349;LUCY
. 215,230;MARY,251
. MICHAEL,284,296,351
. NANCY,283,296;ORNAN
. 296,370;POLLY,250
. RANSON,348;REBEKAH
. 264,285;RICHARD,311
. ROBERT,284,370;SALLY
. 370;SHURLEY,296
. TABITHA,253;THOMAS W
. 284;WILLIS,296,340
. WILSON,370;WYATT,284
. WYTHE,297
WHATTLEY,ELIZABETH,370
WHEALIS,JOHN,82
WHEALY,JOHN,284
WHEAT,ELI,166;H,329
. HARVEY,166,186
. JONATHAN,284;JOS,329
. JOSEPH,321,329;WESLEY
. 166
WHEATLEY,229
WHEATON,WM H,420
WHEELAS,JOAB,284
WHEELER,ABNER,311;AVERY
. 284;CHARLES,201
. CHARLES A,420;ELIGAR
. 313;ELIJAH,284;ELIZA
. 43;GIDEON R,84,87,96
. HARDY,284;LAURENCE F
. 284;LOTT,35;MARY,45
. MARY ANN,199;MARY C
. 241;RAMELIA N,251
. SARAH F,268;SARAH M
. 415;SHADRACK,201;WM J
. 420
WHEELES,289
WHEELIN,JOHN,314
WHEELIS,HARDY,303
WHEELOUS,WM,284
WHELAN,PETER,238
WHELLIS,ISHAM,291

WHETSONE,JOHN A,284
WHETT,ADALINE,262
WHIDBY,DANIEL,420
WHIDDEN,WILLIAM,20
WHIEFIELD,BENJA,306
WHIEHEAD,AMOS,4
WHIGHAM,ASCAMITITY,379
. WILLIAM,13
WHINKLEY,JOHN,56
WHIT,MARY,165
WHITAKER,BENJ,1;GEORGE
. 115;HUDSON,1;JOHN B
. 340;MARRIAH,394;MARY
. 263;WM,284,420
WHITCOMB,NO,183
WHITCOMBE,NOTLEY,183;WM
. 420
WHITE,92,94,101;A B,98
. 116;ALVA B,124
. ALVENUS,125;ANDREW
. 284;ANN H,333,340
. ANNA E,389;ARMSTEAR
. 164;ARTHUR,6,35
. BENEDICK,420;BENEDICT
. 420;BENJAMIN,60
. CATHERINE C,248;CELEA
. 249;CHRISTOPHER,70
. CLARA H,400;CLEM,165
. COLEMAN,284;CONSTANCE
. 13;CONSTANT,35;D A
. 284;DANIEL,13,56-57
. DANL,7;DAVID,243,343
. 344;DAVID M,284
. EDMUND,284;ELBERT,374
. ELEANOR N,392;ELIZA
. 236,248,271;ELIZA P
. 410;ELIZABETH,253,371
. EZEKIEL,35;G G,89
. GEORGIA ANN,250;HENRY
. 13,35,56;ISABELLA,419
. J M,314;JAMES,3,284
. JAMES I,284;JANSEY
. BARTON,374;JESSE,9,35
. 329;JNO,302;JOHN,122
. 142,284,291,330,333
. 340;JOS,233;JOSEPH
. 224,291,303,340,353
. KATHARINE,156;KITTY
. 416;LILEY,401;LUCIUS
. 340;LYDIA,251;MARY
. 165;MARY A,409
. MARY ANN D,402;MARY
. ELIZ,410;MARY N,269
. MELINDA,165;MICAJAH
. 322;NEHEMIAH B,340
. NICHOLAS M,165;P H,91
. 96;PARMELIA,276;PETER
. 211;PEYTON H,102,104
. PHEBE,286;PLEAS,295
. PLEASANT,299;POLLY
. BARTON,374;R,263,286
. REUBEN,275-278
. 284;ROBERT,8,35,68
. 108,116,119,147;ROSA
. C,37;SALLY,251;SAMUEL
. 8,284,340;SARAH,295
. 309,409;SHORT,184
. SYDNEY,268;THOMAS,155
. 156,159,165,170,184
. 193,340,353,365
. THOMAS M,164-165;THOS
. 154;URETHEA,283;W G
. 97;WADE,147
. WASHINGTON,420;WIDOW
. 311;WILEY,374;WILEY M
. 284;WILLIAM,8-9,13,21
. 22,25,35,165,225
. WILLIAM H,88,116;WM

. 284-285,420;WM H,285
. WM PARKER,420
WHITEACRE,RACHEL,420
WHITEAKER,JOHN,420
. MAHALY,392;MARK,420
WHITECOMBE,RELETHA,390
WHITEFIELD,BENJA,309
. BENJAMIN,298,307,309
. JAMES,157
WHITEHEAD,A P,8;ABY,46
. AMOS,1,5,420;AMOS G
. 56,420;AMOS P,35
. ANNIE,46;AUGUSTUS,46
. CATHRINE B,44;CHARLES
. 56;EASTER,41;ELIZA A
. 420;ELIZABETH,52
. FRANK,211;GEORGE,115
. 291;HENRY W,420;J,56
. J C,56;JAMES,35;JNO
. BERRIEN,420;JOHN,35
. 56,420;JOHN W,285
. JUDY,41;JULIA A,41
. LOHAMIA,202;MALVINA
. 394;MARIA E,403;MARY
. A,57;PRINES,46
. REBECCA B,390;ROBERT
. W,420;SARAH,410;SARAH
. G,39;VIRGINIA L,407
. WILLIAM,211;WM S,313
. ZEMULA,419
WHITEHURST,JOHN,302,308
. 329,341
WHITELEY,SARAH,408
WHITELY,
. RICHARD HENRY,285
WHITENMOE,NOTLEY,158
WHITER,ROBERT,79
WHITESIDE,ANDREW J,285
WHITFIELD,ANN,199;ARTER
. 46;ASA B,46;BENJ,325
. BENJA,215;BENJAMIN
. 217,219,224,329;BENJN
. 348;BRYAN,35,50
. BRYANT W,46;CHARITY
. 199;EMILY,44;FRIDAY
. 46;HENRY,46;IVY I,285
. JAMES A,285;JOHN B
. 340;LEWIS,35,50,56
. MATTHEW,333,340
. MATTHEW C,340;MILES
. 214;ROBERT,201;SAMUEL
. 201;WILLIAM,50
WHITING,WILLARD,420
WHITLAW,JAMES H,285
WHITLEY,JESSE,85
WHITLOCK,J W,420;JAMES
. 420;JOHN,230;JOSIAH
. 230;JOSIASH,230;MARY
. 230,279;POLLY,284
. SALLY,275;SARAH M,230
. WILLIAM A,229;WILLIAM
. S,420;WM A,285
WHITSON,HENRY,13
. WILLIAM,13
WHITSTONE,CAROLINE L
. 286
WHITTED,GIDEON,72
WHITTENTON,ALLEN,8
WHITTINGTON,BARNETT,183
. 190;ELIZ,380
. ELIZABETH,190;EPHRAIM
. 420;EPHRIAM,190;MARIA
. 394;SARAH,183,190
WHITTLE,ELIZ AMELIA,413
. JAMES,420;L H,312
WHLLINGHAM,109
WICKER,ANNE,396;LINNY
. 388

WIDDON,WILLIAM,19
WIER,MARGARET S,239
WIESSINGER,SARAH,383
WIG,FRANCES,208
WIGANS,WM,420
WIGGANS,DORIAN,196
WIGGENS,ABIGAL,197;AMOS
. W,211
WIGGINS,AMOS,8,35,50,56
. AMOS W,201;ASHLEY E
. 214;BENJ,285;CLARISA
. 202;DANIEL W,211
. ELIZABETH,196
. EMMALINE,269;FRANCIS
. 44;GRAREY,36;J M,211
. JANE,199,384;JESSE,7
. 35;JESSE A,211;JOHN
. 52,213,285,420;JOHN C
. 211;JOHN E,211;JOSEPH
. 211;JOSIAH,211;LEWIS
. 223;LIGE,211;LIZZIE
. 203;LUCINDA,204
. MARGARET,209,213
. MARTHA ANN,201;MARTHA
. G,211;MARY B,199;MARY
. C,242;MELVINA,200
. MICHAEL,35,52;OLIFF
. 203;PETER,10;PLEASANT
. 201;RICHD,8;ROBERT
. 420;ROXEY NN,202
. SALLIE,210;SALLY,257
. SARAH,197;SARAH M,270
. STEPHEN,420;WADE,340
. WHITTENTON,285
. WILLIAM,35,51;WM,285
. 420
WIGHTMAN,H S,409;JOHN
. 420;LOUISA A,421
. THOMAS,420
WIGINS,ELIZ,396
WIKSTOOM,CHARLES,211
. CHARLEY W,211
WILBORN,CURTIS,217
. EDWARD,217;ELIZABETH
. 217;JOHNSON,349
. JOSHUA,217;REUBEN,189
. SUSANAH,189;THOMAS
. 350
WILBOURN,EDWARD,216
. MATTHUS,216;THOMAS
. 216
WILBURN,HERMAN H,340
. LEONIDAS C,340
WILCHER,ADAM,213;ELIZ
. 413;MARY,362
WILCOX,AMANDA,419;ELIZ
. 419;H A,145;ISAAC,420
. JANE E,418;JOHN,420
. JONATHAN SAMUEL,420
. MARTIN,420;MARY,420
WILCOXEN,THOMAS,306
WILCOXON,THOMAS,311
WILDE,DAVID,21,23,25
. JOHN W,420;R H,420
. RICHARD D,46
WILDER,DREAD,309;DRED
. 298,340;ISAAC,340
WILDES,ELIZ,384
WILDON,ANDREW,359
WILDS,SAMUEL,8-9;THOMAS
. 420
WILERKSON,SMITH,69
WILES,CHAS,420
WILEY,EDWARD,212
. ELIZABETH,185;HARRIET
. 46;JAMES,364;LINNA
. 156;MOSES,290-291,302
. T,168;TAYLOR,178

WILEY(cont)
. WILLIAM,185;WM,168
. 185
WILFORD,WALTER,285
WILIE,MOSES,317
WILILAMS,BEDFORD,46;ED
. 46;EMIT,46;FRANK R,46
. HENRY,46;HENRY H,46
. HERRINGTON,46;JAMES
. 46;PETER,46;PRASPER
. 46;RANDOLPH,46
. RICHARD,46;RICHMOND
. 46;SAMUEL M,46;THOMAS
. 46
WILKERSON,232;DEMPSEY
. 285;ELIZ,379;FATHEX
. 281;HARMON,340;JAMES
. 20;JAMES R,421;JNO B
. 421;MICAJAH,421;S,149
. SAMUEL,82,90,93,100
. 131
WILKES,137,219
. ELIZABETH,200;JAMES
. 201;JOHN,201;MARY,199
. 384,403;MAUNDAY,196
. SALLY,419;T W,242
. WILEY,212
WILKESON,EZEKIEL,321
WILKINS,DRURY,333,340
. J W,129;JAMIMA,408
. JOHN,285,342;JOICIS
. 41;LEMENDAR,392;LUCY
. 258;MARGAN,393;MARY
. 45,58;S M,275;THOS
. 176;W,189;WHIT,50
. WILLIAM,340,342
. WILLIS,149;WM,193;WM
. D,187
WILKINSON,ABNER,285;ANN
. 410;ANNE,326;BETSEY
. 255;EZEKIEL,326,328
. HENRY,285;JAMES,19
. 326;JOHN,35,227,326
. 328;KELLA,418;LUCY
. 245;MILLA,326;MINGO
. 212;NANCY,279;STEPHEN
. 326;THOMAS,328
. WILLIAM,326
WILKS,ELIAS,212
. ELIZABETH,195,202
. ISRAEL,212;JANE,205
. JOHN,214;JOHN A,285
. JORDAN B,212;MALCOM
. 214;MARY,210;NANCY
. 205;PETER,212
WILL,DAVID,364
WILLAIMS,ELIZABETH,108
. MARTHA T,108;MARY ANN
. 108;NANCY O,108
WILLAMSON,WILLIAM,214
WILLARD,JOHN,95;ROSWELL
. 340;ROYAL,95,118
WILLCOX,ABIGAL,411
. CAROLINE,389;ELIZ,381
. ELIZA,410;JOHN,421
. TOLIVER,421
WILLCOXAN,TOMAS,306
WILLEBEE,WM,421
WILLET,J E,312
WILLEY,ANNA MARIA,407
. JAMES H,285;JAS,3
WILLIAM,J W,140;JOHN W
. 119;O B,94;RACHEL,40
. SCHLEY O,48;SUSANNAH
. 5
WILLIAMS,145;AARON,8,35
. 52,56;ALBERT,285
. ALEXANDER,60;ALFRED

. 340;ALLEY,195,204
. ANDERSON,285,347;ANN
. 392,406;ANNA,217
. ARMIETTA,236;ARTHUR
. 354,362;AUGUSTIN,289
. AUGUSTUS L,340;BENJ
. 152,285;BENJAMIN,160
. 328;BETHANIA,303
. BETSEY,36;BRITTON,324
. C A,86,99,111,123
. CHARLES,361;CHARLOTTE
. 35;CHAS D,421
. CHRISTIAN,38
. CHRISTOPHER,291,303
. 304;CHRLES,233
. CRAWFORD,285;DARCUS
. 202;DAVID,285;DICEY
. 195;E,86;E S,242,244
. 250,253,270;E T,243
. EASTER,303;ED G,285
. EDWARD W,421;EDWD,367
. ELISHA,285;ELIZ,406
. ELIZA,44,208
. ELIZABETH,99,123,211
. 248,271,303,397
. EMALIZA,275;EMILY,400
. ESTHER,270;ESTHER E
. 280;EVELINE B,259
. EXELINE,199;EZEKIEL
. 51,56,285;EZEKIEL L
. 237;EZEKIEL S,268
. FANNIE C,271;FANNY
. 258;FANNY H,42;FATIMA
. 197;FLORA,278;FLOYD T
. 47;FRANCES,259
. FRANCES E,237;FRANCIS
. KEY,285;FRANCIS M,340
. FREDERICK H,285;GEO
. 310;GEO W,421;GEORGE
. 221,319;GERO,299;H,81
. 86,88,100,113,131,142
. 362;HARRIET,40
. HARRIET E,417;HENRY
. 421;HENRY I G,421
. HENRY P,285;HESTER,35
. HEZEKIAH,56,421
. HOLSTON,421;HUBBARD
. 93,126,142;HULDY,250
. I A,245,247,260,273
. 274,281-282;INDIANA
. 398;ISAAC,219,239,285
. 363,421;J,287;J A,241
. J D,267;J P,118-119
. 121,126,137,143;J R
. 104;J S,287;J W,81,93
. 99,104,138;JACK,117
. JAMES,26,79,212-213
. 285,329,421;JAMES B
. 285;JAMES D,285;JAMES
. M,86,101,108,123,333
. 340;JANE,35,50,205
. 249,270;JAS,329;JESSE
. 285,311;JNO,421;JO
. 285;JOANNA,43;JOHN,19
. 35,56,212,231,278,285
. 324,421;JOHN H,118
. JOHN R,90,99,123;JOHN
. S,297;JOHN W,79,85,90
. 109,127,141;JONATHAN
. 217,222,285;JOSEPH
. 285,303;JOSEPH JOHN
. 378;JOSIAH,421;JOTHN
. 222;JULIA ANN,268;L
. 56;L A,277;LAURA,264
. LAURA L,395;LAVINIA
. 277;LEAH,263;LETITIA
. 273;LEWIS,421
. LITTLEBERRY,285

. LOUISA M,411;LUCINDA
. 245;LUKE,82;M H,421
. MALISSA,238;MARGARET
. 51,231,303;MARGATE
. 303;MARGET,311;MARTHA
. 238-239,417
. MARTHA ANN ELIZABETH
. 248;MARTHA T,123;MARY
. 195,203,231,243,265
. 270-271,303-304,378
. 410,418,422;MARY A
. 392,408;MARY ANN,123
. MATILDA,37;MILLIE,247
. N,111,341;N A,101;N H
. 86,101,111,113,123
. 141;N M,340;N O,101
. NANCY,236,244,250,260
. 266,271,283;NANCY O
. 86,93,99,109,123
. NATHAN,99,101,108,123
. 141,344,352,355
. NATHAN H,86,90,102
. 107,134;NATHANIEL,360
. 421;NICHOLAS,341
. OLLIVER,47;ORRIN,285
. PATIENCE,255,258
. PATRICK,285;PATSEY
. 231;PETER,285;PHEBE
. 265;PHILLIP,212
. PLEASANT,285;POLEMAN
. 285;R W,212;REBECCAH
. 285;REBEKAH,284
. REUBEN,212;RICHARD S
. 285;ROBERT,60,285,288
. 293,304,319;ROBERT B
. 285;ROBERTS,309;ROBT
. 421;ROLAND,86;RUBIN M
. 201;SALLIE,208;SALLY
. 262,304;SAMUEL,10,35
. 421;SARAH,182,205,275
. 283,303,387,398;SARAH
. A,269;SCOTT,47;SHUGAR
. 353;SIMEON,421;SUSAN
. 196,269;SUSAN A,282;T
. 115-116,144;T H,13
. THEAPHELUS,122
. THEOPHILUS,111,115
. 119;THOMAS,35,48,285
. 288,293,421;THOMAS R
. 340;THOPHILUS,93;W M
. 141;WASHINGTON A,421
. WELL,47;WILLIAM,35
. 108,303-304,319,328
. 349;WILLIAM L,340
. WILLIAM P,212;WILLIAM
. S,86,101,123;WILLIS
. 285;WILSON,285;WINNEY
. 420;WM,247,276,285
. 299,348;WM A,285;WM B
. 285;WM N,285;WM S,86
. 99;WM T J,285;WRIGHT
. 35;ZACHARIAH,79,99
. 340,421
WILLIAMSON,220-221;A J
. 212;AMELIA E,411;AMY
. 201;CASSIE,208
. CHARLES,212;D S,212
. DICY A,209;ELEZEAR
. 201;ELIAS,421
. ELIZABETH,209;F H,212
. GREEN,293-294;GREENE
. 288;ISAAC,340;ISAAC B
. 85;J C,118;JAMES R
. 212;JNO,3;JOHN,51
. JOHN A,212;JOHN G,212
. M A,201;MALVINA C,399
. MARTHA J,269;MARY,381
. MARY RUTH,412;MATHEW